Ireland

Fionn Davenport
Catherine Le Nevez, Etain O'Carroll,
Ryan Ver Berkmoes, Neil Wilson

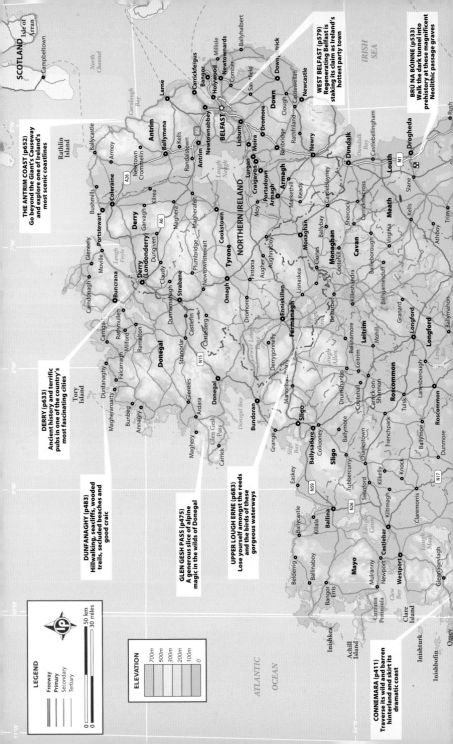

THE ANTRIM COAST (p552)
Go beyond the Giant's Causeway and explore one of Ireland's most scenic coastlines

WEST BELFAST (p579)
Regenerating Belfast is staking its claim as Ireland's hottest party town

BRÚ NA BÓINNE (p533)
Walk the dark tunnel into prehistory at these magnificent Neolithic passage graves

DERRY (p633)
Ancient history and terrific pubs in one of the country's most fascinating cities

DUNFANAGHY (p483)
Hillwalking, seacliffs, wooded trails, secluded beaches and good craic

GLEN GESH PASS (p475)
A generous slice of alpine magic in the wilds of Donegal

UPPER LOUGH ERNE (p683)
Lose yourself amongst the reeds and the birds of these gorgeous waterways

CONNEMARA (p411)
Traverse its wild and barren hinterland and skirt its dramatic coast

LEGEND

Freeway
Primary
Secondary
Tertiary

0 ————— 50 km
0 ————— 30 miles

ELEVATION

700m
500m
300m
200m
100m
0

ATLANTIC OCEAN

IRISH SEA

NORTHERN IRELAND

SCOTLAND

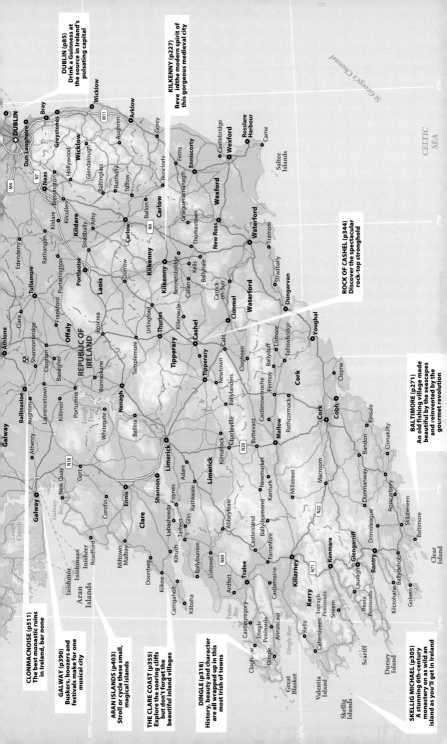

DUBLIN (p85)
Drink a Guinness at the source in Ireland's pulsating capital

KILKENNY (p227)
Revel in the modern spirit of this gorgeous medieval city

ROCK OF CASHEL (p344)
Discover the spectacular rock-top stronghold

BALTIMORE (p271)
An old fishing village made beautiful by the seascapes and reinvented by the gourmet revolution

SKELLIG MICHAEL (p305)
A stunning 6th-century monastery on as wild an island as you'll get in Ireland

DINGLE (p318)
History, beauty and character are all wrapped up in this most Irish of towns

THE CLARE COAST (p355)
Explore the soaring cliffs but don't forget the beautiful inland villages

ARAN ISLANDS (p403)
Stroll or cycle these small, magical islands

GALWAY (p390)
Buskers, boozers and festivals make for one musical city

CLONMACNOISE (p511)
The best monastic ruins in Ireland, bar none

On the Road

FIONN DAVENPORT Coordinating Author
Most people know how pretty Howth (p153) is, and that it's home to one of the best weekend gourmet markets in Dublin (see the boxed text, p135), but I must confess it takes a guidebook update or an insistent girlfriend to get me off my Sunday-sports couch. Thanks to Caroline for a) dragging me out there and b) taking the photo.

RYAN VER BERKMOES I made some new friends at a little nameless inlet I discovered along Greatman's Bay on the craggy Connemara Peninsula (see p413). It was a beautiful Sunday and the donkeys were more than happy to accept some offers of grass from the side of the wall they couldn't reach. Who can resist a friendly donkey?

NEIL WILSON Every time I come back to Northern Ireland I try to squeeze in a hike in the Mourne Mountains (p620). Usually it's cold and wet, but this time I was lucky – I climbed onto the summit ridge of Slieve Binnian and emerged above a sea of cloud into a world of blue sky and sunshine, with granite hills poking through like rugged islands.

ETAIN O'CARROLL I grew up by the Shannon and spent many summer days discovering small islands and tiny bays on my brother's boat. There wasn't much time for that on this trip, but I did squeeze in some thorough research on the waterway's thriving food scene and the region's untouched traditional pubs (see the boxed text, p523).

CATHERINE LE NEVEZ The best thing about travelling is finding yourself in the right place at the right time. I'd been meaning to pick up a bodhrán again, and when I visited the Coleman Irish Music Centre (p457), five-time All-Ireland bodhrán champion Junior Davey happened to drop by and give me an impromptu refresher.

For full author biographies see p732.

Ireland Highlights

Ireland's highlights are difficult to pinpoint because there are just so many of them: a history so rich and deep that a lot of the early bits are made up, a landscape so beautiful that it's hard to describe in words, and people so friendly and warm that each visit will inevitably add to your Facebook friends list. But we thought we'd give it a go...

OLIVER S

1 PUBS

Ireland's social heart beats loudest in the pub (p80), still the best place to discover what makes the country tick – and drink some fine beer in the process.

TRADITIONAL MUSIC

Let your inevitable love affair with Europe's most vibrant folk music begin by sitting in on a traditional *seisiún* (p83); you won't be asked to play, but you won't have to stop your feet from tapping or your hands from clapping.

3

HOLGER LEUE

2

DUBLIN

Ireland's capital (p85) has all of the distractions and dressings of a major international metropolis, but retains the friendliness, intimacy and feel of a provincial town.

JOHN ELK III

4

CASTLES & STATELY HOMES

The Anglo-Norman stamp is best seen in the country's collection of handsome homes, grand demesnes and impressive castles, many of which have been converted into luxury hotels with all the trimmings (see the boxed text, p697).

JOHN SONES

OLIVER STR...

5 FOOD & DRINK

Blessed with a bounty of local produce, Ireland's homegrown cuisine has finally come of age, offering up some outstanding dishes to tease and surprise even the most discerning palate (see the boxed text, p66).

RICHARD CUMM...

6 STROLLING ALONG THE BARROW, COUNTIES CARLOW & KILKENNY

Ireland has countless challenging hikes, but for something gentler you'll love the towpath stretching out along the River Barrow between St Mullins in County Carlow (p226) and Graiguenamanagh in County Kilkenny (p238). The short distance and flat terrain means a round trip is easy…if you don't get waylaid in one of Graigue's extraordinary old-school pubs, that is.

JULIET COOMBE

BALTIMORE, COUNTY CORK

The coast of County Cork is dotted with little old fishing villages, such as Baltimore (p271), that have shaken off their workaday past and blossomed in the modern age. Often-sunny weather, beautiful seascapes and amazing food sourced from the land and sea make for pleasurable days and nights here.

8

7

CLARE COAST

The coast of County Clare (p355) alternates long beaches with soaring cliffs, but the real appeal lies inland, in the myriad tiny villages where traditional Irish culture persists, oblivious to the demands of tourism. Everyone might have heard of Doolin, but you really need to hear about Kilfenora (p386), Ennistymon (p374), Corofin (p387)...

9 **GLENDALOUGH, COUNTY WICKLOW**

Wicklow's nickname is the 'Garden of Ireland', but there's nothing genteel or tame about the wild beauty of the monastic ruins of Glendalough (p163), which are strung along a glacial valley on the edge of two stunning lakes and surrounded by some of the best walking in the country.

CORK CITY

An appealing waterfront location, great food, lively craic and a vibrant 'Dublin? Where?' dynamic make County Cork's namesake city (p242) hard to resist. Surprises abound on the busy narrow streets that weave around the River Lee and its canals.

11

RICHARD CUM

10

RICHARD CUMMINS

DINGLE, COUNTY KERRY

Everybody has heard of Dingle (p317) and it seems that they all want to go there. But this is one place that transcends the crowds with its allure. Sure, you may be stuck behind a bus, but this rocky, striated land that seems to dissolve into the sea has a history as compelling as its beauty.

JOHN E

12

ROCK OF CASHEL, COUNTY TIPPERARY

The Rock of Cashel (p344) never ceases to startle when first seen rising from the otherwise mundane plains of Tipperary. And this ancient fortified home of kings is just the tip of the iceberg for moody and forlorn ruins hidden away in the surrounding green expanse.

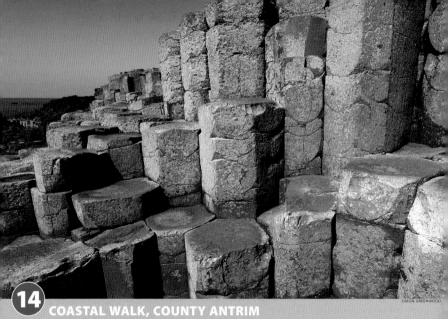

SIMON GREENWOOD

14 COASTAL WALK, COUNTY ANTRIM

Put on your walking boots, shoulder your rucksack and set off along one of Ireland's finest coastal walks, stretching for 16 scenic kilometres between the swaying rope bridge of Carrick-a-Rede and the grand geological flourish of the Giant's Causeway (p656).

HOLGER LEUE

13 SHANNON–ERNE WATERWAY, THE MIDLANDS

There's a wonderfully languid charm about meandering along Ireland's rivers by boat, and the Shannon–Erne Waterway (p521) is an ideal place to just kick back and relax. The pace of life is far slower here, the lush fields greener, the villages untouched and the Guinness even sweeter after a day spent on the water.

BLACK TAXI TOUR, BELFAST

Learn about Northern Ireland's troubled history as you tour the political murals and peace lines of West Belfast in the back of a black taxi (p585), leavened with a touch of black humour from the wise-cracking driver.

16

DAMIAN TULLY /

15

SEAN CAFFREY

BRÚ NA BÓINNE, COUNTY MEATH

It's hard to comprehend just how old the ancient burial sites of Brú na Bóinne (p533) really are. The building techniques and precise alignment with the heavens are highly sophisticated, yet no one really understands what these tombs were for – a tantalising mystery that makes this ancient site so compelling.

NEIL SETC

17 GALWAY CITY, COUNTY GALWAY

City or country? That's the choice in County Galway, but the secret is simply not to choose. Wandering the tuneful streets and alleys of Galway city (p390) will keep you busy for a month's worth of nights; wandering the narrow roads of gorgeous Connemara Peninsula (p411) will keep you busy for a month's worth of days.

Contents

Regional Map Contents

County Donegal p463

Counties Derry & Antrim p634–5

Counties Fermanagh & Tyrone p678–9

Belfast p570–1

Counties Down & Armagh p604–5

Counties Mayo & Sligo p428–9

Counties Meath, Louth, Monaghan & Cavan p532–3

County Galway p390–1

The Midlands p502

Dublin p88

Counties Wicklow & Kildare p158–9

County Clare p356–7

Counties Limerick & Tipperary p332–3

County Kerry p289

Counties Wexford, Waterford, Carlow & Kilkenny p188–9

County Cork p242–3

Destination Ireland

In 2008 an ad for a local bread manufacturer ran on Irish TV, featuring two men building an old-style, traditional stone wall in Connemara. As they work, a woman approaches with a tray of avocado-and-prawn sandwiches, also doling out a green tea and a skinny latte. When one of the men takes a phone call on his mobile, he turns down a request saying he has his Pilates class that evening.

The ad captured the Irish Zeitgeist perfectly, portraying the two distinct sides of a country that has undergone huge, transformative change yet remained largely the same. On the one hand, there's the New Ireland, a land of motorways and multiculturalism, planned and developed in between double decaf lattes and time out at the latest spa for a thermal mud treatment. The economy may have taken a massive hit in the last year or so, but the country has found a new level of cosmopolitanism and sophistication that it's not likely to lose anytime soon. Ireland's *other* personality, however, is a little more traditional and, if the regular polls of departing tourists are to be believed, still holds the key to Ireland's draw as a tourist destination.

At the heart of it all is the often-breathtaking scenery, still gorgeous enough to make your jaw drop, despite the best efforts of developers to scar some of the most beautiful bits with roundabouts, brutal suburbs and summer bungalows. From the lonely, wind-lashed wilderness of Donegal to the postcard landscapes of western Cork, Ireland is one of the world's most beautiful countries, and worth every effort you make to explore it. And we mean, of course, the whole island, including the North – for so long scarred by conflict but now finally engaged in the process of recovery, able to once again parade its stunning self to a world that for so long only heard about the province's troubles on the evening news.

But the overwhelming popularity of scenic superstars like Connemara and Kerry has seen the emergence of quieter idylls as the preferred destination of the discerning traveller, who has discovered the beauty of the lakes of Roscommon and the villages of Waterford, of rarely visited counties like Westmeath. These are the areas where you can come into contact with a more genuine Ireland, the kind removed from the slick machinery of the tourist trail.

Ireland is a complex, often contradictory country, and those contradictions are evident everywhere you go, from the thatched rural pub advertising its wi-fi connection and imported Australian wines to the group of Polish-born school kids chatting away to each other in Irish. No sooner do you make an assumption about the place than something will confound you completely, leaving you no wiser than before you began. But don't worry, you're in good company: most of the Irish are as perplexed about it as you are.

All of this confusion hardly fits the traditional, time-worn view of a nation of affable people made happy by the conviviality of a drink among friends, but the Irish have always mocked the fanciful notions of Irish Americans and other 'hyphenated Irish', who return to the land of their ancestors hoping to find a version of the iconic film *The Quiet Man*. The Irish love their humour, but they usually prefer it served black and ironic, all the better to deal with the difficulties that surround them.

And these are unquestionably difficult times for Ireland. By now, we're all wearily familiar with the story of the pinstriped bozos who brought the world to its knees by throwing bits of paper up in the air and calling them 'derivatives'. But Ireland's is that much more shocking because the collapse of the global financial system triggered the virtual disintegration of an economy that was blindly, blithely – and ultimately disastrously – dependent on a property bubble that burst in late 2008, leaving the country to once again confront the fears of its past: spiralling unemployment, economic paralysis and the slow bleed of emigration.

Then, six months later, just as the country was beginning to come to terms with the harsh new realities of its economic fortunes, its *annus horribilis* was compounded with the publication of the 3000-page report of the Commission to Inquire into Child Abuse, which revealed in all its stark, unspeakable horror the fate of so many of the almost 170,000 children who passed through the industrial school system in the middle decades of the 20th century – and the complicity of both the Church and the State in their workhouse hell. In 2009 one question was on everybody's lips: how did it all go so horribly wrong?

You'll hear a lot of theories from Irish people during your travels, as well as a few no-nonsense solutions: throw all the bankers in jail, defrock the clergy and, above all, get rid of that awful show of liars and incompetents in government. But they know, too, that none of those things are likely to happen, so they'll shake their heads in resignation and *sure, isn't that just the way of things?* Then they'll offer you a drink and talk about Ireland's problem with the stuff – how it's both the nurse and curse of the people – all the while making sure that your glass never gets empty.

For all of Ireland's very real problems and confusing contradictions, the fact remains that the Irish warmth and welcome is the real deal, and millions of visitors testify to the sheer ease with which they made friends here. Someone *will* stop and help you find your way when you're standing on a corner gawking at a map; you *will* strike up a conversation if you're sitting alone in a pub; and there *is* a very good chance that if you're stuck somewhere a local will volunteer a lift to wherever you need to go. The Irish love complaining about their country – the crappy weather, the horrible traffic, the corruption and, increasingly, the horrors of the past – and will swear to you that you're the luckiest person on earth because you don't have to live here. But that they only do because this is the greatest country on the planet. Make sense? Well, it does here.

Getting Started

Compact, relatively homogenous and *theoretically* crossed by car in less than four hours, Ireland doesn't pose any major challenges to the visitor other than the ones set by the often inclement weather; the horrendous traffic that can make getting through a two-dog town a 45-minute struggle against road rage; and what might generously be called *inconsistent* pricing, where value for money isn't always apparent. Otherwise, Ireland is a doddle.

WHEN TO GO

The Irish weather works on the 'four seasons in a day' principle, which basically means that you can't predict a thing when it comes to the behaviour of the sky. Some basic assumptions, however, can be made.

In summer, from June to August, the days are reasonably warm and – most importantly – very long: at the height of summer you won't need to turn on the lights until after 10pm. It is also peak tourist season, which means there are far more people just about everywhere but the most remote corners of the island, and prices are at their highest. Not surprisingly, most of the yearly festivals occur during these times so as to take advantage of the crowds and the more favourable weather.

See Climate Charts (pp701-2) for more information.

Spring (March to May) and autumn (September to November) make good alternatives, although the country's ever-growing popularity as a tourist destination can often blur the lines between mid- and high-season tourism. Still, you have a better chance of some peace and quiet, and the weather can be surprisingly better in April and September than in mid-July – again, it's all part of the uncertainty principle. Spring festivities include the ever-popular St Patrick's Day festival.

Although temperatures will barely venture below freezing, winter (December to February) can be brutal, but huge parts of the country – the west and northwest in particular – are at their savage and beautiful best in the cold winter light. Crowds are at their thinnest, but many of the country's tourist attractions and services close down in October and don't reopen until Easter, which paradoxically leaves visitors with a more convincing taste of how Ireland is experienced by most of the Irish: it's cold, grey and dark by 5pm, but there's always a pub to escape into when the rain starts sheeting down.

COSTS & MONEY

The collapse of the economy in the space of six short months over late 2008 and early 2009 has left the country in a state of flux: prices are coming down

---

DON'T LEAVE HOME WITHOUT...

Ireland won't test your survival skills unless you're the worse for wear in the middle of nowhere, but there are a few essentials you won't want to leave behind:

- Good walking shoes
- Raincoat
- UK/Ireland electrical adapter
- A finely honed sense of humour
- A hollow leg
- Decent Irish-themed playlists for your iPod – see p60 for our recommendations.

in many areas, but they're coming down from such a height that to many visitors Ireland remains a pretty expensive destination. For a decade, Irish wallets were at the mercy of a rip-off culture that stung everybody, including visitors, who felt it most when it came to bed and board.

In Dublin, the bare minimum to survive is about €50 a day: €20 to €25 for a hostel and €20 for sustenance, which leaves just enough for a pint. If your purse strings are a little more relaxed, you can get a decent bed for around €80 in the capital, €60 outside of it. For €120 you can sleep pretty luxuriously most anywhere except those *very* special places. Outside the capital things are a little better, but not much: if you're in a tourist hot zone, it'll be reflected in the prices, which are only marginally better than in Dublin.

Although restaurants are closing down all over the country, the new economy hasn't resulted in a marked decrease in the price of food. For less than €10, don't expect much more than soup and what comes between two slices of bread. Very ordinary meals will cost €20 or more; the better restaurants won't blink twice when charging €35 for fish in a fancy sauce.

In Northern Ireland, the bite isn't as deep. The 'rip-off Republic' tag that for so long dogged the south isn't as much of an issue north of the border, but it certainly hurts anyone from Northern Ireland if they go south: exchange rates make the eurozone very expensive for anyone using pounds sterling (as they do in Northern Ireland, which is part of the UK).

Once in the north, though, you can get by on £35 a day without too much bother if you're on a budget and limit yourself to hostels or self-catering accommodation. Accommodation costs generally mirror the Republic, but you'll find real savings in food – you can get excellent two-course lunches in lots of good restaurants for £10 or less, while main courses in Belfast's best eateries range from £14 to £18.

Car rental is costly throughout the island. Be sure to check your car insurance policy back home before accepting the exorbitant insurance policies offered at car-rental agencies. If your credit card usually covers car-rental insurance, confirm that the policy applies in Ireland.

TRAVELLING RESPONSIBLY

The government coalition may include the Green Party, but of Ireland's 40 shades of green the eco kind is surely one of the faintest. It's not that the Greens are ineffectual (which they are, but mostly because they're the very junior partner in a coalition), nor is it that the Irish are especially indifferent to the needs of the environment. No, it's down to that awkward truth known as history: it's hard to tell a nation that got wealthy a wet week ago after pissing potless for centuries that they *shouldn't* buy an SUV or go on four foreign holidays a year. Somehow, the fact that in 2007 Ireland's carbon footprint was 5.0 global hectares per person – more than double the global average – didn't really have the kind of impact the European Environment Agency hoped it would have, which meant that the country would have to pay for its emissions, a total of 3.6 million tonnes of carbon *per year*.

Enter the economic collapse of 2008–9. All of a sudden, production has dropped across a range of industries and the Environmental Protection Agency has altered its forecast, guessing that the country would be liable for about half the amount of carbon credits, between 1.3 million and 1.8 million tonnes of carbon. Such improvements notwithstanding, Ireland will still struggle to meet its obligations under the Kyoto Protocol and the EU's own binding targets, scheduled for 2020.

The real saving grace for the small band of eco-activists has been the queue, which has done more than an Al Gore movie to remind the Irish that life needs to get a little more sustainable. Endless traffic jams, snaking queues at

HOW MUCH?

Irish Times €1.80

1km taxi fare €1.60

Cinema ticket €9.50

Admission to Gaelic football match €12-18

Aran sweater €55

overburdened airports and just general waiting in line to get stuff drives most Irish people crazy. So when they're informed that becoming eco-responsible will go some way toward restoring a sense of sanity, they react positively.

As so many visits to Ireland begin in Dublin, you could start your trip by dropping into **Cultivate** (☎ 01-674 5773; www.cultivate.ie; 15-19 West Essex St) in Temple Bar, Ireland's only sustainability-focused living and learning centre. The centre has an eco-shop, lots of information stands, and hosts workshops and classes on everything from composting to green building. Also worth checking out are **Sustainable Energy Ireland** (www.sei.ie), the country's national energy centre, and the Irish branch of **Friends of the Earth** (www.foe.ie).

Throughout this book we have endeavoured to highlight any accommodation or project that puts green issues at the forefront of their planning; for more, see the Environment chapter (p74); the itinerary 'An Eco Kind of Green' (p29); our Top 10 Green Projects (p24); and our Greendex (p761).

Offsetting

Paying someone else to offset your greenhouse gas emissions isn't the perfect solution to the major issue of global warming, but it is a step in the right direction. The most popular offsetting program involves tree planting, but there are other schemes such as methane collection and combustion. **Carbon Neutral Ireland** (www.carbonneutralireland.ie) can help you calculate your emissions and advise you how to offset them.

Planning

Create an itinerary that allows you to explore and experience the best of Ireland while maintaining some level of eco-responsibility. Your aim should be to benefit locally owned businesses and any venture that preserves the local culture.

This means choosing locally owned accommodation over the big, multinational chain hotels (see opposite for our selection of green-friendly accommodation); restaurants that make an effort to use local produce; and activities that benefit the local community rather than exploit it. A good example is golf, where you should endeavour to play the older established courses rather than the newer megaresorts designed to draw in wealthy players with a mix of US-style course design and on-course houses that are nothing more than a huge drain on local resources. Throughout this book we have endeavoured to keep all of these considerations uppermost in our thinking.

GREEN WEBSITES

Check out the following online resources for in-depth info on how to travel in Ireland without being an environmental bully or leaving too large a carbon footprint:

www.cultivate.ie Sustainable living centre in Dublin's Temple Bar.

www.sustourism.ie All-Ireland project committed to building a sustainable tourist infrastructure.

www.greenbox.ie An integrated 'green zone' that includes Fermanagh, Leitrim, West Cavan, North Sligo, South Donegal and North West Monaghan

www.enfo.ie Ireland's public information service on environmental matters, including sustainable development.

www.sei.ie Ireland's national energy centre was set up in 2007 to promote and assist the development of sustainable energy.

www.foe.ie The world's largest network of environmental groups has its own Irish branch.

www.friendsoftheirishenvironment.net A network of independent environmentalists that has logged close to 10,000 environment-related stories.

www.thevillage.ie Ireland's first ecofriendly and sustainable urban plan is an extension of the village of Cloughjordan, County Tipperary.

TOP 10 GREEN SLEEPS

Anna's House B&B Strangford Lough, County Down; p612.

Ardtarmon House Drumcliff, County Sligo; p460.

Errigal Hostel Dunlewey, County Donegal; p488.

Jampa Ling Buddhist Centre Bawnboy, County Cavan; p562.

Omagh Independent Hostel Omagh, County Tyrone; p690.

Dolphin Hotel & Restaurant Inishbofin, County Galway; p420.

Phoenix Vegetarian Restaurant & Accommodation Mt Caherconree, County Kerry; p325.

Rocky View Farmhouse Fanore, County Clare; p383.

Rua Castlebar, County Mayo; p448.

Shiplake Mountain Hostel Dunmanway, County Cork; p280.

Sustainable Tourism Ireland (www.sustourism.ie) is a handy starting point with a list of enterprises, from B&Bs to urban planning projects, that put eco-responsibility and sustainability at the fore.

Fly Less

There are numerous boat companies serving Ireland from Britain and France, and return fares often don't cost that much more than one-way fares – not to mention the plethora of special offers designed to challenge the cheap flight hegemony. Boats arrive in Dublin, Belfast, Larne and Wexford; for more details, see the Transport chapter (p717).

Use Less Plastic

The Republic has a levy of €0.22 on all plastic bags at the point of sale, and it has proven remarkably effective, reducing the use of these noxious carriers by up to 90%. Northern Ireland introduced a 5p levy in July 2007. We urge you to use as few plastic bags as possible; most shops sell cloth bags that can be stashed away when not in use.

Stay Longer

An extended visit, as opposed to the rush-in, rush-out limitations of city-break travel, is preferable because it allows for 'slow travel' – the kind of exploratory travel that allows you to take your time and get to know a place without needing to rush (and find the fastest form of transport) to get you around. The ideal form of slow travel is a bike tour – throughout the book we have included details of bicycle rental agencies. Some organisations also run bike tours (see p718).

TRAVEL LITERATURE

Travel in Ireland seems to inspire writers, some of whom seem obsessed with using Guinness as a metaphor for Irish life. As irritating as that is to the Irish and anyone else with an aversion to bad metaphors, some manage the job with cleverness and humour.

Ireland – In a Glass of Its Own by Peter Biddlecombe is a hilarious trip around Ireland, based on the premise that the 32 counties can be said to represent the constituent parts of a pint of the black stuff.

Pint-Sized Ireland by Evan McHugh is the story of the ultimate Aussie pilgrimage: a journey the length and breadth of Ireland to find the perfect pint. The entertaining means do justify the ridiculous ends.

McCarthy's Bar has sold millions of copies thanks to the colourful account of author Pete McCarthy's attempt to rediscover Ireland by having a pint in every pub that bears his name. His follow-up, *The Road to McCarthy,* is a look at the Irish diaspora.

TOP 10

Dublin
United Kingdom
REPUBLIC OF IRELAND
Wales

TOP GREEN PROJECTS

There's nothing more satisfying than helping, participating in, visiting or even just being aware of projects that are working to protect the very environment that drew you here in the first place.

1 Ecos Environmental Centre (Ballymena, County Antrim; p668) is a visitor centre dedicated to alternative energy sources and sustainable technology.

2 Copper Coast GeoPark (Tramore, County Waterford; p211) is an Anglo-Irish enclave with the dubious distinction of being the only village in Ireland without a pub.

3 Cork English Market (Cork city, County Cork; p248) is where locally and organically produced food is displayed so alluringly, sold so bounteously and tastes so good.

4 Jampa Ling Buddhist Centre (Bawnboy, County Cavan; p562) has Galupa Buddhism, philosophy and meditation.

5 T Bay (Tramore, County Waterford; p212), Ireland's biggest surf school, runs eco-walks around one of Europe's largest intertidal lagoons.

6 Sonairte (Laytown, County Meath; p537), also called the National Ecology Centre, is devoted to promoting ecological awareness and sustainable living.

7 Bog of Allen Nature Centre (Lullymore, County Kildare; p180), tells the history of Ireland's bogs through a get-your-hands-dirty interactive program of learning.

8 Coosan Cottage Eco-Guesthouse (Athlone, County Westmeath; p526) is an ecofriendly guest cottage, utilising wind-generated electricity and sawdust-pellet heating.

9 Donegal Craft Village (Donegal town, County Donegal; p466) is a cluster of craft studios showcasing locally produced pottery, ironwork, hand-woven fabrics, jewellery and more.

10 Rossinver Organic Centre (Rossinver, County Leitrim; p524) has courses on organic horticulture and sustainable living.

TOP IRISH FICTION

Getting stuck into some fiction is the best way to gain insight into Irish issues and culture, for there's no greater truth in Ireland than the story that's been made up. Here are the essentials to kick-start a lifelong passion; for more information, see p55.

1 *Dubliners* (1914) by James Joyce

2 *The Book of Evidence* (1989) by John Banville

3 *The Butcher Boy* (1992) by Patrick McCabe

4 *Paddy Clarke Ha Ha Ha* (1993) by Roddy Doyle

5 *The Ballroom of Romance & Other Stories* (1972) by William Trevor

6 *The Third Policeman* (1967) by Flann O'Brien

7 *Amongst Women* (1990) by John McGahern

8 *All the Names Have Been Changed* (2009) by Claire Kilroy

9 *Brooklyn* (2009) by Colm Toibin

10 *Angela's Ashes* (1996) by Frank McCourt

MUST-SEE IRISH MOVIES

Predeparture planning is always more fun if it includes a few flicks to get you in the mood. The following films are available on video or DVD. For more information about Irish cinema and TV, see p57.

1 *Bloody Sunday* (2002; Paul Greengrass)

2 *The Dead* (1987; John Huston)

3 *My Left Foot* (1989; Jim Sheridan)

4 *The Crying Game* (1992; Neil Jordan)

5 *Garage* (2008; Lenny Abrahamson)

6 *Inside I'm Dancing* (2004; Damien O'Donnell)

7 *Once* (2007; John Carney)

8 *Adam & Paul* (2004; Lenny Abrahamson)

9 *The Magdalene Sisters* (2002; Peter Mullan)

10 *Michael Collins* (1996; Neil Jordan)

Silver Linings by Martin Fletcher is a compelling portrait of Northern Ireland at odds with its bruised and tarnished image as a war-scarred region. Northerners on both sides of the divide are friendly, funny and as welcoming as anyone else on the island.

Vitali's Ireland by Vitali Vitaliev is a minutely observed account of 21st-century Ireland, contrasted with the country a century earlier: the country appears to have changed beyond all recognition, but upon close inspection, much remains the same – for good and ill!

A Secret Map of Ireland is Rosita Boland's brilliantly insightful tale of her travels across the 32 counties, uncovering stories, myths and fascinating details about the counties, towns and villages she comes across.

The Oxford Illustrated Literary Guide to Great Britain and Ireland traces the movements of famous writers who have immortalised various towns and villages in Ireland.

The Height of Nonsense by Paul Clements is a fascinating story of Irish quirks, eccentrics and oddities, and travelling the GMRs (Great Mountain Roads) in search of the truth about druids, banshees, highwaymen and loose women.

INTERNET RESOURCES

The internet has become an indispensable planning tool for travellers. Ireland is well wired, so there's a lot of useful information available online. Here are a few sites to get you started.

Blather (www.blather.net) Its motto is 'talking shite since 1997', and this wry webzine delivers, dishing out healthy portions of irreverent commentary on all things Irish. It's a savvy way to get up to date on current events and attitudes.

Entertainment Ireland (www.entertainmentireland.ie) Countrywide listings for clubs, theatres, festivals, cinemas, museums and much more. It's well worth consulting this site as you plan your next move in Ireland.

Fáilte Ireland (www.discoverireland.ie) The Republic's tourist board information site has heaps of practical info. It features a huge accommodation database with photos.

Fine Gael (www.ripoff.ie) Not the website of the actual political party, but an antigovernment website sponsored by the main opposition party, whose aim is to win favour by appearing onside with the poor consumer; we don't buy it, but it does tell it like it is in relation to prices.

Irish Election (www.irishelection.com) The best of Irish political blogging, this is a great site to familiarise yourself with the issues dominating the Irish scene.

Irish Times (www.irishtimes.com) Ireland's newspaper of record online, this has all the latest news, features and reviews.

Lonely Planet (www.lonelyplanet.com) Comprehensive travel information and advice.

Northern Ireland Tourism (www.discovernorthernireland.com) Northern Ireland's official tourism information site is particularly strong on activities and accommodation.

Itineraries
CLASSIC ROUTES

GO WEST!
One Week/Mayo to West Cork

Begin at the excavated **Céide Fields** (p444) in Mayo. Wind your way round the coast, stopping at some of Ireland's wildest beaches, to the pretty village of **Pollatomish** (p443). Head to the pub-packed heritage town of **Westport** (p435), continuing past **Croagh Patrick** (p434) and through **Leenane** (p421) – situated on Ireland's only fjord – to **Connemara National Park** (p421). Take the beautiful coastal route, passing **Kylemore Abbey** (p420) and Clifden's scenic **Sky Road** (p418) through pretty **Roundstone** (p416), or else try the stunning wilderness of the inland route through Maam Cross to **Galway** (p390). Move on to the fishing villages of **Kinvara** (p423) and **Ballyvaughan** (p383) in the heart of **the Burren** (p376) and visit the ancient **Aillwee Caves** (p385). Explore the **Dingle Peninsula** (p317) before following the **Ring of Kerry** (p300), ending in **Killarney National Park** (p295). Continue down the **Beara Peninsula** (p281) to the Italianate **Garinish Island** (p282), with its exotic flowers. Follow the coast to **Cork** (p242) through Castletownshend and the fishing village of **Union Hall** (p268).

This tourist trail takes you past some of Ireland's most famous attractions and through spectacular countryside. It's only about 300km so you could manage it in two days, but what's the point? You won't be disappointed on this route.

THE LONG WAY ROUND

Three Weeks/Starting & Ending in Dublin

Start your loop just north of Dublin at the **Casino at Marino** (p121) – not a place to cash in your chips but a 19th-century Italianate trompe l'oeil mansion. Continue north to the mind-blowing Neolithic necropolis at **Brú Na Bóinne** (p533), built before the Great Pyramids were even a twinkle in a Pharaoh's eye. Continue north to **Mellifont Abbey** (p552), Ireland's first Cistercian abbey, and on to the pretty village of **Carlingford** (p555) on the lough, with its 16th-century buildings. Work your way through the Mourne Mountains – hiking to the top of **Slieve Donard** (p619) – to the **Ards Peninsula** (p608) and **Strangford Lough** (p612). Take a Black Taxi tour in **Belfast** (p585) before moving northwest to the Unesco World Heritage site of **Giant's Causeway** (p656), best enjoyed at sunset. Continue around the stunning coastline of north Donegal, stopping at gorgeous **Killyhoey Beach** (p483), then on to beautiful **Glenveagh National Park** (p489). Head south through the monastic ruins of **Glencolumbcille** (p474) and into lively **Sligo** (p450), where you can climb the Stone Age passage grave **Carrowkeel** (p457) for panoramic views of Lough Arrow. For the west coast as far as Cork, follow the Go West! route (opposite). From Cork, head east to **Fota Wildlife Park** (p255) for a picnic and then on to **Dungarvan Castle** (p213), with its unusual 12th-century shell. Drive around the picturesque **Hook Peninsula** (p197), stopping for ice cream in the seaside town of **Dunmore East** (p210). Spot the unusual varieties of geese in the famous **Wexford Wildfowl Reserve** (p193) before moving on to County Wicklow and **Wicklow Mountains National Park** (p157). Head back to Dublin and settle into a well-deserved pint of Guinness at the **Long Hall** (p142).

A loop to give you a real feel for Ireland's savage and spectacular coastline, as well as the heart of its long history. Four days will see you complete the 750km that make the full circle, but little else, so it's best done in a couple of weeks.

TIP TO TOE
Two Weeks/Derry to Wexford

Begin by walking the city walls of **Derry** (Londonderry; p633) and exploring its fascinating history. Delve deeper at one of Ireland's best museums, the **Ulster American Folk Park** (p690), which reproduces a typical 19th-century Ulster village at the time of mass emigration to America. Just south of here, the town of **Omagh** (p690), site of one of the worst single atrocities in the North's history (a car bomb), acts as a stark reminder of the region's tragic political history. From here, head south to **Castle Coole** (p683), a National Trust–restored 18th-century mansion, before spending an afternoon boating or fishing on **Lough Erne** (p683). For more watery pastimes you can't beat **County Cavan** (p557), which has a lake for every day of the year. Hire a boat in Mountnugent and fish on **Lough Sheelin** (p560) before moving on to **Tullynally Castle's** (p530) Chinese and Tibetan gardens in Westmeath. The **Seven Wonders of Fore** (p530), Westmeath's answer to the Seven Wonders of the World, are less awe-inspiring but will keep you entertained for an hour or two before a wander around the splendid **Belvedere House** (p528), which overlooks Lough Ennell, with its fascinating (if somewhat chequered) history. Place a bet at **Kilbeggan Races** (p528) while emboldened by a tipple of fine whiskey from **Locke's Distillery** (p527). Hike up the beautiful **Slieve Bloom Mountains** (p503) for the best view of the midlands before moving south to the delightful village of **Inistioge** (p237) in County Kilkenny, with its quaint village square and rambling estate, Woodstock Park. In County Wexford have a picnic in the **John F Kennedy Arboretum** (p201) before a visit to the tranquil Cistercian **Tintern Abbey** (p198).

This 400km north–south route covers it all: from Ulster's fine architecture and heritage, through the midlands and its abundance of lakes, to the beautiful countryside of the sunny southeast. You will enjoy this selection of different tastes.

ROADS LESS TRAVELLED

AN ECO KIND OF GREEN
One Week/Dublin to Tramore

Start at Dublin's **Cultivate** (p22), Ireland's only sustainable living information centre, or the National Ecology Centre, **Sonairte** (p537), in Laytown. For some eco-R&R, stop by – or even stay at – the **Jampa Ling Buddhist Centre** (p562). Get tips on organic horticulture at the beautiful gardens of the **Rossinver Organic Centre** (p524) in north Leitrim. Up north, stay at **Anna's House B&B** (p612), Strangford Lough, County Down, or the **Omagh Independent Hostel** (p690), County Tyrone. Out west, bed down at **Ardtarmon House** (p460), in the shadow of Ben Bulben, County Sligo, and tuck into some eco-nosh at **Rua** (p448), down the road in Castlebar, before a visit to the New Agey **Brigit's Garden** (p415). Offshore on the Aran Islands, Inishmaan's **Tig Congaile** (p409) might be the only place in Ireland with freshly ground Guatemalan coffee and sea-vegetable soup on the same menu. To the south, in West Cork, organic local produce is almost a way of life. A great ecofriendly sleeping option is the **Shiplake Mountain Hostel** (p280), while the superb **Ballymaloe House's cookery school** (p258), home to Ireland's most famous chef, Darina Allen, is the best place to learn the basics of Irish cooking (see also p70). Moving east, see the ancient geological formations at the beaches of the **Copper Coast European GeoPark** (p211), in Annestown. Finally, stop by the cheap 'n' cheerful beach resort of Tramore, which has become a haven for New-Age Californians, one of whom runs **T-Bay** (p212), Ireland's biggest surf school and a nonprofit organisation promoting eco-awareness through surfing and guided walks.

Ireland's eco-credentials are only just being established, but here is a selection spread over 500km to prove that travelling sustainably can still bring you the best the country has to offer, from the surprisingly rich midlands through the rugged west to the scenic south.

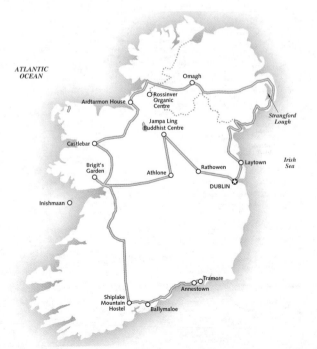

BEST OF THE ISLANDS   Three Weeks/Tory to West Cork

Ireland's outlying islands are many and varied, and offer the visitor an insight into a traditional lifestyle rarely seen in the Western world. Start at the barren and remote **Tory Island** (p480), off Bloody Foreland in Donegal, a Gaeltacht (Irish-speaking) area with a school of naive painters and a wonderful spot for birdwatching. Joined to the mainland by a bridge, **Achill Island** (p439), in County Mayo, features a deserted Famine village and dramatic cliffs; Ireland's largest offshore island, it is renowned for its water sports. **Inishturk** (p434), just south of Achill, has fewer than 100 inhabitants and gets very little tourist traffic, despite its sheltered sandy beaches. Off the coast of Galway, the three Aran Islands are probably Ireland's most visited. The largest, **Inishmór** (p404), has some fine archaeological remains, including the magical fort of Dún Aengus. The middle island, **Inishmaan** (p407), favourite of the writer JM Synge, is a pleasure to walk around, with its stone walls and tiny fields. The smallest and least visited, **Inisheer** (p409), best accessed from Doolin in County Clare, has some wonderful wild walks. Some other very special islands to visit are Europe's most westerly. Uninhabited since 1953, the **Blasket Islands** (p327), off the Kerry coast, offer the chance for spotting puffins, seals and porpoises. **Skellig Michael** (p305), off Caherciveen in Kerry, is a Unesco World Heritage site and home to a 7th-century monastery – it's a breathtaking, truly spiritual place and a highlight of any trip to Ireland. Ornithologists and orators alike will enjoy **Clear Island** (p272), off the western coast of Cork, famous for its Manx shearwaters and its lively Storytelling Festival in September.

If you're one to appreciate the cultural experience and simple pleasures of island life, you won't want to hurry along this trail. Take three weeks if you can spare it and experience the unique differences of Ireland's islands properly. Otherwise, try to get in at least a day trip to a few of them.

Tory Island

ATLANTIC OCEAN

Achill Island

Inishturk Island

Irish Sea

Inishmór
Inishmaan
Inisheer

Blasket Islands

Skellig Michael

Clear Island

TAILORED TRIPS

ADRENALINE ADVENTURES

If you like your Irish visits served with a shot of adrenaline, start nice and easy with some sail-powered beach buggying, better known as **blokarting** (p212), on the beach in Tramore, County Waterford. Alternatively, test your skills with some **quad biking** (p225) in Borris, County Carlow, before heading west to County Kerry, where you can engage in a spot of **horse riding** (p320) in Dingle. Pick the pace up and take flight with some white-knuckle **kitesurfing** (p323) in Castlegregory. Next, stay firmly on the water and learn the difference between goofy and regular with a **surf lesson** (p374) in Lahinch, County Clare – you'll need the lessons later on! Get back on dry land and cross the wilderness of Connemara by hiring a **mountain bike** in Clifden (p419) or Inishbofin (p420). Afterwards, head for Glassillaun Beach, County Galway, to go **scuba diving** (p422) in some of the country's clearest waters, full of colourful marine life brought north by the Gulf Stream. Down the road in Leenane, scramble down on foot to Killary Harbour to sail its sheltered waters in a **catamaran** (p421). Finally, try out your newly acquired skills and **surf** on world-class, near-perfect 3m tubes at Bundoran (p469), County Donegal.

IRELAND OF THE ANCIENTS

Begin at the stunning Neolithic tombs of **Newgrange** (p534) and **Knowth** (p535) in County Meath, in the heart of Brú na Bóinne (the Boyne Palace), where the legendary Irish hero Cúchulainn was conceived. Nearby, stand at the top of the celebrated **Hill of Tara** (p539), a site of immense folkloric significance and seat of the high kings of Ireland until the 11th century. Across the plain is the **Hill of Slane** (p537), where St Patrick lit a fire in 433 to proclaim Christianity throughout the land. Venture west to **Kells** (p545) on the road travelled by Queen Medbh herself in the Irish Stone Age epic, the Táin Bó Cúailnge, pausing to explore the monastic ruins and high crosses before continuing to County Roscommon. Just outside Tulsk village is **Cruachan Aí** (p516), the most important Celtic site in Europe, with 60 scattered megalithic tombs and burial sites. Head south to **Clonmacnoise Abbey** (p511), the 6th-century monastic site in County Offaly. Continue south through the heart of the country to the impressive monastic site that sits atop the craggy **Rock of Cashel** (p344) in County Tipperary. Turn east and head through County Kilkenny, stopping at the Cistercian **Jerpoint Abbey** (p237), at the pretty village of Thomastown. From here, travel northeast to Wicklow and magnificent **Glendalough** (p163), where the substantial remains of a monastic settlement linger by two lakes – it's as atmospheric a site as you'll ever find.

CHILDREN ON BOARD

Ireland has plenty to offer kids beyond the dubious pleasures of a visit to a museum under the promise, 'you'll appreciate this someday.' Get them **surfing** (p326) the waves in Dingle, County Kerry. Let them get up close and personal

with abandoned beasts of burden at a **donkey sanctuary** (p287) in County Cork. If you want to give them a history lesson, make it fun at the **Irish National Heritage Park** (p193), just outside of Wexford Town. Explore their inner Viking with a **Viking tour** (p525) in Athlone, County Westmeath, or explore the ruins and assorted wonderments at **Lough Key Forest Park** (p517) in Boyle, County Roscommon. In nearby County Mayo, watch the kids get harrrdy in the **Pirate Adventure Park** (p435) at Westport House. Cross the border and go back in time to the 18th and 19th centuries in the **Ulster American Folk Park** (p690), outside Omagh in County Tyrone. Then return to the 21st century – and beyond – at Belfast's fun-filled interactive science centre **W5** (p577).

THE IRISH PANTRY

There's some great eatin' in Ireland these days, with culinary surprises waiting to reveal themselves in the unlikeliest corners of the country. If you fancy a gourmet itinerary, start in Belfast with the award-winning French menu at **Shu** (p592). In neighbouring County Down, tuck into five types of oyster at the **Mourne Seafood Bar** (p619) in Dundrum, or at **Jeffers at the Marina** (p607) in the seaside resort of Bangor. Just across the border in County Louth, Carlingford's **Ghan House** (p556) is renowned for its exquisite classical cuisine, while dedicated foodies should make the pilgrimage to

Blacklion's **MacNean House & Restaurant** (p561) in County Cavan. Head to the southeast to sample the slow food delights at **Arlington Lodge** (p208) in Waterford City and the crafted fare at the **Tannery Restaurant & Cookery School** (p214) in seaside Dungarvan. Then, head into the spiritual home of the Irish gourmet movement and cross the border into County Cork. Halfway between Youghal and Cork, Midleton is home to the excellent **Farmgate Restaurant** (p257), surely one of Ireland's best. Further west, Kinsale is just full of top nosh, including the **Fishy Fishy Cafe** (p263), which is only open during the day. Finish up in the slightly shambolic looking but utterly mouth-watering **Out of the Blue** (p322) in Dingle, County Kerry.

History

WHO THE HELL ARE THE IRISH?

Our turbulent tale begins about 10,000 years ago, as the last ice caps melted and the rising sea level cut Ireland off from Britain. Hunters and gatherers may first have traversed the narrowing land bridge, but many more crossed the Irish Sea in small hide-covered boats. Farming did not reach Ireland until around 4000 BC. Bronze Age goldworking was of a very high quality in Ireland and stimulated trade with the rest of Europe.

In the 8th century BC, the island came to the attention of the fearsome Celts, who, having fought their way across Central Europe, began making steady forays onto these shores – the last of these tribes, commonly known as the Gaels (which in the local language came to mean 'foreigner'), came ashore in the 3rd century BC and proceeded to divide the island into five provinces – Leinster, Meath, Connaught, Ulster and Munster (Meath later merged with Leinster) – that were themselves subdivided into territories controlled by as many as 100 minor kings and chieftains, all of whom nominally paid allegiance to a high king who sat at Tara, in County Meath (p539). But their support was fraught and fluid, given when it suited and withdrawn just as quickly when it didn't.

Despite the constantly shifting political situation, the Celts set about creating the basics of what we now term 'Irish' culture: they devised a sophisticated code of law called the Brehon Law, which remained in use until the early 17th century; and their swirling, mazelike design style, evident on artefacts nearly 2000 years old, is considered the epitome of Irish design. Some excellent ancient Celtic designs survive in the Broighter hoard in the National Museum in Dublin (p106). The Turoe Stone in County Galway is another fine representative of Celtic artwork.

For a concise, 10-minute read on who the Celts were see www.ibiblio. org/gaelic/celts.html.

GETTING INTO THE HABIT

Arguably the most significant import into Ireland came between the 3rd and 5th centuries AD, when Christian missionaries first brought the new religion of Rome. Everyone has heard of St Patrick (see the boxed text, p34), but he was merely the most famous of many, who converted the local pagan tribes, with their strong tradition of druidism, by cleverly fusing traditional pagan rituals with the new Christian teaching, which created an exciting hybrid known as Celtic (Insular) Christianity – the presence on some early Christian churches of such decorative elements as the sheila-na-gig, a lewd female fertility symbol, is but one example.

Irish Christian scholars excelled in the study of Latin and Greek philosophy and Christian theology in the monasteries that flourished at, among other

TIMELINE

10,000–8000 BC	4500 BC	700–300 BC
After the last ice age ends, humans arrive in Ireland during the mesolithic era, originally crossing a land bridge between Scotland and Ireland. Few archaeological traces remain of this group.	The first Neolithic farmers arrive in Ireland by boat from as far afield as the Iberian peninsula, bringing cattle, sheep, and crops, marking the beginnings of a settled agricultural economy.	Iron technology gradually replaces bronze. The Celtic culture and language arrives, ushering in 1000 years of cultural and political dominance and leaving a legacy still visible today.

ST PATRICK

Ireland's patron saint is remembered all around the world on 17 March, when people of all ethnicities drink Guinness and wear green clothing. But behind the hoopla was a real man with a serious mission. For it was Patrick (AD 389–461) who introduced Christianity to Ireland.

The plain truth of it is that he wasn't Irish. This symbol of Irish pride hailed from what is now Wales, which at the time of his birth was under Roman occupation.

Patrick's arrival in Ireland was made possible by Irish raiders who kidnapped him when he was 16, and took him across the channel to work as a slave. He found religion, escaped from captivity and returned to Britain. But he vowed to make it his life's work to make Christians out of the Irish. He was ordained, then appointed Bishop of Ireland. Back he went over the channel.

He based himself in Armagh, where St Patrick's Church of Ireland Cathedral (see p627) stands on the site of his old church. Patrick quickly converted peasants and noblemen in great numbers. Within 30 years, much of Ireland had been baptised and the country was divided up into Catholic dioceses and parishes. He also established monasteries throughout Ireland, which would be the foundations of Irish scholarship for many centuries.

So next St Paddy's Day, as you're swilling Guinness and champing down corned beef and cabbage, think of who the man really was.

places, Clonmacnoise in County Offaly, Glendalough in County Wicklow (see p163) and Lismore in County Waterford. It was the golden age, and the arts of manuscript illumination, metalworking and sculpture flourished, producing such treasures as the *Book of Kells*, ornate jewellery, and the many carved stone crosses that dot the island 'of saints and scholars'.

The nature of Christianity in Ireland was one of marked independence from Rome, especially in the areas of monastic rule and penitential practice, which emphasised private confession to a priest followed by penances levied by the priest in reparation – which is the spirit and letter of the practice of confession that exists to this day. The Irish were also exporting these teachings abroad, setting up monasteries across Europe such as the ones in Luxeuil in France and Bobbio in Italy, both founded by St Columbanus (AD 543–615).

RAPE, PILLAGE & PLUNDER: A VIKING'S DAY OUT

The Celts' lack of political unity made the island easy pickings for the next wave of invaders, Danish Vikings, who first landed their slim, powerful boats at Lambay Island off Dublin in AD 795. They made surprise attacks along the eastern coast and strategic advances up rivers to inland terrain, where they set up bases and began plundering the prosperous monasteries. In self-defence, the monks built round towers, which served as lookout posts and places of refuge during attacks. Surviving examples of these towers can be seen at monastic sites such as Glendalough (see p163). The

300 BC–AD 800	AD 431–2	550–800
Ireland is divided into five provinces, known in Irish as *cúigi* (literally, 'fifth part'): Leinster, Meath, Connaught, Ulster and Munster. Meath later merges with Leinster.	According to medieval chronicles, Pope Celestine I sends Bishop Palladius to Ireland to minister to those 'already believing in Christ'; St Patrick arrives the following year to continue the mission.	The flowering of early monasticism in Ireland. The great monastic teachers begin exporting their knowledge across Europe, ushering in Ireland's 'Golden Age'.

monks' best efforts notwithstanding, inferior Irish weapons and lack of a unified defence – made all the worse when local tribes often sided with the invaders for personal profit – allowed the Norsemen to pretty much have their way with Ireland. Over the course of the 9th and 10th centuries, they established a small Viking kingdom called Dubh Linn (Black Pool), which would later become the city of Dublin, and they founded the towns of Wicklow, Waterford and Wexford.

The biggest challenge to Viking rule in Ireland came in 1014, when Brian Ború, king of Munster, defeated the Vikings (and their Irish allies, led by the king of Leinster, Máelmorda mac Murchada) at Clontarf. Both Ború and mac Murchada lost their lives but, like the Celts before them, the Vikings eventually settled, giving up the rape-rob-and-run policy in favour of integration and assimilation: by intermarrying with the Celtic tribes, they introduced red hair and freckles to the Irish gene pool.

THE ENGLISH ARE COMING!

The '800 years' of English rule in Ireland nominally began in 1169, when an army of English barons (actually Cambro-Norman, being a mix of Welsh and Norman nobles) landed in Wexford and quickly captured the two Hiberno-Viking ports of Wexford and Waterford. But their presence was less of an invasion and more of an invitation, which was the result of a tactical alliance between the barons – led by Richard Fitz Gilbert de Clare, Earl of Pembroke (1130–76; aka Strongbow) – and Dermot MacMurrough (d 1171; Diarmait mac Murchada), the king of Leinster (yes, only this one was, ironically, a direct descendant of Brian Ború), who had been ousted from his throne by an alliance of Irish chieftains spurred on by the high king himself, Turlough O'Connor (1088–1156; Tairrdelbach mac Ruaidri Ua Conchobair). In return for help in defeating his enemies (and capturing the crown of the high king for himself) MacMurrough promised Strongbow the hand in marriage of his daughter Aoife as well as the kingdom of Leinster, and Strongbow duly obliged by capturing Dublin in 1171 and then marrying Aoife the very next day. MacMurrough's plans went awry, though, and he was hardly to guess on his deathbed later that year that he'd determined the course of the next 800 years and cemented his place at the top of the list of great Irish traitors.

In truth, while MacMurrough may have provided the catalyst for the Norman invasion, Henry II had been plotting to get his hands on Ireland since 1155, when the English Pope Adrian IV issued him the Bull Laudabiliter, granting him the right to bring rebel Christian missionaries in Ireland to heel. Armed with the blessing of the pope and uneasy about Strongbow's growing power and independence of mind, Henry sent a huge naval force in 1171, landed at Waterford and declared it a royal city. He assumed a semblance of control, but the Norman lords continued to do pretty much as they pleased. Barons such as de Courcy and de Lacy set up independent power bases.

The Course of Irish History by TW Moody and FX Martin is a hefty volume by two Trinity College professors who trace much of Ireland's history back to its land and its proximity to England.

795–841	1014	1169
Vikings plunder Irish monasteries; their raping and pillaging urges sated, they establish settlements throughout the country, including Dublin, and soon turn it into a centre of economic power.	The Battle of Clontarf takes place on Good Friday (23 April) between the forces of the high king, Brian Ború, and the forces led by the king of Leinster, Máelmorda mac Murchada.	Henry II's Welsh and Norman barons land in Wexford and capture Waterford and Wexford with MacMurrough's help. Although no one knows it at the time, this is the beginning of an 800-year occupation by Britain.

Over the next 300 years, the Anglo-Norman nobles and their hirelings were successfully assimilated into Irish society, provoking the oft-quoted phrase *Hiberniores Hibernis ipsis* (more Irish than the Irish themselves) to describe them, and they built magnificent cities like Kilkenny, which still retains much of its medieval character. And it was in Kilkenny in 1366 that the English sought to halt the absorption of the Anglo-Normans into Irish ways by enacting the infamous statutes that outlawed intermarriage and the Irish language and other customs. It was too late: the Anglo-Normans' power bases were too entrenched and, by the turn of the 16th century, the Crown's direct rule didn't extend any further than a cordon surrounding Dublin known as the Pale.

The expression 'beyond the Pale' came into use when the Pale was the English-controlled part of Ireland. To the British elite, the rest of Ireland was considered uncivilised.

DIVORCE, DISSOLUTION & DESTRUCTION

It all began with Henry VIII's inability to get the pope's blessing for his divorce. By going it alone and breaking with the Catholic Church, he pitted all of Catholic Europe against him, including the Anglo-Irish, who were a little iffy about Henry's course of action.

In 1534 the 10th Earl of Kildare, 'Silken' Thomas Fitzgerald, led an attack on the English garrison in Dublin on the false pretext that his father had been executed by Henry in England. Worried that an Irish rebellion could be of help to Spain and France, Henry retaliated with even greater aggression. The rebellion was squashed and Thomas and his followers were subsequently executed. Within seven years, Henry had confiscated the lands of the most rebellious lords, eliminated the power of the Irish church and had himself declared King of Ireland.

Elizabeth I further consolidated English power in Ireland, establishing jurisdiction in Connaught and Munster, despite rebellions by the local ruling families. Ulster remained the last outpost of the Irish chiefs. Hugh O'Neill, Earl of Tyrone, led the last serious assault on English power in Ireland for centuries. O'Neill – who supposedly ordered lead from England to re-roof his castle, but instead used it for bullets – instigated open conflict with the English, and so began the Nine Years' War (1594–1603). He proved a courageous and crafty foe, and the English forces met with little success against him in the first seven years of fighting.

The Battle of Kinsale, in 1601, spelled the end for O'Neill and for Ulster. Although O'Neill survived the battle, his power was broken and he surrendered to the English Crown. In 1607 O'Neill and 90 other Ulster chiefs sailed to Europe, leaving Ireland forever. This was known as the Flight of the Earls, and it left Ulster open to English rule.

For articles exploring the Irish struggle, check out http://larkspirit.com.

With the native chiefs gone, Elizabeth and her successor, James I, could pursue their policy of Plantation with impunity and, while confiscations took place all over the country, Ulster was most affected because of its wealthy farmlands and as punishment for being home to the primary fomenters

1172	1350–1530	1366
King Henry II invades Ireland, using the 1155 Bull Laudabiliter issued to him by Pope Adrian IV to claim sovereignty, forcing the Cambro-Norman warlords and some of the Gaelic Irish kings to accept him as their overlord.	The Anglo-Norman barons establish power bases independent of the English Crown. Over the following two centuries, English control gradually recedes to an area around Dublin known as 'the Pale'.	The English Crown enacts the Statutes of Kilkenny, outlawing intermarriage, the Irish language and other Irish customs to stop the Anglo-Normans from assimilating too much with the Irish. It doesn't work.

of rebellion. It is here that Ulster's often tragic fate was first begun. The Plantations also marked the final collapse of the Gaelic social and political superstructure and the total conquest of Ireland by the English.

BLOODY RELIGION

At the outset of the English Civil War in 1641, the native Irish and Anglo-Norman Catholics, allied under the Confederation of Kilkenny, plumped for Charles I against the Protestant parliamentarians in the hope that it would lead to the restoration of Catholic power in Ireland. It was a major misjudgement, especially when English royalists regrouped in Ireland following their defeat and Charles' execution in 1649. Faced by a major threat to their newly established authority, the parliamentarians, led by Oliver Cromwell, launched a massive invasion in August 1649.

Cromwell's legendary hostility to the Irish was both political and religious, and his passionate opposition to the Catholic Church and the primacy of the pope determined that his campaign would be especially harsh: his armies besieged towns with little regard for the citizenry and, in the cases of Drogheda and Wexford, were guilty of wholesale massacre. Brutal and unsparing, Cromwell's nine-month campaign was nonetheless effective, even if it took three more years of fighting before Ireland was fully subdued. The Irish paid a heavy toll for their resistance: two million hectares of land were confiscated – more than 25% of the country – and handed over to Protestants loyal to Parliament, and many of the former owners sent into exile.

In 1689, in another attempt to resist the English in the spirit of the Confederation of Kilkenny, Irish Catholic monarchists rallied behind James II after his deposition in the Glorious Revolution and his replacement as king by the Dutch Protestant William of Orange (William III), husband to James' own (also Protestant) daughter Mary! James landed in Kinsale and set about raising an army to regain his throne, attracting local support with his promise to return expropriated lands to Catholic landowners. To this end, his army besieged the walled town of Derry (Londonderry) for 105 days, leading to widespread starvation for the trapped Protestant citizenry inside. The Loyalist slogan 'No Surrender!', which acquired mythical status among Irish Protestants over the following centuries, dates from the siege.

The end for James came at the banks of the River Boyne in County Louth on 12 July 1690, when his forces were roundly defeated by William's 36,000-strong army. James' ignominious defeat (he fled the battlefield and is to this day remembered by the Irish as Seamus a Chaca, meaning 'James the Shit') was a turning point for Irish Catholics: five years later the introduction of oppressive Penal Laws, known collectively as the 'popery code', prohibited Catholics from owning land or entering any higher profession. Irish culture, music and education were banned in the hope that Catholicism would be eradicated. Most Catholics continued to worship at secret locations, but some

Cromwell: An Honourable Enemy by Tom Reilly advances the unpopular view that perhaps the destruction of Cromwell's campaign is grossly exaggerated. You're no doubt familiar with the common view; here's the contrary position. (Yes, Reilly is Irish.)

A History of Ulster by Jonathan Bardon is a serious and far-reaching attempt to come to grips with Northern Ireland's saga.

1534–41	**1585**	**1594**
Henry VIII declares war on the property of the Irish church, as part of his break with the Catholic Church. In 1541 he arranges for the Irish Parliament to declare him King of Ireland.	Potatoes from South America are introduced to Ireland, where they eventually become a staple on nearly every table in the country.	Hugh O'Neill, Earl of Tyrone, orders lead from England to re-roof his castle, but instead uses it for bullets – instigating open conflict with the English in what would eventually be termed the Nine Years' War.

MAKING SENSE OF THE 12TH

The key day in the Northern Loyalist calendar, 12 July, marks the anniversary of William's comprehensive defeat of the Jacobite forces of James II at the Battle of the Boyne. Not quite. According to the Julian calendar, the Battle of the Boyne took place on 1 July 1690; just over a year later, on 12 July 1691 the remaining Jacobite forces were crushed and 7000 were killed at the Battle of Aughrim in County Galway in what is still the bloodiest day in Irish history. For decades thereafter, Irish Protestants marked the 12th as the anniversary of Aughrim, not the Boyne. When the adoption of the Gregorian calendar in 1752 shifted the Battle of the Boyne to the 12th, Protestants, suspicious of anything to do with Rome, refused to alter what they were celebrating and so continued to mark the anniversary of Aughrim. The shift eventually occurred following the foundation of the Orange Order in 1795 and, while it remains unclear why exactly the Boyne was given precedence over Aughrim, it has remained so to this day.

prosperous Irish converted to Protestantism to preserve their careers and wealth. Land was steadily transferred to Protestant owners, and a significant majority of the Catholic population became tenants living in wretched conditions. By the late 18th century, Catholics owned barely 5% of the land.

IF AT FIRST YOU DON'T SUCCEED...

With Roman Catholics rendered utterly powerless, the seeds of rebellion against autocracy were planted by a handful of liberal Protestants, inspired by the ideologies of the Enlightenment and the unrest provoked by the American War of Independence and then the French Revolution.

The first of these liberal leaders was a young Dublin Protestant, Theobald Wolfe Tone (1763–98), who was the most prominent leader of a Belfast organisation called the United Irishmen. They had high ideals of bringing together men of all creeds to reform and reduce Britain's power in Ireland, but their attempts to gain power through straightforward politics proved fruitless, and they went underground, committed to bringing change by any means. Wolfe Tone looked to France for help, and Loyalist Protestants prepared for possible conflict by forming the Protestant Orange Society, which later became known as the Orange Order. The tragic failure of the French to land an army of succour in 1796 left the organisation exposed to retribution and the men met their bloody end in the Battle of Vinegar Hill in 1798.

The Great Hunger by Cecil Woodham-Smith is the classic study of the Great Famine of 1845–51.

The Act of Union, passed in 1801, was the British government's vain attempt to put an end to any aspirations towards Irish independence, but the nationalist genie was well out of the bottle and two distinct forms of nationalist expression began to develop. The first was a breed of radical republicanism, which advocated use of force to found a secular, egalitarian Irish republic; the second was a more moderate movement, which advocated nonviolent and legal action to force the government into granting concessions.

1601	1607	1641
The Battle of Kinsale is fought between Elizabeth's armies and the combined rebel forces led by Hugh O'Neill. O'Neill surrenders and the back of the Irish rebellion against the Crown is broken.	O'Neill and 90 other Ulster chiefs sail to Europe, leaving Ireland forever. Known as the Flight of the Earls, it leaves Ulster open to English rule and the policy of Plantation.	During the English Civil War, the native Irish and Anglo-Norman Catholics support Charles I against the Protestant parliamentarians in the hope of restoring Catholic power in Ireland.

The most important moderate was a Kerry-born Catholic called Daniel O'Connell (1775–1847). In 1823 O'Connell founded the Catholic Association with the aim of achieving political equality for Catholics. The association soon became a vehicle for peaceful mass protest and action: in the 1826 general election it supported Protestant candidates who favoured Catholic emancipation. Two years later, O'Connell himself went one better and successfully stood for a seat in County Clare. Being a Catholic, he couldn't actually take his seat, so the British government was in a quandary. To staunch the possibility of an uprising, the government passed the 1829 Act of Catholic Emancipation, allowing some well-off Catholics voting rights and the right to be elected as MPs.

O'Connell continued to pursue his reform campaign, turning his attention toward the repeal of the Act of Union. His main weapon was the monster rally, which attracted hundreds of thousands of people eager to hear the 'Liberator' (as he was now known) speak. But O'Connell was unwilling to go outside the law, and when the government ordered the cancellation of one of his rallies at Clontarf, he meekly stood down and thereby gave up his most potent weapon of resistance.

For the Cause of Liberty: A Thousand Years of Ireland's Heroes by Terry Golway vividly describes the struggles of Irish nationalism.

THE GREAT FAMINE

As a result of the Great Famine of 1845–51, a staggering three million people died or were forced to emigrate from Ireland. This great tragedy is all the more inconceivable given that the scale of suffering was attributable to selfishness as much as to natural causes. Potatoes were the staple food of a rapidly growing, desperately poor population and, when a blight hit the crops, prices soared. The repressive Penal Laws ensured that farmers, already crippled with high rents, could ill afford the few subsistence potatoes provided. Inevitably, most tenants fell into arrears with little or no concession given by the mostly indifferent landlords and were evicted or sent to the dire conditions of the workhouses.

Shamefully, during this time there were abundant harvests of wheat and dairy produce – the country was producing more than enough grain to feed the entire population and it's said that more cattle were sold abroad than there were people on the island. But while millions of its citizens were starving, Ireland was forced to export its food to Britain and overseas.

The Poor Laws, in place at the height of the Famine, deemed landlords responsible for the maintenance of their poor and encouraged many to 'remove' tenants from their estates by paying their way to America. Many Irish were sent unwittingly to their deaths on board the notoriously scourged 'coffin ships'. British prime minister Sir Robert Peel made well-intentioned but inadequate gestures at famine relief, and some – but far too few – landlords did their best for their tenants.

Mass emigration continued to reduce the population during the next 100 years and huge numbers of Irish emigrants who found their way abroad, particularly to the USA, carried with them a lasting bitterness.

1649–53	**1688–90**	**1695**
Cromwell lays waste throughout Ireland after the Irish support Charles I in the English Civil Wars; this includes the mass slaughtering of Catholic Irish and the confiscation of two million hectares of land.	Following the deposition of King James II, James' Catholic army fights William's Protestant forces, resulting in William's victory at the Battle of the Boyne, 12 July 1690.	The Penal Laws (aka the 'popery code') prohibit Catholics from owning a horse, marrying outside their religion, building churches out of anything but wood, and from buying or inheriting property.

AMERICAN CONNECTIONS

Today more than 40 million Americans have Irish ancestry – a legacy of successive waves of emigration, spurred by events from the Potato Famine of the 1840s to the Depression of the 1930s. Many of the legendary figures of American history, from Davy Crockett to John Steinbeck, and 16 out of the 42 US presidents to date are of Irish descent.

Here's a list of places covered in this guide that have links to past US presidents or deal with the experience of Irish emigrants to the USA:

- Andrew Jackson Centre (p666), County Antrim
- Arthur Cottage (p668), County Antrim
- Dunbrody Heritage Ship (p200), County Wexford
- Grant Ancestral Homestead (p694), County Tyrone
- Kennedy Homestead (p201), County Wexford
- Queenstown Story Heritage Centre (p255), County Cork
- Ulster American Folk Park (p690), County Tyrone

O'Connell's failure to defy the British was seen as a terrible capitulation as the country was in the midst of the Potato Famine (see the boxed text, p39), and the lack of urgency on the part of the authorities in dealing with the crisis served to bolster the ambitions of the more radical wing of the Nationalist movement, led in the 1840s by the Young Irelanders, who attempted a failed rebellion in 1848, and later by the Fenians, architects of yet another uprising in 1867.

The Irish may have been bitterly angry at the treatment meted out by the British, but they weren't quite ready to take up arms en masse against them. Instead, the Nationalist cause found itself driven by arguably the most important feature of the Irish struggle against foreign rule: land ownership. Championed by the extraordinary Charles Stewart Parnell (1846–91), the Land League initiated widespread agitation for reduced rents and improved working conditions. The conflict heated up and there was violence on both sides. Parnell instigated the strategy of 'boycotting' (named after one particularly unpleasant agent called Charles Boycott) tenants, agents and landlords who didn't adhere to the Land League's aims: these people were treated like lepers by the local population. The Land War, as it became known, lasted from 1879 to 1882 and was momentous. For the first time, tenants were defying their landlords en masse. The Land Act of 1881 improved life immeasurably for tenants, creating fair rents and the possibility of tenants owning their land.

The other element of his two-pronged assault on the British was at Westminster where, as leader of the Irish Parliamentary Party (IPP) he led the

In 1870, after the Great Famine and ongoing emigration, more than a third of all native-born Irish lived outside Ireland.

1795	1798	1801
Concerned at the attempts of the Society of United Irishmen to secure equal rights for non-Establishment Protestants and Catholics, a group of Protestants create the Orange Institution.	The flogging and killing of potential rebels sparks a rising led by the United Irishmen and their leader, Wolfe Tone. Wolfe Tone is captured and taken to Dublin, where he commits suicide.	The Act of Union unites Ireland politically with Britain. The Irish Parliament votes itself out of existence following a campaign of bribery. Around 100 Members of Parliament move to the House of Commons in London.

fight for Home Rule, a limited form of autonomy for Ireland. Parliamentary mathematics meant that the Liberal Party, led by William Gladstone, was reliant on the members of the IPP to maintain a majority over the Conservatives and Parnell pressed home his advantage by forcing Gladstone to introduce a series of Home Rule bills – in 1886 and 1892 – which passed the Commons but were defeated in the House of Lords. Parnell's ascendency, however, came to a sudden end in 1890 when he was embroiled in a divorce scandal – not acceptable to puritanical Irish society. The 'uncrowned king of Ireland' was no longer welcome. Parnell's health deteriorated rapidly and he died less than a year later.

IRELAND GETS ITS OWN SET OF KEYS

As the 20th century dawned, Ireland was overwhelmingly committed to achieving Home Rule. A new Liberal government under Prime Minister Asquith had removed the House of Lords' power to veto bills and began to put another Home Rule for Ireland bill through Parliament. The bill was passed (but not enacted) in 1912 against strident Unionist opposition, epitomised by the mass rallies organised by the recently founded Protestant vigilante group, the Ulster Volunteer Force (UVF).

The outbreak of WWI in July 1914 merely delayed Irish ambitions as a majority of the Irish Volunteers – founded by academic Eoin MacNeill as a Nationalist answer to the UVF – heeded the call to arms and enlisted in the British army. It was felt that just as England had promised Home Rule to Ireland, so the Irish owed it to England to help her in her hour of need: the Home Rule Act was suspended and for a time the question of Ulster was left unresolved.

A few, however, did not heed the call. Two small groups – a section of the Irish Volunteers under Pádraig Pearse and the Irish Citizens' Army led by James Connolly – conspired in a rebellion that took the country by surprise. A depleted Volunteer group marched into Dublin on Easter Monday 1916, and took over a number of key positions in the city, claiming the General Post Office on O'Connell St as its headquarters. From its steps, Pearse read out to passers-by a declaration that Ireland was now a republic and that his band was the provisional government. Less than a week of fighting ensued before the rebels surrendered to the superior British forces. The rebels weren't popular and had to be protected from angry Dubliners as they were marched to jail.

The Easter Rising would probably have had little impact on the Irish situation had the British not made martyrs of the rebel leaders. Of the 77 given death sentences, 15 were executed, including the injured Connolly, who was shot while strapped to a chair. This brought about a sea change in public attitudes, and support for the Republicans rose dramatically.

By the end of WWI, Home Rule was far too little, far too late. In the 1918 general election, the Republicans stood under the banner of Sinn Féin and won a large majority of the Irish seats. Ignoring London's Parliament,

The Irish in America by Michael Coffey takes up the history of the Famine where many histories leave off: the turbulent experiences of Irish immigrants in the USA.

1828–29	1845–51	1879–82
Daniel O'Connell exploits a loophole in the law to win a seat in Parliament but is unable to take it because he is Catholic. The prime minister passes the Catholic Emancipation Act giving limited rights to Catholics.	A mould ravages the potato harvest. The British government adopts a laissez-faire attitude, resulting in the deaths of between 500,000 and one million, and the emigration of up to two million others.	The Land War, led by the Land League, sees tenant farmers defying their landlords en masse to force the passing of the Land Act in 1881, which allows for fair rent, fixity of tenure and free sale.

where technically they were supposed to sit, the newly elected Sinn Féin deputies – many of them veterans of the 1916 Easter Rising – declared Ireland independent and formed the first Dáil Éireann (Irish assembly or lower house), which sat in Dublin's Mansion House under the leadership of Éamon de Valera (1882–1975). The Irish Volunteers became the Irish Republican Army (IRA) and the Dáil authorised it to wage war on British troops in Ireland.

A KIND OF FREEDOM

The War of Independence lasted 2½ years and resulted in around 1200 casualties, not considered a large number in the context of the times. Nevertheless, it was a particularly nasty affair, as the IRA fought a guerrilla-style campaign against the British, their numbers swelled by returning veterans of WWI known as 'Black and Tans' (on account of their uniforms, a mix of khaki and black), whose experiences in the trenches had traumatised them to the point that they were prone to all kinds of brutality. The IRA campaign was masterminded by the charismatic and ruthless Michael Collins (1890–1922), whose use of 'flying columns' to ambush British forces eventually led to the truce of July 1921.

To gain some insight into the mind of Michael Collins, read *In His Own Words*, a collection of Collins' writings and speeches.

After months of difficult negotiations in London, the Irish delegation signed the Anglo-Irish Treaty on 6 December 1921. It gave 26 counties of Ireland – now known as the Irish Free State – limited independence and allowed six largely Protestant Ulster counties the choice of opting out. If they did (a foregone conclusion), a Boundary Commission would decide on the final frontiers between north and south. But the thorny issue of partition, coupled with the status of the newly established state – still headed by the British monarch, with Irish MPs still having to swear an oath of allegiance to the Crown – was, at best, a bad compromise. Even the signatories of the Treaty knew it: as he was affixing his signature, Collins commented that he was signing his own death warrant.

Yet Collins wasn't entirely naive. He regarded the issue of the monarchy and the oath of allegiance as largely symbolic and hoped that the six northeastern counties wouldn't be a viable entity and would eventually become part of the Free State. During the Treaty negotiations he was convinced that the Border Commission would decrease the size of the part of Ireland remaining outside the Free State. Alas, a series of inflammatory press leaks meant that the eventual findings of the commission in 1925 – basically redividing the frontier so as to include more Nationalists in the Free State – were never instituted and to this day Northern Ireland's borders are as they were in 1921, when the Northern Ireland Parliament first sat with James Craig as the first prime minister. From the start, Northern Ireland was an entity divided along strictly religious grounds, with Catholic Nationalists taking up seats in the new Parliament with great reluctance.

1916	1919–21	1921
The Easter Rising: a group of Republicans take Dublin's General Post Office and announce the formation of an Irish Republic. After less than a week of fighting, the rebels surrender to the superior British forces.	Irish War of Independence, aka the Black and Tan War on account of British irregulars wearing mixed police (black) and army (khaki) uniforms, begins in January 1919.	Two years and 1200 casualties later, the war ends in a truce on 11 July 1921 that leads to peace talks. After negotiations in London, the Irish delegation signs the Anglo-Irish Treaty on 6 December.

The situation was hardly better in the Irish Dáil. The Anglo-Irish Treaty was eventually ratified after a bitter debate and the elections of June 1922 resulted in victory for the pro-Treaty forces. But the anti-Treaty forces, united behind de Valera's leadership, refused to recognise the new state and, within two weeks of the elections, the first clashes between the two sides occurred.

Almost immediately, a bitter civil war broke out between comrades who, a year previously, had fought alongside each other. The most prominent casualty was Collins himself, who was shot in an ambush in his native County Cork. De Valera was briefly imprisoned by the new Free State government, formed by the new Cumann na Gael (Society of Gaels) party under Prime Minister William Cosgrave, which went so far as to execute 77 of its former comrades. By the time the conflict ground to an exhausted halt in 1923, a legacy of bitter division had been created that would last until the end of the century.

Defeated but unbowed, de Valera boycotted the Dáil before regrouping and founding a new party in 1926 called Fianna Fáil (Warriors of Ireland), which proceeded to win nearly half the seats in the 1927 election.

Fianna Fáil went one better in 1932, winning a majority and remaining in power for the next 16 years. A new constitution in 1937 did away with the oath of allegiance to the Crown, reaffirmed the special position of the Catholic Church within Irish society and once again laid claim to the six counties of the north. De Valera's decision to stop paying land annuities to the British, as per the terms of the Anglo-Irish agreement, provoked a trade war with Britain that may have done much to assert Ireland's growing spirit of independence but severely crippled Irish agricultural exports for more than a decade.

Fianna Fáil lost the 1948 general election to Fine Gael (as Cumann na Gael were now known), who proceeded to gazump the Republican credentials of their political rivals by leaving the British Commonwealth and officially declaring the Free State a republic. After 800 years, Ireland – or at least a big chunk of it – was finally independent.

GROWING PAINS & ROARING TIGERS

Unquestionably the most significant figure since independence, Éamon de Valera's contribution to an independent Ireland was immense but, as the 1950s stretched into the 1960s, his vision for the country was mired in a conservative and traditional orthodoxy that was patently at odds with the reality of a country in desperate economic straits, where chronic unemployment and emigration were but the more visible effects of inadequate policy. De Valera's successor as Taoiseach was Sean Lemass, whose tenure began in 1959 with the dictum 'a rising tide lifts all boats'. By the mid-1960s his economic policies had halved emigration and ushered in a new prosperity that was to be mirrored 30 years later by the Celtic Tiger.

Neil Jordan's motion picture *Michael Collins*, starring Liam Neeson as the revolutionary, depicts the Easter Rising, the founding of the Free State and Collins' violent demise.

A History of Ireland by Mike Cronin summarises all of Ireland's history in less than 300 pages. It's an easy read, but doesn't offer much in the way of analysis.

1921–22	1922–23	1932
The treaty gives 26 counties of Ireland independence and allows six largely Protestant Ulster counties the choice of opting out. The Irish Free State is founded in 1922.	Unwilling to accept the terms of the treaty, forces led by Éamon de Valera take up arms against their former comrades, led by Michael Collins. A brief but bloody civil war ensues, resulting in the death of Collins.	After 10 years in the political wilderness, de Valera leads his Fianna Fáil party into government and goes about weakening the ties between the Free State and Britain.

In 1972 the Republic (along with Northern Ireland) became a member of the European Economic Community (EEC), which brought an increased measure of prosperity thanks to the benefits of the Common Agricultural Policy, which set fixed prices and guaranteed quotas for Irish farming produce. Nevertheless, the broader global depression, provoked by the oil crisis of 1973, forced the country into yet another slump and emigration figures rose again, reaching a peak in the mid-1980s.

Nevertheless, European aid was to prove instrumental in kick-starting the Irish economy in the early 1990s. Huge sums of money were invested in education and physical infrastructure, while the renewal of Lemass' industrial policy of incentivising foreign investment through tax breaks and the provision of subsidies made Ireland very attractive to high-tech businesses looking for a door into EU markets. In less than a decade, Ireland went from being one of the poorest countries in Europe to one of the wealthiest: unemployment fell from 18% to 3.5%, the average industrial wage somersaulted to the top of the European league and the dramatic rise in GDP meant that the government had far more money than it knew what do with. Ireland became synonymous with the Celtic Tiger, an economic model of success that was the envy of the entire world.

Coupled with Ireland's economic growth was a steady social shift away from the Catholic Church's overwhelmingly conservative influence, which was felt virtually everywhere, not least in the state's schools and hospitals and over every aspect of social policy. From the 1980s onwards, steady campaigning resulted in new laws protecting gay rights, access to contraception and a successful referendum on divorce. One major issue to remain unresolved, however, is the thorny question of abortion: in theory, abortion is legal if there is risk to the life of the woman, but the cloudy legal status does nothing for the thousands of women who still go to Britain every year for termination.

The dramatic decline in the influence of the Church over the last two decades is primarily the result of global trends and greater prosperity in Ireland, but the devastating revelations of clerical abuse of boys and girls in the care of the Church over the last half century have defined an almost vitriolic reaction against the Church, particularly among the younger generation. The Church's perceived reluctance to confront its own responsibilities in these shocking scandals – including reports of a number of senior members knowing about paedophiliac priests and consequently shuffling them from parish to parish – has heightened a sense of deep betrayal among many of the faithful.

Ireland Since the Famine by FSL Lyons is a standard text for all students of modern Irish history.

IT'S (NOT SO) GRIM UP NORTH

On 8 May 2007 the Northern Ireland Assembly, the devolved legislature of the province, finally met again for the first time since October 2002. The first minister, the Rev Ian Paisley, smiled, shook hands and posed for photos with the deputy first minister, Martin McGuinness.

1948	1969	1972
Fianna Fáil loses the 1948 general election to Fine Gael in coalition with the new Republican Clann an Poblachta. The new government declares the Free State to be a republic at last.	Marches by the Northern Ireland Civil Rights Association are disrupted by Loyalist attacks and police action, resulting in rioting. Culminating in the Battle of the Bogside, it is the beginning of the Troubles.	The Republic (and Northern Ireland) become members of the EEC. On Bloody Sunday, 13 civilians are killed by British troops; Westminster suspends the Stormont government and introduces direct rule.

This was no straightforward meeting. Even if you'd only kept a lazy eye on Irish affairs these last 30 years, you'd know that the sight of a Loyalist firebrand like Paisley – who has a history of deep-rooted, often vicious enmity towards Irish Nationalism and Republicanism – and an ex-IRA commander like McGuinness shaking hands was nothing short of highly improbable. Needless to say, this historic agreement was the culmination of a painstakingly long road of domination, fighting, negotiation, concession and political posturing that began…

Well, it began in the 16th century, with the first Plantations of Ireland by the English Crown, whereby the confiscated lands of the Gaelic and Hiberno-Norman gentry were awarded to English and Scottish settlers of good Protestant stock. The policy was most effective in Ulster, where the newly arrived Protestants were given an extra leg-up by the Penal Laws, which successfully reduced the now landless Catholic population to second-class citizens with little or no rights. Interestingly, from 1707 the Penal Laws also applied to Presbyterians (of which Paisley is one, albeit the founder of his own Free Presbyterian Church), who were considered not much better than Catholics.

But let us fast-forward to 1921, when the notion of independent Ireland moved from aspiration to actuality. On 22 June the Northern Ireland Parliament came into being, with James Craig as the first prime minister. His Ulster Unionist Party (UUP) was to rule the new state until 1972, with the minority Catholic population (roughly 40%) stripped of any real power or representative strength by a Parliament that favoured the Unionists through economic subsidy, bias in housing allocations and gerrymandering: Derry's electoral boundaries were redrawn so as to guarantee a Protestant council, even though the city was two-thirds Catholic. To keep everyone in line, the overwhelmingly Protestant Royal Ulster Constabulary (RUC) and their militia, the B-Specials, made no effort to mask their blatantly sectarian bias. To all intents and purposes, Northern Ireland was an apartheid state.

The first challenge to the Unionist hegemony came with the long-dormant IRA's border campaign in the 1950s, but it was quickly quashed and its leaders imprisoned. A decade later, however, the authorities met with a far more defiant foe, in the shape of the Civil Rights Movement, founded in 1967 and heavily influenced by its US counterpart as it sought to redress the blatant sectarianism in Derry. In October 1968 a mainly Catholic march in Derry was violently broken up by the RUC amid rumours that the IRA had provided 'security' for the marchers. Nobody knew it at the time, but the Troubles had begun.

In January 1969 another civil rights movement, called People's Democracy, organised a march from Belfast to Derry. As the marchers neared their destination, they were attacked by a Protestant mob. The police first stood to one side and then compounded the problem with a sweep through the

The events leading up to the Anglo-Irish War and their effect on ordinary people are movingly and powerfully related in JG Farrell's novel *Troubles*, first published in 1970.

Many films depict events related to the Troubles, including *Bloody Sunday* (2002), *The Boxer* (1997; starring Daniel Day-Lewis) and *In the Name of the Father* (1994; also starring Day-Lewis).

1973–74	1981	1993
The Sunningdale Agreement results in a new Northern Ireland Assembly. Unionists oppose the agreement and the Ulster Workers' Council calls a strike that paralyses the province and brings an end to the Assembly.	Ten Republican prisoners die from going on a hunger strike. The first to die, Bobby Sands, had three weeks earlier been elected to Parliament on an Anti–H-Block ticket. Over 100,000 people attend Sands' funeral.	Downing Street Declaration is signed by British prime minister John Major and Irish prime minister Albert Reynolds. It states that Britain has no 'selfish, strategic or economic interest in Northern Ireland'.

predominantly Catholic Bogside district. Further marches, protests and violence followed and, far from keeping the two sides apart, the police were clearly part of the problem. In August British troops went to Derry and then Belfast to maintain law and order. The British army was initially welcomed in some Catholic quarters, but soon it too came to be seen as a tool of the Protestant majority. Overreaction by the army actually fuelled recruitment into the long-dormant IRA. IRA numbers especially increased after Bloody Sunday (30 January 1972), when British troops killed 13 civilians in Derry.

Northern Ireland's Parliament was abolished in 1972, although substantial progress had been made towards civil rights. A new power-sharing arrangement, worked out in the 1973 Sunningdale Agreement, was killed stone dead by the massive and overwhelmingly Protestant Ulster Workers' Strike of 1974.

Brendan O'Brien's popular *Pocket History of the IRA* summarises a lot of complex history in a mere 150 pages, but it's a good introduction.

While continuing to target people in Northern Ireland, the IRA moved its campaign of bombing to mainland Britain. Its activities were increasingly condemned by citizens and parties on all sides of the political spectrum. Meanwhile, Loyalist paramilitaries began a sectarian murder campaign against Catholics. Passions reached fever pitch in 1981 when Republican prisoners in the North went on a hunger strike, demanding the right to be recognised as political prisoners. Ten of them fasted to death, the best known being an elected MP, Bobby Sands.

The waters were further muddied by an incredible variety of parties splintering into subgroups with different agendas. The IRA had split into 'official' and 'provisional' wings, from which sprang more extreme Republican organisations such as the Irish National Liberation Army (INLA). Myriad Protestant, Loyalist paramilitary organisations sprang up in opposition to the IRA, and violence was typically met with violence.

In the 1990s external circumstances started to alter the picture. Membership of the EU, economic progress in Ireland and the declining importance of the Catholic Church in the South started to reduce differences between the North and South. Also, American interest added an international dimension to the situation.

A series of negotiated statements between the Unionists, Nationalists and the British and Irish governments eventually resulted in the historic Good Friday Agreement of 1998. The new assembly, led by First Minister David Trimble of the UUP and Deputy First Minister Seamus Mallon of the nationalist Social Democratic and Liberal Party (SDLP), was beset by sectarian divisions from the outset, which resulted in no less than four suspensions, the last from October 2002 until May 2007.

During this period, the politics of Northern Ireland polarised dramatically, resulting in the falling away of the more moderate UUP and the emergence of the hardline Democratic Unionist Party (DUP), led by Ian Paisley; and, on the Nationalist side, the emergence of the IRA's political wing, Sinn Féin,

Mid-1990s	1994	1998
Low corporate tax, restraint in government spending, transfer payments from the EU and a low-cost labour market result in the 'Celtic Tiger' boom, transforming Ireland into one of Europe's wealthiest countries.	Sinn Féin leader Gerry Adams announces a 'cessation of violence' on behalf of the IRA on 31 August. In October the Combined Loyalist Military Command also announces a ceasefire.	On 10 April negotiations culminate in the Good Friday Agreement, under which the new Northern Ireland Assembly is given full legislative and executive authority.

as the main torch-bearer of Nationalist aspirations, under the leadership of Gerry Adams and Martin McGuinness.

The hardening of political opinion was almost inevitable. While both sides were eager to maintain an end to the violence, neither side wanted to be accused of having a soft underbelly, especially if both sides' aspirations could not, despite what was promised, be realised by purely political means. Consequently, the DUP and Sinn Féin dug their heels in, with the main sticking points being decommissioning of IRA weapons and the identity and composition of the new police force ushered in to replace the RUC. Paisley and the Unionists made increasingly difficult demands of the decommissioning bodies (photographic evidence, Unionist witnesses etc) as they blatantly refused to accept anything less than an open and complete surrender of the IRA, while Sinn Féin refused to join the police board that monitored the affairs of the Police Service of Northern Ireland (PSNI), effectively refusing to change their policy of total noncooperation with the security forces. In the background, now inactive members of the paramilitary groups on both sides were revealed to be involved in all kinds of murky dealings such as drug dealing and turf wars – the most spectacular moment of all came in December 2004 when a £26.5m bank robbery saw the finger of blame pointed directly at Republicans.

But Tony Blair and Bertie Ahern were not about to see their political legacy ruined by northern stubbornness. They continued to turn the screws on both sides, urging them to continue negotiating just as everyone else had begun to despair of ever seeing a resolution. In an effective bit of strong-arming, they set a deadline for resolution and made vague threats to both sides about the consequences of not meeting the deadline. But in a typically Irish bit of face-saving, the Unionists baulked at the deadline of 26 March 2007 and, in a deal agreed with Sinn Féin, announced that they would take their seats in the assembly on 8 May. It was a classic case of 'we'll do it, but we'll do it our way'.

1998	2005	2007
The 'Real IRA' detonates a bomb in Omagh, killing 29 people and injuring 200. It is the worst single atrocity in the history of the Troubles, but public outrage and swift action by politicians prevent a Loyalist backlash.	The IRA issues a statement ordering its units not to engage in 'any other activities' apart from assisting 'the development of purely political and democratic programmes through exclusively peaceful means'.	The Northern Ireland Assembly resumes after a five-year break when talks between Unionists and Republicans remain in stalemate. They resolve their primary issues.

The Culture

THE NATIONAL PSYCHE

Being Irish, he had an abiding sense of tragedy, which sustained him through temporary periods of joy.

William Butler Yeats

The Irish are justifiably renowned for their easygoing, affable nature. They're famous for being warm and friendly, which is just another way of saying that the Irish love a bit of a chat, whether it be with friends or strangers. They will entertain you with their humour, alarm you with their willingness to get stuck into a good debate and cut you down with their razor-sharp wit. Slagging – the Irish version of teasing – is an art form, which may seem caustic to unfamiliar ears, but is quickly revealed as an intrinsic element of how the Irish relate to one another. It is commonly assumed that the mettle of friendship is proven by how well you can take a joke rather than by the payment of a cheap compliment.

The Irish aren't big on talking themselves up, preferring their actions to speak for themselves. They also admire the peculiar art of self-deprecation, known locally as *an beál bocht a chur ort,* or 'putting on the poor mouth', the mildly pejorative practice of making out that things are far worse than they really are in order to evoke sympathy or the forbearance of creditors, of vital importance in the days when the majority of the Irish were at the mercy of an unforgiving landlord system. As a result, the Irish also have the trait of begrudgery – although it's something only recognised by them and generally kept within the wider family. It's kind of amusing, though, to note that someone like Bono is subject to more intense criticism in Ireland than anywhere else in the world.

> The most popular names in Ireland are Thomas and Sarah.

Beneath all of the garrulous sociability and self-deprecating twaddle lurks a dark secret, which is that at heart the Irish are low on self-esteem. They're therefore very suspicious of praise and tend not to believe anything nice that's ever said about them. The Irish wallow in false modesty like a sport.

This goes some way towards explaining the fractious relationship Ireland has with alcohol. The country regularly tops the list of the world's biggest binge drinkers, and while there is an increasing awareness of, and alarm at, the devastation caused by alcohol to Irish society (especially to young people), drinking remains the country's most popular social pastime, with no sign of letting up; spend a weekend night walking around any town in the country and you'll get a firsthand feel of the influence and effect of the booze.

Some experts put Ireland's binge-drinking antics down to the dramatic rise in the country's economic fortunes, but statistics have long revealed that Ireland has had an unhealthy fondness for 'taking the cure', although the acceptability of public drunkenness is a far more recent phenomenon: the older generation are never done reminding the youngsters that they would *never* have been seen staggering in public.

Whatever the truth of it, there is no denying that the last couple of decades have transformed Irish society in ways no one could have foreseen, with this generation of under-30s only now having to confront the realities of a previous age, when unemployment, emigration and a cap on ambition were basic facts of life – although it must be stressed that whatever the current state of the economy, the Irish have truly come to believe that they are deserving of a seat at anyone's table.

Prosperity has served the country well, and while a huge question mark still remains over the equitable distribution of the wealth accrued during the last decade, there is no doubt that the island has seen some dramatic shifts in traditional attitudes. Not so long ago, Roman Catholicism was a central pillar of everyday life in Ireland; today, the Church's grip on society has slackened to the point that a recent survey revealed that one-third of Irish youth didn't know where Jesus was born or what was celebrated at Easter.

LIFESTYLE

The Irish may like to grumble – about work, the weather, the government and those *feckin' eejits* on reality TV shows – but if pressed will tell you that they live in the best country on earth. There's loads *wrong* with the place, but isn't it the same way everywhere else?

Traditional Ireland – of the large family, closely linked to church and community – is quickly disappearing as the increased urbanisation of Ireland continues to break up the social fabric of community interdependence that was a necessary element of relative poverty. Contemporary Ireland is therefore not altogether different from any other European country, and you have to travel further to the margins of the country – the islands and the isolated rural communities – to find an older version of society.

Ireland has long been a pretty homogenous country, but the arrival of thousands of immigrants from all over the world – 10% of the population is foreign-born – has challenged the mores of racial tolerance and integration. To a large extent it has been successful, although if you scratch beneath the surface, racial tensions can be exposed. So long as the new arrivals take on the jobs that many Irish wouldn't bother doing anymore, everything is relatively hunky dory; it's when the second generation of immigrants begin competing for the middle-class jobs that Ireland's tolerance credentials will truly be tested.

POPULATION

The total population of Ireland is around 6 million: 4.3 million in the Republic and 1.7 million in Northern Ireland. There has been a steady increase in population since 1961, but the figures have a way to go before they

An Irish birthday tradition for kids is 'the bumps', where the celebrants are lifted by their limbs and swung up and down by a number corresponding to their age plus one.

The average number of children per family has fallen to 1.4, the lowest in Irish history.

GAY-FRIENDLY IRELAND

The best things that ever happened to gay Ireland were the taming of the dictating church and the enactment of protective legislation against any kind of sexual discrimination. According to Brian Merriman, the Artistic Director of the International Dublin Gay Theatre Festival, the collapse of church authority and the shocking revelations of priestly abuse, coupled with the liberalisation of the divorce law, helped Ireland come to terms with its own sexual and social honesty.

'Ireland is no longer talking about "them" when referring to anyone who is vaguely unconventional; they're talking about "us" and that every family has the potential to be different,' he says with great conviction. 'It's not just "them" who have the gay in the closet. They're everywhere!'

But it's not all good. There is a huge difference still between attitudes in urban and rural Ireland, he says, and while legislation and liberalisation have been very important, there is still a legacy of internalised homophobia.

'Our enemies are no longer as clearly visible, so it's hard to know sometimes who exactly thinks what.'

He believes, however, that gays and lesbians need to be more visible in Irish society, if only to continue the struggle for parity of esteem and respect. Merriman says that, 'The fight will not stop until the constitutional ban on gays getting married is lifted and there are no second-class citizens in 21st-century Ireland'.

reach their pre-Famine levels. Before the tragedy of 1845–51 the population was in excess of eight million. Death and emigration reduced the population to around five million, and emigration continued at a high level for the next 100 years.

Although the effects of emigration have been tempered by a slowdown in the rate and an increase in the rate of immigrant arrivals, Ireland still loses proportionally more of its native children to emigration than any other European country; in 2005 more than 20,500 left the country to seek their fortunes elsewhere.

Dublin is the largest city and the capital of the Republic, with about 1.2 million people (about 40% of the population) living within commuting distance of the city centre. The Republic's next largest cities are Cork, Galway and Limerick. Ireland's population is relatively young: almost half the population is under 44, 15% is under 24 and only 11% of the population is over 65.

In Northern Ireland, Belfast is the principal city, with a population of around 267,000. It has the youngest population in the UK, with 24% aged under 16. These figures (and population counts throughout the book) are based on the last census of 2006.

SPORT

Ireland, by and large, is a nation of sports enthusiasts. Whether it's shouting the team on from the sideline or from the bar stool, the Irish have always taken their sport seriously.

Gaelic Football & Hurling

Gaelic games are at the core of Irishness; they are enmeshed in the fabric of Irish life and hold a unique place in the heart of its culture. Their resurgence towards the end of the 19th century was entwined with the whole Gaelic revival and the march towards Irish independence. The beating heart of Gaelic sports is the Gaelic Athletic Association (GAA), set up in 1884 'for the preservation and cultivation of National pastimes'. The GAA is still responsible for fostering these amateur games and it warms our hearts to see that after all this time – and amid the onslaught of globalisation and the general commercialisation of sport – they are still far and away the most popular sports in Ireland.

Gaelic games are fast, furious and not for the faint-hearted. Challenges are fierce, and contact between players is extremely aggressive. Both Gaelic football and hurling are played by two teams of 15 players whose aim is to get the ball through what resembles a rugby goal: two long vertical posts joined by a horizontal bar, below which is a soccer-style goal, protected by a goalkeeper. Goals (below the crossbar) are worth three points, whereas a ball placed over the bar between the posts is worth one point. Scores are shown thus: 1-12, meaning one goal and 12 points, giving a total of 15 points.

Gaelic football is played with a round, soccer-size ball, and players are allowed to kick it or hand-pass it, like Aussie Rules. Hurling, which is considered by far the more beautiful game, is played with a flat stick or bat known as a hurley or *camán*. The small leather ball, called a *slíothar*, is hit or carried on the hurley; handpassing is also allowed. Both games are played over 70 action-filled minutes.

Both sports are county-based games. The dream of every club player is to represent his county, with the hope of perhaps playing in an All-Ireland final in September at Croke Park in Dublin, the climax of a knockout championship that is played first at a provincial and then interprovincial level.

Females outnumber males in Dublin by 20,000.

You can find out more about the history and rules of Gaelic sports on the Gaelic Athletic Association website at www.gaa.ie.

Star hurler Sean Og O'Hailpin was born in 1977 to an Irish father and Fijian mother on the tiny island of Rotuma, an isolated atoll about 400 miles north of Fiji.

ERIN GO BROKE

In early 2009 a joke was doing the rounds: 'Q. What's the difference between Ireland and Iceland? A. One letter and about six months.' The Irish fondness for gallows humour has never been so propitious, as Iceland's spectacular collapse in the face of the global financial crisis was a portend of what was to come: by the end of October 2008 the six main Irish banks had seen their share prices collapse and the government had to step in with a massive bailout. Although Ireland wasn't alone in its exposure to financial crisis, it was in deeper trouble than most because of its dangerous over-reliance on a property bubble that was about to run out of air.

Ireland's dirty economic secret was that ever since 2002 the Celtic Tiger – that indomitable feline that transformed the country into the poster-child for the boundless possibilities of untrammelled economic development and dynamic entrepreneurialism – had run out of steam. There was a marked slowdown in growth in all industrial sectors but one: the construction industry, which was growing at a dizzying rate, reaching its peak in 2006 when an astonishing 90,000 new homes were built (compared to 85,000 during the same period in the UK, which has nearly 14 times the population). Between 2000 and 2006, house prices tripled as employment in the construction sector increased from 8% to 13% of the total workforce – more than 40% above the European average – and investment in housing as a percentage of GNP rose from around 6% in 1996 to almost 15% in 2006. These were staggering numbers, everyone agreed, but they were also unsustainable, and it seemed *nobody* wanted to hear that.

And so the developers continued to build, borrowing vast amounts from banks whose coffers were swollen with cheap credit from major international financial institutions whose *own* coffers were swollen thanks to an out-of-control derivatives market. The Irish property market got its first major warning in 2007, when demand for residential housing finally began to recede in the face of high prices and over-saturation, but it wasn't until the end of 2008 – after Lehmann Brothers and the other giants of finance went to the wall – that the credit lines shrivelled up and the banks' massive exposure to the developers threw the whole economy into turmoil.

The government bailout may have prevented a total collapse of the Irish banking system, but the economy remains on some kind of life support: the unemployment rate doubled in the space of one year (it's forecasted to reach 17% by 2010) and the deficit is expected to be a whopping 12% of GDP by the end of 2009. The Nobel Prize–winning economist Paul Krugman reckons that it'll take the country up to 10 years to get out of this economic hole. The Celtic Tiger is truly dead: what now, pussycat?

Rugby & Football

Rugby and football (soccer) enjoy considerable support all over the country, particularly around Dublin; football is very popular in Northern Ireland.

Although traditionally the preserve of Ireland's middle classes, rugby captures the mood of the whole island in February and March during the annual Six Nations Championships, because the Irish team is drawn from both sides of the border and is supported by both Nationalists and Unionists. In recognition of this, the Irish national anthem is no longer played at internationals, replaced by the slightly dodgy but thoroughly inoffensive *Ireland's Call*, a song written especially for the purpose – although nobody seemed to mind it in 2009 when Ireland won its first Grand Slam (a clean sweep of victories in one campaign) since 1948.

There is huge support in Ireland for the 'world game', although fans are much more enthusiastic about the likes of Manchester United, Liverpool and the two Glasgow clubs (Rangers and Celtic) than the struggling pros and part-timers who make up the **National League** (www.fai.ie) in the Republic and the **Irish League** (www.irishfa.com) in Northern Ireland. It's just too difficult for domestic teams to compete with the multimillionaire glitz and glamour of the English Premiership, which has always drawn off the cream of Irish talent. The current crop of local lads playing across the water includes John

O'Shea (Manchester United), Robbie Keane (Spurs), Aiden McGeady (Celtic) and Stephen Ireland (Manchester City).

At an international level, the Republic and Northern Ireland field separate teams; in 2009 both were performing adequately, but it was all a far cry from their relative moments of glory – the 1980s for Northern Ireland and 1988 to 2002 for the Republic. International matches are played at the **Aviva Stadium** (☎ 01-238 2300; Lansdowne Rd), Dublin (aka the new Lansdowne Road) and **Windsor Park** (☎ 9024 4198; off Lisburn Rd), Belfast.

Horse Racing & Greyhound Racing

A passion for horse racing is deeply entrenched in Irish life and comes without the snobbery of its English counterpart. If you fancy a flutter on the gee-gees you can watch racing from around Ireland and England on the TV in bookmakers shops every day. No money ever seems to change hands in the betting, however, and every Irish punter will tell you they 'broke even'.

Ireland has a reputation for producing world-class horses for racing and other equestrian events like showjumping, also very popular albeit in a much less egalitarian kind of way. Major annual races include the Irish Grand National (Fairyhouse, April), Irish Derby (the Curragh, June) and Irish Leger (the Curragh, September). For more information on events contact **Horse Racing Ireland** (☎ 045-842 800; www.hri.ie; Thoroughbred County House, Kill, Co Kildare).

Traditionally the poor-man's punt, greyhound racing ('the dogs'), has been smartened up in recent years and partly turned into a corporate outing. It offers a cheaper, more accessible and more local alternative to horse racing. There are 20 tracks across the country, administered by the **Irish Greyhound Board** (☎ 061-316 788; www.igb.ie; 104 Henry St, Limerick).

Golf

Golf is enormously popular in Ireland and there are many fine golf courses. The annual Irish Open takes place in June or July and the Irish Women's Open in September. For details of venues, contact the **Golfing Union of Ireland** (☎ 01-269 4111; www.gui.ie; 81 Eglinton Rd, Donnybrook, Dublin 4). Ireland's best include Rory McIlroy, Graeme McDowell and, of course, the triple–Major winner Padraig Harrington – Ireland's only Major winner since Fred Daly in 1947.

Cycling

Cycling is a popular spectator sport and major annual events include the gruelling **FBD Insurance Rás** (www.fbdinsuranceras.com), formerly known as the Milk Rás – an eight-day stage race held in May that sometimes approaches 1120km (700 miles) in length, and the Tour of Ulster – a three-day stage race held at the end of April. For more information on events see www.irishcycling.com.

Athletics

Athletics is popular and the Republic has produced a few international stars, particularly in middle- and long-distance events. Current stars of the track include hurdler Derval O'Rourke, distance-runner Mary Cullen and sprinters David Gillick and Paul Hession. In Ireland, the main athletic meets are held at Morton Stadium, Dublin. The **Belfast Marathon** (www.belfastcitymarathon.com) runs on the first Monday in May and the **Dublin Marathon** (www.dublincitymarathon.ie) is run on the last Monday in October.

Boxing

Boxing has traditionally had a strong working-class following. Irish boxers have often won Olympic medals or world championships. Barry McGuigan and Steve Collins, both now retired, were world champions in their day; the

Jim Sheridan's authentic drama *The Boxer* (1998) is a film about a former IRA member's emergence and readjustment from a Belfast prison, to discover everyone, including his girlfriend, has moved on.

best of the current crop is Dublin boxer Bernard Dunne, who defeated Ricardo Cordoba in 2009 to become WBA Super Bantamweight World Champion.

Road Bowling

The object of this sport is to throw an 800g cast-iron ball along a public road (normally one with little traffic) for a designated distance, usually 1km or 2km. The person who does it in the least number of throws is the winner. The main centre is Cork, which has 200 clubs, and, to a lesser extent, Armagh. Competitions take place throughout the year, attracting considerable crowds. The sport has been taken up in various countries around the world, including the USA, Germany and the Netherlands, and a world championship competition has been set up (see www.irishroadbowling.ie).

Handball

Handball is another Irish sport with ancient origins and, like Gaelic football and hurling, is governed by the GAA. It is different from Olympic handball in that it is played by two individuals or two pairs who use their hands to strike a ball against a forecourt wall, rather like squash.

MEDIA
Newspapers

Five national dailies, six national Sundays, stacks of Irish editions of British publications, hundreds of magazines, more than a dozen radio stations, four terrestrial TV stations and more digital channels than you could shake the remote control at…Ireland just doesn't run out of subjects to discuss.

Visit www.medialive .ie for everything you wanted to know about Irish media, but were afraid to ask.

The dominant local player is Independent News & Media, owned by Ireland's primo businessman, Tony O'Reilly, although his title is under threat by the *other* media supremo, Denis O'Brien (see Radio, p54). Its newspapers – the *Irish Independent, Sunday Independent* and *Evening Herald* – are by far the biggest sellers in each market.

The massive overspill of British media here, particularly in relation to the saturated Sunday market, is the biggest challenge facing the Irish media. Rupert Murdoch's News International recognised the importance of the Irish market early, established an office in Dublin and set about an assault of the newspaper racks with its main titles, the *Irish Sun, News of the World* and *Sunday Times*. Every UK tabloid paper now has an Irish edition, leading to accusations by media speculators that Irish culture is being coarsened by the widespread availability of even more tasteless tabloid tat. The traditions of the UK tabloids, which have built circulation on the back of celebrity buy-ups and salacious stories about sex and crime, have inevitably been exported and are beginning to influence the editorial position of the Irish titles, particularly on Sunday.

What this means, of course, is that local papers lacking Murdoch's mammoth resources will struggle even more than they already do; the country's best newspaper, the *Irish Times*, is constantly worried about circulation. All of this goes a way towards explaining how all the English newspapers cost less than a euro while the three Irish national dailies all cost €1.80.

In the north, the three main papers are the *Belfast Telegraph*, with the highest circulation, followed by the pro-Unionist *Newsletter* – Europe's oldest surviving newspaper having begun publication in 1737 – and the equally popular pro-Nationalist *Irish News*.

TV

Irish TV is small fry, it always has been. It lacks the funding and the audience available to behemoths like the BBC. But – and this is a huge but – compared to that of most other European countries it is actually quite good. However,

---

TOP PICKS – BLOGS

Some of the finest and most fearless – not to mention funniest – reporting is done by bloggers, the best of which will reveal what is *really* going on in the country:

- **Blurred Keys** (www.blurredkeys.com) A superb blog that focuses on the media and how it covers current affairs – a watchdog for the watchdogs.
- **Half-Arsed Blog** (www.ricksbreakfastblog.blogspot.com) Radio presenter Rick O'Shea on whatever irks/pleases/interests Rick and his audience on any particular day.
- **Irish Election** (www.irishelection.com) The best political blog, featuring comprehensive analysis of all the major issues.
- **Sinead Gleeson** (www.sineadgleeson.com) An excellent cultural blog.
- **Twenty Major** (www.twentymajor.net) An award-winning blog regularly considered the best in the country for its in-your-face, hilarious commentary.

---

the national broadcaster, RTE, gets its fair share of abuse for being narrow-minded, conservative, boring, short-sighted and way behind the times – and that's just for turning down the chance to produce the enormously successful comedy-drama series *Father Ted* (a gentle and hilarious poke at conservative Ireland, which was then commissioned by Britain's Channel 4).

There are four terrestrial TV channels in Ireland. RTE's strengths are its widespread sports coverage and news and current affairs programming – it's thorough, insightful and often hard-hitting. Programs like *Today Tonight* and *Prime Time* are as good as, or better than, as anything you'll see elsewhere in the world; the reporting treats the audience like mature responsible adults who don't need issues dumbed down or simplified. But let's not forget the Angelus, Ireland's very own call to prayer: 18 sombre hits of a church bell heard at 6pm on RTE1 (and at noon on radio). Undoubtedly out of step with a fast-paced and secular society, it is a daily reminder of the state-encouraged piety of not so long ago.

The purely commercial TV3 has a lightweight programming philosophy, with second-string US fluff to complement its diet of reality TV shows and celebrity nonsense – although its *Nightly News with Vincent Browne* is an intelligent barometer of the day's affairs. The Irish-language station TG4 has the most diverse and challenging output, combining great movies (in English) with an interesting selection of dramas and documentaries *as gaeilge* (in Irish with English subtitles). The main British TV stations – BBC, ITV and Channel 4 – are also available in most Irish homes, through cable.

The big players in the digital TV business are the homegrown NTL and the behemoth that is Sky, who continue to make solid progress in bringing the multichannel revolution into Irish homes.

Radio

The Irish love radio – up to 85% of the population listen in on any given day. The majority tend to stick with RTE, the dominant player with three stations: Radio 1 (88.2-90FM; mostly news and discussion), Radio 2 (90.4–92.2FM; lifestyle and music) and Lyric FM (96–99FM; classical music). In Northern Ireland, the BBC rules supreme, with BBC Radio Ulster flying the local flag in addition to the four main BBC stations.

Independent competitors to RTE are owned by telecommunications impresario Denis O'Brien and include Today FM (100–102FM; music, chat and news) and the talk radio Newstalk (106–108FM; news, current affairs and lifestyle). The rest of the radio landscape is filled out by the 25 or so local radio stations that represent local issues and tastes: the northwest's Highland

Radio – heard in Donegal, Sligo, Tyrone and Fermanagh – is Europe's most successful local radio station, with an 84% market share!

RELIGION

About 3.7 million residents in the Republic call themselves Roman Catholic, followed by 3% Protestant, 0.5% Muslim and the rest an assortment of other beliefs including none at all. In the North, the breakdown is about 53% Protestant and 44% Catholic (with about 3% other or no religion). Most Irish Protestants are members of the Church of Ireland, an offshoot of the Church of England, and the Presbyterian and Methodist churches.

Statistics don't tell the whole story, though, and the influence of the Catholic Church has waned dramatically in the last decade. Most young people see the Church as irrelevant and out of step with the major social issues of the day including divorce, contraception, abortion, homosexuality and cohabitation. The terrible revelations of widespread abuse of children by parish priests, and the untidy efforts of the Church authorities to sweep the truth under the carpet, have provoked a seething rage among many Irish at the Church's gross insensitivity to the care of its flock, while many older believers feel an acute sense of betrayal that has led them to question a lifetime's devotion to their local parishes.

And then there's money: increased prosperity means that the Irish have become used to being rewarded in *this* life, and so many have replaced God with Mammon as a focus of worship. But old habits die hard, and Sunday Mass is still a feature of the weekly calendar, especially in rural communities. Oddly enough, the primates of both the Roman Catholic Church (Archbishop Sean Brady) and the Church of Ireland (Archbishop Robert Eames) sit in Armagh, Northern Ireland, the traditional religious capital of St Patrick. The country's religious history clearly overrides its current divisions.

ARTS
Literature

Of all their national traits, characteristics and cultural expressions it's perhaps the way the Irish speak and write that best distinguishes them. Their love of language and their great oral tradition have contributed to Ireland's legacy of world-renowned writers and storytellers. And all this in a language imposed on them by a foreign invader; the Irish responded to this act of cultural piracy by mastering a magnificent hybrid – English in every respect but flavoured and enriched by the rhythms, pronunciation patterns and grammatical peculiarities of Irish.

Before there was anything like modern literature there was the Ulaid (Ulster) Cycle – Ireland's version of the Homeric epic – written down from oral tradition between the 8th and 12th centuries. The chief story is the Táin Bó Cúailnge (Cattle Raid of Cooley), about a battle between Queen Maeve of Connaught and Cúchulainn, the principal hero of Irish mythology. Cúchulainn appears in the work of Irish writers right up to the present day, from Samuel Beckett to Frank McCourt.

Zip forward 1000 years, past the genius of Jonathan Swift (1667–1745) and his *Gulliver's Travels*; stopping to acknowledge acclaimed dramatist Oscar Wilde (1854–1900); *Dracula* creator Bram Stoker (1847–1912) – some have optimistically claimed that the name of the count may have come from the Irish *droch fhola* (bad blood); and the literary giant that was James Joyce (1882–1941), whose name and books elicit enormous pride in Ireland (although we've yet to meet five people who have read all of *Ulysses*!).

The majority of Joyce's literary output came when he had left Ireland for the artistic hotbed that was Paris, which was also true for another

According to a poll, 73% of Irish citizens believe in God and 22% believe in some kind of spirit or life-force. Only 4% declared themselves non-believers.

John McGahern's simple, economical piece *Amongst Women* centres on well-drawn and complex yet familiar characters, in this case a west-of-Ireland family in the social aftermath of the War of Independence.

The Pulitzer Prize–winning *Angela's Ashes*, by Frank McCourt, tells the relentlessly bleak autobiographical story of the author's poverty-stricken Limerick childhood in the Depression of the 1930s.

great experimenter of language and style, Samuel Beckett (1906–89). Influenced by the Italian poet Dante and French philosopher Descartes, his work centres on fundamental existential questions about the human condition and the nature of self. He is probably best known for his play *Waiting for Godot*, but his unassailable reputation is based on a series of stark novels and plays.

Reading in the Dark by Seamus Deane (the Guardian Fiction Prize winner) is thoughtful prose and recounts a young boy's struggles to unravel the truth of his own history growing up during the Troubles of Belfast.

Of the dozens of 20th-century Irish authors to have achieved published renown, some names to look out for include playwright and novelist Brendan Behan (1923–64), who wove tragedy, wit and a turbulent life into his best works including *Borstal Boy, The Quare Fellow* and *The Hostage*. Inevitably, Behan died young of alcoholism.

Belfast-born CS Lewis (1898–1963) died a year earlier, but he left us *The Chronicles of Narnia*, a series of allegorical children's stories, two of which have been made into films, with a third (*The Voyage of the Dawn Treader*) scheduled for release in 2010. Other Northern writers have, not surprisingly, featured the Troubles in their work: Bernard McLaverty's *Cal* (also made into a film) and his more recent *The Anatomy School* are both wonderful.

Contemporary writers are plentiful, including superstar Roddy Doyle (b 1958), author of the Barrytown trilogy *The Commitments, The Snapper* and *The Van*, as well as a host of more serious books; the Booker–prize winning John Banville (b 1945), who nabbed the prestigious award with *The Sea*; and the wonderful Colm Tóibín (b 1955), whose *The Master* (2004), about Henry James, won the *Los Angeles Times*' Novel of the Year award, as well as the first IMPAC award (see below) for an Irish author.

The Booker Prize–winning novel *The Sea* by John Banville is an engrossing meditation on mortality, grief, death, childhood and memory.

Ireland has produced its fair share of female writers. The 'come here and I'll tell you a story' style of Maeve Binchy (b 1940) has seen her outsell many of the greats of Irish literature, including Beckett and Behan, and her long list of bestsellers includes *Light a Penny Candle* (1982) and *Circle of Friends* (1990); both have been made into successful films.

Circle of Friends, by the queen of Irish popular fiction, Maeve Binchy, captures the often hilarious lives of two country girls in the 1940s who go to Dublin in search of romance.

Nuala O'Faolain (1940–2008), former opinion columnist for the *Irish Times*, 'accidentally' wrote an autobiography when a small publisher asked her to write an introduction to a collection of her columns. Her irreverent, humorous and touching prose struck a chord with readers and the essay was republished as *Are You Somebody?* (1996), followed by *Almost There: The Onward Journey of a Dublin Woman* (2003), which both became international bestsellers.

Ireland can boast four winners of the Nobel Prize for Literature: George Bernard Shaw in 1925, WB Yeats in 1938, Samuel Beckett in 1969 and Seamus Heaney in 1995. The prestigious annual IMPAC awards, administered by Dublin City Public Libraries, accept nominations from public libraries around the world for works of high literary merit and offer a €100,000 award to the winning novelist. Previous winners have included David Malouf (Australian) and Nicola Barker (English).

Poetry

Ireland has always had a way with verse, none better than Nobel laureate WB Yeats (1865–1939), whose poetry far outshines his work as a playwright. His *Love Poems*, edited by Norman Jeffares, makes a suitable introduction for anyone new to his writing.

Three of the executed leaders of the Easter Rising – Pádraig Pearse (1879–1916), Joseph Plunkett (1879–1916) and Thomas McDonagh (1878–1916) – were noted poets, but while they (along with Yeats) evoked a vision of a greater Gaelic Ireland, the emerging poets of the latter half of the 20th century found their themes in the narrowness and frustrations of contemporary Irish life; this is best explored in the work of Patrick Kavanagh (1905–67), whose *The Great Hunger* and *Tarry Flynn* evoke the atmosphere and often grim

THE GAELIC REVIVAL

While Home Rule was being debated and shunted, something of a revolution was taking place in Irish arts, literature and identity. The poet William Butler Yeats and his coterie of literary friends (including Lady Gregory, Douglas Hyde, John Millington Synge and George Russell) championed the Anglo-Irish literary revival, unearthing old Celtic tales and writing with fresh enthusiasm about a romantic Ireland of epic battles and warrior queens. For a country that had suffered centuries of invasion and deprivation, these images presented a much more attractive version of history.

Similarly, Hyde and Eoin MacNeill did much to ensure the survival of the Irish language and the more everyday Irish customs and culture, which they believed to be central to Irish identity. They formed the Gaelic League (Conradh na Gaeilge) in 1893, which, among other things, pushed for the teaching of Irish in schools. Meanwhile, the strongly politicised Gaelic Athletic Association (GAA) promoted Irish sport and culture.

realities of life for the poor farming community. You'll find a bronze statue of him in Dublin, sitting beside his beloved Grand Canal (see p121).

Northern Ireland has unsurprisingly been a rich breeding ground for the poetic muse. Of a host of top-class poets who belong to the Northern School founded by John Hewitt (1907–87), the most renowned is Seamus Heaney (b 1939), Nobel Prize winner in 1995. His most recent collection is *District and Circle* (2006).

Cork-born Irish-language poet Louis de Paor has twice won Ireland's prestigious Sean O'Riordan Prize with collections of his poetry. Tom Paulin (b 1949) writes memorable poetry about the North (try *The Strange Museum*) as does Ciaran Carson (b 1948). Many of Paula Meehan's (b 1955) magical, evocative poems speak of cherished relationships.

Contemporary poets are in a rich vein of form, with the likes of Justin Quinn (b 1968) and Caitriona O'Reilly (b 1973) offering a thoughtful and perceptive critique of modern Ireland in all its complexities. Eavan Boland (b 1944) is a prolific and much-admired writer who combines Irish politics with outspoken feminism; *In a Time of Violence* (1995) and *The Lost Land* (1998) are two of her most celebrated collections.

If you're interested in finding out more about poetry in Ireland, visit the website of the excellent **Poetry Ireland** (www.poetryireland.ie), which showcases the work of new and established poets. For a taste of modern Irish poetry in print, try *Contemporary Irish Poetry* edited by Fallon and Mahon. *A Rage for Order,* edited by Frank Ormsby, is a vibrant collection of the poetry of the North.

Double Drink Story by Caitlin Thomas (née MacNamara), wife of Welsh poet Dylan Thomas, is an eloquent, self-deprecating account of their debauched life, their love-hate relationship and the burden of creativity, making a brilliant literary memoir.

Cinema

Ireland's film-making tradition is pretty poor, largely because the British cinema industry drained much of its talent and creative energies and the Irish government pleaded poverty any time a film-maker came looking for some development cash. The last decade has seen a change in the Irish government's attitudes, but what has long been true is that the country has contributed more than its fair share of glorious moments to the silver screen, as well as a disproportionate number of its biggest stars.

Hot on the heels of such luminaries as Gabriel Byrne *(Miller's Crossing, The Usual Suspects),* Stephen Rea *(The Crying Game, The End of the Affair),* and the Oscar-winning Liam Neeson (for *Schindler's List*), Daniel Day-Lewis and Brenda Fricker (both for *My Left Foot*), are the late-arriving but always excellent Brendan Gleeson, who has had supporting roles in literally dozens of films; the very handsome Cillian Murphy (*Breakfast on Pluto* and *The Wind That Shakes the Barley,* among several others) and the reformed

John Boorman's film *The General* (1998) about Dublin's most notorious crime boss is both horrific and uneasily funny in its portrayal of the mindless brutality and childlike humour of Martin Cahill.

The Oscar statuette handed out at the Academy Awards was conceived by set designer Cedric Gibbons, born in Dublin in 1893 and winner of his own statuette 12 times.

bad-boy Brando-wannabe himself, Colin Farrell, whose recent personal best in an up-and-down career was the well-received *In Bruges*. Close behind him is Jonathan Rhys-Meyers, whose most notable work to date is his Henry VIII on the TV hit *The Tudors*, but has also been seen in Woody Allen's *Match Point* (2005) and 2009's *From Paris With Love*.

The re-establishment of the Irish Film Board in 1993 was part of the government's two-pronged effort to stimulate the local film industry. Big international productions (*Braveheart, Saving Private Ryan* etc) were tempted here with generous tax incentives in order to spread expertise among Irish crews, while money was pumped into the local film industry – with mixed critical results.

Ireland has been working hard to cast off its 'Oirland' identity – that sappy we're-poor-but-happy version so loved by Hollywood's plastic Paddys – but the local film industry is under phenomenal pressure to come up with the goods. And in film, the 'goods' means a commercial success. Exit the creative space to make really insightful films about a host of Irish subjects, enter the themed film designed to make a commercial splash in Britain and the US. Favourite themes include Mad and Quirky – *The Butcher Boy, Disco Pigs* and *Breakfast on Pluto*; Smart-arse Gangsters – *I Went Down* and *Intermission*; and Cutesy Formulaic Love Story – *When Brendan Met Trudy*. Never mind the Irish Welles or Fellini, where's the local equivalent of Loach, Leigh or Winterbottom?

Patrick McCabe's *The Butcher Boy* is a brilliant, gruesome tragicomedy about an orphaned Monaghan boy's descent into madness. It has received several awards and was made into a successful film.

Well, say the film board, they're called Jim Sheridan (*In the Name of the Father, My Left Foot*) and Neil Jordan. The latter is undoubtedly Ireland's greatest director: *The Company of Wolves, Mona Lisa, The Crying Game* and *Michael Collins* are but four examples of his rich filmography.

New directors include the young-but-well-connected Kristen Sheridan (b 1977), daughter of Jim and director of *Disco Pigs* (2001) and *August Rush* (2007), and John Crowley (b 1968), who followed up *Intermission* (2003) with the excellent *Is Anybody There?* (2008), starring Michael Caine. Another bright talent is Damien O'Donnell, who debuted with *East is East* (1999) and went from strength to strength with *Heartlands* (2002) and the outstanding Irish film of 2004, *Inside I'm Dancing*. That same year saw the release of *Adam & Paul*, written by Mark O'Hallorahan and directed by Lenny Abrahamson, a half-decent portrayal of two Dublin junkies and their quixotic quest for a fix. It was a roaring success at the Irish box office, as was John Carney's low-budget film *Once* (2006), starring musician Glen Hansard (whose last appearance on celluloid was as Outspan Foster in 1991's *The Commitments*) as a busker who falls for the elusive Markéta Irglová.

John Crowley's pacey, well-scripted drama *Intermission* (2003) follows a host of eccentric characters in pursuit of love, starring Colin Farrell, Colm Meaney and Ger Ryan.

See p704 to find out when film festivals are held throughout the year.

Music
TRADITIONAL & FOLK

Irish music (known here as traditional music, or just trad) has retained a vibrancy not found in other traditional European forms, which have lost out to the overbearing influence of pop music. Although Irish music has retained many of its traditional aspects, it has itself influenced many forms of music, most notably US country and western – a fusion of Mississippi Delta blues and Irish traditional tunes that, combined with other influences like Gospel, is at the root of rock and roll. Other reasons for trad music's current success include the willingness of its exponents to update the way it's played (in ensembles rather than the customary *céilidh* – communal dance – bands), the habit of pub sessions (introduced by returning migrants) and the economic good times that encouraged the Irish to celebrate their culture rather than trying to replicate international trends. And then, of course, there's *Riverdance*, which made Irish dancing sexy and became a worldwide phenomenon, despite the fact that most aficionados of traditional music are seriously underwhelmed by its musical worth. Good stage show, crap music.

Traditionally, music was performed as a background to dancing, and while this has been true ever since Celtic times, the many thousands of tunes that fill up the repertoire aren't nearly as ancient as that; most aren't much older than a couple of hundred years. Because much of Irish music is handed down orally and aurally, there are myriad variations in the way a single tune is played, depending on the time and place of its playing. The blind itinerant harpist Turlough O'Carolan (1680–1738) wrote more than 200 tunes – it's difficult to know how many versions their repeated learning has spawned.

If you want to hear musical skill that will both tear out your heart and restore your faith in humanity, go no further than the fiddle-playing of Tommy Peoples on *The Quiet Glen* (1998), the beauty of Paddy Keenan's uillean pipes on his eponymous 1975 album, or the stunning guitar playing of Andy Irvine on albums like *Compendium* (2000).

US *Late Show* host David Letterman once described the uillean pipes as 'a sofa hooked up to a stick'.

More folksy than traditional, the Dubliners, fronted by the distinctive gravel voice and grey beard of Ronnie Drew (1934–2008), made a career out of bawdy drinking songs that got *everybody* singing along, but their finest moment was a solo performance of *Scorn Not His Simplicity* by band member Luke Kelly (1940–84), surely one of the saddest, most beautiful songs ever recorded. Other popular bands include the Fureys, comprising four brothers originally from the travelling community (no, not like the Wilburies) along with guitarist Davey Arthur. And if it's rousing renditions of Irish rebel songs you're after, you can't go past the Wolfe Tones.

Since the 1970s, various bands have tried to blend traditional with more progressive genres, with mixed success. The first band to pull it off was Moving Hearts, led by Christy Moore, who went on to become the greatest Irish folk musician ever (see the boxed text, p182).

While traditional music continues to be popular in its own right both in Ireland and abroad, it also continues to provide the base for successful new genres. Think of ambient music with a slightly mystical tinge and invariably Enya will come to mind. As for the stars of tomorrow, the line-up has yet to be finalised, but it will surely include a young piper from Dublin called Sean McKeown and his sometimes playing partner, the fiddler Liam O'Connor.

See p704 for details on when traditional music festivals are held.

POPULAR MUSIC

From the bland but supremely fashionable showbands of the 1960s, popular music took off towards the end of the decade with Van Morrison, whose blues-infused genius really put Irish music on the map. The 1970s were dominated by rock and punk: Thin Lizzy, Celtic rockers Horslips and punk poppers the Undertones were very popular, as were Belfast's own Stiff Little Fingers (SLF), Ireland's answer to the Clash and as good a punk band as there ever was, and the Boomtown Rats, fronted by Bob Geldof.

And then a supernova was born in North Dublin. The world and her sister have an opinion about U2 and, especially, their shy, un-opinionated lead singer Bono, but there's no denying that the band are without question Ireland's most important musical export and a rival to the likes of the Rolling Stones for megastardom and longevity. If we had to pick just one album, it would be the simply magnificent *Joshua Tree* (1987), although *Achtung Baby* (1991) is quite something, too. Their musical output of late has dipped, as inevitably it would with a band whose members are comfortably middle-aged: their last album, *No Line on the Horizon* (2009), was released to very mixed reviews.

Of all the Irish acts that followed in U2's wake during the 1980s and early 1990s, a few managed to comfortably avoid being tarred with 'the next U2' burden. The Pogues' mix of punk and Irish folk kept everyone going for a while, but the real story there was the empathetic songwriting of Shane McGowan, whose genius has been overshadowed by his chronic drinking – but he still managed to pen Ireland's favourite song, 'A Fairytale of New York', sung with emotional fervour by just about everyone around Christmas time. Sinead O'Connor thrived by acting like a U2 antidote – whatever they were into she was not – and by having a damn fine voice; the raw emotion on *The Lion and the Cobra* (1987) makes it a great offering. And then there was My Bloody Valentine, the pioneers of late 1980s guitar-distorted shoegazer rock: *Loveless* (1991) is one of the best Irish albums of all time.

Hot Press (www.hotpress .com) is a fortnightly magazine featuring local and international music interviews and listings.

The 1990s were largely dominated by DJs, dance music and a whole new spin on an old notion, the boy band. Behind Ireland's most successful groups (Boyzone and Westlife) is the Svengali of Saccharine, impresario Louie Walsh, whose musical sensibilities seem mired in '60s showband schmaltz. Commercially megasuccessful, but utterly without musical merit, the boy band (and girl band) phenomenon was a compelling reminder that in the world of pop, millions of people *can* be wrong.

The Irish love their sensitive souls, and there's no shortage of the feelings-out-front singer-songwriter. The established crop include Paddy Casey, Damien Rice and the excellent Fionn Regan (his single 'Be Good or Be Gone' was a big hit and featured on *Grey's Anatomy*), while Belfast-born Duke Special followed up on the success of *Songs from the Deep Forest* (2007) with two albums in quick succession: *Orchestral Manoeuvres in Belfast* and *I Never Thought This Day Would Come* (both 2008). Oh, and don't forget a certain Glen Hansard, whose band the Frames were a fixture on the scene for nearly two decades, but achieved international fame only when he (and co-singer Markéta Irglová) won the Oscar for Best Song in 2008 for 'Falling Slowly' from the movie *Once*.

Other names to look out for are Julie Feeney, whose second album *Pages* (2009) is stunning, Cathy Davey (2007's *Tales of Silversleeve* is worth a listen), and Lisa Hannigan, who played for a number of years with Damien Rice before heading out on her own with the superb *Sea Saw* (2009). We're also big fans of the Nick Cave–like Adrian Crowley – *Long Distance Swimmer* (2007) and *Season of the Sparks* (2009) are recommended – and Villagers, the most hotly tipped act of 2009.

Ireland does its bit for alt-rock with the likes of Fight Like Apes, whose debut album *Fight Like Apes and the Mystery of the Golden Medallion* (2008) was very well received, while Jape has wowed audiences all over Ireland with his wonderfully melodic electronica – *Ritual* (2008) is a must. Finally, and only because we have to, we mention Snow Patrol, Ireland's biggest selling act after U2, even if their particular brand of mortgage rock should have white lines painted right down the middle of it.

TOP TRAD ALBUMS

- ▪ *The Quiet Glen* (Tommy Peoples)
- ▪ *Paddy Keenan* (Paddy Keenan)
- ▪ *Compendium: The Best of Patrick Street* (Various)
- ▪ *The Chieftains 6: Bonaparte's Retreat* (The Chieftains)
- ▪ *Old Hag You Have Killed Me* (The Bothy Band)

OUR 10 BEST IRISH ALBUMS

- *Loveless* (My Bloody Valentine) – utterly intoxicating indie classic that just piles on the layers of sound and melody.
- *Boy* (U2) – best debut album of all time? We think so.
- *The End of History* (Fionn Regan) – too early to say if it's a classic, but it's bloody good.
- *Live & Dangerous* (Thin Lizzy) – released in 1978, it remains one of the greatest live albums ever recorded.
- *I Do Not Want What I Haven't Got* (Sinead O'Connor) – try listening to the Prince-penned 'Nothing Compares to U' and not feel her pain.
- *St Dominic's Preview* (Van Morrison) – everyone knows *Astral Weeks,* but this 1972 album is every bit as good.
- *O* (Damien Rice) – with millions of record sales, we're not going to argue with its merit.
- *Inflammable Material* (Stiff Little Fingers) – forget the Sex Pistols; this album about the life in the Troubles gets our vote for best punk album ever.
- *The Book of Invasion* (Horslips) – this totally catchy album is Celtic rock at its best.
- *Pages* (Julie Feeney) – sublime follow-up to her Choice Music Award–winning debut.

See p704 for details on when music festivals are held.

Architecture

Ireland is packed with prehistoric graves, ruined monasteries, crumbling fortresses and many other solid reminders of its long, often dramatic, history. The principal surviving structures from Stone Age times are the graves and monuments people built for the dead, usually grouped under the heading of megalithic (great stone) tombs. Among the most easily recognisable megalithic tombs are dolmens, massive three-legged structures rather like giant stone stools, most of which are 4000 to 5000 years old. Good examples are the Poulnabrone Dolmen (p385) in the Burren and Browne's Hill Dolmen (p224) near Carlow town.

Passage graves such as Newgrange (p534) and Knowth (p535) in Meath are huge mounds with narrow stone-walled passages leading to burial chambers. These chambers are enriched with spiral and chevron symbols and have an opening through which the rising sun penetrates on the winter or summer solstice, thus acting as a giant celestial calendar.

The Irish names for forts – *dún, ráth, caiseal/cashel* and *caher* – have ended up in the names of countless towns and villages. The Irish countryside is peppered with the remains of over 30,000 of them. The earliest known examples date from the Bronze Age, most commonly the ring fort, with circular earth-and-stone banks, topped by a wooden palisade fence to keep out intruders, and surrounded on the outside by a moatlike ditch. Outside Clonakilty in County Cork, the ring fort at Lisnagun (Lios na gCon) has been reconstructed to give some idea of its original appearance (see p265).

Some forts were constructed entirely of stone; the Iron Age fort of Dún Aengus (p404) on Inishmór is a superb example.

After Christianity arrived in Ireland in the 5th century, the first monasteries were built. The early stone churches were often very simple, some roofed with timber, such as the 6th-century Teampall Bheanáin (Church of St Benen) on Inishmór of the Aran Islands, or built completely of stone, such as the 8th-century Gallarus Oratory (p329) on the Dingle Peninsula. Early hermitages include the small beehive huts and buildings on the summit of Skellig Michael (p305) off County Kerry.

As the monasteries grew in size and stature, so did the architecture. The 12th-century cathedral at Glendalough (p164) and the 10th- to 15th-century cathedral at Clonmacnoise (p513) are good examples, although they're tiny compared with European medieval cathedrals.

Round towers have become symbols of Ireland. These tall, stone, needle-like structures were built largely as lookout posts and refuges in the event of Viking attacks in the late 9th or early 10th centuries. Of the 120 thought to have originally existed, around 20 survive intact; the best examples can be seen at Cashel (p345), Glendalough (p164) and Devenish Island (p685).

With the Normans' arrival in Ireland in 1169 came the Gothic style of architecture, characterised by tall vaulted windows and soaring V-shaped arches. Fine examples of this can be seen in the 1172 Christ Church Cathedral in Dublin (p110) and the 13th-century St Canice's Cathedral in Kilkenny (p229).

The thatched roof cottage is the oldest extant building style in Ireland, dating back nearly 9000 years.

Authentic, traditional Irish thatched cottages were built of limestone or clay to suit the elements, but weren't durable and have become rare, the tradition dying out around the middle of the 20th century.

In Georgian times, Dublin became one of the architectural glories of Europe, with simple, beautifully built Georgian terraces of red brick, with delicate glass fanlights over large, elegant, curved doorways. From the 1960s, Dublin's Georgian heritage suffered badly, but you can still see fine examples around Merrion Square (p109).

The Anglo-Irish Ascendancy built country houses such as the 1722 Castletown House (p178) near Celbridge, the 1741 Russborough House (p168) near Blessington and Castle Coole (p683), which are all excellent examples of the Palladian style, with their regularity and classical correctness. Prolific German architect Richard Cassels (also known as Richard Castle) came to Ireland in 1728 and designed many landmark buildings including Powerscourt House (p159) in County Wicklow and Leinster House (p106; home to Dáil Éireann, the Irish government) in Dublin.

Ireland has little modern architecture of note. For much of the 20th century the pace of change was slow, and it wasn't until the construction of Dublin's Busáras Station in the 1950s that modernity began to really express itself. It was designed by Michael Scott, who was to have an influence on architects in Ireland for the next two decades. The poorly regulated building boom of the 1960s and 1970s, however, paid little attention to the country's architectural heritage and destroyed more than it created. From that period Paul Koralek's 1967 brutalist-style Berkeley Library in Trinity College, Dublin, has been hailed as Ireland's best example of modern architecture.

Since the 1980s more care has been given to architectural heritage and context, the best example of which has been the redevelopment of Dublin's previously near-derelict Temple Bar area (p103). Ireland's recent boom at the turn of the last century spawned a huge growth of building work, of mixed quality, around Dublin. Some good examples in the Docklands area include the imposing Financial Services Centre and Custom House Square; further downriver in the Grand Canal Docks, the centrepiece of the whole area will be a 2000-seat performing arts centre designed by the world's hottest architect, Daniel Libeskind.

Probably the most controversial piece of modern architecture to be unveiled in recent years has been the Monument of Light (p114; rechristened simply the Spire) on Dublin's O'Connell St. At seven times the height of the GPO (120m in total), the brushed steel hollow cone was always going to face opposition, but since its unveiling in spring 2003, the awe-inspiring structure and beautifully reflective surface have won over all but a few hardened cynics.

Visual Arts

Ireland's painting doesn't receive the kind of recognition that its literature and music do. Nevertheless, painting in Ireland has a long tradition dating back to the illuminated manuscripts of the early Christian period, most notably the *Book of Kells*.

The National Gallery (p106) has an extensive Irish School collection, much of it chronicling the people and pursuits of the Anglo-Irish aristocracy.

Like other European artists of the 18th century, Roderic O'Conor featured portraits and landscapes in his work. His post-impressionist style stood out for its vivid use of colour and sturdy brush strokes. James Malton captured 18th-century Dublin in a series of line drawings and paintings.

In the 19th century there was still no hint of Ireland's political and social problems in the work of its major artists. The most prominent landscape painter was James Arthur O'Connor, while Belfast-born Sir John Lavery became one of London's most celebrated portrait artists.

Just as WB Yeats played a seminal role in the Celtic literary revival, his younger brother, Jack Butler Yeats (1871–1957), inspired an artistic surge of creativity in the early 20th century, taking Celtic mythology and Irish life as his subjects. (Their father, John Butler Yeats, had also been a noted portrait painter.) William John Leech (1881–1961) was fascinated by changing light, an affection reflected in his expressionistic landscapes and flower paintings. Born to English parents in Dublin, Francis Bacon (1909–92) emerged as one of the most powerful figurative artists of the 20th century with his violent depictions of distorted human bodies.

The stained-glass work of Harry Clarke (1889–1931) is also worth a mention in the canon of modern Irish art: heavily influenced by contemporary styles including art nouveau and symbolism, Clarke's work was primarily for church windows (see p369 and p565).

The pioneering work of Irish cubist painter Mainie Jellett (1897–1944) and her friend, modernist stained-glass artist Evie Hone (1894–1955), had an influence on later modernists Barrie Cooke (b 1931) and Camille Souter (b 1929). Together with Louis Le Brocquy (b 1916), Jellett and Hone set up the Irish Exhibition of Living Art in 1943 to foster the work of nonacademic artists. Estella Solomons (1882–1968) trained under William Orpen and Walter Osborne in Dublin and was a noted portrait and landscape painter. The rural idyll of the west of Ireland was also a theme of Paul Henry's (1876–1958) landscapes. In the 1950s and 1960s, a school of naive artists, including James Dixon, appeared on Tory Island, off Donegal (see the boxed text, p481).

James Dixon, Tory Island's first 'naive' painter, used boat paint and brushes that he made from donkey hair.

Contemporary artists to watch out for include Nick Miller, New York–based Sean Scully and Fionnuala Ní Chíosáin. Also worth looking out for are Grace Weir and Dorothy Cross, whose works are exhibited in the country's top galleries.

Experimental photographer Clare Langan's work has gained international recognition with her trademark ethereal images of elemental landscapes.

Murals have been an important way of documenting Ireland's more recent political history. Powerful political murals can be seen in West Belfast (p582) and Derry (p639).

Theatre

Dublin and Belfast are the main centres, but most sizeable towns, such as Cork, Derry, Donegal, Limerick and Galway, have their own theatres. Ireland has a theatrical history almost as long as its literary one. Dublin's first theatre was founded in Werburgh St in 1637, although it was closed only four years later by the Puritans. Another theatre, named the Smock Alley Playhouse or Theatre Royal, opened in 1661 and continued to stage plays for more than a century. The literary revival of the late 19th century resulted in the establishment of Dublin's Abbey Theatre (p147), now Ireland's national theatre. Its role is to present works by historical greats such as WB Yeats, George Bernard Shaw (1856–1950), JM Synge (1871–1909) and Sean O'Casey (1880–1964), as well as to promote modern Irish dramatists. Also in Dublin, the Gate Theatre (p147) produces classics and comedies, while the Gaiety and Olympia Theatres (p148) present a range of productions, as does the Grand Opera House (p574) in Belfast. Dublin's Project Arts Centre (p148) offers a more experimental program.

The word 'quiz' was allegedly made up in the 1830s by a Dublin theatre owner called Richard Daly who bet that he could introduce a nonsense word into common parlance in 48 hours.

Under pressure to justify itself as a going concern, Irish theatre has subconsciously turned more and more toward the fizz-bang-wallop of spectacle, often at the expense of quality. Some of the most successful plays of recent years seem obsessed with recreating the high-paced neurotic energy of the action thriller on the stage, as though the audience isn't patient enough to be engrossed by the slow build-up usually associated with theatrical drama. More noise, more guns and sharp dialogue out of an American pulp novel might keep the audience laughing, but it doesn't make for lasting, quality theatre.

Theatre's tattered flag is still kept flying, however, by some excellent writers and companies. Brian Friel (b 1929) and Tom Murphy (b 1935) are the country's leading established playwrights, but the future has been enlivened by a bunch of new writers, including Michael Collins, John Comiskey, Oonagh Kearney, Gina Moxley and Arthur Riordan, playwrights who have been helped on to the stage by innovative production companies like Rough Magic. The present is also pretty shiny for the likes of Enda Walsh, author of *Disco Pigs* (1996) and *Bedbound* (2000), with the former made into a film starring Cillian Murphy. Mark O'Rowe, who presented an electrifying picture of gangland Dublin in his award-winning *Howie the Rookie* (1999) and followed it with *Made in China* (2001) and *Crestfall* (2003), is one of the very hot names in the contemporary scene, but he too has made the move into film writing, cowriting *Intermission* (2003); his latest play, *Terminus* (2007), was very well received. Eugene O'Brien's excellent *Eden* (2001) was followed by the disappointing *Savoy* (2004), which reminded us a bit of Cinema Paradiso, only set in a provincial Irish town. O'Brien has since moved on to some questionable TV work.

See p704 for details on when various arts and theatre festivals are held.

Dance

The most important form of dance in Ireland is traditional Irish dancing, performed communally at *céilidh,* often in an impromptu format and always accompanied by a traditional Irish band. Dances include the hornpipe, jig and reel. Irish dancing has received international attention and success through shows such as *Riverdance* and its offshoots, and while this glamorised style of dance is only loosely based on traditional dancing, it has popularised the real art and given a new lease of life to the moribund Irish dancing schools around the country.

Ireland doesn't have a national dance school, but there are a number of schools and companies teaching and performing ballet and modern dance. The Dance Theatre of Ireland and the Irish Modern Dance Theatre are based in Dublin, while the Firkin Crane Centre in Cork is Ireland's only venue devoted solely to dance.

See p704 for information on when dance festivals are held.

Food & Drink

Generations of travellers who visited these shores during bleaker times typically mused that Irish food is great until it's cooked. They advised getting drunk before eating, or complained that a meal was more a flavourless penance rather than a pleasurable repast. Those days are long gone, and that small-but-growing creation known as Irish cuisine is actually drawing visitors to these shores.

The culinary renaissance has taken place, and the Irish are now enjoying the fine cuisine that they have long deserved. The island has always been blessed with a wealth of staples and specialities, with meat, seafood and dairy produce that are the envy of the world. At the twilight of the 20th century, a new wave of cooks began producing what is sometimes promoted as 'New Irish Cuisine'.

In truth, the new cuisine is more a confident return to the traditional practice of combining simple cooking techniques with the finest local ingredients. Many of the new chefs merely strive to offer their patrons the sort of meals that have always been taken for granted on well-run Irish farms. Whatever you want to call it, it has aroused the nation's taste buds, and you'll find local produce on menus across the country, from Dublin Bay prawns and Connemara salmon to Skeaghanore duck and Kilbrittain lamb.

But gastronomes have more than rediscovered traditions to thank. The Irish diners of today – generally a more affluent and worldly bunch than their forebears – have become more discerning and adventurous. To meet their demands, restaurants are continually springing up on city streets and in old country homes, their menus spruced up with all sorts of international touches. Luckily, excellent food isn't reserved for urbanites and the rich – small restaurants, delis and cafes the country over have fallen in love with good, fresh Irish produce and it's easy to find well-cooked, homely food far from the tourist trail.

Of course, you can still find leathery meat, shrivelled fish and overcooked vegetables, if that's what you're looking for. But why punish yourself, when hearty fare that will make your palate sing is so readily available?

Visit www.ravensgard. org/prdunham/irish food.html for a highly readable and complete history of Irish cuisine, with fascinating chapters such as 'The Most Widely Used Cooking Methods in Pre-Potato Ireland' and 'Collecting of Blood for Pudding Making'.

STAPLES & SPECIALITIES
Potatoes

It's a wonder the Irish retain their good humour amid the perpetual potato-baiting they endure. But, despite the stereotyping, and however much we'd like to disprove it, potatoes are still paramount here and you'll see lots of them on your travels. The mashed potato dishes colcannon and champ (with cabbage and spring onion respectively) are two of the tastiest recipes in the country.

Meat & Seafood

Irish meals are usually meat based, with beef, lamb and pork common options. Seafood, long neglected, is finding a place on the table in Irish homes. It's widely available in restaurants and is often excellent, especially in the west. Oysters, trout and salmon are delicious, particularly if they're direct from the sea or a river rather than a fish farm. The famous Dublin Bay prawn isn't actually a prawn but a lobster. At its best, the Dublin Bay prawn is superlative, but it's priced accordingly. If you're going to splurge, do so here – but make sure you choose live Dublin Bay prawns because once these fellas die, they quickly lose their flavour.

Over 10,000 oysters are consumed each year – accompanied by an equal number of pints of Guinness – at the exuberant Galway Oyster International Festival (www.galwayoysterfest. com; p397).

Bread

The most famous Irish bread, and one of the signature tastes of Ireland, is soda bread. Irish flour is soft and doesn't take well to yeast as a raising agent, so Irish bakers of the 19th century leavened their bread with bicarbonate of soda. Combined with buttermilk, it makes a superbly light-textured and tasty bread, and is often on the breakfast menus at B&Bs.

If you want to know your natural-rind goat's cheese from your semisoft washed-rind cow's cheese, you'll find enlightenment and a complete list of Irish cheesemakers at www .irishcheese.ie.

The Fry

Perhaps the most feared Irish speciality is the fry – the heart attack on a plate that is the second part of so many B&B deals. In spite of the hysterical health fears, the fry is still one of the most common traditional meals in the country. Who can say no to a plate of fried bacon, sausages, black pudding, white pudding, eggs and tomatoes? For the famous Ulster fry, common throughout the North, simply add fadge (potato bread).

DRINKS
Nonalcoholic Drinks
TEA

The Irish drink more tea, per capita, than any other nation in the world and you'll be offered a cup as soon as you cross the threshold of any Irish home. It's a leveller and an ice-breaker, and an appreciation for 'at least a cup in your hand' is your passport to conviviality here. Preferred blends are very strong, and nothing like the namby-pamby versions that pass for Irish breakfast tea elsewhere.

RED LEMONADE

This product, basically a regular glass of lemonade with colouring, has been produced in Ireland since the end of the 19th century and is still made to

---

FINDING THE BEST IRISH FOOD & DRINK

Unearthing the best of Ireland's food and drink will add to your enjoyment of the country as a whole. Try and visit one of the artisan producers, like a cheesemaker's, smoke house or brewery-pub; most producers are happy to talk you through the process and offer tastings.

The next best thing is to go to a farmers market and get a real insight into what's being grown in the area and what's in season. Ask the stallholders, often the producers themselves, what the best local food is and which restaurants are doing it justice.

If you keep your eyes open, you'll realise there's more to Irish beer than just the popular mainstream brands. Look out for those pubs serving speciality beers on draught – it shows they're serious about their brews (see the boxed text, p68).

We've included details of local producers in the regional chapters, but these are just the tip of the iceberg. Use the following resources and ask in local shops to track down others. Be sure to phone before turning up so the producers can set aside time to show you around.

www.bestofbridgestone.com Extensive coverage of artisan producers plus the best restaurants serving their produce.

www.bordbia.ie Irish food board website, with a few local producers listed, as well as a comprehensive list of farmers markets.

Good Food in Cork Excellent annual booklet detailing artisan producers in Cork, established by Myrtle Allen; pick it up from the Farmgate Café (p248) in Cork city; also available online at www.corkfreechoice.com.

www.irishcheese.ie The farmhouse cheesemakers' association, with every small dairy covered.

www.slowfoodireland.com Organisation supporting small producers, with social events across Ireland.

Finally, get off the beaten track – wander away from the main tourist centres and you'll find some delightful hidden pubs, farm shops and restaurants waiting to be discovered.

> **TOP FIVE IRISH CHEESES**
> **Ardrahan** Flavoursome farmhouse creation with a rich, nutty taste.
> **Corleggy** Subtle, pasteurised goats cheese from County Cavan (p560).
> **Durrus** A creamy, fruity cheese, beloved of fine-food fans (p278).
> **Cashel Blue** Creamy blue cheese from Tipperary.
> **Cooleeney** Award-winning Camembert-style cheese.

virtually the same recipe today. Always more popular in the Republic than the North, it's a favourite for adults and children alike. It's commonly used as a mixer with brandy and whiskey.

Alcoholic Drinks

Drinking in Ireland is no mere social activity: it's the foundation on which Irish culture is built. Along with its wonderful drinks, this fact helps to explain why, through centuries of poverty and oppression, the Irish have always retained their reputation for unrivalled hospitality and good humour.

STOUT

Of all Ireland's drinks, the 'black stuff' is the most celebrated. While Guinness has become synonymous with stout the world over, few outside Ireland realise that there are two other major producers competing for the favour of the Irish drinker: Murphy's and Beamish & Crawford, both based in Cork city. More exciting still is the recent re-emergence of independent Irish brewers (Guinness, Murphy's and Beamish & Crawford are no longer Irish owned) – see the boxed text, p68, to whet your appetite.

OTHER IRISH BEERS

Beamish Red Ale This traditional-style red ale, brewed in Cork city by Beamish & Crawford, is sweet and palatable.

Caffrey's Irish Ale One of the most exciting additions to Ireland's beer map, this creamy ale has only been around since 1994. Brewed in County Antrim, it's a robust cross between a stout and an ale.

Kinsale Irish Lager Brewed in the eponymous County Cork town, this golden-coloured lager has a slightly bitter taste that fades after a few sips.

McCardles Traditional Ale This wholesome, dark, nutty ale is hard to come by, but worthy of an exploration.

Smithwick's Smithwick's is a lovely, refreshing full scoop with a charming history. It's brewed in Kilkenny (see p234), on the site of the 14th-century St Francis Abbey in what is Ireland's oldest working brewery.

WHISKEY

While whiskey shares only equal billing with stout as the national drink of Ireland, in the home it is paramount. At last count, there were almost 100 different types of Irish whiskey, brewed by only three distilleries – Jameson's, Bushmills and Cooley's. A visit to Ireland reveals a depth of excellence that will make the connoisseur's palate spin, while winning over many new friends to what the Irish call *uisce beatha* (water of life).

IRISH COFFEE

Stories about the origin of Irish coffee abound but the most common one credits Joe Sheridan, a barman at Shannon airport, with the creation in the 1940s. All travellers arriving in Ireland from the USA would stop over in Shannon for an hour or two before heading on to their final destination. Landing in the bracing cold, shivering passengers used to approach Sheridan

My Goodness! *The Book of Guinness Advertising*, by Jim Davies, is a collection of Guinness' finest posters from the 1920s to the end of the 20th century.

Guinness Is Guinness: The Colourful Story of a Black and White Brand by Mark Griffiths delves into the origins and eventual worldwide dispersion of the great stout. Guinness devotees will find it colourful and insightful.

Established in 1608, Bushmills in County Antrim is the world's oldest legal distillery (see p655). By the time of Bushmills' official opening, whiskey was already exceedingly popular among the common people of Ireland.

looking for an alcoholic drink and something that might heat them up. He hit upon the winning blend of Irish whiskey and piping hot coffee, topped with rich cream. It was just the trick then, and still is today.

POITÍN

Making *poitín* (illicit whiskey) has a folkloric respect in Ireland. Those responsible came to be regarded as heroes of the people, rather than outlaws of the land as the authorities tried to brand them. In tourist and duty-free shops, you'll see a commercial brand of *poitín*, which is strictly a gimmick for tourists. Don't bother: it's just an inferior spirit with little to credit it. There are still *poitín* makers plying their trade in the quieter corners of Ireland. It is not uncommon in Donegal, the *poitín* capital, for deals to be sealed or favours repaid with a drop of the 'cratur'. In the quiet, desolate, peaty bogs of Connemara, a plume of smoke rising into the sky may not just be a warming fire. Or in West Cork, one of the most fiercely patriotic and traditional pockets of Ireland, a friend of a friend may know something about it.

The Bridgestone guides (www.bestofbridgestone.com) are a well-respected series of Irish food guides written by a husband-and-wife team. Books include the *Vegetarian Guide to Ireland*, *Food Lover's Guide to Northern Ireland* and the annual *100 Best Restaurants*.

WHERE TO EAT & DRINK

It's easy to eat well in the cities and you'll be able to find any kind of cuisine your taste buds desire, from Irish seafood to foreign fusion. Along the west coast, you'll be spoilt for choice when it comes to seafood and local produce.

If you ask a local for 'somewhere to eat', you'll probably be directed to his or her favourite pub because, outside the cities, the best place for a feed, particularly lunch, *is* often the pub. Virtually every drinking house will offer the simple fare of soup, potatoes, vegetables, steaks and chicken. Some extend

---

MICROBREWERIES FIGHT BACK

Up until the 1980s the outlook for Ireland's brewing industry looked even bleaker than it did for its food. Sure, everyone knows about Guinness, but over the previous 100 years it had developed at the expense of hundreds of smaller breweries. Ironically, Ireland has clung on to its reputation as a country with a strong beer heritage, but until recently the modern reality was severely lacking – all Irish beer came from only three breweries, none of which is currently Irish owned.

The experience of the Carlow Brewing Company (p220) is typical of the revival of interest in microbrewing. Says founder Seamus O'Hara, 'I had the opportunity to travel in Europe, and it opened my eyes to the fact that there was a lot more to beer than the two or three brands available in Ireland. I went to the US and the microbrewery scene there that had started up in the 1980s led us to believe that we could set up a small brewery and be commercially successful too.' In the mid-'90s other small breweries started up and a pioneering industry developed.

The commercial environment was loaded against new companies, though, with high customs and excise levied against the smaller breweries. 'Many breweries were driven by passion and an interest in brewing, and we were all a bit wide-eyed about the commercial side of the business,' says Seamus. Some breweries have fallen by the wayside since those pioneering first days, and now there are nine left from an original 12.

Carlow Brewing Company survived those early years by exporting up to 75% of its produce. 'Overseas, people are more used to trying different beers, so there was always going to be a market for a genuine Irish beer at the speciality end in terms of quality and flavour.' As with food, extensive lobbying of the industry regulators reaped rewards, and the excise has now been reduced by 50% for small producers. The market is still dominated by the big breweries, but people's attitudes are changing: the number of speciality beers coming into the country and being produced are educating beer drinkers and broadening the market. 'The Irish beer drinker is more discerning and demanding now that they're aware there are other choices. It's similar to what happened with Irish food – there's just a bit of a lag with beer.'

A SNIFTER OF WHISKEY HISTORY

Nobody really knows whether whiskey was first made in Scotland or Ireland, but for the purpose of this book we'll just go along with the Irish version of the story. Whiskey has been made here since the 10th century, when monks brought the art of distillation back from their ecclesiastical jaunts to the Middle East. In Arabia, the technique had been used to distil perfume from flowers, but the monks evidently saw a very different use for it. As the legend maintains, they soon developed a method of distilling whiskey from barley. The monks then fiercely protected their secret for several centuries.

Incidentally, Irish monks did have a solid reputation as hard drinkers. Monastic protocol limited monks to a mere gallon (4.5L) of ale a day. Another rule insisted that they be able to chant the Psalms clearly, so we might reasonably assume the monks managed to build up a sturdy tolerance in order to walk this fine line.

Had the monks not been so secretive, their claim to being the inventors of whiskey might not be disputed today. The Scots make an equally valid, if much later claim, dating to the 15th century. By the way, Scotch whisky is not only spelled differently, it is also distilled twice rather than the three times preferred by the Irish. American bourbon is distilled but once.

---

themselves and have separate dining rooms where you can get fresh soda bread and hearty meals, like shepherd's pie, casseroles and seafood dishes.

For breakfast, you're most likely to be eating at your accommodation, as most lodgings in Ireland offer B&B.

Standard restaurant hours in Ireland are from noon to around 10.30pm, with many places closed one day of the week, usually Monday, or sometimes Sunday.

VEGETARIANS & VEGANS

Veggies can take a deep breath. And then exhale. Calmly. For Ireland has come a long, long way since the days when vegetarians were looked upon as odd creatures; nowadays, even the most militant vegan will barely cause a ruffle in all but the most basic of rustic kitchens. Which isn't to say that travellers with plant-based diets are going to find the most imaginative range of options on menus outside the bigger towns and cities – or in the plethora of modern restaurants that have opened in the last few years – but you can rest assured that the overall quality of the homegrown vegetable is top-notch and most places will have at least one dish that you can tuck into comfortably.

Café Paradiso Cookbook and *Paradiso Seasons* are creative and modern vegetarian cookbooks with ne'er a brown lentil stew in sight; from the eponymous Cork restaurant (p251).

EATING WITH KIDS

You can bring *na páiste* (the children) to just about any Irish eatery, including the pub. However, after 7pm, kids are banished from most boozers and the smarter restaurants. You will sometimes see children's menus, but normally small portions of the adult fare will do. For more information on travelling with children, see p701.

The renowned Georgina Campbell's guides (www .ireland-guide.com) are annual publications with over 900 recommendations for munching, supping and snoozing on the Emerald Isle.

HABITS & CUSTOMS
How the Irish Eat

The Irish have hefty appetites and eat almost 150% of the recommended daily calorie intake, according to the EU. This probably has as much to do with their penchant for snacks as the size of their meals (which *are* big).

When Ireland was predominantly agricultural, breakfast was a leisurely and communal meal shared with family and workers around midmorning, a few hours after rising. As with most of the developed world, it's now a fairly rushed and bleary-eyed affair involving toast and cereals. The traditional fry is a weekend indulgence, while the contracted version of bacon and eggs is still popular whenever time allows. The day's first cup of tea comes with breakfast and most people will admit to not being themselves until they've had it.

Elevenses is the next pit stop and involves tea and snacks to tide over appetites until the next main meal. Afternoon tea takes the same form and serves the same function, also breaking up the afternoon.

Lunch is traditionally the biggest meal of the day, which is probably a throwback to farming Ireland, when the workers would return home ravenous after a morning's work. However, the timing of the main meal today is one of the most visible rural/urban divides. Outside the cities, lunch is still usually the most substantial meal every day of the week, while the workers in urban areas have succumbed to the nine-to-five drudgery and usually eat lunch on the run. However, at weekends, everybody has dinner mid-afternoon, usually around 4pm on Saturday and before 2pm Sunday. They might call it 'lunch' but don't be deceived – it's the most substantial meal of the week.

'Supper' is increasingly becoming the main meal for urbanites, and it takes place as soon as the last working parent gets home.

Etiquette

Conviviality is the most important condiment at the Irish table. Meal times are about taking the load off your feet, relaxing and enjoying the company of your fellow diners. There is very little prescribed or restrictive etiquette. In fact, the only behaviour likely to cause offence could be your own haughtiness. The Irish will happily dismiss any faux pas, but if they think you have ideas above your station, they're quick to bring you back down to earth.

COOKING COURSES

Cooking has regained its sex appeal in Ireland and plenty of schools are finding their classes increasingly popular. The teaching is usually relaxed and sociable, and takes place in beautiful settings. A stint at one of these cookery schools could quite easily be the highlight of your trip:

Ballymaloe (p258; ☎ 021-464 6785; www.cookingisfun.ie; Ballycotton, Co Cork) From half-day sessions to 12-week certificate courses. Classes are held in an old apple-storage house, and there are cottages in the grounds for overnight students.

Ballyknocken (p173; ☎ 0404-69274; www.ballyknocken.com; Glenealy, Ashford) Full-day cooking classes by Ballymaloe graduate Catherine Fulvio that run throughout the year. Classes are held in a converted milking parlour.

Belle Isle School of Cookery (p683; ☎ 028-6638 7231; www.irish-cookery-school.com; Enniskillen, Co Fermanagh) A range of cookery and wine courses lasting from one day to four weeks. Luxurious accommodation in Belle Isle Castle and its estate cottages.

Berry Lodge (☎ 065-708 7022; www.berrylodge.com; Annagh, Co Clare) Offering in-depth instruction, often over more than one day. Packages including classes, accommodation and meals are available.

Castle Leslie (p564; ☎ 047-88109; www.castleleslie.com; Glaslough, Co Monaghan) Offering a program of year-round courses with master chef Noel McMeel. Themed courses cover everything from 'Irish cooking by seasons' to 'death by chocolate' and 'food and erotica'.

Fiacri Country House Restaurant (☎ 0505-43017; www.fiacrihouse.com; Roscrea, Co Tipperary) Course are run year-round, and range from one day to five weeks in length.

Ghan House (p556; ☎ 042-937 3682; www.ghanhouse.com; Carlingford, Co Louth) Offers hands-on cooking classes and cooking demonstrations. Accommodation is also available.

Good Things Café (p278; ☎ 027-61426; www.thegoodthingscafe.com; Durrus, Co Cork) Runs cookery courses year-round, including a two-day 'miracle' program for beginners.

Pangur Ban (☎ 095-41243; www.pangurban.com; Connemara, Co Galway) Two-day weekend courses, covering specific themes such as 'bread and cakes'.

Visit www.foodisland .com, run by state food board Bord Bia, for recipes, a short culinary history of Ireland and links to producers of Irish food, from whom you can purchase that prized farmhouse cheese or whiskey-flavoured fruit cake.

The Ballymaloe series of cookbooks by various members of Ireland's first family of cooking, the Allens, have an extraordinary reputation in Ireland and abroad. The emphasis is on using top-quality ingredients simply and with love.

The *Avoca Café Cookbooks*, by Hugo Arnold, contain hearty, wholesome recipes from the family-run Avoca Handweaver restaurants, originally based in Wicklow (see p149) and now with 10 establishments across the Republic.

MARKETS

There are few better ways to eat well in Ireland than to fill your shopping basket with local, seasonal produce at a farmers market. The markets have seen a real resurgence in recent years and most Irish towns now host one at least once a week. Check out www.irelandmarkets.com or www.bordbia .ie/markets for a definitive list.

EAT YOUR WORDS
Food Glossary

bacon and cabbage – slices of boiled bacon or gammon with boiled cabbage on the side, served with boiled potatoes

barm brack – spicy, cakelike bread, traditionally served at Halloween with a ring hidden inside (be careful not to choke on it!)

blaa – soft and floury bread roll

black-and-white pudding – black pudding is traditionally made from pigs' blood, pork skin and seasonings, shaped like a big sausage and cut into discs and fried; white pudding is the same without the blood

boxty – potato pancake, becoming rarer on menus

carrigeen – seaweed dish

champ – Northern Irish dish of potatoes mashed with spring onions (scallions)

coddle – Dublin dish of semithick stew made with sausages, bacon, onions and potatoes

colcannon – mashed potato, cabbage and onion fried in butter and milk

crubeens – dish of pigs' trotters from Cork

drisheen – another Cork dish of intestines stuffed with sheep or pigs' blood and bitter tansy, boiled in milk

dulse – dried seaweed that's sold salted and ready to eat, mainly found in Ballycastle, County Antrim

fadge – Northern Irish potato bread

farl – general name for triangular flat-bread and cakes common to Northern Ireland

Guinness cake – popular fruitcake flavoured with Guinness

Irish stew – quintessential stew of mutton (preferably lamb), potatoes and onions, flavoured with parsley and thyme and simmered slowly

potato bread – thin bread made out of spuds

soda bread – wonderful bread, white or brown, sweet or savoury, made from very soft Irish flour and buttermilk

yellowman – hard, chewy toffee made in County Antrim

Slowfood Ireland (www .slowfoodireland.com) is an organisation committed to local and artisan food production. It runs various sociable events throughout the country, from bangers 'n mash parties to cheese-and-wine evenings.

Environment

THE LAND

It is clear, from the literature, songs and paintings of Ireland, that the Irish landscape exerts a powerful sway on the people who have lived in it. The Irish who left, especially, have always spread this notion that the old sod was something worth pining for, and visitors still anticipate experiencing this land's subtle influence on perception and mood. Once you've travelled the country, you can't help but agree that the vibrant greenness of gentle hills, the fearsome violence of jagged coasts and the sombre light of so many cloudy days is an integral part of experiencing Ireland.

The entire island stretches a mere 486km north to south and 275km east to west, so Ireland's impressive topographical variety may come as a surprise. The countryside does indeed have an abundance of the expected greenery. Grass grows nearly everywhere in Ireland, but there are notable exceptions, particularly around the dramatic coasts.

Massive rocky outcrops, like the Burren (p376), in County Clare, are for the most part inhospitable to grass, and although even there the green stuff does sprout up in enough patches for sheep and goats to graze on, these vast, otherworldly landscapes are mostly grey and bleak. Nearby, the dramatic Cliffs of Moher (p375) are a sheer drop into the thundering surf below. Similarly, there is no preparing for the extraordinary hexagonal stone columns of the Giant's Causeway (p656) in County Antrim or the rugged drop of County Donegal's Slieve League (p473), Europe's highest sea cliffs. Sand dunes buffer many of the more gentle stretches of coast.

The boglands, which once covered one-fifth of the island, are more of a whiskey hue than green – that's the brown of heather and sphagnum moss, which cover uncut bogs. Travellers will likely encounter a bog in County Kildare's Bog of Allen (p181) or while driving through the western counties – much of the Mayo coast is covered by bog, and huge swaths also cover Donegal. The rural farms of the west coast have a rugged, hard-earned look to them, due mostly to the rock that lies so close to the surface. Much of this rock has been dug up to create tillable soil and converted into stone walls that divide tiny paddocks. The Aran Islands (p403) stand out for their spectacular networks of stone walls.

Smaller islands dot the shores of Ireland, many of them barren rock piles supporting unique ecosystems – Skellig Michael (p305) is a breathtakingly jagged example just off the Kerry coast. The west of Ireland is also the country's most mountainous area. Much of the west coast is a bulwark of cliffs, hills and mountains. The highest mountains are in the southwest; the tallest mountain in Ireland is Carrantuohil (1039m) in County Kerry's Macgillycuddy's Reeks (p298).

But topography in Ireland always leads back to the green. The Irish frequently lament the loss of their woodlands, much of which were cleared by the British (during the reign of Elizabeth I) to build ships for the Royal Navy. Little of the island's once plentiful oak forests survive today, and much of what you'll see is the result of relatively recent planting. Instead, the countryside largely comprises green fields divided by hedgerows and stone walls. Use of this land is divided between cultivated fields and pasture for cattle and sheep.

WILDLIFE

Ireland's flora and fauna is, by and large, shy and subtle, but as in any island environment, travellers who set out on foot will discover a countryside that is resplendent with interesting species.

Of the nine counties that originally comprised the province of Ulster, six are now part of Northern Ireland while three are part of the Republic.

In 1821 the body of an Iron Age man was found in a bog in Galway with his cape, shoes and beard still intact.

Animals

Apart from the fox and badger, which tend to shy away from humans and are rarely seen, the wild mammals of Ireland are mostly of the ankle-high 'critter' category, such a rabbits, hedgehogs and shrews. Hikers often spot the Irish hare, or at least glimpse the blazing-fast blur of one running away. Red deer roam the hillsides in many of the wilder parts of the country, particularly the Wicklow Mountains, and in Killarney National Park, which holds the country's largest herd.

For most visitors, the most commonly sighted mammals are those inhabiting the sea and waterways. The otter, rarely seen elsewhere in Europe, is thriving in Ireland. Seals are a common sight in rivers and along the shore, as are dolphins, which follow the warm waters of the Gulf Stream towards Ireland. Some colonise the coast of Ireland year-round, frequently swimming into the bays and inlets off the western coast.

Many travellers visit Ireland specifically for the birding. Ireland's westerly location on the fringe of Europe makes it an ideal stopover point for birds migrating from North America and the Arctic. In autumn, the southern counties become a temporary home to the American waders (mainly sandpipers and plovers) and warblers. Migrants from Africa, such as shearwaters, petrels and auks, begin to arrive in spring in the southwestern counties.

The reasonably rare corncrake, which migrates from Africa, can be found in the western counties, in Donegal and around the Shannon Callows, and on islands such as Inishbofin in Galway. In late spring and early summer, the rugged coastlines, particularly cliff areas and islands, become a haven for breeding seabirds, mainly gannet, kittiwake, Manx shearwater, fulmar, cormorant and heron. Puffins, resembling penguins with their tuxedo colour scheme, nest in large colonies on coastal cliffs.

The lakes and low-lying wetlands attract large numbers of Arctic and northern European waterfowl and waders such as whooper swans, lapwing, barnacle geese, white-fronted geese and golden plovers. The important Wexford Wildfowl Reserve (p193) holds half the world's population of Greenland white-fronted geese, and little tern breed on the beach there, protected by the dunes. Also found during the winter are teal, redshank and curlew. The main migration periods are April to May and September to October.

The magnificent peregrine falcon has been making something of a recovery and can be found nesting on cliffs in Wicklow and elsewhere. In 2001, 46 golden eagle chicks from Scotland were released into Glenveagh National Park in Donegal in an effort to reintroduce the species. So far, the project's success has been down to the efforts of one pair of eagles: after successfully rearing a chick in 2007, they hatched two more in 2009, a welcome contrast to the deliberate poisoning of an eagle earlier that same year. Some of the eagles have expanded their range well beyond the park – frequent sightings have been reported in Counties Mayo and Antrim.

Plants

Although Ireland is sparsely wooded, the range of surviving plant species is larger here than in many other European countries, thanks in part to the comparatively late arrival of agriculture.

There are remnants of the original oak forest in Killarney National Park and in southern Wicklow near Shillelagh. Far more common are pine plantations, which are growing steadily. Hedgerows, planted to divide fields and delineate land boundaries throughout Ireland, actually host many of the native plant species that once thrived in the oak forests – it's an intriguing example of nature adapting and reasserting itself. The Burren in County

The illustrated pocket guide *Animals of Ireland* by Gordon D'Arcy is a handy, inexpensive introduction to Ireland's varied fauna.

Irish Birds by David Cabot is a pocket guide describing birds and their habitats, and outlines the best places for serious birdwatching.

See the excellent Birds of Ireland News Service website at www.birds ireland.com.

CONNEMARA PONIES

Ireland's best-known native animal is the Connemara pony – the largest of the pony breeds. The Connemara's ancestors, possibly introduced to Ireland by the Celts, developed the sturdiness and agility for which they are known while roaming the wilds of Connemara. According to legend, the breed also inherited some Spanish blood from the Spanish Armada's stallions, who swam ashore from galleons shipwrecked in 1588 and apparently survived to mate with local mares.

The compact and powerful Connemara pony was highly valued by farmers, who tamed wild mares and used them to plough cropland and haul rocks from the fields. Breeding did not become selective until 1923, when the Connemara Pony Breeders' Society was founded by a group based in Clifden. The Connemara pony, it seems, had been weakened by life in the stables and by indiscriminate breeding. Since then, it has been developed and refined, transforming the old work horse into a show horse. Connemara ponies are known for their gentle disposition and are great riding horses – for both adults and children alike.

Clare is home to a remarkable mixture of Mediterranean, alpine and arctic species.

Look for *Reading the Irish Landscape* by Frank Mitchell and Michael Ryan for info on Ireland's geology, archaeology, urban growth, agriculture and afforestation.

The bogs of Ireland are home to a unique flora adapted to wet, acidic, nutrient-poor conditions and whose survival is threatened by the depletion of bogs for energy use. Sphagnum moss is the key bog plant and is joined by other species such as bog rosemary, bog cotton, black-beaked sedge (whose spindly stem grows up to 30cm high) and various types of heather and lichen. Carnivorous plants also thrive, such as the sundew, whose sticky tentacles trap insects, and bladderwort, whose tiny explosive bladders trap aquatic animals in bog pools.

NATIONAL PARKS

Ireland has six national parks: the Burren (p376), Connemara (p421), Glenveagh (p489), Killarney (p295), Wicklow Mountains (p157) and the newest, Ballycroy National Park (p442), which opened in the summer of 2009. These have been developed to protect, preserve and make accessible areas of significant natural heritage. All the parks are open year-round and have information offices.

Forests & Forest Parks

Coillte Teoranta (Irish Forestry Board; ☎ 01-661 5666; www.coillte.ie; Leeson La, Dublin) administers about 3500 sq km of forested land, which includes designated picnic areas and 12 forest parks. This constitutes about 70% of the Republic's forest land. These parks open year-round and have a range of wildlife and habitats. Some also have chalets and/or caravan parks, shops, cafes and play areas for children.

For information on parks, gardens, monuments and inland waterways see www.heritageireland.ie.

National Nature Reserves

There are 66 state-owned and 10 privately owned National Nature Reserves (NNRs) in the Republic, represented by Dúchas (the government department in charge of parks, monuments and gardens). In Northern Ireland there are over 40 NNRs, which are leased or owned by the Department of the Environment. These reserves are defined as areas of importance for their special flora, fauna or geology, and include the Giant's Causeway (p656) and Glenariff (p663) in Antrim, and North Strangford Lough (p612) in County Down. More information is available from the **Northern Ireland Environment Agency** (☎ 0845 302 0008; www.ni-environment.gov.uk).

ENVIRONMENTAL ISSUES

Ireland does not rate among the world's biggest offenders when it comes to polluting the environment, but the country's recent economic growth has led to an increase in industry and consumerism, which in turn generate more pollution and waste. While the population density is among Europe's lowest, the population is rising. The last 10 years have seen the untrammelled expansion of suburban developments around all of Ireland's major towns and cities; the biggest by far is, inevitably, around Dublin, especially in the broadening commuter belt of Counties Meath and Kildare. The collapse of the construction bubble in 2008 has put an end to much of this development, but the rows of semi-detached houses still remain. As more people drive cars and fly in planes, Ireland grows more dependent on nonrenewable sources of energy. The amount of waste has risen substantially since the early 1990s.

Needless to say, concern for the environment is growing and the government has taken some measures to offset the damage that thriving economies can cause. In 2007 the Irish Energy Centre was renamed **Sustainable Energy Ireland** (SEI; www.sei.ie) and charged with promoting and assisting the development of sustainable energy. On a more practical level, a number of recycling programs have been very successful, especially the 'plastax' – a €0.22 levy on all plastic bags used within the retail sector, which has seen their use reduced by a whopping 90%.

Another successful project has been the **Village** (www.thevillage.ie), a 67-acre lot next to the village of Cloughjordan, in North Tipperary, purchased in 2005

CLIMATE CHANGE & OTHER LOOMING CONCERNS

It remains to be seen what's in store for Ireland as the earth's oceans and atmosphere warm up, but scientists have offered a long list of possible scenarios. The gentlest of forecasts has the weather of Northern Ireland resembling the current conditions in County Cork, while Cork turns into Ireland's version of the Côte d'Azure.

By mid-century, winter temperatures are expected to rise by 1°C (1.8°F) on average, while rainfall is predicted to increase, especially in the already wet northwest. Flooding may pose more of a problem in the Shannon River Basin. Summer temperatures may rise by as much as 2.5°C (4.5°F) on average, while rainfall is likely to drop significantly during these months. Seasonal drought may become a problem, wildfires may be a growing concern, and due to new irrigation costs, the potato may cease to be a viable cash crop in much of Ireland.

The rise in sea level will have a direct effect on Ireland's coasts. Gently sloped beaches along the west coast will disappear as higher waves erode sand and tides extend further inland. Already, climatologists are advising against development within 100m of flat coastlines. Many cities, including Dublin, Cork, Limerick and Galway, will be at increased risk of inundation in the event of storm surges unless seawalls are built.

The impact on biodiversity is a huge question mark, since it is difficult to estimate how well various plant and animal species will adapt to climate change and related side effects. Heath and peatlands, of which Ireland has a large proportion, are considered sensitive to extended periods of dryness. Ireland is currently at the southern extent of the range of salmon, which may stay further north (and hence be difficult to farm) if the island's streams warm too much for their breeding. New bird species may migrate to Ireland as their habitats elsewhere change or shrink, which will likely have a dramatic effect on delicate ecosystems.

One hotly debated question is the effect of global warming on the North Atlantic Drift, also known as the Gulf Stream, which carries warm waters north from the Gulf of Mexico and the west coast of Africa. Some scientists argue the Gulf Stream is already losing strength, and may stop circulating altogether within the next few decades. If that happens, Arctic waters may exert a greater influence on Ireland, dramatically cooling things off – at least until global warming brings up the temperature of the Arctic region. In that scenario, Ireland can forget about a Mediterranean climate – Scandinavian would be more like it. The weakening of the Gulf Stream is not universally accepted, and its possible effects are questioned. But, needless to say, folks will be talking a lot about the weather in the near future.

by Sustainable Projects Ireland Ltd who proceeded to develop the site as an entirely sustainable community. The government has jumped on board, too – in 2009, Enterprise Ireland announced grant funding for eco-enterprises located within the Village project. Meanwhile, the Republic has established 67 wind farms in an effort to reduce the country's reliance on fossil fuels.

To see a growing list of low-impact holiday options in Ireland (and elsewhere), visit www .responsibletravel.com.

While these are positive signs, they don't really put Ireland at the vanguard of the environmental movement. Polls seem to indicate the Irish are slightly less concerned about the environment than are the citizens of most other European countries, and the country is a long way from meeting its Kyoto Protocol requirement for reduced emissions. The government isn't pushing the environmental agenda much beyond ratifying EU agreements, although it must be said that these have established fairly ambitious goals for reduced air pollution and tighter management of water quality.

The annual number of tourists in Ireland far exceeds the number of residents (by a ratio of about 1.5 to one), so travellers can have a huge impact on the local environment. Tourism is frequently cited as potentially beneficial to the environment – that is, responsible visitor spending can help stimulate ecofriendly sectors of the economy. Ecotourism is not really burgeoning in a formalised way, although an organisation called the Greenbox has established standards for ecotourism on the island and promotes tour companies that comply to these standards. The rising popularity of outdoor activities such as diving, surfing and fishing create economic incentives for maintaining the cleanliness of Ireland's coasts and inland waters, but increased activity in these environments can be harmful if not managed carefully.

The Greenbox (www .greenbox.ie) offers a range of ecofriendly activities and tours in northwest Ireland.

Ireland's comprehensive and efficient bus network makes it easy to avoid the use of a car, and the country is well suited to cycling and walking holidays. Many hotels, guest houses and hostels tout green credentials, and organic ingredients are frequently promoted on restaurant menus. It's not difficult for travellers to minimise their environmental footprint while in Ireland. See p21 for more information on travelling sustainably.

Irish Culture

The Celtic harp, one of Ireland's most enduring symbols

MARTIN MOOS

THE LANDSCAPE

Can you tell the story of what Ireland looks like? Can you do it without using the words of the comfortable, easy clichés – the many types of green made so by a blanket of rain – that *sound* just about right but hardly do the place justice? Ireland is a temperate, modest place – neither harsh nor extreme – but it has always defied easy description, never more so than for the artists and writers whose very lives were devoted to capturing it on canvas or on the page.

There are few people so attached to the land of their birth as the Irish, as much because of their peasant legacy as for the fact that, for a lot of their history, they were not owners of it but harshly treated tenants. The architects of the Gaelic Revival of the late 19th century – WB Yeats, Lady Gregory et al – understood this troubled relationship all too well and sought to repair the fissure by focusing their artistic attentions on the lands and the people who worked them in an effort to capture both the beauty and the tragedy of the land. And so Yeats urged the playwright John Millington Synge to 'go to the Aran Islands [and] live there as if you were one of the people themselves; express a life that has never found expression'.

Sunlight breaking over Macgillycuddy's Reeks (p298)

GARETH MCCO

Glassillaun Beach, Connemara, County Galway (p422)

GARETH MCCORMACK

Synge took Yeats' advice and out of the tough, uncompromising beauty of the islands were born his most powerful works: *Riders to the Sea, The Shadow of the Glen* and his masterpiece, *The Playboy of the Western World.*

If Ireland of the memorable postcards – those thatched country cottages dotting a brown-green patchwork of fields marked by stone walls – had a creator, then it was surely Paul Henry (1876–1958), the most important Irish painter of the 1920s and 1930s. Like Synge before him, he went west, to Connemara and Achill Island, where he found the Irish version of Gauguin's premodern Arcadia. Henry's sympathetic, yet unromantic portraits have endured to this day, mostly because there is no trace of the chocolate box colleen or the cheeky car driver with his stock of amusing stories; absent is the glamour of false romance in favour of the stark sincerity of the landscape as it truly was.

This hard, loving relationship with the land is common to many Irish writers, but its expression in the work of poet Patrick Kavanagh is especially stark. He was addressing the county of his birth when he wrote the following quatrain – the bane of many an Irish schoolchild:

> O stony grey soil of Monaghan
> The laugh from my love you thieved;
> You took the gay child of my passion
> And gave me your clod-conceived.

The remarkable fact is not that Kavanagh had a stormy relationship with rural Ireland but that so many Irish know exactly what he meant.

Ireland has modernised and urbanised, to be sure, but the relationship with the land endures. It cannot be otherwise, for the journey to full and final ownership has been too wrought with difficulty – something worth considering as you soak in its beauty.

The 'black stuff': Guinness stout (p67)   MICAH WRIGHT

THE ROUNDS SYSTEM

Nothing will hasten your fall from social grace like the failure to uphold one simple law: the rounds system. This simple custom – whereby someone buys you a drink and you buy one back – is the bedrock of Irish pub culture, summed up in the Irish saying 'It's impossible for two men to go to a pub for one drink.' And remember, the next round starts when the first person is about to finish their drink, not you yours. It doesn't matter if you're only halfway through your pint: if it's your round, get them in.

THE PUB

We're not just talking about a place to get a drink. Oh, no. You can get a drink in a restaurant or hotel, or wherever there's someone with a bottle of something strong. The pub is something altogether more than that. It is the broadest window through which you can examine and experience the very essence of the nation's culture, in all its myriad forms. It's the great leveller, where status and rank hold no sway, where generation gaps are bridged, inhibitions lowered, tongues loosened, schemes hatched, songs sung, stories told and gossip embroidered. It's a unique institution: a theatre and a cosy room, a centre stage and a hideaway, a debating chamber and a place for silent contemplation. It's whatever you want it to be, and that's the secret of the great Irish pub.

Talk – whether it is frivolous, earnest or incoherent – is the essential ingredient. Once tongues are loosened and the cogs of thought oiled, your conversation can go anywhere and you should follow it to its natural conclusion. While it's a myth to say you can walk into any Irish pub and make a friend, you probably won't be drinking on your own for long – unless that's what you want, of course. There are few more spiritual experiences than a solitary pint in a quiet country pub in the midafternoon.

But remember that banter is the fibre of sociability. 'Slagging' (teasing) is the country's favourite pastime and a far more reliable indicator of the strength of friendship than virtually any kind of compliment: a fast, self-deprecating wit and an ability to take a joke in good spirits will win you plenty of friends.

Aesthetically, there is nothing better than the traditional haunt, populated by flat-capped pensioners bursting with delightful anecdotes and always ready to dispense a kind of wisdom distilled through generations' worth of experience. The best pubs have stone floors and a peat fire; the chat barely rises above a respectful murmur, save for appreciative laughter; and, most importantly of all, there's no music save the kind played by someone sitting next to you. Pubs like these are a disappearing breed, but there's still plenty of them around to ensure that you will find one, no matter where you are.

IRISH SYMBOLS & ICONS
Shamrock

Ireland's most enduring symbol is the shamrock, a three-leafed white clover known diminutively in Irish as *seamróg*, which was anglicised as 'shamrock'. Ac-

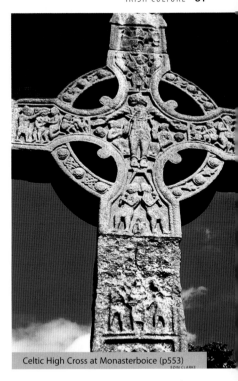

Celtic High Cross at Monasterboice (p553)
EDIN CLARKE

cording to legend, when St Patrick was trying to explain the mystery of the Holy Trinity to the recently converted Celtic chieftains, he plucked the modest little weed and used its three leaves to explain the metaphysically challenging concept of the Father, the Son and the Holy Spirit being separate but part of the one being. This is why the shamrock is a ubiquitous part of the St Patrick's Day celebrations.

The three-leafed shamrock, symbol of the Holy Trinity
JOHN SONES

Celtic Cross

Everywhere you go you will see examples of the Celtic cross – basically a cross surrounded by a ring. Its origins weren't simply a question of aesthetic design, but more one of practical necessity. The cross was a clever fusing of new Christian teaching (the cross itself) with established pagan beliefs, in this case sun worship (marked by the circle).

The most famous crosses in Ireland are in Kells, County Meath (p545), Ardboe, County Tyrone (p693), Monasterboice, County Louth (p553), and Clonmacnoise, County Offaly (p511).

Leprechaun

The country's most enduring cliché is the myth of the mischievous leprechaun and his pot of gold, which he jealously guards from the attentions of greedy humans. Despite the twee aspect of the legend, its origin predates the Celts and belongs to the mythological Tuatha dé Danann (peoples

Harp players at a music festival

RICHARD CUMMINS

of the goddess Danu), who lived in Ireland 4000 years ago. When they were eventually defeated, their king Lugh (the demigod father of Cúchulainn) was forced underground, where he became known as Lugh Chromain, meaning 'little stooping Lugh' – the origin of the leprechaun.

The Irish can get visibly irritated if asked whether they believe in leprechauns (you might as well ask them whether they're stupid), but many rural dwellers are a superstitious lot. They mightn't necessarily *believe* that malevolent sprites who dwell in faerie forts actually exist, but they're not especially keen to test the theory either, which is why there still exist trees, hills and other parts of the landscape that are deemed to have…supernatural qualities, and so will never be touched.

Harp

The Celtic harp, *cláirseach* in Irish, is said to represent the immortality of the soul, which is handy given that it's been a symbol of Ireland since the days of Henry VIII and the first organised opposition to English rule. The harp was the most popular instrument at the Celtic court, with the harpist (usually blind) being ranked behind only the chief and bard in order of importance. In times of war, the harpist played a special, jewel-encrusted harp and served as the cheerleading section for soldiers heading into battle.

During the first rebellions against the English, the harp was once again an instrument of revolutionary fervour, prompting the Crown to ban it altogether. This eventually led to its decline as the instrument of choice for Irish musicians, but ensured its status as a symbol of Ireland.

Claddagh Ring

The most famous of all Irish jewellery is the Claddagh ring, made up of two hands (symbolising friendship) clasping a heart (love) and usually surmounted by a crown (loyalty). Made in the eponymous fishing village in County Galway since the 17th century, its symbolic origins are much older and it belongs to a broader family of rings, popular since Roman times, known as *fede* rings (from *mani in fede*, meaning 'hands in trust'), which were used to symbolise marriage. Nevertheless, their popularity is relatively recent, and almost entirely due to their wearing by expat Americans, who use them to demonstrate their ties to Ireland (see p401).

TRADITIONAL MUSIC

A traditional *seisiún* in a pub? Perish the thought. Traditional music in Ireland may have retired to the smoky atmosphere of the traditional pub, but 'tis far from there that it was reared. Until the latter half of the 20th century, the jigs, reels, polkas and myriad other styles of Irish music were heard only in the music houses of Ireland – yes, literally the private homes of musicians or music lovers in the locality.

Traditional music can be heard in pubs and festivals all over Ireland   DOUG MCKINLAY

Traditional *seisiún*, Hughes' Bar, Dublin (p142)
DOUG MCKINLAY

The entire music-loving community was welcome to gather around the kitchen stove, tapping their feet on the stone floors in appreciation of the genius playing before them: a fiddler playing in the fast-paced style of his native Donegal; an accordionist intoning a polka, for which County Kerry is renowned; or a *sean nós* singer performing in the lyrical style of County Clare.

The music was never written down: it was passed on from one player to another and so endured and evolved. Regional 'styles' developed only because local musicians sought to play just like the one who

THE MUSICAL DIASPORA

'Traditional music' is merely the music of a parish or a locality, whatever that music may be, and, in Ireland's case, the role of the emigrant cannot be overstated. The first recordings of Irish music were made by Jim 'Professor' Morrison (1893–1947), who emigrated to the United States in 1915 and took with him a fiddle that he played in the style of his native north Sligo. The single biggest innovation, however, was made by musicians who escaped the bleak economic landscape of the 1930s and made their way to London. Away from the network of music houses where they could play for their local communities, the best of them found solace in the pubs of London, where in 1947 the first session took place in the Devonshire Arms in Camden Town.

seemed to play better than everybody else. The characteristic of fluidity is key to an appreciation of traditional music, and explains why it is such a resilient form today.

Irish music has successfully absorbed influences as diffuse as blues, rock and folk styles from a host of other countries, but it has influenced other forms just as much – not least American folk music. Yet instead of a multicultural melange unrecognisable from what came before, the old style of playing and performing is stronger than ever – just find a music pub in Miltown Malbay (see p373) and see for yourself.

Dublin

Form is temporary, but class is permanent: the good times may have gone, but Dublin still knows how to have a good time. Sure, the bling has been toned down and Dubliners aren't taking *quite* as many foreign holidays, but it takes more than a global financial crisis and the unparalleled crash of the construction industry to knock this city out of stride.

Prosperous or not, Dublin has always been unflappable in its commitment to the belief that you don't need piles of money to enjoy yourself. Still, the transformation of the last few years – the most radical in its thousand-plus-year history – has raised some challenging questions for many Dubliners, who welcomed the city's fortunes but were suspicious of the crass commercialism that came with it.

But the last couple of decades have done wonders for the city too. Dubliners take it as given that their city is a multicultural melting pot where Russians shop for tinned caviar, Nigerian teenagers discuss the merits of hair extensions and Koreans hawk phone cards from their cars. They are confident in the knowledge that their city is so hip that travellers from all over the world can't wait to get here and indulge in the many pleasures it has to offer.

Because pleasure is something Dublin knows all about – from its music, art and literature to the legendary nightlife that has inspired those same musicians, artists and writers, Dublin knows how to have fun and does it with deadly seriousness. As you'll soon find out.

HIGHLIGHTS

- **Antiquated Scholars** Stroll the Elizabethan cobbled grounds of Trinity College (p100)
- **Book-Bound Serenity** Pore over ancient books and other printed wonders from all around the world in the Chester Beatty Library (p105)
- **Choice Addresses** Enjoy Georgian gems surrounding the landscaped Merrion Square (p109) and St Stephen's Green (p108)
- **History Lesson** See the past up close and personal at Kilmainham Jail (p113)
- **Mine's a Guinness** Quaff a pint or five in one of Dublin's many pubs and clubs (p140)

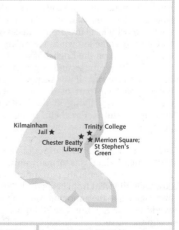

Kilmainham Jail ★

Chester Beatty Library ★

Trinity College ★

★ Merrion Square; St Stephen's Green

■ TELEPHONE CODE: 01   ■ POPULATION: 1.3 MILLION   ■ AREA: 921 SQ KM

HISTORY

Dublin celebrated its official millennium in 1988, but there were settlements here long before AD 988. The first early Celtic habitation, around 500 BC, was at a ford over the River Liffey, giving rise to the city's Irish name, Baile Átha Cliath (Town of the Hurdle Ford).

The Celts went about their merry way for 1000 years or so, but it wasn't until the Vikings showed up that Dublin was urbanised in any significant way. By the 9th century raids from the north had become a fact of Irish life, and some of the fierce Danes chose to stay rather than simply rape, pillage and depart. They intermarried with the Irish and established a vigorous trading port at the point where the River Poddle joined the Liffey in a *dubh linn* (black pool). Today there's little trace of the Poddle, which has been channelled underground and flows under St Patrick's Cathedral to dribble into the Liffey by the Capel St (Grattan) Bridge.

Fast-forward another 1000 years, past the arrival of the Normans in the 12th century and the slow process of subjugating Ireland to Anglo-Norman (then British) rule, a process in which Dublin generally played the role of bandleader. Stop at the beginning of the 18th century, when the squalid city packed with poor Catholics hardly reflected the imperial pretensions of its Anglophile burghers. The great and the good – aka the Protestant Ascendancy – wanted big improvements, and they set about transforming what was in essence still a medieval town into a modern, Anglo-Irish metropolis. Roads were widened, landscaped squares laid out and new town houses built, all in a proto-Palladian style that soon became known as Georgian (after the kings then on the English throne). For a time, Dublin was the second-largest city in the British Empire and all was very, very good – unless you were part of the poor, mostly Catholic masses living in the city's ever-developing slums. For them, things stayed pretty much as they had always been.

The Georgian boom came to a sudden and dramatic halt after the Act of Union in 1801, when Ireland was formally united with Britain and its separate parliament closed down. Dublin went from being the belle of the imperial ball to the annoying cousin who just wouldn't take the hint, and slid quickly into economic turmoil and social unrest. During the Potato Famine (1845–51), the city's population was swollen by the arrival of tens of thousands of starving refugees from the west, who joined the ranks of an already downtrodden working class. As Dublin entered the 20th century, it was a dispirited place plagued by poverty, disease and more social problems than anyone cared to mention. It's hardly surprising that the majority of Dublin's citizenry were pissed off and eager for change.

The first fusillade of transformation came during the Easter Rising of 1916, which caused considerable damage to the city centre. At first, Dubliners weren't too enamoured of the rebels, who caused more chaos and disruption than most locals were willing to put up with, but they soon changed their tune when the leaders were callously executed – Dubliners are natural defenders of the underdog.

As the whole country lurched radically towards full-scale war with Britain, Dublin was, surprisingly, not part of the main theatre of events. In fact, although there was an increased military presence, the odd shooting in the capital and the blowing up of some notable buildings – such as the Custom House in 1921 – it was business as usual for much of the War of Independence. People went to work and socialised in pretty much the same way as when there wasn't a war.

A year later, Ireland – minus its northern bit – was independent, but it then tumbled into the Civil War, which led to the burning of more notable buildings, this time the Four Courts in 1922. Ironically the war among the Irish was more brutal than the struggle for independence – O'Connell St became 'sniper row' and the violence left deep scars that are only today beginning to disappear.

When the new state finally started doing business, Dublin was an exhausted capital. Despite slow and steady improvements, the city – like the rest of Ireland – continued to be plagued by rising unemployment, high emigration rates and a general stagnation that hung about the place like an impenetrable cloud. Dubliners made the most of the little they had, but times were tough. Then, in the 1960s, a silver lining appeared in the shape of an economic boom: Dublin went suburban and began the outward expansion that continues unabated today.

A boom ain't a miracle, however, and Dublin trudged along for another couple of decades with pretty much the same age-old problems (high unemployment, emigration) and some new ones (drug addiction, gangland criminality) before everything began to change in 1994 and a terrible beauty known as the Celtic Tiger was born. Fifteen years later, Dublin is a place transformed, a capital in more than name and a city that has finally taken its rightful place as one of the most vibrant in Europe.

ORIENTATION

Greater Dublin sprawls around the arc of Dublin Bay, bounded to the north by the hills at Howth and to the south by the Dalkey headland. Small and compact, the city centre (which has traditionally been defined as within the boundaries of the Royal Canal, to the north, and the Grand Canal, to the south) has a clear focus and is a walker's delight. It is split in two by the unremarkable River Liffey, which traditionally marks a psychological and social break between the affluent southside and the poorer northside.

South of the river, over O'Connell Bridge, is the Temple Bar area and the expanse of Trinity College. Nassau St, along the southern edge of the campus, and pedestrianised Grafton St are the main shopping streets. At the southern end of Grafton St is St Stephen's Green. About 2km west, beside the river, is Heuston Station, one of the city's two main train stations.

North of the Liffey are O'Connell St and, just off it, Henry St, the major shopping thoroughfares. Most of the northside's B&Bs are on Gardiner St, which becomes rather run-down as it continues north. At the northern end of O'Connell St is Parnell Sq. The main bus station, Busáras, and the other main train station, Connolly Station, are near the southern end of Gardiner St.

The postcodes for central Dublin are Dublin 1 (immediately north of the river) and Dublin 2 (immediately south). The Dublin 4 postcode, covering the swanky neighbourhoods of Ballsbridge, Donnybrook and Sandymount, is synonymous with affluence and often used as a descriptive term. A handy tip to remember is that even numbers apply to the southside and odd ones to the north.

See p150 for information on transport to/from the airport and train stations.

INFORMATION
Bookshops
Books Upstairs (Map p101; ☎ 679 6687; www .booksirish.com; 36 College Green) Top-notch independent bookshop with lots of Irish-interest titles.

Cathach Books (Map p96; ☎ 671 8676; www.rare books.ie; 10 Duke St) A rich and remarkable collection of second-hand Irish-interest books, including 1st editions.
Connolly Books (Map p94; ☎ 670 8707; www .communistpartyofireland.ie/cbooks; 43 East Essex St) Left-wing bookshop beloved of Marxists and radicals.
Dublin Writers Museum (Map pp92-3; ☎ 872 2077; 18 North Parnell Sq) As you'd expect, a good range of Irish and Irish-interest titles.
Dubray Books (Map p96; ☎ 677 5568; www.dubray books.ie; 36 Grafton St) Excellent local shop with a good Irish-interest section.
Eason (Map p94; ☎ 873 3811; www.easons.ie; 40 Lower O'Connell St) Has one of the biggest magazine inventories in Ireland.
Hodges Figgis (Map p96; ☎ 677 4754; 56-58 Dawson St) Dublin's largest bookshop, with the widest selection of titles.
Hughes & Hughes Dublin Airport (Map p88; ☎ 814 4034); St Stephen's Green (Map p96; ☎ 478 3060; St Stephen's Green Shopping Centre) Magazines, bestsellers and new titles.
Irish Museum of Modern Art (IMMA; Map p90; www .imma.ie; ☎ 612 9900; Royal Hospital Kilmainham) Contemporary art and Irish-interest books.
Library Book Shop (Map p101; ☎ 608 1171; Trinity College) Irish-interest books, including ones on the *Book of Kells*.
Murder Ink (Map p96; ☎ 677 7570; 15 Dawson St) Mystery titles.
National Gallery (Map p96; ☎ 678 5450; Merrion Sq West) Traditional art and Irish-interest books.
Sinn Féin Bookshop (Map pp92-3; ☎ 872 7096; 44 West Parnell Sq) Main bookshop and information centre for the country's Republican party (which once maintained close links with the IRA).
Stokes Books (Map p96; ☎ 671 3584; 19 George's St Arcade) Irish historical books, old and new.
Waterstone's Dawson St (Map p96; ☎ 679 1415; 7 Dawson St); Jervis St Centre (Map p94; ☎ 878 1311; Jervis St) The big British chain bookshop has two branches, north and south of the river.
Winding Stair (Map p94; ☎ 872 6576; www.winding -stair.com; 40 Lwr Ormond Quay) The most atmospheric of Dublin's bookshops, with a fine selection of quirky titles and Irish books.

Cultural Centres
Alliance Française (Map p96; ☎ 676 1732; www .alliance-francaise.ie; 1 Kildare St)
British Council (Map p90; ☎ 676 4088; www.british council.org; Newmount House, 22-24 Lower Mount St)
Goethe Institute (Map p96; ☎ 661 1155; www .goethe.de; 37 North Merrion Sq)
Instituto Cervantes (Map p101; ☎ 631 1500; http:// dublin.cervantes.es; Lincoln House, Lincoln Pl)

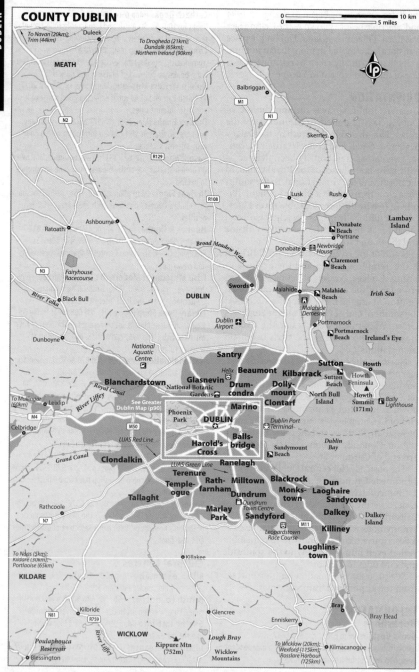

COUNTY DUBLIN

0 _____ 10 km
0 _____ 5 miles

DUBLIN IN...

Two Days

Kick-start your day the right way with breakfast at **Honest to Goodness** (p134) in the wonderful **George's St Arcade** (p148) – and when you're done have a ramble through the arcade's collection of stalls and funky stores. A stone's throw away is **Trinity College** (p100), where the walking tour includes entry to the **Book of Kells** (see the boxed text, p103). Head up to Grafton St to catch the buskers and splurge on Dublin's most exclusive shopping street. Round it off with a cocktail, dinner and outdoor movie on the terrace at **Eden** (p137), one of Dublin's trendiest restaurants, located in **Temple Bar** (p103), before falling into bed at the **Irish Landmark Trust** (p129), which you and six friends have made your home. The next day marvel at the art of the **Chester Beatty Library** (p105) before strolling up to the **Guinness Storehouse** (p112) for a tour that ends with a glass of 'plain' in the Gravity Bar, which has stunning 360-degree views of the city.

Four Days

Follow the two-day itinerary, then wander around the historic **Glasnevin Cemetery** (p120) before moseying into the peaceful **National Botanic Gardens** (p120). Back in town, browse the **designer shops** (p149) in Temple Bar and grab a bite at **L'Gueuleton** (p136), then go on the **Dublin Literary Pub Crawl** (p125). The following day take the Dublin Area Rapid Transport (DART) along the coast to the pretty village of **Dalkey** (p152). On your return, gather your strength with a fine meal at **Town Bar & Grill** (p137) before taking in a gig at **Vicar Street** (p147).

Italian Cultural Institute (Map pp92–3; ☎ 662 0509; www.iicdublino.esteri.it; 11 Fitzwilliam Sq East)

Emergency

For national emergency numbers, see the inside front cover.

Confidential Line Freefone (☎ 1800 666 111) *Garda* (police) confidential line to report crime.

Drugs Advisory & Treatment Centre (Map p90; ☎ 677 1122; Trinity Ct, 30-31 Pearse St)

Rape Crisis Centre (Map p90; ☎ 1800 778 888, 661 4911; 70 Lower Leeson St)

Samaritans (☎ 1850 609 090, 872 7700) Help line for people who are depressed or suicidal.

Internet Access

Global Internet Café (Map p94; ☎ 878 0295; 8 Lower O'Connell St; per hr €5; ⏱ 8am-11pm Mon-Fri, from 9am Sat, from 10am Sun)

Internet Exchange (Map p94; ☎ 670 3000; 3 Cecilia St; per hr €5; ⏱ 8am-2am Mon-Fri, 10am-midnight Sat & Sun)

Internet Resources

www.balconytv.com Interviews and music from a balcony in central Dublin.

www.beaut.ie A superb blog ostensibly about beauty tips but really a great commentary on the Irish and their wants.

www.dublincity.ie Dublin City Council's own website has a great link to live traffic cams

www.dublinks.com One-stop guide for all manner of goings-on in the capital.

www.ireland.ie Official website of Discover Ireland, the public face of the Irish Tourist Board.

www.lecool.com/cities/Dublin Up-to-date online guide that launched its Dublin city module in May 2009.

www.nixers.ie Good place to check for casual work over the summer.

www.overheardindublin.com Proof that the general public are better than any scriptwriter.

www.philpankov.com Great black-and-white photos of the city by a great photographer.

www.thedubliner.com Gossip, features and other Dublin-related titbits.

www.visitdublin.com Official website of Dublin Tourism.

Laundry

Laundry facilities can be found quite easily in the city centre, with prices starting at about €7.50 per load; ask at your accommodation for the nearest one. Alternatively most hostels, B&Bs and hotels will provide laundry service. In hostels, laundry starts at around €6 and is generally self-service.

All-American Laundrette (Map p96; ☎ 677 2779; Wicklow Ct, South Great George's St)

Laundry Shop (Map pp92–3; ☎ 872 3541; 191 Parnell St)

(Continued on p98)

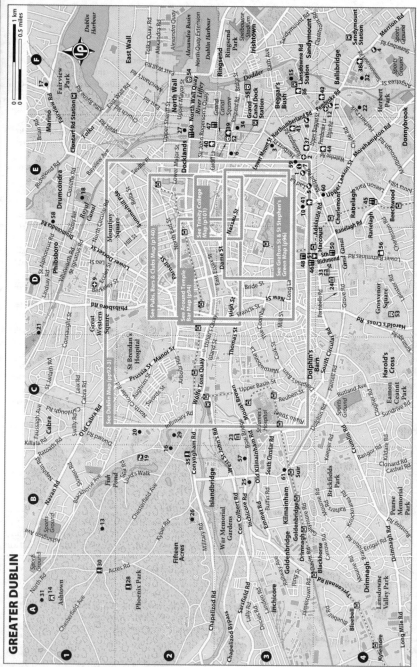

GREATER DUBLIN

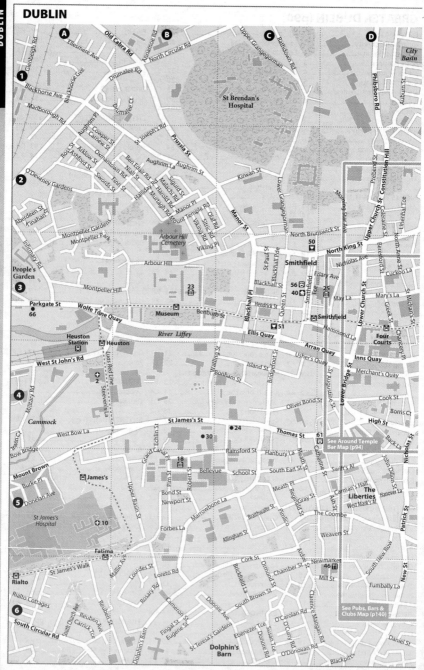

DUBLIN

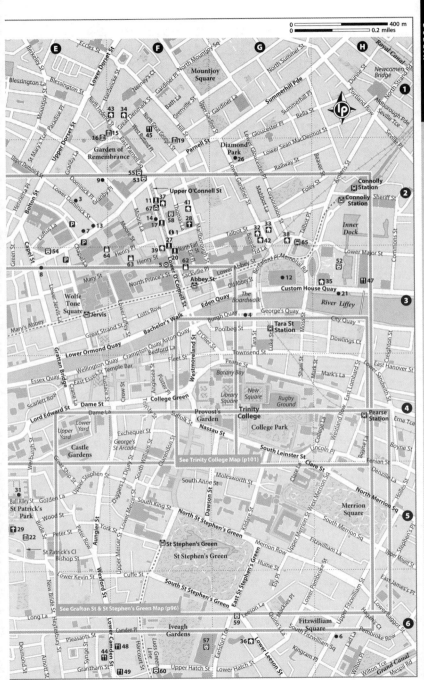

AROUND TEMPLE BAR

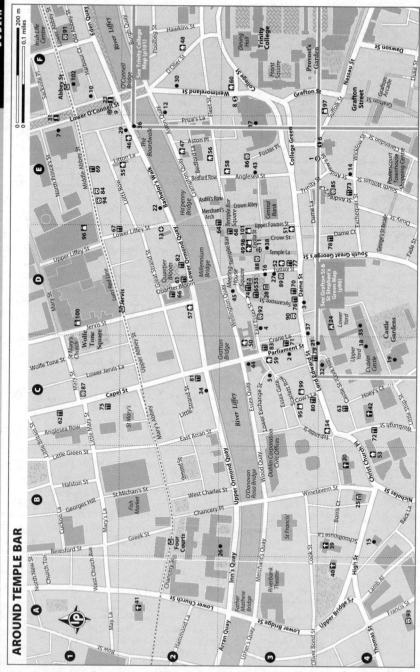

AROUND TEMPLE BAR (p94)

DUBLIN

GRAFTON ST & ST STEPHEN'S GREEN

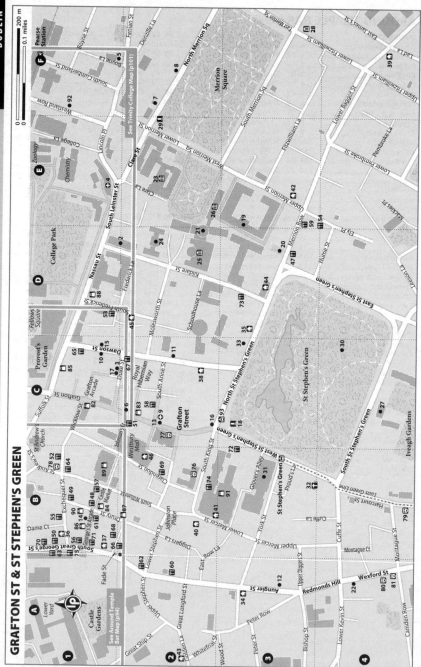

GRAFTON ST & ST STEPHEN'S GREEN (p96)

DUBLIN

(Continued from p89)

Left Luggage

Left-luggage facilities are available at all transport centres, including the airport.

Busáras (Map pp92-3; ☎ 703 2434; locker per 24hr €5-10; ⊙ 7am-10.30pm) Main bus station north of the River Liffey.

Connolly Station (Map pp92-3; ☎ 703 2363; bag per 24hr €3; ⊙ 7am-10pm Mon-Sat, 8am-10pm Sun) The main train station on the northside.

Dublin Airport (Map p88; ☎ 814 4633; Greencaps Left Luggage & Porterage, Dublin airport; per bag per 24hr €5-11; ⊙ 6am-11pm Mon-Sat, 8am-11pm Sun)

Libraries

Dublin City Council (Map p96; ☎ 661 9000; Cumberland House, Fenian St; ⊙ 9.30am-5pm Mon-Fri) Offers information on public libraries.

ILAC Centre Public Library (Map pp92-3; ☎ 873 4333; ILAC Centre, Henry St; ⊙ 10am-8pm Mon-Thu, to 5pm Sat) One of the city's largest public libraries.

Media

Besides the national dailies (see p696), there are a number of Dublin-specific publications and media outlets.

NEWSPAPERS & MAGAZINES

Dublin Event Guide (free) Fortnightly coverage of all things entertainment throughout the city.

Dubliner (€3.99) Monthly magazine that mixes city-related offerings with interviews and features.

Evening Herald (€1) Evening tabloid with thorough entertainment listings and a terrific flat-finder section.

In Dublin (free) A monthly ad rag.

RADIO

98 FM Pop and chart music all day long

Phantom 105.2 FM Alternative music, from mod to metal.

Spin 103.8 FM Chart music and chat for 18-to-24-year olds.

WI-FI HOT SPOTS

Wi-fi (wireless internet) is a handy mobile alternative to plugging into a local area network (LAN). Many public places offer access to wi-fi networks so that customers can use the internet on the move. Try the following hot spots for free access: Chester Beatty Library (p105), Market Bar (p135) or the Globe (p143).

Medical Services

Should you experience an immediate health problem, contact the casualty section (emergency room) of the nearest public hospital; in an emergency, call an ambulance (☎ 999). There are no 24-hour pharmacies in Dublin; the latest any stay open is 10pm.

Baggot St Hospital (Map p90; ☎ 668 1577; 18 Upper Baggot St; ⊙ 7.30am-4.30pm Mon-Fri) Southside city centre.

City Pharmacy (Map p94; ☎ 670 4523; 14 Dame St; ⊙ 9am-10pm)

Dental Hospital (Map p96; ☎ 612 7200; 20 Lincoln Pl; ⊙ 9am-5pm Mon-Fri, from 8am for pre-booked appointments) If you need to get those choppers looked at; if you don't have an appointment, head in after noon.

Doctors on Call (☎ 453 9333; ⊙ 24hr) Request a doctor to come out to your accommodation at any time.

Eastern Regional Health Authority (Map pp92-3; ☎ 679 0700, 1800 520 520; www.erha.ie; Dr Steevens' Hospital, Steeven's Lane; ⊙ 9.30am-5.30pm Mon-Fri) Central health authority with Choice of Doctor Scheme, which can advise you on a suitable GP from 9am to 5pm Monday to Friday. Information services for those with physical and mental disabilities.

Grafton Medical Centre (Map p96; ☎ 671 2122; www.graftonmedical.ie; 34 Grafton St; ⊙ 8.30am-6.30pm Mon-Thu, to 6pm Fri) One-stop shop with male and female doctors, physiotherapists and a tropical medicine bureau.

Mater Misericordiae Hospital (Map p90; ☎ 830 1122; Eccles St) Northside city centre, off Lower Dorset St.

O'Connell's Pharmacy Grafton St (Map p96; ☎ 679 0467; 21 Grafton St; ⊙ 9am-10pm); O'Connell St (Map p94; ☎ 873 0427; 55-56 Upper O'Connell St; ⊙ 9am-10pm)

St James's Hospital (Map pp92-3; ☎ 453 7941; James St) Southside.

Well Woman Centre Lower Liffey St (Map p94; ☎ 872 8051; www.wellwomancentre.ie; 35 Lower Liffey St; ⊙ 9.30am-7.30pm Mon, Thu & Fri, 8am-7.30pm Tue & Wed, 10am-4pm Sat & 1-4pm Sun); Pembroke Rd (Map p90; ☎ 660 9860; 67 Pembroke Rd, Ballsbridge; ⊙ 10am-7.30pm Mon-Wed, 8am-7.30pm Thu & Fri, 10am-4pm Sat) For female health issues. Supplies contraceptives, including the morning-after pill (€65).

Money

There are currency-exchange counters at Dublin airport in the baggage-collection area, and on the arrival and departure floors. The counters are open 5.30am to 11pm.

There are numerous banks around the city centre with exchange facilities, open during regular bank hours.

First Rate (Map p94; ☎ 671 3233; 1 Westmoreland St; ◷ 8am-9pm Mon-Fri, 9am-9pm Sat, 10am-9pm Sun Jun-Sep, 9am-6pm Mon-Sat Oct-May)

Post

An Post (Map p94; ☎ 705 8206; www.anpost.ie; St Andrew's St)

General Post Office (Map pp92-3; ☎ 705 7000; O'Connell St; ◷ 8am-8pm Mon-Sat) Dublin's famed general post office has a free poste-restante service, a philatelic counter and a bank of telephones.

Telephone

Talk Shop (◷ 9am-11pm); Temple Lane (Map p94; ☎ 672 7212; The Granary, 20 Temple Lane) For cheap international phone calls.

Tourist Information

No tourist information offices in Dublin provide any information over the phone – they're exclusively walk-in services.

All telephone bookings and reservations are operated by Gulliver, a computerised information and reservation service that is available at all walk-in offices or from anywhere in the world. It provides up-to-date information on events, attractions and transport, and can also book accommodation. You can book via www.visitdublin.ie or www.gulliver.ie, or via telephone: in Ireland call ☎ 1800 668 668; from Britain call ☎ 00800 6686 6866; from the rest of the world call ☎ 66-979 2030.

Dublin Tourism (www.visitdublin.com); Dublin Airport (arrivals hall; ◷ 8am-10pm); Dun Laoghaire (Dun Laoghaire ferry terminal; ◷ 10am-1pm & 2-6pm Mon-Sat); O'Connell St (Map pp92-3; 14 Upper O'Connell St; ◷ 9am-5pm Mon-Sat); Wilton Tce (Map p90; Wilton Tce; ◷ 9.30am-noon & 12.30-5.15pm Mon-Fri)

Dublin Tourism Centre (Map p94; ☎ 605 7700; www.visitdublin.com; St Andrew's Church, 2 Suffolk St;

◷ 9am-7pm Mon-Sat, 10.30am-3pm Sun Jul & Aug, 9am-5.30pm Mon-Sat Sep-Jun) Dublin's main tourist office. There's a booking fee of €4.50 for serviced accommodation or €7.50 for self-catering accommodation, and a 10% deposit that is refunded through your hotel bill.

Fáilte Ireland head office (Map p90; ☎ 1850 230 330; www.ireland.ie; Wilton Tce; ◷ 9am-5.15pm Mon-Fri)

Travel Agencies

American Express (Amex; Map p94; ☎ 605 7709; Dublin Tourism Centre, St Andrew's Church, 2 Suffolk St; ◷ 9am-5pm Mon-Sat)

Thomas Cook (Map p94; ☎ 677 1721/1307; 118 Grafton St; ◷ 9am-5.30pm Mon, Tue, Fri & Sat, 10am-5.30pm Wed, 9am-7pm Thu)

USIT (Map p94; ☎ 602 1904; www.usit.ie; 19 Aston Quay; ◷ 9.30am-6.30pm Mon-Wed & Fri, 9.30am-8pm Thu, 9.30am-5pm Sat) Travel agency of the Union of Students in Ireland.

DANGERS & ANNOYANCES

Dublin's city centre is generally safe, even if petty crime of the bag-snatching, pickpocketing and car-break-in variety can be a low- to mid-level irritant. Be sensible: guard your belongings, don't leave anything in your car and consider the use of supervised car parks for overnight parking. Remember also that insurance policies often don't cover losses from cars.

The only consistent trouble in Dublin is alcohol-related: where there are pubs and clubs there are worse-for-wear revellers looking to get home and/or get laid, and sometimes the frustrations of getting neither can result in a trip to the casualty department of the nearest hospital – hospitals are clogged to bursting with drink-related cases throughout the weekend.

The area north of Gardiner St, O'Connell St and Mountjoy Sq is not especially salubrious – gangs of disaffected youths and drug addicts on the make are a recipe for trouble and sometimes violence.

SIGHTS
Grafton St & Around

Dublin's most celebrated shopping street is the elegant, pedestrianised spine of the southern city centre: at its northern end is Trinity College, the country's oldest and most beautiful university, which stretches its leafy self across a healthy chunk of south-city real estate. A few steps northwest is the area called Temple Bar, where bacchanalia and bohemia scrap it out for supremacy – when the sun sets, Bacchus is king. Grafton Street's southern end runs into the main entrance to St Stephen's Green, Dublin's perennially popular green lung; surrounding and beyond it is the capital's exquisite Georgian heritage, a collection of galleries, museums, and private and public buildings as handsome as any you'll see in Europe.

TRINITY COLLEGE

On a summer's evening, when the bustling crowds have gone for the day, there's hardly a more delightful place in Dublin than the grounds of Ireland's most prestigious **university** (Map p101; ☎ 896 1000, walking tours ☎ 896 1827; tour €5, incl Long Room €10; ☺ tours every 40min 10.15am-3.40pm Mon-Sat, 10.15am-3pm Sun mid-May–Sep), a masterpiece of architecture and landscaping beautifully preserved in Georgian aspic. Not only is it Dublin's most attractive bit of historical real estate, but it's also home to one of the world's most famous – and most beautiful – books, the gloriously illuminated *Book of Kells*. There is no charge to wander around the gardens on your own between 8am and 10pm.

Officially, the university's name is the University of Dublin, but Trinity is its sole college. Its charter was granted by Elizabeth I in 1592 – on grounds confiscated from an Augustinian priory that was dissolved in 1537 – with the hope that young Dubliners would desist from skipping across to Continental Europe for their education and becoming 'infected with popery'. The 16-hectare site is now in the centre of the city, but when it was founded it was described as 'near Dublin' and was bordered on two sides by the estuary of the River Liffey. Nothing now remains of the original Elizabethan college, which was replaced in the Georgian building frenzy of the 18th century. The most significant change, however, is the student population: the university was exclusively Protestant until 1793, but today most of its 15,000-odd students are Catholic (although until 1970 their own church forbade them from attending on pain of excommunication). All of this would surely have horrified Archbishop Ussher, one of the college's founders, whose greatest scientific feat was the precise dating of the act of creation to 4004 BC. (Darwin, Schmarwin.)

Facing College Green, the Front Gate (Regent House entrance) to the college grounds was built between 1752 and 1759 and is guarded by **statues** of the poet Oliver Goldsmith (1730–74) and the orator Edmund Burke (1729–97). The summer walking tours of the college depart from here.

The open area reached from Regent House is divided into Front Sq, Parliament Sq and Library Sq. The area is dominated by the 30m-high **Campanile**, designed by Edward Lanyon and erected between 1852 and 1853 on what was believed to be the centre of the monastery that preceded the college. To the left of the Campanile is a **statue** of George Salmon, college provost from 1888 to 1904, who fought bitterly to keep women out of the college. He carried out his threat to permit them 'over my dead body' by promptly dropping dead when the worst came to pass.

Clockwise round Front Sq from the Front Gate, the first building is the **chapel** (☎ 896 1260; Front Sq; admission free), built in 1798 to plans made in 1777 by the architect Sir William Chambers (1723–96) and, since 1972, open to all denominations. It's noted for its extremely fine plasterwork by Michael Stapleton, its Ionic columns and its painted (rather than stained-glass) windows. The main window is dedicated to Archbishop Ussher.

Next to the chapel is the **dining hall** (Parliament Sq; ☺ closed to public), originally designed in 1743 by Richard Cassels (aka Castle) but dismantled 15 years later because of problems caused by inadequate foundations. The replacement was completed in 1761 and may have retained

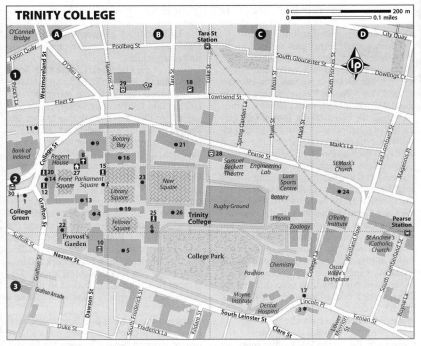

some elements of the original design. It was extensively restored after a fire in 1984.

The 1892 **Graduates' Memorial Building** (Botany Bay; closed to public) forms the northern side of Library Sq. North of it are tennis courts in the open area known as Botany Bay. The legend behind this name is that the unruly students housed around the square were suitable candidates for the British penal colony at Botany Bay in Australia.

At the eastern side of Library Sq, the red-brick **Rubrics Building** dates from around 1690, making it the oldest building in the college.

It was extensively altered in an 1894 restoration and then underwent major structural modifications in the 1970s.

To the south of the square is the **Old Library** (896 2320; Library Sq), built in a rather severe style by Thomas Burgh between 1712 and 1732. Despite Ireland's independence, the Library Act of 1801 still entitles Trinity College Library, along with four libraries in Britain, to a free copy of every book published in the UK. Housing this bounty requires nearly another 1km of shelving every year and the collection amounts to around 4.5 million books. Of course, these cannot all be kept at the college library, so there are now additional library storage facilities dotted around Dublin.

Trinity's greatest treasures are kept in the Old Library's stunning 65m **Long Room** (☎ 896 2320; East Pavilion, Library Colonnades; adult/student/child €9/8/ free; ☺ 9.30am-5pm Mon-Sat year-round, noon-4.30pm Sun Oct-Apr, 9.30am-4.30pm Sun May-Sep), which houses about 250,000 of the library's oldest volumes, including the breathtaking **Book of Kells** (see the boxed text, opposite). Your entry ticket includes admission to temporary exhibitions on display in the East Pavilion. The ground-floor Colonnades was originally an open arcade, but was enclosed in 1892 to increase the storage area. A previous attempt to increase the room's storage capacity had been made in 1853, when the Long Room ceiling was raised. Other displays include a rare copy of the Proclamation of the Irish Republic, which was read out by Pádraig Pearse at the beginning of the Easter Rising in 1916. Also here is the so-called **harp of Brian Ború**, which was definitely not in use when the army of this early Irish hero defeated the Danes at the Battle of Clontarf in 1014. It does, however, date from around 1400, making it one of the oldest harps in Ireland.

Continuing clockwise around the Campanile, there's the **1937 Reading Room** and the **Exam Hall** (Public Theatre), which dates from 1779 to 1791. Like the chapel, it was the work of William Chambers and also has plasterwork by Michael Stapleton. The Exam Hall has an oak chandelier rescued from the Houses of Parliament (now the Bank of Ireland) across College Green, and an organ supposedly salvaged from a Spanish ship in 1702, though evidence indicates otherwise.

Behind the Exam Hall is the 1760 **Provost's House**, a very fine Georgian house where the provost (college head) still resides. The house and its adjacent garden are not open to the public.

To one side of the Old Library is Paul Koralek's 1967 **Berkeley Library** (Fellows' Sq; ☺ closed to public). This solid, square, brutalist-style building has been hailed as the best example of modern architecture in Ireland, though it has to be admitted the competition isn't great. It's fronted by Arnaldo Pomodoro's 1982 sculpture **Sphere Within Sphere**. George Berkeley was born in Kilkenny in 1685, studied at Trinity when he was only 15 years old and went on to a distinguished career in many fields, particularly philosophy. His influence

spread to the new colonies in North America where, among other things, he helped to found the University of Pennsylvania. Berkeley, California, and its namesake university are named after him.

South of the Old Library is the 1978 **Arts & Social Science Building**, which backs on to Nassau St and forms the alternative entrance to the college. Like the Berkeley Library, it was designed by Paul Koralek; it also houses the **Douglas Hyde Gallery of Modern Art** (☎ 896 1116; www.douglashydegallery.ie; admission free; ☺ 11am-6pm Mon-Wed & Fri, 11am-7pm Thu, 11am-4.45pm Sat).

Trinity's newest attraction is the **Science Gallery** (☎ 896 4091; www.sciencegallery.ie; Pearse St; admission free; ☺ exhibitions usually noon-6pm Tue-Sun, cafe 8am-8pm Tue-Fri, noon-6pm Sat & Sun), a refreshingly lively and informative exploration of the relationship between science, art and the world we live in. Past exhibits have touched on a range of fascinating topics, including whether antidepressants really work and how technology can make clothing 'think'. The ground-floor Flux Café, bathed in floor-to-ceiling light, is a pretty good spot to take a load off.

Behind the Rubrics Building, at the eastern end of Library Sq, is New Sq. The highly ornate **Victorian Museum Building** (☎ 896 1477; New Sq; admission free; ☺ by prior arrangement), built from 1853 to 1857, has the skeletons of two enormous Giant Deer just inside the entrance, and the **Geological Museum** upstairs.

The 1734 **Printing House**, designed by Richard Cassels to resemble a Doric temple, and now used for the microelectronics and electrical engineering departments, is on the northern side of New Sq.

At the eastern end of the college grounds are the rugby ground and College Park, where cricket is played. There are a number of science buildings here also. The **Lincoln Place Gate** at this end is usually open and makes a good entrance or exit from the college, especially if you're on a bicycle.

BANK OF IRELAND

The imposing **Bank of Ireland** (Map p94; ☎ 671 1488; College Green; admission free; ☺ 10am-4pm Mon-Wed & Fri, 10am-5pm Thu), directly opposite Trinity College, was originally built in 1729 to house the Irish Parliament. When the Parliament voted itself out of existence by the Act of Union in 1801, it became a building without a role. It was sold in 1803 with instructions that the interior be altered to prevent its being used as a debating chamber in the future; consequently, the large central House of Commons was remodelled, but the smaller chamber of the House of Lords survived. After independence the Irish government chose to make Leinster House the new parliamentary building and ignored the possibility of restoring this fine building to its original use.

Inside, the banking mall occupies what was once the House of Commons, but it offers little indication of its former role. The Irish House of Lords is a much more interesting place, with Irish-oak woodwork, a late-18th-century chandelier of Dublin crystal, tapestries and a 10kg silver-gilt mace.

Éamon MacThomás, a Dublin historian and author, runs **tours** (admission free; ⊙ 10.30am, 11.30am & 1.45pm Tue) of the House of Lords, which also include an informal talk as much about Ireland, and life in general, as the building itself.

TEMPLE BAR

There's been many a wild night had within the cobbled precincts of Temple Bar (Map p94), Dublin's most visited neighbourhood, a maze of streets and alleys sandwiched between Dame St and the Liffey, running from Trinity College to Christ Church Cathedral. But it's not all booze and infamy: you can browse for vintage clothes, check out the latest art installations, get your nipples pierced and nibble on Mongolian barbecue. In good weather you can watch outdoor movies in one square or join in a pulsating drum circle in another – just a few slices of life in Dublin's Cultural Quarter.

There is plenty of culture in Temple Bar, but the title is hardly deserved and worn with ill-concealed discomfort. It's the inevitable consequence of an overbearing effort to sell at all costs that unquantifiable thing that is the 'Dublin Experience', as if the combination of African head masks made in China and jaded traditional music is the embodiment of Dublin's multicultural and global identity.

During the day and on weekday nights Temple Bar does have something of a bohemian bent about it – if you ignore the crappy tourist shops and dreadful restaurants serving bland, overpriced food – but at weekends, when the party really gets going, it all gets very

THE PAGE OF KELLS

More than half a million visitors stop in each year to see Trinity's top show-stopper, the world-famous **Book of Kells**. This illuminated manuscript, dating from around AD 800 and therefore one of the oldest books in the world, was probably produced by monks at St Colmcille's Monastery on the remote island of Iona, off the western coast of Scotland. Repeated looting by marauding Vikings forced the monks to flee to the temporary safety of Kells, County Meath, in AD 806, along with their masterpiece. Around 850 years later, the book was brought to the college for safekeeping and has remained here since.

The Book of Kells contains the four Gospels of the New Testament, written in Latin, as well as prefaces, summaries and other text. If it were merely words, the Book of Kells would simply be a very old book – it's the extensive and amazingly complex illustrations that make it so wonderful. The superbly decorated opening initials are only part of the story, for the book has smaller illustrations between the lines.

And here the problems begin. Of the 680 pages, only two are on display – one showing an illumination, the other showing text – which has led to it being dubbed the *page* of Kells. No getting around that one, though: you can hardly expect the right to thumb through a priceless treasure at random. No, the real problem is its immense popularity, which makes viewing it a rather unsatisfactory pleasure. Punters are herded through the specially constructed viewing room at near lightning pace, making for a there-you-see-it, there-you-don't kind of experience.

To really appreciate the book, you can get your own reproduction copy for a mere €22,000. Failing that, the library bookshop stocks a plethora of souvenirs and other memorabilia, including Otto Simm's excellent *Exploring the Book of Kells* (€12.95), a thorough guide with attractive colour plates, and a popular DVD-ROM (€31.95) showing all 800 pages. Kids looking for something a little less stuffy might enjoy the animated *Secret of Kells* (2009), which is more fun than accurate in its portrayal of how the gospel was actually put together.

DUBLIN

HANDEL WITH CARE

In 1742 the nearly broke GF Handel conducted the very first performance of his epic work *Messiah* in the since demolished Dublin Music Hall, on the city's oldest street, Fishamble St. Jonathan Swift – author of *Gulliver's Travels* and dean of St Patrick's Cathedral – had suggested that his own and Christ Church's choirs take part, but revoked his invitation when he discovered that the sacred music would be performed in a common music hall rather than in the more appropriate setting of a church, and vowed to 'punish such vicars [who allowed their choristers to participate] for their rebellion, disobedience and perfidy'. The concert went ahead nonetheless, and the celebrated work is performed at the original spot in Dublin annually – now a hotel that bears the composer's name.

---

sloppy. The huge, characterless bars crank up the sounds and throw their doors open to the tens of thousands of punters looking to drink and score like the end of the world is nigh. By 3am, the only culture on display is in the pools of vomit and urine that give the whole area the aroma of a sewer – welcome to Temple Barf.

Temple Bar Information Centre (Map p94; ☎ 677 2255; www.templebar.ie, www.visit-templebar.ie; 12 East Essex St; ✆ 9am-5.30pm Mon-Fri) publishes the TASCQ cultural guide to Temple Bar, which gives information on attractions and restaurants in the area. It's available from the information centre or at businesses around Temple Bar. It's best to check the websites for details of events.

Meeting House Square (Map p94) is one of the real success stories of Temple Bar. On one side is the excellent **Gallery of Photography** (Map p94; ☎ 671 4653; admission free; ✆ 11am-6pm Mon-Sat), hosting temporary exhibitions of contemporary local and international photographers. Staying with the photography theme, the other side of the square is home to the **National Photographic Archive** (Map p94; ☎ 671 0073; admission free; ✆ 11am-6pm Mon-Sat, 2-6pm Sun), a magnificent resource for anyone interested in a photographic history of Ireland. On Saturdays it hosts a popular **food market** (see the boxed text, p135).

At the western end of Temple Bar, in the shadow of Christ Church Cathedral, is

Fishamble Street (Map p94), the oldest street in Dublin. It dates back to Viking times – not that you'd know that to see it now.

On Parliament St, which runs south from the river to the City Hall and Dublin Castle, the **Sunlight Chambers** (Map p94) beside the river has a beautiful frieze around its facade. Sunlight was a brand of soap manufactured by the Lever Brothers, who were responsible for the late 19th-century building. The frieze shows the Lever Brothers' view of the world: men make clothes dirty, women wash them!

To the east, buildings on interesting **Eustace Street** (Map p94) include the 1715 Presbyterian Meeting House, now the **Ark** (Map p94; ☎ 670 7788; www.ark.ie; 11A Eustace St), an excellent children's cultural centre. The Dublin branch of the Society of United Irishmen, who sought Parliamentary reform and equality for Catholics, was first convened in 1791 in the Eagle Tavern, now the **Friends Meeting House** (Map p94; Eustace St). (This should not be confused with the other Eagle Tavern, which is on Cork St.)

Merchant's Arch leads to the **Ha'penny Bridge** (Map p94), named after the ha'penny (halfpenny) toll once needed to cross. The **Stock Exchange** (Map p94) is on Anglesea St, in a building dating from 1878.

DUBLIN CASTLE

The centre of British power in Ireland for most of 800 years, **Dublin Castle** (Map p94; ☎ 645 8813; www.dublincastle.ie; Cork Hill) sits atop Cork Hill, behind City Hall. It was originally built on the orders of King John in 1204, but it's more higgledy-piggledy palace than castle. Only the **Record Tower**, completed in 1258, survives from the original Norman construction. Parts of the castle's foundations remain and a visit to the excavations is the most interesting part of the castle tour. The moats, now completely covered by more modern developments, were once filled by the River Poddle. The castle is also home to one of Dublin's best museums, the Chester Beatty Library (p105).

The castle's beautiful **State Apartments** – easily the standout attraction – are still used for government business, so **tours** (full tour adult/student/child €4.50/3.50/2, undercroft & Chapel Royal only adult/student/child €3.50/2.50/free; ✆ every 20 mins, 10am-4.45pm Mon-Fri, 2-4.45pm Sat & Sun) are tailored around meetings and conferences; if the State Apartments are unavailable the discounted tour takes in only the undercroft and the Chapel Royal.

CHESTER BEATTY LIBRARY

The world-famous **Chester Beatty Library** (Map p94; ☎ 407 0750; www.cbl.ie; Dublin Castle, Cork Hill; admission free; ☾ 10am-5pm Mon-Fri, 11am-5pm Sat, 1-5pm Sun year-round, closed Mon Oct-Apr) houses the collection of mining engineer Sir Alfred Chester Beatty (1875–1968), bequeathed to the Irish State on his death. And we're immensely grateful for Chester's patronage: spread over two floors, the breathtaking collection includes more than 20,000 manuscripts, rare books, miniature paintings, clay tablets, costumes and other objects of artistic, historical and aesthetic importance. The library runs tours at 1pm on Wednesdays and at 3pm and 4pm on Sundays.

The **Artistic Traditions Gallery** on the 1st floor begins with memorabilia from Beatty's life, before embarking on an exploration of the art of Mughal India, Persia, the Ottoman empire, Japan and China. Here you'll find intricately designed little medicine boxes and perhaps the finest collection of Chinese jade books in the world. The illuminated European texts are also worth examining.

The **Sacred Traditions Gallery** on the 2nd floor gives a fascinating insight into the rituals and rites of passage of the major world religions – Judaism, Christianity, Islam, Buddhism and Hinduism. There are audiovisual explorations of the lives of Christ and the Buddha, as well as the Muslim pilgrimage to Mecca.

Head for the collection of Qur'ans from the 9th to the 19th centuries, considered to be among the best illuminated Islamic texts. You'll also find ancient Egyptian papyrus texts (including Egyptian love poems from around 1100 BC), scrolls and exquisite artwork from Burma, Indonesia and Tibet – as well as the second-oldest biblical fragment ever found (after the Dead Sea Scrolls).

The comprehensive **Reference Library** (☾ by appointment only), complete with a finely lacquered ceiling that Beatty himself had installed in his own London home, is a great resource for artists or students.

The library regularly holds specialist workshops, exhibitions and talks on everything from origami to calligraphy, and admission is free. It's easy to escape from the rigours of Western life on the serene rooftop **Japanese garden** or at the Silk Road Café (p136) on the ground floor, which serves delicious Middle Eastern cuisine.

BEDFORD & RECORD TOWERS

Directly across the Upper Yard from the main entrance to the castle is the **Bedford Tower** (Map p94; Dublin Castle, Cork Hill). In 1907 the collection known as the Irish Crown Jewels was stolen from the tower and never recovered.

The entranceway to the castle yard, beside the Bedford Tower, is topped by a statue of Justice that has always been a subject of mirth. She faces the castle and has her back to the city – seen as a sure indicator of how much justice the average Irish citizen could expect from the British. The scales of justice also had a distinct tendency to fill with rain and tilt in one direction or the other, rather than assuming the approved level position. Eventually a hole was drilled in the bottom of each pan so the rainwater could drain out.

The chunky medieval **Record Tower** (Map p94), between the lower yard and Castle Gardens, is not just the oldest bit of the whole place (built in the 13th century), but it's also the last remaining medieval tower in Dublin. Today it is home to the small **Garda Museum** (☎ 666 9998; admission free; ☾ 9.30am-4.30pm Mon-Fri, weekends by prior arrangement only), which tells the story of the various Irish police forces, beginning with the Royal Irish Constabulary, founded in 1822 by order of Robert Peel.

CITY HALL

Fronting Dublin Castle on Lord Edward St, **City Hall** (Map p94; ☎ 222 2204; www.dublincity.ie; Cork Hill; adult/student/child €4/2/1.50; ☾ 10am-5.15pm Mon-Sat, 11am-5pm Sun) was built by Thomas Cooley between 1769 and 1779 as the Royal Exchange, and later became the offices of Dublin Corporation (now called Dublin City Council). It's on the site of the Lucas Coffee House and the Eagle Tavern, in which Dublin's infamous Hell Fire Club was established in 1735. Founded by Richard Parsons, Earl of Rosse, it was one of a number of gentlemen's clubs in Dublin where less-than-gentlemanly conduct took place. It gained a reputation for debauchery and black magic, but there's no evidence that such things took place.

The Story of the Capital is a multimedia exhibition in the basement, tracing the history of Dublin from its earliest beginnings.

The 1781 **Municipal Buildings**, just west of the City Hall, were built by Thomas Ivory

(1720–86), who was also responsible for Bedford Tower (p104) in Dublin Castle.

NATIONAL MUSEUM OF IRELAND – ARCHAEOLOGY & HISTORY

Designed by Sir Thomas Newenham Deane and completed in 1890, the star attraction of this branch of the **National Museum of Ireland** (Map p96; ☎ 677 7444; www.museum.ie; Kildare St; admission free; ☺ 10am-5pm Tue-Sat, 2-5pm Sun) is the Treasury, home to the finest collection of Bronze Age and Iron Age gold artefacts in the world, and the world's most complete collection of medieval Celtic metalwork.

The centrepieces of the Treasury's unique collection are Ireland's most famous crafted artefacts, the **Ardagh Chalice** and the **Tara Brooch**. Measuring 17.8cm high and 24.2cm in diameter, the 12th-century Ardagh Chalice is made of gold, silver, bronze, brass, copper and lead. Put simply, this is the finest example of Celtic art ever found. The equally renowned Tara Brooch was crafted around AD 700, primarily in white bronze but with traces of gold, silver, glass, copper, enamel and wire beading, and was used as a clasp for a cloak.

The Treasury includes many other stunning pieces, many of which are grouped together in 'hoards', after the manner in which they were found, usually by a farmer digging up a field or a bog. Be sure not to miss the Broighter and Mooghaun hoards.

An upstairs exhibition illustrates Dublin's Viking era, with items from the excavations at Wood Quay – the area between Christ Church Cathedral and the river, where Dublin City Council plonked its new headquarters. Other exhibits focus on the 1916 Easter Rising and the struggle for independence between 1900 and 1921. Frequent short-term exhibitions are also on offer.

NATIONAL GALLERY

A magnificent Caravaggio and a breathtaking collection of works by Jack B Yeats – William Butler's younger brother – are the main reasons to visit the **National Gallery** (Map p96; ☎ 661 5133; www.nationalgallery.ie; West Merrion Sq; admission free; ☺ 9.30am-5.30pm Mon-Wed, Fri & Sat, 9.30am-8.30pm Thu, noon-5.30pm Sun), but not the only ones. Its excellent collection is strong in Irish art, but there are also high-quality collections of every major European school of painting. There are free tours at 3pm on Saturdays and at 2pm, 3pm and 4pm on Sundays.

The gallery has four wings: the original Dargan Wing, the Milltown Rooms, the North Wing and the impressive Millennium Wing. On the ground floor of the **Dargan Wing** (named after railway magnate and art lover William Dargan, whose statue graces the front lawn) is the imposing **Shaw Room** (named after writer George Bernard, another great benefactor; his bronze statue keeps Dargan company outside), lined with full-length portraits and illuminated by a series of spectacular Waterford crystal chandeliers. Upstairs, a series of rooms is dedicated to the early and high Italian Renaissance, 16th-century northern Italian art, and 17th- and 18th-century Italian art. Fra Angelico, Titian and Tintoretto are among the artists represented, but the highlight is undoubtedly Caravaggio's *Taking of Christ* (1602), which lay for over 60 years in a Jesuit house in Leeson St and was accidentally discovered by chief curator Sergio Benedetti.

The central **Milltown Rooms** were added between 1899 and 1903 to hold Russborough House's art collection, which was presented to the gallery in 1902. The ground floor displays the gallery's fine Irish collection, plus a smaller British collection, with works by Reynolds, Hogarth, Gainsborough, Landseer and Turner. Absolutely unmissable is the **Yeats Collection** at the back of the gallery, displaying more than 30 works by Irish impressionist Jack B Yeats (1871–1957), Ireland's most important 20th-century painter.

Upstairs are works from Germany, the Netherlands and Spain. There are rooms full of works by Rembrandt and his circle, and by the Spanish artists of Seville. The Spanish collection also features works by El Greco, Goya and Picasso.

The **North Wing** was added only between 1964 and 1968, but has already undergone extensive refurbishment. It houses works by British and European artists.

With its light-filled, modern design, the **Millennium Wing** can also be entered from Clare St. It houses a small collection of 20th-century Irish art, high-profile visiting collections (for which there are admission charges), an art reference library, a lecture theatre, a good bookshop and Fitzer's Café.

LEINSTER HOUSE

Dublin's grandest Georgian home, built by Richard Cassels between 1745 and 1748 for the very grand James Fitzgerald, Earl of Kildare, is now the seat of both houses of the Oireachtas na Éireann (Irish Parliament) – the Dáil (Lower House) and Seanad (Upper House). Originally called Kildare House, it was changed to **Leinster House** (Map p96; ☎ 618 3000, tour information 618 3271; www.oireachtas.ie; Kildare St; admission free; ☺ observation gallery 2.30-8.30pm Tue, 10.30am-8.30pm Wed, 10.30am-5.30pm Thu Nov-May; tours 10.30am, 11.30am, 2.30pm & 3.30pm Mon-Fri when parliament is not in session) after the earl assumed the title of Duke of Leinster in 1766.

Leinster House's Kildare St frontage was designed by Richard Cassels to look like a town house, whereas the Merrion Sq frontage was made to look like a country house. Hard to imagine it now, but when Cassels built the house it was in the wild expanses south of the Liffey, far from the genteel northern neighbourhoods where Dublin's aristocracy lived. Never short of confidence, the earl dismissed his critics, declaring, 'Where I go, society will follow.' There's no doubt about it: Jimmy Fitz had a nose for real estate.

The Dublin Society, later named the Royal Dublin Society, bought the building in 1814 but moved out in stages between 1922 and 1925, when the first government of an independent Ireland decided to establish Parliament here. The obelisk in front of the building is dedicated to Arthur Griffith, Michael Collins and Kevin O'Higgins – the architects of independent Ireland.

The Seanad meets in the north-wing saloon, while the Dáil meets in a less interesting room, originally a lecture theatre, which was added to the original building in 1897. When Parliament is sitting, visitors are admitted to an observation gallery. You'll get an entry ticket from the Kildare St entrance on production of some identification. Bags can't be taken in, nor can notes or photographs be taken. Free guided tours are available (by appointment) on weekdays when parliament is not in session.

NATIONAL MUSEUM OF IRELAND – NATURAL HISTORY

The wonderful and slightly creepy 'dead zoo' that is the Victorian **natural history museum** (Map p96; ☎ 677 7444; www.museum.ie; Merrion St; ☺ closed until 2011) had scarcely changed since 1857, when Scottish explorer Dr David Livingstone delivered the opening lecture. But this redoubtable building and its extraordinary collection of two million items (of which only 10,000 were on display) was in need of a makeover, which will keep its doors shut until 2011 at the earliest. We await its reopening with bated breath.

GOVERNMENT BUILDINGS

Dublin's domed **Government Buildings** (Map p96; ☎ 662 4888; www.taoiseach.gov.ie; Upper Merrion St; admission free; ☺ tours 10.30am-1.30pm Sat) were opened for business in 1911. Architecturally, they are a rather heavy-handed Edwardian interpretation of the Georgian style. Each free, 40-minute tour accommodates about 15 people, so you may have to wait a while for a big enough group to assemble. Tours can't be booked in advance, but if you go in on Saturday morning you can put your name down for one later in the day. You get to see the office of the *taoiseach* (prime minister), the cabinet room, the ceremonial staircase – with a stunning stained-glass window designed by Evie Hone (1894–1955) for the 1939 New York Trade Fair – and innumerable fine examples of modern Irish arts and crafts. Tickets for the tours are available from the ticket office of the **National Gallery** (Map p96; ☎ 661 5133; www.nationalgallery.ie; West Merrion Sq; ☺ 9.30am-5.30pm Mon-Wed, Fri & Sat, 9.30am-8.30pm Thu, noon-5.30pm Sun).

NATIONAL LIBRARY

Flanking the Kildare St entrance to Leinster House is the **National Library** (Map p96; ☎ 603 0200; www.nli.ie; Kildare St; admission free; ☺ 10am-9pm Mon-Wed, 10am-5pm Thu & Fri, 10am-1pm Sat), which was built between 1884 and 1890 by Sir Thomas Newenham Deane and his son Sir Thomas Manly Deane, at the same time and to a similar design as the National Museum. Leinster House, the library and museum were all part of the Royal Dublin Society (formed in 1731), which aimed to improve conditions for the poor and to promote the arts and sciences. The library's extensive collection has many valuable early manuscripts, 1st editions, maps and other items; its reading room was featured in James Joyce's *Ulysses*. Temporary displays are often held in the entrance area.

On the 2nd floor is the **Genealogical Office** (Map p96; ☎ 603 0200; 2nd fl, National Library, Kildare St; ☺ 10am-4.30pm Mon-Fri, 10am-12.30pm Sat), where you can obtain information on how best to trace your Irish roots. A genealogist can do the trace for you (at a fee dependent on research) or simply point you in the right direction (for free).

ST STEPHEN'S GREEN & AROUND

While enjoying the nine gorgeous, land-scaped hectares of Dublin's most popular square, consider that once upon a time **St Stephen's Green** (Map p96; admission free; ☸ dawn-dusk) was an open common used for public whippings, beatings and hangings. Activities in the green have quieted since then and are generally confined to the lunchtime picnic-and-stroll variety. Still, on a summer's day it is the favourite retreat of office workers, lovers and visitors alike, who come to breathe a little fresh air, feed the ducks and cuddle on the grass.

Although a stone wall was erected in the 17th century when Dublin Corporation sold off the surrounding land to property develop-ers, railings and locked gates were added only in 1814, when an annual fee of one guinea

was charged to use the green – a great way to keep the poor out. In 1877 Arthur Edward Guinness pushed an act through Parliament that opened the green to the public once again. He also paid for the green's lakes and ponds, which were added in 1880.

The fine Georgian buildings around the square date mainly from Dublin's mid- to late 18th-century Georgian prime. At that time the northern side was known as the Beaux Walk and it's still a pretty fancy stretch of real estate; drop in for tea at the imposing 1867 **Shelbourne Hotel** (p130) and you'll see what we mean. Just beyond the hotel is a small **Huguenot cemetery** (Map p96) dating from 1693, when many French Huguenots fled here from persecu-tion under Louis XIV.

The main entrance to the green is through **Fusiliers' Arch** (Map p96) at the northwestern corner. Modelled on the Arch of Titus in Rome, the arch commemorates the 212 sol-diers of the Royal Dublin Fusiliers who died in the Boer War (1899–1902).

CATHY KELLY

With 11 bestselling novels under her belt and a hectic worldwide schedule that keeps her con-stantly on the move, it's a wonder that author Cathy Kelly gets the time to enjoy the city she grew up in. Asked to describe Dublin in one sentence, she takes a breath and declares that 'Dublin is a city that feels like a village – where you can meet the same person twice in one day, where you can go from beautiful Georgian architecture to Viking remains with only a couple of miles on a modern road in between, and where something that will happen, or someone you meet, will make you laugh at some point. There is a phenomenal Dublin sense of humour and it's alive, actually, and living in the city, ready to grab you.'

Cathy moved out of the city about 10 years ago, but she didn't go far, choosing the County Wicklow town of Enniskerry because 'it's got a rural feel, but the centre of Dublin is perhaps forty minutes away by car'. And when she's in back in Dublin, she's pretty adamant about what to do.

'Get walking,' she says firmly. 'One of Dublin's joys is that it is a compact city and, weather permitting, you can walk to most places.' Surprisingly (for a native), she strongly recommends the Viking Splash Tour (p125) – 'It's like being on a school tour again and with a mad hat on, a latent childishness comes out and you can yell to your heart's content – and travel around the city yelling at Celts and seeing the main historic sights from your growly vehicle' – but warns, 'If you go in November, like I did, wear lots of warm clothes. There are no walls or windows.'

But Cathy's greatest love is for the city's Georgian heritage, especially Merrion Square (opposite) and the National Gallery (p106). 'Just dip in for an hour,' she says, 'and stand in front of a few paintings to ground yourself. I can't even say what I love most: sometimes it's the pure energy of the [works of] Jack B Yeats, and other times I want to marvel at the fire inside Caravaggio's *Taking of Christ*.' She also recommends visiting the weekend gallery that takes place along Merrion Square's railings, 'where many talented artists, who can't afford the gallery commissions, sell their paintings off the rails'.

Dublin is best enjoyed outdoors, she believes, and with this being Ireland, the downside is the weather. But don't let that put you off, she laughs: 'As a practised Dubliner, I always have a hat, flat shoes and a raincoat. Umbrellas whack off other people on narrow streets. It'll only be soft rain, so with the hat, you'll be fine!'

LITERARY ADDRESSES

Merrion Square has long been the favoured address of Dublin's affluent intelligentsia. Playwright Oscar Wilde (1854–1900) spent much of his youth at 1 North Merrion Sq. Poet WB Yeats (1865–1939) lived at 52 East Merrion Sq and later, between 1922 and 1928, at 82 South Merrion Sq. George ('Æ') Russell (1867–1935), the self-proclaimed 'poet, mystic, painter and cooperator', worked at No 84. Political leader Daniel O'Connell (1775–1847) was a resident of No 58 in his later years. The Austrian Erwin Schrödinger (1887–1961), cowinner of the 1933 Nobel Prize for Physics, lived at No 65 between 1940 and 1956. Dublin also seems to attract writers of horror stories: Joseph Sheridan Le Fanu (1814–73), who penned the vampire classic *Carmilla*, was a resident of No 70.

Across the road from the western side of the green are the 1863 **Unitarian Church** (Map p96; ⌚ worship 7am-5pm) and the **Royal College of Surgeons** (Map p96), with a fine facade. During the 1916 Easter Rising, the building was occupied by the colourful Countess Markievicz (1868–1927), an Irish Nationalist married to a supposed Polish count. The columns still bear bullet marks.

On the southern side of the green is **Newman House** (Map p96; ☎ 716 7422; 85-86 St Stephen's Green; adult/child €5/4; ⌚ tours noon, 2pm, 3pm & 4pm Tue-Fri Jun-Aug), now part of University College Dublin. These two buildings have some of the finest plasterwork in the city. The Catholic University of Ireland, predecessor of University College Dublin, acquired No 85 in 1865, then passed it to the Jesuits. Some of the plasterwork was too detailed for Jesuit tastes, however, so cover-ups were prescribed. On the ceiling of the upstairs saloon, previously naked female figures were clothed in what can best be described as furry swimsuits. One survived the restoration process.

Attached to Newman University Church is the **Newman Chapel**, built between 1854 and 1856 with a colourful neo-Byzantine interior that attracted a great deal of criticism at the time. Today it's one of the most fashionable churches in Dublin for weddings.

One of Dublin's most beautiful parks is the landscaped **Iveagh Gardens** (admission free; ⌚ dawn-dusk year-round), directly behind Newman House and reached via Clonmel St, just off Harcourt St. The imposing walls give the impression that they are private gardens, but they are one of the nicest places to relax on a summer's day or before a show in the National Concert Hall.

MERRION SQUARE

St Stephen's Green may win the popularity contest, but tranquil **Merrion Square** (Map p96; admission free; ⌚ dawn-dusk) is our choice for favourite city park. Surrounding the well-kept lawns and beautifully tended flower beds are some of Dublin's most exceptional Georgian frontages, with fine doors, peacock fanlights, ornate door knockers and foot scrapers (used by gentlemen to scrape mud from their boots before venturing indoors).

Despite the air of affluent calm, life around here hasn't always been a well-pruned bed of roses. During the Famine, the lawns of the square teemed with destitute rural refugees who lived off the soup kitchen organised here. The British embassy was located at 39 Merrion Sq East until 1972, when it was burnt out in protest against the killing of 13 innocent civilians in Derry on Bloody Sunday.

That same side of Merrion Sq once continued into Lower Fitzwilliam St in the longest unbroken series of Georgian houses anywhere in Europe, but in 1961 the Electricity Supply Board (ESB), in a myopic crime against history and aesthetics, knocked down 26 of the houses in order to build an office block that is now one of the city's worst eyesores.

Enthusiasts should visit the **Oscar Wilde statue** at the northwestern corner of the square, as it is adorned with the witty one-liners for which Wilde was famous.

Just to prove that it was not entirely unmindful of Dublin's priceless architectural heritage, the ESB had the decency to preserve one fine old Georgian house, **No 29 Lower Fitzwilliam St** (Map pp92-3; ☎ 702 6165; www .esb.ie/education; 29 Lower Fitzwilliam St; adult/student/child €5/2.50/free; ⌚ 10am-5pm Tue-Sat, 1-5pm Sun, closed late Dec) at the southeastern corner of Merrion Sq. It has been restored to give a good impression of genteel home life in Dublin between 1790 and 1820. A short film on its history is followed by a 30-minute guided tour for groups of up to nine.

The Liberties & Kilmainham

At the top of a small hill, just west of Dublin Castle, is the most impressive monument of medieval Dublin, Christ Church Cathedral. It stood firmly inside the city walls, unlike that other great place of worship, St Patrick's, which lay just outside them. Beneath both of them, to the west, is the Liberties (Map pp92–3), Dublin's oldest surviving neighbourhood. The western end of the Liberties has a curious aroma in the air: it is the smell of roasting hops, used in the production of Guinness – Dublin's black gold and, for many visitors, the epitome of all things Irish. Further along St James's St is Kilmainham (Map p90), home to the old prison that was central to the struggle for Irish independence (now a city highlight) and an ancient soldiers' hospital, now the country's most important modern art museum.

CHRIST CHURCH CATHEDRAL

The mother of all of Dublin's churches is **Christ Church Cathedral** (Church of the Holy Trinity; Map p94; ☎ 677 8099; www.cccdub.ie; Christ Church Pl; adult/senior/student €6/4/3; ☉ 9.45am-4.15pm Mon-Sat, 12.30-2.30pm Sun Sep-May, 9.45am-6.15pm Mon-Tue & Fri, to 4.15pm Wed-Thu & Sat, 12.30-2.30pm & 4.30-6.15pm Sun Jun–mid-Jul, 9.45am-6.15pm Mon-Fri, to 4.15pm Sat, 12.30-2.30pm & 4.30-6.15pm Sun mid-Jul–Aug), just south of the river and west of Temple Bar. It was founded in 1030 on what was then the southern edge of Dublin's Viking settlement. It was later smack in the middle of medieval Dublin: Dublin Castle, the Tholsel (Town Hall; demolished in 1809) and the original Four Courts (demolished in 1796) were all close by. Nearby, on Back Lane, is the only remaining guildhall in Dublin. The 1706 Tailors Hall was due for demolition in the 1960s, but survived to become the office of **An Taisce** (National Trust for Ireland; Map p94).

The original wooden church in this spot wasn't really a keeper, so the Normans rebuilt the lot in stone from 1172, mostly under the impetus of Richard de Clare, Earl of Pembroke (better known as Strongbow), the Anglo-Norman noble who invaded Ireland in 1170.

Throughout much of its history, Christ Church vied for supremacy with nearby St Patrick's Cathedral (opposite) but, like its neighbour, it fell on hard times in the 18th and 19th centuries – earlier, the nave had been used as a market and the crypt had housed taverns – and was virtually derelict by the time restoration took place. Today, both Church of Ireland cathedrals are outsiders in a largely Catholic nation.

From the southeastern entrance to the churchyard you walk past ruins of the chapter house, which dates from 1230. The entrance to the cathedral is at the southwestern corner and as you enter you face the northern wall. This survived the collapse of its southern counterpart but has also suffered from subsiding foundations.

The southern aisle has a monument to the legendary Strongbow. The armoured figure on the tomb is unlikely to be Strongbow (it's more probably the Earl of Drogheda), but his internal organs may have been buried here. A popular legend relates that the half figure beside the tomb is Strongbow's son, who was cut in two by his father when his bravery in battle was suspect.

The southern transept contains the superb baroque tomb of the 19th Earl of Kildare (died 1734). His grandson, Lord Edward Fitzgerald, was a member of the United Irishmen and died in the abortive 1798 Rising.

An entrance just by the southern transept descends to the unusually large arched crypt, which dates back to the original Viking church. Curiosities in the crypt include a glass display case housing a mummified cat chasing a mummified mouse, which were trapped inside an organ pipe in the 1860s! From the main entrance, a bridge, part of the 1871–78 restoration, leads to Dvblinia (below).

DVBLINIA & THE VIKING WORLD

A must for the kids, the old Synod Hall attached to Christ Church Cathedral is home to the seemingly perennial **Dvblinia** (Map p94; ☎ 679 4611; www.dublinia.ie; adult/student/child €6/5/3.50; ☉ 10am-5pm Apr-Sep, 11am-4pm Mon-Sat & 10am-4.30pm Sun Oct-Mar), a kitschy and lively attempt to bring medieval Dublin to life. Models, streetscapes and somewhat old-fashioned interactive displays do a fairly decent job of it, at least for kids. The model of a medieval quayside and a cobbler's shop are both excellent, as is the scale model of the medieval city. The newly added **Viking World** tells the story of Dublin's 9th- and 10th-century Scandinavian invaders and the city they built – but the real treat is finding out what life was like aboard their longboats and why they pillaged so many monasteries. Finally, you can climb neighbouring **St Michael's Tower** for views over the city to the Dublin Hills.

Your ticket gets you into Christ Church Cathedral for free (via the link bridge).

ST PATRICK'S CATHEDRAL

It was at this **cathedral** (Map pp92-3; ☎ 475 4817; www .stpatrickscathedral.ie; St Patrick's Close; adult/senior & student/ child €5.50/4.50/free; ☑ 9am-6pm Mon-Sat, 9-11am, 12.45-3pm & 4.15-6pm Sun Mar-Oct, 9am-6pm Mon-Fri, 9am-5pm Sat, 10-11am & 12.45-3pm Sun Nov-Feb), reputedly, that St Paddy himself dunked the Irish heathens into the waters of a well, so the church that bears his name stands on one of the earliest Christian sites in the city and a pretty sacred piece of turf. Although there's been a church here since the 5th century, the present building dates from 1190 or 1225 (opinions differ) and it has been altered several times, most notably in 1864 when the flying buttresses were added, thanks to the neo-Gothic craze that swept the nation. **St Patrick's Park**, the expanse of green beside the cathedral, was a crowded slum until it was cleared and its residents evicted in the early 20th century.

Like Christ Church Cathedral (opposite), the building has suffered a rather dramatic history of storm and fire damage. Oliver Cromwell, during his 1649 visit to Ireland, converted St Patrick's to a stable for his army's horses, an indignity to which he also subjected numerous other Irish churches. Jonathan Swift, author of *Gulliver's Travels,* was the dean of the cathedral from 1713 to 1745, but prior to its restoration it was very neglected.

Entering the cathedral from the southwestern porch you come almost immediately, on your right, to the graves of Swift and his longtime companion Esther Johnson, aka Stella. On the wall nearby are Swift's own Latin epitaphs to the two of them, and a bust of Swift.

The huge, dusty **Boyle Monument** to the left was erected in 1632 by Richard Boyle, Earl of Cork, and is decorated with numerous painted figures of members of his family. The figure in the centre on the bottom level is the earl's five-year-old son Robert Boyle (1627-91), who grew up to become a noted scientist. His contributions to physics include Boyle's Law, which relates the pressure and volume of gases.

The cathedral's choir school dates back to 1432, and the choir took part in the first performance of Handel's *Messiah* in 1742 (see the boxed text, p104). You can hear the choir sing matins at 9.40am and evensong at 5.35pm Monday to Friday (except Wednesday evening) during the school year. The carols performed around Christmas are a real treat; call ☎ 453 9472 for details of how to obtain a hard-to-get ticket.

To get to the cathedral, take bus 50, 50A or 56A from Aston Quay, or bus 54 or 54A from Burgh Quay.

MARSH'S LIBRARY

One of the city's most beautiful open secrets is **Marsh's Library** (Map pp92-3; ☎ 454 3511; www.marsh library.ie; St Patrick's Close; adult/child/student €2.50/free/1.50; ☑ 10am-1pm & 2-5pm Mon & Wed-Fri, 10.30am-1pm Sat), a barely visited antique library with a look and atmosphere that has hardly changed since it opened its doors to awkward scholars in 1707. It's just around the corner from St Patrick's Cathedral.

Crammed into its elaborately carved oak bookcases are over 25,000 books dating from the 16th to early 18th centuries, as well as maps, numerous manuscripts and a collection of incunabula (books printed before 1500). One of the oldest and finest tomes in the collection is a volume of Cicero's *Letters to His Friends* printed in Milan in 1472.

The building was commissioned by Archbishop Narcissus March (1638-1713) and designed by Sir William Robinson, the creator of the Royal Hospital Kilmainham (now the Irish Museum of Modern Art; p113); today it is one of the few 18th-century buildings in Dublin still used for the purpose for which it was built. In short, it's a bloody gorgeous place and you'd be mad not to visit.

ST WERBURGH'S CHURCH

Of undoubtedly ancient but imprecise origin, **St Werburgh's** (Map p94; ☎ 478 3710; Werburgh St; admission by donation; ☑ 10am-4pm Mon-Fri) has undergone numerous facelifts: in 1662, 1715 and, with some elegance, in 1759 (after a fire in 1754). The church's tall spire was dismantled after Robert Emmet's uprising in 1803 for fear that rebels might use it as a vantage point for snipers. The church is closely linked with the history of uprisings against British rule; interred in the vault is Lord Edward Fitzgerald, a member of the United Irishmen, the group that led the 1798 Rising. In what was a frequent theme of Irish rebellions, compatriots gave him away and he died as a result of the wounds he received during his capture. Ironically, his captor Major Henry Sirr is buried in the adjacent graveyard. In the porch you will notice two fire pumps that date from the time when Dublin's fire department was composed of church volunteers.

You will need to phone or visit the Sexton at 8 Castle St to see inside.

ST AUDOEN'S CHURCHES

St Audoen, the 7th-century bishop of Rouen and patron saint of Normandy, must have had a few friends in Dublin to have two churches named after him. Both are just west of Christ Church Cathedral. The more interesting of the two is the smaller **Church of Ireland** (Map p94; ☎ 677 0088; Cornmarket, High St; admission free; ☼ 9.30am-4.45pm Jun-Sep), the only surviving medieval parish church still in use in Dublin. It was built between 1181 and 1212, though recent excavations unearthed a 9th-century burial slab, suggesting that it was built on top of an even older church. Its tower and door date from the 12th century and the aisle from the 15th century, but the church today is mainly a 19th-century restoration.

As part of the tour, you can explore the ruins, as well as the present church and the visitor centre in **St Anne's Chapel**, which houses a number of tombstones of leading members of Dublin society from the 16th to the 18th centuries. At the top of the chapel is the tower, which houses the three oldest bells in Ireland, dating from 1423. Although the church's exhibits are hardly spectacular, the building itself is very beautiful and a genuine slice of medieval Dublin.

The church is entered from the north through an arch off High St. Part of the old city wall, this arch was built in 1240 and is the only surviving reminder of the city gates.

Joined onto the older Protestant St Audoen's is the newer and larger **St Audoen's Catholic Church** (Cornmarket, High St; admission free; ☼ 9.30am-5.30pm Jun-Sep, 10am-4.30pm Oct-May), a large church whose claim to local fame is Father 'Flash' Kavanagh, who used to read Mass at high speed so that his large congregation could head off to more absorbing Sunday pursuits, such as football.

GUINNESS STOREHOUSE

The most popular visit in town is the beer-lover's Disneyland, a multimedia bells-and-whistles homage to the country's most famous export and the city's most enduring symbol. The **Guinness Storehouse** (Map pp92-3; ☎ 408 4800; www.guinness-storehouse.com; St James's Gate Brewery; adult/child/student under 18yr/student over 18yr & senior €15/5/9/11; ☼ 9.30am-5pm Sep-Jun, 9.30am-7pm Jul-Aug), the only part of the massive, 26-hectare St James's Gate Brewery open to the public, is a suitable cathedral in which to worship the black gold; shaped like a giant pint of Guinness, it rises seven impressive storeys high around a stunning central atrium. At the top is the head, represented by the **Gravity Bar**, with a panoramic view of Dublin.

The Gravity Bar is also the best place to get an idea of how big the brewery actually is. From the time Arthur Guinness (1725–1803) founded the St James's Gate Brewery in 1759, the operation has expanded down to the Liffey and across both sides of the street; at one point, it had its own railway and there was a giant gate stretching across St James's St, hence the brewery's proper name. At its apogee in the 1930s, it employed over 5000 workers, making it the largest employer in the city. Increased automation has reduced the workforce to around 600, but it still produces 2.5 million pints of stout *every day*.

You'll get to drink one of those pints at the end of your tour, but not before you have walked through the extravaganza that is the Guinness floor show, spread across 1.6 hectares and involving an array of audiovisual, interactive displays that cover pretty much all aspects of the brewery's history and the brewing process. It's slick and sophisticated, but you can't ignore the man behind the curtain: the extensive exhibit on the company's incredibly successful history of advertising is a reminder that for all the talk of mysticism and magic, it's all really about marketing and manipulation.

The point is made deliciously moot when you finally get a pint in your hand and let the cream pass your lips in the vertiginous heights of the Gravity Bar. It's the best pint of Guinness in the world, claim the cognoscenti (while there's no arguing with how good it tastes, give us a pint among friends in a spit-and-sawdust pub closer to the ground any day of the week).

Around the corner at **No 1 Thomas St** (Map pp92-3; ☼ closed to public) a plaque marks the house where Arthur Guinness lived. In a yard across the road stands **St Patrick's Tower** (Map pp92-3; ☼ closed to public), Europe's tallest smock windmill (with a revolving top), which was built around 1757.

To get to the Storehouse, take bus 21A, 78 or 78A from Fleet St, or the Luas Red Line to James's.

IRISH MUSEUM OF MODERN ART
Ireland's most important collection of modern and contemporary Irish art is housed in the elegant, airy expanse of the Royal Hospital at Kilmainham, which in 1991 became the **Irish Museum of Modern Art** (IMMA; Map p90; ☎ 612 9900; www.imma.ie; Military Rd; admission free; ☒ 10am-5.30pm Tue-Sat, noon-5.30pm Sun).

The Royal Hospital Kilmainham was designed by William Robinson (who also designed Marsh's Library; see p111), and was built between 1680 and 1687 as a home for retired soldiers. It fulfilled this role until 1928, after which it languished for nearly 50 years until a 1980s restoration. At the time of its construction, it was one of the finest buildings in Ireland and there were mutterings that it was altogether too good a place for its residents.

The gallery's 4000-strong collection includes works by artists such as Picasso, Miró and Vasarely, as well as works by more contemporary artists, including Iran do Espírito Santo, Philip Taaffe and Kathy Prendergast. The gallery displays ever-changing shows from its own works, and hosts regular touring exhibitions.

Modern Irish art is always on display, and Irish and international artists live and work on site in the converted **coach houses** behind the south wing. The **New Galleries**, in the restored Deputy Master's House, should also not be missed. There are free guided tours (2.30pm Wednesday, Friday and Sunday) of the museum's exhibits throughout the year, but we strongly recommend the free seasonal heritage tours (hourly from 11am to 4pm Tuesday to Saturday, and from 1pm to 4pm Sunday) of the building itself, which run from July to September. To get there catch bus 24, 79 or 90 from Aston Quay.

KILMAINHAM JAIL
If you have *any* desire to understand Irish history – especially the juicy bits about resistance to English rule – then a visit to **Kilmainham Jail** (Map p90; ☎ 453 5984; www.heritageireland.com; Inchicore Rd; adult/student/child €6/2/2; ☒ 9.30am-5pm Apr-Oct, 9.30am-4pm Mon-Sat, 10am-4pm Sun Nov-Mar) is an absolute must. This threatening grey building, built between 1792 and 1795, has played a role in virtually every act of Ireland's painful path to independence.

The uprisings of 1798, 1803, 1848, 1867 and 1916 ended with the leaders' confinement here. Robert Emmet, Thomas Francis Meagher, Charles Stewart Parnell and the 1916 Easter Rising leaders were all visitors, but it was the executions in 1916 that most deeply etched the jail's name into the Irish consciousness. Of the 15 executions that took place between 3 May and 12 May after the revolt, 14 were conducted here. As a finale, prisoners from the Civil War were held here from 1922. The jail closed in 1924.

An excellent audiovisual introduction to the building is followed by a thought-provoking tour of the eerie prison, the largest unoccupied building of its kind in Europe. Sitting incongruously outside in the yard is the *Asgard,* the ship that successfully ran the British blockade to deliver arms to Nationalist forces in 1914. The tour finishes in the gloomy yard where the 1916 executions took place.

To get here, catch bus 23, 51, 51A, 78 or 79 from Aston Quay.

WAR MEMORIAL GARDENS
By our reckoning, the most beautiful patch of landscaped greenery in Dublin is the **War Memorial Gardens** (Map p90; ☎ 677 0236; www.heritageireland.ie; South Circular Rd, Islandbridge; admission free; ☒ 8am-dusk Mon-Fri, from 10am Sat & Sun), if only because they're as tranquil a spot as any you'll find in the city. Designed by Sir Edwin Lutyens, they commemorate the 49,400 Irish soldiers who died during WWI; their names are inscribed in the two huge granite bookrooms that stand at one end. A beautiful spot and a bit of history to boot.

Take bus 25, 25A, 26, 68 or 69 from the city centre to get here.

O'Connell Street & Around
After decades of playing second fiddle to Grafton St and the other byways of the southside, the northside's grandest thoroughfare is finally getting its mojo back, even if it hasn't quite recaptured the grandeur that once made it Dublin's finest avenue. Still, the evidence of O'Connell St's 18th-century glory lines the street in the shape of a bunch of fabulous buildings, fascinating museums and a fair few of the city's cultural hot spots too – just a handful of reasons to cross O'Connell Bridge and take on the northside.

O'CONNELL STREET STATUARY

Although overshadowed by the Spire, O'Connell St is lined with statues of Irish history's good and great. The big daddy of them all is the 'Liberator' himself, **Daniel O'Connell** (Map p94), whose massive bronze bulk soars high above the street at the bridge end. The four winged figures at his feet represent O'Connell's supposed virtues: patriotism, courage, fidelity and eloquence.

O'Connell is rivalled for drama by the spread-armed figure of trade-union leader **Jim Larkin** (1876–1947; Map p94), just south of the General Post Office; you can almost hear the eloquent tirade.

Looking on with a bemused air from the corner of pedestrianised North Earl St is a small statue of **James Joyce** (Map pp92–3), whom wagsters like to refer to as 'the Prick with the Stick'. Joyce would have loved the vulgar rhyme.

Further north is the statue of **Father Theobald Mathew** (1790–1856; Map pp92–3), the 'Apostle of Temperance' – a hopeless role in Ireland. This quixotic task, however, also resulted in a Liffey bridge bearing his name. The northern end of the street is completed by the imposing statue of **Charles Stewart Parnell** (1846–91; Map pp92–3), Home Rule advocate and victim of Irish morality.

O'CONNELL STREET

It's amazing what a few hundred million euros and a new vision will do to a street plagued by years of neglect, a criminally blind development policy and a history as a hothouse of street trouble. It's difficult to fathom why O'Connell St (Map pp92–3), once so proud and elegant, could have been so humbled that the street's top draws were amusement arcades and fast-food outlets. Poker machines and burger joints on the street that was the main stage for the Easter Rising in 1916? How could it all go so wrong?

It's a far cry from the 18th-century days of empire, when as Drogheda St (after Henry, Viscount Moore, Earl of Drogheda) it cut a swath through a city brimming with Georgian optimism. It became O'Connell St in 1924, but only after spending a few decades as Sackville St – a tribute to a lord lieutenant of Ireland. Whatever its name, it was always an imposing street, at least until the fast-food joints and the crappy shops started invading the retail spaces along it. Thankfully, Dublin City Council is committed to a thorough reappraisal of the street's appearance: a lot done, more to do.

The first project was the impressive **Spire** (the Monument of Light; Map pp92–3), which graced the spot once occupied by a statue of Admiral Nelson (which disappeared in explosive fashion, thanks to the IRA, in 1966). Soaring 120m into the sky, it is, apparently, the world's tallest sculpture, although that hardly impresses the locals, who refer to it as the 'biggest needle around', in reference to the drug blight of the north inner city. Other projects have seen the widening of the pavements and the limiting of traffic, although the street will truly be grand when the plethora of fast-food joints are given the elbow.

GENERAL POST OFFICE

Talk about going postal. The **GPO building** (Map pp92–3; ☎ 705 7000; www.anpost.ie; O'Connell St; ☻ 8am-8pm Mon-Sat) will forever be linked to the dramatic and tragic events of Easter Week 1916, when Pádraig Pearse, James Connolly and the other leaders of the Easter Rising read their proclamation from the front steps and made the building their headquarters. The building – a neoclassical masterpiece designed by Francis Johnston in 1818 – was burnt out in the subsequent siege, but that wasn't the end of it. There was bitter fighting in and around the building during the Civil War of 1922; you can still see the pockmarks of the struggle in the Doric columns. Since its reopening in 1929 it has lived through quieter times, but its central role in the history of independent Ireland has made it a prime site for everything from official parades to personal protests.

ST MARY'S PRO-CATHEDRAL

Dublin's most important **Catholic church** (Map pp92–3; ☎ 874 5441; Marlborough St; admission free; ☻ 8am-6.30pm) is not quite the showcase you might expect. For one, it's in a cramped street rather than in its intended spot on O'Connell St, where the GPO Building (p104) is now located: the city's Protestants had a fit and insisted that it be built on a less conspicuous side street. And less conspicuous it certainly was, unless you were looking for purveyors of the world's oldest profession. Then you were smack in the middle of Monto – as Marlborough St was then known – the busiest red-light district in Europe, thanks to the British army stationed here. After independence and the departure of the British, Monto became plain old Marlborough St and the only enduring evidence is in the writings of James Joyce, who referred to the area where he lost his virginity as 'Nighttown'.

The area mightn't be the hot spot it used to be, but at least you won't be distracted while admiring the six Doric columns of the cathedral, built between 1816 and 1825 and modelled on the Temple of Theseus in Athens. The best time to visit is Sunday at 11am for the Latin Mass sung by the Palestrina Choir, the very choir in which Count John McCormack, Ireland's greatest singing export (sorry, Bono), began his career in 1904.

Finally, a word about the term 'pro' in the title. It roughly means 'unofficial cathedral', due to the fact that church leaders saw this building as an interim cathedral that would do until funds were found to build a much grander one. Which has never happened, leaving this most Catholic of cities with two incredible but underused Protestant cathedrals and one fairly ordinary Catholic one. Irony, one; piety, nil.

DUBLIN CITY GALLERY – THE HUGH LANE

Whatever reputation Dublin has a repository of world-class art has a lot to do with the simply stunning collection at the **Hugh Lane Gallery** (Map pp92-3; ☎ 874 1903; www.hughlane.ie; 22 North Parnell Sq; admission free; ◷ 10am-6pm Tue-Thu, 10am-5pm Fri & Sat, 11am-5pm Sun), which is not only home to works by some of the brightest stars in the modern and contemporary art world both foreign and domestic, but is also where you'll find one of the most singular exhibitions to be seen anywhere: the actual studio of one of the 20th century's truly iconic artists, Francis Bacon.

It's all contained within the fabulous confines of the 18th-century **Charlemont House** and a recent modernist extension that has more than doubled the gallery's capacity. The new building, based in the old **National Ballroom**, spans three floors and includes 13 bright galleries showing works from the 1950s onwards, a specialist bookshop and chic restaurant in the basement. The gallery's remit neatly spans the gap between the old masters of the National Gallery (p106) and the contempo-

rary works exhibited in the Irish Museum of Modern Art (p113).

All the big names of French Impressionism and early 20th-century Irish art are here. Sculptures by Rodin and Degas, and paintings by Corot, Courbet, Manet and Monet sit alongside works by Irish greats Jack B Yeats, William Leech and Nathaniel Hone.

The gallery's **Francis Bacon Studio** was painstakingly moved, in all its shambolic mess, from 7 Reece Mews, London, where the Dublin-born artist lived for 31 years. Bacon, who claimed that chaos suggested art to him and famously hated Ireland, would no doubt have found it amusing that a team of conservators spent years cataloguing scraps of newspaper, horse whips, old socks, dirty rags, jars of pickle and mouse droppings, to reverently reassemble it all in Dublin.

The gallery was founded in 1908 by wealthy art dealer Sir Hugh Lane, who died in 1915 on the *Lusitania* after that ship was torpedoed by a German U-boat. Following his death, a bitter row erupted between the National Gallery in London and the Hugh Lane Gallery over the jewels of his collection; even now, after years of wrangling, half of the works are displayed in Dublin and half in London on a rotating basis, but for the time being the Hugh Lane will hold on to its most prized possession, Renoir's *Les Parapluies*.

DUBLIN WRITERS MUSEUM

You'd think that Dublin's rich literary tradition would ensure that a museum devoted to Ireland's greatest scribblers would be a real treat. But somehow the **Dublin Writers Museum** (Map pp92-3; ☎ 872 2077; www.writersmuseum.com; 18 North Parnell Sq; adult/child/student €7.50/4.70/6.30; ◷ 10am-5pm Mon-Sat Sep-May, to 6pm Jun-Aug, 11am-5pm Sun year-round) is something of a damp squib, unless Samuel Beckett's phone from his Paris apartment or Brendan Behan's union card will tickle your fancy. The museum is full of vaguely literary ephemera and gewgaws associated with some of the city's most recognisable names, but the list stops in the 1970s and no account at all is given to contemporary writers who would be more popular with today's readers; the museum's decision to omit *living* writers limits its appeal in our book.

The museum also has a bookshop and an outstanding restaurant, Chapter One (p139). Admission includes taped guides with readings from relevant texts in English and other languages. If you plan to visit the James Joyce Museum (p153) and the Shaw Birthplace (p122), bear in mind that a combined ticket (adult/student/child €12/10/7.40) is cheaper than three separate ones.

While the museum concerns itself with dead authors, the Irish Writers' Centre, next door at No 19, provides a meeting and working place for their living successors.

JAMES JOYCE CULTURAL CENTRE

Denis Maginni, the exuberant, flamboyant dance instructor immortalised by James Joyce in *Ulysses*, taught in this house. In 1982 Senator David Norris, a renowned Joycean scholar and leading gay-rights activist, bought the run-down house and restored it before opening it as a **cultural centre** (Map pp92-3; ☎ 878 8547; www.jamesjoyce.ie; 35 North Great George's St; adult/child/student €5/free/4; ☾ 10am-5pm Tue-Sat) for the study of Joyce and his books, as well as a small museum devoted to the author and his times.

There isn't much period stuff, but its absence is more than made up for by the superb interactive displays, which include three documentary films on various aspects of Joyce's life and work and – the centre's highlight – computers that allow you to explore the content of *Ulysses* episode by episode and Joyce's life year by year. It's enough to demolish the myth that Joyce's works are an impenetrable mystery and render him as he should be to the contemporary reader: a writer of enormous talent who sought to challenge and entertain his audience with his breathtaking wit and use of language.

Some of the fine plaster ceilings are restored originals, others careful reproductions of Michael Stapleton's designs. For information on a James Joyce–related walking tour departing from the centre, see p125.

Docklands

No urban development program is complete without some kind of docklands revamp, and Dublin is no different: after decades of neglect the eastern banks north and south of the River Liffey (Map p90) have been given a serious once-over. The result is an impressive array of contemporary buildings, including the snazzy National Convention Centre, designed by Kevin Roche (slated to open in 2010–11; Map p90); the new home of the Abbey Theatre (Map pp92-3), a 24,000-sq-metre behemoth

on George's Dock that will include three separate theatres; and, most impressive of all, the Grand Canal Theatre (Map p90), a 2000-seater venue designed by Daniel Libeskind that is slated to open in 2010. Also in the area is Dublin's most impressive indoor arena, the totally refurbished O2 arena (formerly the Point Depot; p146).

Regrettably, the economic crash of 2008–09 put paid to some plans for the area, including the long-expected U2 Tower and a gigantic sculpture by Antony Gormley, as well as a raft of new bars and restaurants. Still, there's enough to keep you occupied and sustained, including a stunning new five-star hotel designed by Portuguese architect Manuel Aires Mateus.

CUSTOM HOUSE

James Gandon (1743–1823) announced his arrival on the Dublin scene with the stunning, glistening white building that is the **Custom House** (Map pp92–3), one of the city's finest Georgian monuments. It was constructed between 1781 and 1791, in spite of opposition from city merchants and dockers at the original Custom House, upriver in Temple Bar.

In 1921, during the independence struggle, the Custom House was set alight and completely gutted in a fire that burned for five days. The interior was later extensively redesigned, and a further major renovation took place between 1986 and 1988.

The best complete view of a building that stretches 114m along the Liffey is obtained from across the river, though a close-up inspection of its many fine details is also worthwhile. The building is topped by a copper dome with four clocks. Atop stands a 5m-high statue of Hope.

Beneath the dome is the **Custom House Visitor Centre** (☎ 888 2538; Custom House Quay; admission €1; ☾ 10am-12.30pm Mon-Fri, 2-5pm Sat & Sun mid-Mar–Oct, closed Mon-Tue & Sat Nov–mid-Mar), which features a small museum on Gandon himself, as well as information on the history of the building.

JEANIE JOHNSTON

One of the city's most original tourist attractions is an exact, working replica of a 19th-century 'coffin ship', as the sailing boats who transported starving emigrants away from Ireland during the Famine were gruesomely known. The good news is that the **Jeanie Johnston** (☎ 1800 532 643, 066-712 9999; www.jeaniejohnston.ie; Custom House Quay; adult/child €5/3; ☾ 10.30am-5pm Sat & Sun Oct-Apr), a three-masted barque originally built in Quebec in 1847, made 16 transatlantic voyages carrying more than 2500 people and never suffered a single death. A small museum on board details the harrowing plight of a typical journey, which usually took around 47 days. The ship also operates as a Sail Training vessel, with journeys taking place from May to September. If you are visiting during these times, check the website for details of when it will be in dock.

WATERWAYS VISITOR CENTRE

If you absolutely must know about the construction and operation of Ireland's canals, the bad news is that the **Waterways Visitor Centre** (Map p90; ☎ 677 7510; www.waterwaysireland.org; Grand Canal Quay), on the Grand Canal Basin, is currently closed for renovations. But you can still admire the 'Box on the Docks' – as this modern building is nicknamed – from the outside (usually good enough for the average enthusiast of artificial waterways).

Smithfield & Phoenix Park

Flanking the northern shore of the Liffey west of O'Connell St is Smithfield, once a vibrant market district and latterly an urban debutante, eagerly anticipating the day when it would take over from Temple Bar as the city's hippest district. A huge construction boom has resulted in an enlivened neighbourhood centred on a handsome square surrounded by modern apartments and office blocks – as well as our favourite cinema in town – that hasn't quite obliterated *every* trace of old Dublin. Further west is Dublin's grandest public park, home of both the president and the zoo; on the way is one of the city's best museums.

SMITHFIELD

Smithfield (Map pp92–3) has been a work-in-progress since the mid-1990s, when it was earmarked for major residential and cultural development. Shoehorning 'culture' into any neighbourhood is never going to really work and in Smithfield it was merely a polite way of saying that the culture that was *already* there – based on the old hay, straw, cattle and horse marketplace of Smithfield Market – wasn't quite good enough for the developers and their creditors. Still, what emerged isn't half-bad; its success is largely due to the efforts of the Historic Area Rejuvenation Project (HARP), whose brief is to restore the northwest inner city.

Bordering the eastern side of Smithfield Plaza is the Old Jameson Distillery (p118). In keeping with the area's traditional past, the old fruit and vegetable market still plies a healthy wholesale trade on the square's western side, where amid the new developments is the excellent Lighthouse Cinema (see p144).

NATIONAL MUSEUM OF IRELAND – DECORATIVE ARTS & HISTORY

So much for the austere life of a soldier. Until it was decommissioned over a decade ago, Collins Barracks, built in 1704 on the orders of Queen Anne, was the largest military barracks in the world. In 1997 the early neoclassical grey stone building on the Liffey's northern bank was given a sparkling, modern makeover and now houses the decorative arts and history collection of the **National Museum of Ireland** (Map pp92–3; ☎ 677 7444; www.museum.ie; Benburb St; admission free; ☿ 10am-5pm Tue-Sat, 2-5pm Sun). The exhibits are good, but the building is stunning: at its heart is the huge central square surrounded by arcaded colonnades and blocks linked by walking bridges. While wandering about the plaza, imagine it holding up to six regiments in formation. The whole shebang is the work of Thomas Burgh (1670–1730), who also designed the Old Library (p101) in Trinity College and St Michan's Church (p118).

Inside the imposing exterior lies a treasure trove of artefacts ranging from silver, ceramics and glassware to weaponry, furniture and folk-life displays. Some of the best pieces are gathered in the 'Curator's Choice' exhibition, a collection of 25 objects hand-picked by different curators, displayed with an account of why they were chosen.

The museum itself offers a glimpse of Ireland's social, economic and military history over the last millennium. It's a big ask – too big, say its critics – but well-designed displays, interactive multimedia and a dizzying array of disparate artefacts make for an interesting and valiant effort. On the 1st floor is the museum's **Irish silver collection**, one of the largest collections of silver in the world; on the 2nd floor you'll find **Irish period furniture** and **scientific instruments**, while the 3rd floor has simple and sturdy **Irish country furniture**.

Lovers of modern furniture and design will enjoy the exhibition on iconic Irish designer Eileen Gray (1878–1976), a museum highlight. Gray was one of the most influential designers of the 20th century, and the exhibition documents her life and work, with examples of her most famous pieces. The fascinating exhibit 'The Way We Wore' displays Irish clothing and jewellery from the past 250 years. An intriguing sociocultural study, it highlights the role of jewellery and clothing in communicating messages of mourning, love and identity.

As it was once a barracks, it's fitting that military history should be a feature: one exhibition chronicles Ireland's Easter 1916 Rising, while the new 'Soldiers & Chiefs: The Irish at War Home & Abroad 1550–2001' explores the civil impact of conflict through original artefacts, audio accounts and replicas. At times harrowing and visceral, these exhibits bring to life these poignant episodes of Irish history with remarkable force.

OLD JAMESON DISTILLERY
Smithfield's biggest draw is the **Old Jameson Distillery** (Map pp92-3; ☎ 807 2355; www.jameson.ie; Bow St; adult/child/student €13.50/8/10; ⊙ tours every 35min 9am-5.30pm), a huge museum devoted to *uisce beatha* (the water of life). To its more serious devotees, that is precisely what whiskey is, although they may be put off by the slickness of the museum, which shepherds visitors through a compulsory tour of the re-created factory and into the ubiquitous gift shop.

On the way, however, there's plenty to discover. Beginning with a short film, the tour runs through the whole process of distilling, from grain to bottle. There are plenty of interesting titbits, such as what makes a single malt, where whiskey gets its colour and bouquet, and what the difference is between Irish whiskey and Scotch (other than the spelling, which prompted one Scot to comment that the Irish thought of everything: they even put an 'e' in 'whisky').

Then it's straight to the bar for a drop of the subject matter; eager drinkers can volunteer for the tasting tour, where you get to sample whiskies from all over the world and learn about their differences. Finally, you head to the almighty shop. If you're buying whiskey, go for the stuff you can't buy at home, such as the excellent Red Breast or the super-exclusive Midleton, a very limited reserve that is appropriately expensive.

FOUR COURTS
Appellants quake and the accused may shiver, but visitors are only likely to be amazed by James Gandon's imposing **Four Courts** (Map p94;

☎ 872 5555; Inn's Quay; admission free; ⊙ 9am-5pm Mon-Fri), Ireland's uppermost courts of law. Gandon's Georgian masterpiece is a mammoth structure incorporating a 130m-long facade and a collection of statuary. The Corinthian-columned central block, connected to flanking wings with enclosed quadrangles, was begun in 1786 and not completed until 1802. The original four courts (Exchequer, Common Pleas, King's Bench and Chancery) all branch off of the central rotunda.

The Four Courts played a brief role in the 1916 Easter Rising without suffering damage, but the events of 1922 were not so kind. When anti-Treaty forces seized the building and refused to leave, it was shelled from across the river. As the occupiers retreated, the building was set on fire and many irreplaceable early records were burned – an event that sparked off the Civil War. The building wasn't restored until 1932.

Visitors are allowed to wander through the building, but not to enter courts or other restricted areas. In the lobby of the central rotunda you'll see bewigged barristers conferring and police officers handcuffed to their charges.

ST MICHAN'S CHURCH
The macabre remains of the ancient dead are the attraction at **St Michan's Church** (Map p94; ☎ 872 4154; Lower Church St; adult/child/student €4/3/3.50; ⊙ 10am-12.45pm & 2-4.45pm Mon-Fri, 10am-12.45pm Sat May-Oct, 12.30-3.30pm Mon-Fri Nov-Apr), near the Four Courts, founded by the Danes in 1095 and named after one of their saints. Incredibly, it was the *only* church on the north side of the Liffey until 1686. The original church has largely disappeared beneath several additions, most dating from the 17th century (except for the battlement tower, which dates from the 15th century). It was considerably restored in the early 19th century and again after the Civil War, during which it had been damaged.

The very unchurchlike interior – it looks a bit like a courtroom – contains an organ from 1724 that Handel may have played for the first performance of his *Messiah*. A skull on the floor on one side of the altar is said to represent Oliver Cromwell. On the opposite side, a penitent's chair was where 'open and notoriously naughty livers' did public penance.

The big draw is the tour of the subterranean crypt, where you'll see bodies between 400 and 800 years old, preserved not by mummification but by the constant dry atmosphere. Tours are organised on an ad hoc basis depending on how many people there are. Catch bus 134 or the Luas Red Line to Smithfield from the city centre to get here.

PHOENIX PARK

Measuring 709 glorious hectares, **Phoenix Park** (Map p90; admission free) is Europe's largest city park: a green lung that is more than double the size of New York's Central Park (a paltry 337 hectares), and larger than all of London's major parks put together. Here you'll find gardens and lakes; pitches for all kinds of British sports from soccer to cricket to polo (the dry original one, with horses); the second-oldest zoo in Europe; a castle and visitor centre; the headquarters of the Garda Síochána (police); the Ordnance Survey offices; and the homes of both the president of Ireland and the US ambassador, who live in two exquisite residences more or less opposite each other. There's even a herd of some 500 fallow deer.

The deer were first introduced by Lord Ormond in 1662, when lands once owned by the Knights of Jerusalem were turned into a royal hunting ground. In 1745 the viceroy Lord Chesterfield threw it open to the public and it has remained so ever since. (The name 'Phoenix' has nothing to do with the mythical bird; it is a corruption of the Irish *fionn uisce*, meaning 'clear water'.)

In 1882 the park played a crucial role in Irish history, when Lord Cavendish, the British chief secretary for Ireland, and his assistant were murdered outside what is now the Irish president's residence by an obscure Nationalist group called the Invincibles. Lord Cavendish's home is now called Deerfield and is used as the official residence of the US ambassador.

Near the Parkgate St entrance to the park is the 63m-high **Wellington Monument**. This took from 1817 to 1861 to build, mainly because the Duke of Wellington fell from public favour during its construction. Nearby is the **People's Garden**, dating from 1864, and the **bandstand** in the Hollow.

Established in 1830, the 12-hectare **Dublin Zoo** (Map p90; ☎ 677 1425; www.dublinzoo.ie; Phoenix Park; adult/child/family €14/9.50/40; ❤ 9.30am-6pm Mon-Sat, 10.30am-6pm Sun Mar-Sep, 9.30am-dusk Mon-Fri, 9.30am-dusk Sat, 10.30am-dusk Sun Oct-Feb) is one of the oldest in the world, but is mainly of interest to

children. It used to be a run-down zoo where depressed animals used to depress visitors, but a substantial facelift has made it a much more pleasant place for animals to live and for visitors to stroll around.

The large Victorian building behind the zoo, on the edge of the park, is the **Garda Síochána Headquarters**. It was designed by Benjamin Woodward in the 19th century. His work also includes the Old Library in Trinity College (p101).

In the centre of the park, the **Papal Cross** marks the site where Pope John Paul II preached to 1.25 million people in 1979. The **Phoenix Monument**, erected by Lord Chesterfield in 1747, looks very un-phoenix-like and is often referred to as the Eagle Monument. The southern part of the park is a 200-acre stretch (about 81 hectares) known as the **Fifteen Acres** (don't ask, nobody knows), which is given over to a large number of football pitches – winter Sunday mornings are the time to come and watch. To the west, the rural-looking **Glen Pond** corner of the park is extremely attractive.

Back towards the Parkgate entrance is **Magazine Fort** on Thomas' Hill. Built at a snail's pace between 1734 and 1801, the fort has served as an occasional arms depot for the British and, later, the Irish armies. It was a target during the 1916 Easter Rising and again in 1940, when the IRA made off with the entire ammunitions reserve of the Irish army (they retrieved it after a few weeks).

The residence of the Irish president, **Áras an Uachtaráin** (Map p90; ☎ 617 1000; Phoenix Park; admission free; ❤ guided tours hourly 10.30am-4.30pm Sat) was built in 1751 and enlarged in 1782, then again in 1816, this time by noted Irish architect Francis Johnston, who added the Ionic portico. From 1782 to 1922 it was the residence of the British viceroys or lord lieutenants. After independence it became the home of Ireland's governor general until Ireland cut ties with the British Crown and created the office of president in 1937.

Tickets for the tour can be collected from the **Phoenix Park Visitor Centre** (☎ 677 0095; adult/concession/family €2.75/1.25/7; ❤ 10am-6pm daily Apr-Sep, 10am-5pm daily Oct, 10am-5pm Mon-Sat Nov & Dec, 10am-5pm Sat & Sun Jan-Mar), the converted former stables of the papal nunciate, now devoted to the park's history and ecology over the last 3500 years. Next door is the restored four-storey **Ashtown Castle**, a 17th-century tower house 'discovered' inside the 18th-century nuncio's mansion when the latter was demolished in 1986 due to dry rot. You can visit the castle only on a guided tour from the visitor centre.

Take bus 10 from O'Connell St, or bus 25 or 26 from Middle Abbey St to get to Dublin's beloved playground. The best way to get around the park is to hop on the new **Phoenix Park Shuttle Bus** (Map pp92-3; ☼ hourly 7am-5pm Mon-Fri, 10am-5pm Sat & Sun; adult/child €2/1), which goes from just outside the main gate on Parkgate St and loops around to the visitor centre.

Beyond the Royal Canal

These days it makes for a lovely walk, but when 'Long' John Binns put his money into the construction of the Royal Canal (Map p90) from 1790, it was an exercise in misplaced optimism and self-flagellating revenge. The usefulness of such waterways was already on the wane, and he invested in the project only because when he was a board member for the Grand Canal (opposite) a colleague mocked his day job as a shoemaker. Sure enough, the canal was a massive bust; Binns lost a pile of money and became a figure of fun.

Binns' catastrophe is the stroller's good fortune and the towpath alongside the canal is perfect for a walk through the heart of the city. You can join it beside Newcomen Bridge at North Strand Rd (Map pp92-3), just north of Connolly Station, and follow it to the suburb of Clonsilla and beyond, more than 10km away. The walk is particularly pleasant beyond Binns Bridge in Drumcondra. At the top of Blessington St a large pond, once used when the canal also supplied drinking water to the city, attracts water birds.

Beyond the Royal Canal lie the suburbs and an authentic slice of north city life. There are also some beautiful gardens, the country's biggest stadium, a historic cemetery and one of the most interesting buildings in all of Dublin.

CROKE PARK

It's a magnificent stadium – if you're impressed by them – that is Ireland's largest and the fourth largest in Europe, but **Croke Park** (Map p90; ☎ 819 2323; Clonliffe Rd) is about much more than 82,000-plus sporting butts on plastic seats. No, Croker – as it's lovingly known in Dublin – is the fabulous fortress that protects the sanctity and spirit of Gaelic games in Ireland, as well as the administrative HQ of the Gaelic Athletic

Association (GAA), the body that governs them. Sound a little hyperbolic? Well, the GAA considers itself not just the governing body of a bunch of Irish games but also the stout defender of a cultural identity that is ingrained in Ireland's sense of self. To get an idea of just how important the GAA is here, a visit to the **Croke Park Experience** (☎ 855 8176; www.gaa.ie; New Stand, Croke Park, Clonliffe Rd; adult/child/student museum €5.50/3.50/4, museum & tour €9.50/6/7; ☼ 9.30am-5pm Mon-Sat, noon-5pm Sun Apr-Oct, 10am-5pm Tue-Sat, noon-4pm Sun Nov-Mar) is a must, though it will help if you're any kind of sporting enthusiast. The twice-daily tours (except match days) of the impressive stadium are excellent.

To get to Croke Park, catch bus 3, 11, 11A, 16, 16A or 123 from O'Connell St.

NATIONAL BOTANIC GARDENS

Founded in 1795, the 19.5-hectare **National Botanic Gardens** (Map p88; ☎ 837 7596; Botanic Rd, Glasnevin; admission free; ☼ 9am-6pm Mon-Sat, 11am-6pm Sun Apr-Oct, 10am-4.30pm Mon-Sat, 11am-4.30pm Sun Nov-Mar) are directly north of the centre, flanked to the north by the River Tolka.

In the gardens is a series of curvilinear glass-houses, dating from 1843 to 1869, created by Richard Turner, who was also responsible for the glasshouse at Belfast Botanic Gardens and the Palm House in London's Kew Gardens. Within these Victorian masterpieces you will find the latest in botanical technology, including a series of computer-controlled climates reproducing environments of different parts of the world. Among the pioneering botanical work conducted here was the first attempt to raise orchids from seed, back in 1844; pampas grass and the giant lily were also first grown in Europe in these gardens.

To get here, catch bus 13, 13A or 19 from O'Connell St, or bus 34 or 34A from Middle Abbey St.

GLASNEVIN CEMETERY

Ireland's largest and most historically important burial site is **Prospect Cemetery** (Map p90; ☎ 830 1133; www.glasnevin-cemetery.ie; Finglas Rd; admission free; ☼ 24hr, tours 2.30pm Wed & Fri), better known simply as Glasnevin Cemetery, after the north Dublin suburb it lies in – it's an easy walk from the National Botanic Gardens. It was established in 1832 as a burial ground for Catholics, who were increasingly prohibited from conducting burials in the city's Protestant cemeteries. Not surprisingly, the cemetery's monuments and memorials have staunchly patriotic overtones, with numerous high crosses, shamrocks, harps and other Irish symbols. The cemetery is mentioned in *Ulysses* and there are several clues for Joyce enthusiasts to follow.

The most interesting parts of the cemetery are at the southeastern Prospect Sq end. The single most imposing memorial is the colossal monument to Cardinal McCabe (1837–1921), archbishop of Dublin and primate of Ireland, while a modern replica of a round tower acts as a handy landmark for locating the tomb of Daniel O'Connell, who died in 1847 and was reinterred here in 1869 when the tower was completed. Charles Stewart Parnell's tomb is topped with a huge granite rock. Other notable people buried here include Sir Roger Casement, who was executed for treason by the British in 1916 and whose remains weren't returned to Ireland until 1964; the Republican leader Michael Collins, who died in the Civil War; the docker and trade unionist Jim Larkin, a prime force in the 1913 general strike; and the poet Gerard Manley Hopkins.

There's also a poignant 'class' memorial to the men who have starved themselves to death for the cause of Irish freedom over the century, including 10 men from the 1981 H Block hunger strikes.

The watchtowers in the cemetery were once used to keep watch for body snatchers.

To get to the cemetery, take bus 40, 40A or 40B from Parnell St.

CASINO AT MARINO

It's not the roulette-wheel kind of casino but the original Italian kind, the one that means 'summer home' (it literally means 'small house'), and this particular **casino** (Map p90; ☎ 833 1618; Malahide Rd; adult/child/senior €3/1/2; ☒ 10am–6pm May-Sep) is one of the most enchanting constructions in all of Ireland. Entrance is by guided tour only; the last tour is 45 minutes before closing.

It was built in the mid-18th century for the Earl of Charlemont, who returned from his grand tour of Europe with more art than he could store in his own home, Marino House, which was on the same grounds but was demolished in the 1920s. He also came home with a big love of the Palladian style – hence the architecture of this wonderful folly.

The exterior of the building, with a huge entrance doorway, and 12 Tuscan columns forming a templelike facade, creates the expectation that its interior will be a simple single open space. But instead it is an extravagant convoluted maze: flights of fancy include chimneys for the central heating that are disguised as roof urns, downpipes hidden in columns, carved draperies, ornate fireplaces, beautiful parquet floors constructed of rare woods, and a spacious wine cellar. A variety of statuary adorns the outside but it's the amusing fakes that are most enjoyable. The towering front door is a sham – a much smaller panel opens to reveal the secret interior. The windows have blacked-out panels to hide the fact that the interior is a complex of rooms, not a single chamber.

To get to the casino, take bus 20A, 20B, 27, 27B, 42, 42C or 123 from the city centre, or travel on the Dublin Area Rapid Transport (DART) to Clontarf Rd.

Beyond the Grand Canal

The more attractive of Dublin's two canals is the Grand Canal (Map p90), built to connect Dublin with the River Shannon. It makes a graceful 6km loop around the south city centre and has a lovely path running alongside it that's perfect for a pleasant walk or cycle. At its eastern end the canal forms a harbour connected with the Liffey at the area called Ringsend, through locks that were built in 1796. The large Grand Canal Dock, flanked by Hanover and Charlotte Quays, is now used by windsurfers and canoeists and is the site of a major new development, including Dublin's first real skyscraper, which will be home to U2's purpose-designed recording studios.

At the northwestern corner of the dock is Misery Hill, once the site of the public execution of criminals. It was once the practice to bring the corpses of those already hung at Gallows Hill, near Upper Baggot St, to this spot, to be strung up for public display for anything from six to 12 months.

The loveliest stretch of the canal is just southwest, between Mount St Bridge and Baggot St. The grassy, tree-lined banks were a favourite haunt of the poet Patrick Kavanagh, whose difficult love affair with the city is echoed in the hauntingly beautiful 'On Raglan Road', later put to music by Van Morrison. Another Kavanagh poem requested that he be commemorated by 'a canal bank seat for passers-by', and his friends obliged with a seat beside the lock on the southern side of the canal. A little further along on the northern side you can sit down beside Kavanagh himself, cast in bronze, comfortably lounging on a bench and watching his beloved canal.

Just southeast of the city centre, beyond the canal, is **Ballsbridge** (Map p90), the epitome of posh Dublin and home to most of the embassies and a batch of luxurious B&Bs. The main attractions around it are the Royal Dublin Society Showground and the newly rebuilt **Lansdowne Road rugby stadium** (Map p90), reopening in 2010 and renamed the Aviva Stadium, though **Herbert Park** (Map p90) is also a favourite spot for sport, walking or just sitting around.

ROYAL DUBLIN SOCIETY SHOWGROUND

The **Royal Dublin Society Showground** (RDS Showground; Map p90; ☎ 668 9878; Merrion Rd, Ballsbridge), about 15 minutes from the city centre by bus 7 from Trinity College, is used for various exhibitions throughout the year. The society was founded in 1731 and has had its headquarters in a number of well-known Dublin buildings, including Leinster House (p106) from 1814 to 1925. The society was involved in the foundation of the National Museum (p106 and p117), National Library (p107), National Gallery (p106) and National Botanic Gardens (p120). The most important annual event at the showground is the August **Dublin Horse Show** (☎ tickets 668 0866), which includes an international showjumping contest. Ask at the tourist office or consult a listings magazine for other events.

SHAW BIRTHPLACE

OK, so it's technically on the city side of the canal, but only just. Noted playwright George Bernard Shaw was born and lived until the age of 10 in what is now home to a **museum** (Map p90; ☎ 475 0854; 33 Synge St; adult/child/student €6/4/5; ☉ 10am-1pm & 2-5pm Mon-Sat year-round, plus 11am-1pm & 2-5pm Sun May-Sep) dedicated to him and the times he grew up in. The museum has an audio presentation of Shaw's life, re-creating a Victorian household.

Note that it's possible to buy a combination ticket (adult/student/child €11.50/9.50/7.50) that also gives you access to the Dublin Writers' Museum (p115) and the James Joyce Museum (p153) in Sandycove.

To get to the museum, take bus 16, 19 or 122 from Trinity College.

IRISH-JEWISH MUSEUM

Just around the corner from the Shaw House is the **Irish-Jewish Museum** (Map p90; ☎ 453 1797; 4 Walworth Rd; admission free; ☉ 11am-3.30pm Tue, Thu & Sun May-Sep, 10.30am-2.30pm Sun only Oct-Apr). Located in an old synagogue, the museum was opened in 1985 by the then Israeli president, Chaim Herzog, who was actually born in Belfast. Dublin's small but culturally important Jewish population is remembered through photographs, paintings, certificates, books and other memorabilia.

ACTIVITIES
Beaches & Swimming

Dublin is hardly the sort of place to work on your suntan, and even a hot Irish summer day is unlikely to raise the water temperature much above freezing. However, there are some pleasant beaches. Many Joyce fans feel compelled to take a dip in **Forty Foot Pool** at Sandycove (p153). Sandy beaches to the north of Dublin include **Sutton** (11km), **Portmarnock** (15km), **Malahide** (17km), **Claremount** (14km) and **Donabate** (21km). Although the beach at **Sandymount** is nothing special, it is only 5km southeast of central Dublin. Take bus 3 from Fleet St.

The **National Aquatic Centre** (Map p88; ☎ 646 4300; www.nationalacquaticcentre.ie; Snugborough Rd, Blanchardstown; adult/child & student €14/12; ☉ 6am-10pm Mon-Fri, 9am-8pm Sat & Sun) is the largest indoor water park in the country. Besides its Olympic-size competition pool, it has water rollercoasters, wave and surf machines, a leisure pool and all types of flumes. It's a great day out for the family but at weekends be prepared to join the line of shivering children queuing for slides. Take bus 38A from Hawkins St to Snugborough Rd.

There is a dearth of quality pools in the city centre – most are small, crowded and not very hygienic. An excellent exception is the **Markievicz Leisure Centre** (Map p101; ☎ 672 9121; cnr Tara & Townsend Sts; adult/child €6/3; ☉ 7am-8.45pm Mon-Fri, 9am-5.45pm Sat, 10am-3.45pm Sun), which has a 25m pool, a workout room and a sauna. For the admission price you can swim pretty much as long as you like; children are allowed only at off-peak times (ie any time except for 7am to 9am, noon to 2pm and 5pm to 7pm Monday to Friday).

Cycling

Compact and flat, Dublin *should* be ideal cycling territory, but traffic congestion, road works and the limited, poorly thought-out network of cycle lanes – cars and buses encroach with impunity – make pedalling your way round the city something of a dodgy obstacle course. Still, if you keep your wits about you it's the fastest way to get around the increasingly congested centre.

Bike theft is a major problem, so be sure to park on busier streets, preferably at one of the myriad U-shaped parking bars. Overnight street parking is dodgy; most hostels and hotels offer secure bicycle-parking areas.

Irish Cycling Safaris (☎ 260 0749; www.cyclingsafaris .com; University College Dublin, Belfield; tour €25; 10.30am Sat, Apr–early Oct) organises a Dublin cycling tour taking in the full scope of Dublin Bay from north to south. They also organise nine highly recommended, week-long **themed tours** (€670, Apr–early Oct) of the countryside. Each group cycles at its own pace, with a guide following in a backup vehicle. The price also includes bike hire and hotel and B&B accommodation.

Recommended bike shops:

Cycle-Logical (Map p94; ☎ 872 4635; 3 Bachelor's Walk) A shop for serious enthusiasts, with top-quality gear and info on cycling events throughout the country. It does not do repairs.

Square Wheel Cycleworks (Map p94; ☎ 679 0838; South Temple Lane) Quick, friendly and excellent for repairs.

Bike hire has become increasingly more difficult to find because of crippling insurance costs. Typical hire costs for a mountain bike are between €15 and €25 a day or up to €90 per week. Raleigh Rent-a-Bike agencies can be found through the following businesses:

Cycleways (Map pp92–3; ☎ 873 4748; www.cycleways .com; 185-186 Parnell St) Dublin's best bike shop, with expert staff who pepper their patter with all the technical lingo. Top-notch rentals.

Eurotrek (☎ 456 8847; www.raleigh.ie) Rentals, repairs, advice and guidance for all cycle-related affairs.

MacDonald Cycles (Map p96; ☎ 475 2586; 38 Wexford St) Friendly and helpful, great for the amateur enthusiast.

WALKING TOUR

Dubliners of old would assure their 'bitter halves' that they were 'going to see a man about a dog' before beating a retreat to the nearest watering hole. Visiting barflies need no excuse to enjoy the social and cultural education – ahem – of a tour of Dublin's finest, most charming and most hard-core bars.

Start in the always excellent **Anseo** (**1**; p143) on Camden St, which pulls a seriously hip and unpretentious crowd on the strength of its fabulous DJs. Head deep into the city centre and stop at Dublin's smallest pub, the **Dawson Lounge** (**2**; p141), for an appropriately diminutive tipple, before sinking a pint of plain in the snug at South Anne St's **Kehoe's** (**3**; p142), one of the city centre's most atmospheric bars. Discuss the merits of that unwritten masterpiece with a clutch of frustrated writers and artists in **Grogan's Castle Lounge** (**4**; p142) on Castle Market, a traditional haunt that admirably refuses to modernise. A couple of streets away is one of the latest contenders for coolest bar in town, the appropriately named **Bar with No Name** (**5**; p143) – even though insiders call it No 3 (on account of its street address); there's

---

WALK FACTS

Start Lower Camden St
Finish Ormond Quay
Distance 2.5km
Duration One hour to two days!

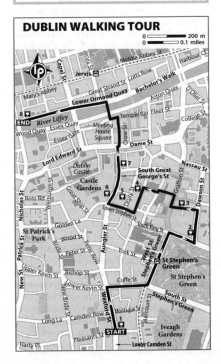

DUBLIN WALKING TOUR

no sign but it's up the stairs from the doorway next door to L'Gueuleton restaurant. If it's more conversation you require, make your way to the **Long Hall** (**6**; p142), where the vicissitudes of life are discussed in a sombre Victorian setting. Shake that booty down the road at the **Globe** (**7**; p143). Cross the Liffey and make a beeline for Ormond Quay and **Sin É** (**8**; p143), a small bar with a big reputation for top-class music and a terrific night out. If you've followed the tour correctly, it's unlikely that you'd now be referring to this guide. How many fingers?

DUBLIN FOR CHILDREN

Sometimes holidaying with small children requires the organisation of an army boot camp, boundless energy and patience, bottomless pockets and a sense of humour, so it really helps when the facilities and goodwill are there to back up your efforts.

All but a few hotels will provide cots and many have baby-sitting on request (normally €7 to €10 per hour). While waiters may not act like your baby is the first they've ever seen, you'll still find a warm reception for junior travellers in Dublin, at least during the day. Frustratingly, many city-centre restaurants are unwilling to accommodate diners under 12, especially babies, after 6pm. You'll need to check before making a booking. Most restaurants – even exclusive ones – have highchairs and will gladly heat bottles and baby food, but so-called kiddie menus lack imagination and rarely stretch further than the ubiquitous chicken nuggets or sausages with chips. That said, places catering specifically for families who want to eat more nutritious food are cropping up all the time, and the pizza chain Milano has resourcefully added free weekend childcare facilities to its Dublin restaurants.

Travellers will find that baby changing facilities and city-centre playgrounds are remarkably few and far between. Shopping centres and department stores (or a hotel if you're stuck) are good places to try for changing nappies (diapers). There's a reasonably sized playground on Gardiner St (Map pp92–3) and in St Stephen's Green (p96), where you can also feed the ducks. The Iveagh Gardens (p109) doesn't have a playground but has a waterfall and small maze, and is a lovely quiet space to relax while your children play.

The **Ark** (Map p94; ☎ 670 7788; www.ark.ie; 11A Eustace St) is a children's cultural centre that organises plays, exhibitions and workshops for four-to-14-year-olds. You really need to book in advance for events.

You could spend the entire day at the **National Aquatic Centre** (Map p88; ☎ 646 4300; www .nationalacquaticcentre.ie; Snugborough Rd, Blanchardstown; adult/child & student €14/12; ☉ 6am-10pm Mon-Fri, 9am-8pm Sat & Sun) – and if you don't the kids certainly could, as they glide from slide to slide and pool to pool.

Lambert Puppet Theatre (☎ 280 0974; www.lambert puppettheatre.com; Clifton Lane, Monkstown) stages puppet shows for the over-threes in Monkstown, 10km south of Dublin. Take bus 7, 7A, 8, 46A, 46X or 746 to get there.

The National Museum (p106 and p117) and the Irish Museum of Modern Art (p113) run fun, educational programs for children at weekends. A nice spot for a picnic is **Newbridge House** (Map p88; ☎ 843 6534; Donabate; adult/child €3.50/2; ☉ 10am-5pm Tue-Sat, 2-6pm Sun Apr-Sep, 2-5pm Sat & Sun Oct-Mar), with its large traditional farm, which has cows, pigs and chickens, a large park and an adventure playground. It's northeast of Swords at Donabate, 19km from the centre. You can get here on the Suburban Rail service (€2.70, 30 minutes), which departs hourly from either Connolly or Pearse Station in the city centre.

The *Irish Times* runs a column on things to do with kids in its Wednesday edition.

If your hotel doesn't have a baby-sitting service, you could try a couple of agencies that provide professional nannies. It's up to you to negotiate a fee with the nanny, but €13 to €15 per hour is the average, plus taxi fare if the nanny isn't driving. You'll need to sign a form beforehand, which the agency will fax to your hotel.

Recommended agencies:
Belgrave Agency (☎ 280 9341; 55 Mulgrave St, Dun Laoghaire; fee per hr €18)
Executive Nannies (Map pp92-3; ☎ 873 1273; 43 Lower Dominick St; fee per hr €20)

TOURS

Dublin is an easy city to see on foot, so a guided walking tour is an ideal way to double up on a bit of culture and exercise. For longer tours or a cushier ride, there are numerous themed citywide bus tours, and several companies also do day trips further afield.

Bus Tours

City Sightseeing (Map pp92-3; www.city-sightseeing .com; Dublin Tourism, 14 Upper O'Connell St; adult/child/

family €15.50/7/38; ⊙ every 8-15min 9am-6pm) City Sightseeing's time-tested hop-on, hop-off open-top tours. Allow 1½ hours.

Dublin Bus Tours (www.dublinbus.ie; tours €15-25; ⊙ tours daily) O'Connell St (Map pp92-3; ☎ 872 0000; 59 Upper O'Connell St); Suffolk St (Map p94; Dublin Tourism Centre, St Andrew's Church, 2 Suffolk St) Offers a variety of tours, including Dublin City Tour, Ghost Bus Tour, Coast and Castles Tour, and South Coast and Gardens Tour.

Dublin Rock'n'Roll Writers Bus Tour (Map p101; ☎ 620 3929; www.dublinrocktours.ie; 3 Westmoreland St; tours €15; ⊙ noon, 2pm, 4pm & 6pm Wed-Sun) Dublin's rich rock legacy is explored audiovisually from the comfort of a kitted-out tour bus. The bus stop is outside O'Brien's sandwich shop on Westmoreland St; the tour lasts about 90 minutes.

Gray Line Dublin Tour (☎ 872 9010; www.irish citytours.com; adult/child/student/senior/family €15.50/7/13/13/38; ⊙ every 15min 9.30am-5.30pm, to 6.30pm Jul & Aug) Bachelor's Walk (Map p94; 33 Bachelor's Walk); Suffolk St (Map p94; Dublin Tourism Centre, St Andrew's Church, 2 Suffolk St) Another hop-on, hop-off tour (1½ hours) of the city's primary attractions.

Wild Wicklow Tour (Map p94; ☎ 280 1899; www .discoverdublin.ie; Dublin Tourism Centre, St Andrew's Church, 2 Suffolk St; adult/child €28/25; ⊙ 9.10am) Award-winning and lots of fun, this top 8½-hour tour leaves from Dublin Tourism Centre and does a quick city run before heading down the coast to Avoca Handweavers, Glendalough and the Sally Gap.

Walking Tours

1916 Easter Rising Walk (Map p94; ☎ 676 2493; www.1916rising.com; International Bar, 23 Wicklow St; adult/child €12/free; ⊙ 11.30am Mon-Sat, 1pm Sun Mar-Oct) A recommended two-hour tour run by graduates of Trinity College, it takes in parts of Dublin that were directly involved in the Easter Rising. Leaves from the International Bar.

Dublin Footsteps Walking Tours (Map p96; ☎ 496 0641; Bewley's Bldg, Grafton St; adult €10; ⊙ 10.30am Mon, Wed, Fri & Sat Jun-Sep) Departing from Bewley's on Grafton St, these excellent two-hour tours weave Georgian, literary and architectural Dublin into a fascinating walk.

Dublin Literary Pub Crawl (Map p96; ☎ 670 5602; www.dublinpubcrawl.com; The Duke, 9 Duke St; adult/student €12/10; ⊙ 7.30pm Mon-Sat, noon & 7.30pm Sun Apr-Nov, 7.30pm Thu-Sun Dec-Mar) An award-winning 2½-hour walk-and-performance tour led by two actors, exploring pubs with literary connections. There's plenty of drink taken, which makes it all the more popular; get to the Duke pub by 7pm to reserve a spot.

Dublin Musical Pub Crawl (Map p94; ☎ 478 0193; www.discoverdublin.com; Oliver St John Gogarty's, 58-59

A WORD IN YOUR EAR

If you fancy a go-it-alone guided walk, why not download one of Pat Liddy's excellent **iWalks** (www.visitdublin.com/iwalks/), which you can play on your iPod or equivalent MP3 player. You can download them from the website or subscribe to them in iTunes. There are a bunch available, from tours of the city's different districts to walks tailored to historical, architectural and activity themes.

Fleet St; adult/student €12/10; ⊙ 7.30pm Apr-Oct, 7.30pm Thu-Sat Nov-Mar) The story of Irish traditional music and its influence on contemporary styles is explained and demonstrated by two expert musicians in a number of Temple Bar pubs. Tours meet upstairs at Oliver St John Gogarty's and take 2½ hours.

James Joyce Walking Tour (Map pp92-3; ☎ 878 8547; James Joyce Cultural Centre, 35 North Great George's St; adult/student €10/8; ⊙ 2pm Tue, Thu & Sat) Excellent 1¼-hour walking tours of northside attractions associated with James Joyce, departing from James Joyce Cultural Centre.

Pat Liddy Walking Tours (Map p94; ☎ 831 1109; www.walkingtours.ie; Dublin Tourism Centre, St Andrew's Church, 2 Suffolk St; adult €6-22, child €5-20) Award-winning themed tours of the city by well-known Dublin historian Pat Liddy, ranging from the 75-min Dublin Experience to the 2-hour Great Guinness Walk, which includes a queue-skipping tour of the Guinness Storehouse. Check the website for details of tour options and times. All tours depart from the Dublin Tourism Centre.

Sandeman's New Dublin Tour (Map p94; ☎ 878 8547; www.newdublintours.com; City Hall; admission free; ⊙ 11am) A high-energy and thoroughly enjoyable three-hour walking tour of the city's greatest hits – and it's free: tip only if you enjoyed the tour. Spanish-language tours are also available.

Boat Tours

River Liffey Cruises (Map p94; ☎ 473 4082; www .liffeyvoyage.ie; Bachelor's Walk; adult/student/child €14/10/8; ⊙ 9am-5.30pm Mar-Oct) Experience the city from the river aboard the (all-important) all-weather *Spirit of the Docklands*. The history of Dublin is told from a watery point of view, from the Vikings to the recent developments of the Docklands.

Viking Splash Tours (☎ 707 6000; www.vikingsplash .ie; adult/child/family from €20/10/60; ⊙ 9am-5.30pm Mar-Oct, 10am-4pm Tue-Sun Nov, 10am-4pm Wed-Sun Feb) Patrick St (Map pp92-3; 64-65 Patrick St); St Stephen's Green (Map p96; North St Stephen's Green) It's hard not to feel a little cheesy with a plastic Viking helmet on your head, but the punters get a real kick out of these amphibious 1¼-hour tours that end up in the Grand Canal Dock.

Carriage Tours

You can pick up a horse and carriage with a driver-commentator at the junction of Grafton St and St Stephen's Green (Map p96). Half-hour tours cost up to €75 and the carriages can take four or five people. Tours of different lengths can be negotiated with the drivers.

FESTIVALS & EVENTS

It wasn't so long ago that a few trucks dressed up as floats, stilt walkers and a flat-bed loaded with peat briquettes were all you'd expect of Dublin's St Patrick's Day Parade. If you wanted a bit of festive glamour, New York's famous parade was the place to go. But then came the economic boom and the realisation that the event was a tourist bonanza waiting to happen. Now 17 March is just part of St Patrick's *Festival*, a four-day extravaganza of activities ranging from street theatre to fireworks, all fuelled by lots and lots of booze.

And therein lies the secret to Dubliners' love of festive events: sure, *officially* it's all about celebrating the city's rich cultural heritage, but really it's an excuse to go a little bit mad.

The following list is by no means exhaustive; for more details check out the website run by **Dublin Tourism** (www.visitdublin.com). For information on special events in Ireland as a whole, see p704.

Temple Bar Trad Festival (☎ 677 2397; www.temple bartrad.com) Traditional music festival in the bars of the cultural quarter over the last weekend in January.

Jameson Dublin International Film Festival (☎ 872 1122; www.dubliniff.com) Local flicks, arty international films and advance releases of mainstream movies make up the menu of the city's film festival, which runs over two weeks in mid-February.

St Patrick's Festival (☎ 676 3205; www.stpatricks festival.ie) The mother of all festivals; 600,000-odd gather to 'honour' St Patrick over four days around 17 March on city streets and in venues.

Convergence Festival (☎ 674 6415; www.sustainable .ie; 15-19 Essex St) Ten-day green festival in late June on sustainable living, with a diverse program of workshops, exhibitions and children's activities.

Dublin Writers Festival (www.dublinwritersfestival.com) Four-day literature festival in early June that attracts Irish and international writers to its readings, performances and talks.

Women's Mini-Marathon (☎ 670 9461; www .womensminimarathon.ie) This 10km road race for

charity (on the second Sunday in June) – the largest of its kind in the world – attracts around 40,000 runners each year.

Diversions (☎ 677 2255; www.templebar.ie) Free outdoor music, children's and film events at weekends from June to September in Temple Bar's Meeting House Sq.

Dun Laoghaire Festival of World Cultures (☎ 271 9555; www.festivalofworldcultures.com) Colourful multicultural music, art and theatre festival on the last weekend of August.

Oxegen (www.oxegen.ie) Three-day mega-music festival in mid-July at Punchestown Racecourse, featuring heavyweight pop, rock and dance acts.

Liffey Swim (☎ 833 2434) Five hundred lunatics swim 2.5km from Rory O'More Bridge to the Custom House in late July – one can't but admire their steel will.

Dublin Theatre Festival (☎ 677 8439; www.dublin theatrefestival.com) Well-established international theatre festival held over a fortnight in late September.

Dublin Fringe Festival (☎ 872 9016; www.fringefest .com) Comedy and alternative fringe theatre from late September to early October.

SLEEPING

If you're looking for evidence of what happens when an economy goes into freefall, book a hotel room in Dublin. The ridiculously expensive room rates of the last decade – which made Dublin one of Europe's most expensive cities to sleep in and rarely (if ever) offered value for money – have largely disappeared as hoteliers try to gauge an appropriate response to an economy in crisis and a pronounced dip in tourist numbers. Their answer (at the time of research, at least) was cheaper beds – as much as 40% cheaper in the middle and upper brackets – as they desperately seek to guarantee the future of their hotels, since many of them built or renovated during the boom at huge costs; although it is difficult to predict what will happen, it is clear that not everyone will survive the lean years.

Which isn't bad news for you, as everyone competes for your euro and is willing to try virtually anything to make sure that you dribble on *their* pillows: there are so many deals on offer that room rates can vary wildly from day to day, never mind season to season. Always check online (see the Booking Services boxed text, p128) and query the rack rate: discounts are more available now than ever before.

What hasn't changed, though, is that Dublin gets busy in summer and it can be

BLOOMSDAY

It's 16 June. There's a bunch of weirdos wandering around the city dressed in Edwardian gear and talking nonsense in dramatic tones. They're not mad – at least not clinically – they're only Bloomsdayers committed to commemorating James Joyce's epic *Ulysses,* which anyone familiar with the book will tell you (and that doesn't necessarily mean that they've *read* the bloody thing) takes place over the course of one day. What they mightn't be able to tell you is that Leopold Bloom's latter-day odyssey takes place on 16 June 1904 because it was on that day that Joyce first 'stepped out' with Nora Barnacle, the woman he had met six days earlier and with whom he would spend the rest of his life. (When James' father heard about this new love he commented that with a name like that she would surely stick to him.)

Although Ireland treated Joyce like a literary pornographer while he was alive, the country (and especially Dublin) can't get enough of him today. Bloomsday is a slightly gimmicky and touristy phenomenon that appeals almost exclusively to Joyce fanatics and tourists, but it's plenty of fun and a great way to lay the groundwork for actually reading what could be the second-hardest book written in the 20th century (the hardest, of course, being Joyce's follow-up blockbuster *Finnegan's Wake,* the greatest book *never* to be read).

In general, events are designed to follow Bloom's progress around town, and in recent years festivities have expanded to continue over four days around 16 June. On Bloomsday proper you can kick things off with breakfast at the James Joyce Cultural Centre (p116), where the 'inner organs of beast and fowl' come accompanied by celebratory readings.

In the morning, guided tours of Joycean sites usually leave from the General Post Office (p114) and the James Joyce Cultural Centre. Lunch-time activity focuses on **Davy Byrne's** (Map p140; Duke St), Joyce's 'moral pub', where Bloom paused to dine on a glass of burgundy and a slice of gorgonzola. Street entertainers are likely to keep you amused through the afternoon as you take guided walks and watch animated readings from *Ulysses* and Joyce's other books; there's a reading at **Ormond Quay Hotel** (Map p94; Ormond Quay) at 4pm and **Harrisons** (Map p94; Westmoreland St) in the late afternoon.

Events also take place in the days leading up to and following Bloomsday. The best source of information about what's on in any particular year is likely to be the James Joyce Cultural Centre or the free *Dublin Event Guide,* close to the date.

tough to get a central bed from around May to September. The south/north divide is also a constant, and you're more likely to get better value for money north of the Liffey – a large-roomed comfortable B&B in the northside suburbs may cost you as little as €50 per person, but the owners of a small, mediocre guesthouse within walking distance of St Stephen's Green won't balk at asking €100 for a room barely bigger than a shoebox. Still, some of the city's most characteristic properties are in the leafy suburbs directly south of the city centre, which is pretty accessible by cab or by public transportation (if you don't fancy a longish walk).

You can pay anything from €80 to €200 for a quality guesthouse or midrange hotel, while the city's top digs usually start their rates at €200; at the other end of the scale, a hostel bed will cost anything from €18 to as much as €34. (Note that hostel rates don't include breakfast; exceptions are noted.)

Grafton St & Around

You can't get more central than the relatively small patch of real estate just south of the Liffey, which has a good mix of options ranging from backpacker hostels to the fanciest hotels. Bear in mind that the location comes with a price.

BUDGET

Abigail's Hostel (Map p94; ☎ 677 9300; www.abigailshostel.com; 7-9 Aston Quay; dm/d from €12.50/38; 🛜) The dorms at this relatively new hostel (converted from an unremarkable hotel) aren't especially big – the eight-bed one is particularly cosy – but they're modern, sunny and well-appointed with all-pine furniture. All rooms are have en suite bathrooms.

Barnacles Temple Bar House (Map p94; ☎ 671 6277; www.barnacles.ie; 19 Lower Temple Lane; dm/d from €15/32; 🖥) Bright, spacious and set in the heart of Temple Bar, this hostel is immaculately clean, and has nicely laid-out dorms with private

---

TOP FIVE SLEEPS

- Best B&B – **Pembroke Townhouse** (p133)
- Best boutique hotel – **Number 31** (opposite)
- Best budget sleep – **Isaacs Hostel** (p130)
- Best luxury hotel – **Merrion** (p130)
- Best view – **Clarence Hotel** (p130)

---

bathrooms and doubles with in-room storage and bathroom. Because of its location, rooms are quieter towards the back. Top facilities, a comfy lounge, and linen and towels are provided.

Avalon House (Map p96; ☎ 475 0001; www.avalon-house.ie; 55 Aungier St; dm/s/d €18/30/60; 💻 🛜) Before there was tourism, this hostel in a gorgeous Victorian building catered to the thin trickle of adventurers who landed in Dublin. They flood in these days – book ahead – but Avalon still takes good care of them, whether they're young backpackers or families. The lounges are great for hanging out, the Bald Barista serves a sublime cappuccino and there's free wi-fi.

Kinlay House (Map p94; ☎ 679 6644; www.kinlayhouse.ie; 2-12 Lord Edward St; dm/d from €19/34; 💻 🛜) A former boarding house for boys, this busy hostel has some massive, 24-bed mixed dorms, as well as smaller rooms. Not for the fainthearted – the hostel has a reputation for being a bit of a party spot. There's a nice TV lounge and a continental breakfast is included.

Ashfield House (Map p94; ☎ 679 7734; www.ashfieldhouse.ie; 19-20 D'Olier St; dm/s/d from €22/36/72; 💻 🛜) A stone's throw from Temple Bar and O'Connell Bridge, this modern hostel in a converted church has a selection of tidy four- and six-bed rooms, one large dorm and 25 private rooms with en suite bathrooms – it's more like a small hotel but without the price tag. A continental-style breakfast is included – a rare beast indeed for hostels. Maximum stay is six nights.

MIDRANGE

Dublin Citi Hotel (Map p94; ☎ 679 4455; www.dublincitihotel.com; 46-49 Dame St; s/d Sun-Thu from €60/80, Fri & Sat €100/140) An unusual, turreted 19th-century building right next to the Central Bank is home to this cheap and cheerful hotel. Its patrons don't mind the small rooms; they're far too busy in the nightclub downstairs. Strictly for those here to party.

Central Hotel (Map p96; ☎ 679 7302; www.centralhotel.ie; 1-5 Exchequer St; s/d from €60/100) The rooms are a little snug for the grand Edwardian-style decor, but it's still a classy joint – no more so than in the wonderful 1st-floor Library Bar: all leather armchairs and sofas, and nothing short of one of the finest spots for an afternoon drink in the whole city. Location-wise, the name says it all.

Grafton House (Map p96; ☎ 679 2041; www.graftonguesthouse.com; 26-27 South Great George's St; s/d from €70/100; 🛜) This slightly offbeat guesthouse in a Gothic-style building gets the nod in all three key categories: location, price and style.

BOOKING SERVICES

If you arrive without accommodation, staff at Dublin Tourism's walk-in booking offices will find you a room for €4 plus a 10% deposit.

If you want to book a hotel from elsewhere in Ireland or abroad, the easiest way is to go through Gulliver, Dublin Tourism's computerised reservations service, via their website www.visitdublin.com, or book directly yourself from the accommodation's own website. See p99 for a list of Dublin Tourism offices and Gulliver contact numbers.

Internet bookings made in advance are your best bet for deals on accommodation. These are just a handful of services that will get you a room at a competitive rate:

All Dublin Hotels (www.all-dublin-hotels.com)
Dublin City Centre Hotels (http://dublin.city-centre-hotels.com)
Dublin Hotels (www.dublinhotels.com)
Go Ireland (www.goireland.com)
Hostel Dublin (www.hosteldublin.com)
Under 99 (www.under99.com)

See the boxed text, p697, for more options, or try www.lonelyplanet.com/hotels.

Just next to George's St Arcade, the Grafton offers the traditional friendly features of a B&B (including a terrific breakfast), coupled with a funky design – check out the psychedelic wallpaper. Hard to beat at this price, especially off-season weekdays, when the deals are at their most interesting.

Mercer Hotel (Map p96; ☎ 478 2179; www.mercerhotel.ie; Lower Mercer St; r from €90; ☎) A stone's throw from Grafton St and behind a plain frontage is a pretty decent hotel; largish rooms are dressed in antiques, giving the whole place an elegant, classic look. The rack rate is strictly for mugs – they have an ever-changing menu of online offers and special deals.

Paramount Hotel (Map p94; ☎ 417 9900; www.paramounthotel.ie; cnr Parliament St & Essex Gate; s/d €105/200) Behind the Victorian facade, the Paramount's lobby is a faithful re-creation of a 1930s hotel, complete with dark wood floors, leather chesterfield couches and heavy velvet drapes. The 70-odd rooms don't quite bring *The Maltese Falcon* to mind, but they're handsomely furnished and very comfortable.

Morgan Hotel (Map p94; ☎ 679 3939; www.themorgan.com; 10 Fleet St; r from €110; ☐ ☎) Designer cool isn't really part of the Temple Bar zeitgeist, but the cream-leather look of this place works surprisingly well considering that fake tan can leave some nasty marks. It might be popular with wannabe WAGs and their gelled-up partners, but the facilities are top-notch. Aromatherapy treatments and massages are extra, as is breakfast (€19).

our pick Number 31 (Map p90; ☎ 676 5011; www.number31.ie; 31 Leeson Close; s/d/t from €115/150/225) This elegant slice of accommodation paradise, designed for his own use by modernist architect Sam Stephenson (of Central Bank fame – or infamy), is unquestionably the most distinctive of Dublin's hotels. Separated by a beautiful garden, its 21 bedrooms are split between the chichi coach house and the more gracious Georgian house, where rooms are individually furnished with French antiques and big beds. Gourmet breakfasts are served in the conservatory. Children under 10 are not permitted.

Trinity Lodge (Map p96; ☎ 617 0900; www.trinitylodge.com; 12 South Frederick St; s/d from €130/170; ☎) Martin Sheen's grin greets you on entering this cosy, award-winning guesthouse. Not that he's ditched movies for hospitality: he just enjoyed his stay (and full Irish breakfast, presumably) at this classically refurbished Georgian pad so

---

UNIVERSITY ACCOMMODATION

From mid-June to late September, you can stay in accommodation provided by the city's universities. Be sure to book well in advance.

Trinity College (Map p101; ☎ 896 1177; www.tcd.ie; Accommodations Office, Trinity College; s/d from €60/125; ☐) Comfortable rooms ranging from basic to with en suite bathrooms in one of the most atmospheric settings in Dublin.

Mercer Court (Map p96; ☎ 478 2179; www.mercercourt.ie; Lower Mercer St; r from €90; ☐) Owned and run by the Royal College of Surgeons, Mercer Court has modern rooms that are up to hotel standard.

---

much that he let them take a mugshot. Room 2 has a lovely bay window.

La Stampa (Map p96; ☎ 677 4444; www.lastampa.ie; 35 Dawson St; r weekday/weekend €135/180; ☐) La Stampa is an atmospheric little hotel on trendy Dawson St, with 29 Asian-influenced rooms in white decorated with rattan furniture and exotic velvet throws. The Ayurvedic spa is a nice treat, but to fully benefit from your restorative treatments ask for a top-floor bedroom away from the revelling at SamSara bar (p143), located below.

Radisson Blu Royal Hotel (Map p96; ☎ 898 2900; www.radissonblu.ie/royalhotel-dublin; Golden Lane; r €160-220; ℗ ✗ ☎) The stunning Dublin flagship of this well-respected Scandinavian group is an excellent example of how sleek lines and muted colours can combine beautifully with luxury to make for a memorable night's stay: from the hugely impressive public areas (the bar alone is worth the visit) to the sophisticated bedrooms – each with flat-screen digital TVs embedded in the wall, to go along with all of the other little touches – this is bound to be one of the most popular options for the business traveller.

Irish Landmark Trust (Map p94; ☎ 670 4733; www.irishlandmark.com; 25 Eustace St; one night/weekend/week €400/800/2000) If you're travelling in a group, instead of renting a bunch of doubles in a hotel that you'll barely remember a week after you've gone home, why not go for this fabulous 18th-century heritage house, gloriously restored to the highest standard by the Irish Landmark Trust? You'll have this unique house all to yourselves. It sleeps up to seven in its double, twin and triple bedrooms.

DUBLIN

Furnished with tasteful antiques, authentic furniture and fittings (including a grand piano in the drawing room), this kind of period rental accommodation is something really special.

TOP END

Bentley's (Map p96; ☎ 638 3939; www.brownesdublin .com; 22 North St Stephen's Green; s/d from €150/200; 💻) Above the superb restaurant (see p137) are 10 exquisitely appointed rooms that offer a 21st-century interpretation of Georgian comfort. For maximum experience, get one of the four rooms overlooking St Stephen's Green; otherwise you'll have to settle for a view from the Aviator Lounge, which serves a mean mojito.

Westbury Hotel (Map p96; ☎ 679 1122; www.doyle collection.com; Grafton St; s/d from €170/260; 🅿 💻) The Westbury sits snugly on a small street just off Grafton St, which suits the high-powered business people and visiting celebs who favour the hotel's finer suites, where they can watch TV from the Jacuzzi before retiring to a four-poster bed. Mere mortals tend to make do with the standard rooms, which are perfectly appointed but lack the sophisticated grandeur promised by the luxurious public spaces.

Merrion (Map p96; ☎ 603 0600; www.merrionhotel .com; Upper Merrion St; r from €455; 🅿 💻 🛎) This is a resplendent five-star hotel set in a terrace of beautifully restored Georgian town houses. Try to get a room in the old house (which has the largest private art collection in the city) – rather than the newer wing – to sample the hotel's truly elegant comforts. Located opposite government buildings, its marble corridors are patronised by visiting dignitaries and the odd celeb. Even if you don't stay, come for the superb afternoon tea (€34), with endless cups of tea served out of silver pots near a raging fire.

Shelbourne (Map p96; ☎ 676 6471; www.theshelbourne .ie; 27 North St Stephen's Green; r from €200; 🅿 💻 🛜) Dublin's most iconic hotel has long been the best address in town – it was good enough for the framers of the Irish Constitution – but since a major refurbishment and its acquisition by the Marriott group there has been steady grumbling that the hotel is not quite at the top of its five-star game. It *looks* pretty impressive, especially the Lord Mayor's Lounge, where afternoon tea is still one of the best experiences in town.

Westin Dublin (Map p94; ☎ 645 1000; www.westin .com; Westmoreland St; s/d €210/260; 🅿 💻 🛜)

Formerly a grand branch of the Allied Irish Bank, this fine old building was gutted and reborn as a stylish upmarket hotel. The rooms, many of which overlook a beautiful atrium, are decorated in elegant mahogany and soft colours: you will sleep on 10 layers of the Westin's own (trademarked) Heavenly Bed, which is damn comfortable indeed. The hotel's most elegant room is the former banking hall, complete with gold leaf plasterwork on the ceiling, now used for banquets. Breakfast will set you back €27.

Clarence Hotel (Map p94; ☎ 407 0800; www.the clarence.ie; 6-8 Wellington Quay; r €390-440, ste €780-2800; 💻 🛜) Dublin's coolest hotel is synonymous with its rock-star owners, Bono and the Edge, so it's hardly surprising that they're used to dealing with celebrity heavyweights. The 50-odd rooms aren't short on contemporary style, but they lack that grandeur you would expect from a top hotel. The hotel was slated to get a megabucks makeover, but the economic downturn has put that on ice for the foreseeable future.

The Liberties & Kilmainham

There's not that much on offer in this part of town, but the following exception is pretty convenient.

Jurys Inn Christchurch (Map p94; ☎ 454 0000; www .jurysinns.com; Christchurch Pl; r from €89; 🛜) A chain hotel that's so generic you may wake up not knowing if you're in Detroit or Darmstadt, let alone Dublin, but it's the perfect choice if you a) wish to remain anonymous, b) don't want to be troubled by personal service, c) get a fantastic deal online or d) just want a place to sleep it off.

O'Connell Street & Around

There are a few elegant hotels around O'Connell St, but the real draw round these parts is just to the east on Gardiner St, Dublin's B&B row. *Caveat emptor:* the further north you go along Gardiner St the dodgier the lodgings and the neighbourhood get, so we've kept our inclusions to the southern end of the street, below Mountjoy Sq.

BUDGET

our pick Isaacs Hostel (Map pp92-3; ☎ 855 6215; www .isaacs.ie; 2-5 Frenchman's Lane; dm/d from €14/62; 🛜) Located in a 200-year-old wine vault, this popular, grungy hostel with loads of character is the place to head if you want one of the

---

HOME AWAY FROM HOME

Self-catering apartments are a good option for visitors staying a few days, for groups of friends, or families with kids. Apartments range from one-room studios to two-bedroom flats with lounge areas, and include bathrooms and kitchenettes. A decent two-bedroom apartment will cost about €100 to €150 per night. Good, central places include the following:

Clarion Stephen's Hall (Map pp92-3; ☎ 638 1111; www.premgroup.com; 14-17 Lower Leeson St) Deluxe studios and suites, with in-room safe, fax, modem facilities and CD player.

Home from Home Apartments (Map p90; ☎ 678 1100; www.yourhomefromhome.com; The Moorings, Fitzwilliam Quay) Deluxe one- to three-bedroom apartments in the southside city centre.

Latchfords (Map p96; ☎ 676 0784; www.latchfords.ie; 99-100 Lower Baggot St) Studios and two-bedroom flats in a Georgian town house.

Oliver St John Gogarty's Penthouse Apartments (Map p94; ☎ 671 1822; www.gogartys.ie; 18-21 Anglesea St) Perched high atop the pub of the same name (p142), these one- to three-bedroom places have views of Temple Bar.

---

cheapest beds in town – without sacrificing the basics of health and hygiene. The lounge area is where it all happens, from summer BBQs to live music, and the easygoing staff are on hand 24/7 for advice and help. Global nomads will feel right at home.

Marlborough Hostel (Map pp92-3; ☎ 874 7629; www .marlboroughhostel.com; 81-82 Marlborough St; dm from €15; ☎) Next to the Pro-Cathedral, this well-located hostel has 76 beds and adequate facilities. High Georgian ceilings make up for small rooms, but the slightly run-down showers in the basement are a bit of a trek from the dorms.

Litton Lane Hostel (Map p94; ☎ 872 8389; www .irish-hostel.com; 2-4 Litton Lane; dm/d from €15/70) True to its origins as a dog-eared recording studio (once patronised by Van Morrison), this friendly hostel could do with a lick of paint but retains a certain grungy charm. Dorms are mixed, and so are the showers, which lends new meaning to its motto: 'Don't Sleep Around; Sleep with Us'.

Abbey Court Hostel (Map p94; ☎ 878 0700; www .abbey-court.com; 29 Bachelor's Walk; dm/d €22/88; ▯) Spread over two buildings on the Liffey quays, this large, well-run hostel has 33 clean dorms with good storage. Doubles with private bathrooms are in the newer building, where a light breakfast is also provided in the cafe.

MIDRANGE

Anchor Guesthouse (Map pp92-3; ☎ 878 6913; www.anchor guesthouse.com; 49 Lower Gardiner St; s/d from €55/75) Most B&Bs round these parts offer pretty much the same sorts of things: TVs, tea- and coffee-making facilities, a half-decent shower and clean linen. The Anchor does all of that,

but it has an elegance you won't find in many of the other B&Bs along this stretch. This lovely Georgian guesthouse, with its delicious wholesome breakfasts, comes highly recommended by readers. They're dead right.

Castle Hotel (Map pp92-3; ☎ 874 6949; www.castle -hotel.ie; 3-4 Great Denmark St; s/d/tr from €70/110/140) In business since 1809, the Castle may be slightly rough around the edges, but it's one of the most pleasant hotels this side of the Liffey. The fabulous palazzo-style grand staircase leads to the 50-odd bedrooms, whose furnishings are traditional and a tad antiquated but perfectly good; check out the original Georgian cornicing around the high ceilings.

Townhouse (Map pp92-3; ☎ 878 8808; www.town houseofdublin.com; 47-48 Lower Gardiner St; s/d/tr from €70/115/132) The ghostly writing of Irish-Japanese author Lafcadio Hearn may have influenced the Gothic-style interior of his former home. A dark-walled, gilt-framed foyer with a jingling chandelier leads into 82 individually designed, comfy rooms. Some rooms in the new wing at the back are larger, with balconies overlooking the small Japanese garden.

Walton's Hotel (Map pp92-3; ☎ 878 3131; www.waltons -hotel.ie; 2-5 North Frederick St; s/d/tr €75/115/155) Better known for its legendary musical instrument shop next door, this friendly hotel was opened by the Walton family in an effort to preserve the traditional Georgian heritage of the building. With the help of the nearby Castle Hotel it's done just that. The 43 rooms are clean and spacious; with a superb location overlooking Findlater's Church and the Rotunda Hospital, Walton's is an excellent choice. Children under 12 stay for free.

Lynam's Hotel (Map pp92-3; ☎ 888 0886; www.lynams -hotel.com; 63-64 O'Connell St; s/d/tr from €80/125/165; ⊛) A midrange hotel smack in the middle of O'Connell St is almost too good to be true. Now that Dublin's premier street is halfway back to its glorious best, Lynam's becomes a rare gem indeed – a smart, friendly hotel with 42 pleasant rooms decorated in country-style pine furniture. Room 41 is a lovely dormer triple with an additional camp bed – handy for groups who want to share. Ask for discounts midweek.

Browns Hotel (Map pp92-3; ☎ 855 0034; www.browns dublinhotel.com; 80-90 Lower Gardiner St; s/d €90/115) The 22 rooms fill up pretty quickly at this small hotel, whose popularity is cemented by neat and tidy rooms replete with modern furnishings. Book early.

Morrison Hotel (Map p94; ☎ 887 2400; www.morrison hotel.ie; Lower Ormond Quay; r from €135, ste from €285; 🖳) Fashion designer John Rocha's loosely Oriental style is evident in the Zen-like furnishings, but extras such as iMac computers, iPod docking stations and Aveda goodies clinch it for us. For a few euro extra, nab a far superior studio den (€415) in the new wing: there's a balcony and enough space to throw a party. This could be the most affordable posh hotel in town.

TOP END

Gresham Hotel (Map pp92-3; ☎ 874 6881; www.gresham -hotels.com; Upper O'Connell St; r €200, ste €450-2500; 🖳) A city landmark and one of Dublin's oldest hotels, the Gresham shed its traditional granny's parlour look with a major overhaul some years ago. Despite its brighter, smarter, modern appearance and a fabulous open-plan foyer, its loyal clientele – elderly groups on shopping breaks to the capital and well-heeled Americans – has stuck firmly. Rooms are spacious and well serviced, though the decor is a little brash.

Docklands

Hotels at the eastern end of the Liffey are aimed almost exclusively at the business traveller, but a highly competitive market means there are some pretty good ones to choose from. A new, much-vaunted five-star hotel designed by Manuel Aires Mateus was scheduled to open at the end of 2009, but that could be delayed into 2010.

MIDRANGE

Maldron Hotel Cardiff Lane (Map p90; ☎ 643 9500; www .maldronhotels.com; Cardiff Lane; r €110-360; 🖳 🖳 ⊛)

On the south side of the Liffey a short walk away from the Grand Canal Dock, this is one of the best midrange options in the city. The rooms are large and extremely comfortable, but the real catch is the amenities: two restaurants, a top-class fitness centre complete with sauna and a 22m swimming pool, the largest hotel pool in town.

TOP END

Clarion Hotel IFSC (Map pp92-3; ☎ 433 8800; www.clarion hotelifsc.com; Custom House Quay; r €265, ste €395-1000; 🅿 🞨 🖳 🖳 ⊛) This swanky business hotel in the heart of the Irish Financial Services Centre has beautiful rooms decorated in contemporary light oak furnishings and a blue-and-taupe colour scheme that is supposed to relax the mind after a long day of meetings. We prefer to relax with a swim in the Sanovitae health club downstairs.

Smithfield & Phoenix Park

It's still an area in development, but Smithfield – especially along the quays – is a good spot to stay as it's close to all the action.

MIDRANGE

Maldron Hotel Smithfield (Map pp92-3; ☎ 485 0900; www .maldronhotels.com; Smithfield Village; r €130-150; 🖳) This modern hotel, with big bedrooms and plenty of earth tones to soften the contemporary edges, is your best bet in this part of town. We loved the floor-to-ceiling windows – great for checking out what's going on below in the square.

Beyond the Grand Canal

You'll get more for your euro in the largely stylish digs dotted throughout the southern city suburb of Ballsbridge, a 30-minute walk from the city centre or a short ride on buses 5, 7, 7A, 8, 18 or 45.

MIDRANGE

Waterloo House (Map p90; ☎ 660 1888; www.waterloo house.ie; 8-10 Waterloo Rd; s/d €70/120; 🅿 ⊛) A short walk from St Stephen's Green, this lovely guesthouse is spread over two ivy-clad Georgian houses off Baggot St. Rooms are tastefully decorated with high-quality furnishings in authentic Farrow & Ball Georgian colours, and all have cable TV and kettles. Home-cooked breakfast is served in the conservatory or in the garden on sunny days.

Ariel House (Map p90; ☎ 668 5512; www.ariel-house
.net; 52 Lansdowne Rd; r €79-250; **P** 🛜) Somewhere
between a boutique hotel and a luxury B&B,
this highly rated Victorian-era property has
28 rooms with en suite bathrooms, all individually decorated in period furniture, which
lends the place an air of genuine luxury. A far
better choice than most hotels.

our pick Pembroke Townhouse (Map p90; ☎ 660
0277; www.pembroketownhouse.ie; 90 Pembroke Rd; s
€90-195, d €115-290; **P** 🛜) This superluxurious
town house is a perfect example of what happens when traditional and modern combine
to great effect. A classical Georgian house
has been transformed into a superb boutique hotel, with each room carefully crafted
and appointed to reflect the best of contemporary design and style, right down to the
modern art on the walls and the handy lift
to the upper floors. May we borrow your
designer?

Schoolhouse Hotel (Map p90; ☎ 667 5014; www
.schoolhousehotel.com; 2-8 Northumberland Rd; s/d from
€99/199; **P**) This is a real beauty: a converted
Victorian schoolhouse that is now a superb
boutique hotel with 31 exquisite rooms, each
named after an Irish writer, and stocked with
luxury toiletries and all sorts of modern amenities. A place ahead of its – ahem – class.

TOP END

Dylan (Map p90; ☎ 660 3001; www.dylan.ie; Eastmoreland Pl;
r from €200; 🀫 🖥 🛜) A genuine contender for favourite celebrity stopover, the Dylan's designer
OTT look – baroque meets Scandinavian sleek
by way of neo-art nouveau and glammed-up
1940s art deco – has nevertheless been a big
hit, a reflection perhaps of a time when too
much was barely enough for the glitterati who
signed contracts over cocktails before retiring
to the crisp Frette linen sheets in the snazzily
appointed rooms upstairs.

Four Seasons (Map p90; ☎ 665 4000; www.fourseasons
.com; Simmonscourt Rd; r from €225; **P** 🖥 🐾 🛜) The
muscular, no-holds-barred style of American
corporate innkeeping is in full force at this
huge hotel that has sought to raise the hospitality bar. Its mix of styles – anyone for faux
Victorian Georgian with a bit of baroque
thrown in for good measure? – has its critics,
but there's no denying the sheer quality of the
place. The spa is superb and the lit basement
pool a treat. For many, this is the best hotel
in town. We're suckers for a slightly more de-
mure luxury, so we'll stick it in the top three.

It's in the grounds of the Royal Dublin Society
Showground.

EATING

The transformation of Dublin from culinary
backwater to gourmet metropolis has resulted
in a city with more restaurants than it knows
what to do with, and a population whose pal-
ates have grown increasingly sophisticated
on a diet of dishes from around the world –
a far cry from the days when the joke held
true that Irish food was wonderful until it
was cooked.

The crash of 2008–09, however, has put a
limit on the sky and there is little doubt that
the future is bleak for many of the city's restaurateurs – it is to be hoped that the cream
will rise to the top and the best ones will survive, but the onus is on the restaurateurs to
consolidate and reimagine their menus to
suit the shrinking budgets of their customers. Which is probably why we've noticed the
dramatic return of the wholesome, filling and
generally affordable burger to menus that a
couple of years ago wouldn't deign to descend
to such unimaginative lows.

The most concentrated restaurant area
is Temple Bar but, apart from a handful of
good places, the bulk of eateries offer bland,
unimaginative fodder and cheap set menus
for tourists. Better food and service can usually be found on either side of Grafton St,
while the top-end restaurants are clustered
around Merrion Sq and Fitzwilliam Sq. Fast-
food chains dominate the northside, though
some fine cafes and eateries are finally appearing there too. The area around Parnell St, in
particular, is worth checking out for the spate
of new exotic restaurants – a reflection of the
increasingly diverse ethnic communities that
have settled in the area.

For many restaurants, particularly those in
the centre, it's worth booking for Friday or
Saturday nights to ensure a table.

Grafton St & Around

If you spent your whole time in this area you
would eat pretty well; the south city centre is
the hub of the best the city has to offer.

BUDGET

Cake Café (Map pp92-3; ☎ 633 4477; Pleasant Pl; mains
€2-8; 🕙 10am-6pm) Dublin's best-kept pastry secret is this great little cafe in a tough-to-find
lane just off Lower Camden St. The easiest

way in is through Daintree stationery shop (61 Camden St); through the back of the Daintree is the self-contained yard, which in good weather is the best spot to enjoy a coffee and a homemade cake.

Gruel (Map p94; ☎ 670 7119; 68a Dame St; breakfast €4, lunch €4.50-8, brunch €5-12, dinner mains €9-15; ☻ 7am-9.30pm Mon-Fri, 10.30am-10.30pm Sat & Sun) For its regulars, Gruel is the best dish in town, whether it's for the superfilling, tasty lunchtime roast-in-a-roll – a rotating list of slow-roasted organic meats stuffed into a bap (large bread roll) and flavoured with homemade relishes – or the exceptional evening menu, where pasta, fish and chicken are given an exotic once-over. Go, queue and share elbow space with the table behind you: it's worth the effort. It doesn't accept bookings.

Simon's Place (Map p96; ☎ 679 7821; George's St Arcade, South Great George's St; mains from €4; ☻ 9am-5.30pm Mon-Sat) Simon hasn't had to change the menu of sandwiches with thick-cut bread and wholesome vegetarian soups since he first opened shop two decades ago – and why should he? His grub is as heartening and legendary as he is. It's a great place to sip a coffee and watch life go by in the old-fashioned arcade.

Queen of Tarts (Map p94; snacks from €4) Cork Hill (☎ 670 7499; 4 Cork Hill; ☻ 7.30am-6pm Mon-Fri); Cow's Lane (☎ 633 4681; 3-4 Cow's Lane; ☻ 7.30am-6pm) Pocket-sized Queen of Tarts was so popular with its mouth-watering array of savoury tarts and filled focaccias, fruit crumbles and wicked pastries that they opened a bigger version around the corner on Cow's Lane. Either is perfect for breakfast or lunch.

Lemon (Map p96; pancakes from €4.25; ☻ 9am-7pm Mon-Sat, 10am-6pm Sun) South William St (☎ 672 9044; 66 South William St); Dawson St (☎ 672 8898; 61 Dawson St) Dublin's best pancake joint is staffed by a terrific bunch who like their music loud and their pancakes good: proper paper-thin

sweet and savoury crêpes smothered, stuffed and sprinkled with a variety of toppings, fillings and sauces. There's a second branch on nearby Dawson St.

Listons (Map p90; ☎ 405 4779; 25 Camden St; lunch €4-9; ☻ 8.30am-7.30pm Mon-Thu, to 6.30pm Fri, 10am-6pm Sat) Lunchtime queues out the door testify that Listons is undoubtedly the best deli in Dublin. Its sandwiches with delicious fillings, roasted vegetable quiches, rosemary potato cakes and sublime salads will have you coming back again and again. The only problem is there's too much to choose from. On fine days it's great to retreat to the solitude of the nearby Iveagh Gardens with your gourmet picnic.

ourpick Honest to Goodness (Map p96; ☎ 677 5373; George's St Arcade; mains €6; ☻ 9am-6pm Mon-Sat, noon-4pm Sun) Wholesome sandwiches (made with freshly baked bread), tasty soups and a near-legendary Sloppy Joe, all made on the premises using produce sourced from local farmers, have earned this lovely spot in the George's St Arcade a bevy of loyal fans who want to keep it all to themselves. No place this good can stay secret for long.

Zaytoon (mains €6-9; ☻ noon-4am) Temple Bar (Map p94; ☎ 677 3595; 14-15 Parliament St); Camden St (Map p90; ☎ 400 5006; 44-55 Lower Camden St) If at the end of the night you need something to absorb the booze, then the Middle Eastern delights at this joint are the thing for you. Just don't expect anything more than what makes up a kebab.

Fallon & Byrne (Map p96; ☎ 472 1000; Exchequer St; deli mains €6-9, brasserie mains €17-28; ☻ deli 9am-8pm Mon-Sat, 11am-6pm Sun, brasserie noon-4.30pm & 6.30-10.30pm Mon-Wed, to 11.30pm Thu-Sat, 11am-4pm Sun) Dublin's answer to New York's much-loved upmarket grocery store Dean & Deluca is this food hall, wine cellar and restaurant. The queues for the delicious deli counter are constant, while the chic, buzzy brasserie upstairs hasn't failed to impress either, with long red banquettes, a diverse menu of creamy fish pie, beef carpaccio and roast turbot, and excellent service.

Larder (Map p94; ☎ 633 3581; 8 Parliament St; mains €6-10; ☻ 8am-6pm) This welcoming cafe-restaurant has a positively organic vibe to it, what with its wholesome porridge breakfasts, gourmet sandwiches such as *serrano* ham, gruyère and rocket (arugula), and speciality Suki teas (try the Gunpowder Green Tea). It's confident about its food – we like the fact that it lists suppliers – and so are we.

Dunne & Crescenzi (Map p96; ☎ 677 3815; 14-16 South Frederick St; mains €9-12; ☻ 9am-7pm Mon & Tue,

---

TOP FIVE BITES

- Best budget eats – **Honest to Goodness** (right)
- Best brunch – **Odessa** (p136)
- Best sandwich to go – **Bottega Toffoli** (right)
- Best lunch – **Yamamori** (p136)
- Best splurge – **Town Bar & Grill** (p137)

FARMERS AND ORGANIC MARKETS

Dublin Food Co-op (Map pp92–3; ☎ 454 4258; www.dublinfoodcoop.com; 12 Newmarket; ☒ 2-8pm Thu, 9.30am-4.30pm Sat) A buzzing community market specialising in organic veg, homemade cheeses and organic wines; there's also a bakery and even baby-changing facilities.

Howth Fishermens & Farmers Market Bar (☎ 611 5016; www.irishfarmersmarkets.ie; West Pier, Howth Harbour; ☒ 10am-5pm Sun & bank holidays) One of the best in Dublin, this is the place to come not only for fresh fish (obviously) but also for organic meat, veg and homemade everything else, including jams, cakes and breads. A great option for Sunday lunch. Take either the DART or bus 32 or 32A to Howth.

People's Park Market (☎ 087-957 3647; People's Park, Dun Laoghaire; ☒ 11am-4pm Sun) Organic meat and veg, local seafood, Irish fruit and farm cheeses are the mainstay at this popular market in the south Dublin suburb of Dun Laoghaire. Grab a burger and sit on the lawn. Take the DART to Dun Laoghaire.

Temple Bar Farmers Market (Meeting House Sq; ☒ 9am-4.30pm Sat) This great little market is a fabulous place to while away a Saturday morning, sampling and munching on organic gourmet goodies bound by the market's only rule: local producers only. From cured meats to wildflowers, you could fill an entire pantry with their selection of delights.

For more info on local markets, check out www.irishfarmersmarkets.ie, www.irishvillagemarkets .com or local county council sites such as www.dlrcoco.ie/markets.

---

to 10pm Wed-Sat) This exceptional Italian eatery delights its regulars with a basic menu of rustic pleasures: panini, a single pasta dish and a superb plate of mixed antipasti drizzled in olive oil. The shelves are stacked with wine, the coffee is perfect and the desserts are sinfully good.

Bottega Toffoli (Map p94; ☎ 633 4022; 34 Castle St; sandwiches & salads €9-12; ☒ 8am-4pm Tue-Wed, 8am-9pm Thu-Fri, 11am-8pm Sat, 1-8pm Sun) Tucked away in the city centre (to the point where you would never find it unless you actually looked for it) is this superb Italian cafe, home of one of the best sandwiches you'll eat in town: beautifully cut prosciutto, baby tomatoes and rocket salad drizzled with imported olive oil, all on homemade *piadina* bread that is just too good to be true.

MIDRANGE

Good World (Map p96; ☎ 677 2580; 18 South Great George's St; dim sum €4-6, mains €8-22; ☒ 12.30pm-2.30am) A hands-down winner of our 'best Chinese restaurant' competition, the Good World has two menus, but to really get the most of this terrific spot, steer well clear of the Western menu and its unimaginative fare. With listings in two languages, the Chinese menu is packed with dishes and delicacies that keep us coming back for more.

Juice (Map p96; ☎ 475 7856; 73 South Great George's St; mains €8-15; ☒ noon-10pm Mon-Thu, noon-11pm Fri & Sat, 10am-10pm Sun) A creative vegetarian restaurant, Juice puts an imaginative, California-type spin on all kinds of dishes. The real treat is the selection of fruit smoothies.

Market Bar (Map p96; ☎ 677 4835; Fade St; mains €8.50-14; ☒ noon-11pm) This one-time sausage factory, now a fashionable watering hole (p143), also has a super kitchen knocking out Spanish tapas and other Iberian-influenced bites. Dishes come in half and full portions, so you can mix and match your dishes and not pig out. Proof that the carvery lunch isn't the height of pub dining.

Gourmet Burger Kitchen (www.gbkinfo.com; burgers €9-13) South William St (Map p96; ☎ 679 0537; 14 South William St; ☒ noon-10pm Sun-Wed, noon-11pm Thu-Sat); South Anne St (Map p96; ☎ 672 8559; 5 South Anne St; ☒ noon-10pm Sun-Wed, noon-11pm Thu-Sat) Temple Bar (Map p94; ☎ 670 8343; Unit 1, Temple Bar Sq; ☒ noon-11pm Mon-Sat, noon-10pm Sun) Burgers are back, and they don't get any better than the ones served at the three city centre branches of this new restaurant. The menu has a big range of choice, from your straight-up beef burger with cheese to something a little more adventurous: how about a Kiwiburger topped with beetroot, egg, pineapple, cheese, salad and relish? They also have decent veggie options.

Café Bardeli (Map p96; www.cafebardeli.ie; mains €9-13; ☒ 7am-11pm) Grafton St (☎ 672 7720; Bewley's Bldg, Grafton St); South Great George's St (☎ 677 1646; 12-13 South Great George's St) With three branches in the city – including a spectacular one in Dublin's most beloved cafe, Bewley's of Grafton St – the folks behind Bardeli have hit the nail firmly on the head: great crispy pizzas with imaginative toppings such as spicy lamb and tzatziki, fresh homemade pastas, and salads such as broccoli, feta and chickpea that you'll dream about for days. All in a buzzing atmosphere at prices that won't break the bank. No reservations, so prepare to wait on a busy night. See also p140.

Green Nineteen (Map pp92-3; ☎ 478 9626; 19 Lower Camden St; mains €10-12; ☺ 10am-11pm Mon-Sat, noon-6pm Sun) The newest addition to Camden St's growing corridor of cool is this sleek restaurant that specialises in locally sourced, organic grub – without the fancy price tag. Braised lamb chump, corned beef, pot-roast chicken and the ubiquitous burger are but the meaty part of the menu that also includes salads and veggie option. We love it.

Shebeen Chic (Map p96; ☎ 679 9667; 5 South Great George's St; mains €10-15; ☺ noon-10pm Sun-Wed, to 11pm Thu-Sat) Cracked chandeliers, paintings hung at odd angles and ne'er a matching table-and-chair set create the suitably ramshackle tone for a restaurant whose name comes from the Irish word for 'illegal drinking establishment'. The menu reads like it was written by Tom Waits: 'spudballs with broccoli, mushrooms and auld cheddar', or 'leek, spud and maybe mud' are representatives of a cuisine best described as 'Irish with attitude'. In the basement is a bar with a speakeasy vibe.

Bistro (Map p96; ☎ 671 5430; 4-5 Castle Market; mains €10-19; ☺ noon-10pm) The real draw at this place in summer is its outdoor seating, set on a lively pedestrianised strip behind the George's St Arcade. An excellent menu of fish, pasta and meat specials, a well-stocked wine cellar and efficient service make this the warm-weather choice for alfresco dining.

Yamamori (Map p96; ☎ 475 5001; 71 South Great George's St; mains €10-28, lunch bento €9.95; ☺ 12.30pm-11pm) This popular Asian restaurant with long communal tables serves filling noodle- and rice-based staples, as well as sushi. The lunch bento is one of the best deals in town, and one of the most delicious to boot. Children are well catered for and service is smart.

Silk Road Café (Map p94; ☎ 407 0770; Chester Beatty Library, Dublin Castle; mains around €11; ☺ 11am-4pm Mon-Fri) Museum cafes don't often make you salivate, but this vaguely Middle Eastern/North African/Mediterranean gem is the exception. The menu is about two-thirds veggie, with house specialities of Greek moussaka and spinach lasagne complementing the deep-fried chickpeas and hummus starters. For dessert, there's Lebanese baklava and coconut *kataïfi* (angel-hair pastry), or you could opt for the juiciest dates this side of Tyre. All dishes are halal and kosher.

Wagamama (Map p96; ☎ 478 2152; South King St; mains €11-18; ☺ 11am-11pm) Production-line rice and noodle dishes served pronto at canteen-style tables mightn't seem like the most inviting way to dine, but boy this food is good. The basement it's served in is surprisingly light and airy – for a place with absolutely no natural light.

Chameleon (Map p94; ☎ 671 0362; 1 Lower Fownes St; mains €12-20; ☺ 6-11pm Tue-Sat, to 10pm Sun) Friendly, characterful and draped in exotic fabrics, Chameleon serves up oodles of noodles and Indonesian classics, including satay, *gado gado* (veggies with peanut sauce), nasi goreng and *mee goreng* (spicy fried noodles). If you can't decide, try the rijsttafel – it's a selection of several dishes with rice.

L'Gueuleton (Map p96; ☎ 675 3708; 1 Fade St; mains €12-25; ☺ noon-3pm & 6-11.30pm Mon-Sat) Dubliners have a devil of a time pronouncing the name (which means 'the Gluttonous Feast' in French) and have had their patience tested with the no-reservations, get-in-line-and-wait policy, but they just can't get enough of the restaurant's take on French rustic cuisine, which makes twisted tongues and sore feet a small price to pay. The steak is sensational, but the Toulouse sausages with *choucroute* (sauerkraut) and Lyonnaise potatoes is a timely reminder that when it comes to the pleasures of the palate, the French really know what they're doing.

Saba (Map p96; ☎ 679 2000; www.sabadublin.com; 26-28 Clarendon St; mains €12-28; ☺ noon-11pm) Southeast Asian cuisine hits Dublin with a stylish bang at this supercool eatery that seeks to impress with its extensive menu and contemporary decor. Both are good without being exceptional, but it's packed every night, so what the hell do we know?

Monty's of Kathmandu (Map p94; ☎ 670 4911; 28 Eustace St; mains €13-21; ☺ 12.30-2.30pm & 6-11.30pm Mon-Sat, 6-11pm Sun) The trade of award-winning Monty's is built on people who keep returning for typical Nepalese dishes such as *gorkhali* (chicken cooked in chilli, yoghurt and ginger) or *kachila* (raw marinated meat). The Shiva beer complements these hearty, spicy dishes. Ethnic food doesn't get much better than this.

Odessa (Map p94; ☎ 670 7634; 13 Dame Ct; mains €13-25) Odessa's lounge atmosphere, with comfy sofas and retro standard lamps, has long attracted the city's hipsters, who flock here for homemade burgers, steaks or daily fish specials. You may not escape the sofa after you've quaffed a few of Odessa's renowned cocktails while playing a game of backgammon. Weekend brunch is *extremely* popular: you have been warned.

Leon (Map p94; ☎ 670 7238; 33 Exchequer St; mains €15-22; ☑ 8am-11pm Mon-Sat, 9am-10pm Sun) French elegance comes to Dublin in the shape of this gorgeous cafe-restaurant. From bouillabaisse to filet of lamb with a *gratin Dauphinois*, the food is classically Gallic, but the real treat here is to linger over a cappuccino with a newspaper by the open fire at the front.

Seagrass (Map p90; ☎ 478 9595; 30 South Richmond St; mains €15-22; ☑ 6-11pm) Utterly unassuming from the outside, this is one of Dublin's best new openings of the last couple of years: the locally sourced, roughly Mediterranean menu (baked seafood penne, pan-fried lambs' livers and a bacon-and-cabbage risotto are typical) is uniformly excellent, the dining room is quietly elegant and the service absolutely perfect.

Jaipur (Map p96; ☎ 677 0999; www.jaipur.ie; 41 South Great George's St; mains €17-20; ☑ noon-10pm) Critics rave about the subtle and varied flavours produced by Jaipur's kitchen, which is down to its refusal to skimp on even the smallest dash of spice. What you get here is as close to the real deal as you'd get anywhere outside Delhi.

TOP END

Eden (Map p94; ☎ 670 5372; Meeting House Sq; mains €15-28; ☑ noon-2.30pm & 6-10.30pm Mon-Fri, noon-3pm & 6-11pm Sat & Sun) Eden is the epitome of Temple Bar chic with its trendy waitstaff, minimalist surroundings, high ceiling, hanging plants and terrace opening onto Meeting House Sq. But the food is the real star: Eleanor Walsh's unfussy modern Irish cuisine uses organic seasonal produce, complemented by a carefully chosen wine list. Seating on the gas-heated terrace is at a premium on summer evenings, when classic films are projected onto the nearby Gallery of Photography.

Bang (Map p96; ☎ 676 0898; www.bangrestaurant .com; 11 Merrion Row; mains €16-36; ☑ 12.30-3pm & 6.30-10.30pm Mon-Sat) The hip and handsome Stoke twins have brought a touch of Denmark to Dublin in appropriately stylish surrounds – and have created a favourite with the 30-somethings who have a little cash to burn. The modern European grub – carefully created by chef Lorcan Cribbin (ex-Ivy in London, don't you know) – is sharp, tasty and very much in demand. Thai baked sea bass, medallions of beef and melt-in-your-mouth roast scallops are just a random selection. Reservations are a must, even for lunch.

Marco Pierre White Steakhouse & Grill (Map p96; ☎ 677 1155; www.fitzers.ie; 51 Dawson St; mains €17-28; ☑ noon-11pm) The long-established Fitzer's restaurant group scored quite a coup when they enlisted bad boy chef Marco Pierre White (he who once made Gordon Ramsay cry) to lend his name to their newest venture, which opened in 2009. Steaks, grilled meats and hunks of fish are the fare, presented with a minimum of fuss but with plenty of taste.

Town Bar & Grill (Map p96; ☎ 662 4724; 21 Kildare St; mains €18-28; ☑ noon-11pm Mon-Sat, to 10pm Sun) On any given night, you're likely to share this low-ceilinged basement dining room with a selection of Ireland's most affluent and influential people, conducting oh-so-important affairs barely above a murmur. But the place's slight stuffiness is swept aside by the simply mouth-watering food, ranging from slow-rotated rabbit to sweet pepper-stuffed lamb. It's how food should be made.

Mermaid Café (Map p94; ☎ 670 8236; 22 Dame St; mains €18-31; ☑ 12.30-2.30pm & 6-11pm Mon-Sat, 12.30-3pm & 6-9pm Sun) The Mermaid is an American-style bistro with natural wood furniture and abstract canvases on its panelled walls. It caters mainly to a hip gourmet crowd, who appreciate the inventive, ingredient-led organic food such as monkfish with buttered red chard or braised lamb shank with apricot couscous. Its informal atmosphere, pure food and friendly staff make it difficult to get a table without booking.

Bentley's Oyster Bar & Grill (Map p96; ☎ 638 3939; www.bentleysdublin.com; 22 North St Stephen's Green; mains €19-35; ☑ noon-2.30pm & 6-11pm Mon-Sat, noon-4pm & 6-10pm Sun) If imitation is the sincerest form of flattery, then the famous original in London will be chuffed at what chef Richard Corrigan has done with the Dublin edition. Modern Irish is the theme of the superb menu, but don't forget the oyster bar, where you can have a selection of shucked delights from Galway or Carlingford presented in a variety of ways.

Thornton's (Map p96; ☎ 478 7000; www.thorntons restaurant.com; 128 St Stephen's Green; midweek 2-/3-course lunch €25/38, dinner mains €45; ☑ 12.30-2pm & 7-10pm Tue-Sat) Kevin Thornton may have lost one

VEGGIE BUDGET BITES

Blazing Salads (Map p96; ☎ 671 9552; 42 Drury St; mains €4-9; 🕙 10am-6pm Mon-Sat, to 8pm Thu) Organic breads (many suitable for special diets), Californian-style salads, smoothies and pizza slices can all be taken away from this delicious vegetarian deli.

Fresh (Map p96; ☎ 671 9552; top fl, Powerscourt Townhouse Shopping Centre, 59 South William St; lunch €6-11; 🕙 9.30am-6pm Mon-Sat, 10am-5pm Sun) This long-standing vegetarian restaurant serves a variety of salads and filling, hot daily specials. Many dishes are dairy- and gluten-free without compromising on taste. The baked potato topped with organic cheese (€5.50) comes with two salads and is a hearty meal in itself.

Cornucopia (Map p96; ☎ 677 7583; 19 Wicklow St; mains from €6; 🕙 9am-7pm Mon-Wed & Fri & Sat, to 9pm Thu) For those escaping the Irish cholesterol habit, Cornucopia is a popular wholefood cafe turning out healthy goodies. There's even a hot vegetarian breakfast as an alternative to muesli.

Govinda's (www.govindas.ie; mains €7-11) Aungier St (Map p96; ☎ 475 0309; 4 Aungier St; 🕙 noon-9pm Mon-Sat) Merrion Row (Map p96; ☎ 661 5095; 18 Merrion Row; 🕙 noon-9pm Mon-Sat) Middle Abbey St (Map p94; 83 Middle Abbey St; 🕙 noon-9pm Mon-Sat, to 7pm Sun) Authentic beans-and-pulses vegetarian place run by the Hare Krishna, now with branches on both sides of the river. The cheap, wholesome mix of salads and Indian-influenced hot daily specials are filling and tasty.

of his two Michelin stars a few years ago, but he has proved somewhat defiantly that Michelin's loss was his customers' gain, and his mouth-watering interpretation of modern French cuisine is as superb as ever, with faultless service in a gorgeous room overlooking St Stephen's Green. Want to watch a grown-up squirm? Ask for ketchup.

Restaurant Patrick Guilbaud (Map p96; ☎ 676 4192; www.restaurantpatrickguilbaud.ie; 21 Upper Merrion St; 2-/3-course set lunch €38/50, dinner mains €38-50; 🕙 12.30-2.30pm & 7.30-10.30pm Tue-Sat) With two Michelin stars on its resumé, this elegant restaurant is one of the best in Ireland, and head chef Guillaume Lebrun does his best to ensure that it stays that way. Next door to the Merrion Hotel, Guilbaud has French *haute cuisine* that is beautifully executed and served in delectable surroundings. The lunch menu is a steal, at least in this stratosphere.

The Liberties & Kilmainham

Fast-food outlets and greasy-spoon diners still dominate the food map in this part of the city, but there's one spot that rises out of the boiling oil and batter-in-a-bucket and takes its place among the legends.

Leo Burdock's (Map p94; ☎ 454 0306; 2 Werburgh St; cod & chips €8.50; 🕙 noon-midnight Mon-Sat, 4pm-midnight Sun) You will often hear that you haven't eaten in Dublin until you've queued in the cold for a cod and chips wrapped in paper from the city's most famous chipper. Total codswallop, of course, but there's something about sitting on the street, balancing the bag on

your lap and trying to eat the chips quickly before they go cold and horrible that smacks of Dublin in a bygone age. It's nice to revisit the past, especially if you don't have to get stuck there.

O'Connell Street & Around

Bar a couple of classy restaurants and one simply outstanding one, the northside's greatest contribution to the city's restaurant map has been in ethnic cuisine: Parnell St and Capel St particularly abound with Chinese, Korean and African eateries; you can spot the good ones by how popular they are with the local immigrant communities.

BUDGET

Epicurean Food Hall (Map p94; Lower Liffey St; lunch €4-12; 🕙 9.30am-5.30pm Mon-Sat) Need to refuel and rest the bag-laden arms? Then this busy arcade with 20-odd food stalls is just the ticket. Quality is hit and miss, but you won't go wrong with a hot bagel with the works from Itsabagel or a finger-licking kebab from Istanbul House, rounded off with an espresso from the excellent El Corte.

Soup Dragon (Map p94; ☎ 872 3277; 168 Capel St; soups €5.30-12.95; 🕙 8am-5.30pm Mon-Fri, 11am-5pm Sat) Eat in or take away one of 12 tasty varieties of homemade soups, including shepherd's pie or spicy vegetable gumbo. Bowls come in three different sizes, and prices include fresh bread and a piece of fruit. Kick-start your day (or afternoon) with a healthy all-day breakfast selection: try fresh smoothies (€3.95) or the generous bowls of yoghurt, fruit and muesli (€4.50).

Cobalt Café & Gallery (Map pp92-3; ☎ 873 0313; 16 North Great George's St; mains €6-10; 🕙 10am-4.30pm Mon-Fri) This gorgeous, elegant cafe in a bright and airy Georgian drawing room is a must if you're in the 'hood. Almost opposite the James Joyce Cultural Centre, Cobalt has a simple menu, but you can enjoy hearty soups by a roaring fire in winter, or fresh sandwiches in the garden on warmer days.

Football-mad developer Mick Wallace has managed to single-handedly create a thriving new Italian quarter, with cafes and eateries popping up all over Quartier Bloom, the lane from Ormond Quay to Great Strand St. **La Taverna di Bacco** (Map p94; ☎ 873 0040; 24 Lower Ormond Quay; mains €8-9; 🕙 12.30-10.30pm Mon-Sat, from 5pm Sun) and **Enoteca Delle Langhe** (Map p94; ☎ 888 0834; Bloom's Lane; 🕙 noon-11pm), a few doors up, serve simple pastas, antipasti and Italian cheeses, along with the delicious produce of Wallace's own vineyard and others in Piemonte.

MIDRANGE

Bar Italia (Map p94; ☎ 874 1000; 28 Lower Ormond Quay; mains €9-18; 🕙 10.30am-11pm Mon-Sat, 1-9pm Sun) One of a new generation of eateries that's showing the more established Italian restaurants how the Old Country *really* eats, Bar Italia's specialities are its ever-changing pasta dishes, homemade risottos and excellent Palombini coffee.

Bon Ga (Map p94; ☎ 872 7934; www.bonga.ie; 52 Capel St; buffet €10-18; karaoke rooms €25-60; 🕙 5.30pm-midnight) Korean barbecue (usually grilled marinated meats) is all well and – in this instance – very good, but there's something extra about this large, friendly place that's always buzzing with locals, visitors and immigrants alike: oh yeah, it's the karaoke rooms, where you can dine and sing to your heart's content. To get the vocal chords going try the *dongdong ju* (rice wine) or *soju*, basically a Korean vodka. Top night out.

Melody (Map p94; ☎ 878 8988; 122 Capel St; buffet €10-18; karaoke rooms €25-60; 🕙 5.30pm-midnight) Lots of red lacquer, black marble, a couple of fish tanks and the biggest TV we've ever seen is clear evidence that this place was designed to suit the sensibilities of the city's substantial Chinese community, but it works for the Irish, too: they come, preferably in big groups, and tuck into the fairly standard Chinese fare.

Downstairs, a warren of tunnels leads to the karaoke dining rooms – probably the real reason this place is so popular.

TOP END

Winding Stair (Map p94; ☎ 873 7320; 40 Lower Ormond Quay; mains €22-27; 🕙 noon-4pm & 6-10pm Tue-Sat, 1-10pm Sun) Housed within a beautiful Georgian building that was once home to the city's most beloved bookshop (the ground floor still is one, see p87), the conversion to elegant restaurant has been faultless. The wonderful Irish menu – creamy fish pie, bacon and organic cabbage, steamed mussels, and Irish farmyard cheeses – coupled with an excellent wine list make for a memorable meal.

Chapter One (Map pp92-3; ☎ 873 2266; www.chapteronerestaurant.com; 18 North Parnell Sq; mains €33-35; 🕙 12.30-2pm Tue-Fri, 6-11pm Tue-Sat) South-side snobs who think fine cuisine ends at the Liffey's edge have never had the pleasure of savouring the classic French cuisine in the best restaurant north of the river, situated in the lovely vaulted basement of the Dublin Writers Museum (p115). That's probably because getting a table here can take months, which is what happens when Monsieur Michelin bestows one of his stars upon you. You'll have to book in advance, but the three-course pre-theatre special (€37.50; served before 7pm) is excellent.

Docklands

Although the crash has put paid to some of the grander plans for restaurant openings in the Docklands, there are a couple of good options that reflect the best of new dining in the city.

MIDRANGE

Quay 16 (Map p90; ☎ 817 8760; www.mvcillairne.com; MV Cill Airne, North Wall Quay; bar food €12-16; mains €19.50-32; 🕙 noon-3pm Mon-Fri, 6-10pm Mon-Sat) The MV *Cill Airne*, commissioned in 1961 as a passenger liner tender, is now permanently docked along the north quays, where it serves the public as a bar, bistro and fine restaurant. The food in the restaurant is surprisingly good – dishes like monkfish on saffron risotto and seared beef fillet are expertly done and served with an excellent choice of wines.

Ely Winebar (www.elywinebar.ie; mains €15-24; 🕙 noon-3pm & 6-10pm Mon-Fri, 1-4pm & 6-10pm Sat); Ely CHQ (Map pp92-3; ☎ 672 0010; Custom House Quay); Ely HQ (Map p90; ☎ 633 9986; Hanover Quay); Ely Place (Map

p96; ☎ 676 8986; 22 Ely Pl) Scrummy homemade
burgers, bangers and mash, and wild smoked-
salmon salad are some of the meals you'll
find in this basement restaurant. Dishes are
prepared with organic and free-range produce
from the owner's family farm in County Clare,
so you can rest assured of the quality. There's
a large wine list to choose from, with over 70
sold by the glass. The original is in Ely Place,
but we prefer the two newer branches on either side of the Liffey.

Beyond the Grand Canal

It's hardly surprising that the chichi southern
suburbs would have their fair share of decent eateries – it's where the city's privileged
classes can turn their collars up and unwind

after a hard day of making money. If you're in
Ranelagh or Ballsbridge, there's always somewhere to get a decent bite.

Café Bardeli (Map p90; ☎ 496 1886; 62 Ranelagh
Rd; mains €9-15; ☟ 12.30-11pm Mon-Sat, to 10pm Sun)
If it ain't broke, do it again: Café Bardeli hit
Ranelagh in 2004 with the same no-fuss menu
that made its big sister such a roaring success
on South Great George's St (see p135) and just
hasn't looked back.

Expresso Bar (Map p90; ☎ 660 0585; 1 St Mary's Rd,
Ballsbridge; mains €9-17; ☟ 7.30am-9.15pm Mon-Fri, 9am-
9.15pm Sat & 10am-5pm Sun) Just across the street
from the Dylan (p133), this bright and cheery
spot does a roaring trade for Sunday brunch –
and you've a good chance to spot an Irish celeb
or two. The eggs Benedict are excellent.

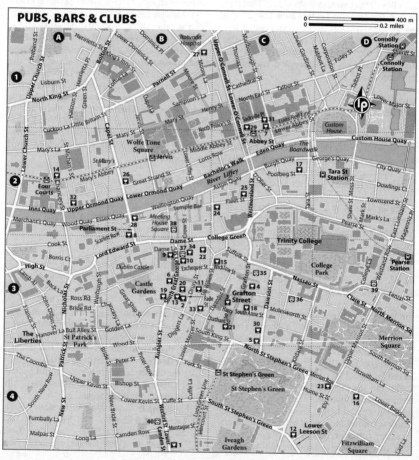

PUBS, BARS & CLUBS

DRINKING

Come hell or high water, Dubliners will always take a drink, and if you don't join them for at least one you will never crack the social code that makes this city tick – and you'll run the risk of being dismissed as a dry shite who really doesn't know how to enjoy themselves. No pressure, then.

It'll hardly come as a surprise that there are some good pubs in Dublin – it's probably one of the main reasons you came here in the first place – but first-time visitors may be taken aback by the protagonist's role the pub has in virtually every Dubliner's social life. The pub is a meeting point for friends and strangers alike, a place to mark a moment and pass the time, a forum for discourse and a temple of silent contemplation. It is where Dubliners are at their friendly and convivial best – and at their drunken and belligerent worst.

There are pubs for every taste and sensibility, although the *truly* traditional haunts populated by flat-capped pensioners bursting with insightful anecdotes are about as rare as hen's teeth: the city has been overwhelmed by designer bars and themed locales that could be found pretty much anywhere else in the world. But despair not, for it is not the spit or sawdust that makes a great Dublin pub (although it can help with the setting) but the patrons themselves.

Most visitors will make a beeline for Temple Bar, the city's concentrated party zone, where giant bars pump out booze and chart-music to a thirsty, animated throng of revellers. It's not so bad for a midweek drink, but come the weekend it's strictly for tourists and visitors with T-shirts advertising themselves as part of a hen or stag group. More discerning party animals favour the strip of supersized bars on Dawson St and the bars along Wexford and Camden Sts, southwest of St Stephen's Green. But don't worry: you can't go too far in the city centre without finding a pub with a bit of life in it.

Last orders are at 11.30pm Monday to Thursday, 12.30am Friday and Saturday and 11pm on Sunday, with 30 minutes' drinking-up time each night. However, many central pubs have licences to serve until 1.30am or 2.30am.

For gay and lesbian bars, see the boxed text, p145.

Traditional Pubs

Dublin still has some good, old-style, traditional establishments.

Flowing Tide (Map p140; ☎ 874 0842; 9 Lower Abbey St) This beautiful and atmospheric old pub is directly opposite the Abbey Theatre (p147) and is predictably very popular with theatre-goers – it can get swamped around 11pm, after the curtain comes down. They blend in with some no-bullshit locals who give the place a vital edge and make it a great place for a drink and a natter.

Patrick Conway's (Map p140; ☎ 873 2687; 70 Parnell St) Although it's slightly out of the way, this place is a true gem of a pub. It has been operating since 1745, and no doubt new fathers have been stopping in here for a celebratory pint since the day the Rotunda Maternity Hospital opened across the road in 1757.

Palace Bar (Map p140; ☎ 677 9290; 21 Fleet St) With its mirrors and wooden niches, Palace Bar is often said to be the perfect example of an old Dublin pub. It's within Temple Bar and is popular with journalists from the nearby *Irish Times*.

Dawson Lounge (Map p140; ☎ 677 5909; 25 Dawson St) To see the smallest bar in Dublin, go through a small doorway, down a narrow flight of steps and into two tiny rooms that always seem to

TOP FIVE PUBS

- Best for a decent pint and a chat – **Grogan's Castle Lounge** (below)
- Best for beats and beatniks – **Anseo** (opposite)
- Best for fiddles and bodhráns – **Cobblestone** (right)
- Best for getting jiggy with it – **Village** (opposite)
- Best to see and be seen – **Bar With No Name** (opposite)

be filled with a couple of bedraggled drunks who look like they're hiding. Psst, here's a secret: a certain sunglassed lead singer of a certain ginormous Irish band is said to love unwinding in here from time to time.

John Mulligan's (Map p140; ☎ 677 5582; 8 Poolbeg St) Outside the eastern boundary of Temple Bar, John Mulligan's is another pub that has scarcely changed over the years. It featured as the local in the film *My Left Foot* and is also popular with journalists from the nearby newspaper offices. Mulligan's was established in 1782 and has long been reputed to have the best Guinness in Ireland, as well as a wonderfully varied collection of regulars.

Stag's Head (Map p140; ☎ 679 3701; 1 Dame Ct) At the intersection of Dame Ct and Dame Lane, just off Dame St, the Stag's Head was built in 1770 and remodelled in 1895. It's sufficiently picturesque to have featured in a postage-stamp series depicting Irish pubs.

Long Hall (Map p140; ☎ 475 1590; 51 South Great George's St) Luxuriating in full Victorian splendour, this is one of the city's most beautiful and best-loved pubs. Check out the elegant chandeliers and the ornate carvings in the woodwork behind the bar. The bartenders are experts at their craft – an increasingly rare experience in Dublin these days.

Kehoe's (Map p140; ☎ 677 8312; 9 South Anne St) This is one of the most atmospheric pubs in the city centre and a real favourite with all kinds of Dubliners. It has a beautiful Victorian bar, a wonderful snug, and plenty of other little nooks and crannies. Upstairs, drinks are served in what was once the publican's living room. And it looks it!

Neary's (Map p140; ☎ 677 8596; 1 Chatham St) A showy Victorian-era pub with a fine frontage, Neary's is popular with actors from the

nearby Gaiety Theatre. The upstairs bar is one of the only spots in the city centre where you stand a chance of getting a seat on a Friday or Saturday night.

Grogan's Castle Lounge (Map p140; ☎ 677 9320; 15 South William St) A city-centre institution, Grogan's has long been a favourite haunt of Dublin's writers and painters, as well as others from the bohemian, alternative set. An odd quirk of the pub is that drinks are marginally cheaper in the stone-floor bar than the carpeted lounge, even though they are served by the same bar!

James Toner's (Map p140; ☎ 676 3090; 139 Lower Baggot St) With its stone floor, Toner's is almost a country pub in the heart of the city, and the shelves and drawers are reminders that it once doubled as a grocery store. Not that its suit-wearing business crowd would ever have shopped here...

Hartigan's (Map p140; ☎ 676 2280; 100 Lower Leeson St) This is about as spartan a bar as you'll find in the city, and it's the daytime home to some serious drinkers, who appreciate the quiet, no-frills surroundings. In the evening it's popular with students from the medical faculty of University College Dublin.

Sackville Lounge (Map p140; Sackville Pl) This tiny one-room, wood-panelled 19th-century bar is discreetly located just off O'Connell St, which perhaps explains why it's so popular with actors, theatregoers and anyone who appreciates a nice pint in a gorgeous old-style bar.

Live-Music Pubs

The following places are excellent venues for catching some traditional Irish and contemporary music.

Sean O'Casey's (Map p140; ☎ 874 8675; 105 Marlborough St) This place has a weekly menu of live rock and some Irish traditional music sessions.

Hughes' Bar (Map p140; ☎ 872 6540; 19 Chancery St) Directly behind the Four Courts, this bar has nightly, if impromptu, sessions that often result in a closed door – that is, they go on long past official closing time. The pub is also a popular lunchtime spot with barristers working nearby.

Cobblestone (Map pp92-3; ☎ 872 1799; North King St) This pub is on the main square in Smithfield, an old northside marketplace. There's a great atmosphere in the cosy upstairs bar, where the nightly music sessions – both traditional and up-and-coming folk and singer-songwriter acts – are superb.

Oliver St John Gogarty's (Map p140; ☎ 671 1822; 58-59 Fleet St) There's live traditional music nightly at this busy Temple Bar pub, catering to a mostly tourist crowd.

International Bar (Map p140; ☎ 677 9250; 23 Wicklow St) The International has live jazz and blues most nights.

Bruxelles (Map p140; ☎ 677 5362; 7-8 Harry St) This place has weekly live rock music, perhaps the only link the now trendy pub has to its heavy-metal past.

O'Donoghue's (Map p140; ☎ 661 4303; 15 Merrion Row) The most famous traditional music bar in Dublin, O'Donoghue's is where world-famous folk group the Dubliners started off in the 1960s. On summer evenings a young, international crowd spills out into the courtyard beside the pub.

Bars

The following modern bars are Dublin's current hot spots.

Anseo (Map p140; ☎ 475 1321; 28 Lower Camden St) Unpretentious, unaffected and incredibly popular, this cosy alternative bar is a favourite with those who live by the credo that to try too hard is far worse than not trying at all. Wearing cool like a loose garment, the punters thrive on the mix of chat and terrific music.

Bar With No Name (Map p140; ☎ 675 3708; 3 Fade St) A low-key entrance just next to L'Gueuleton leads upstairs to one of the nicest bar spaces in town – three huge rooms in a restored Victorian townhouse plus a sizeable heated patio area for smokers. There's no sign or a name – folks just refer to it as the bar with no name or, if you're a real insider, Number 3.

Bernard Shaw (Map p90; ☎ 085-712 8342; www .bodytonicmusic.com; 11-12 South Richmond St) This old-style pub was taken over a couple of years ago by the Bodytonic production crew and restyled as one of the hippest joints in town. There are DJs nightly, playing anything from dub reggae to ambient electronica.

Dice Bar (Map pp92-3; ☎ 674 6710; 79 Queen St) Co-owned by singer Huey from the band Fun Lovin' Criminals, the Dice Bar looks like something you'd find on New York's Lower East Side. Its black-and-red-painted interior, dripping candles and distressed seating, combined with rocking DJs most nights, make this place a magnet for Dublin's beatnik crowds.

No 4 Dame Lane (Map p140; ☎ 679 0291; 4 Dame Lane) This stylish bar across two floors is popular with clubby kids and professionals alike. They come for the modern ambience and the DJ-led entertainment, which is mellow midweek but loud and dancy weekends.

Market Bar (Map p140; ☎ 677 4835; Fade St) This fashionable watering hole is run by the same guys as the Globe (below), around the corner. Little would you know this beautiful, airy Victorian space was a sausage factory in a former life.

Globe (Map p140; ☎ 671 1220; 11 South Great George's St) The granddaddy of the city's hipster bars, the Globe has held on to its groover status by virtue of tradition and the fact that the formula is brilliantly simple: wooden floors, plain brick walls and a no-attitude atmosphere that you just can't fake.

Hogan's (Map p140; ☎ 677 5904; 35 South Great George's St) Hogan's is a gigantic boozer spread across two floors. A popular hang-out for young professionals, it gets very full at the weekend with folks eager to take advantage of its late licence.

Porterhouse (Map p140; ☎ 679 8847; 16-18 Parliament St) Dublin's first microbrewery is our favourite Temple Bar watering hole. Especially popular with foreign residents and visitors, the Porterhouse sells only its own stouts and beers – and they're all excellent.

SamSara (Map p140; ☎ 671 7723; 35-36 Dawson St) This huge, Middle Eastern–themed drinking emporium packs young office types and pre-clubbers in at weekends, when the bar runs late.

South William (Map p140; ☎ 679 3701; South William St) Its star doesn't shine quite as brightly as it did a couple of years ago when it opened, but this remains one of the hippest bars in town. Behind the glass frontage you'll get top-class music, great DJs and a downstairs club.

Sin É (Map p140; ☎ 878 7009; 14-15 Upper Ormond Quay) This excellent quayside bar is proof that the most important quality for any pub is ambience. There's no real decor to speak of, but this place buzzes almost nightly with a terrific mix of students and professionals, the hip and the uncool. It helps that the DJs are all uniformly excellent.

Village (Map p140; ☎ 475 8555; www.thevillagevenue .com; 26 Wexford St) Packed to overflowing every weekend, this large modern bar is where the lovely lads and gorgeous gals show off their plumage in a fun-time courting ritual that has the rest of them queuing up at the door to join in. There are excellent DJs nightly;

the nightclub bit of the venue (p145) opens Thursday through Saturday.

ENTERTAINMENT

Dublin's too small to be the entertainment mecca the tourist authorities and other interested parties would have once had you believe, but it's still a pretty decent burg to have a good time in, with a range of options to satisfy *almost* all desires, from period drama to dog racing and most distractions in between.

For entertainment information, pick up a copy of the *Event Guide* (www.eventguide.ie), a bimonthly freebie available at many locations, including bars, cafes and hostels; the fortnightly music-review *Hot Press* (www.hotpress.com); or the freebie *In Dublin,* also out every two weeks. Friday's *Irish Times* has a pull-out entertainment section called the *Ticket,* which has comprehensive listings of clubs and gigs; the *Irish Independent's* version, also out on Friday, is called *Day & Night.*

Cinemas

Ireland boasts the highest attendances in Europe of young filmgoers. Consequently it's best to book in advance by credit card, or be prepared to queue for up to half an hour for tickets at night-time screenings. Dublin's cinemas are more heavily concentrated on the northern side of the Liffey. Admission prices are generally €6 for early afternoon shows and around €9 for the rest of the day.

Irish Film Institute (Map p94; ☎ 679 5744; 6 Eustace St) The multiscreen cinema shows classics and art-house films. The complex also has a bar, a cafe and a bookshop.

Lighthouse Cinema (Map pp92-3; ☎ 879 7601; www .lighthousecinema.ie; Smithfield Plaza) Classic films and alternative, art-house releases are the staple of this brand-new cinema – easily the most beautiful in town – with four screens and a trendy cafe-bar.

Savoy (Map pp92-3; ☎ 874 6000; Upper O'Connell St; ⊙ from 2pm) A traditional four-screen first-run cinema, Savoy has late-night shows at weekends.

Screen (Map p101; ☎ 671 4988; 2 Townsend St; ⊙ from 2pm) Between Trinity College and O'Connell Bridge, the Screen shows new independent and smaller commercial films on its three screens.

Cineworld (Map pp92-3; ☎ 872 8400; Parnell Centre, Parnell St; ⊙ from 10am) This multiscreen cinema is where you'll get all the mainstream releases.

Nightclubs

Restrictive opening hours, late-night bars offering a free version of the same and the continuing squeeze of the musical mainstream have all had an impact on Dublin clubland. Dublin's population may be increasingly multicultural, but they're a largely conservative bunch whose tastes range from charty stuff to a bit of alternative rock, and from R&B to commercially flavoured dance music. Which doesn't mean you can't get your groove on and have a good time, something Dublin seems particularly adept at.

The seemingly endless list of what's on is constantly changing, so check out the (by no means exhaustive) listings in the *Event Guide* and *In Dublin.* Most clubs open just after pubs close (11.30pm to midnight) and close at 2.30am or 3am. Admission to most costs between €5 and €8 Sunday to Thursday, rising to as much as €15 or €20 on Friday and Saturday.

Academy (Map p94; ☎ 877 9999; 57 Middle Abbey St; ⊙ 10.30pm-3am Fri & Sat) Disco, R&B, alternative rock, hard dance…whatever keeps them dancing, the Academy will play, so long as it's not sellout commercial.

Andrew's Lane Theatre (Map p94; ☎ 478 0766; St Andrew's Lane; ⊙ 10.30pm-3am Thu-Sun) Recently converted from a much-loved theatre, ALT's stripped-down look will please club purists: a huge dancefloor, an amazing sound system and a bar are the essentials to a good night. Add a couple of regular nights (Sunday's Italian Factory is a banging night of European hard house), a regular menu of visiting DJs and live gigs and you've got the makings of a *great* night.

Krystle (Map p96; ☎ 478 4066; www.krystlenightclub .com; Russell Court Hotel, 21-25 Harcourt St; ⊙ 10.30pm-3am Thu-Sat) The favourite venue of many a Celtic cub, Krystle (annoyingly pronounced 'cristal' by its snootiest devotees) is where you'll most likely find the current crop of celebrities and their hangers-on, although you'll have to wade your way through the huge main floor and gain access to the upstairs VIP lounge for maximum exposure. Chart hits and club classics are the mainstay.

Renard's (Map p140; ☎ 677 5876; www.renards.ie; South Frederick St; admission free-€10; ⊙ 10.30pm-2.30am) Not quite as self-regarding as Lillie's Bordello (opposite) and run by Colin Farrell's godfather, this is the actor's (and other celebs') favourite den of iniquity when in town. Renard's is an intimate club with a strict door policy when busy; music is mainly house, with soul, funk and jazz making the odd appearance.

Tripod (Map pp92-3; ☎ 478 0025; www.pod.ie; 35 Harcourt St; admission €5-20; ☺ Mon-Sat) Launched in late 2006 on the site of former club PoD in the atmospheric old Harcourt Street station, Tripod now integrates three venues (geddit?): a state-of-the-art, 1300-capacity live rock and pop venue, a smaller dance club and the intimate live venue Crawdaddy (p146).

Twisted Pepper (Map p94; ☎ 873 4800; www.bodytonicmusic.com; 54 Middle Abbey St; ☺ 8am-midnight Mon-Wed, 10-2.30am Thu-Sat) Dublin's coolest new venue comes in four parts: the basement is where you can hear some of the best DJs in town, the stage is for live acts, the mezzanine is a secluded bar area above the stage and the cafe serves Irish breakfast all day. All run by the Bodytonic crew, one of the most exciting music and production crowds in town. What more could you want?

Village (Map p96; ☎ 475 8555; 26 Wexford St; www.thevillagevenue.com; admission €5-11; ☺ Thu-Sat) When the live music ends (see p143), the club kicks off, taking 600-odd groovers through a consistent mix of new and old tunes, dance-floor

---

GAY & LESBIAN DUBLIN

Dublin's not a bad place to be gay. Most people in the city centre wouldn't bat an eyelid at cross-dressing or public displays of affection between same-sex couples, but discretion is advised in the suburbs.

Information

Gay & Lesbian Garda Liaison Officer (☎ 666 9000) If you encounter any sort of trouble or harassment on the streets, don't hesitate to call. (For sexual assaults, contact the Sexual Assault Unit, below.)

Gay Community News (www.gcn.ie) A useful nationwide news- and issues-based monthly paper. The glossy *Q-Life* and *Free!* are entertainment guides that can be found in Temple Bar businesses and the Irish Film Institute (opposite).

Gay Switchboard Dublin (☎ 872 1055; www.gayswitchboard.ie) A friendly and useful voluntary service that provides information ranging from where to find accommodation to legal issues.

Outhouse (Map pp92-3; ☎ 873 4932; www.outhouse.ie; 105 Capel St) Top gay, lesbian and bisexual resource centre. Great stop-off point to see what's on, check notice boards and meet people. It publishes the free *Ireland's Pink Pages*, a directory of gay-centric services, which is also accessible on the website. They're also good to call in case of trouble.

Sexual Assault Unit (Map pp92-3; ☎ 666 6000) Call or visit the Garda Station on Pearse St.

Festivals & Events

Mardi Gras (www.dublinpride.org) Not the traditional feast that precedes the Catholic Lent but a week-long festival of theatre, performance, music, readings and – inevitably – a high-energy, colourful parade through the city centre for the city's queers, dykes, bis and fetishists. Usually held the last week in June.

International Dublin Gay Theatre Festival (☎ 677 8511; www.gaytheatre.ie) Despite the unwieldy title, the only event of its kind anywhere in the world, with more than 30 gay- and lesbian-themed productions over two weeks in May.

Lesbian & Gay Film Festival (☎ 670 6377; www.irishculture.net/filmfestival) An international film and documentary festival held at the Irish Film Institute in August.

Drinking

Dragon (Map p140; ☎ 478 1590; 64-65 South Great George's St) The latest addition to Dublin's scene, this big disco-bar with colourful Asian decor, comfy booths and small dance floor attracts young pre-George revellers.

George (Map p140; ☎ 478 2983; 89 South Great George's St) You can't miss the bright-purple George, Temple Bar's only overtly gay bar, which has a reputation for becoming ever more wild and wacky as the night progresses. At 6.30pm on Sunday it is packed for an enormously popular bingo night, while Thursday night is the Missing Link game show hosted by Annie Balls.

Front Lounge (Map p140; ☎ 670 4112; 33 Parliament St) A lavish lounge attracting a mixed upmarket clientele. Drag queen Panti runs the cabaret and karaoke night, Casting Couch, on Tuesday.

Panti Bar (Map p140; ☎ 874 0710; www.pantibar.com; 7-8 Capel St) The northside's most outrageous gay bar is almost always packed – they come for the floor shows both on and off the stage. It's open late Friday and Saturday.

classics and whatever else will shake that booty. A great venue, an eager crowd and an overall top night out.

Underground@Kennedy's (Map p140; ☎ 661 1124; 31-32 Westland Row; ⏰ 11.30pm-2.30am Fri & Sat) Beneath this busy pub is a suitably sweaty, darkened room that plays regular host to some top-class local and international DJs playing a variety of styles from house to hip hop.

Lillie's Bordello (Map p140; ☎ 679 9204; www.lillies bordello.ie; Adam Ct; admission €10-20; ⏰ 11pm-3am) Lillie's is strictly for big hairs, wannabes and visiting rock stars. Don't think you'll get to rub shoulders with celebs though, as they'll be whisked out of view and into the VIP room in a flash. As you might expect, the music is mostly safe and commercial.

Think Tank (Map p140; ☎ 670 7655; www.thethinktank .ie; 11 Eustace St; admission €6-15) Dance DJs, Battle of the Bands nights, visiting live acts and assorted other festivities make up the menu at this basement club in Temple Bar. Strictly Handbag, Dublin's longest running club night, takes place on Monday nights and still draws them in with its mixed bag of 80s tunes.

Rí Rá (Map p140; ☎ 677 4835; Dame Ct; admission €5-11; ⏰ Mon-Sat) This long-established club changed hands in 2007, but the new owners are bent on continuing the long-standing commitment to music without frenetic beats – for now, at least. The emphasis has long been on funky stuff, from soul to hip hop, but there's plenty of rock thrown in. Upstairs, the Globe bar (p143) converts into a chilled-out drink and chat area.

Live Music

Bookings can be made either directly at the venues or through **HMV** (Map p96; ☎ 679 5334; 65 Grafton St) or **Ticketmaster** (☎ 0818-719 300, 456 9569; www.ticketmaster.ie), but they charge between 9% and 12.5% service charge *per ticket*, not per booking, on credit-card bookings.

CLASSICAL MUSIC & OPERA VENUES

Classical music concerts and opera take place in a number of city-centre venues. There are also occasional performances in churches; check the press for details.

National Concert Hall (Map pp92-3; ☎ 417 0000; www .nch.ie; Earlsfort Tce) Ireland's premier orchestral hall hosts a variety of concerts year-round, including a series of lunchtime concerts from 1.05pm to 2pm on Tuesdays, June to August.

Gaiety Theatre (Map p96; ☎ 677 1717; www.gaiety theatre.com; South King St) This popular Dublin theatre hosts a program of classical concerts and opera.

Bank of Ireland Arts Centre (Map p94; ☎ 671 1488; Foster Pl) The arts centre hosts a free, regular, midweek lunchtime recital beginning at 1.15pm, as well as an occasional evening program of concerts. Call for details.

Helix (Map p88; ☎ 700 7000; www.thehelix.ie; Collins Ave, Glasnevin) Based in Dublin City University, the Helix hosts, among other things, an impressive array of international operatic and classical recitals and performances. To get there, take bus 11, 13, 13A or 19A from O'Connell St.

Dublin City Gallery – the Hugh Lane (Map pp92-3; ☎ 874 1903; www.hughlane.ie; Charlemont House, Parnell Sq) At noon on Sunday, from September to June, the art gallery hosts up to 30 concerts of contemporary classical music.

Royal Dublin Society Showground Concert Hall (Map p90; ☎ 668 0866; www.rds.ie; Ballsbridge) The huge hall of the RDS Showground hosts a rich program of classical music and opera throughout the year.

ROCK & POP VENUES

Ambassador Theatre (Map pp92-3; ☎ 1890 925 100; O'Connell St) The Ambassador started life as a theatre and then became a cinema. Not much has changed inside, making it a cool retro place to see visiting and local rock acts perform.

Crawdaddy (Map pp92-3; ☎ 478 0225; www.pod.ie; 35A Harcourt St) Named after the London club where the Stones launched their professional careers in 1963, Crawdaddy is an intimate bar/venue that specialises in putting on rootsy performers, from African drum bands to avant-garde jazz artists and flamenco guitarists. It's attached to the nightclub Tripod (p144).

Gaiety Theatre (Map p96; ☎ 677 1717; www.gaiety theatre.com; South King St; ⏰ to 4am) This old Victorian theatre is an atmospheric place to come and listen to late-night jazz, rock or blues on the weekend.

Bleu Note (Map p94; ☎ 878 3371; 61-63 Capel St) Jazz, funk and blues bands perform here nightly; pay your €5 entry, order a Chimay and enjoy the good vibes. Nice.

O2 (Map p90; ☎ 819 8888; www.theo2.ie; East Link Bridge, North Wall Quay) Formerly the Point Depot, a complete overhaul of what was once a rail terminal (built in 1878) has resulted in this superb new venue with a capacity of around

10,000. The acoustics are sublime and the performing acts picked out of the very top drawer: Beyoncé, Britney and Neil Young are just some of the names who played here in 2009.

Olympia Theatre (Map p94; ☎ 677 7744; Dame St) This pleasantly tatty place features everything from disco to country on Friday nights; the eclectic 'Midnight at the Olympia' runs from midnight to 2am on Friday.

Sugar Club (Map pp92-3; ☎ 678 7188; 8 Lower Leeson St) There's live jazz, cabaret and soul music at weekends in this comfortable new theatre-style venue on the corner of St Stephen's Green.

Button Factory (Map p94; ☎ 670 9202; www.button factory.ie; Curved St) A top-class sound system, a carpeted back bar and a big main stage make this an excellent venue to hear some of the more interesting visiting and local acts.

Vicar Street (Map pp92-3; ☎ 454 5533; www.vicar street.com; 58-59 Thomas St) Smaller performances take place at this intimate venue, near Christ Church Cathedral. It has a capacity of 1000, spread between table-serviced group seating downstairs and a theatre-style balcony. It has a varied program of performers, with a strong emphasis on folk and jazz.

Village (Map p96; ☎ 475 8555; www.thevillagevenue .com; 26 Wexford St) An attractive midsize venue that is a popular stop for acts on the way up and down, the Village has gigs virtually every night of the week, featuring a diverse range of rock bands and solo performers. It's also a good showcase for local singer-songwriters.

Whelan's (Map p96; ☎ 478 0766; www.whelanslive .com; 25 Wexford St) Whelan's near-legendary status as the home of the sensitive, soul-searching singer – and where gigs are treated like semi-mystical experiences by their devoted fans – is inevitably the cause of much derision in some Dublin quarters, but there's no denying the venue's special place in the Dublin musical scene. It's a pretty intimate space, perfect if you're looking to 'connect' with your favourite artists, who will most likely be cadging drinks off fans in the bar afterwards.

Sport

Croke Park (Map p90; ☎ 836 3222; www.crokepark.ie; Clonliffe Rd) Hurling and Gaelic football games are held from February to November at Europe's fourth-largest stadium (capacity around 82,000), north of the Royal Canal in Drumcondra; see www.gaa.ie for schedules. Catch bus 19 or 19A to get there.

Aviva Stadium (Map p90; ☎ 647 3800; www.aviva stadium.ie; 11-12 Lansdowne Rd) The beloved Lansdowne Road stadium, the home of Irish rugby and international soccer, has been razed, rebuilt and renamed after its most prominent sponsor. The 50,000-capacity ground is scheduled to open in 2010.

Harold's Cross Park (Map p90; ☎ 497 1081; www.igb .ie; 151 Harold's Cross Rd; adult/child €8/4; ☉ 6.30-10.30pm Mon, Tue & Fri) Greyhound racing takes place near Rathmines in this newly revamped venue. Take bus 16 or 16A from the city centre.

Leopardstown Race Course (Map p88; ☎ 289 3607; www.leopardstown.com; Foxrock) The Irish love of horse racing can be observed about 10km south of the city centre in Foxrock. Special buses depart from the city centre on race days; call the racecourse for details.

Shelbourne Park Greyhound Stadium (Map p90; ☎ 668 3502, on race nights ☎ 202 6601; www.igb.ie; Bridge Town Rd, Ringsend; adult/child €8/4; ☉ 6.30-10.30pm Wed, Thu & Sat) A top-class dog track with terrific vantage points from the glassed-in restaurant, where you can eat, bet and watch without leaving your seat. Take bus 3 from D'Olier St.

Theatre

Dublin's theatre scene is small but busy. Bookings can usually be made by quoting a credit-card number over the phone and tickets collected just before the performance.

Abbey Theatre (Map p94; ☎ 878 7222; www.abbey theatre.ie; Lower Abbey St) It's scheduled to move to a purpose-built location in the Docklands, but for now Ireland's national theatre still resides in a large concrete box by the river. It puts on new Irish works, as well as revivals of classic Irish plays by writers such as WB Yeats, JM Synge, Sean O'Casey, Brendan Behan and Samuel Beckett. Tickets for evening performances cost up to €25, except on Monday, when they're cheaper. The smaller **Peacock Theatre** (Map pp92-3; ☎ 878 7222) is part of the same complex and stages more fringe work.

Ark (Map p94; ☎ 670 7788; 11A Eustace St) A 150-seater venue that stages shows for kids aged between five and 13.

Gaiety Theatre (Map p96; ☎ 677 1717; www.gaiety theatre.com; South King St) Opened in 1871, this theatre is used for modern plays, TV shows, musical comedies and revues.

Gate Theatre (Map pp92-3; ☎ 874 4045; www.gatetheatre .ie; 1 Cavendish Row) To the north of the Liffey, the Gate Theatre specialises in international classics and older Irish works with a touch of comedy by playwrights such as Oscar Wilde, George Bernard Shaw and Oliver Goldsmith, although newer plays are sometimes staged too. Prices vary according to what's on, but they're usually around €20.

Helix (Map p88; ☎ 700 7000; www.thehelix.ie; Collins Ave, Glasnevin) The Helix, Dublin City University's new theatre venue, has already established its reputation as a serious theatre with its mix of accessible and challenging productions. To get here, take bus 11, 13, 13A or 19A from O'Connell St.

International Bar (Map p96; ☎ 677 9250; 23 Wicklow St) This is one of several pubs that host theatrical performances; it also hosts comedy on Wednesday evening at 9.30pm (admission €9).

Olympia Theatre (Map p96; ☎ 677 7744; 72 Dame St) This theatre specialises in light plays and, at Christmastime, pantomimes.

Players' Theatre (Map p101; ☎ 677 2941, ext 1239; Regent House, Trinity College) The Trinity College Players' Theatre hosts student productions throughout the academic year, as well as the most prestigious plays from the Dublin Theatre Festival in October.

Project Arts Centre (Map p94; ☎ 1850-260 027; www .project.ie; 39 East Essex St) This centre puts on excellent productions of experimental plays by up-and-coming Irish and foreign writers.

Tivoli Theatre (Map p94; ☎ 454 4472; 135-136 Francis St) Experimental and less commercial performances take place here.

SHOPPING

In 2007 Europe's busiest shopping street was Dublin's very own Henry St, which saw an average of 16,000 frothing retail junkies *an hour*, each pram-pushing family and consumer couple playing catch-me-if-you-can with the credit card companies. But that was *before* the global credit crunch.

On the surface, nothing seems to have changed. Dubliners still throng the main shopping streets both north and south of the Liffey, even though the overall numbers have dipped, in some cases quite dramatically.

British and US chains dominate the high street and major shopping centres but there are also numerous small, independent shops selling high-quality, locally made goods. Irish designer clothing and streetwear, handmade jewellery, unusual homewares and crafts, and cheeses to die for are readily available if you know where to look.

PASSION FOR FASHION

After years in the wilderness, Irish designers are making a name for themselves on the international fashion stage. John Rocha, whose own-label clothes have been high fashion for the past decade, has branched into hotel design (Morrison, p132) and homewares (available in Brown Thomas, below), as has milliner-to-the-supermodels Philip Treacy, who designed the flamboyant G Hotel in Galway. Irish names currently making a splash internationally include Joanne Hynes, Pauric Sweeney and N&C Kilkenny.

While souvenir hunters can still buy toy sheep, Guinness magnets and shamrock tea towels, a new breed of craft shop offers one-off or limited-edition crafts and art. Traditional Irish products such as crystal and knitwear remain popular choices, and you can increasingly find innovative modern takes on the classics.

Grafton St is the city's most prestigious shopping thoroughfare, but it's largely the domain of the British-style high-street shop, as is busy Henry St, just off O'Connell St. In the warren of streets between Grafton St and South Great George's St, you'll find a plethora of Irish-owned fashion outlets, jewellers and second-hand stores. Francis St in the Liberties is great for antiques and art.

Citizens of non-EU countries can reclaim the VAT paid on purchases made at stores that display a cash-back sticker; ask for details.

Most department stores and shopping centres are open from 9.30am to 6pm Monday to Saturday (open to 8pm Thursday) and noon to 6pm Sunday.

Department Stores & Shopping Centres

Arnott's (Map p94; ☎ 805 0400; 12 Henry St) Occupying a huge block with entrances on Henry, Liffey and Abbey Sts, this formerly mediocre department store has been completely overhauled and is now probably Dublin's best. It stocks virtually everything you could possibly want to buy, from garden furniture to high fashion, and everything is relatively affordable.

Brown Thomas (Map p96; ☎ 605 6666; 92 Grafton St) This is Dublin's most expensive department store, suitably stocked to cater for the city's more moneyed shoppers. You'll find every top label represented here. The 3rd-floor Bottom Drawer outlet stocks the finest Irish linen you'll find anywhere.

Dundrum Town Centre (Map p88; ☎ 299 1700; Sandyford Rd, Dundrum; ☾ 9am-9pm Mon-Fri, 8.30am-7pm Sat, 10am-7pm Sun) Modern Ireland's grandest cathedral is this huge shopping and entertainment complex in the southern suburb of Dundrum. Over 100 retail outlets are represented. To get here, take the Luas to Ballaly, or catch bus 17, 44C, 48A or 75 from the city centre.

George's St Arcade (Map p96; www.georgesstreet arcade.ie; btwn South Great George's St & Drury St; ☾ 9am-6.30pm Mon-Sat, to 8pm Thu; noon-6pm Sun) Dublin's best nonfood market (there's sadly not much competition) is sheltered within an elegant Victorian Gothic arcade. Apart from the shops and stalls selling new and old clothes, second-hand books, hats, posters, jewellery and records, there's a fortune teller, some gourmet nibbles and a fish-and-chipper who does a roaring trade.

Powerscourt Townhouse Shopping Centre (Map p96; ☎ 679 4144; 59 South William St) This absolutely gorgeous and stylish centre is in a carefully refurbished Georgian townhouse, originally built between 1741 and 1744. These days its best known for its cafes and restaurants but it still does a top-end, selective trade in high fashion, art, exquisite handicrafts and other chichi sundries.

St Stephen's Green Shopping Centre (Map p96; ☎ 478 0888; St Stephen's Green) Inside this flash shopping centre you will discover a diverse mixture of chain stores and individual shops.

Jervis St Centre (Map p94; ☎ 878 1323; Jervis St) Just north of the Capel St Bridge, this is an ultra-modern mall with dozens of outlets.

Clery's & Co (Map pp92-3; ☎ 878 6000; O'Connell St) This graceful shop is a Dublin classic. Recently restored to its elegant best, it caters to the more conservative Dublin shopper.

Debenham's (Map pp92-3; ☎ 873 0044; Henry St) This UK giant hit these shores in 2006; it's bold and glass-fronted on the outside and holds street-smart fashion labels such as Zara, Warehouse and G-Star on the inside, as well as the obligatory homewares and electrical sections.

Clothing

Temple Bar and the area around Grafton St are the best places for all kinds of designer gear, both new and second-hand.

Costume (Map p96; ☎ 679 5200; 10 Castle Market) From casuals to sparkly full-length dresses, Costume specialises in stylish contemporary women's wear from young European designers. Its own Costume label sits alongside pieces by Isabel Marant, Anna Sui, Jonathan Saunders and Irish label Leighlee.

Smock (Map p96; ☎ 613 9000; 31 Drury St) This elegant designer shop sells cutting-edge international women's wear from classy 'investment labels' Easton Pearson, Veronique Branquinho and AF Vandevorft, as well as a small range of interesting jewellery and lingerie.

5 Scarlet Row (Map p94; ☎ 672 9534; 5 Scarlet Row) Beautiful, modern, exclusive, minimalist. If that's what you're after, try the creations of Eley Kishimoto, Zero, Irish designer Sharon Wauchob and menswear label Unis at 5 Scarlet Row. Owner Eileen Shields worked with Donna Karan in New York before founding her own gorgeous shoe label, which retails here.

BT2 (Map p96; ☎ 679 5666; 88 Grafton St) This is Brown Thomas' young and funky offshoot, with high-end casuals for men and women and a juice bar upstairs overlooking Grafton St. Brands include DKNY, Custom, Diesel, Ted Baker and Tommy Hilfiger.

Jenny Vander (Map p96; ☎ 677 0406; 50 Drury St) A visit to Jenny Vander is like walking into an

---

DUBLIN MARKETS

Blackberry Fair (Map p90; Lower Rathmines Rd; ☾ 10am-5pm Sat & Sun) You'll have to rummage through a lot of junk to find a gem in this charmingly run-down weekend market that stocks furniture, records and a few clothes stalls. It's cheap, though.

Blackrock Market (Main St, Blackrock; ☾ 11am-5.30pm Sat & Sun) This long-running market, in an old merchant house and yard in the seaside village of Blackrock (Map p88), south of Dublin, has all manner of stalls selling everything from New Age crystals to futons. Take bus 5, 7, 7A, 8, 45 or 46A from city centre to Blackrock.

Cow's Lane Designer Mart (Map p94; Cow's Lane; ☾ 10am-5pm Sat) For the best in new Irish design, artwork and clothing, you'll find everything here, including yarn spun right in front of you and Ireland's only bone jeweller.

exotic 1940s boudoir. The selection of antique clothing, hats and jewellery is pretty wild, although you won't find many bargains.

Urban Outfitters (Map p94; ☎ 670 6202; 4 Cecilia St) Its loyal clientele think it's the funkiest shop in town, and they're not far wrong, with the latest styles complemented by the coolest gift items and even a trendy record store.

Irish Crafts & Souvenirs

Avoca Handweavers (Map p94; ☎ 677 4215; 11-13 Suffolk St) This contemporary craft shop is a treasure trove of interesting Irish and foreign products. The colourful shop is chock-a-block with woollen knits, ceramics, handcrafted gadgets and a wonderful toy selection – and not a tweed cap in sight.

Claddagh Records (Map p94; ☎ 677 0262; 2 Cecilia St) This shop sells a wide range of Irish traditional and folk music.

DesignYard (Map p96; ☎ 474 1011; 48-49 Nassau St) A high-end craft-as-art shop where everything you see – be it glass, batik, sculpture, painting –is one-off and handmade in Ireland. It also showcases contemporary jewellery from young international designers in its exhibition space.

Kilkenny Shop (Map p96; ☎ 677 7066; 6 Nassau St) This shop has a wonderful selection of finely made Irish crafts, featuring clothing, glassware, pottery, jewellery, crystal and silver from some of Ireland's best designers.

GETTING THERE & AWAY
Air

Dublin Airport (Map p88; ☎ 814 1111; www.dublinairport .com), 13km north of the centre, is Ireland's major international gateway airport, with direct flights from Europe, North America and Asia. For information on who flies in and out of here, see p714.

Boat

Dublin has two ferry ports: the **Dun Laoghaire ferry terminal** (☎ 280 1905; Dun Laoghaire), 13km southeast of the city, serves Holyhead in Wales and can be reached by DART to Dun Laoghaire, or bus 7, 7A or 8 from Burgh Quay or bus 46A from Trinity College; and the **Dublin Port terminal** (Map p90; ☎ 855 2222; Alexandra Rd), 3km northeast of the city centre, serves Holyhead and Liverpool.

Buses from Busáras (below) are timed to coincide with arrivals and departures: for the 9.45am ferry departure from Dublin

Port, buses leave Busáras at 8.30am. For the 9.45pm departure, buses depart from Busáras at 8.30pm. For the 1am sailing to Liverpool, the bus departs from Busáras at 11.45pm. All bus trips cost adult/child €2.50/1.25.

See p717 for details of ferry journeys.

Bus

Busáras (Map pp92-3; ☎ 836 6111; www.buseireann.ie; Store St), the main bus station, is just north of the river behind Custom House, and serves as the main city stop for **Bus Éireann** (www.buseireann .ie).

For information on fares, frequencies and durations to various destinations in the Republic and Northern Ireland, see p719.

Car & Motorcycle

A number of hire companies have desks at the airport, and other operators are based close to the airport and deliver cars for airport collection. Listed are some of the main hire companies in Dublin:

Avis (www.avis.com) City (Map p90; ☎ 605 7500; 35-39 Kilmainham Lane); Dublin Airport (☎ 844 5204)

Budget (www.budgetcarrental.ie) City (Map p90; ☎ 837 9802; 151 Lower Drumcondra Rd); Dublin Airport (☎ 844 5150)

Dan Dooley Car Hire (www.dan-dooley.ie) City (Map p96; ☎ 677 2723; 42-43 Westland Row); Dublin Airport (☎ 844 5156)

Europcar (www.europcar.com) City (Map p90; ☎ 614 2800; Baggot St Bridge); Dublin Airport (☎ 844 4179)

Hertz (www.hertz.com) City (Map p90; ☎ 660 2255; 149 Upper Leeson St); Dublin Airport (☎ 844 5466)

Sixt Rent-a-Car (www.icr.ie) City (☎ 862 2715; Old Airport Rd, Santry); Dublin Airport (☎ 844 4199)

Thrifty (www.thrifty.ie) City (Map p90; ☎ 1800 515 800; 125 Herberton Bridge, just off South Circular Rd); Dublin Airport (☎ 840 0800)

Train

For general train information, contact **Iarnród Éireann Travel Centre** (Map p94; ☎ 836 6222; www .irishrail.ie; 35 Lower Abbey St; ⏰ 9am-5pm Mon-Fri, 9am-1pm Sat). **Connolly Station** (Map pp92-3; ☎ 836 3333), just north of the Liffey and the city centre, is the station for trains to Belfast, Derry, Sligo and other northern destinations. **Heuston Station** (Map pp92-3; ☎ 836 5421), just south of the Liffey and well west of the centre, is the station for Cork, Galway, Killarney, Limerick, Wexford, Waterford and other destinations west, south and southwest of Dublin. See p723 for more information.

GETTING AROUND
To/From the Airport

There is no train service to/from the airport, but there are bus and taxi options.

BUS

Aircoach (☎ 844 7118; www.aircoach.ie; one way/return €7/12) Private coach service with two routes from the airport to 18 destinations throughout the city, including the main streets of the city centre. Coaches run every 10 to 15 minutes between 6am and midnight, then hourly from midnight until 6am.

Airlink Express Coach (☎ 872 0000, 873 4222; www .dublinbus.ie; adult/child €6/3) Bus 747 runs every 10 to 20 minutes from 5.45am to 11.30pm between the airport, the central bus station (Busáras) and the Dublin Bus office on Upper O'Connell St; bus 748 runs every 15 to 30 minutes from 6.50am to 10.05pm between the airport and Heuston and Connolly Stations.

Dublin Bus (Map pp92-3; ☎ 872 0000; www.dublinbus .ie; 59 Upper O'Connell St; adult/child €2.20/1) A number of buses serve the airport from various points in Dublin, including buses 16A (Rathfarnham), 746 (Dun Laoghaire) and 230 (Portmarnock); all cross the city centre on their way to the airport.

TAXI

There is a taxi rank directly outside the arrivals concourse. A taxi should cost about €20 from the airport to the city centre, including a supplementary charge of €2.50 (not applied going to the airport). Make sure the meter is switched on.

Bicycle

Dublin is pretty flat and the traffic can be awful, so getting around on a bike can make life a lot easier. Still, though Dublin has an increasing number of rust-red cycle lanes, cyclists share them with drivers who are indifferent to the line markings, making cycling a little more of a challenge than it really ought to be.

In September 2009, Dublin City Council launched **DublinBikes** (www.dublinbikes.ie), a pay-as-you-go bike scheme, similar to the Parisian Vélib' system, with 450 bikes at 40 stations spread throughout the city centre. Cyclists will need to purchase a €10 Smart Card (as well as put down a credit-card deposit of €150) – either online or at any of the stations – before 'freeing' a bike for use, which is then free for the first 30 minutes and €0.50 for each half-hour thereafter.

Car & Motorcycle

Traffic in Dublin is a nightmare and parking is an expensive headache. There are no free spots to park anywhere in the city centre during business hours (7am to 7pm Monday to Saturday), but there are plenty of parking meters, 'pay and display' spots (€2.70 to €5.20 per hour), and over a dozen sheltered and supervised car parks (around €5 per hour).

Clamping of illegally parked cars is thoroughly enforced, with an €80 charge for removal. Parking is free after 7pm Monday to Saturday and all day Sunday in all metered spots and on single yellow lines.

Car theft and break-ins are a problem, and the police advise visitors to park in a supervised car park. Cars with foreign number plates are prime targets; never leave your valuables behind. When booking accommodation, enquire about parking facilities.

Public Transport
BUS

The office of **Dublin Bus** (Map pp92-3; ☎ 872 0000; www .dublinbus.ie; 59 Upper O'Connell St; ✆ 9am-5.30pm Mon-Fri, 9am-2pm Sat) has free single-route timetables of all its services.

Buses run from around 6am (some start at 5.30am) to 11.30pm. Fares are calculated according to stages: one to three stages costs €1.15; four to seven stages, €1.60; eight to 13 stages, €1.80; and 14 to 23 stages, €2.20. You must use exact change for tickets when boarding buses; anything more and you will be given a receipt for reimbursement, which is possible only at the Dublin Bus main office.

LUAS

The **Luas** (www.luas.ie; ✆ 5.30am-12.30am Mon-Fri, from 6.30am Sat, 7am-11.30pm Sun) light-rail system has two lines: the Green Line (trains run every five to 15 minutes), which connects St Stephen's Green with Sandyford in south Dublin via Ranelagh and Dundrum; and the Red Line (trains run every 20 minutes), which runs from Lower Abbey St to Tallaght via the north quays and Heuston Station. There are ticket machines at every stop or you can buy tickets from newsagencies throughout the city centre; a typical short-hop fare will cost you €1.90.

NITELINK

These late-night buses run from the College St, Westmoreland St and D'Olier St triangle (at Trinity College's northwest corner),

DUBLIN

covering most of Dublin's suburbs. Buses leave at 12.30am and 2am Monday to Wednesday, and every 20 minutes between 12.30am and 3.30am Thursday to Saturday. Tickets start at €4.

TRAIN

The **Dublin Area Rapid Transport** (DART; ☎ 836 6222; www.irishrail.ie) provides quick train access to the coast as far north as Howth (about 30 minutes) and as far south as Greystones in County Wicklow. Pearse Station (Map pp92–3) is convenient for central Dublin south of the Liffey, and Connolly Station for north of the Liffey. There are services every 10 to 20 minutes, sometimes even more frequently, from around 6.30am to midnight Monday to Saturday; services are less frequent on Sunday. Dublin to Dun Laoghaire takes about 15 to 20 minutes. A one-way DART ticket from Dublin to Dun Laoghaire or Howth costs €2.20; to Bray it's €2.50.

There are also suburban rail services north as far as Dundalk, inland to Mullingar and south past Bray to Arklow.

You can get fare-saver passes from www .dublinbus.ie or at the Dublin Tourism Office (p99). Some examples:

Adult (Bus & Rail) Short Hop (€10.20) Valid for unlimited one-day travel on Dublin Bus, DART, Luas and suburban rail travel, but not Nitelink or Airlink.

Bus/Luas Pass (1/7 days €7/29) One-day unlimited travel on both bus and Luas.

Family (Bus & Rail) Short Hop (€15.60) Valid for travel for unlimited one-day travel for a family of two adults and four children aged under 16 on all bus and rail services except for Nitelink, Airlink, ferry services and tours.

Rambler Pass (1/3/5 days €6/13.30/20) Valid for unlimited travel on all Dublin Bus and Airlink services, but not Nitelink.

Taxi

From 8am to 10pm, taxi fares begin with a flag-fall of €4.10, followed by around €1 per kilometre thereafter; from 10pm to 8am, it's €4.45 flagfall and €1.35 per km. Extra charges include €1 for each extra passenger and €2 for telephone bookings; there is no charge for luggage.

Taxis can be hailed on the street and found at **taxi ranks** around the city, including O'Connell St, College Green (in front of Trinity College) and St Stephen's Green at the end of Grafton St. There are numerous taxi companies that will dispatch taxis by radio. Some options:

City Cabs (☎ 872 2688)
National Radio Cabs (☎ 677 2222)

Phone the **Garda Carriage Office** (☎ 475 5888) if you have any complaints about taxis or queries regarding lost property.

AROUND DUBLIN

Without even the smallest hint of irony Dubliners will happily tell you that one of the city's best features is how easy it is to get out of it, and they do, whenever they can. But they don't go especially far: for many the destination is one of the small seaside villages that surround the capital. To the north are the lovely villages of Howth and Malahide – slowly and reluctantly being sucked into the Dublin conglomeration – while to the south is Dalkey, which has long since given up the fight but has managed to retain that village vibe.

DALKEY

South of Dun Laoghaire is Dalkey (Deilginis), which has the remains of a number of old castles. On Castle St, the main street, two 16th-century castles face each other: **Archibald's Castle** and **Goat Castle**. Next to the latter is the ancient **St Begnet's Church**, dating from the 9th century. **Bulloch Castle**, overlooking Bullock Harbour, north of town, was built by the monks of St Mary's Abbey in Dublin in the 12th century.

Goat Castle and St Begnet's Church have recently been converted into the **Dalkey Castle & Heritage Centre** (☎ 285 8366; www.dalkeycastle .com; Castle St; adult/child/student €6/4/5; ⊙ 9.30am-5pm Mon-Fri, 11am-5pm Sat & Sun). Models, displays and exhibitions form a pretty interesting history of Dalkey and give an insight into the area during medieval times.

Dalkey has several holy wells, including **St Begnet's Holy Well**, next to the ruins of another church dedicated to St Begnet on the 9-hectare **Dalkey Island**, a few hundred metres offshore from Coliemore Harbour. Reputed to cure rheumatism, the well is a popular destination for tourists and the faithful alike. To get here, you can hire a boat with a small outboard engine in Coliemore Harbour. To get one, simply show up (you can't book them in advance); they cost around €25 per hour.

DETOUR: SANDYCOVE & JAMES JOYCE MUSEUM

About 1km north of Dalkey is **Sandycove**, with a pretty little beach and a **Martello tower** – built by British forces to keep an eye out for a Napoleonic invasion – now housing the **James Joyce Museum** (☎ 280 9265; www.visitdublin.com; Joyce Tower, Sandycove; adult/child/student €6.70/4.20/5.70; ☻ 10am-1pm & 2-5pm Mon-Sat, 2-6pm Sun Apr-Oct, by appointment only Nov-Mar). This is where the action begins in James Joyce's epic novel *Ulysses*. The museum was opened in 1962 by Sylvia Beach, the Paris-based publisher who first dared to put *Ulysses* into print, and has photographs, letters, documents, various editions of Joyce's work and two death masks of Joyce on display.

Below the Martello tower is the **Forty Foot Pool**, an open-air, sea-water bathing pool that took its name from the army regiment, the Fortieth Foot, that was stationed at the tower until the regiment was disbanded in 1904. At the close of the first chapter of *Ulysses,* Buck Mulligan heads off to the Forty Foot Pool for a morning swim. A morning wake-up here is still a local tradition, winter or summer. In fact, a winter dip isn't much braver than a summer one since the water temperature varies by only about 5°C (9°F). Basically, it's always bloody cold.

Pressure from female bathers eventually opened this public stretch of water – originally nudist and for men only – to both sexes, despite strong opposition from the 'forty foot gentlemen'. They eventually compromised with the ruling that a 'Togs Must Be Worn' sign would apply after 9am. Prior to that time nudity prevails and swimmers are still predominantly male.

To the south there are good views from the small park at Sorrento Point and from Killiney Hill. **Dalkey Quarry** is a popular site for rock climbers, and originally provided most of the granite for the gigantic piers at Dun Laoghaire Harbour. A number of rocky **swimming pools** are found along the Dalkey coast.

Queen's (☎ 285 4569; 12 Castle St; lunch €8-10; ☻ noon-4pm & 5-7.30pm Mon-Fri, noon-4pm Sat & Sun) is a Dalkey institution offering a great pub lunch of meat and fish dishes.

OK, so it's not strictly Dalkey, but all self-respecting crustacean-lovers should make the 1km trip to **Caviston's Seafood Restaurant** (☎ 280 9245; Glasthule Rd, Sandycove; mains €14-28; ☻ noon-6pm Tue-Sat) for a meal to remember. Local fish and seafood are cooked simply with imaginative ingredients that enhance, rather than overpower, their flavour.

Dalkey is on the DART suburban train line or, for a slower journey, you can catch bus 8 from Burgh Quay in Dublin. Both cost €2.

HOWTH

The pretty fishing village of Howth (Binn Éadair), built on steep steps that run down to the waterfront, is a popular excursion from Dublin and has developed as a residential suburb of the city. The most desirable properties are on the hill above the village, located on a bulbous head that juts into the northern edge of Dublin Bay. The views from the top are magnificent. Although the harbour's role as a shipping port has long gone, Howth is a major fishing centre and yachting harbour.

In 1914 noted Irish Nationalist Robert Erskine Childers (better known as Erskine) had his yacht, *Asgard,* bring a cargo of 900 rifles into the port to arm the Nationalists. During the Civil War, Childers was court-martialled by his former comrades and executed by firing squad for illegal possession of a revolver. His son, also called Erskine, became the fourth president of Ireland. The *Asgard* is now on display at Kilmainham Jail (p113) in Dublin.

Howth (the name rhymes with 'both') is only 15km from central Dublin and easily reached by DART or by simply following Clontarf Rd out around the northern bay shoreline. En route you pass Clontarf, site of the pivotal clash between Celtic and Viking forces at the Battle of Clontarf in 1014. Further along is North Bull Island, a wildlife sanctuary where many migratory birds pause in winter.

Sights
AROUND THE PENINSULA

Most of the town backs onto the extensive grounds of **Howth Castle**, built in 1564 but much changed over the years, most recently in 1910 when Sir Edwin Lutyens gave it a modernist make-over. Today the castle is divided into four very posh and private residences. The original estate was acquired in 1177 by the Norman noble Sir Almeric Tristram, who changed his surname to St Lawrence after winning a battle at the behest (or so he believed) of his favourite saint. The family has owned the land ever since, though the unbroken chain of male succession came to an end in 1909.

On the grounds are the ruins of the 16th-century **Corr Castle** and an ancient dolmen (tomb chamber or portal tomb made of vertical stones topped by a huge capstone) known as **Aideen's Grave**. Legend has it that Aideen died of a broken heart after her husband was killed at the Battle of Gavra near Tara in AD 184, but the legend is rubbish because the dolmen is at least 300 years older than that.

The **castle gardens** (admission free; 24hr) are worth visiting, as they're noted for their rhododendrons (which bloom in May and June), azaleas and a long, 10m-high beech hedge planted in 1710.

Also within the grounds are the ruins of **St Mary's Abbey** (Abbey St, Howth Castle; admission free), originally founded in 1042 by the Viking King Sitric, who also founded the original church on the site of Christ Church Cathedral. The abbey was amalgamated with the monastery on Ireland's Eye (below) in 1235. Some parts of the ruins date from that time, but most are from the 15th and 16th centuries. The tomb of Christopher St Lawrence (Lord Howth), in the southeastern corner, dates from around 1470. See the caretaker or read instructions on the gate for opening times.

A more recent addition is the rather ramshackle **National Transport Museum** (832 0427; www.nationaltransportmuseum.org; Howth Castle; adult/child & student €3/1.25; 10am-5pm Mon-Sat Jun-Aug, 2-5pm Sat, Sun & bank holidays Sep-May), which has a range of exhibits, including double-decker buses, a bakery van, fire engines and trams – most notably a Hill of Howth electric tram that operated from 1901 to 1959. To reach the museum, go through the castle gates and turn right just before the castle.

Howth is essentially a very large hill surrounded by cliffs, and **Howth Summit** (171m) has excellent views across Dublin Bay right down to County Wicklow. From the Summit you can walk to the top of the Ben of Howth, a headland near the village, which has a cairn said to mark a 2000-year-old Celtic **royal grave**. The 1814 **Baily Lighthouse** at the southeastern corner is on the site of an old stone fort and can be reached by a dramatic cliff-top walk. There was an earlier hilltop beacon here in 1670.

IRELAND'S EYE

A short distance offshore from Howth is Ireland's Eye (Map p88), a rocky sea-bird sanctuary with the ruins of a 6th-century monastery. There's a Martello tower at the northwestern end of the island, where boats from Howth land, while a spectacularly sheer rock face plummets into the sea at the eastern end. As well as the sea birds overhead, you can see young birds on the ground during the nesting season. Seals can also be spotted around the island.

Doyle & Sons (831 4200; return €12) takes boats out to the island from the East Pier of Howth Harbour during the summer, usually on weekend afternoons. Don't wear shorts if you're planning to visit the monastery ruins because they're surrounded by a thicket of stinging nettles. And please bring all your rubbish back with you – far too many island visitors don't.

Further north from Ireland's Eye is **Lambay Island**, an important sea-bird sanctuary that cannot be visited.

Eating

Oar House (839 4562; www.oarhouse.ie; 8 West Pier; tapas €5-12, mains €10-24; 12.30-10pm) A feast-o-fish is what the menu is all about at this newish restaurant – particularly the locally caught variety. Par for the course in a fishing village, but this place stands out for both the way the fish is prepared and that you can get everything on the menu in smaller, tapas–style portions as well as mains.

ourpick **The House** (839 6388; www.thehouse.ie; 4 Main St; mains €16-22; 9am-3pm Mon-Fri, 11.30am-3pm & 6pm-11pm Sat & Sun) One of our favourite new openings in Dublin is this wonderful spot on the main street leading away from the harbour. In the handsome, airy dining room you can feast on dishes like crunchy Bellingham blue cheese polenta or wild Wicklow venison stew, as well as a fine selection of fish.

Aqua (832 0690; www.aqua.ie; 1 West Pier; mains €29-32; 12.30-3.30pm & 5.30-10.30pm Tue-Sat, 4-8.30pm Sun) Another contender for best seafood in Howth, Aqua has been serving top-quality fish dishes in its elegant dining room overlooking the harbour, in a building that was once home to the Howth Yacht Club.

There's also a wonderful organic market every Sunday (see the boxed text, p135).

Getting There & Away

The easiest and quickest way to get to Howth from Dublin is on the DART, which whisks you there in just over 20 minutes for a fare of €2.20. For the same fare, buses 31 and 31A from Lower Abbey St in the city centre run as far as the Summit, 5km to the southeast of Howth.

MALAHIDE

Malahide (Mullach Íde) was once a small village with its own harbour, a long way from the urban jungle of Dublin. The only thing protecting it from the northwards expansion of Dublin's suburbs is Malahide Demesne, 101 well-tended hectares of parkland dominated by a castle once owned by the powerful Talbot family. The handsome village remains relatively intact, but the once-quiet marina has been massively developed and is now a bustling centre with a pleasant promenade and plenty of restaurants and shops. A great way to see Dublin from the sea is by boarding a speedboat run by **Sea Safaris** (☎ 806 1626; www .seasafari.ie; Malahide Marina; per hr €30) and going for an hour-long trip around Dublin Bay.

Sights

MALAHIDE CASTLE

Despite the vicissitudes of Irish history, the Talbot family managed to keep **Malahide Castle** (☎ 846 2184; www.malahidecastle.com; adult/child/student/family €7.50/4.50/6.30/20, incl Fry Model Railway €11.50/7.50/9.50/31; ☯ 10am-5pm Mon-Sat, 11am-6pm Sun Apr-Oct, 11am-5pm Sat & Sun Nov-Mar) under its control from 1185 to 1976, apart from when Cromwell was around (1649–60). It's now owned by Dublin County Council. The castle is the usual hotchpotch of additions and renovations; the oldest part is a three-

storey 12th-century tower house. The facade is flanked by circular towers that were tacked on in 1765.

The castle is packed with furniture and paintings; highlights are a 16th-century oak room with decorative carvings, and the medieval Great Hall, which has family portraits, a minstrel's gallery and a painting of the Battle of the Boyne. Puck, the Talbot family ghost, is said to have last appeared in 1975.

The **parkland** (admission free; ☯ 10am-9pm Apr-Oct, 10am-5pm Nov-Mar) around the castle is a good place for a picnic.

FRY MODEL RAILWAY

Ireland's biggest **model railway** (☎ 846 3779; Malahide Castle; adult/child/student/family €6/4/5/16; ☯ 10am-1pm & 2-5pm Mon-Sat, 2-6pm Sun Apr-Sep, 2-5pm Sat, Sun & holidays Oct-Mar) is 240 sq metres, and authentically displays much of Ireland's rail and public transport system, including the DART line and Irish Sea ferry services, in O-gauge (32mm track width). A separate room features model trains and other memorabilia. Unfortunately the operators suffer from the overseriousness of some grown men with complicated toys; rather than let you simply look and admire, they herd you into the control room in groups for demonstrations.

Getting There & Away

Malahide is 13km north of Dublin. Bus 42 (€2.20) from Talbot St takes around 45 minutes. The DART stops in Malahide (€2.50), but be sure to get on the right train (it's marked on the front carriage) since the line splits at Howth Junction.

Counties Wicklow & Kildare

Bordering Dublin to the south and west are the counties of Wicklow and Kildare, which are themselves neighbours but very different from one another. Wicklow is scenic, stunning and wild, whereas Kildare offers a more sedate, pastoral landscape dotted with wealthy homes and expensive horses.

Wicklow, to the south, has been far more successful in fending off the worst effects of the sprawl, largely due to the county's most imposing natural feature: a gorse-and-bracken mountain spine that is as wildly beautiful as it is impenetrable to the developers. Here, history and geology work together to great effect and preserve one of Ireland's most stunning landscapes, replete with dramatic glacial valleys, soaring mountain passes and some of the country's most important archaeological treasures – from breathtaking early-Christian sites to the elegant country homes of the wealthiest Ireland's 18th-century nobility.

Kildare might not have the dramatic landscapes, but it is one of the most prosperous farming counties in the country and once a key part of the English Pale, as the 'obedient territories' surrounding Dublin were once known. It is also where you'll find some of the most lucrative thoroughbred stud farms in the world, many with links to the horse-breeding centre of Kentucky in the US. Horse breeding is a big deal in Ireland, but in Kildare it's the very lifeblood of the county, generating many millions of tax-free euro.

HIGHLIGHTS

- **Monastic Magic** Evocative ruins and the marvellous slopes and forests of gorgeous Glendalough (p163)
- **Bogged Down** County Kildare's huge tracks of fecund land at the Bog of Allen (p181)
- **The Hills are Alive** Ireland's most popular hiking trail, the Wicklow Way (p166)
- **The Art is Hot** Art and atmosphere of magnificent Russborough House (p168)
- **The Glory of the Garden** Gorgeous Italianate gardens and the impressive waterfall at Powerscourt Estate (p159)

- POPULATION: 300,775
- AREA: 3718 SQ KM

COUNTY WICKLOW

Wicklow (Cill Mhantáin) is Dublin's favourite playground – directly south of the capital and in a long and desperate struggle to stop its northern reaches from being absorbed by the persistent spread of the suburban jungle. Wicklowites have fought the good fight, and the 'Garden of Ireland' has been successful in fending off the worst ravages of the urban expansion, mostly because so much of the county remains defiantly opposed to the planners' bulldozers – although nature also lends a hand, blocking the way with a daunting mountain range.

Linking much of Wicklow's attractions is the 132km-long Wicklow Way, the country's foremost walking trail and – if you've got the legs for it – still the best and most satisfying way to explore the county. From the suburbs of southern Dublin to the rolling fields of County Carlow, the Way leads walkers along disused military supply lines, old bog roads and nature trails over the eastern flanks of the mountains.

National Parks

Wicklow Mountains National Park covers more than 170 sq km of mountainous blanket bogs and woodland. Plans to extend it will eventually see virtually all of the higher ground stretching the length of the mountains fall under the protection of the national park, which will cover more than 300 sq km.

Within the boundaries of the protected area are two nature reserves, owned and managed by the Heritage Service, and legally protected by the Wildlife Act. The larger reserve, west of the Glendalough Visitor Centre, conserves the extensive heath and bog of the Glendalough Valley plus the Upper Lake and valley slopes on either side. The second, Glendalough Wood Nature Reserve, conserves oak woods stretching from the Upper Lake as far as the Rathdrum road to the east.

Most of Ireland's native mammal species can be found within the confines of the park. Large herds of deer roam on the open hill areas, though these were introduced in the 20th century as the native red-deer population became extinct during the first half of the 18th century. The uplands are the preserve of foxes, badgers and hares. Red squirrels are usually found in the pine woodlands – look out for them around the Upper Lake.

The bird population of the park is plentiful. Birds of prey abound, the most common being peregrine falcons, marlins, kestrels, hawks and sparrowhawks. Hen harriers are a rarer sight, though they too live in the park. Moorland birds found in the area include meadow pipits and skylarks. Less common birds such as whinchats, ring ouzels and dippers can be spotted, as can red grouse, whose numbers are quickly disappearing in other parts of Ireland. For information, call in or contact the **National Park Information Point** (Map p163; ☎ 0404-45425; www.wicklownationalpark.ie; Bolger's Cottage, Miners' Rd, Upper Lake, Glendalough; ⊗ 10am-6pm May-Sep, to dusk Sat & Sun Oct-Apr), off the Green Rd that runs by the Upper Lake, about 2km from the Glendalough Visitor Centre. There's usually someone on hand to help, but if you find it closed the staff may be out running guided walks. *Exploring the Glendalough Valley* (Heritage Service; €2) is a good booklet on the trails in the area.

Getting There & Away

It's a cinch to get to Wicklow from Dublin. The main routes through the county are the N11 (M11), which runs north–south from Dublin all the way through to Wexford, taking in all of the coastal towns; and the N81, which runs down the western spine of the county through Blessington and into County Carlow. The Dublin Area Rapid Transport (DART) suburban rail line runs southward from Dublin as far as Bray, and there are regular train and bus connections from the capital to Wicklow town and Arklow.

For Glendalough, **St Kevin's Bus** (☎ 01-281 8119; www.glendaloughbus.com) runs twice daily from Dublin and Bray, also stopping in Roundwood. For the western parts of the county, Dublin Bus 65 runs regularly as far as Blessington. For more details, see the Getting There & Away section for each town.

WICKLOW MOUNTAINS

As you leave Dublin and cross into Wicklow, the landscape changes – dramatically. From Killakee, still in Dublin, the Military Rd begins a 30km southward journey across vast sweeps of gorse-, bracken- and heather-clad moors, bogs and mountains dotted with small corrie lakes.

The numbers and statistics aren't all that impressive. The highest peak in the range, Lugnaquilla (924m), is really more of a very large hill, but that hardly matters here. This

COUNTIES WICKLOW & KILDARE

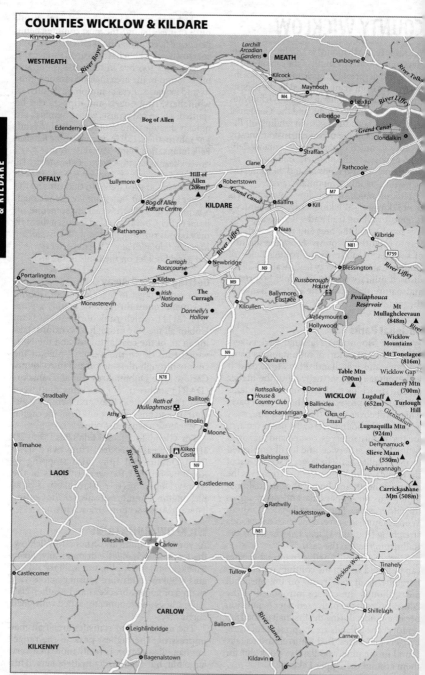

COUNTIES WICKLOW & KILDARE

vast granite intrusion, a welling-up of hot igneous rock that solidified some 400 million years ago, was shaped during the Ice Ages into the schist-capped mountains visible today. The peaks are marvellously desolate and as raw as only nature can be. Between the mountains are a number of deep glacial valleys, most notably Glenmacnass, Glenmalure and Glendalough; while corrie lakes such as Lough Bray Upper and Lower, gouged out by ice at the head of the glaciers, complete the wild topography.

The narrow Military Rd winds its way through the most remote parts of the mountains, offering some extraordinary views of the surrounding countryside. The best place to join it is at Glencree (from Enniskerry). It then runs south through the Sally Gap, Glenmacnass Valley and Laragh, then on to Glenmalure Valley and Aghavannagh.

On the trip south you can divert east at the Sally Gap to look at Lough Tay and Lough Dan. Further south you pass the great waterfall at Glenmacnass before dropping down into Laragh, with the magnificent monastic ruins of Glendalough nearby. Continue south through the valley of Glenmalure and, if you're fit enough, climb Lugnaquilla.

Enniskerry & Powerscourt Estate
pop 2672
At the top of the '21 Bends', as the winding R117 from Dublin is known, the handsome village of Enniskerry is home to art galleries and the kind of all-organic gourmet cafes that would treat you as a war criminal if you admitted to eating battery eggs. Such preening self-regard is a far cry from the village's origins, when Richard Wingfield, Earl of nearby Powerscourt, commissioned a row of terraced cottages for his labourers in 1760. These days, you'd want to have laboured pretty successfully to get your hands on one of them.

The village is lovely, but the main reason for its popularity is the magnificent 64-sq-km **Powerscourt Estate** (☎ 01-204 6000; www.powerscourt .ie; adult/child/student €8/5/7; ☼ 9.30am-5.30pm Feb-Oct, to 4.30pm Nov-Jan), which gives contemporary observers a true insight into the style of the 18th-century super-rich. The main entrance is 500m south of the village square.

The estate has existed more or less since 1300, when the LePoer (later anglicised to Power) family built themselves a castle here. The property changed Anglo-Norman hands a

COUNTIES WICKLOW & KILDARE

COUNTIES WICKLOW & KILDARE

few times before coming into the possession of Richard Wingfield, newly appointed Marshall of Ireland, in 1603 – his descendants were to live here for the next 350 years. In 1731 the Georgian wunderkind Richard Cassels (or Castle) was given the job of building a Palladian-style mansion around the core of the old castle. He finished the job in 1743, but an extra storey was added in 1787 and other alterations were made in the 19th century.

The Wingfields left during the 1950s, after which the house had a massive restoration. Then, on the eve of its opening to the public in 1974, a fire gutted the whole building. The estate was eventually bought by the Slazenger sporting-goods family who have overseen a second restoration, as well as the addition of two golf courses, a cafe, a huge garden centre and a bunch of cutesy little retail outlets as well as a small exhibition on the house's history.

Basically, it's all intended to draw in the punters and wring as many euros out of their pockets as possible in order to finish the huge restoration job and make the estate a kind of profitable wonderland. If you can deal with the crowds (summer weekends are the worst) or, better still, avoid the worst of them and visit midweek, you're in for a real treat. Easily the biggest drawcards of the whole pile are the simply magnificent 20-hectare formal gardens and the breathtaking views that accompany them.

Originally laid out in the 1740s, the gardens were redesigned in the 19th century by Daniel Robinson, who had as much fondness for the booze as he did for horticultural pursuits: he liked (needed?) to be wheeled around in a wheelbarrow after a certain point in the day. Perhaps this influenced his largely informal style, which resulted in a magnificent blend of landscaped gardens, sweeping terraces, statuary, ornamental lakes, secret hollows, rambling walks and walled enclosures replete with more than 200 types of trees and shrubs, all beneath the stunning natural backdrop of the Great Sugarloaf Mountain to the southeast. Tickets come with a map laying out 40-minute and hour-long tours of the gardens. Don't miss the exquisite Japanese Gardens or the Pepperpot Tower, modelled on a three-inch actual pepperpot owned by Lady Wingfield. Our own favourite, however, is the animal cemetery, final resting place of the Wingfield pets and even some of their favourite milking cows. Some of the epitaphs are astonishingly personal.

A 7km walk to a separate part of the estate takes you to the 130m **Powerscourt Waterfall** (adult/child/student €5/3.50/4.50; 9.30am-7pm May-Aug, 10.30am-5.30pm Mar-Apr & Sep-Oct, to 4.30pm Nov-Jan). It's the highest waterfall in Britain and Ireland, and is most impressive after heavy rain. You can also get to the falls by road, following the signs from the estate. A nature trail has been laid out around the base of the waterfall, taking you past giant redwoods, ancient oaks, beech, birch and rowan trees. There are plenty of birds in the vicinity, including the chaffinch, cuckoo, chiffchaff, raven and willow warbler.

TOURS

All tours that take in Powerscourt start in Dublin.

Bus Éireann (01-836 6111; www.buseireann.ie; Busáras; adult/child/student €28.80/22.50/25.20; 10am mid-Mar–Oct) A whole-day tour that takes in Powerscourt and Glendalough (all admissions included), departing from Busáras (Map pp92–3).

Dublin Bus Tours (Map pp92-3; 01-872 0000; www.dublinbus.ie; 59 Upper O'Connell St; adult/child €25/12; 11am) A visit to Powerscourt is included in the four-hour South Coast & Gardens tour, which takes in the stretch of coastline between Dun Laoghaire and Killiney before turning inland to Wicklow and on to Enniskerry. Admission to the gardens is included.

Gray Line Tours (Map pp92-3; 01-872 9010; www.irishcitytours.com; Gresham Hotel, O'Connell St; adult/student/child €35/32/25; 10am Fri-Sun) Incorporating Wicklow's big hits – Powerscourt, Glendalough and the lakes and a stop at Avoca, then takes in Dun Laoghaire and Dalkey (includes admission to Glendalough visitor centre and Powerscourt, but not coffee).

SLEEPING

Coolakay House (01-286 2423; www.coolakayhouse.com; Waterfall Rd, Coolakay; s/d from €40/80; P) A modern working farm about 3km south of Enniskerry (it is signposted along the road), this is a great option for walkers along the Wicklow Way. The four bedrooms are all very comfortable and have terrific views, but the real draw is the restaurant, which does a roaring trade in snacks and full meals (mains around €11).

Summerhill House Hotel (01-286 7928; www.summerhillhousehotel.com; r from €110; P) A truly superb country mansion about 700m south of town just off the N11 is the best place around to lay your head, on soft cotton pillows surrounded by delicate antiques and pastoral views in oils. Everything about the place – including the top-notch breakfast – is memorable.

The nearest youth hostel is in Glencree, 10km west of here.

EATING

Powerscourt Terrace Café (☎ 01-204 6070; Powerscourt House; mains €8-13; ☺ 10am-5pm) The folks at Avoca Handweavers (p171) have applied all their know-how and turned what could have easily been just another run-of-the-mill tourist-attraction cafe into something of a gourmet experience. A slice of quiche on the terrace, overlooking the gardens in the shadow of the Great Sugarloaf? Yes, please.

Emilia's Ristorante (☎ 01-276 1834; www.emilias.ie; Clock Tower, The Square; mains €12-16; ☺ 5-10.45pm Mon-Sat, noon-9.30pm Sun) A lovely 1st-floor restaurant to satisfy even the most ardent craving for thin-crust pizzas. Emilia's does everything else just right too, from the organic soups to the perfect steaks down to the gorgeous meringue desserts.

Poppies Country Cooking (☎ 01-282 8869; The Square; mains around €9; ☺ 8.30am-6pm) If the service wasn't so slow and the organisation so frustratingly haphazard, this pokey little cafe on the main square would be one of the best spots in Wicklow. The food – when you finally get a chance to eat it – is sensational: wholesome salads, filling sandwiches on doorstop-cut bread and award-winning ice cream will leave you plenty satisfied.

Johnnie Fox (☎ 01-295 5647; www.jfp.ie; Glencullen; Hungry Fisherman's seafood platter €29.95; ☺ noon-10pm) Busloads of tourists fill the place nightly throughout the summer, mostly for the knees-up, faux-Irish floorshow of music and dancing. But there's nothing contrived about the seafood, which is so damn good we'd happily sit through yet another chorus of *Danny Boy* and even consider joining in the jig. The pub is 3km northwest of Enniskerry in Glencullen.

GETTING THERE & AWAY

Enniskerry is 18km south of Dublin, just 3km west of the M11 along the R117. **Dublin Bus** (☎ 01-872 0000, 01-873 4222) service 44 (€2.20, every 20 minutes) takes about 1¼ hours to get to Enniskerry from Hawkins St in Dublin. Alternatively, you can take the DART train

to Bray (€2.75) and catch bus 185 (€1.60, hourly) from the station, which takes an extra 40 minutes.

Getting to Powerscourt House under your own steam is not a problem (it's 500m from the town), but getting to the waterfall is tricky. **Alpine Coaches** (☎ 01-286 2547; www.alpinecoaches.ie) runs a shuttle service between the DART station in Bray and the house (€6 return) and the house (€4.50). Shuttles leave Bray at 11.05am (11.30am July and August), 12.30pm, 1.30pm (and 3.30pm September to June) Monday to Saturday, and 11am, noon and 1pm Sunday. The last departure from Powerscourt House is at 5.30pm.

Glencree

Just south of the County Dublin border and 10km west of Enniskerry is Glencree, a leafy hamlet set into the side of the valley of the same name, which opens east to give a magnificent view down to Great Sugarloaf Mountain and the sea.

The valley floor is home to the Glencree Oak Project, an ambitious plan to reforest part of Glencree with the native oak vegetation, mostly broadleaf trees, that once covered most of the country but now covers only 1% of Ireland's landmass.

The village, such as it is, has a tiny shop and a hostel but no pub. There's a poignant **German cemetery** dedicated to 134 servicemen who died in Ireland during WWI and WWII. Just south of the village, the former military barracks are now a retreat house and reconciliation centre for people of different religions from the Republic and the North.

A beautiful converted 18th-century farmhouse with wonderful views over Glencree, **Knockree Youth Hostel** (☎ 01-276 7981; www.knockree youthhostel.com; Knockree, Enniskerry; dm/d €21.50/70; ☐) was recently upgraded to a luxurious, five-star hostel with 76 beds divided across a number of dorm rooms – none with more than six beds. There are also a selection of doubles, including a honeymoon suite. All the rooms have private bathrooms.

Run in tandem with the Knockree Youth Hostel, **EcoAdventure Ireland** (☎ 01-276 7988; www.ecoadventureireland.ie; Knockree, Enniskerry; non-residential programs €25-45) runs all kinds of outdoor activities programs, from pony trekking to ecological field studies. You have the option of residential and non-residential programs; accommodation is in the youth hostel.

Sally Gap

One of the two main east–west passes across the Wicklow Mountains, the Sally Gap is surrounded by some spectacular countryside. From the turn-off on the lower road (R755) between Roundwood and Kilmacanogue near Bray, the narrow road (R759) passes above the dark and dramatic Lough Tay, whose scree slopes slide into **Luggala** (Fancy Mountain). This almost fairy-tale estate is owned by one Garech de Brún, member of the Guinness family and founder of Claddagh Records, a leading producer of Irish traditional and folk music. The small River Cloghoge links Lough Tay with Lough Dan just to the south. It then heads up to the Sally Gap crossroads, where it cuts across the Military Rd and heads northwest for Kilbride and the N81, following the young River Liffey, still only a stream.

Roundwood
pop 589

Reputed to be Ireland's highest village, Roundwood hardly towers above the world at 238m, but it is a handy and popular stop for walkers along the Wicklow Way, which runs past the town about 3km to the west. The long main street leads south to Glendalough and southern Wicklow. Turn-offs lead to Ashford to the east and the southern shore of Lough Dan to the west. Unfortunately, almost all Lough Dan's southern shoreline is private property and you can't get to the lake on this side.

The town has shops and a post office, but not a bank or an ATM. The nearest ATM is at the petrol station in Kilmacanogue, 16km away at the junction of the M11 and the R755.

ACTIVITIES

Guided or self-guided tour options up to eight days in Wicklow (and plenty of other spots in Ireland) are available with **Footfalls Walking Holidays** (☎ 0404-45152; www.walkinghikingireland.com; Trooperstown, Roundwood). A six-day trek through the Wicklow Mountains complete with bed and board will cost €755.

SLEEPING & EATING

Roundwood Caravan & Camping Park (☎ 01-281 8163; www.dublinwicklowcamping.com; campsites per adult/child €8/4; ☻ Apr-Sep) Top-notch facilities, including a kitchen, dining area and TV lounge, make this one of the best camping grounds in all of Wicklow. It is about 500m south of the village and is served by the daily St Kevin's Bus service between Dublin and Glendalough.

Tochar House (☎ 01-281 8247; s/d from €35/64) In the middle of Main St, this handsome house has sizeable, comfortable rooms decorated with plenty of pinewood, which gives the place a bright look. There's a pub downstairs, which can get a little noisy at weekends.

Woodstock (☎ 01-281 8005; woodstockjohn@hotmail .com; s/d from €35/65) At the southern end of town, this pleasant bungalow is popular with walkers along the Wicklow Way – as much for its tidy, comfortable rooms and decent breakfast as for the convenient service of luggage transfer to your next destination along the walkers' route.

Roundwood Inn (☎ 01-281 8107; Main St; bar food €10-16, mains €16-32; ☻ bar noon-9pm, restaurant 7.30-9.30pm Fri & Sat, 1-3pm Sun) This 17th-century German-owned house has a gorgeous bar with a snug open fire, in front of which you can sample bar food with a difference: on the menu are dishes such as Hungarian goulash and Irish stew with a German twist. The more-formal restaurant is the best in town, and has earned praise for its hearty, delicious cuisine. The menu favours meat dishes, including seasonal game, Wicklow rack of lamb and a particularly good roast suckling pig. Reservations are required.

GETTING THERE & AWAY

St Kevin's Bus (☎ 01-281 8119; www.glendaloughbus .com) passes through Roundwood on its twice-daily jaunt between Dublin and Glendalough (one way/return €8/14, 1¼ hours).

Glenmacnass

Desolate and utterly deserted, the Glenmacnass valley, a stretch of wild bogland between the Sally Gap crossroads and Laragh, is one of the most beautiful parts of the mountains, although the sense of isolation is quite dramatic.

The highest mountain to the west is Mt Mullaghcleevaun (848m), and River Glenmacnass flows south and tumbles over the edge of the mountain plateau in a great foaming cascade. There's a car park near the top of the waterfall. Be careful when walking on rocks near **Glenmacnass Waterfall** as a few people have slipped to their deaths. There are fine walks up Mt Mullaghcleevaun or in the hills to the east of the car park.

Wicklow Gap

Between Mt Tonelagee (816m) to the north and Table Mountain (700m) to the southwest, the Wicklow Gap is the second major pass over the mountains. The eastern end of the road begins just to the north of Glendalough and climbs through some lovely scenery northwestwards up along the Glendassan Valley. It passes the remains of some old lead and zinc workings before meeting a side road that leads south and up Turlough Hill, the location of Ireland's only pumped-storage power station. You can walk up the hill for a look over the Upper Lake.

Glendalough

pop 280

If you've come to Wicklow, chances are that a visit to Glendalough (Gleann dá Loch, 'Valley of the Two Lakes') is one of your main reasons for being here. And you're not wrong, for this is one of the most beautiful corners of the whole country and the epitome of the kind of rugged, romantic Ireland that probably drew you to the island in the first place.

The substantial remains of this important monastic settlement are certainly impressive, but the real draw is the splendid setting: two dark and mysterious lakes tucked into a deep valley covered in forest. It is, despite its immense popularity, a deeply tranquil and spiritual place, and you will have little difficulty in understanding why those solitude-seeking monks came here in the first place.

HISTORY

In AD 498 a young monk named Kevin arrived in the valley looking for somewhere to kick back, meditate and be at one with nature. He pitched up in what had been a Bronze Age tomb on the southern side of the Upper Lake and for the next seven years slept on stones, wore animal skins, maintained a near-starvation diet and – according to the legend – became bosom buddies with the birds and animals. Kevin's ecofriendly lifestyle soon attracted a bunch of disciples, all seemingly unaware of the irony that they were flocking to hang out with a hermit who wanted to live as far away from other people as possible. Over the next couple of centuries his one-man operation mushroomed into a proper settlement and by the 9th century Glendalough rivalled

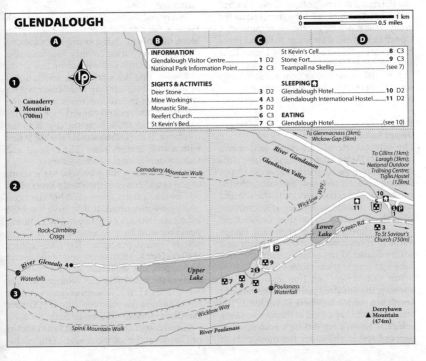

GLENDALOUGH

0 ——— 1 km
0 ——— 0.5 miles

INFORMATION	
Glendalough Visitor Centre	**1** D2
National Park Information Point	**2** C3

SIGHTS & ACTIVITIES	
Deer Stone	**3** D2
Mine Workings	**4** A3
Monastic Site	**5** D2
Reefert Church	**6** C3
St Kevin's Bed	**7** C3

St Kevin's Cell	**8** C3
Stone Fort	**9** C3
Teampall na Skellig	(see 7)

SLEEPING	
Glendalough Hotel	**10** D2
Glendalough International Hostel	**11** D2

EATING	
Glendalough Hotel	(see 10)

Clonmacnoise (p511) as the island's premier monastic city. Thousands of students studied and lived in a thriving community that was spread over a considerable area.

Inevitably, Glendalough's success made it a key target of Viking raiders, who sacked the monastery at least four times between 775 and 1071. The final blow came in 1398, when English forces from Dublin almost completely destroyed it. Efforts were made to rebuild and some life lingered on here as late as the 17th century when, under renewed repression, the monastery finally died.

ORIENTATION & INFORMATION

At the valley entrance, before the Glendalough Hotel, is **Glendalough Visitor Centre** (☎ 0404-45325; www.heritageireland.ie/en/MidlandsEastCoast/Glendalough VisitorCentre; adult/child & student €3/1; ☿ 9.30am-6pm mid-Mar–Oct, to 5pm Nov–mid-Mar). It has a high-quality 17-minute audiovisual presentation called *Ireland of the Monasteries,* which does exactly what it says on the tin.

Coming from Laragh you first see the visitor centre, then the Glendalough Hotel, which is beside the entrance to the main group of ruins and the round tower. The Lower Lake is a small dark lake to the west, while further west up the valley is the much bigger and more impressive Upper Lake, with a large car park and more ruins nearby. Be sure to visit the Upper Lake and take one of the surrounding walks.

A model in the visitor centre should help you fix where everything is in relation to everything else.

SIGHTS
Upper Lake

The original site of St Kevin's settlement, **Teampall na Skellig** is at the base of the cliffs towering over the southern side of the Upper Lake and is accessible only by boat; unfortunately, there's no boat service to the site and you'll have to settle for looking at it across the lake. The terraced shelf has the reconstructed ruins of a church and early graveyard. Rough wattle huts once stood on the raised ground nearby. Scattered around are some early grave slabs and simple stone crosses.

Just east of here and 10m above the lake waters is the 2m-deep artificial cave called **St Kevin's Bed**, said to be where Kevin lived. The earliest human habitation of the cave was long before St Kevin's era – there's evidence that people lived in the valley for thousands of years before the monks arrived. In the green area just south of the car park is a large circular wall thought to be the remains of an early Christian **stone fort** *(caher)*.

Follow the lakeshore path southwest of the car park until you come to the considerable remains of **Reefert Church** above the tiny River Poulanass. It's a small, plain, 11th-century Romanesque nave-and-chancel church with some reassembled arches and walls. Traditionally, Reefert (literally 'Royal Burial Place') was the burial site of the chiefs of the local O'Toole family. The surrounding grave-yard contains a number of rough stone crosses and slabs, most made of shiny mica schist.

Climb the steps at the back of the church-yard and follow the path to the west and you'll find, at the top of a rise overlooking the lake, the scant remains of **St Kevin's Cell**, a small beehive hut.

Lower Lake

While the Upper Lake has the best scenery, the most fascinating buildings lie in the lower part of the valley east of the Lower Lake, huddled together in the heart of the ancient monastic site.

Just round the bend from the Glendalough Hotel is the stone arch of the **monastery gate-house**, the only surviving example of a monastic entranceway in the country. Just inside the entrance is a large slab with an incised cross.

Beyond that lies a **graveyard**, which is still in use. The 10th-century **round tower** is 33m tall and 16m in circumference at the base. The upper storeys and conical roof were reconstructed in 1876. Near the tower, to the southeast, is the **Cathedral of St Peter and St Paul** with a 10th-century nave. The chancel and sacristy date from the 12th century.

At the centre of the graveyard to the south of the round tower is the **Priest's House**. This odd building dates from 1170 but has been heavily reconstructed. It may have been the location of shrines of St Kevin. Later, during penal times, it became a burial site for local priests – hence the name. The 10th-century **St Mary's Church**, 140m southwest of the round tower, probably originally stood outside the walls of the monastery and belonged to local nuns. It has a lovely western doorway. A little to the east are the scant remains of **St Kieran's Church**, the smallest at Glendalough.

Glendalough's trademark is **St Kevin's Kitchen** or Church at the southern edge of the enclosure. This church, with a miniature round towerlike belfry, protruding sacristy and steep stone roof, is a masterpiece. How it came to be known as a kitchen is a mystery as there's no indication that it was anything other than a church. The oldest parts of the building date from the 11th century – the structure has been remodelled since but it's still a classic early Irish church.

At the junction with Green Rd as you cross the river just south of these two churches is the **Deer Stone** in the middle of a group of rocks. Legend claims that when St Kevin needed milk for two orphaned babies, a doe stood here waiting to be milked. The stone is actually a *bullaun* (a stone used as a mortar for grinding medicines or food). Many such stones are thought to be prehistoric, and they were widely regarded as having supernatural properties: women who bathed their faces with water from the hollow were supposed to keep their looks forever. The early churchmen brought the stones into their monasteries, perhaps hoping to inherit some of their powers.

The road east leads to **St Saviour's Church**, with its detailed Romanesque carvings. To the west, a nice woodland trail leads up the valley past the Lower Lake to the Upper Lake.

ACTIVITIES

The Glendalough Valley is all about **walking** and clambering. There are nine marked ways in the valley, the longest of which is about 10km, or about four hours walking. Before you set off, drop by the **National Park Information Point** (☎ 0404-45425; ☼ 10am-6pm daily May-Sep, to dusk Sat & Sun Oct-Apr) and pick up the relevant leaflet and trail map (all around €0.50) or, if you're solo, arrange for walking partners. It also has a number of excellent guides for sale – you won't go far wrong with Joss Lynam's *Easy Walks Near Dublin* (€7.99). A word of warning: don't be fooled by the relative gentleness of the surrounding countryside or the fact that the Wicklow Mountains are really no taller than big hills. The weather can be merciless, so make sure to take the usual precautions, have the right equipment and tell someone where you're going and when you should be back. For Mountain Rescue call ☎ 999.

The easiest and most popular walk is the gentle hike along the northern shore of the Upper Lake to the lead and zinc **mine workings**, which date from 1800. The better route

is along the lakeshore rather than on the road (which runs 30m in from the shore), a distance of about 2.5km, one way, from the Glendalough Visitor Centre. Continue on up the head of the valley if you wish.

Alternatively, you can walk up the **Spink** (from the Irish for 'pointed hill'; 380m), the steep ridge with vertical cliffs running along the southern flanks of the Upper Lake. You can go part of the way and turn back, or complete a circuit of the Upper Lake by following the top of the cliff, eventually coming down by the mine workings and going back along the northern shore. The circuit is about 6km long and takes about three hours – if you feel like going on, check out the boxed text, p166.

The third option is a hike up **Camaderry Mountain** (700m), hidden behind the hills that flank the northern side of the valley. The walk starts on the road just 50m back towards Glendalough from the entrance to the Upper Lake car park. Head straight up the steep hill to the north and you come out on open mountains with sweeping views in all directions. You can then continue up Camaderry to the northwest or just follow the ridge west looking over the Upper Lake. To the top of Camaderry and back is about 7.5km and takes about four hours.

TOURS

If you don't fancy discovering Glendalough under your own steam, there are a couple of tours that will make it fairly effortless. They both depart from Dublin.

Bus Éireann (Map pp92-3; ☎ 01-836 6111; www.bus eireann.ie; Busáras; adult/child/student €28.80/22.50/ 25.20; ☼ departs 10am mid-Mar-Oct) Includes admission to the visitor centre and a visit to Powerscourt Estate in this whole-day tour, which returns to Dublin at about 5.45pm. The guides are good but impersonal.

Wild Wicklow Tour (☎ 01-280 1899; www.discover dublin.ie; adult/student & child €28/25; ☼ departs 9am) Award-winning tours of Glendalough, Avoca and the Sally Gap that never fail to generate rave reviews for atmosphere and all-round fun, but so much craic has made a casualty of informative depth. The first pick-up is at the Dublin Tourism office, but there are a variety of pick-up points throughout Dublin; check the point nearest you when booking. The tour returns to Dublin about 5.30pm.

SLEEPING

Most B&Bs are in or around Laragh, a village 3km east of Glendalough, or on the way there from Glendalough.

Glendalough International Hostel (☎ 0404-45342; www.anoige.ie; The Lodge; dm May-Sep €24, Oct-Apr €20; 🖳) Conveniently, this modern hostel is situated near the round tower, set within the deeply wooded glacial area that makes up the Glendalough Valley. All dorms have en-suite bathrooms and there's a decent cafeteria on the premises.

our pick **Glendalough Hermitages** (☎ 0404-45140, for bookings 45777; www.hermitage.dublindiocese.ie; St Kevin's Parish Church, Glendalough; s/d €45/70) In an effort to recreate something of the contemplative spirit of Kevin's early years in the valley, St Kevin's Parish Church rents out five *cillíns* (hermitages) for folks looking to take time out from the bustle of daily life and

---

WALK: THE WICKLOW WAY – GLENDALOUGH TO AUGHRIM

The Wicklow Way is one of Ireland's most popular long-distance walks because of its remarkable scenery and its relatively fluid and accessible starting and finishing points – there are plenty of half- and full day options along the way.

This section is 40km long and takes you through some of the more remote parts of the Wicklow Mountains and down into the southeastern foothills. There's relatively little road walking but the greater part of the day is through conifer plantations. The walk should take between 7½ and eight hours, with an ascent of 1035m.

From the **National Park Information Point** on the southern side of the Upper Lake, turn left and ascend beside Lugduff Brook and **Poulanass Waterfall**. Veer left when you meet a forest track, then left again at a junction and cross two bridges. The Way leads northeast for about 600m then, from a tight right bend, heads almost directly southwards (via a series of clearly marked junctions), up through the conifer plantations, across Lugduff Brook again and beside a tributary, to open ground on the saddle between **Mullacor** (657m) and **Lugduff** (1¾ hours from Glendalough). From here on a good day, massive Lugnaquilla sprawls across the view to the southwest; in the opposite direction is Camaderry's long ridge above Glendalough, framed against the bulk of Tonelagee. Follow the raised boardwalk down, contour above a plantation and drop into it where a steep muddy and rocky path descends to a forest road; turn left.

If you're planning to stay at Glenmalure Hostel (see p168), rather than go all the way down to the crossroads in Glenmalure, follow the Way from the left turn for about 1km southwards. At an oblique junction where the Way turns southeast, bear left in a westerly direction and descend steeply to the road in Glenmalure. The hostel is about 2km northwest.

To continue straight on along the Way from the left turn, follow forest roads south then southeast for 1.6km to a wide zigzag above open ground, then contour the steep slope, swing northeast and drop down to a minor road beside two bridges. Continue down to an intersection and Glenmalure; it's about 1¼ hours from the saddle.

The Way presses straight on (south) through the crossroads for 500m, across the River Avonbeg and past silent **Drumgoff Barracks**, built in 1803 but long since derelict, then right along a forest track. Keep left past a ruined cottage and start to gain height in two fairly long reaches; go through two left turns then it's down and across a stream. About 800m further on, turn right along a path to start the long ascent almost to the top of **Slieve Maan** (550m) via four track junctions, maintaining a southwesterly to south-southwesterly direction. Back on a forest track, the Way turns left (southeast) close to unforested ground to the west. With a few more convoluted turns, you're out of the trees and on a path between the plantation and the road (mapped as the Military Rd). The Way eventually meets the latter beside a small tributary of the River Aghavannagh (two hours from Glenmalure).

Walk down the road for about 250m, then turn off left along a forest track, shortly bearing left to gain height steadily on a wide path over **Carrickashane Mountain** (508m). Descend steeply to a wide forest road and continue down for about 1km. Bear right to reach a minor road and turn right. Leave the road 500m further on and drop down to another road – Iron Bridge is just to the right (an hour from Military Rd).

Walk 150m up to a road and turn left; follow this road down the valley of the River Ow for 7.5km to a junction – Aughrim is to the left, another 500m. Buses along the Dublin to Wexford line stop here.

reflect on more spiritual matters. In keeping with modern needs, however, there are a few more facilities than were present in Kevin's cave. Each hermitage is a bungalow consisting of a bedroom, a bathroom, a small kitchen area and an open fire supplemented by a storage heating facility. The whole venture is managed by the local parish, and while there is a strong spiritual emphasis here, it is not necessarily a Catholic one. Visitors of all denominations and creeds are welcome, so long as their intentions are reflective and meditative; backpackers looking for a cheap place to bed down are not. The hermitages are in a field next to St Kevin's Parish Church, about 1km east of Glendalough on the R756 to Laragh.

Glendale (☎ 0404-45410; www.glendale-glendalough.com; Laragh East; s/d €70/80, cottage per week €355–480; **P**) This is an immaculately modern and tidy B&B with large, comfortable rooms. Also available are five modern self-catering cottages that sleep six. Every cottage has all the mod cons, from TV and video to a fully equipped kitchen complete with microwave, dishwasher and washer-dryer. The owners will also drop you off in Glendalough if you don't fancy the walk.

Glendalough Hotel (☎ 0404-45135; www.glendaloughhotel.com; s/d €118/164; **P** 🖳) There's no mistaking Glendalough's best hotel, conveniently located next door to the visitor centre. There is no shortage of takers for its 44 fairly luxurious bedrooms.

EATING
Laragh's the place for a bit of grub, as there's only one sit-down spot in Glendalough.

During summer, villagers put out signs and serve tea and scones on the village green.

Glendalough Hotel (☎ 0404-45135; bar mains around €10, 3-course lunch €21; ☽ noon-6pm) The hotel's enormous restaurant serves a very good lunch of unsurprising dishes, usually involving some chicken, beef and fish. The bar menu – burgers, sandwiches, sausages and the like – is also quite filling.

Wicklow Heather Restaurant (☎ 0404-45157; www.thewicklowheather.com; Main St, Laragh; mains €16-26; ☽ noon-8.30pm) This is the best place for anything substantial. The menu offers Wicklow lamb, wild venison, Irish beef and fresh fish (the trout is excellent) – most of it sourced locally and all of it traceable from farm to fork.

GETTING THERE & AWAY
St Kevin's Bus (☎ 0404-481 8119; www.glendaloughbus.com) departs from outside the Mansion House on Dawson St in Dublin at 11.30am and 6pm Monday to Saturday, and 11.30am and 7pm Sunday (one way/return €13/20, 1½ hours). It also stops at the Town Hall in Bray. Departures from Glendalough are at 7.15am and 4.30pm Monday to Saturday. During the week in July and August the later bus runs at 5.30pm, and there is an additional service at 9.45am.

Glenmalure
As you go deeper into the mountains south-west of Glendalough near the southern end of the Military Rd, everything gets a bit wilder and more remote. Beneath the western slopes of Wicklow's highest peak, Lugnaquilla, is Glenmalure, a dark and sombre blind valley flanked by scree slopes of loose boulders. After coming over the mountains into Glenmalure you turn northwest at the Drumgoff bridge. From there it's about 6km up the road beside the River Avonbeg to a car park where trails lead off in various directions.

Glenmalure figures prominently in the national tale of resistance against the British. The valley was a clan stronghold, and in 1580 the redoubtable chieftain Fiach Mac Hugh O'Byrne (1544–97) and his band of merry men actually managed to defeat an army of 1000 English soldiers; the battle cost the lives of 800 men and drove Queen Elizabeth into an apoplectic rage. In 1597 the English avenged the disaster when they captured O'Byrne and impaled his head on the gates of Dublin Castle.

SIGHTS & ACTIVITIES
Near Drumgoff is Dwyer's or **Cullen's Rock**, which commemorates both the Glenmalure battle and Michael Dwyer, a member of the United Irishmen who fought unsuccessfully against the English in the Rising of 1798 (see also p38) and holed up here. Men were hanged from the rock during the Rising.

You can walk up Lugnaquilla Mountain or head up the blind Fraughan Rock Glen east of the car park. Alternatively, you can go straight up Glenmalure Valley passing the small, seasonal An Óige Glenmalure Hostel, after which the trail divides – heading northeast, the trail takes you over the hills to Glendalough, while going northwest brings you into the Glen of Imaal (p169).

TOP FIVE EATS IN WICKLOW

- **Campo de Fiori** (p171)
- **Ballyknocken House** (p173)
- **Tinakilly Country House & Restaurant** (p174)
- **Grangecon Café** (opposite)
- **Organic Life/Marc Michel** (p172)

The head of Glenmalure and parts of the neighbouring Glen of Imaal are off-limits. It's military land, well posted with warning signs.

SLEEPING

Glenmalure Hostel (☎ 01-830 4555; www.anoige.ie; Greenane; dm €15; Jun-Aug, Sat only Sep-May) No phone, no electricity (lighting is by gas), just a rustic two-storey cottage with 19 beds and running water. This place has a couple of heavyweight literary links: it was once owned by WB Yeats' femme fatale, Maud Gonne, and was also the setting for JM Synge's play, *Shadow of a Gunman*. It's an isolated place, but it is beautifully situated beneath Lugnaquilla.

Glenmalure Log Cabin (☎ 01-269 6979; www.glenmalure.com; 11 Glenmalure Pines, Greenane; 2 nights €200-290, 3 nights €350-550) In the heart of Glenmalure, this modern, Scandinavian-style lodge has two rooms with private bathrooms, a fully equipped kitchen and a living room kitted out with all kinds of electronic amusements, including your very own DVD library. Hopefully, though, you'll spend much of your time here enjoying the panorama from the sun deck. There's a two-night minimum stay, except for July and August when it's seven days.

Birchdale House (☎ 0404-46061; tmoylan@wicklowcoco.ie; Greenane; s/d €38/65) and **Woodside** (☎ 0404-43605; www.woodsideglenmalure.com; Greenane; s/d €50/80) are two comfortable, modern homes in Greenane, towards the southern end of the valley.

WESTERN WICKLOW

As you go west through the county, the landscape gets less rugged and more rural, especially towards the borders of Kildare and Carlow. The wild terrain gives way to rich pastures; east of Blessington the countryside is dotted with private stud farms where some of the world's most expensive horses are trained in jealously guarded secrecy.

The main attraction in this part of Wicklow is the magnificent Palladian pile at Russborough House, just outside Blessington but if it's more wild scenery you're after, you'll find it around Kilbride and the upper reaches of the River Liffey, as well as further south in the Glen of Imaal.

Blessington

pop 4018

There's little to see in Blessington; it's basically made up of a long row of pubs, shops and 17th- and 18th-century town houses. It's the main town in the area, and as such makes a decent exploring base. Just outside Blessington is the Poulaphouca Reservoir, created in 1940 to drive the turbines of the local power station to the east of town and to supply Dublin with water.

The **tourist office** (☎ 045-865 850; Blessington Craft Centre, Main St; 9.30am-4pm Mon-Fri) is across the road from the Downshire House Hotel.

SIGHTS

Magnificent **Russborough House** (☎ 045-865 239; www.russborough.ie; Blessington; adult/child/student €10/5/8; 10am-6pm May-Sep, Sun & bank holidays only Apr & Oct, closed rest of year) is one of Ireland's finest stately homes, a Palladian pleasure palace built for Joseph Leeson (1705–83), later the first Earl of Milltown and, later still, Lord Russborough. It was built between 1741 and 1751 to the design of Richard Cassels, who was at the height of his fame as an architect. Poor old Richard didn't live to see it finished, but the job was well executed by Francis Bindon. Now, let's get down to the juicy bits.

The house has always attracted unwelcome attention, beginning in 1798 when Irish forces took hold of the place during the Rising; they were soon turfed out by the British army who got so used to the comforts of the place that they didn't leave until 1801, and then only after a raging Lord Russborough challenged their commander, Lord Tyrawley, to a duel 'with blunderbusses and slugs in a sawpit'. Miaow.

The house remained in the Leeson family until 1931. In 1952 it was sold to Sir Alfred Beit, the eponymous nephew of the co-founder of the de Beers diamond-mining company. Uncle Alfred was an obsessive art collector, and when he died his impressive haul – which includes works by Velázquez, Vermeer, Goya and Rubens – was passed on to his nephew, who brought it to Russborough House. The collection was to attract the interest of more than just art lovers.

In 1974 the IRA decided to get into the art business by stealing 16 of the paintings. They were eventually all recovered, but 10 years later the notorious Dublin criminal Martin Cahill (aka the General) masterminded another robbery, this time for Loyalist paramilitaries. On this occasion, however, only some of the works were recovered and of those, several were damaged beyond repair – a good thief does not a gentle curator make. In 1988 Beit got the picture and decided to hand over the most valuable of the paintings to the National Gallery; in return for the gift, the gallery agreed to lend other paintings to the collection as temporary exhibits. The sorry story didn't conclude there. In 2001 two thieves took the direct approach and drove a jeep through the front doors, making off with two paintings worth nearly €4 million, including a Gainsborough that had been stolen, and recovered, twice before. And then, to add abuse to the insult already added to injury, the house was broken into again in 2002, with the thieves taking five more paintings, including two by Rubens. Incredibly, however, both hauls were quickly recovered.

The admission price includes a 45-minute tour of the house, which is decorated in typical Georgian style, and all the important paintings, which, given the history, is a monumental exercise in staying positive. Whatever you do, make no sudden moves.

ACTIVITIES

Rathsallagh Golf Club (☎ 045-403 316; www.rathsallaghhousehotel.com; green fees hotel guest/visitor from €60/65) is known – somewhat optimistically – as 'Augusta without the Azelias', but it is still one of the best parkland courses in Ireland, stretching over 6.5km amid mature trees, small lakes and shallow streams.

SLEEPING & EATING

Haylands House (☎ 045-865 183; haylands@eircom.net; Dublin Rd; s/d from €40/70; P) We highly recommend this modern bungalow for its lovely rooms (all with en-suite bathrooms), warm welcome and excellent breakfast. It's only 500m out of town on the main Dublin road. As it's popular, book early if you can.

our pick **Rathsallagh House & Country Club** (☎ 045-403 112; www.rathsallaghhousehotel.com; Dunlavin; mains €33-42, s/d from €135/260) About 20km south of Blessington, this fabulous country manor, converted from Queen Anne stables in 1798, is more than just a fancy hotel. Luxury is par for the course here, from the splendidly appointed rooms to the exquisite country-house dining (the food here is some of the best you'll eat anywhere in Ireland) and the marvellous golf course that surrounds the estate. Even the breakfast is extraordinary: it has won the National Breakfast Award three times. Is there anything Irish tourism doesn't have an award for?

Grangecon Café (☎ 045-857 892; Tullow Rd; mains €11-18; 10am-5pm Tue-Sat) Salads, home-baked dishes and a full menu of Irish cheeses are the staples at this tiny, terrific cafe in a converted schoolhouse. Everything here – from the pasta to the delicious apple juice – is made on the premises and many of the ingredients are organic. A short but solid menu represents the best of Irish cooking.

Russborough House hosts a monthly **farmers market** (☎ 087-611 5016; 10am-4pm, first Sun of the month) that goes indoors during the winter months.

GETTING THERE & AWAY

Blessington is 35km southwest of Dublin on the N81. There are regular daily services by **Dublin Bus** (☎ 01-872 0000, 01-873 4222); catch bus 65 from Eden Quay in Dublin (€4.50, 1½ hours, every 1½ hours). **Bus Éireann** (☎ 01-836 6111; www.buseireann.ie) operates express bus 005 to and from Waterford, with stops in Blessington two or three times daily; from Dublin it's pick-up only, and from Waterford drop-off only.

Glen of Imaal

About 7km southeast of Donard, the lovely Glen of Imaal is about the only scenery of consequence on the western flanks of the Wicklow Mountains. It's named after Mal, brother of the 2nd-century king of Ireland, Cathal Mór. Unfortunately, the glen's northeastern slopes are mostly cordoned off as an army firing range and for manoeuvres. Look out for red danger signs.

The area's most famous son was Michael Dwyer, who led rebel forces during the 1798 Rising and held out for five years in the local hills and glens. On the southeastern side of the glen at Derrynamuck is a small whitewashed, thatched cottage where Dwyer and three friends were surrounded by 100 English soldiers. One of Dwyer's companions, Samuel McAllister, ran out the front, drawing fire and meeting his death, while Dwyer escaped into the night. He was eventually deported in 1803 and jailed on Norfolk Island, off the eastern coast of Australia. He became chief constable of Liverpool, near Sydney, before he died in 1825. The cottage is now a small **folk museum** (☎ 0404-45325; Derrynamuck; admission free; ⏰ 2-6pm mid-Jun–Sep) located on the Knockanarrigan–Rathdangan road.

THE COAST

Wicklow's coastline is not nearly as scenic or dramatic as its mountains and inland marvels: its largely unassuming towns and small coastal resorts have a subtle kind of charm that isn't immediately apparent and virtually disappears on a rainy day. Most attractive of all are the fine beaches of Brittas Bay, a wide lazy arc of coastline between Wicklow and Arklow. Running alongside it is the N11 (M11) from Dublin to Wexford, a busy road that cuts through a great glacial rift, the **Glen of the Downs**, carved out of an Ice Age lake by floodwaters. There's a forest walk up to a ruined teahouse on top of the ridge to the east. If you're looking for quieter and more scenic coastal byways, we recommend the coastal route through Greystones, Kilcoole and then along country lanes to Rathnew.

Bray
pop 27,041

Described in its 19th-century heyday as the 'Irish Brighton', Bray's genteel, Victorian charms may have faded, but there is more to this seaside resort than the amusement arcades and ice-cream vans that have fuelled the desperate needs of many an Irish child over the decades. The handsome promenade and wide beach are great for an afternoon stroll, while its proximity to Dublin on the DART line means that there's no reason to overnight here. There's also a great scenic walk from here south to Greystones.

INFORMATION

The **tourist office** (☎ 01-286 7128, 01-286 6796; www.braytourism.ie; h9.30am-1pm & 2-5pm Mon-Sat Jun-Sep, 2-4.30pm Oct-May) is in the courthouse (built in 1841) beside the Royal Hotel at the bottom of Main St.

SIGHTS

Top of the pretty small heap is the **heritage centre** (☎ 01-286 7128; Old Courthouse; admission €3; ⏰ 9am-5pm Mon-Fri, 10am-3pm Sat) above the tour-

ist office, where you can explore Bray's 1000-year history and examine the lengths to which engineer William Dargan (1799–1867) went to bring the railroad to Bray. Your kids will hate you for it.

You can make it up to them at the **National Sealife Centre** (☎ 01-286 6939; www.sealifeeurope.com; Strand Rd; adult/child €10.95/7.50; ⏰ 11am-5pm Mon-Sat, from 10am Sun). The British-run aquarium has a fairly big selection of tanks, stocked with 70 different sea and freshwater species.

About 3km south of Bray on the Greystones road are **Killruddery House & Gardens** (☎ 01-286 3405; www.killruddery.com; Killruddery; house & gardens adult/child €10/3, gardens only €6/2; ⏰ 1-5pm May, Jun & Sep). A stunning mansion in the Elizabethan Revival style, Killruddery has been home to the Brabazon family (earls of Meath) since 1618 and has one of the oldest gardens in Ireland. The house, designed by trendy 19th-century architects Richard Morrisson and his son William in 1820, was *reduced* to its present-day huge proportions by the 14th earl in 1953; he was obviously looking for something a little more bijou. The house is impressive, but the prizewinner here is the magnificent orangery, built in 1852 and chock-full of statuary and plant life. If you like fancy glasshouses, this is the one for you. The TV series *The Tudors*, starring Jonathan Rhys Meyers, is filmed here.

ACTIVITIES

One of the most beautiful **coastal walks** in Wicklow stretches from the southern end of Bray's promenade over Bray Head and down to the tiny commuter town of Greystones, 7km further south. The path is pretty smooth and easy to follow, but you can make a detour and clamber up **Bray Head** (240m) through the pine trees all the way to the large cross, erected in 1950. The head is full of old smuggling caves and railway tunnels, including one that's 1.5km long. From the top, there are fine views of the Great Sugarloaf Mountain. Back on the coastal path, you approach Greystones via a narrow footbridge over the railway, after which the path narrows until you hit the lovely harbour in Greystones. Here you should relax in **Byrne's** (Greystones Pier), better known as Dan's, which serves a gorgeous pint.

FESTIVALS

The **Bray Jazz Festival** (www.brayjazz.com) brings some pretty decent players to the seaside town over the May Bank Holiday – the first weekend of the month.

EATING

The weekly **farmers market** (☎ 087-957 3647; ✹ 11am-3pm Sat) takes place in front of the heritage centre.

Campo de Fiori (☎ 01-276 4257; 1 Albert Ave; mains €15-25; ✹ 5-10.30pm Mon-Tue & Fri & Sat, 2-9pm Sun) One of the best Italian restaurants along the eastern seaboard, everything here has the flavour of authenticity, from the homemade breads and dipping oils to the complimentary shot of *limoncello* liqueur with the bill.

Barracuda (☎ 01-276 5686; www.barracuda.ie; Strand Rd; mains €19-25; ✹ noon-9pm) When you've had your fill of live sea creatures in the National Sealife Centre, head upstairs to this minimalist, metal-and-mirrors restaurant and see what happens to Nemo when a really good chef gets his hands on him…or not. For your newly found love of the sea and all its inhabitants, there's always a good steak.

DRINKING & ENTERTAINMENT

Harbour Bar (☎ 01-286 2274; Seapoint Rd) A strong contender for Ireland's best pub, here you can enjoy an excellent pint of Guinness in a quiet atmosphere of conviviality. There is a separate lounge with velvet curtains, assorted paintings and cosy couches. Sundays see the gay and lesbian community chill to some terrific DJs.

Clancy's Bar (☎ 01-286 3191; Quinnsboro Rd) A real spit-and-sawdust kind of place with a clientele as old as the wood in the bar; it's perfect for a quiet pint and a chat.

Porterhouse (☎ 01-286 0668; Strand Rd) The Bray branch of one of Temple Bar's most popular pubs, this equally popular watering hole does a roaring trade in beers from around the world as well as its own selection of intoxicating brews.

Mermaid Art Centre (☎ 01-272 4030; Main St; admission free; ✹ 10am-6pm Mon-Sat) An art gallery, theatre and cinema. The theatre puts on excellent gigs and modern, experimental-style plays, while the cinema shows art-house movies almost exclusively. Call to check prices. The art gallery has constantly changing exhibitions featuring the latest Irish and European works.

GETTING THERE & AWAY

With the **Dublin Bus** (☎ 01-872 0000) service, buses 45 (from Hawkins St) and 84 (from Burgh Quay) serve Bray (one way €2.50, one hour).

St Kevin's Bus (☎ 01-281 8119; www.glendaloughbus .com) to Dublin departs from Bray Town Hall (€2.50, 50 minutes) at 8am and 5pm Monday to Friday, 10.30am and 5pm Saturday, and 10.30am and 6.30pm Sunday. From Dublin, buses depart from in front of the Mansion House on Dawson St.

Bray train station (☎ 01-236 3333) is 500m east of Main St just before the seafront. The DART (one way €3.50, 30 minutes) runs into Dublin and further north to Howth every five minutes at peak times and every 20 or 30 minutes at quiet times.

The station is also on the main line from Dublin to Wexford and Rosslare Harbour, with up to five trains daily in each direction Monday to Saturday, and four on Sunday.

Kilmacanogue & the Great Sugarloaf
pop 839

At 503m, it's not even Wicklow's highest mountain, but the Great Sugarloaf is one of the most distinctive peaks in Ireland, its conical tip visible for many miles around. The mountain towers over the small village of Kilmacanogue, on the N11 about 4km south of Bray, which would barely merit a passing nod were it not for the presence of the mother of all Irish craft shops just across the road from the village.

Avoca Handweavers (☎ 01-286 7466; www.avoca.ie; Main St) is one hell of an operation, with seven branches nationwide and an even more widespread reputation for adding elegance and style to traditional rural handicrafts. Operational HQ is in a 19th-century arboretum, and its showroom will leave you in no doubt as to the company's incredible success.

Shopping for pashminas and placemats can put a fierce hunger on you, and there's no better place to satisfy it than at the shop's huge and always-busy **restaurant** (mains €12-18; ✹ 9.30am-5.30pm), which puts a premium on sourcing the very best ingredients for its dishes. It is best known for its beef-and-Guinness casserole, but vegetarians are very well catered for as well. Many of the recipes are available in the two volumes of the *Avoca Cookbook*, both on sale for €45 for two.

Bus Éireann (☎ 01-836 6111; www.buseireann.ie) operates bus 133 from Dublin to Wicklow town and Arklow, with stops in Kilmacanogue (one way/return €3.60/5.80, 30 minutes, 10 daily).

WALK: THE GREAT SUGARLOAF

Before you attack the 7km, moderately difficult walk to the summit, we recommend that you get the *Wicklow Trail Sheet No 4* (€1.50) from the tourist office in Bray.

Start your walk by taking the small road opposite **St Mochonog's Church** (named after the missionary who administered the last rites to St Kevin). Ignore the left turn and continue round the bend until you get to a small bridge on your right. To your right, you'll see the expanse of the **Rocky Valley** below, a defile eroded by water escaping from a glacial lake that developed during the last Ice Age, about 10,000 years ago. Continue on the path until you reach a fork: the lower road to the right continues round the mountain, while the left turn will take you up to the summit. As you reach the top, the track starts to drop; turn left and scramble up the rocky gully to the top. Return by the same path and continue southwards until you reach a large grassy area. Cross it, keeping to your left until you reach a gate. With the fence on your right, go downhill until you reach a path of grass and stones. This path takes you around the southern side of the mountain, where you will eventually pass a small wood on your right. Immediately afterwards you will see, on your left, a sports pitch known as the Quill. Beyond it is Kilmacanogue.

Greystones to Wicklow

The resort of Greystones, 8km south of Bray, was once a charming fishing village, and the seafront around the little harbour is idyllic. In summer, the bay is dotted with dinghies and windsurfers. Sadly, the surrounding countryside is vanishing beneath housing developments.

SIGHTS

Horticulturalists from around the world can be found salivating and muttering in approval as they walk around the 8-hectare **Mt Usher Gardens** (☎ 0404-40116; www.mountusher gardens.ie; adult/child/student €7.50/3/6; ⌚ 10.30am-6pm mid-Apr–Oct), just outside the unremarkable town of Ashford, about 10km south of Greystones on the N11. OK, not really, but the gardens are pretty special, with trees, shrubs and herbaceous plants from around the world laid out in Robinsonian style – ie according to the naturalist principles of famous Irish gardener William Robinson (1838–1935) – rather than the formalist style of preceding gardens.

SLEEPING

Hunter's Hotel (☎ 0404-40106; www.hunters.ie; Newrath Bridge, Rathnew; s/d €95/190; **P**) This exquisite property just outside Rathnew on the R761 is an absolute find, with 16 stunning rooms, each decorated with unerringly good taste. The house, one of Ireland's oldest coaching inns, is surrounded by an award-winning garden that is part of the Wicklow Gardens Festival (see the boxed text, p175).

EATING

Three Q's (☎ 01-287 5477; Church Rd; mains €14-20; ⌚ 9am-10pm Tue-Fri, to 3pm Sat & Sun) You'll find a smart menu at this elegant restaurant, with dishes like wood pigeon and duck sharing the space with North African delicacies like baked Moroccan fish with chickpeas, tomato and coriander.

our pick **Organic Life/Marc Michel** (☎ 01-201 1882; Tinna Park, Kilpedder; mains around €17; ⌚ 10am-5pm, restaurant noon-4pm) Our favourite spot in all of Wicklow is this superb organic restaurant attached to the Organic Life shop in the town of Kilpedder, about 2km south of the Greystones turnoff on the N11. All of the vegetables are grown in the fields surrounding you (Ireland's first organically certified farm), while the beef served in the superb burger is bought from a local cattle rancher. The sole pity is that it's only open for lunch.

Hungry Monk (☎ 01-287 5759; Church Rd; mains €19-27; ⌚ 7-11pm Wed-Sat, 12.30-9pm Sun) An excellent 1st-floor restaurant on Greystones' main street. The blackboard specials are the real treat, with dishes like suckling pig with prune and apricot stuffing to complement the fixed menu's classic choices – fresh seafood, Wicklow rack of lamb, bangers 'n' mash and so forth. This is one of the better places to get a bite along the whole of the Wicklow coast.

GETTING THERE & AWAY

Bus Éireann (☎ 01-836 6111; www.buseireann.ie) operates bus 133 from Dublin to Wicklow town and Arklow with stops outside Ashford House, in Ashford (one way/return €5.50/7.90, one hour, 10 daily).

Wicklow Town
pop 6930

Busy Wicklow town has a fine harbour and a commanding position on the crescent curve of a wide bay, which stretches north for about 12km and includes a long pebble beach that makes for a fine walk. One top-notch attraction aside, this is not really a big tourist town and, unless you have your own transport, it doesn't make an especially good base for exploring inland.

The **tourist office** (☎ 0404-69117; www.wicklow.ie; Fitzwilliam Sq; 🕑 9.30am-6pm Jun-Sep, 9am-1pm & 2-5pm Oct-May, closed Sun) is in the heart of town.

SIGHTS
Wicklow's Historic Gaol

Wicklow's infamous **jail** (☎ 0404-61599; www .wicklowshistoricgaol.com; Kilmantin Hill; adult/child/student incl tour €7.30/4.50/6; 🕑 10.30am-4.30pm Mon-Sat, from 11.30am Sun, Apr-Oct), opened in 1702 to deal with prisoners sentenced under the repressive Penal Laws, was renowned throughout Ireland for the brutality of its keepers and the harsh conditions suffered by its inmates. The smells, vicious beatings, shocking food and disease-ridden air have long since gone, but adults and children alike can experience a sanitised version of what the prison was like – and stimulate the secret sadist buried deep within – in the highly entertaining tour of the prison, now one of Wicklow's most popular tourist attractions. Actors play the roles of the various jailers and prisoners, adding to the sense of drama already heightened by the various exhibits on show, including a life-size treadmill that prisoners would have to turn for hours on end as punishment, and the gruesome dungeon.

On the 2nd floor is a model of HMS *Hercules*, a convict ship that was used to transport convicts to New South Wales under the captaincy of the psychotic Luckyn Betts: six months under his iron rule and most began to see death as a form of mercy. The top floor is devoted to the stories of the prisoners once they arrived in Australia. Tours are every 10 minutes except between 1pm and 2pm; on the last Friday of every month there are **adult-only tours** (🕑 every 30 min, 7-9pm; €25) of the prison, complete with ghouls, finger food and a glass of wine.

Other Sights

The few remaining fragments of the **Black Castle** are on the shore at the southern end of town, with pleasant views up and down the coast. The castle was built in 1169 by the Fitzgeralds from Wales after they were granted land in the area by the Anglo-Norman conqueror, Strongbow. It used to be linked to the mainland by a drawbridge, and rumour has it that an escape tunnel ran from the sea cave underneath up into the town. At low tide you can swim or snorkel into the cave.

The walk south of town along the cliffs to **Wicklow Head** offers great views of the Wicklow Mountains. A string of **beaches** – Silver Strand, Brittas Bay and Maheramore – start 16km south of Wicklow. With high dunes, safe bathing and powdery sand, the beaches attract droves of Dubliners in good weather.

FESTIVALS

In mid-May, the **Wicklow Arts Festival** (☎ 086-033 3906; www.wicklowartsfestival.ie) is a five-day extravaganza of music, poetry, comedy and workshops that usually takes place over the two middle weekends of the month.

The long-established **Wicklow Regatta Festival** (☎ 0404-68354; www.wicklowregatta.com) is held every year for 10 days from late July into early August. The extensive program of events and activities includes swimming, rowing, sailing

---

DETOUR: BALLYKNOCKEN HOUSE

As fine a country home as you could ever hope to find, **Ballyknocken House & Cookery School** (☎ 0404-69274; www.ballyknocken.com; Glenealy, Ashford; s/d from €69/118, 3/4-course dinner €35/45) is a beautiful ivy-clad Victorian home, 5km south of Ashford on the R752 to Glenealy. Each of the bedrooms is carefully appointed with original furnishings and have en-suite bathrooms, some with stencilled Victorian claw-foot tubs, which lends the whole place an air of timeless elegance that is becoming increasingly difficult to find. The old milking parlour on the farm grounds has been converted into a tidy two-bedroom loft that sleeps up to six people. Besides the home itself, the big draw is Catherine Fulvio's **cooking classes** (€110), which run throughout the year; check the website for details.

and raft races, singing competitions, concerts and the Festival Queen Ball.

SLEEPING & EATING

Town lodgings are not that great, but if you are planning on staying in the area, you're better off staying in one of the beautiful country homes within a few kilometres of town.

Grand Hotel (☎ 0404-67337; www.grandhotel.ie; Abbey St; s/d from €80/130; **P**) Wicklow town's best accommodation is this mock-Tudor hotel that is quite a bit short of 'grand', but it's a handsome, comfortable place nonetheless. The rooms are immaculate, and the smallish size of the place assures a personalised, friendly service.

Leitrim Bar & Lounge (☎ 0404-67443; www.leitrim lounge.com; 15 Leitrim Pl; mains €12-20; ⊙ 12.30-8.30pm) Above-par bar food with a bit of imagination is the staple at this old-fashioned public house in the middle of town. Burgers, steaks and sandwiches are there, but you'll also find some Asian-influenced stir-fries and duck dishes.

Donelli's (☎ 0404-61333; www.donellis.ie; Market Sq; mains €17-20; ⊙ 9am-4pm Mon-Wed, to midnight Thu-Sat) From great coffee and cakes to an excellent menu of inviting dishes – including the likes of Penang chicken, vegetarian curry and Asian marinated salmon – this is a wonderful place to eat or linger in.

The town hosts a weekly **farmers market** (⊙ 10am-3pm Sat) on Market Square, just off Main St.

GETTING THERE & AROUND

Bus Éireann (☎ 01-836 6111; www.buseireann.ie) runs bus 133, serving Wicklow town from Dublin (€7.90, 1½ hours, 10 daily); Wicklow town is also served by express bus 2 running between Dublin (one hour, 12 daily) and Rosslare Harbour (11/2 hours, €15.80).

Iarnród Éireann (Irish Rail; ☎ 01-836 6222) serves Wicklow town from Dublin on the main Dublin to Rosslare Harbour line (one way/return €13/16, one hour, five daily). The station is a 10-minute walk north of the town centre.

Wicklow Cabs (☎ 0404-66888; Main St) usually sends a few cabs to meet the evening trains from Dublin. The fare to anywhere in town should be no more than €6.

SOUTHERN WICKLOW

South of Wicklow town, the landscape gives way to rolling hills and valleys cut through by rustling rivers and dotted with lovely little hamlets, including the especially beautiful Vale of Avoca, favoured by song and busloads of tourists.

Rathdrum
pop 2123

The quiet village of Rathdrum at the foot of the Vale of Clara comprises little more than a few old houses and shops, but in the late 19th century it had a healthy flannel industry and a poorhouse. It's not what's in the town that's of interest to visitors, however, but what's just outside it.

The small **tourist office** (☎ 0404-46262; 29 Main St; ⊙ 9am-5.30pm Mon-Fri) has leaflets and information on the town and surrounding area, including the Wicklow Way.

SIGHTS

> Woe be to the man by whom the scandal cometh…It would be better for him that a millstone were tied about his neck and that he were cast into the depth of the sea rather than he should scandalise one of these, my least little ones.
> *James Joyce, A Portrait of the Artist as a Young Man*

Joyce's fictional dinner-table argument wasn't about a murderer or any such criminal, but about Charles Stewart Parnell (1846–91), the

---

DETOUR: TINAKILLY COUNTRY HOUSE & RESTAURANT

Wicklow has no shortage of fine country homes converted into luxury manor hotels, but **Tinakilly Country House & Restaurant** (☎ 0404-69274; www.tinakilly.ie; Rathnew; s/d from €150/300, dinner mains €14-22), a magnificent Victorian Italianate house just outside Rathnew (about 5km west of Wicklow town) stands out for sheer elegance. The guest rooms are divided between the period rooms in the west wing, decked out in original antiques, four-poster and half-tester canopy beds; and the shockingly sumptuous suites in the east wing, which have gorgeous views of either the richly colourful garden or the Irish Sea, albeit somewhere in the distance. And then there's the restaurant, which takes country-house cuisine to a whole new level of sophistication.

WICKLOW GARDENS FESTIVAL

More than 40 private and public gardens participate in the yearly **Wicklow Gardens Festival** (☎ 20070; www.visitwicklow.ie), which runs from Easter roughly through to the end of August. The obvious advantage for green thumbs and other garden enthusiasts is access to beautiful gardens that would ordinarily be closed to the public. Some of the larger gardens are open throughout the festival, while other smaller ones open only at specific times; call or check the website for details of entrants, openings and special events, including all manner of horticultural courses.

'uncrowned king of Ireland' and unquestionably one of the key figures in the Irish independence movement. **Avondale House**, a marvellous 209-hectare estate, dominated by a fine Palladian **mansion** (☎ 0404-46111; adult/student & child €6.50/6; 🕐 11am-6pm May-Aug, Sat & Sun only Apr, by appointment only rest of year), designed by James Wyatt in 1779, was his birthplace and Irish headquarters. Of the house's many highlights, the most impressive are the stunning vermilion-hued library (Parnell's favourite room) and beautiful dining room.

From 1880 to 1890 Avondale was synonymous with the fight for Home Rule, which was brilliantly led by Parnell until 1890, when a member of his own Irish Parliamentary Party, Captain William O'Shea, sued his wife Kitty for divorce and named Parnell as co-respondent. Parnell's affair with Kitty O'Shea scandalised this 'priest-ridden' nation, and the ultraconservative clergy declared that Parnell was 'unfit to lead' – despite the fact that as soon as the divorce was granted the two lovers were quickly married. Parnell resigned as leader of the party and withdrew in despair to Avondale, where he died the following year.

Surrounding the house are 200 hectares of forest and parkland, where the first silvicultural experiments by the Irish Forestry Service (Coillte) were conceived, after the purchase of the house by the state in 1904. These plots, about half a hectare in size, are still visible today, flanking what many consider to be the best of Avondale's many walking trails, the Great Ride. You can visit the park during daylight hours year-round.

SLEEPING & EATING

Old Presbytery Hostel (☎ 0404-46930; www.hostels-ireland.com; The Fairgreen, Rathdrum; dm/d €18/48; P) A modern, centrally located IHH hostel that looks more like campus accommodation. There is a mix of large, comfy dorms and well-appointed doubles with en-suite bathrooms, as well as family rooms. A laundry and a TV room round off the facilities. You can also camp in the grounds.

our pick **Brook Lodge & Wells Spa** (☎ 0402-36444; www.brooklodge.com; Macreddin; r/ste from €260/330; P wi-fi) The favourite chill-out spot for Dublin's high-flyers is this luxurious country house about 3km west of Rathdrum in the village of Macreddin. The 39 standard rooms set a pretty high tone, with four-poster and sleigh beds dressed in crisp Frette linen. But the suites sing an altogether more harmonious tune, each a minimalist marvel that wouldn't seem out of place in a New York boutique hotel – massive beds, flat-screen plasma TVs, top-of-the-range sound system and every other style sundry. The accommodation is pure luxury, but it's the outstanding spa that keeps guests coming back for more. Mud and flotation chambers, Finnish and aroma baths, *hammam* (Turkish bath) massages and a full range of Decléor and Carita treatments make this one of the top spas in the country. Your credit card will never have nestled in softer hands.

The village hosts an **organic market** (🕐 10am-5pm Sun, Apr-Oct) on the first Sunday of the month during the summer months.

GETTING THERE & AWAY

Bus Éireann (☎ 01-836 6111; www.buseireann.ie) service 133 goes to Rathdrum from Dublin (one way/return €6.90/9.50, 1¾ hours, 10 daily) on its way to Arklow.

Iarnród Éireann (☎ 01-836 6222) serves Rathdrum from Dublin on the main Dublin to Rosslare Harbour line (one way/return €15.50/19.50, 11/2 hours, five daily).

Vale of Avoca

In summer, tour buses and other interested parties clog the road through the scenic Vale of Avoca on their way to the renowned mills in the eponymous village. En route, tourists *ooh* and *aah* at the gorgeous scenery of the darkly wooded valley that begins where the Rivers Avonbeg and Avonmore come together to form the River Avoca. This is a lovely spot suitably named the **Meeting of the Waters**, made famous by Thomas Moore's 1808 poem of the same name.

The Meeting of the Waters is marked by a pub called the **Meetings** (☎ 0402-35226; www .themeetingsavoca.com; ☽ noon-9pm), which serves food (mains €10 to €15) and has music at weekends year-round. There are *céilidh* (traditional music and dancing sessions) between 4pm and 6pm Sunday, April to October. There's also a guesthouse attached (known as Robin's Nest) with decent, clean rooms (single/double €45/75). Buses to Avoca from Dublin stop at the Meetings, or you can walk from Avoca, 3km south of here.

Avoca
pop 570
The tiny village of Avoca (Abhóca) still trades on being the setting for the now-defunct BBC TV series *Ballykissangel*, but the main reason to visit is to amble about – and hopefully spend loads of money in – the birthplace of the superstar of all Irish cottage industries, **Avoca Handweavers** (☎ 35105; www.avoca.ie; Old Mill, Main St; ☽ 9am-6pm May-Sep, 9.30am-5.30pm Oct-Apr), housed in Ireland's oldest working mill.

It's been turning out linens, wools and other fabrics since 1723, and much of Avoca's much-admired line is produced here. You are free to wander in and out of the weaving sheds.

Just in case you might want some local info, the **tourist office** (☎ 0402-35022; Old Courthouse; ☽ 10am-5pm Mon-Sat) is in the library.

SLEEPING
River Valley Park (☎ 0402-41647; www.rivervalleypark .com; campsites €12, mobile homes €330-620) This well-equipped campsite is about 1km south of the village of Redcross, 7km northeast of Avoca on the R754 country road. It has mobile homes for rent that sleep up to six, and also includes a Secret Garden on the grounds for adults only.

Koliba (☎ /fax 0402-32737; www.koliba.com; Beech Rd; s/d €52/75; ☽ Apr-Oct) A thoroughly modern bungalow with comfortable, well-appointed rooms (all with en-suite bathrooms). Koliba is 3km out of Avoca on the Arklow road.

our pick **Sheepwalk House & Cottages** (☎ 0402-35189; www.sheepwalk.com; Arklow Rd; s/d €60/80, cottages per week €250-660) Built in 1727 for the Earl of Wicklow, this is our favourite place to stay in Avoca (although it's 2km out of town). The main house is splendid, with beautifully appointed rooms, while the converted out-

buildings – complete with beamed ceilings, fireplaces and flagstone floors – are a wonderful option for groups of four or six.

GETTING THERE & AWAY
Bus Éireann (☎ 01-836 6111; www.buseireann.ie) operates bus 133 from Dublin, which serves Avoca via Bray, Wicklow and Rathdrum on its way to Arklow (one way/return €10.60/14.20, two hours, 10 daily).

ARKLOW
pop 9955
Wicklow's biggest and busiest town is a thriving commercial centre built around what was once an important local port. Although this may not inspire you to change route and come here, chances are if you're in this part of the county you'll probably end up here anyway. There's a local belief that the town is included in Ptolemy's 2nd-century map of Europe, but what is absolutely verifiable is that Sir Francis Chichester's prize-winning transatlantic yacht *Gypsy Moth III* was built here.

The town's seafaring past is explored in the small **maritime museum** (☎ 0402-32868; St Mary's Rd; admission €3; ☽ 10am-1pm & 2-5pm Mon-Sat May-Sep, closed Sat rest of year), which features a model of the *Titanic*, some salvaged items from the *Lusitania* and an extraordinary model of a ship – made from 10,000 matchsticks.

For all other info, there's the **tourist office** (☎ 0402-32484; www.arklow.ie; ☽ 9.30am-1pm Mon-Sat Jun-Sep) in the Coach House.

There is a white, sandy beach, but it lies between the docks and a gravel plant; you're better off heading 10km north to **Brittas Bay** or 7km south to the more sheltered **Clogga Beach**.

Sleeping & Eating
Plattenstown House (☎ /fax 0402-37822; Coolgreany Rd; s/d €49/98; **P**) This gorgeous traditional farmhouse is set in 50 acres of land about 5km south of town. Family antiques throughout this elegant 19th-century home, great views of the lovingly tended gardens and comfortable, well-appointed rooms make this place a terrific choice in the area.

Arklow Bay Hotel (☎ 0402-32309; www.arklowbay .com; Sea Rd; r from €69; **P** ☽ ☐) This relatively modern place is the biggest hotel in town and comes with all of the facilities you'd expect from a business hotel, including a conference centre, spa and swimming pool.

Otherwise, there's a fairly broad range f decent B&Bs, each offering comfortable ooms and a decent breakfast. Try **Pinebrook** ☎ 0402-31527; www.pinebrook.net; Ticknock Close, Briggs a; s/d €45/80; **P**).

Kitty's of Arklow (☎ 0402-31669; Main St; lunch €9-17, nner €23-26; ☒ noon-5pm & 6-10.30pm) An Arklow nstitution, Kitty's serves a great version of he usual bar food choices during the day – rom beef burgers to fillets of plaice – while he evening menu tackles some exciting sea-ood dishes and an impressive range of meat ishes. It's not new cuisine, but it's a fine take n the classics.

Jay K's (☎ 0402-32253; Main St; mains €8-13; ☒ noon-.30pm) The best pub in town for a decent meal, ay K's (*not* named after Jamiroquai's front nan) serves up good steaks, chicken dinners nd tasty salads.

ietting There & Away

Bus Éireann (☎ 01-836 6111; www.buseireann.ie) oper-tes bus 133 from Dublin, which serves Avoca ia Bray, Wicklow and Rathdrum on its way o Arklow (one way/return €12.20/16.20, 2¼ ours, 10 daily); Arklow is also served by xpress bus 2 between Dublin and Rosslare Iarbour (one way/return €14.90/20.70, 1½ ours, 12 daily). All buses stop outside the Chocolate Shop.

Iarnród Éireann (☎ 01-836 6222) serves Arklow rom Dublin (one way/return €15.20/18.50, ¼ hours, five daily) on the Arrow suburban ine as well as by Intercity train to Rosslare Iarbour – the price is the same no matter vhich train you take.

COUNTY KILDARE

Once a backwater from Dublin, the lush green pastures of County Kildare (Cill Dara) are prime suburbia, and charming towns like Maynooth and Kildare have become com-muter bedrooms, a reality reflected in the ever-expanding motorway network that seeks to ease the traffic burden.

Still, the county has some of the best farmland in Ireland and is home to some of the country's most prestigious stud farms, many surrounding the sweeping grasslands of the Curragh. The northwest of the county is dominated by a vast swathe of bog. The county isn't especially stuffed with must-see attractions, but there are enough diversions

to justify a day trip from the capital or a stop on your way out west.

MAYNOOTH
pop 10,715

Much of Maynooth's (Maigh Nuad) life comes from the university (National University of Ireland Maynooth; NUIM), which gives this tree-lined town with stone-fronted houses and shops a dynamism that belies its country-town appearance. It's within easy reach of Dublin by public transport, thanks as much to the university as to the legions of barristers and other swells who make the town their home.

Orientation & Information

Main St and Leinster St join and run east–west, while Parson St runs south to the canal and the train station (accessed via a couple of footbridges), and Straffan Rd runs south to the M4.

Sights
ST PATRICK'S COLLEGE

Turning out Catholic priests since 1795, **St Patrick's College & Seminary** (☎ 01-628 5222; www .maynoothcollege.ie; Main St) was founded to ensure that aspiring priests wouldn't skip off to semi-nary school in France and get infected with strains of republicanism and revolution. It be-came a Pontifical University in 1898 (granting control of the college's theological courses to the Holy See) but in 1910 it joined the newly established National University of Ireland (NUI), which governed the university's non-theological studies. Nevertheless, the student body remained exclusively clerical until 1966, when lay students were finally admitted. A restructuring of the NUI in 1997 made St Patrick's College independent of the bigger university, which now has more than 6500 students; there are only a few dozen studying for the priesthood.

The college buildings are impressive – Gothic architect Augustus Pugin had a hand in designing them – and well worth an hour's ramble. You enter the college via Georgian Stoyte House, where the **accommodation office** (☎ 01-708 3576; ☒ 8.30am-5.30pm & 8-11pm Mon-Fri, 8.30am-12.30pm & 1.30-11pm Sat & Sun) sells booklets (€4.50) for guiding yourself around. In sum-mer there's also a **visitor centre** (☒ 11am-5pm Mon-Fri, 2-6pm Sat & Sun May-Sep) and a small **science museum** (admission by donation; ☒ 2-4pm Tue & Thu, to 6pm Sun May-Sep). The college grounds contain a number of lofty Georgian and neo-Gothic buildings, gardens and squares, but the highlight of the tour has to be the **College Chapel**. Pull open the squeaky door and you enter the world's largest choir chapel, with stalls for more than 450 choristers and some magnificent ornamentation.

MAYNOOTH CASTLE

Near the entrance to St Patrick's College you can see the ruined gatehouse, keep and great hall of 13th-century **Maynooth Castle** (☎ 01-628 6744; admission free; ⏰ 10am-6pm Mon-Fri, 1-6pm Sat & Sun Jun-Sep, 1-5pm Sun Oct), home of the Fitzgerald family. The castle was dismantled in Cromwellian times, when the Fitzgeralds moved to Kilkea Castle (p185). Entry is by a 45-minute guided tour only; there's a small exhibition on the castle's history in the keep.

Activities
CANOEING

Leixlip, on the River Liffey between Maynooth and Dublin, is an important **canoeing** centre and the starting point of the annual 28km **International Liffey Descent Race** (www.liffeydescent .com). Usually held in early September, the race attracts more than 1000 competitors. For more information on canoeing in Ireland, try **Canoeing Ireland** (www.canoe.ie).

GOLF

On the edge of town, **Carton House** (☎ 01-651 7720; www.cartonhousegolf.ie; green fees €90 Sun-Wed, €110 Thu-Sat) is home to two outstanding 18-hole championship courses designed by Colin Montgomery and Mark O'Meara respectively. See the following Carton House sleeping review for details of the attached hotel.

Sleeping

Maynooth is quite lacking when it comes to B&B accommodation.

NUI Maynooth (☎ 01-708 6200; www.maynooth campus.com; s €30-100, d €48-126; [P]) The university campus can accommodate 1000 guests in seven types of room, ranging from a traditional college room to doubles in an apartment in the purpose-built university village. Most are in the mid-1970s North Campus, but rooms are better in the South Campus, where the accommodation office is. These are strewn around the courts and gardens of atmospheric St Patrick's College (p177). Availability is best in the summer months.

Glenroyal Hotel & Leisure Club (☎ 01-629 090 www.glenroyal.ie; Straffan Rd; r from €79; [P] [Q] [R] ⓢ This modern 113-room hotel is tailored business travellers and weddings. The desig is bog standard but the rooms are spacio and spotless, with high-speed internet, an there are *two* swimming pools.

Carton House (☎ 01-505 2000; www.cartonhou .com; r from €150; [P] [Q] [R] ⓢ) It really doesn't g any grander than this vast, early 19th-centur estate set on over 1000 acres of lavish ground The interiors belie the Palladian exterior an are stylishly minimalist. As you'd expect, th beautiful rooms come equipped with all th latest high-tech gadgetry. To reach the hote follow the R148 east towards Leixlip alon the Royal Canal.

Eating

Kehoe's (☎ 01-628 6533; Main St; meals €6-10; ⏰ 8am 4pm Mon-Sat) The place for a classic Irish break fast, Kehoe's offers a warm, trad welcome t its small and cosy quarters. There are numer ous daily lunch specials.

Mohana (☎ 01-505 4868; www.mohanaindianrestaurar .com; Main St; mains €13; ⏰ noon-2.30pm & 5-11pm Several cuts above the usual curry joint Mohana has a wide range of excellent Soutl Asian dishes. The dining room has a graciou air and it's a floor above the street. For a kick i the old masala, try the chicken chilli version.

Getting There & Away

Dublin Bus (☎ 01-873 4222; www.dublinbus.ie) runs a service to Maynooth (€3.10, one hour) leaving several times an hour from Pearse St in Dublin.

Maynooth is on the main Dublin–Sligo line, with regular trains in each direction: to Dublin (€2.70, 35 minutes, one to four per hour); to Sligo (€35, two hours 40 minutes, four per day).

AROUND MAYNOOTH
Castletown House

In a country full of elegant Palladian mansions, it is no mean feat to be considered the grandest of the lot, but **Castletown House** (☎ 01-628 8252; www.castletownhouse.ie; Celbridge; adult/child €4.50/3.50; ⏰ 10am-6pm Mon-Fri, from 1pm Sat & Sun Easter-Sep, 10am-5pm Mon-Fri, from 1pm Sun Oct) simply has no peer. It is Ireland's largest and most imposing Georgian estate, and a testament to the vast wealth enjoyed by the Anglo-Irish gentry during the 18th century.

The house was built between the years 1722 and 1732 for William Conolly (1662–1729), peaker of the Irish House of Commons and, at the time, Ireland's richest man. orn into relatively humble circumstances n Ballyshannon, County Donegal, Conolly ade his fortune through land transactions n the uncertain aftermath of the Battle of the oyne (1690; see p37).

The original design of the house was by the talian architect Alessandro Galilei (1691–737), who in 1718 designed the facade of he main block to resemble a 16th-century talian palazzo. Construction began in 1722 ut Galilei didn't bother hanging around to upervise, having left Ireland in 1719. Instead, he project was entrusted to Sir Edward Lovett earce (1699–1733), who returned from his rand tour of Italy in 1724 (where he had ecome friends with Galilei).

Inspired by the work of Andrea Palladio, hich he had studied during his visit to taly, Pearce enlarged the original design of he house and added the colonnades and he terminating pavilions. The interior is as pulent as the exterior suggests, especially he Long Gallery, replete with family portraits nd exquisite stucco work by the Francini rothers. (In the US, Thomas Jefferson be-ame a Palladian acolyte and much of official Washington DC is in this style.)

As always seems the way with these grand rojects, Conolly didn't live to see the com-letion of his wonder-palace. His widow, Katherine, continued to live at the unfin-shed house after his death in 1729, instigat-ng many of the improvements made after he main structure was completed in 1732. Her main architectural contribution was the curious 42.6m **obelisk**, known locally as the Conolly Folly. Designed to her specifica-ions by Richard Cassels and built so as to give employment to the poor after the 1739 famine, it is 3.2km north of the house and visible from both ends of the Long Gallery. Her other offering is the Heath Robinson (or Rube Goldberg, if you prefer)–esque **Wonderful Barn**, six teetering storeys wrapped by an exte-rior spiral staircase, on private property just outside Leixlip. The surrounding 500-house development kills the mood somewhat, but you still can appreciate the barn's eccentric charm.

Castletown house remained in the family's hands until 1965, when it was purchased by Desmond Guinness. He spent vast amounts of money in order to restore the house to its original splendour, an investment that was continued from 1979 by the Castletown Foundation. In 1994 Castletown House was transferred to state care and today it is man-aged by the Heritage Service.

Buses 120 and 123 run from Dublin to Celbridge (€3.50; 30 minutes; every half-hour Monday to Friday, hourly Saturday, six buses Sunday).

Larchill Arcadian Gardens

These **gardens** (☎ 01-628 7354; www.larchill.ie; Kilcock; adult/child €7.50/5.50; ✆ noon-6pm Tue-Sun Jun-Aug, noon-6pm Sat & Sun Sep) are Europe's only example of a mid-18th-century *ferme ornée* (ornamental farm). A 40-minute walk takes you through beautiful landscaped parklands, passing ec-centric follies, classic 18th-century formal plantings, gazebos and a lake. Children will be chuffed with the adventure playground, maze and winsome farm animals.

The gardens are 5km north of Kilcock on Dunsaughlin Rd (R125).

STRAFFAN
pop 439

Teeny Straffan has a few small attractions for the young (or at least the young at heart), and one huge one for golf enthusiasts.

Mechanical fanatics worship at the **Steam Museum & Lodge Park Walled Garden** (☎ 01-627 3155; www.steam-museum.com; adult/concession €7.50/5; ✆ 2-6pm Wed-Sun Jun-Aug), located in an old church, which traces the history of steam power and the Industrial Revolution. The collection in-cludes working steam engines from breweries, distilleries, factories and ships. Next door, the 18th-century walled garden has traditional fruits, flowers and formal plantings.

Just down the road at the **Straffan Butterfly Farm** (☎ 01-627 1109; www.straffanbutterflyfarm.com; Ovidstown; adult/child €7.50/5; ✆ noon-5.30pm Jun-Aug), you can wander through a tropical green-house full of enormous exotic butterflies, or commune with critters like Larry, the leopard gecko.

Two of Ireland's top golf courses can be found at the **K Club** (Kildare Hotel & Country Club; ☎ 01-601 7200; www.kclub.com; Straffan; r from €200; P ☐ ☎ ⬙), a Georgian estate and golfers' paradise. Inside there are 92 well-appointed rooms and lots of public spaces for having a drink and lying about your exploits outside.

There are two golf courses: one, with Arnold Palmer's design imprimatur, is one of the best in Ireland and hosted the PGA European Open until 2008; the second course opened in 2003. Like everywhere else, the K Club is suffering the effects of the recession and has lowered its green fees from a prohibitive €250 to a more interesting €100. Not bad for the course where, in 2006, Europe won its third Ryder Cup in a row.

Bus Éireann (☎ 01-836 6111; www.buseireann.ie) runs buses from Dublin (one way/return €3.80/5.80, 30 minutes, every half hour, six buses Sunday).

ALONG THE GRAND CANAL

Heading west from Straffan, there are some interesting sites as you follow the banks of the Grand Canal, which flows gently from Dublin to tiny, tranquil **Robertstown**, just past Clane and well worth a detour. This picturesque village has remained largely untouched and is dominated by the now-dilapidated Grand Canal Hotel, built in 1801. It's a good place to start a canal walk (see the boxed text, below).

Just southwest of Robertstown and at the centre of the Kildare flatlands, the **Hill of Allen** (206m) was a strategic spot through the centuries due to its 360-degree view. Today the top is marked by a 19th-century folly and the ruins of some Iron Age fortifications said to mark the home of Fionn McCumhaill.

Further west you'll find the wonderfully interpretive **Bog of Allen Nature Centre**

(☎ 045-860 133; www.ipcc.ie; R414, Lullymore; adult/ch €6/free; ⏰ 9.30am-5pm Mon-Fri), a fascinating i⟩ stitution run by the nonprofit Irish Peatlan⟩ Conservation Council. The centre traces th⟩ history of bogs and peat production, and h⟩ the largest carnivorous plant collection i⟩ Ireland, including sundews, butterwort an⟩ other bog-native protein-eaters. Much fund ing comes from the Netherlands, where th⟩ historic bogs are all gone. It's common to fin⟩ dewy-eyed Dutch volunteers assisting in th⟩ ongoing renovations. In an effort to bring th⟩ science of the bog to bear for Irish student⟩ 2008 saw the opening of a dipping pond fo⟩ freshwater invertebrates and facilities for ob⟩ serving how bog 'grows'. A nearby boardwal⟩ extends into the Bog of Allen.

A rather mangy rabbit mascot greets visi⟩ tors to the cheerful **Lullymore Heritage & Discove⟩ Park** (☎ 045-870 238; www.lullymoreheritagepark.con⟩ Lullymore; admission €9; ⏰ 10am-6pm Mon-Sat, from 11a⟩ Sun Easter-Oct, 11am-6pm Sat & Sun Nov-Easter), abou⟩ 1km north of the Bog of Allen Nature Centr⟩ Aimed right at kids, a woodland trail leads yo⟩ past various dwellings (including Neolithi⟩ huts, a not-so-festive Famine-era house an⟩ an enchanting fairy village), and there's craz⟩ golf and a road train. Should the unthinkabl⟩ happen and it rains, the Funky Forest is a vas⟩ indoor playground.

For information on hiring narrow boats o⟩ the canal, see the boxed text, p506.

NEWBRIDGE & THE CURRAGH
pop 17,042

The fairly unremarkable town of Newbridg⟩ (Droichead Nua) is near the junction o⟩ the M7 and M9. Many tourists flock to th⟩ **Newbridge Silverware Showroom** (☎ 045-431 301⟩ www.newbridgecutlery.com), a purely commercia⟩ venture that trades on the area's metalwork⟩ heritage as it peddles vast quantities of silver⟩ plated spoons, forks and whatnots.

Silverware aside, the town is more famou⟩ as the gateway to the Curragh, one of th⟩ country's largest pieces of unfenced fertil⟩ land and the centre of the Irish horse indus⟩ try. It's renowned for its **racecourse** (☎ 045-44⟩ 205; www.curragh.ie; admission €15-60; ⏰ mid-Apr-Oct)⟩ the oldest and most prestigious in the coun⟩ try, which is in the middle of a substantia⟩ spruce-up – thanks in large part to the gen⟩ erosity of the Aga Khan. Even if you're not⟩ a horsey type, it's well worth experiencing⟩ the passion, atmosphere and general craic of⟩

WALKING THE TOWPATH

The Grand Canal towpath is ideal for leisurely walkers and there are numerous access points, none better than Robertstown if you fancy a long-distance ramble. The village is the hub of the Kildare Way and River Barrow towpath trails, the latter stretching all the way to St Mullin's, 95km south in County Carlow. From there it's possible to connect with the South Leinster Way (p240) at Graiguenamanagh, or the southern end of the Wicklow Way (p157) at Clonegal, north of Mt Leinster.

A variety of leaflets detailing the paths can be picked up at most regional tourist offices. **Waterways Ireland** (www.waterways ireland.org) is also a good source.

BOG OF ALLEN

Stretching like a brown, moist desert through nine counties, including Kildare, Laois and Offaly, the Bog of Allen is Ireland's best-known raised bog, and once covered much of the midlands. Unfortunately, in a pattern repeated across Ireland, the peat is rapidly being turned into potting compost and fuel. Once Ireland had almost 17% of its land covered in bogs; today it's less than 2%. Bogs are home to a wide range of plants and animals, including cranberries, insect-eating sundews, all manner of frogs and butterflies. For more information on ways to discover this rich land, enquire at the Bog of Allen Nature Centre (see opposite), found right along the Grand Canal.

day at the races, which can verge on mass ysteria. If you miss the chance to hear the ooves, you can still see some action: if you et up early or pass by in the late evening, ou'll see the thoroughbreds exercising n the wide-open spaces surrounding the acecourse.

The M7 runs through the Curragh (exit 2) and Newbridge from Dublin. There is frequent Bus Éireann service between Dublin's Busáras bus station and Newbridge (€7.90, 90 minutes). From Newbridge, buses continue n to the Curragh racecourse (€1.60, 10 minutes) and Kildare town. There are extra buses n race days.

The Dublin–Kildare **train** (☎ 01-836 6222) uns from Heuston train station and stops n Newbridge (€13, 30 minutes, hourly). Check the timetable for trains that stop at he racecourse.

South Kildare Community Transport (☎ 045-71 916; www.skct.ie) runs a local bus service n two routes that serve Athy, Ballitore, Castledermot, Kildare town and Moone and Newbridge among others (one way €4, up to ive times daily).

KILDARE TOWN
op 7538

Built around a compact, triangular square ronting its impressive cathedral, Kildare is busy enough place, even if there aren't a ot of attractions within the town itself. It is losely associated with Ireland's second-most mportant saint, Brigid.

Information

The **Tourist Office & Heritage Centre** (☎ 045-521 240; www.kildare.ie; Market House, Market Sq; 9.30am-1pm & 2-5.30pm Mon-Sat May-Sep, 10am-1pm & 2-5pm Mon-Fri) has an **exhibition** (admission free) outlining Kildare's history. There's also local art for sale.

Sights
ST BRIGID'S CATHEDRAL

The solid presence of 13th-century **St Brigid's Cathedral** (☎ 045-521 229; Market Sq; admission by donation; 10am-1pm & 2-5pm Mon-Sat, 2-5pm Sun May-Sep) looms over Kildare Sq. Look out for a fine stained-glass window inside that depicts the three main saints of Ireland: Patrick, Brigid and Colmcille. The church also contains the restored tomb of Walter Wellesley, Bishop of Kildare, which disappeared soon after his death in 1539 and was only found again in 1971. One of its carved figures has been variously interpreted as an acrobat or a sheila-na-gig.

The 10th-century **round tower** (admission €5) in the grounds is Ireland's second highest at 32.9m, and one of the few that you can climb, provided the guardian is around. Its original conical roof has been replaced with an unusual Norman battlement. Near the tower is a **wishing stone** – put your arm through the hole and touch your shoulder and your wish will be granted. On the north side of the cathedral are the heavily restored foundations of an ancient **fire temple** (see the boxed text, p183).

IRISH NATIONAL STUD & GARDENS

With highlights like the 'Teasing Shed', the **Irish National Stud** (☎ 045-521 617; www.irish-national-stud.ie; Tully; adult/child €10/5; 9.30am-6pm mid-Feb–Dec, last admission 5pm), about 3km south of town, is the big attraction in the locality. The stud was founded by Colonel Hall Walker (of Johnnie Walker whiskey fame) in 1900. He was remarkably successful with his horses, but his eccentric breeding technique relied heavily on astrology: the fate of a foal was decided by its horoscope and the roofs of the stallion boxes opened on auspicious occasions to reveal the heavens and duly influence the horses' fortunes. Today the immaculately kept centre is owned and managed by the Irish government. It breeds high-quality stallions to mate with mares from all over the world.

There are **guided tours** (many of the guides have a real palaver) of the stud every hour on the hour, with access to the intensive-care unit for newborn foals. If you visit between February and June, you might even see a foal being born. Alternatively, the foaling unit shows a 10-minute video with all the action. You can wander the stalls and go eye-to-eye with famous stallions. Given that most are now geldings, they probably have dim memories of their time in the aforementioned Teasing Shed, the place where stallions are stimulated for mating, while dozens look on. The cost: tens of thousands of euros for a top horse.

After the thrill of seeing such prized stallions up close, the revamped **Irish Horse Museum** is quite disappointing; its celebration of championship horses and the history of horse racing is one step above what you'd expect to see from a really good school project.

Also disappointing are the much-vaunted **Japanese Gardens** (part of the complex), considered to be the best of their kind in Europe – which doesn't say much for other contenders. Created between 1906 and 1910, they trace the journey from birth to death through 20 landmarks, including the Tunnel of Ignorance, the Hill of Ambition and the Chair of Old Age.

When in bloom the flowers are beautiful, bu the gardens are too small and bitty to reall impress.

St Fiachra's Garden is another bucolic feature with a mixture of bog oak, gushing water, rep lica monastic cells and an underground crysta garden of dubious distinction. Both garden are great for a relaxing stroll, though.

The large **visitor centre** houses the obligator cafe, shop and children's play area. A tour c the stud and gardens takes about two hours

Lying outside the site, behind the museum are the ruins of a 12th-century **Black Abbey**; an just off the road back to Kildare is **St Brigid' Well**, where five stones represent different as pects of Brigid's life.

Sleeping

Silken Thomas (☎ 045-522 232; www.silkenthomas.com Market Sq; s/d from €40/65; P) This local institution includes clubs, bars and an 18-room hotel There's a modern wing and an 18th-century town house. Rooms are unfrilly but comfort able; try for one away from the action.

Derby House Hotel (☎ 045-522 144; www.derb househotel.ie; s/d €55/95; P �🛜) This old hotel ha 20 decent rooms right in the centre of town

---

CHRISTY MOORE: A NEW TRADITION FOR TRADITIONAL MUSIC

A native of Newbridge, County Kildare, Christy Moore is one of Ireland's best-known, and certainly best-loved, traditional singers. Combining a ready wit and puckish charm, he has produced more than 23 solo albums of songs that are easy on the ear if not the mind.

The causes he has championed – Travellers, antinuclear protests, South Africa, Northern Ireland – might give one the wrong impression: Christy is equally at home singing tender love songs (Nancy Spain), haunting ballads (Ride On), comic ditties (Lisdoovarna) and bizarre flights of lyrical fancy (Reel in the Flickering Light). He was also influential as a member of Planxty and Moving Hearts, as Ireland experimented during the 1970s and 1980s with its traditional musical forms to combine folk, rock and jazz in a heady and vibrant fusion.

Born in 1945, Moore grew up the son of a grocer and was influenced early in his musical career by a Traveller, John Riley. He was denied the musical opportunities he craved in Ireland and left in 1966 for England, where he quickly became popular on the British folk scene in Manchester and West Yorkshire.

Moore's first big break came with Prosperous (named after the Kildare town), on which he teamed up with the legendary Donal Lunny, Andy Irvine and Liam O'Flynn. They went on to form Planxty and recorded three ground-breaking albums.

Moore has done much to breathe life into traditional music. His work is always entertaining but like any good pub ballad, there's far more to his lyrics than you might first suspect. He's passionate, provocative and distinctive; you'll hear the influences of others as diverse as Jackson Browne and Van Morrison.

Certainly, even as he curtails his live performances to write, he is an iconic figure among Irish trad musicians and fans. He has built an international reputation as a writer and interpreter of a living tradition, at the head of the table of Irish traditional music.

Recommended listening: The Christy Moore Collection, 1981-1991.

COUNTIES WICKLOW & KILDARE

ST BRIGID

St Brigid is one of Ireland's best-known saints, hailed as an early feminist but also known for her compassion, generosity and special ways with barnyard animals. Stories about her are both many and mythical. All agree that she was a strong-willed character: according to one legend, when her father chose her an unwanted suitor, she pulled out her own eye to prove her resolve never to wed. After she had taken her vows, and was mistakenly ordained a bishop rather than nun, her beauty was restored. Another has her being shipped off to a convent after she compulsively gave away the family's wealth to the poor. (One tale even has Brigid being spirited to Ireland from Portugal by pirates.)

Brigid founded a monastery in Kildare in the 5th century for both nuns and monks, which was unusual at the time. One lurid account says it had a perpetual fire tended by 20 virgins that burned continuously until 1220 when the Bishop of Dublin stopped the tradition, citing it as 'un-Christian'. The supposed fire pit can be seen in the grounds of St Brigid's Cathedral where a fire is lit on 1 February, St Brigid's feast day. Nonvirgins are welcome.

Brigid was a tireless traveller, and as word of her many miracles spread, her influence stretched across Europe. Yet another legend claims that the medieval Knights of Chivalry chose St Brigid as their patron, and that it was they who first chose to call their wives 'brides'.

Brigid is remembered by a simple reed cross first woven by her to explain the redemption to a dying chief. The cross, said to protect and bless a household, is still found in many rural homes. She is also the patron of travellers, chicken farms and seamen, among others.

's an easy walk from here to bars, restaurants nd all the St Brigid lore you could hope for.

Martinstown House (☎ 045-441 269; www.martins wnhouse.com; The Curragh; s/d from €125/190; mid-n–mid-Dec; **P**) This beautiful 18th-century ountry manor is built in the frilly Strawberry Hill Gothic style and set in a 170-acre estate nd farm surrounded by trees. The house has our rooms filled with antiques; children are anned – darn. You can arrange for memora-le dinners in advance (€55); ingredients are rawn from the kitchen garden.

ating

he **Whitewater Farmers Market** (10am-4pm Wed & Sat) is held in the Whitewater Shopping Centre twice a week and has a wide range of ocal produce, including cheese, organic fruit nd veg, organic meats and local crafts.

L'Officina by Dunne & Crescenzi (☎ 045-535 850; ildare Retail Village; meals €4-8; 10am-6pm Mon-Wed Fri, to 8pm Thu, to 10pm Sat, 10.30am-6pm Sun) The Dublin-based purveyors of gourmet Italian itbits have spread their wings and landed n the anodyne arms of the relatively new Kildare Retail Village. No matter: the salads, warm focaccias and desserts are as delicious nd authentic as the ones in the capital (see 134).

Agape (☎ 045-533 711; Station Rd; meals €5-10; 9am-6pm Mon-Sat) Just off Market Sq, this rendy little cafe has a fine range of home-made food. There's a full coffee bar and a menu of salads, soups, sandwiches and tasty hot specials.

Chapter 16 (☎ 045-522 232; Market Sq; mains €17-22; 6-10pm) Part of the Silken Thomas empire, this ambitious restaurant serves steaks, seafood and modern Irish fare in an attractive setting. The vast pub has a popular carvery lunch.

Getting There & Away

There is frequent Bus Éireann service between Dublin Busáras and Kildare (€10.30, 1¾ hours). Buses continue on to Limerick (€9.90, 2½ hours, four daily). Some Dublin buses also service the Stud.

The Dublin–Kildare **train** (☎ 01-836 6222) runs from Heuston train station and stops in Kildare (€13.80, 35 minutes, one to four per hour). This is a major junction and trains continue on to numerous places including Ballina, Galway, Limerick and Waterford.

See p181 for information on local bus service provided by South Kildare Community Transport.

ATHY

pop 7943

Strategically placed at the junction of the River Barrow and the Grand Canal, the Anglo-Norman settlement of Athy (Áth Í; a-*thigh*) shows little of its long history.

COUNTIES WICKLOW & KILDARE

DETOUR: BALLYMORE EUSTACE

The village of Ballymore Eustace is home to one of Ireland's best modern pubs, the **Ballymore Inn** (☎ 045-864 585; www.bally moreinn.com; mains €24-29). The richly tiled interior is warmed by small fireplaces, which flicker against the wicker and leather seating. The food ranges from pizza to amazing steaks. You can opt for a more formal experience in the dining room at lunch or dinner or settle back in the large pub, where pub food is served all day. Food is sourced from a stellar cast of local suppliers.

Athy was founded in the 12th century and later became an important defence post. Many of the town's older buildings remain, including the impressive **White's Castle**, a tower built in 1417 to house the garrison. The castle is next to Crom-a-boo Bridge, named after what must be the world's worst battle cry (meaning 'Up Crom!'), hollered by the local Geraldine family.

The **Tourist Office & Heritage Centre** (☎ 059-863 3075; Emily Sq; admission Heritage Centre adult/child €3/2; ⏰ 10am-5pm Mon-Fri, 2-4pm Sat & Sun May-Oct, 10am-5pm Mon-Fri Nov-Apr) gives good walking recommendations. The heritage centre traces the history of Athy and has a fascinating exhibit on Antarctic explorer Sir Ernest Shackleton (1874–1922), who was born in nearby Kilkea. On display is one of Shackleton's sledges, acquired from New Zealand where he sold it to pay off his debts.

Activities

Athy is a popular place for pike, salmon and trout **fishing**. For equipment and information try **Griffin Hawe Hardware** (☎ 059-863 1221; www .griffinhawe.ie; 22 Duke St). There's a wide range of fly rods and gear.

Sleeping & Eating

Carlton Abbey Hotel (☎ 059-863 0100; www.carlton abbeyhotel.com; town centre; r from €50; P ⚑ 🛜) Once as stolid as the morals of its residents, this old convent has been converted into a most inviting boutique hotel. There are 40 rooms with dark woods and light linens and mod cons such as wi-fi throughout. There's a popular pub, a good restaurant and a 21m pool.

Coursetown House (☎ 059-863 1101; fax 863 2740; Stradbally Rd; s/d €70/110; P) This 200-year-old

farmhouse is just east of Athy off the R428. It's set among gorgeous gardens, which provide a lot of the produce that makes the breakfasts here so bountiful in season. The five rooms exude country charm and have powerful showers for washing the grime off after a long walk in the countryside.

The **farmers market** (⏰ 10am-2pm Sun) takes place in Emily Sq.

Getting There & Away

Bus Éireann (☎ 01-836 6111; www.buseireann.ie) has six buses to/from Dublin (€10.80, 1½ hours) and Clonmel (€13.10, two hours).

See p181 for information on local bus service provided by South Kildare Community Transport.

DONNELLY'S HOLLOW TO CASTLEDERMOT

This 25km stretch south towards Carlow contains some interesting detours to tiny towns bypassed by the speedy but unlovely N9.

See p181 for information on local bus service provided by South Kildare Community Transport.

Donnelly's Hollow

Dan Donnelly (1788–1820) is revered as Ireland's greatest bare-knuckle fighter of the 19th century. He's also the stuff of legend – his arms were so long, he could supposedly tie his shoelaces without having to bend down. This spot, 4km west of Kilcullen on the R413, was his favourite battleground, and the obelisk at the centre of the hollow details his glorious career.

Ballitore
pop 338

Low-key Ballitore is the only planned and permanent Quaker settlement in Ireland. It was founded by incomers from Yorkshire in the early 18th century. A small **Quaker Museum** (☎ 059-862 3344; Mary Leadbeater House, Main St; admission by donation; ⏰ noon-5pm Tue-Sat year-round, 2-6pm Sun Jun-Sep), in a tiny restored house, documents the lives of the community (including the namesake former owner who was known for her aversion to war). There's a Quaker cemetery and Meeting House, and a modern **Shaker Store** (☎ 059-862 3372; www.shakerstore.ie; Main St; ⏰ 10am-6pm Mon-Fri, from 2pm Sat & Sun), which sells delightfully humble wooden toys and furniture. It also has a tearoom.

About 2km west is **Rath of Mullaghmast**, an Iron Age hill fort and standing stone where Daniel O'Connell, champion of Catholic emancipation, held one of his 'monster rallies' in 1843.

Moone
pop 380

Just south of Ballitore, the unassuming village of Moone is home to one of Ireland's most magnificent high crosses. The unusually tall and slender **Moone High Cross** is an 8th- or 9th-century masterpiece, which displays its carved biblical scenes with the confidence and exuberance of a comic strip. The cross can be found 1km west of Moone village and the N9 in an atmospheric early Christian churchyard. Old stone ruins add to the mood of the drive.

The solid, stone 18th-century **Moone High Cross Inn** (☎ 059-862 4112; Bolton Hill; s/d from €50/80; P), 2km south of Moone, has five rooms decorated in quaint country-house style. The delightful bar downstairs serves good pub lunches and there's a proper **restaurant** (mains €11-20; ⏱ 6-8.30pm), which uses local and organic ingredients. The inn revolves around a Celtic theme, celebrating pagan festivals and hoarding healing stones, lucky charms and even a 'love stone' in the outside courtyards.

Kilkea Castle

Built in the 12th century, **Kilkea Castle Hotel** (☎ 059-914 5156; www.kilkeacastle.ie; Castledermot; r from €140; P ▢) is Ireland's oldest continuously inhabited castle. It's the kind of place where you'll find a suit of armour in a nook in the hall – it looks like a castle right out of Central Casting. It was once the second home of the Maynooth Fitzgeralds, and the grounds are supposedly haunted by Gerald the Wizard Earl, who rises every seven years from the Rath of Mullaghmast to free Ireland from its enemies – a pretty good trick considering he was buried in London.

The castle was completely restored in the 19th century and is now an exclusive hotel and golf club. Among its exterior oddities is an **Evil Eye Stone**, high up at the back of the castle. Thought to date from the 14th or 15th century, it depicts some very weird goings-on between nightmarish creatures that may be a woman, wolf and cock. Another carving depicts a monkey in bondage; definitely fertile grounds for voyeurs.

De Lacy's (set dinner from €50), the restaurant, serves complex and formal meals in elegant surroundings.

The castle is 5km northwest of Castledermot on the Athy road (R418).

Castledermot
pop 1160

Castledermot was once home to a vast ecclesiastical settlement, but all that remains of St Diarmuid's 9th-century **monastery** is a 20m round tower topped with a medieval battlement. Nearby are two well-preserved, carved, 10th-century granite high crosses; a 12th-century Romanesque doorway; and a medieval Scandinavian 'hogback' gravestone, the only one in Ireland. Reach the ruins by entering the rusty gate on all-too-busy Main St (N9), then walking up the tree-lined avenue to St James' church. At the southern end of town, the ruins of an early 14th-century **Franciscan friary** can be seen alongside the road.

Counties Wexford, Waterford, Carlow & Kilkenny

Counties Wexford, Waterford, Carlow and Kilkenny are (along with the southern chunk of Tipperary) collectively referred to as the 'sunny southeast'. This being Ireland the term is of course, relative. But due to the moderating effect of the Gulf Stream, it *is* the country's warmest, driest region.

Although sun-lounger time might be limited, the coastal counties of Wexford and Waterford are wreathed with wide, sandy beaches, along with thatched fishing villages, genteel seaside towns and remote, windswept peninsulas littered by wrecks – as well as a swashbuckling history of marauding Vikings, lighthouse-keeping monks and shadowy knights sects. You can stick to the coast (hop on a car ferry for a quick shortcut), or head into the hinterland to the beautiful Nire Valley and Comeragh Mountains, where prehistoric remains hide among the heather.

Deeper inland, the gently meandering River Barrow separates the verdant counties of Carlow and Kilkenny. But while County Carlow is a country gal at heart – with romantic country lodgings hidden away in her rolling hills, and flowering estates connected by a garden trail – Kilkenny is her city-slicker cousin. A mighty castle, a magnificent cathedral, narrow, winding medieval lanes and cracking pubs make County Kilkenny's namesake city one of the most visited in the country, while hip eateries, happening clubs and a host of festivals give this spirited little city a worldly sophistication.

Best of all, thanks to that 'sunny southeastern' climate, these four counties have some of Ireland's best outdoors pursuits, including glorious walking and cycling opportunities.

COUNTIES WEXFORD, WATERFORD, CARLOW & KILKENNY

HIGHLIGHTS

- **Storybook Sleeps** Stay in a castle whatever your budget – from a haunted hostel near Ballyragget (p239) to a private island in Waterford city (p208)

- **River Rambles** Amble the towpath linking the charming villages of Graiguenamanagh (p238) and St Mullins (p226)

- **Horror Stories** Learn about Ireland's poignant history at the National 1798 Rebellion Centre in Enniscorthy (p202) and aboard a Famine ship in New Ross (p200)

- **Culinary Creations** Sharpen your cookery skills with top chefs Paul Flynn in Dungarvan (p215) or Kevin Dundon in Arthurstown (p200)

- **Adrenaline Rushes** Surf, sea-kayaking, or spin until you're dizzy on fairground rides at Tramore (p211)

★ Ballyragget

Graiguenamanagh ★

St Mullins ★   ★ Enniscorthy

New Ross ★

Waterford ★   ★ Athurstown

Tramore ★

Dungarvan ★

■ POPULATION: 377,617   ■ AREA: 7147.19 SQ KM

COUNTY WEXFORD

pop 131,749

County Wexford's navigable rivers and fertile land have long lured invaders and privateers. The Vikings founded Ireland's first major towns on the wide, easy-flowing River Slaney, which cuts through the middle of the county. The most enjoyable way for visitors to unwrap Wexford's swashbuckling maritime history is pausing in pretty waterfront villages and sampling catches from the surrounding waves.

WEXFORD TOWN

pop 8931

At first glance, Wexford (Loch Garman) appears a sleepy port town where the silted estuary now sees less traffic than Waterford and Rosslare Harbour. However, there are reminders of its glorious Viking and Norman past in the meandering lanes off Main St – as well as some medieval monuments and a world-class opera festival in autumn, held in the city's state-of-the-art new opera house.

History

The Vikings named it Waesfjord (meaning 'harbour of mud flats') and its handy location near the mouth of the Slaney encouraged landings as early as AD 850. It was captured by the Normans in 1169; traces of their fort can still be seen in the grounds of the Irish National Heritage Park.

Cromwell included Wexford in his destructive Irish tour from 1649 to 1650. Around 1500 of the town's 2000 inhabitants were put to the sword, including all the Franciscan friars. During the 1798 Rising, rebels made a determined, bloody stand in Wexford town before they were defeated.

Orientation

From Wexford Bridge at the north end of the town, the quays lead southeast along the water, via the small kink called the Crescent, home to a statue of Commodore John Barry (1745–1803), who emigrated from Wexford to America and founded the US navy. Most shops are a block inland on North and South Main St.

Information

BOOKSHOPS

Readers' Paradise (☎ 053-912 4400; 2 Slaney St; ☽ 9.30am-6pm Mon-Sat) Good stock of Irish-interest second-hand fiction and nonfiction.

Wexford Book Centre (☎ 053-912 3543; 5 South Main St; ☽ 9am-6pm Mon-Thu & Sat, 9am-7pm Fri, 1-5pm Sun) Lots of new Irish titles plus a limited selection of foreign newspapers and magazines.

INTERNET ACCESS

Tangiers (☎ 053-914 6404; 19 Trimmers La; per hr €3.50; ☽ 9am-10pm Mon-Sat, 10.30am-8pm Sun)
Wexford Library (☎ 053-912 1637; McCauley Car Park, off Redmond Sq; www.wexford.ie/library; ☽ 10.30am-5.30pm Mon-Tue & Thu-Sat, 10.30am-8.30pm Wed) Free internet access (one hour time limit).

LAUNDRY

My Beautiful Laundrette (☎ 053-912 4317; St Peters Sq; ☽ 9.30am-1pm Mon-Sat) Opening hours can vary.

LEFT LUGGAGE

O'Hanrahan Station (☎ 053-912 2522; Redmond Pl; ☽ 6am-9pm Mon-Sat, 8am-9pm Sun) Has left-luggage facilities for €2.50 per item per day at the southern end of the platform.

MEDICAL SERVICES

Wexford General Hospital (☎ 053-915 3000) On the N25, 2.5km west of the centre.

MONEY

There's an AIB bank and a National Irish Bank on North Main St near Common Quay St.

POST

Main post office (☎ 053-914 5314; Anne St)

TOURIST INFORMATION

Tourist office (☎ 053-912 3111; Quayfront; ☽ 9am-6pm Mon-Sat Apr-Oct plus 11am-1pm & 2-5pm Sun Jul & Aug, 9.15am-1pm & 2-5pm Mon-Sat Nov-Mar)

Sights

Originally a beach where provisions were boated into the city, the **Bull Ring** became a centre for bull baiting in medieval times: the town's butchers gained their guild charter by providing a bull each year for the sport. The **Lone Pikeman statue** commemorates the participants in the 1798 Rising, who used the place as an open-air armaments factory.

The only survivor of the six original town gates is the 14th-century **Westgate**. It was originally a tollgate, and the recesses used by the toll collectors are still intact, as is the lockup used to incarcerate 'runagates' – those who tried to avoid paying. Some stretches of the town wall are also in good nick, including

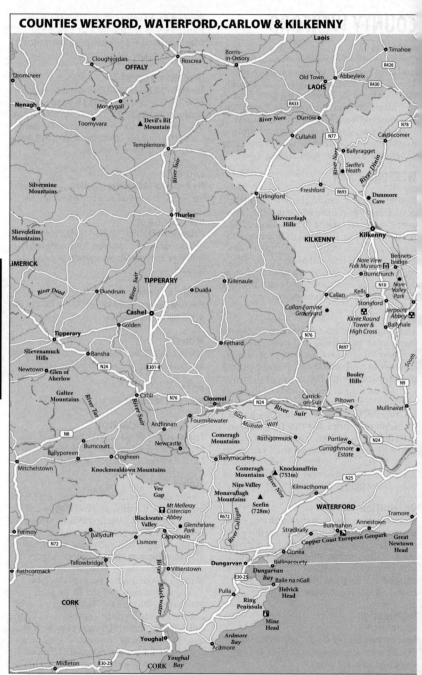

COUNTIES WEXFORD, WATERFORD, CARLOW & KILKENNY

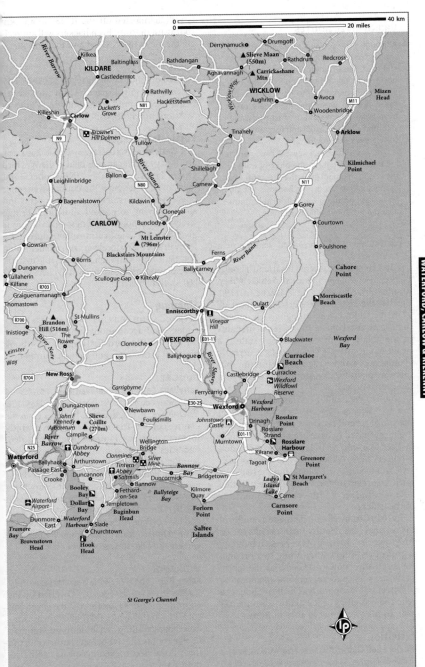

0   40 km
0   20 miles

Derrynamuck   Drumgoff

Kilkea   Rathdangan   Slieve Maan   Rathdrum   Redcross
(550m)

Baltinglass   Aghavannagh   Carrickashane
Mtn

KILDARE   Castledermot   **WICKLOW**   Avoca   Mizen
Head

Rathvilly   Aughrim   **M11**

Killeshin   Hacketstown   Woodenbridge

N81   **Carlow**   *Duckett's*
Grove

N9   *Browne's*   Tinahely   **Arklow**
Hill Dolmen   Tullow

Kilmichael
Point

Leighlinbridge   Ballon   Shillelagh

N80   Carnew   **N11**

Bagenalstown   Kildavin   Clonegal   Gorey

CARLOW   Bunclody   Courtown

Gowran   Mt Leinster   Poulshone
(796m)

Borris   **Blackstairs Mountains**   Ferns   *River Bann*

Dungarvan   Ballycarney   Cahore
Point

Tullaherin   Scullogue Gap   Kiltealy

Kilfane   **R703**   Oulart   Morriscastle
Beach

Graiguenamanagh
Thomastown   St Mullins   **Enniscorthy**   *Wexford*
Bay

R700   **Brandon**   *Vinegar*
Hill (516m)   *Hill*

Inistioge   The   Clonroche   **WEXFORD**   **E01-11**   Blackwater
Rower

Leinster   Ballyhogue
Way   **N30**   **Curracloe**
Beach

R704   **New Ross**   Carrigbyrne   Castlebridge   Curracloe

Dunganstown   Ferrycarrig   *Wexford*
Wildfowl
Reserve

John F   **Slieve**   Newbawn   *Wexford*
Kennedy   **Coillte**   **Wexford**   *Harbour*
Arboretum   (270m)   Foulksmills   *Johnstown*
Castle   **E30-25**

N25   *River*   Campile   Drinagh   **Rosslare**
Barrow   Wellington   Rosslare   **Point**

Waterford   **Dunbrody**   Bridge   Murntown   Strand
Abbey   **Rosslare**
Ballyhack   Arthurstown   *Clonmines*   *Silver*   Kilrane   **Harbour**
Passage East   Duncannon   **Tintern**   *Mine*
Crooke   **Abbey**   *Bannow*   Tagoat   **Greenore**
Saltmills   *Bay*   Bridgetown   **Point**

Booley   Bannow   Duncormick
Bay   *Lady's*   **St Margaret's**
Waterford   Fethard-   *Ballyteige*   Kilmore   *Island*   **Beach**
Airport   **Dollar**   on-Sea   *Bay*   Quay   *Lake*   Carne
Bay   Templetown

Dunmore   **Baginbun**   Forlorn   **Carnsore**
East   *Waterford*   **Head**   Point   **Point**
Harbour   Slade

Tramore   Churchtown   **Saltee**
Bay   **Islands**
Brownstown   **Hook**
Head   **Head**

St George's Channel

LP

COUNTIES WEXFORD,
WATERFORD, CARLOW & KILKENNY

VIKING RIVER ROUTES

Although little remains of Viking Wexford, the *keysers* (meaning 'roads to the quays') still exist. These tiny paths, just one pack-horse wide, fall at right angles to the river and the lifeblood of the city ran through them: honey, wheat and malt were taken from Wexford's warehouses to the water-side, and whale oil, wool and fish came from the harbour into town.

The main road was Keysers Lane, which led from Keysergate in the old city walls to the Viking ship pool (now the Crescent). The gradual silting up of the harbour left the *keysers* as an interesting historical footnote …and a modern traffic nightmare.

---

a particularly well-preserved section near Cornmarket.

After Henry II murdered his friend Thomas Becket, he did penance at **Selskar Abbey**, founded by Alexander de la Roche in 1190. Basilia, the sister of Robert FitzGilbert de Clare (better known as Strongbow), is thought to have married one of Henry II's lieutenants in the abbey. Its present ruinous state is a result of Cromwell's visit in 1649. Currently visitors aren't able to access the interior, but there are plans for its restoration – check with the tourist office.

South of the Bull Ring, **St Iberius' Church** (North Main St; ☿ 10am-3pm Mon-Sat) was built in 1760 on the site of several previous churches (including one reputed to have been founded before St Patrick came to Ireland). Oscar Wilde's forebears were rectors here. The Renaissance-style frontage is worth a look, but the real treat is the Georgian interior with its finely crafted altar rails and set of 18th-century monuments in the gallery.

In 1649 Cromwell's forces made a bonfire of the original 13th-century **Fransiscan Friary** (School St; ☿ 10am-6pm), so most of the present building is from the 19th century. Only two original walls remain. Some parts, such as the taber-nacle, are very modern, creating an appealing architectural incongruity. The friary houses a relic and wax effigy of St Adjutor, a boy martyr slain by his own father in ancient Rome.

Activities

Wexford Golf Club (☎ 053-914 2238; www.wexfordgolf club.ie; Mulgannon; 18 holes weekdays/weekends €40/45)

is well signposted off the R733, about 2km southwest of town. Even hackers will appreci-ate the views of Wexford and the harbour.

Tours

Guided one-hour **walking tours** (☎ 053-916 1155 adult/concession €5/4) leave at 11am Monday to Friday year-round from outside Whites or Wexford hotel (opposite).

Festivals & Events

The **Wexford Festival Opera** (www.wexfordopera.com), an 18-day extravaganza, is held at the Wexford Opera House in October/November. First held in 1951, it's now the country's premier opera event, with rarely performed operas and shows playing to packed audiences. Fringe street theatre, poetry readings and exhibitions give the town a fiesta atmosphere during the festival, and many local bars run amateur song competitions. Although it's advisable to book several months ahead, it's worth checking for last-minute tickets.

Sleeping

Wexford's proximity to Dublin attracts week-enders, and accommodation is often scarce during the Wexford Festival Opera – book ahead at these times and in high summer.

BUDGET

Ferrybank Camping & Caravan Park (☎ 053-914 4378; www.wexfordcorp.ie; Ferrybank; tent/van sites €14/20; ☿ Easter-Sep; P) Right across the river from the centre, council-run Ferrybank is in a windy location but has fantastic views of town. Facilities include a heated pool next door, laundry facilities and a children's play area.

Kirwan House (☎ 053-912 1208; www.wexfordhostel .com; 3 Mary St; dm/s/d/q €22/35/60/100) Occupying a triple-decker Georgian building, some rooms in this IHH hostel are brightened by sky-blue walls and have private bathrooms. The TV room has an open fireplace, and there's a small dishevelled garden and bike storage shed out back.

MIDRANGE

Abbey B&B (☎ 053-912 4408; www.abbeyhouse.ie; 34-36 Abbey St; s €35-45, d €60-80; ☜) Dwarfed by the enormous Whites Hotel across the street, this cute, black-and-white B&B blazes with win-dow boxes trailing red blooms in summer. Its five rooms all have private bathrooms and fresh floral decor; evening meals can be ar-ranged on request.

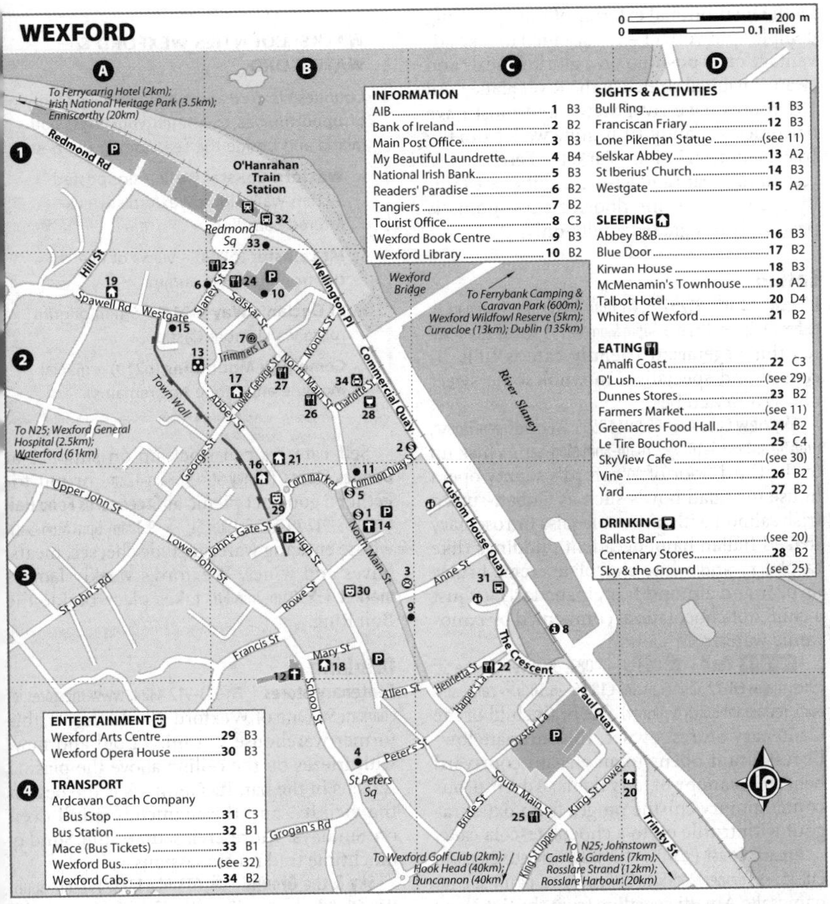
WEXFORD
0 200 m
0 0.1 miles
A
B
C
D
1
2
3
4
To Ferrycarrig Hotel (2km); Irish National Heritage Park (3.5km); Enniscorthy (20km)
Redmond Rd
O'Hanrahan Train Station
Redmond Sq
Hill St
Spawell Rd
Westgate
Slaney St
Selskar St
Trimmers La
Town Wall
Abbey St
Lower George St
North Main St
Monck St
Charlotte St
Wellington Pl
Commercial Quay
Custom House Quay
Wexford Bridge
River Slaney
To Ferrybank Camping & Caravan Park (600m); Wexford Wildfowl Reserve (5km); Curracloe (13km); Dublin (135km)
To N25; Wexford General Hospital (2.5km); Waterford (61km)
George St
Upper John St
Cornmarket
Common Quay St
John's Gate St
Lower John St
High St
St John's Rd
Rowe St
Anne St
Francis St
Mary St
School St
Allen St
Henrietta St
Harper's La
The Crescent
Paul Quay
Oyster La
Peter's St
St Peters Sq
South Main St
King St Lower
Bride St
King St Upper
Trinity St
Grogan's Rd
To Wexford Golf Club (2km); Hook Head (40km); Duncannon (40km)
To N25; Johnstown Castle & Gardens (7km); Rosslare Strand (12km); Rosslare Harbour (20km)
INFORMATION
AIB 1 B3
Bank of Ireland 2 B2
Main Post Office 3 B3
My Beautiful Laundrette 4 B4
National Irish Bank 5 B3
Readers' Paradise 6 B2
Tangiers 7 B2
Tourist Office 8 C3
Wexford Book Centre 9 B3
Wexford Library 10 B2
SIGHTS & ACTIVITIES
Bull Ring 11 B3
Franciscan Friary 12 B3
Lone Pikeman Statue (see 11)
Selskar Abbey 13 A2
St Iberius' Church 14 B3
Westgate 15 A2
SLEEPING
Abbey B&B 16 B3
Blue Door 17 B2
Kirwan House 18 B3
McMenamin's Townhouse 19 A2
Talbot Hotel 20 D4
Whites of Wexford 21 B2
EATING
Amalfi Coast 22 C3
D'Lush (see 29)
Dunnes Stores 23 B2
Farmers Market (see 11)
Greenacres Food Hall 24 B2
Le Tire Bouchon 25 C4
SkyView Cafe (see 30)
Vine 26 B2
Yard 27 B2
DRINKING
Ballast Bar (see 20)
Centenary Stores 28 B2
Sky & the Ground (see 25)
ENTERTAINMENT
Wexford Arts Centre 29 B3
Wexford Opera House 30 B3
TRANSPORT
Ardcavan Coach Company Bus Stop 31 C3
Bus Station 32 B1
Mace (Bus Tickets) 33 B1
Wexford Bus (see 32)
Wexford Cabs 34 B2

Blue Door (☎ 053-912 1047; http://indigo.ie/~bluedoor; 18 Lower George St; s/d from €45/80) Behind the eponymous cobalt-blue door of this 200-year-old townhouse, bright, airy bedrooms are framed by floor-to-ceiling windows, and are quiet despite the central location.

Talbot Hotel (☎ 053-912 2566; www.talbotwexford.ie; Trinity St; s €59-119, d €78-198; P 💻 wi-fi 🏊) A landmark on Wexford's quayfront, this hotel, established in 1905, has water views from many of its well-equipped rooms, and a first-floor pool, steam room, sauna and gym. There's a stylish restaurant open for dinner (three-course menu €33.50) and a popular bar (see p192).

McMenamin's Townhouse (☎ 053-914 6442; www.wexford-bedandbreakfast.com; 6 Glena Tce, Spawell Rd; s/d €65/100; P) Rooms at this red-brick late-Victorian B&B are furnished with period antiques including canopied beds. You are well looked after, not least at breakfast where the menu features homemade breads and jams, rum-laced porridge, and kidneys with sherry.

TOP END

Whites of Wexford (☎ 053-912 2311; www.whitesofwexford.ie; Abbey St; r €98-256; P wi-fi 🏊) With its bars, restaurants and hi-tech spa, Whites is a contemporary colossus. The 157 rooms are all metal right-angles, plasma and glass, gazing across the estuary to Curracloe Beach. Public areas and high-end rooms have wi-fi.

Ferrycarrig Hotel (☎ 053-912 0999; www.ferrycarrighotel.ie; Ferrycarrig; r €99-239; P 💻 wi-fi 🏊) Don't let the institutional exterior of this sprawling complex put you off – it's oriented to take advantage of its position on a glorious seal- and swan-inhabited stretch of the River Slaney. All 102 rooms have river views, and most have balconies. A handy 10-minute walk from the Irish National Heritage Park, the Ferrycarrig's restaurants, bars and leisure facilities are family friendly, but one floor of guestrooms is peacefully designated adults-only.

Eating

D'Lush (☎ 053-912 3795; Wexford Arts Centre, Cornmarket; dishes €5-8; 🕒 10am-5.30pm Mon-Sat) A local favourite, this vegetarian-friendly cafe is fully licensed and specialises in wholesome sweet and savoury crêpes.

SkyView Cafe (☎ 053-914 2598; Wexford Opera House, High St; dishes €5-10; 🕒 10am-5pm Mon-Sat) Whisk up to the third floor of Wexford's snazzy opera house for salad bowls such as Cuban-spiced Irish salmon with pineapple salsa or rosemary-baked Italian ham, decadent puddings (like raspberry and white chocolate crème brûlée or pear and almond frangipane tart), or just a chilli hot chocolate, accompanied by panoramic waterfront views.

our pick Yard (☎ 053-914 4083; 3 Lower George St; lunch mains €8-12, dinner mains €18.50-26.50; 🕒 cafe 9am-6pm, restaurant lunch & dinner) The brainchild of the Centenary Stores' owner, this intimate low-lit restaurant opens to an elegant courtyard beneath a canopy of fairy lights. Adventurous contemporary cuisine ranges from oxtail ragout with truffle oil to a chocolate-cola cake.

Amalfi Coast (☎ 053-912 4330; Henrietta St; mains €18-35; 🕒 dinner Mon-Sat) OK, so you can't see its namesake Amalfi coastline from this 1st-floor restaurant. But it does have glittering views of the illuminated quay, as well as high-level Italian dishes – particularly seafood, such as steamed whole lobster.

Vine (☎ 053-912 2388; 109 North Main St; mains €16-20; 🕒 dinner) Following the creaking dark timber staircase leads you to this land of glimmering mirrors and metal flowers, where fragrant Thai dishes include *mu phad kaprow* (stir-fried pork with chillies and basil) and *gaeng peht ped yang* (roast duck in red curry).

Le Tire Bouchon (☎ 053-9124877; 112-113 South Main St; mains €17.50-31; 🕒 dinner) Above the Sky & the Ground's pub, the 'Corkscrew' serves modern French/Irish cuisine: pan seared duck breast with burnt orange and ginger, griddled ostrich and so on.

> **WALKS: COUNTIES WEXFORD & WATERFORD**
>
> Counties Wexford and Waterford have plenty of opportunities to stretch your legs, both inland and beside the sea. Among the best:
>
> - **Wexford Coastal Walk** – signposted 221km-walk along Wexford's wreck-littered coastline
> - **Mt Leinster** (p204) – views of five counties from its 796m summit
> - **St Declan's Way** (p216) – 94km pilgrim route via Lismore Castle
> - **Comeragh Mountains** (p219) – glacial moraine and Stone Age remains

Self-caterers can stock up on supplies at **Dunnes Stores** (Slaney St; 🕒 8am-12am) or put together a gourmet picnic at **Greenacres Food Hall** (☎ 053-912 2975; 7 Selskar St; 🕒 9.30am-6pm Mon-Sat), whose enticing wares include cheeses, meats, olives and wines. Wexford's weekly **farmers market** (🕒 9am-2pm Fri) takes place beside the Bull Ring.

Drinking

Centenary Stores (☎ 053-912 4424; www.thestores.ie; Charlotte St) One of Wexford's livelier spots, this former warehouse is a mix of old and new, with friezes on the ceiling above the plasma screens in the bar. Its Guinness is the best in the vicinity, and the nightclub is full even on Sundays. More civilised are the Sunday lunchtime trad music sessions.

Sky & the Ground (☎ 053-912 1273; 112-113 South Main St) A longstanding Wexford favourite, the Sky & the Ground's decor is pure old-man's pub, with enamel signage and a roaring fire, but it attracts a youthful clientele. Trad sessions frequently take place on weeknights.

Ballast Bar (☎ 053-912 2566; Talbot Hotel, Trinity St) Taking its cue from the quay out front, this cavernous venue has vaulted ceilings, elaborate woodwork and chunks of ships' ballast mounted on the walls. There's live music at weekends.

Entertainment

The website www.wexlive.com lists gigs, theatre, exhibitions and more.

Wexford Opera House (☎ 053-912 2400; www.wexfordoperahouse.ie; High St) Opened in 2008 on the site of the old Theatre Royal, Wexford's gleaming new opera house packs more architectural punch inside than out. In addition to opera, it stages drama and concerts by local and touring artists.

Wexford Arts Centre (☎ 053-912 3764; www.wexford artscentre.ie; Cornmarket) In an 18th-century market hall, this centre hosts exhibitions, theatre (including occasional productions in Irish), dance and music.

Getting There & Around
BUS

Bus Éireann (☎ 053-912 2522; www.buseireann.ie) buses leave from O'Hanrahan train station on Redmond Sq and travel to Rosslare Harbour (€4.50, 30 minutes, at least nine daily), Waterford (€7.20, one hour, six daily Monday to Saturday, three Sunday) and Dublin (€13.10, three hours, at least nine daily), normally via Enniscorthy (€5.80, 25 minutes). Tickets are available across the street at the Mace newsagency.

Wexford Bus (☎ 053-914 2742; www.wexfordbus .com) operates seven services daily to/from Dublin airport (€19, two hours, 35 minutes) via Enniscorthy and Ferns, though it doesn't stop in Dublin city centre.

Ardcavan Coach Company (☎ 053-912 2561; www .ardcavan.com) runs one to three buses per day between Dublin airport (€15, three hours) and Dublin city centre (€11, 2½ hours) and Wexford. Bicycles can be transported for €5.

TRAIN

O'Hanrahan Station (☎ 053-912 2522; Redmond Pl) is at the northern end of town. Wexford is on the Dublin Connolly Station (€22.50, 2½ hours) to Rosslare Europort (€4.70, 25 minutes) line (via Enniscorthy and Rosslare Strand), serviced by three trains daily in each direction.

TAXI

For a 24-hour taxi service, call **Wexford Cabs** (☎ 053912 3123; 3 Charlotte St) or **AA Cabs** (☎ 053-914 0222). Most fares around the centre are €6 to €7.

AROUND WEXFORD TOWN
Irish National Heritage Park

This **heritage park** (☎ 053-912 0733; Ferrycarrig; adult/under 13yr/13-16yr/family incl 90min guided tour €8/4/6.50/20; ⊙ 9.30am-6.30pm Apr-Sep, 9.30am-5.30pm Oct-Mar) successfully squashes 9000 years of Irish history, up to the Normans, into an entertaining and informative visit. Costumed actors guide you past a recreated Neolithic farmstead, stone circle, ring fort, monastery, *crannóg* (lake settlement on an artifical island), Viking shipyard and Norman castle, while sound effects and smoking fires add to the realism.

The park is 3.5km northwest of Wexford town on the N11. A taxi from Wexford town costs about €7.

Johnstown Castle & Gardens

Parading peacocks guard this splendid 19th-century castellated house, the former home of the once-mighty Fitzgerald and Esmonde families.

The empty castle overlooks a small lake and is surrounded by 20 hectares of wooded **gardens** (car & passengers May-Sep €6; ⊙ 9am-5pm). The outbuildings house the **Irish Agricultural Museum** (☎ 053-917 1247; adult/child €6/4; ⊙ 9am-5pm Mon-Fri, 11am-5pm Sat & Sun Apr-Nov, 9am-5pm Mon-Fri Dec-Mar). It has an interesting collection of farm machinery and Irish country furniture, a horse-drawn caravan and a small Famine exhibition.

The castle is 7km southwest of Wexford town en route to Murntown.

Wexford Wildfowl Reserve

The Slobs may not sound inspiring (the name derives from the Irish *slab*, meaning 'mud, mire or a soft-fleshed person'), but this swathe of low-lying land reclaimed from the sea certainly inspires awe among birdwatchers. Each winter, it's home to one-third of the world's population of Greenland white-fronted geese – some 10,000 in total. Winter is also a good time to spot the brent goose from Arctic

---

THIRST FOR KNOWLEDGE

During a hunting trip to the Slobs in the 1950s, the Guinness Brewery's managing director, Sir Hugh Beaver, shot at but missed a golden plover. A spirited debate ensued among his hunting party over whether it, or the red grouse, was Europe's fastest game bird. Sir Hugh realised similar debates regularly cropped up in pubs, and that publishing definitive answers could resolve them (over pints of Guinness, of course). He was right on that score (today the *Guinness Book of World Records* is a record-holder itself, as the biggest-selling copyrighted book in the world), but wrong about Europe's fastest game bird (it's the spur-wing goose).

Canada. Throughout the year you'll see numerous species of wader and wildfowl.

The **Wexford Wildfowl Reserve** (☎ 053-912 3129; North Slob; admission free, guided tours on request; ⚓ 9am-6pm mid-Apr–Sep, 10am-5pm Oct–mid-Apr), which protects the birds' feeding grounds, has an observation tower, assorted hides and a visitor centre with detailed exhibits. From Wexford, head north for 3km on the R741 towards Dublin and take the signposted right-hand turn; the visitor centre is another 2km along the lane.

Trivia buffs may also know the Slobs and its birds as the inspiration for the *Guinness Book of World Records* – see p193.

Curracloe

The opening carnage of *Saving Private Ryan* (1997) wasn't filmed in Normandy, but here at Curracloe's 11km-long, Blue Flag–rated beach –one of a string of deserted beaches north of Wexford town. Many of the birds found at the Wexford Wildfowl Reserve can also be seen at Curracloe's **Raven Nature Reserve**. It's signposted 13km northeast of Wexford (from Wexford, take the R741). If you're discreet you can pitch a tent in the sheltered dunes.

A 30-minute walk from the beach, **Hotel Curracloe** (☎ 053-913 7308; www.hotelcurracloe.com; s €40-45, d €70-80; P) is a small family-run hotel with a staid but snug interior, a restaurant, and traditional sessions on Friday, Saturday and Sunday nights.

Morriscastle

Some 16km north of Curracloe, Morriscastle's beach also has a Blue Flag rating. Right beside the sand dunes, facilities at the **Morriscastle Strand Holiday Park** (☎ 053-913 0212, 087 773 7637; www.morriscastlestrand.com; campsite €20-24; ⚓ Easter-Oct) include washing machines and dryers, and coveted tent sites (€8 to €11 if you're travelling without a car). Electricity costs €4; showers are €1.

ROSSLARE STRAND
pop 1359

Surrounded by suburban-style homes, Rosslare (Ros Láir) town, 12km northwest of Rosslare Harbour, is rather soulless but opens onto a glorious Blue Flag beach. In summer, the beach is the habitat of hordes of ice cream–fuelled children. In winter, the empty sands billow at the feet of the occasional solitary walker.

The long shallow bay is perfect for windsurfing. During the summer months, gear hire and windsurfing, kayaking, sailing and surfing tuition is available at **Rosslare Watersports Centre** (☎ 053-913 2202; www.rosslareholidayresort.com). **Rosslare Golf Links** (☎ 053-913 2203; www.rosslaregolf.com; green fee weekdays/weekends €50/70) runs along the beach road, and there are gentle walks towards Rosslare Point, 7km north.

Sleeping & Eating

Killiane Castle (☎ 053-915 8885; www.killianecastle.com; Drinagh; s/d €75/100, 1-/2-bedroom apt per week from €300/450; P) Northeast of the N25 en route to Wexford, this farmhouse B&B is in a 17th-century house attached to a 13th-century Norman castle – guests can climb its tower for panoramas of the surrounding countryside and coastline. Self-catering apartments are set in the leafy grounds (weekend-only rental possible outside high summer), which also accommodate a golf range, tennis court, croquet lawn and nature trails.

YE OLDE LANGUAGE

Keep your ears open for remnants of a dialect called Yola, which hangs on in County Wexford's two southeasternmost baronies, Forth and Bargy. Yola stands for 'ye olde language' and is a mix of Irish with old French, English, Welsh, Danish and Flemish brought over by new settlers following the arrival of the Normans.

It's likely that the Yola language would have disappeared altogether were it not for wealthy local landowner and philanthropist Jacob Poole (1774–1827), who compiled a glossary of some 1700 words. First published 40 years after his death, Poole's 'mini-dictionary' can still be found in libraries today.

Yola is characterised by drawled vowels and endings, and initial Fs pronounced as Vs and initial Ss pronounced as Zs. Some of our favourite examples of the language include: *raimais* (talking rubbish), *sleeveen* (sly person), *stouk* (a truculent woman) and *aar's dhurth a heighe* (there's dirty weather above).

Kelly's Resort Hotel (☎ 053-913 2114; www.kellys .ie; s €77-95, d €154-190, full board per person €127-154; ⓟ 🖥 🖀 🖀) Established in 1895 and run by the fourth generation of the same family, this seaside family resort is an Irish institution. While the service remains delightfully old-fashioned and personal, the property has been thoroughly modernised, with bright, contemporary rooms and every conceivable facility: tennis, crazy golf, snooker, table tennis, badminton, yoga, croquet, restaurants, bars, and a pampering SeaSpa.

Rosslare is short on good restaurants, but **La Marine** (☎ 053-32114; lunch mains €11-16, dinner mains €18-25; ☽ noon-10pm), the wonderful Gallic bistro-bar at Kelly's, welcomes nonguests.

Getting There & Away

Wexford Bus (☎ 053-914 2742; www.wexfordbus.com) runs four buses a day (two on Sunday) to Wexford (€4, 40 minutes).

On the main Dublin–Wexford–Rosslare Europort line, three **trains** per day in each direction call at Rosslare Strand (from Dublin €22.50, three hours; from Wexford €4.70, 19 minutes; from Rosslare Europort €4.70, 11 minutes). There is one train daily Monday to Saturday in each direction between Rosslare Strand and Waterford (€15, 1¼ hours).

ROSSLARE HARBOUR
pop 1041

Busy, functional Rosslare Harbour has connections to Wales and France from the monolithic Europort ferry terminal, where you will also find Rosslare Europort train station. A road leading uphill from the harbour becomes the N25 and takes you to B&Bs and hotels. Further along this road are Kilrane and Tagoat, where there are more sleeping and eating options. There's a **Bank of Ireland** (St Martin's Rd) just off the N25, and an ATM inside the shopping centre on the main road, where you'll also find a supermarket and pharmacy.

Sights

Farm animals and flapping birds roam the reconstructed 18th-century thatched cottages, working windmill and tiny, four-pew church at **Yola Farmstead folk park** (☎ 053-913 2610; Tagoat; adult/child/family €6/4.50/15; ☽ 10am-7pm Jul & Aug, 10am-4.30pm May-Jun & Sep-Oct, 10am-4.30pm Mon-Fri Nov-Apr). The name of this small heritage centre comes from the local dialect, which

still survives today – see opposite. Common surnames of the Yola people include Barry, Condon, Doyle, Fleming, Grace, Hay, Keating, Lambert, Larkin, Power, Stafford, Talbot and Walsh. If you're tracing your ancestors, contact the onsite **genealogy centre** (wexgen@eircom.net; searches from €30; ☽ 10am-4pm Mon-Fri), which can search parish and census records. The park is just outside Tagoat, on the N25.

Sleeping & Eating

St Martin's Rd is lined with B&Bs that cater for ferry-catchers with early breakfasts.

our pick **O'Leary's Farmhouse B&B** (☎ 053-913 3134; www.olearysfarm.com; Killilane, Kilrane; s €35-45, d €70-90; ⓟ) The O'Leary family have been rearing rare breeds of sheep and beef cattle at this working organic farm since the 1800s, and have renovated six airy, whitewashed guestrooms with honey-coloured hardwood floors and crisp linens. If you're lucky enough to get an east-facing room (and fine weather), you'll wake to unforgettable views of the sun rising over the Irish Sea. Breakfast includes vegan options like Quorn sausages, which you can work off on a 10-minute stroll to the beach. Turn off the N25 onto the road separating Kilrane's pair of pubs, the Kilrane Inn and Culleton's Pub, from where it's a clearly signposted 3km.

Harbour View Hotel (☎ 053-916 1450; www .harbourviewhotel.ie; s €60-75, d €90-120; ⓟ) Service at this buttercup-yellow hotel melts away the Europort's hulking presence, as do its sprightly, colourful rooms.

Churchtown House (☎ 053-913 2555; www.church townhouse.com; Tagoat; r €110-150; ☽ Mar-Nov; ⓟ) Set back from the R736 on the northern side of Tagoat, this 17th-century manor house has uncluttered, flowing guestrooms decorated in autumn hues. Evening meals are available on request.

Seasons Restaurant (☎ 053-916 1450; Harbour View Hotel; mains €9.50-21.50, ☽ dinner) Despite the nautical-style interior of the Harbour View Hotel's restaurant, it serves an extensive range of Chinese fare (sizzling king prawns in black bean sauce, aromatic duck with steamed pancakes, vegetable chop suey), as well as Thai and European dishes. The wine list stretches to Argentina, Chile and South Africa.

Getting There & Away
BOAT

Stena Line (☎ 053-913 3115; www.stenaline.ie) sails between Rosslare Harbour and Fishguard

COUNTIES WEXFORD, WATERFORD, CARLOW & KILKENNY

in Wales (adult foot passenger €30, bicycle €8, motorbike and driver €55 to €65, car and driver €85 to €189, two to four sailings per day). The crossing takes 3½ hours (two hours on Express ferry services, operating mid-May to mid-September).

Irish Ferries (☎ 053-913 3158; www.irishferries .com) sails to Pembroke in Wales (3¾ hours, twice daily). Single fares start at €28 for a foot passenger, €59 for a motorbike and driver, and €85 for a car and driver. Between late February and mid-December there are ferries to Cherbourg, France (19½ hours, up to three a week) and, between mid-May and September, less frequent sailings to Roscoff, France (18 hours). Single fares are from €56 for a foot passenger, €10 for a bicycle, €89 for a motorbike and driver, and €99 for a car and driver.

For more information see p717.

BUS
Buses and trains depart from the Rosslare Europort station, located at the ferry terminal.

Bus Éireann (☎ 053-912 2522) has services to numerous Irish towns and cities, including Dublin (€16.70, three hours, at least nine daily) via Wexford (€4.50, 30 minutes), and Cork (€21.20, four hours, five daily Monday to Saturday, three Sunday) via Waterford (€14.90, 1½ hours).

CAR
Budget (☎ 053-913 3318) has an outlet in the ferry terminal.

TRAIN
Three trains daily in each direction operate on the Rosslare Europort–Rosslare Strand–Wexford–Dublin route (to Rosslare Strand €4.70, 10 minutes; to Wexford €4.70, 25 minutes; to Dublin Connolly Station €22.50, three hours). Trains on the Rosslare Europort–Limerick route stop in Waterford (€17, 1¼ hours, two daily Monday to Saturday).

SOUTH OF ROSSLARE HARBOUR
About 9km south of Rosslare Harbour is Carnsore Point, home to the east coast's first wind farm. Ireland's first nuclear power stations would also be here had not cost (and protests) aborted the scheme.

The village of **Carne** has a few pretty, white-washed, thatched cottages and a fine beach.

Locals and visitors alike pack the **Lobster Pot** (☎ 053-913 1110; Carne; lunch dishes around €12, dinner mains €21-35; ☯ restaurant dinner Tue-Sun, bar food noon-7.30pm Tue-Sun, closed Jan-early Feb) in summer (at which time it doesn't take bookings), but it's worth the squeeze to get at the super-fresh seafood. The chowder – brimming with cockles, mussels, prawns, salmon, crab and cod – is among the best on the planet.

Heading back up the road takes you past Lady's Island Lake containing **Our Lady's Island**, site of an early Augustinian priory and still a centre of devotion. Fervent pilgrims used to crawl round the island; people still walk it barefoot. Look out for the stump of the Norman tower, which tilts more than the Leaning Tower of Pisa. When it's not waterlogged, you can drive out to the castle on the island and walk a 2km circuit taking in the shrine.

On the lake's eastern shore, the catch-all **Castle View Heights** (☎ 053-913 1140; www.castleview heights.com) complex has a restaurant, craft shop and minigolf, as well as self-catering cottages (€200 to €600 per week).

St Margaret's Beach Caravan & Camping Park (☎ 053-913 1169; stmarg@eircom.net; St Margaret's Beach; campsites €18-20; ☯ mid-Mar–Sep), is a well-equipped campsite 500m from the beach.

There's no public transport to this area.

KILMORE QUAY
pop 396
Dotted with thatched cottages, Kilmore Quay is a small, working fishing village whose harbour is the jumping-off point for Ireland's largest bird sanctuary, the Saltee Islands (see opposite), which are clearly visible out to sea.

Mussel in on the four-day **Seafood Festival** (☎ 053-912 9918) in mid-July for music, dancing and, of course, tastings.

Sights & Activities
To charter a boat for sea angling, contact **Kilmore Quay Boat Charters** (☎ 053-912 9704).

Sailing Ireland (☎ 053-913 9163; www.sailingireland .ie) offers five-day live-aboard courses (from €750 per person) and skippered boat charters (per boat €300/550 per half-day/day).

Sandy beaches stretch northwest and northeast from Forlorn Point (Crossfarnoge). There are some signposted walking trails behind the peaceful dunes, circled by serenading skylarks. Look out for **St Patrick's Bridge causeway**, which stretches towards Little

Saltee. A Dutch trawler ran aground there in 2006.

Wrecks like SS *Isolde* and SS *Ardmore*, both dating back to the 1940s, and extraordinary marine life keep divers occupied. Contact **Wexford Sub Aqua Club** (www.divewexford.org) for advice.

About 9km north of Kilmore Quay, **Ballycross Apple Farm** (☎ 053-913 5160; www.bally cross.com; Bridgetown) sells its apples, apple juices, chutneys and jams direct to the public and also bakes yummy waffles. It's open from 2pm to 6pm on Saturday and Sunday during apple season (variously mid-August to March).

Sleeping & Eating

Mill Road Farm (☎ 053-912 9633; www.millroadfarm.com; R739; s/d €45/70; ✺ closed late Dec; P) About 2km northeast of Kilmore Quay on the R739, this working dairy farm offers simple rooms and breakfasts featuring homemade bread and free-range eggs.

Hotel Saltees (☎ 053-912 9601; www.hotelsaltees .ie; Kilmore Quay; s/d €80/140; P) Although rooms here are typical motel-style, they're generously sized and enlivened by painterly canvases and fresh colours. Its restaurant, Le Saffron, is open for dinner from Friday to Sunday and for Sunday lunch, and sticks to well-cooked surf and turf classics, with a handful of vegetarian options (mains €17 to €28).

Silver Fox Seafood Restaurant (☎ 053-912 9888; Kilmore Quay; mains €18-32; ✺ noon-9.30pm Jun-Aug, 5-9.30pm Mon-Sat, 12.30-2.30pm & 5-9.30pm Sun Sep-May) Inside a brown-painted building just back from the quay, the Silver Fox's fresh-from-the-ocean offerings include a potato-crusted fisherman's pie filled with prawns, monkfish, salmon and cod in Pernod cream sauce, while land-based options include guinea fowl and wok-fried egg noodles.

Kehoe's (☎ 053-912 9830; Kilmore Quay) Decorated with nautical equipment, right down to the beer garden built from a trawler mast and boom, this inviting pub has regular live music at weekends.

Getting There & Away

The Viking Shuttle Bus, operated by **Wexford Bus** (☎ 053-914 2742; www.wexfordbus.com), runs to/from Wexford up to four times daily (€5.50, 45 minutes). **Bus Éireann** (☎ 053-912 2522) service 383 covers the same route on Wednesday and Saturday (two services in each direction).

SALTEE ISLANDS

Once the haunt of privateers, smugglers and 'dyvars pyrates', the **Saltee Islands** (www.saltee islands.info) now have a peaceful existence as one of Europe's most important bird sanctuaries. Over 375 recorded species make their home here, 4km offshore from Kilmore Quay, principally the gannet, guillemot, cormorant, kittiwake, puffin, aux and the Manx shearwater. The best time to visit is the spring and early-summer nesting season. The birds leave once the chicks can fly, and by early August it's eerily quiet.

The two islands, the 90-hectare Great Saltee and the 40-hectare Little Saltee, feature some of Europe's oldest rocks, dating back over 2000 million years, and were inhabited as long ago as 3500 to 2000 BC. From the 13th century until the dissolution of the monasteries, they were the property of Tintern Abbey, after which various owners were granted the land.

Two of the Wexford rebel leaders, Bagenal Harvey and John Colclough, hid here after the failed 1798 Rising. They were betrayed by a paid informer, tracked down in a six-hour manhunt, taken to Wexford, hanged, and their heads stuck on spikes.

Boats make the trip from Kilmore Quay harbour, but docking depends on the wind direction and is often impossible. Contact local boatmen such as **Declan Bates** (☎ 053-912 9684, 087 252 9736; day trip €25), who also runs a 1½-hour trip around the islands (€20).

For more information read *Saltees: Islands of Birds and Legends* by Richard Roche and Oscar Merne (O'Brien Press).

HOOK PENINSULA & AROUND

The road shadowing the long, tapering finger of the Hook Peninsula is signposted as the Ring of Hook coastal drive. Around every other bend is a quiet beach, a crumbling fortress, a stately abbey or a seafood restaurant, and the world's oldest working lighthouse is flung out at its tip.

Strongbow (Robert FitzGilbert de Clare, Earl of Pembroke) landed here on his way to capture Waterford in 1170, reputedly instructing his men to land 'by Hook or by Crooke', the latter referring to the nearby settlement of Crooke in County Waterford across the harbour.

Duncormick to Wellington Bridge

The promontory east of the Hook Peninsula, signposted as the Bannow Drive, is littered

---

PRINCE OF THE SALTEES

The Saltees were bought in 1943 by Michael Neale, who immediately proclaimed himself 'Prince of the Saltees'. Something of a strange one, he erected a throne and obelisk in his own honour on Great Saltee, and had a full-blown coronation ceremony there in 1956. Although the College of Arms in London refuted Neale's claim to blue blood, he won a small victory when Wexford County Council began addressing letters to 'Prince Michael Neale'.

The prince broadcast his intention to turn Great Saltee into a second Monte Carlo, but was distracted by a war right on his doorstep. In an escalation of hostilities, he released two ferrets, then a dozen foxes, then 46 cats onto the island to kill the rabbits that he hated so.

Prince Michael died in 1998, but before his death decreed: 'All people, young and old, are welcome to come, see and enjoy the islands, and leave them as they found them for the unborn generations to come, see and enjoy.'

---

with Norman ruins. The invaders founded a town at **Bannow**, yet nothing of it remains other than a ruined church. Enthusiastic historians, eyeing the uneven ground in front of the church and the shifting sands of the estuary, speak of the 'buried city of Bannow'.

Bannow Bay is a sanctuary for wildfowl including brent geese, redshank, wigeon and teal, and is also a cultivation site for Irish oysters. The remains of the medieval village of **Clonmines**, which fell into decline when its estuary silted up, are southwest of Wellington Bridge. The ruins are on private land, but there's a good view just south of the bridge as you head north into town. The redbrick chimney in a roadside paddock on the other side of the bridge is an old **silver mine**. It was in operation from the 1530s to 1851, and supplied the Irish mint.

Tintern Abbey

In better structural condition than its Welsh counterpart, from where its first monks hailed, Ireland's **Tintern Abbey** (☎ 051-562 650; Saltmills; admission free; ☺ 10am-6pm mid-Jun–Sep, 10am-5pm Oct) is secluded amid 100 acres of woodland. William Marshal, Earl of Pembroke, founded the Cistercian abbey in the early 13th century after he nearly perished at sea and swore to establish a church if he made it ashore.

Allow time to explore the **Tintern Trails**, a series of short woodland and coastal tracks around the abbey estate. Free walking maps are available from the tourist office in Fethard-on-Sea.

Fethard-on-Sea
pop 326
Continuing south towards the Head, Fethard is the largest village in the area. It's home

to the scant ruins of 9th-century church **St Mogue's** and a 15th-century **castle** (too unstable to walk inside), which belonged to the bishop of Ferns. There's a small community-run **tourist office** (☎ 051-397 502; www.thehook-wexford .com; Main St; ☺ 9.30am-5pm Mon-Fri) opposite the castle.

About 1km north of town, the quiet little **Ocean Island Camping & Caravan Park** (☎ 051-397 148; campsites €24; ☺ Apr-Sep) has a shop, a playground, and laundry and games rooms.

Hook Head & Around

The journey from Fethard to Hook Head takes in a hypnotic stretch of horizon, with few houses between the flat, open fields on the tapering peninsula. Views extend across Waterford Harbour and, on a clear day, as far as the Comeragh and Galtee Mountains.

On its southern tip, Hook Head is capped by the world's oldest working **lighthouse** (☎ 051-397 055; adult/child €6/3.50 incl guided tour; ☺ 9.30am-6pm Jun-Aug, 9.30am-5.30pm May & Sep, 9.30am-5pm Nov-Feb, closed mid-late Dec), staffed until 1996. It's said that monks lit a beacon on the head from the 5th century and that the first Viking invaders were so happy to have a guiding light that they left them alone. In the early 13th century William Marshal erected a more permanent structure, which has remained largely unchanged. Traces of the lighthouse keepers' lives remain inside the black-and-white-striped tower. Access is by half-hour guided tour. The visitor centre has a decent cafe/restaurant.

There are brilliant, blustery **walks** on both sides of the head, but beware the freak waves and numerous blowholes on the western side of the peninsula. The rocks around the lighthouse are Carboniferous limestone, rich in **fossils**. Search carefully and you may find

350-million-year-old shells and tiny disclike pieces of crinoids, a type of starfish. A good place to hunt is Patrick's Bay, on the southeast of the peninsula. Hook Head visitor centre has a free map of the area's accessible beaches. At low tide, there's a good walk between Grange and Carnivan beaches, past caves, rock pools and **Baginbun Head**, which, surmounted by the 19th-century **Martello tower**, is where the Normans first landed (1169) for their conquest of Ireland. It's a good vantage point for **birdwatching**: over 200 species have been recorded passing through. You might even spot dolphins or whales in the estuary, particularly between December and February.

Caves, crevasses and gullies are part of the underwater scenery at diving sites out from the inlet under the lighthouse and from the rocks at the southwestern corner of the head, with a maximum depth of 15m. If it's too rough, try Churchtown, 1km north of the point on the western side of the peninsula. The rocks south of Slade Harbour are another popular area. Contact Ray Forlong at the **Hook Sub Aqua Club** (☎ 087 678 1636; rfurlong@bolandcars .ie) for advice.

About 5km northeast of the Hook Head lighthouse, ghostly Loftus Hall (closed to the public), built by the Marquis of Ely in the 1870s, gazes across the estuary at Dunmore East. The English-owned Loftus estate once covered much of the peninsula.

About 3km further on, turning left at a small roundabout brings you to the village of **Slade**, where the most activity is in the swirl of seagulls above the ruined castle and harbour.

Driving from Hook Head towards Duncannon brings you past the ruins of a fortified **medieval church**. In 1172 Henry II granted land hereabouts to the Knights Templar; they made nearby Templetown their headquarters and built various churches. The 13th-century structure they built here was later added to by the Knights Hospitaller and the Loftus estate. On the ground to the left of the church, a stone slab bears a Templar seal: a lamb and crucifix.

Across the street from the church, the roadside pub **Templar's Inn** (☎ 051-397 162; Templetown; mains €10-22; ⏰ restaurant 12.30-9pm Mar-Oct, noon-8pm Thu-Sun Nov-Mar, pub noon-late daily), opens to a panoramic outdoor terrace overlooking the church, fields and ocean beyond. Inside, the dark-timber interior looks like a wayfarers' tav-

ern, but is a cosy place for a steak or seafood. Owner Nancy is a fount of info on the area.

Just beyond Templetown en route to Duncannon are two small, delightfully secluded beaches: **Dollar Bay** and **Booley Bay**.

Duncannon & Around
pop 291

The small, laidback holiday town of Duncannon slopes down to a sandy beach that's transformed into a surrealist canvas during July's **Duncannon International Sand Sculpting Festival** (www.visitduncannon.com).

To the west of the village, star-shaped **Duncannon Fort** (☎ 051-389 454; www.duncannonfort .com; adult/child/family €5/3/12; ⏰ 9.30am-5.30pm Jun-mid-Sep, rest of yr by appointment) was used as a set for *The Count of Monte Cristo* starring Richard Harris and Guy Pearce (2001). The fort was built in 1588 to stave off a feared attack by the Spanish Armada, and later used by the Irish army as a WWI training base. There's a small maritime museum and a cafe; guided tours (included in admission) depart at 11am and 3pm. A military re-enactment weekend takes place here over the June bank holiday.

About 4km northwest of Duncannon is pretty **Ballyhack**, from where a car ferry travels to Passage East in County Waterford (see p211). It's dominated by the 15th-century **Ballyhack Castle** (☎ 051-389 468; admission free; ⏰ 10am-6pm mid-Jun–mid-Sep), a Knights Hospitallers tower house, containing a small exhibition on the Crusades.

Beside the R733, some 9km north of Duncannon, the ruined **Dunbrody Abbey** (☎ 051-388 603; www.dunbrodyabbey.com; Campile; adult/child €2/1; ⏰ 11am-5pm mid-May–mid-Sep) is a remarkably intact Cistercian abbey founded by Strongbow in 1170 and completed in 1220. The adjoining **Dunbrody Abbey Visitor Centre** (adult/child €6/3) provides access to the ruins of Dunbrody Castle, a craft shop, a museum with a huge doll's house, minigolf, and a yew-hedge maze made up of over 1500 trees.

SLEEPING & EATING
Aldridge Lodge Restaurant & Guesthouse (☎ 051-389 116; www.aldridgelodge.com; Duncannon; s €55, d €100-110; ⏰ dinner Tue-Sun Jul & Aug, Wed-Sun Sep-Jun; **P**). In a wind-blown spot on open fields above Duncannon, Aldridge takes a bit of finding, but it's worth it for its elegant, contemporary guestrooms and fresh local seafood like Hook Head crab claws or Kilmore cod (dinner

€38.50). Two caveats: call ahead for periodic closures, and kids under seven aren't allowed. Heading out of Duncannon village towards Hook Lighthouse, turn right at Wallace's Mobile Homes; it's 500m ahead on your left.

Glendine Country House (☎ 051-389 500; www.glendinehouse.com; Arthurstown; s/d from €60/120; **P**) This vine-covered 1830s-built former dower house is wonderfully homey. Bay windows overlook the estuary and grounds populated by deer, cattle and sheep. The Crosbie family lay on organic fare and home-baked treats such as cream teas.

Squigl Restaurant & Roche's Bar (☎ 051-389 188; Quay Rd, Duncannon; bar food €6.50-14.50, restaurant mains €19.50-23.50; ☷ bar food 10.30am-10pm, restaurant dinner Wed-Sat Feb-Easter, Tue-Sun Easter-Dec) Local produce is the mainstay of Squigl, where dishes range from honey-glazed ham to spring lamb (bookings essential). The same kitchen serves Roche's Bar next door, which is adorned with vintage advertising posters and seamen's knots. Trad sessions take place on Friday, Saturday and, during summer, midweek.

ourpick Dunbrody Country House Hotel, Restaurant & Cookery School (☎ 051-389 600; www.dunbrodyhouse.com; Arthurstown; 2-/3-course restaurant meal €52/65, tasting menu with paired wines €80; **P** ☷) Chef Kevin Dundon is a familiar face on Irish TV, and the author of cookbooks *Full On Irish* and *Great Family Food*. His spa hotel (single/double room from €145/240), in a period-decorated 1830s Georgian manor on 300-acre grounds, is the stuff of foodies' fantasies, with a gourmet restaurant and cookery school (1-/2-day courses €175/320 excluding accommodation).

Getting There & Away
There's public transport as far as Fethard, but none to Hook Head.

BUS
West Coast Wexford Rural Transport (☎ 051-389 679; www.wexfordruralbus.com; Ramsgrange Centre, New Ross) has at least one service per week to towns throughout the upper Hook Peninsula. Return fares are €5 to €8; €3 for students and under-16s.

On Monday and Thursday, **Bus Éireann** (☎ 053-912 2522) service 370 runs between Waterford, New Ross, Duncannon, Templetown, Fethard, Wellington Bridge and Wexford. The entire journey takes 2¾ hours. The same bus links Waterford, New Ross

and Duncannon from Monday to Saturday (departing in the evening), and Waterford, New Ross, Wellington Bridge and Wexford on Wednesday and Saturday. In all cases there is one service in each direction (none on Sunday).

FERRY
If you're travelling directly to Waterford city, the Ballyhack–Passage East car ferry (see p211) saves detouring via New Ross.

NEW ROSS
pop 4677

The big attraction at New Ross (Rhos Mhic Triúin), 34km west of Wexford town, is the opportunity to board a 19th-century Famine ship. But New Ross' historical links stretch back much further – to the 12th century, when it developed as a Norman port on the River Barrow. A group of rebels tried to seize the town during the 1798 Rising. They were repelled by the defending garrison, leaving 3000 dead and much of the place in tatters. Today its eastern bank retains some intriguing steep, narrow streets and the impressive ruins of a medieval abbey.

The **tourist office** (☎ 051-421 857; The Quay; ☷ 9am-6pm Apr-Sep, 9am-5pm Oct-Mar) doubles as the entrance to the Dunbrody Heritage Ship, and also has a small cafe and internet terminals (€2 per 20 minutes). Alternatively, surf the net across the street at **Solaak Inventures** (☎ 051-420 807; The Quay; per hr €4; ☷ 10am-11pm Mon-Sat, 1pm-midnight Sun).

Sights & Activities
Emigrants' sorrowful yet often-inspiring stories are brought to life by actors during a 30-minute tour of the **Dunbrody Heritage Ship** (☎ 051-425 239; www.dunbrody.com; The Quay; adult/child €7.50/4.50; ☷ 10am-6pm Apr-Sep, 10am-5pm Oct-Mar), a full-scale replica 1845 Famine ship (also known as a 'coffin ship', due to the number of passengers who didn't survive the journey). Prior to the tour, a 10-minute film gives you background on the original three-masted barque and the construction of the new one. Admission includes access to the onsite database of Irish emigration to America from 1845 to 1875, containing over two million records.

By the time you're reading this, New Ross' answer to France's Bayeux tapestry is due to have opened across the Quay from the

COUNTIES WEXFORD, WATERFORD, CARLOW & KILKENNY

Dunbrody Heritage Ship. The **Ros Tapestry** (☎ 051-445 396; www.rosexpo.ie; The Quay) will weave together the story of the Normans' influence on Ireland via fifteen panels created by volunteer embroiderers, and incorporate a cafe and craft shop.

Two- and three-hour cruises on the **Galley River Cruising Restaurant** (☎ 051-421 723; www .rivercruises.ie; North Quay; cruise & tea/lunch/dinner from €12/25/40; ☒ 12.30pm, 3pm & 7pm May-Oct) drift slowly up the River Barrow, past rolling fields and peaceful farmlands. You can enjoy the ride over a cuppa or local fare like Wexford lamb or poached salmon, followed by local strawberries and cream.

The roofless ruin on Church Lane is **St Mary's Abbey**, one of the largest medieval churches in Ireland. It was founded by Isabella of Leinster and her husband William in the 13th century. Ask at the tourist office for access.

Sleeping & Eating

MacMurrough Farm Hostel (☎ 051-421 383; www .macmurrough.com; MacMurrough, New Ross; dm €16-18, d €40-44, 2-person cottage per night €60-70, per week €350; ☒ mid-Mar–Oct; ℗ ☎) A strutting rooster serves as an alarm clock at Brian and Jenny's remote hilltop hostel. The farm's cheery bedrooms and stove-warmed common area have a rustic charm, as does the two-person self-catering cottage in the old stables. There's also a family-size two-storey, two-bedroom cottage (ask for prices). Follow the hand-painted signs up a series of tracks 3.5km northeast of town.

Brandon House Hotel (☎ 051-421 703; www .brandonhousehotel.ie; New Ross; s €125-150, d €190-260; ℗ ☐ ☎ ☎) Up a steep driveway 2km south of New Ross, with river views, this 1865-built redbrick manor certainly lives up to its reputation as family friendly, with kids happily bounding around the place. Winning elements include open log fires, a library bar and large rooms, as well as spa treatments. Wi-fi in the public areas extends to some nearby rooms.

Sid's Diner (☎ 051-421 973; Marsh Meadows; mains €8.50-10.50; ☒ 7am-7pm Mon-Fri, 7am-4pm Sat) Worth a stop for its sheer eclecticness, Sid's, 1.5km south of the centre, serves sturdy Irish classics in an American-style diner (complete with red-vinyl booths and licence plates) by Renault-branded staff (it's next to the showroom).

Upper Deck Cafe (☎ 051-425 391; 8 Mary St; mains €9-15; ☒ 9am-5.30pm Mon-Sat) Tucked up a wooden staircase inside the general store Ann McDonald's Deli, this arty cafe adds a modern twist to the wholefood formula with dishes like a four-cheese quiche and grilled salmon marinated in ginger, honey and lime.

Cafe Nutshell (☎ 051-422 777; 8 South St; mains €12-16; ☒ 9am-5.15pm Mon-Sat Jun-Sep, 9am-5.15pm Tue-Sat Oct-May) It's a shame that Nutshell closes of an evening, as New Ross' town centre is short on places of this calibre. Scones, breads and buns are all baked on the premises, hot lunch specials utilise local produce and there's a great range of smoothies, juices and organic wines.

Getting There & Away

Bus Éireann (☎ 053-912 2522) buses depart from Dunbrody Inn on the Quay and travel to Waterford (€5.40, 30 minutes, 11 daily Monday to Saturday, seven Sunday), Wexford (€6.30, 40 minutes, four daily Monday to Friday, three Saturday), Rosslare Harbour (€12.20, one hour, four daily Monday to Saturday, three Sunday) and Dublin (€12.20, three hours, four daily).

AROUND NEW ROSS

About 7km south of New Ross, the **Kennedy Homestead** (☎ 051-388 264; www.kennedyhomestead .com; Dunganstown; adult/child/family €5/2.50/15; ☒ 10am-5pm Jul & Aug, 11.30am-4.30pm Mon-Fri May, Jun & Sep, by appointment rest of yr) was the birthplace of Patrick Kennedy, great-grandfather of John F Kennedy, who left Ireland for the USA in 1848. When JFK visited the farm in 1963 and hugged the current owner's grandmother, it was his first public display of affection according to his sister Jean. Jean later unveiled the plaque here. The outbuildings have been turned into a museum that examines the Irish-American dynasty's history on both sides of the Atlantic.

Containing 4500 species of trees and shrubs in 252 hectares of woodlands and gardens, the **John F Kennedy Arboretum** (☎ 051-388 171; New Ross; adult/child/family €2.90/1.30/7.40; ☒ 10am-8pm May-Aug, 10am-6.30pm Apr & Sep, 10am-5pm Oct-Mar) is the promised land for families on a sunny day. The park, 2km southeast of the Kennedy Homestead, has a small visitor centre, tearooms and a picnic area; a miniature train tootles around in the summer months. **Slieve Coillte** (270m), opposite the park entrance, has a viewing point from where you can see the arboretum and six counties on a clear day.

On the N25, 15km east of New Ross, **Cedar Lodge Hotel and Restaurant** (☎ 051-428 386; www .cedarlodgehotel.ie; Carrigbyrne, Newbawn; s from €90, d €120-160; 🕒 bar food lunch; restaurant dinner; P 🖥 🛜) sits amid orchards and backs onto the Carrigbyrne Forest, with beautiful wooded walking trails. Although the hotel has 30 flowing rooms (with enormous bathrooms), it feels like staying in a private home, thanks to ceramic ducks lining the staircase and fluffy teddy bears in the reception area. Veal in white wine, scallops in vermouth, and homemade honey ice cream are among the highlights of its excellent restaurant (bar mains from €13, dinner mains €25 to €35).

ENNISCORTHY
pop 3241

County Wexford's second-largest town, Enniscorthy (Inis Coirthaidh) has a warren of steep streets descending from Augustus Pugin's cathedral to the Norman castle and the River Slaney. Enniscorthy is inextricably linked to some of the fiercest fighting of the 1798 Rising, when rebels captured the town and set up camp at Vinegar Hill.

Information

The **tourist office** (☎ 053-923 4699; Mill Park Rd; 🕒 9.30am-5pm Mon-Fri, noon-4pm Sat & Sun Jun-Aug, 9.30am-4pm Mon-Fri Sep-May), inside the National 1798 Rebellion Centre, can book accommodation (€4).

At the bottom of Castle Hill, on and around Abbey Sq, are the main post office and two banks. **Internet Cafe Plus** (☎ 053-924 3676; Templeshannon; per hr €2; 🕒 10am-10pm Mon-Fri, noon-10pm Sat & Sun Apr-Oct, 10am-10pm Mon-Fri, noon-8pm Sat & Sun Nov-Mar) overlooks Enniscorthy Bridge.

Sights

Visiting the excellent **National 1798 Rebellion Centre** (☎ 053-923 7198; www.iol.ie/~98com; Mill Park Rd; adult/child €6/3.50; 🕒 same hr as tourist office) before climbing Vinegar Hill greatly enhances its impact. The centre's exhibits cover the French and American revolutions that sparked Wexford's abortive uprising against British rule in Ireland, before chronicling what was one of the most bloodthirsty battles of the 1798 Rebellion, and a turning point in the struggle. A month later, English troops attacked and forced the rebels to retreat, massacring hundreds of women and children in the 'follow-up' operation. Interactive displays include a chessboard with pieces representing key figures in the Rising, and a multiscreen re-creation of the finale atop a virtual Vinegar Hill. It's chilly inside – bring a jacket. From Abbey Sq walk out of town along Mill Park Rd, then take the first right after the school.

To reach **Vinegar Hill** itself, follow the brown sign from Templeshannon on the eastern side of the river. It takes about 45 minutes to walk to the top of the hill (or five minutes to drive). At the summit there's a memorial to the uprising.

During the 1798 Rising, rebels used the **Enniscorthy Castle** as a prison. The stout, four-towered keep was built by the Normans; Queen Elizabeth I awarded its lease to the poet Edmund Spenser for the flattering things he said about her in his epic *The Faerie Queene*. Rather ungratefully, he sold it to a local landlord. Like everything else in these parts, the castle was attacked by Cromwell in 1649.

Restored to its original glory (check out the star-spangled roof), the dazzling Roman Catholic **St Aidan's Cathedral** (1846) was designed by Augustus Pugin, the architect behind the Houses of Parliament in London.

Activities

Eighteen-hole **Enniscorthy Golf Club** (☎ 053-923 7600; New Ross Rd; green fee weekday/weekend €30/40) is 2.5km southwest of town.

Fishing is possible through **Danny's Bait & Tackle** (☎ 053-924 3571; St Senan's Rd).

Festivals & Events

Enniscorthy holds its weekend-long **Strawberry Fair** (www.enniscorthystrawberryfestival.com) in June, when pubs extend their hours, and strawberries and cream are laid on heavily.

Sleeping

Old Bridge House (☎ 053-923 4222; oldbridgehouse bnb@eircom.net; Slaney Pl; s/d €45/80) Overlooking the Slaney, the Redmonds' comfortable guesthouse, with bohemian artefacts, pot plants and prints, is the perfect antidote to big-hotel blandness and B&B tweeness.

Treacy's Hotel (☎ 053-923 7798; www.treacyshotel .com; Templeshannon; r €150; P 🛜) With spruced-up rooms in streamlined, woodsy colours, Treacy's also scores with two bars, two restaurants (one international, one Thai) and a nightclub. Entertainment includes live bands and Irish dancing, and guests can use the leisure centre opposite for free.

COUNTIES WEXFORD, WATERFORD, CARLOW & KILKENNY

Monart (☎ 053-923 8999; www.monart.ie; The Still; from €175; P ⍟) Hidden in woodland 2km west of Enniscorthy, rooms at this discreet spa resort surround a pond. Modern touches such as a glass walkway have been added to the main house without lessening its stately grandeur. You can be sure of peace and quiet, as kids aren't allowed.

Eating

De Olde Bridge (☎ 053-923 8624; Templeshannon; snacks €2.50-4, meals €6-11.50; ☼ 8am-4pm Mon-Sat, 9am-4pm Sun) With its worn booths and vinyl table-cloths, this dusty cafe is the kind of place you thought had long disappeared. Old-fashioned stomach-stokers include lamb cutlets, mixed grills and traditional full Irish breakfasts.

Baked Potato (☎ 053-923 4085; Rafter St; dishes €5.50-8.50; ☼ 8am-6pm Mon-Sat) One of a cluster of cafes doing a brisk trade in homemade cakes, pies, sandwiches and daily specials.

Bailey (☎ 053-923 0353; www.thebailey.ie; Barrack St; lunch mains €9-14, dinner mains €13-26.50; ☼ 10am-10pm) Leather armchairs lurk between Jurassic pot-ted plants in this converted riverside grain store. Dishes range from finely honed pub grub to more interesting options like Cajun salmon steak.

Galo Chargrill Restaurant (☎ 053-923 8077; 19 Main St; 2-/3-course menus from €19/23; ☼ lunch & dinner Tue-Sat, noon-9pm Sun) Fame seems to have gone to the head of this Portuguese restaurant, whose spicy chargrills like double chicken fillets with chilli are overpriced for what you get. Still, you can wash them down with a fine Portuguese beer or wine.

Enniscorthy's **farmers market** (Abbey Sq; ☼ 9am-2pm Sat) sells local and organic veg, bacon, cheese, bread, fish and fruit.

Drinking & Entertainment

Antique Tavern (☎ 053-923 3428; 14 Slaney St) Slanted on the side of a hill, this creaky black-and-white pub has traditional live music most weekends in summer.

Bailey (above) This riverside landmark also in-corporates a venue staging local and national music and comedy.

Slaney Plaza Cinema (☎ 053-923 7060; www.slaney plaza.net; Templeshannon; adult/child €8/5.50) Screens mainstream and art-house films.

Shopping

The Enniscorthy area has been a centre of pottery since the 17th century. Continuing the tradition, **Kiltrea Bridge Pottery** (☎ 053-923 5107; www.kiltreapottery.com; ☼ 10am-1pm & 2-5.30pm Mon-Sat) creates handthrown terracotta pots including some stunning oversized conversa-tion pieces. It's 6.5km west of Enniscorthy off the Kiltealy Rd (R702).

Getting There & Away

BUS

Bus Éireann (☎ 053-912 2522) stops on the Shannon Quay on the eastern bank of the river, outside the **Bus Stop Shop** (☎ 053-923 3291; ☼ 9am-10pm) where you can buy tickets. There are nine daily buses to Dublin (€10.50, 2½ hours), and eight to Rosslare Harbour (€9.30, one hour) via Wexford (€5.80, 25 minutes).

TRAIN

The **train station** (☎ 053-923 3488) is on the eastern bank of the river. The one line serves Dublin Connolly Station (€22.50, 2¼ hours), Wexford (€6.50, 25 minutes) and Rosslare Europoort (€7.70, 45 minutes) three times daily.

FERNS

pop 954

It's hard to believe that this workaday vil-lage was once the powerhouse of the kings of Leinster, in particular Dermot MacMurrough (1110–71), who is forever associated with bringing the Normans to Ireland (see p35). The Normans left behind a cathedral and a doughty castle, later smashed to pieces by Cromwell. An hour or so will allow you to take in the town's major sites.

Chief among them, **Ferns Castle** (☎ 053-936 6411; admission free; ☼ 10am-6pm mid-Jun–mid-Sep) was built around 1220. A couple of walls and part of the moat survive; you can climb to the top of the one complete tower. Parliamentarians destroyed the castle and executed most of the local population in 1649. The ruins are thought to stand on the site of Dermot MacMurrough's old fortress. In the visitor centre are a cafe and a tapestry depicting local history.

At the eastern end of the main street is **St Edan's Cathedral**, built in early Gothic style in 1817. Its graveyard contains a ruined **high cross**, said to mark the resting place of Dermot MacMurrough.

Behind the cathedral are two medieval ruins: the Norman-built **Ferns Cathedral** and, with an unusual square-based round tower, **St Mary's Abbey**. Dermot MacMurrough founded it in

1158, inviting Augustinian monks to run a monastery here. An earlier Christian settlement founded here by St Aedan (also known as St Mogue) in 600 was destroyed by the Vikings.

Further out of town is **St Peter's Church**, built from stones taken magpie-like from Ferns Cathedral and St Mary's Abbey.

Ferns is an easy 12km drive northeast of Enniscorthy on the N11. **Wexford Bus** (☎ 053-914 2742; www.wexfordbus.com) operates seven services daily between Dublin airport and Wexford, which stop in Ferns.

MT LEINSTER

The highest peak in the Blackstairs Mountains, **Mt Leinster** (796m) has magnificent views of Counties Waterford, Carlow, Kilkenny and Wicklow from the top. It's home to some of Ireland's best hang-gliding: contact the **Irish Hang Gliding & Paragliding Association** (www.ihpa .ie) for further information.

The car park at the foot of the mountain is signposted from Bunclody, 16km northwest of Ferns. From here, it's a steep 1½-hour return walk. See p226 if you're coming from the western side of the mountains. Ordnance Survey's Discovery map number 68 covers the Blackstairs Mountains region.

COUNTY WATERFORD

pop 107,961

Diverse County Waterford harbours seaside resorts of all flavours along its sandy coastline; a warren of walking trails in the beautiful Nire Valley, concealed by the Comeragh and Monavullagh Mountains; and rejuvenated Waterford city, with its winding medieval lanes, open-air plazas soundtracked by buskers, and well-preserved Georgian architecture.

WATERFORD CITY

pop 45,775

Ireland's oldest city, Waterford (Port Láirge) is first and foremost a busy port. Some parts of the city still feel almost medieval, though, with narrow alleyways leading off larger streets. A great introduction to the area is Waterford's state-of-the-art museum on the quayfront, which uses multimedia wizardry to convey the city's extensive history.

History

In the 8th century Vikings settled at Port Láirge, which they renamed Vadrafjord and turned into a booming trading post. Their ferocity made Waterford the most powerful and feared settlement in the country. Local tribes paid a tribute known as *Airgead Sróine* (nose money), and defaulters had their noses cut off.

Anglo-Normans attacked the strategically situated town in 1170, defeating a combined Irish–Viking army and hurling 70 prominent citizens to their deaths off Baginbun Head. Strongbow (the Earl of Pembroke) then finished the takeover with 200 soldiers and 1000 archers, and married local chief Dermot MacMurrough's daughter.

King John extended the original Viking city walls in 1210 and Waterford became Ireland's most powerful city. In the 15th century it resisted the forces of two pretenders to the English Crown, Lambert Simnel and Perkin Warbeck, earning the motto *Urbs Intacta Manet Waterfordia* (Waterford city remains unconquered). The city defied Cromwell in 1649, but in 1650 his forces returned and Waterford surrendered. Although the town escaped the customary slaughter, Catholics were either exiled to the west or shipped as slaves to the Caribbean, and the population declined.

In recent years the city has received a facelift, with pedestrianised streets and public artworks.

Orientation

Waterford lies on the tidal reach of the River Suir, 16km from the coast. The main shopping street runs directly south from the Suir, beginning as Barronstrand St and passing through John Roberts Sq before becoming Broad St, Michael St and John St, which intersects with Parnell St; this then runs northeast back up to the quay-lined river, becoming The Mall on the way. Most sights and shops lie within this triangle.

Information
BOOKSHOPS
Waterford Book Centre (☎ 051-873 823; 25 John Roberts Sq; ☺ 9am-6pm Mon-Thu & Sat, 9am-9pm Fri, 1-5pm Sun) Three floors of books, foreign papers and magazines, and a cafe.

INTERNET ACCESS
Waterford e-Centre (☎ 051-878 448; 10 O'Connell St; per hr €4.50; ☺ 9.30am-9pm Mon-Thu, 9.30am-8pm Fri, 9.30am-6pm Sat, 11am-6pm Sun)

COUNTIES WEXFORD, WATERFORD, CARLOW & KILKENNY

WATERFORD

0   320 m
0   0.2 miles

INFORMATION
AIB	1	C4
Left Luggage	(see 41)	
Main Post Office	2	C4
Snow White Laundrette	3	B5
Tourist Office	4	B4
Waterford Book Centre	5	B4
Waterford e-Centre	6	B4

SIGHTS & ACTIVITIES
Beach Tower	7	B4
Bishop's Palace	8	C5
Christ Church Cathedral	9	C5
City Hall	10	D5
Clock Tower	11	C4
Edmund Rice International Heritage Centre	12	B6
French Church	13	C4
Half Moon Tower	14	B5
Holy Trinity Cathedral	15	C4
Reginald's Tower	16	D5
Theatre Royal	(see 39)	
Waterford Heritage Services	17	B4
Waterford Museum of Treasures	18	B4

SLEEPING
Arlington Lodge	19	C6
Granville Hotel	20	B4
Mayor's Walk House	21	B5
Portree Guesthouse	22	A4

EATING
47 The Bistro	23	B5
Bodéga!	24	B5
Cafe Lucia	25	C5
Harlequin	26	B5
La Bohème	27	B4
Saturday Market	28	B4

DRINKING
Downes Bar	29	A4
Geoff's	30	C5
Katty Barry's	31	D5
Munster Bar	32	C5
T&H Doolan's	33	B4

ENTERTAINMENT
Forum	34	A4
Garter Lane Art Gallery	35	A4
Garter Lane Arts Centre	36	B4
Kazbar	37	B5
Ruby's	38	C6
Theatre Royal	39	C5

TRANSPORT
Altitude (Bicycle Hire)	40	A5
Bus Éireann Station	41	A4
Eurolines	(see 41)	
Suirway	(see 41)	
Taxi Stand	42	C5
Taxi Stand	43	A3
Taxi Stand	44	C4

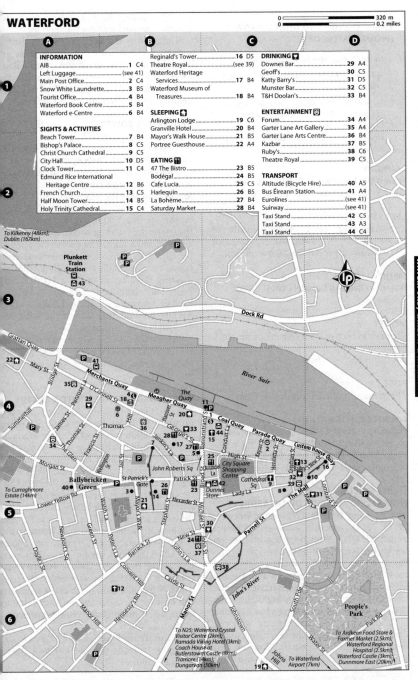

To Kilkenny (48km); Dublin (167km)

Plunkett Train Station

Dock Rd

River Suir

Grattan Quay

Mary St

Merchants Quay

O'Connell St

Meagher Quay

The Quay

Coal Quay

Parade Quay

Custom House Quay

Summerhill

James St

Thomas St

Francis St

The Glen

Morgan St

Thomas

George's St

Jenkins La

High St

Arundel La

City Square Shopping Centre

Cathedral Sq

Ballybricken Green

St Patrick's Gate

Patrick St

Dunnes Store

Lady La

The Mall

Lombard St

Wellington St

Mayor's Walk

Stephen St

Alexander St

Michael St

Parnell St

Newport's Sq

Green St

Peter's La

Barrack St

New St

John's La

John's River

Doyle St

Convent Hill

Castle St

Manor Hill

Hennessy's Rd

Manor St

Johnstown

John's Hill

South Pde

Water Rd

People's Park

Park Rd

To Curraghmore Estate (14km)

Lower Yellow Rd

To N25; Waterford Crystal Visitor Centre (2km); Ramada Viking Hotel (3km); Coach House at Butlerstown Castle (8km); Tramore (14km); Dungarvan (50km)

To Waterford Airport (7km)

To Ardkeen Food Store & Farmer Market (2.5km); Waterford Regional Hospital (2.5km); Waterford Castle (3km); Dunmore East (20km)

COUNTIES WEXFORD, WATERFORD, CARLOW & KILKENNY

> ### THREE THINGS YOU DIDN'T KNOW ABOUT WATERFORD
>
> ■ Ireland's first frog was released here.
>
> ■ A shellicky boo-ky is a Waterford garden snail.
>
> ■ To save on grave diggers and gallows, prisoners of the 1798 Rebellion were hung from a lifting bridge, then cut down into the river once they were dead.

LAUNDRY

Snow White Laundrette (☎ 051-858 905; Mayor's Walk; ◷ 9.15am-1.30pm & 2.30-6pm Mon-Sat)

LEFT LUGGAGE

The sweet shop (candy counter) inside the **bus station** (p209; ◷ 8am-7pm) stores luggage for €2.40 per item, per day (€4.80 overnight).

MEDICAL SERVICES

Waterford Regional Hospital (☎ 051-848 000; Dunmore Rd)

MONEY

There's a branch of the AIB bank by the clock tower on the quayfront, and ATMs throughout the town.

POST

The main post office is on Parade Quay.

TOURIST INFORMATION

Waterford city tourist office (☎ 051-875 823; www .discoverireland.ie/southeast; Merchants Quay; ◷ 9am-6pm Mon-Sat, 11am-5pm Sun Jul & Aug, 9.30am-5.30pm Mon-Fri, 10am-6pm Sat May & Jun, 9.15am-5pm Mon-Sat Sep-Apr)

Sights & Activities

WATERFORD MUSEUM OF TREASURES

The dazzling **Waterford Museum of Treasures** (☎ 051-304 500; www.waterfordtreasures.com; Hanover St; adult/child €7/3.20; ◷ 9am-6pm Mon-Sat, 11am-5pm Sun Jun-Aug, 10am-5pm Mon-Sat, 11am-5pm Sun Sep-May) is one of Ireland's widest-ranging and most high-tech museums. An audio-guide leads you through exhibitions navigating the town's 1000-year history. A highlight is the 'Viking longship', a rocking ride narrated by Waterford's Nordic forebears, who call themselves 'children of the raven' but sound more like comedic Scotsmen. You can also attend the marriage of Strongbow and local

princess Aiofe, who promises to teach he Anglo-Norman lord how the Irish feast.

Though they can feel a little lost under the weight of 21st-century technology, there are some beautiful 'real' exhibits. Golden Viking brooches, jewel-encrusted Norman crosses, the magnificent 1372 Great Charter Roll and 18th century church silver are among the booty.

REGINALD'S TOWER

The oldest complete building in Ireland and the first to use mortar, 12th-century **Reginald' Tower** (☎ 051-304 220; The Quay; adult/child €2.10/1.10 ◷ 10am-6pm Easter-Oct, 10am-5pm Wed-Sun Oct-Easter is an outstanding example of medieval de fences, and was the city's key fortification The Normans built its 3m- to 4m-thick wall on the site of a Viking wooden tower. Ove the years, the building served as an arsenal a prison and a mint. The exhibits relating to the latter role are interesting: medieval silve coins, a wooden 'tally stick' with notches in dicating the amount owed, a 12th-century piggy bank (smashed), and a coin balance used to determine weight and bullion value Architectural oddities include the toilet tha drained halfway up the building.

Behind the tower, a section of the old wal is incorporated into the Bowery bar. The two arches were sally ports, to let boats 'sally forth into the inlet.

WATERFORD CRYSTAL VISITOR CENTRE

The city's famed Waterford Crystal was no immune to Ireland's economic woes. In 2009 the nation was shocked when this civic icon went into receivership. (The factory has previously ridden out hard times: the firs Waterford glass factory was established at the western end of the riverside quays in 1783 but closed 68 years later because of punitive taxes imposed by the British before its revival las century.) Despite a sit-in by workers, who symbolically kept the furnaces burning, the future of manufacturing here remained uncertain when this book went to press. However you can still stop by the **Waterford Crystal Visitor Centre** (☎ 051-332 500; www.waterfordvisitorcentre.com Cork Rd; ◷ 9am-5pm), 2km south of the centre. In lieu of its previous factory tours, it's due to house a new multimedia 'visitor experience' by the time you're reading this, including live demonstrations. Buses 1C and 3C run to the visitor centre from opposite the Clock Tower every 15 minutes (€1.60).

CHURCHES

Christ Church Cathedral (☎ 051-874 757; www waterford-cathedral.com, Cathedral Sq; ☼ 10am-6pm Mon-Fri, 10am-4pm Sat) is Europe's only neoclassical Georgian cathedral. Designed by local architect John Roberts, it was built on the site of an 11th-century Viking church, also the site where the 12th-century marriage of Strongbow and Aiofe took place. The highlight is the 15th-century **tomb of James Rice**, seven times lord mayor of Waterford: sculpted worms and frogs crawl out of the statue of his decaying body. Guided tours (adult/child €6/5) take place at 11.30am and 3.30pm. The cathedral also acts as a **concert venue** with wonderful acoustics – its broad program of performances features everything from choirs to pop quartets.

The sumptuous interior of the Catholic **Holy Trinity Cathedral** (☎ 051-874 757; Barronstrand St) boasts a carved-oak baroque pulpit, painted pillars with Corinthian capitals and 10 Waterford Crystal chandeliers. It was built between 1792 and 1796 by John Roberts, who, unusually, also designed the Protestant Christ Church Cathedral.

The elegant ruin of the **French Church** is on Greyfriars St, announced by a statue of Luke Wadding, the Waterford-born Franciscan friar who persuaded the Pope to negotiate with Charles I on behalf of Irish Catholics. Hugh Purcell gave the church to the Franciscans in 1240, asking them in return to pray for him once a day. The church became a hospital after the dissolution of the monasteries, and was then occupied by French Huguenot refugees between 1693 and 1815. John Roberts is buried here. Ask the staff at Reginald's Tower to let you in.

Edmund Ignatius Rice, founder of the Christian Brothers, established his first school at Mt Sion on Barrack St. A whiz-bang interactive museum, the **Edmund Rice International Heritage Centre** (☎ 051-874 390; www.edmundrice.ie; Barrack St; adult/child €7/4; ☼ 10am-6pm Mon-Sat, 2-6pm Sun Apr-Sep, 10am-5pm Mon-Sat Oct-Mar) recreates life in 18th-century Waterford. It incorporates a chapel, where Edmund Rice's tomb takes pride of place, awaiting the anticipated canonisation of its occupant.

OTHER BUILDINGS

The Mall, a wide 18th-century street built on reclaimed land, was once a tidal inlet. From the river end, its stateliest buildings are John Roberts' **City Hall** (1788) and beautifully refurbished **Theatre Royal**, arguably Ireland's most intact 18th-century theatre, and Richard Cassels' austere **Bishop's Palace** (1741), now the city engineering offices.

Crumbling fragments of the old city wall include **Beach Tower** at the top of Jenkin's Lane and **Half Moon Tower** (both are just off Patrick St). One impossible-to-miss building in Waterford is its landmark 1860s **clock tower**.

GENEALOGICAL CENTRE

If you have ancestors from the county, **Waterford Heritage Services** (☎ 051-876 123; www .iol.ie/~mnoc; Jenkin's La; ☼ 9am-1pm & 2-5pm Mon-Thu, 9am-2pm Fri) may have the details you need to complete your family tree.

Tours

A must for anyone visiting Waterford is Jack Burtchaell's **guided walking tour** (☎ 051-873 711; tour €7; ☼ 11.45am & 1.45pm). Jack's 'gift of the gab' brings Waterford's nooks and crannies alive, effortlessly squeezing 1000 years of history into one hour. Tours leave from the reception area inside the Waterford Museum of Treasures, picking up walkers from the Granville Hotel en route.

Festivals & Events

Now over 50 years old, Waterford's **International Light Opera Festival** (☎ 051-874 402; The Mall; ☼ Nov) is cheaper and more easily accessible than the better-known Wexford Festival Opera (p190), but booking is still advisable.

Sleeping
BUDGET

The city has scant budget accommodation (and no hostels), but frequent buses to Tramore allow you to base yourself at one of its budget options.

Mayor's Walk House (☎ 051-855 427; www.mayors walk.com; 12 Mayor's Walk; s/d €28/50) This respectable four-room B&B is in a tall, thin building. The landing bathrooms are shared, but the large (if dated) rooms have washbasins.

MIDRANGE

Portree Guesthouse (☎ 051-874 574; www.portree guesthouse.ie; Mary St; s/d €55/90; **P**) This friendly Georgian B&B is on a quiet street – a bonus in noisy Waterford. Kids under 12 stay for half price, but reserve ahead as it's popular with groups.

Ramada Viking Hotel (☎ 051-336 933; www.ramada vikinghotel.ie; Cork Rd; r €69-139; P ⌨) For easy access to the coast without having to contend with city traffic, this efficient hotel 3km from the centre is an excellent bet. Neutral-toned rooms are white-glove-test clean, and there's a quality onsite restaurant and staff so welcoming you'd swear they owned the place. It's set well back from the N25, so you don't hear passing traffic.

Coach House at Butlerstown Castle (☎ 051-384 656; www.butlerstowncastle.com; Butlerstown; s/d €70/110; P) A 10-minute drive from town, this 19th-century stone B&B is as appealing inside as it is out, with deep, studded leather armchairs to sink into, toasty open fires to warm up by, canopied beds to drift off in, and pancakes to wake up to.

Granville Hotel (☎ 051-305 555; www.granville-hotel .ie; Meagher Quay; s/d from €80/99; P ⌘) The floodlit 18th-century building overlooking the river is the Granville, one of Ireland's oldest hotels. Brocaded bedrooms maintain a touch of Georgian elegance, as do the public areas, including a fine restaurant and bar. The hotel's had its share of famous guests: Charles Stewart Parnell gave a speech from a 1st-floor window.

TOP END

Arlington Lodge (☎ 051-878 584; www.arlingtonlodge .com; Johns Hill; s/d €150/€230; ⏾ restaurant dinner Mon-Sat, lunch Sun; P ⌨ ⌘) Bon vivant Maurice Keller rescued this 1760-built former bishop's residence from dereliction and transformed it into a warm, intimate boutique establishment. Many of the beautifully wallpapered guestrooms have ornate tiling and stained-glass leadlights. Guests and nonguests can dine on Maurice's locally sourced creations like organic chicken in tarragon and Grand Marnier soufflé (three-course menu €37.50 to €45). A combined gourmet deli-cafe is due to have opened onsite by the time you're reading this.

ourpick Waterford Castle (☎ 051-878 203; www .waterfordcastle.com; The Island, Ballinakill; s €245, d €335-450, cottages per night from €300; P ⌨ ⌘) Getting away from it all is an understatement at this mid-19th-century turreted castle, which is located on its own 310-acre island roamed by deer. A free, private car ferry signposted just east of the Waterford Regional Hospital provides round-the-clock access. All 19 castle rooms have clawfoot baths, and some have

poster beds. There are also 48 contemporary self-catering cottages on the island. Breakfast is available for €18 to €22, and both guests and nonguests can dine on organic fare in chef Michael Quinn's sublime oak-panelled restaurant (menus from €65), or play a round of golf (green fees midweek/weekend €44/52).

Eating

Waterford's hotels and pubs offer some good dining prospects.

Bodéga! (☎ 051-844 177; 54 John St; lunch mains €7-15, dinner mains €17-26; ⏾ lunch Mon-Fri, dinner Mon-Sat) The exclamation mark in the name clues you in to the effusive nature of this Mediterranean cantina. Sun-inspired, seasonally changing dishes might include garlicky pan-fried calamari or succulent duck.

Harlequin (☎ 051-877 552; 37 Stephen St; lunch mains €7.50-10.50, dinner mains €10-14; ⏾ 8.30am-8.30pm Mon-Wed, 8.30am-10.30pm Thu & Fri, 9.30am-10.30pm Sat) Run by young, charismatic Italian duo Simone and Alessandro, this authentic little trattoria morphs throughout the day from a cappuccino and pastry stop to a busy dining spot to a candlelit wine bar. House speciality antipasti platters are laden with cheeses, marinated vegetables and/or finely sliced cured meats.

Cafe Lucia (☎ 051-854 023; 2 Arundel Lane; mains €8-11; ⏾ 9.30am-5pm Mon-Sat) This bright, funky cafe dishes up homemade soups, salads, panini, wraps and Thai fish cakes, but it's especially popular with city workers for its sweet treats like banana crêpes, mixed berry and apple crumble, and rich chocolate fudge cake.

47 The Bistro (☎ 051-844 774; 47 Patrick St; mains €10.50-17.50; ⏾ 11.30am-9.30pm Mon-Sat, noon-9pm Sun) Looking like an interior design magazine spread, elevated, S-shaped walnut seating and glossy maple floors provide an unlikely backdrop for comfort food like shepherds pie and stew.

La Bohème (☎ 051-875 645; 2 George's Street; mains €29-32, 7-course tasting menu €75; ⏾ dinner Tue-Sat) Down a short flight of steps in the Georgian 'Port of Waterford' vaults, this romantic gem combines French flair with fresh Irish produce, resulting in mains such as mustard-and-honey rack of lamb or seaweed-encrusted scallops, and desserts like Tahitian vanilla crème brûlée.

SELF-CATERING

Fresh food is sold at Waterford's weekly **Saturday market** (George's St; ⏾ 10am-2pm Sat) along-

de local crafts. On the second and fourth
unday of each month, there's a mouth-
atering **farmers market** (9.30am-2pm) outside
dkeen Food Store (051-874 620; www.ardkeen.com;
nmore Rd; 8am-9pm Mon-Sat, 9am-6pm Sun).

rinking

eoff's (051-874 787; 9 John St) This cavernous
cal with creaky wooden floors and rock
usic pumping from the speakers is a home
way from home for Wexford's alternative
owd.

Downes Bar (051-874 118; Thomas St; from 5pm)
or a change from stout, drop into Downes,
hich has been brewing its No 9 Irish whis-
ey for over two centuries. Have a dram in
s series of character-filled rooms, or buy a
ottle to take away.

T&H Doolan's (051-841 504; 32 George's St) A
censed establishment for over 300 years,
Doolan's hosts traditional music every night
f the week.

Katty Barry's (051-855 095; Mall La) Don't be
scouraged by the plain exterior and side-
treet location; this small, friendly place serves
smooth Guinness, and has trad sessions
very Wednesday.

Munster Bar (051-874 656; Bailey's New St) Dating
rom 1822, this wonderful old pub has long
een a cosy spot for a pint by its roaring open
re. Of late, it's also been attracting attention
or its gourmet pub grub.

ntertainment

he town's nightlife relies heavily on the stu-
ents at the Waterford Institute of Technology,
nany of whom disappear home at weekends.
Clubs concentrate around the Apple Market
rea. The best are Ruby's and Kazbar, both
n John St.

Garter Lane Arts Centre (051-855 038; www.garter
ane.ie; 22a O'Connell St) This much-complimented
heatre stages art-house films, music, dance
nd plays in an atmospheric 18th-century
uilding.

Garter Lane Art Gallery (5 O'Connell St) Just down
he road, this affiliated gallery hosts regular
xhibitions and workshops.

Theatre Royal (051-874 402; The Mall) Now re-
plendently refurbished, Waterford's flagship
heatre stages plays, musicals and dance.

Forum (051-871 111; www.forumwaterford.com;
he Glen) The mighty Forum hosts everything
rom gay club nights to the Irish kick-boxing
hampionships.

Shopping

Crystal aside, Waterford has a wealth of local
craftspeople creating textiles, paintings, jewellery, pottery, papier-mâché, candles, and
furniture built from recycled materials. The
website www.waterforddesignermakers.com
maintains an updated list, including contact
details to arrange appointments.

Getting There & Away

AIR

Waterford Airport (051-875 589; www.flywaterford
.com) is 9km south of the city centre at Killowen.
AerArann (in the UK 0800 587 2324, in the Republic
0818 210 210; www.aerarann.com) flies twice daily to
London's Luton airport and five days a week
to Birmingham and Manchester year-round,
and has summer-only services to Lorient and
Bordeaux, France; Faro, Portugal; and Malaga,
Spain.

BUS

The **Bus Éireann** (051-879 000) station is on
the waterfront at Merchant's Quay. There are
frequent daily services to Tramore (€2.70, 30
minutes); Dublin (€12.20, three hours) via
Enniscorthy or Carlow; Wexford (€7.20, 1½
hours); Killarney (€21.20, 4¼ hours) via Cork
(€17.10, 2¼ hours); and Dungarvan (€10.30,
50 minutes).

Eurolines (051-879 000; www.eurolines.ie) runs
daily buses to London (€58, 13 hours).

Suirway (051-382 209; www.suirway.com) buses
depart to Dunmore East (€4, 30 minutes,
at least seven daily Monday to Saturday),
Passage East (€4, 30 minutes, at least three
daily Monday to Saturday) and Portlaw (€4,
30 minutes, at least four daily Monday to
Saturday) from opposite the tourist office,
next to the Bus Éireann station.

TRAIN

Plunkett train station (051-873 401) is north of
the river. There are four to six daily services
to/from Dublin's Heuston Station (€27 to
€34.50, 2¾ hours), Kilkenny (€14.90 to €19,
45 minutes) and Limerick (€34, 2¾ hours) via
Limerick Junction or Kildare.

Getting Around

There is no public transport to the airport. A
taxi (051-858 585 or 051-777 10) will cost around
€15. There are taxi ranks at Plunkett train
station, Coal Quay and outside Dunnes Store
supermarket.

Altitude (☎ 051-870 356; www.altitude.ie; 22 Ballybricken; ✆ 9.30am-6pm Mon-Fri & 9.30am-5.30pm Sat) rents bicycles for €15 per day. Hiring a bike for four days gets you a fifth day for free.

CURRAGHMORE ESTATE

Lord and Lady Waterford dwell at the 2500-acre **Curraghmore Estate** (☎ 051-387 102; www .curraghmorehouse.ie; Portlaw; admission €5; ✆ 1-5pm Thu Easter–mid-Oct), which has belonged to the family since the 12th century. Its lavish **gardens** incorporate the whimsical **shell house** built by Catherine Countess of Tyrone in 1754, who arranged for sea captains docking at Wexford's port to bring her seashells from distant shores. By prior appointment, the fine Georgian **house** (admission €15; ✆ 9am-1pm Mon-Fri Feb & May-Jul, plus 1st & 3rd Sun of month May-Jul), containing some superior plaster work, is open to visitors. Lord Waterford normally conducts the tours.

Curraghmore is 14km northwest of Waterford town, 3.5km east of the pretty village of Portlaw. **Suirway** (☎ 051-382 209; www .suirway.com) buses from Waterford can drop you 1km from the estate entrance.

SOUTHEAST COUNTY WATERFORD

This hidden corner of the county makes an easy daytrip from Waterford city, but it's also easy to fit in as part of an onward journey.

Some 19km southeast of Waterford, **Dunmore East** (Dún Mór) is strung out along a coastline of red sandstone cliffs full of screaming kittiwakes and concealed coves. In the 19th century, the town was a station for the steam packets that carried mail between England and the south of Ireland. Legacies left from the era include thatched cottages lining the main street and an unusual Doric lighthouse (1825) overlooking the working harbour.

Less than 14km east of Waterford is the estuary village of **Passage East**, from where car ferries yo-yo to Ballyhack in County Wexford. A pretty little fishing village, it's also lined with thatched cottages surrounding its neat harbour.

Although the main roads (and thus public transport) involve returning to Waterford, a little-travelled 11km-long **coast road** wiggles between Dunmore East and Passage East. Single-vehicle-width, steep and poorly signed in parts (don't worry, you won't get lost), it offers mesmerising views of the ocean and undulating fields that you won't see from the main thoroughfares.

In the opposite direction, it's a 16.5k drive west from Dunmore East to the seasid frivolities of Tramore (opposite).

Information on the area is available a www.discoverdunmore.com.

Activities

The area slumbers in winter but wakes u in summer when bathers head to Dunmor East's Counsellor's Beach, beneath the cliffs and Ladies Cove in its village.

Sea Safari (☎ 086 813 1437; www.seasafariwaterfor .com; adult/child from €30/20; ✆ Easter-Sep), run b the vivacious winner of RTÉ reality TV show *Cabin Fever*, Elaine Power, offers one-hou trips in a high-powered 10m 'rib' past cave shipwrecks, fishermen and seals.

Dunmore East Adventure Centre (☎ 051-38. 783; www.dunmoreadventure.com) hires out equip ment for windsurfing, canoeing, surfing an snorkelling, and also runs sailing and power boating courses and land-based activities lik archery and rock climbing.

If you fancy shark fishing or diving wrecks off the southeastern coast, contact **Dunmore East Angling Charters** (☎ 051-383 397).

Sleeping & Eating

Avon Lodge B&B (☎ 051-385 775; www.avonlodgebandb .com; Lower Dunmore East; s\d €60/80; Ⓟ) Although the exterior of this large suburban-style house looks rather bland, it's in a great location near the sea. Run by traditional musician Richie Roberts, homey rooms are clean, comfortable and brightened by beachy colour schemes.

Haven Hotel (☎ 051-383 150; www.thehavenhotel .com; Dunmore East; s €65, d €110-130; ✆ Mar-Oct; Ⓟ) Built in the 1860s as a summer house for the Malcolmson family, whose coat of arms can still be seen on the fireplaces, the Haven is now run by the Kelly family and remains an elegant retreat with wood-panelled bathrooms and, in two rooms, four-poster beds. Local produce underpins dishes in the restaurant (mains €12.50 to €23, open from 4pm Monday to Saturday and from 12.30pm Sunday) and the low-lit crimson-toned bar (dishes €4.50 to €8.50, open from noon to 4pm).

Parkswood (☎ 051-380 863; www.parkswood.com; Passage East; s €95, d €160-180; ✆ Easter-Nov; Ⓟ 🛜) Storytelling evenings and themed food nights are among the events that take place at this rather pricey but commendably eco-conscious four-room B&B situated on 6 acres on the River Suir. Breakfasts and table d'hôte–style evening meals (€25) are sourced from the gardens, including homemade jams and eggs fresh from the resident hens. Hosts Theresa and Roger can also arrange bike hire for guests (€20 per day).

Bay Cafe (☎ 051-383 900; Dock Rd, Dunmore East; mains €7-11; ☺ 9am-6pm) With harbour views so good there's a whale-watching guide stuck to the window, this artsy cafe serves interesting twists on local produce like mackerel pâté on homemade brown bread, and Scandinavian-tyle open-faced seafood sandwiches.

Drinking & Entertainment

Toe-tapping trad sessions take place on Tuesday nights year-round at the butter-yellow corner pub **Power's Bar** (☎ 051-383 318; Dock Rd, Dunmore East). It's nicknamed 'the Butcher's' after its former incarnation as a meat and grocery store.

Summer regularly sees live music in full swing at the **Spinnaker Bar** (☎ 051-383 133; Lower Dunmore East), filled with rustic maritime artefacts. Its excellent locally caught seafood (mains €18 to €28) makes its kitchen one to watch.

Getting There & Away

BUS

Suirway (☎ 051-382 209; www.suirway.com) buses connect Waterford with Dunmore East and Passage East.

FERRY

If you're going to travel between Counties Waterford and Wexford along the coast, you can cut out a long detour around Waterford Harbour and the River Barrow by taking the five-minute **car ferry** (☎ 051-382 480; www.passageferry.ie; ☺ 7am-10pm Mon-Sat, 9.30am-10pm Sun Apr-Sep, 7am-8pm Mon-Sat, 9.30am-8pm Oct-Mar) between Passage East and Ballyhack in County Wexford. Single/return tickets for pedestrians or cyclists cost €2/3 and for cars €8/12. Return tickets are valid for an unlimited time.

TRAMORE
pop 9200

In summer the seafront spread out below the steep town of Tramore (Trá Mhór in Irish, meaning 'big beach') is a whirl of fairground rides, amusement arcades, sand castles and fast-food outlets galore. (In winter, it's considerably quieter.)

Tramore's eponymous wide, 5km-long beach is capped by 30m-high sand dunes at the eastern end, and is a premier surfing spot. Local activities companies are successfully developing the area as an ecotourism destination, aiming to curb damage inflicted by the beach-going hordes.

The **tourist office** (☎ 051-381 572; www.tramoretourism.net; Railway Sq; ☺ 10am-5pm Mon-Sat mid-Jun–Aug) has a free brochure detailing six walks around town, and can also point you in the direction of the area's **megalithic tombs** and **standing stones** and the town's beautiful Holy Cross Church (1860).

Sights

Tramore Bay is hemmed in by **Great Newtown Head** to the southwest and **Brownstown Head** to the southeast. Their 20m-high concrete pillars were erected by Lloyds of London in 1816 after a shipping tragedy: 363 lives were lost when the *Seahorse* mistook Tramore Bay for Waterford Harbour and was wrecked.

Some of the best views of the heads extend from the delightful, sheltered swimming spot, **Guillamene Cove**, where a sign dating back over 60 years decrees that the beach is for 'men only' (it no longer is, of course).

Atop Great Newtown Head, the **Metal Man**, a 12ft sailor made from iron in 1819. In white breeches and blue jacket, he points dramatically seawards as a warning to approaching ships. It's one of four made from the same mould – another is in Rosses Point, County Sligo, but the other two are missing. Legend has it that if a girl hops around the base of the statue three times on one leg, she will be married within a year. Local wits reckon that hopping around backwards will secure a divorce within the year. Alas, neither theory can be tested at present as the land is off-limits to the public – check with the tourist office for access updates.

Regular art exhibitions take place at the cliff-top 19th-century **Coast Guard Station** (☎ 051-393 833; Love La; ☺ 9am-4.30pm Mon-Fri), which has been turned into a community arts centre.

Stretching 25km west of Tramore, the rugged coastline of the **Copper Coast European Geopark** (☎ 051-396 686; www.coppercoastgeopark.com; ☺ park office 9.30am-5pm Mon-Fri) takes its name from the 19th-century copper mines outside Bunmahon. Among the area's scalloped coves and beaches are geological formations dating back 460 million years, including quartz blocks, fossils, and former volcanoes. Free one-hour guided walks are available in July and August, or you can pick up a map from the park office in Bunmahon. The park encompasses Annestown, which has the dubious distinction of being the only village in Ireland without a pub.

Activities

Tramore's beach break is great for surfers of all levels, including beginners, thanks to slow-forming waves. The town has three year-round **surf schools** which also offer eco-walks around the Back Strand, one of Europe's largest intertidal lagoons, and various other activities. Surfing lessons cost around €45 for a group class and €120 for private tuition. Equipment hire is around €25 including wetsuits and (much-needed) boots, gloves and hoods during winter.

Oceanics (☎ 051-390 944; www.oceanics.ie; Red Cottage, Riverstown, Tramore) Run by husband-and-wife hippie surfers.

T-Bay Surf & Wildlife Centre (☎ 051-391 297; www .surftbay.com) Ireland's largest.

Freedom Surf School (☎ 086 391 4908; www .freedomsurfschool.com; The Gap, Riverstown, Tramore) Also runs lessons in blokarting (sail-powered beach buggying).

To explore the Copper Coast's caves, coves and cliffs in sea kayaks, contact friendly Mick O'Meara at **Sea Paddling** (☎ 051-393 314; www .seapaddling.com; one-/two-day tour from €95/165).

Roaring rapids, splash slides and pirate ships are all part of the water park **Splashworld** (☎ 051-390 176; www.splashworld.ie; Railway Sq; adult/child €10/7.50), as well as 'balmy temperatures all year-round'. It's open for about three hours a day during the week, and six at weekends.

The first European horserace meeting of the year takes place on 1 January at **Tramore Racecourse** (☎ 051-381 425; www.tramore-racecourse .com; Graun Hill), one of many events throughout the year. To saddle up yourself, contact Tramore's pony trekking and riding centre, **Lake Tour Stable** (☎ 051-381 958).

Sleeping

Newtown Caravan & Camping Park (☎ 051-381 979; www.newtowncove.com; Dungarvan Coast Rd; campsites €8-15; ⏰ Easter-Sep) About 2km out of town, this family-run affair is the best local campsite. Electricity is an extra €4; showers cost €1.

Beach Haven House B&B & Hostel (☎ 051-390 208; www.beachhavenhouse.com; Waterford Rd; hostel dm/

d €20/50, B&B s €30-60, d €40-80, studio €70-90; 🅿 🛜) One of the *very* few B&Bs in town to ope year-round, Californian Avery and his Iris wife Niamh's B&B has eight, cream-coloure rooms with skylights, private bathroom and seashell decorations. Next door, thei well-equipped hostel has spotless room and dorms, a common area opening onto BBQ patio, books and board games for rain days, and laundry facilities. Adjoining th hostel are six stylish studio apartments witl kitchenettes.

O'Shea's Hotel (☎ 051-381 246; www.osheas-hot .com; Strand St; s/d from €55/110) O'Shea's rooms while attractive, are not as classy as the flower emblazoned, black-and-white exterior sug gests. Still, this family-run hotel near th beach offers good value and a coveted locatio close to the beach.

Also recommended:

Atlantic Breeze B&B (☎ 051-330 095; Lower Branch Rd; s €50-70, d €70-90; ⏰ approx May-Sep; 🅿) Vine-covered 200-year-old Georgian house with original period features.

Glenart House B&B (☎ 051-381 236; Tivoli Rd; s €50-60, d €70-100; ⏰ approx May-Sep; 🅿 🛜) Cream coloured 1920s home handy for the beach.

Eating

Chips and candyfloss are Tramore's staple diet, but there are also a handful of gourme options.

Vee Bistro (☎ 051-386 144; 1 Lower Main St; lunch mains €10.50-12, dinner mains €16.50-28; ⏰ breakfast lunch & dinner daily, hours may vary outside summer) In a port-wine-coloured building with tribal ar and abstract canvases on the walls, the Vee's French-accented dishes include confit of duck on Toulouse sausage and mussels in white wine with juniper berries. Live acoustic music plays on Saturday nights.

Esquire (☎ 051-381 324; Little Market St; mains €15-25 ⏰ bar food noon-7pm, restaurant lunch & dinner) Located behind the post office, this gastro-pub with the feel of a smugglers' haunt serves locally caught fish as well as traditional meaty dishes like duck, lamb and veal, and a veggie option. Hours fluctuate outside summer.

Pine Room (☎ 051-381 683; Turkey Rd; mains €16-28; ⏰ 6-9.45pm) Tramore's classiest restaurant is found inside a Georgian house with seascapes decorating the walls and a rustic feel. The emphasis is on meat, with some great chicken dishes on the menu as well as a vegetarian dish of the day.

COUNTIES WEXFORD, WATERFORD, CARLOW & KILKENNY

A weekly **farmers market** (🕙 9am-1pm Sun) sets up outside the Coast Guard Station.

Getting There & Away

Bus Éireann (☎ 051-879 000) runs frequent buses daily between Waterford and Tramore (€2.50, 30 minutes). The main bus stop is opposite the Majestic Hotel.

DUNGARVAN

pop 7813

With its pastel-shaded buildings ringing the picturesque bay where the River Colligan meets the sea, Dungarvan (Dún Garbhán) resembles Galway in miniature. St Garvan founded a monastery here in the 7th century, but most of the centre dates from the early 19th century when the Duke of Devonshire rebuilt the streets around Grattan Sq. Overlooking the bay are a dramatic ruined castle and an Augustinian abbey, as well as lively pubs. The Waterford county town, Dungarvan is also becoming a foodie haven, with outstanding restaurants, a state-of-the-art cookery school and the annual Waterford Festival of Food.

Orientation & Information

Dungarvan's main shopping area is Grattan Sq, southwest of the river. Main St (also called O'Connell St) runs along the square's southern edge and turns into Parnell or Lower Main St, which leads to the harbour.

The **tourist office** (☎ 058-41741; www.dungarvan tourism.com; TF Meagher St; 🕙 9.30am-5pm Mon-Fri year-round, plus 10am-5pm Sat May-Sep) is next to the post office.

Most banks are on Grattan Sq. Internet access is available at the **library** (☎ 058-41231; The Quay; internet free; 🕙 10am-5pm Tue-Sat, plus 6-8pm Wed & Thu) and at **Sip & Surf** (☎ 058-48658; Davitt's Quay; internet per hr €5; 🕙 8.30am-8pm Mon-Fri, 10.30am-5pm Sat, 2-6pm Sun), which also serves healthy, homemade dishes like pasta bakes (€4 to €7).

Sights & Activities

The colourful 18th-century **Davitt's Quay** is an idyllic spot to grab a pint and watch the boats sail in.

A major renovation project is returning **Dungarvan Castle** (☎ 058-48144; admission free; 🕙 10am-6pm Jun-Sep) to its former Norman glory. Once inhabited by King John's constable Thomas Fitz Anthony, the oldest part of the complex is the unusual 12th-century

shell keep, built to defend the mouth of the river. The 18th-century British army barracks house a visitor centre with various exhibits. Admission is by guided tour.

Waterford County Museum (☎ 058-45960; www .waterfordcountymuseum.org; St Augustine St; admission free; 🕙 9am-5pm Mon-Fri, 2-5pm Sat Jun-Sep) is small but nicely presented. It covers maritime history (with relics from shipwrecks), Famine history, local personalities and various other titbits, all displayed in a former wine store.

The solitary **St Augustine's Church** on the eastern side of the bridge overlooks Dungarvan Harbour. It was built in 1832 and once had a thatched roof. There are features incorporated from the original 13th-century abbey, including a well-preserved tower and nave. The abbey was destroyed during the Cromwellian occupation of the town, but the church remains in use today.

The **Old Market House Arts Centre** (☎ 058-48944; Lower Main St; admission free; 🕙 11am-5pm Tue-Sat) hosts regularly changing local exhibitions.

Near Dungarvan, back towards Tramore, is **Clonea Strand**, a beautiful patch of pristine beach.

Festivals & Events

The area's abundant fresh produce is celebrated during mid-April's **Waterford Festival of Food** (www.waterfordfestivaloffood.ie), featuring cookery workshops and demonstrations, talks by local producers at their farms, and a food fair.

Over the early May bank-holiday weekend, Dungarvan pubs and hotels host the **Féile na nDéise** (www.feilenandeise.com), a lively traditional music and dance festival that attracts around 200 musicians.

Sleeping

Cairbre House (☎ 058-42338; www.cairbrehouse.com; Abbeyside; s/d €46-56, d €84-100; 🕙 closed mid-Dec–mid-Jan; P 🛜) Blazing with red flowers in summer, this oft-recommended B&B is set on an acre of riverside gardens a 1km stroll from the town centre. The gardens come into their own at breakfast, providing many of the ingredients including fragrant herbs.

Mountain View House (☎ 058-42588; www.mountain viewhse.com; O'Connell St; s €55-75, d €90-110; P 🛜) This beautiful Georgian house, built in 1815 and set in walled grounds, has great high-ceilinged rooms and views of the Comeragh Mountains. Rates drop if you forego breakfast (though with choices like porridge drizzled with warm honey on the menu, you may not want to). Walk for five minutes down O'Connell St from Gratton Sq; it's signposted on the left before the technical college.

our pick Powersfield House (☎ 058-45594; www .powersfield.com; Ballinamuck West; s €60-70; d €100-110; P) Energetic mother, chef and cookery instructor Eunice Power lives in one half of this Georgian home with her family, and has opened four beautifully decorated rooms in the other for guests. Breakfast is a veritable feast of Eunice's jams, chutneys and other delicacies from her garden, as are her three-course evening meals (€25 to €35, by arrangement). It's a five-minute drive north of town on the road to Clonmel.

Tannery Townhouse (☎ 058-45420; www.tannery .ie; Church St; s €60-80, d €100-120; Feb-Dec; P 🖥) The Tannery Restaurant (right) has applied its impeccable taste to this boutique guesthouse, which spans two buildings in the town centre. Its 14 rooms are small but perfectly formed, and have fridges stacked with juices, fruit and pastries so you can eat a continental breakfast in peace.

Lawlor's Hotel (☎ 058-41122; www.lawlorshotel .com; TF Meagher St; s €60-80, €90-150; P) Across the road from the tourist office, the landmark, lemon-yellow Lawlor's was praised by William Makepeace Thackeray in 1843 as a 'very neat and comfortable inn'. Today, its swish renovations extend from its intimate, artfully lit restaurant (mains €15 to €25) to its contemporary, creamy-toned bedrooms, many of which have harbour views.

Seahorse Suites (☎ 058-41153; www.seahorsesuites .com; Grattan Sq; r per night 1/2/3 nights €120/80/60; 🖥) Overlooking the action on Grattan Sq, these three apartments are equipped with kitchenettes; alternatively, nip downstairs to the cobalt-blue Ormond's Cafe (mains €7.50 to €11; 8am to 5pm Monday to Saturday) for breakfast. Each apartment occupies a whole floor: two have two double beds, and one a single and a double. Limited private parking can be arranged nearby.

Eating

Cakes & Bakes (☎ 058-48858; Davitt's Quay; dishes around €6.50; 10am-6pm Mon-Fri, 11am-6pm Sat) The aroma of baked goods straight from the oven is likely to entice you inside this cosy little cafe, whether to snack on the premises or pick up items to take away.

Nude Food (☎ 058-24594; O'Connell St; mains €7.5(14.50; 9am-6pm Mon-Wed, 9am-9.30pm Thu-Sat) Jaz provides a soulful soundtrack for sipping Ill coffee or tucking into a wholesome plough man's platter or veggie burger. Deli items in cluding artisan breads made on the premises marinated vegetables and salads and organi juices are perfect for a gourmet beach picnic

Interlude (☎ 058-45898; Davitt's Quay; mains €12 22; 10.30am-9pm Tue & Wed, 10.30am-9.30pm Thu-Sa 10.30am-6pm Sun) Weird knobbly furniture an(indie music gives this Irish–European quay front cafe an underground vibe.

our pick Tannery Restaurant and Cookery Schoo (☎ 058-45420; www.tannery.ie; 10 Quay St; mains €18-2⁹ 12.30-2.30pm Tue-Fri & Sun, 6.30-9.30pm Tue-Sat, 6.3(9pm Jul & Aug) An old leather tannery now houses this innovative restaurant, where Pau Flynn (opposite) creates seasonally changin(dishes like quail and foie gras pie or pan fried potato gnocchi with red wine butter followed by roasted fruits with cinnamo custard or warm chocolate mousse wit violets. Everything is served so beautifull that it's almost – almost – a shame to eat it Looking like a futuristic kitchen showroom Flynn's cookery school (demonstration/clas including meal from €60/150) adjoins a frui vegetable and herb garden. Some courses in clude foraging for ingredients, while market gardening classes (from €95) with fun-lovin horticulturalist Tim Yorke cover soil prepa ration, seed germination, bed maintenanc and more.

Mill Restaurant (☎ 058-45488; Davitt's Quay; main €19-30; from 5pm Wed-Sat, from 3pm Sun) From the moment you walk in the door, you feel at ease staff are patient with kids, the place is smar but relaxed, and it's clear everyone's having a good time. Seafood, such as pistachio encrusted cod, is the main speciality, but it also serves succulent steaks and crispy pizzas.

Breads, cheeses, chocolate and hot food to eat on the spot are available at Dungarvan' weekly **farmers market** (www.dungarvanfarmersmarke .com; Grattan Sq; 9am-2pm Thu).

Entertainment

On the quayfront, live music and DJs perform regularly at the laidback **Moorings** (☎ 058-4146 Davitt's Quay), which has beautiful original timbe cabinetry and a snug, and – sticking with the nautical theme – the **Anchor Bar** (☎ 058-41249 Davitt's Quay). The latter is also a good spot t catch sport on the big screen.

FRESH FARE, FROM THE GROUND UP

For top Irish chef Paul Flynn of the **Tannery Restaurant and Cookery School** (opposite), his new market garden in his native Dungarvan has 'turned food on its head. Rather than thinking up dishes in a kitchen then ordering the ingredients,' he says, 'I now see ingredients growing, like asparagus, and come up with ways to put them on the menu. It's true seasonal food – you can pick a salad and 10 minutes later it's on your plate.'

Well known for his cookbooks *The Tannery Cookbook: An Irish Adventure with Food* and *Second Helpings: Further Irish Adventures with Food* and his three-year stint as a food writer for the *Irish Times*, Flynn believes Dungarvan's budding reputation as a foodie hub is due to 'a discerning public with a down-to-earth attitude. It's a "real town", not just done up for tourism; it's rooted in farming. The **farmers market** (opposite) is the pulse of the town and creates a real sense of community. And the **Waterford Festival of Food** (p213) was a huge success the first year in 2008. Following up its success the second year was like trying to put out a difficult second album, but people flocked.'

When not cooking or teaching – 'I really enjoy it' – behind the stoves himself, Flynn says, 'It's a real treat to eat in a nice restaurant.' His picks in the southeast include '**Cliff House** (p216) in Ardmore – to eat a bowl of soup in the bar and look out at the sea, **Nude Food** (opposite) here in [Dungarvan] town – I really, really like their food. It's proper food, full of flavour, and **Campagne** (p233) in Kilkenny city – it's my favourite restaurant in the country at the moment.' Flynn's hottest tip hadn't even opened at the time of writing (but will have by the time you're reading this): 'Justin and Jenny Green, who own Ballyvolane House in Fermoy, County Cork, are opening **O'Brien's Chophouse** (p219) in Lismore. I can't wait – they're a really cool couple and really talented. I'll be eating there a lot.'

That is, too, when Flynn isn't in his pride and joy. 'I'm privileged to have this garden. A big creamery [dairy] had closed down; it was an empty site in the middle of town. The creamery still has its offices in Dungarvan and agreed to lease me the plot and sponsor the garden. Having the garden attached to the cookery school gives it soul. The economic downturn means more people want to grow their own produce; we also help local special-needs schools set up gardens. A lot of people want to be celebrity chefs for the sake of being a celebrity chef, but the ones I really admire, like Jamie Oliver and Rick Stein, are the ones who stand for something. I want to give something back.'

SGC Cinema (☎ 058-45796; www.sgcdungarvan.net; ngarvan Shopping Centre; adult/child €8/5.50) screens ollywood flicks in the centre of town.

etting There & Away

s Éireann (☎ 051-879 000) buses pick up and rop off on Davitt's Quay on the way to and om Waterford (€10.30, one hour, 11 daily) d Cork (€14.90, 1½ hours, 13 daily).

Parking in the town centre is metered, but u'll find free parking by the castle.

NG PENINSULA
p380

st 15 minutes' drive from Dungarvan, e Ring Peninsula (An Rinn, meaning 'the eadland') is one of Ireland's best-known aeltacht areas. En route, views of the omeragh Mountains, Dungarvan Bay and e Copper Coast drift away to the northeast. t the peninsula's tip, the small working har- our in Helvick Head has a **monument** to the rew of *Erin's Hope*. The crew brought guns

from New York in 1867, intending to start a Fenian uprising, but were arrested when they landed here. Follow signs to An Rinn then Cé Heilbhic, passing Baíle na nGall ('village of strangers'; it was founded by fishermen from elsewhere).

Ex-Waterford Crystal worker Eamonn Terry returned home to the peninsula to set up his own workshop, **Criostal na Rinne** (☎ 058-46174; www.criostal.com; ☽ by appointment), where you can buy deep-prismatic-cut, full-lead crystal vases, bowls, clocks, jewellery and even chandeliers.

Sleeping & Eating

Seaview (☎ 058-41583; www.seaviewdungarvan.com; Pulla; s €45-65, d €60-110; P ☎) Handy for the wonderful An Seanachaí and the Marine Bar, this light-filled guesthouse has comfy rooms (one wheelchair accessible) and sweeping views of Dungarvan and the Comeragh Mountains.

Dùn Ard (☎ 058-46782; www.ringbedandbreakfast.ie; Gaotha, Dungarvan; s/d from €55/90; P ☎) Perched high above Dungarvan Bay, this sophisticated B&B has three cool, contemporary rooms and exceptionally helpful hosts.

An Seanachaí (☎ 058-46755; www.seanachai.ie; Pulla; carvery lunch €10, dinner mains €12.50-21, set menu €25; ☺ 11am-9pm Mon-Sat, 12.30-9pm Sun) The rough-hewn walls of the 'Old Storyteller' could certainly tell a few stories of their own. Parts of this thatched-roof pub date back to the 14th century from its earliest incarnation as a farm. It's an atmospheric spot for a pint, a meal (try the house-specialty fish pie) or regular live music. On the grounds, a dozen brand-new self-catering cottages are finished in high-quality timbers (rates on request).

Marine Bar (☎ 058-46520; www.marinebar.com; Pulla) Sure, there's good food at this two-century-old pub, but the real reason to stop by is the craic. Year-round, traditional sessions rock the place on Monday and Saturday nights, while locals contest the traditional Irish card game '45' on Wednesday evenings (anyone can join in). There's music every night (except card night) in summer.

There's a small **supermarket** in Ringville.

Getting There & Around

Bus Éireann (☎ 051-879 000) stops in Ring en route to Ardmore (30 minutes) and Waterford (€12.70, 1¼ hours) via Dungarvan. The buses stop once daily in July and August; Friday and Saturday only in other months.

Pubs, accommodation and shops are scattered along the peninsula; you really need a car or bicycle to get around.

ARDMORE

pop 415

The seaside village of Ardmore may look pretty but insignificant, but it's claimed that St Declan set up shop here between 350 and 420. This brought Christianity to southeast Ireland long before St Patrick arrived from Britain. Today's visitors come mainly for its beautiful strand, water sports and superb places to eat and/or sleep.

Tourist info is available at **Ardmore Pottery** (☎ 024-94152; ☺ 10am-6pm Mon-Sat, 2-6pm Sun May-Oct, by appointment Sat & Sun Nov-Apr).

Sights & Activities

In a striking position on a hill above town, the ruins of **St Declan's Church** stand on the site of St Declan's original monastery alongside a cone-roofed, 29m-high, 12th-century **round tower**, one of the best examples of these stru tures in Ireland.

On the outer western gable wall of t 13th-century church, weathered 9th-centu carvings set in unusual arched panels sho the Archangel Michael weighing souls, th adoration of the Magi, Adam and Eve, and clear depiction of the judgement of Solomo Inside the church are two Ogham stones fea turing the earliest form of writing in Irelan one with the longest such inscription in th country. Local lore claims St Declan was bu ied in the 8th-century Oratory (Beannachán which was re-roofed and modernised in 171 Inside is an empty pit beneath a missing flag stone, the result of centuries of relic collection The site was leased to Sir Walter Raleigh i 1591 after the dissolution of the monasterie In 1642 the building was occupied by Royali troops, 117 of whom were hanged here.

Pilgrims once washed in **St Declan's Well**, lo cated in front of the ruins of Dysert Church behind the new hotel development abov Ardmore Pottery. A 5km, cobweb-banishin **cliff walk** leads from the well. On the one-hou round trip you'll pass the wreck of a crane shi that was blown ashore in 1987 on its from Liverpool to Malta.

At the southern end of the beach is **S Declan's Stone**, different geologically from the rocks in the area. It was perhaps brought b glacier from the Comeragh Mountains bu according to legend, St Declan's bell, whic he is often pictured with in his hand, drifte across the sea from Wales on the stone afte his servant forgot to pack it. He decreed tha wherever the stone came to rest would be th place of his resurrection.

The 94km **St Declan's Way** mostly trace an old pilgrimage route from Ardmore to the Rock of Cashel (County Tipperary) vi Lismore. Catholic pilgrims walk along it on St Declan's Day (24 July).

Sleeping & Eating

Newtown Farm Guesthouse (☎ 024-94143; Grange www.newtownfarm.com; s/d €53/80; P ⓢ) Fresh eggs homemade scones, local cheeses and smoked salmon are on the breakfast menu at this stylish B&B on a working sheep farm. Coming from Dungarvan on the N25, go past the Ardmore turn-off and take the next left 1km further on from where it's 100m up the road.

Cliff House Hotel (☎ 024-87800; www.thecliff househotel.com; r €225-265, ste €300-450; ☺ closed Jan;

P 🖥 📶 📺) Built into the cliff-face, all uestrooms at this ultra-contemporary new 'difice overlook the bay, and most have balonies or terraces. Some suites even have wo-person floor-to-ceiling glass showers strategically frosted in places) so you don't niss those sea views. There are also sea views rom the indoor swimming pool, outdoor acuzzi and spa, the bar (meals €18.50 to .28.50) and the restaurant (menu €62.50). Staff can organise sea kayaking, canoeing, cuba diving, fly- and deep-sea fishing and ock climbing. Seasonal closures can vary.

Olde Forge (☎ 024-94750; Main St; dishes €5-20; noon-9pm May-Sep) Quality not quantity is rue of the variety at this seasonally opening afe. There are only four or five dishes on the nenu at any given time, such as gourmet-style ish and chips.

White Horses (☎ 024-94040; Main St; lunch mains €8-3, dinner mains €13-24; 11am-4pm & 6-11pm Tue-Sun 1ay-Sep, 6-10pm Fri, 11am-4pm & 6-11pm Sat, noon-4pm Sun ct-Dec & mid-Feb–Apr) Energetically run by three sisters, this smashing bistro serves nourishing are like fresh seafood chowder or fried brie with tomato chutney on plates handmade in he village. Kids can order half-portions from the adult menu if they fancy something more adventurous than burgers.

There is a small **supermarket** attached to he post office.

Getting There & Away
Bus Éireann (☎ 051-879 000) operates two buses daily Monday to Friday, three Saturday and one Sunday from Cork (€13.80, 1¾ hours) to Ardmore. In July and August there are two buses daily Monday to Saturday to Waterford (€15, two hours) via Ring and Dungarvan; on Friday and Saturday only in other months. Buses stop outside O'Reilly's pub on Main St.

CAPPOQUIN & AROUND
pop 740
Slinking up a steep hillside, the small market town of Cappoquin sits at the foot of the rounded, heathery Knockmealdown Mountains. To the west lies the picturesque Blackwater Valley, where traces of the earliest Irish peoples have been discovered, dating back over 9000 years.

The **Dromana Drive** to Cappoquin from Villierstown (An Baile Nua), 6km south, traces the River Blackwater through the Dromana Forest. At the bridge over the River Finisk is a remarkable **Hindu-Gothic gate**, inspired by the Brighton Pavilion in England and unique to Ireland.

Permits for the area's excellent fishing are available from **Titelines** (☎ 058-54152; Main St, Cappoquin) tackle shop.

The beautiful **Mt Melleray Cistercian Abbey** (☎ 058-54404; admission free; 7am-8pm) is a fully functioning monastery with 28 Trappist monks, but welcomes visitors wishing 'to take time for quiet contemplation'. The abbey was founded in 1832 by 64 monks who were expelled from a monastery near Melleray in Brittany, France. There are tearooms (closed Monday) and a heritage centre. It's signposted 6km north from Cappoquin in the Knockmealdown foothills.

Turn right off the road to Mt Melleray for the forest walks and picnic spots at **Glenshelane Park**.

Cappoquin House and Gardens (☎ 058-54004; house & garden €10, garden only €5; 9am-1pm Mon-Sat May-Jul, by appointment rest of yr) is a magnificent 1779-built Georgian mansion and 5 acres of formal gardens overlooking the River Blackwater. It's the private residence of the Keane family who've lived here for 200 years. The entrance to the house is just north of the centre of Cappoquin; look for a set of huge black iron gates.

ourpick **Richmond House** (☎ 058-54278; www.richmondhouse.net; N72; s €95-140, d €150-240; restaurant dinner nightly Apr-May, Tue-Sat Oct-Mar), which dates back even further to 1704, was built by the Earl of Cork, and is set on 14 acres of woodlands. All the same, its nine guestrooms – furnished with countrified plaids, prints and mahogany – are cosy rather than imposing, and service is genuinely friendly. Nonguests are welcome at its restaurant, where local produce includes West Waterford lamb and Helvick monkfish (mains €25 to €40, five-course menu €58).

Barron's Bakery (☎ 058-54045; The Square; dishes €2.60-7.50, 8.30am-5.30pm Mon-Sat) has used the same Scotch brick ovens since 1887. Sandwiches, light meals and a mouth-watering selection of cakes and buns baked on the premises are available in its spearmint-green-painted cafe, while its breads are also sold in shops and markets throughout the area.

Getting There & Away
Bus Éireann (☎ 051-879 000) services stop in Cappoquin en route to Lismore (€2.60) and Dungarvan (€5, 20 minutes) on Monday,

Thursday and Saturday. There's a Sunday bus to Dublin (€19.40, 4¼ hours) at 3.55pm. On Friday there are buses to Waterford (€14.30, one hour 10 mins) at 5.50pm and Cork (€14.30, one hour 20 minutes) at 9.40am. Cork is also served on Sunday at 6.10pm except in July and August. Buses stop outside Morrissey's pub.

LISMORE

pop 790

Today, Lismore's enormous 19th-century castle seems out of proportion to this quiet, elegant town on the River Blackwater. Most of its existing buildings date from the early 19th century, but Lismore once had over 20 churches – many of which were destroyed during 9th- and 10th-century Viking raids. Over the centuries, statesmen and luminaries have streamed through Lismore, the location of a great monastic university founded by St Carthage in the 7th century. King Alfred of Wessex attended the university, Henry II visited the papal legate Bishop Christian O'Conarchy (Gilla Crist Ua Connairche) here in 1171, and even Fred Astaire dropped by when his sister Adele married into the Cavendish family, who own the castle.

Between doses of history and legend, you can picnic in the **Millennium Gardens**, beside the castle car park, or take a 20-minute riverside stroll along **Lady Louisa's Walk** to the cathedral with its Edward Burne-Jones window.

Information

The locally – and enthusiastically – run **tourist office** (☎ 058-54975; www.lismoreheritage.ie; Main St; ☺ 9.30am-5.30pm Mon-Fri, 10am-5.30pm Sat, noon-5.30pm Sun mid-Mar–Christmas, 9.30am-5.30pm Mon-Fri Jan–mid-Mar) is inside the Lismore Heritage Centre.

Sights

'One of the neatest and prettiest edifices I have seen', commented William Thackeray in 1842 about the striking **St Carthage's cathedral** (1679). And that was before the addition of the Edward Burne-Jones **stained-glass window**, which features all the Pre-Raphaelite hallmarks: an effeminate knight and a pensive maiden against a sensuous background of deep-blue velvet and intertwining flowers. Justice, with sword and scales, and Humility, holding a lamb, honour Francis Currey, who helped to relieve the suffering of the poor during the Famine. Among the cathedral's oddities and wonders are some noteworthy **tombs**,

including the elaborately carved MacGrath family crypt dating from 1557 and fossils in the pulpit.

From the Cappoquin road there are stunning glimpses of the riverside **Lismore Castle** which is closed to day-trippers but available fo groups to hire. You can visit the 3 hectares o **gardens** (☎ 058-54424; www.lismorecastle.com; adult/chil €8/4; ☺ 11am-4.45pm mid-Mar–Sep), thought to be the oldest in Ireland, divided into the walled Jacobean upper garden and less formal lowe garden. There are brilliant herbaceous borders magnolias and camellias, and a splendid yev walk where Edmund Spenser is said to have written The Faerie Queen. The contemporary sculptures dotting the gardens have been joined by a contemporary **art gallery** (☎ 058-54061; www .lismorecastlearts.ie) in the west wing of the castle.

The original castle was erected by Prince John, lord of Ireland, in 1185. After a stint as the local bishop's residence, it was presented to Sir Walter Raleigh in 1589 along with 200 sq km of the surrounding countryside. He later sold it to the Earl of Cork, Richard Boyle, whose son Robert, known as the 'father of modern chemistry' for devising Boyle's Law, was born here.

Most of the current castle was constructed in the early 19th century. During its rebuilding workmen discovered the 15th-century Book of Lismore and 12th-century Lismore Crozier both in the National Museum in Dublin. The book not only documents Irish saints lives but also has an account of Marco Polo's voyages. The castle is owned by Peregrine Cavendish, 12th Duke of Devonshire.

In the old courthouse, the **Lismore Heritage Centre** (☎ 058-54975; www.discoverlismore.com; Main St, adult/child €5/3.50; ☺ same hr as tourist office) features a 30-minute audiovisual presentation taking you from the arrival of St Carthage in AD 636 to the present day via the discovery of the Book of Lismore behind a wall in the castle in 1814 and John F Kennedy's visit in 1947.

Tours

The tourist office runs 45-minute guided walking tours (€5) of the town year-round on request, or you can pick up the info-packed Lismore Walking Tour Guide (€3).

Sleeping & Eating

Beechcroft B&B (☎ 058-54273; beechcroftbandb@eircom .net; Deerpark Rd; d with/without bathroom from €70/60; ☒) Homey touches at this central B&B just off East Main St include electric blankets.

Glencairn Inn & Pastis Bistro (☎ 058-56232; www glencairninn.com; Glencairn, Lismore; s/d €60/95; res-aurant dinner Thu-Sat, lunch Sun, inn & restaurant closed nid-Nov–mid-Jan; P) Painted the colour of churned butter, this south-of-France-style country inn has four rooms with brass beds, French cuisine like pear and Roquefort salad, and *steak-frites* with whiskey-peppercorn sauce (mains €22 to €29), and a quintessen-cially Provençal pétanque pitch. Follow the signposts 4km west of town.

Lismore House Hotel (☎ 058-72966; www.lismore housshotel.com; Main St; r €99-139; P) Directly op-posite the Heritage Centre, Ireland's oldest pur-pose-built hotel was built in 1797 by the Duke of Devonshire. He'd still recognise the exterior, but inside rooms have had a contemporary makeover with sleek dark timber furniture and cream-and-gold fabrics. Breakfast costs extra. You'll often get astounding room rates online (as low as €29 midwinter). The onsite restau-rant offers meals from €12.50 to €23.

Saffron (☎ 058-53778; Main St; mains €8-15; lunch & dinner) Low lighting and plum-coloured walls give this impressive Indian restaurant an in-timate, classy ambience. The spicy chickpea *chana massala* is highly recommended.

Foley's (☎ 058-53671; Main St; mains €10-24; 9am-9pm) This inviting traditional pub serves ex-cellent steaks, fish and homemade burgers in its interior replete with peacock wallpaper, leather-backed benches and an open fire, or in the floodlit beer garden out back.

O'Brien's Chophouse (☎ 058-53810; www.obrienchop house.ie; Main St; mains €13.50-23.50; 10:30am-10pm Mon-Sat, from 11:30am Sun) This new restaurant in an old Victorian pub serves locally sourced dishes, including – yes – chops. They also offer traditional Sunday roasts from noon to 5pm.

There's a small **supermarket** on Main St.

Shopping

Summerhouse (☎ 058-54148; Main St; 10am-5.30pm Tue-Sun) If you want to create that 'heritage' look in your own home (with a stylised, contemporary twist), check out the unusual glassware, fabrics, ceramics and ironwork at this gallery-style shop. It also sells handmade jewellery, and has an aromatic cafe and bakery onsite (dishes €4.75 to €11).

Getting There & Away

There are **Bus Éireann** (☎ 051-879 000) services in both directions between Lismore and Dungarvan (€6.40, 30 minutes) via Cappoquin

on Monday, Thursday and Saturday, and a Sunday bus to Dublin (€19.50, 4½ hours) at 3.45pm. On Friday there are buses to Waterford (€15.00, 1¼ hours) at 5.40pm and Cork (€13.80, 1¼ hours) at 9.50am. Buses stop outside O'Dowd's on West St. Cork is also served by **Hallahan's Coaches** (☎ 058-54065; john@ hallahans.com) on Saturday (one in each direc-tion; €10 return) from outside the Heritage Centre.

NORTHERN COUNTY WATERFORD

Some of the most scenic parts of County Waterford are in the north around Bally-macarbry and in the Nire Valley, which runs between the Comeragh and Monavullagh Mountains. While not as rugged as the west of Ireland, with which it shares the same 370-million-year-old red sandstone, this mountain scenery has a stark beauty and doesn't attract much tourist traffic. It's also a great area to catch traditional music and dancing.

Sights & Activities

Rolling hills and woodland stuffed with megalithic remains make the county's north a superb area for walkers. The Comeragh Mountains, where there are ridges to trace and loughs to circle, are named after their many *coums* (valleys, often of glacial origin). Coumshingaun and Coum Iarthair – next to Crotty's Lough, and named after an outlaw who lay low in a cave there – are some of Ireland's finest.

Stop for a pint and panino in **Melody's Nire View** (☎ 052-36169; Ballymacarbry), where the genial folk have info on local walks and activities.

Otherwise make sure you're around for the **Nire Valley Walking Festival** (☎ 052 36134), which takes place on the second weekend in October, with guided walks for all and traditional music in the pubs.

The **East Munster Way** walking trail (p352) covers some 70km between Carrick-on-Suir in County Tipperary and the northern slopes of the Knockmealdown Mountains. Access is at Fourmilewater, about 10km northwest of Ballymacarbry.

From March to September, the Rivers Nire and Suir are great for **fishing**. Permits (from €30 per day) can be arranged through Hanora's Cottage (p220) or the **fly-fishing cen-tre** (☎ 052-36765; www.flyfishingireland.com; Clonanav, Ballymacarbry), which also has a school and guest-house, and leads guided trips.

Sleeping

Powers the Pot (☎ 052-23085; www.powersthepot.net; Harney's Cross; campsites €15; ☯ May-Sep) An intimate little camping ground run by archaeology and hiking buff Niall. Filling meals are served in the thatched bar (mains €10 to €15), which has great acoustics for musicians to jam around the peat fire. It's in the hills 9km southeast of Clonmel in county Tipperary, signposted from the road to Rathgormuck and from Ballymacarbry.

Glasha Farmhouse B&B (☎ 052-36108; www .glashafarmhouse.com; Ballymacarbry; s €50-60, d €60-120; ☯ restaurant dinner Mon-Sat by reservation; P 🛜) Olive O'Gorman takes meticulous pride in maintaining the plaid- and brocade-decorated bedrooms at her working dairy farm. Some wonderful loop walks fan out around the farm; afterwards, reward yourself with dinner served by candlelight (€25 to €45) and breakfast served in a glass conservatory. The farm is signposted 2km northwest of Ballymacarbry.

our pick **Hanora's Cottage** (☎ 052-36134; www.hanoras cottage.com; Nire Valley, Ballymacarbry; s/d incl packed lunch €95, d €170; ☯ restaurant dinner Mon-Sat; P) This 19th-century ancestral home next to Nire Church houses one of the country's best B&Bs. All 10 rooms have Jacuzzis (try for one overlooking the River Nire swirling under the stone bridge out front). You won't be disturbed by the patter of little feet as kids aren't permitted. Everything in the gourmet restaurant, even the crackers, is made on the premises and gluten-free meals are a specialty (dinner €40 to €50). Take the road east from Ballymacarbry, opposite Melody's; it's signposted 5km further on.

Getting There & Away

Bus Éireann (☎ 051-879 000) runs Tuesday services from Ballymacarbry to Dungarvan (€6.80, 45 minutes) at 3pm, and Clonmel in Tipperary (€5.40, one hour) at 9.40am. There are also two buses between Clonmel and Ballymacarbry on Friday afternoon. A taxi from Clonmel to Ballymacarbry costs around €30.

COUNTY CARLOW

pop 50,349

Strings of quietly picturesque villages wind through Carlow (Ceatharlach), Ireland's second-smallest county after Louth. The scenic Blackstairs Mountains dominate the southeast, while the region's most dramatic

chunk of history is Europe's biggest dolmen just outside vibrant Carlow town. A ruined Gothic mansion and a reputedly haunted castle form the backdrop to two of the county's best flower-filled gardens – see p223 for more blooming information.

CARLOW TOWN

pop 13,623

The narrow streets and lanes of Carlow have enough heritage to keep you wandering for an afternoon, and a ripple of trendy cafes and solid nightlife may keep you in town past dusk. But, unlike its more famous neighbour Kilkenny, you're unlikely to be besieged by tour bus hordes. An increasingly popular dormitory for commuters to Dublin, less than an hour's drive away following the M9 motorway's extension, the town is also etching out a place on the international arts map with the opening of its futuristic contemporary art museum.

Orientation & Information

Dublin St is the city's principal north-south axis, with Tullow St, the main shopping street, running off it at a right angle.

Chartbusters (☎ 059-914 2747; Carlow Shopping Centre, Kennedy Ave; per hr €3; ☯ noon-10pm) Full internet services.

Post office (cnr Kennedy Ave & Dublin St)

Tourist office (☎ 059-913 1554; www.carlowtourism .com; cnr Tullow & College Sts; ☯ 9.30am-1pm & 2-5pm Mon-Fri year-round, plus 10am-5pm Sat Jun-Aug) A useful source of county-wide information. From early 2010 the adjoining building will house the county's new museum (www.carlowcountymuseum.com).

Sights

Follow the walking tour (opposite) to hit central Carlow's highlights.

As of late 2009 Carlow's cultural claim to fame is its new **Visual Centre for Contemporary Art**, a glowing opaque-white cube-like space on the grounds of St Patrick's College (opposite). British architect Terry Pawson scooped the international competition for the purpose-built centre with his factory-inspired industrial design of concrete, steel and glass. Its five separate galleries include the 'cathedral', the largest single exhibition space in Ireland, and an upstairs 'digital' (multimedia) gallery, as well as a studio for artists-in-residence. The centre has no permanent collection, instead hosting specially commissioned works and major travelling exhibitions, as well as art and drama workshops. Under the same roof are the 353-seat George Bernard Shaw Theatre and a cafe–restaurant.

Incongruously hidden in an industrial estate on the northern edge of town, the 2.5-acre **Delta Sensory Gardens** (☎ 059-914 3527; www.delta centre.org; Strawhall Estate, Cannery Rd; adult/under 13yr €5/free; 9am-5pm Mon-Fri, noon-5pm Sat & Sun) incorporate 16 interconnecting, themed gardens spanning the five senses – from sculpture garden to a formal rose garden, water and woodland garden, willow garden and a musical garden with mechanical fountains – which are tended by the long-term unemployed under the guidance of professional horticulturalists. Admission proceeds benefit the adjoining Delta Centre, which provides services and respite for adults with learning disabilities.

Activities

The River Barrow is awash with canoeists, kayakers and rowers. **Go with the Flow River Adventures** (☎ 087 252 9700; www.gowiththeflow.ie) runs daily guided trips that tackle the relatively tame white-water (from €49; advance bookings essential) and, for multiday use only, can rent out canoes (prices on request).

Walking Tour

The tourist office has established a new walking trail around town complete with interpretive panels, but it's just as easy to start from the tourist office on College St and then hit the highlights as follows. Just to the right of the tourist office is the elegant Regency Gothic **Cathedral of the Assumption (1)**, which dates from 1833. The cathedral was the brainchild of Bishop Doyle, a staunch supporter of Catholic emancipation. His statue inside includes a woman said to represent Ireland rising up against her oppressors. The church also has an elaborate pulpit and some fine stained-glass windows.

Next door is **St Patrick's College (2)**, officially known as Carlow College (www.carlow college.ie), Ireland's first post-penal seminary. Opened in 1793, it is thought to have been in use for longer than any other seminary in the world, and today specialises in humanities and social studies. Its president, Father Kevin O'Neill, is an avid art collector, which

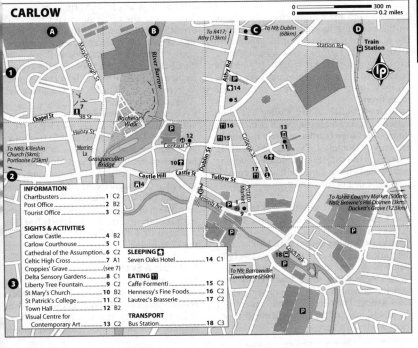

CARLOW

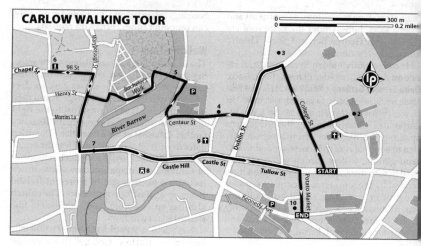

WALK FACTS

Start Tourist office
Finish Liberty Tree fountain
Distance 2.5km
Duration One hour

explains both the sumptuous collection of works adorning its walls and the fact that the college donated part of its grounds to accommodate Carlow's new Visual Centre for Contemporary Art (p220). It's usually possible to get a free, informal tour of the campus – pop into the admin office in the main foyer.

Walking north along College St then turning left on Dublin St, you'll come to the impressive **Carlow Courthouse** (3), at the northern end of Dublin St. Designed by William Morrisson in 1830, this colonnaded building is modelled on the Parthenon and is considered to be one of the most impressive courthouses in the country.

Continue down Dublin St and turn right into Centaur St and past the **Town Hall** (4), dating from 1884. When you reach the river, cross the **Millennium Bridge** (5) and walk across the park to 98 St where you'll find the **Celtic high cross** (6) that marks the mass Croppies' Grave. Here 640 United Irish rebels were buried following the bloodiest fighting of the 1798 Rising. The name 'croppie' came from the rebels' habit of cropping their hair to indicate their allegiance.

From here turn back into Maryborough St and walk south to the five-arched **Graiguecullen Bridge** (7), also known as Wellington Bridge, which is thought to be the oldest and lowest bridge over the River Barrow. Cross the bridge and continue east to the ruins of 13th-century **Carlow Castle** (8), built by William de Marshall on the site of an earlier Norman motte-and-bailey fort. The castle survived Cromwell's attentions but succumbed to the grand plans of a certain Dr Middleton, who decided to convert it into a lunatic asylum. Proving the cliché about the lunatics running the asylum, he blew up much of the castle in 1814 in order to 'remodel' it. All that is left is a single wall flanked by two towers.

Continue up Castle Hill and take the fork to your left onto Castle St. On your left you will see **St Mary's Church** (9), built in 1727 (the tower and spire were added later, in 1834), with a number of statues by Richard Morrison.

Walk on up Tullow St, the town's principal shopping thoroughfare, and take the second right into Potato Market. At the end of the lane is a small square. The bronze statue in the middle of the fountain is the **Liberty Tree** (10), designed by John Behan to commemorate the 1798 Rising.

Festivals & Events

Every summer (usually in mid-June) Carlow town celebrates the 10-day **Éigse Carlow Arts Festival** (☎ 059-914 0491; www.eigsecarlow.ie), when musicians, writers, actors and street performers take over the town. Artists and groups ome from across Ireland and as far away as South Korea and India. Late August heralds the nine-day **Floral Festival** (www.carlowfloralfestival .com), featuring talks by Irish gardening personalities; while you can get your hiking boots muddy during Carlow's **Autumn Walking Festival** (www.carlowtourism.com/walking_festival.html), held on the second weekend in October.

Sleeping

Diminutive County Carlow's abundance of charming inns means it's easy to stay out in the lovely countryside (see listings throughout the County Carlow section) and pop into town for food and culture. There are some worthwhile options in the centre, though little in the way of budget accommodation.

Barrowville Townhouse (☎ 059-914 3324; www .barrowville.com; Kilkenny Rd; s €55-70, d €110-130; P 🛜) This whitewashed 18th-century townhouse has been meticulously converted into a classy B&B, under five minutes' walk south of town. The seven rooms vary in size, but are all perfectly atmospheric for curling up with a book. Enjoy local free-range eggs for breakfast in the airy conservatory.

Seven Oaks Hotel (☎ 059-913 1308; www.seven oakshotel.com; Athy Rd; s €60-75, d €80-150; P 🛜 🏊) Warmed by open fires, the richly carpeted lobby and book-lined library of this grand three-star hotel are a local gathering point for a cuppa, as are its timber bar and adjoining restaurant, TD Molloy's, serving Irish favourites like oak-smoked salmon (lunch menu €20, dinner menus €30 to €37). The autumnal-hued decor extends to the spacious bedrooms, while the health and leisure club incorporates a high-tech gym. To lose the kids (at least temporarily), babysitting can be arranged.

Eating & Drinking

The town is the nightlife hub for those out in the sticks; ask around to find out what the clubs of the moment are. There's usually something along on Tullow St and Thursday night is popular for live music. Restaurants and cafes dishing up cuisines from around the globe proliferate throughout the town centre.

Caffe Formenti (☎ 059-914 0533; 20 Dublin St; mains €9.50-12.50; ⊗ 8am-6pm, to 4pm Jan & Feb) This buzzing cafe combines the talents of an Irish–Italian husband-and-wife team. In addition to daily lunch specials and wholesome soups, there's a tempting selection of Italian pastries, freshly made gelati and aromatic coffees.

Hennessy's Fine Foods (☎ 059-913 2849; 26 Dublin St; dishes around €10; ⊗ 8am-3pm Mon-Sat) A worthy stop for a meal or gourmet grocery shopping (local cheeses, red onion marmalade, chilli jam, red pepper pesto and so on), Hennessy's also runs regular cooking classes from 7pm to 10pm (€65).

Lautrec's Brasserie (☎ 059-914 3455; 115 Tullow St; meals €17-30; ⊗ 5-9pm) The Carlow branch of the Kilkenny original, the candlelit Lautrec's is named after the artist (replete with his poster of the red-scarf-clad *chansonnier* Aristide Bruant mounted on the roof). Creative bistro fare includes monkfish and tiger prawn curry, or Cajun blackened salmon.

Carlow's **farmers market** (⊗ 9am-2pm Sat) fittingly sets up on the Potato Market – look out for Tom Malone's mouth-watering freshly made jams and juices.

On Fridays, over 20 producers sell breads, tarts and preserves, free-range and duck eggs, butter, fruit and veg, flowers, and arts and

---

CARLOW IN BLOOM

County Carlow is renowned for its gardens, 16 of which form part of Ireland's first dedicated **garden trail** (www.carlowgardentrail.com). Our top five:

- **Delta Sensory Gardens** (p221) – a multisensory, not-for-profit oasis.
- **Huntington Castle and Gardens** (p226) - rambling, overgrown grounds in the shadow of a haunted castle, incorporating a canopy of yew trees planted by monks over 700 years ago.
- **Duckett's Grove** (p224) – restored walled gardens behind a ruined Gothic mansion.
- **Kilgraney House Herb Gardens** (p225) – aromatic gardens filled with medicinal and kitchen plants.
- **Altamont Gardens** (p224) – Heritage-listed Victorian splendour, hosting a weeklong Snowdrop Festival in February.

Green thumbs also shouldn't miss County Carlow's summertime **Floral Festival** (opposite).

crafts at the **Askea Country Market** (Askea Paris Centre; ☒ 10am-noon Fri).

Getting There & Away
BUS
Bus Éireann (☎ 051-879 000) runs buses to Dublin (€11, two hours, nine daily), to Cork (€21.50, 3½ hours, one daily) via Kilkenny (€8.20, 35 minutes), and to Waterford (€9.90, 1½ hours, seven daily).

JJ Kavanagh & Sons (☎ 059-914 3081; www.jj kavanagh.ie) has 12 buses per day to Dublin (€12, two hours) and Dublin Airport (€16, three hours). There are two buses per day Monday to Saturday to Kilkenny (€6, 50 minutes) and Portlaoise (€7.50, one hour).

Buses leave from the bus station located at the eastern end of Kennedy Ave.

TRAIN
The **train station** (☎ 059-913 1633; Station Rd) is to the northeast of town. Carlow is located on the Dublin–Waterford line with five trains daily in each direction Monday to Saturday (four Sunday). One way to Dublin's Heuston Station or to Waterford (both 1¼ hours) costs €14.90.

TAXI
Carlow Cabs (☎ 059-914 0000) operate taxis around town and further afield.

AROUND CARLOW TOWN
Browne's Hill Dolmen
This 5000-year-old granite monster is Europe's largest **portal dolmen** and one of Ireland's most famous. The capstone alone weighs well over 100 tonnes. It's signposted 3km east of town on the R726 Hacketstown Rd; a 300m path leads round the field to the dolmen. There's no public transport. A cab will charge about €10 to €15 from Carlow, including a 20-minute wait.

Duckett's Grove
Adjoining a foreboding ruined Gothic mansion, the original high brick garden walls of **Duckett's Grove** (admission free; ☒ 10am-5.30pm Apr-Oct, 10am-4pm Nov-Mar) frame two sprawling, interconnected formal gardens. Filled with the scents of lavender and fruit blossom in spring and summer, they adjoin a shaded woodland area, covering some 11 acres all up. The remains of the 18th-century mansion – derelict since a fire in 1933 – may become accessible in the future. For now, facilities include toilets and wheelchair access; plans are underway for craft studios, a nursery and a cafe in the stables and outbuildings. Check with Carlow's tourist office for the gardens program of events including a Christmas market, midsummer night celebration, concerts and outdoor plays. There's no public transport; the gardens are signposted 12.5km northeast of Carlow.

Killeshin Church
Once the site of an important monastery with one of the finest round towers in the country, this medieval marvel was destroyed early in the 18th century by a philistine farmer worried that it might collapse and kill his cows. The **ruins** of a 12th-century church remain, including a remarkable Romanesque doorway dating from the 5th century. Look for the wonderful bearded face on the capstone. Killeshin is 5km west of Carlow on the R430. There's no public transport. A cab will charge about €10 to €15 from Carlow, including a 20-minute wait.

BALLON
pop 596
Grand estates and gardens envelop the small village of Ballon on the N80.

Altamont Gardens (☎ 059-915 9444; www.heritage ireland.ie; admission free; ☒ 10am-6pm Mon-Fri, 11am-6pm Sat & Sun Jan-Nov, 10am-6pm Mon-Fri Dec; P) is one of Ireland's most magnificent old walled formal gardens. Run by the Heritage Service, the 40-acre garden has a design dating to Victorian times. To recreate the look in your own backyard, there's a small onsite nursery selling plants. The gardens are 5km east of Ballon.

Just 600m south of Altamont Gardens, **Sherwood Park House** (☎ 059-915 9117; www .sherwoodparkhouse.ie; Kilbride, Ballon; s/d from €60/100; P) is a greystone Georgian manor dating from 1730. The five rooms are huge and boast such period niceties as satin- and velvet-adorned four-poster beds. You can make arrangements for dinner (€40 per person; BYO wine). This is prime walking country.

Reached by a long, stately driveway through sheep-flecked paddocks off the N80 on the northern edge of town, **Ballykealey Manor Hotel** (☎ 059-915 9288; www.ballykealeymanorhotel.com; Ballon; s/d from €90/150, cottages $300; ☒ restaurant lunch Sun year-round, dinner Thu-Sat Mar-Oct, Fri & Sat Nov-Feb, hotel & restaurant closed Tue-Thu winter; P) is an 1830s-uilt pastiche of Tudor and Gothic detail. he stone manor's 12 antique-filled rooms nclude a bridal suite with a four-poster bed nd sunken bathroom. On the grounds, 15 ownhouse-style cottages (one of which has vheelchair access) sleep up to five people and re equipped with stainless-steel kitchens. The nanor's former library now houses a high-nd restaurant, the Oak Room, which also velcomes nonguests (five-course menu €55).

If strolling around Altamont Gardens has eft you peckish, pop into the **Forge Restaurant** (☎ 059-915 9939; Kilbride Cross, Ballon; dishes €5-11; ☼ 9.30am-5.30pm Mon-Sat, 11am-6pm Sun), where Mary Jordan cooks up steaming soups (served on a wooden bread board) and hot lunches, as vell as baked goods to take away, and also sells local art and crafts. There's often a wait for a able at weekends, but hang in there.

BORRIS & AROUND
op 582

This seemingly untouched hillside Georgian village has a dramatic mountain backdrop and traditional main street. A huge stone railway viaduct on the edge of town has been disused since the line closures of the 1950s.

Borris is full of character, with plenty of atmospheric bars hosting summertime trad music.

Sights & Activities
Borris is a starting point for the 13km **Mt Leinster Scenic Drive** (it can also be walked) and is also on the South Leinster Way (see p240). Alternatively, there's a lovely 10km walk along the **River Barrow towpath** to pictur-esque Graiguenamanagh (County Kilkenny) and on to St Mullins.

To the south of town, quad bikes can be rented from **Country Quads** (☎ 059-972 4624; www .countryquads.net; Maloney's Farm, Tinnecarrig, Borris; per hr adult €50, child €32-40; ☼ by appointment), which also has a fun computer-simulated indoor shooting range (€100 per group per hour) where you can fend off attacking bears, flying pheasants and more.

Continuing south, **Carrigleade Golf Course** (☎ 059-972 4370; carrigleade@gmail.com; Carrigleade; green fees weekday/weekend €10/12) is a wonderfully informal 18-hole golf course in a beautiful country setting with mountain views.

Heading north from Borris, the R705 fol-lows the scenic River Barrow Valley 12km to Bagenalstown, the new home of the successful

microbrewery **Carlow Brewing Company** (☎ 059-913 4356; www.carlowbrewing.com; Royal Oak Rd, Bagenalstown; tours €8 by reservation). Its award-winning O'Hara's Irish Stout bursts with flavour and certainly holds its own against that *other* Irish stout.

Also in Bagenalstown, **Kilgraney House Herb Gardens** (☎ 059-977 5283; www.kilgraneyhouse.com; ad-mission €6; ☼ 2-5pm Thu-Sun Apr-Sep) boasts a heady cocktail of medicinal and kitchen plants.

Sleeping & Eating
our pick **Step House Hotel** (☎ 059-977 3209; www.step househotel.ie; 66 Main St; s/d from €65/130; ☼ restaurant dinner; **P**) Right in the centre of town, this Georgian home has undergone a stunning makeover in elegant shades of pistachio green. Its 23 rooms all boast balconies with picture-perfect garden views framed by Mt Leinster. In the house's old kitchens, tables in the Cellar Restaurant are tucked in romantic corners beneath vaulted ceilings. Classy fare ranges from grilled Ardsallagh goat's cheese to roast cushion of venison with chocolate fig purée (mains €26 to €30).

Lorum Old Rectory (☎ 059-977 5282; www.lorum .com; s/d from €95/150; ☼ Mar-Nov; **P**) Halfway be-tween Borris and Bagenalstown off the R705, this historic manor house sits on a prominent knoll east of the road. The gardens stretch in all directions, offering peaceful views from each of the five rooms. The largely organic cooking here is renowned; confirm dining arrangements when you book.

Kilgraney Country House (☎ 059-977 5283; http:// indigo.ie/~kilgrany; s/d from €100/130; ☼ Mar-Nov; **P**) The River Barrow burbles down the shallow valley from this six-room Georgian manor. The owners, veteran travellers, have created a fabulous interior with artefacts collected from far-away places like the Philippines. Unwind in the spa, the herb gardens (above) or over a six-course meal (€48 to €56). It's off the R705 halfway between Borris and Bagenalstown.

M O'Shea (☎ 059-977 3106; Main St) Surprises abound in this warren of rooms that combines a general store, modern grocery store and old-fashioned pub where spare parts and bits of machinery still hang from the ceiling.

Getting There & Away
Borris is on the east-west R702, which links the N9 with the N11 in County Wexford.

Six trains a day travel between Carlow town and Bagenalstown (14 min; €7) en route to/ from Kilkenny (18 min; €7).

DETOUR: CLONEGAL

The minute village of Clonegal is the southern terminus of Ireland's inaugural long-distance walking trail, the Wicklow Way. Non-hikers can reach it by driving along a series of sign-posted winding local roads 5km east of Kildavin and the N80.

Accessed by a long driveway off the main street, **Huntington Castle** (☎ 053-937 7552; Clonegal; castle & gardens tour adult/concession €7/5; ☒ 2-6pm Jun-Aug, by appt rest of yr) is a spooky, dusty old keep built in 1625 by the Durdin-Robertson family, who still own it and live here today. The family conduct hour-long tours of the property, which, they claim, is haunted by two ghosts: Bishop Leslie (a former bishop of Limerick) and Ailish O'Flaherty (the granddaughter of Grace O'Malley, the Pirate Queen). Descending to the castle's basement brings you to the Temple of Isis, where the Fellowship of Isis, worshipping the ancient Egyptian goddess, was founded by the family in 1963.

A traditional stop for Wicklow Way walkers, **Osborne's pub** (☎ 054-77359; Main St) is also slightly eerie thanks to its bar made from coffin lids.

ourpick **Sha-Roe Bistro** (☎ 053-937 5636; Main St; mains €18-26.50; ☒ lunch Sun, dinner Wed-Sat), tucked inside an 18th-century building, serves standout contemporary cuisine like potato, parmesan and herb gnocchi with roast butternut squash, followed by desserts like a fig *tarte tatin* with toffee ice cream, or Irish cheeses with rhubarb chutney and homemade crackers. The menu lists local suppliers who provide ingredients fresh from the surrounding orchards and farms. Book at least two weeks ahead.

MT LEINSTER

To reach this mighty mountain (p204) from Borris, follow the Mt Leinster Scenic Drive signposts 13km towards Bunclody in County Wexford. The last few kilometres are on narrow, exposed roads with steep fall-offs. It takes a good two hours on foot or 20 minutes by car. On the northern slopes of Mt Leinster, the tiny village of Kildavin is the starting point of the South Leinster Way (p240).

ST MULLINS

Tranquil little St Mullins sits 6km downstream from Graiguenamanagh in County Kilkenny. The village is the maternal home of Michael Flatley of Riverdance fame. Sure enough, the river snakes through here in the shadow of Brandon Hill, as does the River Barrow towpath (p225). From the river, a trail winds uphill to the ruined hulk of an old **monastery** surrounded by the graves of 1798 rebels. A 9th-century Celtic cross, badly worn down over the centuries, still stands beside the monastery. Nearby, St Moling's Well is a holy well that seems to attract spare change.

Overlooking the weir at the river's edge, Martin and Emer O'Brien have eschewed corporate life to convert St Mullins' **Old Grain Store** (☎ 051-424 4440; www.oldgrainstorecottages.ie, Old Grain Store, St Mullins; cottages €300-480 per week; ☒ cafe opening hr vary) into a fabulous cafe serving Irish-roasted coffee, and three self-catering cottages sleeping two to four people, set in the coach house, the forge and the stables. The cottages interiors are stylish yet homey, with shelves of books and wood-burning stoves. Shorter stays are sometimes possible on request. Martin and Emer also lend guests bikes and kayaks free of charge.

Just up the hill from the river, **Mulvarra House** (☎ 051-424 936; www.mulvarra.com; St Mullins; s/d €50/80; P) is a modern, comfortable B&B with guestrooms opening to balconies taking in the glorious setting. Dinner (€30) is available by arrangement, and you can also indulge in body treatments such as hot stone massages.

COUNTY KILKENNY

pop 87,558

County Kilkenny's centrepiece is, of course, its namesake city. An enduring gift of the Normans, it mesmerises visitors with its medieval alleys that wind past its castle, cathedral, ruined abbeys and dynamic modern-day buildings.

But the appeal of the county as a whole shouldn't be underestimated. It's a place of rolling hills, where you'll soon run out of adjectives for green. Tiny roads navigate the valleys alongside swirling rivers, moss-covered stone walls and relics of centuries of Irish religious history. Wanderers and ramblers are rewarded by characterful pubs and fine resaurants. Shamrock-cute Inistioge may be star of many movies, but it's the real deal, as are towns like Graiguenamanagh, Bennettsbridge and Thomastown, where you'll find skilled artists and craftspeople busy creating in their studios.

KILKENNY CITY
pop 8661

Kilkenny (Cill Chainnigh) is the Ireland of many visitors' imaginations. Its majestic riverside castle, tangle of 17th-century passageways, rows of colourful, old-fashioned shopfronts and centuries-old pubs with traditional live music all have a timeless appeal, as does its splendid medieval cathedral. But Kilkenny is also awash with contemporary eateries, and is a hotbed of arts, crafts and cultural activities.

Kilkenny's architectural charm owes a huge debt to the Middle Ages, when the city was a seat of political power. It's also sometimes called the 'marble city' because of the local black limestone, which resembles a slate-coloured marble and is used on floors and in decorative trim all over town.

To avoid the crowds, try to visit on a weekday or sometime out of season, when you're better able to appreciate the elegance and vibrancy that give the town (oops, locals insist on 'city') a timeless appeal. You can cover pretty much everything on foot in a couple of hours, but sampling its many delights will take much longer.

History

In the 5th century, St Kieran is said to have visited Kilkenny and, on the site of the present Kilkenny Castle, challenged the chieftains of Ossory to accept the Christian faith. Subsequently, St Canice established his monastery here. Kilkenny consolidated its importance in the 13th century under William Marshall, the Earl of Pembroke and son-in-law of the Anglo-Norman conqueror Strongbow. Kilkenny Castle was built to secure a crossing point on the River Nore.

In the Middle Ages, Kilkenny was intermittently the unofficial capital of Ireland, with its own Anglo-Norman parliament. In 1366 the parliament passed the so-called Statutes of Kilkenny aimed at preventing the assimilation of Anglo-Normans into Irish society. Anglo-Normans were prohibited from marrying the native Irish, taking part in Irish sports, speaking or dressing like the Irish or playing any Irish music. Although the laws remained theoretically for over 200 years, they were never enforced with any great effect and did little to halt the absorption of the Anglo-Normans into Irish culture.

During the 1640s Kilkenny sided with the Catholic royalists in the English Civil War. The 1641 Confederation of Kilkenny, an uneasy alliance of native Irish and Anglo-Normans, aimed to bring about the return of land and power to Catholics. After Charles I's execution, Cromwell besieged Kilkenny for five days, destroying much of the southern wall of the castle before Ormond surrendered. The defeat signalled a permanent end to Kilkenny's political influence over Irish affairs.

Today, tourism is Kilkenny's main economic focus, but it's also the regional centre for more traditional pursuits like agriculture – you'll see farmers on tractors stoically dodging tour buses.

Orientation

At the junction of several major highways, Kilkenny straddles the River Nore, which flows through much of the county. St Canice's Cathedral sits on the northern side of the River Bregagh (a tributary of the Nore) to the northwest of the town centre outside the town walls. Kilkenny's main thoroughfare, Parliament and High Sts, runs southeast from the cathedral. Kilkenny Castle, on the banks of the River Nore, dominates the town's southern side. John St is the main road on the east side of the River Nore and links up with Dublin Rd at MacDonagh train station with its vast new shopping mall.

Information

BOOKSHOPS

Kilkenny Book Centre (☎ 056-776 2117; 10 High St) The largest bookshop in town, stocking plenty of Irish-interest fiction and nonfiction, periodicals and a big range of maps. There's a good cafe upstairs.

EMERGENCY

Police station (☎ 056-22222; Dominic St)

INTERNET ACCESS

Mobile Connections (☎ 056-772 3000; 10 Rose Inn St; per hr €2.40; ⏱ 10am-6pm Mon-Sat) Central and cheap.

LAUNDRY

Bretts Launderette (☎ 056-63200; Michael St; per small/large load €18/24; ⏱ 8.30am-8pm Mon-Sat)

KILKENNY

0		300 m
0		0.2 miles

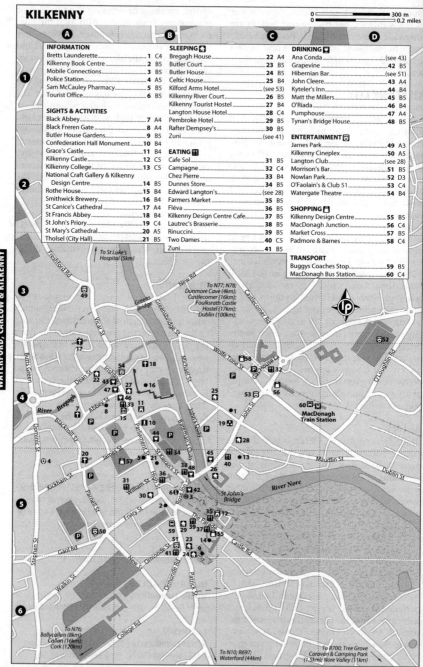

INFORMATION
Bretts Launderette	1 C4
Kilkenny Book Centre	2 B5
Mobile Connections	3 B5
Police Station	4 A5
Sam McCauley Pharmacy	5 B5
Tourist Office	6 B5

SIGHTS & ACTIVITIES
Black Abbey	7 A4
Black Freren Gate	8 A4
Butler House Gardens	9 B5
Confederation Hall Monument	10 B4
Grace's Castle	11 B4
Kilkenny Castle	12 C5
Kilkenny College	13 C5
National Craft Gallery & Kilkenny Design Centre	14 B5
Rothe House	15 B4
Smithwick Brewery	16 B4
St Canice's Cathedral	17 A4
St Francis Abbey	18 B4
St John's Priory	19 C4
St Mary's Cathedral	20 A5
Tholsel (City Hall)	21 B5

SLEEPING
Bregagh House	22 A4
Butler Court	23 B5
Butler House	24 B5
Celtic House	25 B4
Kilford Arms Hotel	(see 53)
Kilkenny River Court	26 B5
Kilkenny Tourist Hostel	27 B4
Langton House Hotel	28 C4
Pembroke Hotel	29 B5
Rafter Dempsey's	30 B5
Zuni	(see 41)

EATING
Cafe Sol	31 B5
Campagne	32 B5
Chez Pierre	33 B4
Dunnes Store	34 B5
Edward Langton's	(see 28)
Farmers Market	35 B5
Fléva	36 B5
Kilkenny Design Centre Cafe	37 B5
Lautrec's Brasserie	38 B5
Rinuccini	39 B5
Two Dames	40 C5
Zuni	41 B5

DRINKING
Ana Conda	(see 43)
Grapevine	42 B5
Hibernian Bar	(see 51)
John Cleere	43 A4
Kyteler's Inn	44 B4
Matt the Millers	45 B5
O'Riada	46 B4
Pumphouse	47 A4
Tynan's Bridge House	48 B5

ENTERTAINMENT
James Park	49 A3
Kilkenny Cineplex	50 A5
Langton Club	(see 28)
Morrison's Bar	51 B5
Nowlan Park	52 D3
O'Faolain's & Club 51	53 C4
Watergate Theatre	54 B4

SHOPPING
Kilkenny Design Centre	55 B5
MacDonagh Junction	56 C4
Market Cross	57 B5
Padmore & Barnes	58 C4

TRANSPORT
Buggys Coaches Stop	59 B5
MacDonagh Bus Station	60 C4

To St Luke's Hospital (5km)

Fishford Rd

Greens Bridge

To N77; N78;
Dunmore Cave (4km);
Castlecomer (16km);
Foulksrath Castle
Hostel (17km);
Dublin (100km)

Castlecomer Rd

Greensbridge St

New Rd

Vicar St

Butts Green

Dean St

Irishtown

Michael St

Wolfe Tone St

Gas House La

O'Loughlin Rd

MacDonagh
Train Station

River Breagagh

Abbey St

Parliament St

Blackmill St

Dominic St

Maudlin St

Dublin St

James's St

St Kieran's St

John St

River Nore

St John's
Bridge

Maudlin St

Kickham St

Parnell St

William St

High St

Rose Inn St

The Parade

St John's
Bridge

Castle Rd

Friary St

Stephen St

Gaol Rd

New St

Ormonde St

Patrick St

Walkin St

College Rd

To N76;
Ballycallan (8km);
Callan (16km);
Cork (120km)

To N10; R697;
Waterford (44km)

To R700; Tree Grove
Caravan & Camping Park
(1.5km); Nore Valley (11km)

MEDICAL SERVICES

t Luke's Hospital (☎ 056-778 5000; Freshford Rd)
am McCauley Pharmacy (☎ 056-775 0122; 33 High
t) The largest of High St's many pharmacies.

MONEY

reland's major banks have branches with
ATMs on High St.

TOURIST INFORMATION

Tourist office (☎ 056-775 1500; Rose Inn St; www
discoverireland.ie; 🕑 9am-7pm Mon-Sat, 11am-5pm Sun
ul & Aug, 9.15am-1pm & 2-5pm Mon-Sat Sep-Jun) County
Kilkenny's only tourist office, stocking excellent guides and
walking maps, set in Shee Alms House, built in local stone
n 1582 by local benefactor Sir Richard Shee to provide
elp for the poor.

Sights

KILKENNY CASTLE

Rising above the Nore, **Kilkenny Castle** (☎ 056-
772 1450; www.kilkennycastle.ie; adult/child €6/2.50;
🕑 9.30am-5.30pm Jun-Aug, 9.30am-5.30pm Apr-May & Sep,
9.30am-5pm Mar, 9.30am-4.30pm Oct-Feb) is one of
Ireland's most visited heritage sites. The first
structure on this strategic site was a wooden
tower built in 1172 by Richard de Clare, the
Anglo-Norman conqueror of Ireland better
known as Strongbow. In 1192, Strongbow's
son-in-law, William Marshall, erected a stone
castle with four towers, three of which survive.
The castle was bought by the powerful Butler
family in 1391, and their descendants continued to live there until 1935. Maintaining such
a structure became a big financial strain and
most of the furnishings were sold at auction.
The castle was handed over to the city in 1967
for the princely sum of £50.

One glance tells you that the castle has
been modified through the centuries. First
of all it's missing a wall – a key defensive de-
ficiency. Second, there's all those windows –
perfect targets, say, for a catapult. Most of
the changes visible today date from the 19th
century when efforts were made to banish the
gloom and bring in the cheer. By then the only
real defensive worry was a peasant flinging a
rotten potato.

Regular 40-minute guided tours focus on
the **Long Gallery**, in the wing of the castle nearest the river. The gallery, which showcases
stuffy portraits of the Butler family members
over the centuries, is an impressive hall with
high ceilings vividly painted with Celtic and
Pre-Raphaelite motifs.

The castle basement is also home to the
Butler Gallery (☎ 056-776 1106; www.butlergallery
.com; admission free), one of the country's most
important art galleries outside Dublin. Small
exhibitions featuring the work of contemporary artists are held throughout the year. Also
in the basement, the castle kitchen houses
a popular summertime cafe. You can head
directly to either the Butler Gallery or the cafe
without paying the tour admission price.

About 20 hectares of **parkland** (admission free;
🕑 daylight hr) extend to the southeast, with a
Celtic cross-shaped rose garden, a fountain to
the northern end and a children's playground
to the south. The castle's former stables are
now home to the Kilkenny Design Centre
(p235).

ST CANICE'S CATHEDRAL

Soaring over the north end of the centre is
Ireland's second-largest medieval cathedral (after St Patrick's in Dublin), **St Canice's
Cathedral** (☎ 056-776 4971; www.stcanicescathedral.ie;
St Canice's Pl; adult/child €4/3, combo ticket with Rothe House
€6; 🕑 9am-6pm Mon-Sat, 2-6pm Sun Jun-Aug, 10am-1pm &
2-5pm Mon-Sat, 2-5pm Sun Apr-May & Sep, 10am-1pm & 2-
4pm Mon-Sat, 2-4pm Sun Oct-Mar). This Gothic edifice
with its iconic round tower has had a long and
fascinating history. Legend has it that the first
monastery was built here in the 6th century
by St Canice, Kilkenny's patron saint. Records
show that a wooden church on the site was
burned down in 1087.

The existing structure was raised between
1202 and 1285, but then endured a series of ca-
tastrophes and resurrections. The first disaster,
the collapse of the church tower in 1332, was
the consequence of Dame Alice Kyteler's conviction for witchcraft. Her maid was also con-
victed, and her nephew, William Outlawe, was
implicated. The unfortunate maid was burned
at the stake, but Dame Alice escaped to London
and William spared himself by offering to re-
roof part of St Canice's Cathedral with lead
tiles. His new roof proved too heavy, however,
bringing the church tower down with it.

In 1650 Cromwell's forces defaced and
damaged the church, using it to stable their
horses. Repairs began in 1661 and are still
ongoing. The beautiful roof in the nave was
completed in 1863. Also worth a look is a
model of Kilkenny as it was in 1642 – things
haven't changed that much.

Inside, highly polished ancient **grave slabs**
are set on the walls and the floor. On the

northern wall, opposite the entrance, a slab inscribed in Norman French commemorates Jose de Keteller, who died in 1280; despite the difference in spelling he was probably the father of Alice Kyteler. The stone chair of St Kieran embedded in the wall dates from the 13th century. The fine 1596 monument to Honorina Grace at the western end of the southern aisle is made of beautiful local black limestone. In the southern transept, a handsome **black tomb** has effigies of Piers Butler, who died in 1539, and his wife, Margaret Fitzgerald. Tombs and monuments (listed on a board in the southern aisle) to other notable Butlers crowd this corner of the church.

Outside the cathedral, a 30m-high **round tower** (adult/child €3/2.50; ☽ Apr-Oct) rises amid an odd array of ancient tombstones and is the oldest structure within the grounds. It was built sometime between AD 700 and 1000 on the site of an earlier Christian cemetery. Apart from missing its crown, the round tower is in excellent condition and those aged over 12 can admire a fine view from the top. It's a tight squeeze and you'll need both hands to climb the 100 steps up steep ladders. The approach to the cathedral on foot from Parliament St leads you over Irishtown Bridge and up St Canice's Steps, which date from 1614; the wall at the top contains fragmentary medieval carvings. The leaning tombstones scattered about the grounds prompt you to look at the very least for a black cat.

ROTHE HOUSE

Ireland's best surviving example of a 16th-century merchant's house is the Tudor **Rothe House** (☎ 056-772 2893; www.rothehouse.com; Parliament St; adult/child €5/4, combo ticket with cathedral €6; ☽ 10.30am-5pm Mon-Sat, 3-5pm Sun Apr-Oct, 10.30am-4.30pm Mon-Sat Nov-Mar). Built around a series of courtyards, it now houses a museum with local artefacts including a well-used Viking sword found nearby and a grinning head sculpted from a stone by a Celtic artist. The king-post roof of the 2nd floor is a meticulous reconstruction.

In the 1640s the wealthy Rothe family played a part in the Confederation of Kilkenny, and Peter Rothe, son of the original builder, had all his property confiscated. His sister was able to reclaim it, but just before the Battle of the Boyne (1690) the family supported James II and so lost the house permanently. In 1850 a Confederation banner was discovered in the house; it's now in the National Museum in Dublin.

BLACK ABBEY

This Dominican **abbey** (Abbey St; ☽ open daily for Mass) was founded in 1225 by William Marshall and takes its name from the monks' black habits. In 1543, six years after Henry VIII's dissolution of the monasteries, it was turned into a courthouse. Following Cromwell's visit in 1650, it remained a roofless ruin until restoration in 1866. Much of what survives dates from the 18th and 19th centuries, but remnants of more ancient archways are still evident within the newer stonework. Look for the 13th-century coffins near the entrance.

NATIONAL CRAFT GALLERY & KILKENNY DESIGN CENTRE

Contemporary Irish crafts are showcased at this imaginative **gallery** (☎ 056-776 1804; www.ccoi .ie; Castle Yard; admission free; ☽ 10am-6pm Mon-Sat, plus 11am-6pm Sun Apr-Dec) in the former castle stables that also house the Kilkenny Design Centre (p235). Ceramics dominate, but exhibits often feature furniture, jewellery and weaving from the members of the Crafts Council of Ireland. There are regular classes in pottery and jewellery making.

Behind the complex, look for the walkway that extends into the beautiful **gardens** of Butler House (p232), whose most unusual feature is a fountain constructed from remnants of the British-built Nelson Column, blown up by nationalists in Dublin around a century ago.

OTHER SIGHTS

The **Tholsel** (City Hall) on High St was built in 1761 on the spot where Dame Alice Kyteler's maid, Petronella, was burned at the stake in 1324.

With its arched entry and stone steps, **Butter Slip**, a narrow and dark walkway connecting High St with St Kieran's St (previously called Low Lane) is the most picturesque of Kilkenny's many narrow medieval corridors. It was built in 1616 and once was lined with the stalls of butter vendors.

Black Freren Gate on Abbey St is the only gate from the old Norman city walls still standing, albeit with the help of metal bracing to ensure the safety of those who pass through. Crumbling sections of the old walls remain throughout the central city.

On the corner of Parliament St and the road leading down to Bateman's Quay, the **Confederation Hall monument** (really just a fragment) beside the Bank of Ireland marks the site where the national Parliament met from 1642 to 1649. Nearby is the ramshackle **Grace's Castle**, originally built in 1210, but lost to the family and converted into a prison in 1568, and then in 1794 into a courthouse, which it remains today. Rebels from the 1798 Rising were executed here.

The 19th-century **St Mary's Cathedral** is visible from most parts of town. A plaque at the entrance notes: 'The construction of the cathedral began in 1843 and continued during the Famine years, the years of emigration, coffin ships, starvation, and even despair because of the many thousands of our people who died of hunger and disease…', before going on to list yet more tribulations.

Across the river stand the ruins of **St John's Priory**, which was founded in 1200 and was noted for its many beautiful windows until Cromwell's visit. Nearby **Kilkenny College**, on John St, dates from 1666. Its students included Jonathan Swift and the philosopher George Berkeley, but it now houses Kilkenny's county hall.

Tours

Tynan Tours (☎ 087 265 1745; adult/student €6/5.50; ✆ 2 to 4 tours daily mid-Mar–Oct) conducts entertaining, informative hour-long walking tours that meander Kilkenny's narrow lanes, steps and pedestrian passageways.

Festivals & Events

Kilkenny hosts several world-class events throughout the year that attract revellers in the thousands.

Kilkenny Rhythm & Roots (☎ 056-779 0057; www .kilkennyroots.com; ✆ early May) Over 30 pubs and other venues participate in hosting Ireland's biggest music festival, with an emphasis on country and 'old-timey' American roots music.

Cat Laughs Comedy Festival (☎ 056-776 3416; www.thecatlaughs.com; ✆ late May-early Jun) Acclaimed gathering of world-class comedians in Kilkenny's hotels and pubs.

Kilkenny Arts Festival (☎ 056-775 2175; www .kilkennyarts.ie; ✆ mid-Aug) The city comes alive with theatre, cinema, music, literature, visual arts, children's events and street spectacles for 10 action-packed days.

Kilkenny Celtic Festival (www.celticfestival.ie; ✆ late Sep-early Oct) A weeklong celebration of all things trad Irish, especially the language, spanning performances, exhibits, seminars and more.

Sleeping

If you're arriving in town with no room booked (an unwise move at weekends, in summer and during festivals), the tourist office runs an efficient accommodation booking service (€4).

BUDGET

Tree Grove Caravan & Camping Park (☎ 056-777 0302; www.treegrovecamping.com; New Ross Rd; campsites €15-20; ✆ Mar–mid-Nov) This camping ground in a small park is 1.5km south of Kilkenny off the R700. Tent sites for hikers or cyclists travelling without a car cost €7.50. Showers are free, and there's a camp kitchen, TV room with a pool table, and a laundry. Bike hire can be arranged.

Kilkenny Tourist Hostel (☎ 056-776 3541; www .kilkennyhostel.ie; 35 Parliament St; dm €17-19, tw 40-42; ⌨) Inside an ivy-covered 1770s Georgian townhouse, this cosy, 60-bed independent hostel has a sitting room warmed by an open fireplace, and a timber- and leadlight-panelled dining room adjoining the self-catering kitchen. Staff keep a list of pub gigs, most of which are within stumbling distance.

Atmospheric Foulksrath Castle Hostel (p239) is just 17km north of town.

MIDRANGE

Rafter Dempsey's (☎ 056-772 2970; www.accommodation kilkenny.com; 4 Friary St; r €45-130) While worn, this good-natured pub's 16 basic B&B rooms are perfectly clean and just footsteps from the town centre and castle.

Bregagh House (☎ 056-772 2315; www.bregaghhouse .com; Dean St; s €50-60, d €76-100; Ⓟ) If you want the cosiness that comes with staying in a family home, this B&B is a good bet for its convenient location opposite the cathedral, friendly hosts, and filling hot breakfasts. There's ample onsite parking and a pretty back garden.

Kilford Arms Hotel (☎ 056-776 1018; www .kilfordarms.ie; John St; s €50-85, d €90-160; Ⓟ ⌨ 🛜) Mounted in the lobby, a stuffed 150-year-old Bengal tiger (somewhat mangy, but in better shape than the Celtic Tiger) sets the tone at this slightly offbeat hotel, which has 70 colourful rooms and an equally offbeat bar (O'Faolain's; p234).

Pembroke Hotel (☎ 056-778 3500; Patrick St; www .pembrokekilkenny.com; r from €69; 🛜) Wake up to

---

KILKENNY CATS

There once were two cats of Kilkenny
Each thought there was one cat too many
So they fought and they hit
And they scratched and they bit
'Til (excepting their nails
And the tips of their tails)
Instead of two cats there weren't any!

The origins of this little ditty, with or without its optional extra couplet, and the phrase 'fighting like a Kilkenny cat' (fighting tooth and nail) have been lost over time (most theories relate to soldiers' mistreatment of felines at various points in history). To this day, Kilkenny's citizens are dubbed 'Kilkenny cats'; its hurling team (consistently Ireland's best) wears black-and-orange tom-cat colours and are called 'the Cats'; and it inspired the name of the Cat Laughs Comedy Festival (p231).

---

castle views (from some of the 74 rooms) at this new epicentral hotel. The Pembroke's decor has a retro-funky feel, there's a leather-sofa-filled bar onsite, and free parking and use of swimming and leisure facilities are just around the corner.

Celtic House (☎ 056-776 2249; www.celtic-house-bandb.com; 18 Michael St; r €80-90; P) Artist Angela Byrne extends one of Ireland's warmest welcomes at her spick-and-span B&B. Some of the bright rooms have sky-lit bathrooms, others have views of the castle, and Angela's landscapes adorn many of the walls. Guests return time and again – definitely book ahead.

Butler Court (☎ 056-776 1178; www.butlercourt.com; Patrick St; r €80-130; 🖳 🛜) Not to be confused with the grand Butler House a few doors up-hill (right), this was originally the mail coach yard for Kilkenny Castle. Wrapping around a flower-filled courtyard, contemporary rooms have Canadian-cherry parquet floors and king-size beds. A continental breakfast, including fresh fruit and filtered coffee, is stocked in your in-room fridge. Ask about parking arrangements.

Zuni (☎ 056-772 3999; www.zuni.ie; 26 Patrick St; r €99-150; P 🛜) This former playhouse now houses one of the city's chicest restaurants (opposite) and 13 townhouse-style rooms. Rooms are decked out with contemporary art, angular furniture and soft-glowing lamps.

TOP END

Langton House Hotel (☎ 056-776 5133; www.langtons.ie; 67 John St; s €75-125, d €130-200; P 🖳 🛜) In the same family since the 1930s, but constantly evolving, this Kilkenny icon has some 30 rooms of varying styles – from clubby, leather-upholstered affairs to futuristic ones with 16-jet, computerised showers complete with double bench-seats, in-shower lighting and an in-shower radio to drown out your singing. There's also a fine restaurant (Edward Langton's; opposite) and a sophisticated nightclub (Langton Club; p234).

Kilkenny River Court (☎ 056-772 3388; www.kilrivercourt.com; John St; r €95-200; P 🖳 🛜 🐾) When not unwinding in your lavishly appointed room, you can dine at the respected restaurant, swim laps in the award-winning health club's sunlit indoor pool, or sip a cocktail on the cobblestone terrace of the wraparound bar overlooking the bridge and castle. Staff are consistently helpful.

ourpick Butler House (☎ 056-772 2828; www.butler.ie; 16 Patrick St; s €120-155, d €170-225; P 🖳 🛜) You can't stay in Kilkenny Castle, but this historic mansion is surely the next best thing. Once the home of the earls of Ormonde, who built the castle, these days it houses a boutique hotel with aristocratic trappings including sweeping staircases, marble fireplaces, an art collection and impeccably trimmed gardens (see p230). The 13 generously sized rooms are individually decorated including brand-new bathrooms.

Eating

Kilkenny has some 40 restaurants – the hard part is choosing.

CAFES

Two Dames (☎ 085 175 5005; 80 John St; dishes €3-7; ⏰ 8.30am-4.30pm Mon-Fri, 10am-4.30pm Sat) Organic orridge, granola with organic yoghurt and CYO' (create your own) sandwiches that night feature brie, cranberry, grape and rispy bacon are just a few of the reasons locals queeze into this hole-in-the-wall cafe.

Chez Pierre (☎ 056-776 4655; 17 Parliament St; daytime ishes €4.50-13, dinner mains €20; ☉ 10am-5pm Mon-Sat, lus dinner Thu-Sat) This sunny-sweet French spot loes great *tartines* (open-faced sandwiches), oups and sweets plus blackboard specials.

Cafe Sol (☎ 056-776 4987; William St; lunch mains €9-5, dinner mains €17-29; ☉ 11.30am-10pm Mon-Sat, noon-pm Sun) Leisurely lunches stretch until 5pm at his cafe–restaurant. Local produce includes Kilkenny beef and Carlow free-range chicken, out vegetarians aren't an afterthought, with hoices like oven-baked goat's cheese with nango and plum chutney, and pecan, veg-table and hazelnut roast.

Kilkenny Design Centre Cafe (☎ 056-772 2118; astle Yard; dishes €10-13; ☉ 10am-7pm Mon-Sat year-ound, plus 11am-7pm Sun Apr-Dec) Upstairs from he arty shops, this equally arty, organic-riented cafe is one of the best places in town or home-baked breads and scones, salads uch as warm chicken with smoked bacon nd feta, and sumptuous desserts.

RESTAURANTS

Zuni (☎ 056-772 3999; www.zuni.ie; 26 Patrick St; lunch mains 7-13, dinner mains €21-27; ☉ lunch & dinner) Dark leath-ers contrasting with lighter tables and walls at his one-time theatre provide a stylised back-drop for chef Maria Rafferty's show-stopping cooking in the open kitchen. Irish produce takes on pan-European flavours in dishes like wild Wicklow venison with potato gratin.

Fléva (☎ 056-777 0021; 84 High St; lunch mains €9.50-12.50, dinner mains €18.50-27; ☉ lunch & dinner Tue-Sun) There's a postmodern sense of experimen-tation at this art-filled restaurant. Locally sourced produce is complemented by fla-voursome accompaniments like wholegrain mustard, minted peas and celeriac purée.

Rinuccini (☎ 056-776 1575; 1 The Parade; lunch mains €10-20, dinner mains €19-30; ☉ lunch & dinner) Follow a short flight of steps down to a candlelit basement to bliss out on Antonio Cavaliere's classical Italian cuisine, including his sub-lime *Spaghetti al Astice* – lobster tossed with pasta, shallots, cream, brandy and black truf-fle, doused with fresh parmesan, and served in the shell. The restaurant's named for Giovanni Rinuccini, a Florentine noble who was ap-pointed papal nuncio to Kilkenny in 1650.

Edward Langton's (☎ 056-776 5133; 67 John St; mains €15-28; ☉ noon-10pm) The restaurant within this enormous, snazzy pub seems able to seat much of the town (certainly most everybody's here for Sunday lunch). The food is quality trad Irish: never-ending bowls of boiled pota-toes and desserts like toffee and brown bread pudding with hot butterscotch sauce. Regular dinner-and-show specials for around €40 are popular with locals and tourists alike.

Lautrec's Brasserie (☎ 056-776 2720; 9 St Kieran's St; mains €16-26; ☉ dinner daily, lunch Sat & Sun) Romantics can hold hands at the tiny tables in the tiny dining room and partake of the dispropor-tionate wine selections at this seductive, rose-coloured French bistro. It's spawned a second restaurant in Carlow town (p223).

Campagne (☎ 056-777 2858; The Arches, 5 Gashouse Lane; lunch 2-/3-course set menu €24/28, dinner mains €24-29; ☉ lunch Fri & Sun, dinner Wed-Sun) Chef Garrett Byrne has returned home from the capital's Michelin-starred Chapter One restaurant to open this bold, stylish new restaurant in his native Kilkenny. Dubliners now commute to feast on specialities like chestnut and pheasant soup, and goose terrine with apple marmalade.

SELF-CATERING

Over 20 stalls selling local produce set up at Kilkenny's **farmers market** (Mayors Walk, The Parade; ☉ 9am-2pm Thu). Otherwise, picnickers can pick up groceries from **Dunnes Store** (St Keiran's St; ☉ 24hr).

Drinking

Tynan's Bridge House (☎ 056-772 1291; St John's Bridge) Looking like it might fall down at any mo-ment, this wonky Georgian pub is the best trad bar in town. To be sure, the 300-year-old building has settled a bit over the years, but then so have many of the customers.

John Cleere (☎ 056-776 2573; 22 Parliament St) One of Kilkenny's finest venues for live music, this long bar has blues, jazz and rock, as well as trad music sessions.

Grapevine (☎ 056-772 956; 6 Rose Inn St) If yet another pint in an atmospheric pub is just one too many, take refuge at this smart new tapas and wine bar. There's also a stellar range of craft beers and, joy of joys, Moretti coffee, air-freighted from Italy, and quite possibly the best coffee you'll ever taste.

O'Riada (27 Parliament St) The lowest-key bar in Kilkenny gets pretty lively when there's

---

LOCAL BREW?

For foreigners, Kilkenny is synonymous with its namesake ale. But locally, 'Kilkenny' is known as **Smithwick's**.

John Smithwick opened the brewery in Kilkenny city in 1710 on the site of **St Francis Abbey** (the abbey's ruins remain within the complex). But it wasn't until the 1980s that it started selling overseas under the Kilkenny name. This was to avoid pronunciation pitfalls with the silent W in the word 'Smithwick's', and to provide a stronger taste catering to its offshore market. Today 'Kilkenny' refers to a similar yet distinctly different beer – it is more bitter and has a creamy, Guinness-like head (Smithwick's retains a thinner head and smoother taste).

Ireland's oldest working brewery, Smithwick's is now owned by drinks giant Diageo (Guinness, Harp et al), and primarily brews Budweiser under licence. It was slated to close when Diageo decided to relocate to newer, bigger premises. However, at the time of writing, Ireland's economic downturn had placed this move under review. Stay tuned...

---

a hurling match screening. But most of the time you can ponder your pint and strike up a conversation with anyone – including yourself.

Kyteler's Inn (☎ 056-772 1064; 27 St Kieran's St) Dame Alice Kyteler's (p229) old house was built back in 1224 and has seen its share of history: the Dame had four husbands, all of whom died in suspicious circumstances, and she was charged with witchcraft in 1323. Today, tourists of all ages whoop it up in the dungeon-like basement.

Also recommended:

Ana Conda (☎ 056-777 1657; Parliament St) Local favourite featuring regular *céilidh* sessions and rock shows.

Pumphouse (☎ 056-776 3924; 26 Parliament St) Frequent live rock groups plus pool tables, big TVs and a rooftop terrace.

Hibernian Bar (☎ 056-777 1888; Hibernian Hotel, Patrick St) Civilised lounge bar with deep, comfy leather banquettes and a long list of proper cocktails.

Matt the Millers (☎ 056-776 1696; 1 John St) Tangerine-coloured medieval mill with four bars over four floors, crowd-pleasing bands and DJs, and good pub grub.

Entertainment

For information on local events, check out the weekly *Kilkenny People* newspaper (www .kilkennypeople.ie). Events are listed on the tourist office website, and on www.whazon .com.

CINEMA & THEATRE

Kilkenny Cineplex (☎ 056-772 3111; Fair Green, Gaol Rd) Four screens blare the latest Hollywood releases.

Watergate Theatre (☎ 056-776 1674; www.water gatekilkenny.com; Parliament St) Recently spiffed up, this theatre hosts drama, comedy and musi-

cal performances. If you're wondering why intermission lasts 18 minutes, it's to allow patrons time to nip into John Cleere's pub for a pint.

NIGHTCLUBS

Ask around to see what's hot now. Clubs close at 2am.

O'Faolain's and Club 51 (☎ 056-776 1018; Kilford Arms Hotel, John St) Built on three levels around a 16th-century stone church that was brought over in crates from Wales and painstakingly rebuilt here, numbered stone by numbered stone, O'Faolain's is a lively night-time spot year-round. Between approximately Easter and October, Club 51 (admission €6 to €10) in a strobe-lit space out back, sees dancers getting sweaty on Saturday nights.

Morrison's Bar (☎ 056-777 1888; 1 Ormonde St) In the belle époque cellar of the Hibernian Hotel, DJs spin an eclectic mix for an upmarket crowd that actually cares about getting spilled on.

Langton Club (admission free Tue, free before 11pm, €5 after 11pm Thu, €5 before 11pm, €10 after 11pm Sat; ☑ Tue, Thu & Sat) A massive wave-design bar made from turquoise volcanic rock is the centrepiece of this local nightlife magnet.

SPORT

You can go to the dogs (as it were) at James Park (☎ 056-772 1214; Freshford Rd; ☑ races 8pm Wed & Fri).

One of the unique pleasures of a trip to Ireland is catching a game of hurling at the Cats' hallowed home stadium, **Nowlan Park** (☎ 056-775 1500; www.kilkennygaa.ie; O'Loughlin Rd) Hurling and Gaelic football schedules are listed in *Kilkenny People*.

Shopping

An interesting mix of local stores concentrates on High St and in **Market Cross**, a multilevel mall behind a row of High St shops.

In a vast converted factory, the family-run outdoors store **Padmore & Barnes** (☎ 056-772 1037; Wolfe Tone St; 9am-6pm Mon-Sat, 2-6pm Sun) has an unbeatable selection of well-priced camping equipment, hiking boots, wet-weather clothing and sports gear.

The whopping new chain-store-filled shopping mall **MacDonagh Junction** is the largest in the region.

Getting There & Away

BUS

Bus Éireann (☎ 056-776 4933) operates from a shelter about 200m east of John St adjacent to the train station. Bus Éireann also picks up and drops off passengers on St Patrick's St in the centre of town. There are services to Carlow (€7.40, one hour, 12 daily), Clonmel (€8.10, one hour, 12 daily), Cork (€16.10, three hours, two daily), Dublin (€10.80, 2¼ hours, five daily) and Waterford (€9, one hour, two daily).

JJ Kavanagh & Sons (☎ 056-883 1106; www.jjkavanagh.ie) has regular services to destinations including Carlow town, Portlaoise and Dublin airport, with wi-fi available in some vehicles.

Buggys Coaches (☎ 056-444 1264; www.buggy.ie) runs services to the north of the county.

CRAFTY KILKENNY

At least 130 full-time craftspeople and artists work commercially in the county – one of the highest concentrations in Ireland – thanks to its fine raw materials and inspirational scenery.

Across the Parade from Kilkenny Castle, the 1760-built former castle stables have been extensively renovated and now house the **National Craft Gallery** (p230), as well as a number of local craftspeople such as silversmiths. The front building contains the gallery-like shops of the **Kilkenny Design Centre** (☎ 056-772 2118; www.kilkennydesign.com; Castle Yard), where top-end Irish crafts and artwork for sale includes items by artisans county-wide.

Pick up a free **craft trail brochure** from the tourist office.

TRAIN

On the eastern side of the new shopping mall of the same name, MacDonagh train station (☎ 056-772 2024) has five trains daily to/from Dublin's Heuston Station (from €10, 1¾ hours) and Waterford (from €10, 50 minutes).

GETTING AROUND

There are large car parks off both sides of High St, and numerous others throughout the city.

For a taxi, call **Kilkenny Cabs** (☎ 056-775 2000).

CENTRAL KILKENNY

The area south – and most notably southeast – of Kilkenny city is laced with country roads and dotted with cute villages overlooking the rich, green Barrow and Nore valleys. This is fine walking country and is also home to some of the county's most notable craftspeople, whose workshops can be visited.

Much of the area is easily visited on a daytrip from the city, but you really need your own wheels, as public transport is limited.

Kells & Around

Kells (not to be confused with Kells in County Meath) is a mere hamlet with a fine stone bridge on a tributary of the Nore. However, in Kells Priory, the village has one of Ireland's most impressive and romantic monastic sites. The village is 13km south of Kilkenny city on the R697. A taxi from Kilkenny city costs about €25 one-way.

KELLS PRIORY

This is the best sort of ruin, where visitors can amble about whenever they like, with no tour guides, tours, set hours or fees. At dusk on a vaguely sunny day the old priory is simply beautiful. Most days you stand a chance of exploring the site alone (apart from bleating sheep).

The earliest remains of this gorgeous monastic site date from the late 12th century, while the bulk of the present ruins are from the 15th century. In a sea of rich farmland, a carefully restored protective wall connects seven dwelling towers. Inside the walls are the remains of an **Augustinian abbey** and the foundations of some chapels and houses. It's unusually well fortified for a monastery and the heavy curtain walls hint at a troubled history. Indeed, within a single century from

1250, the abbey was twice fought over and burned down by squabbling warlords. It slid into permanent decline beginning when it was suppressed in 1540.

The ruins are 800m east of Kells on the Stonyford road.

KILREE ROUND TOWER & HIGH CROSS

About 2km south of Kells (signposted from the priory car park) there's a 29m-high round tower and a simple early high cross, which is said to mark the grave of a 9th-century Irish high king, Niall Caille. He's said to have drowned in the King's River at Callan some time in the 840s while attempting to save a servant, and his body washed up near Kells. His final resting place lies beyond the church grounds because he wasn't a Christian.

CALLAN FAMINE GRAVEYARD

West of Kilree, and signposted off the main road 2km south of Callan, is a **cemetery** where the local victims of the Great Famine (p39) are buried. It isn't much to look at, but the unmarked graves are a poignant reminder of the anonymity of starvation.

Bennettsbridge & Around
pop 685

Just 7km south of Kilkenny city on the R700, Bennettsbridge is an arts-and-crafts treasure chest, although these treasures are scattered throughout the town, rather than within a concentrated area.

In a big mill by the river west of town, pottery shop **Nicholas Mosse Irish Country Shop** (☎ 056-772 7105; www.nicholasmosse.com; ☷ 10am-6pm Mon-Sat, 1.30-5pm Sun) specialises in handmade spongeware – creamy-brown pottery decorated with sponged patterns. It also sells linens and other handmade craft items (although some hail from lands of cheap labour far from Ireland). A seconds shop yields huge savings. Its cafe is the best choice locally for lunch, with a creative line-up of soups, sandwiches, hot dishes and its renowned scones.

Signposted up the road, **Keith Mosse Bespoke** (☎ 056-772 7948; www.keithmosse.com; ☷ 11am-6pm Wed-Sat, noon-6pm Sun) is home to the eponymous craftsman, who takes fine woods from five continents and turns them into elegant furniture and decorator items.

Another few hundred metres away, by the bridge, **Moth to a Flame** (☎ 056-772 7826; mothtoa flame@iolfree.ie; ☷ 10am-6pm Mon-Sat year-round, plus 10am-6pm Sun May-Dec) creates elaborate candles.

For fine leather, check out the factory boutique of **Chesneau** (☎ 056-772 7456; www.chesneau design.com; ☷ 9am-6pm Mon-Fri, 10am-6pm Sat, noon-6pm Sun), near the village centre. Stylish bags and accessories are on offer in a rainbow of colours - emerald-green numbers are big sellers. Most of the designs are created locally and sold internationally.

On a small road above Nicholas Mosse the **Nore View Folk Museum** (☎ 056-27749; Danesfort Rd; admission free) is not your average museum. Seamus Lawlor is a passionate chronicler of Irish life and is full of fascinating facts about his private collection of local items, including farming tools, kitchen utensils and other wonderful old bric-a-brac.

Nore Valley Park (☎ 056-972 7229; www.nore valleypark.com; Annamult; day admission €5.20, campsites from €12; ☷ park 9am-6pm Mon-Sat Mar-Oct, campground Mar-Oct) is a 2-hectare farm where you can also camp (electricity is an additional €3, but showers are free). Kids can caress goats, cuddle rabbits, navigate a maze and jump on a straw bounce. There's a tearoom and picnic area. If you're coming into Bennettsbridge from Kilkenny along the R700, turn right just before the bridge.

Opposite the church, **Italian Affair** (☎ 056-770 0988; 4 Chapel St; mains €8-25; ☷ lunch & dinner Tue-Sun summer, lunch Sun, dinner Tue-Sun rest of yr) serves up good pizzas, pastas and coffee.

Thomastown & Around
pop 1837

The busy N9 runs right through the centre of this small market town but it's worth stopping the car for a short stroll around its compact centre. Named after Welsh mercenary Thomas de Cantwell, Thomastown has some fragments of a medieval wall and the partly ruined 13th-century **Church of St Mary**. Down by the bridge, **Mullin's Castle** is the sole survivor of the 14 castles once here.

Like the rest of Kilkenny, the area has a vibrant craft scene. Look out for **Clay Creations** (☎ 056-772 4977; Low St; ☷ 10am-1pm & 2-5pm Tue-Sat) displaying the quixotic ceramics and sculptures of local artist Brid Lyons.

Just 4km southwest of Thomastown, highfliers tee off at the Jack Nicklaus–designed **Mount Juliet** (☎ 056-777 3000; www.mountjuliet.com; Thomastown; green fees €90-120; P 🖥). Set over 1500 wooded acres, it also has its own equestrian entre, a gym and spa, two restaurants, wine naster-classes, and palatial rooms catering to very whim, right down to the pillow menu accommodation from €169).

In town, the pistachio-and-cream-painted **lackberry Cafe** (☎ 087 053 7858; Market St, Thomastown; **shes** €4.50-7.50, ⏰ 9.30am-5.30pm Mon-Fri, 10.30am-.30pm Sat) does superb thick-cut sandwiches nd warming soups (the tomato and basil s delicious) served with pumpkin-seed-peckled soda bread. Between noon and 2pm, ireat-value multicourse hot lunches see the •lace squeezed to bursting.

ERPOINT ABBEY

)ne of Ireland's finest Cistercian ruins, **erpoint Abbey** (☎ 056-24623; www.heritageireland e; Hwy N9; adult/child €2.90/1.30; ⏰ 9.30am-6pm Jun-ep, 9.30am-5.30pm Oct, 10am-4pm Nov, 10am-5pm Mar-lay, closed Dec-Feb, last tour 1hr before closing) is about .5km southwest of Thomastown on the N9. t was established in the 12th century and ias been partially restored. The tower and 'loister are late 14th or early 15th century. .ook for the series of often amusing figures :arved on the cloister pillars, including a knight. There are also stone carvings on the :hurch walls and in the tombs of members of he Butler and Walshe families. Faint traces of a 15th- or 16th-century painting remain on the northern wall of the church. This :hancel area also contains a tomb thought o belong to hardheaded Felix O'Dulany, 'erpoint's first abbot and bishop of Ossory, vho died in 1202.

According to local legend, St Nicholas or Santa Claus) is buried near the abbey. While retreating in the Crusades, the knights of Jerpoint removed his body from Myra in nodern-day Turkey and reburied him in the **Church of St Nicholas** to the west of the abbey. The grave is marked by a broken slab deco-rated with a carving of a monk.

STONYFORD

On the N10, a few kilometres northwest of the abbey and Thomastown, is the small village of Stonyford. The local highlight, the nation-ally renowned **Jerpoint Glass Studio** (☎ 056-24350; www.jerpointglass.com; ⏰ studio 10am-4.30pm Mon-Thu, 10am-2pm Fri, shop 10am-6pm Mon-Sat, noon-5pm Sun), is housed in an old stone-walled farm build-ing where you can watch workers craft mol-ten glass into exquisite artistic and practical items.

KILFANE

The village of Kilfane, 3km north of Thomastown on the N9, has a small, ruined **13th-century church** and **Norman tower**, 50m off the road and signposted. The church has a remarkable stone carving of Thomas de Cantwell called the Cantwell Fada or Long Cantwell. It depicts a tall, thin knight in detailed chain-mail armour brandishing a shield decorated with the Cantwell coat of arms.

Kilfane Glen & Waterfall (☎ 056-24558; ⏰ 11am-6pm Jul & Aug only) is a pretty spot with wooded paths winding through its wild 6-hectare gar-dens, which date from the 1790s. An elabo-rately decorated thatched cottage is worth hiking to. Kilfane Glen is 2km north of town along the N9.

GOWRAN

Some 14km northeast of Thomastown on the N9 (and 14km east of Kilkenny), the small village of Gowran is notable for the Heritage Service–run **St Mary's Church** (☎ 056-772 6894; www.heritageireland.ie; admission free; ⏰ 9.30am-6pm mid-Jun–mid-Sep), a 13th-century house of wor-ship for clerics living in a loose community. Much modified through the years, it has a 19th-century church grafted onto one side.

Brave souls can handle some of the slith-ering creatures at the indoor (ie rainy-day friendly) **Reptile Village** (☎ 056-772 6757; www .reptilevillage.net; The Demesne, Gowran; adult/child/family €8.90/5.70/26; ⏰ 10am-6pm); the less brave can peer at them through glass.

GETTING THERE & AWAY

There are bus services operated by **Kilbride Coaches** (☎ 051-423 633) and **JJ Kavanagh & Sons** (☎ 056-883 1106; www.jjkavanagh.ie), however, the **train** offers the most frequent public transport to/from Thomastown. Five trains daily (four on Sunday) stop on the Dublin–Waterford route via Kilkenny (€7, 12 minutes). The sta-tion is 1km west of town.

Inistioge
pop 263

The little village of Inistioge (*in-ish-teeg*) is a picture. Its 18th-century, 10-arch **stone bridge** spans the River Nore and vintage shops face its tranquil square. Somewhere so inviting could hardly hope to escape the attention of movie-location scouts: Inistioge's film credits include *Widow's Peak* (1993), *Circle of Friends*

(1994) and *Where the Sun is King* (1996). There are picnic tables on the river.

With a scenic stretch of the South Leinster Way coursing through town, this is a good base for exploring the region. The R700 from Thomastown makes for a lovely **scenic drive** through the river valley. Better yet, try the **hiking trails** that follow the river and side trails leading up into the hills.

Approximately 3km south, on Mt Alto, is the heavily forested **Woodstock Gardens** (☎ 056-779 4000; parking €4; ☼ 9am-8pm Apr-Sep, 10am-4pm Oct-Mar), a beauty of a park with expansive gardens, picnic areas and trails. The panorama of the valley and village below is spectacular. Coming from town, follow the signs for Woodstock Estate and enter the large gates (despite appearances, it's a public road) then continue along the road for about 2km until you reach the car park.

SLEEPING & EATING

Woodstock Arms (☎ 056-775 8440; www.woodstock arms.com; Inistioge; s/d/tr €45/75/96) This friendly pub has tables outside overlooking the square and seven simple rooms that are freshly painted and squeaky clean. The three triples are particularly spacious. Breakfast is served in a pretty little room out back with wooden tables and blue-and-white china.

Circle of Friends (☎ 056-775 8800; dishes €4.50-16; ☼ at least noon-6pm winter, to 9pm summer, may close one day per week) Also with tables overlooking the square, this cheerful apple-green cafe with strawberry-motif table cloths has flavoured coffees (mint, caramel and so on), hot dishes like beer-battered cod and chips and – the reason everyone's really here – gargantuan servings of homemade desserts like pavlova.

Bassetts at Woodstock (☎ 056-775 8820; www .bassetts.ie; lunch mains €9-14, dinner mains €19.50-27.50; ☼ lunch Wed-Sun, dinner Wed-Sat) Adjacent to Woodstock Gardens, John Bassett has turned his family home into an inspired dining experience. Dinner from Wednesday to Friday is à la carte, while Saturday nights feature tasting menus (€9.50 per course) paired with wines (from €5 per glass) served at set intervals from 7.30pm. The food is fresh, local and inventive (think duck with vanilla risotto, or chocolate fondant with pink peppercorn sorbet). Future meals graze right outside the door.

Motte Restaurant (☎ 056-775 8655; Plas Newydd Lodge; lunch menu €28.50, 2-/3-course dinner menu €36.50/42.50; ☼ lunch Sun, dinner Thu-Sat) On the northern edge of the village, this aubergine trimmed cottage is illuminated inside by an open fire and candles. Beef in cracked peppe and brandy cream sauce is a highlight of it Irish menu.

GETTING THERE & AWAY

This is primarily car, hiking or biking terri tory, but buses run by **Kilbride Coaches** (☎ 051 423 633) connect Inistioge and Kilkenny.

Graiguenamanagh
pop 1376

Graiguenamanagh (greg-*na*-muh-na; know locally simply as Graigue) is the kind of place where you could easily find yoursel staying longer than planned. Spanning the Barrow, an ancient six-arch stone bridge i illuminated at night and connects the village with the smaller township of Tinnahinch on the County Carlow side of the river (look for the darker stones on the Carlow side – a legacy from being blown up during the 179? rebellion).

SIGHTS & ACTIVITIES

Some picturesque **walks** pass through and nea town – see p240.

Dating back to 1204, **Duiske Abbey** (☎ 059 24238; ☼ 8am-6pm) was once Ireland's larges Cistercian abbey. What you see today is the result of 800 years of additions and changes and it is very much a working parish (come at the right time and you'll interrupt the kids choir practice, much to their delight). The simple exterior and whitewashed interior only hint at its long history. To the right of the entrance look for the Knight of Duiske, a 14th century, high-relief carving of a knight in chain mail who's reaching for his sword. On the floor nearby, a glass panel reveals some of the original 13th-century floor tiles, now 2m below the present floor level. In the grounds stand two early **high crosses** (7th century and 9th century), brought here for protection in the last century. The smaller Ballyogan Cross has panels on the eastern side depicting the crucifixion, Adam and Eve, Abraham's sacrifice of Isaac, and David playing the harp The western side shows the massacre of the innocents.

Around the corner, the **Abbey Centre** (☼ 9am-1pm Mon-Fri, some days longer) houses a small exhibition of Christian art, plus pictures of the abbey in its unrestored state.

COUNTIES WEXFORD, WATERFORD, CARLOW & KILKENNY

Friendly Philip Cushen is 'at least the sixth ¡eneration' to produce knitting yarns, blanets, tweed and winter woollies at **Cushendale Voollen Mill** (☎ 059-972 4118; www.cushendale e; ⏱ 8.30am-12.30pm & 1.30-5.30pm Mon-Fri, 9.30am-2.30pm Sat) and can give you an informal,)ehind-the-scenes peek at the mill's century-•ld machinery in action.

Also in the village centre, **Duiske Glass** ☎ 059-972 4174; www.duiskeglass.ie; ⏱ 9am-5pm Mon-ri, 10am-1pm & 2-5pm Sat) creates contemporary ι nd traditional crystal.

ESTIVALS & EVENTS

)uring late September, Graiguenamanagh's ιarrow streets spill over with booksellers, authors and bibliophiles during the three-day 'own of Books Festival (www.booktownireland.com). •lans are underway for Graiguenamanagh to •ecome a year-round 'book town' in the same 'ein as Wales' Hay-on-Wye – check the festiνal website for updates. Meanwhile, there's a ¡ood antiquarian bookshop on Abbey St.

SLEEPING & EATING

)own by the boats tied up along the river, the nviting guesthouse and restaurant **Waterside** ☎ 059-972 4246; www.watersideguesthouse.com; Quay ;raiguenamanagh; s/d €59/98; ⏱ restaurant lunch Sun, dinner Mon-Sat Apr-Sep, lunch Sun, dinner Fri & Sat Oct-Apr) occupies ι converted solid granite 19th-century corn store. Its 10 renovated rooms have exposed timber beams and brand-new bathrooms. Hosts Brian and Brigid Roberts can point out the village's hidden nooks and crannies. The restaurant is well regarded for its interesting modern Irish menu and its regular 'After Dinner Live' music acts featuring anything from jazz to bluegrass (mains from €19 to €26.50).

During the day, healthy wraps, soups, salads and organic teas are available at **Coffee on High** (☎ 059-972 5725; High St; dishes €3.80-8; ⏱ 10am-5pm Mon-Fri, 10am-3pm Sat).

DRINKING & ENTERTAINMENT

One of Graiguenamanagh's hidden treasures is its pair of unchanged-in-generations old pubs. **Mick Doyle's** and **Mick Ryan's**, both on Abbey St, still sell everything from fishing tackle to pitch forks to dusty tins of baked beans along with pints of stout. The former still has its sheep-dipping sign; the latter has an equally untouched timber snug.

On the corner of the Quay and Abbey Street, another cosy, old-time pub, **Murray's**,

is the life and soul of the village during its cracking Sunday evening trad sessions; listen out for songs featuring local landmarks.

GETTING THERE & AWAY

Graiguenamanagh is 23km southeast of Kilkenny city on the R703. **Kilbride Coaches** (☎ 051-423 633) runs two buses Monday to Saturday to/from Kilkenny.

NORTHERN KILKENNY

The rolling green hills of northern County Kilkenny are idyllic for leisurely drives along the back roads with the makings of a picnic stowed in the boot. There's not a whole lot going on in this part of the county; it's best enjoyed by simply taking in the scenery and discovering peaceful little villages.

Castlecomer & Around

pop 1531

Castlecomer is on the gentle River Dinin, some 18km north of Kilkenny. The town became a centre for anthracite mining after the fuel was discovered nearby in 1636; the mines closed for good in the mid-1960s. The anthracite, a very hard form of coal, was widely regarded as being Europe's best, containing very little sulphur and producing almost no smoke.

Coal-mining exhibits are set among lush woodlands at the new **Castlecomer Discovery Park** (☎ 056-444 0707; www.discoverypark.ie; Estate Yard; adult/child €8/5; ⏱ 9.30am-6pm May-Aug, 10am-5pm Sep-Oct & Mar-Apr, 10.30am-4.30pm Nov-Feb), including some rare fossils predating dinosaurs, found here. Anglers can hook trout at the adjacent **Rainbow Trout Lakes** (per 4 hr €20; ⏱ 10am-dusk); you're allowed to keep two fish and must release the rest.

About 10km southwest of Castlecomer is **Swifte's Heath**, home to Jonathan Swift during his school years in Kilkenny. The 'e' was evidently dropped from the name before the satirist gained notoriety as the author of *Gulliver's Travels* and *A Modest Proposal*.

ourpick **Foulksrath Castle Hostel** (☎ 056-67674; www.anoige.ie; Ballyragget; dm incl linen €19; ⏱ reception 5-10pm; Ⓟ) All the storybooks you read as a kid come to life at this reputedly haunted castle. Dating from 1320 and modified in the 16th century, it's the oldest building in the world to operate as a hostel. A heart-stoppingly steep, worn-smooth spiral stone staircase leads to 42 beds in rustic dorms inside the tower, while a secret passageway leads to the rooftop with

---

WALKS: COUNTIES CARLOW & KILKENNY

The **South Leinster Way** slices through the hilly southern part of County Kilkenny, from Graiguenamanagh through Inistioge, down to Mullinavat and westward to Piltown. By far the prettiest part, a stretch of some 13km, begins on the River Barrow. It links Graiguenamanagh and Inistioge, two charming villages with amenities for travellers. In either village you can reward yourself with a top-notch meal.

Alternatively, along this path, you can branch off onto **Brandon Way** (4km south of Graiguenamanagh), which scales **Brandon Hill** (516m). The broad moorland summit is easily reached and affords a lovely view of the Blackstairs Mountains and Mt Leinster to the east. A return trip from Graigue is a fairly relaxed 12km walk.

The trail down **River Barrow** from Graiguenamanagh to St Mullins in County Carlow is equally beautiful, with a firm path wending past canals and through some wooded country and pleasant grassy picnic areas.

---

views over the woods. Modern concessions include new bathrooms and a stainless-steel kitchen; after cooking, hostellers usually dine by candlelight in the stone banquet hall. Stock up on supplies beforehand as there are no shops nearby and breakfast isn't included.

GETTING THERE & AWAY

Bus Éireann (☎ 056-64933) has five buses daily to Kilkenny (€5, 20 minutes). **Buggys Coaches** (☎ 056-444 1264; www.buggy.ie) has one bus daily (€4) between Kilkenny (outside the castle) and a stop 300m from Foulksrath Castle Hostel.

Dunmore Cave

Striking calcite formations enliven **Dunmore Cave** (☎ 056-67726; www.heritageireland.ie; Ballyfoyle; adult/child/family €2.90/1.30/7.40; ☷ 9.30am-6.30pm Jun-Sep, 10am-5pm Mar-Jun & Sep-Oct, 10am-5pm Nov-Mar), some 6km north of Kilkenny on the Castlecomer road (N78). According to sources, marauding Vikings killed 1000 people at two ring forts near here in 928. When survivors hid in the caverns, the Vikings tried to smoke them out by lighting fires at the entrance. It's thought that they then dragged off the men as slaves and left the women and children to suffocate. Excavations in 1973 uncovered the skeletons of at least 44 people mostly women and children. They also found coins dating from the 920s, but none from a later date. One theory suggests that the coins were dropped by the Vikings (who often carried them under the arms, secured with wax) while enthusiastically engaged in the slaughter. However, there are few marks of violence on the skeletons, lending weight to the theory that suffocation was the cause of death.

Admission to the cave is via a compulsory but highly worthwhile guided tour. After a steep descent you enter caverns full of stalactites, stalagmites and columns, including the 7m **Market Cross**, Europe's largest freestanding stalagmite. Although well lit and spacious, it's damp and cold (it's a cave, after all); bring warm clothes.

Buggys Coaches (☎ 056-444 1264) runs one bus daily (€3.50) from outside Kilkenny castle. **JJ Kavanagh & Sons** (☎ 056-883 1106; www.jjkavanagh.ie) also has a service here.

County Cork

Any hard edges to Ireland are lost in County Cork, unless you're talking about the fantastically eroded rocky coast, that is. Here lush land meets the roiling sea, the weather is often balmy (by Emerald Island standards) and scores of little seaside villages offer up days of languor and idyll, enjoying the good life.

Cork city is the centre and has a certain understated confidence as it thrives far from any shadow of Dublin. Food – from the incredible choices in its markets to an ever-changing cast of creative eateries – fuels the city. Pubs, entertainment and culture provide a depth of fun, and evocative old precincts provide reason to stroll. Kinsale, to the south, combines fine food with ancient charms in one beguiling package.

Further afield, you'll want to do just that: go further afield. In fact, you'll want to cross fields while walking the twists, turns and inlets of the eroded coasts and its multitude of perfectly charming old fishing villages, such as Clonakilty and Baltimore.

The county's three fingers jut out into the sea – you're in for some amazing views and many a ramble. Mizen Head caps a peninsula that is battered by waves on all sides, yet has some beautiful beaches and perfect little quayside pubs. Out on the lonely, windswept Sheep's Head Peninsula, it may feel like it's just you and the sheep. The thumb of the bunch, the Beara Peninsula, is the place to settle in. Tackle mountain passes and touch Ireland's ancient past.

Once you've uncorked Cork, you won't be able to get it back into the bottle.

HIGHLIGHTS

- **City Spectacular** Buzzing Cork city, with its intriguing selection of restaurants (p250), pubs (p251), music (p252) and theatres (p252)

- **Land Fall** The stunning Beara Peninsula coastal road around Allihies (p285)

- **Perfect Package** Medieval streets, mammoth forts, shoreline walks and lovely seafood pubs in Kinsale (p259)

- **Going Down** Reliving the age of ocean liners, good and bad, in Cobh (p255)

- **Ahoy There!** Unspoilt fishing villages, including Union Hall (p268), Glandore (p268), Castletownshend (p269), Castletownbere (p284) and Baltimore (p271)

- POPULATION: 485,000
- AREA: 7508 SQ KM

CORK CITY

pop 120,000

Cork over Dublin? That's what the locals cheerfully believe and what many travellers think as well. The city has much to recommend: great restaurants fed by a solid foodie scene, a walkable centre surrounded by interesting waterways, and a location that is close to the tourist mecca of the Irish west coast. If it's a tad weak in the 'atmospheric old boozer' department, it makes up for it with appealing modern cafes and bars.

The River Lee flows around the centre, an island packed with grand Georgian parades, cramped 17th-century alleys and modern masterpieces, such as the opera house. The flurry of urban renewal that began with the city's stint in 2005 as European Capital of Culture continues apace, with new buildings, bars and arts centres springing up all over town. The best of the city is still happily traditional, though – snug pubs with live music sessions most of the week, excellent local produce in an ever-expanding list of restaurants and a genuinely proud welcome from the locals.

HISTORY

Cork has a long and bruising history, inextricably linked with Ireland's struggle for nationhood.

COUNTY CORK

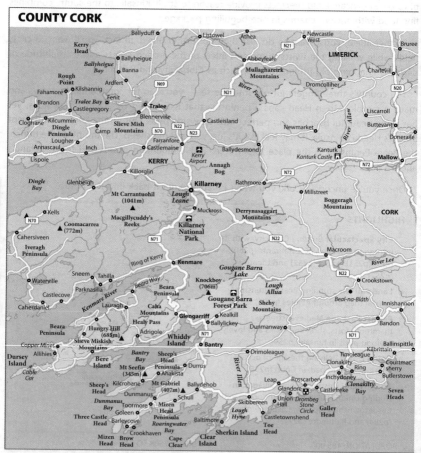

The story begins in the 7th century, when St Finbarre founded a monastery on a *corcach* (marshy place). By the 12th century the settlement had become the chief city of the Kingdom of South Munster, having survived raids and sporadic settlement by Norsemen. Irish rule was short-lived and by 1185 Cork was under English rule. Thereafter it changed hands regularly during the relentless struggle between Irish and Crown forces. It survived Cromwellian assault only to fall to that merciless champion of Protestantism, William of Orange.

During the 18th century Cork prospered, with butter, beef, beer and whiskey exported round the world from its port. A mere century later famine devastated both county and city,

and robbed Cork of millions of its inhabitants by death or emigration.

The 'Rebel City's' deep-seated Irishness ensured that it played a key role in Ireland's struggle for independence. Mayor Thomas MacCurtain was killed by the Black and Tans in 1920. His successor, Terence MacSwiney, died in London's Brixton prison after a hunger strike. The British were at their most brutally repressive in Cork – much of the centre, including St Patrick's St, the City Hall and the Public Library, was burned down. Cork was also a regional focus of Ireland's self-destructive Civil War in 1922–23.

ORIENTATION

The city centre lies on an island in the River Lee, which is crisscrossed by bridges. St Patrick's St runs from St Patrick's Bridge on the North Channel of the Lee, through the city's main shopping and commercial area, to the Georgian Grand Pde, which leads to the river's South Channel. North and south of St Patrick's St lie the city's most entertaining quarters: webs of narrow streets crammed with pubs, cafes, restaurants and shops.

Across St Patrick's Bridge is an equally bustling area, focused around MacCurtain St, with its own spread of pubs, restaurants and shops. East of MacCurtain St, you'll find Kent Train Station and budget B&Bs. West of Bridge St is Shandon, which has a village atmosphere, especially in the narrow lanes around its hilltop churches.

From midway down Grand Pde, Washington St leads southwest to the university.

INFORMATION
Bookshops

Connolly's Bookshop (☎ 021-427 5366; Rory Gallagher Pl, Paul St) Great chat and masses of second-hand books.

Eason's (☎ 021-427 0477; 113 St Patrick's St; ⏲ 9am-7pm Mon-Sat, noon-6pm Sun) Lots of magazines; good stationery on the 2nd floor.

Liam Ruiséal Teo (☎ 021-427 0981; 49-50 Oliver Plunkett St) New and second-hand books, including plenty on Cork.

Vibes & Scribes (☎ 021-450 5370; 3 Bridge St; ⏲ 10am-6.30pm Mon-Sat, 12.30-6.30pm Sun) Four floors of books, CDs and DVDs. Also on Lavitt's Quay.

Waterstone's (☎ 021-427 6522; 69 St Patrick's St; ⏲ 9am-7pm Mon-Thu & Sat, 9am-8pm Fri, noon-6pm Sun) Has the best travel section in the southwest.

Map of County Cork showing Tipperary, Waterford, and surrounding towns including Cork, Kinsale, Youghal, Blarney, Midleton, Cobh Island, Cork Harbour, and the Atlantic Ocean. Scale: 0–20 km / 0–12 miles.

COUNTY CORK

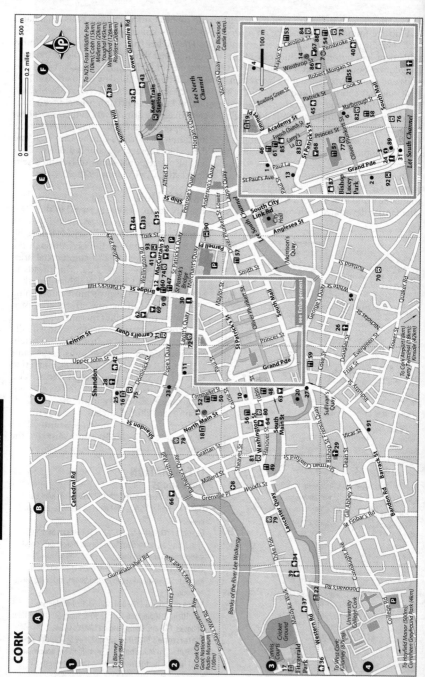

Emergency

Mercy University Hospital (☎ 021-427 1971; www
.muh.ie; Grenville Pl)

Internet Access

Netspresso (16 Bridge St; per hr €1; 🕑 10am-10pm)
Full service.

Webworkhouse.com (☎ 021-427 3090; www.web
workhouse.com; 8A Winthrop St; per hr €1.50-3; 🕑 24hr)
Also offers low-cost international phone calls.

Wired to the World (☎ 021-453 0383; www.wired
totheworld.ie; 28 North Main St; per hr €1; 🕑 9am-
midnight Mon-Sat, 10am-midnight Sun)

Left Luggage

There's no left-luggage facility at the train
station.

Cork Bus Station (☎ 021-450 8188; cnr Merchant's Quay &
Parnell Pl; per item for 24hr €3.50; 🕑 7.45am-7pm)

Libraries

Cork City Library (☎ 021-492 4900; www.corkcity
libraries.ie; 57-61 Grand Pde; 🕑 10am-5.30pm Mon-Sat)

Money

The banks on St Patrick's St have ATMs and
currency exchange. There are bureaux de
change in the tourist office and at the bus
station.

Post

Main post office (☎ 021-485 1042; Oliver Plunkett St;
🕑 9am-5.30pm Mon-Sat)

Tourist Information

Cork City Tourist Office (☎ 021-425 5100; www
.cometocork.com; Grand Pde; 🕑 9am-6pm Mon-Sat,
10am-5pm Sun Jul-Aug, 9.15am-5pm Mon-Fri & 9.30am-
4.30pm Sat Sep-Jun) Souvenir shop and information desk

COUNTY CORK

with plenty of brochures and books about the city and county, as well as Ordnance Survey maps. Stena Line ferries (see p717) has a desk here.

People's Republic of Cork (www.peoplesrepublicof cork.com) Picking up on the popular nickname for this liberal-leaning city, this indie website has excellent info.

DANGERS & ANNOYANCES

Cork cherishes its reputation as being a less hard-skinned place than Dublin, but watch out for drunken scenes around central pubs and clubs late at night.

SIGHTS

The best sight in Cork is the city itself as you wander its streets. Note that the once hugely popular former **Beamish & Crawford Brewery** was closed by owners Heineken in 2009. The fate of the beautiful half-timbered headhouse is uncertain.

Crawford Municipal Art Gallery

Cork's public **gallery** (☎ 021-490 7855; www.crawford artgallery.com; Emmet Pl; admission free; ۞ 10am-5pm Mon-Sat) houses a small but excellent permanent collection, featuring works by Irish artists, such as Jack Yeats and Seán Keating. Look out for Keating's *Men of the South* (1921), a fine piece of historical romanticism depicting members of the North Cork Battalion of the IRA.

The Sculpture Galleries contain snow-white plaster casts of Roman and Greek statues, given to King George IV by the pope in 1822. George didn't like the present and stuck the sculptures in the cellar until someone suggested that Cork might appreciate them.

The downstairs exhibition hall hosts superior temporary displays.

St Finbarre's Cathedral

Spiky spires, gurning gargoyles and rich sculpture make up the exterior of Cork's Protestant **cathedral** (☎ 021-496 3387; www.cathedral.cork.anglican .org; Bishop St; adult/child €3/1.50; ۞ 9.30am-5.30pm Mon-Sat & 12.30pm-5pm Sun Apr-Sep, 10am-12.45pm & 2-5pm Mon-Sat Oct-Mar), an attention-grabbing mixture of French Gothic and medieval whimsy. Local legend says that the golden angel on the eastern side will blow its horn when the Apocalypse is due to start… Yikes!

The grandeur continues inside, with marble floor mosaics, a colourful chancel ceiling and a huge pulpit and bishop's throne. Quirky items on display include a cannonball blasted into an earlier medieval spire during the Siege of Cork (1690).

Most of the ostentation is the result of a competition, held in 1863, to choose an architect for the building. William Burges was the hands-down winner, and once victory was assured he promptly redrew all his plans – with an extra choir bay and taller towers – and his £15,000 budget went out the window. Luckily, the bishop understood such perfectionism and spent the rest of his life fundraising for the project.

The cathedral sits at an aloof distance south of the centre, on the spot where Cork's patron saint, Finbarre, founded his monastery in the 7th century.

Lewis Glucksman Gallery

The **Glucksman** (☎ 021-490 2760; www.glucksman.org; University College Cork; admission free; ۞ 10am-5pm Tue, Wed, Fri & Sat, 10am-8pm Thu, noon-5pm Sun), a startling limestone, steel and timber construction, is a visible symbol of Corkonian optimism. Opened in 2004, the award-winning building has three huge display areas, which host ever-changing art exhibitions and installations. If you're in town, don't miss the free fortnightly curatorial tours; the website has details. The gallery's situation in the grounds of the UCC means it's always buzzing with people coming to attend lectures, view the artwork or procrastinate in the basement cafe (see p250).

Cork Public Museum

Located in a pleasant Georgian house in Fitzgerald Park, this **museum** (☎ 021-427 0679; www.corkcitycouncil.ie/amenities; Fitzgerald Park; admission free; ۞ 11am-1pm & 2.15-5pm Mon-Fri, 11am-1pm & 2.15-4pm Sat year-round, 3-5pm Sun Apr-Sep) recounts Cork's history from the Stone Age right up to local football legend Roy Keane with a diverse collection of local artefacts. There's a cafe next door.

Take bus 8 to the main gates of the UCC and follow the signs.

Cork City Gaol

Faint-hearted souls may find **Cork City Gaol** (☎ 021-430 5022; www.corkcitygaol.com; Convent Ave; adult/child €7/3.50; ۞ 9.30am-5pm Mar-Oct, 10am-4.30pm Nov-Feb, last admission 1hr before closing) a little grim, but it's certainly a highly unusual and worthwhile attraction. An audio tour guides you around the restored cells, which feature models of suffering prisoners and sadistic-looking guards.

COUNTY CORK

It's very moving, bringing home the harshness of the 19th-century penal system. The most common crime was that of poverty; many of the inmates were sentenced to hard labour for stealing loaves of bread.

The prison closed in 1923, reopening in 1927 as a radio station. The change of use is reflected in the upstairs **National Radio Museum** (adult/child €7/3.50; ☺ 9.30am-5pm Mar-Oct, 10am-4.30pm Nov-Feb, last admission 1hr before closing) where, alongside collections of beautiful old radios, you can hear the story of Guglielmo Marconi's conquest of the airwaves.

To get there, walk from the city centre, or take bus 8 from the bus station to the University College Cork (UCC); walk north across Fitzgerald Park, over Mardyke Bridge, along the Banks of the River Lee Walkway and follow the signs up the hill.

Cork Vision Centre

There's a model exhibition at the **Cork Vision Centre** (☎ 021-427 9925; www.corkvisioncentre.com; St Peter's Church, North Main St; admission free; ☺ 10am-5pm Tue-Sat) – literally. A huge and intriguing model of the city and its surrounds dominates the centre of this old church. Special exhibits include local art and engaging historical photographs.

Shandon

Galleries, antique shops and cafes along the old lanes and squares of **Shandon** make it a good stroll. Perched on a hillside overlooking the city centre, it's a great spot for the views alone. Those tiny old row houses, where generations of workers raised huge families in very basic conditions, are now sought-after urban pieds-à-terre.

Shandon is dominated by the 1722 **St Anne's Church** (☎ 021-450 5906; www.shandonbells .org; John Redmond St; ☺ 10am-5pm Mon-Sat), aka the 'Four-Faced Liar', so called as each of the tower's four clocks used to tell a different time. Wannabe campanologists can ring the **bells** (adult/child €6/5) on the 1st floor of the 1750 Italianate tower and continue the 132 steps up to the top for 360-degree views of the city.

Cork had the largest butter market in the world during the 1860s, exporting butter as far as India, South America and Australia. The Butter Exchange was in Shandon and you can still spot dairy motifs throughout the area: look out for the cow above the **old butter market** (O'Connell Sq), which was being used as a souvenir centre but is now closed. The **Cork Butter Museum** (☎ 021-430 0600; www.corkbutter .museum; O'Connell Sq; adult/child €4/3; ☺ 10am-5pm Mar-Jun & Sep-Oct, 10am-6pm Jul-Aug, by arrangement Nov-Feb) has interesting displays showing how the Irish butter industry took a commodity item (butter) and created a brand (Kerry Gold) that has allowed farmers to sell the spreadable stuff at a premium. The square in front of the museum – with its butter-coloured walls – is dominated by the striking **Firkin Crane**, a round building that was central to the old butter market and which now houses a dance centre (p252).

Other Sights

One of Cork's most famous figures was Father Theobald Mathew, the 'Apostle of Temperance', who went on a short-lived crusade against alcohol in the 1830s and 1840s – a quarter of a million people took the 'pledge', and whiskey production halved. The **Holy Trinity Church** (Fr Mathew Quay) was designed by the Pain brothers in 1834 in his honour, and the Father Mathew Bingo Hall around the corner also celebrates his memory. Mathew's **statue** stands on St Patrick's St.

Red Abbey Tower (Red Abbey St), the only medieval building left in Cork, is all that remains of a 14th-century Augustinian priory. Its location is fairly anonymous, but a bit of imagination will help create a stirring sense of antiquity.

On Grand Pde, near the tourist office, is the ornate **Nationalist Monument**, erected in memory of the Irish patriots who died during the 1798 and 1867 Risings. Just to the southeast, a mournful **war memorial** ably captures the loss of generations of Irish soldiers who died as conscripts fighting for the British. Nearby, memories of the bloody past continue at the **small stone bridge** at the bottom of South Main St. Heads of miscreants were displayed on the ends of pikes here in medieval times.

On the other side of the centre is a bridge that's much more salubrious. The pedestrian-only **Millennium Bridge** over the River Lee at the top of Cornmarket St is a modern gem. Its graceful arched design has won scores of awards; at night it is lit up like a jewellery store.

Bishop Lucey Park, off Grand Pde, is a popular and green place of urban respite.

Some 4km east along the Lee, **Blackrock Castle** (☎ 021-435 7917; Blackrock; adult/child €6/4; ☺ 10am-5pm Mon-Fri, 11am-5pm Sat & Sun) is a restored

COUNTY CORK

THE ENGLISH MARKET

It could just as easily be called the Victorian Market for its ornate vaulted ceilings and columns, but the **English Market** (⏱ 9am-5.30pm Mon-Sat) is a true gem, no matter what you name it. Scores of vendors sell some of the very best local produce, meats, cheeses and takeaway food to go in the region. On decent days, take your lunch to nearby Bishop Lucey Park, a popular alfresco eating spot. A few favourites:

Joup (☎ 021-422 6017) Has a range of soups and Med-flavoured salads, plus sandwiches on a variety of home-made breads.

On the Pig's Back (☎ 021-427 0232) Boasts house-made sausages and incredible cheeses, many ready to munch.

Sandwich Stall Has a drool-worthy display of remarkable and creative sandwiches.

On a mezzanine overlooking part of the market is one of Cork's best eateries. **our pick Farmgate Café** (☎ 021-427 8134; English Market; lunch €4-13, dinner €18-30; ⏱ 8.30am-10pm Mon-Sat) is an unmissable experience. Like its sister restaurant in Midleton (see p257), this cafe has mastered the magic art of producing delicious meals without fuss or faddism. The food, from rock oysters to the lamb for an Irish stew, is sourced from the market below. There are tables but the best seats are at the balcony counter, where you can ponder the passing parade of shoppers. We still have memories of the seafood chowder and the raspberry crumble.

16th-century castle that now, rather incongruously, hosts a science centre and observatory. But kids love it and the pastoral location is worth the jaunt. Take bus 2 to get there.

TOURS

Arrangements Unlimited (☎ 021-429 3873; www.arrangements.ie) Organises walking tours on request.

Bus Éireann (☎ 021-450 8188; www.buseireann.ie; adult/child €11/7.50; ⏱ departs 10.30am & 2.45pm Jun-Aug) Three-hour open-top bus tour of Cork and Blarney Castle from the bus station.

our pick Cork City Tour (☎ 021-430 9090; adult/child €14/5; ⏱ 10am-5.30pm Apr-Oct, last bus starts at 4pm) Hop-on-hop-off open-top bus linking the city's main areas of interest. The Outer Limits Tour takes you outside the centre.

Cork Historic Walking Tours (☎ 085 100 7300; www.walkcork.ie; adult/child €10/5; ⏱ 10am & 2pm Mon-Fri Apr-Sep) Runs 90-minute tours from the tourist office.

Cork Literary Tour A free audio walking tour of Cork; pick up a copy or download one onto your MP3 player at the Cork City Library (p245).

FESTIVALS & EVENTS

Book well in advance, particularly for the October jazz and film festivals.

Cork Film Festival (www.corkfilmfest.org) Eclectic week-long program of international films held in October/November.

Cork Pride (www.corkpride.com) Week-long gay-pride celebrations in May/June.

Cork World Book Fest A huge book festival with loads of authors in late April; sponsored by the Cork City Library (p245).

Guinness Jazz Festival (www.corkjazzfestival.com) All-star line-up in venues across town, held in October.

International Choral Festival (www.corkchoral.ie) A major event held from late April to early May in the City Hall and other venues.

SLEEPING
Budget

Brú Bar & Hostel (☎ 021-455 9667; www.bruhostel.com; 57 MacCurtain St; dm €12-24, r from €50; P 💻) This buzzing hostel has its own internet cafe, with free web access for guests, and a fantastic bar, popular with backpackers and locals alike. The dorms (each with a bathroom) have 4 to 6 beds and are both clean and stylish – ask for one on the upper floors to avoid bar noise. Breakfast is free.

Sheila's Hostel (☎ 021-450 5562; www.sheilashostel.ie; 4 Belgrave Pl, Wellington Rd; dm €13-18, d €44-52; P 💻 🛜) Sheila's heaves with young travellers, and it's no wonder given its excellent central location. Facilities include a sauna, free internet access, a pool table and barbecue. Staff can arrange bicycle and car hire. Breakfast is €3 extra.

Kinlay House (☎ 021-450 8966; www.kinlayhousecork.ie; Bob & Joan's Walk; dm €13-20, d €44-54; 💻) This labyrinthine hostel is in a bucolic spot near St Anne's Church in Shandon. It has a fun, laid-back atmosphere; services include bureau de change, laundry and luggage storage. Guests can use the next-door gym at a discount.

Cork International Hostel (☎ 021-454 3289; www.anoige.ie; 1 & 2 Redclyffe, Western Rd; dm €13-20, d €54-58; **P** 🖳) Housed in a stolid and attractive red-brick building near the university, this 98-bed An Óige hostel has bright dorms and cheerful staff, who do a great job coping with the constant stream of guests. The drawback is the 2km walk (or bus 8 ride) to the centre along a busy road.

Near the train station the roads are busy and the area is filled with workmen. There's a handful of basic but clean B&Bs, including the following:

Aaran House Tourist Hostel (☎ 021-455 1566; 4 Woburn, Lower Glanmire Rd; dm €15-17, d €44; **P**) Reilly the dog greets all guests.

Oakland B&B (☎ 021-450 0578; 52 Lower Glanmire Rd; s/d from €45/70) In an 18th-century row house.

Midrange

Western Rd has the biggest choice of B&Bs; walk to the city on less busy Dyke Parade.

Auburn House (☎ 021-450 8555; www.auburnguesthouse.com; 3 Garfield Tce, Wellington Rd; s €38-58, d €64-80; **P**) There's a warm family welcome at this neat B&B, which has smallish but well-kept rooms brightened by window boxes. Try to bag one of the back rooms, which have sweeping views over the city. Breakfast has meat-free choices; the location near the fun of MacCurtain St is a plus.

Emerson House (☎ 021-450 3647; www.emersonhousecork.com; 2 Clarence Tce, North Summer Hill; s/d from €60/80; **P** 🛜) Near the top of busy Summer Hill is this gay and lesbian B&B tucked away on a quiet terrace. The accommodation, in a Georgian house retaining many original features, is comfortably elegant, and host Cyril is a mine of information on the area.

Victoria Hotel (☎ 021-427 8788; www.thevictoriahotel.com; Patrick St; r €60-180; 🛜) You can't get better value for such a central location than this 1810 hotel; it's popular with large groups. Staff proudly tell you that Charles Stewart Parnell gave speeches from the upper balcony; another resident was Stephen Dedalus in James Joyce's *Portrait of the Artist as a Young Man* (his dad had drisheen for breakfast). The 29 rooms are smartly decorated; some have broadband internet.

Blarney Stone Guesthouse (☎ 021-427 0083; www.blarneystoneguesthouse.ie; Western Rd; r €60-150; **P** 🖳) A standout from this close-knit row of B&Bs –

if for no other reason than its brilliant white paint scheme out front – the Blarney Stone will make you want to kiss something after you settle into one of its eight rooms. Decor is lavish in a way that harks back to the time when vinyl roofs were popular on cars; there's lots of frill and curlicues.

Isaac's Hotel (☎ 021-450 0011; www.isaacs.ie; 48 MacCurtain St; r €60-160; 💱 🖳 🛜) Location is the real selling point at this grand old hotel housed in what once was a Victorian furniture warehouse. The 47 rooms are decorated in a faded salmon-rust scheme and service can be a bit spotty. Also, be sure to get a room away from the busy street. Non-fan rooms can get steamy on sunny days, no matter what you get up to…

our pick **Garnish House** (☎ 021-427 5111; www.garnish.ie; Western Rd; r €60-200; **P** 🛜) Every attention is lavished upon guests at this award-winning B&B. The legendary breakfast menu (30 choices!) includes fresh fish, French toast, omelettes and a whole lot more. Typical of the touches here is the freshly cooked porridge, which comes with creamed honey and your choice of whiskey or Baileys. Enjoy it out on the garden terrace. The 14 rooms are very comfortable; reception is open 24 hours.

Crawford House (☎ 021-427 9000; www.crawfordguesthouse.com; Western Rd; r €80-120; **P** 💱 🖳) You'll have no problem getting wet at Crawford House, a luxurious B&B: power showers and large spa baths feature in the 12 rooms, which include king-size beds and gracious yet restrained wooden furnishings. The standard is that of a contemporary hotel (24-hour reception); the atmosphere, that of a family home.

Top End

Imperial Hotel (☎ 021-427 4040; www.flynnhotels.com; South Mall; r €90-220; **P** 🖳) Fast approaching her bicentenary, the Imperial knows how to age gracefully. Public spaces resonate with opulent period detail such as marble floors, elaborate floral bouquets and more. The 130

COUNTY CORK

CORK FOR ADULTS…

Looking for a night out away from your little travelling companions? The **Sitters Bureau** (☎ 021-427 5369; www.sittersbureau.ie) in Cork has child-minders who will watch over them in your hotel room.

rooms are of four-star hotel standards: writing desk, restrained decor and modern touches, like a digital music library. A posh Aveda spa is a recent addition – something unheard of when Charles Dickens stayed here.

Hayfield Manor (☎ 021-484 9500; www.hayfieldmanor .ie; Perrott Ave, College Rd; r €200-400; **P** ⛽ 💻 🛜) Roll out the red carpet and pour yourself a sherry for *you have arrived*. A mile from the city centre but with all the ambience of a country house, Hayfield combines the luxury and facilities of a big hotel with the informality and welcome of a small one. The 88 beautiful bedrooms (choose from traditional or contemporary styling) enjoy 24-hour room service, although you may want to idle the hours away in the library.

EATING

Cork's food scene is reason enough to visit. The English Market (see p248) is a local – no, make that national – treasure.

Restaurants
BUDGET

Cafe Antigua (☎ 021-427 4644; www.triskelart.com; Tobin St; lunch €5-9; ⏱ 8.30am-5pm Mon-Sat, 3-7pm Sun, 8pm-late Fri & Sat) Attached to the Triskel Arts Centre, this cool cafe has creative takes on standards, such as full Irish breakfasts, sandwiches and salads. There's a range of fresh burritos and specials of the day, including soup. Tapas are served at nights when it's open for salsa and swing music.

Idaho Café (☎ 021-427 6376; 19 Caroline St; dishes €7-12; ⏱ 8.30am-5pm) It looks like a trad old caff from the outside, but take a gander at the menu and you'll find all sorts of creative takes on Irish standards. The tea selection includes scads of herbal numbers and there's a good per-glass wine menu. Tight seating means nothing is private. Idaho Café makes a good place to regroup while touring or shopping.

Café Glucksman (☎ 021-490 1848; www.glucksman .org; Lewis Glucksman Gallery, University College Cork; dishes €7-12; ⏱ 10am-4pm Mon-Sat & noon-4pm Sun) The cafe at the Lewis Glucksman Gallery has sweeping views of the university grounds; there's a Miesian simplicity to the clean lines of the interior. The food is modern European; expect creative pastas, salads and the frequent appearance of Irish smoked salmon.

Quay Co-op (☎ 021-431 7026; www.quaycoop.com; 24 Sullivan's Quay; mains €8-12; ⏱ 9am-9pm Mon-Sat) A gathering spot for the People's Republic of Cork

---

EATING IN THE HUGUENOT QUARTER

The narrow, nearly lightless pedestrianised streets north of St Patrick's St throng with cafes and restaurants, and the place hops day and night. A plethora of options await – all have outside tables and many serve till late, so the best advice is go for a wander and find somewhere that suits your mood and budget. Among the best picks:

Amicus Café & Restaurant (☎ 021-427 6455; 23 Paul St Plaza) Bistro fare overlooking a small and vibrant square, where Cork's fresh-faced goths gather on Saturdays.

Strasbourg Goose (☎ 021-427 9534; 17-18 French Church St) Excellent food, although the French accent is illusory: le bacon cheeseburger?

---

proletariat, this nonflash cafe offers a range of self-service veggie options (all organic), including big breakfasts, hearty soups and casseroles. There's daily specials; dishes cater for gluten-, dairy- and wheat-free needs. The bulletin board has news for and of the masses.

MIDRANGE

Boqueria (☎ 021-455 9049; www.boqueria.ie; 6 Bridge St; breakfast €4-8, tapas €4-15; ⏱ breakfast 8.30am-noon daily, tapas noon-late Mon-Sat & 5pm-late Sun) The flavours of Spain shine (even if the sun doesn't) at this ever-popular tapas bar. In addition to the usual onion-garlic-tomato combinations, the chefs use local creations, such as sourdough, Gubbeen cheese and salmon, to create tasty Irishified tapas. It's a dusky, intimate spot, favoured by couples in the evenings, and at lunch by friends seeking a civilised glass of wine.

ourpick Nash 19 (☎ 021-427 0880; www.nash19 .com; Princes St; mains €8-20; ⏱ 7.30am-5.30pm Mon-Fri) A sensational bistro with a small market; local foods are honoured from breakfast to lunch and on to tea. Fresh scones draw in the crowds early; daily fresh specials (soups, salads, desserts, etc) and an incredible burger keep them coming throughout the rest of the day.

Café de la Paix (☎ 021-427 9556; 16 Washington St; www.cafedelapaixcork.com; mains €8-15; ⏱ 8am-10pm) An unassuming red exterior hides this chilled-out wine bar backing on to the River Lee. Picture windows make the most of the view and there's a fabulous riverside deck. Global favourites grace the menu, from Thai curries to daily pasta specials.

Liberty Grill (☎ 021-427 1049; www.libertygrill cork.com; 32 Washington St; mains €7-20; ☻ 8am-10pm) A gleaming white outpost on an otherwise faded street of brick facades, the Liberty Grill is popular for its locally sourced menu of crowd-pleasers, like trad breakfasts, burgers, sand-wiches, salads and slightly more ambitious dinner fare. Think of it as a diner for foodies.

Star Anise (☎ 021-455 1635; 4 Bridge St; mains €10-20; ☻ noon-2pm, 6-10pm Mon-Sat) Fresh and creative cooking is the hallmark at this narrow lit-tle shopfront bistro. There are steaks for the masses but also treats like tiger prawns on chickpea salad and a killer vegetarian lasagne. The wine list is both superb and affordable. Three-course specials are a fine deal at €28.

our pick Market Lane (☎ 021-427 4710; www.market lane.ie; 5 Oliver Plunkett St; mains €10-26; ☻ noon-late Mon-Sat, 1-9pm Sun) It's always hopping at this bright corner bistro with an open kitchen. Service is quick and attentive, but you may want to pause at the long wooden bar anyway. The menu is broad, and changes often to reflect what's fresh. Smoked haddock perched on creamy potatoes is better here than it ever was back in the day. Steaks come with awesome aioli. At lunch, however, you might just get enraptured by the bacon sandwich. Lots of wines by the glass.

Cornstore (☎ 021-427 4777; www.cornstorecork.com; 40A Cornmarket St; mains €10-28; ☻ noon-11pm) Bustling and buzzy day and night, this modern res-taurant has a swish bar, where you can enjoy creative cocktails while waiting for a table. Some tables are minute but, if you're having the amazing house special of lobster, hold out for a large one so your elbows and shells can fly. There's also excellent fresh fish, steaks and pasta.

TOP END

Jacques Restaurant (☎ 021-427 7387; http://jacques restaurant.ie; 9 Phoenix St; mains €22-27; ☻ 6-10pm Mon-Sat) With almost three decades in the business, Jacqueline and Eithne Barry have built up a terrific network of local suppliers to help them realise their culinary ambitions – the freshest Cork food cooked simply. The menu, served in an elegant dining room, changes daily: we loved the fennel risotto with beef short ribs. Clattering dishes in the upstairs kitchen echo down this spot's tiny lane.

Les Gourmandises (☎ 021-425 1959; www.les gourmandises.ie; 17 Cook St; mains €20-30; ☻ 6-9.30pm Tue-Sat) Remember those beautiful fresh fish you saw in the English Market (p248)? Many of them end up at this cute little restaurant that reminds you of that perfect place you stumbled upon in Paris once… The talented kitchen turns out an array of local fish, and meats also get their due: the rack of lamb is a perennial fave. Service is gracious and calm.

Self-Catering

In addition to the English Market (see the boxed text, p248), the **Quay Co-op Organic & Wholefood Shop** (Sullivan's Quay; ☻ 9am-6.15pm Mon-Sat) is an excellent place to find interesting and fresh picnic fare. The **farmers market** takes over much of Cornmarket St on Saturdays.

DRINKING

In Cork pubs, drink Guinness at your own peril, even though Heineken now owns both of the local stout legends, Murphy's and Beamish (and closed down the latter's brew-ery). Cork's microbrewery, the Franciscan Well Brewery, makes quality beers, including Friar Weisse, popular in summer.

An Spailpín Fánac (☎ 021-427 7949; South Main St) 'The Wandering Labourer' really hangs on to its character, with exposed brickwork, stone-flagged floors, snug corners and open fires. There are good trad sessions most nights.

Sin É (☎ 021-450 2266; Coburg St) You could eas-ily while away an entire day at this great old place, which is everything a craic-filled pub should be. There are no frills or fuss here – just a comfy, sociable pub, long on atmosphere and short on pretension. There's music most nights, much of it traditional, but with the odd surprise.

Dan Lowry's (☎ 021-450 5071; 13 MacCurtain St) Genial is the word as you first enter this time-less family pub and are greeted by the genera-tions of regulars. It's cosy in more ways than one; you can often get a seat on a Saturday night and enjoy an intimate chat.

Mutton Lane Inn (☎ 021-427 3471; Mutton Lane) Tucked down the tiniest of laneways off St Patrick's St, this inviting pub, lit by candles and fairy lights, is one of Cork's most intimate drink-ing holes. It's minuscule and much admired, so try to get in early to bag the snug, or join the smokers perched on beer kegs outside.

Long Valley (☎ 021-427 2144; Winthrop St) A Cork institution that dates from the mid-19th cen-tury and is still going strong. Some of the furnishings hail from White Star Line ocean liners that used to call at Cobh.

COUNTY CORK

GONE TO THE DOGS

If you tire of the pubs, the live music and the theatre, there's always the dogs. Greyhound racing is big news in Ireland, particularly with families, and **Curraheen Greyhound Park** (☎ 021-454 3095; www.igb.ie/cork; Curraheen Park; adult/child €10/5; ☼ from 6.45pm, days vary) is one of the country's poshest stadiums. There are 10 races a night, plus a restaurant, bar and live music to keep you entertained in between. Curraheen is 5.5km from the centre; to get there, take bus 8. A free bus drops you back between 10.30pm and 12.30am.

Franciscan Well Brewery (☎ 021-421 0130; www.franciscanwellbrewery.com; 14 North Mall) The copper vats gleaming behind the bar give the game away: the Franciscan Well brews its own beer. The best place to enjoy it is in the enormous beer garden at the back. The pub holds regular beer festivals with other small (and often underappreciated) Irish breweries – check the website for details.

Abbot's Ale House (☎ 021-450 7116; Devonshire St) A low-key 1st-floor pub, whose small size contrasts with a huge beer list. There are always several on tap and another 300 in bottles. Good for preclubbing.

Pubs are Cork's best asset but, if you hanker after a cocktail, there's a booming bar scene, too:

Chambers (☎ 021-422 2860; Washington St; ☼ late Thu-Sun) A haberdasher swallowed a copy of *Wallpaper*, and Chambers was born.

Cornstore (p251) The buzzy bistro's bar is a swishy place for a cocktail.

Crane Lane Theatre (right) Their courtyard beer garden is a central Cork oasis.

ENTERTAINMENT

For listings of Cork's vibrant scene, pick up a copy of the free *WhazOn?* (www.whazon.com).

Theatre

Cork's cultural life is as fine as any in Ireland and attracts numerous internationally renowned performers.

Cork Arts Theatre (☎ 021-450 5624; www.corkartstheatre.com; Camden Court, Carroll's Quay) An excellent theatre putting on thought-provoking drama and new works.

Cork Opera House (☎ 021-427 0022; www.corkoperahouse.ie; Emmet Pl; ☼ box office 9am-8.30pm, to 5.30pm nonperformance nights) This leading venue has been entertaining the city for more than 150 years with everything from opera and ballet to stand-up and puppet shows. Performances are as varied as *Carmen*, Brian Kennedy and the drama *Jane Eyre*.

Everyman Palace Theatre (☎ 021-450 1673; www.everymanpalace.com; 15 MacCurtain St; ☼ box office 10am-7.30pm Mon-Sat, to 6pm nonperformance nights) Acclaimed musical and dramatic productions are the main bill of fare here, but there's also the occasional band, comedy act, etc.

Firkin Crane (☎ 021-450 7487; www.firkincrane.ie; Shandon) One of Ireland's premier centres for modern dance. Located in part of the old butter market (p247).

Granary (☎ 021-490 4275; www.granary.ie; Dyke Pde) Contemporary and experimental works are staged at the Granary by the University College Cork drama group and visiting companies.

Half Moon Theatre (☎ 021-427 0022; www.halfmoontheatre.ie; Emmet Place) One of Cork's best venues for live theatre, comedy and music. It's at the back of the Cork Opera House.

Triskel Arts Centre (☎ 021-472 2022; www.triskelart.com; Tobin St; tickets around €15) Expect a varied program of live music, installation art, photography and theatre at this intimate venue. There's also a great cafe (Cafe Antigua; p250).

Cinemas

Gate Multiplex (☎ 021-427 9595; North Main St) Multiscreen cinema showing mainstream films.

Kino Cinema (☎ 021-427 1571; www.kinocinema.net; Washington St) Shows art-house flicks.

Live Music

Cork overflows with tunes. As well as the pubs with music mentioned earlier (p251), the following places are either dedicated music venues or bars known particularly for their live events. For full listings, refer to *WhazOn?*, Plugd Records (opposite) and www.corkgigs.com. Buy tickets at the venues themselves or from Plugd.

An Cruiscín Lán (☎ 021-484 0941; www.cruiscin.com; Douglas St) Trad bands and world, blues and pop musicians all play at this acclaimed bar south of the river.

Crane Lane Theatre (☎ 021-427 8487; www.cranelanetheatre.com; Phoenix St) An excellent venue for live music, Crane Lane also has a great beer garden during the day. Acts include pianist/vocalist Max Greenwood, Jeffrey Lewis and the Junkyard and numerous top Cork bands.

Fred Zeppelins (☎ 021-427 3500; www.fredzeps.com; 8 Parliament St) There's a hard edge to this dark den of a bar, popular with goths, rockers and anyone who feels uncomfortable leaving the house without a packet of Rizlas.

Liquid Lounge (Clancy's; ☎ 021-427 6097; www.liquidlounge.ie; 29 Marlborough St; ☣ Wed-Sat) Dialled down several notches from the megaclubs, regular gigs here feature bands signed to Irish labels, and DJ sets covering music from Celtic rock to everything current. Mondays see folk dancing, including free lessons. There's a rooftop terrace and a popular restaurant to boot.

Pavilion (☎ 021-427 6230; www.pavilioncork.com; 13 Carey's Lane; ☣ noon-late) This modern-day coffee house has java by day, which you can enjoy at long tables; by night, it has one of Cork's best mixes of bands, musicians and vocalists. Jazz, blues, rock, alternative and more are on the line-up.

Nightclubs

Cork's club life really does rival Dublin's, in quantity if not in quality. Most clubs go all guns blazing for pissed students and 20-somethings on the pull. If this is your scene, several clubs of the moment (they change constantly) will keep you happy; try **G2** (74 Oliver Plunkett St).

Entry ranges from free to €15 and most of these places are open until 2am on Friday and Saturday.

Scotts (☎ 021-422 2779; www.scotts.ie; Caroline St; ☣ Fri & Sat) This scenester venue, all dark wood and moody lighting, has a fine restaurant downstairs and an upstairs club featuring mainstream floor fillers for well-groomed over-20s.

Havana Browns (☎ 021-427 1969; www.havana-browns.com; Hanover St; ☣ nightly) Long-running

Havana Browns has three bars, a VIP room, an outdoor terrace and a fine line in neon and amber backlighting. The music doesn't stray far from MTV's current playlist.

SHOPPING

St Patrick's St is the retail heart of Cork, housing all the major department stores and malls. But pedestrianised Oliver Plunkett St is the retail spine; it and nearby narrow lanes are lined with interesting small shops.

O'Connaill (☎ 021-437 3407; 16B French Church St) Don't leave Cork without sampling the Chocolatier's Hot Chocolate (€4) at O'Connaill confectioners' tiny counter. The foolhardy can stagger away with 2.5kg slabs of chocolate, but there are subtler concoctions on offer.

P Cashell (☎ 021-427 5824; 13 Winthrop St) A timeless and jammed antique and curio shop that seems entirely out of place amid the glitz of central Cork. It's like a treasure hunt.

Plugd Records (☎ 021-427 6300; 4 Washington St) A terrific music shop that stocks everything from techno to nu-jazz beats. You can buy tickets for gigs and pick up the very latest info on the club scene.

Pro Musica (☎ 021-427 1659; Oliver Plunkett St) The heart of Cork's world for musicians: sheet music, instruments and a notice board with ads by and for musicians.

GETTING THERE & AWAY
Air

Cork Airport (ORT; ☎ 021-431 3131; www.cork-airport.com) is 8km south of the city on the N27. Facilities include ATMs and car-hire desks (p254). Airlines servicing the airport include Aer Lingus, BMI, Ryanair and Wizz. There are flights to Dublin, London Heathrow and a few cities in Europe.

See p254 for information on getting into town.

COUNTY CORK

Boat
Brittany Ferries (☎ 021-427 7801; www.brittanyferries
.ie; 42 Grand Pde) sails to Roscoff (France) weekly
from the end of March to October. The crossing takes 15 hours and fares are widely variable. The ferry terminal is at Ringaskiddy.

See below for information on getting into
town.

Bus
Bus Éireann (☎ 021-450 8188; www.buseireann.ie) operates from the bus station on the corner of
Merchant's Quay and Parnell Pl. You can get
to most places in Ireland from Cork, including
Dublin (€12, 4¼ hours, six daily), Killarney
(€16, 1¾ hours, 14 daily), Kilkenny (€17, three
hours, three daily) and Waterford (€18, 2¾
hours, 14 daily).

Citylink (☎ 1890 280 808; www.citylink.ie) operates
services to Galway (3¼ hours) and Limerick.
Buses are frequent and fares are as low as €10.

Train
Kent Train Station (☎ 021-450 4777) is north of
the River Lee on Lower Glanmire Rd. Bus 5
runs into the centre (€1.60) and a taxi costs
from €9 to €10.

The train line goes through Mallow, where
you can change for the line to Tralee, and
Limerick Junction, for the line to Ennis (and
the new extension to Galway), then on to
Dublin (€36, three hours, 16 daily).

GETTING AROUND
To/From the Airport
SkyLink (☎ 021-432 1020; www.skylinkcork.com; adult/
child €5/2.50; ☽ hourly) buses pick around central
Cork and take up to 30 minutes.

A taxi into town costs €15 to €20.

To/From the Ferry Terminal
The ferry terminal is at Ringaskiddy, 15 minutes by car southeast of the city centre along
the N28. Taxis cost €28 to €35. Bus Éireann
runs a service from the bus station to link up
with sailings (bus 223; adult/child €5.50/3.50,
50 minutes). Confirm times. There's also a
service to Rosslare Harbour (bus 40; adult/
child €23.50/16; four to five hours).

Bicycle
You can rent bikes and glean cycling tips from
Rothar Cycles (☎ 021-431 3133; www.rotharcycletours
.com; 55 Barrack St; per day/week €25/80). It offers a one-
way pick-up service from other towns for €30

(with a €100 refundable deposit) and runs
frequent summer cycling tours.

Bus
Most places are within easy walking distance
of the centre. A single bus ticket costs €1.60.
A day pass is €4.40.

Car
PARKING
Streetside parking requires scratch-card
parking discs (€2 per hour), obtained from
the tourist office and some newsagencies. Be
warned – the traffic wardens are ferociously
efficient and the cost of retrieving your vehicle
is hefty. There are several signposted car parks
around the central area, with charges of €2 per
hour and €12 overnight.

RENTAL
The following companies have desks at the
airport.
Alamo/National (☎ 021-431 8623; www.carhire.ie)
Avis (☎ 021-432 7460; www.avis.ie)
Budget (☎ 021-431 4000; www.budget.ie)
Hertz (☎ 021-496 5849; www.hertz.ie)
Sixt (☎ 021-431 8644; www.e-sixt.ie)
Thrifty (☎ 021-434 8488; www.thrifty.ie)

Taxi
For taxi hire, try **Cork Taxi Co-op** (☎ 021-427 2222)
or **Shandon Cabs** (☎ 021-450 2255).

AROUND CORK CITY

BLARNEY CASTLE
One of the most inexplicably popular tourist
stops in Ireland is **Blarney Castle** (☎ 021-438 5252;
www.blarneycastle.ie; Blarney; adult/child €10/3.50; ☽ 9am-
7pm Mon-Sat & 9am-5.30pm Sun Jun-Aug, 9am-6.30pm
Mon-Sat & 9.30am-5.30pm Sun May & Sep, 9am-sundown
Sun Oct-Apr, last admission 30min before closing). Crowds
flock here to kiss the **Blarney Stone**, a cliché that
has entered every lexicon and tour route.

The stone is perched at the top of the 15th-
century castle, reached by a steep climb up
slippery spiral staircases. On the battlements,
you bend backwards over a long, long drop
(with safety grill and attendant to prevent
tragedy) to kiss the stone; as your shirt rides
up, coach loads of onlookers stare up your
nose. Once you're upright, don't forget to
admire the stunning views before descending.
Try not to think of the local lore about all the

fluids that drench the stone *other* than saliva. Better yet, just don't do it.

The custom of kissing the stone (which supposedly gives one the gift of gab – if not other things) is a relatively modern one, but Blarney's association with smooth talking goes back a long time. Queen Elizabeth I is said to have invented the term 'to talk blarney' out of exasperation with Lord Blarney's ability to talk endlessly without ever actually agreeing to her demands.

Be warned: this place gets mobbed. If it all gets too much, vanish into the **Rock Close**, part of the beautiful and often ignored gardens. And a hint: Barryscourt Castle (p257), east of Cork, is more impressive and much less crowded.

Blarney is 8km northwest of Cork and buses run frequently from Cork bus station (adult/child €3.10/1.80, 30 minutes).

FOTA

Fota Wildlife Park (☎ 021-481 2678; www.fotawildlife .ie; Carrigtwohill; adult/child €13.50/9; 10am-6pm Mon-Sat & 10am-6pm Sun mid-Mar–Oct, 10am-3pm Mon-Sat & 11am-3pm Sun Nov–mid-Mar, last admission 1hr before closing) is a huge outdoor zoo, where animals roam without a cage or fence in sight. Here you can see kangaroos bound past; monkeys and gibbons leap and scream on wooded islands; and cheetahs run.

A tour train runs a circuit round the park every 15 minutes in high season (one way/return €1/2), but the 2km circular walk offers a more close-up experience.

From the wildlife park, you can take a stroll down to the Regency-style **Fota House** (☎ 021-481 5543; www.fotahouse.com; Carrigtwohill; adult/child €6/3; 10am-5pm Apr-Oct, last admission 1hr before closing). The mostly barren interior contains a fine kitchen and ornate plasterwork ceilings; interactive displays bring the rooms to life.

Attached to the house is the 150-year-old **arboretum**, which has a Victorian fernery, a magnolia walk and some beautiful trees, including giant redwoods and a Chinese ghost tree.

Fota is 10km east of Cork. The hourly Cork–Fota train (€3, 13 minutes) goes on to Cobh. A car park (€3) is shared by the park and the house.

COBH

pop 6800

In the wake of the Famine, 2.5 million people emigrated from the port of Cobh (pronounced cove) – go on a grey day, and the sense of loss is still almost palpable. When the sun shines and the crowds flock in, though, you'll see another side to this hilly little town. The spectacular cathedral looks down over brightly coloured houses, the wide seaside promenade and the glittering estuary, and Cobh seems to shake off its sad past.

History

For many years Cobh was the port of Cork, and it has always had a strong connection with Atlantic crossings, including many fateful ones. In 1838 the *Sirius*, the first steamship to cross the Atlantic, sailed from Cobh. The *Titanic* made its last stop here before its fateful journey in 1912, and, when the *Lusitania* was torpedoed off the coast of Kinsale in 1915, it was here that many of the survivors were brought and the dead buried. Cobh was also the last glimpse of Ireland for the people who emigrated during the Famine.

In 1849 Cobh was renamed Queenstown after Queen Victoria paid a visit. The name lasted until Irish independence in 1921 when, unsurprisingly, the local council reverted to the Irish original.

The world's first yacht club, the Royal Cork Yacht Club, was founded here in 1720, but now operates from Crosshaven on the other side of Cork Harbour.

Orientation

Cobh is on Great Island, which fills much of Cork Harbour, and is joined to the mainland by a causeway. It faces Haulbowline Island (once the base of the Irish Naval Service) and the greener Spike Island (which houses a prison). The waterfront comprises the broad Westbourne Pl and West Beach, from where steep streets climb inland. A delightful waterside park with a bandstand and playground lie next to the tourist office.

Information

The Old Yacht Club contains a **tourist office** (☎ 021-481 3301; www.cobhharbourchamber.ie; 9.30am-5.30pm Mon-Fri, 1-5pm Sat & Sun) and arts centre.

Sights

COBH, THE QUEENSTOWN STORY

The howl of storms almost blows your hair, there's a bit of fake vomit and the people in the pictures all look pretty miserable. That's just one room at **ourpick Cobh Heritage Centre**

(☎ 021-481 3591; www.cobhheritage.com; adult/child €8/4; ☺ 10am-6pm May-Oct, 10am-5pm Nov-Apr, last admission 1hr before closing). Housed in the old train station, this interactive museum is far above average. The room described above deals with the mass Famine emigrations across the Atlantic: trips where the people were green – and not with envy. Displays show how conditions improved – except for the *Titanic* or *Lusitania*, which have fateful links to Cobh.

There's also some shocking stuff on the fate of convicts, shipped to Australia in transport 'so airless that candles could not burn'. Scenes of sea travel in the 1950s, however, might actually make you wistful for a more gracious way of transiting the world. There's a genealogy centre attached and an adjoining cafe (see right).

ST COLMAN'S CATHEDRAL

Standing dramatically above Cobh on a hillside terrace, the massive French Gothic **St Colman's Cathedral** (☎ 021-481 3222; Cathedral Pl; admission by donation) is out of all proportion to the unassuming town. Its most exceptional feature is the 47-bell carillon, the largest in Ireland, with a range of four octaves. The biggest bell weighs a stonking 3440kg – about as much as a full-grown elephant! You can hear carillon recitals at 4.30pm on Sundays between May and September.

The cathedral, designed by EW Pugin, was begun in 1868 but not completed until 1915. Much of the funding was raised by nostalgic Irish communities in Australia and the USA.

COBH MUSEUM

A small but lively **museum** (☎ 021-481 4240; www.cobhmuseum.com; High Rd; adult/child €4/2; ☺ 11am-1pm Mon-Sat & 2-5.30pm daily Apr-Oct) is housed in the 19th-century Scottish Presbyterian church overlooking the train station. It holds model ships, paintings, photographs and curious artefacts tracing Cobh's history.

Tours

Marine Transport Services (☎ 021-481 1485; www.scottcobh.ie) One-hour boat tours (€8/4 per adult/child) daily June to September.

Titanic Trail (☎ 021-481 5211; www.titanic-trail.com; adult/child €9.50/4.75; ☺ 11am year-round, 2pm Jun-Aug) Michael Martin's 1¼-hour guided walk leaves from the Commodore Hotel on Westbourne Pl, with a free sampling of stout at the end. Martin also runs a ghoulish Ghost Walk (€17.50).

Sleeping

Westbourne House (☎ 021-481 1391; 12 Westbourne Pl; s/d €30/60) The friendly owner of this historical house (an old shipping agent's) provides good value beyond the reasonable price. Lavish it ain't, but the rooms are big and sunny and the many yachting pictures go with those harbour views.

Commodore Hotel (☎ 021-481 1277; www.commodorehotel.ie; Westbourne Pl; s/d €57/96; 🖳 🛜 🖳) A classic seaside hotel with soaring chandeliered hallways and 42 modern and attractive rooms (it's worth paying extra for one with a sea view). The pool is indoors and a roof garden offers yet more views.

Amberleigh (☎ 021-481 4069; www.amberleigh.ie; West End Terrace; s/d €60/90) You'll receive a warm welcome at this beautiful Victorian house perched on a hill overlooking the harbour. It has just four guest rooms, all of them enormous with high ceilings and a refreshingly white decor. There's also a guest lounge, with a coal fire on chilly evenings.

Knockeven House (☎ 021-481 1778; www.knockevenhouse.com; Rushbrooke; s/d €75/120) Knockeven is a splendid, relaxed Victorian house, 1.5km north of Cobh. Huge bedrooms are done out with period furniture and overlook a magnificent garden full of magnolias and camellias. Breakfasts are great too – homemade breads and fresh fruit – and are served in the sumptuous dining room. The decor takes you back to 1st-class passage on a vintage liner.

Eating & Drinking

A **farmers market** is held on the seafront every Friday from 10am to 1pm.

Queenstown Restaurant (☎ 021-481 3591; lunch €4-7; ☺ 10am-5pm) Inside the old train station with the heritage centre, this simple cafe is best right when the doors open and the scones are emerging from the oven, warm and fragrant. Other times the food is fine but akin to what you might have had shipboard in 2nd class.

Kelly's (☎ 021-481 1994; Westbourne Pl; meals €7-12) Sunny Kelly's is filled with sociable punters day and night. The pub's two rooms are decked out with pew-style seating, chunky wooden furniture, a wood-burning stove and, curiously, a stag's head. Seating outside is good for a pint and a sandwich.

Jack Doyles (☎ 021-420 1932; Midleton St) Named for a famous local boxer *and* tenor, this sportsmad pub, a short walk uphill from the cathedral, is a fine place to meet residents of Cobh.

SMOKIN'

Two kilometres out of Midleton on the N25 towards Fota, the effervescent Frank Hederman runs **Belvelly** (☎ 021-481 1089; www.frankhederman.com), the oldest natural smoke house in Ireland – and indeed the only one. Seafood and cheese are smoked here, but the speciality is fish – in particular, salmon. In a traditional process that takes 24 hours from start to finish, the fish is filleted and cured before being hung in the tiny smoke house to smoke over beech woodchips. No trip to Cork is complete without a visit to an artisan food producer, and Frank is more than happy to show you around; phone or email to arrange. Or stop by his booth at the Midleton farmers market.

Getting There & Away

Cobh is 15km southeast of Cork, off the main N25 Cork–Rosslare road. Hourly trains connect it with Cork (€3.50, 24 minutes).

Getting Around

All of Cobh's sites are within walking distance of the town centre.

BARRYSCOURT CASTLE

Immigrants from Wales in the 12th century, the Barry family quickly began intermarrying with important Irish families of the time. Soon they had huge tracts of land and real wealth. In order to protect their fortune, the clan began building a vast fortification in the 15th century. Today much of the **castle** (☎ 021-488 3864; www.heritageireland.ie; admission free; ⊙ 10am-6pm Jun-Sep) survives in remarkably good condition (albeit with a lot of restoration). An authentic 16th-century kitchen and decorative gardens have been re-created.

The castle is just off the N25, 2km east of the road to Cobh and near Carrigtwohill.

MIDLETON & AROUND
pop 3900

Most visitors sweep through the Midleton area on their way east or west on the N25, but it's worth a bit more of your time. Rather ambitiously named the 'Irish Riviera' by the tourist board, the region is nonetheless full of pretty villages, craggy coastline and some heavenly rural hotels. Midleton itself is a pleasant and bustling market town, though, with plenty of accommodation in the surrounding area, there's no real reason to stay here.

The **tourist office** (☎ 021-461 3702; www.eastcorktourism.com; ⊙ 9.30am-1pm & 2-5.15pm Mon-Sat May-Sep) is by the entrance gate to the distillery.

Sights

The big attraction in town is the **Old Jameson Distillery** (☎ 021-461 3594; www.jamesonwhiskey.com; tours adult/child €13.50/8; ⊙ shop 9am-6.30pm, tour times vary). Coachloads pour in to tour the restored 200-year-old building and purchase bottles from the gift shop. Exhibits and tours explain the process of taking barley and creating whiskey (Jameson is today made in a modern factory in Cork).

Sleeping & Eating

Midleton has several attractive cafes in its centre, making it worth wandering in off the bypass. The **farmers market** is one of Cork's best markets, with bushels of local produce on offer and producers who are happy to chat. It's on every Saturday morning behind the courthouse on Main St.

Loughcarrig House (☎ 021-463 1952; www.loughcarrig.com; Ballinacurra; s/d €50/80) Right on Cork Harbour, this gracious old Georgian house has four rooms available, ideal for those looking for a restful country retreat. Walks and birdwatching on the beautiful land here are prime activities. The owners can also set you up for some angling in the fish-filled waters. Breakfasts are suitably hearty.

ourpick Farmgate Restaurant (☎ 021-463 2771; The Coolbawn; ⊙ coffee & snacks 9am-5.30pm, lunch noon-3.30pm Mon-Sat, dinner 6.30-9.30pm Thu-Sat) The original and sister establishment to Cork's Farmgate Café (p248), the Midleton restaurant offers the same superb blend of traditional and modern Irish in its approach to cooking. In the front is a shop selling amazing baked goods and local produce, including organic fruit and vegetables, cheeses and preserves. Behind is the farmhouse-style cafe-restaurant, where you'll eat as well as anywhere in Ireland.

Getting There & Away

Midleton is 20km east of Cork. There are buses every 30 minutes from Monday to Saturday (hourly on Sunday) from Cork bus station (€6, 25 minutes). There are no buses between Cobh and Midleton, and you'll need a car to explore the surrounding area.

COUNTY CORK

POSH RETREAT: BALLYMALOE

Drawing up at wisteria-clad **Ballymaloe House** (☎ 021-465 2531; www.ballymaloe.ie; Shanagarry; s/d from €175/260; 🚗 🛜), you know you've arrived somewhere special. The Allen family has been running this superb hotel and restaurant in the old family home for more than 40 years now; Myrtle is a living legend, acclaimed internationally for her near single-handed creation of fine Irish cooking. The rooms have been individually decorated with period furnishings and are a pleasing mass of different shapes and sizes. Guests enjoy beautiful grounds and amenities, which include a tennis court, a swimming pool, a shop, minigolf and public rooms. And don't forget the celebrated **restaurant**, whose menu is drawn up daily to reflect the availability of produce from Ballymaloe's extensive farms and other local sources. The hotel also runs wine and gardening weekends; check the website for details.

A few kilometres down the road on the R628, TV personality Darina Allen runs a famous **cookery school** (☎ 021-464 6785; www.cookingisfun.ie). Lessons, from half-day sessions (€55 to €105) to 12-week certificate courses (around €9800), are often booked well in advance. There are pretty cottages amid the 100 acres of grounds for overnight students.

YOUGHAL

pop 6500

The ancient seaport of Youghal (Eochaill; pronounced yawl), at the mouth of the River Blackwater, has a rich history that may not be instantly apparent, especially if you coast past on the N25. In fact, even if you stop, it may just seem like a humdrum Irish market town. But take a little time and you'll sniff out some of its once-walled past and enjoy views of the wide River Blackwater estuary.

The town was a hotbed of rebellion against the English in the 16th century, and Oliver Cromwell wintered here in 1649 as he sought to drum up support for his war in England and quell insurgence from the pesky Irish. Youghal was granted to Sir Walter Raleigh during the Elizabethan Plantation of Munster, and he spent brief spells living here in his house, Myrtle Grove.

Orientation & Information

Youghal Visitor Centre (☎ 024-20170; www.east corktourism.com; Market Sq; ⏰ 9am-5.30pm Mon-Fri, 10am-5pm Sat & Sun), housed in an attractive old market house on the waterfront, contains a small **heritage centre**. Pick up the free leaflet *Youghal Town Map* or the excellent booklet *Youghal: Historic Walled Port* (€5) to learn more.

Guided tours (€6/3 per adult/child) lasting 1½ hours leave the visitor centre at 11am Monday to Friday during July and August.

Sights & Activities

In 1956 the harbour stood in for New Bedford, Massachusetts, in the US for the filming of *Moby Dick*, starring Gregory Peck in one of his best roles. Today it is very quiet.

Youghal has two Blue Flag **beaches**, ideal for building sandcastles modelled after the Clock Gate. Claycastle (2km) and Front Strand (1km) are both within walking distance of town, off the N25. Claycastle has summer lifeguards.

Whale of a Time (☎ 086 328 3256; www.whaleofa time.ie) runs sea and river cruises (€20/15 per adult/child), including whale-watching trips.

Dinky **Fox's Lane Folk Museum** (☎ 024-20170, 024-291 145; www.tyntescastle.com/fox; North Cross Lane; adult/child €4/2; ⏰ 10am-1pm & 2-6pm Tue-Sat Jul-Aug) contains more than 600 household gadgets, dating from 1850 to 1950, and a Victorian kitchen.

Walking Tour

Youghal's history is best understood through its landmarks. Heading through town from south to north, this tour details the more prominent sights.

The curious **Clock Gate** was built in 1777, and served as a clock tower and jail concurrently; several prisoners taken in the 1798 Rising were hanged from its windows.

The beautifully proportioned brick **Red House**, on North Main St, was designed in 1706 by the Dutch architect Leuventhen, and features some Dutch Renaissance details. Main St has an interesting curve that follows the original shore; many of the shopfronts are from the 19th century. A few doors further up the street are six **almshouses** built by Englishman Richard Boyle, who bought Raleigh's Irish estates and became the first Earl of Cork in 1616 in recognition of his work in creating 'a very excellent colony'. The almshouses were given to ex-soldiers, along with an annual pension of £5.

Across the road is the 15th-century tower house **Tynte's Castle** (www.tyntescastle.com), which originally had a defensive riverfront position. When the River Blackwater silted up and changed course in the 17th and 18th centuries, the castle was left high and dry. It's currently under renovation.

Built in 1220, **St Mary's Collegiate Church** incorporates elements of an earlier Danish church dating back to the 11th century. Inside there's a monument to Richard Boyle, portrayed with his wife and 16 kids. The Earl of Desmond and his troops, rebelling against English rule, demolished the chancel roof in the 16th century; Cromwell is believed to have given a funerary speech inside for a fallen general in 1650. The churchyard is bounded by a fine stretch of the 13th-century **town wall** and one of the remaining turrets.

Beside the church, **Myrtle Grove** is the former home of Sir Walter Raleigh. Local tradition claims that he smoked the first cigarette and planted the first potatoes here, but historians (the spoilsports) tend to disagree. His **gardens**, on the other side of St Mary's, have recently been restored and are open to the public.

Sleeping

Clonvilla Caravan & Camping Park (☎ 024-98288; clonvilla@hotmail.com; Clonpriest; campsites from €20; ☺ Mar–Oct) Facilities are basic at this small site 4km out of town, but it's quiet enough.

Roseville (☎ 024-92571; www.rosevillebb.com; New Catherine St; r €50-70) In the heart of Youghal, deep-red Roseville, with its own walled garden, has the mood of a country house. The rooms have big comfy beds and are decorated in restful shades of beige. The garden is a fine place for lounging on a summer evening.

Avonmore House (☎ 024-92617; www.avonmore youghal.com; South Abbey; s/d from €50/70) This grand Georgian house near the clock tower was built in 1752 on the site of a Franciscan abbey destroyed by Cromwellian troops. Avonmore belonged to the earls of Cork before passing into private hands in 1826. Rooms are basic and multicoloured.

Aherne's (☎ 024-92424; www.ahernes.net; 163 North Main St; s/d from €130/150; ▣) The 12 rooms above the popular restaurant (see right) are well appointed, with broadband internet; larger ones have small balconies, where you can get a whiff of the sea air.

Eating

You'll find a few cafes and pubs in the centre near the Clock Gate.

Aherne's Seafood Bar & Restaurant (☎ 024-92424; 163 North Main St; bar food €10-40, dinner €24-40; ☺ bar food noon-10pm, dinner 6.30-9.30pm) Three generations of the same family have run Aherne's, an award-winning restaurant, justifiably famous for its terrific menu. Besides the restaurant there is a stylish, cosy bar and a much larger one popular with locals. The pub food is excellent.

Drinking

For an end-of-day pint and traditional live music, nowhere beats **Treacy's** (The Nook; 20 North Main St), Youghal's oldest boozer.

Getting There & Away

Bus Éireann (☎ 021-450 8188; www.buseireann.ie) runs frequent services to Cork (€11, 50 minutes, 14 daily) and Waterford (€15, 1½ hours, 11 daily).

WESTERN CORK

The Irish coast begins the slow build of beauty that culminates in counties even further west and north, but what you find here in Cork is already quite lovely. Kinsale is a superb little waterside town and there are many smaller ones almost as charming along the craggy coast to the Ring of Beara. It's perfect for aimless wandering as roads criss-cross the area like lace made by a deranged person.

KINSALE

pop 4100

Kinsale (Cionn tSáile) may be the perfectly sized Irish coastal town. Narrow winding streets, tiny houses and bobbing fishing boats and yachts give it a seductive picture-postcard feel. Its sheltered bay is guarded by a huge and engrossing fort, just outside the town at Summercove.

Kinsale enjoys a food reputation beyond its size and boasts numerous good restaurants, including one excellent seafood bistro. The compact centre is good for walking and there are artsy little shops aplenty. More walks wander off along the shore in both directions.

COUNTY CORK

History

In September 1601 a Spanish fleet anchored at Kinsale was besieged by the English. An Irish army from the north, which had appealed to the Spanish king to help it against the English, marched the length of the country to liberate the ships, but was defeated in battle outside the town on Christmas Eve. For the Catholics, the immediate consequence was that they were banned from Kinsale; it would be another 100 years before they were allowed back in. Historians now cite 1601 as the beginning of the end of Gaelic Ireland.

After 1601 the town developed as a shipbuilding port. In the early 18th century, Alexander Selkirk left Kinsale Harbour on a voyage that left him stranded on a desert island, providing Daniel Defoe with the idea for *Robinson Crusoe*.

Orientation

Most of Kinsale's hotels and restaurants are situated near the harbour and within easy walking distance of the town centre; Scilly, a peninsula to the southeast, is barely a 10-minute walk away. A path continues from there to Summercove and Charles Fort.

Information

Pearse St has a post office and banks with ATMs. Public toilets are next to the tourist office.

Bookstór (☎ 021-477 4946; www.bookstor.ie; 1 Newman's Mall) An excellent indie bookshop; top-notch recommendations of the best modern Irish fiction.

Castle Cleaners (☎ 021-477 2875; Market St; per load drop-off €12 ☼ 9am-6pm Mon-Fri)

Elasnik Web Café (☎ 021-477 7356; Market Sq; per 60min €5; ☼ 10am-7pm) Free coffee thrown in with the hourly rate.

Kinsale Bookshop (☎ 021-477 4244; 8 Main St) Another excellent indie shop; has poetry readings.

Tourist office (☎ 021-477 2234; www.kinsale.ie; cnr Pier Rd & Emmet Pl; ☼ 9.15am-5pm Tue-Sat Nov-Mar, Mon Apr-Jun, Sep & Oct, 10am-5pm Sun Jul-Aug) Has a good map detailing walks in and around Kinsale.

Sights

The best way to see Kinsale is on foot. You can spend an enjoyable day just walking the local environs.

A nifty **Regional Museum** (☎ 021-477 7930; Market Sq; adult/concession €3/1.50; ☼ 10am-5pm Wed-Sat, 2-5pm Sun) is based in the 17th-century courthouse that was used for the inquest into the sinking of the *Lusitania* in 1915. The museum contains information on the disaster, as well as curiosities as diverse as Michael Collins' hurley stick and shoes belonging to the eight-foot-tall Kinsale Giant.

Kinsale's roots with the old wine trade are on display at **Desmond Castle** (☎ 021-477 4855; www.heritageireland.ie; Cork St; adult/child €3/1; ☼ 10am-6pm Tue-Sun Easter-Sep, last admission 45min before closing), an early 16th-century fortified house that was occupied by the Spanish in 1601. Since then it has served as a custom house, as a prison for French and American captives and as a workhouse during the Famine. There are lively exhibits detailing its history and a small **wine museum** (www.winegeese.ie) that tells the story of the Irish wine-trading families, including names like Hennessy (of brandy fame), who fled to France because of British rule.

St Multose is the patron saint of Kinsale, and the Church of Ireland **church** (St Multose Church; ☎ rectory 021-477 2220; Church St) is one of Ireland's oldest, built around 1190 by the Normans on the site of a 6th-century church. Not much of the interior is original but the exterior is preserved beautifully. The graveyard has some interesting large family tombs, and several victims of the *Lusitania* sinking are also buried there. Inside, a flat stone carved with a round-handed figure was traditionally rubbed by fishermen's wives to bring their husbands home safe from the sea.

CHARLES FORT

One of the best-preserved 17th-century star-shaped forts in Europe, **Charles Fort** (☎ 021-477 2263; adult/child €4/2; ☼ 10am-5pm; P) would be worth a visit for its spectacular views alone. But there's much more here: ruins inside the vast site date from the 18th and 19th centuries and make for some fascinating wandering. Displays explain the typically tough lives led by the soldiers who served here and the comparatively comfortable lives of the officers. Built in the 1670s to guard Kinsale Harbour, the fort was in use until 1921, when much of it was destroyed as the British withdrew. The best way to get here is to walk – follow the signs on the lovely walk around the bay from Scilly to Summercove, 3km east of Kinsale.

Activities

For sailings to Charles Fort, James Cove and up the River Bandon, you can phone **Kinsale Harbour Cruises** (☎ 021-477 8946, 086 250 5456;

www.kinsaleharbourcruises.com; adult/child €12.50/6). Departure times vary throughout the year and are weather dependent; check the website or with the tourist office for details. The boats leave from near Vista Wine Bar on Pier Rd towards the marina.

Whale of a Time (☎ 086 328 3250; www.whaleofatime .ie) offers coastal cruises and whale-watching

trips from €35 per person for 90 minutes on fast speedboats.

Kayak Kinsale's beautiful harbour and the surrounding shores with **H2O Sea Kayaking** (☎ 021-477 8884; www.h2oseakayaking.com). Half-day tours start at €40.

For those interested in fishing, tackle can be hired at **Mylie Murphy's** (☎ 021-477 2703; 14 Pearse St)

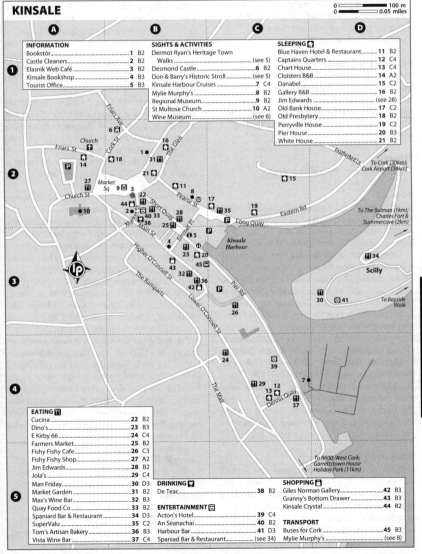

KINSALE

0   100 m
0   0.05 miles

INFORMATION	
Bookstór	**1** B2
Castle Cleaners	**2** B2
Elasnik Web Café	**3** B2
Kinsale Bookshop	**4** B3
Tourist Office	**5** B3

SIGHTS & ACTIVITIES	
Dermot Ryan's Heritage Town Walks	(see 5)
Desmond Castle	**6** B2
Don & Barry's Historic Stroll	(see 5)
Kinsale Harbour Cruises	**7** C4
Mylie Murphy's	**8** B2
Regional Museum	**9** B2
St Multose Church	**10** A2
Wine Museum	(see 6)

SLEEPING	
Blue Haven Hotel & Restaurant	**11** B2
Captains Quarters	**12** C4
Chart House	**13** C4
Cloisters B&B	**14** A2
Danabel	**15** C2
Gallery B&B	**16** B2
Jim Edwards	(see 28)
Old Bank House	**17** C2
Old Presbytery	**18** B2
Perryville House	**19** C2
Pier House	**20** B3
White House	**21** B2

EATING	
Cucina	**22** B2
Dino's	**23** B3
E Kirby 66	**24** C4
Farmers Market	**25** B2
Fishy Fishy Cafe	**26** C3
Fishy Fishy Shop	**27** A2
Jim Edwards	**28** B2
Jola's	**29** C4
Man Friday	**30** D3
Market Garden	**31** B2
Max's Wine Bar	**32** B3
Quay Food Co	**33** B2
Spaniard Bar & Restaurant	**34** D3
SuperValu	**35** C2
Tom's Artisan Bakery	**36** B3
Vista Wine Bar	**37** C4

DRINKING	
De Teac	**38** B2

ENTERTAINMENT	
Acton's Hotel	**39** C4
An Seanachai	**40** B2
Harbour Bar	**41** D3
Spaniad Bar & Restaurant	(see 34)

SHOPPING	
Giles Norman Gallery	**42** B3
Granny's Bottom Drawer	**43** B3
Kinsale Crystal	**44** B2

TRANSPORT	
Buses for Cork	**45** B3
Mylie Murphy's	(see 8)

To Cork (30km); Cork Airport (34km)

To The Bulman (1km); Charles Fort & Summercove (2km)

Kinsale Harbour

Scilly

To Bayside Walk

To R600; West Cork; Garrettstown House Holiday Park (11km)

COUNTY CORK

for €10 per day. For those hooked on fishing trips, contact **Kinsale Angling Co-op** (☎ 021-477 4946; www.kinsale-angling.com).

Tours

Two outfits offer excellent walking tours of Kinsale; both leave from the tourist office.

Dermot Ryan's Heritage Town Walks (☎ 021-477 2729; www.kinsaleheritage.com; adult/child €5/free; ⏱ 10.30am & 4.30pm) Authoritative; lasts one hour.

Don & Barry's Historic Stroll (☎ 021-477 2873; www.historicstrollkinsale.com; adult/child €7/1; ⏱ 11.15am) Good natured; 90 minutes.

Festivals & Events

Gourmet Festival (www.kinsalerestaurants.com) Tastings, meals and harbour cruises in early October add to the town's foodie reputation.

Kinsale Fringe Jazz Festival (www.kinsale.ie) Chilled-out entertainment over the late-October bank-holiday weekend.

Sleeping

There are many charming options.

BUDGET

Kinsale is geared towards the well heeled. There are good bus links to Cork city, so you might consider staying in one of the city's hostels (see p248) and busing it to Kinsale.

Garrettstown House Holiday Park (☎ /fax 021-477 8156; www.garrettstownhouse.com; campsites €14; ⏱ Apr–mid-Sep; P) This is the closest campsite to Kinsale, and is located in the grounds of an 18th-century estate. It's near an excellent beach but can get rowdy with families in summer (maybe it's the 'Crazy Golf' or the disco). The park is 1.3km southwest of Ballinspittle (11km southwest of Kinsale) on the R600.

Captains Quarters (☎ 021-477 4549; www .captains-kinsale.com; 55 Dennis Quay; r €50-100) You'll feel like an admiral at this good-value B&B near the centre and slightly up the hill from the harbour. The six rooms have a certain 1970s charm and are decorated with prints of old sailing ships, many with poop decks.

MIDRANGE

Danabel (☎ 021-477 4087; www.danabel.com; Sleaveen; s/d from €60/80; P) Just off Featherbed Lane (we're not making this up), this modern home has comfortable rooms with large private bathrooms and nice hardwood floors; some have views of the harbour. It's a brief walk to the centre.

Cloisters B&B (☎ 021-470 0680; www.cloisters kinsale.com; Friars St; s €70, d €80-110) Little touches make the difference at this delightful B&B near Desmond Castle. Inside the vermilion walls, chocolates await your arrival, and the orthopaedic mattresses are so comfy that only the creative breakfasts will tempt you out of bed. It's right across from St John the Baptist Church.

White House (☎ 021-477 2125; www.whitehouse -kinsale.com; Pearse St; r €75-180; P ⌨) A classic pub on the outside, a stylish inn on the inside. The White House may not make you feel presidential, but at least you'll feel like a cabinet secretary. The 10 rooms have warm shades of creams and browns and large, firm beds.

Chart House (☎ 021-477 4568; www.charthouse -kinsale.com; 6 Dennis Quay; s €80-130, d €120-170; P) There's a relaxed elegance about this Georgian town house; the four rooms have period pieces but not the fussiness that often accompanies them. The large dining room is so nice for breakfast you might want to stay for lunch.

Old Presbytery (☎ 021-477 2027; www.oldpres.com; Cork St; s €90, d €90-170; ⏱ closed Jan–mid-Feb; ☎) The Old Presbytery has gracefully moved into the 21st century with a careful refurbishment that maintains its character without pushing it into the 'batty old dowager' category. The timeless pine furniture contrasts with the refitted bathrooms. Stay in room 6 only if you have plans to see nothing of Kinsale: with its sunroom and balcony, you'll never want to leave. The breakfasts, cooked by landlord and former chef Phillip, are the stuff of legend.

Pier House (☎ 021-477 4475; www.pierhousekinsale .com; Pier Rd; r €120-140; ☎) This superb guesthouse, set back from the road in a sheltered garden, is a lovely place to rest your head. Pristine rooms, decorated with shell-and-driftwood sculptures, have black-granite bathrooms with power showers and underfloor heating. Four of the rooms also have balconies and views of the milling mobs outside.

Other recommendations:

Gallery B&B (☎ 021-477 4558; www.gallerybnb.com; The Glen; r €60-120) Musical instruments dominate the common rooms of this self-described 'funky' B&B with genial owners.

Jim Edwards (☎ 021-477 2541; www.jimedwards kinsale.com; Short Quay; r €60-100) These seven basic rooms couldn't be more central, at one of the town's best restaurants (see opposite).

TOP END

Old Bank House (☎ 021-477 4075; www.oldbankhouse
kinsale.com; 11 Pearse St; r €120-220; 🖳) Georgian elegance and style give a timeless quality to this
top-of-the-range 18-room hotel. Beautiful objets d'art and paintings grace the walls, and the
luxurious public rooms add a country-house
ambience. Although room decor is lavish, it
manages to avoid pretension through subtle
whimsy. Breakfasts, with homemade breads
and jams, are superb.

Perryville House (☎ 021-477 2731; www.perryville
house.com; Long Quay; r €130-250; 🅿 🛜) It's top-to-
bottom grandeur at family-run Perryville,
whether you're pulling up outside its imposing wrought-iron-clad facade or taking afternoon tea in the drawing room. All the 26
rooms exude comfort; move up the rate card
and the beds go from queen to king, while
balconies and sea views appear. Bathrooms
are huge. Eggs at breakfast are laid by a staff
member's chickens.

Also recommended:

Blue Haven Hotel & Restaurant (☎ 021-477 2209;
www.bluehavenkinsale.com; 3 Pearse St; €140-230; 🖳)
Boutique hotel with 17 posh rooms and good public spaces
and bar. Has the same owners as Old Bank House.

Eating

Kinsale fully deserves its billing as a foodie
haven and you can eat wonderfully on every
budget. Its busy fishing fleet provides a steady
supply of seafood, which the local restaurants
have a particularly good reputation for preparing. There's a weekly **farmers market** (Short Quay;
🕙 9.30am-1.30pm Tue) in front of Jim Edwards' restaurant. Lower O'Connell St is worth a stroll as
new restaurants have been appearing there.

RESTAURANTS
Budget

Cucina (☎ 021-470 0707; www.cucina.ie; 9 Market St; meals
€4-14; 🕙 9am-5pm Mon-Sat, last orders 4pm) Laid-back
jazz sets the mood at this modern little cafe.
Healthy bruschetta, salads and soups, and
not-so-healthy but very delicious cup cakes
are served in a simple setting.

Vista Wine Bar (☎ 021-470 6866; Shearwater, Pier
Rd; lunch €5-15, tapas €5-9) This shiny modern bar
has spectacular views over the marina, and
diners can enjoy the rhythmic clank, clank,
clank of rigging banging on boats. Come for
quiches and the baking at lunch, tapas in the
evening (from 6pm) and wine and coffee any
time of day.

Spaniard Bar & Restaurant (☎ 021-477 2436; www
.thespaniard.ie; Scilly; bar meals €6-18; restaurant mains €18-
24) This is a classic pub on Scilly, with low
ceilings and a peat fire, so why not crack open
some crab claws or settle for a sandwich at
the bar. Prices for most dishes at the bar are
around €10; there's a pricier restaurant upstairs. See p264 for more details on the pub.

Fishy Fishy Shop (☎ 021-477 4453; Guardwell; meals
€8-15; 🕙 noon-9pm Apr-Oct) The casual retail outlet
for the vaunted restaurant (below), you can
pause here on your Kinsale ramble for *just* a
superb coffee but, really, you'll want some of
the best fish and chips in town, or one of the
other treats. Tables are located both inside
and out.

Dino's (☎ 021-477 4561; Pier Rd; mains €9-12; 🕙 8am-
10.30pm) People happily spill out over the surrounding sidewalks at this nautically themed
chippy and family restaurant. Besides fish and
chips, Dino's does breakfasts (€7). Plop down
on the low wall and enjoy marina views.

Midrange

our pick **Jim Edwards** (☎ 021-477 2541; www.jim
edwardskinsale.com; Market Quay; bar meals €7-20, restaurant
meals €15-30; 🕙 bar 12.30-10pm, restaurant 6-10pm) Like
many places in Kinsale, this much-frequented
eatery has bar food of a high standard. The
restaurant has a traditional vibe that is thoroughly calming. Steaks feature but – as always in this area – the seafood shines. Service
couldn't be more sparkly.

E Kirby 66 (☎ 021-470 0488; 66 Lower O'Connell St;
mains €11-17; 🕙 noon-9pm) An old neighbourhood
pub has been reborn and has a welcoming
dinner menu of Italian classics. It's great for
when you want to say no to mussels and say
yes to spaghetti and meatballs. There's excellent pizza and, in a nod to local tradition, fine
seafood ravioli. By day this charmer is good
for a coffee and a pause along the gentrifying street.

our pick **Fishy Fishy Cafe** (☎ 021-470 0415; www
.fishyfishy.ie; Crowley's Quay; mains €13-33; 🕙 noon-4pm
Mon-Fri, noon-4.30pm Sat & Sun) Fishy Fishy is a superb place for fish. The setting is beautifully
understated, with stark white walls splashed
with bright artwork and a terrific decked terrace at the front. All the fish is caught locally;
have the cold seafood platter, a tasty spectacle
that's a concert of what's fresh. Scallops are
dollops of goodness. Front-of-house staff are
charmers, but waitstaff can look as tired as
week-old haddock.

COUNTY CORK

Bulman (☎ 021-477 2131; www.thebulman.com; Summercove; mains €16-21; ☺ 12.30-9.30pm) This is seaside eating at its best. Escape from central Kinsale to this gastro pub in an unspoilt harbourside venue, where salty informality is a style in its own right. Seafood excels here, whether swimming in chowder or laid out seductively on a platter. Much of everything is sourced locally; herbs are right from the kitchen garden.

Top End

Jola's (☎ 021-477 3322; www.jolasrestaurant.com; 18-19 Lower O'Connell St; lunch €6-10, dinner €20-25; ☺ noon-3.30pm & 6pm-late, cafe open noon-late) With double-height ceilings, exposed brick walls and a stunning chandelier, Jola's brings a dash of metropolitan style to Kinsale. The food is equally adept, confidently marrying Eastern European and Irish cuisine. The blini are our favourite, but nothing on the menu will disappoint you, from the veal with horseradish mash to the lamb shank with *boczek* (Polish pork belly).

Max's Wine Bar (☎ 021-477 2443; 48 Main St; mains €20-28; ☺ noon-2pm & 6-10pm Tue-Sun, shorter hours in winter) Behind the brilliant red traditional wooden facade is a restaurant popular with locals that combines French influences with the best Irish produce and seafood. The menu changes regularly but the wine list doesn't (at least in concept): it's always vast and alluring.

Man Friday (☎ 021-477 2260; www.man-friday.net; cnr River & High Rds, Scilly; mains €21-30; ☺ 6.30-10pm) Around the harbour walk in relaxing Scilly, this veteran seafood restaurant has outdoor seating with views back across the harbour to Kinsale. Book if you want a terrace table on balmy evenings. Just the walk down to the entrance is magical.

SELF-CATERING

Kinsale has a **SuperValu** (Pearse St; ☺ 8.30am-9pm Mon-Sat, 10am-9pm Sun) and the **Quay Food Co** (☎ 021-477 4000; www.quayfood.com; Market Quay; sandwiches €4-6; ☺ 9am-6pm daily Apr-Sep, 9.30am-5.30pm Mon-Sat Oct-Mar) for local produce and little luxuries. Also good for picnickers is **Market Garden** (☎ 021-477 574; The Glen; 9am-7pm Mon-Sat), a low-ceilinged warren of organic and local fruit and veg. Window displays at **Tom's Artisan Bakery** (☎ 021-477 3561; 46 Main St; ☺ 8am-5pm Mon-Sat) are suitably artful.

Drinking & Entertainment

Harbour Bar (☎ 021-477 2528; Scilly; ☺ from 6pm) Romping home in Kinsale's 'most unusual bar' stakes, this is like being in someone's front room. Battered old sofas, a fire stoked in the hearth, characters in every corner and benches with water views in the garden are all part of the charm.

Spaniard Bar & Restaurant (☎ 021-477 2436; www.thespaniard.ie; Scilly; ☺) The food is good (p263), but the real appeal of this old pub (it feels like it dates back to the Armada) lies in the quiet corners, where you can smell the peat fire and catch fragments of hushed conversations that could be about smuggling but are likely to be about sport.

Acton's Hotel (☎ 021-477 2135; www.actonshotel kinsale.com; Pier Rd) The modern hotel is charm-challenged, but its Waterfront Bar stages terrific Sunday lunchtime jazz sessions (April to October) featuring the famous Cork City Jazz Band.

De Teac (☎ 021-477 4602; 1 Main St) The pub menu has gone a hair upmarket, but this is still a rollicking local boozer, where locals prance in and out as if it were their living room (actually it is) and the regulars all their family.

Also recommended:

An Seanachai (☎ 021-477 7077; 6 Market St) This cavernous, barnlike pub has trad music sessions most nights.
Bulman (☎ 021-477 2131; Summercove) Always worth the stroll, the pub matches the restaurant (left) in salt-tinged allure.

Shopping

There is no shortage of places ready to reel in the browser.

Giles Norman Gallery (☎ 021-477 4373; 45 Main St) There's a big selection of evocative black-and-white imagery of Ireland here, from a master of the genre. Prints start at €30/45 (unframed/framed).

Granny's Bottom Drawer (☎ 021-477 4839; 53 Main St) A great range of exquisite Irish linen, damask and vintage-style homewares is sold at this cheerful shop with the perfect name.

Kinsale Crystal (☎ 021-477 4493; Market St) Sells exquisite work by an ex-Waterford craftsman who stands by the traditional 'deep-cutting, high-angle style'. A million tiny sparkles greet you as you enter.

Getting There & Away

Bus Éireann (☎ 021-450 8188) services connect Kinsale with Cork (€7, 50 minutes, 14 daily Monday to Friday, 11 Saturday and five Sunday) via Cork airport. The bus stops on Pier Rd, near the tourist office.

DETOUR: KINSALE & CLONAKILTY

The coastal road (R600) between Kinsale and Clonakilty is a much preferable route to the no-nonsense N71. During your meander, you'll encounter a lot of seaside scenery, the Michael Collins Centre (p267) and two excellent restaurants. If you enjoy good Irish food, plan to make a detour. Further along you'll come to a fine old pub that's at the centre of a good walking area.

Casino House (☎ 023-884 9944; www.casinohouse.ie; Kilbrittain; mains €19-27; ☷ dinner Thu-Mon, closed Jan–mid-Mar) The bright, simply decorated farmhouse overlooking the sparkling bay is the perfect setting for the modern Irish cuisine of Casino House. Local produce is used in every dish; we are already planning our next visit for lobster risotto. It's just off the R600.

Dillons (☎ 023-884 6390; Timoleague; mains €18-24; ☷ dinner Thu-Sun) Bright, inviting Dillons serves interesting variations on Irish staples in its bistro-style dining room. The emphasis is on meat (for example, Skeaglianore duck breast and roast quail), but there are interesting fish and veggie options too. Credit cards are not accepted.

O'Neill's Pub (☎ 023-884 0228; Butlerstown) A country pub straight from Central Casting, where peat fires are ready to warm you on the coldest days, while you can take your perfectly poured pint into the sunshine on nice days. The bar is long and mahogany, the walls are covered with old photos and the clientele spin yarns. Butlerstown is located down a warren of little lanes off the R600. It's the hub of walks around the dramatic coastal bluffs otherwise known as the Seven Heads.

Getting Around

You can hire bikes from **Mylie Murphy's** (☎ 021-477 2703; 14 Pearse St; per day €10; ☷ 9.30am-6pm Mon-Sat). For a taxi call **Kinsale Cabs** (☎ 021-477 2642).

CLONAKILTY
pop 4200

Cheerful, brightly coloured Clonakilty is a bustling market town that serves as a hub for the score of beguiling little coastal towns that surround it. You'll find smart B&Bs, top restaurants and cosy pubs alive with music. Little waterways coursing through add a drop of charm.

Clonakilty is famous as the birthplace of Michael Collins (see the boxed text, p267), a matter of extreme pride to the community; a large **statue** of the Big Fella stands on the corner of Emmet Sq.

History

Clonakilty received its first charter in 1292 but was refounded in the early 17th century by Richard Boyle, the first Earl of Cork. He settled it with 100 English families and planned a Protestant town from which Catholics would be excluded. His plan ultimately failed: Clonakilty is now very Irish and very Catholic – the Presbyterian chapel has been turned into a post office.

From the mid-18th to mid-19th centuries, more than 10,000 people worked in the town's linen industry. The fire station stands on the site of the old linen market.

Orientation

Roads converge on Asna Sq, dominated by a **1798 Rising monument** commemorating the event. Also in the square is the **Kilty Stone**, a piece of the original castle that gave Clonakilty (Clogh na Kylte in Irish, meaning 'castle of the woods') its name.

Information

The post office is in the old Presbyterian chapel on Bridge St. There are public toilets on the corner of Connolly and Kent Sts.

AIB Bank (cnr Pearse & Bridge Sts) Has an ATM.

Clon Business Solutions (☎ 023-883 4515; 32 Pearse St; per hr €6; ☷ 9am-6pm Mon-Fri, 10am-5pm Sat) Internet access.

Clonakilty Bookshop (☎ 023-883 3661; 12 Pearse St) Small, like perfect prose.

Kerr's Bookshop (☎ 023-883 4342; www.kerr.ie; 18 Ashe St) Sells fiction and guidebooks.

Tourist office (☎ 023-883 3226; info@corkkerrytourism .ie; Ashe St; ☷ 9.30am-5.30pm Mon-Sat Sep-Jun, 9am-7pm Mon-Sat & 10am-5pm Sun Jul-Aug) Has a good, free map.

Wash Basket (☎ 023-883 4821; Spillers Lane; ☷ 9am-6pm Mon-Sat) Has same-day laundry service (€8 to €10).

Sights & Activities

Wandering the centre is good for a couple of hours; Georgian Emmet Square attests to the area's traditional wealth. Spillers Lane has nifty little shops.

Of the more than 30,000 ring forts scattered across Ireland, **Lisnagun** (Lios na gCon; ☎ 023-883 2565; www.liosnagcon.com; adult/child €5/3; ☷ tours noon-4pm summer) is the only one that's been reconstructed on its original site. Complete with souterrain and central thatched hut, it gives a vivid impression of life in a 10th-century farmstead. To get there, take the turn signposted to Bay View House B&B at the roundabout at the end of Strand Rd. Follow the road uphill to the T-junction, turn right, then continue for about 800m before turning right again (signposted).

You can't help but smile at the **West Cork Model Railway Village** (☎ 023-883 3224; www.model village.ie; Inchydoney Rd; adult/child €8/4.25; 11am-5pm Sep-Jun, 10am-5pm Jul-Aug). It features a vast out-door recreation of the West Cork Railway as it was during the 1940s and superb miniature models of the main towns in western Cork. Less fun, the **road train** (adult/child incl admission to Railway Village €12/6.25; daily summer, weekends winter) leaves from the Railway Village on a 20-minute circuit of Clonakilty. It's good if you like being cooped up and stared at.

The bay is good for **swimming**, albeit in a bracing sort of way. The sandy Blue Flag **beach** at Inchydoney Island, 4km from town, is good, too, but watch out for the dangerous rip tide; when lifeguards are on duty, a red flag indicates danger. The **West Cork Surf School** (☎ 086 869 5396; www.westcorksurfing.com) is riding the wave of Irish surfing's recent popularity. A two-hour lesson will set you back €35. In town, **Jellyfish Surf Co** (☎ 023-883 5890; Spillers Lane) can advise surfers where to go locally.

Sleeping

Stay in town to enjoy the range of nightlife.

Desert House Caravan & Camping Park (☎ 023-883 3331; deserthouse@eircom.net; Coast Rd; campsite from €10, r per person €35; Easter & May-Sep;) This attractive 36-pitch park, 1.5km southeast of town on the road to Ring, is on a dairy farm overlooking the bay. B&B rooms inside are an orgy of patterned carpets and floral wallpaper.

Tudor Lodge (☎ 023-883 3046; www.tudorlodgecork .com; McCurtain Hill; r €50-80) If you want Tudor-ish visions of Henry VIII, you'll have to don a fat suit. But apart from that, this modern family home sits pleasantly above it all a short walk from the town centre. Standards are kept up to scratch in impeccably smart, peaceful rooms.

Bay View House (☎ 023-883 3539; www.bayview clonakilty.com; Old Timoleague Rd; r €50-90;) This

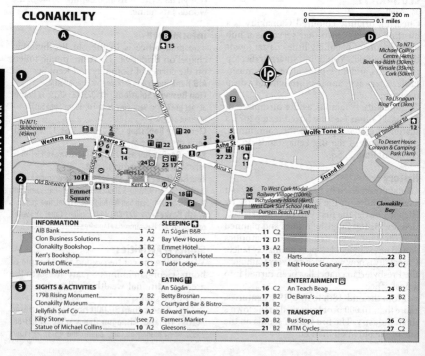

MICHAEL COLLINS – THE 'BIG FELLA'

County Cork, and especially the Clonakilty area, has a deeply cherished association with Michael Collins, the 'Big Fella', commander-in-chief of the army of the Irish Free State, which won independence from Britain in 1922.

Collins was born on a small farm at Woodfield near Clonakilty as the youngest of eight children, and went to school in the town. He lived and worked in London from 1906 to 1916, returning to Ireland to take part in the Easter Rising, after which he became a key figure in Irish Nationalism. He revolutionised the way the Irish rebels fought, organising them into guerrilla-style 'flying columns', and was the main negotiator of the 1921 Anglo-Irish Treaty that led to the Irish Free State. The mixed reaction to the treaty, with many thinking Ireland had made too many concessions to the British, plunged the country into a brutal civil war.

On a tour of western Cork, Michael Collins was ambushed and killed by anti-Treaty forces on 22 August 1922 at Beal-na-Bláth, near Macroom. Each year, a commemorative service is held on the anniversary of the killing. To visit the site, follow the N22 west from Cork for about 20km, then take the left turn (R590) to Crookstown. From there turn right onto the R585 to Beal-na-Bláth. The ambush site is on the left after 4km.

The useful map and leaflet *In Search of Michael Collins* (€4) is available at the Clonakilty tourist office, outlining places in the district associated with him. A visit to the **Michael Collins Centre** (☎ 023-884 6107; www.michaelcollinscentre.com; adult/child €6/3; ⏰ 10.30am-5pm Mon-Fri, 11am-2pm Sat mid-Jun–Sep) is an excellent way to make sense of his life and that period of Ireland's history. A tour reveals photos, letters and a reconstruction of the 1920s country lane where Collins was killed, complete with armoured vehicle. The centre runs tours of the crucial locations in Collins' life on occasion. The centre is signposted off the R600 between Timoleague and Clonakilty.

The **Clonakilty Museum** (Western Rd; admission €3; ⏰ Jun–Sep) has some more memorabilia, including Collins' weapons and uniform. The museum is run on a voluntary basis; contact the tourist office for exact opening hours.

---

frothy pink house offers immaculate B&B standards, a genial welcome and great breakfasts. Rooms 5 and 6, and the cosy landing lounge, offer fantastic views over the fields that slope down to Clonakilty Bay.

An Súgán B&B (☎ 023-883 3719; www.ansugan.com; Sand Quay; r €50-70; ⏰ mid-Mar–Oct) There are few frills at this B&B, but you do get a relaxed atmosphere and enormous rooms in a great location a couple of doors down from An Súgán restaurant (p268).

O'Donovan's Hotel (☎ 023-883 3250; www.odonovans hotel.com; Pearse St; s/d €50/100; 🅿 🛜) Behind the vintage vivid-red exterior beats the heart of a classic old hotel. Service is simple but friendly. Rooms are straightforward and you can't beat the central location. A WWII plaque out front will intrigue Americans.

Emmet Hotel (☎ 023-883 3394; www.emmethotel .com; Emmet Sq; r €75-120; 🛜) This lovely Georgian accommodation option on the elegant square happily mixes period charm and old-world service with the perks of a modern hotel. The 20 rooms are large and plush; O'Keeffe's restaurant on site serves up tasty Irish food made from organic and local ingredients.

Eating

Clonakilty is the source of the best black pudding in Ireland. It features on many local restaurant menus and you can buy varieties based on 19th-century recipes from **Edward Twomey** (☎ 023-883 3733; www.clonakiltyblackpudding .ie; 16 Pearse St; puddings from €2.50). Try to pay a visit to the twice-weekly **farmers market** (McCurtain Hill; ⏰ 10am-2pm Thu & Sat).

Harts (☎ 023-883 5583; 8 Ashe St; meals €5-10; ⏰ 10am-5pm Mon-Sat) Always busy, this classic city-centre caff surprises with creative takes on standards. Ciabatta sandwiches, fine baked goods, local cheese plates and homemade preserves set the tone.

Betty Brosnan (☎ 023-883 4011; 58 Pearse St; meals €5-13; ⏰ 9am-5pm Mon-Sat) A prime place for lunch, this historic cafe offers lots of breakfast choices (including a 14-inch cooked Irish feast for the 'very hungry'), sandwiches, lasagne, smoothies and puddings. The upstairs gallery displays black-and-white travel photography by owner Dermot Brosnan.

Courtyard Bar & Bistro (☎ 023-883 5802; 3-4 Harte's Courtyard; mains €5-15; ⏰ 10am-9pm) Tables out back overlook the brook, out front they are sheltered from the rain and have heaters. Inside a fire burns and you'll enjoy the scents of excellent baked goods, fine sandwiches and other comfort foods. Superb coffees.

An Súgán (☎ 023-883 3719; 41 Wolfe Tone St; bar meals €5-28, restaurant mains €13-28; 🕑 meals noon-10pm) This snug little oasis exudes idiosyncratic style. The bar and restaurant are crammed with knick-knacks – jugs dangle from the ceiling, patrons' business cards are stuffed beneath the rafters, and lanterns and even ancient fire-extinguishers dot the walls. Seafood is the thing here – try the chowder and anything with the smoked salmon.

Malt House Granary (☎ 023-883 4355; 30 Ashe St; mains €18-25; 🕑 5-10pm Mon-Sat) You'll be able to check out the Clonakilty black pudding, Boilie goat's cheese, Gubbeen chorizo and Bantry Bay mussels among other ingredients on the menu at the Malt House, as everything on your plate originates from West Cork. The interior design is a hotchpotch of stylish and kitsch. The seafood platter is a classic.

Gleesons (☎ 023-882 1834; www.gleesons.ie; 3-4 Connolly St; dinner €19-29; 🕑 6.30-9.30pm Mon-Fri, 6-10pm Sat) Gleesons is a temple of fine dining that melds Irish produce with continental technique. The surrounds are nicely understated, with a wood and slate decor. The seafood, not surprisingly, is tasty. Early diners can enjoy a good-value three-course set menu (€35).

Entertainment

our pick De Barra's (☎ 023-883 3381; www.debarra.ie; 55 Pearse St) A marvellous atmosphere, walls splattered with photos, press cuttings, masks and musical instruments, plus the cream of live music every night of the week (starting around 9.30pm) make this a busy pub.

An Teach Beag (☎ 023-883 3883; 5 Recorder's Alley) This intriguing pub, out back from O'Donovan's Hotel, has all the atmosphere necessary for good traditional music sessions. You might even catch a *scríocht* (a session by storytellers and poets) in full flow. There's music nightly during July and August; at weekends, the rest of the year. Check out the historical plaque at the start of the alley – times have changed…

Getting There & Away

There are eight daily buses Monday to Saturday and seven Sunday to Cork (€11.50, 65 minutes) and Skibbereen (€8, 40 minutes). Buses stop across from Harte's Spar shop on the bypass going to Cork. Note the alternative way to Kinsale on the R600; see the boxed text, p265, for details.

Getting Around

MTM Cycles (☎ 023-883 3584; 33 Ashe St) hires bikes for €10 per day. A nice ride is to Duneen Beach, about 13km south of town.

CLONAKILTY TO SKIBBEREEN

Picturesque villages, a fine stone circle and calming coastal scenery mark the less-taken route from Clonakilty to Skibbereen. Rather than follow the main N71 all the way, when you get to Rosscarbery, turn left onto the R597 at the far end of the causeway (signposted Glandore); or, even better, take twice as long and freelance your way along narrow roads near the water the entire way.

Drombeg Stone Circle

On an exposed hillside, with fields sweeping away towards the coast and bothered cattle braying in the distance, the Drombeg stone circle is superbly atmospheric. Its 17 uprights once guarded the cremated bones of an adolescent, discovered during a 1960s excavation. The 9m-diameter circle probably dates from the 5th century AD, representing a sophisticated Iron Age update of an earlier Bronze Age monument.

Just beyond the stones are the remains of a hut and an Iron Age cooking pit, known as a *fulachta fiadh*. Experiments have shown that its heated rocks would boil water and keep it hot for nearly three hours – enough time to cook hunks of meat. Generally quiet, there's usually a few vestiges of private rituals held here.

To get there, take the signposted left turn off the R597, approximately 4km west of Rosscarbery.

Glandore & Union Hall

pop 250

The pretty waterside villages of Glandore (Cuan Dor) and Union Hall burst into life in summer when fleets of yachts tack into the shelter of the Glandore Harbour inlet. A tangle of back roads meander across the area; you should, too.

Union Hall, accessible from Glandore via a long narrow causeway over the estuary, was named after the 1800 Act of Union, which abolished the separate Irish parliament. The

1994 film *War of the Buttons*, about two battling gangs of youngsters, was filmed here.

There's an ATM, post office and general store in Union Hall and food is available in both villages. Union Hall has the most choice, with a deli, coffee shop and several pubs, two of which have fantastic waterside terraces.

SIGHTS & ACTIVITIES

Delightful Theresa O'Mahoney runs the **Ceim Hill Museum** (☎ 028-36280; adult/child €4/2; ⏰ 10am-7pm) from her farmhouse off Castletownshend Rd. The small collection of Iron Age bits in the 'Independence' room are worth a glance if you're passing.

You can splash round the coast with **Atlantic Sea Kayaking** (☎ 028-21058; www.atlanticseakayaking.com; Union Hall; half-day trip €50; ⏰ year-round), which offers many tours and classes.

Two outfits offer whale and dolphin tours year-round from Reen Pier, about 3km beyond Union Hall. Prices average €50/30 per adult/child for half-day cruises. **Whale Watch West Cork** (☎ 028-33357; www.whalewatchwestcork.com) **Whale Watch with Colin Barnes** (☎ 086 327 3226; www.whalewatchwithcolinbarnes.com)

SLEEPING & EATING

Meadow Camping Park (☎ 028-33280; meadowcamping@eircom.net; Rosscarbery Rd, Glandore; campsites €17; ⏰ Easter & May–mid-Sep) This small idyllic site, in a garden filled with trees and flowers, is 2km east of Glandore on the R597 to Rosscarbery.

Ardagh House (☎ 028-33571; www.ardaghhouse.com; Union Hall; s/d €45/70; 💻) You're soon made to feel part of the family at this restored farmhouse by the harbour. The rooms, many with sea views, are bright and sunny, and there's a garden. The house itself is a bit of a star, having made an appearance in *War of the Buttons*.

Shearwater B&B (☎ 028-33178; www.shearwaterbandb.com; Union Hall; s/d €50/70; ⏰ Apr-Oct) On a small hill about 500m from the centre of Union Hall, rooms are comfy and there is a large terrace with killer views.

Bay View House (☎ 028-33115; Glandore; s/d €50/80) The truth: Bay View House has *spectacular* views across the bay. Try to snag room 1 for the best view of all. Bright citrus colours, tidy pine furniture and gleaming bathrooms add to the appeal. Local pubs are a stumble away.

Hayes Bar (☎ 028-33214; The Square, Glandore; meals €8-20; ⏰ kitchen noon-9pm) The food – and the

decor – at this perfect portside pub will put you in the pink. Soups, tapas, sandwiches and more are best enjoyed at the picnic tables outside.

Also here: **Glandore Inn** (☎ 028-33468; The Square, Glandore) A seamen's haunt, with plenty of picnic tables.

GETTING THERE & AWAY

Buses stop in nearby Leap (3km north), from where most B&B owners will pick you up if you arrange it in advance.

Castletownshend

pop 160

With its grand houses and higgledy-piggledy stone cottages dating back to the 17th and 18th centuries tumbling down the precipitously steep main street, Castletownshend is one of Ireland's most enigmatic villages. At the bottom of the hill is a small quayside and the castle (really a crenellated mansion) after which the village is named. Once you've seen these, you can just put your feet up and relax: you've ticked all the boxes.

The **castle** (☎ 028-36100; www.castle-townshend.com; r €110-170), sitting imposingly on the waterfront, is a rocky fantasy. Huge mullioned windows obviate any authenticity of the decorative defensive touches. The seven guest rooms range from one with an old four-poster, where you can play 'royal and consort' games, to small but bright rooms, some with terraces and views.

The only way here is by car down the R596 for 8km. A **taxi** (☎ 028-21258) from Skibbereen costs about €15.

SKIBBEREEN

pop 2300

Skibbereen (Sciobairín) was once a typical market town: unvarnished, down to earth and warm-hearted. It's still all those things but there is now an overlay of glitz, which attests to the wealth of the weekending swells and yachties from Dublin.

It's a good West Cork pit stop, and an hour's stroll is a nice diversion.

History

Skibbereen was one of the most badly affected towns in Ireland during the Famine. Huge numbers of the local population emigrated or died of starvation or disease. 'The accounts are not exaggerated – they cannot be exaggerated –

nothing more frightful can be conceived.' So wrote Lord Dufferin and GF Boyle, who journeyed from Oxford to Skibbereen in February 1847 to see if reports of the Famine were true. Their eyewitness account makes horrific reading; Dufferin was so appalled by what he saw that he contributed £1000 (about €100,000 in today's money) to the relief effort.

Orientation

The main landmark in town is a statue in the central square, dedicated to heroes of Irish rebellions against the British. From here, three roads branch off: Market St heads south to Lough Hyne and Baltimore; Main St, the principal shopping street, becomes Bridge St before heading west over the river to Ballydehob and Bantry; and North St heads towards the main Cork road.

Information

The **tourist office** (☎ 028-21766; www.skibbereen.ie; North St; ☿ 10am-5pm Mon-Fri Sep-May, Sat & Sun Jun-Aug) can book accommodation in Baltimore and on Sherkin and Clear Islands, advise on local walks, and provide ferry timetables to the islands.

There's an AIB Bank with an ATM on Bridge St. For internet access head to **Skibbereen Business Services** (☎ 028-23287; 27A Main St; per 10 min €1; ☿ 9.30am-6pm Mon-Fri, 10am-5pm Sat).

Sights

Constructed on the site of the town's old gasworks, the **Skibbereen Heritage Centre** (☎ 028-40900; www.skibbheritage.com; Old Gasworks Bldg, Upper Bridge St; adult/child €6/3; ☿ 10am-6pm Tue-Sat Oct-May, daily Jun-Sep) houses a haunting exhibition about the Famine, with actors reading heartbreaking contemporary accounts. A visit here puts Irish history into harrowing perspective. There's also a smaller exhibition about nearby Lough Hyne, the first marine nature reserve in Ireland, and a genealogical centre.

Guided evening **historical walks** (adult/child €5/2.50), lasting 1½ hours, leave from the Heritage Centre. Call ahead to confirm times.

The **Abbeystrewery Cemetery** is a 1km walk east of the centre, on the N71 to Schull, and holds the mass graves of 8000 to 10,000 local people who died during the Famine.

A beautiful and disused **old railway bridge** crosses the river near Ilen St. A **cattle market** on Fridays at the showgrounds is a frenetic, smelly glimpse of rural life.

Sleeping

our pick **Bridge House** (☎ 028-21273; monabestbridge house@yahoo.com; Bridge St; s/d €40/70) Mona Best has turned her entire house into a work of art, filling the rooms with fabulous Victorian tableaux and period memorabilia. The whole place bursts at the seams with cherished clutter, crazed carvings, dressed-up dummies and fragrant fresh flowers. Guests can request black satin sheets.

Ilenroy House (☎ 028-22751; ilenroyhouse@ocean free.net; North St; s/d €50/70) Right in the centre of town, the Ilenroy offers modest B&B accommodation. It's nothing fancy, but the price is right.

West Cork Hotel (☎ 028-21277; www.westcork hotel.com; Ilen St; r €60-150) This stolid veteran has 30 comfortable and recently redone rooms next to the river and old railway bridge. The bar is a good retreat; rooms at the back have pastoral views.

Eating

There's a **county market** (☿ 12.30-2.30pm) every Friday and a **farmers market** (☿ 10am-1.30pm) every Saturday on Old Market Sq. If you're in town in mid-September, don't miss the **Taste of West Cork Food Festival** (www.atasteofwestcork .com), with a lively market and events at local restaurants.

Kalbo's Bistro (☎ 028-21515; 26 North St; breakfast & lunch €4-11, dinner €17-30; ☿ 9am-9pm Mon-Sat year-round, plus 5.30-9.30pm Sun Jul-Aug) This local favourite recently downsized to give the owners a slight break for their well-deserved popularity. But the simply prepared classic meals continue. Locally sourced produce and a deft hand in the kitchen mean that pancakes in the morning and bacon sandwiches at lunch are tops. Dinners are creative.

Over the Moon (☎ 028-22100; 46 Bridge St; lunch €8-14, dinner mains €25; ☿ noon-2pm & 6-9pm Wed-Mon, closed Sun lunch) The classic deep-blue and white exterior plus the beguiling logo make you want to walk inside; you should. Locally sourced foods (purveyors are listed) star on a creative and changing menu of fresh fare. Local ham, cheese and seafood star.

Getting There & Away

Bus Éireann (☎ 021-450 8188; www.buseireann.ie) runs buses to Cork nine times daily Monday to Saturday, and five on Sunday (€15, 1¾ hours); and to Schull eight times daily Monday to Saturday and six times Sunday (€6, 30 minutes) from outside the former Eldon Hotel on Main St.

BALTIMORE
pop 400

Picturesque Baltimore has its sailing hat wedged at a jaunty angle and a merry whistle on its lips. Sitting on the broad terrace at the centre of town and watching the boats, boats, boats everywhere with a pint of stout in your hand is indulgently somnolent.

Besides idlers, Baltimore attracts sailing folk, anglers, divers and visitors to Sherkin and Clear Islands, meaning that the population hits force 10 during summer months.

Information

There's an information board at the harbour, or check out www.baltimore.ie. The nearest ATM is in Skibbereen. There's internet access (€3.50 per hour) at Casey's hotel.

Sights

The pretty harbour is dominated by the remains of the **Dun na Sead** (Fort of the Jewels; ☎ 028-20735; adult/child €3/free; ☒ 11am-6pm Jun-Sep). Inside are seasonal art displays, but the best way to appreciate this 13th-century survivor is from a distance.

Activities

There's some excellent diving to be had on the reefs around Fastnet Rock; the waters are warmed by the Gulf Stream and a number of shipwrecks lie nearby. **Aquaventures Dive Centre** (☎ 028-20511; www.aquaventures.ie; Stonehouse B&B, Lifeboat Rd) charges €65 for a full day's diving, and also offers diving and accommodation packages in the attached B&B; contact the centre for prices.

Baltimore Sailing School (☎ 028-20141; www.baltimoresailingschool.com) provides courses (five days for €340) from May to September for beginners and advanced sailors.

For a shorter taste of the sea, set sail with **Baltimore Yacht Charters** (☎ 028-20160; www.baltimoreyachtcharters.com), which has a variety of cruises on its yachts starting at €50. Also leaving from the harbour, **Baltimore Sea Safari** (☎ 028-20753) has various sailing adventures starting at €25 for 1½ hours.

Information about other diving, sailing and angling operators is posted by the harbour.

A white-painted landmark beacon (aka Lot's Wife) stands on the western headland of the peninsula and makes for a pleasant **walk**, especially at sunset.

Ten kilometres from Baltimore, on the R585 towards Skibbereen, there's good **walking** around Lough Hyne and the Knockamagh Wood Nature Reserve. Well-marked trails lead round the lake and up a steep hill through the forest. You're rewarded with stunning views at the top.

Festivals & Events

The town goes nuts in May.

Fiddle Fair (www.fiddlefair.com) The second weekend of May, with sessions from international and local musicians.

Seafood Festival (www.baltimore.ie) Over the last full weekend of May, jazz bands perform and pubs bring out the mussels and prawns; wooden boats parade.

Walking Festival (www.westcork.ie) Guided walks of Baltimore and the region in mid-May.

Sleeping

Top of the Hill Hostel (☎ 028-20094; www.topofthehillhostel.ie; dm/d €15/44) Everything, from the exterior to the duvets, is white at this beautiful hostel, which is exactly where you'd think but still close to the centre. Sleep securely on sturdy steel bunks. The (white) communal areas consist of a lounge, dining room and kitchen, and there's a lovely garden to the side.

Rolf's Country House (☎ 028-20289; www.rolfsholidays.eu; Baltimore Hill; s €50-60, d €80-100; ☒ ☒) Upmarket Rolf's, in a much-restored old farmhouse in restful gardens on the outskirts of town, does the lot: there are 14 excellent-value, smartly decorated private rooms, self-catering cottages (from €500 per week), helpful staff and a charming restaurant.

Fastnet House (☎ 028-20515; fastnethouse@eircom.net; Main St; s/d from €50/90) This early 19th-century house, up from the main harbour, is another good option. Stone steps lead up to uncluttered rooms with big windows. Window boxes add colour to the vintage stuccoed facade.

our pick Waterfront (☎ 028-20600; www.waterfronthotel.ie; r €60-120; ☒ ☒) Truly the heart of town, Youen Jacob and his family run what seems to be half the town – and run it well they do. This three-storey 13-room guesthouse has stylish, clean-lined rooms with huge bathrooms. Opt for one with a view: it's intoxicating.

Casey's of Baltimore (☎ 028-20197; www.caseysofbaltimore.com; Skibbereen Rd; s/d €110/182; ☒) Ten of the 14 bedrooms here have estuary views and spiffy rooms with huge beds. Eating is a delight as well (see below). The hotel is right at the entrance to town.

Eating

La Jolie Brise (☎ 028-20600; mains €12-20; ⊙ 10am-10pm) Part of the Youen Jacob empire, this casual restaurant does excellent food. Enjoy meals (excellent thin-crust pizza and fish and chips) at the plethora of picnic tables on the square in front of the Waterfront guesthouse.

Casey's of Baltimore (☎ 028-20197; lunches €4-10, mains €14-30; ⊙ 12.30-3pm & 6.30-9pm, bar meals all day) At Casey's your food comes with fantastic views, whether you call in for breakfast, sandwiches or a tasty dinner. Seafood includes mussels fresh from the hotel's own shellfish farm in Roaringwater Bay and the hotel specialty, crab claws in garlic butter.

Glebe Gardens & Café (☎ 028-20232; www.glebe gardens.com; meals €15-30; ⊙ 10am-10pm Wed-Sat, 10am-6pm Sun Apr-Oct) The beautiful gardens here are an attraction in themselves; lavender and herbs add fragrant aromas that waft over the tables inside and out. Food is simple and fresh, sourced from the gardens and a list of local purveyors.

Chez Youen (☎ 028-20136; The Quay; dinner from €30; ⊙ 6-10pm, closed Nov & Feb) Where it all started and still excellent, terrific seafood is the rule in this Breton-inspired restaurant. The luscious shellfish platter, containing lobster, prawns, brown crab, velvet crab, shrimps and oysters, offers the chance to sample shellfish at its unadorned best.

Drinking

Bushe's Bar (☎ 028-20125; www.bushesbar.com; The Quay) Seafaring paraphernalia literally drips from the ceiling at this genuinely character-filled old bar. The benches outside on the main square are the best spots in town for a sundowner and you can watch sailors get misty at the nautical views. Famous crab sandwiches are served at times.

Getting There & Away

There are four daily buses weekdays and three times over the weekend between Skibbereen and Baltimore (€3.50, 20 minutes).

CLEAR ISLAND
pop 150

With its lonely inlets, pebbly beaches, gorse- and heather-covered cliffs, Clear Island (Oileán Chléire; Cape Clear Island) is an escapist's heaven. But that's just as well, as you'll want time to appreciate this small, rugged Gaeltacht (Irish-speaking) area, the southernmost inhabited island in the country. It's a place for quiet walks, hunting down standing stones and birdwatching. Soon you'll catch the alternative, independent vibe of the place.

Facilities are few, but there are a couple of B&Bs, one shop and three pubs.

Orientation & Information

The island is 5km long and just over 1.5km wide at its broadest point. It narrows in the middle when an isthmus divides the northern and southern harbours. There's a **tourist information post** (☎ 028-39100; ⊙ 11am-1pm & 3-6pm May-Aug) beyond the pier, next to the coffee shop. There are various leaflets available. You'll find toilets at the harbour.

The island's website (www.oilean-chleire .ie) is useful, and has links to a surprising number of books written about the island.

Sights

The small **heritage centre** (☎ 028-39119; admission €3; ⊙ 2.30-5pm Jun-Aug) has exhibits on the island's history and culture, and fine views north across the water to Mizen Head.

The ruins of 14th-century **Dunamore Castle**, the stronghold of the O'Driscoll clan, can be seen perched on a rock on the northwestern side of the island (follow the track from the harbour). The great hall lives up to its name and is sometimes open for tours (€3) when visitors turn up.

Activities
BIRDWATCHING

Cape Clear is one of the top birdwatching spots in Ireland, particularly known for sea birds, including Manx shearwater, gannet, fulmar and kittiwake. Guillemot breed on the island, but other birds head to and fro on hunting trips from the rocky outposts of the western peninsulas. Tens of thousands of birds can pass hourly, especially in the early morning and at dusk. The best time of year for twitching here is October.

The white-fronted **bird observatory** is by the harbour (turn right at the end of the pier and it's 100m along). It's worth calling in to ask about any planned birdwatching trips. For details on courses, see opposite.

WALKING

There are marked trails all over the island, and B&Bs and the tourist information post can advise on other walks. For **guided walks** covering historical, archaeological or ecological aspects of the island, phone ☎ 028-39157 (during summer); for walks focused on literature and culture, phone ☎ 028-39190.

Courses

Once you're this isolated, you might as well learn something.

Ionad Foghlama Chléire (Cape Clear Island Language Services; ☎ 028-39190; www.cleire.com) runs Irish-language programs for adults.

Besides running the bird observatory, **BirdWatch Ireland** (www.birdwatchireland.ie) runs birdwatching field courses to Cape Clear. Details are on the website and the group has a small house so birdwatchers can stay the night.

For everything you need to know about goat husbandry, contact Ed Harper at **Chléire Goats** (☎ 028-39126; www.oilean-chleire.ie/english/goats .htm), based at a farm west of the church. He makes ice cream and cottage cheese, available for tastings, and runs half-day (€35) to week-long courses on goat keeping.

Festivals

The **Cape Clear Island International Storytelling Festival** (☎ 028-39157; www.capeclearstorytelling.com; weekend ticket €65) brings hundreds of people to Clear Island for storytelling, workshops and walks, as summer wanes in early September.

Sleeping & Eating

Accommodation on the island is satisfyingly unfancy. Book ahead, especially between May and September. Ask for directions to all of the following:

Chléire Haven (☎ 028-39119; www.yurt-holidays -ireland.com; per person €10; ⊗ Jun-Sep) There's campsites here and also yurts and tepees. The latter require multiple-day stays (a good thing) and start at €170 for three nights.

Cluain Mara (☎ 028-39153, 028-39172; www.cape clearisland.com; North Harbour; per person €28-35) There are self-catering cottages here at the isolated end of the already isolated island. The pub does home-cooked meals (€8 to €12) throughout the year.

Also recommended:

Cape Clear Island Hostel (☎ 028-41968; www .mamut.net/anoigecapeclear; Old Coastguard Station, South Harbour; dm from €20; ▯) In a large white building at the south harbour, amid lovely gardens.

Ard Na Gaoithe (☎ 028-39160; www.oilean-chleire .ie/english/leonard.htm; The Glen; per person from €35) Has restful rooms in a simple sturdy house.

Getting There & Away

From Baltimore, the ferry **Naomh Ciarán II** (☎ 028-39153; www.capeclearferry.com; adult/child return €15/7) takes 45 minutes to cover the 11km journey to Clear Island and it's a stunning trip on a clear day. There are four sailings daily from June to mid-September, with the earliest leaving at 11am and the latest returning at 7pm, and at least two per day the rest of the year. Bicycles travel free.

From Schull, the **Clear Island ferry** (☎ 028-28278; www.capeclearferries.com; ⊗ 10.30am, 2.30pm & 4.30pm Jun-Aug, 2.30pm Sep; adult/child return €14/7) leaves from the pier.

GOUGANE BARRA FOREST PARK

Gougane Barra (www.gouganebarra.com) is a truly magical part of inland County Cork. It's almost alpine in feel, with spectacular vistas of craggy mountain, silver stream and pine forest sweeping down to a mountain lake, the source of the River Lee. St Finbarre, the founder of Cork, established a monastery here in the 6th century. He had a hermitage on the island in **Gougane Barra Lake** (Lough an Ghugain), which is now approached by a short causeway. The small **chapel** on the island has fine stained-glass representations of obscure Celtic saints. A road runs through the park in a loop, but you're better off slowing down and walking the well-marked network of paths and **nature trails** through the forest.

The area cries out for a hostel, but the only place to air your hiking boots is the pricy **Gougane Barra Hotel** (☎ 026-47069; www.gougane barrahotel.com; per person from €72). There's an on-site restaurant (serving a hearty dinner for €42), a cafe and a pub next door; the hotel runs a summer theatre festival.

Getting There & Away

Bus connections to the park will make you feel like an explorer. Call the hotel for details and possible pick-up part way.

The Macroom **tourist office** (☎ 026-43280; ⊗ summer only) can help with accommodation in town if needed. Alternatively, take a **taxi** (☎ 026-41152) from Macroom for around €35, or possibly organise a tour from Bantry.

The park is signposted on the R584 after Ballingeary. Returning to the main road afterwards and continuing west, you'll travel over the Pass of Keimaneigh and emerge on the N71 at Ballylickey, midway between the Beara Peninsula and the Sheep's Head Peninsula.

MIZEN HEAD PENINSULA

From Skibbereen the road rolls west through Ballydehob, the gateway to the Mizen, and then on to the pretty village of Schull. Travelling on into the undulating countryside takes you through ever-smaller settlements to the village of Goleen.

Even here the Mizen isn't done. Increasingly narrow roads head further west to spectacular Mizen Head itself and to the hidden delights of Barleycove Beach and Crookhaven. Without a decent map you may well reach the same crossroads several times.

Heading back from Goleen, you can bear north to join the scenic coast road that follows the edge of Dunmanus Bay for most of the way to Durrus. At Durrus, one road heads for Bantry while the other turns west to Sheep's Head Peninsula.

SCHULL

pop 700

Schull (pronounced skul) is a small fishing village where a few vessels still keep the trade alive. The harbour has the satisfying clutter of a working port, and water sports play their part in making Schull a busy tourist attraction. It's particularly crowded during Calves Week, a sailing regatta usually held after the August bank holiday. Out of season the village is even more attractive in some ways, with a strong local community and curving, appealing Main St.

Orientation & Information

Most shops and B&Bs line the long Main St.

There's no tourist office, but a very useful booklet, *Schull Visitor's Guide*, can be obtained from hotels, some shops and @Your Service, and there's an excellent **website** (www.schull.ie).

AIB Bank on Main St has an ATM and bureau de change.

@Your Service (☎ 028-28600; Main St; per 30/60min €3/6; ⏰ 10am-10pm summer, shorter hours winter) The de-facto community centre has internet access and tourist info.

Chapter One (☎ 028-27606; www.chapterone.ie; Main St; ⏰ daily) A good indie bookshop.

Sights

This is another one of those atmospheric Irish seaside towns that is best enjoyed simply walking the streets and down to the docks.

The Republic's only planetarium, the **Schull Planetarium** (☎ 028-28552; www.schullcommunitycollege.com; Colla Rd; adult/child €5/3.50), on the grounds of Schull Community College, has an 8m dome and a video and slide show. It was founded by a German visitor who was charmed by the town. A 45-minute **star show** starts at 4pm or 8pm during the rather complex opening hours; call to confirm times.

The planetarium is at the Goleen end of the village on Colla Rd. You can also reach it by walking along the foreshore path from the pier.

Activities

There are a number of **walks** in the area, including a 13km return trip up Mt Gabriel. It was once mined for copper, and there are Bronze Age remains and 19th-century mine shafts and chimneys. For a gentler stroll try the short 2km foreshore path from the pier out to Roaringwater Bay and a view of the nearby islands. These and other walking routes are outlined in *Schull Visitor's Guide*.

The **Schull Watersport Centre** (☎ 028-28554; The Pier) hires out sailing dinghies (€60 per half-day) and snorkelling gear (€15 per day), and can arrange sea-kayaking sessions (a two-hour session costs €30) plus other activities, like sailing lessons.

In addition to runing courses and dives to wreck and reef sites, **Divecology** (☎ 028-28943; www.divecology.com; Cooradarrigan) offers guided walks along the shore looking for spiny critters. Check around the dock for charter boats going out fishing.

Horse- and pony-trekking and trap rides are available at the **Ballycumisk Riding School** (☎ 028-37246, 087 961 6969; Ballycumisk), outside Schull on the way to Ballydehob, for €30 per hour.

Sleeping

Stanley House (☎ 028-28425; www.stanley-house.net; off Colla Rd; s/d €50/78) Just outside of town on a little knoll, this modern B&B has sweeping views of the water from its front lawn. The four rooms are comfortable and somehow the owners resisted the urge to use the rust-shaded colour scheme found elsewhere; here's it soothing coffees and creams.

Harbour View Hotel (☎ 028-28101; www.harbourview hotelschull.com; Main St; r €60-160; 🖥) Schull's swish new hotel has 30 modern rooms with flat-screen TVs and the like. Run by a local family, it has comfortable furniture, all produced in Cork, plus a relaxed vibe that prevents it from being a too-posh kind of place.

Corthna-Lodge Guesthouse (☎ 028-28517; www .corthna-lodge.net; Airhill; s/d from €65/90; 🖥) The pleasures come aplenty at this rambling modern home just outside the centre. There's an outdoor hot tub, sauna house and gym. Should you just need to pass out, the seven rooms have a sprightly decor and attractive furniture that will help you reawaken.

Grove House (☎ 028-28067; www.grovehouseschull .com; Colla Rd; s €75-120) This beautifully restored ivy-covered mansion is an elegant option. The house has lovely pine floors and is exquisitely decorated in an easygoing antiques-and-homemade-rugs style. It also has a restaurant (right). Enjoy time in the countrified gardens.

Eating

Schull has a popular **Sunday Country Market** (www .schullmarket.com; Pier Car Park; 🕑 Easter-Dec), which draws producers and purveyors from around the region.

`our pick` **Hackett's** (Main St; 🕑 lunch daily year-round, dinner Wed-Thu Jul-Aug, Fri & Sat year-round; bar meals €4-9, dinner €15-20) The town's social hub, Hackett's

rises above the norm with a creative pub menu of organic dishes prepared from scratch. Black-and-white photos and tin signs adorn the pub's crooked walls and there's a mishmash of old kitchen tables and benches on the worn stone floor. It's a democratic place, where swells mingle with crusty locals inside or out front on the sunny benches.

Newman's West (☎ 028-27776; www.tjnewmans.com; Main St; dishes €6-15; 🕑 9am-11pm; 🖥) This sailor-filled wine bar (with many good choices by the glass) and art gallery serves soup and salads and enormous chunky sandwiches filled with local cheese and salami. The daily Western Seaboard specials might include Bantry Bay mussels and chowder. The original pub, TJ Newman's, is a charmer.

Grove House (mains €15-24; 🕑 Wed-Mon Jul-Aug, Thu-Sat Sep-Jun) Meals are the real stars at this B&B (see left), which is open to nonguests for dinner. You might be surprised to see Swedish influences on the menu, until you realise the family has Swedish roots. Who knew herring could be this good? However, France is also represented in the vast hand-picked wine list.

Waterside Inn (☎ 028-28203; Main St; mains €17-28; 🕑 11am-9pm) The dark interior is a bit of a throwback to the '70s, but locals love this place and changes might cause a revolution. The menu makes a tour through local meat and seafood, many used in timeless preparations. If you shrink at the thought of another shrimp, have the well-marbled rib-eye steak.

FASTNET LIGHTHOUSE

The pictures will curl your toes: a huge lighthouse seemingly ready to be engulfed by a wave one might associate with something biblical, like Noah or the parting of the Red Sea.

The subject of these photos is the Fastnet Lighthouse, a huge structure that, despite a name that sounds like an internet cafe, has been shrugging off huge waves and general inundation since 1904. Widely considered the most perfectly engineered lighthouse in the world, Fastnet shines its light from a nub of rock in the middle of the ocean 15km south of Schull and 7km west of Clear Island. You can see its 48.5 height from large swaths of coast between Baltimore and Mizen Head.

One of the reasons so many remain in awe of the lighthouse is the ingenious design. It's built out of Cornish granite blocks, each a different shape from the next and each designed to lock into its neighbour. It's an amazing achievement for a time when all design was done by hand. That the lighthouse has remained unscathed in the face of Atlantic gales for over 100 years (previous lighthouses here were flops) is simply remarkable.

You can see photos of Fastnet Lighthouse under oceanic assault at **Tom Newman Photography** (☎ 028-28110; Post Office, Main St) in Schull, or look online. The **Mizen Head Signal Station** (p277) has excellent displays on the construction of the lighthouse and an example of one of the enormous custom-carved stones.

Getting There & Away

There are two buses daily from Cork to Schull (€17, 2½ hours), via Clonakilty and Skibbereen.

Getting Around

Parking in Schull is difficult in summer. There are three car parks: opposite the Harbour View Hotel, behind AIB Bank, and at Pier Rd.

For bus and taxi services, try **Betty Johnson's Bus Hire** (☎ 028-28410, 086 265 6078).

WEST OF SCHULL TO MIZEN HEAD

If you're driving or cycling, take the undulating coastal route from Schull to Goleen. On a clear day there are great views out to Clear Island and the Fastnet lighthouse (p275). The landscape becomes wilder around the hamlet of Toormore. From Goleen, roads run out to thrilling Mizen Head and to the picturesque harbour village of Crookhaven.

Take time to admire the old local houses that are made of stone, many now derelict in fields. While there's obviously no shortage of materials, building these houses to withstand Atlantic gales required enormous amounts of labour on the part of locals, already challenged by the unreliable fertility of the land.

Goleen

Tourism in the Goleen area is handled well by the local community, with the intriguing **Mizen Head Signal Station** (opposite) being a token of their commitment and imagination. In summer it hums with holidaymakers.

SLEEPING & EATING

Heron's Cove (☎ 028-35225; www.heronscove.com; Goleen; s/d €50/80) A delightful location, on the shores of the tidal inlet of Goleen Harbour, makes this fine restaurant and B&B a top choice. Rooms have been refurbished to a restful style and several have balconies overlooking the inlet. The small restaurant has an excellent menu of organic and local food. It's open from 7pm to 9.30pm April to October (and year-round for guests staying at the Heron's Cove). Mains are between €18 and €25. Book in summer.

Fortview House (☎ 028-35324; www.fortviewhouse.ie; Gurtyowen, Toormore; s/d €62/100; Mar-Nov) Out on its own, in terms of location, warmth *and* quality, this lovely house has five antique-filled, flower-themed bedrooms. Hospitable hostess Violet has the most infectious laugh ever, and her breakfast choice is gourmet standard, with eggs from cheerfully clucking hens in the garden. To get there, head along the road that turns off the R592 for Durrus about 1km northeast of Goleen.

Rock Cottage (☎ 028-35538; www.rockcottage.ie; Barnatonicane, Schull; s/d €100/140) This slate-clad Georgian hunting lodge has three rooms, which stylishly mix antique furniture and modern textiles for an elegant yet cheery effect. Rock Cottage is also a working 17-acre farm (you can commune with a sheep) and many of the ingredients on the evening set menu (€50) come from the surrounding fields. To find it, continue 1km up the road from Fortview House and go through the gate on your left.

GETTING THERE & AWAY

Bus Éireann (www.buseireann.ie) has two buses a day from Skibbereen (€9.50, 70 minutes) via Schull. Goleen is the end of the line for bus service on the peninsula.

Crookhaven

Onwards from Goleen, the westerly outpost of Crookhaven feels so remote that you imagine it's more easily reached by boat than by road. And so it is for some people – in summer there's a big yachting presence and Crookhaven bustles with life. Off season it's quiet.

In its heyday Crookhaven's natural harbour was an important anchorage. Mail from America was collected here, and sailing ships and fishing vessels found ready shelter. On the opposite shore the gaunt remains of quarry buildings, closed in 1939, lie embedded in the hillside, and are the source of many dubious yarns by locals in response to curious questions from visitors.

SLEEPING & EATING

Pints in the sunshine are the reward for venturing out on the crooked road to Crookhaven. (If it's raining, make that 'Pints by the fireplace…').

Galley Cove House (☎ 028-35137; www.galleycovehouse.com; s/d €55/90) A cheerful welcome complements the secluded location of this modern home, 2km from Crookhaven and with terrific views across the ocean. It's handy for Barleycove Beach, and the pine-floored rooms are clean, airy and filled with light.

O'Sullivan's Bar (☎ 028-35319; meals €5-15; kitchen noon-8pm) is a timeless building right on the harbour. Several generations' worth of picnic tables draw several generations of punters when there's even a hint of sun. Pub food like seafood chowder and fried shrimp is popular – and good.

Crookhaven Inn (☎ 028-35309; mains €5-20; ☼ 12.30-8pm Apr-Oct) Set discreetly back from the water, this stone cottage of a pub also has a bulwark of picnic tables outside. The food here is more ambitious; seafood, of course, is tops. In summer there are trad sessions many nights.

Brow Head

This is the southernmost point on the Irish mainland and is well worth the walk. As you leave Crookhaven, you'll notice a turn-off to the left marked 'Brow Head'. If travelling by car, park at the bottom of the hill – the track is very narrow and there's nowhere to pull over should you meet a tractor coming the other way. After 1km the road ends. Continue on a path to Brow Head where you'll see an **observation tower**, from which Guglielmo Marconi transmitted his first message (to Cornwall) that received a reply.

Barleycove

Simply spectacular! Vast sand dunes hemmed in by two long bluffs dissolve into the surf, forming western Cork's finest beach. Rarely crowded, it's a great place for youngsters, with gorgeous stretches of golden sand, a safe bathing area where a stream flows down to the sea, lifeguards in July and August, and a Blue Flag award marking the cleanliness of the water. Access is via a long boardwalk and pontoon, which protect the surrounding wetlands from the impact of visitors' feet. There's a car park at the edge of the beach, on the south side of the causeway on the road to Crookhaven.

Barleycove Beach Hotel (☎ 028-35234; www.barley covebeachhotel.com; Barleycove; r from €80, 2-bedroom self-catering per week €500) is a conundrum: it's a modern aberration spoiling the beautiful view but, then again, it's already built. A mere 200m away from the sand, the rooms are simply finished, with beach views, and there's a bar-restaurant with outdoor seating. Bring ear plugs – the bedroom walls are thin.

Near the beach on the other side of the bay, **Barleycove Holiday Park** (☎ 028-35302; Barleycove; campsite €20; ☼ mid-Apr–mid-Sep) is an ideally located camping ground with bike rental, shop and children's club.

Mizen Head Signal Station

Don't miss Ireland's most southwesterly point, the **Mizen Head Signal Station** (☎ 028-35225, 028-35115; www.mizenhead.ie; Mizen Head; adult/child €6/3.50; ☼ 10am-6pm daily Jun-Sep, 10.30am-5pm daily mid-Mar–May & Oct, 11am-4pm Sat & Sun Nov–mid-Mar), a complex built over 100 years ago to help warn ships off the rocks, which appear in the water around here like crushed ice in a cola.

Like many Victorian-era public works, it exudes the pride of the builders. From the visitors centre, you can take various pathways out to the station, culminating in the crossing of a spectacular **arched bridge** that spans a vast gulf in the cliffs. The views are simply stunning, with spurting plumes of white water in every direction. Beyond the bridge, and at the far point of the outer rock island, is the **signal station**, containing the keeper's quarters, engine room and radio room of the Mizen Head Fog Signal Station, completed in 1909 and destaffed and automated in 1993. You can see how the keepers lived and how the station worked, but the real rush (even among crowds on a busy day) is the sense of so much Atlantic beneath vast skies.

Back at the visitors centre is **Fastnet Hall**, with plenty of information about local ecology, history and the namesake lighthouse (p275). There's also a modest cafe.

NORTHSIDE OF THE PENINSULA

Although the landscape is less dramatic on this side of the peninsula, it's well worth driving along the coast road here for the great views out to Sheep's Head Peninsula and beyond to the magnificent Beara Peninsula.

Durrus
pop 900

Durrus is a perky little crossroads at the head of Dunmanus Bay and is a popular access point for both the Mizen Head and Sheep's Head Peninsulas.

Travel a world of plants at **Kilravock Garden** (☎ 027-61111; Ahakista Rd; adult/child €6/3; ☼ 10am-6.30pm Mon-Sat May-Sep), which has been transformed over two decades from a field of scrag and stone to a feast of exotic plants by one green-fingered couple.

Set in five acres of land, Georgian country house **Blairs Cove House** (☎ 027-61127; www.blair scove.ie; r €105-230; ☼ Mar-Jan) is centred around an exquisite courtyard. Rooms and self-catering apartments display elegance and style; you

COUNTY CORK

DURRUS CHEESE

If we were cows, we would be happy grazing in the rugged green fields of West Cork. Irish bovines must agree, because the area is a centre of excellence for artisan dairy production. If you want to see cheese-making in action, call in at **Durrus Cheese** (☎ 027-61100; www.durruscheese.com). Founder Jeffa Gill is happy to talk visitors through the process of making her much-lauded creamy, rich rounds, which are for sale. Be sure to call ahead if you want to visit (the best times are 10.30am to noon Thursday and Friday). Follow the Ahakista road out of Durrus for 500m; turn right at the church and keep going for 3km until you see the dairy's sign.

might think it belongs in a magazine. The **restaurant** (☒ dinner Tue-Sat, lunch Sunday Mar-Oct), in a chandeliered hall, offers a superb set three-course dinner (€56) with local produce given international treatment. Booking is advised.

Located on Dunmanus Bay, **Good Things Café** (☎ 027-61426; www.thegoodthingscafe.com; Ahakista Rd; lunch mains €10-20, dinner mains €21-38; ☒ 12.30-3pm & 7-9pm Thu-Mon mid-Jun–Dec) is a haven for foodies. The restaurant serves great contemporary dishes made with organic, locally sourced ingredients; think everything from a fluffy omelette with locally smoked haddock to grilled lobster. Tables on a vast terrace have views of nervous sheep. Popular cooking courses include a two-day 'miracle' program (€375) for those whose cooking skills stop after reading the microwave directions on the frozen meal.

BANTRY
pop 3300

Vast Bantry Bay, framed by the craggy Caha Mountains, draws your eye no matter where you are in Bantry. The tidy town has been on a long upswing from the 19th century, when poverty and mass emigration left entire swaths of land depopulated.

The last several decades have been more prosperous, thanks to commerce and the bay: you'll see Bantry oysters and mussels on menus throughout County Cork. Today it is a small and compact community that makes an essential break on your coastal journey.

The town narrowly missed a place in history in the late 18th century, when storms prevented Wolfe Tone's French fleet landing to join the United Irishmen's rebellion. A local Englishman, Richard White, was rewarded with a peerage for alerting the British military. His grand home is now Bantry's main attraction.

Orientation & Information

The two main roads into Bantry converge on Wolfe Tone Sq, where the pedestrianised central concourse boasts a **statue of Wolfe Tone** (see p38).

There's a **post office** on Blackrock Rd and an **AIB ATM** on Wolfe Tone Sq.

Bantry Bookshop (☎ 027-55946; Marino St) Large shop.

Bantry Laundrette (☎ 027-55858; ☒ 9.30am-6pm Mon-Fri, to 5.30pm Sat) In a small courtyard off Barrack St.

Fast.Net Business Services (☎ 027-51624; Bridge St; per 10/60 min €1/5; ☒ 9am-6pm Mon-Fri, 10am-5pm Sat).

Tourist office (☎ 027-50229; Wolfe Tone Sq; ☒ 9.15am-5pm Mon-Sat Apr-Oct) Based in the old courthouse.

Sights

With its melancholic air of faded gentility, 18th-century **Bantry House** (☎ 027-50047; www .bantryhouse.com; Bantry Bay; adult/child €10/3; ☒ 10am-6pm mid-Mar–Oct) makes for an intriguing visit. The house has belonged to the White family since 1729 and every room brims with treasures brought back from each generation's travels since then. The entrance is paved with mosaics from Pompeii, French and Flemish tapestries adorn the walls, and Japanese chests sit next to Russian shrines. Upstairs, worn bedrooms look out wanly over an astounding view of the bay – the 18th-century Whites had ring-side seats to the French armada. Experienced pianists are invited to tinkle the ivories of the ancient piano in the library. It's possible to stay the night in the wings (see p280).

The **gardens** of Bantry House are its great glory. Lawns sweep down from the front of the house towards the sea, and the formal Italian garden has an enormous 'stairway to the sky', offering spectacular views.

In the former stables you'll find the **1796 French Armada Exhibition Centre**, with its powerful account of the doomed French invasion of Ireland. The fleet was torn apart by storms; one frigate, La Surveillante, was scuttled by its own crew and today lies 30m down at the bottom of the bay.

Bantry House is 1km southwest of the town centre (a 10-minute walk) on the N71.

COUNTY CORK

Festivals

West Cork Chamber Music Festival (www.westcork music.ie) Held at Bantry House for a week in June/July, when the house closes to the public. The garden, craft shop and tearoom remain open.

Sleeping
BUDGET

Eagle Point Camping (☎ 027-50630; www.eaglepoint camping.com; Glengarriff Rd, Ballylickey; campsites from €28; ☺ May-Sep) An enviable location at the end of a filigreed promontory 6km north of Bantry makes this a popular site. Most of the 125 spots have sea views, and there's direct access to the pebbly beaches nearby.

MIDRANGE

Atlanta House (☎ 027-50237; www.atlantahouse.ie; Main St; s/d €40/70; ☐) You won't get a more central stay than in this town house, which has good-sized rooms and firm beds piled high with pillows, perfect for tossing at your companion. It's the best-value place in town; all rooms have high-speed internet access.

Mill B&B (☎ 027-50278; Glengarriff Rd; www.the-mill.net; s/d from €50/80; ☺ Easter-Oct) This modern house, on the immediate outskirts of town, oozes individuality. The irrepressible landlady, Tosca, is just part of it. The rooms are a riot of knick-knacks, and the spacious dining room has a wonderful collection of Indonesian puppets and Tosca's art to accompany solid breakfasts.

Bantry Bay Hotel (☎ 027-50062; www.bantrybayhotel .ie; Wolfe Tone Sq; r €50-140; ☐) Most of the 14 rooms overlook the square, with glimpses of the bay. Nothing about the decor will surprise and, in fact, there's nothing to keep you in your room and forgo local explorations. The bar's maritime theme may put you in the mood to hoist the mizzen-mast.

Ballylickey House (☎ 027-50071; www.ballylickey manorhouse.com; Ballylickey; r €90-160; ☺ Mar-Nov; ☺) Possessing a name that rolls off the tongue, Ballylickey is a beautiful manor house with manicured lawns overlooking the bay. There are two choices for the night: rooms in the house or cute cottages set round a swimming pool. All are spacious and comfortably furnished.

TOP END

Sea View House Hotel (☎ 027-50073; www.seaview househotel.com; Ballylickey; s €85-95, d €150-170) You'll

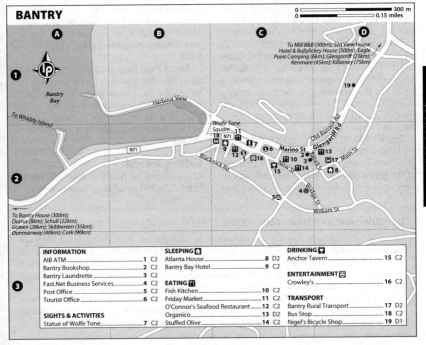

find everything you'd expect from a luxury hotel here: country-house ambience, tastefully decorated public rooms, expansive service and 25 cosy, posh bedrooms. The hotel is on the N71, 5km northeast of Bantry.

Bantry House (☎ 027-50047; www.bantryhouse.com; Bantry Bay; r €140-250; ♈ Apr-Oct) Bantry House's guest rooms, decorated in pale hues and a mixture of antiques and contemporary furnishings, are luxurious places to while away the hours. Rooms 22 and 25 are double winners, with views of both the garden and the bay. Enhance the dream by playing croquet, lawn tennis or billiards and lounging in the house's library once the doors are shut to the public. And if you see French ships offshore, go and tell someone immediately!

Eating

Wolfe Tone Sq takes on a heady mix of aromas for the **Friday Market**, which draws in the masses – both vendors and shoppers – from a wide area.

Stuffed Olive (☎ 027-55883; New St; meals €4-7; ♈ 8am-5pm Mon-Sat) This exquisite bakery and deli has a fine coffee bar and stools along a narrow counter in the sunny front window. Luscious baked goods are displayed like, well, a bunch of tarts. Find your picnic lunch here and nab one of the excellent bottles of wine.

O'Connor's Seafood Restaurant (☎ 027-50221; www.oconnorseafood.com; Wolfe Tone Sq; lunch €7-15, dinner €20-30; ♈ lunch & dinner daily Mar-Oct, Tue-Sat Nov-Feb) The tank full of lobsters and the three wooden yachts in the window give the game away – award-winning O'Connor's offers Bantry seafood at its posh best. It's an exquisite experience and one to savour.

Organico (☎ 027-51391; 2 Glengarriff Rd; lunch €8-15; ♈ 9.30am-5.30pm Mon-Sat; 🛜) The milk in the organic latte here is fairtrade – just one example of the green ethos prevalent throughout this very attractive bakery–deli–cafe. Enjoy fine baked goods throughout the day; at lunch there's an array of daily specials. The soups are hearty and fresh, the salads innovative. Everything is meat-free but not dairy-free: cheese lovers, enjoy!

our pick Fish Kitchen (☎ 027-56651; New St; mains €8-20; ♈ noon-9pm Tue-Sat) Fittingly located above Bantry's fish vendors, the Fish Kitchen is a welcome addition to town. Everything is unfussy, from the decor to the food styles to the prices, but one thing is exacting: the care shown in the kitchen. The finest mussels, scallops, haddock and more are prepared perfectly.

Drinking & Entertainment

Crowley's (☎ 027-50029; Wolfe Tone Sq) One of the best bars for music, Crowley's has traditional bands on Wednesday nights.

Anchor Tavern (☎ 027-50012; New St) Old salts literally anchor the bar; enjoy a pint and ponder the many old nautical instruments on display – although they may not help you get home after a few.

Getting There & Away

Bus Éireann (www.buseireann.ie) has eight buses daily Monday to Saturday (four on Sunday) between Bantry and Cork (€15.50, two hours). There's one or two daily to Glengarriff. Heading north to the Ring of Beara, Kenmare and Killarney require backtracking through Cork.

Bantry Rural Transport (☎ 027-52727; www.ruraltransport.ie; 5 Main St) runs a useful series of circular routes to Dunmanway, Durrus, Goleen, Schull, Skibbereen and outlying villages. There's a set price of €4/6 one-way/return. Service is not frequent; check the website for details.

Getting Around

Bicycles can be hired at **Nigel's Bicycle Shop** (☎ 027-52657; Glengarriff Rd; per day/week €15/60).

DETOUR: SHIPLAKE MOUNTAIN HOSTEL

Far up a twisting track lies one of Cork's most unusual hostels. The IHH-affiliated **Shiplake Mountain Hostel** (☎ 023-884 5750; www.shiplakemountainhostel.com; Dunmanway; campsite €7, dm €18, d €45-50; ♈ Apr-Oct) consists of three brightly coloured gypsy caravans, each with a double bed squeezed in, two dorm rooms in an old stone cottage and a yurt. The owners take their environmental responsibility seriously – the showers use local spring water and you can have the hostel's own duck eggs for breakfast. They can pick you up from nearby Dunmanway, which has an ATM and grocery shops. Once here, chase the ducks, go for walks (scads of maps and advice available), borrow a bike (free) or gather round the stove in the common room for a good yarn.

WALK: MT SEEFIN

Make time for an exhilarating 1km stride to the summit of Mt Seefin (345m). It's not challenging, but this is open country, where mist can easily descend, so go properly equipped. There's a path, but it fades out in places.

The ascent begins at the top of the Goat's Path Rd, about 2km between Gortnakilly and Kilcrohane. On the roadside is an out-of-place imitation of Michelangelo's *Pietà* – follow the track that starts opposite the parking area on the south side of the sculpture. Keep to the path along the rocky spine of the hill until you reach a depression. Follow a path up a short gully to the right of a small cliff and then continue, again on the rocky spine of the broad ridge, to a trig point on the summit. Retracing your steps can be challenging. From the trig point it's best to keep high along the broad ridge and not drift too far to the left.

SHEEP'S HEAD PENINSULA

The least visited of Cork's three peninsulas, Sheep's Head Peninsula has a charm all its own – and plenty of sheep. There are good seascapes to appreciate from the loop road running along most of its length. A good link road with terrific views, called the Goat's Path Rd, runs between Gortnakilly and Kilcrohane (on the north and south coasts respectively), over the western flank of Mt Seefin.

Ahakista (Atha an Chiste) consists of a couple of pubs and a few houses stretched out along the R591. An ancient **stone circle** is signposted at the southern end of Ahakista; access is via a short pathway. The peninsula's other village is **Kilcrohane**, 6km to the southwest, beside a fine **beach**. You can get pub food in both villages.

For more information about the area, take a look at the **website** (www.thesheepshead.com).

Walking & Cycling

Walkers and cyclists will relish the chance to stretch their legs and enjoy the windswept moors, wild gorse, foxgloves and fuchsias in beautiful solitude. On the Goat's Path Rd, the steep Bantry–Kilcrohane section requires firm thighs; the Ahakista–Durrus stretch is more gentle. Bantry's tourist office (see p278) can book accommodation along the Sheep's Head Way, has lots of info on the peninsula and sells a map and guide (€12.50).

The **Sheep's Head Way** is an 88km-long walking route around the peninsula, on roads and tracks where possible. Use Ordnance Survey maps 85 and 88 to navigate your way around (see www.osi.ie to purchase maps). There are no campsites on Sheep's Head Peninsula; camping along the route is allowed with permission from the landowner.

The 120km **Sheep's Head Cycle Route** runs anticlockwise from Ballylickey (north of Bantry), round the coastline of Sheep's Head Peninsula, back onto the mainland and down to Ballydehob. There are opportunities to take short cuts or alternative routes (eg over the Goat's Path Rd, or along the coast from Ahakista to Durrus). The widely available brochure, *The Sheep's Head Cycle Route,* has full details.

Getting There & Away

Bantry Rural Transport (☎ 027-52727; www.ruraltransport.ie; 5 Main St, Bantry) buses run a circular route on various days, going via the Goat's Path Rd to Kilcrohane and Durrus (one-way/return €4/6).

BEARA PENINSULA (RING OF BEARA)

The Beara Peninsula is the third major 'ring' in the west. Dingle and Kerry are comfortably in the number one and two spots respectively, leaving Beara in third place, which is just about right.

The south side, along Bantry Bay, is a series of interesting working fishing villages and scenery that's mild on the eyes. The north side, in contrast, is often a stunner, with craggy drives in and out of the nooks and crannies of the peninsula. A plus is that many of these roads are off the tourist trail.

Other highlights include a thrillingly wobbly cable car at the tip of the peninsula, which

---

BEARA WAY

This moderately easy, 196km walk forms a loop around the Beara Peninsula. The peninsula is relatively unused to mass tourism and makes a pleasant contrast with the Iveragh Peninsula to the north.

Part of the walk, between Castletownbere and Glengarriff, follows the route taken by Donal O'Sullivan and his band after the English took his castle following an 11-day siege in 1602. At Glengarriff, O'Sullivan met up with other families and set out on a journey north, hoping to reunite with other remaining pockets of Gaelic resistance. Of the 1000 or so men who set out that winter, only 30 completed the trek. Bundle up.

The Beara Way mostly follows old roads and tracks and rarely rises above 340m. There's no official start or finish point and the route can be walked in either direction. It could easily be reduced to seven days by skipping Bere and Dursey Islands and, if you start at Castletownbere, you could reach Kenmare in five days or less.

There's a good downloadable guide to the walk (and the peninsula itself) at www.beara tourism.com.

---

takes you and the sheep out to tiny Dursey Island and exhilarating hill walking requiring some skill and commitment, as well as proper clothing and navigational experience.

The 196km **Beara Way** is a signposted walk linking Glengarriff with Kenmare (in Kerry) via Castletownbere, Bere Island, Dursey Island and the north side of the peninsula; for more details, see above. The 138km **Beara Way Cycle Route** takes a similar direction, passing through all the villages on Beara via small lanes.

Orientation & Information

A small part of the peninsula lies in Kerry, but is dealt with here for the convenience of people travelling the Ring of Beara. Castletownbere in Cork and Kenmare in Kerry make good bases for exploring the area.

You can easily drive the 137km around the coast in one day, but you would miss the spectacular **Healy Pass** road (R574), which cuts across the peninsula from Cork to Kerry. In fact, if pressed for time, skip the rest and do the pass.

The following towns are described in a route that assumes you're starting from Glengarriff and working your way clockwise to Kenmare.

GLENGARRIFF
pop 1100

Hidden deep in the Bantry Bay area, Glengarriff (Gleann Garbh) is an attractive village that snares plenty of passers-by in need of sweaters.

The rough, rocky Caha Mountains make for good hill walking. There are plenty of gen-

tler strolls, too, in mature oak woodlands and through the coastal Blue Pool Amenity Area, where seals, perched on submerged rocks, appear to levitate on the water.

In the second half of the 19th century, Glengarriff became a popular retreat for prosperous Victorians, who sailed from England, took the train to Bantry, then chugged over to the village in a paddle steamer. By 1850 the road to Kenmare had been blasted through the mountains and the link with Killarney was established. Today Glengarriff lies on the main Cork to Killarney road (N71).

Information

There's a **Fáilte Ireland tourist office** (☎ 027-63084; Main St; ⏰ 9.30am-1pm & 2-5pm Jun-Aug) and a privately run **tourist office** (⏰ 10am-1pm & 2-6pm Mon-Sat Jun-Aug) beside the Blue Pool Ferry ticket booth. See www.glengarriff.ie for more local info.

Sights

If you're becalmed in town, wander down past the Blue Ferry pier and enjoy good **nature walks** along the coast. Signs with maps show you your options. Try to spot a seal.

GARINISH (ILNACULLIN) ISLAND

The magical Italianate **garden** (☎ 027-63040; adult/senior & child €4/2.50; ⏰ 9.30am-6.30pm Mon-Sat & 11am-6.30pm Sun Jul-Aug, 10am-6.30pm Mon-Sat & 11am-6.30pm Sun Apr-Jun & Sep, 10am-4.30pm Mon-Sat & 1-5pm Sun Mar & Oct, last admission 1hr before closing) on Garinish Island is the top sight in Glengarriff. Subtropical plants flourish in the rich soil and warm climate. The camellias, magnolias and rhododendrons especially provide a seasonal blaze of colour. There are good views from a **Grecian temple** at the end of a cypress avenue, and a spectacular panorama from the top of the 19th-century **Martello tower**, built to watch out for a possible Napoleonic invasion.

This little miracle of a place was created in the early 20th century, when the island's owner, Annan Bryce, commissioned the English architect Harold Peto to design him a garden on the then-barren outcrop.

Garinish Island is reached by taking a 10-minute boat trip past islands and colonies of basking seals. The ferry companies leave every 20 to 30 minutes when the garden is open. The return boat fare (adult €10 to €12, child €6) doesn't include entry to the gardens.

Blue Pool Ferry (☎ 027-63333) From a little cove near the centre of the village.

Harbour Queen Ferries (☎ 027-63116, 087 234 5861; www.harbourqueenferry.com) From the pier opposite the Eccles Hotel.

BAMBOO PARK
Bamboo Park (☎ 027-63570; www.bamboo-park.com; adult/child €5/free; ⏱ 9am-7pm) flourishes thanks to

Glengarriff's mild, frost-free climate. It has 12 hectares of exotic plants, including palm trees and tree ferns, and coastal woodland walks.

GLENGARRIFF WOODS NATURE RESERVE
The 300-hectare ancient **woodland** lining Glengarriff's glacial valley was owned by the White family of Bantry House in the 18th century. The thick tree cover maintains humid conditions that allow ferns and mosses to flourish.

The woodlands and bogs are also home to Ireland's only arboreal ant and the rare and protected Kerry slug. If you're lucky (have camera ready so you can share your slug with friends and family), you'll see these spotty cream-coloured gastropods on the lichen carpet munching after rainfall.

There are four marked trails through the reserve, separately covering woodland, mountain, river and meadow, and you can combine them to form one big walk (8.5km, three to four hours).

To get to the woods, leave Glengarriff on the N71 towards Kenmare. The entrance is about 1km along on the west.

BEARA PENINSULA (RING OF BEARA)

Sleeping

Dowlings Caravan & Camping Park (☎ /fax 027-63154; Castletownbere Rd; campsites from €12; ☺ Easter–Oct) This well-set-up park, 4km west of Glengarriff on the road to Castletownbere, enjoys a woodland setting. Amenities include a games room and a licensed bar staging traditional music most nights from June to August.

Murphy's Village Hostel (☎ 027-63555; Main St; dm/d €15/50; ☺ Jun–Sep) Right at the heart of Glengarriff, Murphy's is a quiet little place that's about as low-key as you can get. Rooms are clean and are furnished with wooden bunk beds.

Casey's Hotel (☎ 027-63010; www.caseyshotelglen garriff.ie; Main St; s/d from €60/100; ☐) Old-fashioned Casey's has been welcoming guests since 1884 and is proud of such past visitors as Éamon de Valera. The 19 rooms have been modernised a bit but are still small. It's got gobs of atmosphere, though, and the vast terrace is a treat.

Eccles Hotel (☎ 027-63003; www.eccleshotel.com; Glengarriff Harbour; r €100-140; ☐) Just east of the centre, the Eccles has a long and distinguished history (since 1745), counting the British War Office, Thackeray, George Bernard Shaw and WB Yeats as former occupants. The decor is blandly modern, but the 66 rooms are big and bright and a pleasant air of nostalgia hangs about the place. Ask for a bayside room on the 4th floor.

Eating & Drinking

Hawthorne Bar (☎ 027-63440; Main St; bar meals €5-10, dinner €14-20) This agreeable pub may not have changed in about 40 years. Its dining room, the Rainbow Restaurant, serves the same menu in a more formal setting. Sitting on the streetside benches and tucking into Bantry Bay mussels or seafood chowder with soda bread is a fine way to spend a sunny evening.

P Harrington's (☎ 027-63021; Main St) This pub has a prime position at the junction of the N71 and the Beara Rd. Settle into one of the comfy outside benches with a pint and watch addled tourists freeze up and bring transport for this region of Ireland to a halt.

Getting There & Away

Bus Éireann (www.buseireann.ie) has up to three buses daily to Bantry and on to Cork (€17, 2½ hours).

GLENGARRIFF TO CASTLETOWNBERE

The striations of the peninsula's underlying bedrock become evident as you drive west from Glengarriff towards Castletownbere. On the highest hills, Sugarloaf Mountain and Hungry Hill, rock walls known as 'benches' snake backwards and forwards across the slopes. They can make walking on these mountains quite challenging, and dangerous in fog. Take a map (Ordnance Survey Discovery series 84 and 85 cover the area) and compass if venturing into the hills, and seek local advice.

Adrigole is a scattered strip of houses. The **West Cork Sailing Centre** (☎ 027-60132; www.westcork sailing.com; The Boat House, Adrigole) offers numerous ways to get out on the water. A half-day on a skippered sailing boat costs €160; kayak rental is €12 per hour.

Hungry Hill Lodge (☎ 027-60228; www.hungryhill lodge.com; Adrigole; campsites €15, dm €15, s/d €25/44; ☺ Mar–Dec) is a well-situated hostel with excellent facilities, just beyond Adrigole village. It's in a peaceful location; amenities include bike hire, scuba trips, an adjoining trad pub and a nearby minimarket.

CASTLETOWNBERE & AROUND
pop 850

Castletownbere (Baile Chais Bhéara) is a fishing town first and a pause in the road for tourists second. And that gives it a real appeal for those looking for the 'real' Ireland. That's not to say it doesn't have its popular sights, like a bar famous to millions.

The **tourist office** (☎ 027-70054; www.bearatourism .com; Main St; ☺ Tue–Sat) is just outside the Church of Ireland. On Main St and The Square, you'll find ATMs as well as cafes, pubs and grocery stores.

Sights

On a lonely hill 2km from Castletownbere, the impressive **Derreenataggart Stone Circle**, consisting of 10 stones, can be found close to the roadside. It's signposted at a turn-off to the right at the western end of town. There are a number of other standing stones in the surrounding area.

Looming offshore, **Bere Island** is a place that makes Castletownbere seem like the big city. Only 12km by 7km, it has a couple of hundred permanent residents but attracts scores more to summer holiday homes. There are bits of old ruins and some craggy coves good for swimming. A **ferry** (☎ 027-75009; www.bereisland ferries.com; passenger/car return €8/25; ☺ hourly Mon-Sat Jun-Aug, less often Sun & Sep-May) leaves from town.

Activities

Bike N Beara Bike Hire (☎ 027-74898, 086 128 0307; per day from €15) Can drop off bikes to your accommodation; enquire at SuperValu on Main St.

Sea Kayaking West Cork (☎ 027-70692, 086 309 8654; www.seakayakingwestcork.com) Will take you out for a paddle for €45 per half-day.

Sleeping & Eating

Rodeen B&B (☎ 027-70158; www.rodeencountryhouse .com; s/d €45/70; ⊗ Mar–Oct) A delightful six-room haven, tucked away above the eastern approach to town. The musical-instrument-filled house has stunning sea views and is surrounded by gardens full of crumbling Delphic columns. Flowers from the garden grace the breakfast table, and there are home-baked scones with honey from landlady Ellen's bees.

Jack Patrick's (☎ 027-70319; Main St; mains €8-20; ⊗ noon-3pm) Run by one of the top local butchers – the shop is next door – this simple restaurant is just the choice if you want to get out of your shell and have some meat. Steaks and chops and other meaty mains, like bacon and cabbage, are on offer here.

Olde Bakery (☎ 027-70869; Castletown House; mains €13-21; ⊗ 5.30-9.30pm daily, plus noon-4.30pm Sun) One of the best restaurants in town, the Olde Bakery serves hearty portions of top regional seafood to locals who won't settle for seconds – unless it's a second helping. A few tables out front are just the place to be on a long evening.

Taste (☎ 027-71842; Main St; ⊗ 9.30am-6pm Mon-Fri, 10am-5pm Sat) A wide range of local foods, including creamy Milleens cheese, are on offer. There are creative sandwiches to take away from this inviting shop just off The Square.

Drinking

our pick **McCarthy's Bar** (☎ 027-70014; Main St) If you're carrying a copy of the late Pete McCarthy's bestseller, *McCarthy's Bar*, you'll be excited to see the front-cover photo sitting in three dimensions on Main St. McCarthy's is a grocery as well as a pub, so if you fancy a tin of peaches and a can of corn (check the sell-by date) to go with your Beamish, you've come to the right place. There's frequent live music and a wicked wee snug inside the door.

Getting There & Away

Bus Éireann (www.buseireann.ie) has up to three buses daily to Bantry and on to Cork (€19;

3¼ hours). Check signage at the bus stop on The Square for occasional private buses along the peninsula or ask at the tourist office.

DURSEY ISLAND

pop 60

Tiny Dursey Island, at the end of the peninsula, is reached by Ireland's only **cable car** (adult/child return €4/1; ⊗ 9-11am, 2.30-5pm & 7-8pm Mon-Sat, 9-10am, 1-2.30pm & 7-7.30pm Sun year-round, plus 4-5pm Sun Jun-Aug), which sways 30m above Dursey Sound. In a perfect photo op, livestock take precedence over humans in the queue. The later times shown above are for returning only; bikes are not allowed.

The island, just 6.6km long by 1.5km wide, is a wild bird and whale sanctuary, and dolphins can sometimes be seen swimming in the waters around it. There's no accommodation, but it's easy to find somewhere to camp.

The **Beara Way** loops round the island for 11km, and the signal tower is an obvious destination for a short walk.

NORTHSIDE OF THE BEARA

The entire north side is the scenic highlight of the Beara Peninsula. A series of roads, some single-lane tracks, snake around the ins and outs of the weathered, rugged coast. Boulder-strewn fields tumble dramatically towards the ocean and it's blissfully remote – your only company along some stretches are flocks of sheep and the odd sheepdog.

Allihies

This edge-of-the-world village has dramatic vistas and plenty of walks, where you will get lungfuls of bracing air.

Copper-ore deposits were first identified on the far Beara in 1810. While mining quickly brought wealth to the Puxley family who owned the land, it brought low wages and dangerous, unhealthy working conditions for the labour force, which at one time numbered 1300. Experienced Cornish miners were brought into the area, and the dramatic ruins of engine houses replicate those of Cornwall's coastal tin mines. As late as the 1930s, more than 30,000 tonnes of pure copper were exported annually, but by 1962 the last mine was closed.

You'll see the most **mine ruins** along the R575 north of the village; signs mark the spots. In town the **Allihies Copper Mine Museum** (☎ 027-73218; adult/child €5/3; ⊗ 10am-5pm daily May-Sep, Sat

& Sun Oct-Apr) is the result of years of work by the community and has engaging exhibits plus a summer cafe housed in an old wooden church.

There are inviting pubs and B&Bs in Allihies (Na hAilichí), and a small tourist information kiosk, beside the church, opens in summer.

The **Allihies Village Hostel** (☎ 027-73107; www .allihieshostel.net; dm/d from €18/50), run by father-and-daughter team Michael and Sarah, is a model hostel. Gleaming from top to bottom, it has smart wood-floored dorms and public areas, a courtyard and a barbecue area. Michael is a mine of information on the area and can advise on local walks and pony trekking.

Also in town, **Sea View B&B** (☎ 027-73004; www .seaviewallihies.com; s/d €45/75) has 10 cosy rooms in a tidy yellow building. Many have views north over the waters and some are quite large. The spread at breakfast will help fuel your rambles.

Among the several pubs, **O'Neil's** (☎ 027-73008; meals €7-15; ☺ kitchen noon-9pm) is the most appealing, with a tidy red and blue facade and some polished wooden benches and picnic tables out front for enjoying the views. Pub food intermingles with fresh local seafood.

Eyeries to Lauragh

Heading north and east from Allihies, the beautiful coastal road (R575), with hedges of fuchsias and rhododendrons, twists and turns for about 12km to **Eyeries**. This cluster of brightly coloured houses overlooking Coulagh Bay is often used as a film set. The town is also home to **Milleens cheese** (☺ 027-74079; www .milleenscheese.com), from pioneering producer Veronica Steele. She welcomes visitors to her farm; phone ahead.

From Eyeries, forsake the R571 for the even smaller coast roads (lanes really) to the north and east. This is the Beara at its most spectacular – and intimate. Tiny coves are like pearls in a sea of rocks, the views of the Ring of Kerry to the north sublime.

Rejoin the R571 at the crossroads of **Ardgroom** (Ard Dhór). As you head east towards Lauragh, look for signs pointing to the Ardgroom **stone circle**, an unusual Bronze Age monument with nine tall, thin uprights. There's muddy parking at the end of a 500m-long narrow approach lane. The circle is visible about 200m away and a path leads to

it across bogland. A crude sign says simply 'money' and a US dollar under a rock gives a hint.

Lauragh (Laith Reach), situated northeast of Ardgroom, is in County Kerry. It's home to the **Derreen Gardens** (☎ 064-83103; adult/child €6/3; ☺ 10am-6pm Apr-Oct), planted by the fifth Lord Lansdowne around the turn of the 20th century. Mossy paths weave through an abundance of interesting plants, including spectacular New Zealand tree ferns and red cedars, and you may see seals on the shore.

From Lauragh, a serpentine road travels 11km south across the other-worldly **Healy Pass** and down to Adrigole, offering spectacular views of the rocky inland scenery. About 1km west of Lauragh, along the R571, is a road to **Glanmore Lake**, with the remains of an old hermitage on a tiny island in the middle. There are walking opportunities in the area, but gaining access can be problematic: ask locally for advice.

SLEEPING & EATING

The small road just west of Lauragh off the R575 leads into a lovely valley along Glanmore Lake.

Glanmore Lake Hostel (☎ 064-83181; www.anoige .ie; Glanmore Lake; dm adult/child from €17/14; ☺ end-May-end-Sep) A rural atmosphere and an engaging location at the heart of Glanmore make this remote An Óige hostel an appealing place. It's in Glanmore's old boarding school, 5km from the R571.

Josie's Lakeview House (☎ 064-83155; Glanmore Lake; lunch €6-15, dinner mains €15-25) Captivating lake views accompany your food. Josie's sits on a hill overlooking Glanmore Lake. Choose from salads and sandwiches for lunch, cakes at tea or heartier rack of lamb and local seafood specials at night. Josie's is 4km from the R571; follow the signs.

GETTING THERE & AWAY

The bus service in this area is limited. Contact **Bus Éireann** (☎ 021-450 8188; www.buseireann.ie) for times and prices of the summer services between Kenmare and Castletownbere via Lauragh.

Lauragh to Kenmare

Leaving Lauragh, take the R573, which hugs the coast, rejoining the more no-nonsense R571 at Tuosist for the 16km run east to Kenmare in Kerry (p309).

NORTHERN CORK

Northern Cork lacks the glamour and romance of the county's coastal regions, but the area's towns and villages have a refreshing rural integrity.

DONKEY SANCTUARY

Reason enough to head this way, the **our pick** Donkey Sanctuary (☎ 022-48398; www .thedonkeysanctuary.ie; Liscarroll; admission free; ☼ 9am-4.30pm Mon-Fri, 10am-5pm Sat & Sun) is a wonderful nonprofit institution dedicated to Ireland's iconic beasts of burden. Naturally bedraggled looking, the small, sturdy steeds of the Irish countryside are also often abused by thoughtless owners either out of meanness or simply because economic conditions have made it too hard to care for them properly.

At this large farm, abandoned and abused donkeys are given a home for life. There are pastures, food, medical care and virtually no demands on them. It's a splendid operation and one most visitors end up supporting – especially after they've seen one of the winsome critters up close through the self-guided tour of the pastures and barns.

The sanctuary is in the small town of Liscarroll, which is on the R522, 13km west of Buttevant on the main N20 highway to Cork. There are some scenic ruins of a castle close to the sanctuary.

MALLOW

Mallow (Mala) is a prosperous town located in the Blackwater Valley on the main N20 highway. Visitors to its spa in the 19th century christened it the 'Bath of Ireland'. The comparison is far-fetched these days, though the architecture in the town centre hints at its former grandeur.

The **tourist office** (☎ 022-42222; www.eastcork tourism.com; ☼ 9.30am-1pm & 2-5.30pm Mon-Fri) can help with accommodation and activities.

In the town itself, you can spot white fallow deer around the imposing ruins of **Mallow Castle** (Bridge St), which dates back to 1585. Also look out for the distinctive **Clock House** (Bridge St), designed by an amateur architect after an Alpine holiday – you'd never guess.

AROUND MALLOW

At Buttevant, about 20km north of Mallow on the N20, are the ruins of a 13th-century **Franciscan abbey**. Between Mallow and Killarney, you might want to divert to see the well-preserved remains of 17th-century **Kanturk Castle**. Inhabited only by crows these days, the castle acted as both fortification and country house from the early 17th century to 1906.

Red deer scamper around the 400 acres of landscaped gardens at **Doneraile Park** (☼ dawn-8pm), 13km northeast of Mallow. There are woodland walkways, cascades and playgrounds to keep the kids happy.

COUNTY CORK

County Kerry

Kerry is the destination of choice for legions of travellers each year, drawn to Ireland's most iconic sights: impossibly crenulated coasts, endless fields of green criss-crossed by stone walls, and misty peaks and bogs where *anything* might be sheltering.

Killarney is where many start. Well schooled in serving visitors' needs, it can shroud tourists in a jet-lagged blur of fine seafood, trad sessions in pubs and the occasional dawn discovery that one is wearing a new sweater from the night before. But Killarney is also a place of remarkable beauty, boasting one of Ireland's most scenic national parks right out the back door.

Heading to the coast poses the first great Kerry decision: Dingle Peninsula or Ring of Kerry? The fortunate simply say 'both'. But for most travellers on a schedule it comes down to one or the other. The Ring of Kerry around the Iveragh Peninsula is the larger of the two and has the greater sweep of land, with windswept coasts and islands with ancient histories, such as Valentia and Skellig Michael.

In contrast, the compact little Dingle Peninsula is like much of Ireland's coast boiled down to a reduction of ancient sites, evocative beauty and little glimpses of a hard and always unforgiving land. Here, the namesake town of Dingle is the centre of everything. Its seafood restaurants vie for attention with its ancient yarn-filled pubs.

How to enjoy Kerry is up to you. And when you need to escape from everyone else who flocks here in summer and faces the same question, remember there's always a mountain pass, an isolated cove or an untrodden trail where you can find your own answers.

HIGHLIGHTS

- **Placid Sheep** The sheep are oblivious to the perilous beauty of the Dingle Peninsula (p317)

- **Setting Sail** Heading out for the Upper Lake in Killarney National Park (p295)

- **Island Hopping** The rocky Skelligs (p305) and evacuated Blaskets (p327)

- **Oceans Infinity** Dingle town's array of superb seafood restaurants (p318)

- **Tenors & Spoons** Impromptu trad music and singing in a Ring of Kerry pub (p300) and the county's many storytellers

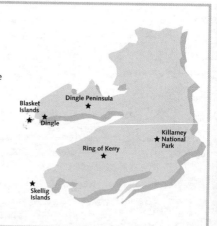

- Blasket Islands
- Dingle Peninsula
- Dingle
- Killarney National Park
- Ring of Kerry
- Skellig Islands

■ POPULATION: 140,000   ■ AREA: 4746 SQ KM

KILLARNEY

pop 16,900

Killarney is a well-oiled tourism machine in the middle of the sublime scenery of its namesake national park. Its studied twee-ness is renowned. However, it has many charms beyond the obvious proximity to lakes, waterfalls, woodland and moors dwarfed by 1000m-plus peaks. In a town that's been practising the tourism game for over 250 years, competition keeps standards high, and visitors on all budgets can expect to find good restaurants, fine pubs and plenty of accommodation.

Mobbed in summer, Killarney is perhaps at its best in the late spring and early autumn when the weather allows enjoyment of its outdoor charms and the crowds have thinned.

HISTORY

Killarney and its surrounds have been inhabited probably since the Neolithic period and were certainly important Bronze Age settlements, based on the copper ore mined on Ross Island. Killarney changed hands between warring tribes, the most notable of which were the Fir Bolg ('bag men'), expert stonemasons who built forts (including Staigue) and developed Ogham script.

In the 7th century St Finian founded a monastery on Inisfallen Island, and Killarney became a focus for Christianity in the region. The O'Donoghue clan later ousted the Gaels,

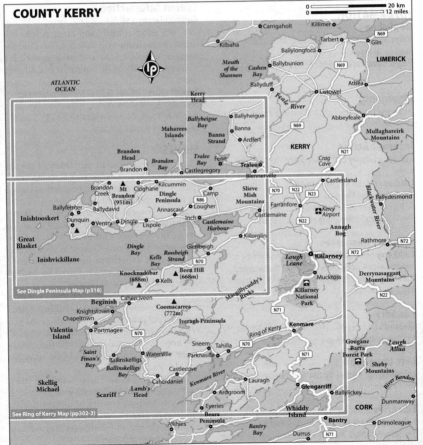

before building Ross Castle (in the 15th century).

It wasn't until much later, in the 17th century, that Viscount Kenmare developed the town as a tourist centre, an Irish version of England's Lake District. Among its many notable 19th-century visitors were Queen Victoria and the Romantic poet Percy Bysshe Shelley, who began *Queen Mab* here.

ORIENTATION

The centre of Killarney is the T-junction where New St meets High and Main Sts. As it heads south, High St becomes Main St, then turns east into Kenmare Pl and East Ave Rd, where the large hotels are. The national park is to the south, while the bus and train stations are east of the centre.

INFORMATION
Bookshops

Killarney Bookshop (☎ 064-663 4108; 32 Main St) Good for hiking maps.
Pages Bookstore (064-662 6757; 20 New St) Lots of fiction.

Emergency

For emergencies (ambulance, fire or police) dial ☎ 999.

Internet Access

Killarney Library (☎ 064-663 2655; Rock Rd) Free access.
Leaders (☎ 064-663 9635; Beech Rd; per 30 min €2; ☿ 9.30am-5pm Mon-Sat)
Rí Rá (☎ 064-663 8729; Plunkett St; per 30 min €2; ☿ 11am-9pm) Offers cheap phone calls abroad.

Internet Resources

CorkKerry (www.corkkerry.ie) A useful resource for accommodation & information throughout the southwest.
Killarney (www.killarney.ie) Official site for the town; lots of tourism links.

Laundry

Gleeson's (☎ 064-663 3877; Brewery Lane; per 6kg €12; ☿ 9am-6pm Mon-Sat)

Left Luggage

Left-luggage office (☎ 064-663 7509; per bag €2; ☿ 7am-6pm) At the bus station shop, inside the mall.

Libraries

Killarney Library (☎ 064-663 2655; Rock Rd; ☿ 10am-5pm Mon, Wed, Fri & Sat, 10am-8pm Tue & Thu)

Medical Services

The closest accident and emergency unit is at Tralee General Hospital (p312).
SouthDoc (☎ 1850-335 999; Upper Park Rd) Doctors outside surgery hours; 500m east of the centre.

Money

Many banks have a bureau de change, an ATM, or both. The tourist office has a bureau de change.

Post

Killarney Post Office (☎ 064-663 1461; New St; ☿ 9am-5.30pm Mon & Wed-Sat, from 9.30am Tue)

Toilets

There are public toilets on Kenmare Pl.

Tourist Information

Guide Killarney (☎ 064-663 1108; www.guidekillarney.com) is a good annual local guide filled with artful maps (form over function) and mountains of excellent info and background. It's marked '€5' but can be found for free all over town.
Tourist office (☎ 064-663 1633; www.corkkerry.ie; Beech Rd; ☿ 9am-8pm Jun-Aug, 9.15am-5pm Sep-May) Busy, but efficient; can handle almost any query, especially dealing with transport intricacies.

SIGHTS

The real attraction in Killarney, and the reason to come, is Killarney National Park (p295). The town itself can be easily explored on foot in an hour or two.

Built between 1842 and 1855, **St Mary's Cathedral** (☎ 064-663 1014; Cathedral Pl), which sits at the western end of New St, is a superb example of neo-Gothic revival architecture. The cruciform building, designed by Augustus Pugin, was inspired by Ardfert Cathedral (p314), near Tralee.

At the northern end of High St is a **memorial** to those who fought for the Republic, erected by the Republican Graves Association in 1972. With a determination reflecting the implacable hope for a united Ireland, the inscription reads: 'This memorial will not be unveiled until Ireland is free.'

On Fair Hill is an 1860s **Franciscan friary**, displaying an ornate Flemish-style altarpiece, some impressive tile work and stained-glass windows by Harry Clarke. The Dublin artist's organic style was influenced by art nouveau, art deco and symbolism.

ACTIVITIES

You can fish for trout and salmon in the Rivers Flesk (per day €10) and Laune (per day €25); a state salmon licence is needed. Or you can fish for brown trout for free in Killarney National Park's lakes. Information, permits, licences and hire equipment can be obtained at **O'Neill's** (☎ 064-663 1970; 6 Plunkett St),

which looks like a gift shop but is a long-established fishing centre.

Killarney Riding Stables (☎ 064-663 1686; www .killarney-reeks-trail.com; Ballydowney; rides from €35) is 1.5km west of the centre on the N72. The well-run complex offers short rides as well as two- and five-day rides through the Iveragh Peninsula for more experienced riders.

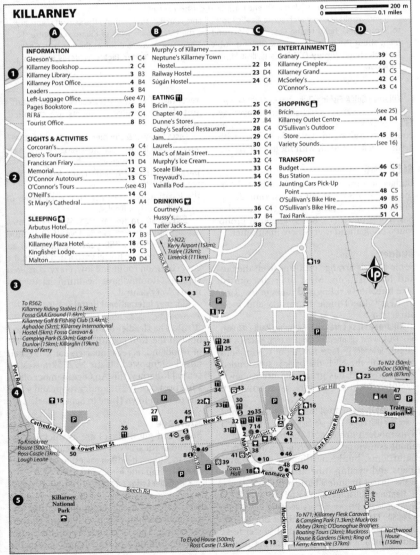

KILLARNEY

0 ————— 200 m
0 ————— 0.1 miles

INFORMATION	
Gleeson's	**1** C4
Killarney Bookshop	**2** C4
Killarney Library	**3** B3
Killarney Post Office	**4** B4
Leaders	**5** B4
Left-Luggage Office	(see 47)
Pages Bookstore	**6** B4
Rí Rá	**7** C4
Tourist Office	**8** B5

SIGHTS & ACTIVITIES	
Corcoran's	**9** C4
Dero's Tours	**10** C5
Franciscan Friary	**11** D4
Memorial	**12** C3
O'Connor Autotours	**13** C5
O'Connor's Tours	(see 43)
O'Neill's	**14** C4
St Mary's Cathedral	**15** A4

SLEEPING	
Arbutus Hotel	**16** C4
Ashville House	**17** B3
Killarney Plaza Hotel	**18** C5
Kingfisher Lodge	**19** C3
Malton	**20** D4

Murphy's of Killarney	**21** C4
Neptune's Killarney Town Hostel	**22** B4
Railway Hostel	**23** D4
Súgán Hostel	**24** C4

EATING	
Bricín	**25** C4
Chapter 40	**26** B4
Dunne's Stores	**27** B4
Gaby's Seafood Restaurant	**28** C4
Jam	**29** C4
Laurels	**30** C4
Mac's of Main Street	**31** C4
Murphy's Ice Cream	**32** C4
Sceale Eile	**33** C4
Treyvaud's	**34** C4
Vanilla Pod	**35** C4

DRINKING	
Courtney's	**36** C4
Hussy's	**37** B4
Tatler Jack's	**38** C5

ENTERTAINMENT	
Granary	**39** C5
Killarney Cineplex	**40** C5
Killarney Grand	**41** C5
McSorley's	**42** C4
O'Connor's	**43** C4

SHOPPING	
Bricín	(see 25)
Killarney Outlet Centre	**44** D4
O'Sullivan's Outdoor Store	**45** B4
Variety Sounds	(see 16)

TRANSPORT	
Budget	**46** C5
Bus Station	**47** D4
Jaunting Cars Pick-Up Point	**48** C5
O'Sullivan's Bike Hire	**49** B5
O'Sullivan's Bike Hire	**50** A5
Taxi Rank	**51** C4

To N22;
Kerry Airport (15km);
Tralee (32km);
Limerick (111km)

To R562;
Killarney Riding Stables (1.5km);
Fossa GAA Ground (1.6km);
Killarney Golf & Fishing Club (3.4km);
Aghadoe (5km); Killarney International
Hostel (5km); Fossa Caravan &
Camping Park (5.5km); Gap of
Dunloe (15km); Killorglin (19km);
Ring of Kerry

To N22 (50m);
SouthDoc (500m);
Cork (87km)

Train Station

To Knockreer
House (500m);
Ross Castle (3km);
Lough Leane

Town Hall

Killarney
National
Park

Beech Rd

Countess Rd

Countess Gve

To N71; Killarney Flesk Caravan
& Camping Park (1.3km); Muckross
Abbey (2km); O'Donoghue Brothers
Boating Tours (2km); Muckross
House & Gardens (5km); Ring of
Kerry; Kenmare (37km)

Northwood
House
(150m)

To Elyod House (500m);
Ross Castle (1.5km)

COUNTY KERRY

FOOTBALL CRAZY

Gaelic football clubs are as common in Ireland as green fields and pub signs bearing the 'G' word. However, among Kerrymen, the obsession with the sport reaches fever pitch. Forget about soccer or even hurling; this obsession is akin to rugby in New Zealand and soccer in Brazil.

Run by the GAA (Gaelic Athletic Association), the 15-a-side game is played with a heavy leather ball on a rectangular grass pitch with H-shaped, net-backed goals. Teams score through a confusing combination of kicking, carrying, hand-passing and *soloing* (dropping and toe-kicking the ball into the hands). The game, which closely resembles Australian Rules football, dates back to the 16th century, but took its current form in the 19th century.

If you would like to watch some Gaelic football and you're in town during the season (February to September), head to the Fossa GAA Ground on the N72, 1.6km west of Killarney's centre. To learn about the game from some lifelong pub commentators, have a drink at the bar-cum-Gaelic football shrine **Jimmy O'Brien's** (College St) in Fair Hill. Nearby **Tatler Jack's** (p294) is also a big GAA bar.

Killarney Golf & Fishing Club (☎ 064-663 1034; www .killarney-golf.com; Mahony's Point; green fees per person from €40), 3.4km west of town on the N72, has three courses: two alongside Lough Leane, one with artificial lakes, and all with mountain views.

SLEEPING

Budget accommodation tends to be right in the centre; B&Bs are often just outside on Rock, Lewis and Muckross Rds. The latter also has scores of generic hotels aimed at group tours. Book ahead everywhere in summer.

Budget

Some hostels arrange pick-ups from the bus and train stations. Most offer discounted bike hire, horse riding and tours of the Ring of Kerry, the Dingle Peninsula and local attractions.

Killarney Flesk Caravan & Camping Park (☎ 064-663 1704; www.killarneyfleskcamping.com; Muckross Rd; campsites from €10; ⏰ Easter-Sep) About 1.3km south of town on the N71, the park is surrounded by woods and has great mountain views. Facilities include bike hire, a supermarket, bar and cafe.

Railway Hostel (☎ 064-663 5299; www.killarneyhostel .com; Fair Hill; dm €13-22, s/d from €38/52; P ⏰) This modern hostel near the train station is about as inviting as hostels get, with private bathrooms, bunks nestling in nooks, and maps and cycling itineraries adorning the walls. Prices include a basic breakfast.

Neptune's Killarney Town Hostel (☎ 064-663 5255; www.neptuneshostel.com; Bishop's Lane, New St; dm €14-20, d €40-50; ⏰) Neptune's mixed dorms can sleep over 150, but the central hostel feels much smaller thanks to the roaring fire in

reception, free internet access, and the staff's unfailing helpfulness. Sheets are supplied, towels aren't.

Fossa Caravan & Camping Park (☎ 064-663 1497; www.camping-holidaysireland.com; Fossa; dm €15, campsites from €16; ⏰ Easter-Sep). The better of two parks on the N72 to Killorglin, found 5.5km west of Killarney, it has a restaurant, and the location is a relaxing spot with views of Macgillycuddy's Reeks.

our pick **Súgán Hostel** (☎ 064-663 3104; www .killarneysuganhostel.com; Lewis Rd; dm/d €16/40) Behind its publike front, 250-year-old Súgán is an amiably eccentric hostel with a turf fire in the cosy common room and low, crazy-cornered ceilings. Rooms have beautiful hardwood floors. Very central.

Killarney International Hostel (☎ 064-663 1240; www.anoige.ie; Aghadoe House, Fossa; dm €16-23, d from €46; P ⏰) The Headley barons' former residence, built in the 18th century and set in 75 acres of woodland, is regal quarters for a 170-bed hostel. Signposted off the N72, 5km west of central Killarney, this An Óige member offers a full breakfast (€7), laundry room and a free bus to/from town (June to September).

Midrange

B&Bs and guesthouses are as thick on the ground in Killarney as jaunting cars. But from June to August it's often easiest to let the tourist office find one for you (€4).

Kingfisher Lodge (☎ 064-663 7131; www.kingfisher lodgekillarney.com; Lewis Rd; r €50-100; P ⏰) Lovely back gardens are a highlight at this immaculate B&B on a strip with others close to the centre. The 11 rooms are slightly posh. Walkers will be especially happy here as the owner, Donal Carroll, is a certified guide with years of experience walking and hiking in the region. Much local knowledge is on offer.

Elyod House (☎ 064-663 6544; www.elyodhouse.ie; Ross Rd; r €60-80; **P**) This quietly located modern house is on the road to Ross Castle and a few minutes' walk from town. Rooms are fresh and clean, and the welcome is friendly. The good location balances leafy charms with urban fun.

Ashville House (☎ 064-663 6405; www.ashvillekillarney. com; Rock Rd; r €60-90; ☽ Mar-Dec; **P** ☎) One of several on this strip close to town, Ashville is spotless. The owners take deep pride in their place and the 18 rooms are comfortable and well equipped. It's very quiet.

Northwood House (☎ 064-663 7181; www.northwood house.com; 5 Muckross View; r €64-80; **P**) This B&B in a quiet location to the southeast of town, reached along Countess Rd, has modern rooms with TVs, private bathrooms and wonderful views, some from breezy balconies.

Murphy's of Killarney (☎ 064-663 1294; www .murphysofkillarney.com; College St; r €70-150) Recently refurbished, Murphy's is owned by a real Murphy who takes real pride in his 20 stylish rooms in the heart of town. If it's pissing down you won't have to leave as the restaurant, bar and pub all win praise.

Top End

Arbutus Hotel (☎ 064-663 1037; www.arbutuskillarney .com; College St; s/d from €80/150; ☽ Feb-Nov; ▨) The 34 bedrooms range from those with 1920s Celtic deco furniture to more modern rooms with black-and-white bathrooms and the bath in a sweeping alcove. Trad sessions fire up in Buckley's Bar on many nights and Sunday lunchtimes.

Killarney Plaza Hotel (☎ 064-662 1111; www .killarneyplaza.com; Kenmare Pl; r €120-250; **P** ▨ ☎) Dominating the view of the south end of Main St, this large, 198-room hotel is built in a brilliant white traditional style. Rooms come in several grades but all have a restrained style with just a touch of élan. Public facilities are in keeping with its class; besides the beautifully tiled indoor pool, there's a sauna, steam room and spa.

Malton (☎ 064-663 8000; www.themalton.com; r €120-300; **P** ▨ ☎) So commanding it doesn't need an address, the Malton is pillared, ivy-covered and a throwback to Victorian elegance – at least from the outside. The inside has been thoroughly refurbished, much to the disdain

of Colonel Blimp types, though most others find the stylish surrounds a breath of fresh air. Of the 172 rooms, those in the 1852 wing are best, retaining their period opulence.

EATING

Killarney's eating options at first seem geared to the visiting mobs (complete with early dining times and specials for groups checking out early in the am) but look a little closer ands you'll find loads of interesting options popular with locals.

Budget

Murphy's Ice Cream (☎ 064-915 2644; Main St; ☽ 11am-9pm) For superlative homemade ice cream.

Dunne's Stores (☎ 064-6635888; New St) Has a well-stocked supermarket with a lovely self-serve salad and pasta counter bar.

Jam (☎ 064-663 1441; Old Market Lane; snacks & meals €2-8; ☽ 8am-5pm Mon-Sat) This charmer of a cafe is a local hideout. Duck down an alley for a changing menu of hot meals, deli items, and coffee and cake. It's all made with locally sourced produce and there's a few tables under an awning out front.

Vanilla Pod (☎ 064-662 6559; Old Market Lane; snacks & meals €2-12; ☽ 9am-6pm Mon-Sat) Gavin Gleeson's gem of a little cafe has a range of locally sourced fresh and organic foods. The menu changes daily, but there are build-your-own sandwiches, salads and more elaborate fare like roasted fish. Bakery items can be enjoyed as a treat all day, especially at the tables out front.

Sceale Eile (☎ 064-663 5066; 73 High St; mains €6-12; ☽ 9.30am-5pm Mon-Sat) This bakery–cafe, with Irish literary memorabilia decorating the walls upstairs, energises Killarney's workforce with baguettes, bagels, burgers, lasagne and roasts. The big BLT is famous locally; tarts abound.

Midrange

our pick Treyvaud's (☎ 064-663 3062; 62 High St; lunch mains €8-15, dinner mains €15-30; ☽ noon-10pm) Michael Treyvaud's modish restaurant has a strong reputation for subtle dishes that merge trad Irish with seductive European influences. The seafood chowder at lunch is a seductive repast; dinner mains include the best of local lamb and a winsome bacon and cabbage plate.

Mac's of Main Street (☎ 064-663 5213; Main St; mains €8-20; ☽ 10.30am-10pm) With possibly the latest serving hours of a restaurant in Killarney, Mac's is a big, buzzy, casual place that sees loads of traffic through the day. The menu isn't long but features good renditions of standards like shepherd's pie, fish and chips, and burgers. Pints are poured, there's wine by the glass, and big booths to sit in; many can't resist the special sundaes.

Chapter 40 (☎ 064-667 1833; New St; mains €11-30; ◷ 5-10pm Mon-Sat) Popular with Killarney's stylish bounders, this beautiful dining room is all polished wood and cream leather. Very popular is the daily list of tapas plates made with what's fresh locally. Trad mains veer into top-end territory but are superbly executed examples of meats and seafood. The wines by the glass show a deft hand in the cellar.

Laurels (☎ 064-663 1149; Main St; mains €16-25; ◷ 12-3pm & 6-9.30pm) Tasty but pricey pub grub such as burgers, steaks and pizzas with inventive toppings. Sit in the bar rather than the slightly formal restaurant to enjoy a setting that mixes a traditional feel with good service. Champ (potatoes mashed with spring onions) is a house speciality.

Brícín (☎ 064-663 4902; 26 High St; mains €18-20; ◷ 12.30-3pm & 6-9pm Tue-Sat) Decorated with fittings from a convent, an orphanage and a school, this Celtic deco restaurant doubles as the town museum, with Jonathan Fisher's 18th-century views of the national park taking pride of place. The McGuire brothers (Johnny up front, Paddy in the kitchen) welcome all with simple and excellent food. Try the house speciality, boxty (potato pancake).

Top End

Gaby's Seafood Restaurant (☎ 064-663 2519; 27 High St; mains €18-50; ◷ 6-10pm Mon-Sat) Gaby's is a refined dining experience for those who want superb seafood served in a traditional manner. Peruse the menu by the fire before drifting past the wine cellar to the low-lit dining room, where you'll savour exquisite Gallic dishes such as lobster in a sauce that includes cognac and cream. Specials are legion depending on what's fresh. The wine list is long and the advice unerring.

DRINKING & ENTERTAINMENT

Most pubs put on live music, and most nights are lively here – even Mondays, when many of the town's hospitality staff are released to the fun side of the bar. Plunkett and College Sts are lined with pubs. The tourist office has a handy night-by-night listing of sessions.

Traditional Pubs

O'Connor's (☎ 064-663 0977; High St) Typically, this tiny pub with leaded glass doors is one of Killarney's most popular haunts. There's entertainment every night, from trad sessions to stand-up comedy, storytelling and pub theatre.

Killarney Grand (☎ 064-663 1159; Main St; music 9pm-2.45am) There's free entry before 11pm to this busy Killarney institution, where trad music gives way to live bands, set dancing on Wednesdays and a nightclub at weekends.

Courtney's (Yer Man's; ☎ 064-663 2689; Plunkett St) Timeless trad pub with trad sessions many nights year-round. This is where locals come to see their old mates perform.

Hussy's (☎ 064-663 5472; High St) Escape the tourist mobs and muse over a pint in this small pub sporting a snug at the entrance and genial drinkers within.

Tatler Jack's (☎ 064-663 2361; Plunkett St) Sports photos of proud local teams line the walls at this surprisingly large pub, which features pool tables, the comfiest stools in town and merciless craic.

Bars & Clubs

Granary (☎ 064-662 0075; Touhills Lane) Hidden down the alley next to the Killarney Grand, this bar–restaurant, with low lighting, exposed stone walls and leather sofas, is favoured by local scenesters. Bands and DJs play at weekends.

McSorley's (☎ 064-663 7280; College St) A popular, clubby bar with multicoloured lighting and kilt-clad cover bands.

Cinemas

Killarney Cineplex (☎ 064-663 7007; Kenmare Pl; adult/child €12/6) This four-screener has current releases.

SHOPPING

Variety Sounds (☎ 064-663 5755; College St) An eclectic music shop with a good range of traditional music, instruments, sheet music and hard-to-find CDs.

Killarney Outlet Centre (☎ 064-663 6744; Fair Hill) This mall in renovated old train sheds has a number of shops including Lowe Alpine and Blarney Woollen Mills, all selling brand-name clothing and other products at discounts.

O'Sullivan's Outdoor Store (☎ 064-662 6927; New St) There's a general selection of activity gear at O'Sullivan's branches. They cram a vast amount into a small space.

COUNTY KERRY

Brícín (☎ 064-663 4902; 26 High St) Interesting items such as local craftwork seek your attention alongside touristy fare.

GETTING THERE & AWAY
Air
Kerry Airport (KIR; ☎ 066-976 4644; www.kerryairport .com) is at Farranfore, about 15km north of Killarney along the N22 and then about 1.5km along the N23. **Ryanair** (☎ 0818 303 030; www.ryan air.com) rules the roost with daily flights to Dublin, London's Luton and Stansted airports, Grenoble in France and Hahn in Germany.

The small airport has a cafe, bureau de change, an ATM and wi-fi. Virtually all the major car-hire firms have desks at the airport.

Bus
Bus Éireann (☎ 064-663 0011; www.buseireann.ie) operates from the east end of the Killarney Outlet Centre, offering regular links to Cork (€16, two hours, 15 daily); Dublin (€23, six hours, six daily); Galway (€22, seven hours, seven daily) via Limerick (€16.50, 2¼ hours); Tralee (€8, 40 minutes, hourly); and Waterford (€21.50, 4½ hours, hourly).

Train
Killarney's train station is behind the Malton Hotel, just east of the centre. **Irish Rail** (☎ 064-6631067; www.irishrail.ie) has up to three direct trains a day to Cork (€20, 1½ hours) and nine to Tralee (€9.50, 45 minutes). There are direct trains to Dublin (€36, 3½ hours), but you usually have to change at Mallow.

GETTING AROUND
To/From the Airport
Bus Éireann services between Killarney and the airport run roughly two hourly (adult/child €5/2.50, 20 minutes).

A taxi to Killarney costs about €35.

Bicycle
Bicycles are ideal for exploring the scattered sights of the Killarney area, many of which are accessible only by bike or on foot.

O'Sullivan's Bike Hire (☎ 064-663 1282; per day €15) has branches on New St, opposite the cathedral, and on Beech Rd, opposite the tourist office.

Car
The centre of Killarney can be thick with traffic at times. **Budget** (☎ 064-663 4341; Kenmare Pl) is the only car-hire outfit with an office in town. Otherwise contact the companies at the airport.

There is a sizeable, free car park next to St Mary's Cathedral. The central car parks cost €1 per hour, 8.30am to 6.30pm Monday to Saturday.

Jaunting Car
If you're not on two wheels, Killarney's traditional transport is the horse-drawn **jaunting car** (☎ 064-663 3358; www.killarneyjauntingcars.com), also known as a trap, which comes with a driver known as a jarvey. The pick-up point, nicknamed 'the Ha Ha' or 'the Block', is on Kenmare Pl. Trips cost €40 to €70, depending on distance; traps officially carry four people. Jaunting cars also congregate in the N71 car park for Muckross House and Abbey, and at the Gap of Dunloe.

Taxi
The town taxi rank is on College St.

AROUND KILLARNEY

Castles, gardens, lake adventures and more are part of a visit to Killarney National Park, immediately south of the city. Just beyond, there's surprisingly rugged scenery including the too-lovely-for-words Gap of Dunloe, with its babbling brooks and alpine lakes, plus even more rugged scenery beyond.

KILLARNEY NATIONAL PARK
You can escape Killarney for the surrounding wilderness surprisingly quickly. Buses rumble up to Ross Castle and Muckross House, but it's possible to find your own refuge in the 10,236 hectares, among Ireland's only wild herd of native red deer, the country's largest area of ancient oak woods and views of most of its major mountains.

The glacial Lough Leane (the Lower Lake or 'Lake of Learning'), Muckross Lake and the Upper Lake make up about a quarter of the park. Their peaty waters are as rich in wildlife as the surrounding soil: cormorants skim across the surface, deer swim out to graze on the islands, and salmon, trout and perch prosper in a pike-free environment. The Lower Lake has vistas of reeds and swans.

Designated a Unesco Biosphere Reserve in 1982, the park extends to the southwest of

COUNTY KERRY

town. There are pedestrian entrances opposite St Mary's Cathedral (Map p291), with other entrances (for drivers) off the N71.

Knockreer House & Gardens

Near the St Mary's Cathedral entrance to the park stands Knockreer House, with gardens featuring a terraced lawn and a summerhouse. The original 1870s structure burned; the present incarnation dates from 1958. The house isn't open to the public, but its gardens have views across the lakes to the mountains. From the St Mary's Cathedral entrance, follow the path immediately to your right uphill for about 500m.

Ross Castle

Restored by Dúchas, **Ross Castle** (☎ 064-663 5851; www.heritageireland.ie; Ross Rd; adult/child €6/2; ⏰ 9am-6.30pm Jun-Aug, 9.30am-5.30pm Sep–mid-Oct & mid-Mar–May) dates back to the 15th century, when it was a residence of the O'Donoghues. It was the last place in Munster to succumb to Cromwell's forces, thanks partly to its cunning spiral staircase, every step of which is a different height, in order to break an attacker's stride.

According to a prophecy, the castle would be captured only from the water, so in 1652 the Cromwellian commander Ludlow had floating batteries brought to Lough Leane from Castlemaine Harbour along the River Laune. Seeing the prophecy about to be fulfilled, the defenders, having resisted the English siege from the land for months, promptly surrendered.

The castle is a lovely 3km walk from the St Mary's Cathedral pedestrian park entrance; you may well see red deer. If you're driving from Killarney, turn right opposite the Texaco petrol station at the start of Muckross Rd. Access is by guided tour only.

Inisfallen Island

The first monastery on Inisfallen Island (at 22 acres, the largest of the national park's 26 islands) is said to have been founded by St Finian the Leper in the 7th century. The island's fame dates from the early 13th century when the Annals of Inisfallen were written here. Now in the Bodleian Library at Oxford, they remain a vital source of information on early Munster history. On Inisfallen ('island')

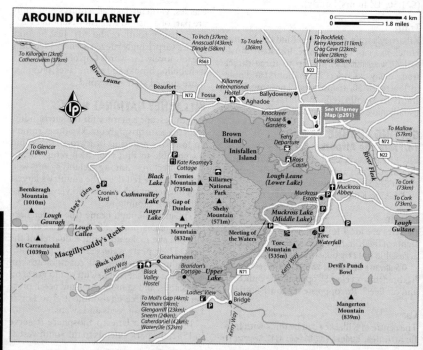

AROUND KILLARNEY

DETOUR: AGHADOE

On a hilltop 5km west of town, Aghadoe's views of Killarney, the lakes and Inisfallen Island have drawn tourists for centuries. At the eastern end of the meadow, in front of the Aghadoe Heights Hotel, are the ruins of a **Romanesque church** and the 13th-century **Parkavonear Castle**. Parkavonear's keep, still standing, is one of the few cylindrical rather than rectangular keeps built by the Normans in Ireland. Unsurprisingly, its name translates as 'field of the meadow'.

If driving from Killarney, turn right off the N72 after the turn for Killarney Riding Stables. Between Monday and Saturday, June to September, four daily buses link Killarney and Aghadoe. Some tours stop there.

are the ruins of a 12th-century **oratory** with a carved Romanesque doorway and a **monastery** on the site of St Finian's original.

You can hire boats from Ross Castle to row to the island. Alternatively, boaters charge passengers around €7.50 each for the crossing. Some Gap of Dunloe boats and bus tours also stop here.

Muckross Estate

The core of Killarney National Park is the Muckross Estate, donated to the state by Arthur Bourn Vincent in 1932. **Muckross House** (☎ 064-667 0144; www.muckross-house.ie; adult/child €7/3, combined ticket with farms €12/6; 🕑 9am-7pm Jul & Aug, to 6pm Sep-Jun) is a 19th-century mansion, restored to its former glory and packed with contemporaneous fittings. Entrance is by guided tour.

The beautiful gardens slope down, and a block behind the house contains a restaurant, craft shop and studios where you can see potters, weavers and bookbinders at work. Jaunting cars wait to run you though deer parks and woodland to Torc Waterfall and Muckross Abbey (about €10 each return).

our pick **Garden Restaurant** (☎ 064-663 1440; meals €4-10; 🕑 9am-5pm), in the visitor centre (which also has excellent maps and books), is one of the region's best places for lunch. It serves an array of fresh and interesting dishes from snacky to full-on. It's all cafeteria style so you can wander around choosing from the array of organic and locally sourced foods.

Immediately east of Muckross House are the **Muckross Traditional Farms** (☎ 064-663 1440; adult/child €7/4, combined ticket with Muckross House €12/6; 🕑 10am-6pm Jun-Sep, 1-6pm May, 1-6pm Sat, Sun & public holidays mid-Mar-Apr & Oct). These reproductions of 1930s Kerry farms, complete with chickens, pigs, cattle and horses, show farming and living conditions when people had to live off the land.

Muckross House is 5km south of town, signposted from the N71. The house is included in some half-day tours of Killarney, and it would be possible to work it into a circuit of the park and the Gap of Dunloe.

If you're walking or cycling to Muckross, there's a cycle track alongside the Kenmare road for most of the first 2km. A path then turns right into Killarney National Park. Following this path, after 1km you'll come to **Muckross Abbey**, which was founded in 1448 and burned by Cromwell's troops in 1652. William Thackeray called it 'the prettiest little bijou of a ruined abbey ever seen'. Muckross House is another 1.5km from the abbey ruins.

Cycling around Muckross Lake (Middle Lake) is easier and more scenic when done in an anticlockwise direction.

Gap of Dunloe

Geographically, the Gap of Dunloe is outside the Killarney National Park, but most people include it in their visit to the park. The land is ruggedly beautiful, and fast-changing weather conditions add drama.

In the winter, it's an awe-inspiring mountain pass, overshadowed by Purple Mountain and Macgillycuddy's Reeks. In high summer, though, it's a bottleneck for the tourist trade, with buses depositing countless visitors at Kate Kearney's Cottage for the one-hour horse-and-trap ride through the Gap.

In the south, **Brandon's Cottage** (snacks €3-6; 🕑 9am-4pm Apr-Oct) is a simple old 19th-century hunting lodge with a fine open-air cafe and a dock for boats crossing the Upper Lake. It is surrounded by lush, green pastures. From here a narrow road weaves up the hill to the Gap. Heading down towards the north the scenery is a fantasy of rocky bridges over clear mountain streams and lakes.

Eventually you reach the 19th-century pub **Kate Kearney's Cottage** (☎ 064-664 4146; lunch €10.50-13), where many drivers park in order to walk up to the Gap.

Getting There & Around

The best way to see the Gap is to hire a bike in Killarney and cycle to Ross Castle. Get there

---

MUNROS AND HEWITTS

Macgillycuddy's Reeks is the magnificent group of mountains southwest of Killarney, concentrated to the west of the Gap of Dunloe. The name derives from the ancient Mac Gilla Muchudas clan; *reek* means 'pointed hill'. In Gaeltacht they're known as Na Crucha Dubha (the black tops).

The red sandstone mountains were carved by minor glaciers into elegant forms, such as Carrantuohil's curved outline – referred to in its name, which translates as 'reversed reaping hook'. The mountains are studded with awesome cliffs, the summits are buttressed by ridges of purplish rock and the cupped valleys between are filled with glittering lakes.

The Reeks are Ireland's highest mountain range, featuring nine of its 12 *munros* (a Scottish term meaning a mountain over 900m). These include the country's seven highest peaks, towering alongside roughly half of Ireland's 211 *hewitts* (hills in England, Wales and Ireland that are over 2000ft, or 610m).

---

before 11am to catch a boat up the lakes to Brandon's Cottage, then cycle through the Gap and back to town via the N72 and a path through the golf course (for bike hire and boat trip, about €30).

The 1½-hour boat ride alone justifies the trip. It crosses all the lakes, passing islands and bridges and winding between the second two lakes via Meeting of the Waters and the Long Range.

On land, walking, pony or four-person trap can be substituted for cycling. The Gap pony men charge €50 per hour or €80 for the two-hour trip between Brandon's Cottage and Kate Kearney's Cottage.

Note that it is hard to do the Gap as part of a walking loop. You can get as far as Kate Kearney's, but from there back to Killarney it is a long slog on busy roads – no fun at all. Your best bet would be to call a cab from there. See right for tours of the Gap.

You can also drive this route, but really only outside summer and even then walkers and cyclists have the right of way. On the plus side, to reach Brandon's Cottage by car you have to drive a long, scenic detour on the N71 to the R568 and then come back down a gorgeous rugged valley. It takes about 45 minutes.

WALKING & CLIMBING

Climbing and walking opportunities abound around Killarney, including the four-hour circuit of Muckross Lake. The Killarney tourist office and local bookshops stock trekking guides and the map (Ordnance Survey Map Discovery Series No 78) for several mountains, including Carrantuohil (1039m), Ireland's highest peak.

Ascending **Macgillycuddy's Reeks** and their neighbours (Purple, Tomies and Shehy mountains, between the Gap of Dunloe and Lough Leane, and Torc and Mangerton mountains, southeast of Muckross Lake) should never be attempted without having the skills to use a map and compass. Weatherproof and waterproof footwear and clothing are essential at all times of the year. Seek advice locally before attempting mountain walks.

There are several ways up Carrantuohil. Some require reasonable hill-walking ability, others are serious scrambling or rock-climbing routes. Get a taste of the Reeks at close quarters by walking up Hag's Glen, the beautiful approach valley that leads to the Callee and Gouragh lakes below the north face of Carrantuohil.

The best approach is from **Cronin's Yard** (☎ 064-663 4963; www.croninsyard.com; Mealis), where there's a tearoom, showers and toilets, a public telephone, and packed lunches available on request. It's at the road's end (OS ref 836873), reached from the N72 via Beaufort, west of Killarney. You may be asked to pay a small fee for using the car park. From there, the way lies alongside the Gaddagh River, which you need to ford in places; great care is required if it's in flood. It's just over 3km to the lakes.

The popular but hair-raising way to summit Carrantuohil from the lakes is via **Devil's Ladder**, a gruelling trudge up a badly eroded gully path, southwest of the lakes. The ground is loose in places, and in wet conditions the way becomes muddy. This takes six hours return from Cronin's Yard.

TOURS

Guided two-hour **national park walks** (☎ 064-663 3471, 087 639 4362; www.killarneyguidedwalks.com; adult/

child €9/5) leave at 11am daily from opposite St Mary's Cathedral at the western end of New St. Tours meander through Knockreer gardens, then to spots where Charles de Gaulle holidayed, David Lean filmed *Ryan's Daughter* and Brother Cudda slept for 200 years. Trips are available at other times on request.

Two companies offer customisable itineraries to see the Gap of Dunloe (€30 to €50):

O'Connor's Tours (☎ 064-663 0200; www.gapofdunloe tours.com; High St)

O'Donoghue Brothers Boating Tours (☎ 064-663 1068; www.killarneydaytour.com; Old Weir Lodge, Muckross Rd)

Glass-enclosed boats for the masses (adult/child €10/5) do one-hour lake circuits, usually from Ross Castle:

Destination Killarney (☎ 064-663 2638)
Killarney Watercoach Cruises (☎ 064-663 1068)

The **open boats** (☎ 087 689 9241) you can charter at Ross Castle offer more appealing trips with boatmen who define 'character'. It costs €10 from Ross Castle to the Muckross (Middle) Lake and back; €15 for a tour of all three lakes.

A number of Killarney companies run daily day trips by bus around the Ring of Kerry (€27) and Dingle Peninsula (€27). Half-day

WALK: REEKS RIDGE

Experienced walkers with confidence over steep ground could consider the longest and most sustained ridge walk in Ireland, a seven-hour, 13km trek with wide-ranging views. The demanding trek scales six 900m-plus peaks – including Knocknapeasta and Maolán Buí, Ireland's fourth- and fifth-highest summits – with a total ascent of 1050m.

The exposed walk should be avoided in windy conditions. In poor weather, or when there is a chance of encountering snow and ice (much of the year), it is a serious undertaking. An ice axe, and perhaps other mountaineering equipment, should be carried; only those with winter mountaineering experience should attempt it.

From Cronin's Yard (opposite), pass through a gate on the right of the yard. Skirt a field on a grass track, cross a stile and follow the stony track that climbs gently above the Gaddagh River. Leave the track where it crosses a tributary of the Gaddagh and head southeast across open ground, climbing the increasingly steep slopes towards the conspicuous summit of **Cruach Mór** (932m). Aim slightly east of the summit to find easier ground. The top, marked by a stone grotto, has impressive views south across the Iveragh Peninsula (1½ to two hours from the start).

However, your attention is likely to be drawn by the rock ridge running south towards the **Big Gun** (939m). Huge blocks of rock (gendarmes) adorn the crest of the ridge, making it initially difficult to keep to the top. Follow informal paths below and to the west of the ridge, being careful not to lose too much height. Scramble back up to the ridge at a notch, then climb – carefully – directly along the exciting rocky arête to reach the Big Gun. The ridge now swings southwest towards Knocknapeasta. Stick to the crest as you descend to a col, but where the ridge becomes difficult again you can drop south (left) of the arête before rejoining it just beneath the summit of **Knocknapeasta** (988m; one hour from Cruach Mór).

The views from the highest point on the walk are tremendous, taking in Ireland's three highest summits to the west and, to the east, the serrated ridge you have traversed. To the north, wild cliffs fall away into the dark waters of Lough Cummeenapeasta, with the patchwork fields of north Kerry beyond. Southward, the mountain falls away to Black Valley, and ridge after ridge of mountains extend towards the Atlantic.

Head south from Knocknapeasta along a broad, stony ridge, then bear southwest as you drop to a col and climb a short distance to the summit of **Maolán Buí** (973m). Cross an unnamed top at 926m to reach **Cnoc an Chuillin** (958m), the last major peak on the ridge. Now descend to a col and climb onto another unnamed summit. It is best to descend directly into Hags Glen from here, keeping to the west of steep ground, though some walkers brave Devil's Ladder (opposite) further to the west. Once in Hags Glen, follow the stony track for 4km to the finish (one to 1½ hours).

An alternative route (eight to 10 hours, 15km, 1450m ascent) for very fit walkers extends the route west across Ireland's two highest peaks – Carrauntuohil (1039m) and Beenkeragh (1010m) – before descending to Hags Glen.

tours (€17), taking in Aghadoe, Ross Castle, Muckross House and Torc Waterfall also operate, as do bike tours and lake cruises.

Operators include:

Corcoran's (☎ 064-663 6666; 8 College St)

Dero's Tours (Map p291; ☎ 064-663 1251; www.deros tours.com; Main St)

O'Connor Autotours (Map p291; ☎ 064-663 4833; Ross Rd)

KILLARNEY TO KENMARE

The vista-crazy N71 to Kenmare (32km) winds between rock and lake, with plenty of lay-bys to stop and admire the views. Watch out for the buses squeezing along the road. About 2km south of the entrance to Muckross House, a path leads 200m to the pretty **Torc Waterfall**. After another 8km on the N71 you come to **Ladies' View**, where the fine views along Upper Lake were much enjoyed by Queen Victoria's ladies-in-waiting. There are cafes here and 5km further on at **Moll's Gap**, another good viewpoint.

RING OF KERRY

The second of Ireland's big circle drives (number one Dingle, number three Beara), the Ring of Kerry is the longest and the most diverse. It combines jaw-dropping coastal scenery with more mundane stretches of land that's simply emerald green and sort of blissful.

This 179km circuit of the Iveragh Peninsula pops up on tourist itineraries for a good reason. The road winds past pristine beaches, the island-dotted Atlantic, medieval ruins, mountains and loughs (lakes). Even locals stop their cars to gawk at the rugged coastline – particularly between Waterville and Caherdaniel in the southwest of the peninsula. And even in summer the remote Skellig Ring can be uncrowded and serene (starkly beautiful too).

And for many, the Ring is simply music to their ears as traditional pubs with music sessions dot the villages.

Getting Around

Although you can tour it in one day by car or three by bicycle, the more time you take, the more you'll enjoy it. Tour buses travel the Ring in an anticlockwise direction. Getting stuck behind one is tedious, so consider driving clockwise; just watch out on blind corners.

There's little traffic on the Ballaghbeama Gap, which cuts across the peninsula's central highlands with some spectacular views: it's perfect for a long cycle, as is the longer Ballaghisheen Pass to Waterville. The 214km Kerry Way (below) starts and ends in Killarney.

From June to mid-September, **Bus Éireann** (☎ 064-663 0011; www.buseireann.ie) circumnavigates the Ring of Kerry daily (bus 280). Stops include Killorglin, Glenbeigh, Caherciveen, Waterville and Caherdaniel. From Monday to Saturday during the same period, bus 279 links Killarney with Waterville and Caherciveen via stops including Killorglin. Outside summer, transport on the Ring is not good.

A number of Killarney tour companies run daily bus trips around the Ring (see p298).

KERRY WAY

The 214km Kerry Way is the Republic's longest way-marked footpath and is usually walked anticlockwise. Starting and ending in Killarney, it stays inland for the first three days, winding through the spectacular Macgillycuddy's Reeks and past 1039m Mt Carrantuohil, Ireland's highest mountain, before continuing around the Ring of Kerry coast through Cahirciveen, Waterville, Caherdaniel, Sneem and Kenmare.

You could complete the walk in about 10 days, provided you're up to a good 20km per day. With less time it's worth walking the first three days, as far as Glenbeigh, from where a bus or a lift could return you to Killarney.

Accommodation isn't a problem, but you need to book in July and August. Places to eat are few, however; consider carrying your own food. Ordnance Survey Discovery Series maps 78, 83 and 84 cover the walk. The website www.kerryway.net has info, and local tourist offices and bookshops have specialised guidebooks and maps. **Go Ireland** (www.govisitireland.com) offers a seven-day self-guided walk from €640.

KILLORGLIN

pop 3900

Travelling anticlockwise from Killarney, the first town on the Ring is Killorglin (Cill Orglan). The town is quieter than the waters of the River Laune that lap against the eight-arched bridge, built in 1885. In August, there's an explosion of time-honoured ceremonies and libations at the famous pagan festival, the Puck Fair. A winsome statue (and photo op) of King Puck (a goat) can be seen on the Killarney side of the river. Author Blake Morrison documents his mother's childhood here in *Things My Mother Never Told Me*.

The **tourist office** (☎ 066-976 1451; Library Pl; 9am-5pm Mon-Sat) has maps, walking guides, fishing licences and souvenirs for sale, and free internet access at the **library** (☎ 066-976 1272; Library Pl; 10am-5pm Tue-Sat). The name **Books & Gifts** (☎ 066-979 6006; Upper Bridge St) says it all.

Festivals

The lively **Puck Fair Festival** (Aonach an Phuic; ☎ 066-976 2366; www.puckfair.ie) takes place 1012 August. First recorded in 1603, its origins are hazy. It is based around the custom of installing a billy goat (a poc, or puck), the symbol of mountainous Kerry, on a pedestal in the town, its horns festooned with ribbons. Other entertainment ranges from the horse fair and bonny baby competition to street theatre and the pubs staying open until 3am. Accommodation is as hard to find as a goat in a tin-can factory.

Sleeping & Eating

Killorglin's got good eats. A bunch of old-boozer-style pubs line Upper Bridge St.

West's Holiday Park (☎ 066-976 1240; enquiries@westcaravans.com; Killarney Rd; campsites from €18; Apr-Oct) This small site has views of Carrantuohil across tree-lined fields. On the N72, just under 2km east of the bridge.

our pick **Bianconi** (☎ 066-976 1146; www.bianconi.ie; Annadale; r €65-100; restaurant 5-9pm Mon-Sat) The rooms are as good as the food at this classic 15-room guesthouse right in the centre. Everything is gracious here, including the restaurant, where you'll find lively takes on local seafood (mains €12 to €25) like the killer prawns in a creamy garlic and green onion sauce, mussels in garlic sauce and much more.

Jack's Bakery (☎ 066-976 1132; Lower Bidge St; snacks €2-6; 8am-6pm Sat-Mon) Serving the weekend swells who enjoy the Ring, Jack Healy bakes amazing breads and also makes patés and beautiful sandwiches. Think picnic. Sunday is hot apple tart day.

Sol Y Sombra (☎ 066-976 2347; Lower Bridge St; dishes €5-13; Wed-Mon Jun-Aug, Wed-Sun Sep-Jan & Mar-May, closed Feb) This tapas bar, in a beautifully renovated church, transports you to Mediterranean soil with its tapas and larger *raciones* dishes (for sharing), such as grilled squid, marinated anchovy fillets and an array of tostadas. Bands play at weekends; dancing is fuelled by the huge wine list.

Nick's Seafood Restaurant (☎ 066-976 1219; info@nicks.ie; Lower Bridge St; mains €20-38; 6.30-9.30pm daily Jun-Sep, Wed-Sun other times) French-Irish flair makes this classic restaurant an enduring favourite. Dishes such as *moules* (mussels) and shellfish mornay get the first-class preparation they deserve; or choose the best Kerry beef and lamb or great vegetarian dishes.

KERRY BOG VILLAGE MUSEUM

On the N70 between Killorglin and Glenbeigh, the **Kerry Bog Village Museum** (☎ 066-976 9184; www.kerrybogvillage.ie; adult/child €6/4; 9am-7pm Easter-Oct, to 6pm rest of year) re-creates a 19th-century bog village, typical of the small communities that carved out a precarious living in the harsh environment of Ireland's ubiquitous peat bogs. You'll see the homes of the turfcutter, blacksmith, thatcher and labourer, and a dairy. Commune with the Kerry Bog ponies.

ROSBEIGH STRAND

This unusual **beach**, 1.6km west of Glenbeigh, is a tendril of sand protruding into Dingle Bay, with views of Inch Point and the Dingle Peninsula. On one side the sea is ruffled by Atlantic winds; on the other it's sheltered and calm.

Burke's Activity Centre (☎ 066-976 8872; Rosbeigh) offers horse trekking, crazy golf, a hedge maze and a working farm.

CAHERCIVEEN

pop 1300

Caherciveen's population, over 30,000 in 1841, was decimated by the Great Famine and emigration to the New World. A sleepy outpost remains, overshadowed by the 688m peak of Knocknadobar. It looks rather dour compared with the peninsula's other settlements, but it's close to a cool castle and some good accommodation. In many ways this village does more to recall the tough 1930s in Ireland than any other you'll see in Kerry. The town makes a good staging area for the ferry to Valentia Island (p304).

Information

Caherciveen has a post office and banks with ATMs. AIB has a bureau de change.

Tourist office (☎ 066-947 2589; Community Centre; Ⓨ Apr-Oct) Opens sporadically. The Old Barracks Heritage Centre also has information.

Sights

O'CONNELL'S BIRTHPLACE

The ruined cottage on the eastern bank of the Carhan River, on the left as you cross the bridge en route from Kells, is the humble birthplace

of Daniel O'Connell, 'the Great Liberator' (see p39). On the opposite bank there's a stolid bust of O'Connell. Paths along the river have boards explaining the area's wildlife.

BARRACKS

The **Old Barracks Heritage Centre** (☎ 066-947 2777; www.theoldbarracks.com; off Main St; adult/child €4/2; Ⓨ 10am-4.30pm Mon-Fri, noon-4.30pm Sat & Sun Jun-Sep, other times variable) is housed in a tower of the former Royal Irish Constabulary (RIC) barracks. Anti-Treaty forces burnt it down in 1922 and today it looks over-restored, like an oddball confection.

Topped by a spiral staircase ascending to a lookout (best suited for those who don't care to see anything), the museum covers

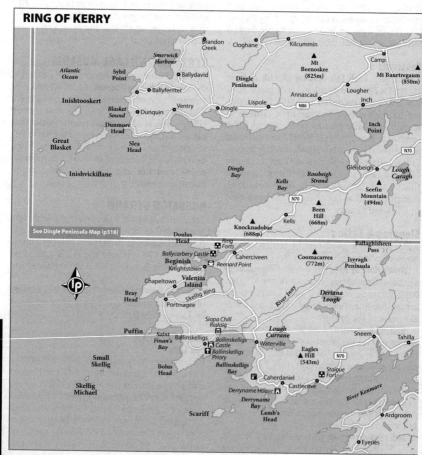

RING OF KERRY

subjects of local and national interest, such as the Fenian Rising, Daniel O'Connell and Caherciveen's other great son, Gaelic football star Jack O'Shea. There are re-creations of a local dwelling at the time of the Famine and of the barracks during the 1916 Easter Rising.

BALLYCARBERY CASTLE & RING FORTS
The best attraction locally is the ruins of Ballycarbery Castle, 2.4km along the road to White Strand Beach from the barracks. The 16th-century castle was inhabited by the McCarthy More chieftains and, later, Sir Valentine Brown, surveyor general of Ireland under Elizabeth I. Today the atmospheric remains are surrounded by green pastures inhabited by cows who like to get in the pictures.

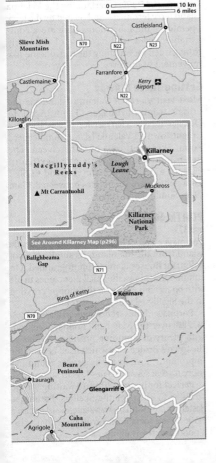

Along the same road are two stone ring forts. **Cahergall**, the larger one, dates from the 10th century and has stairways on the inside walls, a *clochan* (beehive hut), and the remains of a house. The smaller, 9th-century **Leacanabuile** has the entrance to an underground passage. Their inner walls and chambers give a strong sense of what life was like in a ring fort. If driving, leave your car in the parking area next to a stone wall and walk up the footpaths.

Activities
Local **walks** include the 5½-hour Killelan Mountain circuit and the less strenuous foreshore walk to the castle and ring forts. Ask at the tourist office for info on local guided walks and boat rides.

Festivals
Celtic music is a major component of the **Caherciveen Festival of Music & the Arts** (☎ 066-947 3772; www.celticmusicfestival.com), which takes place over the bank holiday weekend at the beginning of August and features cover bands, busking competitions and set dancing.

Sleeping
Mannix Point Camping & Caravan Park (☎ 066-947 2806; www.campinginkerry.com; Mannix Point; campsites per person €10; ☼ Mar-Oct) Mortimer Moriarty's award-winning coastal site has an inviting kitchen, a barbecue area and even a bird-watching platform.

Sive Hostel (☎ 066-947 2717; sivehostel.ie; 15 East End; dm/d €15/40) Simple and sweet, this IHH affiliate is a good walking base. The jaunty yellow exterior and pink sheets will put vim in your vigour.

O'Shea's B&B (☎ 066-947 2402; www.osheasbnb.com; Church St; s/d €45/70) Four rooms (with private bathrooms) in a comfortable family house with views of the castle and barracks. A good source of local information, the O'Sheas organise walking and boat trips.

Eating & Drinking
Trad sessions are held in An Bonnán Buí, the Anchor and among the fishing tackle in Mike Murts.

Helen's Coffee Shop (☎ 066-947 2056; Main St; snacks €4-6) A perfect stop: Helen's can restore you with a range of coffees, tasty soups and sandwiches, homemade cakes and candy. Yeah!

Fertha (☎ 066-947 2023; 20 Main St; bar food €7-12) A classic Guinness sign hanging out front sets the tone for this classic old pub, which offers a range of hearty dishes including roasts.

our pick **QCs** (☎ 066-947 2244; 3 Main St; mains lunch €5-10, dinner €17-25; ⊗ kitchen noon-2pm & 6-9.30pm) A sure sign that Caherciveen is about to turn a corner, QCs is a modern take on a classic pub and as such is open usual pub hours for pints and craic. But when the kitchen's open, some of the finest food on the Ring pours forth (locally sourced seafood, meats etc). Hours are short in winter, but in summer you'll need to book; the word is out.

VALENTIA ISLAND
pop 720

Crowned by Geokaun Mountain, 11km-long Valentia Island (Oileán Dairbhre) is an altogether homier isle than the brooding Skelligs to the southwest. Like the Skellig Ring it leads to, Valentia's an essential, coach-free detour from the Ring of Kerry. Some lonely ruins are worth exploring. Knightstown, the only town, has a good pub.

Valentia was chosen as the site for the first transatlantic telegraph cable. When the connection was made in 1858, it put Caherciveen in direct contact with New York, although without connection with Dublin. The link worked for 27 days before failing, but went back into action years later. The telegraph station operated until 1966.

The island makes for an ideal driving loop. There's a frequent, quick ferry trip at one end and a bridge to Portmagee (right) on the mainland at the other end.

Sights & Activities

Immediately across the bridge from Portmagee is an interesting building with turf-covered barrel roofs. The **Skellig Experience** (☎ 066-947 6306; www.skelligexperience.com; adult/child €5/3; ⊗ 10am-7pm Jun-Aug, to 6pm Apr, May & Sep-Nov, last admission 45min before closing) contains exhibitions on the life and times of the Skellig Michael monks, the history of the island's lighthouses and the wildlife. If you're planning a trip to the Skelligs, this is an essential stop for background information; if the weather's bad, it may be the closest you get to the islands.

Out in the boggy west, with its lonely vistas worthy of some lost world, look for signs for **St Brendan's Well**, an ancient religious site that still attracts a smattering of pilgrims. Although evidence is rather thin, legend has it that St Brendan sailed here from Dingle, scaled the cliffs (in the 5th century), found a couple of dying pagans and anointed them. Things haven't changed here much since then. From a narrow track, walk to the sacred well, with statues and recent offerings.

In Knightstown, see if the quirky little **museum** is open.

Sleeping & Eating

If you want to stay on the island, tiny Knightstown is a good base: it has pubs, food, walks, the ferry and Skellig Island boats.

Royal Valentia (☎ 066-947 6144; www.theroyalvalentia.com; Knightstown; r 35-75) This gingerbreaded old holiday resort has basic rooms and a pub (meals €6 to €20) that's the centre of local life year-round.

Spring Acre (☎ 066-947 6141; www.springacrebb.com; Knightstown; s/d €40/70) Overlooking the Valentia Island ferry terminal – and owned by the ferry operator – the four rooms here are a comfortable respite and have use of the lovely front garden for watching the metronome-like movement of the ferry.

Getting There & Away

Most visitors reach Valentia Island via the bridge from Portmagee. From April to October, there is a **ferry service** (☎ 066-947 6141) to Knightstown on Valentia Island from Reenard Point, 5km southwest of Caherciveen. The five-minute crossing costs one way/return €5/8 for a car, €2/3 for a cyclist and €1.50/2 for a pedestrian. It operates between 8.15am (9am Sunday) and 10pm.

PORTMAGEE
pop 375

Portmagee overlooks the south side of Valentia Island from the mainland. Its single street of colourful houses is much photographed. On summer mornings, the small pier comes to life with boats embarking on the choppy crossing to the Skellig Islands (opposite).

Portmagee holds **set-dancing workshops** (☎ 066-947 7108) over the May bank holiday weekend, with plenty of stomping practice sessions in the town's Bridge Bar, which itself is good for impromptu music by the locals year-round and more formal sessions Tuesdays in summer.

Perfect for hanging around waiting for the weather to clear for the Skelligs, **Portmagee Hostel** (☎ 066-948 0018; www.portmageehostel.com; dm/d €15/46-52) is a sociable, no-frills place that's also a good hub for walking.

The **Moorings** (☎ 066-947 7108; www.moorings.ie; s €70-100, d €100-140) is a friendly local gathering point, with 16 rooms split between modern sea-view choices and simpler options, most refreshingly white. The nautical-themed restaurant (meals €20 to €35) specialises in excellent seafood.

SKELLIG ISLANDS
gannet pop 45,000
The Skellig Islands (Oileáin na Scealaga) are impervious to the ever-pounding Atlantic. George Bernard Shaw said Skellig Michael was 'the most fantastic and impossible rock in the world'. A visit is a test of endurance for your stomach, bladder and brain, the latter because the sheer magnificence of the natural beauty and ancient ruins is mind-blowing.

You'll need to do your best grisly sea-dog impression ('argh!') on the 12km crossing, which can be rough. There are no toilets or shelter on Skellig Michael, the only island visitors are permitted to land on. Bring something to eat and drink and wear stout shoes and weatherproof clothing. (Boat operators can often lend passengers old waterproof duds for the crossing.)

Activities
The Skelligs are a **birdwatching** paradise. Keep a sharp lookout during the boat trip and you may spot diminutive storm petrels (also known as Mother Carey's chickens) darting above the water like swallows. Gannets are unmistakable with their savage beaks, imperious eyes, yellow caps and 100cm-plus wing spans. They dive like tridents into the sea, from up to 30m at well over 100km per hour, to snatch fish below the surface. Kittiwakes – small, dainty seabirds with black-tipped wings – are easy to see and hear around Skellig Michael's covered walkway as you step off the boat. They winter at sea then land in their thousands to breed between March and August.

Further up the rock you'll see stubby-winged fulmars, with distinctive bony 'nostrils' from which they eject an evil-smelling green liquid if you get too close. Look also for razorbills, black-and-white guillemots and the delightful puffins with their multicoloured beaks and waddling gait. In May, puffins come ashore to lay a solitary egg at the far end of a burrow, and parent birds can be seen guarding their nests. Puffins stay only until the first weeks of August.

Skellig Michael
The jagged, 217m-high rock of **Skellig Michael** (Archangel Michael's Rock; like St Michael's Mount in Cornwall and Mont Saint Michel in Normandy) is the larger of the two islands and a Unesco World Heritage site. It looks like the last place on earth where anyone would try to land, let alone establish a community, yet early Christian monks survived here from the 6th until the 12th or 13th century. Influenced by the Coptic Church (founded by St Anthony in the deserts of Egypt and Libya), their determined quest for ultimate solitude led them to this remote, windblown edge of Europe.

The monastic buildings are perched on a saddle in the rock, some 150m above sea level, reached by 600 steep steps cut into the rock face. The astounding 6th-century oratories and beehive cells vary in size; the largest cell has a floor space of 4.5m by 3.6m. You can see the monks' south-facing vegetable garden and their cistern for collecting rainwater. The most impressive structural achievements are the settlement's foundations – platforms built on the steep slope using nothing more than earth and drystone walls.

Little is known about the life of the monastery, but there are records of Viking raids in AD 812 and 823. Monks were kidnapped or killed, but the community recovered and carried on. Legend even has it that the monks converted one of the raiders, Olaf Tryggvesson, and he became Norway's first Christian ruler. In the 11th century a rectangular oratory was added to the site, but although it was expanded in the 12th century, the monks abandoned the rock around this time, perhaps because of particularly ferocious Atlantic storms.

After the introduction of the Gregorian calendar in 1582, Skellig Michael became a popular spot for weddings. Marriages were forbidden during Lent, but since Skellig used the old Julian calendar, a trip to the islands allowed those unable to wait for Easter to tie the knot.

In the 1820s two lighthouses were built on Skellig Michael, together with the road that runs around the base.

The guides on the island ask you to do your picnicking on the way up to the monastery, or at Christ's Saddle just before the last flight of steps, rather than among the ruins. This is to keep sandwich-loving birds and their droppings away from the monument.

Small Skellig

While Skellig Michael looks like two triangles linked by a spur, Small Skellig is longer, lower and much craggier. From a distance it looks as if someone battered it with a feather pillow that burst. Close up you realise you're looking at a colony of over 20,000 pairs of breeding gannets, the second-largest breeding colony in the world. Most boats circle the island so you can see the gannets, and you may see basking seals as well. Small Skellig is a bird sanctuary; no landing is permitted.

Getting There & Away

Skellig Michael's fragility places limits on the number of daily visitors. The 15 boats are licensed to carry no more than 12 passengers each, for a maximum of 180 people there at any one time. So it's wise to book ahead in July and August, bearing in mind that if the weather's bad the boats may not sail (about two days out of seven). Trips usually start running around Easter, depending, again, on weather.

Boats leave around 10am and return at 3pm, and cost about €45 per person. You can depart from Portmagee, Knightstown, Caherciveen, Ballinskelligs or Derrynane. The boat owners try to restrict you to two hours on the island, which is the bare minimum, on a good day, to see the monastery, look at the birds and have a picnic. The crossing takes about 1½ hours from Portmagee, one hour from Ballinskelligs and 1¾ hours from Derrynane.

Local pubs and B&Bs will point you in the direction of operators, including:

Casey's (☎ 066-947 2437; www.skelligislands.com; Portmagee)

Dan & Donal McCrohan (☎ 066-947 6142; Valentia Island)

John O'Shea (☎ 087 689 8431; johnoshea33@hotmail.com; Caherdaniel)

Sea Quest (☎ 066-947 6214; www.skelligsrock.com; Valentia Island, Reenard Point)

If you just want to see the islands up close and avoid actually having to clamber out of the boat, the Skellig Experience (p304) runs two-hour cruises daily in summer (adult/child €28/15), usually about 3pm.

SKELLIG RING

This 18km detour from the Ring of Kerry (N70) links Portmagee and Waterville via a Gaeltacht (Irish-speaking) area centred on Ballinskelligs (Baile an Sceilg). Ballinskelligs'

name translates as 'town of the crag', which may elicit sniggers from fans of *Father Ted* and his Craggy Island pals (see the boxed text, p406). The area is as wild and beautiful as anything on Ted's fictional isle, with the ragged outline of Skellig Michael never far from view.

Besides the desolate scenery, the Skellig Ring's narrow roads are tour-bus free.

Sights

SIOPA CHILL RIALAIG

On the site of a village abandoned during the Famine, this contemporary **art gallery** (☎ 066-947 9297; cillrialaig@easatclear.ie; Dun Geagan; 10am-7pm Jul-Aug, 11am-5pm rest of year) is packed with work by local artists and talent from around Ireland and the world. It is the shop window of the Cill Rialaig Project, which provides a retreat for creative people who pay for their stay with art.

The gallery is by the R566 at the northeastern end of Ballinskelligs. You'll spot its circular, thatched roofs and the sculpture that resembles a hallucinogenic mushroom. There is a cafe inside.

BALLINSKELLIGS PRIORY & BAY

The sea and salty air are eating away at the atmospheric ruins of this **medieval priory**, a monastic settlement that was probably built by the Skellig Michaels monks after they fled their isolated outpost in the 12th century. To reach it, follow the sign to the pier at the western end of town and you will see it on the left.

Another sign points to the fine little Blue Flag **beach**. At the western end of the beach are the last remnants of the 16th-century **castle** stronghold of the McCarthys, built on the isthmus as a defence against pirates.

Activities

St Finian's Bay is good for surfing. **Ballinskelligs Watersports** (☎ 086 389 4849; www.skelligsurf.com) hires out surfboards, kayaks and windsurfers, and gives lessons (per two hours €35 to €45).

Sleeping & Eating

Skellig Hostel (☎ 066-947 9942; www.skellighostel.com; Ballinskelligs; dm/d €15/46-52) This modern building exudes all the character of an auditor at work but inside the pink bedding is worthy of Barbie's dream house. The common spaces are comfortable and the elevated location provides good sea views.

Ballinskelligs Inn (☎ 066-947 9106; www.ballin skelligsinn.com; s/d from €50) A classic rural establishment where the conversation is in Gaeilge. An addition has brought the room count to 14, all with various iconic views. The simple restaurant does simple meals (€10 to €20) or you can hit the small shop for crisps. They will organise diving and activities for you.

Café Coistrá (☎ 066-947 9323; snacks €1-3; ☉ 9am-6pm) At the car park for Ballinskelligs strand, this beach-hut cafe and craft shop is a great place for a coffee. Locals flock here for their morning jolt. Photos seem to go back to Famine times.

WATERVILLE
pop 550

Waterville, a line of colourful houses strung on the N72 between Lough Currane and Ballinskelligs Bay, is charm-challenged in the way of many such mass-consumption beach resorts. A vast golf resort hopes to give the town an élan it once had when Charlie Chaplin visited – a statue of him in costume leers along the seafront.

There is tourist information and a bureau de change at **Waterville Craft Market** (☎ 066-947 4212; ☉ 9am-9pm Jun-Aug, 10am-6pm Sep-May).

Sights & Activities

At the north end of Lough Currane, **Church Island** has the ruins of a medieval church and beehive cell. Reputedly founded as a monastic settlement by St Finian in the 6th century, it's a dry-land alternative to the Skelligs in choppy weather.

Sleeping & Eating

O'Dwyer's (☎ 066-947 4248; Main St; s/d from €35/70) A central budget option, above a remarkably clean pub. Rooms are tight from the bathrooms to the beds, but the value is big. A sign downstairs: 'Avoid hangovers, stay drunk.'

Clifford's B&B (☎ 066-947 4283; www.cliffordbandb .com; Main St; s/d from €40/76; ☉ Mar-Oct) A pink house right in the town and across from the shore, rooms here are purely functional and comfortable; some have sea views. Walkers in the often stormy conditions are accommodated with a drying room for their clothes, boots, underwear… Good breakfasts, too.

CAHERDANIEL
pop 350

Hiding between Derrynane Bay and the foothills of Eagles Hill, Caherdaniel barely qualifies as a tiny hamlet. Businesses are scattered about the undergrowth like smugglers, fitting since this was once a haven for same.

This is the ancestral home of Daniel O'Connell, 'the Liberator' (see p39), whose family made money smuggling from their base by the dunes. The area boasts a Blue Flag beach, plenty of activities, good hikes and some pubs where you may be tempted to break into pirate talk and boast about your love for Arrrgh-gentina. Lines of wind-gnarled trees add to the wild air.

Sights
DERRYNANE NATIONAL HISTORIC PARK

Derrynane House (☎ 066-947 5113; Derrynane; adult/ child €3/1; ☉ 9am-6pm Mon-Sat, 11am-6pm Sun May-Sep, 1-5pm Tue-Sun Apr & Oct, 1-5pm Sat & Sun Nov-Mar, last admission 45 min before closing) is the family home of Daniel O'Connell, the campaigner for Catholic emancipation. His ancestors bought the house and surrounding parkland, having grown rich on smuggling with France and Spain. It's largely furnished with O'Connell memorabilia, including the restored triumphal chariot in which he lapped Dublin after his release from prison in 1844.

The gardens, warmed by the Gulf Stream, hold palms, 4m-high tree ferns, gunnera ('giant rhubarb') and other South American species. A walking track through them leads to wetlands, beaches and clifftops. You can spot wild pheasants and other birds, whose musical calls add a note of contrast to the dull roar of the surf. The **chapel**, which O'Connell added to Derrynane House in 1844, is a copy of the ruined one on **Abbey Island**, which can usually be reached on foot across the sand.

Look out for the **Ogham stone** on the left of the road to the house. With its carved notches representing the simple Ogham alphabet of the ancient Irish, the stone has several missing letters, but may represent the name of a local chieftain.

Activities

As it has for centuries (although now it tends to be legal), most of the activity here centres on the beach. Popular **Derrynane Sea Sports** (☎ 087 908 1208; derrynaneseasports@eircom.net) organises sailing, canoeing, windsurfing and waterskiing for all levels, operating from the beach between June and August. **Eagle Rock Equestrian Centre** (☎ 066-947 5145; www.eaglerockcentre.com) offers beach, mountain and woodland treks for all levels (from €30 per hour).

Walkers should head to **Bunavalla Pier**, 3.2km downhill from the N70, west of Caherdaniel. Walk there and you'll descend towards 'Ireland's best known view' (according to the Scarriff Inn's sign at the top) along what could be Ireland's windiest, steepest lane. Keep left and conserve your energy for the slog back uphill.

The Kerry Way passes through here (see p300) and goes on to a megalithic tomb at the base of Farraniaragh Mountain, 248m above sea level.

The dunes are a good place for shags, which birders know are another name for cormorants, a very common bird here.

Sleeping

Wave Crest (☎ 066-947 5188; www.wavecrestcamping .com; campsites from €12; ⊗ mid-Mar–mid-Oct; ⏾) Just 1.6km southeast of Caherdaniel, this cliffside compound has a superb setting and well-kept facilities. Book during peak season.

Glenbeg Caravan & Camping Park (☎ 066-947 5182; glenbeg@eircom.net; campsites €17; ⊗ mid-Apr–early Oct) Some 2.5km east of Caherdaniel on the N70, Glenbeg has an unbeatable seaside location, overlooking a sandy beach with views of the Beara Peninsula.

Travellers' Rest Hostel (☎ 066-947 5175; dm/d from €17/40) All low ceilings, board games and dried flowers in the grate, Travellers' Rest has the quaint feel of a country cottage. If you buy into the local funky charm, you'll love this place. Call at the garage opposite if there's nobody about.

Olde Forge (☎ 066-947 5140; www.theoldeforge.com; s/d from €40/74) This B&B has six comfortable and undramatic rooms; the excitement comes from the fantastic views of Kenmare Bay and the Beara Peninsula. It's 1.2km southeast of town on the N70.

Eating & Drinking

Courthouse Cafe (☎ 066-947 5834; dinner €10; ⊗ 11am-4pm & 6-10pm Jun-Sep) Pizza is just one of the crowd-pleasers at this cafe near the Blind Piper. Fish cakes and chips are among the other filling feeds on the card.

Blind Piper (☎ 066-947 5126; bar food €10-18; ⊗ noon-9.30pm Jun-Aug, to 8.30pm rest of year) This local institution with tables outside is a great family pub during the day, serving expensive but quality grub. Deep-fried monkfish gives

the idea that they're striving for more here. After dark, locals and visitors crowd inside and music sessions happen.

Freddy's (☎ 066-947 5125) A profusion of beer steins hangs over the small bar at this perfectly realised little haunt of sailors and drinkers. It's a mere stumble from the Blind Piper.

STAIGUE FORT

This ring fort at the head of a valley is an imposing sight, and a powerful evocation of late Iron Age Ireland. Its circular stone wall, up to 6m high and 4m thick, is surrounded by a protective bank and ditch. Steps criss-cross the interior of the wall, which contains two small rooms and a narrow entrance tunnel.

Staigue probably dates from the 3rd or 4th century. The building's sophistication suggests it belonged to a powerful chieftain. Despite having sweeping views down to the coast, it's not visible from the sea. It may have been a communal place of refuge, or a cultural and commercial centre where people came to celebrate, exchange goods and stage ceremonies.

The fort is near the village of Castlecove, about 4km off the N70, reached by a battered country lane that narrows as it climbs to a road-end car park beside the site.

The battered building that would look at home in Havana is the **exhibition centre** (⊗ 10am-9pm Easter-Sep), which has a cafe and an interpretative display.

A scrawled sign, before it descends into a stream of consciousness about trespassing, asks for €1 for access to the Dúchas site across private land.

SNEEM

Halfway between Caherdaniel and Kenmare, Sneem (An tSnaidhm) is a good place to pause for something restorative, especially if you're travelling anticlockwise, as the remaining 27km to Kenmare the N70 drifts away from the water and coasts along under a soothing canopy of trees.

The village's Gaeilge name translates as 'the knot', which is thought to refer to the River Sneem that swirls, knot-like, into nearby Kenmare Bay. Sneem is nicknamed 'the knot in the Ring of Kerry'. Other local puns include one about Charles de Gaulle, who holidayed here when Paris was burning in 1968. The statue commemorating this is called 'Le Gallstone'.

Take a gander at the town's two cute squares, then pop into the **Blue Bull** (☎ 064-664 5382), a perfect little old stone pub where you can probably learn more local puns.

KENMARE
pop 2500

The copper-covered limestone spire of Holy Cross Church, drawing the eye to the wooded hills above town, may make you forget that Kenmare is a seaside town for a split second. But with rivers named Finnihy, Roughty and Sheen emptying into Kenmare Bay, you couldn't be anywhere other than southwest Ireland.

Kenmare is an ideal stop, whether your itinerary includes the Ring of Beara, the Ring of Kerry or both. Elegant streets with beguiling restaurants and shops fan out from Fair Green in a handy triangular loop. It gets busy in summer, but it's less hectic than Killarney.

Orientation

In the 18th century, Kenmare was laid out on an X-plan, with a triangular market square in the centre. Today the inverted V to the south is the focus. Henry and Main Sts are the main shopping and eating and drinking thoroughfares; Shelbourne St links their southern ends. Kenmare Bay stretches out to the southwest, and there are glorious views of the mountains.

Information

The post office on the corner of Henry and Shelbourne Sts sells local walking maps and guides, as well as internet access (€1 for 15 minutes). For info, try www.kenmare.com. Banks and ATMs are common.

Finnegan's Taxis & Tours (☎ 064-664 1491) Located above the tourist office.

Kenmare Bookshop (☎ 064-664 1578; Shelbourne St) Has a wide range of books, including a strong Irish section with maps and guides.

Live Wire (☎ 064-664 2714; Rock St; per 30min €2; ☑ 10am-6pm Mon-Sat) Just off Main St.

O'Shea's Laundry (☎ 064-664 1394; Kenmare Business Park; ☑ 8.30am-6pm Mon-Fri, to 5.30pm Sat; self-service €1) Located 2km north of town on the N71.

Public toilets (Old Killarney Rd) Opposite the Holy Cross Church, next to a car park.

Tourist office (☎ 064-663 1633; The Square; ☑ 9am-5pm Easter-Oct) Gives out free maps detailing a heritage trail around town and longer walks of up to 13km.

Sights

The **Kenmare Heritage Centre** (☎ 064-664 1233; The Square; adult/child €3/1.50; ☑ 9am-5pm Easter-Oct), reached through the tourist office, tells the history of the town from its founding as Neidín by the swashbuckling Sir William Petty in 1670. The centre also relates the story of the Poor Clare Convent, founded in 1861, which is still standing behind Holy Cross Church. Local women were taught needlepoint lace-making at the convent, and their lacework catapulted Kenmare to international fame.

Upstairs, the **Kenmare Lace and Design Centre** (☎ 064-664 2978; ☑ 10.15am-5.30pm Mon-Sat Easter-Oct, 10.30am-1.30pm Nov-Mar) has displays including designs for 'the most important piece of lace ever made in Ireland' (in a 19th-century critic's opinion). It's run by lace-maker Nora Finnegan, who was taught by the Poor Clare nuns. Also interesting is the story of Margaret Anna Cusack (1829–99), the Nun of Kenmare and an early advocate of women's rights. She was hounded out of Kenmare, converted to Protestantism and died, embittered, in Leamington, England.

Signposted southwest of the Square is an early Bronze Age **stone circle**, one of the biggest in southwest Ireland. Fifteen stones ring a boulder dolmen, a burial monument rarely found outside this part of the country.

Built in 1862, the **Holy Cross Church** on Old Killarney Rd boasts a splendid wooden roof with 14 angel carvings. Fine mosaics adorn the aisle arches and edges of the stained-glass window over the altar. The architect was Charles Hansom, collaborator and brother-in-law of Augustus Pugin (the architect behind London's Houses of Parliament).

Activities

Star Sailing (☎ 064-664 1222; www.staroutdoors.ie; Dauros), on the R571, offers activities including sailing, sea kayaking, diving, windsurfing, pony trekking, cycling and hillwalking for novices and experts.

Warm yourself on tea, coffee, rum and the captain's sea shanties on a two-hour spotting voyage to see seal pups and other marine life with **Seafari** (☎ 064-664 2059; www.seafariireland.com; Kenmare Pier; adult/child €20/12.50). Book ahead.

The tourist office has details of walks around Kenmare Bay and into the hills, on sections of the Kerry Way (see p300) and Beara Way (p282).

Sleeping

B&Bs abound, especially on Henry St.

BUDGET

Ring of Kerry Caravan & Camping Park (☎ 064-664 1648; Reen; campsites from €15; ☺ Apr-Sep) Mountains and sea surround this beautiful site in wooded country, 3.5km west of town and 1km down a side road, off the north side of the Sneem road.

Kenmare Lodge (☎ 064-664 0662; www.kenmare hostel.com; 27 Main St; dm/d from €17/50; ▯ ⧉) Perfectly located, this pleasant, modern hostel has a patio, laundry facilities and a roomy kitchen and dining area.

MIDRANGE

Greenville B&B (☎ 064-664 1769; Killowen Rd; s/d from €45/70) Just 100m east of Main St, this modern house has eye-catching gardens and ancient stone walls, as well as four comfy bedrooms with private bathrooms. Breakfasts are hearty and the bucolic scene is enhanced by views of the golf course.

Whispering Pines (☎ 064-664 1194; wpines@eircom .net; s/d from €45/80; ☺ Easter-Nov) In a quiet location near the pier, with four immaculate rooms and a cheerful welcome. Town is a short walk and the location out here near the brine is fantastic.

ourpick Virginia's Guesthouse (☎ 064-664 1021; www.virginias-kenmare.com; Henry St; r from €50/80; ⧉) You can't get more central than this award-winning B&B, whose creative breakfasts celebrate organic local produce (rhubarb and blueberries in season, for example). Its eight excellent rooms are perfectly comfortable but not posh. Excellent value.

Hawthorn House (☎ 064-664 1035; www.hawthorn housekenmare.com; Shelbourne St; s/d from €55/90; ⧉) This stylish house has seven spacious rooms, including a majestic family room, all named after local towns and decked out in light pine. It is set back from busy Shelbourne St behind a low wall.

Rose Cottage (☎ 064-664 1330; The Square; d €70-80) This countrified B&B is almost a cliché and it's even right in the centre. The rooms are timeless as is the experience (although they are sold as doubles only). The Poor Clare nuns stayed here when they arrived in Kenmare, then had to leave just as the apples were ripening in the orchard.

D'Arcy's (☎ 064-664 1589; www.darcys.ie; r from €80) Antiques and simple decor mingle in the seven rooms above one of Kenmare's best restaurants (see opposite). Besides enjoying a dinner discount, guests can partake in an included full breakfast with some lovely baked goods.

TOP END

Sheen Falls Lodge (☎ 064-664 1600; www.sheenfallslodge .ie; r from €350; ☺ Feb-Dec; ⧉ ▯ ⧉) The Marquis of Landsdowne's former summer residence still feels like an aristocrats' playground. The lodge is an elegant and luxurious retreat with a spa and 66 rooms with DVD players and Italian marble bathrooms. With views of the falls and across Kenmare Bay to Carrantuohil, it's a beautiful escape. Amenities are many (clay-pigeon shooting, anyone?).

Eating

Choices, whether snacks, picnic, lunch or dinner, are many – and good. For self-catering options, the **farmers market** (☺ 10am-4pm Wed) is on the Square, the **SuperValu** (☎ 064-664 1307; Main St) supermarket has a wide selection, and **Truffle Pig** (☎ 064-664 2953; The Square; ☺ 9am-5pm Mon-Sat) offers fine meats, cheeses and other deli items from the region.

BUDGET

Jam ☎ 064-664 1591; Henry St; meals & snacks €2-9; ☺ 8am-5pm) Funky, comfy Jam offers organic baked goods, picnic joy and elaborate coffees. Veggies can go silly for the lentil and nut loaf.

Purple Heather Bistro (☎ 064-664 1016; Henry St; meals & snacks €5-15; ☺ 10.45am-6pm Mon-Sat) With a great atmosphere and comfy traditional decor, this Kenmare favourite serves a great range of creative sandwiches and Irish dishes with a dash of European flair. The homemade desserts are the bomb.

Whartons (☎ 064-664 2622; 35 Main St; meals €8-12; ☺ 11am-9pm) Traditional fish and chips are the big deal – and almost the only deal – at this spiffy chipper. Dine upstairs or out front.

MIDRANGE

ourpick Prego (☎ 064-664 2350; Henry St; mains €8-25; ☺ 8.30am-9pm, to 10.30pm summer) A restaurant for all seasons – and times. Local and organic produce is the basis of this all-day restaurant. The breakfast menu is long and varied and the antidote to every bit of dodgy black pudding you've avoided on your B&B plate; lunches feature many specials and are known for their soups and salads. At dinner, the Italian zest here shines with a lot of Med flavours on pastas and seafood.

PF McCarthy's (☎ 064-664 1516; 14 Main St; dinner €13-27; ⊗ noon-3pm Mon-Sat, plus 5-9pm Tue-Sat) This well-mannered spot offers meals about three notches above the pub-grub norm. Numerous sandwiches and hot specials are complemented by a varied selection of beers on tap – more than the Coors Light/Heineken juggernaut.

Horseshoe (☎ 064-664 1553; 3 Main St; mains €17-28; ⊗ 5-10pm) Ivy frames the entrance to this gastropub, which has a short but excellent menu that runs from Kerry's best burger to luscious scallops and hearty steaks. Vegetarian specials appear daily.

TOP END

D'Arcy's Oyster Bar and Grill (☎ 064-664 1589; www
.darcys.ie; mains €19-32; ⊗ 6.30-9.30pm) 'Eat fish – your heart will love you for it' reads the sign in the window. It could also say, eat fresh! Local purveyors supply the best in organic produce, cheeses and fresh seafood, all served in modern, low-key surrounds. Needless to say the raw oysters capture the elusive scent of the bay. The accommodation is good also (see opposite).

Drinking & Entertainment

For good trad sessions try **Crowley's** (Henry St), while **Florry Batt's** (Henry St) sees a cheerful crowd and occasional singalongs. A wide range of acts plays **PF McCarthy's** (☎ 064-664 1516; 14 Main St) Thursday to Saturday.

Shopping

Kenmare has many quality craft shops. On 15 August every year, marketers from throughout Ireland descend on town with crafts, local produce, ponies, cattle, sheep, bric-a-brac etc.

PFK Gold & Silversmith (☎ 064-664 2590; pfkelly@
indigo.ie; 18 Henry St) Minimalist jewellery by Paul Kelly and contemporary Irish designers. Check out the salt servers with enamel linings by West Cork designer Marika O'Sullivan. Prices start at €80; Kelly also takes commissions.

Soundz of Muzic (☎ 064-664 2268; 9 Henry St) Has a selection of Irish and contemporary music.

Noel & Holland (☎ 064-664 2464; 3 Bridge St) Find that elusive favourite at this excellent second-hand bookshop, which sells some rare editions and also has a terrific range of paperbacks, all neatly collated.

The **farmers market** (⊗ 10am-4pm Wed) also draws many artisans.

Getting There & Away

The 32km drive on the N71 to Killarney is surprisingly dramatic with tunnels and stark mountain vistas.

Twice-daily buses serve the transport hub of Killarney (€9, 50 minutes). See p295 for service to Castletownbere, County Cork and other points during the summer. Buses stop outside Roughty Bar (Main St).

Getting Around

Finnegan's Cycle Centre (☎ 064-664 1083; Shelbourne St) rents bikes for €15/85 per day/week. There's free parking throughout town, with a two-hour limit between 9am and 6pm.

NORTHERN KERRY

The landscape of Northern Kerry is often dull compared with the glories of the Ring of Kerry and the Dingle Peninsula, Killarney and Kenmare. But there are some interesting places that should give you pause on your drive. Tralee has a great museum while Ballybunion and the blustery beaches south of the Shannon estuary are worth a look.

TRALEE
pop 22,100

Despite being the county town, Tralee is dismissed in the rest of Kerry as an overflow valve for Limerick and its social problems. It's certainly a down-to-earth place, more engaged with the business of everyday life than the tourist trade. Stop in for a stroll of an Irish town where you *might* have a hard time buying a shamrock-clutching teddy bear.

Founded by the Normans in 1216, Tralee has a long history of rebellion. In the 16th century the last ruling earl of the Desmonds was captured and executed here. His head was sent to Elizabeth I, who spiked it on London Bridge. The Desmond castle once stood at the junction of Denny St and the Mall, but any trace of medieval Tralee that survived the Desmond Wars was razed during the Cromwellian period.

Orientation

You'll find most things you need along the Mall and its continuation, Castle St. Elegant Denny St and Day Pl are the oldest parts of town, with 18th-century buildings. Ashe St is home to the circular Courthouse, a solemn, fortresslike building. The tourist office is at the southern end of Denny St. The bus and train stations are a five-minute walk northeast of the town centre. The Square, just south of the Mall, is a pleasant open space with a contemporary style.

Information

Castle St has banks with ATMs and bureaux de change.

Internet Cafe (☎ 066-719 1441; 40 Bridge St; per hr €2) For internet access, cheap international calls, Western Union transfers, photocopying and mobile top-up.

Luggage storage (per item €4; ☷ 7am-5pm) At the train station.

Polymaths (☎ 066-712 5035; 1-2 Courthouse Lane) Bookshop with a good selection of books on the region.

Post office (Edward St)

Public toilets (Denny St)

Tourist office (☎ 066-712 1288; Denny St; ☷ 9am-5pm) Below Kerry County Museum.

Tralee General Hospital (☎ 066-712 6222; Boherbee) Has an accident and emergency unit.

Sights & Activities

An absolute treat, the **Kerry County Museum** (☎ 066-712 7777; Denny St; adult/child/family €8/5/22; ☷ 9.30am-5.30pm) has excellent interpretive displays on Irish historical events and trends, with an emphasis on County Kerry. The **Medieval Experience** re-creates life (smells and all) in Tralee in 1450. Check out the deranged

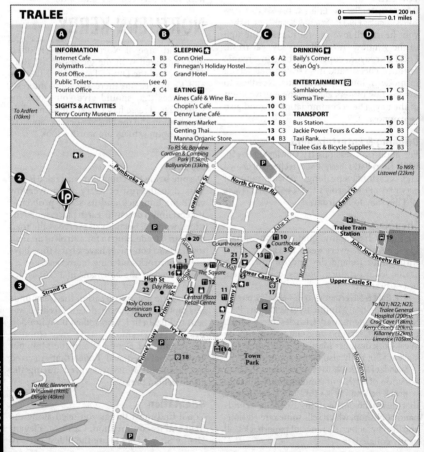

TRALEE

INFORMATION		
Internet Cafe	1	B3
Polymaths	2	C3
Post Office	3	C3
Public Toilets	(see 4)	
Tourist Office	4	C4

SIGHTS & ACTIVITIES		
Kerry County Museum	5	C4

SLEEPING		
Conn Oriel	6	A2
Finnegan's Holiday Hostel	7	C3
Grand Hotel	8	C3

EATING		
Aines Café & Wine Bar	9	B3
Chopin's Café	10	C3
Denny Lane Café	11	C3
Farmers Market	12	B3
Genting Thai	13	C3
Manna Organic Store	14	B3

DRINKING		
Baily's Corner	15	C3
Séan Óg's	16	B3

ENTERTAINMENT		
Samhlaíocht	17	C3
Siamsa Tíre	18	B4

TRANSPORT		
Bus Station	19	D3
Jackie Power Tours & Cabs	20	B3
Taxi Rank	21	C3
Tralee Gas & Bicycle Supplies	22	B3

To Ardfert (10km)

To R556; Bayview Caravan & Camping Park (1.5km); Ballyunion (33km)

To N69; Listowel (22km)

Pembroke St

North Circular Rd

Edward St

Ashe St

Tralee Train Station

John Joe Sheehy Rd

Russell St

Lower Rock St

Courthouse La

Courthouse

The Mall

The Square

Lower Castle St

McCowan's St

Upper Castle St

High St

Bridge St

Day Place

Denny St

Strand St

Holy Cross Dominican Church

Prince's St

Central Plaza Retail Centre

Ivy Tce

To N21; N22; N23; Tralee General Hospital (200m); Crag Cave (18km); Kerry County (20km); Killarney (32km); Limerick (105km)

Prince's Quay

Moyderwell

Town Park

To N86; Blennerville Windmill (1km); Dingle (40km)

0 ——— 200 m
0 ——— 0.1 miles

COUNTY KERRY

nights, a vision of horror right out of Monty Python. Children love strolling the medieval streets and there's a commentary in various languages. The **Tom Crean Room** celebrates the local hero, an early-20th-century explorer who accompanied both Scott and Shackleton on epic Antarctic expeditions. It's housed in the neoclassical Ashe Memorial Hall.

Blennerville, 1km southwest of Tralee on the N86, used to be the city's chief port, though the harbour has long since silted in. A 19th-century flour **windmill** there has been restored and is the largest working mill in Ireland and Britain. Its modern **visitor centre** (☎ 066-712 1064; adult/child €5/3; ☺ 9am-6pm Jun-Aug, 9.30am-5.30pm Apr-May & Sep-Oct) houses an exhibition on grain-milling, and on the thousands of emigrants who boarded 'coffin ships' from what was then Kerry's largest embarkation point. There's also a database of the Irish émigrés who flocked to America. Admission includes a 30-minute guided tour of the windmill.

Between 1891 and 1953 a narrow-gauge **steam railway** connected Tralee with Dingle. A 3km Tralee–Blennerville section has been restored but at the time of research it was indefinitely closed for repair.

Sleeping

Denny St has places to stay at all price ranges.

Bayview Caravan & Camping Park (☎ 066-712 6140; bayviewtralee@eircom.net; Killeen; campsites €14; ☺ Apr-Oct) This small park has good facilities and a pleasant tree-lined location. It's 1.5km north of the centre on the R556.

Finnegan's Holiday Hostel (☎ 066-712 7610; www .finneganshostel.com; 17 Denny St; dm/s/d €17/30/50; ⌨) The elegant Georgian facade leads to a hostel and hotel. The grandeur has faded, but there are a sizeable kitchen and lounge. The dorms, named after Irish scribblers, have their own bathrooms as do the private rooms (which have high-speed internet).

Conn Oriel (☎ 066-712 5359; www.connoriel.com; 6 Pembroke Sq, Pembroke St; s/d €40/70; P) One of a line of B&Bs, this friendly mother-daughter operation has cheery decorative art on pastel walls; if nightlife's a dud, enjoy the satellite TV in every room.

Grand Hotel (☎ 066-712 1499; www.grandhoteltralee .com; Denny St; r €85-150; P ⌨ ☜) Built in 1928, the Grand is just that. At night, it's lit up like a beckoning refuge, which it is, but it main-

tains the feel of a proper county-town hotel in its public rooms. The 44 rooms have had a stylish refit.

Eating

For a snack or a meal, Tralee has popularly priced food for the masses.

Denny Lane Café (☎ 066-719 4319; Denny Lane; meals €4-10; ☺ 8am-5pm Mon-Sat) 'Simple quality food prepared with care' says the sign, and it's true. Enjoy Cuban coffees, a plethora of cakes and excellent sandwiches, soups, salads and hot specials at this big, modern lunch spot.

Chopin's Café (☎ 066-711 7539; 8 Ashe St; meals €5-12; ☺ 8am-6pm) This cute little box of a cafe has cliché-busting breakfasts from chocolate brioche to savoury omelettes. Lunch sees many specials, including popular daily soups and plates like crab claws and many pastas.

Áines Café & Wine Bar (☎ 066-718 5388; The Square; meals €6-18; ☺ 8am-10pm) Where Tralee's glitterati try to affect boredom while their kids go nuts playing football metres away on the Square. Lots of salads, steaks, hot specials and cute little sandwiches. Heaters over tables outside make trying to affect that Continental lifestyle palatable.

our pick **Genting Thai** (☎ 066-719 4285; 11 Courthouse Lane; mains €8-18; ☺ noon-9pm Mon-Sat) It's the real deal here at this little bistro as well-mannered as a Thai dancer. The menu is actually Thai (without a lot of masses-friendly Chinese numbers like sweet and sour pork) and is both perfectly spiced and often spicy; people's tongues deadened by Irish cooking will thrill to the many dishes rated with three chillies on the menu.

Manna Organic Store (☎ 066-711 8501; New Rd; ☺ 8am-6pm Mon-Sat) has organic produce, groceries and various feel-good potions and lotions. Wheatgrass grows in the window. The **farmers market** (☺ 10am-4pm) sprawls across the main square.

Drinking & Entertainment

The local arts group **Samhlaíocht** (☎ 066-712 9934; www.samhlaiocht.com; Old Presbytery, Lower Castle St) stages exhibitions and special events such as the **Kerry Film Festival** (www.kerryfilmfestival.com) in early November.

PUBS

Castle St is thick with mass-market pubs, many of them offering live entertainment. There are some reasonable cafe-bars on the

Square where you could easily pass an afternoon watching Tralee coming and going.

Baily's Corner (☎ 066-712 6230; Ashe St) Baily's is deservedly popular for its traditional sessions, with local musicians performing original material most weeknights.

Seán Óg's (☎ 066-712 8822; Bridge St) Fair diddling trad is on at this rambling and raucous bar from Sunday to Thursday.

THEATRE

Siamsa Tíre (☎ 066-712 3055; www.siamsatire.com; Town Park; shows per person €15-30; booking office ☉ 9am-6pm Mon-Sat) In a pleasant location in the town park, near the tourist office, Siamsa Tíre, the National Folk Theatre of Ireland, re-creates dynamic aspects of Gaelic culture through song, dance, drama and mime. There are several shows a week from May to September at 8.30pm. Winter shows range from dance to drama and mainstream musicals.

Getting There & Away

Bus Éireann (☎ 066-716 4700; www.buseireann.ie) has buses from the **bus station** next to the train station, east of the town centre. Eight daily services run to Dublin (€23, six hours), going via Listowel (€7, 30 minutes) and changing in Limerick (€15, two hours). There are hourly buses to Waterford (€20.50, 5½ hours), Killarney (€8, 40 minutes) and Cork (€17, 2½ hours).

Irish Rail (☎ 066-712 3522; www.irishrail.ie) has services from the train station, including three direct daily services to Cork (€32, 2¼ hours), nine to Killarney (€9.50, 45 minutes) and one direct to Dublin (€36, four hours) and others requiring a change in Mallow.

Getting Around

There's a taxi rank on the Mall, or try **Jackie Power Tours & Cabs** (☎ 066-712 9444; 2 Lower Rock St). **Tralee Gas & Bicycle Supplies** (☎ 066-712 2018; Strand St) hires out bikes (€12 per day).

AROUND TRALEE
Crag Cave

This **cave** (☎ 066-714 1244; www.cragcave.com; Castleisland; adult/child €12/5; ☉ 10am-6pm daily mid-Mar–Dec, 10am-6pm Wed-Sun Jan & Feb) was discovered in 1983, when problems with water pollution led to a search for the source of the local river. In 1989, 300m of the 4km-long cave were opened to the public; admission is by 30-minute guided tour. The remarkable rock formations include a stalagmite shaped like a statue of the Madonna, at least to some.

The cave is signposted from both Castleisland and the Abbeyfeale–Castleisland stretch of the N21. Castleisland is well connected with both Tralee and Killarney by bus.

Ardfert
pop 950

Ardfert (Ard Fhearta), about 10km northwest of Tralee on the Ballyheigue road, is most notable for the soaring **Ardfert Cathedral** (☎ 066-713 4711; www.heritageireland.ie; adult/child €3/1; ☉ 9.30am-6pm Easter-Sep, last admission 45min before closing). Most of the building dates back to the 13th century, but it incorporates elements of an 11th-century church. Set into one of the interior walls is an effigy, said to be of St Brendan the Navigator, who was educated in Ardfert and founded a monastery here. The grounds contain the ruins of two other churches, 12th-century Templenahoe and 15th-century Templenagriffin.

Turning right in front of the cathedral and going 500m down the road brings you to the extensive remains of a **Franciscan friary**, dating from the 13th century, but with 15th-century cloisters.

LISTOWEL
pop 3900

The late writer Bryan MacMahon said of Listowel: 'I harbour the absurd notion of motivating a small town in Ireland, a speck on the map, to become a centre of the imagination.' Listowel certainly has more literary credentials than your average provincial town, with connections to such accomplished scribes as John B Keane, Maurice Walsh, George Fitzmaurice and Brendan Kennelly.

Outside these connections and a few venues, however, the town is little more than some tidy Georgian streets and a riverside park.

Orientation & Information

The Square is the main focus of the town. At its centre is the St John's Theatre and Arts Centre, formerly St John's Church. Most pubs and restaurants are on Church and William Sts, north from the Square, while a short walk southeast along Bridge Rd takes you to the River Feale and Childers Park. The river can also be reached down the road alongside the castle.

There's metered parking in the main square, and free parking downhill to the right of the castle.

Bank of Ireland (the Square) Has an ATM and bureau de change.

North Kerry Together (☎ 068-23429; 58 Church St; 15min/1hr €1/3; ☺ 9.30am-5pm Mon-Fri) Internet access and wi-fi.

Post office (William St) At the northern end of the street.

Tourist office (☎ 068-22590; www.listowel.ie; ☺ 9.30am-1pm & 2-5.15pm Mon-Sat Jun-Sep) Housed in the St John's Theatre & Arts Centre.

Woulfe's Bookshop (☎ 068-21021; 7 Church St) A good place for works by local literary luminaries. The Kerry Literary & Cultural Centre bookshop also stocks titles by local writers.

Sights & Activities

Kerry Literary & Cultural Centre, with its audio-visual **Writers' Exhibition** (Seanchaí; ☎ 068-22212; www.kerrywritersmuseum.com; 24 the Square; adult/child €5/3; ☺ 9.30am-5.30pm daily Jun-Sep, Mon-Fri Oct-May), is an absolute gem that gives due prominence to Listowel's heritage of literary observers of Irish life. Rooms are devoted to local greats such as John B Keane and Bryan MacMahon, with simple, haunting tableaux narrating their lives and recordings of them reading their work. There is a cafe and a performance space where events are sometimes staged.

Keane, who is remembered with a **statue** in which he seems to be hailing a cab, wrote with wry humour about subjects ranging from Limerick's beggars to the perils of giving up

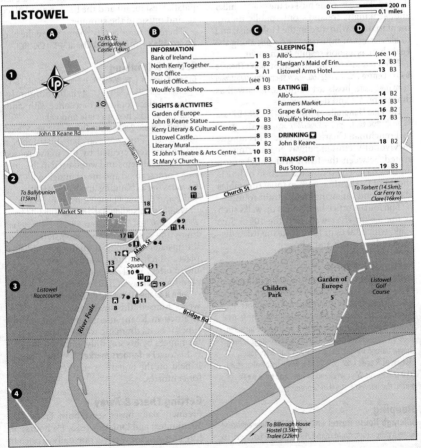

LISTOWEL

To R552;
Carrigafoyle
Castle (14km)

John B Keane Rd

William St

To Ballybunion
(15km)

Market St

Church St

To Tarbert (14.5km);
Car Ferry to
Clare (16km)

Main St

The
Square

Listowel
Racecourse

River Feale

Bridge Rd

Childers
Park

Garden of
Europe

Listowel
Golf
Course

To Billeragh House
Hostel (3.5km);
Tralee (22km)

0 — 200 m
0 — 0.1 miles

COUNTY KERRY

porter as a New Year's resolution. On Church St there is a **literary mural** depicting the local writers and their pronouncements.

The 12th-century **Listowel Castle** (☎ 086 385 7201; www.heritageireland.ie; admission free; ◷ 9.30am-5.30pm late May-Aug), behind the Kerry Literary & Cultural Centre, was once the stronghold of the Fitzmaurices, the Anglo-Norman lords of Kerry. The castle was the last in Ireland to succumb to the Elizabethan attacks during the Desmond revolt. What remains of the castle has been thoroughly restored.

St Mary's Church, in the Square, was built in 1829 in the neo-Gothic style. It has some lovely mosaic work over the altar and a vaulted roof with timber beams. In Childers Park is the **Garden of Europe** (☑), opened in 1995. Its 12 sections represent the 12 members of the EU of the day. There is a fine bust of the poet Schiller and, strikingly, Ireland's only public monument to those who died in the Holocaust, and to all victims of injustice. The walk along the Feale here is a good respite from town.

Loctated in a former church, **St John's Theatre & Arts Centre** (☎ 068-22566; www.stjohnstheatrelistowel .com; The Square) hosts art exhibitions as well as drama, music and dance events.

Lartigue Monorailway (☎ 068-24393; John B Keane Rd; adult/child €6/3; ◷ 1-4.30pm May-Sep) was designed by Frenchman Charles Lartigue. This unique survivor of Victorian railway engineering operated between the town and Ballybunion on the coast. The renovated section of line is short but fascinating, with manual turntables at either end for swinging the train round.

The tourist office has leaflets on **walks** such as the 3.5km river walk and the 10km Sive walk, which takes in John B Keane Rd, a disused railway track and a bog.

Festivals & Events

Writers' Week (☎ 068-21074; www.writersweek.ie; 24 the Square) Takes place in late May. Readings, poetry, music, drama, seminars, storytelling and many other events are held at various places around town. The festival attracts an impressive list of writers, which have included Booker Prize–winning Colm Toibin, John Montague, Jung Chang, Damon Galgut, Rebecca Miller and Terry Jones.

Listowel Races (☎ 068-21144; www.listowelraces.ie) Take place over Whit weekend in June and for a week during the harvest festival in September.

Sleeping

Billeragh House Hostel (☎ 068-40321; billeraghhouse hostel@yahoo.com; dm/d from €20/45; ☑) Housed in

an ivy-clad Georgian hall, this hostel is 3.5km south of Listowel on the N69. Facilities include private bathrooms, a kitchen and dining room, and a laundry room.

Flanigan's Maid of Erin (☎ 068-21321; www.maid oferin.ie; Main St; s/d from €40/70) The comely and statuesque redhead with harp and dog looming over the door here is a local architectural landmark. Fortunately the rooms are not so distracting: the simple decor is restful.

Listowel Arms Hotel (☎ 068-21500; The Square; www .listowelarms.com; r from €90-150; ☑ ☑) Listowel's only full-service hotel is a family-run affair in a Georgian building that balances touches of grandeur with country charm. Antiques, marble sinks, high-speed internet and power showers highlight the 42 rooms, which overlook the river and the racecourse. There's a palatial restaurant and the bar is a good place to find music in the summer.

There are three comfy rooms above the bar-bistro **Allo's** (☎ 068-22880; Church St; s/d €50/100).

Eating & Drinking

Grape & Grain (☎ 068-23001; Church St; meals €6-15; ◷ 10am-6pm Mon-Sat) A stylish, burgundy-coloured place for lunch or a coffee with sandwiches, salads, hot specials and cakes.

Allo's (☎ 068-22880; Church St; mains €12-30; ◷ noon-9pm Tue-Sat) This popular bar–bistro has a traditional feel created by the many reused architectural items and wood used in the interior. Local seafood and meats mingle with Med flavours for a changing array of sprightly and satisfying dishes. The wine list is excellent.

Woulfe's Horseshoe Bar (☎ 068-21083; 14 Lower William St; bar food €13-20, dinner €18-28; ◷ noon-9pm) Enjoy the cosiness of the downstairs bar or the upstairs restaurant at this long-established place, which features window gnomes. The menu offers a full range of pub standards including an array of daily roasts.

John B Keane (37 William St) Once run by the late writer himself, this small, unassuming bar is swathed in Keane memorabilia. At various times it hosts dramatic works including performances by his son Billy in the summer.

Listowel's **farmers market** (◷ 10am-1pm Thu) is held on the Square as markets have been for centuries.

Getting There & Away

Frequent daily buses serve both Tralee (€7, 40 minutes) and Limerick (€15, 1½ hours). In July and August there is one daily service to the Cliffs of Moher and Galway. The bus stop is on the northern side of the Square.

AROUND LISTOWEL
Ballybunion

There are a surprising number of reasons to visit this one-seahorse beach town 15km northeast of Listowel on the R553. Beyond the statue of a club-swinging Bill Clinton, commemorating his visit to the local golf course in 1998, there are two Blue Flag **beaches**.

Overlooking the southern beach are the remains of **Ballybunion Castle**, the 16th-century seat of the Fitzmaurices. There's an underground passage leading from the castle to the cliff.

The **Ballybunion Bachelor Festival** takes place in June. The event sees 15 tuxedo-clad bachelors from across Ireland vying to impress the judges, while the town enjoys a long weekend of street entertainment and celebrations.

One bus (two in summer) runs from Listowel to Ballybunion Monday to Saturday (€3.50, 25 minutes).

Carrigafoyle Castle

A lonely location on the Shannon Estuary adds to the romantic drama of this late-medieval **castle** (☎ 068-43304; 9am-6pm May-Sep). Its name comes from Carragain Phoill (Rock of the Hole); it's built in a channel between the mainland and Carrig Island. Built by the O'Connors, who ruled most of northern Kerry, the castle was besieged by the English in 1580, retaken by O'Connor, and finally destroyed by Cromwell's forces in 1649. You can climb the spiral staircase to the top for a good view of the estuary.

The castle is 2km west of the village of Ballylongford (Bea Atha Longphuirh).

Tarbert
pop 810

Tarbert is 16km north of Listowel on the N69. **Shannon Ferry Limited** (☎ 068-905 3124; www .shannonferries.com; one way/return bicycle & foot passengers €5/7, motorcycles €9/14, cars €18/28; ☼ 9am-9pm Jun-Aug, to 7pm Sep-May) runs a half-hourly ferry between Tarbert and Killimer in County Clare, a salvation if you want to avoid congested Limerick city. The ferry dock is 2.2km west of Tarbert and clearly signposted. If you must go through Limerick from here, the N69 is pretty (see the boxed text, p342) and Foyne is a diverting town.

If you have some time before you catch your ferry, you should visit the renovated **Tarbert Bridewell Jail & Courthouse** (☎ 068-36500; adult/child €6/3; ☼ 10am-5pm Apr-Oct), which has exhibits (including stoic mannequins) on the rough social and political conditions of the 19th century. From the jail, the 3.8km **John F Leslie Woodland Walk** runs along Tarbert Bay towards the mouth of the Shannon.

There are buses on Tuesday and Thursday mornings and Friday night to Tralee (one hour) and Sunday afternoon to Limerick (1¼ hours).

DINGLE PENINSULA

The northernmost promontory in Kerry and Cork's proud collection, the Dingle Peninsula is first among stiff competition. Its ever-varied and multihued landscape is one of green hills and golden sands, and culminates in Europe's westernmost point, gazing across the sound at the ghost town on Great Blasket Island. Mt Brandon, the Connor Pass and other high areas add drama, but it's where the land meets the ocean – either in conflict at whitewater-pounded rocks or in little coves where it just dissolves away – that Dingle's beauty is unforgettable.

Centred on charming Dingle town, the peninsula has a high concentration of ring forts and other ancient ruins. Activities on offer range from diving to playing the bodhrán. There's an alternative way of life here, lived by the artisans and idiosyncratic characters and found at trad sessions and folkloric festivals across Dingle's tiny settlements.

DINGLE WAY

This 168km walk in County Kerry loops round one of the most beautiful peninsulas in the country (see above). It takes eight days to complete, beginning and ending in Tralee, with an average daily distance of 21km. The first three days offer the easiest walk but the first day, from Tralee to Camp, is the least interesting; it could be skipped by taking the bus to Camp and starting from there. Ordnance Survey Discovery Series map 70 covers the peninsula. **Go Ireland** (www.govisitireland.com) offers a seven-day self-guided walk from €640.

The classic loop drive around the peninsula from Dingle town is 50km. Base yourself in Dingle for two nights (at least) and take a day to do the drive.

Tours

A number of Killarney companies run daily day trips by bus around the Dingle Peninsula (see p298). Alternatively, Dingle-based companies operate guided minibus tours of the peninsula daily from May to September.

O'Connor's Slea Head Tours (☎ 087 248 0008; tour €20; ⏰ 11am & 2pm daily) Departs from Dingle pier.

Sciúird (☎ 066-915 1606; tour €20; ⏰ 10.30am & 2pm daily) Has two-hour archaeological tours exploring the prehistoric sites, Ogham stones and monastic ruins in the western part of the peninsula. Check for departure point when booking.

Getting Around

Regular buses serve Dingle town from Tralee via the N86 (see p323), but service to the rest of the peninsula is limited to community buses running once or twice a week. You'll want your own car or bike, or else you can join one of the many tours that leave from Dingle.

DINGLE
pop 1800

Wandering the hilly streets in this naturally quaint town, you quickly realise that the peninsula's capital is a very special place indeed. It's one of Ireland's largest Gaeltacht towns; many pubs double as shops, so you can enjoy Guinness and a singalong among screws and nails, wellies and horseshoes. These charms have long drawn runaways from across the world, making the port town a surprisingly cosmopolitan, creative place. In summer it can be mobbed, there's no way around it; in the other seasons its authentic charms are yours for the savouring. Excellent seafood restaurants can be enjoyed year-round.

Note that although this is Gaeltacht country, the locals have voted to retain the name Dingle rather than go by the officially sanctioned – and dictated – An Daingean.

Information

The banks on Main St have ATMs and bureaux de change. The post office is off Lower Main St. Parking is free throughout town and €1 per hour in the car park at the harbour.

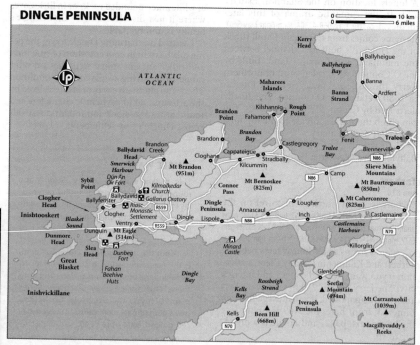

DINGLE PENINSULA

ALL YOUR EGGS IN ONE DOLPHIN

In 1984 a bottlenose dolphin swam into Dingle Bay and local tourism hasn't been the same since. Showing an unnatural affinity for humans, it swam around with the local fishing fleet. Eventually somebody got the idea of charging tourists to go out on boats and see the friendly dolphin. Today up to 12 boats at a time and over 1000 tourists a day ply the waters with Dingle's mascot, the cornerstone of the local economy.

A few Fungie facts:

■ **His name.** One of the first fisherman to take an interest in Fungie was nicknamed Fungie because his efforts to grow a beard looked like fungus. His name became the dolphin's name.

■ **His nature.** Bottlenose dolphins are migratory, Fungie isn't. Some suspect he escaped from a dolphin show and made Dingle Bay his new home.

■ **His sex.** Fungie is a boy. There are loads of stories told in local pubs about a friend's cousin who swam with Fungie and found him to be very much a him and *very* friendly.

■ **His powers.** Promoters arrived in the early 1990s claiming that swimming with Fungie would produce miraculous health benefits, not unlike a trip to Lourdes.

■ **His future.** Bottlenose dolphins have an average lifespan of 25 years, which is about as long as Fungie's been in Dingle. (Uh-oh.)

An Café Liteártha (☎ 066-915 2204; Dykegate Lane) Bookshop specialising in Irish history.

Dingle Bookshop (☎ 066-915 2433; Green St) Has a good collection of new and used books, including books on travel and local interest.

Dingle Cleaners (☎ 066-915 0680; Mail Rd; ⏱ 9.30am-6pm Mon-Sat)

Dingle Internet Café (☎ 066-915 2478; Lower Main St; per hr €4; ⏱ 10am-10pm Mon-Fri May-Sep, to 6pm rest of year; 📶) Burns disks, cheap calls etc.

Olde Forge (☎ 066-915 0523; Holyground; per hr €4; ⏱ 10.30am-7.30pm Mon-Sat, 9.30am-10pm Jun-Aug, 12.30pm-7.30pm Sun) Internet cafe; also cheap calls.

Tourist office (☎ 066-915 1188; www.dingle-penin sula.ie; The Pier; ⏱ 9am-7pm Jul-Aug, 9am-1pm & 2-6pm May-Jun & Sep, to 5pm Oct-Apr) Busy but helpful, this place has maps, guides and plenty of information on the entire peninsula. It books accommodation for a €4 fee.

Sights

Dingle is one of those towns whose very fabric is the sight. Wander up and down hills, poke around back alleys, head off across the docks, and amble into shops and pubs at random and see what you find.

FUNGIE THE DOLPHIN

Boats leave the pier daily for one-hour dolphin-spotting trips of Dingle's famous tourism patron, Fungie (see the boxed text, above); the **Dingle Boatmen's Association** (☎ 066-915 2626; The Pier; adult/child €16/8) is the cooperative running things. It's free if Fungie doesn't show, but

he usually does. The association also runs a daily two-hour boat trip for enthusiasts who want to **swim with Fungie** (per person €25, plus wetsuit hire adult €25, child €15-20; ⏱ 8am Jun-Aug, 9am rest of the year). Organise it in advance through **Brosnan's** (☎ 066-915 1967; Cooleen), where you can hire wetsuits and snorkelling gear.

DINGLE OCEANWORLD

This **aquarium** (☎ 066-915 2111; www.dingle-ocean world.ie; Dingle Harbour; adult/child/€12/7; ⏱ 10am-5pm) is a lot of fun. Psychedelic fish (how many of them are jealous of Fungie?) glide through tanks that re-create such environments as Lake Malawi, the River Congo and the piranha-filled Amazon. Reef sharks and stingrays cruise the shark tank; water is pumped from the harbour for the spectacularly ugly wreck fish. There's a walk-through tunnel and a touch pool.

OTHER SIGHTS

Next to **St Mary's Church** on Green St is the **Trinity Tree**, a sculpture representing the Holy Trinity, made from an unusual three-trunked sycamore. With its carved faces, it looks like something out of a fairy tale.

On the other side of the church, in the former convent, is the Celtic culture centre **Díseart** (☎ 066-915 2476; adult/child €3.50/2; ⏱ 9am-1pm & 2-5pm), which has stained-glass windows by Harry Clarke (see Franciscan Friary, p290) depicting 12 scenes from the life of Christ.

COUNTY KERRY

Activities

Mountain Man Outdoor Shop (☎ 066-915 2400; www .irishadventures.net; Strand St) is a shopfront for **Irish Adventures**, which offers all sorts of adventure packages including rock climbing, kayaking (half-day €50) and boat trips to the Blaskets. It also takes bookings for **Dingle Horse Riding** (☎ 066-915 2199; Ballinaboola; 1hr €30), which organ-

ises mountain treks, beach rides and peninsula tours.

Snorkelling and scuba diving in Dingle Bay and around the Blasket Islands, courses and wreck dives can be arranged at **Dingle Marina Diving Centre** (☎ 066-915 2789, 915 2422; www .divingdingle.ie; The Wood). A single-tank boat trip with all gear provided costs €70.

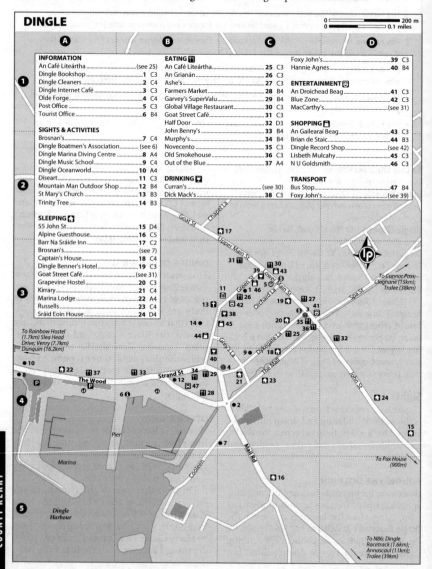

DINGLE

INFORMATION	
An Café Liteártha	(see 25)
Dingle Bookshop	1 C3
Dingle Cleaners	2 C4
Dingle Internet Café	3 C3
Olde Forge	4 C3
Post Office	5 C3
Tourist Office	6 B4

SIGHTS & ACTIVITIES	
Brosnan's	7 C4
Dingle Boatmen's Association	(see 6)
Dingle Marina Diving Centre	8 A4
Dingle Music School	9 C4
Dingle Oceanworld	10 A4
Díseart	11 C3
Mountain Man Outdoor Shop	12 B4
St Mary's Church	13 B3
Trinity Tree	14 B3

SLEEPING	
55 John St	15 D4
Alpine Guesthouse	16 C5
Barr Na Sráide Inn	17 C2
Brosnan's	(see 7)
Captain's House	18 C4
Dingle Benner's Hotel	19 C3
Goat Street Café	(see 31)
Grapevine Hostel	20 C4
Kirrary	21 C4
Marina Lodge	22 A4
Russells	23 C4
Sráid Eoin House	24 D4

EATING	
An Café Liteártha	25 C3
An Grianán	26 C3
Ashe's	27 C3
Farmers Market	28 B4
Garvey's SuperValu	29 B4
Global Village Restaurant	30 C3
Goat Street Café	31 C3
Half Door	32 D3
John Benny's	33 B4
Murphy's	34 B4
Novecento	35 C3
Old Smokehouse	36 C3
Out of the Blue	37 A4

DRINKING	
Curran's	(see 30)
Dick Mack's	38 C3

Foxy John's	39 C3
Hannie Agnes	40 B4

ENTERTAINMENT	
An Droichead Beag	41 C3
Blue Zone	42 C3
MacCarthy's	(see 31)

SHOPPING	
An Gailearaí Beag	43 C3
Brian de Staic	44 B3
Dingle Record Shop	(see 42)
Lisbeth Mulcahy	45 C3
N U Goldsmith	46 C3

TRANSPORT	
Bus Stop	47 B4
Foxy John's	(see 39)

To Rainbow Hostel (1.7km) Slea Head Drive; Ventry (7.7km) Dunquin (16.2km)

To Connor Pass; Cloghane (15km); Tralee (38km)

The Wood

To Pax House (900m)

Marina

Pier

Dingle Harbour

To N86; Dingle Racetrack (1.6km); Annascaul (11km); Tralee (39km)

In July and August, **Dingle Music School** (☎ 086 319 0438; Dykegate Lane) offers beginners' workshops in bodhrán and tin whistle (€25; 11am Mon). Bodhráns are supplied.

Festivals & Events

During these events, crowded Dingle gets just plain sick with visitors.

Dingle Races (www.dingleraces.ie) Held every second weekend in August, these races bring crowds from far and wide. The racetrack is 1.6km east of town on the N86.

Dingle Regatta A race in the harbour in traditional Irish *currach* (or *naomhóg*) canoes, this is Kerry's largest such event, held at the end of August.

Sleeping
BUDGET

Rainbow Hostel (☎ 066-915 1044; www.rainbow hosteldingle.com; campsite per person €9, dm/d €16/40; P) Hardwood and bright-blue sheets abound in this rural, houselike hostel some 1.5km west of Dingle town centre. It's a good choice when a) the in-town budget places are packed out, and b) you want to wake up to the smell of nature.

Grapevine Hostel (☎ 066-915 1434; www.grapevine dingle.com; Dykegate Lane; dm €16-18, d €21) Tucked away near the centre of town, this dinky hostel has eight-, four- and two-bed rooms with wooden bunks, private bathrooms (with minimalist sliding doors) and a fire-lit lounge. Book well ahead.

Goat Street Café (☎ 066-915 2770; www.thegoatstreet cafe.com; Goat St; d from €40) Enjoy one of Dingle's most delightful restaurants (see p322) and then bed down upstairs. Rooms are simple and breakfast is extra, but the value is superb. It's at the top of Main St.

Brosnan's (☎ 066-915 1146; www.dinglebrosnans accommodation.com; Cooleen; s/d €40/70; P) Flowery decor spans the rainbow at this friendly, great-value B&B.

MIDRANGE

This tourist town has plenty of midrange B&Bs, many resting on their laurels. There are, however, some first-class places.

Kirrary (☎ 066-915 1606; Avondale; collinskirrary@ eircom.net; s/d from €50/90; P) You'll get plenty of info and chat from Eileen at this cheerful place. Rooms are a reasonable size and the breakfast has fresh options. Enjoy tea and refreshments in the lovely garden, screened by a hedge.

Russells (☎ 066-915 1747; maryr@iol.ie; The Mall; s/d from €50/90; P) Who can resist this location set back

from a tiny babbling brook coursing through town? The modern rooms are tastefully decorated and an extensive breakfast menu includes kippers, salmon and French toast.

55 John St (Stella Doyle's; ☎ 066-915 2378; www.stella doyle.com; 55 John St; s/d €55/75; May-Sep) A surprise awaits as you enter the plain-fronted, plum-coloured facade here: a vision of colour and light from the back garden, which, while small, is alive with blooms. The two rooms are plainly comfortable; breakfast is a challenge as Stella, a chef, will cook whatever you want. Go on, order.

Sráid Eoin House (☎ 066-915 1409; www.sraideoin bnb.com; John St; s/d €60/80; Mar-Oct; P) Above a travel agency at the quiet end of town, the four rooms are comfy; the buffet breakfast allows contemplative and caloric browsing in the am.

Alpine Guesthouse (☎ 066-915 1250; www.alpine guesthouse.com; Mail Rd; s/d from €60/110; P) This nearly five-decade old favourite has bright rooms and a good selection of breakfasts, including free-range eggs, Kerry bacon and locally smoked salmon. Friendly owner Paul O'Shea is a mine of Fungie trivia.

Barr Na Sráide Inn (☎ 066-915 1331; barrnasraide @eircom.net; Upper Main St; r €60-120; P 🖳 🛜) The bar by the entrance has a style that only beautifies the crusty regulars and their hearts of gold. Rooms sprawl over three floors and are mostly good sized and comfortable. One of the best amenities is up on the 3rd floor: a guest self-serve laundry.

Marina Lodge (☎ 066-915 0800; www.dinglemarina lodge.com; The Wood; s/d from €60/120; P 🖳) A clean-cut, purpose-built B&B on the waterfront with a neat, modern interior. Power showers can blast off residue from any interactions with Fungie.

TOP END

Pax House (☎ 066-915 1518; www.pax-house.com; Upper John St; s/d from €90/120; P 🖳) From its highly individual decor (all bold colours and bright paintings) to the outstanding views over the estuary from room balconies and the terrace, Pax House is a treat. It's 1km from the town centre.

Captain's House (☎ 066-915 1531; captigh@eircom .net; The Mall; s/d €60/100; mid-Mar–mid-Nov; P) A streamside garden and beautiful interior furnishings make this handsome house a great choice. Snuggle in one of the eight rooms or by the peat fire.

COUNTY KERRY

Dingle Benner's Hotel (☎ 066-915 1638; www
.dinglebenners.com; Main St; s €100-110, d €140-180; **P**)
A Dingle institution melding old-world el-
egance, local touches and modern comforts
in the quiet rooms, lounge, library, bar and
restaurant. Rooms in the 300-year-old wing
have the most character; those in the new
parts are quieter.

Eating
BUDGET

Novecento (☎ 066-915 0663; Lower Main St; pizza slice €3;
☼ 3.30-9.30pm) Follow the basil and garlic scents
wafting from this beacon of affordable goodness occupying a tidy central storefront. Pizzas
are classically styled: thin and wonderful.

An Grianán (☎ 066-915 1910; Green St; lunch €4-8;
☼ 9am-5pm) The cafe at this organic grocery
serves soups with wondrous soda bread,
goats cheese burgers, salads and lovely chocolate cake. Get sandwiches to go for your
adventures.

An Café Liteártha (☎ 066-915 2204; Dykegate Lane;
snacks €3-6; ☼ 9am-6pm) Curl up with a book and
a cup of tea at this delightful spot at the back
of a bookshop, and relax engulfed in the spirit
of literary Dingle.

Goat Street Café (☎ 066-915 2770; Goat St; snacks &
mains €4-12; ☼ 10.30am-5pm Mon-Sat, to 9pm Thu-Sat) A
budget mecca, the perennially popular Goat
Street Café gets mobbed in summer with folks
seeking out its tasty salads, tarts and tagine.
Dinner brings fresh seafood. It's at the top
of Main St.

For self-catering, try the big **Garvey's
SuperValu** (☎ 066-915 1397) near the Strand.
Dingle's **farmers market** (☼ 9am-3pm Fri) is by
the bus stop. Ice cream in tourist towns can
be a cliché but **Murphy's** (☎ 066-915 2644; Strand St;
cones from €2; ☼ 11am-10pm summer, shorter hours winter)
breaks the mould. Amazingly good flavours
here include honeycomb and an impossibly
cooling mint chip.

MIDRANGE

Old Smokehouse (☎ 066-915 1061; Lower Main St; lunch
€6-10, dinner €15-23; ☼ 12.30-10pm Jun-Aug, 6.30-10pm
Apr-May & Sep-Oct) The food, like the decor and
service, is unfussily pleasant. The menu is
classically Atlantic Irish: seafood chowder,
lamb stew, steak pie etc. Get there early to
grab a table in the conservatory overlooking
the stream.

Ashe's (☎ 066-915 0989; Main St; mains €16-29;
☼ noon-3pm & 6-9pm Mon-Sat) Owned by a distant

relation of Gregory Peck (really, aren't we
all?), this elegantly fronted gastropub serves
modern takes on seafood in old-fashioned
surrounds. The tempura of pollack with coriander aioli is mighty fine.

Global Village Restaurant (☎ 066-915 2325; Main
St; mains €18-25; ☼ 6-9.30pm Mar-Oct, later in summer)
With the sophisticated feel of a continental
bistro, this restaurant offers a fusion of global
recipes gathered by the well-travelled owner-
chef, whose CD and art collections are, well,
global. Seafood is the base for many a dish.
The wine list is excellent.

Half Door (☎ 066-915 1600; John St; mains €22-50; set
menu €25; ☼ 12.30-2.30pm Mon-Sat, plus 5.30-10pm daily)
Fish and shellfish are superbly presented at this
outstanding seafood restaurant, which exudes a
dignified, genteel air. The menu reflects what's
fresh down at the docks; the local shrimp and
larger crustaceans are especially good here.

our pick **Out of the Blue** (☎ 066-915 0811; The Wood;
lunch €10-20, dinner mains €15-30; ☼ 12.30-3pm & 6-9.30pm
Thu-Tue mid-Mar–mid-Nov) The funky blue-and-
yellow exterior might make you think 'chipper'. Wrong! Dingle's best restaurant has an
intense devotion to local seafood; if they don't
like the catch, they don't open. Dishes are creative and change nightly. The surrounds are
slightly shambolic – have a glass of wine from
the tiny, overwhelmed bar and chill. Booking
for dinner is essential. Lunchtime choices are
simple and can be enjoyed outside.

Drinking

Dingle has over 50 pubs, many of them mon-
grel affairs that still have vestiges of their lives
as shops. Two examples of this on Main St are
Foxy John's (☎ 066-915 1316) and **Curran's** (☎ 066-
915 1110), which respectively have old stock of
hardware and outdoor clothing lying about.
Don't expect an exuberant welcome from the
flinty-eyed locals.

our pick **Dick Mack's** (☎ 066-915 1960; Green St)
Announced by stars in the pavement bearing
the names of its celebrity customers, Dick
Mack's has an irrepressible sense of self.
Ancient wood and ancient snugs dominate
the interior, which is lit like the inside of a
whiskey bottle. Out back there's a warren of
tables, chairs and characters.

Hannie Agnes (☎ 087 949 0832; Green St) Local
haunt that's known for its smooth Guinness
and, during the summer, trad sessions and
Irish coffee. The windows are frosted and the
interior is spare – like a good pint.

Entertainment
The first three places listed are also prime pub pint venues.

MacCarthy's (☎ 066-915 1205; www.maccacrthyspub .com; Goat St) Popular bar containing one of Ireland's smallest venues. There is music at the weekends; check the website.

John Benny's (☎ 066-915 1215; Strand St) Lively trad, set dancing and singing are on offer from 9.30pm Monday, Wednesday, Friday and Saturday.

An Droichead Beag (Small Bridge Bar; ☎ 066-915 1723; Lower Main St) Traditional music kicks off at 9.30pm nightly at this raucous pub by the bridge.

Blue Zone (☎ 066-915 0303; Green St; ☽ 6pm-1am Tue-Thu, to 2am Fri & Sat, to 12.30am Sun) Late-night hang-out with Corona, San Miguel and pizzas on the menu and live music on Tuesday and Thursday.

Shopping
Amid Fungie flotsam there are shops with beautiful goods by local artisans.

An Gailearaí Beag (☎ 066-915 2976; Main St) A showcase for the work of the West Kerry Craft Guild, selling ceramics, paintings, wood carvings, photography, batik, jewellery, stained glass and much more.

Brian de Staic (☎ 066-915 1298; www.briandestaic .com; Green St) This local jewellery designer's exquisite modern Celtic work includes symbols, crosses and standing stones.

Dingle Record Shop (☎ 087 298 4550; Green St) Tucked under jazz venue Blue Zone, this crammed and jammed music store has all the good stuff you can't download yet.

Lisbeth Mulcahy (☎ 066-915 1688; Green St) Beautiful scarves, rugs and wall hangings are created on a 150-year-old loom by this long-established designer. Also sold here are ceramics by her husband, who has a workshop at Louis Mulcahy Pottery (p328), west of Dingle.

N U Goldsmith (☎ 066-915 2217; Green St) Original jewellery by Niamh Utsch is on display at this stylish little gallery. Individual pieces start at €40 and keep rising.

Getting There & Away
Bus Éireann (www.buseireann.ie) buses stop outside the car park behind the supermarket. To Tralee, where you can connect across Ireland or hop on the train, there are four buses Monday to Saturday and three on Sunday (€11; 80 minutes). Check for additional summer services.

There are eight buses a week to Dunquin and Ballydavid, on Monday, Tuesday, Thursday and Friday.

Getting Around
Dingle is easily navigated on foot. For a taxi call **Dingle Co-op Cabs** (☎ 087 222 5777), which can also give private tours of the peninsula.

Bike-hire places include **Foxy John's** (☎ 066-915 1316; Main St; per day €10), where you can abandon your energetic ideas and simply have a pint. The regulars will approve.

NORTHSIDE OF THE PENINSULA
There are two routes from Tralee to Dingle, both following the same road out of Tralee past the Blennerville Windmill. Near the village of Camp, a right fork heads to the Connor Pass, while the N86 via Annascaul takes you to Dingle more quickly. The former is much more beautiful. At Kilcummin, a road heads west to the quiet villages of Cloghane and Brandon, and finally to Brandon Point and its fine views of Brandon Bay.

Castlegregory & Around
pop 950

Castlegregory (Caislean an Ghriare), which once rivalled Tralee as a busy local centre, is a quiet village, with a highlight being views back to the often snowy hills to the south (a lowlight is the growing number of philistine holiday homes).

However, things change when you drive up the sandstrewn road along the Rough Point peninsula, the broad spit of land between Tralee Bay and Brandon Bay. Up here, it's a playground. Not content with being a prime windsurfing location, the peninsula sees strange new sports like wave-sailing and kitesurfing. Divers can glimpse pilot whales, orcas, sunfish and dolphins. In the pub, the many-accented babble tells of a community of people who came for a day and couldn't face ever going home.

Jamie Knox Watersports (☎ 066-713 9411; www .jamieknox.com; Brandon Bay) offers surf, windsurf, kitesurf (rental €50 per day), canoe and pedaloe hire and lessons. Look for the garish yellow trailers.

Beyond Rough Point are the seven **Maharees Islands**. The largest of the 'hogs', as the islands are known locally, is Illauntannig. The remains of a 6th-century monastic settlement there include a stone cross, a church and bee-hive huts. Two small adjoining islands can be reached on foot from Illauntannig at low tide, but make sure you know exactly what the tide is doing.

The islands are privately owned, but trips (taking about 10 minutes) can be arranged through Harbour House (below) or on a **scuba diving** trip with **Waterworld** (☎ 066-713 9292; www.waterworld.ie; Rough Point; 2-tank dive €70), a top-end dive shop based at Harbour House (below). The great underwater visibility makes this one of Ireland's best diving areas.

SLEEPING & EATING

O'Donnell's Old Ship Inn (☎ 066-713 9927; www.oldshipinn.ie; W Main St, Castlegregory; s/d from €60/80) An old pub has had a swab of the poop deck and emerged ship-shape. The B&B has rooms with modern, elegant style. The restaurant is really a gastropub, with simple preparations of local seafood and meats. The bar is ideal for a cultured pint.

Harbour House (☎ 066-713 9292; www.maharees.ie; Rough Point; s/d from €60/100; 🖳 🖳 🛜) This busy B&B and its attached restaurant are in a great position overlooking the Maharees Islands, 5km north of Castlegregory near the end of the peninsula. It's home to Waterworld dive centre (above); the 15 very comfortable rooms have what is accurately described as 'epic views'. Food in the pub is solid, Lucy the mascot a drooling charmer.

Spillane's (☎ 066-713 9125; Fahamore; bar meals €6-25, mains €10-25; 🕙 1-9pm Jun-Aug, 4-9pm Apr, May, Sep & Oct, 6-9pm Nov-Mar) Outside tables overlook the beach, bay and mountains; inside, the usual bar-propping Guinness-swillers look on as feral children tear past waitresses serving pub stalwarts. In summer you'll need to act like a kid to be heard.

GETTING THERE & AWAY

This is driving country. Buses are weekly at best.

Cloghane & Around
pop 280

Cloghane (An Clochán) is another little piece of beauty tucked away on the Dingle Peninsula. The village's friendly pubs and accommodation nestle between Mt Brandon and Brandon Bay, with views across the water to the Stradbally Mountains. If you don't fancy scaling Mt Brandon, there are plenty of coastal strolls.

On the last weekend in July, Cloghane celebrates the ancient Celtic harvest festival **Lughnasa** with events – especially bonfires – both in the village and atop Mt Brandon. In late August, the **Brandon Regatta** is a race in traditional *currach* canoes.

The 5km drive out to **Brandon's Point** from Cloghane follows ever-narrower single-track roads, culminating in cliffs with fantastic views north and east. Sheep wander the constantly eroding rocks oblivious to their tenuous positions.

You can get tourist info in Cloghane from the shop and post office near the hostel and pub. Pick up copies of the local walking and hiking guides from the shop or your accommodation.

The vacuum-silent **St Brendan's Church** has a stained-glass window showing the Gallarus Oratory and Ardfert Cathedral.

SLEEPING & EATING

Mount Brandon Hostel (☎ 066-713 8299; www.mountbrandonhostel.com; dm/s/tw €20/30/50; 🕙 Mar-Jan; 🖳) A small, simple hostel with scrubbed wooden floors and furniture, and a patio overlooking the bay. Treatments such as shiatsu massage are available.

Mullally's (☎ 066-713 8154; mullallysbar@eircom.net; s/d from €35/70) A big old place where the turf fires in the pub never seem to go out, Mullally's has basic B&B rooms in addition to a decent kitchen that turns out the kind of meaty, hearty fare that keeps hikers hiking.

O'Connors (☎ 066-713 8113; www.cloghane.com; s from €50, d €70-90; 🖳) Book ahead to bag a room or a table in this welcoming village pub, which serves evening meals (€14 to €18) made with local produce, ranging from salmon to steak, between 7pm and 9.30pm. Landlord Michael is a fount of local information and can also explain why there's an airplane engine out front.

Crutch's Hillville House Hotel (☎ 066-713 8118; Connor Pass Rd, Kilcummin; s/d from €60/100) Built in 1833 by alcoholic aristocracy and later tinkered with by a retired army captain who used railway tracks for beams, this blue-and-white, creeper-covered hotel is a surviving bastion of upper-crust eccentricity. The style here is unique, perfect if perfection is irritating. A much-loved breakfast is included in the room rate; dinner (mains €17 to €23) is available in the restaurant overlooking the sycamore-ringed lawn.

WALK: MT BRANDON

At 951m, **Mt Brandon** (Cnoc Bhréannain) is Ireland's eighth-highest peak. It's made up of a beautiful series of high summits that lie along the edge of a spectacular series of east-facing cliffs and steep ridges above a rocky, lake-filled valley. An ascent of the mountain is a serious all-day trip. You should be well equipped with weatherproof clothing and mountain boots, even in summer. Above all you should be experienced in the use of a map (Ordnance Survey Map No 70) and compass because thick mist can develop quickly, as can wind and rain. Allow at least six to seven hours return.

A popular route from the west is the Saint's Rd, which starts at Kilmalkedar Church (p329). To avoid 274m-high Reenconnell, start the trail at the large Mt Brandon car park, signposted from the Dingle–Feohanagh road. It's a straightforward 6km slog there and back, well marked with 14 crosses interspersed with white markers, and takes five hours return.

The classic way up Mt Brandon starts from Faha (OS reference 493120) above Cloghane. (You can drive there. If you walk, the steep 2km adds a couple of hours to the six-hour there-and-back climb from Faha.) To reach Faha, take the turn left (signposted 'Cnoc Bhréanainn'), about 200m northeast of Cloghane school, and follow the narrow lane to a T-junction. Turn left again and carry on until you reach the Faha road-end parking area. From here, it's a fairly tough 7km to the summit and back.

Walk left up the track above the car park and follow the obvious path past a grotto onto the open mountain. The rocky path is very clear. Occasional guide poles mark the way along a rising grassy ridge, with a magnificent line of cliffs and ridges ahead. The path contours around rocky slopes before descending into the glaciated wilderness at the valley head, from where it winds between great boulders and slabs. Yellow arrows on the rocks point the way.

When the back wall is reached, the path zigzags very steeply to the rim of the great cliffs. Turn left at the top and head for the summit of Mt Brandon, marked by a trigonometry point or pillar, a wooden cross and the remains of Teampaillin Breanainn (St Brendan's Oratory). The views in clear weather from the summit are reverie-inducing, but be alert to the sudden edge of the cliffs. You can continue along the cliffs' edge to the subsidiary summits and Brandon Peak, 2km south, but this will add a couple of hours. Retracing your steps requires care and concentration on the initial steep zigzags. The rest of the way back to Faha is free-wheeling.

CONNOR PASS

At 456m, the Connor (or Conor) Pass is the highest in Ireland and offers spectacular views of Dingle Harbour to the south and Mt Brandon to the north. On a foggy day you'll see nothing but the road just in front of you. The road is in very good shape, excepting that it is very narrow and very steep (large signs portend doom for buses and trucks).

The summit car park yields **views** down to two lakes in the rock-strewn valley below plus the remains of walls and huts where people once lived impossibly hard lives. When visibility is good, the 10-minute climb to the summit is well worthwhile for the kind of views that inspire mountain-climbers.

TRALEE TO DINGLE VIA ANNASCAUL

For drivers, the N86 has little to recommend it other than being faster than the Connor Pass route. By bike it's less demanding. On foot, the Dingle Way (p317) runs near the road for the first three days.

The main reason to pause in Annascaul (Abhainn an Scáil), also spelled Anascaul, is to visit the **South Pole Inn** (☎ 066-915 7388; Main St; bar meals €8-20; ☺ noon-8pm). Antarctic explorer Tom Crean ran the pub in his retirement. Now it's a regular Crean museum and gift shop, as well as a cracking pub serving hearty dishes worthy of an explorer. Ask to have the 'polar experience'.

Buses stop here on the Dingle to Tralee run.

KILLARNEY TO DINGLE VIA CASTLEMAINE

The quickest route from Killarney to Dingle passes through Killorglin and Castlemaine. At Castlemaine, head west on the R561. You'll soon meet the coast, then go through the beachy seaside town of Inch before joining the N86 to Dingle.

If you'd rather not stay in one more orderly, generic B&B, try **Phoenix Vegetarian Restaurant & Accommodation** (☎ 066-976 6284; www.thephoenix organic.com; Shanahill East, Castlemaine; campsites €18,

COUNTY KERRY

DETOUR: MT CAHERCONREE

About 11km west of Castlemaine is the turn-off for Mt Caherconree (825m), signposted as the scenic drive to Camp. About 4km along this road coming from the south is an Iron Age promontory fort that may have been built by Cúror MacDáine, king of Munster.

Whichever direction you come from, there are stunning views of Caherconree's sweeping slopes and the surrounding countryside, which at the top is a land of bogs and springs. Brown on the south slope, it's green and lush on the north slope. Watch out for drivers who don't get the concept of the narrow, rough, twisting road.

---

r €35-80; ☙ Easter-Oct) The owner runs a dance centre here and there's a film club. The restaurant, open year-round, specialises in vegetarian dishes using produce from the organic gardens (lunch €6 to €15, dinner €20 to €30). Rooms are quirkily interesting, but be sure to inspect the gypsy caravans and toilets before you commit.

Castlemaine is well connected with Tralee, Killorglin, and Limerick via Killarney, but there are no buses from Castlemaine to Annascaul via Inch.

Inch

Inch's 5km-long **sand spit** was a location for both *Ryan's Daughter* and *Playboy of the Western World*. Sarah Miles, love interest in the former film, described her stay here as 'brief but bonny'.

The dunes are certainly bonny, scattered with the remains of shipwrecks and Stone Age and Iron Age settlements. The west-facing beach is also a hot surfing spot; waves average 1m to 3m. **Westcoast Surf School** (☎ 086 836 0271; www.westcoastsurfschool.ie) offers lessons and five-day kids' camps.

Cars are allowed on the beach, but don't end up providing others with nonstop laughs by getting stuck.

Sammy's (☎ 066-915 8118; 💻), at the entrance to the beach, is the nerve centre of the village. The beach-facing bar–restaurant serves a vast range of dishes from sandwiches and pasta to fresh oysters and mussels. There's a shop, tourist information and trad sessions during the summer. Camping (sites from €10) is offered in a field above the beach.

Foley's (☎ 066-915 8117) is another popular watering hole overlooking grassy dunes.

Inch Beach Guest House (☎ 066-915 8333; www.inch beachguesthouse.com; s/d from €60/80) is all skylights, sea views and *Ryan's Daughter* memorabilia. The general breeziness is completed by attractive modern fittings.

WEST OF DINGLE

At the tip of the peninsula is the Slea Head drive along the R559. It has the greatest concentration of ancient sites in Kerry, if not the whole of Ireland. Specialist guides on sale in An Café Liteártha (p318) and the tourist office (p319) in Dingle list the most interesting and accessible sites.

This part of the peninsula is a Gaeltacht area. The landscape is dramatic, especially in shifting mist, although full-on sea fog obliterates everything. For the best views, follow the Slea Head drive in a clockwise direction. Cross the bridge west of Dingle and keep straight on to Ventry (below). Beyond Ventry the road hugs the coast past Dunbeg Fort (opposite), then round the rocky outposts of Slea Head (p326) and Dunmore Head (p327). Continuing along the coast to Dunquin (opposite), then turning east to Ballyferriter (p328), the views of the Blasket Islands (p327) give way to views of 951m-high Mt Brandon (p325) and its neighbours. Beyond Ballyferriter is the Gallarus Oratory (p329) and numerous other historic sites, not to mention a confusing clutter of lanes. From Gallarus, the R599 circles back to Dingle.

Although a mere 50km in length, doing this drive justice will require a full day, at least.

Ventry
pop 410

The village of Ventry (Ceann Trá) is next to a wide sandy bay.

A great base for exploring the area is **Ceann Trá Heights** (☎ 066-915 9866; www.iol.ie/~ventry; s/d from €45/70; ☙ Mar-Nov), a comfortable, modern three-room guesthouse overlooking Ventry Harbour.

Near Ceann Trá Heights is **Long's Riding Stables** (☎ 066-915 9723; www.longsriding.com; 1hr/day from €30/130), which offers mountain and beach treks.

Slea Head & Dunmore Head

Overlooking the mouth of Dingle Bay, Slea Head has fine beaches, good walks and views of Mt Eagle and the Blasket Islands. It's understandably popular with coach parties, and cake vendors stand at the ready. But it's also an excellent area to see some well-preserved structures from Dingle's ancient past.

Dunmore Head is the westernmost point on the Irish mainland and the site of the wreckage in 1588 of two Spanish Armada ships.

About 7km southwest of Ventry on the road to Slea Head is the Iron Age **Dunbeg Fort**, a dramatic example of a promontory fortification, perched atop a sheer sea cliff. The fort has four outer walls of stone. Inside are the remains of a house and a beehive hut, as well as an underground passage.

The Slea Head area is dotted with **beehive huts**, **forts**, **inscribed stones** and **church sites**. The **Fahan huts**, including two fully intact huts, are 500m west of Dunbeg Fort on the inland side of the road.

When the kiosks are open in summer, you'll be charged about €2 to €3 for entrance to the sights.

Dunquin

Yet another pause on a road of scenic pauses, Dunquin is a scattered village beneath Mt Eagle and Croaghmarhin. It's a hub for all things Blasket. The local website (www.dunchaoin .com) notes that it is the next parish to America.

The **Blasket Centre** (Ionad an Bhlascaoid Mhóir; ☎ 066-915 6444; www.heritageireland.ie; adult/child €4/2; ☺ 10am-7pm Jul & Aug, to 6pm mid-Mar–Jun, Sep & Oct, last admission 45min before closing) is a wonderful interpretive centre in a long, white hall ending in a wall-to-ceiling window overlooking the islands. Great Blasket's rich community of storytellers and musicians is profiled along with its literary visitors like John Millington

Synge, writer of *Playboy of the Western World*. The more prosaic practicalities of island life are covered by exhibits on shipbuilding and fishing. There's a cafe with Blasket views, and a useful bookshop.

Dunquin Hostel (☎ 066-915 6121; www.anoige.ie; dm €15-19, tw €42; ☺ Feb-Nov) has a terrific location, near the Blasket Centre and not too far from Dunquin Pier. There are stunning views. This An Óige member closes between 10am and 5pm.

Mustard-coloured **De Mórdha B&B** (☎ 066-915 6276; www.demordha.com; s/d from €45/70; ☺ Easter-Oct) is a pleasant little B&B with all mod cons and great views. The pub is under a 1km walk away.

An Portán (☎ 066-915 6212; www.anportan.com; meals €12-25; ☺ Easter-Sep) serves traditional Irish meals with an international flavour. It has a separate guesthouse with 14 modern, large and fairly unadorned rooms.

Blasket Islands

The Blasket Islands (Na Blascaodaí), 5km out into the Atlantic, are the most westerly in Ireland. At 6km by 1.2km, Great Blasket (An Blascaod Mór) is the largest and most visited, and mountainous enough for strenuous walks, including a good one detailed in Kevin Corcoran's *Kerry Walks*. All of the Blaskets were inhabited at one time or another; there is evidence of Great Blasket being inhabited during the Iron Age and early Christian times. The last islanders left for the mainland in 1953 after they and the government agreed that it was no longer feasible to live in such isolated and harsh conditions.

You could camp on the islands, but there are no facilities. There's accommodation in

---

THE BLASKET WEAVER

The deserted village on Great Blasket might not look like the most inviting place to live, but for some 20 years Welsh immigrant Sue Redican has occupied one of the cottages between April and October.

Europe's westernmost resident has no electricity or phone line, but has candles for light, gas for cooking, and a mobile phone and VHF radio for communication. She stays there for as much of the year as she can, and once stayed for 10 months, although bad weather can cut her off from the mainland. 'I'd rather get stuck in than stuck out,' she says. Blasket inhabitants traditionally speak of going 'out' to the mainland and coming 'in' to the island.

'I feel alone rather than lonely here,' she says. 'You can have 400 seals on the beach sitting up and watching you, and in the past few weeks we've seen basking sharks and killer whales.' Sue also gets plenty of human company during the summer, when she sells her weaving to day-trippers and delivers her scones to the Blasket Islands Eco Ventures boat.

Dunquin, although a few people make their home out here for part of the year (see the boxed text, p327).

Weather can cause ferry cancellations; otherwise the options for getting there and away are similar:

Blasket Island Ferries (☎ 066-915 1344, 066-915 6422; www.blasketisland.com; adult/child €20/10; ☿ 10.30am-3.30pm Easter-Sep) Boats depart hourly and take 20 minutes; add €15 for an ecotour of the island.

Blasket Islands Ferry (☎ 066-915 4864, 087 231 6131; www.blasketislands.ie; adult/child €20/10; ☿ 9.55am-4.55pm Easter-Oct) Boats depart hourly and take 15 minutes; add €15 for an ecotour of the island.

There are also options from Dingle; check at the tourist office (p319) for the latest details. Some outfits simply cruise past the islands and don't stop.

Ballyferriter

Continuing north from Dunquin, stop at **Clogher Head**, where a short walk takes you out to the head with views down to a perfect little beach at Clogher. It's a prime resting spot for seals and other mammals with thick layers of insulating blubber not affected by the frigid waters.

Follow the road another 500m around to the crossroads at **Clogher**. Leave the loop road here and follow a narrow paved track down to the **beach** you viewed from the head. The rugged surf is intoxicating, ceaselessly pounding this perfect crescent of sand. One normally cynical friend said: 'It's the most beautiful place I've ever seen.'

Back on the loop road, follow the road as it turns inland to reach **Ballyferriter** (Baile an Fheirtearaigh). It's named after Piaras Ferriter, a poet and soldier who emerged as a local leader in the 1641 rebellion and was the last Kerry commander to submit to Cromwell's army. The entire landscape is a rocky patchwork of varying shades of green, delineated by miles and miles of ancient stone walls.

One of the most interesting potteries on the peninsula, **Louis Mulcahy Pottery** (☎ 066-915 6229; Clogher; ☿ 9am-5.30pm Mon-Fri, 10am-5.30pm Sat, 11am-5.30pm Sun Easter-Nov) has all sorts of clay creations and a cafe.

About 2.5km northeast of Ferriter's Cove is **Dún an Óir Fort** (Fort of Gold), the scene of a hideous massacre during the 1580 Irish rebellion against English rule. The fort was held by Sir James Fitzmaurice, who commanded an

---

GET A MAP

The thicket of lanes on the north side of the peninsula is matched only by the even thicker network of walking paths. Locals, possibly driven mad from fumes while being stuck behind sclerotic caravans of tour buses, tend to drive with abandon when they can. To avoid becoming a hood ornament, and to simply have a more bucolic experience, get the Ordnance Survey Discovery series no 70, which shows every last path on the peninsula in exhaustive detail.

---

international brigade of Italians, Spaniards and Basques. On 7 November English troops under Lord Grey attacked the fort; within three days the defenders surrendered. 'Then putt I in certeyn bandes who streight fell to execution. There were 600 slayne,' said the poet Edmund Spenser, who was secretary to Lord Grey and patently not in a lyrical mood at the time.

All that remains of the fort is a network of grassy ridges, but it's a pretty spot overlooking Smerwick Harbour, which has relatively sheltered waters that lack the sense of impending doom of those facing due west. About 2.5km north of Ballyferriter, near the golden Beal Bán beach, it's reasonably signposted from the main loop road.

In **Ballyferriter** itself (a tiny village with a couple of shops and a pub – all the essentials really), the **Dingle Peninsula Museum** (Músaem Chorca Dhuibhne; ☎ 066-915 6100; adult/child €4/2; ☿ 10am-6pm Apr-Oct, by appointment rest of year) is housed in the 19th-century schoolhouse. It has displays on the archaeology and ecology of the peninsula. Across the street there's a lonely, lichen-covered church.

If you're not ready to do the loop in a day, or you just want a fine base for explorations on foot, **An Speice** (☎ 066-915 6254; www.anspeice.com; Ballyferriter; s/d from €50/70) has sunny rooms exhibiting an attractive modern style that would flummox most Irish B&B owners: where are the garish patterns? The mismatched linen? The colours usually seen these days only on rusting '70s appliances?

Free camping is possible near Ferriter's Cove but there are no facilities; ask locally before pitching.

In **Murphy's Bar** (Tigh Uí Mhurchú; ☎ 066-915 6224; snacks & mains €4-11; ☿), a stuffed fox with a pheasant in its jaws looks down on Gaeilge-speaking locals of all ages tucking into basic pub grub.

Riasc Monastic Settlement

The remains of this 5th- or 6th-century monastic settlement are one of the peninsula's more impressive and haunting sites, particularly the pillar with beautiful Celtic designs. Excavations have also revealed the foundations of an oratory first built with wood and later stone, a kiln for drying corn and a cemetery. The ruins are signposted as 'Mainistir Riaisc' along a narrow lane off the R559, about 2km east of Ballyferriter.

Gallarus Oratory

This dry-stone oratory is quite a sight, standing in its lonely spot beneath the brown hills as it has done for some 1200 years. It has withstood the elements perfectly, apart from a slight sagging in the roof. Traces of mortar suggest that the interior and exterior walls may have been plastered. Shaped like an upturned boat, it has a doorway on the western side and a round-headed window on the eastern side. Inside the doorway are two projecting stones with holes that once supported the door.

The **oratory** (☎ 066-915 6444; www.heritageireland .ie; admission free) is signposted off the R559, about 2km further on from the Riasc Monastic Settlement turn-off. Parking by the site is extremely limited and tends to become a mess in summer. There is a nearby private parking area with a **visitor centre** (☎ 066-915 5333; adult/child €3/free; 9am-9pm Jun-Aug, 10am-6pm Feb-May & Sep-10 Nov) that shows a 15-minute audio-visual display and offers up clean toilets.

Ballydavid

About 2km from Gallus Oratory, this little nub of civilisation has a fine setting on a sheltered cove and old coastguard breakwater. Europe's westernmost camping ground, **Oratory House Camping** (Campaíl Teach An Aragail; ☎ 066-915 5143; www .dingleactivities.com; Gallarus; campsites from €18; Apr-Sep), is nearby. It's a source of much local information on a mass of activities, especially walking.

The pub, **Tigh TP** (☎ 066-915 5300; www.tigh-tp.ie; meals €8-15), is a good place for a waterside pint. Next door it runs the Coast Guard Lodge, which has six rooms that sleep three to four people each in military comfort for €75 (or €50 for more than one night) per room.

Kilmalkedar Church

This 12th-century church was once part of a complex of religious buildings. The characteristic Romanesque doorway has a tympanum with a head in the centre. There is an **Ogham stone**, pierced by a hole, in the grounds as well as a very early sundial. Nearby is a restored two-storey building known as **St Brendan's House**, believed to have been the residence of the medieval clergy. The track to the right of this is the **Saint's Rd**, the traditional approach to Mt Brandon (p325). Parking is limited.

From Gallarus Oratory, the R559 goes north to the little village of Murreagh. The church is about 2km east of the village.

Following the R559 southeast for 8km from Kilmalkedar takes you back to Dingle.

Counties Limerick & Tipperary

From marching ditties to bad puns on bathroom walls, the names Tipperary and Limerick are part of the lexicon. But, as is so often the truth, the reality bears little relationship to the lore.

Limerick is a city with a history as dramatic as Ireland's. In a nation of hard knocks, it seems to have had more than its fair share. This is a city that generations of people fled as soon as they could, and that even today is a place dismissed by people elsewhere in Ireland. But Limerick's streets are rich with tangible links to the past and a gritty, honest vibrancy. The rest of County Limerick is closely tied to its namesake city, which doesn't always thrill the folks in twee Adare.

In contrast, Tipperary city is minor – here it's the county that matters. Pastorally beautiful, the rolling hills, rich farmland and river valleys bordered by soaring mountains make for satisfying exploration. This is a place to get near the ground – to follow a river to its source or to climb a stile to see that lonely ruin.

Both counties are places to revel in the Irish past. Ancient Celtic sites, medieval abbeys and other relics endure in solitude, waiting for discovery. Sights like the monumental Rock of Cashel and Cahir Castle are on many an itinerary, but still have a rough dignity that moves and inspires.

As you explore these two counties you just might find yourself whistling a merry tune – just make sure you leave those bathroom walls alone.

HIGHLIGHTS

■ **Surprising City** Discover the cafe culture in Limerick (p337) and the amazing Limerick City Gallery of Art (p336)

■ **Twist & Turn** Enjoy the narrow roads and Shannon vistas while wandering the back roads of Limerick, from Kilmallock (p340) to Foynes (p342)

■ **Over Hill and Dale** Explore the wilds of Tipperary, from the Glen of Aherlow (p343) to the River Suir Valley (p349)

■ **Boiling Oil** Walk the walls and keep of Cahir's authentic and well-preserved castle (p348)

■ **World View** Look out over County Tipperary from the ancient monuments on the Rock of Cashel (p344)

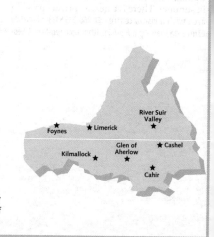

■ POPULATION: 263,000 ■ AREA: 6989 SQ KM

COUNTY LIMERICK

Limerick's low-lying farmland is framed on its southern and eastern boundaries by swelling uplands and mountains. Limerick City is boisterously urban in contrast and has enough historic and cultural attractions for a day's diversion. About 15km south of the city are the haunting archaeological sites around Lough Gur, while around the same distance southwest of the city is the tourist-pleasing village of Adare.

LIMERICK CITY

pop 56,000

Hardscrabble and Limerick city will always be linked. And why shouldn't they? Efforts at glitz and gloss only try to obscure an unflinchingly honest town that doesn't shy away from a tough past as portrayed in Frank McCourt's *Angela's Ashes*.

Schemes to polish Limerick's image by making the city more upmarket come and go (during the present economy they've vanished). But that doesn't mean you should pass by the Republic's fourth largest city. It has an intriguing castle, a lively art museum and even a bit of cafe culture to go with its uncompromised pubs. Most importantly that old cliché about friendly people really does apply here. Locals are glad to see you; just pause on a street corner and people will almost certainly start asking if you need directions.

History

Viking adventurers established a settlement on an island in the River Shannon in the 9th century. They fought with the native Irish for control of the site until Brian Ború's forces drove them out in 968 and established Limerick as the royal seat of the O'Brien kings. Brian Ború finally destroyed Viking power and presence in Ireland at the Battle of Clontarf in 1014. By the late 12th century, invading Normans had supplanted the Irish as the town's rulers. Throughout the Middle Ages the two groups remained divided, with the oppressed Irish clustering to the south of the River Abbey in Irishtown and the Anglo-Normans walling themselves in to the north, in Englishtown.

From 1690 to 1691, Limerick acquired heroic status in the endless saga of Ireland's struggle against occupation by the English. After their defeat in the Battle of the Boyne in 1690, Jacobite forces withdrew west behind the famously strong walls of Limerick town. Months of bombardment followed and eventually the Irish Jacobite leader Patrick Sarsfield sued for peace. The terms of the Treaty of Limerick (1691) were then agreed, and Sarsfield and 14,000 soldiers were allowed to leave the city for France. The treaty guaranteed religious freedom for Catholics, but the English later reneged on it and enforced fierce anti-Catholic legislation, an act of betrayal that came to symbolise the injustice of British rule.

During the 18th century, the old walls of Limerick were demolished and a well-planned and prosperous Georgian town developed. Such prosperity had waned by the early 20th century, as traditional industries fell on hard times. Several high-profile nationalists hailed from here, including Éamon de Valera. These days, technological and service industries are major employers. Call a helpline from anywhere in the world and you may be speaking to someone in Limerick (or India).

Orientation

Limerick straddles the Shannon's broadening tidal stream, where the river swings west to join the Shannon Estuary. The city has a clearly defined grid of main streets. The central thoroughfare runs roughly north to south, changing names from Rutland St in the north to Patrick St, O'Connell St, the Crescent and Quinlan St, and finally exiting south along O'Connell Ave onto the Cork and Killarney roads. The main places of interest are clustered to the north on King's Island (the oldest part of Limerick and once part of Englishtown); to the south around the Crescent and Pery Sq (the city's noteworthy Georgian area); and along the riverbanks. The joint train and bus station lies southeast, off Parnell St.

Traffic is often coagulated. A welcome new bypass south of town will join the N7 (itself being improved), N18, N20 and N24.

Information
BOOKSHOPS

Celtic Bookshop (☎ 061-401 155; 2 Rutland St) A fine addition to the local scene with books on local and Irish topics.

Eason (☎ 061-419 588; 9 O'Connell St) Good place for magazines, fiction and guidebooks.

O'Mahony's (☎ 061-418 155; 120 O'Connell St) Ireland's largest independent bookshop has occupied these

COUNTIES LIMERICK & TIPPERARY

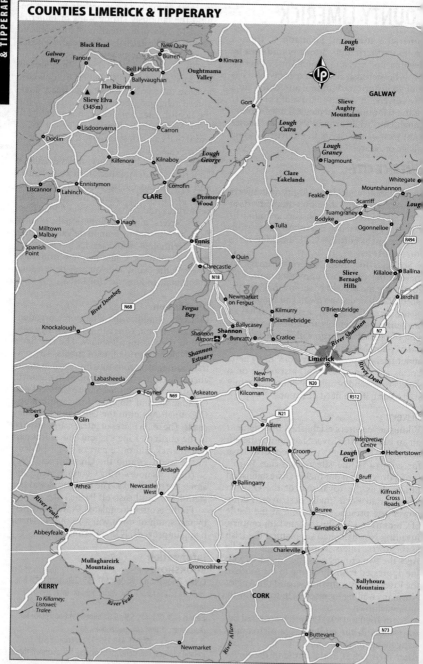

premises for over 100 years, with an excellent selection of books of local and regional interest.

INTERNET ACCESS

Check at the tourist office for new access points. There's also internet access at Limerick City Library, right.

Limerick Online (LOL; William St; per 30min €1; 8am-8pm) Cheap calls and internet.

LAUNDRY

Launderette (☎ 061-315 345; Thomas St; per load €12; 9am-5pm Mon-Sat)

LEFT LUGGAGE

Limerick Train Station (☎ 061-217 331; Colbert Station, Parnell St; per item 24hr €3; 8am-6pm & 6.30-8.30pm Mon-Fri, 9.30am-6pm Sat & Sun)

LIBRARIES

Limerick City Library (☎ 061-407 501; The Granary, Michael St; 10am-5.30pm Mon & Tue, to 8pm Wed-Fri to 1pm Sat)

MEDICAL SERVICES

Both of the following hospitals have accider and emergency departments:

Midwestern Regional Hospital (☎ 061-482 219, 061-482 338; Dooradoyle)

St John's Hospital (☎ 061-415 822; St John's Sq)

MONEY

ATMs are common. Both of these banks als have bureaux de change.

AIB Bank (☎ 061-414 388; 106/108 O'Connell St)

Ulster Bank (☎ 061-410 200; 95 O'Connell St)

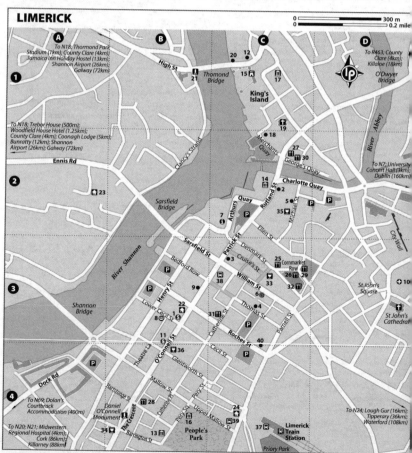

OST

Main Post Office (☎ 061-316 777; Lower Cecil St)

OILETS

Toilets (Arthur's Quay; admission €0.20)

OURIST INFORMATION

Limerick Tourist Office (☎ 061-317 522; www
hannonregiontourism.ie; Arthurs Quay; ⊗ 9.30am-1pm
2-5.30pm Mon-Fri, 9.30am-1pm Sat) A large, impressive
facility with amazingly helpful staff; open longer hours in
summer. Ask here about *Angela's Ashes* tours. Also look
round town for red-clad 'street ambassadors' offering
advice and info.

Dangers & Annoyances

Reputation and the unfortunate nickname
'Stab City' aside, central Limerick is not any
less safe than other urban Irish areas. Keep
alert at night and you should be fine.

Sights

The streets of Limerick's centre are lined with
stark, plain-fronted Georgian facades – city
hallmarks that augment its hardscrabble aura.
It's as if even a frilly mullion might have been
beyond the budget. Even today, trees and other
urban amenities are few in town.

KING JOHN'S CASTLE

The massive curtain walls and towers of
Limerick's showpiece **castle** (☎ 061-360 788;
www.shannonheritage.com; Nicholas St; adult/child
€9.50/5.50; ⊗ 10am-5pm Mon-Fri, till 5.30pm Sat & Sun,
last admission 1hr before closing) are best viewed
from the west bank of the River Shannon.
The castle was built by King John of England
between 1200 and 1212 on the site of an
earlier fortification. It served as the mili-

tary and administrative centre of the rich
Shannon region.

Inside there are recreations of brutal medieval
weapons like the trebuchet, as well as excavated
Viking sites, reconstructed Norman features
and other artefacts. Walk the walls and pretend
you're carrying a bucket of boiling oil.

Across medieval Thomond Bridge, on the
other side of the river, the **Treaty Stone** marks
the spot on the riverbank where the Treaty
of Limerick was signed. Before you cross the
bridge, look out for the 18th-century **Bishop's
Palace** (☎ 061-313 399; Church St; ⊗ 10am-1pm & 2-4pm
Mon-Fri) and the ancient **toll gate**.

HUNT MUSEUM

Although named for its benefactors, this
museum (☎ 061-312 833; www.huntmuseum.com;
Palladian Custom House, Rutland St; adult/child €8/4.25, free
Sun; ⊗ 10am-5pm Mon-Sat, 2-5pm Sun) might well
be named for the kind of hunt you do for
treasure. Visitors are encouraged to open
drawers and otherwise poke around the finest collection of Bronze Age, Iron Age and
medieval treasures outside Dublin. The 2000-
plus items are from the private collection of
the late John and Gertrude Hunt, antique
dealers and consultants, who championed
historic preservation throughout the region.
Look out for a tiny but exquisite bronze horse
by da Vinci, and a Syracusan coin thought to
have been one of the 30 pieces of silver paid
to Judas for his betrayal of Christ. Cycladic
sculptures, a Giacometti drawing and paintings by Renoir, Picasso and Jack B Yeats add
to the feast. Guided tours from the dedicated
and colourful volunteers are available.

The museum has an excellent in-house
restaurant, DuCarts (see p338).

FRANK MCCOURT

No recent person has been as closely linked to Limerick as Frank McCourt (1930–2009). His autobiographical novel *Angela's Ashes* was a surprise publishing sensation in 1996, bringing him fame and honours (including the Pulitzer Prize).

Although he was born in New York City, McCourt's immigrant family returned to Limerick four years later, unable to survive in America. His childhood was filled with the kinds of deprivations that were all too common at the time: his father was a drunk who later vanished, three of his six siblings died in childhood and at age 13 he dropped out of school to earn money to help his family survive.

At age 19, McCourt returned to New York and later worked for three decades as a teacher in the city's high schools. Among the subjects he taught was writing. He dabbled in writing and theatre with his brother Malachy beginning in the 1970s. He got started on *Angela's Ashes* only after he retired from teaching in 1987. Its early sales success was thanks to a bevy of enthusiastic critics, but in Limerick the reaction was much more mixed, with many decrying the negative portrait it painted of the city.

Today McCourt's legacy in Limerick is more celebrated. There's an exhibit about the Limerick of the book at the Georgian House & Garden (below), and you can visit one of the pubs mentioned in the book, South's (p338). The tourist office (p335) has information about tours of sights related to the book.

GEORGIAN HOUSE & GARDEN

There is an engaging eeriness about the lofty, echoing rooms of the restored **Georgian House** (☎ 061-314 130; 2 Pery Sq; adult/child €8/4; ☼ 10am-4pm Mon-Fri), a recreation showing how Limerick's swells once lived. Lavish marble, stucco and wall decorations adorn the main rooms, while things are decidedly downscale when you reach the bare boards and dusty furnishings of the servants' quarters. You'll say 'Brace yourself, Bridget!' reading the hackneyed but entertaining limericks on various wall plaques. The restored back garden is an antidote – and beautiful contrast – to the plain fronts on the street. It leads to a coach house that contains a photographic memoir of Limerick. A small **Ashes Exhibition** linked to novelist Frank McCourt was under renovation at the time of writing.

LIMERICK CITY GALLERY OF ART

A mix of traditional paintings from the last 300 years covers every inch of wall space in the **Limerick City Gallery of Art** (☎ 061-310 633; www.limerickcitygallery.ie; Carnegie Bldg, Pery Sq; admission free; ☼ 10am-6pm Mon-Wed & Fri, to 7pm Thu, to 5pm Sat, 2-5pm Sun). The gallery is beside the peaceful People's Park, at the heart of Georgian Limerick. The permanent collection features work by Sean Keating and Jack B Yeats. Check out Keating's atmospheric *Kelp Burners* and Sir John Lavery's *Stars in Sunlight*; both infuse their traditional subjects with inner light and a certain joy. The gallery also stages changing exhibitions of often pseudo-scandalous works and is the home of **ev+a** (www.eva.ie) a long-running city-wide contemporary art exhibition held each spring.

ST MARY'S CATHEDRAL

Limerick's ancient **cathedral** (☎ 061-310 293; Bridge St; admission free; ☼ 9.30am-4.30pm Mon-Sat May-Nov, to 1pm Sat Dec-Apr) was founded in 1168 by Donal Mór O'Brien, king of Munster. Parts of the 12th-century Romanesque western doorway, nave and aisles survive, and there are splendid 15th-century black-oak misericords (support ledges for choristers), unique examples of their kind in Ireland. It's worth checking if there are any musical events scheduled.

LIMERICK CITY MUSEUM

This small **museum** (☎ 061-417 826; Castle Lane; admission free; ☼ 10am-1pm & 2.15-5pm Tue-Sat) is beside King John's Castle. Exhibits include Stone Age and Bronze Age artefacts, the civic sword, Limerick silverwork, and examples of Limerick's lace and kid-glove manufacturing. Tough times in the late 19th century are also covered.

THOMOND PARK STADIUM

From 1995 until 2007, the **Munster rugby team** (www.munsterrugby.ie) was undefeated in this legendary stadium, which was massively rebuilt

2008, the year they won the Heineken uropean Cup for the second time. You can sit the **museum** (☎ 061-421 100; www.thomondpark ; adult/child €7/5; ⏱ 9.30am-5pm Mon-Fri) and go on **tour** (combined ticket adult/child €12/10) of what is lled the 'hallowed ground' (a phrase used by lot of stadiums worldwide). During matches ae stadium is known a) for its noise and b) r its deathly quiet when someone is about to ick for goal. It is an easy 1km walk northwest f the centre along High St.

ours

. local development group runs two-hour **alking tours** (☎ 087 635 3648; per person €10). One popular tour visits locations mentioned in ngela's Ashes, starting and ending at the ourist office on Arthur's Quay (tour starts at .30pm). The second historical tour begins at 1am. Confirm both with the tourist office.

One-hour **open-top bus tours** (☎ 061-430 9090, 61-317 522; adult/child €12/5; ⏱ hourly 9.15am-3.45pm lar-Oct) depart from in front of the Court Iouse on Merchant's Quay.

leeping

ry to find a place to stay near the city centre, o you can walk around and enjoy the night-ife. Otherwise you'll be on or near approach oads, in which case you may opt for some-hing further afield in, for example, Bunratty p365), which will be more bucolic.

BUDGET

amaica Inn Holiday Hostel (☎ 061-369 220; www amaicainn.ie; Mount Levers, Sixmilebridge, Co Clare; dm €19-0, d €60; P 🖳) A good option 13km northwest f the city. Rooms range from singles with orivate bath to six-bed dorms. There are bus connections daily (except Sunday) to Limerick nd Shannon Airport.

Courtbrack Accommodation (☎ 061-302 500; www courtbrackaccom.com; Courtbrack Ave; dm/s/d €24/30/52; ⏱ Jun-Aug; P 🖳) A few minutes' walk along Dock Rd from the Shannon Bridge. Rates at this spiffy, red-hued place include a light breakfast, and there's a kitchen and aundry.

MIDRANGE

Alexandra Tce on O'Connell Ave (which runs south from O'Connell St) has several mid-range B&Bs. Ennis Rd, leading northwest to-wards Shannon, also has a selection, although most are at least 1km from the centre.

Glen Eagles (☎ 061-455 521; gleneaglesbandb@eircom .net; 12 Vereker Gardens, Ennis Rd; r €45-70; ⏱ Feb-Nov; P) Across the river from the city centre, Glen Eagles is on a peaceful cul-de-sac and has four decent-sized, comfortable rooms and a cheerful welcome.

Woodfield House Hotel (☎ 061-453 022; www.wood fieldhousehotel.com; Ennis Rd; r €45-90; P 🖳 🛜) The 26 rooms here are of a typical modern motel standard (aka blandly comfortable) and the location, only a 1.25km walk from the cen-tre is a plus (although the road is busy). The real treat are the picnic tables for enjoying a refreshment outside.

Coonagh Lodge (☎ 061-327 050; www.coonaghlodge .com; s/d from €45/65; P 🖳 🛜) A cute little B&B with a traditional high-pitched roof. The six rooms here vary from singles to rather size-able family rooms. It's in Coonagh, a small town off the N18, 5km west of Limerick.

Trebor House (☎ 061-454 632; www.treborhouse .com; Ennis Rd; s/d from €45/70; ⏱ May-Sep; P) The McSweeney family offer a warm welcome in this classic suburban town house (note the pebble-dash exterior), a 10-minute walk from the city centre. The five rooms have a pastel-green charm.

Railway Hotel (☎ 061-413 653; www.railwayhotel .ie; Parnell St; s/d from €45/80; P) Right across from the bus and train station, this long-established hotel is busy and shows the wear, although the location is as central as you can get. The 30 rooms are not huge and will remind you of a time when everybody smoked.

George (☎ 061-460 400; www.thegeorgeboutiquehotel .com; O'Connell St; s/d from €80/90; P 🖳 🛜) This sleek place has a popular atrium lobby and small terrace above the busy streets of the city centre. The design looks like something out of a Sunday supplement – all warm colours with luxurious touches. The 127 rooms have wi-fi, iPod docks, evening cordials and more.

Eating

Seafood is the thing in Limerick and there are a few notable options. At weekends be sure to book for the better places. George's Quay has some continental flair and tables along the water. Locals call it 'first-date row'.

Pick from organic produce and local foods like cheese at the **Milk Market** (☎ 061-415 180; Cornmarket Row; ⏱ 8am-2.30pm), a traditional farm-ers market held in Limerick's old market buildings. Look for the soups by Forbidden Food.

BUDGET

Cafe Noir (☎ 061-411 222; Robert St; snacks & meals €3-12; ◷ 8am-6pm) Gorgeous tarts lead the way at this bakery and lunch place, which also offers gem-like pastries, salads, quiches and more. The coffees are just what you need when it rains.

DuCarts (☎ 061-312 662; Hunt Museum, Rutland St; meals €5-12; ◷ 10am-5pm Mon-Sat, 2-5pm Sun) Window seats overlooking a grassy verge and the Shannon are bathed with light even on the gloomiest of days. The food does the cultural surroundings proud, with a changing selection of salads, soups, sandwiches and hot dishes.

Wild Onion (☎ 061-440 055; High St; mains €7-10; ◷ 8am-4pm Tue-Sat) Get your American on at this blue-fronted cafe and bakery known for its full-bore American breakfasts (that means no black pudding, but plenty of hash browns). It's popular with local expats who know that once you've gone Reuben you never go back.

MIDRANGE

ourpick Sage Cafe (☎ 061-409 458; 67-68 Catherine St; meals €7-15; ◷ 9am-6pm Mon-Sat) Hardscrabble my arse. After you've followed the crowds to this amazing lunch spot, you'll enjoy some of the best food in Ireland. The decor says it all: superb taste that doesn't call attention to itself. Breakfast treats and baked goods give way to a changing line-up of lunch sandwiches, salads and hot plates. And then there are those desserts…

Locke Bar (☎ 061-413 733; George's Quay; mains €9-15) When the Atlantic gusts abate, enjoy the tables waterside at this sprawling cafe-cum-bar or get lost in the maze of rooms and bars. Enjoy the pub menu of pasta, fish and chips, burgers and more amid the scrum, or in more refined quarters upstairs.

Copper & Spice (☎ 061-313 620; 2 Cornmarket Row; meals €12-20; ◷ 5-10pm Tue-Sun) Your first thought on entering: 'What an incredible smell!' Spice indeed. Indian and Thai dishes team up to bring some much-needed spice to town. The surrounds are stylish.

Moll Darby's (☎ 061-411 511; George's Quay; mains €12-30; ◷ noon-2pm Mon-Fri, 5.30-10pm daily) Exposed brick, dark wood and bundles of nautical schlock make Moll's an attractive and atmospheric choice on George's Quay. The red-checked tablecloths add a jaunty air, which will only intensify as you slurp down the superb oysters and other seasonal seafood delights.

TOP END

Market Square Brasserie (☎ 061-316 311; 74 O'Conn St; mains from €20; ◷ 6-10pm Tue-Sat) Tucked awa in the basement of an attractive Georgia house, the food here is creatively prepare and artfully presented. Local purveyors sup ply the best produce, meats and seafood fo an ever-changing menu. Service is smoot the wine list long and the setting intimat Book in advance.

Drinking & Entertainment

Limerick nightlife features local acts and visit ing headliners; you'll find everything from tra Irish to trash rock, indie, chart, soul, reggae drum 'n' bass, jazz and classical, as well a theatre and stand-up comedy. Most clubs hav strict door checks. The free *Limerick Even Guide* (LEG; www.eightball.ie) can be found i pubs, eateries and hotels all over town.

PUBS & CLUBS

Dolan's (☎ 061-314 483; www.dolanspub.com; 3/4 Doc Rd) Limerick's best venue for live music prom ises an unbeatable gig list as well as cutting edge stand-ups. The Warehouse nightclub i grafted on to the atmospheric Dolan's Pub where you're guaranteed authentic trad musi sessions most nights. There's usually live jazz by up-and-comers upstairs.

Trinity Rooms (☎ 061-411 177; www.trinityrooms.ie The Granary, Michael St) Three venues in one reflec the name of this vast club in a 300-year-old waterside building. The Green Room front-of-house bar is open for food and drink all day, and has DJs and live bands after dark. The Quarter Club is a late-night chill-out lounge with R&B emphasis, while the Main Room blasts into the early hours with a hot list of DJs. Courtyards rock on mild nights.

Nancy Blake's (☎ 061-416 443; Upper Denmark St) There's sawdust on the floor and peat on the fire in the cosy front pub of this old standby. Out back is a vast covered drinking zone that often features live music or televised matches.

ourpick White House Pub (☎ 061-412 377; 52 O'Connell St) A classic right in the centre, this corner pub has good seating outside (under a rare tree) and a good beer list. On some nights it has live acoustic, on others it helps lead a rebirth of local poetry through readings (www.whitehousepoets.blogspot.com).

South's (☎ 061-318 850; 4 Quinlan St) The *Angela's Ashes* connection is played up here (the loos are named Frank and Angela). But the current oscale mirror-and-glass motif bears little resemblance to the pub where Frank's father nocked 'em back. Enjoy a traditional pint in posh setting.

ENUES

niversity Concert Hall (UCH; ☎ 061-322 322; www.uch ; University of Limerick) Permanent home of ish Chamber Orchestra, the UCH adds lus- e to Limerick's cultural scene with visits om world-class performers and regular con- rts, opera, drama and dance events. Look for omedy, too, from the likes of Jon Kenny.

etting There & Away

IR

hannon Airport (see p363) in County Clare andles domestic and international flights. taxi from Limerick city to the airport costs round €35.

US

us Éireann (☎ 061-313 333; www.buseireann.ie; Parnell t) services operate from the bus and train tation near the city centre. There are regular uses to Cork (€14, 1¾ hours), Tralee (€16, wo hours) and Dublin (€10, 3½ hours), as vell as to Galway, Killarney, Rosslare, Ennis, hannon, Derry, and most other centres. You an also get off in Limerick at the bus stop on)'Connell St.

Citylink (☎ 1890 280 808; www.citylink.ie) has up to even buses a day to Galway (€12, 1½ hours) nd Cork (€14, two hours). Buses stop on Jpper Mallow St.

RAIN

rish Rail (www.irishrail.ie) offers regular trains rom **Limerick Railway Station** (☎ 061-315 555; 'arnell St) including eight trains daily to Ennis €9, 40 minutes) and six trains daily to Dublin leuston (€26, 2½ hours). The line was slated o extend to Galway in 2009. Other routes ncluding Cork, Tralee, Tipperary, Cahir and Waterford involve changing at Limerick unction, 20km southeast of Limerick.

Getting Around

Regular buses connect Limerick's bus and train station with Shannon Airport (€7), while a taxi from the city centre to the airport costs €35. The airport is 26km northwest of Limerick, about 30 minutes by car.

Limerick is small enough to get around easily on foot or by bike. To walk across town

from St Mary's Cathedral to the train station takes about 15 minutes.

Taxis can be found outside of the tourist office, at the bus and train stations, and in Thomas St.

There are numerous parking garages around the city at varying rates.

Bikes can be hired at **Emerald Alpine** (☎ 061-416 983; www.irelandrentabike.com; Roches St; per day/week €20/80). The company will also retrieve or deliver a bike from anywhere in Ireland for €25.

AROUND LIMERICK CITY

To the south of the city there's a clutch of outstanding historic sites that reward a day visit by car or a couple of days by bike. Only the larger villages are served by bus.

Lough Gur

The area around this horseshoe-shaped lake has dozens of intriguing archaeological sites. **Grange Stone Circle**, known as the Lios, is a superb 4000-year-old circular enclosure made up of 113 embanked uprights. It is the largest stone circle of its kind in Ireland. There's roadside parking and access to the site is free. To get there, leave Limerick on the N24 road south towards Waterford. Look for a sign to Lough Gur indicating a right turn at the roundabout outside town. This takes you onto the R512. In about 16km you reach the stone circle.

Around 1km further south along the R512, at Holycross garage and post office, a left turn takes you towards Lough Gur, past a ruined 15th-century **church**, and a **wedge tomb** on the other side of the road.

Another 2km leads to a car park by Lough Gur and the thatched replica of a Neolithic hut containing the **Lough Gur Stone Age Centre** (☎ 061-360 788; www.shannonheritage.com; adult/child €5/3; ☼ 10am-5pm early May-Sep). The centre has a good exhibit on prehistoric Irish farms (meaning pre–potato era) and a small **museum** displaying Neolithic artefacts and a replica of the Lough Gur shield that's now in the National Museum in Dublin. Other displays explain recent emigration from the area, which included a number of future American mobsters.

Short walks along the lake's edge lead to burial mounds, standing stones, ancient enclosures and other points of interest. Admission to these sites is free. The whole area is ideal for picnics.

Kilmallock
pop 1400

Ireland's third-largest town during the Middle Ages (after Dublin and Kilkenny) still has a smattering of medieval buildings that are well worth a visit.

Kilmallock developed around a 7th-century abbey, and from the 14th to the 17th centuries was the seat of the Earls of Desmond. The village lies beside the River Lubach, 26km south of Limerick and a world away from the city's urban racket.

Coming into Kilmallock from Limerick, the first thing you'll see (to your left) is a **medieval stone mansion** – one of 30 or so that housed the town's prosperous merchants and landowners. Further along, the street dodges around the four-storey **King's Castle**, a 15th-century tower house with a ground-floor archway through which the pavement now runs. Across the road, a lane leads down to the tiny **Kilmallock Museum** (☎ 063-91300; Sheares St; admission free; ⏰ 11am-3pm). It houses a random collection of historical artefacts and, more fun, a model of the town in 1597 so you can get an idea of what you missed (besides the smells, diseases etc). The museum is the base for the **history trail**, which has stops around town for info and context.

Beyond the museum and across the River Lubach are the moody and extensive ruins of a 13th-century **Dominican priory**, which boasts a splendid five-light window in the choir.

Returning to the main street, head back towards Limerick city, then turn left into Orr St, which runs down to the 13th-century **Collegiate Church**. This has a round tower dating probably to an earlier, pre-Norman monastery on the site.

Further south along the main street, turn left (on foot, the road is one-way against you) into Wolfe Tone St. On the right, just before the bridge, you'll see a plaque marking the house where the Irish poet Aindrias Mac Craith died in 1795. Across the road, one of the pretty, single-storey cottages (the fifth one from the bridge) preserves a 19th-century interior. Obtain the key from next door.

Off the other side of the main street, in Emmet St, is **Blossom Gate**, the one surviving gate of the original medieval town wall.

Kilmallock has an excellent facility in its **Friars' Gate Theatre & Arts Centre** (☎ 063-98727; www.friarsgate.ie; Main St), where you can also find tourism information about the village. The centre hosts art exhibitions and has a fine little theat in which it stages plays and music events.

Two Bus Éireann buses run Monday Saturday from Limerick to Kilmallock (€8.7 one hour).

ADARE & AROUND
pop 1150

Tourists are drawn to Adare by the busloa which is sort of a shame as the roads are a ready pretty clogged. But suffer the traff (especially in high season) and you'll be re warded by a couple of star medieval building pleasant walks and an agreeable village wit some thatched cottages that look, ahem, lik they are right out of an English village (blam the 19th-century English landlord, the Ea of Dunraven). Underneath the crowds is a attractive Irish town and during slack time its inherent charm is undeniable.

Located on the River Maigue, Adare lie 16km southwest of Limerick on the busy N21 There's street-side parking in the village, bu the best bet is a free car park behind the herit age centre.

Information

AIB Bank (☎ 061-396 544) Near the tourist office; has an ATM and bureau de change.

Tourist office (☎ 061-396 255; Adare Heritage Centre, Main St; ⏰ 9am-1pm & 2-5pm Mon-Sat, closed Jan) Open longer in summer.

Website (www.adarevillage.com)

Sights
ADARE HERITAGE CENTRE

In the middle of the village is the **heritage centre** (☎ 061-396 666; www.adareheritagecentre.ie; Main St; adult/child €5/3.50; ⏰ 9am-6pm summer, 9.30am-5pm winter). Its exhibits explain the history and the medieval context of Adare's buildings in an entertaining way (note the happy horse). Try picking up the longbow (have you had your spinach today?). Admission includes entry fee and a tour of Adare Castle (opposite).

RELIGIOUS HOUSES

Before the Tudor dissolution of the monasteries (1536–39), Adare had three flourishing religious houses, the remains of which can still be seen. In the village itself, next to the heritage centre, the dramatic tower and southern wall of the **Church of the Holy Trinity** date from the 13th-century Trinitarian priory that was restored by the first Earl of Dunraven. Holy rinity is now a Catholic church. There's a restored 14th-century **dovecote** down the side-turning next to the church.

The ruins of a **Franciscan friary**, founded by the Earl of Kildare in 1464, stand in the middle of Adare Manor golf course beside the River Maigue. Public access is assured, but let them know at the clubhouse that you intend to visit. A track leads away from the clubhouse car park for about 400m – watch out for flying golf balls. There's a handsome tower and a fine sedilia (row of seats for priests) in the southern wall of the chancel.

North of the village, on the N21 and close to the bridge over the River Maigue, is the Church of Ireland parish church, once the **Augustinian priory**, founded in 1315. It was also known as the Black Abbey. The interior of the church is agreeably cavernous, but the real joy is the atmospheric little cloister.

A pleasant, signposted **riverside path**, with wayside seats, starts from just north of the priory gates. Look for a narrow access gap and head off alongside the river. After about 250m, turn left along the road to reach the centre of Adare, where the main road intrudes noisily.

ADARE CASTLE

Dating back to around 1200, this picturesque **feudal ruin** (admission & tour incl with Heritage Centre admission; [clock] tour hourly 10am-5pm Jun-Sep) saw rough usage until it was finally wrecked for good by Cromwell's troops in 1657. By then it had already lost its strategic importance. Restoration work is ongoing; look for the ruined great hall with its early-13th-century windows. When tours are not on, you can view the castle from the busy main road, or more peacefully from the riverside footpath or the grounds of the Augustinian priory.

Sleeping

There's no shortage of B&Bs about. There are also a few large hotels with plenty of room for bus parking.

Adare Camping & Caravan Park ([phone] 061-395 376; www.adarecamping.com; Adare; campsites €20) This sheltered, uncrowded site is about 4km south of Adare off the N21 and R519. Percolate your pains away in the hot tub.

Adare Village Inn ([phone] 061-251 7102; www.adarevillageinn.com; Main St; s/d from €45/60; [wifi]) Excellent-value rooms are cosy, come with a fruit basket and are dead centre in town near the crossroads and village hall.

Smithfield House ([phone] 061-64114; gklowe@eircom.net; Croagh, Rathkeale; s/d €50/70; [P]) Some 4km west of Adare on the N21, this three-storey 1780 Georgian farmhouse has four comfy rooms and a bucolic farm setting. The main staircase is a vintage wonder. Be sure to pet the pony.

Berkeley Lodge ([phone] 061-396 857; www.adare.org; Station Rd; r from €55-80; [wifi]) One of several modern B&Bs on Station Rd close to the village, this six-room house has TVs in the rooms, great breakfasts and welcomes early arrivals from Shannon Airport. It is a three-minute walk to the centre.

Dunraven Arms ([phone] 061-396 633; www.dunravenhotel.com; Main St; s/d from €135/155; [computer] [wifi] [bar]) The high-class choice of Adare, this 1792 inn sits discreetly behind extensive plantings. All 86 rooms have a high standard of traditional luxury. The leisure centre boasts a pool and other watery delights.

Eating & Drinking

In summer you may have to book to beat the mobs, otherwise stroll Main St to choose what fancies. The iconic thatched cottages at the east entrance to town hold much dining joy.

Dovecot ([phone] 061-396 449; Adare Heritage Centre, Main St; lunch €4-12; [clock] 9am-5pm) This bright and airy cafeteria packs 'em in for typical, but good, breakfast and lunch fare.

Seán Collins ([phone] 061-396 400; Killarney Rd; meals €5-12) Adare's most traditional pub – despite a recent refurbishment – has a good menu of pub favourites. On Monday there's trad music (more often in summer).

Good Room Cafe ([phone] 061-396 218; Main St; meals €6-12; [clock] 8am-5pm Mon-Sat) Where you'd go if you lived here, this is a bakery with excellent scones, soda bread and homemade jams. The soups, salads and sandwiches are better than you'd expect from the hackneyed thatched-cottage location.

Wild Geese ([phone] 061-396 451; Main St; mains €20-30; [clock] 6.30-10pm Mon-Sat, Sun summer only) In a town where upmarket competition is downmarket fierce, this cottage-based bistro may be the winner. The ever-changing menu celebrates the best of Southwest Ireland's foods, from scallops to sumptuous racks of lamb. The preparations are imaginative, the service genial and the wine list inspirational.

Bill Chawke Lounge Bar ([phone] 061-396 160; Main St) There's trad music every Thursday night and a singalong on Friday nights (or any other

---

DETOUR: SCENIC N69

Narrow and generally peaceful, the N69 road follows the Shannon Estuary west from Limerick for 65km to Listowel, County Kerry (see p314). You'll enjoy some great views of the water and seemingly endless rolling green hills laced with stone walls. You'll also discover a number of tiny heritage museums and gardens (most usually only open in the peak season). However, at Foynes there's a major attraction in the **Foynes Flying Boat Museum** (☎ 069-65416; www .flyingboatmuseum.com; adult/child €9/5; ☒ 10am-6pm Apr-Oct, till 5pm Mar & Nov). From 1939 to 1945 this was the landing place for the flying boats that linked North America with the British Isles. Big Pan Am clippers – there's a replica here – would set down in the estuary and refuel. The flights were often filled with wartime intrigue.

---

night that the pints loosen up the baritones). There's a beer garden, too.

Getting There & Away

Hourly Bus Éireann services link Limerick to Adare (€5, 25 minutes). Many continue on to Tralee (€16, 1¾ hours). Others serve Killarney (€16, 1¾ hours). Pick up a timetable from the tourist office or check at the bus stop.

COUNTY TIPPERARY

Landlocked Tipperary boasts the sort of fertile soil that farmers dream of. There's still an upper-crust gloss to traditions here. Local fox hunts are in full legal cry during the winter season and the villages can look like something out of the English shires. The central area of the county is low-lying, but rolling hills spill over from adjoining counties. There's good walking and cycling, especially in the Glen of Aherlow near Tipperary town.

But the real crowd-pleasers are iconic Cashel, and Cahir and its castle. In between, you'll find delights along pretty much any country road you choose.

TIPPERARY TOWN
pop 4600

Tipperary (Tiobrad Árann) has a storied name, largely due to the WWI song. And indeed, you may find it a long road to Tipperary as the N24 and a web of regional roads converge on the centre and traffic often moves at the same speed as the armies at the Somme. The town itself has few pretensions and there's no need to detour here.

The **tourist office** (☎ 062-80520; Excel Heritage Centre, Mitchell St; ☒ 9.30am-5.30pm Mon-Sat) is reached via St Michael's St, a side street leading 200m off the northern side of Main St. There's a car park alongside the heritage centre, which also has a small gallery, a movie theatre, a goo **genealogy centre** (☎ 062-80552; ☒ 9.30am-4.40pm Mon-Fri) and **internet access** (per 10min €1).

Banks, ATMs, bureaux de change and a manner of shops can be found along Main S

Midway along Main St, there's a **statue** c **Charles J Kickham** (1828–82), a local novelis (author of *Knocknagow*, a novel about rura life) and Young Irelander. He spent four year in London's Pentonville Prison in the 1860 for treason.

There's a regular food market in and aroun the Excel Heritage Centre's parking lot.

Tipp's Sporting Pub (☎ 062-51716; 50 Main St; main €7-15) is also known as the Kirkham House i honour of the local patriot. This old pub ha carvery lunches that include smoked haddoc and cod pie.

Tipperary Racecourse (☎ 062-51357; www.tipperar races.ie; Limerick Rd) is one of Ireland's leading tracks. It's 3km out of town and has regu lar meetings during the year; see the loca press for details. The course is within walk ing distance of Limerick Junction station. On race days there are minibus pick-ups from Tipperary town; phone for details.

Getting There & Away
BUS

Most buses stop on Abbey St beside the river. **Bus Éireann** (www.buseireann.ie) runs up to eight buses daily on the Limerick (€7.50, 40 minutes) to Waterford route via Cahir and Clonmel. **Bernard Kavanagh** (☎ 062-51563; www .bkavcoaches.com) runs one service daily to Dublin via Cahir and Cashel (€7, 50 minutes). Buses leave from outside the Marian Hall at the northern end of St Michael's St.

TRAIN

To get to the train station, head south along Bridge St. Tipperary is on the Waterford–

imerick Junction line. There are two daily ervices to Cahir (25 minutes), Clonmel, Carrick-on-Suir, Waterford and Rosslare Harbour, and multiple connections to Cork, erry and Dublin from **Limerick Junction** (☎ 062-51406), barely 3km from Tipperary tation along the Limerick road.

etting Around
pringhouse Bicycle Hire (☎ 062-31329; gmrbailey@ rcom.net; Kilshane; rental day/week €20/80) has bikes, an offer cycling advice for the region, and will ick up and drop off bikes at the bus and train tations. It has a small B&B and is located on he N24, just southeast of Tipperary.

LEN OF AHERLOW & ALTEE MOUNTAINS
outh of Tipperary are the shapely lievenamuck Hills and Galtee Mountains, eparated by the broad, chequered val- ey of the Glen of Aherlow. A 25km scenic rive through the Glen is signposted from Tipperary town. At the eastern end of the Glen, between Tipperary and Cahir, is Bansha (An Bháinseach). The village marks the start f a 20km trip west to Galbally, an easy bike ide or scenic drive along the R663 that takes n the best of the county's landscapes.

The R663 from Bansha and the R664 outh from Tipperary converge at Newtown t the **Coach Road Inn** (☎ 062-56240), a fine old ub that's popular with walkers and a good ource of information on the area. Another good resource is the local visitor information website at www.aherlow.com, which lists rural 3&Bs in the area.

The terrain through the region ranges from he lush riverbanks of the Aherlow to pine orests in the hills and windswept, rocky grass- ands that seem to stretch on forever.

There's also excellent walking throughout the area, and the views from the hills across the Glen are always spectacular (when it's not raining that is). A popular **lookout** and historic **statue of Christ** can be found 1.6km north of Newtown on the R664.

Sleeping
There's a good range of rural accommodation – much of it catering to walkers. Most places also have self-catering accommodation for longer stays.

Ballinacourty House Camping Park & B&B (☎ 062- 56559; www.camping.ie, www.ballinacourtyhse.com; Glen

of Aherlow; campsites €16, s/d €52/70; mid-Apr–Sep) Set against a great backdrop of the Galtees, this attractive site is 10km west from Bansha, and past Newtown. It has excellent facili- ties, as well as a fine garden, restaurant, wine bar and tennis court. An old stone house has been renovated and now offers B&B accommodation.

Homeleigh Farmhouse (☎ 062-56228; www.homeleigh farmhouse.com; Newtown; s/d €55/80) Just west of Newtown and the Coach Road Inn on the R663, this working farm rents out rooms in a modern home. Furnishings are traditional and you can arrange for dinner. This is really ground zero for local hiking.

Bansha House (☎ 062-54194; www.tipp.ie/banshahs .htm; Bansha; s/d €60/90) Period elegance and high ceilings characterise this Georgian country house in spacious grounds. Set amid farmland and close to walking paths, it's a great getaway. The house is signposted and is 250m along a lane at the western entrance to Bansha.

Aherlow House Hotel (☎ 062-56153; www.aherlow house.ie; Newtown; s/d from €90/160;) This 1928 hunting lodge has been turned into a luxuri- ous retreat complete with self-catering chalets. In the 1970s it was developed into a hotel and has been much improved upon since. The 29 palatial rooms have traditional furniture. It's often the host to local walking festivals.

Getting There & Away
The frequent Bus Éireann link from Tipperary to Waterford stops in Bansha. From here it's a walk or bike ride into the hills. See left for bike rental information, otherwise a rental car will let you explore far and wide between walks.

CASHEL
pop 2500
With one of the finest 1000-year-old castles around looming over town, it's no wonder that Cashel (Caiseal Mumhan) is popular. The iconic Rock of Cashel and the clutch of historical religious buildings that crown its breezy summit seem like a magical extension of the rocky landscape itself. Despite mobs of visitors, Cashel manages to maintain a certain charm as a smallish market town.

Orientation
A bypass on the Dublin–Cork route eases some of the town's congestion. The Rock and its inspiring buildings stand loftily above it all.

Reasonable photo opportunities for framing the Rock can be had on the road into town from the Dublin Rd roundabout or the little roads just west of the centre. Much better is to shoot from inside the ruins of Hore Abbey (opposite).

Parking in Cashel can be tight. Avoid the parking lot closest to the Rock as it's a bit of a scam: one all-day price with no option for less time. Better are the street spots nearby and throughout town that allow you to pay for only as much time as you need.

Information

Banks and ATMs are in the centre.

Book Nook (☎ 062-64947; 79 Main St) Has a good selection of local-interest, general and travel books.

Cashel Heritage Town Centre (☎ 062-62511; www .cashel.ie; Town Hall, Main St; ⏰ 9.30am-5.30pm mid-Mar–Sep, closed weekends Oct–mid-Mar) Helpful staff make this a great place to get information and purchase walking maps. It also has a museum (opposite).

Online (☎ 062-64062; 102 Main St; per 20min €1; ⏰ 10am-8pm) On the back side of Main St.

Police station (☎ 062-62866) Behind the post office at the bottom of Main St.

Sights

ROCK OF CASHEL

The **Rock of Cashel** (☎ 062-61437; www.heritageireland .com; adult/child €6/2; ⏰ 9am-5.30pm mid-Mar–mid-Oct, to 4.30pm mid-Oct–mid-Mar, last admission 45min before closing) is one of Ireland's most spectacular archaeological sites. The 'Rock' is a prominent green hill, banded with limestone outcrops. It rises from a grassy plain on the outskirts of the town and bristles with ancient fortifications – the word 'cashel' is an anglicised version of the Irish word *caiseal,* meaning 'fortress'. Sturdy walls circle an enclosure that contains a complete round tower, a roofless abbey and the finest 12th-century Romanesque chapel in Ireland. For more than 1000 years the Rock of Cashel was a symbol of power, and the seat of kings and churchmen who ruled over the region.

It's a five-minute stroll from the town centre to the Rock and you can take some pretty paths including the Bishop's Walk, which ends in the gardens of the Cashel Palace Hotel. Sheep grudgingly allow you to pass. There are a couple of parking spaces for visitors with disabilities at the top of the approach road to the ticket office; otherwise see p343 for details on Cashel parking. The Rock is a major draw

for coach parties for most of the year and extremely busy during July and August. Th sweeping views allow you to see a tour bu approaching from any direction like a raiding party. The scaffolding moves from plac to place each year as part of the never-endin struggle to keep the Rock caulked.

History

In the 4th century the Rock of Cashel wa chosen as a base by the Eóghanachta cla from Wales, who went on to conquer muc of Munster and become kings of the region For some 400 years it rivalled Tara (p539) a a centre of power in Ireland. The clan wa associated with St Patrick, hence the Rock' alternative name of St Patrick's Rock.

In the 10th century, the Eóghanachta los possession of the rock to the O'Brien (or Dá gCais) tribe under Brian Ború's leadership. I 1101, King Muircheartach O'Brien presente the Rock to the Church, a move designed t curry favour with the powerful bishops an to end secular rivalry over possession of th Rock with the Eóghanachta, by now know as the MacCarthys. Numerous buildings mus have occupied the Rock over the years, but i is the ecclesiastical relics that have survive even the depredations of the Cromwellia army in 1647.

Hall of the Vicars Choral

The entrance to the Rock of Cashel is through this 15th-century building, once home to th male choristers who sang in the cathedral. I houses the ticket office. The exhibits in th adjoining undercroft include some very rar silverware, Bronze Age axes and St Patrick' Cross – an impressive, although eroded, 12th-century crutched cross with a crucifixion scene on one face and animals on the other. A replica stands outside, in the castle courtyard. The kitchen and dining hall upstairs contain some period furniture, tapestries and paintings beneath a fine carved-oak roof and gallery. A 20-minute audiovisual presentation on the Rock's history runs every half hour. Showings are in English, French, German and Italian.

Cathedral

This 13th-century Gothic structure overshadows the other ruins. Entry is through a small porch facing the Hall of the Vicars Choral. The cathedral's western location is formed y the **Archbishop's Residence**, a 15th-century, our-storey castle that had its great hall built ver the nave. Soaring above the centre of the athedral is a huge square tower with a turret n the southwestern corner.

Scattered throughout are monuments, panls from 16th-century altar tombs, and coats f arms. If you have binoculars, look for the umerous stone heads on capitals and corbels igh above the ground.

Round Tower

On the northeastern corner of the cathedral s an 11th- or 12th-century round tower, the arliest building on the Rock of Cashel. It's 28m tall and the doorway is 3.5m above the ground – perhaps for structural rather than defensive reasons.

Cormac's Chapel

f the Rock of Cashel boasted only Cormac's Chapel, it would still be an outstanding place. This compelling building dates from 1127, and the medieval integrity of its trans-European architecture survives. It was probably the first Romanesque church in Ireland. The style of the square towers that flank it to either side may reflect Germanic influences, but there are haunting similarities in its steep stone roof to the 'boat-hull' shape of older Irish buildings, such as the Gallarus Oratory in County Clare and the beehive huts of the Dingle Peninsula.

The true Romanesque splendour is in the detail of the exquisite doorway arches, the grand chancel arch and ribbed barrel vault, and the outstanding carved vignettes that include a trefoil-tailed grotesque and a Norman-helmeted centaur firing an arrow at a rampaging lion. The chapel's interior is tantalisingly dark, but linger for a while and your eyes will adjust. Inside the main door, on the left, is the sarcophagus said to house King Cormac, dating from between 1125 and 1150. Frescoes once covered the walls, but only vestiges of these survive. The southern tower leads to a stone-roofed vault and a croft above the nave (no access).

HORE ABBEY

Cashel throws in another bonus for the heritage lover. This is the formidable ruin of 13th-century Hore Abbey, located in flat farmland just under 1km north of the Rock. Originally Benedictine and settled by monks from Glastonbury in England at the end of the 12th century, it later became a Cistercian house. It was gifted to the order by a 13th-century archbishop who expelled the Benedictine monks after dreaming that they planned to murder him. The complex is enjoyably gloomy, and from its interior there are superb photo ops of the Rock of Cashel with creative foregrounds, if you get it right.

BRÚ BORÚ

Cashel's heritage and cultural centre, **Brú Ború** (☎ 062-61122; www.comhaltas.ie/locations/detail/bru_boru; ◷ 9am-5pm Jun-Sep, closed Sat & Sun Oct-May) is in a modern building next to the car park below the Rock of Cashel. The centre offers an absorbing insight into Irish traditional music, dance and song. It has a shop and cafe, but its main daytime attraction is **Sounds of History**, an exhibition in a subterranean chamber where the story of Ireland and its music is told through imaginative audio displays. In the summer there is a traditional show at night in the centre's theatre. There are also daytime theatrical performances. Admission to events varies from €10 for daytime events to over €40 for the dinner shows.

OTHER SIGHTS

Cashel Heritage Town Centre (☎ 062-62511; www.casheltc.ie; Town Hall, Main St; admission free; ◷ 9.30am-5.30pm mid-Mar–Sep, closed Sat & Sun Oct–mid-Mar), located in the town hall, has displays and a scale model showing how Cashel looked in the 1640s.

The **Cashel Folk Village** (☎ 062-62525; Dominic St; adult/child €6/3; ◷ 9.30am-7.30pm May-Oct, 10am-6pm Mar & Apr) is an engaging exhibition of old buildings and shopfronts from around the town, plus local memorabilia and a 'penal chapel'. It's a bit slipshod in a heart-warming way: one sign says 'Ponder around our unique Museum'.

In a forbidding 1836 stone building, the **Bolton Library** (☎ 062-61944; John St; adult/child €4/2; ◷ 10am-4.30pm Mon-Fri) houses a splendid 18th-century collection of books, maps and manuscripts from the dawn of printing onwards. There are works by writers from Chaucer to Swift.

Sleeping

BUDGET

Cashel Lodge and Camping Park (☎ 062-61003; www.cashel-lodge.com; Dundrum Rd; campsites per person €8, dm/s/d €20/40/65; **P**) This first-class IHH

SISTER FIDELMA'S CREATOR

Cashel's most famous resident is a fictional 7th-century nun. Sister Fidelma, the star of more than 18 novels by Peter Tremayne (including the recent *Dove of Death*), is a crimefighter of the distant past, a sort of Sherlock Holmes in heavy robes.

Legions of fans visit Cashel every year looking for tangible links to a character whose next exploits they eagerly await. Home to kings from at least the 4th century, the ancient town inspires not only fans but the author himself. 'I still catch my breath when, approaching Cashel from any direction, coming round the hills on the road, I see the great Rock with its ancient buildings rising 200ft above the plain', says Tremayne. 'It is iconic, an immediately recognisable symbol that is never forgotten.'

Although his roots to the area may not go back as far as the good sister's, they do go back. 'My father's family are an old Munster family. They were recorded in the Awbeg Valley in north County Cork in the 13th century,' he says. 'I was very young when he first pointed out the Rock and told me stories of the Eóghanacht kings', the true-to-life rulers to whom the fictional Fidelma is related.

Tremayne says there are tangible ways people can live the Fidelma experience, even if the structures on the rock post-date her days solving mysteries by up to 1000 years. Not surprisingly he suggests staying at the Cashel Town B&B (below), with its Sister Fidelma motifs. He also recommends asking at the visitors centre for advice. And he suggests exploring the countryside including the 'wild scenery of the nearby Glen of Aherlow (p343)', scene of many a Fidelma exploit.

'Intrepid walkers [can even] set off along the ancient roadway that Fidelma rode many times from Cashel to Knockgraffon, to Ardfinnan, across the Knockmealdon Mountains to Lismore and from Lismore to Ardmore on the coast. This is called Rian Bò Pádraig, the track of St Patrick's Cow – parts of which have been excavated showing how ancient it is.'

hostel, in a converted coach house northwest of town, is friendly, relaxing and well equipped. It has high-standard dorms and rooms, and a campsite. Terrific views of the Rock and Hore Abbey are bonuses, as is the attractive bare stone and wood interior.

Cashel Holiday Hostel (☎ 062-62330; www.cashel hostel.com; 6 John St; dm €16-18, s/d from €30/50; 🛜) This is a friendly and central budget option in a vivid safety-orange-coloured three-storey Georgian terrace off Main St. It has 52 beds in four- to eight-bed rooms as well as a recreation room, kitchen and laundry.

MIDRANGE & TOP END

The sweet spot for Cashel accommodation is right in the middle of town, and you'll find a huge range of choices, all an easy walk to the Rock.

Cashel Town B&B (Sister Fidelma B&B; ☎ 062-62330; www.cashelbandb.com; 5 John St; s/d €50/80; 🅿 🖳) 'The chief poet of the tribe earns 21 cows…' is but one of the multitude of old Irish bromides that adorn the walls of this seven-room B&B, which has a startling new exterior colour that would send you to the doctor if you emitted it. Interior decor includes rooms taking their cues from Sister Fidelma, the crime-

fighting nun (see boxed text, above). It is run by the same cheerful management as the Cashel Holiday Hostel next door.

Kearney's Castle Hotel (☎ 062-61044; Main St; s/d from €50/80) Located right across from the Cashel Heritage Town Centre. The owners modestly dismiss their building as 'just an old house' even though parts comprise a medieval fortified tower. The 12 simple rooms are sprightly decorated in blue and beige, and have TVs.

Ashmore House (☎ 062-61286; www.ashmorehouse .com; John St; s/d €60/70; 🅿 🛜) Look for the vivid yellow door on this Georgian town house, which has five big, high-ceilinged rooms filled with antiques. It's located on a quiet street just off Main St. The owner is a retired merchant seaman and has as many stories as he has mementos of his voyages.

Hill House (☎ 062-61277; www.hillhousecashel.com; Palmershill; r €60-120; 🅿 🖳) It actually could be called Amazing View House, as this Georgian charmer has magnificent views across to the Rock. Set back in gardens, the house is about 400m uphill from Main St. Rooms have a traditional style and come with four-poster beds.

Ladyswell House (☎ 062-62985; www.ladyswellhouse .com; Ladyswell St; s/d €65/90) Barely a five-minute walk to the Abbey, this five-room B&B is spotless. Some bathrooms have skylights. The owners and their dog are total charmers and will organise custom tours as well as Shannon Airport pick-ups.

Cashel Palace Hotel (☎ 062-62707; www.cashel palace.ie; Main St; r from €70-200; P 🖳 🛜) The Cashel Palace, a handsome red-brick, late-Queen Anne house, is a local landmark. Fully restored, it has 23 rooms oozing with luxuries like trouser presses (as if you wouldn't have someone else attend to that); some rooms have soaking tubs you'll leave only after you're totally prunified. Built in 1732 for a Protestant archbishop, the rooms are in the gracious main building or quaint mews. The bar is a place to talk about your upcoming hunt.

Eating

Cashel has eating choices up and down the price scale, some excellent. The superb local blue cheese can be found on many menus.

Henry's Fine Foods (☎ 086 894 3707; 5 Main St; meals from €5; 🕑 9am-6pm) And fine it is. Local ham and cheese features in many a lunch item; definitely partake. The eggs are free range and there are homemade jellies, jams and chutneys for sale.

Bake House (☎ 062-61680; 7 Main St; meals €5-8; 🕑 9am-5.30pm) Head for this busy cafe for tea and coffee, breakfast, or a light lunch. Try the tasty Cashel blue-cheese quiche. Across from the Cashel Heritage Town Centre, ponder the passing parade at tables out front.

our pick Cafe Hans (☎ 062-63660; Dominic St; mains €10-20; 🕑 noon-5pm Tue-Sat) Competition for the 32 seats is fierce at this casual cafe run by the same family who run Chez Hans (below). There's a terrific selection of salads (the Caesar is always a winner), open sandwiches and fish, shellfish, lamb and vegetarian dishes, with a discerning wine selection and mouth-watering desserts. Get there early or after the rush, or expect to queue.

Chez Hans (☎ 062-61177; www.chezhans.net; Dominic St; 3 courses €40-60; 🕑 6-10pm Tue-Sat) Since 1968 this former church has been a place of worship for foodies from all over Ireland and, for that matter, the world. Still as fresh and inventive as ever, the superb restaurant gives its blessing to all manner of local foods, which are prepared simply and with elegance. Some of the wines come from Chef Hans' own vineyards in Germany. Book ahead.

Drinking

Cashel has a number of quality pubs.

Davern's (☎ 062-61121; 20 Main St) This bar is popular for a good chat. There's live music some nights, which you may or may not hear tucked away in one of the many crags and corners of this old, old pub.

Ryan's (☎ 062-62688; Ladyswell St) Locals chew the fat, share the gossip and gulp the pint at this congenial place with a large beer garden that really is a garden.

Getting There & Away

Bus Éireann (www.buseireann.ie) runs eight buses daily between Cashel and Cork (€12, 1½ hours) via Cahir (€4.50, 20 minutes, six to eight daily) and Fermoy. There is one bus daily to Thurles (€6, 30 minutes) where you can connect to trains on the Dublin–Limerick line. The bus stop for Cork is outside the Bake House on Main St. The Dublin stop (€12, three hours, six daily) is opposite. Tickets are available from the nearby Spar shop or you can buy them on the bus.

Bernard Kavanagh (☎ 062-51563; www.bkav coaches.com) runs one evening service Monday to Saturday to Tipperary (€7, 50 minutes) and a service to Thurles and Clonmel (€7, 30 minutes).

AROUND CASHEL

The atmospheric – and, at dusk, delightfully creepy – ruins of **Athassel Priory** sit in the shallow and verdant River Suir Valley, 7km southwest of Cashel. The original buildings date from 1205, and Athassel became one of the richest and most important monasteries in Ireland. What survives is substantial: the gatehouse and portcullis gateway, the cloister and stretches of walled enclosure, as well as some medieval tomb effigies.

To get there take the N74 to the village of Golden, then head south, along the narrow road signed Athassel Abbey, for 2km. Roadside parking is limited and very tight. The Priory is reached across often-muddy fields. The welter of lanes back here is good for cycling.

CAHIR

pop 2850

Cahir (An Cathair; pronounced care) is a compact and attractive town that encircles its namesake castle, which doesn't rise to the heights of the Rock of Cashel but does do a

---

DETOUR: FAMINE WARHOUSE

A relic of one of Ireland's darkest chapters, the **Famine Warhouse** (☎ 087-908 9972; www.heritage
ireland.ie; admission free; ☟ 2.30-5.30pm Wed-Sun Apr-Sep, 2-4pm Sat & Sun Oct-Mar) sits seemingly benignly
today amid typical farmland near Ballingarry. During the 1848 rebellion, rebels led by William
Smith O'Brien besieged police who had barricaded themselves inside and taken children hostage. Things did not go well and this incident marked the effective end of the rebellion. Besides
exhibits about the incident, there are also displays detailing the famine and the mass exodus
of Irish emigrants to America.

The warhouse is 30km northeast of Cashel on the R691 about midway to Kilkenny. Be careful
navigating as County Tipperary has two Ballingarrys; the wrong one is over by Roscrea.

---

good job of looking like every castle you ever
tried building at the beach. Towers, a moat
and various battlements hit every fortified
cliché you can think of – except it is missing a
long-haired blonde in the highest window.

Cahir's town square is lined with pubs and
simple cafes. Serene walking paths follow the
banks of the River Suir; watch for lazy brown
trout. And look for signs marking the Cahir
Heritage Trail, which hits a number of buildings that feature from the town's various hey-
days. You can easily spend a couple of hours
wandering about.

Orientation

Cahir is 15km south of Cashel, at the eastern
tip of the Galtee Mountains.

Buses stop in Castle St near a large car park
alongside the river and castle (car parking
here costs €1 for two hours). East of Castle
St is the centre of town, eponymously named
the Square. There's street parking throughout
the town.

Information

AIB Bank (Castle St) Has an ATM and bureau de change.
Post office (Church St) North of the Square.
Public toilets Located next to the tourist office.
Tourist office (☎ 052-744 1453; www.cahirtourism.ie;
Main St; ☟ 9.30am-5pm Mon-Sat Jun-Sep) Has leaflets
and information about the town and region.

Sights

CAHIR CASTLE

Cahir's awesome **castle** (☎ 052-744 1011; www
.heritageireland.ie; Castle St; adult/child €3/1; ☟ 9am-6.30pm
mid-Jun–Aug, 9.30am-5.30pm mid-Mar–mid-Jun & Sep–mid-
Oct, to 4.30pm mid-Oct–mid-Mar) is feudal fantasy
in a big way. A river-island site with moat,
rocky foundations, massive walls, turrets and
towers, defences and dungeons are all there.
This castle is one of Ireland's largest. Founded

by Conor O'Brien in 1142, it was passed to
the Butler family in 1375. In 1599 it lost the
arms race of its day when the Earl of Essex
used cannons to shatter the walls, an event
explained with a huge model.

The castle was surrendered to Cromwell in
1650 without a struggle; its future usefulness
may have discouraged the usual Cromwellian
'deconstruction'. It is largely intact and formidable still, and was restored in the 1840s
and again in the 1960s when it came under
state ownership.

A 15-minute audiovisual presentation puts
Cahir in context with other Irish castles. The
buildings within the castle are sparsely furnished, although there are good displays. The
real rewards come from simply wandering
through this remarkable survivor of Ireland's
medieval past. There are frequent guided
tours, and several good printed guides are
for sale at the entrance.

SWISS COTTAGE

A pleasant riverside path from behind the
town car park meanders 2km south to Cahir
Park and the **Swiss Cottage** (☎ 052-744 1144; www
.heritageireland.ie; Cahir Park; adult/child €3/1; ☟ 10am-
6pm mid-Apr–mid-Oct), an exquisite, thatched
cottage surrounded by roses, lavender and
honeysuckle. It's the best thatched fantasy
in Ireland, and was built in 1810 as a retreat
for Richard Butler, 12th Baron Caher, and
his wife. The design was by London architect
John Nash, creator of the Royal Pavilion at
Brighton and London's Regent's Park. The
cottage-orné style emerged during the late
18th and early 19th centuries in England in
response to the prevailing taste for the picturesque. Thatched roofs, natural wood and
carved weatherboarding were characteristics,
and most examples were built as ornamental
features on estates.

There could not be a more lavish example of Regency Picturesque than the Swiss Cottage. It is more of a sizable house than a cottage and has extensive facilities. The 30-minute (compulsory) guided tours are thoroughly enjoyable, although you may have to wait for one in the busier summer months.

Sleeping

Apple Caravan & Camping Park (☎ 052-744 1459; www.theapplefarm.com; Moorstown, Cahir; campsite per adult/child 7/5; ☺ May-Sep) This quiet and spacious campsite on a farm of apple orchards is on the N24 between Cahir (6km) and Clonmel (9km). The place has a delightful fruity ambience and there's free use of a tennis court and racquets. The juice is worth the trip.

Lisakyle (☎ 052-744 1963; Ardfinnan Rd; dm/s/d 18/20/40) Some 2km south of town, past the Swiss Cottage on the R670, this charmer of a hostel also offers tent space (€10) amid pretty gardens. Maurice offers a warm welcome and 21 beds. And how do you get here from town? 'You just call, we'll come and get you.'

Tinsley House (☎ 052-744 1947; www.tinsleyhouse.com; The Square; r €40-70; ☺ May-Sep) This mannered house has a great location and four well-furnished rooms. There's a roof garden and the owner, Liam Roche, is an expert on local history and can recommend walks and other activities.

Cahir House Hotel (☎ 052-744 3000; www.cahirhouse hotel.ie; The Square; €60/90; 🖳 🤶) On a prominent corner of the centre, this landmark hotel has a relaxed vibe. The 42 rooms have a rather bold yellow-and-red decor – think of it as a visual wake-up call. A new spa offers a full range of waxing for your debut on the Irish shore.

Eating

Lazy Bean Cafe (☎ 052-744 2038; The Square; snacks €3-7; ☺ 9am-6pm Mon-Sat, 10.30am-6pm Sun) Busy, breezy little cafe that dishes out loads of tasty sandwiches, snacks and ice cream. Its motto: 'Chocolates, coffee, men. Some things are just better rich.'

River House (☎ 052-744 1951; 1 Castle St; meals €6-12; ☺ 9am-5pm) A change in ownership has turned this icon by the river into just another caff, but the patio still has fine castle views. Enjoy them with your burger and chips.

Cahir's **farmers market** (Craft Yard; ☺ 9am-1pm Sat) attracts the region's best food vendors.

Shopping

Hundreds of locals toiled away in a notorious linen mill during the 19th century.

Almost 200 years later, the once ominous stone building has been reborn as the **Cahir Craft Granary** (☎ 052-744 1473; www.craftgranary .com; Church St; ☺ 10am-5pm Mon-Fri, 9am-5pm Sat). Ceaseless slaving over looms has been replaced by local artists creating and selling a huge range of works. Pottery, carving, painting, sculpting, collectable books and quite a bit more are available from dozens of artisans and dealers.

The Granary is just north of the Square, past the post office.

Getting There & Away

BUS

Cahir is a hub for several Bus Éireann routes, including Dublin–Cork, Limerick–Waterford, Galway–Waterford, Kilkenny–Cork and Cork–Athlone. There are eight buses per day Monday to Saturday (six buses on Sunday) to Cashel (€4.50, 20 minutes). Buses stop in the car park beside the tourist office.

TRAIN

From Monday to Saturday, the Limerick Junction–Waterford train stops three times daily in each direction.

MITCHELSTOWN CAVES

While the Galtee Mountains are mainly sandstone, a narrow band of limestone along their southern side has given rise to the **Mitchelstown Caves** (☎ 052-746 7246; www.mitchelstowncave.com; Burncourt; adult/child €7/2; ☺ 10am-5.30pm, earlier outside summer). Superior to Kilkenny's Dunmore

---

WALK: TIPPERARY HERITAGE TRAIL

Extending a distance of 55km from a place called the Vee in the south to Cashel in the north, the **Tipperary Heritage Trail** takes in some beautiful river valleys and ruins. The 30km segment running north from Cahir to Cashel is the best segment as it takes in the verdant lands around the River Suir and passes close to highlights such as Athassel Priory. The best stretches around Golden are off roads. Expect to see a fair amount of wildlife as the paths and very minor roads follow the waters and pass through woodlands. You can use public transport to return to either Cashel or Cahir when you're done. Ordnance Survey Discovery series maps 66 and 74 cover the route.

Cave (p240) and yet less developed for tourists, these caves are among the most extensive in the country with nearly 3km of passages, and spectacular chambers full of textbook formations with names such as the Pipe Organ, Tower of Babel, House of Commons and Eagle's Wing. Tours take about 30 minutes.

The caves are near Burncourt, 16km southwest of Cahir and signposted on the N8 to Mitchelstown (Baile Mhistéala).

Sleeping

Mountain Lodge Hostel (☎ 052-746 7277; www.anoige.ie; Burncourt; dm €16; May-Sep) This 24-bed An Óige hostel (housed in an attractive former shooting lodge), is 6km north of the caves, and is a handy base for wandering the Galtee Mountains. It lies to the north of the N8 Mitchelstown–Cahir road, and is electricity-free, being lit by gas.

Getting There & Away

Frequent **Bus Éireann** (☎ 062-51555) buses from Dublin to Cork or Athlone drop off at the Mountain Lodge Hostel gate.

CLONMEL

pop 16,000

Clonmel (Cluain Meala; 'Meadows of Honey') is Tipperary's largest and most bustling town. It's worth a stop for a stroll along the wide River Suir, a browse of the many shops (the timeless market town feel is so tangible that you keep looking for someone in stocks), and a chance to load up on supplies.

Laurence Sterne (1713–68), author of *A Sentimental Journey* and *Tristram Shandy*, was a native of the town. However, the commercial cheerleader for Clonmel was Italian-born Charles Bianconi (1786–1875), who, at the precocious age of 16, was sent to Ireland by his father in an attempt to break his liaison with a woman. Bianconi later channelled all his frustrated passion into setting up a coach service between Clonmel and Cahir; his company quickly grew to become a nationwide passenger and mail carrier. For putting Clonmel on the map, Bianconi was twice elected mayor.

Orientation

Clonmel's centre lies on the northern bank of the River Suir. Set back from the quays and running parallel to the river, the main street runs east-west, starting off as Parnell St and becoming Mitchell St and O'Connell St before passing under West Gate, where it changes to

Irishtown and Abbey Rd. Running north from this long thoroughfare is Gladstone St, which has a number of hotels and pubs.

There's a confounding system of one-way streets; you'll find refuge in the vast parking lot off Gladstone and Mary Sts.

Information

AIB Bank (O'Connell St) Has an ATM and bureau de change.
Circles Internet (☎ 052-612 3315; 16 Market St; per 10min €1; 11am-11pm)
Post office (Emmet St)
Sophie's Bookshop (☎ 052-618 0752; 15 Mitchell St) Cute; has a good selection of general and travel books, as well as books of local interest.
Tourist office (☎ 052-612 2960; St Mary's Church, Mary St; 9.30am-1pm & 2-4.30pm Mon-Fri) Set in quiet church grounds; the free town map available here has excellent details on local sights and history.

Sights

At the junction of Mitchell and Sarsfield Sts is the beautifully restored **Main Guard** (☎ 052-612 7484; www.heritageireland.ie; Sarsfield St; admission free; 9.30am-6pm mid-Apr–Sep), a Butler courthouse dating from 1675 and based on a design by Christopher Wren. The columned porticos are once again open (after renovations) and exhibits include the ubiquitous model of Clonmel as a walled 17th-century town.

In Nelson St, south of Parnell St, is the refurbished **County Courthouse**, designed by Richard Morrison in 1802. It was here that the Young Irelanders of 1848, including Thomas Francis Meagher, were tried and sentenced to transportation to Australia.

West along Mitchell St (past the town hall with its statue commemorating the 1798 Rising) and south down Abbey St is the **Franciscan friary**. Inside, near the door, is a 1533 Butler tomb depicting a knight and his lady. There's some fine modern stained glass, especially in St Anthony's Chapel to the north.

Turn south down Bridge St and cross the river, following the road round until it opens out at **Lady Blessington's Bath**, a picturesque stretch of the river that is just right for picnicking.

The **South Tipperary County Museum** (☎ 052-613 4550; www.southtippcoco.ie; Mick Delahunty Sq; admission free; 10am-5pm Tue-Sat) has displays on the history of County Tipperary from Neolithic times to the present, and hosts changing exhibitions.

Near the museum, look for the life-size **Frank Patterson Statue**, which portrays the son of Clonmel and Ireland's 'Golden Tenor' in full-throated glory. If only it had sound. Among his long list of accomplishments was performing 'Danny Boy' in the Coen Brothers 1990 film *Miller's Crossing*.

Sleeping

There are several B&Bs on Marlfield Rd, due west of the centre.

Fennessy's Hotel (☎ 052-612 3680; www.fennessys hotel.com; Gladstone St; r from €45-80; **P**) Sts Peter and Paul Church, across from this hotel, will provide courage should you have impure thoughts in any of the 10 rooms at this attractive four-storey central hotel.

Befani's (☎ 052-617 7893; www.befani.com; 6 Sarsfield St; s/d €55/90; 💻) Between the Main Guard and the Suir, this new guesthouse run by locally popular tapas restaurant of the same name (right) balances good value with style. Rooms aren't huge, but they are attractive and are nicely fitted out in the sunny colours of Spain.

our pick Hotel Minella (☎ 052-612 2388; www.hotel minella.ie; Coleville Rd; r €90-250; **P** 💻 🛜 🖵) What can you say about a luxury hotel that has a sheep dog named Sparky to greet you at the door? Unpretentious yet refined, this family-run place sits amid extensive grounds on the south bank of the River Suir, 2km east of the centre. The 90 rooms are divided between those in an 1863 mansion and those in a new wing. The latter boast almost every kind of convenience, including luxurious private hot tubs on terraces overlooking the river.

Eating

Honey Pot (☎ 052-612 1457; 11 Abbey St; 🕑 9am-6pm Mon-Sat) It's like a farmers market every day at this organic deli and health food store. The fairtrade provenance of goods on sale is explained in detail. The biggest problem with the picnics prepared-to-go is waiting to get to your picnic spot.

Niamh's (☎ 052-612 5698; 1 Mitchell St; meals €5-15; 🕑 8am-6pm Mon-Sat) A smart deli and cafe with a wide range of appealing lunch options. Eat in the popular cafe or get one of the creative sandwiches takeaway and head to the banks of the Suir.

Sean Tierney (☎ 052-612 4467; 13 O'Connell St; meals €7-20; 🕑 kitchen noon-9pm) Ketchup red at street level and mustard yellow for the two floors above, this narrow old pub churns out vast portions of pub classics like roasts, lasagne and more. Wander the warren of rooms and floors until you find a table that's just right.

Befani's (☎ 052-617 7893; 6 Sarsfield St; meals €15-30; 🕑 9am-9.30pm) Just down the street from the Main Guard, Befani's brings the Mediterranean to Clonmel. Brightly flavoured dishes delight from breakfast to dinner. Throughout the day there's a tapas menu highlighted by locally sourced organic produce, perfect for accompanying a sherry from the small bar. Breakfasts are a cure for the black-pudding blues. The €16 tapas platter is a bargain.

Drinking

Sean Tierney (left) has trad sessions some nights; the ground-level bar is always alive with craic.

Two traditional pubs almost next to each other on Parnell St (near Nelson St) are the diminutive **Phil Carroll** (☎ 052-612 5215), Clonmel's most atmospheric old boozer, and the **Coachman** (☎ 052-612 1299), which has also escaped the crimes of modernisation.

Entertainment

There's an excellent program of art exhibitions, plays and films at the **South Tipperary Arts Centre** (☎ 052-612 7877; www.southtippparts.com; Nelson St), the focus of the arts in the region.

Getting There & Away

BUS

Bus Éireann (www.buseireann.ie) has buses to Cahir (€5, 30 minutes, eight daily), Cork (€16, two hours, three daily), Kilkenny (€8.50, one hour, 12 daily), Waterford (€7, one hour, eight daily), and a number of other places. Tickets can be bought at the train station on Prior Park Rd, where the buses stop.

TRAIN

The **train station** (☎ 052-612 1982) is on Prior Park Rd. Head 1km north along Gladstone St, past the Oakville Shopping Centre and it's just after the petrol station. Monday to Saturday, the Limerick Junction–Waterford train stops three times daily in each direction.

AROUND CLONMEL

Directly south of Clonmel, over the border in County Waterford, are the Comeragh Mountains. There's a scenic route south to Ballymacarbry and the Nire Valley. For more details, see p219.

The East Munster Way (p352) passes through Clonmel.

WALK: EAST MUNSTER WAY

This 70km walk travels through forest and open moorland, along small country roads and a river towpath. It's clearly laid out with black markers bearing yellow arrows, and could be managed in three days, starting at Carrick-on-Suir (opposite) in County Tipperary and finishing at Clogheen in County Waterford.

The first day takes you to Clonmel following the old towpath on the Suir for significant portions of the route. At Kilsheelan Bridge, you leave the river to Harney's Crossroads, then wander through Gurteen Wood and the Comeraghs to Sir Thomas Bridge where you rejoin the river.

For the second day to Newcastle the way first leads south into the hills and then descends to Newcastle and the river once more. The third day sees a lot of very atmospheric walking along the quiet River Tar to Clogheen.

Ordnance Survey Discovery series maps 74 and 75 cover the route.

FETHARD
pop 1400

Fethard (Fiodh Ard) is a quiet, cute little village with a surprising number of medieval ruins scattered about its compact, linear centre. Located 14km north of Clonmel on the River Clashawley, it has a good slice of its old walls still intact. Driving north on the R689 you cross a small ridge and see Fethard in the emerald valley below, looking much as it would have to travellers centuries ago. Its wide main street testifies to its historic role as an important market town.

You can get information from the cheery office of the **Tirry Community Centre** (☎ 052-613 1000; Barrack St; 9am-5pm Mon-Fri). Ask for the walking-tour leaflet. You can also find good information at www.fethard.ie.

There's an ATM in Kenny's Foodmarket, about 50m northeast along the road from the Tirry Community Centre.

Sights

Fethard's **Holy Trinity Church** and **churchyard** (☎ 052-612 6643; Main St; admission free) lie within a captivating little time warp. The church is right off Main St and is reached through a cast-iron gateway. Getting inside is part of the adventure: get the keys from the XL Stop & Shop (aka Whyte's) on Main St, 50m west of the gate.

The main part of the building dates from the 13th century, but its ancient walls have been rather blighted by being covered with mortar for weatherproofing. The handsome west tower was added later and has had its sturdy stonework uncovered. It looks more like a fortified tower house and has savage-looking finials on its corner turrets. The interior of the church has an aisled nave and a chancel of typical medieval style, but is sparsely furnished. A ruined chapel and sacristy adjoin the south end of the church. It is the context of the entire churchyard that is the real winner. Old gravestones descend in ranks to a refurbished stretch of medieval wall complete with a guard tower and a parapet, from where you can look down on the gentle River Clashawley between its horse-trod banks.

Close to the church in Main St is the 17th-century **town hall**, with some fine coats of arms mounted on the facade.

Fethard's main concentration of medieval remains (some of which have been incorporated into later buildings) are just south of the church at the end of Watergate St. Beside Castle Inn are the ruins of several fortified 17th-century **tower houses**. Just under the archway to the river bank and Watergate Bridge is a fine **sheila-na-gig** (a sexually explicit medieval depiction of a woman) embedded in the wall to your left. You can stroll the river bank, provided the resident geese are feeling friendly. From here, the backs of the Abbey St houses, although much added to and knocked about in places, once again display the pleasing irregularities of typical medieval building style.

East along Abbey St is the 14th-century **Augustinian friary**, which is now a Catholic church, with some fine, medieval stained glass and another in-your-face **sheila-na-gig** in its east wall.

Eating & Drinking

McCarthy's (☎ 052-613 1149; Main St; lunch €5-10) A classic that deserves national acclaim and preservation, McCarthy's proclaims itself as Pub, Restaurant and Undertaker – and not necessarily in that order. This timeless joint has closely spaced wooden booths and tables amid a thicket of treasures dating back to 1840

hat will prod your imagination. And yes, it s an efficient set-up for wakes; arrangements are made downstairs.

Getting There & Away

There's no public transport to Fethard but it would make a pleasant cycle from Cashel (p343), 15km to the west.

CARRICK-ON-SUIR

pop 5700

The unassuming market town of Carrick-on-Suir (Carraig na Siúire), 20km east of Clonmel, boasted twice its present population during the late-medieval period, when it was a centre of the brewing and wool industries. The modern town makes a good pit stop – if for no other reason than to escape the local traffic and Byzantine traffic patterns.

Carrick-on-Suir was quick to honour local boy Sean Kelly, one of the world's greatest cyclists, in the late 1980s. The town square bears his name, as does the sports centre. Carrick is also the birthplace of the singing Clancy Brothers, who, with Tommy Makem and assorted Aran Island sweaters, did much to popularise folk music in the 1960s.

From Carrick-on-Suir, the East Munster Way (opposite) winds west to Clonmel before heading south into Waterford.

Information

Main St has banks, ATMs and other services ranged along it.

The **tourist office** (☎ 051-640 200; www.carrick onsuir.ie; ⌚ 10am-5pm Mon-Fri May-Sep, to 4pm Tue-Fri Oct-Apr) is off Main St, through a narrow entranceway. An old church houses this helpful office as well as a Heritage Centre. Get info here on the East Munster Way.

Sights

Carrick-on-Suir was once the property of the Butlers, the Earls of Ormond, who built **Ormond Castle** (☎ 051-640 787; www.heritageireland.ie; Castle St; admission free; ⌚ 10am-6pm May-Sep) on the banks of the river in the 14th century. Anne Boleyn, the second of Henry VIII's wives, may have been born here, though other castles also claim this worthy distinction, possibly hoping to boost their own sales of knick-knacks celebrating the beheaded. The Elizabethan mansion next to the castle was built by the 10th Earl of Ormond, Black Tom Butler, in long-term anticipation of a visit by his cousin,

Queen Elizabeth I, who rather thoughtlessly never turned up.

Some rooms in this Dúchas-owned edifice have fine 16th-century stuccowork, especially the Long Gallery with its depictions of Elizabeth and the Butler coat of arms.

Sleeping & Eating

Main St has numerous lunch cafes, and pubs with food.

Fatima House (☎ 051-640 298; www.fatimahouse .com; John St; s/d from €40/75) Located about 500m west of the Greenside bus stop, this B&B is housed in a stark-fronted 100-year-old town house. Furnishings have been accumulating in the rooms for that entire time.

Carraig Hotel (☎ 051-641 455; www.carraighotel.com; Main St; s/d from €70/100; ⌨) Dominating the centre of town, the Carraig is one of those classic Irish hotels of an undefinable age that has spread over a few buildings and sprawls from room to room. Its bars and eating areas are done up in timeless wood; the 24 rooms are surprisingly modern. Food focuses on simple presentations of steaks, roasts and fresh fish (meals €8 to €25).

The local **farmers market** (⌚ 10am-2pm Fri) is held weekly in the Heritage Centre yard, off of Main St.

Getting There & Away

BUS

Buses stop at Greenside, the park beside the N24 road. Follow New St north from Main St, then turn right.

Bus Éireann (☎ 051-879 000; www.buseireann.ie) has numerous buses serving Carrick-on-Suir. The Limerick–Waterford line serves Cahir and Clonmel (€6, 25 minutes) up to nine times daily. There's also a frequent service to Kilkenny (€8, 45 minutes).

TRAIN

The station is north of Greenside, off Cregg Rd. From Monday to Saturday, the Limerick Junction–Waterford train stops three times daily in each direction.

THURLES & AROUND

pop 6900

Thurles (Durlas) is a busy market town, 22km north of Cashel. It was founded by the Butler family during the 13th century. It is a down-to-earth place holding little reason for an inordinate pause. In 1884, the Cumann

Lúthchleas Gael (Gaelic Athletic Association; GAA) was founded here, and today the town's famous Semple Stadium rivals Croke Park Stadium in Dublin as a holy ground of Gaelic sports like hurling and Gaelic football.

The centre of town is the long, spacious and traffic-choked Liberty Sq. The **visitor centre** (☎ 0504-22702; www.tipperary.gaa.ie; exhibits adult/child €4/2; ☯ 10am-5.30pm) can be found at **Lár na Páirc** (Slievenamon Rd), the shop of the GAA, which is sick with the blue, black and gold of the local team.

The highlight of the area is the Cistercian **Holy Cross Abbey** (☯ 9am-8pm), 6km southwest of Thurles beside the River Suir. The large buildings that survive today date from the 15th century, although the abbey was founded in 1168. Look for the ornately carved sedilia near the altar and pause to appreciate the early form of 'stadium seating'. The abbey contains two relics of the True Cross of varying pedigree. A bookshop is open irregular hours.

Your only reason to visit Thurles may be to pass through the **train station** on the busy Dublin–Limerick Junction train line as part of a trip to Cashel (p343).

ROSCREA
pop 5600

A castle is the star of this pleasant little town on the journey between Dublin and the west on the N7. Roscrea owes its beginnings to a 5th-century monk, St Cronan, who set up a way station for the travelling poor. Most of the historical structures are on or near the main street, Castle St. The town is rescued from the busy traffic of the N7 by a bypass.

Roscrea Castle, a 13th-century stone edifice right in the town centre, was started in 1213 and is remarkably intact. There are two fortified stone towers, surrounded by walls. Look closely and you can see where the original drawbridge was installed. Inside the courtyard stands **Damer House**, the Queen Anne–style residence of the Damer family. Built in the early 18th century, it no doubt had few problems with burglars owing to its location.

Inside you'll find the **Roscrea Heritage Centre** (☎ 0505-21850; www.heritageireland.ie; Castle St; adult/concession €4/2; ☯ 10am-6pm Apr-Aug, 9.30am-4.30pm Sat & Sun Sep-Mar), which contains some interesting exhibitions, including one on the medieval monasteries of the midlands and another on

early-20th-century farming life. There's a peaceful walled garden by the house.

Up to 12 **Bus Éireann** (www.buseireann.ie) buse stop at Roscrea between Dublin (€10, 2 hours) and Limerick (€7, 1½ hours). Thre buses daily serve Cashel (€10.50, 1¼ hours) Dublin trains require a connection i Ballybrophy.

NENAGH & AROUND

Nenagh is a pretty place with a violent past. was a garrison town in the 19th century an before that it was the site of a dominant castle You can see evidence of all this just north o the centre on O'Rahilly St; look for the tal steeple of St Mary's of the Rosary church **Nenagh Castle** looks like the prototype for the rook in chess and is surrounded by cawing crows and coughing teens. The tower date from the 13th century and has impossibly thick walls.

Nearby, the civic centre is an imposing complex of dark-stone buildings from the 19th century, including an old **gaol**. Next doo stands the 1840 **Round House**, a pretty stone building that holds the **Nenagh Heritage Centre** (☎ 067-31610; www.nenagh.ie; ☯ 9.30am-5pm Mon-Fri also 10am-5pm Sat May-Aug), which has tourist info and genealogy services.

There are some excellent places for food in Nenagh.

our pick **Country Choice** (☎ 067-32596; 25 Kenyon St; meals €6-12; ☯ 9am-5pm Mon-Sat) is a place of pilgrimage for lovers of really great Irish artisan foods. Sample the beautiful lunch menu in the cafe or just have a coffee but ready yourself to browse the extensive deli area with homemade preserves, farmhouse cheeses and myriad other treats. Baskets of fruit and even eggs sit out front of the store, luring you in. A chat with the owners, Peter and Mary, is like a grad-school course in Irish foods.

Nenagh is the gateway to the eastern shore of **Lough Derg**, a popular boating and fishing area. About 9km northwest on the R495 is the waterfront hamlet of **Dromineer**, a good place to sample lakeside life. There are plenty of visiting boats in summer and you can swim, fish or rent a sailing boat. Enquire at **Shannon Sailing** (☎ 067-24499; www.shannonsailing.com).

An interesting, scenic lakeside drive from Nenagh is the 24km R494 that winds around to Killaloe and Ballina (p365).

County Clare

Clare is one of Ireland's sweetest spots. It combines the stunning natural beauty of its long and meandering coastline with unique windswept landscapes and a year's worth of dollops of Irish culture.

Rugged nature and the timeless ocean meet on the county's coast. The Atlantic relentlessly pounds year-round, eroding the rocks into fantastic landscapes, and forming sheer cliffs like those at the iconic Cliffs of Moher, strange little islands like those off lone Loop Head and craggy bluffs like those found in Fenore. There are even stretches of beach where surfers have found new world hotspots for riding the (chilly) waves. Rocks are a theme throughout Clare. The Burren, an ancient region of tortured stone and alien vistas, stretches down to the coast and right out to the Aran Islands.

But if the land is hard, Clare's soul is not. There's a song in every heart here, as traditional Irish culture and music flourish. And it's not just a show for tourists, either. In little villages like Miltown Malbay, Ennistymon and Kilfenora you'll find pubs where sessions of trad music and evening dancing happen throughout the year. Doolin, visitor-mad and all the rage, effortlessly hosts scores from around the world. The main town of Ennis has more traditional pubs than you could visit in a week.

Wandering the many back lanes of Clare or hiking its awesome landscapes then sitting down to a warm bowl of seafood chowder in a peat-fire-heated pub isn't a cliché. Here, it's a way of life.

HIGHLIGHTS

- **The Real Deal** Swoon to the music in the uncompromised traditional pubs of Kilfenora (p386), Lisdoonvarna (p382) and Corofin (p387)

- **Pounding Sand** Lose yourself on the vast sweep of beach at White Strand (p372)

- **Rural Escape** Delight in the amazing drives, walks and villages of Loop Head (p372)

- **Barren Burren** Find lost dolmens and abandoned abbeys among the rocky expanse of the Burren at Carron (p385)

- **Village Idyll** Become part of the scene in the artful, tuneful town of Ennistymon (p374)

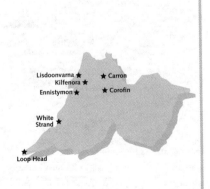

- POPULATION: 106,000
- AREA: 3147 SQ KM

ENNIS & AROUND

ENNIS
pop 19,000
Ennis (Inis) is the busy commercial centre of Clare. It lies on the banks of the smallish River Fergus, which runs east, then south into the Shannon Estuary.

It's the place to stay if you want a bit of urban flair; from Ennis, you can reach any part of Clare in under two hours. Short on sights, the town's strengths are its food, lodging and traditional entertainment. The town centre, with its narrow, pedestrian-friendly streets, is home to large stores.

History
The town's medieval origins are indicated by its irregular, narrow streets. Its most important historical site is Ennis Friary, founded in the 13th century by the O'Briens, kings of Thomond, who also built a castle here in the 13th century. Much of the wooden town was destroyed by fire in 1249 and again in 1306, when it was razed by one of the O'Briens.

Orientation
The old town centre is on the Square, and the principal streets of O'Connell St, High St (becoming Parnell St), Bank Pl and Abbey St, radiate from there. There has been an effort to create some pedestrian quarters around

COUNTY CLARE

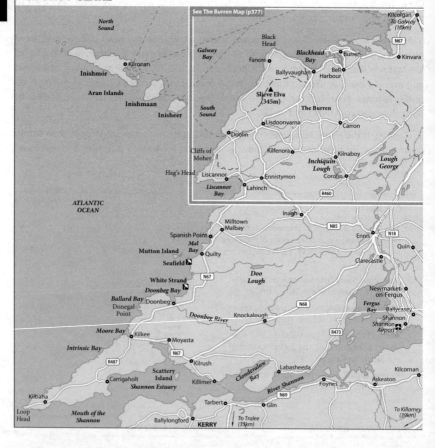

Parnell St with mixed results. The large but fairly mundane cathedral (1843) is at the southern end of O'Connell St; its spire is a useful landmark from afar.

The N18 bypass east of the city lets traffic between Limerick and Galway whiz right past, although trips to the coast still take you through the centre.

Information
BOOKSHOPS
Abbey News Agency (36 Abbey St) Good selection of newspapers. Also sells Ordnance Survey maps.
Ennis Bookshop (☎ 065-682 9000; 13 Abbey St) Excellent independent shop for maps and books of local interest.

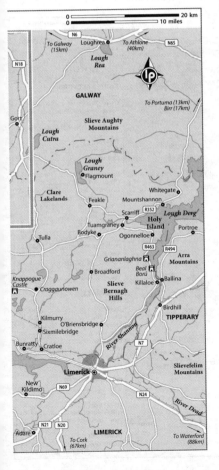

O'Mahony's (☎ 065-682 8355; Merchant Sq) Large local branch of 100-year-old Limerick store.

INTERNET ACCESS
Linkserve (☎ 065-689 3767; 4A Lower Market St; per hr €2; ☻ 10.30am-9pm) Head upstairs for surfing and internet calling.

LIBRARIES
De Valera Library (☎ 065-682 1616; www.clare library.ie; Harmony Row; ☻ 10am-5.30pm Mon, Wed & Thu, to 8pm Tue & Fri, to 2pm Sat) Offers one hour of free internet access. Also has dedicated email screens for short-term use.

MEDICAL SERVICES
Cassidy's Pharmacy (☎ 065-682 8765; 10 O'Connell St; ☻ 8am-6pm)

MONEY
Banks on the Square change money; ATMs are common.

POST
The post office is on Bank Pl, northwest of the Square.

TOURIST INFORMATION
Ennis tourist office (☎ 065-682 8366; www.visit ennis.ie; Arthur's Row; ☻ 9.30am-5.30pm daily Jul & Aug, 9.30am-1pm & 2-5.30pm Mon-Sat Mar-Jun & Sep-Dec, 9.30am-1pm & 2-5.30pm Mon-Fri Jan & Feb) Very helpful and efficient. Can book accommodation for a €4 fee; lots of shamrock-embellished gifts.

Sights
MONUMENTS & SCULPTURES
In the town centre (the Square) is a **Daniel O'Connell monument**. His election to the British parliament by a huge majority in 1828 forced Britain to lift its bar on Catholic MPs and led to the Act of Catholic Emancipation a year later. The 'Great Liberator' stands on an extremely high column, so far above the rest of us you would hardly know he was there.

Éamon de Valera was the parliamentary representative for Clare from 1917 to 1959; a **bronze statue** of him stands near Ennis courthouse.

Numerous **modern sculptures** can be found scattered around the town centre. Works include the *Weathered Woman* on Old Barrack St, which is both interesting and provides a handy place to sit. Get the *Ennis Sculpture Trail* map from the tourist office.

ENNIS FRIARY

Just north of the Square is **Ennis Friary** (☎ 065-682 9100; Abbey St; adult/child €2/1; ☉ 9.30am-6.30pm May-Sep). It was founded by Donnchadh Cairbreach O'Brien, king of Thomond, sometime between 1240 and 1249, but a lot of what you see now was completed in the 14th century. Although it pales against the ruins found elsewhere in Clare, it does have a graceful five-section window dating from the late 13th century, and a McMahon tomb (1460) with alabaster panels depicting scenes from the Passion.

CLARE MUSEUM

Sharing the same building as the tourist office is this diverting little **museum** (☎ 065-682 3382; Arthur's Row; admission free; ☉ 9.30am-5.30pm Tue-Sat Oct-May, 9.30am-5.30pm Mon-Sat, 9.30am-1pm Sun Jun-Sep). The 'Riches of Clare' exhibition tells the story of Clare from 8000 years ago to the present day using original artefacts grouped into four themes: earth, power, faith and water. It also recounts the development of the submarine by Clare-born JP Holland, who's good for at least two of the themes.

Tours

The best way to explore Ennis is on foot and the best way to appreciate it is with an expert. **Ennis Walking Tours** (☎ 087 648 3714; www.enniswalking tours.com; tour €8; ☉ 11am Mon, Tue, Thu-Sat May-Oct) offers excellent walks that leave from in front of the tourist office (p357).

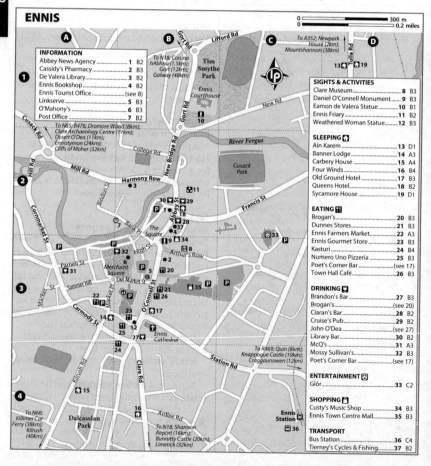

ENNIS

0–300 m
0–0.2 miles

INFORMATION
Abbey News Agency	1	B2
Cassidy's Pharmacy	2	B3
De Valera Library	3	B2
Ennis Bookshop	4	B2
Ennis Tourist Office	(see 8)	
Linkserve	5	B3
O'Mahony's	6	B3
Post Office	7	B2

SIGHTS & ACTIVITIES
Clare Museum	8	B3
Daniel O'Connell Monument	9	B3
Eamon de Valera Statue	10	B1
Ennis Friary	11	B2
Weathered Woman Statue	12	B3

SLEEPING
Ain Karem	13	D1
Banner Lodge	14	A3
Carbery House	15	A4
Four Winds	16	B4
Old Ground Hotel	17	B3
Queens Hotel	18	B2
Sycamore House	19	D1

EATING
Brogan's	20	B3
Dunnes Stores	21	B3
Ennis Farmers Market	22	A3
Ennis Gourmet Store	23	B3
Kasturi	24	B4
Numero Uno Pizzeria	25	B3
Poet's Corner Bar	(see 17)	
Town Hall Café	26	B3

DRINKING
Brandon's Bar	27	B3
Brogan's	(see 20)	
Cíaran's Bar	28	B3
Cruise's Pub	29	B3
John O'Dea	(see 27)	
Library Bar	30	B2
McQ's	31	A3
Mossy Sullivan's	32	B3
Poet's Corner Bar	(see 17)	

ENTERTAINMENT
Glór	33	C2

SHOPPING
Custy's Music Shop	34	B3
Ennis Town Centre Mall	35	B3

TRANSPORT
Bus Station	36	C4
Tierney's Cycles & Fishing	37	B2

To A352; Newpark House (2km); Mountshannon (38km)

To N18; Cóis na hAbhna (1.5km); Gort (12km); Galway (48km)

To N85; R476; Dromore Wood (8km); Clare Archaeology Centre (11km); Dysert O'Dea (11km); Ennistymon (24km); Cliffs of Moher (32km)

To R469; Quin (8km); Knappogue Castle (10km); Craggaunowen (12km)

To N68; Killimer Car Ferry (38km); Kilrush (40km)

To N18; Shannon Airport (16km); Bunratty Castle (20km); Limerick (32km)

Festivals & Events

Fleadh Nua (☎ 065-682 4276; www.fleadhnua.com) A lively traditional music festival held in late May, with singing, dancing and workshops.

Ennis Trad Festival (www.ennistradfestival.com) Traditional music is performed in venues across town for one week in early November.

Sleeping

Ennis has a great variety of places to stay. There are modest B&Bs on most of the main roads into town, some an easy walk to the centre. Many people come here straight from Shannon Airport, which is less than 30 minutes to the south.

Alas, the long-running Abbey Tourist Hostel on Harmony Row closed in 2006 and there's no sign of a replacement for the budget market.

MIDRANGE

Aín Karem (☎ 065-682 0024; ainkaremennis@eircom .net; 7 Tulla Rd; s/d from €45/70; P) Northeast of the centre, this modern two-storey house is pleasantly furnished and rooms are standard size. The neighbourhood has several other B&Bs; it's a 10-minute walk to the centre.

Sycamore House (☎ 065-682 1343; smsfitz@gofree .indigo.ie; Tulla Rd; s/d from €45/70; P) Right across from Aín Karem, there are four modest rooms in this B&B in a modern, unassuming, typical one-storey Irish house. It's clean and friendly – what more do you want?

Banner Lodge (☎ 065-682 4224; www.bannerlodge .com; Market St; s/d from €45/80) You can't really get more central than this, and at great value. Some of the eight rooms are pretty tight, but given the location it is a fair trade-off. The decor in the second-storey inn is dominated by the bold blue carpet. Service is minimal.

Carbery House (☎ 065-682 4046; Kilrush Rd; s/d from €50/90; P) About a 10-minute walk south from the centre, this orderly and very modern B&B has two fireplaces to provide atmosphere. Early arrivals from the airport are OK, space permitting, and credit cards are accepted.

Four Winds (☎ 065-682 9831; fourwinds.ennis @eircom.net; Clare Rd; s/d from €50/80; mid-Mar–mid-Oct; P) This is a pleasant two-storey house with decent rooms. There's a nice back garden, while the front is screened by a low wall and hedge.

Queens Hotel (☎ 065-682 8963; www.irishcourthotels .com; Abbey St; s/d from €65/90; P 💻 🛜) This corner hotel is perfect for those seeking an anonymous stay. The 48 modern rooms are standard-hotel in design, with a timeless red and beige motif. The exterior hints at the building's grand past.

Newpark House (☎ 065-682 1233; www.newpark house.com; s/d from €65/120; Easter-Oct; P) A vine-covered country house dating from 1650, Newpark is 2km north of Ennis. The six rooms have a mix of furnishings old and new; garden views are a fine thing to wake up to. To get here, go along Tulla Rd to Scarriff road (R352) and turn right at the Roselevan Arms.

TOP END

our pick Old Ground Hotel (☎ 065-682 8127; www.flynn hotels.com; O'Connell St; s/d from €90/150; P 💻 🛜) The lobby at this local institution is always a scene: old friends sprawl on the sofas, deals are cut at the tables and ladies from the neighbouring church's altar society exchange gossip over tea. Parts of this rambling landmark date back to the 1800s. The 83 rooms vary greatly in size and decor – don't hesitate to inspect a few.

Eating

Ennis has a good mix of restaurants, cafes and bars that serve food.

Puccino's (☎ 065-689 1665; 41 O'Connell St; snacks €2-6; 8am-6pm Mon-Sat) This tiny nook on the main drag has a full coffee bar and blends up fresh fruit smoothies and juices that may help digest that lump of black pudding from breakfast.

Ennis Gourmet Store (☎ 065-684 3314; 1 Old Barrack St; snacks €4-10; 9am-7pm Mon-Sat, noon-6pm Sun) Enjoy a warm drink from the full coffee and tea bar at one of this little gem's outside tables. There's a range of soups, sandwiches and hot specials plus a deli case of Irish cheeses, preserves, good wines and more.

Poet's Corner Bar (☎ 065-682 8127; Old Ground Hotel, O'Connell St; meals €6-14; 12.30-9pm) This famous old bar has a deserved reputation for its traditional dishes, especially the oh-so-fresh fish and chips. Service is slick.

Numero Uno Pizzeria (☎ 065-684 1740; 3 Barrack St; meals €8-16; noon-10pm) You expect the wine to come in bottles covered with straw at this timeless pizza and pasta joint. The pies are thin and loaded up with traditional ingredients. The pastas are hearty and filling. Watch half of Ennis pop in for a pizza-to-go from the dining area.

our pick Brogan's (☎ 065-682 9859; 24 O'Connell St; meals €8-20; 10am-10pm) The peas at this popular old pub are always well cooked, and the supply of spuds never-ending. Standards like roasts get top billing although you can ferret out more modern fare. Three-course specials cost €12.

Kasturi (☎ 065-684 8060; Carmody St; meals €10-20; ✍ noon-2.30pm & 6-11pm Mon-Sat, 1-4pm Sun) Indian cuisine is excellent at this most accommodating of restaurants. The staff are gracious, constantly serving the large dining room with a mannered feel. Classics such as tandoori chicken are two cuts above the norm.

Town Hall Cafe (☎ 065-682 8127; O'Connell St; lunches €6-14, dinners €20-35; ✍ 10am-5pm & 6-9.30pm) Adjacent to, and affiliated with, the Old Ground Hotel, this excellent bistro is in the stylishly resurrected old town hall. High ceilings allow large artwork, while the spare settings don't compete with the food on the ever-changing menu. Look for local ingredients, especially seafood, taking front and centre stage.

The enormous **Dunnes Stores** (☎ 065-684 0700; Ennis Town Centre Mall; ✍ 24hr) has everything from prepared foods to groceries, while the **Ennis farmers market** (Upper Market St car park; ✍ 8am-2pm Fri) lures some of Clare's best producers.

Drinking & Entertainment

As the capital of a renowned music county, Ennis is not short of pubs with trad music. In fact, this is the best reason to stay here. Where's best changes often; check the weekly *Clare People* for good listings.

PUBS

our pick Ciaran's Bar (☎ 065-684 0180; Francis St) Slip into this small place by day and you can be just another geezer pondering a pint. At night there's usually trad music. We bet you wish you had a copy of the Guinness mural out front!

Brogan's (☎ 065-682 9859; 24 O'Connell St) On the corner of Cooke's Lane, Brogan's sees a fine bunch of musicians rattling even the stone floors from about 9pm Monday to Thursday, plus even more nights in summer. It's a big pub that stretches a long way back from the street.

Brandon's Bar (☎ 065-682 8133; O'Connell St) This place still holds its own for trad sessions, on Monday nights especially (from about 9.30pm). Brandon's also stages other live music, including blues and rock.

John O'Dea (☎ 065-682 4539; 66 O'Connell St) Close to Brandon's, this plain-tile-fronted pub is

a hideout for local musicians serious about their trad sessions.

Cruise's Pub (☎ 065-684 1800; Abbey St) This friendly bar has a long side courtyard that's perfect for enjoying a fresh-air pint in the shadow of the old friary. There are trad music sessions most nights from 9.30pm.

McQ's (☎ 065-682 4608; 78 Parnell St) Aromatic peat fires warm this cosy pub that's a haven on a rainy day. There's good food and a few simple B&B rooms upstairs.

Poet's Corner Bar (☎ 065-682 8127; Old Ground Hotel, O'Connell St) The old hotel pub can have some massive trad sessions on Fridays.

Mossy Sullivan's (15 Parnell St) Behind the green door lies an old pub that's quiet for much of the day. The candlelit tables are perfect for planning your journey in convivial climes.

Library Bar (Abbey St) Trendy bar/club with a small patio sheltered by shrubs where you can text your crew to come join you. A few books really are placed around the edgy, moody interior, with lots of primary-colour backlights behind the bar. Open till 2am at weekends.

VENUES

Cois na hAbhna (☎ 065-682 0996; www.coisnahabhna .ie; Gort Rd) This pilgrimage point for traditional music and culture is housed in a custom-built pentagonal hall 1.5km north of town along the N18. It has frequent performances and a full range of classes in dance and music. The archive is a resource centre and a library of Irish traditional music, song, dance and folklore relating mainly to County Clare; books and recordings are on sale.

Glór (☎ 065-684 3103; www.glor.ie; Friar's Walk) Clare's cultural centre is in a striking modern building. Art, traditional music, theatre, dance, photography and film are some of the programs offered. There's a strong Irish bias, but international influences are celebrated.

Shopping

Ennis has the best shopping in the county; stock up on essentials in the vast **Ennis Town Centre Mall**, with its Dunnes Stores, just behind O'Connell St. Look for a discreet passage in. On Saturday morning, there is a market at Market Pl. For the best selection of shops, head to O'Connell St.

Down a little alley, browse the terrific stock of **Custy's Music Shop** (☎ 065-682 1727; www.custys music.com; off O'Connell St) for Irish music, instruments, other musical items and general info

---

DETOUR: REAL BEER

A splendid antidote to Ireland's dismal beer scene (yeah, we know about Guinness but what about some variety, huh?) can be found right at the intersection of the Ennistymon (N85) and the Kilfenora (R481) roads in Inagh, 16km northeast of Ennis. **Biddy Early Brewery** (☎ 065-683 6742; www.beb.ie) is a rarity for the Emerald Isle: a great microbrewery serving its own range of beers. The Black Biddy Irish Stout recalls every bit of bold flavour that's been mass-marketed out of the corporate stouts. All beers are made with natural ingredients and there's often seasonal specials like Buzzy Biddy, an organic honey beer perfect for long summer nights. Enjoy a pint in the airy pub or outside at tables; there's food most months. Ask about the Biddy Early legend and you'll understand why this detour could be a one-way trip.

---

about the local scene. Has a shop on the web as well.

Getting There & Away
BUS
Bus Éireann (☎ 065-682 4177; www.buseireann.ie) services operate from the bus station beside the train station. Buses run from Ennis to Cork (€14, three hours, nine daily); Doolin (€11, 1½ hours, three daily) via Corofin, Ennistymon, Lahinch and Liscannor; Galway (€9, 1½ hours, hourly) via Gort; Limerick (€8.50, 40 minutes, hourly) via Bunratty; and Shannon Airport (€6.50, 50 minutes, hourly). To reach Dublin, connect through Limerick.

TRAIN
Irish Rail (www.irishrail.ie) trains from **Ennis station** (☎ 065-684 0444) comprise nine daily to Limerick (€9, 40 minutes), where you can connect to trains to places further afield like Dublin. At time of research it was expected that the line between Ennis and Galway would be reopened in late 2009 after a massive rebuilding program.

Getting Around
Call **Burren Taxis** (☎ 065-682 3456) for a taxi, or catch one at the stands by the train station and beside the Daniel O'Connell Monument.

Tierney's Cycles & Fishing (☎ 086 803 0369; 17 Abbey St; ☒ 9am-6pm Mon-Sat) has well-maintained mountain bikes costing €20/80 per day/week to hire, including helmet, lock and repair kit. Staff will recommend routes where trucks are less likely to squash you.

Most people get their rental cars at Shannon Airport (p363). Parking is fairly good in Ennis. There's a big car park behind the tourist office in Friar's Walk and one alongside the river just off Abbey St. It's pay and display for about €1 per hour.

AROUND ENNIS
North of Ennis is the early Christian site of Dysert O'Dea; to the southeast are several fine castles. Note that much of the county can be enjoyed as a day trip from Ennis.

Local and express buses cover most areas around Ennis, but their frequency varies; many buses run only May to September (some only July and August) and on certain days. Before making plans confirm times and destinations with **Bus Éireann** (☎ 065-682 4177; www.buseireann.ie) at the Ennis bus station.

Dysert O'Dea
You can feel the past as you navigate the narrow tracks with grass in the middle to **Dysert O'Dea** (Map p377), where St Tola founded a monastery in the 8th century. The church and high cross, the White Cross of St Tola, date from the 12th or 13th century. The cross depicts Daniel in the lion's den on one side and a crucified Christ above a bishop carved in relief on the other. Look for carvings of animal and human heads in a semicircle on the southern doorway of the Romanesque church. There are also the remains of a 12m-high round tower.

In 1318 the O'Briens, who were kings of Thomond, and the Norman de Clares of Bunratty fought a pitched battle nearby, which the O'Briens won, thus postponing the Anglo-Norman conquest of Clare for some two centuries. The 15th-century O'Dea Castle nearby houses the **Clare Archaeology Centre** (☎ 065-683 7401; www.dysertcastle.com; adult/child €4/2.50; ☒ 10am-6pm May-Sep). A 3km history trail around the castle passes some two-dozen ancient monuments – from ring forts and high crosses to a prehistoric cooking site. A further 5km walk along a medieval road takes you to another stone fort.

East of Dysert O'Dea, you can wander along a lovely river in **Dromore Wood** (Map p377;

☎ 065-683 7166; www.heritageireland.ie; Ruan; admission free; ☷ visitor centre 10am-6pm mid-Jun–mid-Sep). This Dúchas nature reserve encompasses some 400 hectares as well as the ruins of the 17th-century O'Brien Castle, two ring forts and the site of Kilakee church.

GETTING THERE & AWAY

Dysert O'Dea is 1.7km off the Corofin road (R476), 11km north of Ennis. Dromore Wood is 8km east of Dysert, off the N18.

Bus Éireann (☎ 065-682 4177) generally runs one bus daily from Ennis to Doolin, which will stop along the R476.

Quin
pop 460

Quin (Chuinche), a tiny village 10km south-east of Ennis, was the site of the Great Clare Find of 1854 – the most important discovery of prehistoric gold in Ireland. Greed and need beat out any good deeds, and only a few of the several hundred torcs, gorgets and other pieces, discovered by labourers working on the Limerick–Ennis railway, made it to the National Museum in Dublin; most were sold and melted down. The source of this treasure, and much of ancient Ireland's gold, may have been the Wicklow Mountains on the east coast.

The Franciscan friary **Quin Abbey** (☎ 065-684 4084) was founded in 1433 using part of the walls of an older de Clare castle built in 1280. Despite many periods of persecution, Franciscan monks lived here until the 19th century. The last friar, Father Hogan, who died in 1820, is buried in one corner. The splendidly named Fireballs MacNamara, a notorious duellist and member of the region's ruling family, is also buried here. An elegant belfry rises above the main body of the abbey, and you can climb the narrow spiral staircase to look down on the fine cloister and surrounding countryside. The site is always open and you can ponder the encroaching modern graves.

Beside the friary is the 13th-century Gothic **Church of St Finghin**.

Numerous cafes and pubs line the quiet streets near the ruins. On the Ennis side of the village, look for **Zion Coffee House** (☎ 065-682 5417; Ennis Rd; meals €6-20; ☷ 8am-5pm Mon-Wed, to 10pm Thu-Sat). There are good views of the back of the abbey and you can fortify yourself with excellent coffees, teas and juices. During the

day breakfast and fresh, creative lunches are available.

Knappogue Castle

About 3km southeast of Quin is **Knappogue Castle & Walled Garden** (☎ 061-368 103; www.shannonheritage .com; adult/child €8/3.50; ☷ 10am-5pm early May-Sep). It was built in 1467 by the MacNamaras, who held sway over a large part of Clare from the 5th to the mid-15th century and like early fast-food franchisers littered the region with 42 castles. Knappogue's walls are intact, and it has a fine collection of period furniture and fireplaces. The formal gardens have been restored.

When Oliver Cromwell came to Ireland in 1649, he used Knappogue as a base, which is one of the reasons it was spared from destruction. The MacNamara family regained the castle after the Restoration in 1660, and since then windows and other features have been added to make it more 'liveable'.

Knappogue also hosts touristy **medieval banquets** (☎ 061-360 788; adult/child €57/28.50; ☷ 6.30pm May-Oct). Unlike Bunratty Castle (p364), Knappogue provides knives and forks.

Craggaunowen

For more ancient Irish heritage tarted up for the masses, visit **Craggaunowen** (☎ 061-367 178; www .shannonheritage.com; adult/child €9.40/5.50; ☷ 10am-5pm Mon-Fri, till 6pm Sat & Sun mid-May–mid-Sep). Around 6km southeast of Quin, the complex includes re-created ancient farms, dwellings such as a *crannóg* (artificial island) and a 5th-century ring fort, plus real artefacts including a 2000-year-old oak road. Craggaunowen Castle is a small, well-preserved MacNamara fortified house. With lots of animals like snot-nosed boars, this is a good place for kids who like dirty critters.

Craggaunowen has a pleasant little cafe. Nearby Cullaun Lake is a popular boating and picnic spot, and there are forest trails nearby.

EASTERN & SOUTHEASTERN CLARE

Away from the Atlantic coast and the rugged Burren uplands, Clare rolls gently eastward through low-lying green countryside given emphasis by the occasional range of smooth hills. The county's eastern boundary is the River Shannon and the long, wriggling inland waterway of Lough Derg, which stretches

3km from Portumna in County Galway to ist south of Killaloe. Lakeside villages such as Mountshannon seem in a different world from the rugged, evocative west of Clare, but this a delightful, intimate countryside of water, oods and panoramic views. Southeastern lare, where the Shannon swells into its broad stuary, is a plain landscape dotted with farms nd small villages. Overhyped Bunratty Castle a major attraction and nearby Shannon irport is an important entry point.

This part of Clare, along with portions of ounty Limerick, is marketed by Shannon Ieritage, which has an excellent website – ww.shannonheritage.com – for info.

HANNON AIRPORT

reland's second-largest airport used to be a ital fuelling stop for piston-engine planes acking the range to make it between the North American and European mainlands. 'oday Shannon (Sionainn) is a low-stress ateway to the region. It's an ideal entry point or counties Clare, Galway, Kerry, Limerick nd others in the region.

About 3km from the airport, **Shannon town**, uilt to serve airport workers, has the feel of ne of those old planned Soviet industrial ities – albeit with more reliable hot water. Don't linger.

nformation

hannon Town Centre, an enclosed shopping nall off the N19, has banks, basic stores and ast food.

The **airport terminal** (☎ 061-742 6666; www shannonairport.com) has many facilities, including a nice, free observation area for those stuck waiting. Almost everything is on one level. You can park close to the terminal (€1 per 15 minutes); more remote areas are much cheaper.

Aer Rianta (☎ 061-712 000) This desk provides airport and flight information.

Bank of Ireland (☎ 061-471 100) Open from the first flight (about 6.30am) to 5.30pm; there are also currency exchanges and ATMs.

Internet access The terminal has free wi-fi throughout. Terminals are available outside the Hughes & Hughes Bookshop (€1.50 per 15 minutes).

Tourist office (☎ 061-471 664; www.shannon regiontourism.ie; ⏱ 6.30am-6pm May-Sep, 7am-5.30pm Oct-Apr) Near the arrivals area, it's a great first stop, with plenty of regional info, plus useful books and maps for sale. It also books rooms (€4 fee).

Sleeping & Eating

There's B&B accommodation 3km from the airport in Shannon town but Ennis, Limerick and much prettier towns – even Bunratty – can be reached in 30 minutes. The airport terminal has one big, and often crowded, buffet-style restaurant.

Moloney's B&B (☎ 061-364 185; 21 Coill Mhara St; s/d from €45/70) The four rooms at this cheery B&B in Shannon town offer a hassle-free welcome after a long flight. Coming from the airport, turn right off the N19 at the big roundabout by the town centre. Keep on past the centre and at a crossroads go left down a slip road. Continue left past a school and the Shannon Leisure Centre (which has a public pool). At the next junction go right, and then take the first left.

Park Inn Shannon Airport (☎ 061-471 122; www .parkinns.com; r €155; 🖵 🛜) Wake up in one of the 114 generic hotel rooms here and you could be anywhere, which is the idea as the terminal is just across the parking lot. This is an option if you have an early flight and want to lose the rental car. Look for specials.

Getting There & Around
AIR
There are limited services across the Atlantic to North America, but travellers to the US can enjoy the great convenience of pre-clearance for customs and immigration before they leave Ireland, so there's no waiting in queues once you arrive on the other side of the pond.

Airlines with direct flights to/from Shannon:

Aer Lingus (☎ 0818 365 000; www.aerlingus.ie) Dublin, Boston, New York JFK, Chicago and London Heathrow.

Air France (www.airfrance.ie) Paris CDG.

Continental (☎ 1890 925 252; www.continental.com) Newark.

Delta Air Lines (☎ 1800 768 080; www.delta.com) New York JFK.

Ryanair (☎ 0818 303 030; www.ryanair.com) London Stansted and Gatwick, Glasgow and numerous secondary and obscure European airports such as Frankfurt-Hahn.

US Airways (www.usairways.com) Philadelphia.

BUS
Bus Éireann (☎ 061-474 311; www.buseireann.ie; ⏱ 8am-5pm May-Sep, Mon-Fri Oct-Apr) has a ticket office near the arrivals area in the terminal. If it's closed you can buy tickets from the machine by the driver. Destinations served by direct buses include Cork (€15, 2½ hours, hourly), Ennis

(€7, 50 minutes, hourly), Galway (€13, 1¾ hours, hourly) and Limerick (€7, 30 to 55 minutes, two per hour). Some frequencies are reduced on Sundays.

Citylink (www.citylink.ie) has five daily services to/from Galway (from €16, 1¼ hours).

TAXI

A taxi to the centre of Limerick or Ennis costs about €35 if booked at the taxi desk inside the airport. You may pay more at the outside rank. The taxi desk opens with first flights.

BUNRATTY

Conveniently located beside the N18 motorway and with plenty of bus-sized parking, Bunratty (Bun Raite) – home to government schemes for hawking tourism hard – draws more tourists than any other place in the region. The namesake castle has stood over the area for centuries. In recent decades it's been spiffed up and surrounded by attractions. A theme park recreates a clichéd Irish village of old (where's the horseshit, lash and disease we ask?) and each year more and more shops crowd the access roads – many selling authentic Irish goods just out of the container from China. There are some rather pricey group-dining options that are big with the bus crowd.

Buses and groups lay siege to Bunratty from April to October. With all the hoopla, it's easy to overlook the actual village, which is at the back of the theme park. It is a pretty place and has numerous leafy spots to stay and eat. It's good if you want something close to Shannon Airport, only 5km west.

There's a small **visitor information office** (☎ 364 321; ⊙ 9am-5.30pm Mon-Fri Oct–Mid-May, daily mid-May–Sep) in Bunratty Village Mills, a strip mall near the castle. There are also ATMs and exchange services.

Bunratty Castle & Folk Park

There's a joint-entry-fee ticket to this **castle & folk park** (☎ 061-360 788; www.shannonheritage .com; adult/child €16/10). You can get separate entrance tickets to the park when the castle is closed; all prices are slightly reduced in the low season.

A gift shop guarding the entrance has an especially garish selection of green schlock including a 'Top of the Morning' alarm clock. (A sign inside the park reads 'Exit to Car Park through shop'.)

BUNRATTY CASTLE

Square and hulking **Bunratty Castle** (⊙ 9am-4pm) is only the latest of several constructions to occupy its location beside the River Ratty. Vikings founded a settlement here in the 10th century, and other occupants included the Norman Thomas de Clare in the 1270s. The present structure was put up in the early 1400s by the energetic MacNamara family, falling shortly thereafter to the O'Briens, kings of Thomond, in whose possession it remained until the 17th century. Admiral Penn, father of William Penn, who was the Quaker founder of the US state of Pennsylvania and the city of Philadelphia, lived here for a short time.

A complete restoration was carried out more recently, and today the castle is full of fine 14th- to 17th-century furniture, paintings and wall hangings. Most aren't original to the place, but are similar to objects you would have found in the day (sadly, they include no pots of boiling oil).

BUNRATTY FOLK PARK

The **folk park** (⊙ 9am-6pm Jun-Aug, 9am-5.30pm Sep-May, last admission 45min before closing) adjoins the castle. It is a reconstructed traditional Irish village with cottages, a forge and working blacksmith, weavers and pie-makers. There's a complete village street with a post office, pub and small cafe.

A few of the buildings were brought here from elsewhere, but most are recreations of the real thing. In peak season, four or five employees in period garb can be found explaining the more family-friendly aspects of the late 19th century (there are no workhouses, trigger-happy English soldiers etc). The entire place is attractive in the way that Disneyland has its own charm. But you'll find far more surviving authenticity of rural village Ireland in a place like Ennistymon than you will here.

The **Traditional Irish Night** (☎ 061-360 788; adult/child €50/25; ⊙ 7-9.30pm Apr-Oct) is held in a corn barn in the folk park. Lots of red-haired (real or fake, it's clearly a big help in securing employment) servers dish up trad music, dancing, Irish stew, apple pie and soda bread. There's non-traditional wine as well, which may put you in the mood for the singalong.

MEDIEVAL BANQUETS

If you skip the high-jinks in the corn barn, you may opt for a **medieval banquet** (☎ 061-360 788; adult/child €57.50/28.75; ⊙ 5.30pm & 8.45pm), replete with harp-playing maidens, court jesters and food with a medieval motif (lots of meaty items, but somehow we think the real stuff would empty the place right out). It's all washed down with mead – a kind of honey wine – and you eat with your fingers. The banquets are very popular with coach parties, so it's advisable for independent travellers to book well ahead. Various actors interact with choral singers.

The banquets at Knappogue Castle (p362) and Dunguaire Castle (in Galway; p423) are similar but more sedate.

Sleeping

Bunratty has a few hotels and dozens of B&Bs. A big map by the park entrance shows locations; most are away from the castle, park and shop scrum. All are good choices if you are coming or going from Shannon Airport.

Bunratty Camping & Caravan Park (☎ 061-369 190; Low Rd; campsites from €18; ☩ Mar-Oct) Set in a typically leafy and green pasture near the castle (five-minute walk) and airport, there are the usual services and a small cafe.

Briar Lodge (☎ 061-363 388; www.briarlodge.com; Hill Rd; s/d from €50/75; ☩ mid-Mar–mid-Oct; ☐) On a quiet cul-de-sac 1.6km from the castle, this traditionally styled house makes for a good refuge. All five rooms have little extras like curling irons (for that grand banquet entrance!) and some have huge king-size beds.

Cahergal Farmhouse (☎ 061-368 358; www.cahergal .com; Newmarket-on-Fergus; s/d from €65/100) Wake up to the gentle, distant cluck of a chicken at this luxurious B&B on a working farm mid-way between Bunratty and the airport. Rooms are posh, with king-size beds and bucolic views. The food is farm-hearty with famous baked treats.

Eating & Drinking

Most of the food choices – especially in the malls – are geared to the masses.

Durty Nelly's (☎ 061-364 861; Bunratty House Mews; pub meals €5-15, restaurant mains from €20) Thronging with tourists all summer long, Nelly's manages to provide some charm amid the hubbub, right across from the castle. Meals are better than you'd expect, although the pub is more enjoyable than the restaurant upstairs. There are trad sessions many nights, but we could do without the pricey 'pull your own pint' schtick.

Creamery Bar (☎ 061-364 114; Bunratty; meals €7-20) An old utility building has been converted

into an agreeable pub right near the folk park entrance. It's never going to be authentic, but it's not a bad stop if you're here. If nothing else you can learn about local culture from the food menu: eg chicken-nugget-like creations are called 'goujons of chicken' in Ireland.

Mac's Bar (MacNamara's; ☎ 061-361 511; Bunratty Folk Park) This engaging place is actually part of the folk park village. It has traditional music many evenings from June to September, and at weekends the rest of the year. Ignore it during the day, but after the park closes (you can still get in) it starts to feel real.

Getting There & Away

Bunratty is on the busy **Bus Éireann** (☎ 061-313 333) Limerick–Shannon Airport route. Service to both is at least hourly and trips take less than 30 minutes and cost under €5. There are at least five direct buses daily to Ennis (€6.20, 30 minutes). Buses stop outside the Fitzpatrick Bunratty Shamrock Hotel near the castle.

KILLALOE & BALLINA

pop 1750

Facing each other across a narrow channel, Killaloe and Ballina are really one destination, even if they have very different personalities (and counties). A fine old 13-arch one-lane bridge spans the river, linking the pair. You can walk it in five minutes or drive it in about 20 (a Byzantine system of lights controls traffic).

Killaloe (Cill Da Lúa) is picturesque Clare at its finest. It lies on the western banks of lower Loch Deirgeirt, the southern extension of Lough Derg, where the lough narrows at one of the principal crossings of the River Shannon. The village lies snugly against the Slieve Bernagh Hills that rise abruptly to the west. The Arra Mountains create a fine balance to the east and all of Lough Derg is at hand. The village is also on the 180km East Clare Way.

Not as quaint as Killaloe, Ballina is in County Tipperary and actually manages to have some of the better pubs and restaurants. It lies at the end of a scenic drive from Nenagh (p354) along Lough Derg on the R494.

From Killaloe and Ballina, the Shannon is navigable all the way north to Lough Key in County Sligo; in summer the towns are jammed with weekend sailors.

Orientation & Information

In Ballina, Main St is the focus; it's up the hill from the water. The busy narrow street running from the river on the Killaloe side is Bridge St, which turns right and becomes Main St.

The **tourist office** (☎ 061-376 866; Brian Boru Heritage Centre; ✆ 10am-6pm May-Oct) is on a tiny island off the bridge on the Killaloe side and shares space with the heritage centre and the **library** (☎ 061-376 062; ✆ 10am-1.30pm & 2.30-5.30pm Mon, Tue & Thu, 10am-5.30pm & 6.30-8pm Wed & Fri, 10am-2pm Sat), which has free internet access. For local info, try the **town website** (www.killaloe.ie).

The AIB bank at the bottom of Church St in Killaloe has an ATM.

There's parking on both sides of the river and that's just what you'll want to do as soon as you arrive. Pretty as it is, the bridge is really a traffic nightmare, so park and walk. There are toilets on the Killaloe side in the car park.

Sights & Activities

Killaloe Cathedral (St Flannan's Cathedral; ☎ 061-376 687; Limerick Rd) dates from the early 13th century and was built by the O'Brien family on top of a 6th-century church. Inside, magnificent carvings decorate the Romanesque southern doorway, next to which is the shaft of a stone cross, known as Thorgrim's Stone. It dates from the early Christian period and is unusual in that it bears both the old Scandinavian runic and Irish Ogham scripts. In the cathedral grounds is St Flannan's Oratory, of 12th-century Romanesque design.

The **Brian Ború Heritage Centre** (☎ 061-376 866; www.shannonheritage.com; Lock House, Killaloe; adult/child €3.35/1.75; ✆ 10am-5pm May-Sep) is named for the local boy who made good as the king who purportedly both unified Ireland and freed it from the Viking scourge. (Recently such claims have been ascribed to political spinmeisters.) The centre does much to celebrate the legends and has good displays about the nautical heritage of this patchwork of lakes and rivers.

For all your fishing needs go to **TJ's Angling Centre** (☎ 061-376 009; Main St, Ballina). You can rent fishing tackle for €10 per day and catch your limit in free advice. It also organises fishing trips, although you can hook trout and pike right here in town.

The **Spirit of Killaloe** (☎ 086 814 0559; Bridge St, Killaloe; adult/child €10/6; ✆ 2.30pm May-Sep) does hour-long cruises of the waters.

Sleeping

B&Bs abound in the area, especially on the roads along the lough. Book ahead in summer.

Arkansas B&B (☎ 061-376 485; arkans@eircom.net; Main St, Ballina; s/d from €45/70) There are four basic rooms at this B&B only 300m from the bridge. And the name? The lovely owner says she once saw a fishing trawler named Arkansas and liked the sound of it.

Kincora House (☎ 061-376 149; www.kincorahouse .com; Church St, Killaloe; s/d from €45/70) Set in a town house that's centuries old, this B&B is right in the heart of Killaloe. The traditional-style rooms have a simple, older feel and could belong to a favoured aunt.

Lakeside Hotel (☎ 061-376 122; www.lakesidehotel.ie; Ballina; s/d from €70/120; 🖥 🗩) In a great location on the Ballina side of the bridge, this gentrified waterfront hotel has several attractive public areas and good grounds for strolling. The 46 rooms vary greatly, prices work in direct ratio to view. All, however, let you use the way-fun 40m water slide.

Kincora Hall Hotel (☎ 061-376 000; www.kincorahall .com; Killaloe; s/d from €80/120) This handsome hotel sits right on the water and has its own marina. There's a comfy away-from-it-all feel to everything; rooms are big and stylishly furnished, and there's a plush library for relaxing (away from the weekend wedding parties). It's 1.3km north of the bridge.

Eating & Drinking

our pick **Crotty's** (☎ 061-376 965; Bridge St, Killaloe; meals €8-18) The most atmospheric spot on the Clare side of the water, Crotty's has picnic tables outside that you won't want to leave, especially on long summer nights. Inside it could be the model for the perfect old pub anywhere (and it's the real deal). Fish and chips and burgers rise above the norm, and the purveyors of the foods are listed.

Molly's Bar & Restaurant (☎ 061-376 632; Ballina; meals €8-24; ✆ food served noon-10pm) Guarding the east flank of the bridge, this riverside pub has an alluring rooftop deck that puts you high above the coagulated traffic, and can get very busy. It offers Irish standards such as bacon and cabbage, plus pub classics like pizza and burgers. Weekend nights there's a festival of live music and DJs.

River Run (☎ 061-376 805; www.riverruncafe.com; Main St, Ballina; mains €10-25; ✆ noon-10pm Tue-Sat, noon-3pm Sun) Small, smart and stylish, this blue-fronted bistro has food as creative as the local art for sale on the walls. The selections are kept short, but always include good seafood (we like the roasted monkfish wrapped in Parma ham), meat and veggie options. The more casual lunch menu is served until closing.

Gooser's Bar & Eating House (☎ 061-376 791; Main St, Ballina; dinner mains €18-28; ☻ noon-10pm Mon-Sat, 12.30-9.30pm Sun) Only the masses of fun-seekers on busy weekends diminish the Gooser's experience. This is a hugely popular thatched pub, noted for its big selection of fish. Sailors make mirth and plough into the hefty seafood platter. Want to avoid a wait? Dine at the bar (meals €9.50 to €24).

Liam O'Riains (☎ 061-376 722; Main St, Ballina) At this grizzled, stone-faced old veteran, you're greeted by a cow-eyed, 12kg pike mounted on a wall near the entrance – he's an ugly mother. Everything else here, however, is lovely. Candles glow softly and windows overlook the river below.

The twin towns also have their **farmers market** (☻ 9am-4pm Sun) on the islet off the bridge on the Killaloe side. Get picnic goods all week long at the Italian-flavoured deli **Ponte Vecchio** (☎ 061-622 845; Killaloe; ☻ 11am-7pm Tue-Sat, 11am-3pm Sun), which makes darn good sandwiches and sells bottles of wine ready to be uncorked. It's near the cathedral.

Getting There & Away

There are four **Bus Éireann** (☎ 061-313 333) services a day Monday to Saturday from Limerick to Killaloe (€6.50, 45 minutes). The bus stop is outside the cathedral.

KILLALOE TO MOUNTSHANNON

The journey north to Mountshannon along Lough Derg weaves along the placid waters; there are good viewpoints and picnic spots. To get to Mountshannon from Killaloe take the R463 to Tuamgraney, then turn east on the R352.

About 2km north of Killaloe, **Beal Ború** is an earthen mound or fort said to have been Kincora, the fabled palace of the famous Irish king Brian Ború, who, besides lending his name to bad Irish bars the world over, took on the Vikings at the Battle of Clontarf in 1014. Traces of Bronze Age settlement have been found. With its commanding view over Lough Derg, this was obviously a site of strategic importance (and if you see a big splash out in the lough it could be a cousin of the record 32.6kg pike that was caught here).

About 3.5km north of Killaloe is the **University of Limerick Activity Centre** (☎ 061-376 622; www.ulac.ie; Two Mile Gate). Here individuals and groups learn such water-based skills as canoeing, sailing and windsurfing. Land-based activities include archery, orienteering and forest games. Kayaking on Lough Derg is the top activity.

About 4.5km north of Killaloe is Cragliath Hill, which has another fort, **Griananlaghna**, named after Brian Ború's great-grandfather, King Lachtna.

Tuamgraney, at the junction of the road to Mountshannon (R352), has an interesting old church, St Cronan's, with a small museum, the **East Clare Heritage Centre** (☎ 061-921 351; www.east clareheritage.com). Although the museum keeps erratic hours, the surrounding moody parish cemetery is a fascinating look into Irish genealogy.

If the serene waters have you feeling snoozy, you can hit the hay at **Lantern House** (☎ 061-923 034; www.lanternhouse.com; Scarriff Rd, Ogonnelloe; s/d from €50/80). About 10km north of Killaloe, and in a hillside location overlooking a sweep of Lough Derg, this glass-fronted six-room house is beautifully encircled by gardens of heather. At times, you can book evening meals.

MOUNTSHANNON & AROUND

pop 330

More than just a 'Tidy Town' award-winning village, Mountshannon (Baile Uí Bheoláin) is good for an agreeable pause on the southwestern shores of Lough Derg. It was founded in 1742 by an enlightened landlord to house a largely Protestant community of flax workers.

The harbour is host to a fair number of fishing boats, and visiting yachts and cruisers in summer. It is the main centre for trips to Holy Island, one of Clare's finest early Christian settlements.

There's some great fishing around Mountshannon, mainly for brown trout, pike, perch and bream. Ask at your lodging about boat hire and equipment.

Holy Island

Lying 2km offshore from Mountshannon, Holy Island (Inis Cealtra) is the site of a **monastic settlement** thought to have been founded by St Cáimín in the 7th century. On the island you will see a round tower that is more than 27m tall (though missing its top storey). You'll also find four old chapels, a hermit's cell and some early Christian gravestones dating from the 7th to 13th centuries. One of the chapels has an elegant Romanesque arch and, inside, an Old Irish inscription that translates as 'Pray for Tornog, who made this cross'.

The Vikings treated this monastery roughly in the 9th century, but under the crowd-pleasing protection of Brian Ború and others, it flourished.

At Mountshannon harbour in summer, you may find **boats** (☎ 086 874 9710) willing to take you over to the island or at least sail around it. The usual cost for this is adult/child €10/5. Look for a small kiosk offering boat rides and rentals.

Trips can also be arranged from Mountshannon by the staff at the East Clare Heritage Centre (p367) in Tuamgraney, when it is open.

Sleeping & Eating

Lakeside Holiday Park (☎ 061-927 225; www.lake sideireland.com; campsites €18; ☺ May-Oct) This spacious park has a fine lakeside location with 35 campsites and a few holiday trailers (€160 per two nights). It hires out boats and equipment for windsurfing, rowing and sailing. From Mountshannon, head north along the Portumna road (R352) for 2km and take the first turn-off on the right.

Hawthorn Lodge (☎ 061-927 120; www.mount shannon-clare.com; s/d from €50/70) Just 1km from the tidy joy that is Mountshannon, this equally tidy cottage is a modern and relaxed retreat. Set your electric blanket on high and you may never emerge into the chilly albeit fresh morning air.

Mountshannon Hotel (☎ 061-927 162; www.mount shannon-hotel.ie; Main St; s/d from €50/80; ☺ Mar-Oct) A big ol' hound lies in the street in front of this old inn, which lies equally low in the quiet centre of town. The 14 rooms are as timeless as the dog out front, but smell much better. The pub is perfect for a relaxed pint and fish stories. The food is of the chicken kiev and lasagne school (mains €10 to € 20).

Sunrise B&B (☎ 061-927 343; www.sunrisebandb.com; Mountshannon; s/d from €55/80) The breakfast room at this rural B&B 300m from the village is worthy of an architecture award. Windows wrap around – literally as it's round. A soaring wood ceiling with skylights brings in cheer even on the dimmest of days. The bedrooms are not as dramatic, but are comfortable with their warm quilts.

Bourke's the Galley (☎ 061-927 214; Main St, Mountshannon; snacks €2-10; ☺ 9am-5pm) The sign at this sparkling cafe across from the church reads: Be warm, be welcome, be at home. Of course, home never had such cupcakes. Attached to a deli, Bourke's offers rich coffees, alluring baked goods and fresh light meals.

An Cupán Caifé (☎ 061-927 275; Main St; meals €8-18; ☺ 6-9.30pm Wed-Sun, plus Sun 11am-3pm) This cafe-restaurant has a Continental atmosphere and a daily menu of steaks and lake trout plus a few pastas. Presentation is slightly formal and the specials are a draw.

Getting There & Away

Driving (or swimming) is your best way to reach Mountshannon. **Bus Éireann** (☎ 061-313 333) runs one bus here each Saturday from Limerick.

NORTH TO GALWAY

North of Mountshannon, the R352 follows Lough Derg to Portumna (p426) in Galway. It's just one of several not-quite-two-lane country roads that weave through the fertile landscapes under arching trees. Another is the R461 from Scarriff, which heads right to the heart of the Burren.

SOUTHWESTERN & WESTERN CLARE

One look at the map and you can see that Loop Head on Clare's southwestern tip is giving the finger to the Atlantic. OK, it's a stubby finger, but still it's emblematic of the never-ceasing titanic struggle between land and sea along this stretch of Irish coast.

The soaring cliffs south of the beach resort of Kilkee to Loop Head are both striking and underappreciated by many visitors. Most save their energies for the much-visited Cliffs of Moher. Marching in geologic lockstep, the formations are undeniably stunning, although in summer you will be marching in lockstep with hordes of other visitors.

South of the cliffs to Kilkee are the low-key beach towns of Lahinch, Miltown Malbay and Doonbeg. No part of this coast is remotely tropical, but there's a stark windblown beauty that stretches to the horizon. Many a hapless survivor of the Spanish Armada washed ashore here 400 years ago. Tales of their progeny still spice local gossip.

Your best days here may be spent on the smallest roads you can find. Make your own discoveries, whether it's a stretch of lonely beach or something more settled, like the charming heritage town of Ennistymon.

Getting There & Away

BOAT

Shannon Ferry Limited (☎ 065-905 3124; www.shannon ferries.com; one way/return bicycle & foot passengers €5/7, motorcycles €9/14, cars €18/28; ☒ 9am-9pm Jun-Aug, 9am-7pm Sep-May) runs a half-hourly ferry between Tarbert in County Kerry (p317) and Killimer in County Clare. It's a real time-saver over detouring through Limerick, and puts you close to the Dingle Peninsula.

BUS

You can usually count on a **Bus Éireann** (www .buseireann.ie) service or two linking all the main towns in the region each day. From Limerick routes run along the Shannon to Kilrush and Kilkee, as well as up through Corofin, Ennistymon, Lahinch, Liscannor and on to the Cliffs of Moher and Doolin. Buses from Ennis follow the same pattern. On the coast between Lahinch and Kilkee services average twice daily in summer. A few other, non-daily routes are geared to schoolkids.

KILRUSH

pop 2700

Kilrush (Cill Rois) is a small, interesting town that overlooks the Shannon Estuary and the hills of Kerry to the south. The main street, Frances St, runs directly to the harbour. It is more than 30m wide, reflecting Kilrush's origins as a port and market town in the 19th century when there was much coming and going between land and sea. It has the western coast's biggest **marina** (www.kilrushcreekmarina.ie) at Kilrush Creek, and a centre for the research and viewing of dolphins living in the Shannon.

Tourist info (☎ 065-905 1577; Francis St; ☒ varies) can be found at Katie O'Connor's Holiday Hostel (right).

In Market Sq there's an ACC bank with an ATM and on Frances St you'll find the post office and an AIB ATM. **KK Computing** (☎ 065-905 1806; Frances St; per hr €5; ☒ 10am-10pm, shorter hr in winter) has internet access.

Sights & Activities

St Senan's Catholic church (Toler St) contains eight detailed examples of stained glass by well-known early 20th-century artist Harry Clarke. East of town is **Kilrush Wood**, which has some fine old trees and a picnic area.

Vandeleur Walled Garden (☎ 065-905 1760; adult/child €5/2; ☒ 10am-6pm Apr-Oct, to 5pm Nov-Mar) is a remarkable 'lost' garden. It was the private domain of the wealthy Vandeleur family – merchants and landowners who engaged in harsh evictions and forced emigration of local people in the 19th century. The gardens lie within a large walled area and have been re-designed and planted with colourful tropical and rare plants. Woodland trails wind around the area, and there's also a cafe.

Near the marina, **Shannon Dolphin & Wildlife Centre** (☎ 065-905 2326; www.shannondolphins.ie; Merchants Quay; ☒ 10am-4pm May-Sep) is a research facility that monitors the 100 or so dolphins swimming out in the Shannon. Look for the mural of the dolphin on the front of the building, which houses exhibits on the playful cetaceans. It's also a stop on the well-marked **Kilrush Shannon Dolphin Trail**, which ends 3km out of town at **Aylevarro Point**, where signs have more info and where you can often see dolphins frolicking offshore. Follow the road south of the harbour to get here.

The local flora and fauna are the inspiration at **Naturequest Gallery** (☎ 065-905 1309; Burton St; ☒ 1-4pm Thu-Sat), an artist-run gallery just off the Butter Market.

Sleeping & Eating

B&Bs are about as common here as driftwood on a beach.

Katie O'Connor's Holiday Hostel (☎ 065-905 1133; katieoconnors@eircom.net; Frances St; dm/d from €19/40; ☒ mid-Apr–Oct) This fine old main-street house dates from the 18th century, and was one of the town houses of the Vandeleur family. There are 16 beds in two rooms at this delightfully funky IHH-affiliated hostel.

our pick Crotty's (☎ 065-905 2470; www.crottyspub kilrush.com; Market Sq; s/d from €45/70) Brimming with character, Crotty's has an old-fashioned high bar, intricately tiled floors and a series of snugs decked out with traditional furnishings. You can enjoy music many nights in summer. Food is served daily (meals €6 to €16) and includes high-end versions of pub fare. Upstairs are seven small, traditionally decorated rooms.

Hillcrest View (☎ 065-905 1986; www.hillcrestview .com; Doonbeg Rd; s/d from €60/80; ☒) This large house, at the top of the hill where the Doonbeg road climbs out of Kilrush, is about 1km from the centre. Its six rooms have vaguely posh furnishings, and breakfast is served in a bright conservatory.

LAST CALL FOR THE WEST CLARE RAILWAY?

Running on a roundabout route from Ennis to Kilrush and Kilkee, the narrow-gauge West Clare Railway was the line that barely could. It operated from 1892 until 1961 and during that time reached its greatest notoriety when popular early 20th-century musician Percy French mocked it in the song *Are Ye Right There Michael*. It seems the perennially late WCR caused French to miss a paying gig in Kilkee. After French took his revenge via song, the railway management – so the oft-told tale goes – sued for libel. Percy triumphed when, late for a court appearance, he was asked by the judge for an explanation. His reply: 'I took the West Clare Railway, your honour.' The case was thrown out and he was awarded costs.

Today a 2km vestige of the **line** (☎ 065-905 1284; www.westclarerailway.ie; adult/child €6/3; ☻ 10am-6pm May-Sep) survives near Moyasta on the Kilkee Rd (N67) 6km northwest of Kilrush. Run by volunteers, the steam-powered trains shuttle back and forth over the open land. And if some local boosters get their way the line will be restored between Kilrush and Kilkee. However, there's one obstacle: like seemingly everywhere else in Ireland, the route is under threat from new home construction.

The local **farmers market** (☻ 9am-2pm Thu) is held on the Butter Market square.

Getting There & Around

Bus Éireann has one or two buses daily to Limerick (1¾ hours), Ennis (one hour) and Kilkee (15 minutes). Fares average €7.

You can hire bikes at **Gleeson's Cycles** (☎ 065-905 1127; Henry St; per day/week €20/80).

SCATTERY ISLAND

This uninhabited, windswept, treeless island, 3km southwest of Kilrush in the estuary was the site of a Christian settlement founded by St Senan in the 6th century. Its 36m-high **round tower** is one of the tallest and best preserved in Ireland, and the entrance is at ground level instead of the usual position high above the foundation. The remains of five **medieval churches** include a 9th-century cathedral. This is a moody and evocative place to wander about.

An exhibition on the history and wildlife of the Heritage Service–administered island is housed in the **Scattery Island Visitor Centre** (www .heritageireland.ie; admission free; ☻ 10am-6pm Jun-Sep).

Scattery Island Ferries (☎ 065-905 1327; Kilrush Creek Marina; adult/child €12/6; ☻ Jun-Sep) runs boats from Kilrush to the island. There's no strict timetable as the trips are subject to tidal and weather conditions. There's a stay of about 1hr on the island. You can buy tickets at the small kiosk at the marina.

KILKEE

pop 1300

During the summer, Kilkee's wide beach is thronged with day trippers and holiday mak-

ers. The semicircular bay has high cliffs on the north end and tidal rocks to the south. The sea puts on a show anytime as large breakers pound the shore.

Kilkee (Cill Chaoi) first became popular in Victorian times when rich Limerick families built seaside retreats here. Today, it is well supplied with guesthouses, amusement arcades and takeaways, although good taste – mostly – prevails.

Information

Bank of Ireland (O'Curry St) Has an ATM.
Post office (O'Connell St) Across from the library.
Tourist office (☎ 065-905 6112; O'Connell St; ☻ 9.30am-5.30pm Jun-Aug) Near the seafront.

Sights & Activities

Many visitors come for the fine sheltered **beach** and the **Pollock Holes**, natural swimming pools in the Duggerna Rocks. **St George's Head**, to the north, has good cliff walks and scenery, while south of the bay, the **Duggerna Rocks** form an unusual natural amphitheatre. Further south is a huge **sea cave**. These sights can be reached by driving to Kilkee's West End area and following the coastal path.

Kilkee is a well-known **diving** centre. There are shore dives from the Duggerna Rocks fringing the bay and boat dives on the Black Rocks further out. Experience and local knowledge or guidance are strongly advised. Right at the tip of the Duggerna Rocks is the small inlet of Myles Creek, out from which lies excellent underwater scenery. **Oceanlife Ireland** (☎ 065-905 6707; www.diveireland.com; George's Head, Kilkee), by the harbour, has tanks and other equipment for hire and runs a range of courses.

Sleeping

Kilkee has plenty of guesthouses and B&Bs, though during the high season rates can soar and you may have a problem finding a vacancy.

Green Acres Caravan & Camping Park (☎ 065-905 7011; Doonaha, Kilkee; campsites €20; ☼ Apr-Sep) Beside the Shannon, 6km south of Kilkee on the R487, this is a small, open and peaceful park with 40 sites.

Lynch's B&B (☎ 065-905 6420; www.lynchskilkee.com; O'Connell St; s/d from €45/70; ☎) The three-masted model in the window tells you that things are shipshape in this perfectly located B&B in the centre. Guest rooms have hardwood floors and bedspreads with designs that will bring a smile to aunties everywhere.

Strand Guest House (☎ 065-905 6177; www.the strandkilkee.com; The Strand; s/d from €55/90) Right across from the water, this six-room guesthouse is a veteran of many a summer. The rooms are simply decorated, but do have telephones. Some have great views as does the lounge, which has picnic tables outside for a little salt-spray in your stout.

Stella Maris Hotel (☎ 065-905 6455; www.stella marishotel.com; O'Connell St; s/d from €65/120; ☐) There are 20 modern rooms in the year-round choice for lodging in Kilkee. Some on the top floor have views of the surf, some have high-speed internet and some have king-size beds. The hotel is right in the centre and serves good food.

Halpin's Townhouse Hotel (☎ 065-905 6032; www .halpinsprivatehotels.com; Erin St; s/d from €70/120; ☼ mid-Mar–mid-Nov; ☐ ☎) A smart Georgian town house has been turned into a plush 12-room hotel. Close to the centre, it eschews the salt-stained furnishings of many a beach-town place for a minimalist look. Residents enjoy the basement bar with its good wine list.

Eating & Drinking

Kilkee has a number of markets; in summer the ranks of eateries swell with several that win plaudits as far away as Dublin.

Pantry (☎ 065-905 6576; O'Curry St; meals €6-12; ☼ 8am-6pm) This seemingly simple caff is filled with surprises and treasure. The scones are plainly the best in Clare and pretty much everything else you order from the seemingly typical menu will have you going, 'That's the best…I ever had.'

Stella Maris (☎ 065-905 6455; O'Connell St; meals €10-25; ☼ noon-9pm) This popular hotel has a good menu of local seafood on offer through the day. Enjoy quality ocean salmon and shellfish or one of many daily specials in the bright and simple dining room or in the usually crowded pub.

Naughton's Bar (☎ 065-905 6597; 46 O'Curry St; meals €10-25; ☼ kitchen 5-9.30pm) The terrace alone is enough to make Naughton's a mandatory stop, but the food is even better. Fresh local produce and seafood combine for some mighty fine pub meals at this family-run place, and they're further complemented by a good wine and beer selection.

Murphy Blacks (☎ 065-905 6854; The Square; mains €16-28; ☼ 5-9.30pm Wed-Sun Apr-Oct) How do you ensure that you're getting the best fish? Go to a place owned by an ex-fisherman. This deservedly popular dinner spot is booked up solid night after night for its carefully crafted dishes. Tables outside are a summer-night treat.

Getting There & Away

Bus Éireann has one to two buses daily to Kilkee from Limerick (€11, two hours) and Ennis (€12.50, 1¼ hours). Both routes pass through Kilrush.

KILKEE TO LOOP HEAD

While others are dodging sweater vendors at the Cliffs of Moher, discriminating travellers are coming here for coastal views that in many ways are more dramatic (p372).

The land from Kilkee south to Loop Head has subtle undulations that suddenly end in dramatic cliffs falling off into the Atlantic. It's a windswept place with timeless striations of old stone walls. You can see literally for miles and there's a rewarding sense of escape from the mainstream. It's good cycling country and offers coastal walks – which is just as well as there's no public transport.

Carrigaholt
pop 100

On 15 September 1588, seven tattered ships of the Spanish Armada took shelter off Carrigaholt (Carraig an Chabaltaigh), a tiny village inside the mouth of the Shannon Estuary. One, probably the *Anunciada*, was torched and abandoned, sinking somewhere out in the estuary. Today Carrigaholt has one of the simplest and cutest main streets you'll find. The substantial remains of a 15th-century McMahon castle with a square keep overlook the water.

COUNTY CLARE

DETOUR: CLIFFS OF AMAZEMENT

On the south side of Kilkee's bay, look for a sign that reads 'Scenic Loop'; it's an understatement. A narrow track curves south around the coast for 10km until it joins the R487, the Loop Head Rd. Along the way you will be struck by one stunning vista of soaring coastal cliffs after another. Some have holes blasted through by the surf, others have been separated from land and now stand out in the ocean as lonely sentinels. One even has an old house perched on top – how in the world did that get there and who built it? Plan on puttering along, zoning out staring at the sea and pausing for passing cows.

To view resident bottlenose dolphins (there are more than 100 in the Shannon Estuary), head for **Dolphinwatch** (☎ 065-905 8156; www.dolphinwatch.ie; Carrigaholt; adult/child €24/12), next to the post office. It runs two-hour trips in the estuary from April to October, weather permitting. Ask about Loop Head sunset cruises. For more on these broguish relatives of Flipper, see p369.

Long Dock (☎ 065-905 8106; West St; meals €6-24; food served 11am-9pm) is an atmospheric pub-restaurant combo. Stone walls and floors and a welcoming fire are only the start. Fresh fish is the thing here; you'll see the purveyors out working in the estuary or even drinking at the bar. Nab a table outdoors on a summer night.

Like Carrigaholt, **Morrissey's Village Pub** (☎ 065-905 8041; West St) hasn't changed much in a long time and is all the better for it. Get your feet ready for music and dancing many nights through the year. Other boozy vets are nearby.

Kilbaha
pop 50

The land at this minute waterfront village is as barren as the soul of the 19th-century landlord who burned down the local church so his workers wouldn't waste productive hours praying. Even today the scars are felt. Gazing at the ruins of the landlord's house far up the hillside, a local says: 'Yeah, we got rid of him', as if the events of 150 years ago were yesterday.

You can learn more about this story and other aspects of local life from a unique modern-day **scroll**, an open-air sculpture that relates the area's history.

The **Lighthouse Inn** (☎ 065-905 8358; www.the lighthouseinn.ie; s/d from €40/70) is a stolid place right on the water, with 11 basic rooms. The pub serves sandwiches and the like through the year and more complex seafood dinners (from €12) in summer. Trad sessions some nights are a bonus.

Loop Head

On a clear day, Loop Head (Ceann Léime), Clare's southernmost point, has magnificent views south to the Dingle Peninsula crowned by Mt Brandon (951m), and north to the Aran Islands and Galway Bay. There are bracing walks in the area and a long hiking trail runs along the cliffs to Kilkee. A working **lighthouse** (complete with Fresnel lens) is the punctuation on the point.

The often deserted wilds of the head are perfect for a little DIY fun. **Loop Head Adventures** (☎ 065-905 8875; loopheadsports@eircom.net; May-Oct) rents gear and gives advice for cycling (bikes €15 per day), fishing (rods and gear €15 per day) and snorkelling (drysuits and gear €35 per day). It's located a short distance from the lighthouse.

KILKEE TO ENNISTYMON

North of Kilkee, the land flattens, with vistas that sweep across pastures and dunes. The N67 runs inland for some 32km until it reaches Quilty. Take the occasional lane to the west and search out unfrequented places such as **White Strand**, north of Doonbeg. **Ballard Bay** is 8km west of Doonbeg, where an old telegraph tower looks over some fine cliffs. **Donegal Point** has the remains of a promontory fort. There's good fishing all along the coast, and safe beaches at Seafield, Lough Donnell and Quilty. Off the coast of Quilty, look for **Mutton Island**, a barren expanse sporting an ancient tower.

Doonbeg
pop 610

Doonbeg (An Dún Beag) is a tiny seaside village about halfway between Kilkee and Quilty. Another Spanish Armada ship, the *San Esteban*, was wrecked on 20 September 1588 near the mouth of the River Doonbeg. The survivors were later executed at Spanish Point. Note the surviving wee little 16th-century **castle tower** next to the graceful seven-arch stone bridge over the river.

White Strand (Trá Ban) is a quiet beach, 2km long and backed by dunes. It's north of town and hard to miss, as it's now been surrounded by the snooty – and hulking – Doonbeg Golf Resort and Lodge. From the public car park (protected from the adjacent resort hotel by a stout fence, no doubt so the swells won't steal your hubcaps), you follow a break in the dunes to a perfect sweep of sand.

Doonbeg also has some decent **surfing** for those who want to get away from the crowds in Lahinch (right).

SLEEPING & EATING

For campers there are often spots on the side roads around Doonbeg that make a good pitch, with glorious sunsets as a bonus. The town has two popular rural pubs where locals celebrate anything they can think of.

Whitestrand B&B (☎ 065-905 5347; www.white strand-bnb.com; Killard; s/d €35/70) This large, modern house looks over a perfect little cove of beach across to the sweep of the White Strand. Its two comfortable rooms have views. Remote – at times you can hear cows mooing over the surf – the B&B is just south of town, then 2km to the water.

Morrissey's (☎ 065-905 5304; www.morrisseysdoonbeg .com; Main St; s/d €70/100; ☾ Mar-Oct; 🖳 🛜) Under its fourth-generation owner, this old pub has been transformed into a stylish coastal haven. The seven rooms feature king-size beds, flat-screen TVs and large soaking tubs. The pub's restaurant is renowned for its casual but enticing seafood, from fish and chips to barbecued salmon. Outside there's a terrace overlooking the river, while inside colours reminiscent of a box of good bonbons mingle with stark white walls. Meals range from €12 to €22.

Miltown Malbay
pop 1600

Like Kilkee, Miltown Malbay was a resort favoured by well-to-do Victorians, though the town isn't actually on the sea: the beach is 2km south at Spanish Point. A classically friendly place in the chatty Irish way, Miltown Malbay has a thriving music scene. Every year it hosts the Willie Clancy Irish Music Festival (right), one of Ireland's great trad music events.

For local information, drop by **An Ghiolla Finn Gift Shop** (☎ 065-688 9239; Main St; ☾ 10.30am-6pm Mon-Sat). The wonderful Maureen Kilduff knows everything and everybody.

Possibly the friendliest welcome in town is at **An Gleann B&B** (☎ 065-708 4281; angleann@oceanfree .net; Ennis Rd; s/d €45/80). Off the R474 about 1km

from the centre, the rooms here are basic and comfy and owner Mary Hughes is a delight. Cyclists are catered for.

Across the road from the gift shop, **Baker's Cafe** (☎ 065-708 4411; Main St; meals €4; ☾ 7am-7pm Mon-Sat) has excellent baked goods and creates enormous sandwiches – perfect for seaside picnics. Nearby, the **Old Bake House** (☎ 065-708 4350; Main St; meals €6-15; ☾ noon-9pm) serves a more ambitious menu and does so well.

O'Friel's Bar (Lynch's; ☎ 065-708 4275; The Square) is one of a couple of genuine old-style places with occasional trad sessions. The other is the dapper **Hillery's** (Main St).

Bus Éireann service is paltry. Expect one or two buses daily north and south along the coast and inland to Ennis.

Lahinch
pop 650

Surf's up, dude! This scruffy old holiday town is now one of the centres of Ireland's hot surfing scene. Schools and stores dedicated to riding the waves cluster here, like surfers waiting for the perfect set.

Lahinch (Leacht Uí Chonchubhair) has always owed its living to beach-seeking tourists. The town sits on protected Liscannor Bay and has a fine beach. Free-spending mobs descend in summer, many wielding golf clubs for play at the famous, traditional-style **Lahinch Golf Club** (☎ 065-708 1003; www.lahinchgolf.com; greens fees from €100).

The tourist office, **Lahinch Fáilte** (☎ 065-708 2082; www.lahinchfailte.com; The Dell; ☾ 9am-8pm Jun-Aug, 10am-5pm Sep-May), is off the northern

---

A FESTIVAL FOR EVERYONE

Half the population of Miltown Malbay seems to be part of the annual **Willie Clancy Irish Music Festival** (☾ 065-708 4148), a tribute to a native son and one of Ireland's greatest pipers. The eight-day festival usually begins in the first or second week in July, when impromptu sessions occur day and night, the pubs are packed, and Guinness is consumed by the barrel. Workshops and classes underpin the event; don't be surprised to attend a recital with 40 noted fiddlers. Asked how such a huge affair has happened for almost four decades, a local who teaches fiddle said: 'No one knows, it just does.'

end of Main St and is part of a well-stocked gift shop. There's an ATM outside. **Lahinch Bookshop** (☎ 065-708 1300; Main St) is the best outside Ennis.

Like swells after a storm, the surfing scene keeps getting bigger. You can get lessons from about €40 per two-hour session. Local outfits:

Ben's Surf Clinic (☎ 086 844 8622; www.benssurf clinic.com) Offers lessons plus rents out boards and wetsuits (essential!).

Lahinch Surf School (☎ 087 960 9667; www.lahinch surfschool.com; Beach Hut, Lahinch Prom) Offers lessons and various multi-day packages.

Lahinch Surf Shop (☎ 065-708 1108; www.lahinch surfshop.com; Church St) Sells gear from a dramatic surfside location.

Ocean Scene Surf School (☎ 065-708 1108; www .oceanscene.ie; Church St) Gives lessons plus has a good live surf-cam on the website.

SLEEPING & EATING

The tourist office has good links to local B&Bs.

Lahinch Hostel (☎ 065-708 1040; lahinchok@eircom .net; Church St; dm €17, r €30-50) This well-run IHH hostel has clean, bright rooms with a total of 55 beds. It's close to the beachfront and has surfboard and bicycle storage.

Atlantic Hotel (☎ 065-708 1049; www.atlantichotel .ie; s/d from €95/140; 💻) There's still a pleasant air of bygone times in the reception rooms and bars at this town-centre classic with 14 well-appointed rooms. The restaurant offers fine seafood choices (mains from €15) and the pub is the perfect spot for nursing a pint on a blustery day.

Barrtra Seafood Restaurant (☎ 065-708 1280; Miltown Malbay Rd; mains €16-28) The 'Seafood Symphony' menu item says it all at this rural repose 3.5km south of Lahinch. Enjoy views over pastures to the sea from the homey dining rooms. The cooking eschews flash and lets the inherent tastiness of the food shine.

GETTING THERE & AWAY

Bus Éireann runs one or two buses daily through Lahinch on the Doolin–Ennis/ Limerick routes and one or two daily south along the coast to Doonbeg in summer.

ENNISTYMON

pop 880

Ennistymon (Inis Díomáin) is a timeless country village located just 4km inland from Lahinch, but worlds away in terms of atmosphere. People go about their business (which involves a lot of cheerful chatting, barely noticing the characterful buildings lining Main St. And behind this facade there's a surprise: the roaring **Cascades**, the stepped falls of the River Inagh. After heavy rain they surge, beer-brown and foaming, and you risk getting drenched on windy days in the flying drizzle. You'll find them through an arch by Byrne's Hotel.

The **library** (☎ 065-707 1245; 🕙 10am-1.30pm & 2.30-5.30pm Mon, Tue & Thu, 10am-5.30pm & 6.30-8pm Wed & Fri, 10am-2pm Sat), just down from the Square, offers free internet access.

Besides excellent pubs and good sleeping options, Ennistymon has a burgeoning arts scene. **Courthouse Studios & Gallery** (☎ 065-707 1630; Parliament St; 🕙 noon-4pm Tue-Sat) is an impressive new facility with ever-changing exhibitions by local and international artists.

On the first Monday of each month is one of Clare's great spectacles: the **Ennistymon Horse Market** literally takes over the town's streets as people from around the region come to buy and sell donkeys, mares, thoroughbreds and even a few plain old nags.

Sleeping & Eating

Byrne's (☎ 065-707 1080; Main St; r €80-120) The Cascades are just out back at this historic guesthouse and restaurant. When the air is not heavy with mist, you can enjoy a drink at a back-deck table. The menu is substantial, with plenty of seafood specials (mains €15 to €25). Six comfortable rooms await up the creaky heritage stairs.

Falls Hotel (☎ 065-707 1004; www.fallshotel.ie; s/d from €85/120; 💻 🐾) This handsome and sprawling Georgian house, built on the ruins of an O'Brien castle, has 140 modern rooms. Fittings throughout are heavy and traditional. The view of the Cascades from the entrance steps is breathtaking, and there are walks around the 20 hectares of wooded gardens.

Holywell Italian Restaurant (☎ 065-707 2464; Church St; mains €10-12; 🕙 noon-11pm May-Sep) At the north end of the centre, this dark and casual restaurant fills up during the summer months. Fresh pastas and thin-crust pizzas are not your bog-standard spag-bol slop.

There is also a local **farmers market** (🕙 11am-3pm Sun), which spreads its fertile wealth on Market Sq.

THE POET & THE PRIESTS

Ennistymon has more than its fair share of cultural associations. The Welsh poet Dylan Thomas lived at what is now the Falls Hotel when the house was the family home of his wife Cáitlín McNamara. There's plenty of Thomas memorabilia and a Dylan Thomas Bar at the hotel. At the other end of the scale is *Father Ted,* the enduring British TV comedy set around the high jinks of three Irish priests living on the fictional Craggy Island (p406). Most of the locations used in the show are around Ennistymon (Eugene's pub was used as a location and the cast drank here) and nearby Kilfenora. The lonely *Father Ted* house is near Kilnaboy.

Entertainment

Eugene's (☎ 065-707 1777; Main St) Not to be missed, Eugene's is a classic pub that defines craic. It's intimate, cosy and has a trademark collection of visiting cards covering its walls, alongside photographs of famous writers and musicians. The inspiring collection of whiskey (Irish) and whisky (Scottish) will have you smoothly debating their relative merits.

Cooley's House (☎ 065-707 1712; Main St) Another great old pub, but with music most nights in summer and on Wednesday (trad night) in winter.

Getting There & Away

Bus Éireann runs one or two buses daily through Ennistymon on the Doolin–Ennis/Limerick routes and one or two daily south along the coast via Lahinch to Doonbeg in summer. Buses stop in front of Aherne's on Church St.

LISCANNOR & AROUND
pop 380

This small seaside village overlooks Liscannor Bay, where the road (R478) heads north to the Cliffs of Moher and Doolin. Liscannor (Lios Ceannúir) has given its name to a type of local stone – slatelike and with a rippled surface – that is used for floors, walls and even roofs.

John Philip Holland (1840–1914), the inventor of the submarine, was born in Liscannor. He emigrated to the USA in 1873, and dreamed that his invention would be used to sink British warships. There's a rather silly statue of the man (or is it a walrus?) in front of the Cliffs of Moher Hotel.

Sleeping & Eating

Moher Lodge Farmhouse (☎ 065-708 1269; www .cliffsofmoher-ireland.com; s/d €50/75; ⊙ Apr-Oct) This big bungalow is in a great position overlooking the owner's open farmlands and the sea. The four rooms are welcoming after a day rambling; there's much to ramble to. It's 3km northwest of Liscannor, 1.6km from the Cliffs of Moher.

Cliffs of Moher Hotel (☎ 065-708 6770; www.cliffs ofmoherhotel.ie; Main St; s/d from €60/100; ☐) A modest yet modern inn right in the centre, this hotel has 23 nicely furnished and comfortable rooms. Local icons above and below the sea are recalled in the Puffin Bar and Submarine Restaurant.

Vaughan's Anchor Inn (☎ 065-708 1548; Main St; mains €12-25; ⊙ kitchen noon-9.30pm) Noted for its excellent seafood (yes to the scallops and halibut), Vaughan's packs 'em in – and out. When it rains, you can settle in by a peat fire, when it shines (sometimes 15 minutes later) you can take in the air at a picnic table.

Joseph McHugh's Bar (☎ 065-708 1163; Main St) Next to Vaughan's, lots of courtyard tables and regular trad sessions make this old pub a winner.

Getting There & Away

Bus Éireann runs one to three buses daily through Liscannor on the Doolin–Ennis/Limerick routes.

HAG'S HEAD

Forming the southern end of the Cliffs of Moher, Hag's Head is a dramatic place from which to view the cliffs.

There's a huge sea arch at the tip of Hag's Head and another arch visible to the north. The signal tower on the Head was erected in case Napoleon tried to attack on the western coast of Ireland. The tower is built on the site of an ancient promontory fort called Mothair, which has given its name to the famous cliffs to the north. A walking trail links the head with the cliffs and Liscannor.

CLIFFS OF MOHER

Star of a million tourist brochures, the Cliffs of Moher (Aillte an Mothair, or Ailltreacha Mothair) are one of the most popular sights in Ireland. But like many an ageing star, you have to look beyond the famous facade to appreciate the inherent attributes behind the postcard image.

The entirely vertical cliffs rise to a height of 203m, their edge falling away abruptly into the constantly churning sea. A series of heads, the dark limestone seems to march in a rigid formation that amazes, no matter how many times you look.

Such appeal comes at a price: mobs. This is check-off tourism big time and busloads come and go constantly in summer. A vast visitor centre handles the hordes. Set back into the side of a hill, it's impressively unimpressive – it blends right in. As part of the development, however, the main walkways and viewing areas along the cliffs have been surrounded by a 1.5m-high wall. It's lovely stone, but it's also way too high and set too far back from the edge. The entire reason for coming here (the view – unless you're a bus-spotter) is obscured.

But, like so many oversubscribed natural wonders, there's relief and joy if you're willing to walk for 10 minutes. Past the end of the 'Moher Wall' south, there's still a trail along the cliffs to Hag's Head – few venture this far. There's also a path heading north, but you're discouraged from it, so use your common sense. With binoculars you can spot the more than 30 species of birds – including darling little puffins – that make their homes among the fissure-filled cliff faces. On a clear day you'll channel Barbra Streisand as you can see forever; the Aran Islands stand etched on the waters of Galway Bay, and beyond lie the hills of Connemara in western Galway.

For uncommon views of the cliffs and wildlife you might consider a cruise. The boat operators in Doolin (p381) offer popular tours of the cliffs.

Information

The **visitor centre** (Map p377; ☎ 065-708 6141; www.cliffs ofmoher.ie; ☒ 8.30am-9pm Jun-Aug, 8.30am-7pm May & Sep, 9am-6pm Mar, Apr & Oct, 9.30am-5pm Nov-Feb) – actually, revealingly, it's called the 'Cliffs of Moher Visitor Experience' – has glitzy exhibitions about the cliffs and the environment called the 'Atlantic Edge' (adult/child €5/3). Staff lead tours outside and answer questions.

The car park costs €8. Vendors of 'authentic' sweaters and other tat have stalls near the cars and buses. The basement cafe seems designed to urge you up to the views at the pricier restaurant. Careful readers will note by now that if you don't need to park or see the exhibits, this natural wonder is free.

Getting There & Away

Bus Éireann runs one to three buses daily past the cliffs on the Doolin–Ennis/Limerick routes. Waits between buses may exceed your ability to enjoy the spectacle so you might combine a bus with a walk.

The Doolin area is 6km away. If walking stick to the minor road right near the cliffs that runs for the final half. Liscannor is under 2km along a path that is part of the Burren Way (p378).

THE BURREN

The Burren region is rocky and windswept, an apt metaphor for the hardscrabble lives of those who've eked out an existence here. Stretching across northern Clare, from the Atlantic coast to Kinvara in County Galway, it's a unique limestone landscape that was shaped beneath ancient seas, then forced high and dry by a great geological cataclysm. The sea is not muted here by offshore islands or muffled promontories, as it sometimes is on the coasts of Kerry and Galway. In the Burren, land and sea seem to merge into one vast, exhilarating space beneath huge skies.

Boireann is the Irish term for 'rocky country', a plain but graphic description of the Burren's acres of silvery limestone karst pavements. Known as 'clints', these lie like huge, scattered bones across the swooping hills. Between the seams of rock lie narrow fissures, known as 'grikes'. Their humid, sheltered conditions support exquisite wildflowers in spring, lending the Burren its other great charm: brilliant, if ephemeral, colour amid so much arid beauty. There are also intriguing villages to enjoy, especially along the coast and in the south Burren. These include Doolin on the west coast, Kilfenora inland and Ballyvaughan in the north, on the shores of Galway Bay. The Burren's coastline is made up of rocky foreshores, occasional beaches and bare limestone cliffs, while inland lies a haunting landscape of rocky hills peppered with ancient burial chambers and medieval ruins. If driving, take any road – the smaller the better – and see what you discover: you'll never be lost for long.

Large areas of the Burren, about 40,000 hectares in all, have been designated as Special Areas of Conservation. Apart from being against the law, it makes ecological sense not to remove plants or to damage walls, ancient monuments or the landscape itself. Visitors are also asked to resist the temptation to erect 'sham' replicas of dolmens and other monuments, however small, including *Spinal Tap Stonehenge* size.

Information

There is a wealth of literature about the Burren, and it's best to trawl the bookshops of Ennis and any local heritage centres for long-standing, but still relevant, publications such as Charles Nelson's *Wild Plants of the Burren and the Aran Islands*. The Tír Eolas series of foldout maps, *A Rambler's Guide & Map*, shows antiquities and other points of interest. The *Burren Journey* books by George Cunningham are excellent for local lore, but you may have to search for them. The visitor centre in Ennis is another good source; the booklet *The Burren Way* has good walking routes. Look for wonderfully detailed maps

by Tim Robinson. Ordnance Survey Discovery series maps 51 and 57 cover most of the area.

The **Burrenbeo Trust** (www.burrenbeo.com) is a non-profit dedicated to promoting the natural beauty of the Burren and increasing awareness. Its website is a tremendous resource.

Archaeology

The Burren's bare limestone hills were once lightly wooded and covered in soil. Towards the end of the Stone Age, about 6000 years ago, nomadic hunter-gatherers began to develop a settled lifestyle of farming and hunting. They cleared the woodlands and used the hills for grazing. Over the centuries, much soil was eroded and the limestone bones of the country became increasingly exposed.

Despite its apparent harshness, the Burren supported quite large numbers of people in ancient times, and has more than 2500 historic sites. Chief among them is the 5000-year-old Poulnabrone Dolmen, the framework of a Neolithic/Bronze Age chamber tomb, and one of Ireland's iconic ancient monuments.

Around 70 such tombs are in evidence today. Many are wedge-shaped graves, stone

COUNTY CLARE

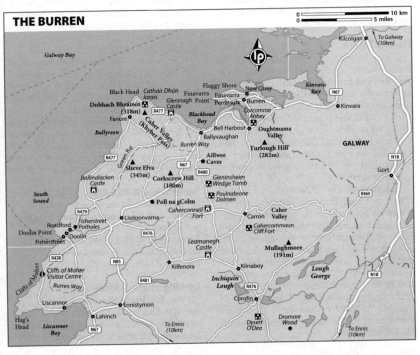

THE BURREN

WALK: BURREN WAY

This 35km walk traverses the Burren limestone plateau in County Clare. It presents a strange, unique landscape to the walker. There's very little soil and few trees, but a surprising abundance of flora. The way stretches between Ballyvaughan, on the northern coast of County Clare, and Liscannor to the southwest, taking in the village of Doolin, famous as a traditional-music centre. The trail south of Doolin to the dramatic Cliffs of Moher is a highlight of the route. From the cliffs a new path has been developed inland towards Liscannor (older maps may show a route, now closed, along the cliffs).

The best time for this walk is late spring or early summer. The route is pretty dry, but walking boots are useful as the limestone can be sharp.

boxes tapering both in height and width, and about the size of a large double bed. The dead were placed inside, and the whole structure covered in earth and stones. Gleninsheen, south of Aillwee Caves, is a good example.

Ring forts dot the Burren in prodigious numbers. There are almost 500, including Iron Age stone forts such as Cahercommaun near Carron.

In later times, many castles in the area were built by the region's ruling families, including Leamanegh Castle near Kilfenora, Ballinalacken Castle near Doolin, and Gleninagh Castle on the Black Head road.

Many ring forts and stone walls have been bulldozed out of existence.

Flora & Fauna

Soil may be scarce on the Burren, but the small amount that gathers in the cracks is well drained and rich in nutrients. This, together with the mild Atlantic climate, supports an extraordinary mix of Mediterranean, Arctic and alpine plants. Of Ireland's native wildflowers, 75% are found here, including a number of beautiful orchids, the creamy-white burnet rose, the little starry flowers of mossy saxifrage and the magenta-coloured bloody cranesbill.

The Burren is a stronghold of Ireland's most elusive mammal, the weasel-like pine marten. It's rarely seen, although there are certainly some living in the Caher Valley. Badgers, foxes and even stoats are common throughout the region. Otters and seals haunt the shores around Bell Harbour, New Quay and Finavarra Point.

The estuaries along this northern coast are rich in bird life and frequently attract brent geese during the winter. More than 28 of Ireland's 33 butterfly and moth species are found here, including one endemic species, the Burren green.

As they have elsewhere, modern farming and 'land improvement' grants have had their effect on the Burren. Weedkillers, insecticides and fertilisers favour grass and little else, often fatally undermining fragile ecological systems.

Walking

'Green roads' are the old highways of the Burren, crossing hills and valleys to some of the remotest corners of the region. Many of these unpaved ways were built during the Famine as part of relief work, while some date back possibly thousands of years. They're now used mostly by hikers and the occasional farmer. Some are signposted, but there is an element of footpath blockage and neglect these days, in spite of much publicity being given to walking and to 'official' walking routes.

The Burren Way (see above) runs down through the Burren from Ballyvaughan to Doolin and then inland along mainly paved lanes, since cliff access around the Cliffs of Moher has been discouraged.

Guided nature, history, archaeology and wilderness walks are great ways to appreciate the Burren. Typically the cost of the walks starts at €15 and there are many options, including individual trips. Recommended guides:

Burren Guided Walks & Hikes (☎ 065-707 6100, 088 265 4810; www.burrenguidedwalks.com; Fanore) Long-time guide Mary Howard leads groups on a variety of itineraries.

Burren Wild (☎ 087 877 9565; www.burrenwalks.com; Bell Harbour) John Connolly offers a broad range of walks (from €10) and packages.

Getting There & Away

Various Bus Éireann (www.buseireann.ie) buses pass through the Burren. The main routes include one from Limerick and Ennis to Corofin, Ennistymon, Lahinch, Liscannor, the Cliffs of

Moher, Doolin and Lisdoonvarna; another connects Galway with Ballyvaughan, Lisdoonvarna and Doolin. Usually there are one to three buses daily, with the most in summer.

Getting Around
By car you can cover a fair amount of the Burren in a day and have a chance to explore some of the many unnamed back roads. Mountain bikes are an excellent means of getting off the main roads; ask about rentals at your accommodation. Finally, walking is a superb way to appreciate the area's subtle beauty and dramatic landscapes.

DOOLIN
pop 250
Doolin gets plenty of press and chatter as a centre of Irish traditional music, owing to a couple of pubs that have sessions through the year. It's also known for its setting – 6km north of the Cliffs of Moher and down near the ever-unsettled sea, the land is windblown, with huge rocks exposed by the long-vanished top soil.

Given all its attributes, you might be surprised when you realise that Doolin as it's known barely exists. Rather, when you arrive you might be forgiven for exclaiming, 'There's no *there* here!' For what's called Doolin is really three infinitesimally small neighbouring villages. **Fisherstreet** is right on the water, **Doolin** itself is about 1km east on the little Aille River and **Roadford** is another 1km east. None has more than a handful of buildings, which results in a scattered appearance, without a centre.

Still, the area is hugely popular with backpackers and more affluent travellers (ex-backpackers with jobs). There are scores of excellent-value hostels and B&Bs widely spread about the rough landscape, and a pretty good scene – usually with music – develops in the local pubs at night. It's also a place to get boats to the Aran Islands offshore.

Orientation
Doolin's three parts are easily reached. From the north and Black Head the R479 first hits Roadford, with its hostels and two pubs. From the east, the R479 heads down into Doolin village from a junction with the R478, where there's a market. Doolin village has new upmarket hotels and developments (all looking nervous due to the economy). From the south, take a small road off the R478 north of the Cliffs of Moher and follow it down to Fisherstreet, with its postcard-perfect row of shops and pub. From here the harbour and ferries are 1.5km.

Information
There is no post office or bank. The closest ATM is in Ennistymon. Many places offer internet access and will change money. Try **Doolin Internet Cafe** (per 30min €3; ⌚ 8am-7pm; 🛜) in the Doolin Activity Lodge (p380). It also does laundry and rents bikes (€15 per day).

For tourist info, ignore the sign outside the Hotel Doolin and check the **tourism website** (www .doolin-tourism.com) instead.

Activities
One of the most enjoyable ways to pass your time in Doolin is by walking the windswept country. Tracks and paths radiate in all directions; the Cliffs of Moher are 6km south.

The Doolin area is popular with cavers. The **Fisherstreet Potholes** are nearby, and **Poll na gColm**, 5km northeast of Lisdoonvarna, is Ireland's longest cave, with more than 12km of mapped passageways; see www.cavingireland .org for more details. A little over 1km north of Roadford you'll find **Doolin Cave** (☎ 065-707 5761; www.doolincave.ie; adult/child €15/8; ⌚ 10am-5pm mid-Feb–Nov), which boasts an enormous stalactite that looks like a giant squid. The main entrance is at the Fisherstreet Potholes; tour times vary by season.

The rocks to the north of Doolin Harbour are honeycombed with an unusual system of undersea caves called the **Green Holes of Doolin**. They're the longest known undersea caves in temperate waters. Nondivers can look, with care, into Hell, a large gash in the rocks, north of the harbour and about 50m from the sea. The gash is about 6m wide, and the heaving water at the bottom leads to a maze of submarine passages.

The unguided caves mentioned here require experience and full equipment.

Sleeping
Although a new place to stay seems to open in Doolin about as often as a drunken tourist yells, 'One more time!' after hearing 'Danny Boy' at a trad music session, you should still book ahead in summer.

BUDGET
The Doolin area has an excellent range of hostels, best in the west.

Rainbow Hostel (☎ 065-707 4415; www.rainbow hostel.net; Roadford; dm €16-19, d from €50; 🛜) Many a friendship has started in the cosy lounge here. IHH-affiliated, this hostel has 30 beds and is in an old farmhouse by the road.

Nagles Doolin Caravan & Camping Park (☎ 065-707 4458; www.doolincamping.com; campsites from €17; 🕓 Apr-Sep) With full-on views of the Cliffs of Moher, and Doolin only a short distance away, this is an appealing location. The 60 sites are open to the elements, so pin those pegs down.

Paddy's Doolin Hostel (☎ 065-707 4421; www .doolinhostel.com; Fisherstreet, Doolin; from €17, d from €50; 🛜) A modern, IHH-affiliated hostel. There are 90 beds in four- and eight-bed rooms; private rooms with bathrooms are also available. The sweaty indoor charms of Fisherstreet are steps away.

Aille River Hostel (☎ 065-707 4260; ailleriver@esat clear.ie; Roadford; dm €18-25, d €50; 🕓 mid-Mar–Dec; 🖳 🛜) In a picturesque spot by the river in the upper village, this converted 17th-century farmhouse is a great choice. There are turf fires, hot showers and a free laundry. This award-winning IHH hostel has 30 beds, along with campsites from €16.

MIDRANGE

Most places to stay in this price range are in houses on large plots of land. There are many choices: all of the following are well located for walking to the various permutations of Doolin. Without exception all are family run.

Doolin Cottage (☎ 065-707 4762; caroldoolin@ hotmail.com; Roadford; s/d from €40/65; 🕓 Mar-Nov) This charming little old house has a peaceful and friendly atmosphere and is good value. The three rooms vary greatly in size.

Doolin Activity Lodge (☎ 065-707 4888; www .doolinlodge.com; Fisherstreet; s/d from €45/70; 🖳 🛜) This impressive purpose-built guesthouse occupies a large compound; the solid stone buildings are quite attractive. There are 14 nicely furnished rooms, some with skylights for watching the rain blow past, as well as self-catering apartments.

Riverfield House (☎ 065-707 4113; www.doolinlink .com/riverfield.html; Doolin; s/d from €45/70) Standing sturdy and back from the lane, this two-storey modern farmhouse offers stolid comfort. It has a few trees, too (most don't). Rooms are large – you can have a king-size bed to roll around in all day.

O'Connors Guesthouse (☎ 065-707 4498; www .oconnorsdoolin.com; Doolin; s/d from €50/70; 🕓 Feb-Nov)

On a bend in the Aille, this working farm has 10 rooms of varying sizes in a rather plush farmhouse. Fresh-baked breads in the morning may put you in the mood to clean the barn (not possible actually). Commune with cattle instead. There are also campsites (€20).

Dubhlinn House (☎ 065-707 4770; www.dubhlinn house.com; Doolin; s/d from €50/75; 🛜) This gleaming white B&B has good views down towards the water. The three rooms are simply decorated, while the breakfasts are lavish; American urbanites will recognise and appreciate the bagel BLT.

Atlantic View B&B (☎ 065-707 4189; www.doolin ferries.com; Doolin Point; s/d €50/80) The perfect spot for guests who want their ocean up close and personal. This modern 12-room lodge is built right near the water, not far from the dock. Fisherstreet is a five-minute walk.

Cullinan's Guest House (☎ 065-707 4183; www .cullinansdoolin.com; Doolin; s €50-80, d €80-100; 🛜) The eight B&B rooms here are all of a high standard, with power showers and comfortable fittings. Right on the Aille (two rooms have balconies), it has a lovely back terrace for enjoying the views. The restaurant is one of the village's best. The owner is a well-known local musician (see the boxed text, opposite).

Sea View House (☎ 065-707 4826; www.ireland -doolin.com; Fisherstreet; r €60-100; 🛜) On high ground right above Fisherstreet village, this big house and its terrace have sweeping ocean views. The common lounge has a telescope for enjoying the vantage point. The four rooms have solid mahogany furnishings.

Eating

Doolin Cafe (☎ 065-707 4795; Roadford; mains €7-24; 🕓 noon-3pm, 6-10pm) The cottage is small, but the flavours are big at this much-loved bistro. Salads, soups and sandwiches are the deal at lunch, while at night there's a range of meats and seafoods with fusion preparations.

Cullinan's (☎ 065-707 4183; 1-/2-/3-courses €25/32/40; Doolin; 🕓 6-9pm Thu-Tue) Attached to the guesthouse of the same name, this excellent restaurant offers delicious seafood as well as meat and poultry dishes. The short menu changes depending on what's fresh, but is always creative. Bold combinations are favoured and there's a long wine list.

For self-catering, the well-stocked **Doolin Deli** (Fisherstreet) is just down from O'Connor's pub in Fisherstreet on the road to the pier. The pubs listed under Drinking all do good and

JAMES CULLINAN, DOOLIN MUSICIAN

James Cullinan has been playing the fiddle for 35 years. He's a noted musician in County Clare and can often be heard playing in Doolin's pubs. 'It's a bit impromptu', he says, 'I'll be out with friends, have two or three pints, hear some music and the next thing you know I've run home, got the fiddle and I'm back playing music.' Unplanned, pint-fuelled sessions aside, his playing is kept in check by his work as chef and owner of the well-regarded guesthouse and restaurant that bears his name. Outside of summer, however, he's a regular at the area's music festivals. He took a few moments to answer our questions about music.

How did Doolin become known for music? In the 1970s Michael Russell and his brothers really began reviving the old songs. They had a farm here but weren't very good farmers – if they heard of a session, they'd go play and leave the hay in the field. Pretty soon they had a reputation and people started coming here to hear them. Over time people began to expect music here, so publicans would pay a few guys each night just to get something going. It was a good way to get free pints.

How did you start playing? I had a great music teacher. It was the early 1970s and Irish music was becoming cool again. He gave everybody a tin whistle and if you showed any talent you got a fiddle.

Why did you stick with the fiddle? It has endless possibilities for how you play it. I can play the same song at every session here, but each time will be different. It can depend on where you sit, who else is playing, what the crowd's like and more.

What kind of crowd is best? Loud. You just want to feel like you're playing amongst people.

Does Doolin or Clare have a unique style? Yes, we do a lot of jigs and reels here. In other counties you'll hear more polkas or other influences, but Clare musicians are pretty conservative. Older people come here and know everything we play. We play around with the old stuff and have fun with that.

What's the worst thing that can happen in a pub session? Somebody starts to sing. We keep the jigs and reels going because otherwise after a few pints everybody thinks they can sing and they take over. We're there playing for ourselves, not to back up drunks.

The second worst thing? Some guy always comes up and asks for 'Devil Came Down to Georgia'. They must play it a lot in bad Irish bars in America.

reasonably priced versions of Irish classics like roasts, stews, fish and chips etc.

Drinking & Entertainment

Doolin's rep is largely based on music. A lot of musicians live in the area, and they have a symbiotic relationship with the tourists: each desires the other and each year things grow a little larger. But given the heavy concentration of visitors it's inevitable that standards don't always hold up to those in some of the less-trampled villages in Clare. In summer, the antics of the tourists (joining in with musicians uninvited, trying to sing, ceaselessly demanding 'When Irish Eyes are Smiling', sending blurry cell-phone snaps worldwide etc) can be as entertaining as the sessions. Still, in the low season, Doolin is where you'll always be able to hear a trad session.

Doolin's three main pubs (others are recent interlopers) are listed here in order of their importance to the music scene.

O'Connor's (☎ 065-707 4168; Fisherstreet) Right on the water, this sprawling favourite packs them in and has a rollicking atmosphere when the music and drinking are in full swing. The food's good, too.

McGann's (☎ 065-707 4133; Roadford) McGann's has all the classic touches of a full-on Irish music pub; the action often spills out onto the street. Food is also served here and there's a small outside covered area.

MacDiarmada's (☎ 065-707 4700; Roadford) Also known as McDermott's, this simple red-and-white old pub can be the rowdy favourite of locals. Music sessions are up to the best Doolin standards.

Getting There & Away

BOAT

Doolin is one of two ferry departure points to the Aran Islands (p403) from April to October. Three ferry companies offer numerous departures in season. It takes around 20 to 30 minutes to cover the 8km to Inisheer (€30 return), the closest of the three islands. A boat to Inishmór takes one to 1½ hours with an Inisheer stop (€40 return). Ferries to Inishmaan are infrequent. Sailings are often cancelled due to high seas. Call and confirm times and book in advance.

Cliffs of Moher Cruises (☎ 065-707 5949; www .mohercruises.com; Doolin Pier; ☒ Apr–Oct) Offers combined Aran Islands trips with Cliffs of Moher cruises on the *Jack B.*

Doolin Ferries (☎ 065-707 4455, 065-707 4466; www .doolinferries.com; Doolin Pier) Offers frequent sailings to the islands and the cliffs.

O'Brien Line (☎ 065-707 5555; www.obrienline.com; Doolin Pier) Also offers cliff cruises.

BUS
Bus Éireann runs one to three buses daily to Doolin from Ennis (€11, 1½ hours) and Limerick (€15, 2½ hours) via Corofin, Lahinch and the Cliffs of Moher. Buses also go to Galway (€14, 1½ hours, one or two daily) via Ballyvaughan.

In the summer, various backpacker shuttles often serve Doolin from Galway and other points in Clare. These are amply marketed in hostels.

Getting Around
Besides the Doolin Activity Lodge (p380), several hostels and B&Bs rent bikes; ask around.

LISDOONVARNA
pop 950
Lisdoonvarna (Lios Dún Bhearna), often just called 'Lisdoon', is well known for its mineral springs. For centuries people have been visiting the local spa to swallow its waters. Posh in the Victorian era, the town is now a much more plebeian and friendly place. Away from the coast, it's not overrun like Doolin and is a good base for exploring the Burren.

The town was once a centre for *basadóiri* (matchmakers) who, for a fee, would fix up a person with a spouse. Most of the (mainly male) hopefuls would hit town in September, feet shuffling, cap in hand, after the hay was in. Today, true matchmaking is unlikely, but the ever-expanding **Lisdoonvarna Matchmaking Festival** (www.matchmakerireland.com), held throughout September and early October, is a great excuse for daftness, drinking, merrymaking, music and, of course, moneymaking.

Orientation & Information
Lisdoonvarna is essentially a one-street town with a square in the centre from where you turn west for Doolin and the coast. It has shops, pubs, B&Bs and hotels with some fine restaurants. Change money at the post office on Main St to the north.

There's internet access at the **Internet Shop** (☎ 065-707 5005; Main St; per 20min €2; ☒ 9am-6pm Mon-Sat May-Sep).

Sights & Activities
At the southern end of town is a **spa well**, with a sulphur spring, a Victorian pumphouse and an agreeable, wooded setting. The iron, sulphur, magnesium and iodine in the water are supposed to be good for rheumatic and glandular complaints. Closer to the centre, you can drink the water, even if it's not exactly a vintage wine-tasting experience. Look for a trail beside the Roadside Tavern that runs 400m down to two **wells** by the river. One is high in sulphur, the other iron. Mix and match for a cocktail of minerals.

You can learn about the ancient Irish art of oak-smoking salmon from a video (available in six languages) at the **Burren Smokehouse** (☎ 065-707 4432; www.burrensmokehouse.ie; Kincora Rd; admission free; ☒ 10am-5pm Apr-May, 9am-6pm Jun-Oct, shorter hr in winter). Tasty smoked salmon and other fishies in a myriad of forms are offered for free tasting – perhaps you'll even buy some? Good coffee and tea are sold along with other deli-type foods suitable for picnics. Tourist information is also available. The smokehouse is at the edge of Lisdoonvarna on the Kincora road (N67).

Sleeping & Eating
Book during September's Matchmaking Festival; B&Bs are like mushrooms after the rain.

Sleepzone (☎ 065-707 7168; www.sleepzone.ie; Doolin Rd; dm €15-20, s/d €35/50; ☐ ☎) Housed in a formerly posh hotel, this 124-bed hostel has an unusual grace. The grounds reflect its past and there are all the usual facilities and free continental breakfasts. The hostel is on a private bus route from Galway; ask the staff for details.

ourpick Sheedy's Country House Hotel & Restaurant (☎ 065-707 4026; www.sheedys.com; Sulphur Hill; s/d from €120/180; ☒ mid-Mar–Sep) Take a leek from the kitchen garden – that's just one of the playful bits of fun you can have at this posh yet relaxed 11-room guesthouse just out-side of town. A long porch has comfy chairs for pondering the many gardens or just taking a snooze. Food is excellent. The bar has a huge range of whiskey.

Roadside Tavern (☎ 065-707 4084; meals €6-12) Down by the river, this pub is pure craic. Third-generation owner Peter Curtin knows every story worth telling. There are trad sessions daily in summer and during the weekends in winter. Imbibing musicians can be found here anytime. The trad fun extends to the kitchen, which turns out creamy seafood chowders etc.

Getting There & Around
Bus Éireann runs one to three buses daily to Doolin via Lisdoonvarna from Ennis, and to Limerick via Corofin, Lahinch and the Cliffs of Moher. Buses also go to Galway via Ballyvaughan and Black Head.

FANORE
pop 150
Fanore (Fan Óir), 5km south of Black Head, is less a village and more a stretch of coast with a shop, a pub and a few houses scattered along the main road (R477). It has a fine sandy beach with an extensive backdrop of dunes. You'll find good parking and there are toilets open in summer.

Surfers flock here throughout the year. **Aloha Surf School** (☎ 087 213 3996; www.surfschool .tv; lessons from €35) offers classes for all ages and abilities.

There's a well-stocked shop, **Siopa Fan Óir** (☎ 065-707 6131; ☼ 9am-9pm summer, to 7pm winter), just across from O'Donohue's pub, where you can buy fishing tackle, walking maps, boogie boards and cheap sand buckets.

One of the Fanore area's few accommodation/eating options, **Rocky View Farmhouse** (☎ 065-707 6103; www.rockyviewfarmhouse.com; s/d €45/80), is a charming house at the heart of the coastal Burren. Its six open and airy rooms are suited to this especially barren end of the region. Organic food is grown and used in the breakfasts, which are served in a glassed-in room.

In many ways the community centre, **O'Donohue's** (☎ 065-707 6119; meals €6-15; ☼ Apr-Oct), 4km south of the beach, offers no-nonsense soup, hot dishes and sandwiches along with its genuine local character. Done up in bright blue and white, it looks out over the grey sea.

Bus Éireann runs one to three buses daily from Galway via Black Head and through Fanore to Lisdoonvarna.

BLACK HEAD
Atlantic storms have stripped the land around the unfortunately named Black Head down to bare rock. Grass and the occasional shrub cling to crevices. Standing like sentinels, boulders and the odd cow dot the landscape here, Clare's northwesternmost point.

The main road (R477) curves around the head just above the sea. There's good shore **angling** for pollack, wrasse, mackerel – and sea bass if you're lucky – from the rocky platforms near sea level. These can be fatally dangerous waters, even for those with long-standing local knowledge. Even in apparently calm conditions, watch for sudden surges.

BALLYVAUGHAN & AROUND
pop 200
Something of a hub for the otherwise dispersed charms of the Burren, Ballyvaughan (Baile Uí Bheacháin), sits between the hard land of the hills and a quiet leafy corner of Galway Bay. It makes an excellent base for visiting the northern reaches of the Burren.

The centre of the village is located at the junction of the N67 and the coastal R477. Going south and inland on the N67 brings you to the centre of the Burren. Turning west leads you to the magnificent coast road (R477) around Black Head and south towards Doolin.

Just west of the junction, on the R477, is the quay, built in 1829 at a time when boats traded with the Aran Islands and Galway, exporting grain and bacon and bringing in turf – a scarce commodity in the windswept rocks of Burren.

A few metres past the harbour, a signposted track leads to a seashore bird shelter offering good views of the tidal shallows.

Information
The **tourist info desk** (☎ 065-707 7464; www.bally vaughantourism.com; ☼ 9am-6pm daily Mar-Oct, Sat & Sun only Nov-Feb) is in a vast gift shop. **Brendan's Boat** (☎ 065-707 7337; www.brendansboat.ie; ☼ 9.30am-6.30pm Apr-Dec) is a renowned local leather maker. On the south side of the centre, it offers internet access and shares the building with a laundry and bike rental place.

WALK: CLIMBING THE AGES

An exhilarating outing is the climb up Black Head to the Iron Age ring fort of **Cathair Dhún Iorais**. There's no path, so it's essential to take a map (Ordnance Survey Discovery Series No 51) and compass. The ground is very rocky in places, so strong footwear is essential. Be prepared for wet, windy and potentially cold conditions, even in summer. It's a steep 1.5km to the fort.

Start from just above the lighthouse on the northern tip of Black Head. There's limited parking on the inland side of the road. Head due south up the rocky hillside from the road, negotiating between rock shelves, to reach an old green track. Cross the track and continue directly to where things level off and Cathair Dhún Iorais stands amid a sea of limestone pavements. It's not the most dramatic of ring forts, but the setting is magnificent. The views to Galway and Connemara are breathtaking in clear weather.

From the fort you can bear southeast to skirt the limestone cliffs that run in an unbroken wall to the west. This takes you onto the broad shoulder that leads south, in 1.3km, to the summit of **Dobhach Bhráinín**, one of the highest points in the Burren at 318m. Again, skilled use of map and compass is essential in case of sudden mist, when careless descent from Dobhach Bhráinín may land you above the cliffs. It's best to return to the fort and descend the way you came.

Sights & Activities

About 6km south of Ballyvaughan on the Lisdoonvarna road (N67) is a series of severe bends up **Corkscrew Hill** (180m). The road was built as part of a Great Famine relief scheme in the 1840s. From the top there are spectacular views of the northern Burren and Galway Bay, with Aillwee Mountain and the caves on the right, Cappanawalla Hill on the left, and the partially restored 16th-century Newtown Castle, erstwhile residence of the O'Lochlains, directly below.

Sleeping & Eating

There are several simple B&Bs close to the centre.

Oceanville House B&B (☎ 065-707 7051; www.bally vaughanbandb.com; s/d from €45/70) Near Monk's, this oceanfront B&B has views across the bay from the dormer windows in its compact upstairs rooms. This is a good spot for walking the village and sampling its pleasures.

Hyland's Burren Hotel (☎ 065-707 7037; www .hylandsburren.com; Main St; s/d €70/90) An appealing place, this central hotel has 30 large rooms and manages to retain a local feel alongside modern hotel schtick. There's a bar and a restaurant. Ask for the hotel's *Walks* leaflet.

Rusheen Lodge (☎ 065-707 7092; www.rusheen lodge.com; Lisdoonvarna Rd; s/d from €70/100; ⏰ Feb-Nov; 🖳 📶) Stylish, imaginative furnishings make this nine-room guesthouse a winner. Enjoy a romp in the colourful gardens. It's about 750m south of the village on the N67.

Monk's Bar & Restaurant (☎ 065-707 7059; Old Pier; mains €10-20; ⏰ kitchen noon-8pm) Famed for its excellent seafood, Monk's is a cheerful, spacious and comfortable place. Peat fires warm in winter, while sea breezes cool you at the outdoor tables in summer. The pub is open late and there are trad sessions some nights in high season.

Ólólainn (Main St) A tiny family-run place on the left as you head out to the pier, Ólólainn (o-*loch*-lain) is the place for a timeless moment or two in old-fashioned snugs. Look for the old whiskey bottles in the window.

Ballyvaughan's **farmers market** (⏰ 10am-2pm Sat) celebrates the huge range of high-quality local produce.

Getting There & Away

Bus Éireann runs one to three buses daily from Galway through Ballyvaughan and around Black Head to Lisdoonvarna and Doolin.

CENTRAL BURREN

The scenery along the R480 as it passes through the heart of the region is harsh but inspiring, highlighting the barren Burren at its best. Amazing prehistoric stone structures can be found throughout this area.

South from Ballyvaughan the R480 branches off the N67 at the sign for Aillwee Caves, passing Gleninsheen Wedge Tomb and Poulnabrone Dolmen before reaching Leamanegh Castle, where it joins the R476, which runs southeast to Corofin. At any point along here, try a small road – especially those to the east – for an escape into otherworldly solitude.

Aillwee Caves

Popular with kids, the **Aillwee Caves** (☎ 065-707 7036; www.aillweecave.ie; Ballyvaughan; adult/child €17/10; ☺ 10am-5.30pm) are a large tourist attraction. The main cave penetrates 600m into the mountain, widening into larger caverns, one with its own waterfall. The caves were carved out by water some two million years ago. Near the entrance are the remains of a brown bear, extinct in Ireland for more than 10,000 years. Often crowded in summer, there's a cafe and other time killers like a cheese factory on site. A large raptor exhibit has captive hawks, owls and more.

Gleninsheen Wedge Tomb

One of Ireland's most famous prehistoric grave sites, Gleninsheen lies beside the R480 just south of Aillwee Caves. It's thought to date from 4000 to 5000 years ago. A magnificent gold torc (a crescent of beaten gold that hung round the neck), found here and dating from around 700 BC, is now on display at the National Museum in Dublin (p106). Note: the access gate to the tomb is sometimes locked, and signage is poor.

Poulnabrone Dolmen

What would a Burren brochure designer do without it? Also known as the Portal Tomb, Poulnabrone Dolmen is one of Ireland's most photographed ancient monuments. The dolmen (a large slab perched on stone uprights) stands amid a swathe of rocky pavements, surprising even the most jaded traveller with its otherworldly appearance; the capstone weighs five tonnes. The site is about 8km south of Aillwee and is visible from the R480. A large free parking area and excellent displays make it visitor friendly.

Poulnabrone was built more than 5000 years ago. It was excavated in 1986, and the remains of 16 people were found, as well as pieces of pottery and jewellery. Radiocarbon dating suggests that they were buried between 3800 BC and 3200 BC. When the dead were originally entombed here, the whole structure was partially covered in a mound of earth, which has since worn away. It's your guess as to how they built it.

Caherconnell Fort

For a look at a well-preserved *caher* (walled fort) of the late Iron Age–Early Christian period, stop at **Caherconnell Fort** (☎ 065-708 9999; www.burrenforts.ie; adult/child €6/4; ☺ 10am-6pm Jul & Aug, 10am-5pm Mar-Jun, Sep & Oct), a privately run heritage attraction that's more serious than sideshow. Exhibits detail how the evolution of these defensive settlements may have reflected territorialism and competition for land among a growing, settling population. The drystone walling of the fort is in excellent condition. The top-notch visitor centre also has information on many other monuments in the area. It's about 1km south of Poulnabrone on the R480.

Carron & Around

The tiny village of Carron (Carran on some maps, An Carn in Gaelic), a few kilometres east of the R480, is a wonderfully remote spot. Vistas of the rocky Burren stretch in all directions from Carron's elevated position.

A must-see stop, the **Burren Perfumery & Floral Centre** (☎ 065-708 9102; www.burrenperfumery .com; Carron; ☺ 9am-7pm Jul-Aug, 10am-5pm Sep-Jun) is a creative treasure. It uses wildflowers of the Burren to produce its scents, and is the only handicraft perfumery in Ireland. There's a free audiovisual presentation on the flora of the Burren, which has a surprising diversity. One example: the fragrant orchid that grows among the rocks. The centre has an organic-tea cafe, and native and herb gardens. Look for perfumery signs at the T-junction near Carron church. Note that tour buses aren't welcome.

Below Carron lies one of the finest turloughs in Ireland. It's known as the **Carron Polje**. Polje is a Serbo-Croatian term used universally for these shallow depressions that flood in winter and dry out in summer, when the lush grass that flourishes on the surface is used for grazing.

Stretching south from Carron almost to Kilnaboy is land best suited for growing rocks. Take any narrow track you find, and every so often you'll see an ancient **dolmen**.

About 3km south of Carron and perched on the edge of an inland cliff is the great stone fort of **Cahercommaun**. It was inhabited in the 8th and 9th centuries AD by people who hunted deer and grew a small amount of grain. The remains of a souterrain (underground passage) lead from the fort to the outer cliff face. To get there, go south from Carron and take a left turn for Kilnaboy. After 1.5km a path on the left leads up to the fort. Look for a good info board at the start of the path.

ROCK LEGENDS

The geology of the Burren may seem like a load of old rocks, but there is immense drama and excitement in the primeval adventures that produced the exquisite landscape we see today. The Burren is the most extensive limestone region, or karst (after the original Karst in Slovenia), in Ireland or Britain. It consists almost entirely of limestone, except for a cap of mud and shale that sits on the higher regions. The rock-faced Aran Islands are part of this same geologic area.

During the Carboniferous period 350 million years ago, this whole area was the bottom of a warm and shallow sea. The remains of coral and shells fell to the seabed, and coastal rivers dumped sand and silt on top of these lime deposits. Time and pressure turned the lower layers to limestone and the upper ones to shale and sandstone.

Massive shifts in the earth's crust some 270 million years ago buckled the edges of Europe and forced the former seabed above sea level. At the same time the stone sheets were bent and fractured to form the long, deep cracks so characteristic of the Burren today, each one a stone trench crammed full of wildflowers nurtured on tenuous soil and a microclimate of sweet, damp air.

During numerous ice ages, glaciers scoured the hills, rounding the edges and sometimes polishing the rock to a shiny finish, and dumping a thin layer of rock and soil over the region. Huge boulders were carried by the ice, incongruous aliens on a sea of flat rock. Seen all over the Burren, these 'glacial erratics' are often a visibly different type of rock.

our pick **Clare's Rock Hostel** (☎ 065-708 9129; www.claresrock.com; Carron; dm/s/d €18/30/44; ☺ May-Sep; ☐ ☎) is an imposing building of grey exposed stone. It has 30 beds, big spacious rooms and excellent facilities. Guests can hire bikes or cavort with the trolls on the outdoor garden-gnome chessboard.

Cassidy's (☎ 065-708 9109; Carron; bar mains €4.50-9.50; ☺ daily May-Sep, Sat & Sun Oct-Apr) serves up a good range of pub dishes, several with witty names reflecting the establishment's previous incarnation as a British Royal Irish Constabulary (RIC) station, and then as a *garda* barracks. Enjoy trad music and dancing some weekends. The views from the terrace are as intoxicating as the drink.

KILFENORA

pop 360

Underappreciated Kilfenora (Cill Fhionnúrach) lies on the southern fringe of the Burren, 8km (a five-minute drive) southeast of Lisdoonvarna (p382). It's a small place, with a diminutive 12th-century cathedral. High crosses adorn the churchyard, and low polychromatic buildings surround the compact centre.

The town has a strong music tradition that rivals that of Doolin, but without the crowds. The **Kilfenora Céili Band** (☎ 065-684 2228; www .kilfenoraceiliband.com) is a celebrated community that's been playing for 100 years. Its traditional music features fiddles, banjos, squeezeboxes and more. It often plays Wednesday nights at Linnane's (opposite).

Sights

The **Burren Centre** (☎ 065-708 8030; www.theburren centre.ie; Main St; adult/child €7/4; ☺ 10am-5pm) has a series of entertaining and informative displays on many aspects of the Burren past and present. There's a tea room and a very large shop that sells local products.

The now-ruined 12th-century **cathedral** at Kilfenora was once an important place of pilgrimage. St Fachan (or Fachtna) founded the monastery here in the 6th century, and it later became the seat of Kilfenora diocese, the smallest in the country. The cathedral is certainly the smallest you're ever likely to see. Only the ruined structure and nave of the more recent Protestant church are actually part of the cathedral. The chancel has two primitive carved figures on top of two tombs.

Kilfenora is best known for its **high crosses**, three in the churchyard and a large one from the 12th century in a field about 100m to the west. Most interesting is the 800-year-old **Doorty Cross**, standing prominently to the west of the church's front door. It lay broken in two until the 1950s, when it was re-erected. A panel in the churchyard does an excellent job of explaining the carvings that adorn the crosses.

Sleeping & Eating

Kilfenora has two fabulous pubs.

Kilfenora Hostel (Shepherd's Rest; ☎ 065-708 8908; www.kilfenorahostel.com; Main St; dm €20-24, d €52-60; ☐ ☎) Affiliated with Vaughan's Pub next door, this guesthouse has 46 beds in nine rooms. There's a laundry and a big kitchen. Weary travellers in the lounge may feel they've fallen into the hand of God.

Murphy's B&B (☎ 065-708 8040; lika@eircom.net; Main St; s/d from €45/70; ☺ mid-Feb–Nov) Right on the main street, Mrs Mary Murphy runs a fine little B&B with the kind of simple rooms you could call your own. She has two more houses nearby.

Linnane's (☎ 065-708 8157; Main St; meals €5-12; ☺ kitchen noon-8pm) Irish standards like smoked salmon and more are fully honoured here. Peat fires warm the almost bare interior; nary a frill in sight. There's trad music many nights in summer.

our pick Vaughan's Pub (☎ 065-708 8004; Main St; meals €9-15; ☺ kitchen 10am-9pm) Seafood, traditional foods and local produce feature on the Vaughan's appealing menu. The pub has a big reputation in Irish music circles. There's music in the bar every night during the summer and on many nights the rest of the year. The adjacent barn is the scene of terrific set-dancing sessions on Thursday and Sunday nights. Have a pint under the big tree out front.

Getting There & Away
Kilfenora does not have a useful bus service.

COROFIN & AROUND
pop 420

Corofin (Cora Finne), also spelt Corrofin, is a traditional village on the southern fringes of the Burren. It's low-key and a classic place to sample the rhythms of Clare life. The surrounding area features a number of turloughs and several O'Brien castles, including two on the shores of nearby Lough Inchiquin.

Corofin is home to the interesting **Clare Heritage Centre** (☎ 065-683 7955; www.clareroots.com; Church St; adult/concession €4/2; ☺ 9.30am-5.30pm Apr-Oct). Housed in an old church, it has a display covering the horrors of the Famine. More than 250,000 people lived in Clare before the Famine; even today the county's population is only about 106,000 – a drop of almost 60%. In a separate building nearby, the **Clare Genealogical Centre** (☎ 065-683 7955; ☺ 9am-5.30pm Mon-Fri) has facilities for people researching their Clare ancestry.

About 4km northwest of Corofin, on the road to Leamanegh Castle and Kilfenora (R476), look for the small town of **Kilnaboy**. The ruined church here is well worth seeking out for the sheila-na-gig over the doorway.

Sleeping & Eating
Corofin Hostel & Camping Park (☎ 065-683 7683; www.corofincamping.com; Main St; campsites €20, dm/s/d €16/25/40) Campsites out back have nice open spaces, and inside there are 30 beds. The large common room at this IHH-affiliated hostel has a pool table. Hot showers are free for all.

Lakefield Lodge (☎ 065-683 7675; lodgebandb.com; Ennis Rd; s/d from €50/70; ☺ Mar-Oct) A well-run place near the southern edge of the village. There are four comfy rooms in a pleasant bungalow surrounded by gardens and well-placed for Burren hikes.

Fergus View (☎ 065-683 7606; www.fergusview.com; s/d from €52/74; ☺ Apr-Oct; ☐ ☐) The name exactly describes the scene: the River Fergus flows right past. A lovely home with six rooms, its breakfasts have achieved fame for being fresh – often organic – and creative. It's 3km north of Corofin on the R476.

our pick Inchiquin Inn (☎ 065-683 7713; Main St; lunch €6-10; ☺ kitchen 9am-6pm) Townsfolk follow the horses at this oh-so-local pub with a great kitchen. The seafood chowder and bacon and cabbage are some of the best you'll find. The former is thick, tangy and redolent with smoked fish. There's trad music some summer nights.

Corofin Arms Restaurant (☎ 065-683 7373; Main St; meals €8-20; ☺ kitchen 5.30-9pm, noon-9pm Sun) This sprightly, always popular little pub offers dishes made with locally sourced foods, including tangy Kilnaboy cheese from just up the road.

Getting There & Away
Bus Éireann has an infrequent service some weekdays between Corofin and Ennis.

NORTHERN BURREN
Low farmland stretches south from County Galway to the bluff limestone hills of the Burren, which begin west of Kinvara and Doorus in County Galway.

From Oranmore in County Galway to Ballyvaughan, the coastline wriggles along small inlets and peninsulas; some, such as Finavarra Point and New Quay, are worth a detour. Here, narrow roads traverse low rocky windswept hills dotted with old stone ruins that have yielded to nature.

Inland near Bell Harbour is the largely intact Corcomroe Abbey, while the three ancient churches of Oughtmama lie up a quiet side valley. Galway Bay forms the backdrop to some outstanding scenery: bare stone hills shining in the sun, with small hamlets and rich patches of green wherever there's soil.

Buses to/from Galway pass through the area on the N67. Just over the border in Galway, Kinvara (p423) makes a good base for this region.

New Quay & the Flaggy Shore

New Quay (Ceibh Nua), on the **Finavarra Peninsula**, is about 1km off the main Kinvara–Ballyvaughan road (N67) and is reached by turning off at Ballyvelaghan Lough 3km north of Bell Harbour.

Smack on the water, **Linnane's Seafood Bar** (☎ 065-707 8120; New Quay; meals €9-25; ☽ noon-8pm), has achieved international cachet as a no-nonsense purveyor of fresh seafood sourced from the trap-covered docks behind the restaurant. For centuries this area was famous for its oysters; shellfish are still processed here and you can sometimes buy them from the little works behind the pub.

The **Flaggy Shore**, west of New Quay, is a particularly fine stretch of coastline where limestone terraces step down to the sea. About 500m west of Linnane's, at a crossroads, the **Russell Gallery** (☎ 065-707 8185; New Quay; ☽ 10am-6pm Mon-Sat, from noon Sun) specialises in *raku* (Japanese lead-glazed earthenware) work. The airy gallery has a range of other works by Irish artists for sale along with books on the region.

Nearby, just off the N67, **Wilde & Wooley** (☎ 065-707 8042; Burren) is the name for Antoinette Hensey's shop, where she makes custom knitwear from exquisitely dyed wool. The designs are complex and beautiful; a sweater costs upwards of €200.

Turn north off the N67 for the Flaggy Shore. The road hugs the shoreline going west, then curves south past **Lough Muiri**, where you're likely to see a number of wading birds, as well as swans. There are said to be otters in the area. At a T-junction just past the lough, a right turn leads to a rather dingy-looking **Martello tower** on Finavarra Point, a relic of the paranoia over the Napoleonic threat.

Bell Harbour

No more than a crossroads with a growing crop of holiday cottages and a pub, Bell Harbour (Beulaclugga) is about 8km east of Ballyvaughan. There's a pleasant walk along an old green road that begins behind the modern Church of St Patrick, 1km north up the hill from the Y-junction at Bell Harbour, and threads north along Abbey Hill.

Inland from here are the ruins of Corcomroe Abbey, the valley and churches of Oughtmama, and the interior road that takes you through the heart of the Burren.

Corcomroe Abbey

Moody and evocative, lonely Corcomroe, a former Cistercian abbey 1.5km inland from Bell Harbour, lies in a small, tranquil valley surrounded by low hills. It is a marvellous building, one of the finest of its kind. The abbey was founded in 1194 by Donal Mór O'Brien. His grandson, Conor na Siudaine O'Brien (died 1267), king of Thomond, is said to occupy the tomb in the northern wall, and there's a crude carving of him below the effigy of a bishop holding a crosier, the pastoral staff that was carried by a bishop or abbot. The surviving vaulting in the presbytery and transepts is very fine and there are some striking Romanesque carvings scattered throughout the abbey, which began a long decline in the 15th century. Often-touching modern graves crowd the ruins.

Oughtmama Valley

Small ancient churches lie hidden in this lonely, deserted valley. To get there turn inland at Bell Harbour, then go left at the Y-junction. In just under 1km you reach a house amid trees, on the right at Shanvally. A rough track leads inland from just beyond the house for about 1.5km to the churches. Roadside parking is very limited, but there is a large roadside area about 400m before Shanvally, back towards the Y-junction, with views of Corcomroe. Monks in search of solitude built the **churches** at Oughtmama in the 12th century. Look for the Romanesque arch in the westernmost – and largest – church. It's a hardy walk up **Turlough Hill** behind the chapels, but the views are tremendous. Near the summit are the remains of a **hill fort**.

County Galway

County Galway presents a major problem: its namesake main city is such a charmer that you might not be able to tear yourself away to the countryside. Conversely (perversely?), the wild and beautiful Aran Islands and Connemara Peninsula might keep you captive such that you'll never have time for the city. What to do? Both, of course!

Galway city is a swirl of enticing old pubs that hum with trad music sessions throughout the year. More importantly, it has an overlaying vibe of fun and frolic that can't help but amuse. Hop aboard for a thrilling ride. Its setting on the wide, tidal bay and the tiny atmospheric fishing villages to the south are bonuses.

Offshore, the eroded, sheer swaths of land known as the Aran Islands have a desolate, windswept aura that entrances. Tiny villages cling to the rocks while soft-hearted locals welcome their modern lifeblood: visitors. Dún Aengus, a mysterious 2000-year-old fortress, evokes an Ireland utterly alien to the clichéd one of merry mirth makers in treacly pubs.

North of Galway city, the Connemara Peninsula matches the beauty of the other Atlantic outcrops to the south, like Dingle. Tiny roads wander along a coastline studded with islands, surprisingly white beaches and intriguing old villages with views over it all. This is the place to don the hiking boots and take to the well-marked network of trails that wander through lonely valleys and past hidden lakes before ending at sprays of surf at the Atlantic.

COUNTY GALWAY

HIGHLIGHTS

- **Go Crawling** Sample Galway city's array of atmospheric pubs (p400)
- **Start Shelling** Enjoy oysters direct from the bay at iconic oyster restaurants in Clarinbridge and Kilcolgan (p423)
- **Get Stoned** Ponder the people who built the enigmatic fort Dún Aengus on Inishmór (p404)
- **Go with the Flow** Marvel at the range of life in Kilkieran Bay (p414)
- **Pound Sand** Frolic on postcard-perfect Glassillaun Beach on Connemara's north coast (p422)

- POPULATION: 210,000
- AREA: 3760 SQ KM

GALWAY CITY

pop 72,400

Arty, bohemian Galway (Gaillimh) is renowned for its entertainment scene. Brightly painted pubs heave with live music, while cafes offer front-row seats from which to observe all manner of street performers.

Steeped in history, the city nonetheless has a contemporary vibe. Students make up a quarter of its population, and remnants of the medieval town walls lie between shops selling Aran sweaters, handcrafted Claddagh rings, and stacks of second-hand and new books. Bridges arc over the salmon-filled River Corrib, and a long promenade leads to the seaside suburb of Salthill, on Galway Bay, the source of the area's famous oysters.

Galway is a very rainy city, even by Irish standards, and water can play a major role in your visit here, whether you're dodging it from the skies, walking along the bayshore or exploring paths along the river, creeks and canals.

In 2009 Galway cast off the economic malaise when it hosted a stop on the Volvo Ocean Race. For two weeks it was a sort of Celtic Monaco, as enormous globe-trotting yachts and accompanying glitterati invaded the city. Besides spending lots of cash, the visitors inspired a general clean-up around town, including the removal of some eyesore oil tanks near the gentrifying harbour.

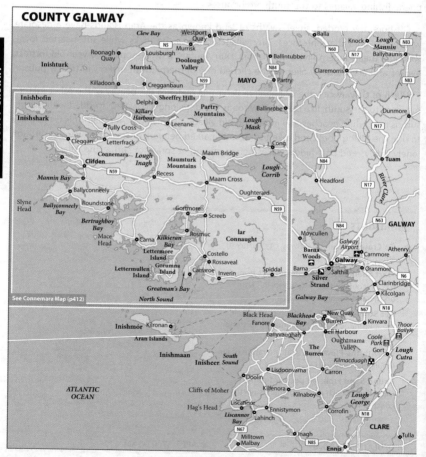

COUNTY GALWAY

Galway is often referred to as the 'most Irish' of Ireland's cities (and it's the only one where you're likely to hear Irish spoken in the streets, shops and pubs), but some locals lament that these may be the last days of 'old' Galway before it, too, becomes globalised. Still, if you ask a local what they're doing next Tuesday, they will look at you puzzled, knowing that anything can happen between now and then.

HISTORY

Galway's Irish name, Gaillimh, originates from the Irish word *gaill,* meaning 'outsiders' or 'foreigners', and the term resonates throughout the city's history.

From humble beginnings as a tiny fishing village at the mouth of the River Corrib, it

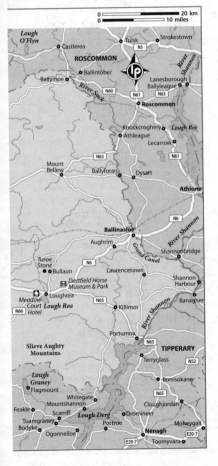

grew into an important town when the Anglo-Normans, under Richard de Burgo (also spelled de Burgh or Burke), captured territory from the local O'Flahertys in 1232. Its fortified walls were built from around 1270.

In 1396 Richard II granted a charter transferring power from the de Burgos to 14 merchant families or 'tribes' – hence Galway's enduring nickname: City of the Tribes. (Each of the city's roundabouts is named for the one of the tribes.) These powerful, mostly English or Norman families clashed frequently with the leading Irish families of Connemara.

A massive fire in 1473 destroyed much of the town but created space for a new street layout, and many solid stone buildings were erected in the 15th and 16th centuries.

Galway maintained its independent status under the ruling merchant families, who were mostly loyal to the English Crown. Its coastal location encouraged a huge trade in wine, spices, fish and salt with Portugal and Spain, rivalling London in the volume of goods passing through its docks. Its support of the Crown, however, led to its downfall; the city was besieged by Cromwell in 1651 and fell the following year. In 1691 William of Orange's militia added to the destruction. Trade with Spain declined and, with Dublin and Waterford taking most sea traffic, Galway stagnated for centuries.

The early 1900s saw Galway's revival as tourists returned to the city and student numbers grew. In 1934 the cobbled streets and thatched cabins of Claddagh were tarred and flattened to make way for modern, hygienic buildings, and construction has boomed since.

Galway's population has grown rapidly – as those estates you see on the outskirts attest – and it is among the fastest-growing cities in Europe.

ORIENTATION

Galway's compact town centre straddles Europe's shortest river, the Corrib, which connects Lough Corrib to the sea. Most shops and services congregate on the river's eastern bank, while some of the city's best music pubs and restaurants are huddled to its west. From this area, known locally as the West Side, a 10-minute walk leads you out to the beginning of the seaside suburb of Salthill.

Running west from grassy Eyre Sq, the city's pedestrianised primary shopping street starts as Williamsgate St, becomes William St and

COUNTY GALWAY

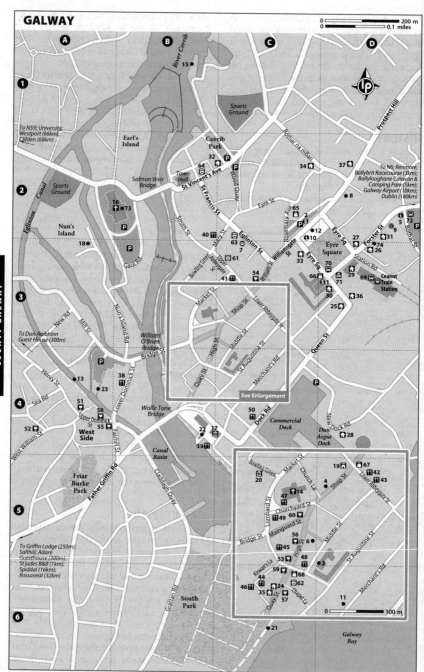

then Shop St, before forking into Mainguard St and High St. Just east of Eyre Sq is the combined bus and train station, half a block northeast of which is the main tourist office.

INFORMATION

Bookshops

Charlie Byrne's (☎ 091-561 766; Cornstore, Middle St) Brilliant collection of second-hand and discounted books (many €1) in a succession of rambling rooms.

Eason's (☎ 091-562 284; Shop St) Superstore with a large selection of travel guides and Galway's biggest periodicals rack.

Internet Access

A plethora of internet cafes around town charge around €5 per hour. Places open up and close down quickly, but you'll have no problems finding somewhere to log on.

Square Eyes (☎ 091-500 688; Forster St; ☯ noon-midnight) Internet access upstairs, Call of Duty grunts downstairs.

Laundry

Olde Malt Laundrette (☎ 091-564 990; High St; drop-off service per load €10; ☯ 8.30am-6pm Mon-Sat).

Prospect Hill Laundrette (☎ 091-568 343; Prospect Hill; self-service per load €7; ☯ 8am-7pm Mon-Sat).

Left Luggage

The transport stations are locker free, but there is a central refuge for your bags while you hunt for a room.

Cara Cabs (☎ 091-563 939; 17 Eyre Sq; ☯ 24hr) Taxi office stores bags for €5 per day.

Money

Irish banks with ATMs abound in the city centre.

AIB (Lynch's Castle, cnr Shop & Upper Abbeygate Sts)
Bank of Ireland (Eyre Sq) Two branches on the square.

Post Office

Post office (☯ 9am-5.30pm Mon-Sat) Also changes money.

Tourist Information

Ireland West Tourism (☎ 091-537 700; www .discoverireland.ie/west; Forster St; ☯ 9am-5.45pm daily Easter-Sep, 9am-5.45pm Mon-Sat Oct-Easter) Large, efficient information centre that can help arrange local accommodation, and regional bus tours and ferry trips.

INFORMATION		
AIB Bank	(see 19)	
Bank of Ireland	1	D3
Bank of Ireland	2	C2
Charlie Byrne's	3	D5
Eason's	4	D5
Ireland West Tourism	5	D2
Olde Malt Laundrette	6	C5
Post Office	7	C3
Prospect Hill Laundrette	8	D2
Square Eyes	9	D2
Tourist Information Booth	10	C2

SIGHTS & ACTIVITIES		
Bold Art Gallery	11	D6
Browne's Doorway	12	C2
Canal Locks	13	A4
Collegiate Church of St Nicholas of Myra	14	C5
Corrib Princess	15	B1
Galway Cathedral	16	B2
Galway City Museum	17	C4
Galway Fisheries	18	A3
Lynch's Castle	19	D5
Nora Barnacle House	20	C5
Prom	21	C6
Spanish Arch	22	B4
Wee Little Stone Bridge	23	A4

SLEEPING		
Barnacle's Quay Street House	24	C6
Claddagh Hostel	25	D3
Galway City Hostel	26	D3
Garvey's Inn	27	D3
Harbour Hotel	28	D4
Hotel Meyrick	29	D3
Kinlay House	30	D3
Park House Hotel	31	D2
Salmon Weir Hostel	32	C2
Skeffington Arms Hotel	33	C3
Sleepzone	34	C2
Spanish Arch Hotel	35	C6
Victoria Hotel	36	D3
Western Hotel	37	D2

EATING		
Abalone Restaurant	38	B4
Ard Bia & Nimmo's	39	B4
Asian Tea House	40	B2
Finnegan's	41	C3
Food 4 Thought	42	D5
Gourmet Tart Co	43	D5
Goya's	44	C6
Kettle of Fish	45	C5
Kirwan's Lane Restaurant	46	C6
Market	47	C5
McDonagh's	(see 35)	
Mustard	48	C5
Quays	(see 57)	
Sheridans Cheesemongers	49	C5
Sheridans on the Docks	50	C4

DRINKING		
Bar No 8	(see 50)	
Bierhaus	51	A4
Crane Bar	52	A4
Front Door	53	C5
Garavan's	54	C3
Monroe's Tavern	55	A4
Murphy's	56	C5
Quays	57	C5
Róisín Dubh	58	A4
Séhán Ua Neáchtain	59	C6
Tig Coílí	60	C5

ENTERTAINMENT		
Central Park	61	C3
Druid Theatre	62	C6
GPO	63	C2
Town Hall Theatre	64	B2

SHOPPING		
Corrib Shopping Centre	65	C2
Eyre Square Centre	66	D3
Kiernan Molony Musical Instruments	(see 6)	
P Powell & Sons	67	D5
Thomas Dillon's Claddagh Gold	68	C6

TRANSPORT		
Bus Station	69	D3
Buses to Salthill	70	D3
Cara Cabs	71	D3
Coach Station	72	D2
Europa Bicycles	73	B2
Island Ferries Office	74	D3

COUNTY GALWAY

ADVICE FROM A COLUMNIST

Every week readers of Galway's *Tribune* newspaper turn to Carlie Adley's column about life and much more in the city and the region. An unabashed fan of the place, Adley's heart still had to be won over originally. He came to Galway 17 years ago after a life in London, San Francisco and elsewhere. He hasn't looked back.

'The city centre is the perfect size for walking around, chilling out and bumping into people', he says from one of his favourite pubs, Séhán Ua Neáchtain's (p400), where he often has his afternoon office, watching the world go by while a movable feast of friends comes and goes.

Later, after the pub? 'Who knows – Galwegians don't make plans. The perfect Galway day is one that takes its own shape.'

Adley's perfect day includes 'sitting on a rock on the beach at Salthill; watching the tide turn; looking out at the ocean and trying to spot one of the Aran Islands; just being calm; and appreciating the volatile light and weather, which truly offer a different view across to County Clare every day of the year.'

Visitors looking for the real Galway, he says, need to do the above, plus 'do the pubs and music and you can't go wrong. Galwegians will reach out to you and have a chat; the craic awaits.'

Tourist Information Booth (Eyre Sq; 1.30-5.30pm Sun Oct-Easter, 9am-5.30pm daily Easter-Sep) Operated by the main tourist office, it dispenses free city maps and local info.

SIGHTS & ACTIVITIES
Collegiate Church of St Nicholas of Myra

Crowned by a pyramidal spire, the **Collegiate Church of St Nicholas of Myra** (091-564 648; Market St; admission by donation; 9am-5.45pm Mon-Sat, 1-5pm Sun Apr-Sep, 10am-4pm Mon-Sat, 1-5pm Sun Oct-Mar) is Ireland's largest medieval parish church still in use. Dating from 1320, the church has been rebuilt and enlarged over the centuries, though much of the original form has been retained.

Christopher Columbus reputedly worshipped here in 1477. One theory suggests that the story of Columbus' visit to Galway arose from tales of St Brendan's 6th-century voyage to America (see p425). Seafaring has long been associated with the church – St Nicholas, for whom it's named, is the patron saint of sailors.

After Cromwell's victory, the church was used as a stable, and damaged stonework is still visible today. But St Nicholas was relatively fortunate: 14 other Galway churches were razed entirely.

Parts of the church's floor are paved with gravestones from the 16th to 18th centuries; the Lynch Aisle holds the tombs of that illustrious Galway family. A large block tomb in one corner is said to be the grave of James Lynch, a mayor of Galway in the late 15th century, who condemned his son Walter to death for killing a young Spanish visitor. As

the tale goes, none of the townsfolk would serve as executioner, so the mayor personally acted as hangman, after which he went into seclusion. Outside on Market St is a stone plaque on the **Lynch Memorial Window**, which relates this legend and claims to be the spot where the gallows stood.

The two church bells date from 1590 and 1630.

Lynch's Castle

Considered the finest town castle in Ireland, the old stone town house **Lynch's Castle** (cnr Shop & Upper Abbeygate Sts; admission free) was built in the 14th century, though much of what you see today dates from around 1600. The Lynch family was the most powerful of the 14 ruling Galway 'tribes', and its members held the position of mayor no fewer than 80 times between 1480 and 1650.

Stonework on the castle's facade includes ghoulish gargoyles and the coats of arms of Henry VII, the Lynches and the Fitzgeralds of Kildare. The castle is now a branch of the AIB Bank, and you can peer into its old fireplace while withdrawing money from the foyer's ATMs.

Spanish Arch & Medieval Walls

Framing the river east of Wolfe Tone Bridge, the Spanish Arch (1584) is thought to be an extension of Galway's medieval walls. The arch appears to have been designed as a passageway through which ships entered the city to unload goods, such as wine and brandy from Spain.

Today it reverberates to the beat of bongo drums, and the lawns and riverside form a gathering place for locals and visitors on any sunny day. Many watch kayakers manoeuvre over the minor rapids of River Corrib.

Although a 1651 drawing of Galway clearly shows its extensive fortifications, depredation by Cromwell and William of Orange and subsequent centuries of neglect saw the walls almost completely disappear. Another surviving portion has been artfully incorporated into the modern shopping mall, Eyre Square Centre, complete with a **tarot-card reader** (☎ 091-556 826; ☙ by appointment) installed in the basement of a former turret.

Galway City Museum

Adjacent to the Spanish Arch, the **Galway City Museum** (☎ 091-567 641; Spanish Pde; admission free; ☙ 10am-5pm Apr-Oct, closed Mon Nov-Mar) is in a glossy, glassy building that reflects the old walls. Exhibits trace aspects of daily life through Galway's history; especially good are the areas dealing with life – smelly and otherwise – during medieval times. When the roof is open, there are sweeping views out to the bay.

Galway Cathedral

Lording over the River Corrib, imposing **Galway Cathedral** (☎ 091-563 577; www.galwaycathedral.org; Gaol Rd; admission by donation; ☙ 8am-6pm) was dedicated by the late Cardinal Richard Cushing of Boston in 1965. The cathedral's unwieldy full name is the Catholic Cathedral of Our Lady Assumed into Heaven and St Nicholas, but its high, curved arches and central dome make a simple, solid elegance, as well as superb acoustics that are best appreciated during an **organ recital**. Program dates are posted on the website.

From the Spanish Arch, a riverside path runs upriver and across the Salmon Weir Bridge to the cathedral.

Eyre Square

Galway's central public square is busy in all but the harshest weather. It's a welcome open green space with sculptures and pathways. Its lawns are formally named Kennedy Park in commemoration of President John F Kennedy's 1963 visit to Galway, though you'll rarely, if ever, hear locals refer to it as anything but Eyre Square.

The street running along the southwestern side of the square is pedestrianised and lined with seating, while the eastern side is taken up almost entirely by the Hotel Meyrick (formerly the Great Southern Hotel), an elegant grey limestone pile restored to its Victorian glory. Guarding the upper side of the square, **Browne's Doorway** (1627), a classy, if forlorn, fragment from the home of one of the city's merchant rulers, looks like the remains from a carpet-bombing raid (at least the English can't be blamed for this…).

Salmon Weir

Upstream from Salmon Weir Bridge, which crosses the River Corrib just east of the cathedral, the river cascades down the great weir, one of its final descents before reaching Galway Bay. The weir controls the water levels above it, and when the salmon are running you can often see shoals of them waiting in the clear waters before rushing upriver to spawn.

The salmon and sea-trout seasons usually span February to September, but most fish pass through the weir during May and June. To obtain fishing permits and book a time, contact the manager at **Galway Fisheries** (☎ 091-562 388; www.wrfb.ie; Nun's Island). A half-day's fishing costs as little as €18.

Bold Art Gallery

There's never a dull moment at the effervescent modern art **gallery** (☎ 091-539 900; www.boldartgallery.com; Merchant's Rd; ☙ 9.30am-6pm Mon-Sat), which seems to have a bottomless pit of inspiration when it comes to wit. Works vary between the profane, the beautiful and the moving but are never mundane. The owner

---

A PERFECT SPOT

A fine footpath runs northwest along the Eglington Canal from the Lower Dominick St Bridge. Passing behind several of Galway's better pubs (nod to the smokers who have ducked out back), the path makes a gentle climb. Look to your right for the spot where two creeks enter the canal, a larger one and a very tiny one. Over the small one is a **wee little stone bridge** that could be the artefact of some leprechaun fantasy or a leftover from a John Ford film. With the water burbling in all directions – and cascading through the **canal locks** just upstream – it's a spot where the sounds of Galway are literally washed away, leaving you to your own contemplation.

GALWAY HOOKERS

Obvious jokes aside, Galway hookers are the iconic small sailing boats that were the basis of local seafaring during the 19th century and part of the 20th century. Small, tough and highly manoeuvrable, these wooden boats are undergoing a resurgence thanks to weekend sailors and hobbyists. The hulls are jet black, due to the pitch used for waterproofing, while the sails flying from the single mast are a distinctive rust colour. Expect to see them all along the Galway coast.

is a fountain of local knowledge; ask to see the card showing what happens before and after you drink Guinness.

Nora Barnacle House

James Joyce courted his future wife Nora Barnacle (1884–1951) at this little **house** (☎ 091-564 743; www.norabarnacle.com; 8 Bowling Green), beginning in 1909. It's now a privately owned museum displaying the couple's letters and photographs among evocatively arranged furniture. Hours are erratic; call ahead or check with the tourist office. Expect to pay around €3 admission.

Salthill

A favourite pastime for Galwegians and visitors alike is walking along the **Prom**, the seaside promenade running from the edge of the city along Salthill. Local tradition dictates 'kicking the wall' across from the diving boards (a 2.5km stroll from town starting at the Wolfe Tone Bridge and following the shoreline path) before turning around. At the time of writing, plans were under way to extend the Prom all the way from Salthill to Silver Strand – about 7.5km all up.

In and around Salthill are plenty of cosy pubs from where you can watch storms roll over the bay. Between May and September, you can also catch the traditional Irish dance and music spectacular, **Trad on the Prom** (☎ 087 238 8489; www .tradontheprom.com; Salt Hill Hotel). The website posts show times and ticket information including various dinner-and-show packages.

TOURS

If you're short on time, bus tours departing from Galway are a good way to see Connemara, the Burren or the Cliffs of Moher, while boat

tours take you to the heart of Lough Corrib. Tours can be booked directly or at the tourist office.

Burren Wild Tours (☎ 087 877 9565; www.burren walks.com; adult/student €25/22) Seasonal bus tours to the Burren and the Cliffs of Moher incorporating an easy 90-minute guided mountain walk.

Corrib Princess (☎ 091-592 447; www.corribprincess .ie; Woodquay; adult/child €16/8; ☼ May-Sep) Two to three 1½-hour cruises on the River Corrib and Lough Corrib per day, departing from Woodquay, just beyond Salmon Weir Bridge.

Lally Coaches (☎ 091-562 905; www.lallytours.com; adult/child €23/14) Entertaining, informative bus tours of Connemara, or the Burren and the Cliffs of Moher with local guides.

O'Neachtain Tours (☎ 091-553 188; www.ontours.biz; adult/child €25/15) Runs coach tours of Connemara, or the Burren and the Cliffs of Moher.

SLEEPING

You'll find B&Bs lining the major approach roads, including many in Salthill, but to take full advantage of Galway's tightly packed attractions, try for a room in the city centre. If you're planning to stay in Galway for an extended period, Wednesday's edition of the free *Galway Advertiser* (www.galway advertiser.ie) lists rental properties.

Galway's festivals (opposite) and easy striking distance from Dublin make it *hugely* popular year-round, especially at weekends. Accommodation often fills far in advance – book ahead!

Most of our accommodation recommendations have private parking or offer discounted parking at nearby car parks. Enquire when you book.

Budget

Galway's many hostels all offer discounted bookings on tours and activities.

Salmon Weir Hostel (☎ 091-561 133; www.salmon weirhostel.com; 3 St Vincent's Ave; dm €14-20, d €44-50; ☐) Galway's hippie vibe finds its spiritual home in the Salmon Weir's guitar-strewn lounge room, where informal jam sessions take place most nights. The hostel has a share-house feel, including shared bathrooms for all rooms. There's no breakfast, although coffee and tea are free. The train and bus stations are a five-minute walk away.

Ballyloughane Caravan & Camping Park (☎ 091-755 338; galwcamp@iol.ie; Ballyloughane Beach, Renmore; campsites from €15; ☼ Jun-Aug) This family-run

COUNTY GALWAY

camping ground is clean and secure, and its beachside location affords sweeping views across the bay. It's off the Dublin road (N6), 5km from Galway.

Galway City Hostel (☎ 091-566 959; www.galwaycityhostel.com; Eyre Sq; dm €19-26, d €50-80; 💻 🛜) This cheery spot directly across from the train station is so close you may just wander over barefoot. Recently renovated, on balmy days (by Galway standards) you can take your breakfast cereal out onto the balcony. Reception is open 24/7.

our pick Kinlay House (☎ 091-565 244; www.kinlayhouse.ie; Merchant's Rd; dm €19-30, d €60-70; 💻 🛜) Easygoing staff, a full range of facilities and a cream-in-the-donut location just off Eyre Sq make this a top choice. Spanning two huge, brightly lit floors, Kinlay House belies the dirty powder-blue exterior. Amenities include two self-catering kitchens and two cosy TV lounges.

Other recommendations:

Sleepzone (☎ 091-566 999; www.sleepzone.ie; Bóthar na mBan; dm €13-28, d €52-76; 💻 🛜) Big (over 200 beds), busy backpacker base has plenty of services, including a pool table and BBQ terrace. Party-goers beware: no alcohol is allowed on the premises. Reception is open 24/7.

Claddagh Hostel (☎ 091-533 555; www.claddaghhostelgalway.com; Queen St; dm €15-30, d €60-80; 💻 🛜) Small, central multilevel terrace house with glassed-in lounge-cum-TV-room. You can rent bikes.

Barnacle's Quay Street House (☎ 091-568 644; www.barnacles.ie; 10 Quay St; dm €15-40, d €64-98; 💻 🛜) Very central, this well-run hostel is housed in a medieval building with a modern extension. The kitchen is spacious and there's a warm common room with a big gas fireplace. Breakfast includes scones and soda bread.

Midrange

Griffin Lodge (☎ 091-589 440; www.irishholidays.com/griffin.shtml; 3 Father Griffin Pl; s €45-60, d €55-80; 🅿 💻) You'll be welcomed like a long-lost friend at this completely renovated B&B, which has eight immaculate rooms in soothing shades of spearmint and moss green. Frills are kept to a minimum, with just a few elegant framed prints and crocheted cotton bedspreads.

Dun Aoibhinn Guest House (☎ 091-583 129; www.dunaoibhinnhouse.com; 12 St Mary's Rd; r €50-120; 🅿 💻 🛜) Pronounced doon-*ay*-ven, this restored town house with original leadlight windows and floorboards is less than five minutes' stroll from the West Side's music pubs. Small antique-filled rooms come with flat-screen satellite TVs, laptop safes and fridges, which are filled with the fixings for making your own continental breakfast.

St Judes B&B (☎ 091-521 619; www.st-judes.com; 110 Lower Salthill; r €50-120; 🅿 💻) You may want to hire a butler to accompany you when you stay at this stone manor house that has the airs of a stately Wayne Manor. The six rooms

---

AND THE FUN NEVER ENDS

Galway's packed calendar of festivals turns the city and surrounding communities into what feels like one nonstop party – streets overflow with revellers, and pubs and restaurants often extend their opening hours.

Highlights include the following:

Cúirt International Festival of Literature (☎ 091-565 886; www.galwayartscentre.ie/cuirt) Top-name authors converge on Galway in April for Ireland's premier literary festival, featuring poetry slams, theatrical performances and readings.

Galway Arts Festival (☎ 091-566 700; www.galwayartsfestival.ie) A two-week extravaganza of theatre, music, art and comedy in mid-July.

Galway Film Fleadh (☎ 091-751 655; www.galwayfilmfleadh.com) One of Ireland's biggest film festivals, held in July around the same time as the arts festival.

Galway International Oyster Festival (☎ 091-522 066; www.galwayoysterfest.com) Oysters are washed down with plenty of pints in the last week in September.

Galway Race Week (☎ 091-753 870; www.galwayraces.com) Horse races in Ballybrit, 3km east of the city, are the centrepiece of Galway's biggest, most boisterous festival of all. Thursday is a real knees-up: by night the swells have muddy knees on their tuxes and are missing random high heels. The week occurs in late July or early August.

Also see p423 for information on Galway hooker boat races, p423 for more oyster-related events, p411 for bodhrán (hand-held goatskin drum) workshops and p406 for the Aran Islands' rollicking *Father Ted* festival, Tedfest.

are much more the accommodation for the masses, however. Furnishings are comfy and very, very white. It's located in Salthill, a lovely 15-minute stroll (follow the Prom) from Galway.

Adare Guesthouse (☎ 091-582 638; www.adarebedand breakfast.com; 9 Father Griffin Pl; s €55-65, d €100-110; ⊚) Overlooking a football pitch and children's playground, this barn-style place has 10 generously sized rooms and service that runs like clockwork. Sift through a dozen menu choices at breakfast including French toast, pancakes, smoked salmon and various combos of black sausage.

ourpick Skeffington Arms Hotel (☎ 091-563 173; www.skeffington.ie; Eyre Sq; r €75-190; 🔀 🖳 ⊚) Rooms at the Skeff, overlooking Eyre Sq, eschew the frilly cliché. In fact the only lace you may find in any of the 24 rooms is on your underwear. Pass through the arched traditional entrance into a minimalist haven. Air-con allows early risers to cut out noise from the frolicsome masses roaming the streets on long summer nights.

Garvey's Inn (☎ 091-562 224; www.garveysinn.com; Eyre Sq; r €80-200; 🖳) Set over an authentic timber pub dating from 1861, this comfortable family-owned hotel lords over Eyre Sq. Walk 10 minutes in any direction and you'll pass a week's worth of fun. The modern rooms have plenty of hotel amenities, like irons and trouser presses. Enjoy!

Western Hotel (☎ 091-562 834; www.thewestern.ie; 33 Prospect Hill; r €80-200; 🅿 🖳 ⊚) Three Georgian buildings have been wedded at this central spot just east of Eyre Sq. The 38 rooms are large, modern and comfortable and there's parking in the basement. Good-sized desks await the work encumbered. The full-on breakfasts are above the always-filling average.

Victoria Hotel (☎ 091-567 433; www.byrnehotels.com; Eyre Sq; r €90-250; 🖳 ⊚) Just down a slight hill from Eyre Sq, the Victoria is a sedate choice for those who want something more anonymous than a B&B. The 57 rooms are mostly bright and have a generic decor. Service is excellent, with most guests' needs readily accommodated.

Spanish Arch Hotel (☎ 091-569 600; www.spanish archhotel.ie; Quay St; r €95-150; 🖳) In a sensational spot on the main drag, this 20-room boutique hotel is housed in a 16th-century former Carmelite convent. Its solid-timber bar has a great line-up of live music, so the rooms at the back, while smaller, are best for a quiet night's sleep. Among the amenities is room service from the restaurant.

Top End

Park House Hotel (☎ 091-564 924; www.parkhousehote .ie; Forster St; r €100-250; 🅿 🔀 🖳 ⊚) Housed in an old farm-feed wholesale warehouse, this hotel offers 84 guest rooms and a sumptuous lobby stuffed with embroidered armchairs. When the lights are out, you won't see the rust-red colour scheme that seems to be employed in half of Ireland's hotel rooms. Air-con muffles exterior noise.

Harbour Hotel (☎ 091-569 466; www.harbour.ie; New Dock Rd; r €100-350; 🅿 🖳 ⊚) Now that Galway is spiffing up its once workman-filled harbour area, you might as well enjoy the view. This modern hotel with 96 rooms is right down near the tidal zone; many rooms let you gaze out over the vast tidal flats at low tide. Should you overdo it on the local oysters, you can restore yourself in the steam room, gym and hot tub.

Hotel Meyrick (☎ 091-564 041; www.hotelmeyrick.ie; Eyre Sq; r €165-250; 🅿 🖳) Known as the Railway Hotel when it opened in 1852, and later as the Great Southern Hotel, this stately showpiece looms large over Eyre Sq. A massive renovation artfully combines traditional decor with savvy modern touches. Note the zebra prints on the lobby chairs. Definitely not original equipment: the rooftop hot tub. All 97 guest rooms include bath-tubs and high-speed internet.

EATING

Seafood is Galway's speciality, be it fish and chips, ocean-fresh chowder or sea bass cooked to perfection. Galway Bay oysters are also found locally. The city's smorgasbord of eating and drinking options ranges from the market – where farmers in wellington boots unload soil-covered vegetables – to adventurous new restaurants redefining Irish cuisine.

Pedestrianised Quay St is lined with restaurants aimed at the tourist throngs. As one local told us, 'I can remember when all you'd get on Quay St was a hard biscuit, then you'd get run down by a bus.'

Restaurants

Ard Bia & Nimmo's (☎ 091-539 897; www.ardbia.com; Spanish Arch; cafe dishes €6-12, lunch mains €10-14, dinner mains €16-30; ⊙ cafe noon-3pm Wed-Sun, restaurant 6.30-10.30pm Wed-Sat) In Irish, Ard Bia means 'High 'ood', and that's somewhat apt, given the ocation in the 18th-century customs house near the Spanish Arch. Local seafood and organic produce feature on the seasonal menu. Nimmo's, on the ground floor, is funkier and has a North African bent.

Mustard (☎ 091-532 752; Bridge Mills; mains €8-12; noon-10pm) In the cellar of an old mill, some tables view the still-turning wheel. Burgers and excellent pizza are the thing here. Go nuts and have the Boxty Burger, a vegetarian treat made from mashed potatoes, green onions and more. Be sure to start with the 'garlic crust', which comes with pesto. Yum.

McDonagh's (☎ 091-565 001; 22 Quay St; fish & chips from €8, restaurant mains €15-25; cafe & takeaway counter noon-midnight Mon-Sat, 5-11pm Sun, restaurant 5-10pm Mon-Sat) A trip to Galway isn't complete without stopping at McDonagh's (something even locals confirm – we heard one exclaim happily, 'I haven't been here in years!'). Divided into two parts, with a takeaway counter and a cafe with long communal wooden tables on one side, and a more upmarket restaurant on the other, Galway's best chippy churns out battered cod, plaice, haddock, whiting and salmon nonstop, all accompanied by homemade tartare sauce.

Finnegan's (☎ 091-564 764; 2 Market St; mains €10; 9am-10pm Mon-Sat, 11am-10pm Sun) Organic, schmorganic. A haven for the masses, Finnegan's warms the soul with timeless comfort food like homemade shepherd's pie. Look for trad standards like Irish stew, roast chicken and all-day Irish breakfasts. Rub elbows with your bus driver and find out the tricks of the trade.

Kirwan's Lane Restaurant (☎ 091-568 266; Kirwan's Lane; lunch mains €10-18, dinner mains €18-30; noon-2pm & 6-10pm) Happily hidden on a tiny square within steps of several busy streets, Kirwan's is not only a refuge but also a heaven for those seeking out the best of local cuisine. The menu proudly lists the provenance of the ingredients used in a variety of creative dishes. On sunny days, get a patio table at lunch.

Quays (☎ 091-568 347; Quay St; mains €12-25; 11am-10pm) This sprawling pub does a roaring business downstairs in its restaurant, which has hearty carvery lunches and more ambitious mains at night. The cold seafood platter is simply a symphony of the bounty from Galway Bay. Students on dates and out celebrating get rowdier as the pints and hours pass.

Asian Tea House (☎ 091-563 749; 13 Mary St; mains €15-25; 5pm-10pm) A stylish addition to Galway's dining scene, this upscale Asian restaurant reflects the owner's years of Eastern travels. Beautiful glazed green tiles set the mood for dishes that range from Malaysia to Vietnam to China. We like the Malaysian sambal chicken, which scores the highest on the hot meter – a rare treat in tongue-sensitive Ireland.

ourpick Sheridans on the Docks (☎ 091-566 905; 3 Dock Rd; mains €17-26; 6.30-10.30pm Tue-Sat) From the talented team behind Sheridans Cheesemongers (p400) comes this excellent restaurant in a vintage stone building overlooking the harbour. The menu changes regularly, but dishes, such as cockle beignets, wild sea bass with purple sprouted broccoli and baked rhubarb, celebrate the best of locally produced foods. In winter (October to April) get a table by the fireplace. Bar No 8 downstairs (p401) is a welcoming pub.

Abalone Restaurant (☎ 091-534 895; 53 Lower Dominick St; mains €20-30; 6-10pm) Just over the bridge from the buzzy heart of Galway, Abalone already feels more relaxed. There's very fine dining in this tiny yet elegant storefront. As you'd expect from the name, seafood is the star here, but you'll also find vegetarian treats, steaks and various global mains.

Cafes

Food 4 Thought (☎ 091-565 854; Lower Abbeygate St; mains €5-7; 8am-6pm Mon-Sat, 11.30am-4pm Sun) Besides providing organic and vegetarian sandwiches, savoury scones, and wholesome dishes such as cashew-nut roast, this New Age-y place is great for finding out about energy workshops and yoga classes around town. (And feel free to cheat – the BLT is excellent.)

Kettle of Fish (☎ 091-569 881; 4 Upper Cross St; mains from €5; 11am-late) A New Age chipper that boasts of its line-caught fish, including salmon. The sides border on the artful, which is fitting given the lovely sea-foam-green interior. Though many weekend patrons fail to appreciate the niceties, they crowd in until 4am.

Goya's (☎ 091-567 010; 2 Kirwan's Lane; dishes €5-10; 9.30am-6pm Mon-Sat) Cupcake love! Cakes in all sizes are supreme at Goya's, a Galway treasure hidden on a small square. Its cool pale-blue decor, Segafredo coffee and sweet treats make it a perfect spot to take some time out. The deli does a booming lunch trade; enjoy a sandwich at a table outside.

HOPPY SALVATION

Irish pubs may be atmospheric places to enjoy a pint and, indeed, many folks fly thousands of miles to sit in a little nook happily quaffing a properly poured creamy Guinness. But once past the stout, things go flat in a hurry. In pub after pub the non-Guinness choices amount to a sad array of bland lagers. What did the Irish ever do to America besides send it some of their finest citizens? In return America has sent the Irish Budweiser, Miller Genuine Draft (MGD) and, horror of horrors, Coors Light. The Dutch haven't done much better by the Emerald Isle, exporting untold hectolitres of Heineken, a beer that inspired a Dutch friend to ask us, 'why do you drink our old man's beer?'

But if the beer situation in much of the country is bleak (what the hell happened to Harp?), in Galway there's an alternative to the lame lagers: Hooker. Named for the iconic local fishing boats, this fine ale is the creation of two cousins, Ronan Brennan and Aidan Murphy (their mothers are identical twins). Providing a local beer for those not wanting a Guinness was a challenge. 'Eventually we found an existing brewery, which had been dormant for five years and needed to be completely recommissioned, including new machinery, which meant a lot of begging, borrowing and stealing', recalls Brennan.

The pair's brew, a tasty pale ale, has won plaudits and, more importantly, a local following. 'We're putting the flavour in the way it's meant to be. There's a love of good beer in this country, but a lack of variety. People are slow to change their drinking habits. We were careful which pubs we put it into – places where people are open-minded and it didn't outlast its keg life [about a month]', notes Murphy.

Ask for a Hooker at pubs across Galway. Not only will you get a superior pint, but you'll earn the respect of the locals around you.

Self-Catering

Galway's **market** (8am-4pm Sat) fills the streets around St Nicholas Church. It's one of the region's best and is the place to see the many briny, earthy and dairy delights of the county.

our pick Gourmet Tart Co (☎ 091-588 384; Lower Abbeygate St; mains €5-10; 10am-5pm Mon-Sat) Food porn is an apt description for the stunning array of dishes on offer here in both the deli case and at the bounteous buffet bar. Luscious salads, salmon, beautiful sandwiches and, yes, tarts that give pastry a good name. It's all take out; enjoy your lunch on the grass by the Spanish Arch.

Sheridans Cheesemongers (☎ 091-564 829; 14 Churchyard St; 9.30am-6pm Mon-Fri, 9am-6pm Sat) Sheridans Cheesemongers is redolent of the superb local and international cheeses and other deli items within, many with a Med bent. Its real secret, however, is up a narrow flight of stairs. Sample from a huge wine list in an airy and woodsy room while enjoying many of the best items from below (open 2pm to 9pm Tuesday to Friday, noon to 8pm Saturday).

DRINKING

Galway's nickname of the City of Tribes sums up its drinking and entertainment scene. For its size the city has surprisingly distinct areas where you'll encounter different crowds: Eyre Sq and its surrounds tends to be the domain of retail and office workers and tourists; the main shopping strip draws hip young professionals; the Woodquay area, near Salmon Weir Bridge, is where salt-of-the-earth rural folk congregate when in town; and the West Side attracts creative types and musicians. Wherever you go, you'll enjoy pubs that are a cut above the norm. The website **Galway City Pub Guide** (www.galwaycitypubguide.com) is a good resource.

Most of Galway's pubs see musicians performing at least a couple of nights a week, whether in an informal session or as a headline act, and many swing to live music every night.

Séhán Ua Neáchtain (☎ 091-568 820; 17 Upper Cross St) Painted a bright cornflower blue, this 19th-century pub, known simply as Neáchtain's (*nock*-tans), has a wraparound string of tables outside, many shaded by a large tree. It's a place where locals plop down and let the world pass them by – or stop and join them for a pint.

Crane Bar (☎ 091-587 419; 2 Sea Rd) An atmospheric old pub west of the Corrib, the Crane is the best spot in Galway to catch an informal *céilidh* (session of traditional music and dancing) most nights. Talented bands play its rowdy, good-natured upstairs bar; downstairs at times it seems right out of *The Far Side.*

Róisín Dubh (☎ 091-586 540; Upper Dominick St) From the rooftop terrace you can see sweeping views of Galway; inside you can see emerging acts before they hit the big time.

Bar No 8 (☎ 091-565 111; 3 Dock Rd) Bentwood chairs and overstuffed sofas provide comfort in this at once funky and stylish bar overlooking the harbour. Art by patrons is on display; order from the long drinks list and debate the merits.

our pick **Tig Cóilí** (Mainguard St) Two live *céilidh* a day draw the crowds to this authentic fire-engine-red pub, just off High St. It's where musicians go to get drunk or drunks go to become musicians…or something like that. A gem.

Murphy's (☎ 091-564 589; 9 High St) A complete anomaly amongst the partying throngs in the centre, Murphy's is a timeless haven where locals still explore the limits of the art of conversation. The sign on the door says it all: 'No hen parties'.

Monroe's Tavern (☎ 091-583 397; Upper Dominick St) Often photographed for its classic, world-weary facade, Monroe's delivers traditional music and ballads, plus it remains the only pub in the city with regular Irish dancing. A pizza joint buried within turns out good pies.

Bierhaus (☎ 091-587 766; 2 Henry St; 🤶) The imported beer here won't insult your sensibilities. Good brews from across Europe are on offer along with Hooker. At night DJs provide a Euro beat.

Other good places:

Front Door (☎ 091-563 757; High St) Heated balconies and cosy timber booths make this a popular spot for a pint, especially among local women on the 'lap circuit' checking out the male talent.

Garavan's (☎ 091-562 537; 46 William St) A genteel old boozer in the city centre that is a place of refuge for those in search of a pint *and* a seat on a busy Saturday night.

Quays (☎ 091-568 347; Quay St) Enormous tavern with endless timber-panelled rooms and passageways, and great vantage points from which to watch live music (ranging from traditional to pop) most nights. Good sidewalk tables.

ENTERTAINMENT
Most pubs in Galway have live music at least a couple of nights a week. Thursday's edition of the free *Galway Advertiser* (www.galwayadvertiser.ie) lists what's on in the city. A new film centre is set to open near the Galway City Museum later in 2010.

Nightclubs
Clubs generally get cranking around 11pm and wind down around 2am. Admission prices vary according to the nightly program.

Central Park (☎ 091-565 976; www.centralparkclub.com; 36 Upper Abbeygate St; ⏰ 11pm-2am) With seven bars and a capacity of 1000 people, CPs is a Galway clubbing institution.

GPO (☎ 091-563 073; www.gpo.ie; 21 Eglinton St; admission €6-10) On Wednesday, GPO cranks out '80s and '90s tunes; the rest of the week, it's house, R&B, indie and hip hop. It's a favourite with students, who get free admission most nights.

Theatre
Druid Theatre (☎ 091-568 617; www.druidtheatre.com; Chapel Lane) This long-established theatre is famed for showing experimental works by young Irish playwrights, as well as new adaptations of classics. Its home is an old tea warehouse, which was renovated in 2009.

Town Hall Theatre (☎ 091-569 777; www.tht.ie; Courthouse Sq) The Town Hall Theatre features Broadway and West End shows, and visiting singers.

COUNTY GALWAY

CLADDAGH RINGS
The fishing village of Claddagh once had its own king as well as its own customs and traditions. Now subsumed into the Galway city centre, virtually all remnants of the original village are gone, but Claddagh rings survive as both a timeless reminder and a timeless source of profits.

Popular with people of real or imagined Irish descent everywhere, the rings depict a heart (symbolising love) between two outstretched hands (friendship), topped by a crown (loyalty). Rings are handcrafted at jewellers around Galway, and start from about €20 for a silver band to well over €1000 for a diamond-set blinged-up version worthy of Tony O'Soprano.

Jewellers include Ireland's oldest jewellery shop, **Thomas Dillon's Claddagh Gold** (☎ 091-566 365; www.claddaghring.ie; 1 Quay St), which was established in 1750. It has some vintage examples in its small back-room 'museum'.

SHOPPING

Galway has an array of speciality shops dotting its narrow streets, stocking cutting-edge fashion, Irish woollens (including Aran sweaters), outdoor clothing and equipment, local jewellery, art and, of course, music. Galway's market (p400) is not just about artisan foods. Artists of all sorts plus buskers, bakers and all-around schlock pedlars make it a festive event. At times stalls appear here on days other than Saturday.

P Powell & Sons (☎ 091-562 295; powellsmusicshop@ eircom.net; William St) You can pick up tin whistles, bodhráns and other instruments here, as well as sheet music. Backpackers note: they stock bongos.

Kiernan Molony Musical Instruments (☎ 091-566 488; Old Malt Centre, High St) Fiddles abound at this dealer in fine instruments. If your harp has come unglued, they'll fix it.

Besides the good street shopping, shopping centres include the **Eyre Square Centre**, with a large Dunne's supermarket, and **Corrib Shopping Centre**, a flashy modern place with huge department stores.

GETTING THERE & AWAY

Air

Service at **Galway airport** (GWY; ☎ 800 491 492; www .galwayairport.com; Carnmore) is limited to **Aer Arran** (www.aerarran.com), which serves London Luton, Edinburgh and Manchester.

The closest major airport is **Shannon Airport** (SNN; ☎ 061-712 000; www.shannonairport.com), served by domestic and international carriers including Ryanair. **Ireland West Airport** (NOC; ☎ 094-67222; www.irelandwestairport.com), in Knock, is also within easy reach of Galway.

Bus

Bus Éireann (www.buseireann.ie) has services to all major cities in the Republic and the North from the **bus station** (☎ 091-562 000) just off Eyre Sq, near the train station. The one-way fare to Dublin (3¾ hours) is €14.

Several private bus companies are based at the glossy new **coach station** (Bothar St), which is located near the tourist office. They include the following:

Citylink (☎ 1890 280 808; www.citylink.ie) Offers service to Dublin (3¼ hours), Dublin Airport, Cork, Limerick and Connemara. Departures are frequent and fares are as low as €10.

gobus.ie (☎ 091-564 600; www.gobus.ie) Frequent service to Dublin and Dublin Airport. Buses have wi-fi.

Train

From the **train station** (☎ 091-564 222), just off Eyre Sq, there are up to five trains daily to/ from Dublin's Heuston Station (one-way from €35, three hours). Connections with other train routes can be made at Athlone (one hour). In late 2009, it was expected that the line between Galway, Ennis and Limerick would be reopened after a massive rebuilding program.

GETTING AROUND

To/From the Airports

Bus service between Galway airport and Galway is comically useless, with just one or, at best, two buses a day (€3, 15 minutes). A taxi to/from the airport costs about €20, and can be ordered from a bank of free phones at the airport. Some B&Bs and hotels can arrange pick-up.

Bus Éireann (www.buseireann.ie) operates numerous daily services from Shannon Airport to Galway (€13.50, two hours). **Citylink** (www.city link.ie) also runs services between Galway and Shannon Airport (€15). Citylink and gobus. ie serve Dublin Airport.

Bicycle

On Earl's Island, opposite Galway Cathedral, **Europa Bicycles** (☎ 091-563 355; Hunter's Bldg; ☼ 9am-6pm Mon-Sat) hires bikes for €12 for 24 hours.

Bus

You can walk to almost everything in Galway, including out to Salthill, but you'll also find frequent buses departing from Eyre Sq. For Salthill, take bus 1 (€1.50, 15 minutes).

Car

Parking throughout Galway's streets is metered. There are several multistorey and pay-and-display car parks around town.

Galway's unprecedented growth and the resulting lack of infrastructure serving its urban sprawl means that traffic in and out of the city centre can bank up alarmingly. For a stress-free holiday, leave the roads to commuters at peak hours if possible.

Taxi

Taxi ranks are located on Eyre Sq, on Bridge St, and next to the bus-train station. You can also catch a cab at a taxi office. Try **Abbey Cabs** (☎ 091-569 469) or **Cara Cabs** (☎ 091-563 939; 17 Eyre Sq; ☼ 24hr).

ARAN ISLANDS

Easily visible from large swaths of coastal Galway and Clare Counties, the Aran Islands sing their own siren song to thousands of travellers each year who find their desolate beauty beguiling. Day trippers shuttle through in a daze of rocky magnificence, while those who stay longer find places that, in many ways, seem further removed from the Irish mainland than a 40-minute ferry ride or 10-minute flight.

An extension of the limestone escarpment that forms the Burren, the islands have shallow topsoil scattered with wildflowers, and jagged cliffs pounded by surf. Ancient forts such as Dún Aengus on Inishmór and Dún Chonchúir on Inishmaan are some of the oldest archaeological remains in Ireland.

A web of stone walls (1600km in all) runs across all three islands. They also have a smattering of early *clocháns* (drystone beehive huts from the early Christian period), resembling stone igloos.

Inishmór (Árainn in Irish, meaning 'Big Island') is the largest and most easily accessible from Galway. It is home to one of Ireland's most important and impressive archaeological sites, as well as some lively pubs and restaurants, particularly in its little township Kilronan. The smallest island, Inisheer (Inis Oírr, 'Eastern Island'), with a notable arts centre, is also easily reached from Galway year-round and from Doolin in the summer months. Inishmaan (Inis Meáin, 'Middle Island') tends to be bypassed by the majority of tourist traffic, preserving its age-old traditions and evoking a sense of timelessness.

Hardy travellers find that low season showcases the islands at their wild, windswept best.

History

Little is known about the people who built the massive Iron Age stone structures on Inishmór and Inishmaan. Commonly referred to as 'forts', they are believed to have served as pagan religious centres. Folklore holds that they were built by the Firbolgs, a people who invaded Ireland from Europe in prehistoric times.

It is thought that people came to the islands to farm, a major challenge given the rocky terrain. Early islanders augmented their soil by hauling seaweed and sand up from the shore. People also fished the surrounding waters on long *currachs* (rowing boats made of a framework of laths covered with tarred canvas), which remain a symbol of the Aran Islands.

Christianity reached the islands remarkably early, and some of the oldest monastic settlements were founded by St Enda (Éanna) in the 5th century. Enda appears to have been an Irish chief who converted to Christianity and spent some time studying in Rome before seeking out a suitably remote spot for his monastery.

From the 14th century, control of the islands was disputed by two Gaelic families, the O'Briens and the O'Flahertys. The English took over during the reign of Elizabeth I, and in Cromwell's times a garrison was stationed here.

As Galway's importance waned, so did that of the islands, and their isolation meant islanders maintained a traditional lifestyle well into the 20th century. Up to the 1930s, people wore traditional Aran dress: bright red skirts and black shawls for women, baggy woollen trousers and waistcoats with *crios* (colourful belts) for men. The classic heavy creamcoloured Aran sweater, featuring complex patterns, originated and is still hand-knitted on the islands.

MODERNITY HITS THE ISLANDS

Until the last few decades, the islands were, if not centuries from civilisation, then at least a perilous all-day journey in unpredictable seas. Air services began in 1970, changing island life forever, and today fast ferries make a quick (if sometimes still rough) crossing.

All three islands now have secondary schools, but as recently as a decade ago, students on the two smaller islands had to move to boarding school in Galway to complete their education, which involved an abrupt switch from speaking Irish to English. Farming has all but died out on the islands and tourism is now the primary source of income; while Irish remains the local tongue, most locals speak English with visitors and converse with each other in Irish.

Information

Although high summer brings throngs of tourists, services on the islands are few. Only Inishmór has a year-round tourist office as well as a sole ATM; the majority of places don't accept credit cards (always check ahead). Restaurants, including pubs that serve food, often reduce their opening hours or shut completely during low season.

There are a number of books about the islands, most no more than pretty pictures and florid text. However *Monuments of the Aran Islands* (€4) is an excellent recent publication. The official website (www.irelandsislands .com) covers the islands.

Getting There & Away
AIR
All three islands have landing strips. The mainland departure point is Connemara regional airport at Minna, near Inverin (Indreabhán), about 35km west of Galway. **Aer Arann Islands** (☎ 091-593 034; www.aerarannislands .ie) offers return flights to each of the islands several times daily (hourly in summer) for adult/child/student €45/25/37; the flights take about 10 minutes, and groups of four or more can get group rates. Try for the first or second row for stunning views of the scoured bedrock (best is the seat next to the pilot). If you work out some complex timings, you can visit more than one island in a day. A bus from outside Galway's Kinlay House hostel (p397) to the airport costs €3 each way.

BOAT
Weather permitting, there's at least one boat a day heading out to the Aran Islands. Galway has agents selling ferry tickets on and around Eyre Sq as does the tourist office.

Operating year-round, **Island Ferries** (☎ 091-568 903, 572 273; www.aranislandferries.com; 4 Forster St, Galway; adult/child/student €25/13/20) serves all three islands and also links Inishmaan and Inisheer.

Aran Direct (☎ 091-566 535; www.arandirect.com; return adult/child/concession €25/15/20; ☽ April–late Sep) serves Inishmór.

Schedules peak in July and August, when both companies run several boats a day. The crossing can take up to one hour and is subject to cancellation in high seas. Buses from Galway (€6 return) connect with the sailings; ask when you book.

Ferries to Inisheer also operate from Doolin (p381).

Getting Around
Interisland services run in high season only; from October to April connections require a trip back to Rossaveal.

INISHMÓR
pop 1300

Most visitors who venture out to the islands don't make it beyond Inishmór (Árainn) and its main attraction, Dún Aengus, the stunning stone fort perched perilously on the island's towering cliffs. The arid landscape west of Kilronan (Cill Rónáin), Inishmór's main settlement, is dominated by stone walls, boulders, scattered buildings and the odd patch of deep-green grass and potato plants.

Tourism turns the wheels of the island's economy: an armada of tour vans greet each ferry and flight, offering a ride round the sights. As one local said: 'We move 'em through like a conveyor belt.' Happily, you can set your own pace.

The 2010 romantic comedy *Leap Year* starring Amy Adams and Adam Scott was partially filmed on Inishmór. Rather tellingly, it involves a woman bedevilled by travel mishaps.

Orientation
Inishmór is 14.5km long and 4km at its widest stretch. All boats arrive and depart from Kilronan, on the southeastern side of the island. The airstrip is 2km further southeast of town; a shuttle to Kilronan costs €5 return. One principal road runs the length of the island, intersected by small lanes and paths of packed dirt and stone.

Information
The useful **tourist office** (☎ 099-61263; Kilronan; ☽ 11am-7pm Jun-Sep, 11am-2pm & 3-5pm Oct-May), on the waterfront west of the ferry pier in Kilronan, changes money, as does the **post office**. The good-sized **Spar supermarket** (Kilronan; ☽ 9am-6pm Mon-Wed, 9am-7pm Thu-Sat year-round, 10am-5pm Sun Jun-Aug) has an ATM.

Mainistir House Hostel (p406) offers public **internet access** (☽ 9am-1pm, 5-7pm).

Sights
DÚN AENGUS
Three spectacular forts stand guard over Inishmór, each believed to be around 2000 years old. Chief among them is **Dún Aengus** (Dún Aonghasa; ☎ 099-61008; www.heritageireland.ie; adult/child €3/1; ☽ 10am-6pm), which has three nonconcentric walls that run right up to sheer drops to the ocean below. It is protected by remarkable *chevaux de frise*, fearsome and densely packed defensive stone spikes that surely helped deter ancient armies from invading the site.

Powerful swells pound the 60m-high cliff face. A complete lack of rails or other modern additions that would spoil this amazing ancient site means that you can not only go right up to the cliff's edge but also potentially fall to your doom below quite easily. When it's uncrowded, you can't help but feel the extraordinary energy that must have been harnessed to build this vast site.

A small visitor centre has displays that put everything in context. A slightly strenuous 900m walkway wanders uphill through a rocky landscape lined with hardy plants to the fort.

OTHER SIGHTS

Along the road between Kilronan and Dún Aengus you'll find the small, perfectly circu-lar fort **Dún Eochla**. Dramatically perched on a clifftop promontory south of Kilronan is **Dún Dúchathair**.

The ruins of numerous stone churches trace the island's monastic history. The small **Teampall Chiaráin** (Church of St Kieran), with a high cross in the churchyard, is near Kilronan. To the southeast, near Cill Éinne Bay, is the early-Christian **Teampall Bheanáin** (Church of St Benen). Near the airstrip are the sunken remains of a church; the spot is said to have been the site of **St Enda's Monastery** in the 5th century, though whatever is visible dates from the 8th century onwards. Past Kilmurvey is the perfect **Clochán na Carraige**, an early Christian stone hut that stands 2.5m tall, and various small early Christian ruins known

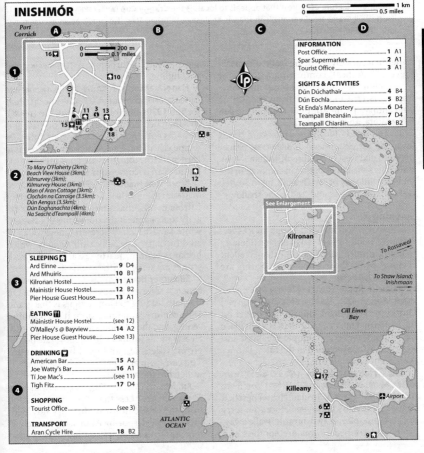

INISHMÓR

INFORMATION	
Post Office	1 A1
Spar Supermarket	2 A1
Tourist Office	3 A1

SIGHTS & ACTIVITIES	
Dún Dúchathair	4 B4
Dún Eochla	5 B2
St Enda's Monastery	6 D4
Teampall Bheanáin	7 D4
Teampall Chiaráin	8 B2

SLEEPING	
Ard Einne	9 D4
Ard Mhuiris	10 B1
Kilronan Hostel	11 A1
Mainistir House Hostel	12 B2
Pier House Guest House	13 A1

EATING	
Mainistir House Hostel	(see 12)
O'Malley's @ Bayview	14 A2
Pier House Guest House	(see 13)

DRINKING	
American Bar	15 A2
Joe Watty's Bar	16 A1
Tí Joe Mac's	(see 11)
Tigh Fitz	17 D4

SHOPPING	
Tourist Office	(see 3)

TRANSPORT	
Aran Cycle Hire	18 B2

Port Corrúch

Mainistir

See Enlargement

Kilronan

To Rossaveal

To Straw Island; Inishmaan

Cill Éinne Bay

Killeany

Airport

ATLANTIC OCEAN

To Mary O'Flaherty (2km);
Beach View House (3km);
Kilmurvey (3km);
Kilmurvey House (3km);
Man of Aran Cottage (3km);
Clochán na Carraige (3.5km);
Dún Aengus (3.5km);
Dún Eoghanachta (4km);
Na Seacht dTeampaill (4km);

DIVINE INSPIRATION

Devotees of the late 1990s cult TV series *Father Ted* might recognise Craggy Island – the show's fictional island setting off Ireland's west coast – from its opening sequence showing the *Plassy* shipwreck (p411) on Inisheer. However, apart from this single shot, the sitcom was mostly filmed in London studios, with additional location shots in Counties Clare, Wicklow and Dublin. Alas, the Parochial House and Vaughan's Pub are nowhere to be found here (instead you'll find them around Lisdoonvarna in County Clare).

This hasn't stopped the Aran Islands from embracing the show as their own. Although there has been some grumbling from its smaller neighbours, Inishmór has seized upon Ted-mania for itself and each year hosts **Tedfest** (www.tedfest.org), a *Father Ted* festival. Held during the purgatory of tourism (late February or March) this three-day carnival of nonsense has been a huge hit.

There are games (hide-and-seek in the dark is, er, big), talent contests, themed meals and drinking – lots of drinking. So popular has the event become that in 2009 it sold out and plans are to hold multiple Tedfests over multiple weekends.

Besides being an excuse to party island-style, the festival was organised to commemorate actor Dermot Morgan (Father Ted), who died in 1998 from a heart attack, aged 45. Proceeds are donated to Croí, the West of Ireland Cardiology Foundation.

A popular feature of Tedfest that appeals to locals is the **Craggy Cup** (www.craggycup.com), which pits football teams from various Irish islands against each other. This also provides an excuse for more drinking and, goodness, gambling.

---

rather inaccurately as the **Na Seacht dTeampaill** (Seven Churches), comprising a couple of ruined churches, monastic houses and some fragments of a high cross from the 8th or 9th century. To the south of the ruins is **Dún Eoghanachta**, another circular fort.

There's an EU Blue Flag white-sand beach (awarded for cleanliness) at **Kilmurvey**, peacefully situated west of bustling Kilronan. Many sunbathers shed their parkas in summer. In the sheltered little bay of **Port Chorrúch**, up to 50 grey seals sun themselves and feed in the shallows.

Sleeping

The tourist office can book rooms for a €4 fee. Advance bookings are advised, particularly in high summer. Many places offer excellent evening meals; those listed under Eating are open to nonguests.

Mainistir House Hostel (☎ 099-61169; www .mainistirhousearan.com; Mainistir; dm/d €17/50; 🖳 🛜) Quirky and colourful, this 60-bed hostel on the main road north of Kilronan is a fun place for young travellers. A simple breakfast and free pick-up are included in the rates. Dinner is an event (see opposite).

ourpick Kilronan Hostel (☎ 099-61255; www .kilronanhostel.com; Kilronan; dm €21-27; 🛜) You'll see the pistachio-green Kilronan Hostel perched above Tí Joe Mac's pub even before your ferry docks at the pier, a two-minute walk away. Four- and six-bed rooms are spotless and

have private bathrooms. A terrace is good for chilling.

Man of Aran Cottage (☎ 099-61301; www.manofaran cottage.com; Kilmurvey; s/d from €60/90; 🌣 Mar-Oct) Built for the 1930s film of the same name (p408), this thatched B&B doesn't trade on past glories – its authentic stone-and-wood interiors define charming. The owners are avid organic gardeners (the tomatoes are famous) and their bounty can become your meal.

Beach View House (☎ 099-61141; www.beachview housearan.com; r €60-100) Located 4km west of Kilronan, this unassuming B&B lives up exactly to its name: it overlooks the EU-flagged white-sand beach. There are good walks in all directions, especially Dún Aengus, which beckons from a nearby escarpment. Fresh scones are served with breakfast.

Kilmurvey House (☎ 099-61218; www.kilmurvey house.com; Kilmurvey; s/d from €65/100; 🌣 Apr-Sep) On the path leading to Dún Aengus is this grand 18th-century stone mansion. It's a beautiful setting, and the 12 rooms are well maintained. Hearty meals (dinner €30) incorporate home-grown vegetables, and local fish and meats. You can swim at a pretty beach that's a short walk from the house.

Ard Mhuiris (☎ 099-61333; ardmhuiris@eircom.net; Kilronan; s/d €70/80) Less than a five-minute stroll from the centre of town, this very tidy B&B hits the sweet spot of Aran Islands accommodation: it's quiet, welcoming and has good sea views if you have to curl up in your room on a rainy day.

Ard Einne (☎ 099-61126; www.ardeinne.com; Killeany; r €90-120) Enjoy broad views of Cill Éinne Bay from this mannered, almost timeless, eight-room guesthouse near various ruins and the airport. It really couldn't be quieter – the perfect surrounds after a day spent walking. There's a restaurant for guests that features fresh local food.

Pier House Guest House (☎ 099-61417; www .pierhousearan.com; Kilronan; r €90-120; ☺ Mar-Oct) You won't have time to lose your sea legs in the 100m walk from the ferry to this two-storey house perched on a small rise. The 10 rooms are bright and comfortable.

Eating
Some of the pubs listed under Drinking offer good bar food.

O'Malley's @ Bayview (☎ 099-61041; Kilronan; mains €7-23; ☺ 11am-9.30pm Mon-Fri, from 9am Sat & Sun) The terrace here has commanding harbour views. The simple menu belies the talents of the kitchen; choices include fine fish chowder, good burgers and pizza, plus fresh fish at night.

Mainistir House Hostel (☎ 099-61169; Mainistir; buffet €16; ☺ from 8pm summer, from 7pm winter) Mainistir House Hostel cooks up renowned organic, largely vegetarian fare featuring dishes redolent with the tastes of summer – pesto is much in evidence. Nonguests are welcome, but be sure to book.

Pier House Guest House (☎ 099-61811; Kilronan; mains €22-30; ☺ noon-10pm) Sitting on the large terrace watching the ferries come and go while grazing your way through a platter of local seafood is one of the island's joys. There's a fireplace inside for when it blows.

Drinking
Tigh Fitz (☎ 099-61213; Killeany) Near the airport, this jovial pub has traditional sessions and set dancing every weekend and does excellent bar food (noon to 5pm) from June to August. It's 1.6km from Kilronan (about a 25-minute walk).

Joe Watty's Bar (☎ 099-61155; Kilronan) This is the best pub in Kilronan, with traditional sessions most nights and pub food (noon to 8pm) from June to August.

Tí Joe Mac's (☎ 099-61248; Kilronan) Informal music sessions and pub food served all year make Tí Joe Mac's a local favourite.

American Bar (☎ 099-61130; Kilronan) Two large rooms fill with happy pint quaffers throughout the year. In low season sloshed locals anticipate the next year of tourists (especially the namesakes of the bar). The room on the right as you enter, with its windows and access to the terrace, is the best bet.

Shopping
Shops around Kilronan mostly sell machine-knitted Aran sweaters. For a much heavier, hand-knitted version, visit **Mary O'Flaherty** (☎ 099-61117; Oat Quarter). Chances are you'll see Mary knitting when you call in. Expect to pay around €100 for a genuine hand-knitted sweater.

The **tourist office** (☎ 11am-7pm Jun-Sep, 11am-2pm & 3-5pm Oct-May) sells greeting cards featuring evocative impressionist paintings by local artist Michaél Ó Ceallaigh, and can give you details about buying original works. Its selection of local books is tops.

Getting Around
Aran Cycle Hire (☎ 099-61132; per day €10), near the pier, hires out hundreds of sturdy bikes, which it'll deliver to your accommodation anywhere on the island. You can also bring your own bicycle on the ferry for free. Most places to stay have bicycles for use or rent.

Year-round, numerous **minibuses** (tours €10) greet each ferry and plane. All offer 2½-hour island tours; some of the drivers are such characters (including Thomas O'Toole, ☎ 087 624 9802) that you'll be laughing too hard to notice the rocky vistas.

To see the island at a gentler pace, **pony traps** (☺ Mar-Nov) with a driver are available for trips between Kilronan and Dún Aengus; the return journey costs between €60 and €100 for up to four people.

INISHMAAN
pop 200
The least-visited of the islands, with the smallest population (a little over 100 in winter, 200 during the summer population boom), Inishmaan (Inis Meáin) is a rocky respite. Early Christian monks seeking solitude were drawn to Inishmaan, as was the author JM Synge, who spent five summers here over a century ago (see the boxed text, p408). The island they knew largely survives today: stoic cows and placid sheep, impressive old forts, and warm-hearted locals, who may tell you

ARTISIC ARAN

The Aran Islands have sustained a strong creative streak, partly as a means for entertainment during long periods of isolation and partly, in the words of one local composer, to 'make sure the rest of the country doesn't forget we're here'. Artists and writers from the mainland have similarly long been drawn to the elemental nature of island life.

Dramatist JM Synge (1871–1909) spent a lot of time on the islands (listening to the local dialect through the floorboards of his room), and his play *Riders to the Sea* (1905) is set on Inishmaan. His book *The Aran Islands* (1907) is the classic account of life here and remains in print. His drama *The Playboy of the Western World* also drew upon his experiences on the Arans.

American Robert Flaherty came to the islands in the early 1930s to film *Man of Aran*, a dramatic account of daily life. He was something of a fanatic about the project and got most of the island's people involved in its production, and even set up an entire film studio. One of the cottages built for the film is today a B&B (Man of Aran Cottage, p406). The film is a classic and is regularly screened in Kilronan on Inishmór.

The map-maker Tim Robinson has written a wonderful two-volume account of his explorations on Aran, called *Stones of Aran: Pilgrimage* and *Stones of Aran: Labyrinthe*. His book *The Aran Islands: A Map and Guide* is superb.

Two other excellent publications are *The Book of Aran*, edited by Anne Korf, consisting of articles by 17 specialists covering diverse aspects of the islands' culture, and *Aran Reader*, edited by Breandán and Ruairí O hEither, with essays by various scholars on the islands' history, geography and culture.

Local literary talent includes the writer Liam O'Flaherty (1896–1984) from Inishmór. O'Flaherty, who wandered around North and South America before returning to Ireland in 1921 and fighting in the Civil War, is the author of several harrowing novels, including *Famine*.

with a glint in their eye that they had a hard night on the whiskey the previous evening (there are no *gardaí* on the island to enforce closing times). Inishmaan's scenery is breathtaking, with a jagged coastline of startling cliffs, empty beaches, and fields where the main crop seems to be stone.

Orientation & Information

Inishmaan is roughly 5km long by 3km wide. Most of its buildings are spread out along the road that runs east–west across the centre of the island. The principal boat landing is on the eastern side of the island, while the airstrip is in the northeastern corner. Inishmaan's down-to-earth islanders are largely unconcerned with the prospect of attracting tourists' euros, so facilities are few and far between. In An Córa, the helpful **Inishmaan Island Co-operative** (☎ 099-73010; 🕑 9am-1pm & 2-5pm Mon-Fri), northwest of the pier and post office, dispenses limited tourist information. There's no ATM; the bank visits on the second Tuesday of each month.

Sights

Glorious views of Inishmaan's limestone valleys extend from the elliptical stone fort **Dún Chonchúir**, which is thought to have been built sometime between the 1st and 7th centuries AD.

Teach Synge (☎ 099-73036; admission €3; 🕑 by appointment), a thatched cottage on the road just before you head up to the fort, is where the writer JM Synge spent his summers between 1898 and 1902.

Cill Cheannannach is a rough 8th- or 9th-century church south of the pier. The well-preserved stone fort **Dún Fearbhaigh**, a short distance west, dates from the same era. On a hill, **St Mary's Church** has excellent stained-glass windows.

At the desolate western edge of the island, **Synge's Chair** is a lookout at the edge of a sheer limestone cliff with the surf from Gregory's Sound booming below. The cliff ledge is often sheltered from the wind, so do as Synge did and find a comfortable seat to take it all in. The formation is two minutes' walk from the parking area; you can leg it around the bleak west side of the island from here in an hour. Note the new windmills providing green electricity.

On the walk out to Synge's Chair, a sign points the way to a **clochán**, hidden behind a house and shed.

In the east of the island, about 500m north of the boat-landing stage, is **Trá Leitreach**, a safe, sheltered beach.

Sleeping & Eating

Most B&Bs serve evening meals, usually using organic local foods. Meals generally cost around €22 to €25.

Máire Mulkerrin (☎ 099-73016; s/d €30/50) Now in her 80s and going strong, Mrs Mulkerrin is a local legend in her skirts and shawls. She keeps a cosy, spick-and-span home, filled with faded family photos, and her stove warms the kitchen all day.

Ard Alainn (☎ 099-73027; s/d with shared bathroom €30/50; ☼ May-Sep) Signposted just over 2km from the pier, thatched Ard Alainn is a vintage fantasy. The five rooms share a bathroom. Breakfasts by hostess Maura Faherty will keep you going all day.

our pick **Tig Congaile** (☎ 099-73085; bbinismeain@ eircom.net; Moore Village; r €45-80) Not far from the pier, Guatemalan-born Vilma Conneely serves guests freshly ground coffee from her native land, but it's her use of local foods that really wins plaudits. Her sea-vegetable soup is famous and best enjoyed – if possible – at a table outside. The dining room is open to nonguests (lunch dishes from €5, dinner from €20; open 10.30am to 9pm). The seven rooms are spacious and have starkly iconic views.

An Dún (☎ 099-73047; www.inismeainaccommodation .com; r €45-100; ☐) Opposite the entrance to Dún Chonchúir, modern An Dún has a sauna and five comfortable rooms with private bathrooms. The restaurant is open to nonguests and serves lauded local cuisine such as pillowy potatoes (fertilised with seaweed), luscious smoked salmon, and seafood chowder (mains €8 to €25). Rooms are available year-round; the restaurant serves lunch and dinner in summer.

Teach Anna (☎ 099-73054; r €60-80) Run by islander Anna Byrne (whom you'll also meet at the post office in a small shop, where she works by day), this cosy B&B is five minutes' walk from the beach and has four rooms. Guests are welcome year-round and Anna cooks good-value evening meals.

Leonard Doyle (☎ 087 248 2673; r €60-90) An islander transplant, Doyle rents out a postcard-perfect thatched cottage with views across much of the island to the east. Should you require spiritual intervention, the church and pub are short walks away. The owner was part of the crew who did initial surveys for the windmills that now make the Arans nearly carbon neutral.

Teach Ósta (☎ 099-73003; mains from €10; ☼ noon-late) The island's perfect pub hums on summer evenings (grab a table outside for the views) and supplies snacks, sandwiches, soups and seafood platters. Though the pub often keeps going until the wee hours, food service generally stops around 7pm and may not be available in the winter months.

Shopping

The knitwear factory **Cniotáil Inis Meáin** (☎ 099-73009) exports fine woollen garments to some of the world's most exclusive shops. You can buy the same sweaters here; call before visiting.

Getting Around

Walking is a fine way to explore the island's sights. A van **tour** (☎ 099-73993) from the ferry or the airport will cost €15 for a relaxed one or two hours.

INISHEER

pop 300

Inisheer (Inis Oírr), the smallest of the Aran Islands, has a palpable sense of enchantment, enhanced by the island's deep-rooted mythology and ethereal landscapes.

The wheels of change turn very slowly here. Electricity wasn't fully reliable until 1997. Given that there's at best six inches of topsoil to eke out a living farming, the slow conversion of the economy to tourism has been welcome. Day trippers from Doolin (p381), 8km across the water, enliven the paths all summer long.

Information

In July and August a small **kiosk** (☼ 10am-6pm Jul-Aug) at the harbour provides tourist information. Like Inishmaan, there's no ATM; bring euros.

Online, www.inisoirr-island.com is a handy resource for planning your trip.

Sights & Activities

The majority of Inisheer's sights are in the north of the island. The 15th-century **O'Brien's Castle** (Caisleán Uí Bhriain), a 100m climb uphill to the island's highest point, has dramatic views over clover-covered fields to the beach and harbour. It was built within the remains of a ring fort called Dún Formna, dating from as early as the 1st century AD. The gate is sometimes locked, but, if it's open, you can explore the remains freely. Nearby is an 18th-century signal tower.

On the Strand (An Trá) is the roofless 10th-century **Teampall Chaoimháin** (Church of St Kevin), named for Inisheer's patron saint, who is buried close by. On the eve of his 14 June feast day, a mass is held here in the open air at 9pm. Those with ailments sleep here for the night to be healed.

Cill Ghobnait (Church of St Gobnait), southwest of Inisheer Heritage House, is a small 8th- or 9th-century church named after Gobnait, who fled here from Clare while trying to escape an enemy who was pursuing her.

About 2km southwest of the church is the **Tobar Éinne** (Well of St Enda). Locals still carry out a pilgrimage known as the *Turas*, which involves, over the course of three consecutive Sundays, picking up seven stones from the ground nearby and walking around the small well seven times, putting one stone down each time, while saying the rosary until an elusive eel appears from the well's watery depths. If, during this ritual, you're lucky enough to see the eel, it's said your tongue will be bestowed with healing powers, enabling you to literally lick wounds.

WALK: INISHEER EXPLORED

This moderate 12km (five-hour) walk takes in many of Inisheer's sights. It virtually circumnavigates the island, taking you through the settled northern fringe, past the stone-walled fields in the centre and south, and around the wild and rocky south coast. For all but 2km along the southern shore, the walk follows quiet lanes. You'll come across yellow markers on some sections of the walk, marking the Inis Oírr Way, which confines itself to the northern two-thirds of the island.

From the Inisheer ferry pier, walk west along the narrow road parallel to the shore and continue past the **Fisherman's Cottage** cafe. At the next junction go on straight ahead to the small fishing pier at the northwest corner of the island. Continue along the road, now with a gravel surface, past another acute-angled junction on the left (where the waymarkers reappear). Here the shingle shore is on one side of the road, and a dense patchwork of fields, enclosed by the ubiquitous stone walls, is on the other.

About 1km from the acute junction, turn left at the painted sign; about 100m along the paved lane is the **Tobar Éinne**.

Return to the coast road and continue southwest as it becomes a rough track. After about 600m, head roughly south across the limestone pavement and strips of grass to the shore. Follow the gently sloping rock platform around the southwestern headland (Ceann na Faochnaí) and walk east to the **lighthouse** near Fardurris Point (two hours from the ferry pier).

Walk around the wall enclosing the lighthouse and use a stile to cross another wall by the entrance gate. Now back on a level surface, follow the road generally northeast as it climbs gradually. Access to Cill na Seacht Niníon (the Church of the Seven Daughters) is from a point 1.5km from the lighthouse, almost opposite two metal-roofed sheds on the right; a pillar next to a gate bears the chapel's name and an arrow points vaguely in its direction. Use stiles to cross three fields to a rusty gate in the ivy-clad walls around the chapel site. In the largest stone enclosure are five weathered grave markers, one of which still has a faint incised cross.

Back on the road, continue northeast to the village of An Formna. Take the right fork, then turn right again at a T-junction and head south along the road above Lough More. Keep left at a track junction and continue to the Atlantic shore with the **wreck of the Plassy** just ahead (one hour from the lighthouse).

Head north, following the track, which then becomes a sealed road at the northern end of Lough More. Continue following the road along the northern shore of the island, past the airstrip.

At the airstrip you can diverge, if you wish, to the sandy hummock that shelters the ancient **Teampall Chaoimháin**. A little further along the road, turn left to reach **O'Brien's Castle**. From here, follow the narrow road northwest, turn right at a T-junction and then make your way to Cnoc Rathnaí, a Bronze Age burial mound (1500 BC), which is remarkably intact considering it was buried under the sand until the 19th century, when it was rediscovered. Continue towards the beach; the **pier** is to your left through a maze of lanes.

The signposted 10.5km **Inis Oírr Way** (Inisheer Way) walking path brings you past the rusting hulk of the **Plassy**, a freighter wrecked in 1960 and thrown high up onto the rocks. Miraculously, all on board were saved; Tigh Ned's pub has a collection of photographs and documents detailing the rescue. An aerial shot of the wreck was used in the opening sequence of the iconic TV series *Father Ted* (see the boxed text, p406). The photogenic **lighthouse** (1857) on the island's southern tip is inaccessible.

Inisheer boasts a large community arts centre, **Áras Éanna** (☎ 099-75150), which sits out on an exposed stretch of the northern side of the island, a 15-minute walk from the village. It has visiting artists programs.

Festivals & Events
One of the island's highlights is the week-long **Craiceann Inis Oírr International Bodhrán Summer School** (☎ 099-75067; www.craiceann.com) in late June, which includes bodhrán masterclasses, lectures and workshops, as well as related events, such as Irish dancing. Craiceann takes its name from the Irish word for 'skin', referring to the goat skin used to make these circular drums, which are held under one arm and played with a wooden beater. The festival – its slogan is 'Lock up your goats!' – is headed up by Inisheer local Micheal O hAlmhain, who has performed with a number of Irish bands, including the Chieftains. During Craiceann, nightly drumming sessions take place in the island's pubs.

Sleeping & Eating
There is camping (with toilets and showers) at the official site by the main beach.

Brú Radharc Na Mara Hostel (☎ 099-75024; radharcnamara@hotmail.com; dm €18, d €50; ☾ Mar-Oct) Handily located next to a pub and by the pier, this spotless hostel has ocean views, a large kitchen, a warming fireplace and bikes for hire. The owners also run the adjacent B&B (rooms €50), with basic rooms with private bathrooms.

Radharc an Chláir (☎ 099-75019; bridpoil@eircom.net; r €45-75) This pleasant, modern B&B near O'Brien's Castle has views of the Cliffs of Moher and Galway Bay. Book several weeks ahead, as hostess Brid Poil's home cooking draws many repeat visitors. Guests can hire bikes (€10 per day) and arrange evening meals (€20). Some rooms share bathrooms.

OUR PICK Fisherman's Cottage & South Aran House (☎ 099-75073; www.southaran.com; s/d €45/70; ☾ Apr-Oct; ☎) Slow-food enthusiasts run this sprightly B&B and cafe that's a mere five-minute walk from the pier. Lavender grows in profusion at the entrance; follow your nose. Food (lunch and dinner, open to nonguests, mains €12 to €20) celebrates local seafood and organic produce. Rooms are simple yet stylish. Kayaking and fishing are among the activities on offer.

Óstán Inis Oírr (☎ 099-75020; r €55-90; ☾ Apr-Sep) The Flaherty family's modern hotel, just up from the Strand, has 14 homey rooms and serves hearty meals in its pub and restaurant (mains €8 to €14, open lunch and dinner). On chilly nights, set your electric blanket to 11.

Drinking
Tigh Ned (☎ 099-75004) Here since 1897, Tigh Ned is a welcoming, unpretentious place, with lively traditional music and inexpensive lunchtime fare. Tables in the garden have harbour views.

Tigh Ruaírí (☎ 099-75020) Rory Conneely's atmospheric digs host live music sessions.

Getting Around
Bikes can be rented from **Rothair Inis Oírr** (☎ 099-75033; per day €10; ☾ May-Sep). Most places to stay also rent bikes to nonguests.

You can take a tour of the island on a **pony trap** (per person per hr €10-15) in summer, or on an atmospheric tractor-drawn, thatched-cottage-style **wagon** (☎ 086 607 3230).

CONNEMARA

Think of the best crumble you've ever had, one with a craggy crust that accumulates hollows of perfect flavour. Similarly, the filigreed coast of the Connemara Peninsula is endlessly pleasing, with pockets of sheer delight awaiting discovery.

The name Connemara (Conamara) is Irish for 'Inlets of the Sea' and the coastal roads bear this out as they wind around small bays and coves, some with hidden beaches. A succession of seaside hamlets entice, including the jewel-like fishing harbour at Roundstone, and sleepy Leenane on Killary Harbour, the country's only fjord. Clifden, Connemara's largest town, is spectacularly sited on a hill, while offshore lies the idyllic island of Inishbofin.

Connemara's interior is a kaleidoscope of rusty bogs, lonely valleys and shimmering black lakes. At its heart are the Maumturk Mountains and the pewter-tinged quartzite peaks of the Twelve Bens mountain range, with a network of scenic hiking and biking trails. Everywhere the land is laced by the seemingly endless stone walls you're glad you didn't have to build. It's dazzling at any time of day but especially when the sky and waters sparkle azure, the hills shine green, and bright yellow blooms abound.

One of the most important Gaeltacht (Irish-speaking) areas in the country begins around Spiddal and stretches along the coast as far as Cashel. It's a centre for Ireland's thriving Irish-language media (opposite).

If you intend any detailed exploration of the area, the excellent *Connemara: Introduction and Gazetteer*, by Tim Robinson, is a must. *Connemara: A Hill Walker's Guide*, written by Robinson and Joss Lynam, is also invaluable.

Galway's tourist office (p393) has a wealth of information on the area. Online, **Connemara** Tourism (www.connemara.ie) and **Go Connemara** (www.goconnemara.com) have regionwide info and links.

Getting There & Around
BUS

Organised bus tours from Galway (p396) are plentiful and offer a good overview of the region, though ideally you'll want more than one day to absorb the area's charms, plus you'll want the freedom to make your own discoveries.

Bus Éireann (☎ 091-562 000; www.buseireann.ie) serves most of Connemara. Services can be sporadic, and many buses operate May to September only, or July and August only. Some drivers will stop in between towns if arrangements are made at the beginning of the trip.

Citylink (☎ 1890 280 808; www.citylink.ie) has several buses a day linking Galway city with Clifden, with stops in Moycullen, Oughterard, Maam Cross and Recess, and on to Cleggan and Letterfrack. If you're going somewhere between towns (a hostel in the countryside,

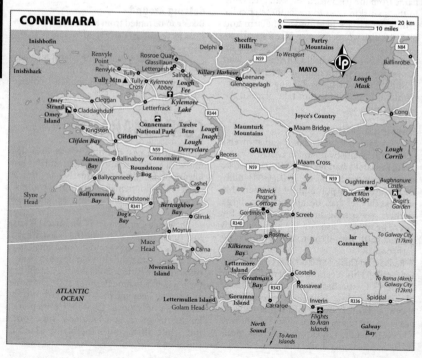

CONNEMARA

TRUE IRISH MEDIA

That spoken Irish is enjoying a renaissance around the country (when posh Dublin parents compete to enrol their kids in Irish-language schools, you know something is up) can be credited in no small part to several media outlets based in Connemara and Galway. From this last refuge of the language, Ireland's national Irish-language radio station, Radio na Gaeltachta (www.rte .ie/rnag) and its Irish-language TV station, TG4 (www.tg4.ie), sprang in the 1990s. So, too, has sprouted the Irish-language weekly newspaper *Foinse* (www.foinse.ie).

Not just for linguists and traditionalists, these media outlets have a national impact. TG4 has funded an entire cottage industry of Irish speakers who dub American TV series, such as *The Wire* and *Curb Your Enthusiasm*. The station also won the exclusive rights to broadcast major sporting events, like the Tour de France. In addition, it produces its own shows, like the popular – and fluffy – *Paisean Faisean,* a reality dating show, which you can see streamed on the website (with subtitles in English!). In fact TG4 has a quiet following among Ireland's (shrinking) immigrant community, who prefer to read the dialog in English rather than cope with rapid-fire brogue.

If you want to join the fun, you can enrol in short courses at the International Summer School of the **National University of Ireland, Galway** (☎ 091-495 442; www.nuigalway.ie/iss) and **Cnoc Suain Cultural Centre** (☎ 091-555 703; www.cnocsuain.com) in Spiddal.

---

for example), you might be able to arrange a drop-off with the driver.

CAR

Your own wheels are the best way to get off this scenic region's beaten track – though watch out for the narrow roads' stone walls, just waiting to scrape the sides of your car.

Keep an eye out, too, for meandering Connemara sheep – characterised by thick creamy fleece and coal-black faces and legs – which frequently wander onto the road. Even Connemara's flattest stretches of road tend to be bumpy due to the uneven bog beneath the tarmac.

Heading west from Galway, you can either take the coast road (R336) through Salthill, Barna and Spiddal, or the direct inland route (N59) through Oughterard. The journey from Maam Cross northwest to Leenane (R336) or northeast to Cong (R345) in County Mayo takes you through the stunning mountainous region of Joyce's country.

Many road signs in this area are in Irish only, so take note of the Irish place names (in parentheses) that are listed in this section.

COASTAL DRIVE – GALWAY CITY TO MACE HEAD

The slow coastal route between Galway and Connemara takes you past pretty seascapes and villages, although the fun doesn't really begin until after Inverin.

Opposite the popular Blue Flag beach **Silver Strand**, 4.8km west of Galway, are the **Barna Woods**, a dense, deep green forest perfect for rambling and picnicking. Conserved by the Galway County Council, the woods contain the last natural growing oaks in Ireland's west.

The once unspoilt village of Barna, a further 3km west, has been inundated by recent development (to the chagrin of locals, who campaigned passionately and, ultimately, futilely against it). Barna is, however, home to some of the greater Galway area's best seafood at **O'Grady's on the Pier** (☎ 091-592 223; www.ogradysonthepier.com; mains €15-30; ☺ from 6pm Mon-Sun & 12.30-2.45pm Sun). Daily specials include many ocean-fresh catches. Long, lazy Sunday lunches attract legions of locals; book ahead.

West again, **Spiddal** (An Spidéal) is a refreshingly untouched little village, and the start of the Gaeltacht region. On your right as you approach the village are the **Spiddal Craft & Design Studios** (☎ 091-553 376; www.ceardlann .com; ☺ hours vary), where you can watch woodworkers, leatherworkers, sculptors and weavers plying their crafts, or have lunch at **Bistro Jackie** (☎ 091-55030), which offers superlative soda bread.

Exceptional traditional music sessions take place at the unassuming **Tigh Hughes** (☎ 091-553 447; Spiddal) – it's not uncommon for major musicians to turn up unannounced and join in the craic. Sessions start at around 9pm on Tuesdays. The pub's just adjacent to the main street; turn right at the town centre's little crossroads next to the bank, and it's a couple of doors up on your right.

COUNTY GALWAY

A few kilometres west of Spiddal, the scenery becomes more dramatic, with parched fields criss-crossed by low stone walls rolling to a ragged shore. **Carraroe** (An Cheathrú Rua) has fine beaches, including the Coral Strand, which is composed entirely of shell and coral fragments. It's worth wandering the small roads on all sides of **Greatman's Bay** to discover tiny inlets and little coves, often watched over by the genial local donkeys.

Lettermore, **Gorumna** and **Lettermullen** islands are low and bleak, with a handful of farmers eking out an existence from minute, rocky fields. Fish farming is big business.

Near Gortmore, along the R340, is **Patrick Pearse's Cottage** (Teach an Phiarsaigh; ☎ 091-574 292; www.heritageireland.ie; adult/child €3/1; ☽ 10am-6pm Easter & Jun-Aug). Pádraig Pearse (1879–1916) led the Easter Rising with James Connolly in 1916; after the revolt he was executed by the British. Pearse wrote some of his short stories and plays in this small thatched cottage.

The scenic R340 swings south along **Kilkieran Bay**, an area that has recently been granted protected status. The intricate and interlinked system of tidal marshes, bogs, swift-flowing streams and elaborate tidal basins contains an amazing diversity of life that biologists are only now beginning to fully understand.

Continuing on, **Carna** is a small fishing village, with pleasant walks out to **Mweenish Island** or north to Moyrus and out to **Mace Head**. This wild headland is best known for its research station (closed to the public), which measures changes in the global atmosphere and their effect on weather and climate.

Sleeping

The following places are worth a stop if you aren't planning to make Roundstone or beyond by nightfall.

Buninvhir B&B (☎ 091-574 238; www.buninvhir.com; Derryrush, Rosmuc; r €45-70; ☽ Easter-Sep) Ignoring its uninterrupted view over Kilkieran Bay from the front terrace, the next best thing about this whitewashed four-room B&B is the fine gardens and serene location out on its tiny peninsula. Tasty evening meals (€25) are served on the terrace in fine weather.

Cloch na Scíth (☎ 091-553 364; www.thatchcottage .com; Kellough, Spiddal; r €45-75, cottages from €250) Set in a story-book garden roamed by ducks and chickens, this century-old thatched cottage has a warm, friendly host, Nancy, who cooks bread in an iron pot over the peat fire (as her

grandmother taught her and as she'll teach you). A separate self-catering thatched cottage on the property makes a great base for families.

our pick Cashel House Hotel (☎ 095-31001; www .cashel-house-hotel.com; Cashel; s €95-140, d €190-310; 🖳 🛜) At the head of Cashel Bay, this flowered fantasy of a country mansion has 32 period rooms surrounded by 17 hectares of woodland and gardens. It also has a stable of Connemara ponies (riding lessons available), a superb dining room and even a small private beach. Potentates who have graced its sheets include Charles de Gaulle.

OUGHTERARD & AROUND
pop 2400

The writer William Makepeace Thackeray sang the praises of the small town of Oughterard (Uachtar Árd), saying, 'A more beautiful village can scarcely be seen'. Fortunately, little has changed in the intervening years. Just 27km along the main road from Galway city to Clifden, near Lough Corrib, this pretty gateway to Connemara is one of Ireland's principal angling centres.

Immediately west of Oughterard, the countryside opens up to sweeping panoramas of lakes, mountains and bogs, which get more spectacular the further west you travel. Nearby attractions include Aughnanure Castle, a spiritual Celtic garden, and the Quiet Man Bridge.

Information

Bank of Ireland (Main St) Has an ATM and bureau de change.
Tourist office (☎ 091-552 808; www.oughterard tourism.com; Main St; ☽ 9.30am-5.30pm Mon-Fri) Also offers internet access at €1 per 15 minutes. The website is excellent.

Sights

If you see tourists wandering around, talking with a drawl and calling people 'pilgrim', it's probably because they are here to relive the iconic film *The Quiet Man*; see the boxed text, opposite, for details.

AUGHNANURE CASTLE

Built around 1500, this bleak **fortress** (☎ 091-552 214; www.heritageireland.com; adult/child €3/1; ☽ 9.30am-6pm early Apr–Sep) was home to the 'Fighting O'Flahertys', who controlled the region for hundreds of years after they fought off the Normans. The six-storey tower house

---

BRIDGING THE QUIET MAN

Whenever an American cable TV station needs a ratings boost (and they've already just shown *Gone With the Wind*), they trot out the iconic 1952 film *The Quiet Man*. Starring John Wayne and filmed in lavish colour to capture the crimson locks of his co-star Maureen O'Hara, the film regularly makes the top-10 lists of film buffs for its high-energy portrayal of rural Irish life, replete with drinking and fighting, fighting and drinking etc.

Director John Ford returned to his Irish roots and filmed the movie almost entirely on location in Connemara and the little village of Cong, just over the border in County Mayo (p429). One of the most photogenic spots from the film, the eponymous Quiet Man Bridge, is just 3km west of Oughterard off the N59. Looking much as it did in the film, the picture-perfect little arched span (whose original name was Leam Bridge) would be a lovely spot even if it hadn't achieved screen immortality. Purists will note, however, that the scene based here had close-ups done on a cheesy set back in Hollywood. That's showbiz.

Hard-core fans will want to buy the superb *The Complete Guide to The Quiet Man* by Des MacHale. It is sold in most tourist offices in the area.

---

stands on a rocky outcrop overlooking Lough Corrib and has been extensively restored. Surrounding the castle are the remains of an unusual double *bawn* (area surrounded by walls outside the main castle, acting as a defence and a place to keep cattle in times of trouble), and underneath the castle the lake washes through a number of natural caverns and caves.

Aughnanure Castle is situated 3km east of Oughterard, off the main Galway road (N59).

GLENGOWLA MINES

For such ugly work, it's amazing that beautiful materials were extracted from this **mine** (☎ 091-552 360; adult/child €8/4; 🕑 10am-6pm Mar-Nov), a 19th-century hole in the ground that yielded all manner of silver, glistening quartz and much more. Visitors learn about the tough lives led here and see some of the beauty left inside. It is 3km west of Oughterard off the N59.

BRIGIT'S GARDEN

Can you feel the power of the crystal? Halfway between the villages of Moycullen and Oughterard is **Brigit's Garden** (☎ 091-550 905; www.galwaygarden.com; Polagh, Roscahill; adult/child €7.50/5; 🕑 10am-5.30pm mid-Apr–Sep), a New Age-y place with lots of lovely plants, yoga classes, Celtic festivals, mythology and a vegetarian cafe.

Sleeping & Eating

Canrawer House (☎ 091-552 388; www.oughterard hostel.com; Station Rd; dm €17-23; 🕑 Feb-Oct) Dorms

and family rooms are bright and clean, and there's an outdoor patio where you can chat with other guests while enjoying views of the 1-hectare rural site, 1km from the centre of town. If you want to catch the area's wild brown trout for dinner, the owner will show you the way for a fee.

Waterfall Lodge (☎ 091-552 168; www.waterfall lodge.net; Glann Rd; s/d €50/80) Decorated in rose-coloured hues and lit by glowing lamps, this double-fronted traditional-style B&B stands amid wooded gardens beside a brook, a brief stroll from the village centre. Breakfast choices are many.

Boat Inn (☎ 091-552 196; www.theboatinn.com; Market Sq; d €90-120) In addition to providing 11 decent rooms, this inn serves traditional Irish stew to warm you up after a day's fishing, as well as other moderately priced, family-friendly fare. The bar hosts regular live music. At the town crossroads, sit outside and watch the tractors go by.

Currarevagh House (☎ 091-552 312; www.currarevagh.com; d €184-198; 🕑 Mar–mid-Oct) You'd be hard pressed to find a more romantic place than this rambling 19th-century mansion, on vast grounds along Lough Corrib. In fact, you might get your romantic vibes from the inn itself: it was given to the ancestors of the owners as a wedding gift in 1846. The food is superlative and features a lot of the locally caught fish, especially trout.

Yew Tree Bakery (☎ 091-866 986; Main St; snacks from €1; 🕑 8am-5pm) This cute little bakery bursts with as much goodness as its luscious pastries do. An ideal snack stop for good coffees and treats.

COUNTY GALWAY

Drinking

Power's Bar (☎ 091-557 047; Market Sq) Head to this thatched pub for a good pint and live music at weekends.

Getting There & Away

Bus Éireann (www.buseireann.ie) and **Citylink** (www.citylink.ie) have regular buses from Galway to Oughterard.

LOUGH CORRIB

The Republic's biggest lake, Lough Corrib, virtually cuts off western Galway from the rest of the country. Over 48km long and covering some 200 sq km, it encompasses more than 360 islands, including Inchagoill, which has a monastic settlement that can be visited from Oughterard or Cong.

Lough Corrib is world-famous for its salmon, sea trout and brown trout. The highlight of the **fishing** calendar is the mayfly season, when zillions of the small bugs hatch over a few days (usually in May) and drive the fish and anglers into a frenzy. Hooks are baited with live flies, which join their cousins dancing on the surface of the lake. Salmon begin running around June. The owner of Oughterard's **Canrawer House** (p415) is a good contact for information and boat hire, as is **Thomas Tuck's Fishing Tackle** (☎ 091-552 335; Main St, Oughterard; ☻ 9am-6.30pm Mon-Sat), an excellent shop teeming with local knowledge.

The largest island on Lough Corrib, **Inchagoill** is a lonely place hiding many ancient remains. Most fascinating is an obelisk called **Lia Luguaedon Mac Menueh** (Stone of Luguaedon, Son of Menueh), which marks a burial site. It stands about 75cm tall, near the Saints' Church, and some people claim that the Latin writing on the stone is the second-oldest Christian inscription in Europe, after those in the catacombs in Rome. **Teampall Phádraig** (St Patrick's Church) is a small oratory of a very early design, with some later additions. The prettiest church is the Romanesque **Teampall na Naoimh** (Saints' Church), probably built in the 9th or 10th century. There are carvings around the arched doorway.

Inchagoill can be reached by boat from Oughterard (or Cong in County Mayo). **Corrib Cruises** (☎ 092-46029; www.corribcruises.com) sail from Oughterard to Inchagoill (adult/child €15/7) and on to Cong (€22/10). Departures are two or three times daily May to October.

LOUGH INAGH VALLEY

Magnificent desolation. If Buzz Aldrin hadn't said it on the moon, we'd say it here. Okay, we will anyway. This stark brown landscape beguiles by its very simplicity. Cloud shadows throw patterns on the jutting peaks; pause and let the ceaseless winds tousle your hair.

The R344 enters the valley from the south, just west of playfully named Recess. The moody waters of Loughs Derryclare and Inagh reflect the colours of the moment. On the western side is the brooding **Twelve Bens** mountain range. At the north end of the valley, the R344 meets the N59, which loops around Connemara to Leenane (p421).

Towards the northern end of the valley, a track leads west off the road up a blind valley, which is well worth exploring.

About 6km from where the R344 enters the valley stands the spotless **Ben Lettery Hostel** (☎ 091-51136; www.anoige.ie/hostels/ben-lettery; Ballinafad; dm €15-20; ☻ Mar-Nov). On the main Clifden road, in the heart of the Connemara wilderness, it has a tidy, homey kitchen and living room, and is an excellent base for exploring the Twelve Bens and Lough Inagh Valley. The hostel is 13km east of Clifden. Citylink buses will stop here if you arrange it with the driver, but note that it's only possible to check in between 5pm and 10pm.

Steeped in Victorian grandeur, the atmospheric **Lough Inagh Lodge** (☎ 091-34706; www.loughinaghlodgehotel.ie; s €104-138, d €168-240, dinner €43; 💻 📶) is midway up the gorgeous Lough Inagh Valley off the R344. Set against a hill, it has a plum position on the water. Turf fires lend the cosy public spaces a scent that says 'country'. You start breathing deeply from the time you enter one of the 13 rooms.

ROUNDSTONE

pop 400

Clustered around a boat-filled harbour, Roundstone (Cloch na Rón) is one of Connemara's gems. Colourful terrace houses and inviting pubs overlook the dark recess of Bertraghboy Bay, which is home to lobster trawlers and traditional *currachs* with tarred canvas bottoms stretched over wicker frames.

Sights & Activities

Wander the short **promenade** for views over the water to ribbons of eroded land.

Just south of the village, in the remains of an old Franciscan monastery, is Malachy

Kearns' **Roundstone Musical Instruments** (☎ 091-35808; www.bodhran.com; Michael Killeen Park; ☺ 9am-7pm Jul-Sep, 9.30am-6pm Mon-Sat Oct-Jun). Kearns is Ireland's only full-time maker of traditional bodhráns. Watch him work and buy a tin whistle, harp or booklet filled with Irish ballads; there's also a small free folk museum and a cafe. Adjacent **craft shops** sell everything from fine pottery to sweaters.

Looming above the stone pier is **Mt Errisbeg** (298m), the only significant hill along this section of coastline. The pleasant walk from Roundstone to the top takes about two hours. Follow the small road past O'Dowd's pub in the centre of the village. From the summit there are wonderful views across the bay to the distant humps of the Twelve Bens.

Sleeping & Eating

Gurteen Beach Caravan & Camping Park (☎ 091-35882; www.gurteenbay.com; Roundstone; campsites €15) This peaceful, well-equipped camping ground is in a great spot 2.5km west of town, near Dog's Bay beach.

Wits End B&B (☎ 091-35813; Main St; r from €60; ☺ Mar-Nov) Right in the centre of town, this pink palace (well, pink modest house) has rooms (with private bathrooms) looking over the road to the water. It's basic but comfortable and is a mere stumble from the fine pubs.

Roundstone House (☎ 091-35864; www.roundstone househotel.com; Main St; r €65-120; ☺ Apr-Oct) A dignified presence lining Main St, this sprawling inn has 13 restful rooms with tea kettles and other creature comforts, plus views across the bay. The pub has trad sessions some nights in summer and you can enjoy pints and local seafood out on the terrace.

O'Dowd's (☎ 091-35809; Main St; mains €15-22; ☺ restaurant noon-10pm Apr-Sep, noon-3pm & 6-9.30pm Oct-Mar) This well-worn, comfortable old pub hasn't lost any of its authenticity since it starred in the Hollywood flick *The Matchmaker*. Specialities at its adjoining restaurant include seafood sourced off the old stone dock right across the street.

ROUNDSTONE TO CLIFDEN

The R341 shadows the coast from Roundstone to Clifden. Beaches along here have such beautiful white sand and turquoise water that, if you added 10°C to the temperature, you could be in St Barts. About 2.5km from Roundstone, look for the turn to **Gurteen Bay** (sometimes spelt Gorteen Bay). After a further 800m there

---

WHERE THERE'S SMOKE, THERE'S SALMON

If you're curious to discover how the area's famous salmon is smoked, you can tour the family-run **Connemara Smokehouse** (☎ 095-23739; www.smokehouse.ie; Bunowen Pier, Ballyconneely; ☺ tours 3pm Wed Jun-Aug). Free tours show you the hand filleting, traditional preparation, slicing and packing of the wild and organic salmon, and shed light on various smoking methods before finishing up with a tasting. Advance reservations are essential. Outside tour times, it's usually possible to stop by the smokehouse and stock up if you call ahead.

---

is a turn for **Dogs Bay**. Together, the pair form the two sides of a dog-bone-shaped peninsula lined with idyllic beaches. Park and enjoy a day strolling the grassy heads and frolicking on the hard-packed sand.

Overlooking the sand, **Errisbeg Lodge** (☎ 091-35807; www.errisbeglodge.com; r €80-120) is a hiker's haven. Let the sea breezes in through your room's window and soon you'll be exploring the area, from hikes up the peaks to beachside ambles. Genial hoofed critters stand placidly in the fields.

Away from the coast, there is an alternate route through protected **Roundstone Bog**, between Roundstone and Clifden. The old road is a bumpy ride, passing through an eerie, rust-collared wilderness. Locals who believe the bog is haunted won't drive this road at night; indeed, the roughness of the road is reason enough to avoid it after dark. In summer, you might see turf being harvested by hand, as blanket bogs cannot be cut mechanically. The road runs west from a junction on the R341 about 4km north of Roundstone. It rejoins the R341 at Ballinaboy.

CLIFDEN & AROUND

pop 1900

Connemara's 'capital', Clifden (An Clochán), is an appealing Victorian-era country town with an imperfect oval of streets offering evocative strolls. It presides over the head of the narrow bay where the River Owenglin tumbles into the sea. The surrounding countryside beckons you to walk through woods and above the shoreline.

Though the summer months clog Clifden's streets with tourists, winter gives the town a

COUNTY GALWAY

GUIDED WALKS IN CONNEMARA

Maps of the myriad walking trails in Connemara are sold at bookshops and tourist offices. However, to really appreciate the region's unique geology, natural beauty and ancient history, you may wish to go with a guide.

Connemara Safari (☎ 095-21071; www .walkingconnemara.com) runs five-day tours in the region that include meals and accommodation. Tour leaders are experts in fields such as archaeology. Routes include some of the deserted islands off the coast and cost from €700.

---

faded, forgotten charm. Year-round, its easily accessed by public or private transport (about 80km from Galway city) and good diversions make it an inviting stop while exploring the region.

Information

There are banks with ATMs around Market Sq, as well as a large supermarket.

Clifden Bookshop (☎ 095-22020; Main St) Good for local titles.

Post office (Main St)

Shamrock Washeteria (☎ 095-21348; Market Sq) Laundrette.

Tourist office (☎ 095-21163; www.clifdenchamber.ie; Galway road; ☼ 10am-5pm Mon-Sat Easter-Jun & Sep, 10am-5pm daily Jul & Aug)

Two Dog Internet Café (☎ 095-22186; Church Hill; per hr €5) Excellent coffee and snacks.

Sights & Activities

The region's past comes to life at the **Connemara Heritage & History Centre** (☎ 095-21808; www.conne maraheritage.com; Lettershea; adult/under 12yr €8/4; ☼ 10am-6pm Apr-Oct). Farmer Dan O'Hara lived here until his eviction from the farm and subsequent emigration to New York, where he ended up selling matches on the street. Its present owners have restored the property, turning it into a window onto lost traditional ways, with demonstrations of bog cutting, thatching, sheep shearing and so on. It's possible to stay at the farmhouse in more comfort than Dan ever enjoyed. The homestead is 7km east of town on the N59.

Heading directly west from Clifden's Market Sq, **Sky Road** traces a spectacular loop out to the township of Kingston and back to Clifden, taking in some rugged, stunningly beautiful coastal scenery en route. The round trip of about 12km can be easily walked or cycled, but, if you're short on time, you can also drive.

Connemara's ponies are a docile bunch. If you'd like to strike up a friendship, try going for a ride with **Errislannan Manor** (☎ 095-21134; www.connemaraponyriding.com; Ballyconneely Rd). Guides provide lessons and lead treks along the beach and up into the hills. Rates start at €35 per hour and depend on the type and length of ride you want to take. The centre is 3.5km south of Clifden on the R341.

You can see the local ponies at their swiftest during the annual **Connemara Pony Show** (www .cpbs.ie) held in late August. It draws punters from across western Ireland.

Sleeping

Numerous attractive choices in the centre allow you to easily partake of Clifden's many charms.

Brookside Hostel (☎ 095-21812; www.brookside hostel.com; Fairgreen; dm €16, d €40-50; ☼ Mar-Oct; ☞) Run by Richard Bartley, who built it from scratch, this sterling IHH hostel is located in a peaceful spot off the bottom of Market St, with the River Owenglin trickling past. Watch the annual pony show from the rooms.

Clifden Town Hostel (☎ 095-21076; www.clifden townhostel.com; Market St; dm €17-21, d €44) Right in the centre of town, this cheery IHH hostel is set in a cream-coloured house framed by big picture windows. Its sunlit rooms hold 34 beds.

Ben View House (☎ 095-21256; www.benviewhouse .com; Bridge St; r €45-80) This central 1848 town house has a vintage charm provided by timber beams, polished floorboards and old-fashioned hospitality. The nine rooms are nutty with antiques. It caters to cyclists, with special storage areas and a tolerance for sweat.

our pick **Dun Ri Guesthouse** (☎ 095-21625; www .dunri.ie; Hulk St; r €50-100; ☞) Just down the hill from the centre, in a quiet spot near the pony track, this appealing modern inn has 13 spacious rooms. The included breakfast offers many choices; the cheese plate was one of the finest we've been served.

Foyles Hotel (☎ 095-21801; www.foyleshotel.com; Main St; s €72, d €114-170; ☼ Jun-Aug) A white-trimmed, Wedgwood-blue landmark in the centre of town, Clifden's oldest hotel has been in the same family for decades. Tradition never went out of fashion here. The carpets seem timeless as do the glowing embers in the lounge fireplace, and the 25 gracious rooms.

Sea Mist House (☎ 095-21441; Market St; www .seamisthouse.com; r €80-120; 🛜) Right in town but opening onto a private fairy-tale garden (which also provides fruit for homemade jam to spread on your freshly baked scones), this stone house has four immaculate rooms.

Quay House (☎ 095-21369; www.thequayhouse.com; Beach Rd; r €90-180; 😍 mid-Mar–mid-Nov) Down by the water, a 10-minute walk from town, this rambling 1820 house has 14 rooms filled with antiques but managing an unfussy style that seems contemporary. Run by an offshoot of the Foyle family of hoteliers, it has pleasures unheard of during past careers as a convent and monastery. Bathrooms have tubs and showers; breakfasts are superb.

Eating & Drinking

Pubs and restaurants cluster around Clifden's town centre. As elsewhere in these parts, seafood reigns supreme.

Lowry's Bar (☎ 095-21347; Market St; meals €4-9; 😍 10.30am-midnight Sun-Thu, 10.30am-1am Fri & Sat) A time-worn local, Lowry's has traditional pleasures, ranging from the age-old, unadorned look of the place to its *céilidh* sessions, which take place at least a couple of nights a week. The food is 'unpretentious Irish' (eg bangers and mash).

Off the Square (☎ 095-22281; Main St; mains €10-22; 😍 9am-10pm) Mediterranean flavours make an appearance at this excellent restaurant, which serves meals throughout the day. Casual fare at lunch gives way to superb meals at night. Local meats star; we had a satiny bacon and cabbage special.

EJ Kings (☎ 095-21330; Market Sq; mains €14-22; 😍 10.30am-11pm Sun-Thu, 10am-12.30am Fri & Sat) A busy old pub established in 1852, EJ Kings has decent though fancy pub food, but it's really the place to quaff some pints on a busy weekend night. Get a tip on the ponies.

Mitchell's (☎ 095-21867; Market St; mains around €17-28; 😍 noon-10pm) Seafood takes centre stage at this elegant spot. From a velvety chowder right through a long list of ever-changing specials, the produce of the surrounding waters is honoured. The wine list does the food justice.

Mullarky's Pub (☎ 095-21801; Main St) Another Foyle family production, this rollicking pub is a riot of local merriment, with live music many nights. Join the fun and you may need to stay in Clifden longer than you thought.

Getting There & Away

Bus Éireann (www.buseireann.ie) and **Citylink** (www .citylink.ie) have several services daily to Galway along the N59. Fares start at €11 and the trip takes 90 minutes, passing many other towns on the way.

Getting Around

The compact town centre is easy to cover on foot. **John Mannion & Son** (☎ 095-21160; Bridge St) hires out bicycles for €15 per day.

CLADDAGHDUFF & OMEY ISLAND

Following the fretted coastline north of Clifden brings you to the tiny village of **Claddaghduff** (An Cladach Dubh), which is signposted off the road to Cleggan. If you turn west here down by the Catholic church, you will come out on **Omey Strand**, and at low tide you can drive or walk across the sand to **Omey Island** (population 20), a low islet of rock, grass, sand and a handful of houses. During summer, horse races are held on Omey Strand.

CLEGGAN
pop 300

Most visitors whiz through Cleggan (An Cloiggean), a small fishing village 16km northwest of Clifden, to hop on the Inishbofin ferry. While here, however, you can experience Ireland's 'wild west' at **Cleggan Riding Centre** (☎ 095-44746; www.cleggandingcentre.com; prices vary), which offers year-round horseback adventures including three-hour treks to Omey Island via the sandy causeway.

Oliver's (☎ 095-44640; mains €18-25; 😍 5-9pm) is a locally loved seafood pub. The classic facade is as black as a pint of Guinness. Specials depend on the catch.

Citylink (www.citylink.ie) buses continue to Cleggan three times daily from Clifden.

INISHBOFIN
pop 200

By day sleepy Inishbofin is a haven of tranquillity. You can walk or bike its narrow, deserted lanes, green pastures and sandy beaches, with farm animals and seals for company. But with no *gardaí* on the island to enforce closing times at the pub, by night – you guessed it – Inishbofin has mighty fine craic.

Information

Inishbofin's small post office has a grocery shop and a currency-exchange facility. Pubs and hotels will usually change travellers cheques. The **tourism association** (☎ 095-45861; www.inishbofin.com) has good info, including detailed online guides to local walks.

Sight & Activities

Situated 9km offshore, Inishbofin is compact – 6km long by 3km wide – and its highest point is a mere 86m above sea level. Just off the northern beach is **Lough Bó Finne**, from which the island gets its name; *bó finne* means 'white cow'.

St Colman exiled himself to Inishbofin in AD 664, after he fell out with the Church over its adoption of a new calendar. He set up a monastery, supposedly northeast of the harbour, where the more recent ruins of a small 13th-century **church** still stand. Grace O'Malley, the famous pirate queen, used Inishbofin as a base in the 16th century, and Cromwell's forces captured the island in 1652, building a star-shaped prison for priests and clerics. Just behind the pier, the small but comprehensive **heritage museum** (☎ 095-45950; www.inishbofin.com; admission free; ☽ hours vary) gives an overview of the island's history. Displays include the contents of a pre-Famine house, photographs, and traditional farming and fishing equipment.

Inishbofin's pristine waters offer superb **scuba diving** (see the boxed text, p422).

Festivals & Events

The island well and truly wakes up during the May **Inishbofin Arts Festival** (☎ 095-45861; www.inishbofin.com), which features accordion workshops, archaeological walks, art exhibitions and concerts by such high-profile Irish bands as the Frames, as well as other events.

Sleeping & Eating

You can pitch a tent on most unfenced ground, but not on or near the beaches.

Inishbofin Island Hostel (☎ 095-45855; www.inishbofin-hostel.ie; camping per person €10; dm €15-18, d €80-90; ☽ early Apr-Sep) In an old farmhouse, this snug 38-bed hostel has glassed-in common areas with panoramic views and equally scenic campsites. It's 500m up from the ferry dock.

Doonmore Hotel (☎ 095-45804; www.doonmorehotel.com; s €60-75, d €100-130; ☽ Apr-Sep) Close to the harbour, Doonmore has comfortable, unpretentious rooms. Lunch (€15) and dinner (€35) in the dining room take advantage of the

abundance of locally caught seafood, and the hotel can pack lunches for you to take while exploring the island.

Dolphin Hotel & Restaurant (☎ 095-45991; www.dolphinhotel.ie; r €70-110; ☐) A panoply of beiges dominates the guest rooms at this stylish study in modern minimalism. Walnut furniture is set off by images of the island's natural beauty. Solar panels on the roof and an organic kitchen garden lend green cred. Local seafood and vegetarian dishes dominate the menu (mains €15 to €25). At weekends there may be a two-night minimum stay.

Getting There & Around

Ferries from Cleggan to Inishbofin take 30 to 45 minutes and cost €20/10 per adult/child.

Dolphins often swim alongside the boats. Confirm ahead, as ferries may be cancelled when seas are rough. Once there, everything is walkable: the island is a mere 3km by 6km.

Island Discovery (☎ 095-45894, 095-45819; www.inishbofinislanddiscovery.com) runs two to three times daily from Cleggan to Inishbofin.

Kings Bicycle Hire (☎ 095-45833), at the pier, hires out bicycles for €15 per day.

LETTERFRACK & AROUND
pop 200

Founded by Quakers in the mid-19th century, Letterfrack (Leitir Fraic) is ideally situated for exploring Connemara National Park, Renvyle Point and Kylemore Abbey. The village is barely more than a crossroads with a few pubs and B&Bs, but the forested setting and nearby coast are a magnet for outdoors adventure seekers. A 4km walk to the peak of Tully Mountain takes 40 minutes and affords wonderful ocean views.

Sights
KYLEMORE ABBEY

A few kilometres east of Letterfrack stands **Kylemore Abbey** (☎ 095-41146; www.kylemoreabbey.com; adult/under 12yr/student €12/free/7; ☽ visitor centre, abbey & church 9am-5pm, gardens 10am-4.30pm mid-Mar–Oct). Magnificently situated on the shores of a lake, this crenellated 19th-century neo-Gothic fantasy was built for a wealthy English businessman, Mitchell Henry, who spent his honeymoon in Connemara. His wife died tragically young.

Admission also covers the abbey's **Victorian walled gardens**. Without paying admission, you

COUNTY GALWAY

can stroll around the lake and surrounding woods.

During WWI, a group of Benedictine nuns left Ypres in Belgium and set up in Kylemore Abbey. They established an exclusive convent boarding school here, but a decision to close the school in 2010 means bad news for local Catholic high-school girls.

Kylemore's tranquillity is shattered in high summer with the arrival of dozens of tour coaches per day, each one followed through the gates by an average of 50 cars (yes, about 2750 cars every day).

CONNEMARA NATIONAL PARK

Immediately southeast of Letterfrack, **Connemara National Park** (☎ 095-41054; www.npws.ie, www.heritageireland.ie; Letterfrack; admission free; ☺ visitor centre & facilities 10am-5.30pm Mar-May & Sep-early Oct, 9.30am-6.30pm Jun-Aug, grounds open year-round) spans 2000 dramatic hectares of bog, mountain and heath. The visitor centre is in a beautiful setting off a parking area 300m south of the Letterfrack crossroads.

The park encloses a number of the **Twelve Bens**, including Bencullagh, Benbrack and Benbaun. The heart of the park is **Gleann Mór** (Big Glen), through which the River Polladirk flows. There's fine walking up the glen and over the surrounding mountains. There are also short, self-guided walks and, if the Bens look too daunting, you can hike up **Diamond Hill** nearby.

The visitor centre offers an introduction to the park's flora, fauna and geology, and visitors can scrutinise maps and various trails here before heading out into the park. Various types of flora and fauna native to the area are explained, including the Mothra-sized elephant hawkmoth.

Guided nature walks (☺ Jul & Aug) depart from the visitor centre. They last two to three hours and cover rough, boggy terrain.

Sleeping & Eating

Letterfrack has some good cafes and pubs.

Letterfrack Lodge (☎ 095-41222; www.letterfrack lodge.com; Letterfrack; campsites from €12, dm €10-20, d €50-60; 🖳 🛜) Personality oozes out of the cracks at this fun hostel close to the Letterfrack crossroads. Dorms come in a variety of sizes, but all are clean and spacious. Doubles are hotel-like in decor and comfort. Mike, the owner, is a great source of info on topics as diverse as local hikes and pubs.

Getting There & Away

Bus Éireann (www.buseireann.ie) and **Citylink** (www.citylink.ie) buses continue to Letterfrack several times daily from Clifden, 15km southwest on the N59.

LEENANE & KILLARY HARBOUR

The small village of Leenane (also spelled Leenaun) drowses on the shore of dramatic Killary Harbour. Dotted with mussel rafts, the harbour is widely believed to be Ireland's only fjord. Slicing 16km inland and more than 45m deep in the centre, it certainly looks like a fjord, although some scientific studies suggest it may not actually have been glaciated. **Mt Mweelrea** (819m) towers to its north.

Leenane boasts both stage and screen connections. It was the location for *The Field* (1989), a movie with Richard Harris based on John B Keane's poignant play about a tenant farmer's ill-fated plans to pass on a rented piece of land to his son. The village's name made it onto the theatrical map with the success in London and New York of Martin McDonagh's play *The Beauty Queen of Leenane*.

The local **website** (www.leenanevillage.com) is a good source of info.

Sights

After surveying the countryside studded with sheep, you can roam among them at the **Sheep & Wool Centre** (☎ 095-42323, 095-42231; www.sheepand woolcentre.com; admission €4; ☺ 9am-6pm Apr-Oct). You can also see spinning and weaving demonstrations, learn about the history of dyeing at the little museum, and feed the farm animals – then dine yourself, on homemade cakes, pies and Irish stew at the cafe. The centre's shop sells locally made handcrafts, as well as topographical walking maps. If you're here in the low season, it's still worth phoning as you may be able to pop by if the family is around.

Activities

Canoeing, sea kayaking, sailing, rock climbing, windsurfing and day hikes are but a few of the activities on offer at **Killary Adventure Centre** (☎ 095-43411; www.killaryadventure.com; ☺ 10am-5pm), approximately 3km west of Leenane on the N59. Rates begin at adult/child €50/32.

From Nancy's Point, about 2km west of Leenane, **Killary Cruises** (☎ 091-566 736; www.killary cruises.com; adult/child €21/10) offers 1½-hour cruises of Killary Harbour. Dolphins leap around the

COUNTY GALWAY

DETOUR: CONNEMARA'S NORTH COAST

Although Connemara is one long series of stunning sights, the north coast is supremely sublime. Its gorgeous beaches compete for your attention with stark, raw mountain vistas and views out to the moody sea.

Eschew the N59 for a series of small roads that follow the twists and turns along the coast for about 15km. Start at **Letterfrack**, where a narrow track leads northwest. Follow various small roads, sticking as close to the water as you can. The land here seems to be in the midst of a beautiful dissolution into the sea. You may find yourself on a road that comes to a dead end at a beach. Good! Get out and take a deep breath.

At **Renvyle** you can pause for the night. **Renvyle Beach Caravan & Camping** (☎ 095-43462; www.renvylebeachcaravanpark.com; Renvyle; campsites €15-20; ☺ Easter-Sep) has campsites on a grassy expanse with direct access to a sandy beach. **Renvyle House Hotel** (☎ 095-43511; www.renvyle .com; Renvyle; r €100-250; ▯ ☉ ☁) is a luxurious 68-room converted country estate that was once owned by the poet Oliver St John Gogarty (among his better lines: 'If anyone thinks that I amn't divine, He gets no free drinks when I'm making the wine').

Continue east, past a couple of fine country pubs at the tiny crossroads of **Tully Cross**. Stick to the coast and stop often – especially on sunny days to marvel at the rich kaleidoscope of colours: rich cobalt sea, cerulean sky, emerald-green grass, brown hills, slate-grey rocks and white-sand beaches. The beach horse-racing sequences for *The Quiet Man* were shot at **Lettergesh**.

Look for a turn to **Rosroe Quay**, where a truly magnificent crescent of sand awaits at **Glassillaun Beach**. If you're drawn to the beauty of the water, **Scuba Dive West** (☎ 095-43922; www.scubadivewest .com) is based at Glassillaun Beach, and runs highly recommended courses and dives around the surrounding coastlines and islands. Rates span the gamut.

Continue southeast along the final 5km stretch of road that runs along **Lough Fee**. In spring when the gorse explodes in yellow bloom, the views here are, again, simply breathtaking. When you reach the N59, you may be ready for a break – maybe a cigarette – after this orgy of beauty.

boat, which passes by a mussel farm and stops at a salmon farm, where you'll see the fish being fed. There are four cruises per day from April to October.

There are several excellent **walks** from Leenane, including one to **Aasleagh Waterfall** (Eas Liath), about 3km away on the northeastern side of Killary Harbour. Also from Leenane, the road runs west for about 2km along the southern shore. Where the highway veers inland, walkers can continue on an old road along the shore to the tiny fishing community of **Rosroe Quay**; see the boxed text, p424 for a detailed route description. For guided day and overnight walks in the region, Gerry Greensmyth from **Croagh Patrick Walking Tours** (☎ 098-26090; www.walkingguideireland.com) has a wealth of local expertise.

Sleeping & Eating

Sleepzone Connemara (☎ 095-42929; www.sleepzone .ie; campsites from €12; dm €20-26, s €50, d €70; ☺ Mar-Oct; ▯ ☁) This renovated 19th-century property has over 100 beds in spotless dorms and private rooms. Popular with walkers, its ameni-

ties include a bar, barbecue terrace, tennis court and bike hire. Ask about the transport scheme with a Galway-based tour company.

Killary House (☎ 095-42254; www.connemara.com/ killaryhouse; Leenane; r €50-80) On a working farm just a short walk from Leenane, this six-room B&B looks out to the bay from its front rooms, and up to the hills in its rear rooms. Cheaper rooms share a bathroom. Ask about on-site meals, including children's menus.

Blackberry Cafe (☎ 095-42240; Leenane; cafe dishes €4.50-11, dinner mains €14-25; ☺ noon-4pm & 6-9pm Easter-Sep) Connemara smoked salmon, chunky chowder, hot smoked trout and rhubarb tarts are some of the treats on offer at this gem of a bistro, conveniently located near the pubs.

Drinking

Farmers and other locals come for quiet pints and warming Irish coffees at the gentle sweep of traditional pubs near the bridge. Savour a pint outside at one of the picnic tables or inside amidst the dark wood panelling and enormous open fireplaces.

SOUTH OF GALWAY CITY

Take time to smell the oysters on the busy seaside route between Galway city and County Clare. At Kilcolgan, veer east off the N18 and you'll be rewarded with villages like Kinvara, whose charms may play havoc with your schedule – if you have one.

CLARINBRIDGE & KILCOLGAN

pop 2100

Some 16km south of Galway, Clarinbridge (Droichead an Chláirin) and Kilcolgan (Cill Cholgáin) are at their busiest during the **Clarinbridge Oyster Festival** (www.clarenbridge.com), held during the second weekend of September. However, the oysters are actually at their best from May through the summer. Clarinbridge is also good for rummaging the antique stores along the main road.

Oysters are celebrated year-round at **Paddy Burke's Oyster Inn** (☎ 091-796 107; www.paddyburkes galway.com; Clarinbridge; 6 oysters €10, mains €10-24; ⏲ 12.30-10pm), a thatched inn by the bridge dishing up heaped servings in a roadside location.

our pick Moran's Oyster Cottage (☎ 091-976 113; www.moransoystercottage.com; The Weir, Kilcolgan; mains €13-22; ⏲ noon-10pm Mon-Sat, 10am-10pm Sun) is an atmospheric thatched pub and restaurant, with a terrace overlooking Dunbulcaun Bay, where the oysters are reared before they arrive on your plate. It's a well-marked 2km west of the noxious N18, in a quiet cove near Kilcolgan.

Clarinbridge is on the main Galway–Gort– Ennis–Limerick road (N18) and is served by numerous Bus Éireann buses from Galway.

KINVARA

pop 400

The small stone harbour of Kinvara (sometimes spelt Kinvarra) sits smugly at the southeastern corner of Galway Bay, which accounts for its Irish name, Cinn Mhara (Head of the Sea). Traditional Galway hooker sailing boats race here each year on the second weekend in August in the **Cruinniú na mBáid** (Gathering of the Boats).

Kinvara's other big date on its annual calendar is **Fleadh na gCuach** (Cuckoo Festival), a traditional music festival in late May that features over 100 musicians performing at upwards of 50 organised sessions. Spin-off events include a parade.

Details of both festivals are available on Kinvara's **website** (www.kinvara.com).

Sights & Activities

The chess-piece-style **Dunguaire Castle** (☎ 091-637 108; adult/child €6/3; ⏲ 9.30am-5pm May-Oct) was erected around 1520 by the O'Hynes clan and is in excellent condition following extensive restoration. It is widely believed that the castle occupies the former site of the 6th-century royal palace of Guaire Aidhne, the king of Connaught. Dunguaire's owners have included Oliver St John Gogarty (1878–1957) – poet, writer, surgeon and Irish Free State senator.

The least authentic way to visit the castle is to attend a **medieval banquet** (☎ 061-360 788; www .shannonheritage.com; banquet adult/child €56/28; ⏲ 5.30pm & 8.45pm May-Oct). Yuck-filled stage shows and shtick provide diversions while you plough through a big group meal.

Sleeping & Eating

Kinvara has several good places to feast on the bounty of its seaside location; a passel of atmospheric pubs only add to the joy. You won't miss at the appropriately named **Fahy's Travellers Inn** (☎ 091-637 116) and nearby **Connolly's** (☎ 091-637 131) on the quay.

Cois Cuain B&B (☎ 091-637 119; r €70-80) Overlooking the harbour, this modest three-room B&B couldn't be any better located for getting into the Kinvara vibe. Imagine you're staying with your genial Irish aunt and you'll feel right at home.

Pier Head (☎ 091-638 188; ⏲ kitchen 5-9.30pm Mon-Sat, noon-3pm Sun) Popular with yachties who tie up out front, this modern restaurant and pub has views over the brine. Food includes local lobster cooked in garlic, mussels and oysters – lots of oysters. The pub has live music at weekends.

Keough's (☎ 091-637 145; Main St, Kinvara; mains €8-15) This friendly local, where you'll often hear Irish spoken, serves up a fresh battered cod; specials are more ambitious. Traditional music sessions take place on Mondays and Thursdays, while Saturday nights swing with old-time dancing.

Getting There & Away

Bus Éireann (www.buseireann.ie) services 50 and 423 link Kinvara with Galway city (30 minutes) and towns in County Clare, such as Doolin, several times daily.

COUNTY GALWAY

WALK: KILLARY HARBOUR

This easy 18km walk (approximately seven hours) takes in the natural splendour and poignant human history of the area around Killary Harbour. The total ascent is 130m; Salrock Pass marks the modest high point of the circuit at 130m, making this route an ideal option if clouds are lying low over higher peaks in the area. The terrain covered is a mixture of quiet tarmac lanes, grassy *boreens* (small lanes or roadways) and rugged paths; boots are a good idea as sections of the trail can become boggy or muddy. Ordnance Survey Ireland's 1:50,000 map 37 covers this area.

The route starts and finishes 3km southwest of **Leenane**, at the quarry situated 20m southwest of the River Bunowen on the main Leenane–Clifden road (N59). There's ample parking at the quarry, but getting here requires your own transport.

When you come out of the quarry, turn left, walk onwards for 400m and then take the first right. Heading down that road, you'll soon come to two gates and a sign that indicates that private vehicles may not proceed further. Pass through the right-hand gate and continue along the lane for a little over 1km. Lines of floats securing mussel beds bob in the harbour to the north and will be a constant presence for the first half of the route. The lane soon becomes a gravel track, and then, after passing through a couple of gates and crossing a bridge that spans a waterfall, it narrows again to become a grassy *boreen*.

This area was badly affected by the Great Famine, and around 3km from the start of the walk you'll come to the first of several ruined stone buildings that once made up the village of Foher, which was depopulated during the Famine. Follow the *boreen* along the front of the ruins, and pass over a stone stile in the wall to the west. The *boreen* now dwindles to a single-file path, and climbs up and around a rock outcrop. The retaining walls of the Famine road, which was constructed by locals in return for rations, are obvious at the side of the path.

The rugged landscape is now dotted with boulders and bands of rock, although the buildings and boats of **Rosroe Quay** soon come into view ahead (1½ to two hours from the start). Pass along the south side of a large stone wall enclosing a field, and exit the *boreen* beside a cottage. Join the minor road leading to Rosroe harbour; the pier is about 200m along the road to the right, and well worth the short detour.

From the pier, retrace your steps along the road, continuing past the point where you came down off the *boreen*. Killary Harbour Little (or Little Killary) is the picturesque inlet to the south, its shape mimicking the larger-scale fjord further north. Follow the road for around 1km, climbing to a sharp right turn. Leave the lane here, continuing ahead (east) through a wooden gate. A short but steep ascent now leads to Salrock Pass, from where Killary Harbour and Little Killary are both visible.

The descent on the eastern side of the pass is even steeper, but you'll soon come to a junction of a fence and stone wall on your right. Head through a wooden gate on the left, and walk along a rough track that runs over Salrock, from where you follow a line of electricity poles all the way to the deserted village of Foher, which you passed on your outward journey. Follow the wall as it descends gradually through the ruins, rejoining the *boreen* at the eastern end of the hamlet. Retrace your initial steps back to the road and your starting point.

EASTERN GALWAY

Lough Corrib separates eastern Galway from the dramatic landscape of Connemara and the county's western coast, and this region is markedly different. This is farm country and there's nary a hint of the geologic drama and cultural excitement that exists in the west of the county. Several diversions provide good reason to pause on the Dublin drive.

Galway East Tourism (☎ 091-850 687; www.galway east.com) has regional information.

Getting There & Away

Bus Éireann (☎ 091-562 000) services connect Galway with Athenry, Ballinasloe and Loughrea. Services from Galway to/from Portumna require a change at Kilbeggan, County Westmeath.

ATHENRY

pop 2200

The name Athenry is synonymous with the stirring song 'The Fields of Athenry', composed by Pete St John in the 1970s, which recounts incarceration resulting from the

Famine. Often thought to be adapted from an 1880s ballad (disputed by St John), it's been covered by countless artists, and is sung by passionate crowds at sporting matches, including in adapted forms such as Liverpool Football Club's anthem, 'The Fields of Anfield Road'. The **town website** (www.athenry.net) lists sleeping and eating options.

The walled town, 16km east of Galway, takes its own name from a nearby ford (*áth* in Irish) that crosses the River Clare east of the settlement and was the meeting point for three kingdoms, hence Áth an Rí (Ford of the Kings).

The fascinating **Athenry Arts & Heritage Activity Centre** (☎ 091-844 661; www.athenryheritagecentre .com; The Square; ⏰ 11am-4pm Mar-Oct) explores the town's medieval sights and can outline walking itineraries.

Touted as Ireland's most intact collection of medieval architecture, the city holds a number of preserved buildings, including a restored **Norman castle**, the **Medieval Parish Church of St Mary's**, a **Dominican priory** with superb masonry on its occupational gravestones, and an original **market cross**.

LOUGHREA & AROUND
pop 4000

Named for the little lake at its southern edge, Loughrea (Baile Locha Riach) is a bustling market town 26km southeast of Galway. Loughrea has Ireland's last functioning medieval **moat**, which runs from the lake at Fair Green near the cathedral to the River Loughrea north of town.

Not to be confused with St Brendan's Church on Church St, which is now a library, **St Brendan's Catholic Cathedral** (☎ 091-841 212; Barrack St; ⏰ 11.30am-1pm & 2-5.30pm Mon-Fri), dating from 1903, is renowned for its Celtic-revival stained-glass windows, furnishings and marble columns.

Near Bullaun, 7km north of Loughrea, is the pillarlike **Turoe Stone**, covered in delicate La Tène–style relief carvings. It dates from between 300 BC and AD 100. The Turoe Stone wasn't set here originally, but was found at an Iron Age fort a few kilometres away.

On the road east to Ballinasloe, 6.5km from Loughrea, the **Dartfield Horse Museum & Park** (☎ 091-843 968; www.dartfieldhorsemuseum.com; adult/child €10/5; ⏰ 9am-6pm) allows horse lovers to learn about horse breeding, carriages, the colourful racing industry and the horse's role in Irish history. There's also a lot here about rural life in Ireland in the 19th century. The pony rides thrill kids.

BALLINASLOE
pop 6000

On the main Dublin–Galway road (N6), Ballinasloe (Béal Átha na Sluaighe) is famed for its historic October **horse fair** (www .ballinasloe.com), which dates right back to the high kings of Tara. Attending the horse fair invariably involves sloshing through muddy fields – bring boots and don't wear white! Don't let the mud deter you, though: the fair has an old-time carnival atmosphere, created by the 80,000-plus horse traders and merrymakers who roll into town. They include Ireland's Traveller community, who camp nearby in traditional barrel-topped wagons. To learn more about Traveller culture, the websites of the **Irish Traveller Movement** (www.itmtrav.ie) and **Pavee Point Travellers Centre** (www.paveepoint.ie) are good sources of information.

Around 6km southwest of town on the N6, **Aughrim** was the site of the bloodiest battle ever fought on Irish soil, which ended in a crucial victory by William of Orange over the Catholic forces of James II. The **Battle of Aughrim Interpretive Centre** (☎ 0509-73939; Aughrim; adult/child €5/3; ⏰ 10am-6pm Tue-Sat, 2-6pm Sun Jun–mid-Sep) helps place it within the context of the War of the Two Kings. Signposts from the interpretive centre indicate the actual battle site.

Auld Shillelagh Hostel (☎ 0509-73734; info@auld shillelagh.com; Aughrim, Ballinasloe; dm €17-20), near the battle site, has just 12 beds, so you'll need to book well ahead for summer or the horse fair. It hires out bikes and can arrange pick-up around the area. The eponymous gnarled wooden walking sticks hang from the walls in profusion.

CLONFERT CATHEDRAL

Heading 21km southeast of Ballinasloe brings you to the tiny and isolated 12th-century **Clonfert Cathedral**. It's on the site of a monastery said to have been founded in AD 563 by St Brendan 'the Navigator', who is believed to be buried here. Although the historical jury is out on whether St Brendan reached America's shores in a tiny *currach,* there are Old Irish Ogham (the earliest form of writing in Ireland) carvings in West Virginia that date from as early as the 6th century, suggesting an Irish presence in America well before Columbus set foot there.

COUNTY GALWAY

DETOUR: GORT & AROUND

If you're a fan of WB Yeats, two sights connected to the great poet near the highway town of Gort are a worthwhile detour on your way to or from Galway.

A 16th-century Norman tower known as **Thoor Ballyle** (☎ 091-631 436; Peterswell; adult/child €6/1.50; ☼ 9.30am-5pm Mon-Sat May-Sep) was the summer home of Yeats from 1922 to 1929, and was the inspiration for one of his best-known works, *The Tower*. The restored 16th-century tower contains the poet's furnishings, and you can see an audiovisual presentation on his life. From Gort take the Loughrea road (N66) for about 3km and look for the sign.

About 3km north of Gort is **Coole Park** (☎ 091-631 804; www.coolepark.ie; admission free; ☼ 10am-5pm). It was the home of Lady Augusta Gregory, cofounder of the Abbey Theatre and a patron of Yeats. An exhibition focuses on the literary importance of the house (demolished by nitwit bureaucrats in 1941), and the flora and fauna of the surrounding nature reserve. The main attraction on the grounds is the autograph tree, on which many of Lady Gregory's literary guests carved their initials.

Lady Gregory is honoured in full at **Kiltartan Gregory Musuem** (☎ 091-632 346; Kiltartan Cross; ☼ 10am-6pm Jun-Aug), close to Coole Park. Housed in an old schoolhouse designed by the same architect as the lost Coole House, it traces the literary patron's life.

In the same area, about 5km southwest of Gort, is the extensive monastic site of **Kilmacduagh**. Beside a small lake is a well-preserved 34m-high round tower, the remains of a small 14th-century cathedral (Teampall Mór MacDuagh), an oratory dedicated to St John the Baptist, and other little chapels. The original monastery is thought to have been founded by St Colman MacDuagh at the beginning of the 7th century. There are fine views over the Burren from here and you can visit any time.

The marvellous six-arch Romanesque doorway, adorned with surreal human heads, is reason enough to visit. The cathedral is off the R356; you'll need your own car to get here.

PORTUMNA
pop 1900

In the southeast corner of the county, the lakeside town of Portumna is popular for boating and fishing. **Lough Derg Holiday Park** (☎ 061-376 329; www.loughderg.net) rents boats for €15/45/65 per hour/half-day/day.

Impressive **Portumna Castle & Gardens** (☎ 0509-41658; www.heritageireland.ie; Castle Ave; adult/child €3/1; ☼ 9.30am-6pm early Apr–Sep) was built in the early 1600s by Richard de Burgo and boasts an elaborate, geometrically laid-out organic garden that would do a French king proud.

Counties Mayo & Sligo

Travelling just a few hours by road from Dublin transports you to Ireland's 'wild west'. And while it might not be the domain of gun-slinging cowboys, John Wayne did film one of his best-known movies here, the enduring 1950s classic *The Quiet Man*.

Far from the beaten track, you'll find remote country lodgings, unhurried drives behind slow-moving tractors and placid, fish-filled lakes strewn across these two northwestern counties, along with warm-hearted country hospitality. And in-the-know surfers from all over the world head to the counties' coastline in search of legendary breaks.

The larger, more rugged of the two, Mayo juts further into the Atlantic, much of it covered by harsh, barren, boggy terrain. The phrase 'to hell or to Connacht' may well have referred to Mayo's brutally tough farming conditions. But this desolate land offers strikingly stark rock formations and subtle hues: orange-streaked sunsets, yellow asphodel flowers, dark-green myrtle, blue-grey rivers reflecting the changing skies above, purple moor grass rolling underfoot.

Sligo's natural wonderment ranges from the flat-top mountains and lush pastoral scenes that inspired the poet William Butler Yeats to compose some of Ireland's most ardent verse here to an improbable bounty of prehistoric sites.

But it's not all wilderness out here: the gentle pace of rural life contrasts with the counties' vibrant towns, including County Mayo's pub-saturated Ballina, busy Castlebar and Georgian jewel Westport, as well as County Sligo's citified oasis, sophisticated Sligo town.

HIGHLIGHTS

- **Wood Carving** Hear Sligo town's woodcarver Michael Quirke (see the boxed text, p454) recount Irish myths and legends as he carves them to life
- **Wave Carvin'** Hit the waves year-round at Easkey (p458)
- **Seaweed Bathing** Do as the Irish have done for centuries and sink into a homeopathic seaweed-filled bath at Enniscrone or Strandhill (see boxed text, p456)
- **Hawk Handling** Learn to handle and fly Harris hawks at aristocratic Ashford Castle (p430), outside Cong
- **'Pilgrimaging'** Follow St Patrick's footsteps up the conical peak of Croagh Patrick (p434), or visit the site of Knock's apparition (p449)

- POPULATION: 184,542
- AREA: 7234 SQ KM

COUNTY MAYO

County Mayo (Maigh Eo, 'Plain of the Yew Trees') is a continuation of Connemara's wild beauty, yet with a fraction of the tourists.

Like Connemara, Mayo's history does not paint a rosy picture of the easy coun-try life. The ravages of the Potato Famine (1845–51) – which provoked the sad refrain 'County Mayo, Mayo, God help us!' – were harshest here. The resulting mass emigration means that many people with Irish ancestry around the world can trace their roots to this once-plagued land. Today, Mayo's haunting landscapes offer untapped opportunities for

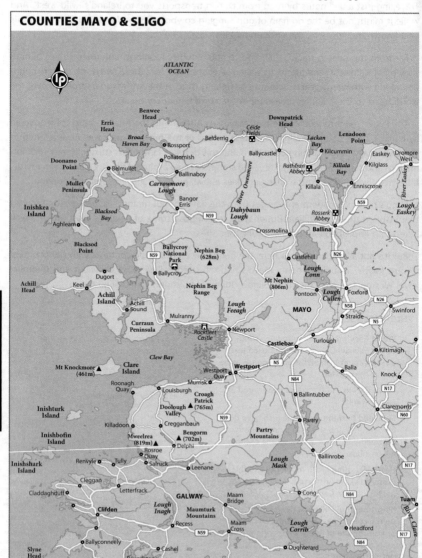

COUNTIES MAYO & SLIGO

explorations, whether by car, foot, bicycle or horseback.

Because County Mayo has such close proximity to Connemara, we've arranged this section going from south to north, starting with the photogenic village of Cong, which can be found just over the border with County Galway.

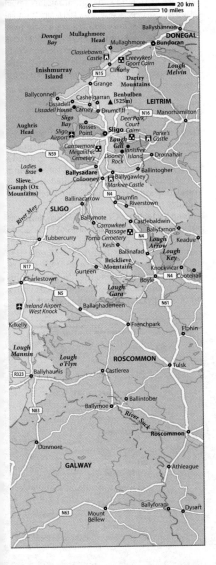

CONG
pop 150
Sitting on a sliver-thin isthmus between Lough Corrib and Lough Mask, Cong complies with romantic notions of a traditional Irish village. Time appears to have stood still ever since the evergreen classic *The Quiet Man* was filmed here in 1951. As such, the arrival of the morning's first tour bus instantly doubles the number of people strolling the town's tiny streets, but the wooded trails between the lovely old abbey and stately Ashford Castle offer genuine quietude.

Information
The **tourist office** (Map430; ☎ 094-954 6542; Abbey St; ☒ 10am-6pm Mar-Nov) is in the old courthouse building opposite Cong Abbey.

There are no banks or ATMs, but you can change money at the post office on Main St, or at the museum (below).

Sights
CONG ABBEY
An evocative reminder of ecclesiastical times past, the weathered shell of Cong's 12th-century **Augustinian abbey** (Map430; admission free; ☒ dawn-dusk) is scored by wizened lines from centuries of exposure to the elements. Nevertheless, several finely sculpted features have survived, including a carved doorway, windows and lovely medieval arches (touched up in the 19th century).

Founded by Turlough Mór O'Connor, high king of Ireland and king of Connaught, in 1120, the abbey occupies the site of an earlier 6th-century church. The community once gathered in the chapter house to confess their sins publicly.

From the abbey, moss-encrusted trees guard a path to the river and the diminutive 16th-century **monk's fishing house** (Map p430), built midway over the river so that the monks could haul their catch straight up through a hole in the floor.

QUIET MAN MUSEUM
Modelled on Sean Thornton's White O' Mornin' Cottage from the film, the **Quiet Man Museum** (Map p430; ☎ 094-954 6089; Circular Rd; adult/student/family €5/4.50/15; ☒ 10am-5pm Mar-Oct) also squeezes in a fascinating regional archaeological and historical exhibition of items from 7000 BC to the 19th century. Film fanatics (or those with a postmodern fascination for

the way reality and fiction blur) can take a 75-minute **location tour** (€10), which includes museum entry.

ASHFORD CASTLE

Just beyond Cong Abbey, the village abruptly ends and the woodlands surrounding **Ashford Castle** (Map p432; ☎ 094-954 6003; www.ashford.ie; admission to grounds €5; 9am-dusk) begin. First built in 1228 as the seat of the de Burgo family, owners over the years included the Guinness family (of stout fame). Arthur Guinness turned the castle into a regal hunting and fishing lodge, which it remains today.

The only way to peek into its immaculately restored interior is to stay or dine here (opposite). But the surrounding estate – 140 hectares of parkland, covered with forests, streams, bridle paths and a golf course – is open to the public. Heading through the Kinlough Woods gets you away from the golfers and out to the shores of Lough Corrib. You can also walk along the riverbanks to the monk's fishing house (p429).

Activities
CRUISES

In the centre of Lough Corrib is the island of Inchagoill. **Corrib Cruises** (Map p432; ☎ 094-954 6029; www.corribcruises.com; Apr-Oct) offers 1½-hour boat tours from the Ashford Castle pier to Inchagoill (€20), with a 30-minute guided tour of the island's monastic sites; and one-hour lake cruises (€20). Cruises taking in Inchagoill and Cong also depart from

Oughterard in County Galway (p414). Tickets can be purchased on-board. The company also runs evening cocktail cruises (€25) with traditional live-music on-board. Sailing times vary depending on demand.

FALCONRY

The medieval splendour of Ashford Castle is a fitting setting to learn the ancient art of falconry at Ireland's inaugural **falconry school** (Map p432; ☎ 094-954 6820; www.falconry.ie; by appointment). The school will teach anyone over the age of seven how to handle and fly Harris hawks. A one-hour introductory lesson costs €70 per person, while a 90-minute 'hawk walk' lesson costs €105. There are reduced rates for two or more people.

Sleeping
BUDGET

Cong Caravan & Camping Park (Map p432; ☎ 094-954 6089; www.quietman-cong.com; Quay Rd, Lisloughrey; campsites €15/25) This agreeable camping ground's thick lawns ensure soft ground for sleeping. It's operated by the same friendly family that runs Cong's hostel, with access to kitchen and laundry facilities.

Cong Hostel (Map p432; ☎ 094-954 6089; www.quietman-cong.com; Quay Rd, Lisloughrey; dm/s/d €17/30/55, linen hire €1.50, breakfast €4, shower €1; P 🖳 🛜) Well run and welcoming, this An Óige and IHH-affiliated hostel has its own *Quiet Man* screening room showing the film *every* night. Between June and mid-September it also hires bikes (€15 per day) and 18ft boats (with/with-

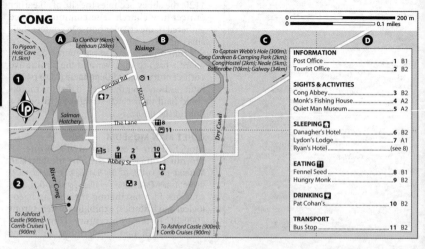

CONG

0 ———————— 200 m
0 ———————— 0.1 miles

To Pigeon Hole Cave (1.5km)
To Clonbur (6km); Leenaun (28km)
Risings
To Captain Webb's Hole (300m); Cong Caravan & Camping Park (2km); Cong Hostel (2km); Neale (5km); Ballinrobe (10km); Galway (34km)

Circular Rd
Main St
Salmon Hatchery
The Lane
Abbey St
River Cong
Dry Canal

To Ashford Castle (900m); Corrib Cruises (900m)
To Ashford Castle (900m); Corrib Cruises (900m)

INFORMATION	
Post Office	1 B1
Tourist Office	2 B2

SIGHTS & ACTIVITIES	
Cong Abbey	3 B2
Monk's Fishing House	4 A2
Quiet Man Museum	5 A2

SLEEPING	
Danagher's Hotel	6 B2
Lydon's Lodge	7 A1
Ryan's Hotel	(see 8)

EATING	
Fennel Seed	8 B1
Hungry Monk	9 B2

DRINKING	
Pat Cohan's	10 B2

TRANSPORT	
Bus Stop	11 B2

COUNTIES MAYO & SLIGO

out motor and fuel €45/20), and operates an adjacent minigolf course (€10).

MIDRANGE

Danagher's Hotel (Map p430; ☎ 094-954 6028; Abbey St; s/d €40/80; 🛜) Upstairs from a comfy old pub in the village centre, some of Danagher's 11 rooms, all with bathroom, have countryside views. It's named for Victor McLaglen's character in the movie (we'll assume you know *which* movie), while its restaurant, Mary Kate's Kitchen (mains €12.50 to €24.50), is named for Maureen O'Hara's character. Traditional music takes place on Thursdays year-round and nightly during summer.

Michaeleen's Manor (Map p432; ☎ 094-954 6089; www.quietman-cong.com; Quay Rd, Lisloughrey; s/d €50/75; 🅿) Margaret and Gerry Collins' large, modern home is something of a shrine to *The Quiet Man*. Each of its 12 sparkling rooms is named after a character in the film and decorated with memorabilia and quotations. There's also a sauna, outdoor hot tub, tennis court, and a large fountain replica of the Quiet Man Bridge (the original is in County Galway; p415).

Ryan's Hotel (Map p430; ☎ 094-954 6243; www.ryanshotelcong.ie; Main St; s/d €55/100; 🅿 🖳 🛜) The social hub of Cong sports revamped plum-coloured rooms with freshly tiled bathrooms and a fine restaurant, Fennel Seed (right).

Lydon's Lodge (Map p430; ☎ 094-46053; lydonslodge@eircom.net; Circular Rd; s/d from €60/90; 🕑 closed Christmas; 🅿 🛜) This rambling riverside lodge has plain but airy rooms and a laid-back bar with an open fire, superb food and regular weekend appearances by DJ King Cong. Bar food is €16 to €29.

TOP END

our pick **Lisloughrey Lodge** (Map p432; ☎ 094-954 5400; www.lisloughrey.ie; The Quay; s €135-165, d €170-230; 🅿 🖳 🛜) The lodge, built in the 1820s by Ashford Castle's owners, has been stunningly renovated in bold, contemporary cranberry and blueberry tones, with 50 guest rooms named for wine regions and champagne houses. Kick back in the bar, billiards room, or beanbag-strewn Wii room.

Ashford Castle (Map p432; ☎ 094-954 6003; www.ashford.ie; r €295-750; 🅿 🖳 🛜) Break the bank to stay here and feel like a film star yourself. Rooms and service are exquisite. Nonguests can book a *table d'hôte* dinner (from €75) in the castle's George V restaurant, but you'll need to dress the part (guys: jacket and tie). Nonguests can also reserve in advance to dine at the less formal Cullen's at the Cottage (mains €15 to €25, 12.30pm to 9.30pm April to October) on the grounds.

Eating & Drinking

Hungry Monk (Map p430; ☎ 094-954 5842; Abbey St; sandwiches €6-8, salads €8-14; 🕑 10am-6pm Wed-Mon Mar-Oct, Fri-Sun Nov-Dec, closed Jan & Feb; 🖳) This cheery little cafe makes fab sandwiches (such as home-baked ham served with mango chutney) and brews the best coffee in town.

Fennel Seed (Map p430; ☎ 094-954 6004; Ryan's Hotel, Main St; bar food €8-12, mains €15-25; 🕑 dinner Mon-Sat, 1-7pm Sun) Michael Crowe and Denis Lenihan used to cook at Ashford Castle and have brought their culinary skills to the village, with great success (don't miss their signature 'smoky bake' pie, filled with trout, salmon, mackerel and haddock). Bar food's served in the adjoining Crowe's Nest Pub until 7pm.

Lisloughrey Lodge (Map p432; ☎ 094-954 5400; www.lisloughrey.ie; The Quay; menus €52-69; 🕑 dinner nightly May-Sep, Thu-Sun Oct-Apr) Book ahead for Wade Murphy's sophisticated twists on Irish cuisine like ham hock and green pea risotto, followed by pan-roasted beef with truffle potato purée, and coffee crème brûlée with whiskey and cinnamon ice cream. Yum.

Pat Cohan's (Map p430; ☎ 087 2259 3824; Abbey St) In a bizarre case of life imitating art, this one-time grocery store was disguised in *The Quiet Man* as the fictional Pat Cohan's. But nearly six decades on, *Quiet Man* craziness refuses to die down, and it has now become that pub.

Getting There & Away

Bus Éireann (☎ 096-71800; www.buseireann.ie) has regular services from Galway (one way/return €10.30/14) and Westport (€11.40/15.20). The bus stops in front of the Quiet Man Coffee Shop on Main St (Map p430).

If you're driving or cycling further into County Mayo, skip the main N84 to Castlebar and head west to Leenane (also spelt Leenaun) then north to Westport via Delphi through the extraordinary Doolough Valley (see p432).

AROUND CONG
Caves

The Cong area is honeycombed with 10 limestone caves, each with a colourful legend or story to its credit.

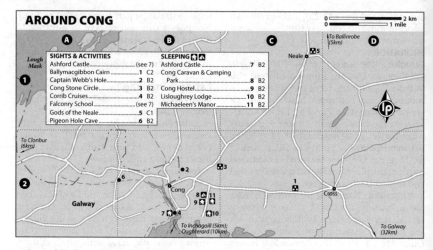

AROUND CONG

SIGHTS & ACTIVITIES	
Ashford Castle...................	(see 7)
Ballymacgibbon Cairn............	**1** C2
Captain Webb's Hole.............	**2** B2
Cong Stone Circle..............	**3** B2
Corrib Cruises.................	**4** B2
Falconry School...............	(see 7)
Gods of the Neale..............	**5** C1
Pigeon Hole Cave..............	**6** B2

SLEEPING	
Ashford Castle.................	**7** B2
Cong Caravan & Camping	
Park.....................	**8** B2
Cong Hostel..................	**9** B2
Lisloughrey Lodge.............	**10** B2
Michaeleen's Manor............	**11** B2

One of the best is **Pigeon Hole** (Map p432), in pine forest about 1.5km west of Cong. It can be reached by road or by the walking track from across the river. Steep, slippery stone steps lead down into the cave, where subterranean water flows in winter. Keep an eye out for the white trout of Cong – a mythical woman who turned into a fish to be with her drowned lover.

Just west of the village is the water-filled **Captain Webb's Hole** (Map p432). Two centuries ago, a local villain nicknamed Captain Webb for the deformity of his hands and feet, is said to have lured a succession of 12 women here, stripped them and hurled them into the hole's soggy depths to die. His would-be 13th victim however was a canny lass. She asked Webb to look away as she undressed, then promptly pushed him to his own watery grave.

Circles & Graves

Weathering the elements since the Early Bronze Age, the **Cong Stone Circle** (Map p432) sticks up from a field about 1.5km northeast of Cong, with a further three stone circles directly behind. About 3.5km east of Cong, north off the Cross road (R346), is the overgrown **Ballymacgibbon Cairn** (Map p432), supposedly the site of the legendary Celtic Battle of Moytura.

Neale

Turning off at the northern end of the village of Neale, 6km northeast of Cong, you'll find the **Gods of the Neale** (Map p432) stone 200m east of the main road, through an unsigned gateway on the left. This mysterious slab,

which is dated 1757, is carved with figures of a human, an animal and a reptile.

DOOLOUGH VALLEY & AROUND

One of Ireland's most poignant drives is through the pristine, desolate Doolough Valley along the R335 scenic route from Leenane (County Galway) to Westport. It was the site of a tragic Famine walk, which took place in 1849. In icy weather, 400 hundred people died along the road as they walked from Louisburgh to Delphi and back. They'd hoped to receive food and aid from a landlord, but were refused.

Most of the valley is untouched by housing, cut turf or even stone walls. Try to drive at a leisurely pace (early morning traffic is usually light), but aim for a dry day, as the narrow, twisting road becomes slippery in wet weather, and curtains of rain can greatly diminish the views.

Fishing (www.delphi-salmon.com; per day €120) is available at Delphi Lodge (opposite).

A host of other activities – including **surfing**, **kayaking**, **ropes courses**, **abseiling** and **archery** – are available at the Delphi Mountain Resort (opposite), costing €60/45 per adult/child for a full day of activity sessions, and €45/25 per half-day.

To the north and west of the valley, side roads lead to often-deserted **beaches**.

Delphi

Geographically *just* inside County Mayo, but administratively in County Galway, this swath

COUNTIES MAYO & SLIGO

of mountainous moorland is miles from any significant population, allowing you to set about the serious business of relaxing.

At the southern extent of the Doolough Valley, the area was named by its most famous resident, the second Marquis of Sligo, who was convinced that it resembled the land around Delphi, Greece. If you can spot the resemblance, you've a better imagination than most, but in many ways it's even more striking than its Mediterranean namesake.

Don't be dissuaded by the 'private' sign at the gate of **Delphi Lodge** (☎ 095-42222; www.delphi lodge.ie; s €133-166, d €200-266, cottages per week from €800; P □), though this Georgian former sporting lodge of the Marquis of Sligo does feel more like a congenial house party than a hotel. You can have your own catch cooked up and served in the communal dining room (guests only); otherwise, you can have it smoked, vacuum-packed and sent on to your address, or swapped for fish that's already packed to take with you. The lunch menu is €20, dinner €50.

The newly reopened, multipurpose establishment **Delphi Mountain Resort** (☎ 095-42987, 095-42208; www.delphiescape.com; dm €40, s/d €134/198; P □), built from rough-cut stone and honey-coloured wood, has standard guest rooms, larger suites (some with enormous timber decks) and some great loft rooms with elevated sleeping areas (strangely, all cost the same), while backpackers can book into one of the (ultrapricey) eight-bed dorms with bathroom. Lunch mains are €12 to €15, dinner mains €15 to €28. Spa treatments use hand-harvested seaweed and the property's own mountain spring water.

Louisburgh
pop 314

The northern gateway to the Doolough Valley, the little village of Louisburgh (Cluain Cearbán), was founded under curious circum-stances in 1795. Based on a simple four-street system known as the Cross, the whole town was designed and built as a living memorial to a relative of the first Marquis of Sligo, Lord Altamont (John Browne): his kinsman was killed at the Battle of Louisburgh in Nova Scotia, 1758.

The **Granuaile Interpretive Centre** (☎ 098-66134; Church St; adult/concession €4/2; ♥ 11am-5pm Jun-Sep, 10.30am-2pm Mon-Fri Oct-May), in the library, offers a quick but illuminating glimpse into the life and times of Grace O'Malley (Gráinne Ní Mháille or Granuaile; 1530–1603) the infamous pirate queen of Connaught.

There are some excellent surf beaches in the vicinity. Contact **Surf Mayo** (☎ 087 621 2508; www .surfmayo.com) for gear rental and lessons.

Old Head Forest Caravan & Camping Park (☎ 087 648 6885; Old Head; campsites €20; ♥ Easter–mid-Sep) is a family-friendly camping park in woodland, 4km from Louisburgh and a short walk from its namesake safe, sandy beach, which has a pier and a lifeguard on duty in summer. Good facilities include free hot showers, a cafe and ice-cream parlour and a tennis court.

Bus Éireann (☎ 096-71800) service 450 links Westport and Louisburgh (€6.40, 35 minutes, up to three times daily Monday to Saturday) via Murrisk.

Killadoon

Panoramic ocean views and vast sandy beaches fan out from tiny Killadoon. The empty beaches are idyllic for horse riding – see p436 for riding stables.

Take the narrow coastal road heading south from Louisburgh, or turn west off the R335 at Cregganbaun. **Bus Éireann** (☎ 096-71800) service 450 from Westport (€8.70) and Louisburgh (€3.40) continues to Killadoon twice daily on Thursdays only. The trip takes about 15 minutes.

COUNTIES MAYO & SLIGO

BOYCOTT BEGINNINGS

It was near the unassuming little village of Neale that the term boycott came into use. In 1880, the Irish Land League, in an effort to press for fair rents and improve the lot of workers, withdrew field hands from the estate of Lord Erne, who owned much of the land in the area. When Lord Erne's land agent, Captain Charles Cunningham Boycott, evicted the striking labourers, the surrounding community began a campaign to ostracise the agent. Not only did farmers refuse to work his land, people in the town refused to talk to him, provide services or sit next to him in church. The incident attracted attention from the London papers, and soon Boycott's name was synonymous with such organised, nonviolent protests. Within a few months, Boycott gave up and left Ireland.

CLARE ISLAND

pop 130

Clew Bay is dotted with some 365 islands, of which the largest is the mountainous Clare Island, 5km offshore at the mouth of the bay. Dominated by rocky **Mt Knockmore** (461m), its varied terrain is terrific for walking and climbing (getting lost is never a worry!), and swimming can be enjoyed at safe, sandy beaches.

The island has the ruins of the Cistercian **Clare Island Abbey** (c 1460) and **Granuaile's Castle**, both associated with the piratical Grace O'Malley. The tower castle was her stronghold, although it was altered considerably when the coastguard took it over in 1831. Grace is said to be buried in the small abbey, which contains a stone inscribed with her family motto: 'Invincible on land and sea'.

The island is also one of the dwindling number of places where you can find choughs (resembling blackbirds but with red beaks).

Sleeping & Eating

Facilities are limited; if you're just going for the day, consider taking your own food.

If you want to stay overnight, for a real 'ends-of-the-earth' feeling, head to the windswept southwestern corner of the island, 5km from the harbour to **Cois Abhainn** (☎ 098-26216; Toremore; s/d €40/70; May-Oct), a cosy B&B with sensational views of Inishturk Island. Not all rooms have private bathrooms, though prices are the same for all. Evening meals (€20) can be arranged.

Getting There & Away

The nearest mainland point is Roonagh Quay, 8km west of Louisburgh. **Clare Island Ferries** (☎ 098-28288, 087 241 4653; www.clareislandferry.com) and **O'Malley's Ferries** (☎ 098-25045, 086 600 0204; www.omalleyferries.com) make the 20-minute trip from Roonagh (adult/child return €15/8). There are around 10 sailings daily in July and August, and around two daily the rest of the year.

Getting Around

Enquire at the pier for taxis and **bikes** (☎ 098-25640; per day €10).

INISHTURK ISLAND

pop 100

Still further off the beaten track is ruggedly beautiful Inishturk, which lies 12km off Mayo's western coast. It's sparsely populated and little visited, despite the two **sandy beaches** on its eastern side, impressive cliffs, wonderful **flora & fauna**, and a rugged, hilly landscape that's ideal for **walking**. In fact, ambling along the island's maze of country roads is a perfect way to adapt to the pace of life here. The island's **website** (www.inishturkisland.com) is a good source of information.

If you want to stay, the scenically positioned **Teach Abhainn** (☎ 098-45510; d with/without bathroom €76/64; dinner €25; Apr-Oct), a working farm 1.5km west of the harbour, has mesmerising views, hearty home cooking and comfy rooms.

John Heanue operates a twice-daily **ferry** (☎ 098-45541, 086 202 9670; adult/child return €25/12.50) from Roonagh Quay, near Louisburgh; the crossing takes 45 minutes. There's also less frequent service to Cleggan in County Galway.

CROAGH PATRICK

Just 8km southwest of Westport, St Patrick couldn't have picked a better spot for a pilgrimage than this conical mountain (also known as 'the Reek'). On a clear day the tough two-hour climb rewards with stunning views over Clew Bay and its sandy islets.

It was on Croagh Patrick that Ireland's patron saint fasted for 40 days and nights, and where he reputedly banished venomous snakes. Climbing the 765m holy mountain is an act of penance for thousands of pilgrims on the last Sunday of July (Reek Sunday). The truly contrite take the original 40km route from Ballintubber Abbey, Tóchar Phádraig (Patrick's Causeway), and ascend the mountain barefoot.

The trail taken by less contrite folk begins in the village of Murrisk (Muraisc) beside a **visitor centre** (☎ 098-64114; www.croagh-patrick.com; 11am-5pm mid-Mar–Oct). Opposite the car park is the **National Famine Memorial**, a spine-chilling sculpture of a three-masted ghost ship wreathed in swirling skeletons, commemorating the lives lost on so-called 'coffin ships' employed to help people escape the Famine (1845–51). The path down past the memorial leads to the scant remains of **Murrisk Abbey**, founded by the O'Malleys in 1547.

Ruth and Myles O'Brien, proprietors of the raspberry-pink-painted pub our pick **The Tavern** (☎ 098-64060; Murrisk; bar food €8.95-21.95, restaurant mains €15-30, set menu €27.50; bar food noon-9pm daily year-round, restaurant lunch Fri & Sat, dinner nightly May-Sep), reckon 'the locals really own the place; we just pay the mortgage', which explains the convival atmosphere around its turf fires. The restaurant's lobsters, cockles, prawns, mussels, scallops and oysters are delivered fresh from their fishermen next-door neighbours.

WESTPORT
pop 5163

Westport (Cathair na Mairt) is exceedingly proud of its Tidy Town status, having won the nation's top honours three times in the past decade alone. To be sure, the town's Georgian streets, lime-tree-shaded riverside mall and colourful pubs are about as photogenic as Ireland gets. A couple of kilometres west on Clew Bay, the town's harbour, Westport Quay, is a picturesque spot for a sundowner.

Westport is Mayo's nightlife hub (though it has clamped down on hen-and-stag revellers), and its central location makes it a convenient and enjoyable base for exploring the county.

Information

Central banks include the **AIB** (Shop St), with an ATM and bureau de change.

Cotton's Laundry (☎ 098-29935; James St; per kilo €2.50; ☯ 9.30am-6.30pm Mon-Fri, 9.30am-6pm Sat)

Gavin's Video & Internet Cafe (☎ 098-26461; Bridge St; per hr €4; ☯ 10am-10pm Mon-Fri, noon-10pm Sat & Sun) Internet access.

The Bookshop (☎ 098-26816; Bridge St) Good selection of OS maps and books on Ireland.

Tourist office (☎ 098-25711; www.discoverireland .ie/west; James St; ☯ 9am-6pm Mon-Sat, 10am-6pm Sun Jul & Aug, 9am-5.45pm Mon-Sat Apr-Jun & Sep, 9am-12.45pm & 2-5pm Mon-Fri rest of year) Mayo's only official tourist office to open year-round.

Sights
TOWN CENTRE

The town's unusual layout unfurls from the octagonal-shaped town square, and slopes down to the River Carrowbeg. The first settlement was built around an O'Malley castle, but it disappeared beneath the demolish-and-build spree that was the Georgian era. The new town was designed by 18th-century architect James Wyatt, with a little help from Georgian superstar Richard Castle.

WESTPORT HOUSE

The charms of this 1730-built country **mansion** (☎ 098-25430; www.westporthouse.ie; Quay Rd; house &

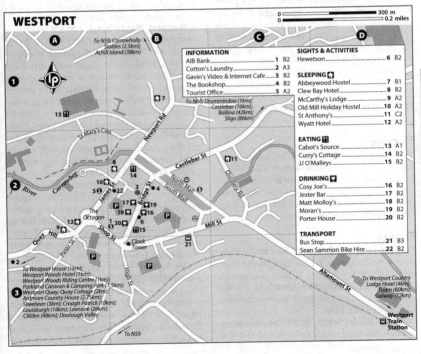

WESTPORT

0 — 300 m
0 — 0.2 miles

INFORMATION	
AIB Bank	**1** B2
Cotton's Laundry	**2** A3
Gavin's Video & Internet Cafe	**3** B2
The Bookshop	**4** B2
Tourist Office	**5** A2

SIGHTS & ACTIVITIES	
Hewetson	**6** B2

SLEEPING	
Abbeywood Hostel	**7** B1
Clew Bay Hotel	**8** B2
McCarthy's Lodge	**9** A2
Old Mill Holiday Hostel	**10** A2
St Anthony's	**11** C2
Wyatt Hotel	**12** A2

EATING	
Cabot's Source	**13** A1
Curry's Cottage	**14** B2
JJ O'Malleys	**15** B2

DRINKING	
Cosy Joe's	**16** B2
Jester Bar	**17** B2
Matt Molloy's	**18** B2
Moran's	**19** B2
Porter House	**20** B2

TRANSPORT	
Bus Stop	**21** B3
Sean Sammon Bike Hire	**22** B2

COUNTIES MAYO & SLIGO

gardens adult/child €12/6.50, house, gardens & Pirate Adventure Park adult/child €21/16.50; ⏷ house & gardens 10am-4pm Sat & Sun Mar, 10am-4pm daily Apr, Jun, Sep & Oct, 10am-5pm daily May, 10am-5.30pm daily Jul & Aug) set in glorious gardens on the ruins of the 16th-century castle built for Grace O'Malley, Ireland's pirate queen, outshines its commercial overhaul of recent years. It's now a kind of stately home theme-park hybrid, incorporating a kid-friendly **Pirate Adventure Park** (⏷ 10am-4pm mid-Apr & Jun, 10am-5pm bank holiday weekend & Sun thereafter May, 10am-5.30pm Jul & Aug, 10am-4pm Sat & Sun Sep) complete with a swinging pirate ship, a 'pirate's playground' and a roller-coaster-style flume ride through a water channel.

To reach Westport House, head out of Westport on Quay Rd towards Croagh Patrick and Louisburgh. Just before Westport Quay, take a small road to the right and through the grand gateway.

Activities

For tackle, camping gear, all-weather clothing and information about fishing, stop into **Hewetson** (☎ 098-26018; Bridge St; ⏷ 10am-5pm Mon-Sat).

Contact **Carrowholly Stables** (☎ 098-27057; www.carrowholly-stables.com; Carrowholly) for details of guided horse and pony treks along trails overlooking Clew Bay. The stables are 3km north of the town centre, next to Westport Golf Club, off the N59 to Newport.

Beach treks (€150) and guided hour-long rides (€60) are available at Westport Woods Riding Centre, at Westport Woods Hotel (right). Rates are one-third cheaper for hotel guests.

Sleeping

Westport is Mayo's major tourist magnet and while there's an abundance of B&Bs and hotels, rooms are in short supply during summer and special events. The tourist office can book rooms for a €4 service fee. Rates drop considerably outside peak periods.

BUDGET

Parkland Caravan & Camping Park (☎ 098-27766; camping@westporthouse.ie; Westport House, Quay Rd; camp-sites €25-32; ⏷ May-early Sep) Wide-open spaces and proximity to Westport House's funfairlike attractions make this site a hit for families with young children.

Old Mill Holiday Hostel (☎ 098-27045; www.oldmill hostel.com; Barrack Yard, James St; dm €18.50-19.30, d €48-50, tr

€66; ⏷ closed late Dec-early Jan; ⏸) Inside a converted stone mill, this central IHH hostel has 58 beds spread across its well-kept rooms, and inviting communal areas that make for a laid-back social vibe. Rates include free tea, coffee and toast.

Abbeywood Hostel (☎ 098-25496; www.abbeywood house.com; Newport Rd; dm €20-24, d €60; ⏷ daily May-Sep, weekends only Oct-Dec & Mar-Apr, closed Jan & Feb; P ▣) Set back from the road at the northern end of town are this characterful old house and gardens, originally part of a monastery. The house still boasts some stained glass, wood floors and high ceilings. Rates include continental breakfast.

MIDRANGE

St Anthony's (☎ 098-28887; www.st-anthonys.com; Distillery Rd; s/d €45/80; P) This genteel B&B sits under cover of a large hedge and thick, twisted vines inhabited by birds' nests. The interior shelters six simple but elegant rooms; two have Jacuzzi-style baths. Call ahead to arrange your arrival time.

McCarthy's Lodge (☎ 098-27050; www.mccarthys lodge.com; Quay Hill; s €45, d €75-80, 2-bed apt €120) Upstairs from a friendly timber-lined pub, McCarthy's eight rooms are as tidy as the town, and as orderly as an Ikea showroom.

Westport Woods Hotel (☎ 098-25811; www .westportwoodshotel.com; Quay Rd; s €75-120, d €100-190; P ▣ ⏸ ⏷) Behind part of Westport House's 1840s-built stone wall, this large mid-20th-century hotel is green and then some. Eco-initiatives include solar power, wood-pellet boilers, reused timber and stone, playground matting made from recycled tyres and running shoes, and even recycled cooking oil fuelling the hotel's vehicles. Skylights fill the neutral-toned interiors with natural light. Service is professional but impressively personalised, too, for a hotel its size.

Wyatt Hotel (☎ 098-25027; www.wyatthotel.com; The Octagon; s €89-99, d €198; P ⏸) Its epicentral position and the bonus of private parking distinguish this sunflower-yellow landmark. Rooms are straightforward but comfortable. There's free guest access to the nearby leisure centre. Wi-fi extends to some but not all rooms.

Clew Bay Hotel (☎ 098-28088; www.clewbayhotel.com; James St; r €210; ▣ ⏸) This revamped 54-room hotel in the centre of town has small but stylish rooms individually decorated with funky wallpaper and all-new mosaic-tiled bathrooms; three have river views. Guests have free access to the gym next door. Mains in the bistro (open

12:30pm to 9:30pm) are €9 to €22; in the restaurant (open for dinner nightly from Easter to September) they're €15 to €26.

TOP END

Ardmore Country House (☎ 098-25994; www.ardmore countryhouse.com; The Quay; s €100-160, d €170-220; ✆ Easter-Oct; **P** 🤝) In a secluded countrified setting overlooking Clew Bay's stunning sunsets, Pat Hoban and his family run Westport's most exquisite guesthouse. Its 13 rooms are luxurious, with sleigh beds, richly textured fabrics and a genuinely warm atmosphere, and its restaurant (right) merits a visit in its own right.

Westport Country Lodge Hotel (☎ 098-56030; www .westportcountrylodge.com; Aghagower; s €110, d €150, green fees €15; **P**) Launched in 2009, this built-from-scratch property still has a showroom quality about it, but Celtic-style prints and padded bedsteads add ready-made comfort to its 21 rooms. It's peacefully set 4km from Westport on the Ballinrobe road overlooking its nine-hole golf course. Its restaurant should be in full swing by the time you're reading this.

Eating

Curry's Cottage (☎ 098-25297; James St; dishes €3.95-6.95; ✆ 9.30am-6pm Tue-Sat) This jovial little tea shop has a toasty open fire and a tempting display of scones, cookies and other baked goodies.

JJ O'Malley's (☎ 098-27307; Bridge St; mains €14-27.50; ✆ dinner) Upstairs from the eponymous trendy meeting place. An 'around the world' menu circumnavigates the globe, with extended excursions to Asia, Mexico and the Med.

our pick Sheebeen (☎ 098-26528; Rosbeg; mains €15-25; ✆ noon-9pm daily mid-Mar–Oct, Sat & Sun only Nov–mid-Mar) Father and son Colm and Simon Cronin have turned this thatched treasure on the shores of Clew Bay into one of the best seafood restaurants in the west. Starters such as steamed mussels in cream and white wine from the bay out front are followed by mains like pan-fried king halibut with crab butter, but there are also inventive meat and vegetarian choices. Save room for the warm ginger and banana cake.

Quay Cottage (☎ 098-26412; Harbour; mains €15.50-26; ✆ dinner mid-Feb–mid-Jan) Serving seafood straight off the boats and steeped in salty-dog charm (including lobster pots hanging from the roof beams), this is the pick of places to eat on Westport's lively harbourfront.

Cabot's Source (☎ 098-50546; The Linen Mill; lunch mains €6-9, dinner mains €18.50-27; ✆ lunch Mon-Fri, dinner Tue-Sun) Charismatic chef Redmond Cabot utilises locally sourced, organic seasonal produce to create a fusion of Italian/Irish cuisine. The hip, open-plan industrial-style space occupies a converted linen mill.

Ardmore Country House (☎ 098-25994; www.ardmore countryhouse.com; The Quay; mains €20-32.50; ✆ dinner guests nightly, nonguests Mon-Sat Apr-Oct) This little gem is where Westport's best chefs dine on their nights off. Superb-value five-course menus cost around €35, depending on what's in season.

Drinking & Entertainment

Matt Molloy's (☎ 098-26655; Bridge St) Matt Molloy, the fife player from the Chieftains, opened this old-school pub years ago and the good times haven't let up. Head to the back room around 9pm and you'll catch live *céilidh* (traditional music and dancing). Or perhaps an old man will simply slide into a chair and croon a few classics.

Moran's (☎ 098-26320; Bridge St) A preserved holdover from the days when a pub was also a shop, and grocery shopping was occasion to have a few pints before heading home, having forgotten about the groceries.

Also recommended:

Porter House (☎ 098-28014; Bridge St) Live music plays every night year-round at the Porter House, as well as weekend afternoons in summer.

Jester Bar (☎ 098-29255; Bridge St) No *céilidhs*, no talk of fishing – urban grooves set the pace at this hipster hang-out.

Cosy Joe's (☎ 098-29403; Bridge St) Beneath a backlit stained-glass ceiling, musicians and DJs entertain the masses at this party-hard pub.

Getting There & Away

Bus Éireann (☎ 096-71800) travels to Achill Island (€12.50, 30 minutes, two daily), Dublin (€18.50, five hours, three daily), Galway (€14.40, two hours, eight daily) and Sligo (€16.70, two hours, two daily). Buses depart from and arrive at the Mill St stop. There are limited services on Sunday.

The **train station** (☎ 098-25253) is 800m from the town centre. There are three daily connections to Dublin (€35 to €48.50, 3½ hours).

Getting Around

For a cab call **Moran's Executive Taxis** (☎ 098-25539) or **O'Toole Taxis** (☎ 087 243 2600). **Sean Sammon** (☎ 098-25471; James St; ✆ 10am-6pm Mon-Sat, by appointment Sun) hires out bikes for €10/55 per day/week.

NEWPORT

pop 590

Newport (Baile Uí Fhiacháin), a wiggling 12km drive north of Westport, is a picturesque 18th-century village in which there really isn't much to do other than fish in streams, lakes or Clew Bay. But the Bangor Trail (p442) and Foxford Trail both end near the town, attracting many walkers, and Achill Island is a short drive away.

The town's most striking feature is a seven-arch viaduct built in 1892 for the Westport–Achill Railway; the trains stopped in 1936 and the bridge has since become a pedestrian walkway.

The post office and bureau de change are across the river. There are no banks.

Sleeping & Eating

Hotel Newport (☎ 098-41155; www.hotelnewportmayo .com; Main St; s €89-99, d €100-140; **P** 🛜) This 2006-built hotel was not only constructed in the same style as the old hotel that stood here, but the original facade was rebuilt numbered stone by numbered stone. All of the spacious rooms have bathtubs (except for the two wheelchair-accessible rooms, which have barrier-free showers). You'll get the best deals by booking packages that include dinner at the hotel's on-site restaurant, which serves good local seafood.

Newport House (☎ 098-41222; www.newporthouse.ie; Main St; s €148-190, d €244-328; 🌙 mid-Mar–Oct; **P** 🖥) Strangled by ivy that turns crimson in autumn, this gorgeous Georgian mansion is one of Ireland's most romantic country retreats. Every room is beautifully appointed (four-poster beds cost an extra €22 per person), but Newport House is especially known for its contemporary Irish cuisine and vintage wine list (dinner €62).

Dominick Kelly's (☎ 098-41149; Main St) If you're self-catering, picnicking or simply want a taste of Newport village life, pop into this much-loved artisan butcher shop, which also sells gourmet deli goods.

Getting There & Away

The frequent **Bus Éireann** (☎ 096-71800) service between Westport (€3.90) and Achill Island (€8.70) passes through Newport.

NEWPORT TO ACHILL ISLAND

If you've time, skip the main road from Newport to Achill Island in favour of the longer and narrower but infinitely more scenic **Atlantic Drive**. It's well signposted along the southern edge of the Curraun Peninsula (also spelt Corraun Peninsula).

Burrishoole Abbey

From a distance, the eerie shell of this wind-battered 1486-built Dominican **abbey** (admission free; 🌙 dawn-dusk) resembles a 2D film set. About 2.5km northwest towards Achill a sign points the way to the abbey, from where it's a further 1km.

Rockfleet Castle

Also known as **Carrigahowley**, this 15th-century tower is one of the most tangible spots associated with 'pirate queen' Grace O'Malley (see p433). She married her second husband, Richard an-Iarrain (impressively nicknamed 'Iron Dick' Burke), to gain control of this castle, and famously fought off an English attack here.

The tower is in a quiet outlet of Clew Bay. Turn south at the sign, about 5km west of Newport on the Achill road.

Mulranny

Rising from a narrow isthmus, the hillside village of Mulranny (An Mhala Raithní), spelt Mulrany on some maps, overlooks a wide Blue Flag beach: take the steps opposite the Park Inn, or the path beside the service station. It's a prime vantage point to try counting the 365 or so saucer-sized islands that grace Clew Bay.

Sleeping

Midrange accommodation is best on Achill (see p441).

Traenlaur Lodge (☎ 098-41358; www.anoige.ie; Lough Feeagh, Newport; dm €17; 🌙 reception 5-10pm Jun-Sep) A gorgeous An Óige hostel in a former fishing lodge with its own harbour on Lough Feeagh. Its summertime-only opening reflects its main clientele: walkers resting their weary feet from the Western Way or Bangor Trail. It's 8km from Newport, signposted from the Achill road.

Park Inn Mulranny (☎ 098-36000; www.parkinn mulranny.ie; N59, Mulranny; s €110-130, d €170-210, apt €225-285; 🌙 Feb-Dec, restaurant closed Sun Feb-May & Sep-Dec; **P** 🖥 🛜 🐾) Established in 1897, this grand building on 17 wooded hectares boasts one of the most magical coastal views in Ireland. Now part of the Park Inn chain, service is haphazard, but room decor is up to date, as are the facilities that include a leisure centre.

THE GREAT WESTERN GHOST TRAIN

A spooky footnote can be added to the Great Western Railway's short-lived history in Achill Sound. Local folklore likes to tell how a 17th-century prophet named Brian Rua O'Cearbhain had a vision that one day 'carts on wheels, blowing smoke and fire' would run here, and that their first and last journeys would carry corpses.

Chillingly, just as work was completed on the rail line to Achill in 1894, tragedy struck when 32 young locals drowned in Clew Bay, and the very first train from Westport to Achill carried the bodies back to their grieving families. The prophecy was completed four decades later when the railway had already ceased to run. Ten migrant workers from Achill were killed in a fire at Kirkintilloch, Scotland in 1937. The railway line was reopened for one last run to bring the bodies back for burial.

ACHILL ISLAND

pop 960

Ireland's largest offshore island, Achill (An Caol), is connected to the mainland by a short bridge. Despite its accessibility, it has plenty of that far-flung-island feeling: soaring cliffs, rocky headlands, sheltered sandy beaches, broad expanses of blanket bog and rolling mountains. It also has its share of history, having been a frequent refuge during Ireland's numerous rebellions.

Achill is at its most dramatic during winter, when high winds and lashing seas make the island seem downright inhospitable. The year-round population, though, remains as welcoming as ever. Few visitors choose to appreciate this temperamental side of Achill, preferring its mild summers, when heather, rhododendrons and wildflowers bloom.

A quiet hamlet known as the Valley, whose rugged terrain is dotted with old stone houses, is the island's most traditional quarter, while the village of Keel is the island's main centre of activity.

Information

Most of the villages have post offices. The supermarkets in Keel and Achill Sound (p442) have ATMs.

Achill Computer Solutions (☎ 098-47940; Cashel; per hr €4; 9.15am-12.30pm & 1.30-5.30pm Mon-Fri, 9.15am-12.30pm & 1.30-4pm Sat) Internet access, hidden behind the Esso petrol station.

Achill Tourism (☎ 098-47353; www.achilltourism.com; Cashel; 9am-6pm Mon-Fri Jul & Aug, 10am-4pm Sep-Jun) One of the best sources for information in all Mayo.

Sights

The signposted **Atlantic Drive** (opposite) continues once you cross the bridge as an alternative route to the main roads along the island's southern shore.

SLIEVEMORE DESERTED VILLAGE

The remains of this deserted village at the foot of Slievemore Mountain are slowly but surely being reduced down to rock piles, and are a poignant reminder of the island's past hardships and a lost way of life. Until the mid-19th century, the village was divided between permanent inhabitants and transhumance farmers (known here as 'booleying'), but as the Potato Famine took grip, starvation forced the villagers to the sea and its sources of food. The adjacent graveyard compounds the desolation.

DOOAGH

This village is where Don Allum, the first person to row across the Atlantic Ocean in both directions, landed in September 1982 in his 6m-long plywood boat, dubbed the *QE3*, after 77 days at sea. Opposite the memorial, the Pub (that's its name) has memorabilia marking the feat.

Activities

Some of Achill's scalloped bays are tame enough for **swimming**. Except in the height of the holiday season, the Blue Flag beaches at Dooega, Keem, Dugort and Golden Strand (Dugort's other beach) are often deserted. The beaches at Dooagh and Dooniver are just as appealing.

The Blue Flag Keel beach is one of Ireland's best **surfing** spots, but there are dangerous rips from its centre to the eastern end (under the Minaun Cliffs). Heed the signs and stick to the western half of the beach. **Achill Adventures** (☎ 098-43148; www.achilladventures.com; Slievemore Rd, Dugort) rents boards on Keel beach during July and August, and also organises canoe, kayak and dinghy rental. **Windsurfing** is also popular; **Wind Wise** (☎ 098-43958; www.windwise.ie) offers instruction and rents equipment.

The island is a wonderful place for **walking**. Mt Slievemore (672m) can be climbed from behind the deserted village for terrific views of Blacksod Bay. A longer climb takes in Mt Croaghaun (668m), Achill Head and a walk atop what locals claim are Europe's highest sea cliffs (though Slieve League in County Donegal is thought to be marginally higher). Achill Tourism produces a *Guide to Walking in Achill* (€3.50) detailing 14 walks in Irish and English, which is also sold at Gielty's Newsagent in Keel.

Sea-angling can be arranged with **Tony Burke** (☎ 098-47257; tmburke@eircom.net; Keel), owner of the 10m *Cuan na Cuime*. With its clear waters Achill is a prime diving spot and **Achill Island Scuba Dive Centre** (☎ 087 234 9884; www.achilldive centre.com; Purteen Harbour, Keel) offers training and equipment hire.

To gallop along Achill's broad beaches, contact **Calvey's Equestrian Centre** (☎ 087 988 1093; www.calveysofachill.com; Slievemore), which also offers riding lessons.

Less energetic activities include summertime painting classes run by **Ó'Dálaigh** (☎ 098-36137; www.achillpainting.com). Instructor Seosamh Ó'Dálaigh will lead you to a scenic spot and offer pointers on how to commit it to canvas.

Festivals

Traditional Irish music resonates for miles in the first two weeks of August during the **Scoil Acla Festival** (www.scoilacla.com), which also has Irish dancing, culture and music workshops.

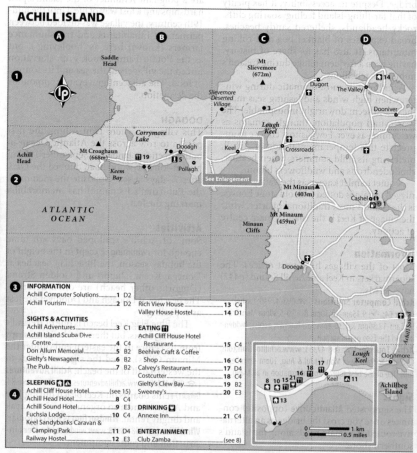

ACHILL ISLAND

INFORMATION
Achill Computer Solutions	1 D2
Achill Tourism	2 D2

SIGHTS & ACTIVITIES
Achill Adventures	3 C1
Achill Island Scuba Dive Centre	4 C4
Don Allum Memorial	5 B2
Gielty's Newsagent	6 B2
The Pub	7 B2

SLEEPING 🏠 🏕
Achill Cliff House Hotel	(see 15)
Achill Head Hotel	8 C4
Achill Sound Hotel	9 E3
Fuchsia Lodge	10 C4
Keel Sandybanks Caravan & Camping Park	11 D4
Railway Hostel	12 E3

Rich View House	13 C4
Valley House Hostel	14 D1

EATING 🍴
Achill Cliff House Hotel Restaurant	15 C4
Beehive Craft & Coffee Shop	16 C4
Calvey's Restaurant	17 D4
Costcutter	18 C4
Gielty's Clew Bay	19 B2
Sweeney's	20 E3

DRINKING 🍷
Annexe Inn	21 C4

ENTERTAINMENT
Club Zamba	(see 8)

Map labels:
Saddle Head; Mt Slievemore (672m); Dugort; The Valley; 14; Slievemore Deserted Village; Dooniver; Lough Keel; 3; Corrymore Lake; Dooagh; Keel; Crossroads; 7; 19; Achill Head; Mt Croaghaun (668m); 5; 6; Pollagh; See Enlargement; Mt Minaun (403m); Cashel; 2; 1; Keem Bay; ATLANTIC OCEAN; Minaun Cliffs; Mt Minaun (459m); Dooega; Achill Sound; Cloghmore; Lough Keel; 17; 18; 16; 8; 10; 15; 21; 11; Keel; 13; 4; Achillbeg Island; 0 1 km; 0 0.5 miles

At the beginning of May, the island hosts a four-day **walking festival** – the tourist office in Westport has details (p435).

Sleeping

Achill is a great budget destination and there are some decent midrange options, but for top-end luxury you'll need to head off-island.

BUDGET

`our pick` **Valley House Hostel** (☎ 098-47204; www.valley -house.com; The Valley; campsites per tent €5, plus per person €5, dm €19-22, s €25, d €50, f from €40; P 🖳 🛜) Amid unruly gardens, this remote, 42-bed hostel in a creaking old mansion has atmosphere to spare. JM Synge based his play *The Playboy*

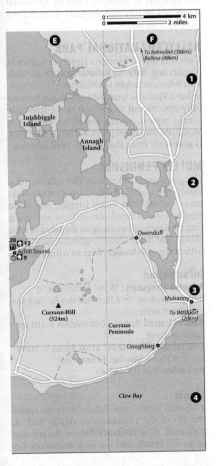

of the Western World on misadventures here (the staff can tell some great stories!), and the subsequent film *Love and Rage* (1999) was also partially shot here. Bonuses include free scones for breakfast and a cosy licensed pub with patio tables (bar food June to August only).

Keel Sandybanks Caravan & Camping Park (☎ 094-903 2054; www.achillcamping.com; Keel; campsites €10; ☽ June–mid-Sep) This camping ground, an easy stroll from town, overlooks Keel Strand and has a sociable lounge and a laundry room.

Railway Hostel (☎ 098-45187; Achill Sound; campsites per person €7.50, dm €15; P) The Railway Hostel was once a train station for the ill-fated Great Western Railway (see boxed text, p439). It's now a social little hostel that sleeps up to 16 people and has toasty open fires in the common and dining rooms. It's just before the bridge you cross to reach the island; ask the bus driver to stop outside.

Rich View House (☎ 098-43462, 086 231 5546; richview hostel@hotmail.com; Keel; dm/s/d €15/18/36) Facilities at this relaxed hostel/home-stay are simple, even scarce, but the jolly live-in owner, musician Shay Kennedy, is extremely knowledgeable about Achill and quick to invite guests to the pub. Shay's daughter has built her house right in front, but it doesn't detract from the eponymous views.

MIDRANGE

Fuchsia Lodge (☎ 098-43350; fuchsialodge@eircom .ie; Keel; s/d €45/70, cottage per week €700; P) This friendly family home is one of very few B&Bs to open year-round. It has three cosy bedrooms, and guests can access the kitchen. The adjacent fisherman's cottage belonged to the owner's grandfather and has been renovated to incorporate three bedrooms, three bathrooms and full kitchen and laundry facilities, but happily retains its original timber ceilings and Irish charm.

Achill Cliff House Hotel (☎ 098-43400; www.achill cliff.com; Keel; s €110-120, d €140-160; ☽ closed Christmas; P) The 10 spacious but unspectacular rooms in this whitewashed hotel that resembles an oversized cottage don't come cheap in high season, but there are often good deals available online and rates drop considerably outside midsummer. You can pay an extra €25 to secure a sea view; alternatively, take advantage of the views from the restaurant (p442).

Also recommended:

Achill Sound Hotel (☎ 098-45245; www.achillsound hotel.com; Achill Sound; s/d €55/100; P) Family-run

COUNTIES MAYO & SLIGO

hotel near the bridge, on the island side, with basic rooms, a bar and restaurant.

Achill Head Hotel (☎ 098-43108; www.achillhead hotel.ie; Pollagh, Keel; s/d €65/90; Ⓨ seasonal opening periods vary; Ⓟ) A 10-minute walk from Keel village and beach. Some of its 19 modern rooms have grandiose four-poster beds and patchwork-style quilts.

Eating

Gielty's Clew Bay (☎ 098-43119; www.gieltys.com; Dooagh; sandwiches €4-7, mains €9-20; Ⓨ food served 10am-9pm) Publican Alan Gielty can fill you in on pretty much anything you need to know about Achill. The building is modern but has a time-honoured atmosphere that's enhanced by open fires and sea views, and good pub grub such as local smoked salmon or beef and red wine casserole. Live music plays every Saturday night year-round, and nightly during July and August.

Beehive Craft & Coffee Shop (☎ 098-43018; Keel; snacks around €7; Ⓨ 10.30am-6pm Apr-Oct) As much a craft shop as a cafe, the Beehive dishes up healthy homemade soups with brown scones, and decadent home-baked cakes.

Calvey's Restaurant (☎ 098-43158; Keel; lunch mains €4-10, dinner mains €10-20; Ⓨ lunch & dinner Easter–mid-Sep) As it's attached to its own organic butchery, it's no surprise that the speciality at this award-winning restaurant is meat (particularly local lamb).

Achill Cliff House Hotel Restaurant (☎ 098-43400; www.achillcliff.com; Keel; mains €21-26; Ⓨ lunch Sun, dinner nightly) Locally caught seafood like black sole on the bone with creamy tarragon sauce or herb-crusted baked cod is the order of the day here, but tasty alternatives include ginger and orange roast duckling.

Supermarkets on the island include Sweeney's, located just across the bridge as you enter Achill, and Costcutter, in Keel.

Drinking & Entertainment

Annexe Inn (☎ 098-43268; Keel; Ⓨ from 6pm) This cosy little pub delivers the best traditional music sessions year-round. It has music almost nightly in July and August, and at weekends the rest of the year.

Club Zamba (Ⓨ seasonal opening periods vary) The DJ at Achill Head Hotel's club (see above) consistently fills the dance floor.

Getting There & Around

Bus Éireann (☎ 096-71800) services run from Ballina and Westport Monday to Saturday

year-round, with nine stops on the island, including at Dooagh, Keel, Dugort, Cashel and Achill Sound.

Call ahead to organise summertime **bike rental** (☎ 098-43125).

BANGOR ERRIS

pop 295

This unexceptional little village is the start or end point for the 48km **Bangor Trail**, which connects Bangor (Bain Gear) and Newport. It's an extraordinary hike that takes walkers through some of the bleakest and most remote countryside in Ireland. Unfortunately, you'll need several 1:50,000 OS maps to cover the trail.

Bus Éireann (☎ 096-71800) runs an evening bus Monday to Saturday (and an additional noon bus in July and August) from Ballina (€11.40, one hour).

BALLYCROY NATIONAL PARK

Covering one of Europe's largest expanses of blanket bog, **Ballycroy National Park** (☎ 098-49888; www.ballycroynationalpark.ie; admission free; Ⓨ visitor centre 8am-5.30pm) was founded in 1998 and became fully operational in 2009. It is a gorgeously scenic region, where the River Owenduff wends its way through intact bogs. The park is accessible from the Bangor Trail (above).

MULLET PENINSULA

Dangling some 30km into the Atlantic, this thinly populated Gaeltacht peninsula feels more cut off than many islands, and has a similar sense of forsakenness. However, you'll find pristine beaches along its sheltered eastern shore. The main settlement is the functional little town of **Belmullet** (Béal an Mhuirthead).

Information

Atlantek Computers (☎ 097-82255; Carter Sq, Belmullet; per hr €6; Ⓨ 9.30am-9pm Mon-Fri, 10am-6pm Sat) Internet access.

Bank of Ireland (Carter Sq, Belmullet) Has an ATM and bureau de change.

Erris tourist office (☎ 097-81500; Barrack St, Belmullet; Ⓨ 9.30am-4.30pm Mon-Fri Easter-Sep)

Post office (Main St, Belmullet)

Sights

The road south from Belmullet loops round the tip of the peninsula to rejoin itself at Aghleam. Near **Blacksod Point** are the remains of an old **church**, and the view across the bay

PIPELINE PROTEST

Mayo's far-flung northwest has made national headlines in recent years. A David-and-Goliath-like battle continues over the construction of a high-pressure raw gas pipeline between Mayo's offshore Corrib gas field (owned by a consortium of Shell, Statoil and Marathon Oil) and refinery at Bellanaboy.

Fearing the pipeline poses health and safety risks to residents, Shell to Sea (Shell chun Sáile) campaigners advocate refining the gas at sea (as it is off County Cork). Offshoot organisation People of Kilcommon (Pobal Chill Chomáin; also known as Gas to Glinsk) proposes moving the refinery to the largely uninhabited Glinsk area to the east. Shell's position is that the pipeline is beneficial for job creation and the nation's gross domestic product and energy supplies.

Protests ensued when local landowners from Rossport, who became known as the 'Rossport Five', rejected compulsory acquisition orders for Shell workers to access their lands, and were jailed for 94 days in 2005. One of the Five, Willie Corduff, later won the European category of the Goldman Environmental Prize for grassroots environmental activists.

Intense media coverage also followed the jailing of another protester in 2009. Keep tabs on developments at Shell to Sea (www.corribsos.com), Shell (www.shell.com) and Mayo County Council (www.mayococo.ie).

takes in the spot where *La Rata Santa Maria Encoronada*, part of the 1588 Spanish Armada, came in and was later burned by its captain.

The road to Blacksod Point passes the Blue Flag beach of **Elly Bay**, a prime spot for bird-watchers and dolphin-watchers, as well as surfers – contact **UISCE** (☎ 097-82111; www.uisce.ie) for the local surf low-down. Further south it passes stunning **Mullaghroe Beach**. In the early 20th century, a whaling station operated at nearby Ardelly Point. The weather centre here determined the eventual date for the D-Day Normandy landing.

Sleeping & Eating

Cheerful cafes ring Belmullet's central roundabout.

Western Strands Hotel (☎ 097-81096; www.western strandshotel.com; Main St, Belmullet; s/d €48/70) A good-time atmosphere predominates in this old-time pub smack-dab in the centre of tiny Belmullet. The bar doubles as the reception desk, and staff (along with pub regulars) can fill you in on the area. Upstairs, it has 10 decent rooms (with four more on the way), all with private bathroom. Satisfying, inexpensive food is available in the bar.

Chez Nous (☎ 097-82167; cheznousbelmullet@yahoo .co.uk; Church Rd, Belmullet; s/d €50/80; ◷ Mar-Dec; ℗ 🛜) You'll find four wonderfully snug, tastefully decorated rooms with private bathroom at this modern B&B. It's opposite the old Church of Ireland, which now hosts occasional art exhibits, and is a five-minute walk from the town centre.

Getting There & Around

Bus Éireann (☎ 096-71800) runs one to two buses from Ballina to Belmullet (€12.50, 1¼ hours) Monday to Saturday, continuing on to Blacksod Point.

POLLATOMISH

pop 150

Irresistibly remote and pretty, Pollatomish (Poll an Tómais), also spelled Pullathomas, drowses in a serene bay some 16km east of Belmullet, signposted on the road to Ballycastle (R314). Those who find their way here often extend their stay to stroll on its sandy **beach** and walk up to **Benwee Head** to take in sensational views.

our pick Kilcommon Lodge Hostel (☎ 097-84621; www.kilcommonlodge.net; Pollatomish; dm/d €16/40; ℗ 🖥 🛜) is a garden-set hostel a short stroll from the beach. It's now headed up by the long-time owners' son, Ciarán, an outdoors enthusiast who can organise surfing, guided walks and rock climbing, as well as Irish-language courses. Less-energetic travellers can curl up with books and board games by the turf fire in the common room. Breakfast is €6, dinner €16.

BALLYCASTLE & AROUND

pop 250

The superbly sited village of Ballycastle (Baile an Chaisil) consists of a sole sloping street. Its main draw (apart from breathtaking coastal scenery) is its megalithic tombs – one of the greatest concentrations in Europe.

Sights

CÉIDE FIELDS

A famous wit once described archaeology as being all about 'a series of small walls'. But it's not often that such walls have had experts hopping up and down with such excitement than at **Céide Fields** (Achaidh Chéide), 8km northwest of Ballycastle.

During the 1930s, local man Patrick Caulfield was digging in the bog when he noticed a lot of piled-up stones buried beneath it. About 40 years later, his son Seamus, who had become an archaeologist on the basis of his father's discovery, began extensive exploration of the area. What he, and later others, uncovered was the world's most extensive Stone Age monument, consisting of stone-walled fields, houses and megalithic tombs – about half a million tonnes of stone. Astonishingly, five millennia ago a thriving farming community lived here, growing wheat and barley and grazing sheep and cattle. The award-winning **Interpretive Centre** (☎ 096-43325; www.heritageireland.ie; R314; adult/child incl tour €4/2; ⌚ 10am-6pm Jun–mid-Oct, 10am-5pm Easter-May & mid-Oct–end Oct, last tour 1hr prior to closing), in a glass pyramid overlooking the site, gives a fascinating glimpse into these times. However, it's a good idea to take a guided tour of the site itself, or it may seem nothing more than, well, a series of small walls.

Activities

The **Heathfield Lodge Stables** (☎ 096-43350; liz@heathfieldstables.com; Ballycastle) offers riding lessons, children's pony rides and trail rides through beautiful coastal hill country near Ballycastle. It's about 1km down the road towards Killala.

Sleeping & Eating

Stella Maris (☎ 096-43322; www.stellamarisireland.com; Ballycastle; s €155-185, d €200-250; ⌚ May-Sep) This salt-spattered building sits on a lonely stretch of coastline 2.5km west of Ballycastle. It was originally a British Coast Guard station, and later a nunnery; now, upmarket rooms combine antiques and stylish modern furnishings, breakfast includes treats like French toast, and the restaurant (open dinner nightly for guests, Tuesday to Sunday for nonguests) is well regarded for locally sourced dishes such as rack of lamb.

Mary's Cottage Kitchen (☎ 096-43361; Lower Main St, Ballycastle; dishes from €2.50; ⌚ 10am-3pm Mon-Fri, 10am-2pm Sat) Cosy stone cottages like this are always appealing, and never more so than when they house a bakery that advertises its wares with the aroma of warm apple pie. During the summer tables are set up out back in a leafy garden. Hours can vary.

Getting There & Away

Bus Éireann (☎ 096-71800) runs between Ballycastle and Ballina (€6, 30 minutes) twice a day, Monday to Friday.

KILLALA & AROUND

pop 569

The town itself is pretty enough, but Killala (Cill Alaidh or Cill Ála) is more famous for its namesake bay nearby, and for its role in the French invasion and rebellion of Wolfe Tone in 1798.

It's claimed that St Patrick founded Killala, and the Church of Ireland cathedral sits on the site of the first Christian church. The 25m round tower still looms over the town's heart; it was struck by lightning in 1800 and the cap was later rebuilt.

Rathfran Abbey

The silence at the remains of this remote Dominican friary, dating from 1274, is broken only by the cawing of crows and the whistling wind. In 1590 the friary was burned by the English, but the resilient monks stayed nearby until the 18th century.

Take the R314 road north out of Killala and, after 5km and crossing the River Cloonaghmore, turn right. After another 2km turn right at the crossroads.

Breastagh Ogham Stone

This lichen-covered stone, the height of a basketball player, is etched with an obscure Ogham script but the weathered markings are all but invisible. It's in a field left of the R314, just past the turning for Rathfran Abbey. Cross the ditch where the sign points to the stone.

Lackan Bay & Kilcummin

Flush with revolutionary fervour and eager to hurt the English in their own backyard, on 22 August 1798 more than 1000 French troops commanded by General Humbert landed at Kilcummin in Killala Bay. It was hoped (or rather promised by Irish patriot Wolfe Tone) that their arrival would inspire the Irish peasantry to revolt against the English.

A right turn off the main R314 is signposted for Kilcummin. On the R314 just after the turning to Lackan Bay a **sculpture** of a French soldier helping a prostrate Irish peasant marks the place where the first French soldier died on Irish soil. Lackan Bay **beach** is a stunning expanse of golden sand. There's good surf here, but you'll need to bring your own equipment.

Getting There & Away
A **Bus Éireann** (☎ 096-71800) bus stops outside McGregor's newsagency in Killala twice a day Monday to Friday between Ballina (€4.20) and Ballycastle (€3.90).

BALLINA
pop 10,409

Mayo's second-largest town, Ballina (Béal an Átha; balli-*nagh*), is synonymous with salmon. If you're there during fishing season, you'll see droves of green-garbed waders, poles in hand, heading for the River Moy – one the most prolific rivers in Europe for catching the scaly critters – which pumps right through the heart of town. You'll also spot salmon jumping in the Ridge (salmon pool), with otters and grey seals in pursuit.

Information
AIB (Pearse St) With ATM and bureau de change.
Chat'rnet (☎ 096-76510; Bridge St; per hr/day €4/10; ☉ 11am-11pm Mon-Fri, noon-11pm Sat, noon-10pm Sun) Central internet access.
Post office (O'Rahilly St) On the southern extension of Pearse St.
Tourist office (☎ 096-70848; Cathedral Rd; ☉ 10am-5.30pm Mon-Sat Apr-Oct, closed Nov-Mar) Across the River Moy from the centre.

Activities
A list of **fisheries** and permit contacts is available at the tourist office. The season is February to September, but the best fishing is June to August. Information, supplies and licences are available at **Ridge Pool Tackle Shop** (☎ 096-72656; Cathedral Rd). Fly-casting lessons can also be arranged.

Pontoon, near Foxford, is a better base for **trout fishing**, in Loughs Conn and Cullen.

Festivals
One of the best outdoor parties in the country, the **Ballina Salmon Festival** (☎ 096-79814; www .ballinasalmonfestival.ie) lasts for two weeks in early July. Festivities include parades, dances, cart racing and more.

Sleeping
Belleek Caravan & Camping Park (☎ 096-71533; www .belleekpark.com; Ballina; campsites €19, apt per week €560, mobile homes per week €395-560; ☉ Mar-Oct) This well-manicured, grassy site, run by a friendly family, is a first-class camping ground with plenty of space for kids to play and good laundry and kitchen facilities. Ask about year-round availability (and cut-price rates) of apartments and mobile homes. It's 2km north of Ballina, 300m off the Killala road.

Loft B&B (☎ 096-21881; www.theloftbar.ie; Pearse St; s €45-50, d €90-100; ☉) In the heart of town, you'll find these nine modern rooms above one of Ballina's livelier pubs. Those in front may get noisy around closing time, but in the back it's quiet, and all have their own bathroom. Reception is at the bar.

Belleek Castle (☎ 096-22400; www.belleekcastle.com; s €100-140, d €160-260; ☉ Apr-Dec; P) A fabulously over-the-top neo-Jacobean manor, set deep in a 400-hectare woodland just over 2km north of town. It's a luxurious romantic getaway, with four-poster beds and loads of historic artefacts. The flamboyant restaurant, Granuaile's, where meals are served with a theatrical flair, and the Armada bar are designed to look like the inside of a Spanish galleon.

Ice House (☎ 096-23500; www.theicehouse.ie; The Quay; r €250; P ☜) This 1800s-built salmon ice store on Ballina's eastern riverbank closed in the 1980s and languished until Dublin architect Joe Kennedy transformed it into an ultra-hip hotel. In a nod to the building's origins, there's a handful of 1800s-styled guest rooms with cedar bathtubs, but most have cutting-edge fit-outs (floor-to-ceiling windows, arctic-white moulded furniture). At the water's edge, the vault where boats once unloaded their catch now houses a sleek bar and restaurant, Pier (right). Upstairs five spa treatment rooms are, somewhat disconcertingly, named after wrecked ships.

our pick **Mount Falcon Country House Hotel** (☎ 096-74472; www.mountfalcon.com; Foxford Rd; d €180-240, 3- to 4-bedroom self-contained chalets per night €400-500; P ☜ ☙) Hidden within 40 hectares between Lough Conn and the River Moy, 5km south of Ballina, this gorgeous 1870s mansion was seamlessly extended a couple of years ago. Rooms in the new wing have forest-inspired colour schemes that appear to morph into the surrounding woodlands, while those in the old house retain some astonishing period features, as does the restaurant (dinner is €49), set in the mansion's original kitchen. Anglers will be hooked by Mount Falcon's own exclusive fishery along the river.

Eating

Gaughan's (☎ 096-70096; O'Rahilly St; lunch €4-18; ☉ 10am-6pm Mon-Sat) Once a dark old local pub, Gaughan's is now solely a restaurant serving its home-cooked staples like baked gammon. You can be sure the salmon's top-notch: Clarke's Salmon Smokery is right next door.

Dillon's Bar & Restaurant (☎ 096-72230; Dillon's Tce; mains €14-25; ☉ food served 5-9pm Mon-Thu, 12.30-9pm Fri-Sun) Easily missed behind a blank concrete archway, Dillon's vine-covered cobbled courtyard with alfresco seating is a diamond find. The menu utilises local produce, there are trad sessions on Wednesdays and DJs Fridays and Saturdays. From the town centre, turn right at the north end of Pearse St; it's on your left.

Pier (lunch mains €7-19, dinner mains €18-34; ☉ lunch & dinner) Chef Gavin O'Rourke heads up this chic waterside spot at the Ice House hotel (left). Organic artisan produce is used in most of his creations, best sampled with an eight-course tasting menu (€79), paired with wines (extra €65).

Drinking

An Bolg Buí (Yellow Belly; ☎ 096-22561; Tolan St) A good place to start a pub crawl of Ballina's dozens of watering holes is this well-worn, all-wood pub by the bridge, where you can savour a pint and swap fishing tales. Traditional music sessions take place on Wednesdays.

Quattro (☎ 096-22750; Pearse St) This multi-purpose restaurant/bar/entertainment hub is onto it, with live bands from Thursday to Monday nights and an excellent Italian-inspired menu (mains €14 to €23).

Getting There & Away

Bus Éireann runs daily express services from the **bus station** (☎ 096-71800; Kevin Barry St) to Westport (€11.50, one hour). Buses also go to Achill Island (€14.90, two to three hours, two daily), Sligo (€12.90, 1½ hours, five daily) and Dublin (€17.10, 3½ hours, six daily).

Trains to Dublin (€35 to €48.50, 3½ hours, three daily) leave from the **train station** (☎ 096-71818; Station Rd), at the southern extension of Kevin Barry St. Ballina is on a branch of the main Westport–Dublin line, so you'll have to change at Manulla Junction.

AROUND BALLINA
Rosserk Abbey

Dipping its toes into the River Rosserk, a tributary of the Moy, this **Franciscan abbey** dates from the mid-15th century. There's an eye-catching double piscina (perforated stone basin) in the chancel: look for the exquisite carvings of a round tower and several angels. Rosserk was destroyed by Richard Bingham, the English governor of Connaught, in the 16th century.

Leave Ballina on the R314 for Killala and after 6.5km turn right at the sign and then left at the next crossroads. Continue for 1km, then turn right.

North Mayo Sculpture Trail

Leading artists from eight different countries were commissioned to create this trail of 14 permanent outdoor sculptures reflecting the beauty and wilderness of the northern Mayo countryside. It essentially follows the R314 for 90km from Ballina to Blacksod Point and can be walked.

Tourist offices and bookshops sell the 60-page *North Mayo Sculpture Trail* (Tír Sáile) book detailing each sculpture.

Errew Abbey & Mt Nephin

It's a rough 800m scramble over farmland to reach the ruined **Errew Abbey**, but it's worth it for the picturesque location cupped on three sides by mirrorlike Lough Conn. The disintegrating remains include a 13th-century house for Augustinian monks built on the site of a 7th-century church.

From the quiet country town of Crossmolina, take the Castlebar road south, and 1km past the heritage centre, turn left at the sign and keep going for 5km. The entrance is by a farm.

To stretch your legs and get your heart pounding a little you can take the scenic two-hour trek up to the top of **Mt Nephin** (806m).

Sleeping & Eating

Healy's Restaurant & Fishing Lodge (☎ 094-56443; www.healyspontoon.com; Pontoon & Foxford; s/d from €55/70; P 🛜) The lakefront Healy's upholds its tradition as an 1840s sporting lodge and rents boats and arranges fishing licences. In addition to its updated hotel rooms, basic self-catering accommodation is available. Two elegant dining rooms (open 8am to 8pm, to 9pm in summer) serve surf-and-turf classics (mains €15 to €30, set menu €45).

Pontoon Bridge Hotel (☎ 094-925 6120; www .pontoonbridge.com; Pontoon; s/d €104/158; bar food €4-10, restaurant mains €15-26.50; 🕑 bar food 1-9pm, restaurant lunch Sun, dinner nightly; P 🖳) Positioned between Loughs Conn and Cullen, this family-run hotel gives you the feeling of being aboard a boat. Its genteel, champagne-coloured 'Grace Kelly' sitting room has some photographs of the actress who was a relative of the hotel's owner. All 58 bedrooms are comfortable (try for one opening on to the panoramic timber deck), but you're unlikely to spend much time in them given the activities on offer: cookery courses (€120 including lunch), painting classes (€95), a fishery school (from €95) and boat hire (with/without engine €40/60 per day; rod and waterproof hire available). Nonguests can also sign up.

Enniscoe House (☎ 096-31112; www.enniscoe.com; Castlehill; r €180-232, 2-bedroom apt per week €450-600, 3-bedroom apt per week €550-800; 🕑 Apr-Oct; P) You can stay in the 1750-built, apricot-coloured Enniscoe House or settle into a self-catering courtyard apartment (also historic). Its Victorian walled garden is only a tiny portion of the sprawling estate, which includes wild woodland walks and large grassy expanses. Dinner costs €50.

CASTLEBAR & AROUND

pop 11,891

Mayo's county town, Castlebar (Caisleán an Bharraigh's), sprawls just 19km east of Westport. As the county's largest town, it's a hub for shops and services, but most places of interest for visitors lie outside the town centre.

Castlebar's place in Irish history was cemented in 1798, when General Humbert's outnumbered army of French revolutionary soldiers and Irish peasants pulled off an astonishing victory here. The ignominious cavalry retreat of the British became known as the Castlebar Races.

Orientation & Information

Central Castlebar has a traffic-choked (and poorly signed) one-way road system. The main thoroughfare changes its name from Ellison St to Main St to Thomas St as you head north.

You'll find banks with bureaux de change on Main St.

Tourist office (☎ 094-902 1207; Linenhall St, Castlebar; 🕑 9.30am-1pm & 2-5.30pm May-Sep) West off the northern end of Main St.

Sights

NATIONAL MUSEUM OF COUNTRY LIFE

This extensive **museum** (☎ 094-903 1755; www .museum.ie; Turlough Park, Turlough; admission free; 🕑 10am-5pm Tue-Sat, 2-5pm Sun) is not a nostalgic remembrance of a worry-free past, but nor is it a gloomy equivalent of *Angela's Ashes*. A branch of the National Museum of Ireland (the other three are all in Dublin), rural traditions and skills celebrated here – from wickerwork to boat building – while not entirely obsolete, are certainly endangered. If there's a point of view, it's one of admiration for the resourcefulness, ingenuity and self-sufficiency of the Irish people. The exhibits concentrate on the period from 1850 to 1950.

The extensive lakeside grounds invite picnics, and part of Turlough's 19th-century manor is open for snooping. The website posts schedules of demonstrations and workshops.

Follow the signs off the N5, 5km northeast of Castlebar.

TURLOUGH ROUND TOWER

With its single lofty window, this impenetrable 9th-century tower calls to mind the fairy tale of Rapunzel. The tower stands on a hilltop by a ruined 18th-century church, a short distance northeast of the National Museum of Country Life.

MICHAEL DAVITT MEMORIAL MUSEUM

Housed in a pre-penal church where the man himself was christened (and next to Straide Abbey, in which he was buried) is this small but passionate **museum** (☎ 094-903 1022; www.museums ofmayo.com; Straide; adult/child/concession €3.20/1.30/2; ☻ 10am-6pm). The man, of course, is Michael Davitt (1846–1906), a Fenian and zealous founding member of the Irish National Land League. Davitt's family was brutally evicted from his childhood home near here.

Take the N5 east and turn left onto the N58 to Straide (Strade on some maps). It's 16km from Castlebar.

BALLINTUBBER ABBEY

The history of this delightful little **abbey** (☎ 094-903 0934; www.ballintubberabbey.ie; Ballintubber; admission free; ☻ 9am-midnight; P) reads like a collection of far-fetched folk tales. Often referred to as 'the abbey that refused to die', this is the only church in Ireland founded by an Irish king that is still in use. It was set up in 1216 next to the site of an earlier church founded by St Patrick after he came down from Croagh Patrick.

The abbey was burned by Normans, seized by James I and suppressed by Henry VIII. The nave roof was only restored in 1965 after the original was burned down by Cromwell's soldiers in 1653. Mass was outlawed and priests hunted down. Yet worship in the roofless remains continued against all the odds.

Take the N84 south towards Galway and after about 13km turn left at the Campus service station; the abbey is 2km along.

Sleeping & Eating

Lough Lannagh Village (☎ 094-902 7111; www.lough lannagh.ie; Old Westport Rd, Castlebar; campsites €18-28, B&B s/d €60/94, cottages per week from €720; ☻ camping ground Easter-Sep, lodge & cottages year-round; P) On the shores of Lough Lannagh, a 10-minute walk from the town centre, this combined camping ground, B&B lodge and self-catering cottages does feel like a bustling little village. You can hit the tennis court or ping-pong table, work out in the gym or arrange bike rental. Lodge guests can use the kitchen facilities.

TF Royal (☎ 094-902 3111; www.tfroyalhotel.com; Old Westport Rd, Castlebar; s €69-105, d €129-170; ☎) First came this family-run hotel, and then came the 2200-capacity TF Royal theatre next door. There's a theatrical feel to the hotel's decor of velour, tasselled drapes and comfy sofas, and some of the 27 rooms have poster beds. The Royal's restaurant get packed when there's a show on, which might be anything from concerts by artists such as Kenny Rogers or Christy Moore to Broadway productions like *Annie*. Carvery fare is €11 to €14; restaurant mains cost €15 to €23.

ourpick **Rua** (☎ 094-928 6072; Spencer St, Castlebar; mains €4-14; ☻ 9am-6pm Mon-Sat) Rua, run by the son of Café Rua's owner, is an inspired new establishment that is reason enough to brave Castlebar's traffic. On the mezzanine, the airy cafe offers a 'taste of the west of Ireland' in its daily changing specials (including numerous vegetarian options), all made from artisan, organic produce such as local duck eggs, Sligo pasta, Carrowholly cheese from Westport and Ballina smoked salmon, and Rua's own bakery. Everything on your plate can be purchased downstairs at the 'farmers market'–style gourmet deli.

Café Rua (☎ 094-902 3376; New Antrim St, Castlebar; dishes €4-14; ☻ 9am-6pm Mon-Sat) This long-time local favourite continues to attract loyal support for its filling, healthy Irish dishes and pastries. On your way in you might catch a whiff of a house speciality: champ (comprising mashed potatoes and onions). It does a mean breakfast, and good coffee, too.

Getting There & Around

Bus Éireann (☎ 096-71800) travels to Westport (€4.50, 20 minutes, 10 daily), Dublin (€17.60, 4½ hours, one daily) and Sligo (€14.90, 1½ hours, three daily). Services on Sunday are less frequent. Buses stop on Market St.

The Westport–Dublin train stops at Castlebar (€38 to €48.50, 3½ hours) three times daily. The station is just out of town on the N84 towards Ballinrobe.

KNOCK

pop 745

Knock (Cnoc Mhuire) was little more than a downtrodden rural village until 1879, when a divine apparition propelled it to become one of the world's most sacred Catholic shrines. Ireland's diminutive equivalent of Lourdes and Fátima is now a serious pilgrimage site for the faithful, particularly the elderly and infirm in search of miracle cures.

The shrine grounds dominate the little village. Across the road you'll find the **tourist office** (☎ 094-938 8193; ⏰ 10am-6pm May-Sep) and a cluster of souvenir shops. The only ATM is at the post office, at the roundabout on Main St.

Sights

The **Knock Marian Shrine** (☎ office 094-938 8100; www .knock-shrine.ie) encompasses churches and a museum in the town centre. The story that led to its development goes thus: on the evening of 21 August 1879, in drenching rain, two young Knock women were startled by a vision of Mary, Joseph, St John the Evangelist and sacrificial lamb upon an altar, freeze-framed in dazzling white light against the southern gable of the parish church. They were soon joined by 13 more villagers, all gazing at the heavenly apparition for around two hours as the daylight faded. A Church investigation confirmed it as a bona fide miracle, and a sudden rush of other Vatican-approved miracles followed as the sick and disabled claimed amazing recoveries upon visiting the spot.

Today, people of all Christian denominations and even other faiths pray at the modern **chapel** enclosing a scene of the apparition carved from snow-white marble, and rubbing a segment of **stone** from the original church mounted on the outside wall (on your right as you're facing the scene of the apparition). Near the church is the 1970s-built, spiky-topped **Basilica of Our Lady, Queen of Ireland**, which can accommodate over 10,000 worshippers.

Across open grasslands from the basilica, the little **Knock Museum** (☎ 094-938 8100; adult/ child/concession €4/3/3.50; ⏰ 10am-6pm May-Oct, noon-4pm Nov-Apr) follows the story from the first witnesses, through the miraculous cures, the repeated Church investigations and finally to the visit of Pope John Paul II on the event's centenary in 1979. One striking photograph shows rows of crutches left behind by miraculously cured pilgrims. It also has an interesting collection of local country life exhibits on how the village was when the apparition occurred.

There's a free **buggy service** around the shrine grounds.

Sleeping & Eating

The Knock Marian Shrine office (left) maintains a list of locals who offer B&B for around €35 to €45 per person, and has advice on the shrine's pilgrims' hostel (single B&B rooms €40 per person), run by nuns; as well as medical-assisted accommodation for infirm visitors. For self-catering cottage rental, check www.mayo rental.com.

Knock Caravan & Camping Park (☎ 094-938 8100; caravanpark@knock-shrine.ie; tent/van sites €11.50/17, plus per person €2.50, caravans per week €426, 2-bedroom bungalows per week €478; ⏰ Apr-Oct; P) A few paces uphill to the west of the shrine (which runs it), campers have plenty of space to stretch out at this well-maintained, grassy site.

Knock House Hotel (☎ 094-938 8088; www.knock househotel.ie; Ballyhaunis Rd; s/d €96/168; bar food €5-9, restaurant mains €15-29.50; P) Knock's only hotel is a modern construction of stone and glass housing 68 rooms and the most reliable places to grab a bite to eat year-round. It's run also by the shrine office (about 500m to the east).

Getting There & Away

Built to serve the influx of pilgrims, **Ireland West Airport Knock** (☎ 094-936 7222; www.irelandwest airport.com), 15km north by the N17, has daily flights to Dublin (Aer Arann) and London Stansted (Ryanair). Less frequent services operate to Alicante, Bristol, East Midlands, Liverpool and London (Luton) with Ryanair, Birmingham and Manchester with Bmi Baby, and London (Gatwick) with Aer Lingus. A €10 development fee is payable on departure.

Bus Éireann (☎ 096-71800) connects Knock's town centre with Westport (€9, one hour), Castlebar (€7, 45 minutes) and Dublin (€16, four hours) three times daily (once on Sunday).

Getting Around

A shuttle bus run by Bus Éireann links Ireland West Airport Knock with Charlestown (€4, 20 minutes), where connections can be made to Knock's town centre.

COUNTY SLIGO

County Sligo (Sligeach) packs as much poetry, myth and folklore into its countryside's lush splendour as any shamrock lover could hope for. It was Sligo that most inspired the Nobel laureate, poet and dramatist William Butler Yeats (1865–1939), who helped cement its pastoral reputation with such verses as 'The Lake Isle of Innisfree', in which he mused about the simple country life. You can still view the lake isle today, along with a cache of prehistoric sites. But it's no complacent backwater: the county town exudes a worldly vitality, and the coast's surf is internationally renowned.

SLIGO TOWN
pop 19,402

Sligo town is in no hurry to shed its cultural traditions but it doesn't sell them out, either. Pedestrian streets lined with inviting shop fronts, stone bridges spanning the River Garavogue, and *céilidh* sessions spilling from pubs contrast with genre-bending contemporary art and glass towers rising from prominent corners of the compact town (which is currently vying for city status).

Sligo's population almost triples each day with workers and shoppers converging on it, and on warm days busy restaurant tables along the quay have the atmosphere of a giant street party.

Information

Bank of Ireland (Stephen St) ATM and bureau de change.

Cafe Online (☎ 071-914 4892; 1 Calry Crt, Stephen St; per hr €3; ☼ 10am-11pm Mon-Sat, noon-11pm Sun) Central internet access.

Keohane's Bookshop (☎ 071-914 2597; Castle St) Great Irish interest section and finely chosen fiction recommendations.

Post office (Wine St)

Tourist office (☎ 071-916 1201; www.discoverireland .ie/northwest; Temple St; ☼ 9am-6pm Mon-Fri, 9am-5pm Sat, 10am-4pm Sun Jun-Aug, 9am-5pm Mon-Fri, 10am-4pm Sat Mar-May & Sep, 9am-5pm Mon-Fri Oct-Feb) Info on the whole northwest region.

Wash & Dry Laundrette (☎ 071-914-1777; Connolly St; small load from €14; ☼ 8.30am-6pm Mon-Sat) Serviced laundry services only; no self-service machines.

Sights
SLIGO COUNTY MUSEUM

The major draw of Sligo's county **museum** (☎ 071-914 1623; Stephen St; admission free; ☼ 10.30am-12.30pm & 2.30-4.30pm Mon-Sat Jun-Sep, 2-5pm Tue-Sat Apr, May & Oct) is the Yeats room, which features photographs, letters and newspaper cuttings connected with the poet WB Yeats, as well as drawings by his brother Jack B Yeats, one of Ireland's most important modern artists (who said he never painted anything without putting a thought of Sligo into it). The room across the hall contains a prison apron dress worn by Countess Constance Markievicz after the 1916 Easter Rising. The upstairs galleries exhibit contemporary artworks, mostly regional.

MODEL ARTS & NILAND GALLERY

Sligo's premier **gallery** (☎ 071-914 1405; www .modelart.ie; The Mall) was undergoing extensive redevelopment at the time of research, and was due to have reopened by the time you're reading this. Once completed, it will also house a new **cultural centre** with a performance space, additional gallery, artists' studios and a destination restaurant.

SLIGO ABBEY

The handsome husk that is Sligo's **abbey** (☎ 071-914 6406; Abbey St; adult/child/concession €3/1/2; ☼ 10am-6pm Easter-Oct, 9.30am-4.30pm Fri-Sun Nov–mid-Dec) has enjoyed the best and worst of luck. It was built by the town's founder, Maurice FitzGerald, around 1252 for the Dominicans, but then burned down in the 15th century and was later rebuilt. Friends in high places saved the abbey from the worst ravages of the Elizabethan era, and rescued the only sculpted altar to survive the Reformation. The abbey's fortunes fell again when it was put to the torch in 1641, and subsequently raided for stone. The doorways reach only a few feet high at the abbey's rear, and the ground around it was swollen by the mass graves from years of famine and war.

YEATS BUILDING

In a pretty setting near Hyde Bridge, the Yeats Building houses the **Sligo Art Gallery** (☎ 071-914 5847; www.sligoartgallery.com; Lower Knox St; admission free), hosting travelling exhibitions; and the **WB Yeats Exhibition** (☎ 071-914 2693; www.yeats-sligo .com; admission free; ☼ 10am-5pm Mon-Fri), which has a video presentation and valuable draft manuscripts; the €2 exhibition catalogue makes a good souvenir of Sligo. The charming **tearoom** (☼ 10am-5pm Mon-Sat) has outdoor tables overlooking the river.

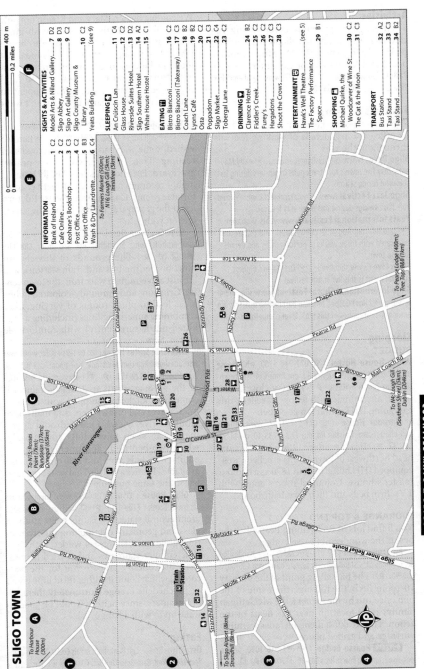

SLIGO TOWN

INFORMATION	
Bank of Ireland	**1** C2
Cafe Online	**2** C2
Keohane's Bookshop	**3** C3
Post Office	**4** C2
Tourist Office	**5** B3
Wash & Dry Laundrette	**6** C4

SIGHTS & ACTIVITIES	
Model Arts & Niland Gallery	**7** D2
Sligo Abbey	**8** D3
Sligo Art Gallery	**9** C2
Sligo County Museum &	
Library	**10** C2
Yeats Building	(see 9)

SLEEPING	
An Crúiscín Lán	**11** C4
Glass House	**12** C2
Riverside Suites Hotel	**13** D2
Sligo Southern Hotel	**14** A2
White House Hostel	**15** C1

EATING	
Bistro Bianconi	**16** C2
Bistro Bianconi (Takeaway)	**17** C3
Coach Lane	**18** B2
Lyons Café	**19** B2
Osta	**20** C2
Poppadom	**21** C3
Sligo Market	**22** C4
Tobergal Lane	**23** C2

DRINKING	
Clarence Hotel	**24** B2
Fiddler's Creek	**25** C2
Furey's	**26** C2
Hargadons	**27** C3
Shoot the Crows	**28** C2

ENTERTAINMENT	
Hawk's Well Theatre	(see 5)
The Factory Performance	
Space	**29** B1

SHOPPING	
Michael Quirke, the	
Woodcarver of Wine St	**30** C2
The Cat & the Moon	**31** C3

TRANSPORT	
Bus Station	**32** A2
Taxi Stand	**33** C3
Taxi Stand	**34** B2

Activities

There are good opportunities for surfing (including several good surf schools at Strandhill, p455), diving (notably off Mullaghmore, p460) and kayaking. For the latter, contact **Paddle Monkey** (☎ 071-913 4977; www.paddlemonkey .info; 2hr trips adult/child €30/20).

Festivals & Events

Sligo knows how to kick up its heels. The tourist office also has details of walking festivals throughout the year.

Sligo Races (www.countysligoraces.com; ◯ early May-early Oct) The town's race track pulls in punters during its colourful racing season.

Sligo Jazz Festival (www.sligojazzproject.com; ◯ mid-Jul) Sligo swings during this three-day festival.

Yeats International Festival (www.yeats-sligo.com; ◯ late Jul–mid-Aug) Irish poetry, music and culture are celebrated with three weeks of performances and events around town.

Sligo Live (www.sligolive.ie; ◯ Oct) Sligo's biggest cultural event is this live music festival.

Sligo International Choral Festival (www.sligochoral fest.org; ◯ Nov) Gospel, folk and barbershop quartets are among the categories of this high-level competition.

Sleeping

BUDGET

White House Hostel (☎ 071-914 5160; whitehouse hostel@gmail.com; Markievicz Rd; dm from €14; ◯ reception 8am-2pm & 5-10pm; P) To stay close to the action and mingle with fellow travellers, this easygoing IHH hostel is a good bet.

Harbour House (☎ 071-917 1547; www.harbour househostel.com; Finisklin Rd; dm €20, s €35-40, d €44-50; P 💻 🛜) If you're after a little budget luxury, head northwest of town to this excellent, well-equipped IHH hostel built in 1870 as a harbour master's house. Colourful rooms come with TVs, firm beds and their own bathroom.

MIDRANGE & TOP END

You'll find lots of B&Bs lining Pearse Rd; the best is the wonderful Pearse Lodge.

An Crúiscín Lan (☎ 071-916 2857; www.bandbsligo .ie; Connolly St; s standard/with private bathroom €35/60, d €60/90; P) The big selling point of the unfussy 10-room B&B 'the full jug' (the name of the pub once run by the owners, the McGettigan family) is its location near the heart of the action. The breakfast menu includes warming porridge and grilled plaice.

ourpick Pearse Lodge (☎ 071-916 1090; pearse lodge@eircom.net; Pearse Rd; s €45-50, d €70-74; P 💻 🛜) Welcoming owners Mary and Kieron not only impeccably maintain the six stylish guest rooms at their cosy B&B but are also up on what's happening in town. Mary's breakfast menu includes smoked salmon, French toast with bananas and homemade muesli (and Illy coffee!). A sunny sitting room opens to a newly landscaped garden. You won't want to leave.

Tree Tops B&B (☎ 071-916 0160; www.sligobandb .com; Cleveragh Rd; s €48-52, d €74; P 🛜) When we visited, some wag had pointed the road sign reading 'Tree Tops Guests' into a nearby graveyard. Fear not: this cosy family home is highly recommended, with attractive, comfortable rooms. Coming from Pearse Rd, turn *left* at the graveyard; it's just before the superette on your left.

Sligo Southern Hotel (☎ 071-916 2101; www.sligo southernhotel.com; Strandhill Rd; s/d from €88/110; P 💻 🛜 🍴) The grounds of this elegant hotel border the bus and train stations, and are just a five-minute walk from the town centre. Crimson- and burgundy-coloured public areas lead to plush rooms of varying sizes, combining superb facilities (including a fully kitted-out leisure centre) with comfortable charm. Service is spot-on.

Riverside Suites Hotel (☎ 071-914 8080; www.river sidesuiteshotelsligo.com; Millbrook; 1-bedroom apt €101-119, 2-bedroom apt €129-159; P 🛜) Riverside's state-of-the-art apartments are fantastic value. All come with kitchens equipped with cookers, microwaves and dishwashers, and many have fabulous river views. One-bedroom apartments can sleep four adults comfortably, while two-bedroom apartments sleep six adults, with kids' cots and roll-out beds also available. There's a stylish Thai restaurant and bar in the same building.

Glass House (☎ 071-919 4300; www.theglasshouse .ie; Swan Point; r €109-130; P 💻) Sligo's boldest architectural statement is this svelte study in glass and geometry overlooking the river. In the public areas, things get wilder, with '70s-style circular staircases and swirled carpets. Even that doesn't prepare you for the bedrooms, which come in either lurid lime green or psychedelic orange (fortunately since neither would be good to wake up to with a hangover).

Eating

Osta (Hyde Bridge, Left Bank; light meals €6.50-10; ◯ 8am-7pm Mon-Wed, 8am-8pm Thu-Sat) Osta is a cafe and a wine bar, and it's well suited to both callings. An array of preserved meats, seafood and Irish farmhouse cheeses accompany its well-chosen wines. It's intimate and well lit, and has a prime quayside location for gazing at the river charging beneath Hyde Bridge.

our pick **Tobergal Lane** (☎ 071-914 6599; Tobergal Lane; lunch dishes €7.50-13, dinner mains €20-21; ☯ 10am-10pm, closed Mon Nov-Easter) Suppliers have top billing on Tobergal Lane's menu, which includes specialities like freshwater Arctic char fish, served pan-fried with hollandaise sauce, or baked on creamed potatoes with almond and lemon-butter sauce. All baking is done in-house. Sligo's creative community heads here for the weekly jazz 'brunch' (3pm to 5pm Sunday), and 'Café Beats': lounge-y DJ sets that take place every second Saturday evening. Alternate Saturday evenings feature 'Penthouse' DJ sets upstairs, with a cover charge of €5.

Poppadom (☎ 071-914 7171; 34 O'Connell St; mains €9.50-20.50; ☯ 5.30-11pm Sun-Thu, 5.30pm-midnight Fri & Sat) Poppadom's atmosphere is a real surprise: minimalist elegance rather than the usual Indian exotica, and the cuisine is excellent. Service is smooth and professional.

Lyons Café (☎ 071-914 2969; Quay St; mains €10; ☯ 9am-6pm Mon-Sat) Sligo's flagship department store, Lyons, opened in 1878, and its airy 1st-floor cafe – with original leadlight windows and squeaky timber floors – has been going strong since 1923. Daily changing hot specials created from locally sourced ingredients might include sautéed lamb's liver, smoky bacon and tomato casserole, or baked red lentil potato gratin with wild mushrooms.

Bistro Bianconi (☎ 071-914 1744; 44 O'Connell St; pizzas €13-18, mains €22.50-29; ☯ lunch Mon-Sat, dinner nightly) Deliberate over Bianconi's 47 varieties of thin-crusted pizza – from grilled chicken and chilli-lime dressing to homemade pesto and caramelised onion. It has an equally wide range of meat and seafood dishes, and a knockout wine list. The O'Connell St bistro is the original location, and has spawned a takeaway outlet (☎ 071-914 7000; 35 High St; open from 5pm), with branches also in Galway and Dublin.

Coach Lane (☎ 071-916 2417; 1-2 Lord Edward St; mains €20-28; ☯ bar food from 3pm, dinner from 5.30pm 'till the cows come home') The place where locals come to celebrate special occasions. Coach Lane shares its kitchen with Donaghy's Pub, but try for a table in the atmospheric dining room. Don't miss the peach and strawberry minestrone for dessert.

Pick up fresh produce at Sligo's central **market** (Market Yard; ☯ 9am-3pm Fri), which also sells crafts, and its **farmers market** (Sligo Institute of Technology; ☯ 9am-1pm Sat).

Drinking

Sligo enjoys some of the best night-time fun in Ireland's northwest, with impromptu sessions striking up at every opportunity.

our pick **Hargadons** (☎ 071-915 3709; O'Connell St; lunch mains €10.50-13, tapas dishes €6.50-9; ☯ from 10am Mon-Sat, from 6pm Sun, lunch Mon-Sat, tapas 4-8pm Thu-Sat) Hargadons has polished up its original 1864 fittings – including its bowed former grocery shelves, snug, uneven stone floors, turf fire, and swivelling 'confession box' frosted-glass panels above the marble bar – without compromising the pub's character. You won't find a TV or DJs here, but you can catch live music on Saturday nights. Tapas dishes range from mussels in white wine to warm crab cake.

Shoot the Crows (☎ 071-916 2554; Castle St) Dark and somewhat dishevelled, this old pub oozes bohemian atmosphere. Early evening draws a good-natured crowd of regulars, and even when the place is packed to the gills it generally has an easygoing vibe. Singalongs and *céilidh* sessions often start up spontaneously.

Also recommended:

Furey's (☎ 071-914 3825; Bridge St) Old-style bar with superb traditional music most nights, as well as jazz and various open mic opportunities for all comers.

Clarence Hotel (☎ 071-914 2211; Wine St) Regular live bands and DJs perform at this local gathering spot.

Fiddler's Creek (☎ 071-914 1866; Rockwood Pde) Riverside pub with a lively atmosphere despite the dark medieval stonework, plus creative pub grub.

Entertainment

Hawk's Well Theatre (☎ 071-61526; www.hawkswell .com; Temple St) This well-regarded theatre presents concerts, dance and drama.

The Factory Performance Space (☎ 071-917 0431; www.blueraincoat.com; Lower Quay St) A once-derelict pork abattoir is home to innovative professional theatre company Blue Raincoat, whose program includes original productions.

Shopping

Michael Quirke, the Woodcarver of Wine St (☎ 071-914 2624; Wine St; ☯ 9.30am-12.30pm & 3-6pm Mon-Sat) Don't miss a chat with Michael Quirke (see the boxed text, p454) as he hand-carves his creations.

MICHAEL QUIRKE: THE WOODCARVER OF WINE ST

The inconspicuous studio (p453) of Michael Quirke, woodcarver, raconteur and local character, is filled with the scents of locally felled timbers and off-cuts of beech stumps. A converted butcher shop, it retains some of the implements of the butcher's trade, including an electric bone saw. Quirke, himself formerly a butcher, began to use his tools for cutting and carving wood in 1968. He divided his time between his twin callings for 20 years, after which he gave up meat, so to speak.

Quirke's art is inspired by Irish mythology, a subject about which he is passionate and knowledgeable, and as he carves he readily chats with the customers and the curious who enter his shop and end up staying for hours. 'Irish mythology, unlike Greek mythology, is alive and constantly changing', he says. 'It's not set in stone, and that's why it's interesting.' He draws unforced connections between Irish myths, music, history, flora, fauna and contemporary events, as well as comparisons in the wider world, such as Australian Aboriginal and Native North American lore. Frequent tangents often debunk misconceptions. For instance: 'You'll hear talk about bunnies in Ireland, but in fact we have hares, which are very different. Bunnies are nervous, skittish animals. That's why they live in holes. On the other hand, the Irish hare has nerves of steel. It does not hide in burrows, and when it runs it does not hesitate. When I walk my dog, if a hare runs by, no more than 20 feet away, my dog will never notice it. It's a grey streak.'

As he talks and carves, Quirke frequently pulls out a county map, pointing to places that spring from the conversation, leading you on your own magical, mystical tour of the county.

The Cat & the Moon (☎ 071-914 3686; www.thecatandthemoon.com; 4 Castle St; ◷ 9am-6pm) Quality Irish crafts and arts sold at this innovative gift shop include designer jewellery.

Getting There & Away

AIR

From **Sligo Airport** (☎ 071-916 8280; www.sligoairport.com; Strandhill Rd) there are direct Aer Arann flights to Dublin twice daily (40 minutes).

BUS

Bus Éireann (☎ 071-916 0066) leaves from the bus station, situated below the train station on Lord Edward St. Destinations include Ballina (€12.90, 1½ hours, five daily), Westport (€16.70, two hours, twice daily) and Dublin (€17.10, four hours, four daily), as well as Galway and Donegal town. Services are less frequent on Sunday.

Feda O'Donnell (☎ 074-954 8114; www.fedaodonnell.com) operates a service between Crolly (County Donegal) and Galway twice daily (four times on Friday). Call to confirm departure points.

TRAIN

Trains leave the **station** (☎ 071-916 9888) for Dublin (€32, 3½ hours, four or five daily) via Boyle, Carrick-on-Shannon and Mullingar.

Getting Around

Local Bus Éireann buses run to Strandhill and to Rosses Point (€3.50, five to seven Monday to Saturday) and sometimes continue to the airport. A taxi to the airport costs about €15.

There are taxi stands on Quay St and on Grattan St. **Zero Cabs** (☎ 071-915 4555) offers regular taxi services as well as tours (two hours per carload from €60) taking in the surrounding countryside and points of interest.

AROUND SLIGO TOWN
Rosses Point
pop 872

Rosses Point (An Ros) is a picturesque seaside resort with grassy dunes rolling down to the strand, birdlife and Benbulben, Sligo's most recognisable landmark, arching skywards in the distance. It holds special appeal for the golf-minded traveller as much of the prime real estate here is dominated by trimmed greens. Accommodation is limited, but Rosses Point is Sligo town's backyard, so you can easily pop by for the day.

Offshore, the 1821-installed **Metal Man** beacon is an exact replica of the one in Tramore, County Waterford.

ACTIVITIES

Established in 1894, **County Sligo Golf Course** (☎ 071-917 7134; www.countysligogolfclub.ie; green fees Mon-Thu €75, Fri-Sun Apr-Oct €90, Mon-Thu €40, Fri-Sun Nov-Mar €50) is one of Ireland's most challenging and renowned links courses, attracting golfers from all over Europe. Its position on the peninsula is breathtaking.

COUNTIES MAYO & SLIGO

SLEEPING & EATING

Greenlands Caravan & Camping Park (☎ 071-917 7113; noelineha@eircom.net; campsites car/hiker or cyclist €20/11; ⏲ Easter–mid-Sep) Peering over the Atlantic from the point's extreme is this windblown site with easy access to the beaches. (Keep your head down if errant golfers are swinging nearby!) Showers cost €1.50; electricity is €5.

Yeats Country Hotel (☎ 071-917 7211; www.yeats countryhotel.com; s/d from €65/130; Ⓟ ⓢ) There isn't a town centre as such, so this huge three-star hotel more or less stands in for the heart of Rosses Point. It has a commanding presence overlooking the beach and the golf course, and attracts golfers and families. Rooms are large and many afford sea views. There's a popular restaurant; food is also served at its two bars.

Parallel to the main road from Sligo (on your right as you come into Rosses Point), the unmissable orange-and-red **Harry's Bar** doesn't serve food, but be sure to stop in for a pint and a peek at its historic well, aquarium and maritime bric-a-brac.

Deer Park Court Cairn

From a nearby car park, a 10-minute walk leads through pine-scented forest to this enigmatic **court tomb** (also called Magheraghanrush). Dating from around 3000 BC, the crumbling structure is comparable to a crude human form, with a large bellylike central court and several protruding burial chambers positioned as though the head and legs.

Take the N16 east from Sligo and turn onto the R286 for Parke's Castle. Almost immediately, turn left at the Y-junction onto a minor road for Manorhamilton. Continue for 3km to the car park, then follow the trail for 50m before veering right up a small hill.

Knocknarea Cairn

Sligo's ultimate rock pile, 2km northwest of Carrowmore, **Knocknarea** is popularly believed to be the grave of legendary Queen Maeve (Queen Mab in Welsh and English folk tales). The 40,000 tonnes of stone have never been excavated, despite speculation that a tomb on the scale of the one at Newgrange lies buried below.

The cairn is perched high atop the limestone plateau (328m) and seems to be looking over your shoulder everywhere you dare tread in its ancestral backyard. It's a 45-minute trek to the top, from which a spectacular panoramic view pulls in Benbulben, Rosses Point and the Atlantic Ocean beyond.

Leave Sligo as though for Carrowmore, then follow signs to Knocknarea. Or from Carrowmore, continue down the road, turn right by a church then follow the signposts.

Carrowmore Megalithic Cemetery

Welcome to the largest Stone Age cemetery in Ireland and the second-biggest in Europe: **Carrowmore** (☎ 071-916 1534; adult/child/concession €3/1/2; ⏲ 10am-6pm Easter-Sep, final admission 5pm; Ⓟ) impresses for its variety and sheer scale. Everywhere you look you'll see rolling hills beaded with stone circles, passage tombs and dolmens – there are about 60, all told.

The conventional wisdom is that the site pre-dates Newgrange in County Meath by some 700 years. Over the centuries, many of the stones have been destroyed, and several remaining stones are on private land.

The delicately balanced dolmens were originally covered with stones and earth, so it requires some effort to picture what this 2.5km-wide area might once have looked like. To help (or some would say hinder) the imagination, Dúchas (which operates the site) has launched a decapitated reconstruction of one cairn, caged by wire and sliced open by a gaping entrance. An exhibit in the roadside visitor centre gives the full low-down on this fascinating site.

To get here, leave town by Church Hill and follow the signposts south for 5km.

Strandhill
pop 1413

The great Atlantic rollers that sweep the shorefront of Strandhill (An Leathras) make this long, red-gold **beach** unsafe for swimming. They have, however, made it a surfing mecca. Its handy 24-hour **surfcam** (www.strandhillsurfcam.com) brings surfers scurrying whenever the surf's up.

Gear hire and lessons can be arranged through **Perfect Day Surf Shop** (☎ 087 202 9399; www.perfectdaysurfing.com; Shore Rd) and **Strandhill Surf School** (☎ 071-916 8483; www.strandhillsurfschool.com; Beach Front), as well as Strandhill Hostel (p456).

Alternatively, take a gentler, warmer dip in the **Voya Seaweed Baths** (see boxed text, p456).

A few kilometres towards Sligo, you can walk – at low tide only! – to **Coney Island**. Its New York namesake was supposedly named by a man from Rosses Point. The island's wishing well is reputed to have been dug by

---

MERMAID DREAMS

Ireland's only native spa therapy is the stuff of mermaid (or merman) fantasies. Part of Irish homeopathy for centuries, steaming your pores open then submerging yourself in a seaweed bath is said to help rheumatism and arthritis, thyroid imbalances, even hangovers. Certainly it leaves your skin feeling baby-soft: seaweed's silky oils contain a massive concentration of iodine, a key presence in most moisturising creams.

Seaweed baths are prevalent along the west coast but two places stand out. **Kilcullen's Seaweed Baths** (☎ 091-36238; www.kilcullenseaweedbaths.com; Enniscrone; s/tw bath €24/32; ☼ 10am-9pm May-Oct, noon-8pm Mon-Fri, 10am-8pm Sat & Sun Nov-Apr) is the most traditional. Set within a grand Edwardian structure, Kilcullen's has loads of character, with original gigantic porcelain baths and stout brass taps still operating. For an altogether more modern setting, try **Voya Seaweed Baths** (☎ 071-916 8686; www.celticseaweedbaths.com; Shore Rd, Strandhill; s/tw €25/35; ☼ 10am-8pm), which has a beachfront location.

If too much relaxation is barely enough, both establishments also offer the chance to indulge in various other seaweed treatments, including body wraps and massages.

St Patrick (who, if all these tales are to be trusted, led a *very* busy life). Check tide times to avoid getting stranded.

SLEEPING

Strandhill Hostel & Knocknarea House (☎ 071-916 8313; www.strandhillaccommodation.com; Shore Rd; hostel dm/s/d €16/20/30, Knocknarea House d €60-70; Ⓟ ☐ ☎) Surfer dudes and dudettes thaw out by the open fire in the common room of this well-run, 34-bed hostel a few paces from the strand. Next door, Knocknarea House is a former B&B that retains its frilly decor, but offers privacy by way of single, double and triple rooms (some with their own bathroom). Breakfast's not included at the hostel or the house, but Knocknarea guests can use the hostel kitchen. The owners operate a surf school, with lessons starting from €30 for two hours, including gear rental.

Strandhill Caravan & Camping Park (☎ 071-916 8111; sxl@iol.ie; campsites car/hiker or cyclist €20/11; ☼ Easter-Sep) Ideally positioned by the long beach, separated only by grassy dunes, this large flat camping ground has 140 sites and good facilities. Showers cost €1.50; electricity is €5.

Dunes Tavern (☎ 071-916 8131; www.accommodation strandhill.com; Top Rd; dm/d from €20/50) Dunes is up the hill from the beach along the main highway and offers the traditional sleeps-over-a-pub combo. All seven rooms have private bathrooms and views of the beach or Knocknarea. The pub, with billiards and the odd *céilidh* session, is a social spot.

EATING & DRINKING

Bella Vista Bar & Bistro (☎ 071-912 2222; Shore Rd; lunch dishes €3.50-12, dinner mains €12-25; ☼ food served 10am-10pm; ☎) The best place to eat in town (amid admittedly limited options) is lively Bella Vista, which prepares a fine rack of Irish lamb, crispy beer-battered cod, and vegetarian dishes including gourmet pizzas, pasta with homemade pesto sauce, and peppers stuffed with aromatic rice.

Venue (☎ 071-916 8167; Top Rd; mains €13.50-26; ☼ food served 12.30-9.15pm) Seafood, fajitas and steaks are part of the decent international menu at this whitewashed pub close to Dunes Tavern. Year-round, you'll catch live music every Thursday, Friday and Saturday in its front bar.

Strand Bar (☎ 071-916 8140; Shore Rd) This old stone pub's decor is worth studying, with proper snugs and cosy corners. Its variety of food options spans bar food to a Chinese restaurant upstairs. Live music plays at weekends.

Getting There & Away

Rosses Point is 8km northwest of Sligo along the R291, while Strandhill is situated 8km due west of Sligo off the R292 airport road. **Bus Éireann** (☎ 071-916 0066) buses run from Sligo to both towns (each €3.50, five to seven Monday to Saturday), but there's no public transport to other places of interest in the area. It's possible to walk to Carrowmore and Knocknarea from town, but it's a *long* day's return trek.

SOUTH OF SLIGO TOWN
Collooney & Riverstown

The endearing **Sligo Folk Park** (☎ 071-916 5001; www.sligofolkpark.com; Millview House, Riverstown; adult/child/family €6/4/20; ☼ 10am-5pm Mon-Sat, 12.30-6pm

Sun mid-Apr–Oct, by appointment Oct-Apr) revolves around a lovingly restored 19th-century cottage. Humble thatched structures complement this centrepiece, along with scattered farm tools and an exhibit that honours the old country life. In December, the park sets up Santa Town, with shows, Santa visits and so on – call for annual opening details.

The three-day **James Morrison Traditional Music Festival** (www.morrison.ie; Aug) includes fun informal seminars on how to sing *sean-nós* ('old-style' songs) or perform traditional Irish reels on instruments such as the button accordion and the fiddle.

SLEEPING & EATING

Gyreum Eco-lodge (071-916 5994; www.gyreum.com; Corlisheen, Riverstown; dm €17-21, d €50-54; P) Horse whisperers are among the volunteers sought by this eco-lodge in exchange for food and lodging, along with less romanticised occupations like plumbing and marketing. Along with a zero-carbon footprint (thanks to wind and geothermal power), the lodge has an organic veggie garden and a Finnish sauna.

Markree Castle (071-916 7800; www.markree castle.ie; Collooney; s €130-165, d €195-260; P) Behind a whimsical Gothic facade, Sligo's oldest inhabited castle has 30 somewhat faded rooms, some named after famous guests, such as number 8 where Johnny Cash stayed (alas, there's no memorabilia). Its thick walls mean wi-fi is available in the public areas only. The restaurant (open for dinner nightly and lunch on Sunday) is a fine excuse to come out this way, but nonguests should book ahead. Lunch costs €27.50; dinner is €45. Follow the N4 to the roundabout in Collooney, then follow the sign to Castle Dargan; the gate to Markree Castle is about 1km up the road, the driveway another 1km through the grounds.

Coopershill House (071-916 5108; www.coopershill .com; Riverstown; s €156-171, d €242-272; Apr-Oct; P) This grey-stone mansion is an idyllic Georgian retreat in an estate alive with wildflowers, birdsong and deer. Most of the eight bedrooms have lovely canopy beds. If you want a small taste of its splendour, the restaurant can accommodate nonguests by prior arrangement. A five-course dinner starts at €59.

Carrowkeel Passage Tomb Cemetery

With a God's-eye view of the county from high in the Bricklieve Mountains, it's little wonder this hilltop site was sacred in pre-historic times. The windswept location is simultaneously eerie and uplifting, dotted with around 14 cairns, dolmens and the scattered remnants of other graves. It's possible to squeeze into at least one limestone chamber, although bigger folk are liable to get stuck. The place has been dated to the late Stone Age (3000 to 2000 BC).

West off the N4 road, Carrowkeel is closer to Boyle than Sligo town. From the latter, turn right in Castlebaldwin, then left at the fork; it's 2km uphill from the gateway. You can take an Athlone bus from Sligo and ask to be dropped off at Castlebaldwin.

Ballymote & Around

pop 1229

This pretty little town merits a visit if only to see the immense ivy-covered shell of **Ballymote Castle**. It was from this early-14th-century castle, fronted by formidable drum towers, that O'Donnell marched to disaster at the Battle of Kinsale in 1601. It's on the Tubbercurry road.

Eagles soar straight over your head at the new volunteer-run research centre **Eagles Flying** (071-918 9310; www.eaglesflying.com; Ballymote; adult/child/student €9/5.50/8; flying demonstrations 11am & 3pm Apr-Oct). Scientists answer questions about these birds of prey during demonstrations; there's also an on-site minizoo with ducks, donkeys and other cute critters.

Around 6km south of Ballymote at Kesh, the **Caves of Kesh** (sometimes spelt Keash) are rich with mythology and are believed to extend for miles (some say as far as Roscommon). Human remains have been found here, as well as those of cave bears, reindeer, Arctic lemmings and Irish elk. Check with the tourist office in Sligo (p450) for current access details, as it can vary.

Just under 10km southwest of Kesh, at the main crossroads of the village of Gurteen (also spelt Gorteen), the **Coleman Irish Music Centre** (071-918 2599; www.colemanirishmusic.com; 10am-5pm Mon-Sat) has multimedia music exhibits and hosts workshops and performances. You can add to your music collection or pick up your own instruments and sheet music at the on-site shop. If you're inspired, contact five-time All-Ireland champion bodhrán player **Andrew 'Junior' Davey** (072-928 3772, 086 301 3567; www .colemanbodhran.com) for private lessons (€25 per hour) or a week-long summer school in late June/early July (€250).

DETOUR: LADIES BRAE

For a DIY adventure well off the beaten track, following the narrow back roads between Ballymote and Aughris Head brings you past the impossibly pretty Ladies Brae. You'll find secluded picnic tables and some superb walks that link with the 74km way-marked **Sligo Way** (www.walkireland.ie).

---

ourpick **Temple House** (☎ 071-918 3329; www.templehouse.ie; Ballymote; s €105-120, d €160-190; ✦ Apr-Nov; **P** ✦), set in 400 hectares of woodlands, overlooks the ruins of a 13th-century Knights Templar castle and a crystalline lake that you can explore by rowboat. The Georgian mansion has been in the same family since the 1600s, and has six shabby-chic period guest rooms (with sparkling new bathrooms), dusty natural-history collections and decapitated hunting trophies. Dinner costs €45. It's signposted 500m south of the small village of Ballinacarrow (also spelt Ballynacarrow), close to the N17.

On Gurteen's main street, the exterior stonework of **Church View B&B** (☎ 071-918 2935; www.thechurchview.com; s/d €40/70; **P**) mirrors St Patrick's church next door. Inside, its rooms are stylish and spotless, with private bathrooms. Breakfast includes steaming potato waffles and homemade marmalade.

Tubbercurry
pop 1421

Sleepy Tubbercurry (Tobar an Choire), also spelt Tobercurry, is shaken awake in mid-July, when the week-long **South Sligo Summer School** (☎ 071-912 0912; www.ssssschool.org) celebrates Irish music and dance with infectious gusto. Try your hand at anything from the tin whistle to an Irish jig, or simply enjoy the eruption of local concerts and recitals.

Year-round, Tubbercurry's town centre comes to life during its weekly **farmers market** (✦ 3-6pm Thu).

Aughris Head

An invigorating 5km **walk** traces the cliffs around remote Aughris Head, where three wild **dolphins** – Oisin, Fionn and Maedbh – have taken to swimming into the bay most days.

In a stupendous setting on the beach by the cliff walk, the **ourpick** **Beach Bar** (☎ 071-917 6465;

mains €10-18.50; ✦ food served daily summer, weekends only winter) is tucked inside a 17th-century thatched cottage, with cracking traditional music sessions and superb seafood including creamy chowder and poached salmon. The owners also operate the B&B **Aughris House** (tent/van sites €10/20, s/d €40/70; **P**) next door, with seven comfy rooms and adjacent campsites.

Easkey & Enniscrone

The town of Easkey (Eascaigh; sometimes spelt Easky) seems blissfully unaware that it's one of Europe's best year-round surfing destinations. Pub conversations revolve around hurling and Gaelic football, and the road to the beach isn't even signposted (turn off next to the childcare centre). Facilities are few; most surfers camp (free) around the castle ruins by the sea. If you're planning on hitting the waves, information and advice are available from **Easkey Surfing & Information Centre** (Irish Surfing Association; ☎ 096-49428; www.isasurf.ie).

Some 14km south at Enniscrone (Innis Crabhann), a stunning beach known as the Hollow stretches for 5km. The town is also famous for its seaweed baths (see boxed text, p456). Surf lessons and board hire are available from Enniscrone-based **Seventh Wave Surf School** (☎ 087 971 6389; www.seventhwavesurfschool.com).

Atlantic Caravan & Camping Park (☎ 096-36132; www.atlanticcaravanpark.com; Enniscrone; campsites €15-20; ✦ Mar-Sep), a sandy two-star camping ground, is spitting distance from Hollow beach. For the tentless, it has furnished caravans that can sleep four or more available for weekly rental.

Getting There & Away

Bus Éireann (☎ 071-916 0066) express service 23 to Sligo from Dublin (€19, 3¾ hours) and service 64 between Galway (€16, 2½ hours) and Derry (€19, 2½ hours) stop outside Quigley's in Collooney. On Saturday only, the Sligo–Castlerea bus 460 stops at Collooney (€3.90, 15 minutes), Ballymote (€6.80, 30 minutes) and Tubbercurry (€9.80, 40 minutes). Buses run from Sligo to Collooney, Monday to Saturday. From Easkey, buses run four times daily (once on Sunday) to Sligo (€10.30, 50 minutes) and Ballina (€7.60, 30 minutes). From Enniscrone, buses also run four times daily (once on Sunday) to Sligo (€12.70, 65 minutes) and Ballina (€4.20, 15 minutes).

The Sligo **train** (☎ 071-916 9888) stops at Collooney and Ballymote (both €7 to €10.20, four to six times daily) en route to Dublin.

LOUGH GILL

The mirrorlike 'Lake of Brightness', Lough Gill is home to as many legends as fish. One that can be tested easily is the story that a silver bell from the abbey in Sligo was thrown into the lough and only those free from sin can hear it pealing. (We didn't hear it…)

The lake, southeast of Sligo town, is an easy day trip from anywhere in the county. Two magical swaths of woodland – **Hazelwood** and **Slish Wood** – have loop trails; there are good views of Innisfree Island from the latter.

Dooney Rock

Immortalised by Yeats in *The Fiddler of Dooney*, this huge fissured limestone knoll bulges awkwardly upward by the lough's southern shore. There's a great lake view from the top.

Leave Sligo south on the N4, but turn left at the sign to Lough Gill. Another left at the T-junction brings you onto the R287 towards Dooney car park.

Innisfree Island

This pint-sized island (Inis Fraoigh) lies tantalisingly close to the lough's southeastern shore, but alas, can't be accessed. Still, it's visible from the shore. Its air of tranquillity so moved Yeats that he famously wrote *The Lake Isle of Innisfree*:

I will arise and go now, and go to Innisfree,
And a small cabin build there, of clay and wattles made;
Nine bean rows will I have there, a hive for the honey bee,
And live alone in the bee-loud glade.

Continue east from Dooney Rock and turn left at the crossroads. After 3km turn left again for another 3km. A small road leads down to the lake.

Getting There & Away

By car and bicycle, leave Sligo east via the Mall past the hospital, and turn right off the N16 onto the R286, which leads to the northern shore of Lough Gill. The southern route is less interesting until you reach Dooney Rock.

NORTH OF SLIGO TOWN
Drumcliff & Benbulben

Visible right along Sligo's northern coast, Benbulben (525m), often written Ben Bulben, resembles a table covered by a pleated cloth: its limestone plateau is uncommonly flat, and its near-vertical sides are scored by earthen ribs. Walking here can be dangerous for the uninitiated – the **Sligo Mountaineering Club** (☎ 071-914 1267) has advice.

Benbulben's beauty was not lost on WB Yeats. Before the poet died in Menton, France in 1939, he had requested: 'If I die here, bury me up there on the mountain, and then after a year or so, dig me up and bring me privately to Sligo'. His wishes weren't honoured until 1948, when his body was interred in the churchyard at Drumcliff (sometimes spelt Drumcliffe), where his great-grandfather had been rector.

Yeats' grave is next to the doorway of the Protestant church, and his youthful bride Georgie Hyde-Lee is buried alongside. Almost three decades her senior, Yeats was 52 when they married. The poet's epitaph is from his poem *Under Ben Bulben*:

Cast a cold eye
On life, on death.
Horseman, pass by!

Visiting the grave is somewhat disturbed by traffic noise along the N15 that no doubt has Yeats rolling over.

In the 6th century, St Colmcille chose the same location for a monastery. You can still see the stumpy remains of the **round tower**, which was struck by lightning in 1936, on the main road nearby. Also in the churchyard is an extraordinary 11th-century **high cross**, etched with intricate biblical scenes.

In summer, the church shows a 15-minute audiovisual on Yeats, St Colmcille and Drumcliff. You can browse books, pick up local ceramics and peruse shamrock souvenirs at its little **tea shop**.

Historic **Lissadell House**, west of Drumcliff off the N15 just past Yeats Tavern, had closed to the public at the time of research, but may reopen – check with the tourist office in Sligo town (p450) for updates.

SLEEPING & EATING

Benbulben Farm (☎ 071-916 3211; www.benbulbenfarm .com; Barnaribbon, Drumcliff; s/d €45/70; ⌛ Apr-Sep; Ⓟ) The two-hour-return mountain walk starts at the gate of this isolated farmhouse B&B at the base of Benbulben. Run by a friendly family, the house has five comfortable rooms with private bathrooms, and uninterrupted views across sheep-flecked paddocks to the sea. It's 2km north of Drumcliff.

our pick **Ardtarmon House** (☎ 071-916 3156; www .ardtarmon.com; Ballinfull; s €64-69, d €88-110; ✕ closed late Dec-early Jan; (P) ✕) In an incomparable location 10km west of the N15 on the Drumcliff to Raghly road, this fifth-generation family-run property has four spacious rooms in the manor house, and five self-contained cottages in converted farm buildings (from €155 for a two-night stay). A 460m stroll through wild-flower-strewn gardens brings you to the beach. Its eco ventures include homegrown produce and woodchip-boiler-powered energy. Dinner (€30) can be arranged.

Laura's (☎ 071-916 3056; Carney; mains €16-34; ✕ lunch Sun, dinner nightly) The heart and soul of the seaside hamlet of Carney is this old-fashioned strawberry-and-cream-painted pub/restaurant, which spills from the bar into a number of rooms as well as a sunny alfresco area. It's run by one of Sligo's best fishmongers, and the all-organic, cooked-to-order menu concentrates almost solely on local catches, from crab claws and calamari starters to baked cod and trout fillet mains.

Henry's Bar & Restaurant (☎ 071-917 3985; Cashelgarran; mains €14-25; ✕ food served noon-9.30pm Mon-Sat, noon-5pm & 6-9.30pm Sun) Since it opened in 2008, this sprawling modern expanse of timber and glass has been a winner with families for its easygoing attitude and solid Irish menu with kid-friendly options.

Yeats Tavern (☎ 071-916 3117; N15; Drumcliff; mains €14.50-26; ✕ food served noon-9.30pm) This smart, contemporary pub/restaurant is popular for a pint or Irish coffee, but especially for its seafood which includes local Drumcliff Bay mussels and Lissadell clams. It's about 300m north of Yeats' grave.

Lough Glencar

Straddling counties Sligo and Leitrim, this picturesque lake is famed for **fishing** as well as its beautiful **waterfall**, and was referred to by Yeats in *The Stolen Child*. The surrounding countryside is best enjoyed by walking east and taking the steep trail north to the valley.

From Drumcliff it's less than 5km to the lake's western shores. There's an infrequent **Bus Éireann** (☎ 071-60066) service from Sligo – call for details.

Streedagh & Grange

From the village of Grange, signs point towards Streedagh Beach, a grand crescent of sand that saw some 1100 sailors perish when three ships from the Spanish Armada were wrecked nearby. Views extend from the beach to the cliffs at Slieve League. Locals regularly swim here, even in winter.

Note that horse riding is currently not allowed on the beach. However, a variety of guided riding opportunities are available at **Island View Riding Stables** (☎ 071-916 6156; www .islandviewridingstables.com; Grange; adult/child per hr €25/18).

Mullaghmore

Sligo's only Blue Flag **beach**, Mullaghmore (An Mullach Mór), is a sweeping arc of dark-golden sand and safe shallow waters. (It wasn't so safe for Lord Mountbatten when the IRA rigged his boat with explosives and assassinated him here in 1979.)

Take time to cycle or drive the scenic road looping around Mullaghmore Head, where wide shafts of rock slice into the Atlantic surf. En route you'll pass **Classiebawn Castle** (closed to the public), a neo-Gothic turreted pile built for Lord Palmerston in 1856 and later home to the ill-fated Lord Mountbatten.

Mullaghmore's clear waters, rocky outcrops and coves are ideal for diving. **Offshore Watersports** (☎ 071-919 4769, 087 610 0111; www.off shore.ie; The Pier) runs dive trips and rents gear.

Would-be explorers might consider a boat trip to uninhabited Inishmurray Island (see boxed text, opposite).

Creevykeel Goort Cairn

Shaped like a lobster's claw, this prehistoric **court tomb** (admission free; ☼ dawn-dusk) encloses several burial chambers. The structure was originally constructed around 2500 BC, with several more chambers added later. Once in the unroofed oval court, smaller visitors can duck under the stone-shielded entrance to reach the site's core.

The tomb is north of Cliffony on the N15.

Sleeping & Eating

Benwiskin Centre (☎ 071-917 6721; www.benwiskin centre.com; Ballintrillick; dm/tw/f €17/50/68; (P)) This 26-bed hostel initially strikes you as somewhat institutional (it's also a community centre), but the staff are wonderful and the setting couldn't be more picturesque. Lime-green dorms are impeccably clean and have their own bathroom, and there's a well-equipped self-catering kitchen and leafy garden. Take the lane by Creevykeel and follow signs 4km east of Cliffony.

Pier Head Hotel (☎ 071-916 6171; www.pierhead hotel.ie; Mullaghmore; s €105-115, d €140-160; (P) 🛜 🖳 ; ☼ closed late Dec) Peering out over the harbour, the contemporary rooms at this hotel are austere but many have magnificent views and some open onto a panoramic rooftop terrace with an outdoor hot tub. There are also great views from the tiny gym, and from the adjoining Quay Bar (mains €11 to €23, food served 12.30pm to 9pm), which has music every Saturday night year-round and pretty much every night in summer; and the more upmarket Clashybann Restaurant (set menu €30, dinner nightly).

Getting There & Away

Bus Éireann (☎ 071-916 0066) buses run from Sligo to Drumcliff (€3.40, 15 minutes), Grange (€5.40, 20 minutes) and Cliffony (€6.40, 25 minutes). In Drumcliff the bus stop is near the church; in Grange it's outside Rooney's newsagency; and in Cliffony it's O'Donnell's Bar.

County Donegal

'Up here it's different', the saying goes, and it's true. County Donegal is the wild child of the Irish family.

In part, this is due to its rugged landscape, where tortuous country roads skirt stark mountains, craggy peninsulas, towering cliffs, thrashing seas, sweeping beaches, sheep-spattered pastures, icy streams and heather-strewn horizons.

In part, too, it's due to its isolation. Ireland's second-largest county (after Cork) feels like its own country. Until the Plantation of Ulster, Donegal was divided between the O'Donnell and O'Neill clans. It was severed from its traditional province when most of Ulster became Northern Ireland, with the extended finger of County Fermanagh cutting it off from the rest of the Republic. Although political turmoil has died down, Donegal remains stubbornly independent and largely ignored by those in Dublin's distant driving seat. Around one-third of the county lies in the Gaeltacht, where Irish is the lingua franca.

Above all, Donegal's character is forged by its impetuous weather. You don't need to set sail to brave the sea – it charges ashore with mists riding stiff winds over fields and into towns. Defying its northerly location, it often tops 25°C (77°F) due to the Atlantic Gulf Stream nudging its coastline. And while the barometer rarely drops below zero, Donegal's howling winds and sheeting rain can feel arctic. Storms arrive unannounced and just as abruptly break into brilliant sunshine that transforms brooding blues and greys into sparkling greenery.

Once you've surrendered expectations for a come-what-may attitude, you'll know you've been tamed by this uncompromising land.

HIGHLIGHTS

- **Getting High** Take in dizzying views from Europe's highest sea cliffs, Slieve League (p473)
- **Getting Higher** Scale scree-scarred Mt Errigal (p488), Donegal's loftiest peak
- **Hunting for Treasures** Collect semiprecious stones from the raised beaches at ends-of-the-earth Malin Head (p495)
- **Doin' the Time Warp** Tour flamboyant Glenveagh Castle (p489) within beautiful Glenveagh National Park
- **Unravelling History** Watch weavers in action in the heritage town of Ardara (p476)

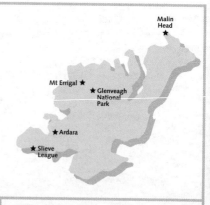

- POPULATION: 146,956
- AREA: 3001 SQ KM

Getting There & Away

Donegal Airport (☎ 074-954 8284; www.donegalairport.ie; Carrick Finn) has flights to/from Dublin (50 minutes, two daily) and flights to Glasgow Prestwick (three per week). It's in the townland of Carrick Finn (Charraig Fhion) about 3km northwest of Annagry along the northwestern coast. There's no public transport to the airport, but there are car-rental desks in the terminal.

The **City of Derry Airport** (☎ 028-7181 0784; www .cityofderryairport.com) is just beyond the county's eastern border, in Northern Ireland.

Getting Around

Donegal is not served by train. The bus is your main transport option if you don't have your own car.

In addition to **Bus Éireann** (www.buseireann .ie), private bus company **Lough Swilly** (☎ in Letterkenny 074-912 2863, in Derry 028-7126 2017; http:// home.clara.net/sjp/nibus/lswilly.htm) traverses the county. Coaches operated by **Feda O'Donnell** (☎ 074-954 8114; www.fedaodonnell.com) serve the western half of the county from Bundoran to Crolly.

This is superb walking and cycling country. Recommended walking guides include *New Irish Walks: West and North* by Tony Whilde and Patrick Simms, *Hill Walkers' Donegal* by David Herman, and Lonely Planet's *Hiking in Ireland*.

When driving, road signs in the Gaeltacht communities are in Irish only – although we use English transliterations, their Irish names

are included in brackets. Be prepared too for signs hidden behind vegetation, signs pointing the wrong way, signs with misleading mileage or no signs at all. Many minor roads are single-vehicle width: stay alert for oncoming vehicles around blind corners. Most of all, prepare yourself for reckless young drivers who put the lives of their fellow motorists at risk.

DONEGAL TOWN

pop 2339

Pretty Donegal town occupies a strategic spot at the mouth of Donegal Bay, on the River Eske in the shadow of the Blue Stack Mountains. It was once a stamping ground of the O'Donnells,

the great chieftains who ruled the northwest from the 15th to 17th centuries, who left behind an atmospheric old castle. Today, despite being the county's namesake, it's neither its largest (Letterkenny), nor the county town (the even smaller town of Lifford), but its compact town centre makes a lively base for exploring the wild coastline nearby.

INFORMATION

Bank of Ireland (The Diamond) One of several banks with ATM and bureau de change.

Blueberry Cybercafe (☎ 074-972 2933; Castle St; per hr €4; ☺ 9am-7pm Mon-Sat) Internet cafe above the Blueberry Tearoom. Check in at the counter downstairs.

Four Masters Bookshop (☎ 074-972 1526; The Diamond) Glass and china ornaments clearly take precedence

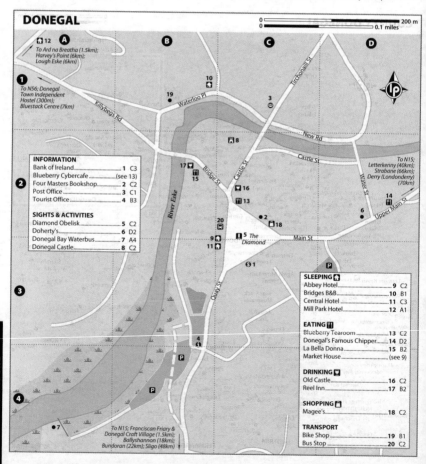

over the out-of-date travel guidebooks, but there's a good range of maps.

Post office (Tirchonaill St) North of the Diamond.

Tourist office (☎ 074-972 1148; donegal@failte ireland.ie; Quay St; 🕙 9am-6pm Mon-Sat, noon-4pm Sun Jul-Aug, 9.30am-5.30pm Mon-Sat Sep-Jun) In the new 'Discover Ireland' building.

SIGHTS
Donegal Castle
Guarding a picturesque bend of the River Eske, **Donegal Castle** (☎ 074-972 2405; Castle St; adult/child €4/2; 🕙 10am-6pm mid-Mar–Oct, 9.30am-4.30pm Thu-Mon Nov-Dec) remains an imperious monument to both Irish and English might. Built by the O'Donnells in 1474, it served as the seat of their formidable power until 1607, when the English decided to be rid of pesky Irish chieftains once and for all. Rory O'Donnell was no pushover, though, torching his own castle before fleeing to France in the infamous Flight of the Earls. Their defeat paved the way for the Plantation of Ulster by thousands of newly arrived Scots and English Protestants, creating the divisions that still afflict the island to this day.

The castle was rebuilt in 1623 by Sir Basil Brooke, along with the adjacent three-storey Jacobean house. Much of the castle is gutted today, but enough has been preserved that it's worth a look-see.

Diamond Obelisk
In 1474 Red Hugh O'Donnell and his wife, Nuala O'Brien, founded Donegal's **Franciscan friary** by the shore south of town. It was accidentally blown up in 1601 by Rory O'Donnell while laying siege to an English garrison, and little remains. Four of its friars, fearing that the arrival of the English meant the end of Celtic culture, chronicled the whole of known Celtic history and mythology from 40 years before the Flood to AD 1618 in *The Annals of the Four Masters* – still one of the most important sources of early Irish history. The obelisk (1937), in the Diamond, commemorates the work, copies of which are displayed in the National Library in Dublin.

ACTIVITIES
Boat Trips
The most enjoyable way to explore the highlights of Donegal Bay is to take one of the boat tours run by **Donegal Bay Waterbus** (☎ 074-972 3666; www.donegalbaywaterbus.com; Donegal Pier; adult/

child €15/7). Aboard a 20m tour boat, the 1¼-hour tour covers everything from historic sites to seal-inhabited coves, admiring an island manor and a ruined castle along the way. The tour runs up to three times daily from Easter to October, and may be possible at other times depending on the weather.

Fishing
Permits are required for fishing in the local rivers. Kits and information are available from **Doherty's** (☎ 074-972 1119; Main St; 🕙 9am-6pm Thu-Tue).

SLEEPING
B&Bs are plentiful around Donegal town, but for high-end luxury you'll need to head into the surrounding countryside.

Budget
Bluestack Centre (☎ 074-973 5564; www.donegal bluestacks.com; Drimarone; dm/f €17/50; 🅿) This remote country hostel/community centre with squeaky-clean rooms and a basketball court is a handy jumping-off point for hikers tackling the Blue Stack Mountains. It's often left unmanned, so call ahead. Follow the signposts 7km northwest of town.

Donegal Town Independent Hostel (☎ 074-972 2805; www.donegaltownhostel.com; Killybegs Rd, Doonan; dm €18, d with/without bathroom €46/42; 🅿 🖳 🛜) Run by an energetic couple, rooms at this IHH hostel 1.2km northwest of town off the Killybegs Rd (N56) have quirky murals – from technicolour landscapes to glow-in-the-dark night skies –and some have water views.

Midrange & Top End
Bridges B&B (☎ 074-972 1082; thebridgesguesthouse@ gmail.com; Waterloo Pl; s without bathroom €40, d with/without bathroom €70/60; 🛜) Overlooking the castle and the river, behind this B&B's crimson-painted door are five simple rooms kept spotless by friendly hosts Bernie and Steve McGrory. Bernie's potato bread is a hit with guests at breakfast.

Ard na Breatha (☎ 074-972 2288; www.ardnabreatha .com; Drumrooske Middle; s €55-74, d €90-110; 🕙 Feb-Oct; 🅿 🛜) In an elevated setting 1.5km north of town, this boutique guesthouse has high-class rooms and organic fare straight from the farm (mains €17 to €28, five-course dinner €48.50), including vegetables, herbs, eggs, and lamb (plus beef from Ard na Breatha's neighbours).

COUNTY DONEGAL

Dinner is available at least Friday to Sunday by reservation.

Mill Park Hotel (☎ 074-972 2880; www.millpark hotel.com; The Mullins; s €75-99, d €118-178, apt from €275; P ⌨ � 🖥) Mill Park's triple-height reception areas with timber and wrought-iron ceilings, gleaming slate floors and open fireplace are a decade old but have a timeless feel, as do the fresh citrus-toned guestrooms. The property also offers lunch (€7 to €14.50) and dinner (€13 to €24.50).

Abbey Hotel (☎ 074-972 1014; www.abbeyhotel donegal.com; The Diamond; s €80-90, d €130-150; P 🖥) Housing 118 rooms, this enormous stone building surprises with its contemporary interior. Rooms out the back overlook the river. The hotel offers access to a gym and has a stylish restaurant and bar.

Central Hotel (☎ 074-972 1027; www.centralhotel donegal.com; The Diamond; s €80-90, d €130-150; P 🖥) Next door to the Abbey, and run by the same owners, the aptly named Central has 112 rooms of its own behind a tomato-red facade, and also offers all mod cons and river views from rear rooms. There is regular live music in the bar. If you're in town for a while, ask about its new self-catering apartments.

EATING

our pick Aroma (☎ 074-972 3222; Donegal Craft Village; dishes €4.50-12; �9.30am-5.30pm Mon-Sat) Hidden in the far corner of Donegal's craft village, the name aptly describes the home baking and Donegal's best coffee wafting through its tiny interior. Blackboard specials utilise seasonal local produce such as white wine risotto with steamed asparagus.

Donegal's Famous Chipper (☎ 074-972 1428; Upper Main St; fish & chips €7-7.60; � 4.30-11.30pm) Its fame spreads as far as the town limit, but this is an excellent place to grab an order of fried cod to eat at the Formica counter or to take to a nearby pub.

Blueberry Tearoom (☎ 074-972 2933; Castle St; mains €7-10; � 9am-7pm Mon-Sat) Piping-hot pies and lunch specials dabbling in flavours from French to Cajun make this snug tearoom a local favourite.

La Bella Donna (☎ 074-972 5790; Bridge St; mains €9-25; �dinner Tue-Sat) Lively and well-dressed crowds congregate at this smart two-storey place for pizza, pasta and its house speciality: fillet steak in rich gorgonzola sauce.

Market House (☎ 074-972 1014; Abbey Hotel, The Diamond; mains €17-28; �lunch & dinner) Replete with tartan carpeting and stone walls, the Market House manages not to feel touristy or old-fashioned. The kitchen tackles surf and turf mainstays with a fresh, light and contemporary ethos.

DRINKING

Reel Inn (Bridge St) The best craic in town is invariably found at this old-school pub. Its owner plays the button-box accordion, and his pals join him in traditional music sessions most nights.

Old Castle (☎ 074-972 1062; Castle St) Built to match the neighbouring castle with attractive stonework, corbel windows and a low wooden ceiling, this grey-stone pub is a relaxing spot to swap banter with locals.

SHOPPING

Donegal Craft Village (☎ 074-972 2225; Ballyshannon Rd; �9am-6pm Tue-Sat, 11am-6pm Sun) You won't find any canned leprechauns or Guinness T-shirts here. Instead, this little huddle of craft studios showcases pottery, ironwork, hand-woven fabrics, jewellery and more. It's signposted 1.5km south of town.

Magee's (☎ 074-972 2660; www.mageedonegal.com; The Diamond) One room of this small department store is devoted to Donegal tweed, which has been produced here since 1866.

GETTING THERE & AWAY

Bus Éireann (☎ 074-913 1008; www.buseireann.ie) services connect Donegal with Sligo (€12.50, 1¼ hours, six daily), Galway (€18.90, 3½ hours, two to three daily) and Killybegs (€6.90, 35 minutes, three daily); Derry (€14.30, 1½ hours, seven Monday to Saturday, three Sunday) and Belfast (€19.50, 3½ hours, frequent); and Dublin (€17.60, four hours, six daily). The bus stop is on the western side of the Diamond.

Feda O'Donnell (☎ 074-954 8114; www.fedaodonnell .com) runs to Galway (single/return €20/30, 3½ hours, twice daily, three on Friday and Sunday) via Ballyshannon, Bundoran and Sligo. Call to confirm departure point. Fares within Donegal range from €7 to €20.

GETTING AROUND

The **Bike Shop** (☎ 074-972 2515; Waterloo Pl; per day €10) rents bikes and has information on cycling in the area. Opening hours vary.

Contact Michael Gallagher for a **taxi** (☎ 074-972 3500).

AROUND DONEGAL TOWN

LOUGH ESKE

Lough Eske translates as 'Lake of the Fish' and, although this hasn't been the case of late, it's due to be restocked with salmon and trout by the time you're reading this. For fishing permits and boat hire, contact the **Northern Regional Fisheries Board** (☎ 074-972 1119; www.nrfb .ie). It's terrific territory for cycling or walking over the majestic Blue Stack Mountains, but there's no public transport.

Sleeping & Eating

Ardeevin Guest House (☎ 074-972 1790; http://ardeevin .tripod.com; Lough Eske; s/d €50/75; **P**) Great views of the lake are just one of this B&B's selling points. In business for 40 years, it has evolved into a large rambling house with charming rooms and an old-fashioned garden. It's 4km north of Donegal town off the Letterkenny road (N15). Take the second left and follow the signs.

Harvey's Point Country Hotel (☎ 074-972 2208; www.harveyspoint.com; Harvey's Point; s €109-210, d €158-320; **Y** closed Sun-Wed Nov-Christmas & early Jan-Mar; **P** **Q** **≈**) At the water's edge, this elegant retreat is privately owned and run, and it's evident in the pride taken by staff – from the kindly concierge through to the chefs at the excellent French restaurant (four-course dinner €59). Rooms range from large to enormous: our pick are the 'standard' rooms opening to a verandah overlooking the lake.

Solis Lough Eske Castle (☎ 074-972 5100; www .solislougheskecastle.com; d €250-275; **Y** closed Sun-Wed Nov-Mar; **P** **Q** **≈** **R**) This slick operation rose from the ashes of the1861-built Lough Eske Castle, which was all but razed by fire. The shell of the ornate turret was salvaged, but most of the complex – minimalist rooms, a decadent spa and smart restaurant (three-course dinner €55) with champagne-coloured velour banquettes – is spanking new.

ROSSNOWLAGH

pop 50

The gentle rollers at the 5km-long Blue Flag **beach** at Rossnowlagh (Ross Neamblach), 17km southwest of Donegal town, are great for learning to surf or honing your skills. Tuition and gear rental is available from **Fin McCool Surf School** (☎ 071-985 9020; www.donegal surfing.com; gear rental per 3hr €25, 2hr lesson incl gear rental €35; **Y** 10am-7pm Easter-Oct, 10am-7pm Sat & Sun mid-Mar–Easter & Nov-Christmas). The school is headed up by Pro Tour surf judge Neil Britton, cousin of four-time Irish women's champion Easkey Britton (who's named after County Sligo's surfing hotspot). In the school's surf shop, flip through four decades of iconic posters drawn by Neil's uncle, Barry Britton, for the **Rossnowlagh Intercounty Surf Contest** (**Y** late Oct), Ireland's largest and most social surf event.

Deep in the adjacent forest is a **Franciscan friary** (☎ 071-985 1342; admission free; **Y** 10am-8pm Mon-Sat) with tranquil gardens; the way of the cross takes you through a hillside smothered with rhododendron to spectacular hilltop views.

The combined pub/restaurant/guesthouse **Smugglers Creek** (☎ 071-985 2367; smugcreek@eircom

---

WALK: BLUE STACK MOUNTAINS

If you're not satisfied with admiring the Blue Stack Mountains from a distance, you can take a rewarding, though difficult, trek along a circuitous 18km path through wild and rugged terrain. A complete circuit takes about seven hours, and entails summiting several peaks. The highest, at 674m, is Blue Stack, from which the views of southern Donegal are spectacular. Alternatively, you can walk the short (though steep) distance to Eas Doonan waterfall, which drops some 30m. This walk can be done in about one hour. Note that in wet weather the trail can be boggy.

The trail head is easy to find, though it sounds complicated. Off the N15 from Donegal town, look for the signs for Lough Eske. There are three turnoffs, all leading to Lough Eske Dr. Follow the road anticlockwise towards the northern end of the lake, where the road hairpins twice. Off the second hairpin, take the small road leading to Edergole, where you'll find a walker sign and space to park your car.

It would be wise to equip yourself with the Ordnance Survey Ireland 1:50,000 map No 11 covering this territory. The **Mountain Views website** (www.mountainviews.ie) is also a useful resource. Donegal's tourist office has stacks of information for walkers.

WILD & WOOLLY

For centuries, Donegal's weavers have been using techniques passed down through generations. The tradition springs from two key ingredients in abundant supply: natural dyes from wild-growing plants including pinky-red fuchsia, orange lichen, yellow gorse, dark-green moss and purple blackberries, and woolly sheep.

Places where you can see weaving in action:

- **Donegal Carpet Factory**, Maritime & Heritage Centre, Killybegs (p471)
- **Studio Donegal**, Kilcar (p473)
- **Glencolumbcille Woollen Mill**, Glencolumbcille (p475)
- **Triona Design**, Ardara (p476)
- **Eddie Doherty**, Ardara (p476)

.net; s/d €60/100; ☺ Easter-Oct; P) perches on the hillside above the bay. It's justifiably popular for its excellent food (mains €15 to €20) and sweeping views (room 4 has the best vantage point and a balcony into the bargain). There's live music on summer weekends.

Smugglers Creek's owners also operate the nearby B&B **Ardeelan Lodge** (☎ 071-985 2367; smugcreek@eircom.net; s/d €50/70; ☺ Easter-Oct) in a cosy salmon-coloured building by the Franciscan friary.

Once an extravagant 19th-century fishing lodge, the beachside **Sandhouse Hotel** (☎ 071-985 1777; www.sandhouse-hotel.ie; d €180-250; ☺ Easter-Dec; P) has a festive atmosphere in its restaurant and bars, and a soothing marine spa. There are good deals on multiday stays.

Rossnowlagh isn't served by public transport.

BALLYSHANNON
pop 2686

Crawling up a steep incline above the River Erne, Ireland's oldest market town, Ballyshannon (Béal Átha Seanaidh), received its royal charter in 1613. But human inhabitation goes back a lot further: archaeological excavations have unearthed Neolithic sites dating to around 4000 BC. The Bank of Ireland, with an ATM, and post office are both on Market St.

As a kid, the poet William Allingham (1824–89), who was born in Ballyshannon, scribbled his first attempts at verse on a window in the AIB bank on Castle St where his dad was the manager. Best remembered for his poem *The Fairies*, Allingham is buried in the graveyard beside **St Anne's Church**, the grave marked simply 'poet'. The church is signposted left off Main St after Dorrian's Imperial Hotel.

In late May, the **Rory Gallagher International Tribute Festival** (www.goingtomyhometown.com) celebrates another native son, rock and blues guitarist Rory Gallagher, with over two dozen Irish and international artists and bands. The exuberant **Ballyshannon Folk & Traditional Music Festival** (www.ballyshannonfolkfestival.com) arrives for the August bank holiday weekend.

Sleeping & Eating

Lakeside Caravan & Camping (☎ 071-985 2822; www .donegalbay.com/caravan.html; Belleek Rd; campsites €18-25, electricity €5, showers €2; ☺ mid-Mar–late Oct) It's worth a few extra euros for a pitch on the shores of beautiful Assaroe Lake at this four-star camping ground, which also has a cafe/restaurant and kayak rental. From Ballyshannon, take the N3 for 1km towards Belleek.

Breesy Centre (☎ 071-982 2925; www.breesycentre .com; Casheland; dm/s/d €20/24/48, breakfast €6; P 🛜) In a remote (read: relaxing) setting 6km northeast of Ballyshannon, this 30-bed hostel has shiny-new rooms, most with private bathroom, and a spiffy kitchen and dining room. Head north on the N15, turn east after 5km (there's a sign for Cashelard) and continue 1km; it's diagonally opposite the Travellers Rest pub.

Cavangarden House (☎ 071-985 1365; www.little ireland.ie/cavangardenhouse; Donegal Rd; s/d €47/70, cottages €100; P 🛜) Amid expansive lawns and trees alive with birdsong, several of the six floral guestrooms at this Georgian house are split-level. Evening meals (€20) are available by arrangement. Take the N15 3km north of town and look for the signs.

Creevy Experience (☎ 071-985 2896; www.creevy experience.com; Creevy, Ballyshannon; cottages per week €585-899; P) For a home away from home, these ecofriendly self-catering cottages are ideal. Each sleeps up to seven and comes with a 'welcome pack' of local produce and fairtrade coffee. Ask about weekend and midweek rates.

Shannon's Corner (☎ 071-985 1180; Main St; mains €10-15; ☺ 8.30am-4.30pm) Locals pile into this unassuming bistro for its home-cooked lunches and smashing sarnies.

Drinking

Thatch Pub (Bishop St; ⏳ approx Jun-Sep) Just off the top of Main St, this postcard-perfect pub is a great place to grab a pint and a few snapshots.

Year-round, traditional pubs that attract a lively local crowd include **Fin McCool's** and **Dicey Rileys**, both on Main St (the latter has an extensive off-licence), and the **Bridge End Bar** on the Port, which regularly hosts live music.

Getting There & Away

There are regular daily **Bus Éireann** (☎ 074-912 1309) services to Bundoran (€2.40, 10 minutes), Donegal (€5.80, 25 minutes), Sligo (€10.30, 50 minutes), Galway (€18.90, 3½ hours) and Dublin (€17.60, 4½ hours; via Enniskillen, Cavan and Navan). The bus station is between the bridge and the Gallogley Jewellers clock tower.

Feda O'Donnell (☎ 074-974 8114) buses depart from opposite the bus station for Donegal (€7, 15 minutes) and Letterkenny (€10, one hour) twice daily, four times on Friday. For Sligo (€9, 45 minutes) and Galway (€20, three hours) they leave from outside Maggie's Bar, south of the river near the roundabout, twice daily, and three times on Friday and Sunday.

BUNDORAN

pop 1964

If you're after ends-of-the-earth wilderness, you'll probably want to skip the blinking amusement arcades, hurdy-gurdy fairground rides and fast-food diners of Bundoran (Bun Dobhráin). But if you're looking for a cheery seaside atmosphere – as well as scenic walks and superb surf – Donegal's best-known seaside resort fits the bill. Outside summer, the carnival atmosphere abates and the town can be very quiet.

Information

Bundoran centres on one long main street just back from the beach. The western end is less commercial.

AIB (Allied Irish Bank; Main St) Has an ATM and bureau de change.

Post office (Main St)

Tourist office (☎ 071-984 1350; bundoran@ireland northwest.ie; The Bridge, Main St; ⏳ Jun-Sep, hr vary annually) Glass-paned kiosk opposite the Holyrood Hotel.

Activities

SURFING

Bundoran has two main surf spots: 'the Peak', an imposing reef break directly in front of the town, which should only be attempted by highly experienced surfers, and the less

---

ON BOARD

Irish surf champion Fergal Smith (www.fergalsmith.com), who won the title in 2007 and 2009, has surfed his way around five continents and numerous paradisaical tropical islands. He admits that 'Ireland's not good on the whole as a surf destination because of the weather', but says, 'when it's working, it's better than anywhere'.

Fergal grew up on his parents' organic farm in County Mayo, hitting the waves with his dad and brother at weekends and holidays at nearby **Achill Island** (p439). 'We surfed by ourselves, so I was blown away when I met professional surfers and realised I was at their level.' He was snapped up for the Irish team and is now a sponsored professional himself, dividing his time between comps and documenting epic rides with two Cornish filmmaker/photographers and fellow surfers, Tom Lowe and Mickey Smith. The climate means that 'Ireland has a different surfing vibe', Fergal says. 'There's no surf industry or surf media or "scene". The waves here are such quality; we don't want to make it a circus.' Instead, documenting it is 'a true reflection of what it takes to get those amazing waves and surf them to their full potential'.

In the northwest, Fergal's top surf spots include **Bundoran** (above): 'it's a built-up area, but when it's good it's world-class'; **Easkey** (p458), 'because it handles all kinds of weather and has loads of types of reefs'; and, 'for fun waves', the beach breaks of **Elly Bay** (p443) and **Louisburgh** (p433), as well as **Dunfanaghy** (p484).

Spring is Fergal's favourite time to surf the Irish coast, because 'the waves are still good, but it's not busy and it stays light until late'. Even in winter, 'the water temperature is usually fine, but it's hard paddling in howling wind and rain. In summer you can use a 3/2 wetsuit, but in winter you need a 6/4 with a built-in hood, good boots and gloves…and hot tea!'

formidable beach break at Tullan Strand, just north of the town centre.

Bundoran hosts the annual **Irish National Surfing Championships** (www.isasurf.ie), which are usually held in April. For Irish surf champ Fergal Smith's insider tips, see p469.

The town has three **surf schools**, each of which rents gear and has its own lodge accommodation:

Bundoran Surf Co (☎ 071-984 1968; www.bundoran surfco.com; surf lessons per 3hr €35, gear rental per day €20, dm/s/d €20/40/50) Offers deals on surf and accommodation packages.

Donegal Adventure Centre (☎ 071-984 2418; www .donegal-holidays.com; Bay View Ave; surf lessons per 3hr €25, gear rental per 2hr €10, dm €20-25) Youth-oriented place that also offers kayaking and gorge walking. The dorm beds are used mainly by groups, but it also owns Homefield Hostel (below), catering for independent travellers.

Turf n Surf (☎ 071-984 1091; www.turfnsurf.ie; Main St; surf lessons per 3hr €35, gear rental per day €20, dm/d €20/50) Also runs hill walking tours (from €15).

HORSE RIDING

The family-run **Donegal Equestrian Holidays** (☎ 071-984 1977; www.donegalequestrianholidays.com), 1km north of the town, offers rides over the dunes and along the beach (two-hour ride per adult/child €48/58) and lessons for all levels (from €30). Reserve ahead.

WATER ACTIVITIES

Bundoran's Blue Flag beach isn't safe for swimming, so the place to do it is **Waterworld** (☎ 071-984 1172; www.waterworldbundoran.com; adult/ child under 8 €10.50/8; ☼ from 10am Sat & Sun mid-Apr–May & Sep, daily Jun-Aug & school holidays), with wave pools and water slides. It's on the waterfront. Also on the premises, **Aquamara** (☎ 071-984 1173; baths from €22.50; ☼ from 11am Sat & Sun mid-Apr–May & Sep, daily Jun-Aug) provides a decidedly more sedate form of bathing in its seaweed baths. See p456 for more on Irish seaweed therapy.

Sleeping

The tourist office here or in Donegal town can help with accommodation across all price ranges. Nonsurfers are welcome at Bundoran's three surf school lodges (above).

Homefield Hostel (☎ 071-984 1288; homefield@ indigo.ie; Bayview Ave; dm €20-25, d €50; P 🖳 🛜) Once Viscount Enniskillen's holiday pad, this 260-year-old building later served as an altogether more restrained convent. It's now closer to its original purpose, housing a 60-bed rock-themed hostel, with vinyl records on the walls and a piano. Rooms are in good nick and there are lots of cosy lounges.

Fitzgerald's Hotel (☎ 071-984 1336; www.fitzgeralds hotel.com; s/d €75/100; ☼ closed Dec–mid-Feb; P 🛜) Awesome ocean views extend from some of the 16 spacious rooms at this stylish boutique hotel across the street from the strand. Lockup parking is a big bonus.

Eating

Gastronomy isn't Bundoran's strong suit, but there are a couple of stand-out places.

Fitzgerald's Bistro (Fitzgerald's Hotel; mains €17.50-24.50; ☼ dinner Wed-Sun, closed Dec–mid-Feb) Opening onto a garden out the back of Fitzgerald's Hotel, this plush bistro looks a little like a hunting lodge. Although seafood is the specialty, the kitchen is equally adept with meat and veg.

La Sabbia (☎ 071-984 2253; Bay View Ave; mains €17.50-25.50; ☼ dinner nightly Jun-Sep, Thu-Sun Oct-May) This colourful cottage decorated with striking contemporary art has tables spilling out onto the front porch and attracts a lively, upbeat crowd. It's run by a Milanese chef, whose hometown specials include delicious risottos as well as crispy pizzas, and pasta dishes like porcini-filled ravioli.

Drinking

Maddens Ould Bridge Bar (☎ 071-984 2050; www .maddensbridgebar.com; Main St) At the western end of town, this surfers' hangout has traditional music sessions on Thursdays (more in summer) and fantastic craic.

Brennan's Criterion Bar (☎ 071-984 1810; Main St) A quiet and neighbourly old pub in the heart of town, Brennan's is a refreshing departure from the brash and spangly places up the street.

Chasin' Bull (☎ 071-41988; www.myspace.com/the chasinbull; Main St) Up-and-coming Irish and international bands gig at this good-time pub.

Getting There & Away

Bus Éireann (☎ 074-912 1309) buses stop twice on Main St, outside the Phoenix Tavern, and the Celtic Bar. Direct daily services include Donegal (€6.90, 40 minutes), Sligo (€8.90, 45 minutes) and Galway (€18.90, 2¼ hours).

Northern Ireland's **Ulsterbus/Translink** (☎ 028-9066 6630; www.translink.co.uk) has up to three buses daily to Belfast (3½ hours) via Enniskillen (1¼ hours).

Feda O'Donnell (☎ 074-974 8114) buses from Crolly (€10, 2½ hours) travelling to Galway (€20, three hours) stop in Bundoran outside the Holyrood Hotel twice daily and three times on Friday and Sunday.

SOUTHWESTERN DONEGAL

MOUNTCHARLES TO BRUCKLESS

Donegal's scenery-o-meter starts to crank up when you reach the coast, just west of Donegal town, and steadily intensifies as you head north. Apart from a scattering of pubs and cafes, there are few places to eat (especially in winter), so stock up before leaving Donegal town or Killybegs.

Mountcharles
pop 497

This hillside village of Mountcharles (Moin Séarlas) is the first settlement along the coastal road (N56) southwest of Donegal town. About 2km south of the village is a safe, sandy beach. The shiny-green **pump** at the top of this hillside village was once the backdrop for stories of fairies, ghosts, historic battles and mythological encounters. It was at this point that native poet and *seanachaí* (storyteller) Séamus MacManus practised the ancient art in the 1940s and 1950s.

Behind century-old stone walls, the contemporary garden design of **Salthill Gardens** (☎ 074-973 5387; www.donegalgardens.com; admission €5; ⏱ 2-6pm Mon-Thu & Sun May-late Sep, Sat May-early Jul) bursts with perennials, vegetables and shrubs. It's 2km southwest of the village.

Dunkineely
pop 363

From dozy little Dunkineely (Dún Cionnfhaolaidh or Dún Cionnaola), a minor road runs down the improbably thin finger of land poking into the sea at St John's Point. There's a beach with a little bit of sand and sweeping coastal views, and the waters around the point are great for diving.

Overlooking the ruins of the 15th-century McSwyne's Castle, **Castle Murray** (☎ 074-973 7022; www.castlemurray.com; St John's Point; s/d €90/150; Ⓟ ⏰) is no castle itself, but a boutique hotel in a rambling old beach house. Each of its 10 individually decorated guestrooms is named

for the townlands contested by 15th-century Scottish clans. It's little wonder breakfast is superb, as it's best known for its French restaurant (four-course lunch/dinner €31/51). You might start with its signature prawns and monkfish in garlic butter, move on to mains like seared Donegal scallops with coconut curry, and finish off with a lime soufflé with gin sorbet. Drop in for lunch on Sunday or dinner any night of the week.

Bruckless
pop 180

Bruckless (An Bhroclais) scatters about 2km west of Dunkineely. You can saddle up at **Deane's Equestrian Centre** (☎ 074-973 7160; www.deanesequestrian.ie; Darney, Bruckless; ⏱ 10am-4pm), which offers five-minute pony rides for children (€5), lessons (from €19/16 per adult/child for 30 minutes) and treks (from €35/30 per adult/child for one hour). You'll need to book ahead.

The luxury, ivy-clad, Georgian B&B **Bruckless House** (☎ 074-973 7071; www.bruckless.com; d €130; ⏱ Apr-Sep; Ⓟ) sprawls over 18 acres of gardens sloping down to the shore. Fronted by a traditional cobbled farmyard, it's home to a stud farm for Connemara ponies. The interior is furnished with antique oriental influences. It's signposted off the main road approximately 3km after Dunkineely.

Getting There & Away

Bus Éireann (☎ 074-913 1008) bus 490 from Donegal to Killybegs (€7.60) stops near the Village Tavern in Mountcharles, the Inver post office in Bruckless and the Dunkineely Furniture Centre in Dunkineely.

KILLYBEGS
pop 1280

The salty scent of fish hauled from the ocean and the sound of cawing seagulls welcome you to Ireland's largest fishing port, Killybegs (Ceala Beaga). A charming working town, Killybegs' oddly angled streets collide at its diamond, a block from the pier. The community-run **tourist office** (☎ 074-973 2346; Quay St; ⏱ hr vary seasonally) is in a cabin near the harbour. The **Bank of Ireland** (Main St) has an ATM and bureau de change.

Sights & Activities

For a good overview of the town's history, visit the not-for-profit **Maritime & Heritage**

Centre (☎ 074-974 1944; www.visitkillybegs.com; Fintra Rd; adult/child €4/2; ☼ 10am-6pm Mon-Fri, plus 1-5pm Sat & Sun Easter-Sep). It's housed in the factory of Donegal Carpets, whose carpets adorn the White House and Buckingham Palace. You can sometimes see its hand-knotting loom (the world's longest of its kind) at work. The fun wheelhouse simulator lets you 'steer' a fishing trawler into the harbour. There's a good cafe/craft shop on site.

Heading up a steep hill in the town centre brings you to **St Mary's Church**, outside which stands the extraordinary **tombstone of Niall Mór MacSweeney** (spelt McSweeney in some documentation) head of the MacSweeney clan, one of Donegal's ruling families before 1607. It clearly depicts a chain-mailed warrior with a plumed helmet, his battleaxe raised and sword at the ready. This warlike figure is a gallowglass, a Scottish mercenary who first came to the north and west of Ireland in the late 13th century.

Several operators offer **fishing** expeditions with the opportunity to catch pollack, cod and whiting. **Killybegs Angling Charters** (☎ 074-973 1144; www.killybegsangling.com; Blackrock Pier) runs fishing charters (€450 for the boat) and rents fishing gear (from €15 per day). Alternatively you can buy rods, reels and tackle at the **Harbour Store** (☎ 074-973 2122; The Harbour), by the wharf.

Secluded **Fintragh Bay**, about 3km west and down a big-dipper of a road, is enchanting to explore and the water is clean and safe for swimming.

Tours

The free *Killybegs Heritage Trail* brochure plots 14 historic points of interest around town. Also free is a map outlining six looped **walks** in the area, ranging from 3.5km to 8km. Both are available from the Maritime & Heritage Centre, tourist office, and from accommodation in town.

Killybegs-based archaeologist **Derek Vial** (☎ 087 275 7183; www.tourdonegal.ie) runs small tours of up to five people around Donegal's southwest, with extensive and entertaining commentary about the area's tombs, forts, thatched cottages and natural history. Four-hour tours cost from €30 per person.

Sleeping

Ritz (☎ 074-973 1309; www.theritz-killybegs.com; Chapel Brae; dm/d/f €20/60/70; P ☑ ☎) The name might be ironic, but this superbly run 38-bed IHO hostel in the town centre has ritzy facilities including an enormous kitchen with an island workbench and dishwasher, colourful rooms with private bath and TVs, and a laundry. Continental breakfast is included.

Seawinds B&B (☎ 074-973 2003; www.seawindsireland .com; The Diamond; s/d €50/70; P ☑) Multitalented host Patricia Faherty paints the watercolours that adorn this cheery B&B's rooms and can organise painting lessons for guests. Patricia is also a trained cook and whips up wholesome evening meals (€12 to €15) by request.

Tara Hotel (☎ 074-974 1700; www.tarahotel.ie; Main St; s €80, d €130-140; ☑) Just a few skips from the harbour, the Tara gives Killybegs an unexpected tinge of minimalist chic. Ask for one of six sea-view rooms with balcony (costing €10 extra in summer).

Eating

Shines Takeaway (☎ 074-973 1996; Killybegs; fish & chips €7.50; ☼ 11am-2pm, 4-11.30pm Mon-Thu, 11am-2am Fri, 4pm-2am Sat, 4pm-midnight Sun) If you're craving something with gills and fins by now, salt down a serve of cod and chips from this spick-and-span chipper and head to the beach.

Kitty Kelly's (☎ 074-973 1925; Kilcar Rd; mains €16-20; ☼ dinner May-Sep) Dining at this restaurant in a 200-year-old, plum-coloured farmhouse feels more like attending an intimate dinner party. The menu is a gourmet take on traditional Irish favourites like rich stew and creamy trifle. It's on the coast road, 5km west of Killybegs. Opening hours vary annually; bookings are essential.

22 Main Street (☎ 074-973 2876; Main St; mains €16.50-24.50; ☼ dinner) Owned by the same local celeb as Kitty Kelly's, TV presenter Noel Cunningham, this Mediterranean-style bistro offers the same quality but a less formal ambience and more reliable opening hours. Piping hot seafood pies and prime Irish beef are among its specialities, along with innovative chocolate or espresso 'martinis' for dessert.

Getting There & Away

Bus Éireann (☎ 074-913 1008) service 492 to Donegal (€7.60, 30 minutes) from Killybegs runs four times daily Monday to Saturday. Bus 490 heads west to Kilcar (€3.90, 20 minutes) and Glencolumbcille (€7.60, 45 minutes) once daily Monday, Wednesday and Friday, and twice on Tuesday, Thursday and Saturday.

KILCAR, CARRICK & AROUND

pop 260

Kilcar (Cill Chártha) and its more attractive neighbour Carrick (An Charraig) make good bases for exploring the breathtaking coastline of southwestern Donegal, especially the stunning sea cliffs at Slieve League.

This is fantastic walking country, particularly if you don't mind hoofing up and down a few hills. Kilcar Tourism has some pointers for walking the Kilcar Way; ask at the **Aísleann Cill Cartha** (☎ 074-973 8376; Main St, Kilcar; 9am-10pm Mon-Fri, 2-6pm Sat), a community centre that provides information for tourists. Just outside Kilcar is a small, sandy beach.

Local information is available at the excellent cultural centre, the **Tí Linn Centre** (☎ 074-973 9077; www.sliabhleague.com; Teelin, Carrick; 10.30am-5.30pm daily Easter-Sep, Fri-Tue Feb-Easter & Oct-Nov), in Teelin (Tí Linn), which also has an artisan cafe, and art and craft gallery.

Sights & Activities

SLIEVE LEAGUE

The Cliffs of Moher get more publicity, but the **sea cliffs** at Slieve League are higher. In fact, these spectacular polychrome cliffs are thought to be the highest in Europe, plunging some 600m to the sea. Looking down, you'll see two rocks nicknamed the school desk and chair by locals for reasons that are immediately obvious. From the lower car park, there's a path skirting up around the near-vertical rock face to the aptly named **One Man's Pass**. You can now also drive all the way to the top, where there's a new car park. Be aware that mist and rain can roll in unexpectedly and rapidly, making conditions treacherous.

Take the turn-off signposted Bunglass from the R263 at Carrick, 5km northwest of Kilcar, and continue beyond the narrow track that's signposted Slieve League to the one that's signposted Bunglass.

The cliffs are, if possible, even more impressive when viewed from the ocean below. Sightseeing boat trips along the Slieve League cliffs can be arranged by contacting **Nuala Star Teelin** (☎ 074-973 9365; www.nualastarteelin.com; Mar-Oct, weather permitting). Prices are €20 to €50 per person, depending on numbers, with reductions for children. The 12-seater boat departs from the Teelin pier approximately every two hours. Sea angling and diving trips can also be arranged.

STUDIO DONEGAL

Beside Kilcar's community centre tweeds are spun and loomed by hand at **Studio Donegal** (☎ 074-973 8194; www.studiodonegal.ie; Glebe Mill, Kilcar; admission free; 9am-5.30pm Mon-Fri year-round plus 9.30am-5pm Sat Easter-Oct). Visitors are often invited upstairs to see spinners and weavers in action.

WALKING

Three walks starting in Kilcar are collectively known as the **Kilcar Way**. From Teelin, experienced walkers can spend a day walking north via Bunglass and the clifftop to Malinbeg, near Glencolumbcille. It shouldn't be attempted in windy conditions or if bad weather is likely to impede visibility.

The Tí Linn Centre (left) organises guided hill walks and archaeological walks. Prices start from €100; it works out cheaper if there are a few of you travelling together.

Sleeping & Eating

Derrylahan Hostel (☎ 074-973 8079; derrylahan@eircom.net; Derrylahan, Kilcar; camping €8 per person, dm/d €16/40; P) On a working farm, this rustic, well-run IHH hostel has comfortable rooms with private bath as well as a 20-person bunk house and plenty of scenic spots to pitch a tent. Bike rental (€20) can be organised if you book ahead. Located 3km west of the village on the coast road. Pick-ups can be arranged.

Dún Ulún House (☎ 074-973 8137; dunulunhouse@eircom.net; Coast Rd; campsites €10, dm €15-20, d €45-50; P) The sweeping view down to a ruined ring fort is what strikes you first about this family-run hostel/B&B. Accommodation is simple but homey, and the family can arrange Irish lessons and help with genealogy. Breakfast (€8) is optional. A little camping ground is ensconced in the tiered hillside. It's 1km west of the village.

Ocean Spray (☎ 074-973 8438; www.littleireland.ie/oceanspray; Muckross, Kilcar; s/d €40/70; P) Following a series of signs through rolling stone-walled green fields brings you to this cosy home with three sparkling rooms. It's a five-minute walk to glorious surf beaches. Heading west, take the first left after the Blue Haven hotel for 3.5km, then left again for 500m.

Blue Haven (☎ 074-973 8090; www.bluehaven.ie; Kilcar-Killybegs Rd; mains €14.50-26; dinner Mon-Fri, noon-9.30pm Sat & Sun late Apr-Oct, noon-9.30pm Sat & Sun Nov-late Apr) Blue Haven's modern restaurant nevertheless focuses on time-honoured 'home

COUNTY DONEGAL

cooking'. The place can be quite festive, and its sunset views are stunning. Views also extend from its 15 guestrooms (single/double €55/100), all of which have access to a communal balcony.

Healthy soups, scones and other homemade fare is available at the **Tí Linn Centre cafe** (p473).

Getting There & Away

Bus Éireann (☎ 074-912 1309) service 490 connects Kilcar (€2.60) and Carrick (€5.40) with Killybegs and Glencolumbcille (€7.60) once daily Monday to Friday and Sunday (twice daily Saturday). In July and August an extra bus runs Monday to Saturday.

GLENCOLUMBCILLE & AROUND
pop 255

'There's nothing feckin' here!', endearingly blunt locals forewarn visitors to Glencolumbcille (Gleann Cholm Cille). But, with some stunning walks fanning out from the three-pub village, scalloped beaches, an excellent Irish language and culture centre, and a fine little folk museum, chances are you'll disagree.

Approaching Glencolumbcille via the Glen Gesh Pass does, however, reinforce just how cut off this starkly beautiful coastal haven is from the rest of the world. You drive past miles and miles of hills and bogs before the ocean appears, followed by a narrow, green valley and the small Gaeltacht village within it.

This spot has been inhabited since 3000 BC and you'll find plenty of Stone Age remains throughout the collection of tiny settlements. It's believed that the 6th-century St Colmcille (Columba) founded a monastery here (hence the name, meaning 'Glen of Columba's Church'), and incorporated Stone Age standing stones called *turas* (after the Irish word for a pilgrimage, or journey) into Christian usage by inscribing them with a cross. At midnight on Colmcille's Feast Day (9 June) penitents begin a walkabout of the *turas* and the remains of Colmcille's church before attending Mass at 3am in the local church.

Sights & Activities
FATHER MCDYER'S FOLK VILLAGE
A museum with a mission, this **folk centre** (☎ 074-973 0017; www.glenfolkvillage.com; Doonalt; adult/child €3/2; ⏰ 10am-6pm Mon-Sat, noon-6pm Sun Easter-

Sep) was established by the forward-thinking Father James McDyer in 1967 to freeze-frame traditional folk life for posterity. It's housed in a huddle of replicated thatched cottages of the 18th and 19th centuries, with genuine period fittings. The *shebeen* (illicit drinking place) sells unusual local wines (made from ingredients such as seaweed and fuchsias) alongside marmalade and whiskey truffles. Admission includes a tour. It's 3km west of the village, by the beach.

BEACHES
There are two sandy beaches with brisk waves in **Doonalt**, immediately west of the village. At **Malinbeg**, a sheltered bay bitten out of low cliffs and filled with firm red-tinged sand, descending 60 steps brings you to another gorgeous little beach just down the coast road.

WALKING
A couple of signed loop walks will get you off into the blustery wilds beyond the town. The **Tower Loop** (10km, two to three hours) takes you up over some stunning coastal cliffs, while the more arduous **Drum Loop** (13km, three to four hours) heads into the hills, northeast of the town. Both walks start and finish at Colmcille's church.

Glencolumbcille's new **walking centre** (☎ 074-973 0302; www.ionadsuil.ie; ⏰ by arrangement), next door to the fire station, offers information and can arrange guided walks.

Courses
Oideas Gael (☎ 074-973 0248; www.oideas-gael.com; ⏰ mid-Mar–Oct), at the Foras Cultúir Uladh (Ulster Cultural Foundation) 1km west of the village centre, offers a range of 'cultural activity holidays' – adult courses in Irish language and traditional culture, including dancing, painting and musical instruments. The centre also leads hill-walking programs in the Donegal highlands. Three-day courses cost from €100. Accommodation can be arranged – you'll have a choice of homestay or self-catering, with prices of around €20 to €40 per person per night.

Sleeping & Eating
The area has some excellent budget accommodation but places to eat are limited.

our pick Dooey Hostel (☎ 074-973 0130; www.dooeyhostel.com; campsites/dm/d €7.50/15/30; **P**) This IHO hostel has character in spades. For one thing, it's owned by an elderly, wild-haired chain-smoker who calls herself 'Mad' Mary O'Donnell. For another, it's literally built *into* the hillside, with a corridor carved out of the plant-strewn rockface, and jaw-dropping views of the ocean and hills below. Facilities are rustic, but clean and comfortable. If you're driving, turn beside the Glenhead Tavern for 1.5km; walkers can take a short cut beside the Folk Village. No credit cards.

Malinbeg Hostel (☎ 074-973 0006; www.malinbeg hostel.com; Malinbeg, Glencolumbcille; dm/s/d €15/25/40; ☺ closed Dec–mid-Jan; ℗) Flung out on a remote stretch of coast, the contemporary Malinbeg hostel sports spotless rooms (some with private bathroom) and scores big for its proximity to the beach and to the grocery store handily situated across the road.

Glencolumbcille Walking Centre (opposite; s/d €35/50; ℗) Overlooking sheep-filled paddocks, this smart new place has 11 immaculate rooms with private bath. Breakfast isn't included but there's an enormous self-catering kitchen. The owners live off site, so call ahead.

An Cistin (Kitchen; ☎ 074-973 0213; Glencolumbcille; mains €10-22; ☺ 9am-9pm Easter-Oct) Attached to Oideas Gael, this cafe/restaurant serves up surprisingly gourmet fare to a soundtrack of mellow jazz.

Shopping

Glencolumbcille Woollen Mill (☎ 074-973 0070; www .rossanknitwear-glenwoolmill.com; Malinmore; ☺ 10am-8pm Mar-Oct, to 5.50pm Nov-Feb) A great place to stock up on Donegal tweed jackets, caps and ties and lambswool scarves and shawls. You can sometimes see weavers in action. It's about 5km southwest of Glencolumbcille, in Malinmore.

John Molloy's (☎ 074-973 0282; www.johnmolloy .com; Glencolumbcille) This Ardara manufacturer's Glencolumbcille factory outlet sells a wide range of woollies made from natural yarns.

Getting There & Away

Bus Éireann (☎ 074-912 1309) service 490 leaves for Killybegs daily (€7.60, 45 minutes) with an extra service on Saturday and in July and August.

MAGHERY & THE GLEN GESH PASS
pop 640

On the northern edge of the peninsula, tiny Maghery has a picturesque waterfront. If you follow the strand westward, you'll get to a rocky promontory full of caves. During Cromwell's 17th-century destruction, 100 villagers sought refuge here but all except one were discovered and massacred.

About 1.5km east of Maghery is the enchanting **Assarancagh Waterfall**, beyond which is the beginning of a 10km marked trail to the **Glen Gesh Pass** (Glean Géis, meaning 'Glen of the Swans'). It's almost alpine in appearance; cascading mountains and lush valleys are dotted with isolated farmhouses and small lakes. If you're driving or cycling, you can get to the pass directly from Glencolumbcille by following the road signs for Ardara.

ARDARA
pop 564

The heart of Donegal's traditional knitwear and hand-woven tweed, Ardara (Árd an Rátha) is a pretty gateway to the switchbacks of Glen Gesh Pass just southwest of the town. Tourist information is available from the **Triona Design visitor centre** (☎ 074-914 1422; www .trionadesign.com; Main St; ☺ 9am-7pm). On the Diamond the Ulster Bank has an ATM; the post office is nearby on Main St.

Festivals & Events

Dancing, storytelling and a school of music are part of the trad-music **Cup of Tae Festival** (www.cupoftaefestival.com), held at the end of April or early May.

Sleeping & Eating

Drumbarron Hostel (☎ 074-954 1200; jfeeneyardara@ eircom.net; The Diamond; dm/d €18/38) In an elevated spot in the town centre, this Georgian-style two-storey house has clean, airy dorms and a large stone-floored kitchen. Knock at the B&B opposite if there's nobody in the hostel. No credit cards.

Drumbarron House (☎ 074-954 1200; jfeeneyardara@ eircom.net; The Diamond; s/d €40/70; ℗ ☺) The artist-owner of the Drumbarron Hostel across the road is the third generation to operate this cosy B&B. All five rooms are spacious and have bright bathrooms. No credit cards.

ᴏᴜʀ ᴘɪᴄᴋ Green Gate (☎ 074-954 1546; www.thegreen gate.eu; Ardvally, Ardara; s/d €70/90; ℗) Finding this idyllic hilltop B&B is something of a treasure hunt (and, at times, obstacle course). Follow a series of tiny pictorial signs of a gate beyond the turn-off to Woodhill House up a series of *steep* dirt tracks. More signs instruct you to enter the gate, and then the main house, where you'll find its gregarious owner, writer and bon vivant, Paul Chatenoud. Accommodation is in small, simple but charming thatched cottages with private bath and, for the ultimate in relaxation, no internet or TV. But you won't miss them anyway – the view over the bay is one of the most magical in Ireland. Phone bookings essential; no credit cards.

Nancy's Bar (☎ 074-954 1187; Front St; mains €6.50-12.50) This pub-restaurant successfully makes its guests feel as though they're sitting in Nancy's living room. It serves superb seafood and chowder, and is also the best place in town for a social pint or two.

Entertainment

Corner House (☎ 074-954 1736; The Diamond) is a good spot to listen to an Irish music session (Friday and Saturday year-round; nightly from June to September). Occasionally, someone will spontaneously break out in song and, if the mood is right, the rest of the pub will join in.

Shopping

Signs in the town centre point you to the town's knitwear producers.

Eddie Doherty (☎ 074-954 1304; www.handwoven tweed.com; Front St) Behind Doherty's bar, you can usually catch Eddie Doherty hand-weaving here on a traditional loom.

John Molloy's (☎ 074-954 1133; www.johnmolloy .com; Ardara) Handmade and machine-knitted woollies are available here at its flagship establishment and at its factory outlet in Glencolumbcille.

Kennedy's (☎ 074-954 1106; Front St) In business for over a century, Kennedy's helped establish Ardara's reputation as a sweater mecca.

Triona Design (☎ 074-914 1422; www.trionadesign .com; Main St) Weavers keep traditional skills alive while demonstrating their techniques for visitors.

Getting There & Around

Bus Éireann (☎ 074-912 1309) service 492 from Killybegs (€3.40, 25 minutes, three daily) stops outside O'Donnell's in Ardara.

Don Byrne's of Ardara (☎ 074-954 1658; Main St; ◷ 9.30am-6pm Jun-Sep, 5.30-8.30pm Mon-Fri, 9.30am-6pm Sat Oct-May), at the eastern edge of the town centre, rents bikes for €15/70 per day/week.

DAWROS HEAD

The outer reaches of beautiful Loughrea Peninsula, north of Ardara, glisten with tiny lakes cupped by undulating hills and the wishbone-shaped Blue Flag beach by the twin set-

tlements of **Narin** and **Portnoo**. The beach's sandy tip points towards **Iniskeel Island**, which you can walk out to at low tide. St Connell, a cousin of St Colmcille, founded a monastery here in the 6th century. Hardly any trace remains, but the island is studded with early-medieval Christian remains.

Another adventurous diversion is to track down **Lough Doon**, 3km south of Narin, in the centre of which sits the 2000-year-old **Doon Fort**, a fortified oval settlement. To reach the fort, you need to hire a rowing boat (around €10) from an adjacent farm. Pick a day that's not too windy.

If the fort whets your appetite for archaeology, the **Dolmen Ecocentre** (☎ 074-954 45010; www.dolmencentre.com; Kilclooney, Portnoo; ◷ 9am-5pm Mon-Fri) can point you towards several other prehistoric sites, including a tortoiselike passage tomb a short walk up a track left of the church.

Also on the peninsula, hemmed in by grassy dunes, is **Tramore Beach**. In 1588 part of the Spanish Armada ran aground here. The survivors temporarily occupied O'Boyle's Island in Kiltoorish Lake, but then marched to Killybegs, where they set sail again in the *Girona*. The *Girona* met a similar fate that year in Northern Ireland, with the loss of over a thousand crew (see p654).

Sleeping

Tramore Beach Caravan & Camping Park (☎ 074-955 1491; campbella@eircom.net; Rosbeg; campsites €14-20; ◷ Easter-Sep) This remote place has 24 sandy campsites sheltered amid dunes, just a short hop from the beach. Take the road from Ardara to Narin then turn left, following the signposts to Tramore Beach.

Lackagh Mor Cottages (☎ 074-954 5935; mgyo@ eircom.net; Lackagh; s/d €35/60; P) A short walk from the ocean, these self-catering stone cottages make a great romantic getaway or family holiday spot. They're signposted 1km southwest of Portnoo.

GLENTIES
pop 811

At the foot of two valleys with a southern backdrop laid on by the Blue Stack Mountains, the proud 'Tidy Town' of Glenties (Na Gleannta) is a good spot for **fishing** and has some cracking **walks** in the surrounding countryside.

A **summer school** (www.patrickmacgill.com) is held in August in honour of plucky Patrick MacGill

(1891–1963), the 'navvy poet' who was sold by his parents at a hiring fair, later escaped and eventually ended up writing for the English *Daily Express*. Glenties is also linked with playwright Brian Friel, whose play (and subsequent film), *Dancing at Lughnasa*, is set in the town.

On the main street there's a Bank of Ireland, with an ATM and bureau de change, and a post office.

St Connell's Museum & Heritage Centre (☎ 074-955 1227; Main St; adult/child €2.50/free; 10am-1pm & 2-4.30pm May-Sep), beside the old courthouse at the western end of town, has a ragbag of local artefacts. Call for (very limited) opening hours during the rest of the year.

Sleeping & Eating
Campbell's Holiday Hostel (☎ 074-955 1491; www.campbellireland.com; dm/d €15/40; Easter-Oct; P) Colour-coding keeps you from getting lost in this mazelike 56-bed hostel. Modern facilities include two kitchens and common areas with open fires, as well as a handy laundry. Look for the signs behind the museum.

Brennan's B&B (☎ 074-955 1235; Main St; s/d/apt €45/70/100; P) The welcome is genuinely warm at this family-run B&B. Its three comfy guestrooms are lovingly tended to, and it's handily situated at the southern end of the main drag among a crop of inviting pubs and shops.

Highlands Hotel (☎ 074-955 1111; www.highlandshotel.com; Main St; mains €13-25) This country hotel at the western end of town is OK for pub grub, but the staff's dismissive attitude is unlikely to inspire you to stay upstairs in its 20 rooms (single/double €60/110).

Entertainment
The thatched **Paddy's Bar** (☎ 074-955 1158; Main St) has been completely remodelled without detracting from its character, and attracts all ages, particularly for its regular traditional music sessions.

Getting There & Away
Bus Éireann (☎ 074-912 1309) service 492 from Donegal stops off in Glenties on the way to Dungloe (€8.20, 45 minutes) one to two times daily Monday to Friday.

FINN VALLEY & AROUND
Off the beaten track, even by Donegal standards, though an easy day trip from Letterkenny, the Finn Valley makes a serene escape for salmon fishing and hill walking or cycling, but you need to be equipped with maps and provisions.

The main town is **Ballybofey** (Bealach Féich), linked to adjoining **Stranorlar** by an arched bridge over the Finn. In its Protestant church is the **grave** of Isaac Butt (1813–79), founder of the Irish Home Rule movement. There's a locally run **tourist office** (☎ 074-913 2377; Main St; 9am-5pm Mon-Fri) in the state-of-the-art **Ballybofey Balor Theatre**, which can help with accommodation if you want to stay in the area.

The county's only operational railway, the **Fintown Railway** (☎ 074-954 6280; www.antraen.com; Fintown; adult/child €8/5), is a charming little tourist train that runs over Easter and during the summer months, plus special trips for Halloween and Christmas. Lovingly restored to its original condition, the red-and-white 1940s diesel railcar runs along a rebuilt 5km section of the former County Donegal Railway track alongside Lough Finn. The return trip, which includes commentary, takes around 40 minutes. Hours of departure vary annually.

Getting There & Away
Bus Éireann (☎ 074-912 1309) express service 64 between Galway (€18.90, 4¾ hours) and Derry (€10, 35 minutes) via Sligo (€13.10, two hours), Donegal (€6.90, 30 minutes) and Letterkenny (€5.40, 25 minutes) stops up to six times daily in Ballybofey. Buses also connect Ballybofey with Killybegs (€10, one hour).

McGeehan Coaches (☎ 074-954 6150; www.mgbus.com) runs services between Glencolumbcille (€9.50, 1¾ hours) and Letterkenny (€6, 35 minutes), with a stop in front of the Fintown post office twice daily Monday to Saturday.

NORTHWESTERN DONEGAL

Few places in Ireland are more savagely beautiful than northwestern Donegal.

Humans have largely been unable to tame the wild and breathtakingly spectacular landscape. The rocky Gaeltacht area between Dungloe and Crolly is known as the Rosses (Na Rossa), and is scattered with shimmering lakes and clean, sandy beaches. Further northwest, between Bunbeg and Dunfanaghy, the scenery is softer but no less stunning.

COUNTY DONEGAL

Offshore, the islands of Arranmore and Tory are fascinating to those eager for a glimpse of a more traditional way of life.

DUNGLOE & AROUND
pop 1068

A number-one pop song from the late 1960s, 'Mary from Dungloe', by Emmet Spiceland, helped put this little pit stop on the map. Each year the town hosts the 10-day **Mary from Dungloe Festival** (☎ 074-952 1254; www.maryfromdungloe.com) in late July/early August, during which a 'new Mary' is crowned, keeping the flame alive after all these years.

Apart from that, though, don't expect too much from Dungloe (An Clochán Liath). Its standout feature is that it's the hub of the Rosses, with ample services for anyone passing through this spectacular locale. The nearby village of **Kincasslagh** is far more picturesque.

The **tourist office** (☎ 074-952 1297; ⌚ Jun-Sep, hr vary annually) is off Main St behind the Bridge Inn. The **Bank of Ireland** (Main St) has an ATM and bureau de change. The **post office** (Quay Rd) is off Main St.

Fishing for salmon and trout in the River Dungloe and Lough Dungloe is popular and you can get tackle and permits from **Bonner's** (☎ 074-952 1163; Main St).

The nearest good beach is 6km southwest of town at **Maghery Bay**. Kevin Tobin, a former national surf champ, runs the local **Dooey Surf School** (Scoil na dTonn; ☎ 074-952 2468; www.dooeysurfschool.com; 2.5hr lesson €30; ⌚ Easter-Oct).

The **country inn** of **Iggy's B&B** (☎ 074-954 3112; Main St, Kincasslagh; d from €50; ⌚ Jun-Sep; **P**) is a real treasure. Rooms are kept up with grandmotherly care and the downstairs pub is a right social spot that also serves seafood dishes. Nothing fancy, just heart-warming.

Rosemary Boyd has won numerous awards for her crafts and her biscuit making, and you'll experience both at homey **Limekiln House** (☎ 074-954 8521; www.limekilnhouse.com; Carrickfin, Kincasslagh; d with/without bathroom €70/60; **P**), which is adorned with her oils, tapestries and embroidery. Two of the four rooms have a private bathroom.

Getting There & Away

McGeehan Coaches (☎ 074-954 6150) runs a service from Dungloe to Dublin (€21.50, 4½ hours, two daily) via Glenties (30 minutes) and Donegal (€8.70, one hour). No transit serves Kincasslagh.

BURTONPORT
pop 345

This pocket-sized port is the embarkation point for Arranmore Island, which looks near enough to wade to. Burtonport (Ailt an Chorráin) has attracted some famously off-the-wall characters over the years. In the 1970s, the Atlantis commune was established here, and practised a primal therapy that earned it the nickname 'the Screamers'. Eventually it relocated to the Colombian jungle. Later, the three Silver Sisters chose Burtonport to live out their Victorian lifestyle, complete with Victorian dress. The village seems perfectly ordinary today, though it is pretty.

For **fishing** and **diving** trips contact **Inishfree Charters** (☎ 074-954 2245; www.burtonport.com). Alternatively, you can check in at the cabins by the pier.

our pick **Lobster Pot** (☎ 074-954 2012; Main St; bar food €10-23.50, dinner mains €17-25; ⌚ bar food noon-6pm, dinner nightly) sports a giant fibreglass lobster clinging precariously to its outer wall as an unsubtle clue to its menu of freshly netted seafood. In the timber-panelled interior, past the life-size pirate statue, jerseys adorning the wall clue you in to its obsession for football. Serious seafood fans can go for the seafood platter (€52.50) that's 'best for two, but one can try if they dare', which is loaded with lobster, crab, mussels, salmon, prawns and more. If you like some turf with your surf, try the 'sink or swim' platter (€58).

Lough Swilly (☎ 074-912 2863) buses from Dungloe (€1.90, 15 minutes, one daily) stop in Burtonport en route to Letterkenny and Derry.

ARRANMORE ISLAND
pop 528

Framed by dramatic cliff faces, cavernous sea caves and clear sandy beaches, Arranmore (Árainn Mhór) lies just 1.5km from the mainland. Measuring just 9km by 5km, the tiny island has been inhabited since the early Iron Age (800 BC), and a prehistoric triangular fort can be seen on the southern side. The west and north are wild and rugged, with few houses to disturb the sense of isolation. The **Arranmore Way** walking path circles the island (allow three to four hours). Off the southwestern tip is **Green Island**, a bird sanctuary for corncrakes, snipes and a variety of seabirds; you can see it from Arranmore (but not visit). Irish is the main language spoken on Arranmore Island, although most inhabitants are bilingual.

The island's pubs put on turf fires and traditional music sessions, and some stay open 24 hours a day to sate thirsty fishermen.

Sleeping & Eating

Arranmore makes an easy day trip but several homes offer B&B accommodation. The island also has the 32-bed **Arranmore Hostel** (☎ 074-952 0015; www.arainnmhor.com; Leabgarrow; dm/d €17/39), a short walk left of the ferry terminal next to a beach in a former post office. Its owners live off site so call ahead.

Getting There & Around

The **Arranmore Ferry** (☎ 074-952 0532; www .arainnmhor.com/ferry) links Burtonport with Leabgarrow (passenger/car and driver €15/30 return, 20 minutes, eight Monday to Saturday, seven Sunday July and August and five Monday to Saturday, three Sunday September to June).

The same route is covered by **Arranmore Fast Ferry** (☎ 087 317 1810) with their fast, passenger-only ferry (€15 return, five minutes, two to three daily) and a car-ferry service (passenger/car and driver €15/30 return; 20 minutes).

Once on the island, you can save your legs by taking a tour with **O'Donnell Taxis** (☎ 087 260 6833). **Bikes** (☎ 087 682 5973) can be rented at the port by calling ahead.

GWEEDORE & AROUND

pop 1390

The Gaeltacht district of Gweedore (Gaoth Dobhair) is a loose assembly of small towns in the shadow of Mt Errigal. It's a good jumping-off point for trips to Tory Island and Glenveagh National Park, but the coast, dotted with white, sandy beaches, has been overrun by holiday homes. Consequently, Derrybeg (Doirí Beaga) and Bunbeg (Bun Beag) virtually run into each other along the R257. A few kilometres east, on the R258, a few hotels are scattered along the roadside – and that's pretty much Gweedore.

Away from the coast, dozens of small fishing lakes break up the bleak, largely uninhabited, landscape.

On the main road in Bunbeg there's a National Irish Bank with an ATM and bureau de change, while Derrybeg has a post office.

CROLLY DOLLS

Christened after the village in which they originated in 1939, Ireland's famous Crolly dolls are beloved by little girls and collectors alike for their masses of silky ringlets, intricate outfits made from local fabrics, and soft-filled bodies with composite porcelain or plastic features. The dolls are now made in a small, private workshop in nearby Annagry. But you can still buy them in their hometown at **O'Donnells of Crolly** (☎ 074-954 8888; www.odonnells.eu), a large petrol station/supermarket/gourmet deli/restaurant/toy shop on the main road.

Activities

The most beautiful walking trail to be found in the area is the **Tullagobegley Walk** (Siúlóid Tullagobegley), a historical trample over **Tievealehid** (Taobh an Leithid; 431m), which was used for centuries by locals carrying corpses to the 13th-century graveyard in Falcarragh. The 5½-hour walk begins at Lough Nacung (Loch na Cuinge), just east of Gweedore off the N56. The path brings you past some 19th-century silver mines to Keeldrum, a small townland on the outskirts of Gortahork, before finishing up at the Tullagobegley graveyard in Falcarragh.

Unfortunately, the walk is not waymarked so an OS Sheet 1 of the area is invaluable.

Sleeping & Eating

Sleepy Hollows Campsite (☎ 074-954 8272; www .sleepyhollows.ie; Meenaleck, Crolly; campsites per adult/ child €10/5; **P**) The 12 grassy tent sites at this friendly, family-run campground are in secluded woods, thoughtfully removed from the five caravan sites. Due to its diminutive size, bookings are essential. Take the airport turn-off from the village of Crolly and follow the signs 200m past Leo's Tavern.

ourpick **Bunbeg House** (Teach na Céidhe; ☎ 074-953 1305; www.bunbeghouse.com; s/d €50/80; guesthouse Easter-Oct, tearoom Jun-Aug; **P**) Reminiscent of Italy's Cinque Terre, this tucked-away guesthouse, in a converted corn mill, sits directly by Bunbeg harbour, within earshot of wooden boats knocking against each other. Nonguests can pop in for home-cooked chowder, fishermen's pie or open crab sandwiches at its summertime tearoom, or soak up the sun on the terrace over a pint.

COUNTY DONEGAL

'LEGOLAND'

Donegal's pre-Christian tombs and other prehistoric titbits date back as far as 9000 years. But it was the arrival of the Celts and their fort-building endeavours that provided the origins of the county's Irish name, Dún na nGall (Fort of the Foreigner).

During the Celtic Tiger years, this took on an altogether different meaning, with cashed-up Dublin developers building holiday homes in some of Donegal's most pristine beauty spots. Stretches of the coastline have fallen prey to a blitz of bungalows (generally a euphemism for two- or three-storey 'McMansion' homes). These rows of identikit houses have clearly diminished the natural beauty of some parts of the county over the past two decades. Areas such as the Bloody Foreland, long celebrated for its stunning sunset views, are now known as 'Legoland'.

An estimated 40% of the county's homes lie empty for much of the year. In an effort to limit the damage to Donegal's natural environment, county officials have pressed for tighter zoning laws that stipulate future development be restricted to full-time residents. However, the downturn of the country's economy is having an even bigger impact. Numerous new-builds (some still unfinished), plastered with 'for sale' and 'for rent' signs, lie vacant year-round for now.

Seaview Hotel (Óstán Radharc na Mara; ☎ 074-953 1159; www.visitgweedore.com/seaview.htm; Bunbeg; s/d from €80/140; P ☎) This 1904-built hotel on the main road was completely revamped a century later. Its beachfront location is unbeatable. It has 36 spacious rooms, as well as good food at its bar, Tábhairne Hughie Tim (mains €13 to €24.50, open from 12.30pm to 9pm) and its stylishly contemporary restaurant, Gola Bistro (three-course menu €35, open for dinner Friday and Saturday).

Leo's Tavern also does good food.

Entertainment

You never know who'll drop by for one of the legendary singalongs at **Leo's Tavern** (☎ 074-954 8143; Meenaleck, Crolly). It's owned by Leo and Baba Brennan, parents of Enya and her siblings Máire, Ciaran and Pól (the core of the group Clannad). The pub glitters with gold, silver and platinum discs and various other mementos of the successful kids. At Crolly, take the R259 1km towards the airport, and look for the signs for Leo's.

Getting There & Away

Feda O'Donnell (☎ 074-954 8114) runs a service twice daily (three Friday and Sunday) from Gweedore to Letterkenny (€7, 1½ hours), Donegal (€10, 1¾ hours), Sligo (€12, 3¼ hours) and Galway (€20, 5½ hours).

Ferries depart Bunbeg for Tory Island (see opposite).

BLOODY FORELAND

Named for the crimson colour of the rocks at sunset, Bloody Foreland (Cnoc Fola) is a spectacular stretch of coast...or at least it was until holiday homes mushroomed across the horizon (see the boxed text, above). Still, the coast road north and south of here remains wonderfully remote and ideal for cycling. Experienced surfers will find plenty of challenging waves, but you'll need to bring your own gear.

TORY ISLAND

pop 170

Swept by sea winds and stung by salt spray, the remote crag of Tory Island (Oileán Thórai) has taken its fair share of batterings. With nothing to shield it from savage Atlantic squalls, it's a tribute to the hardiness of Tory Islanders that the island has been inhabited for over 4500 years. Although it's only 11km north of the mainland, the rough sea has long consolidated the island's staunch independence.

So it's no surprise that Tory is one of the last places in Ireland to hold onto traditional Irish culture instead of simply paying lip service to it. The island has its own dialect of Irish and even has an elected 'king', and over the decades its inhabitants had a reputation for distilling and smuggling contraband *poitín* (a peaty whiskey). However, the island is perhaps best known for its 'naive' (or outsider) artists, many of whom have attracted the attention of international collectors (see the boxed text, opposite).

In 1974, after an eight-week storm that lashed the island mercilessly, the government made plans to evacuate Tory permanently. Father Diarmuid Ó Peícín came to the rescue, spearheading an international campaign to raise funds, create a proper ferry service, establish an electrical supply and more. The demise of the fishing industry has brought its own share of problems, but the community still doggedly perseveres.

The island has just one pebbly beach and two recognisable villages: West Town (An Baile Thiar), containing most of the island's facilities, and East Town (An Baile Thoir). Its eastern end is dominated by jagged quartzite crags like colossal keys, while the southwest slopes down to wave-washed bedrock.

Information is available from the **Tory Island Co-op** (Comharchumann Thoraí Teo; ☎ 074-913 5502; www .oileanthorai.com; ☼ 9am-5pm) near the pier, next to the playground. At the time of research, a new tourist office was also due to open – check with the Co-op for updates.

Sights & Activities
Cottages mingle with ancient ecclesiastical treasures in West Town. St Colmcille is said to have founded a monastery here in the 6th century, and reminders of the early Church are scattered throughout the town. One example is the 12th-century **Tau Cross**, an odd, T-shaped cruciform that suggests the possibility of seafaring exchanges with early Coptic Christians from Egypt. The cross greets passengers disembarking from the ferry. Also nearby is a 6th- or 7th-century **round tower**, with a circumference of nearly 16m and a round-headed doorway high above the ground.

The island is a wondrous place for **birdwatching** – over 100 species of sea bird inhabit the island, and among the cliffs in the northeast you can see colonies of puffins (around 1400 are thought to inhabit the island).

Sleeping & Eating
Teach Bhillie/Tory Hostel (☎ 074-916 5145; www .toraigh.net; West Town; dm/s/d €20/35/50) From the ferry, walk 300m left to find this cheery B&B that also offers shared, hostel-style accommodation. Spotless rooms are enlivened with bright splashes of colour, and linen and a light continental breakfast are included.

Graceanne Duffy's (☎ 074-913 5136; East Town; d with/without bathroom €70/66; ☼ May-Oct) Peacefully situated in the smaller of Tory's two villages, Graceanne's B&B has three simple but comfortable bedrooms (two with private bath). Evening meals (€16, by arrangement) include organic produce.

Caife an Chreagain (☎ 074-913 5856; West Town; mains €10-15, 3-course menu €20; ☼ 10am-10.30pm Easter-Sep) If that sea air has given you an appetite, head for Mary's welcoming cafe/restaurant, offering great value for money. Outside the summer months (June to August), opening times can vary depending on the weather (and, by extension, the ferries).

Entertainment
Club Sóisialta Thórai (Tory Social Club; ☎ 074-916 5121; West Town) The island's social life revolves around this merry spot, which is the island's only pub. Opening times vary, but it usually gets going from around 8pm.

Getting There & Around
Bring waterproofs for the trip – it can be a wild ride. **Donegal Coastal Cruises** (Turasmara Teo; ☎ 074-953 1340) runs boats to Tory (adult/child/student return €26/15/20) from Bunbeg (1½ hours) and Magheraroarty (35 minutes). Sailing times vary according to weather and tides. Check forecasts as it's not uncommon for travellers to be stranded on the island in bad weather.

Magheraroarty is reached by turning off the N56 at the western end of Gortahork near

---

TORY ISLAND 'NAIVE' ART

Tory Island's distinctive school of painters came about in the 1950s when the English painter Derrick Hill began to spend much of his time on the island, producing many paintings. The islanders often watched him as he worked. As the story goes, one of the islanders approached Hill and said, 'I can do that'. He was James Dixon, a self-taught painter who used boat paint and made his own brushes with donkey hairs. Hill was impressed with the 'painterly' quality of Dixon's work and the two formed a lasting friendship. Other islanders were soon inspired to follow suit, forging unique folksy, expressive styles portraying rugged island scenes. Among them were Patsy Dan Rodgers, now elected 'king' of Tory. The islanders' work has been exhibited in Chicago, New York, Belfast, London and Paris, and fetches impressive prices at auctions. You can often see it at the island's **Dixon Gallery** (☎ 074-916 5420; West Town), and the Glebe Gallery (p488) on the mainland.

Falcarragh; the road is signposted Coastal Route/Bloody Foreland.

Bike hire can be arranged with **Rothair ar Cíos** (☎ 074-916 5614; West Town).

FALCARRAGH & GORTAHORK
pop 842

You'll find more tourist amenities up the road in Dunfanaghy, but the small, workaday towns of Falcarragh (An Fál Carrach) and neighbouring Gortahork (Gort an Choirce) afford an opportunity to experience life in the Gaeltacht region, and there's a good beach nearby.

The 19th-century police barracks now house **Falcarragh Visitors Centre** (An tSean Bheairic; ☎ 074-918 0888; ⏰ 10am-5pm Mon-Fri, 11am-5pm Sat), which has tourist information and a cafe. The Bank of Ireland at the eastern end of Main St has an ATM and bureau de change, and the post office is at Main St's western end in Falcarragh.

Sights & Activities

It's 4km to the windswept **beach**; follow the signs marked *Trá* from Falcarragh's Main St. The beach is superb for walking, but currents make swimming unsafe.

The grey bulk of **Muckish Mountain** (670m; p483) dominates the coast between Dunfanaghy and the Bloody Foreland. Ascents from either the north or south are steep but relatively straightforward; the easiest is from southeast of Falcarragh by the inland road through Muckish Gap. Sweeping views to Malin Head and Tory Island unfurl from the summit.

Sleeping & Eating

Cuan Na Mara (☎ 074-913 5327; crisscannon@hotmail.com; Ballyness, Falcarragh; s/d with bathroom €70/35, without €64/32; ⏰ Jun-Sep; **P** 🛜) Behind a neatly clipped box hedge, the painters and decorators were hard at work on the Cannon family's four guestrooms when we visited their whitewashed home. It's about 2km from the centre of Falcarragh – take the turn-off signposted *Trá*.

Óstán Loch Altan (☎ 074-913 5267; www.ostanlochaltan.com; Gortahork; s/d €60/120; **P** 🛜) Gortahork's main landmark is this large cream-coloured hotel on the main street. Some of its 39 neutral-toned rooms with satin-quilted fabrics have sea views. It's one of the few places to stay along this stretch of coast to open all year. Quality bar food (€9 to €19.50) is served from

noon to 9pm year-round, while its restaurant opens for lunch and dinner (mains €21 to €29.50) from June to September.

Maggie Dan's (☎ 074-916 5022; www.maggiedans.ie; An Phanc, Gortahork; pizzas around €10; ⏰ dinner) A little bit of bohemia in the countryside, this excellent pizzeria facing the Market Sq hosts occasional theatre performances.

Drinking & Entertainment

Loistin Na Seamroige (Shamrock Lodge; ☎ 074-913 5057; Main St, Falcarragh) Owner Margaret grew up on these premises, and her pub is the town's living room, especially on Friday mornings, when a market sets up outside the front door, and during July and August when there's traditional music.

Teach Ruairi (☎ 074-913 5428; Beltany, Gortahork) Fronted by red wagon wheels and red shutters, this authentic-as-it-gets pub is tucked 2km west of Gortahork. It is signposted off the Gweedore road and has regular live acoustic music.

Getting There & Away

Feda O'Donnell (☎ 074-954 8114) buses from Crolly stop on Main St, Falcarragh (€7, twice daily Monday to Saturday, three daily Friday and Sunday). From Falcarragh buses continue to Letterkenny (€7, one hour) and Galway (€20, 5¼ hours).

John McGinley (☎ 074-913 5201; www.johnmcginley.com) buses from Annagry to Dublin (€20, five hours) stop at Gortahork and Falcarragh two to four times daily.

DUNFANAGHY & AROUND

pop 316

Clustered around the waterfront, Dunfanaghy's small, attractive town centre has a surprisingly wide range of accommodation and some of the finest dining options in the county's northwest. Glistening beaches, dramatic coastal cliffs, mountain trails and forests are all within a few kilometres.

There are no ATMs in town but the **post office** (Main St) has a bureau de change.

Sights

HORN HEAD

The towering headland of **Horn Head** (Corrán Binne) has some of Donegal's most spectacular coastal scenery and plenty of birdlife. Its dramatic quartzite cliffs, covered with bog and heather, rear over 180m high, and the view from their tops is heart-pounding.

The road circles the headland; the best approach by bike or car is in a clockwise direction from the Falcarragh end of Dunfanaghy. On a fine day, you'll encounter tremendous views of Tory, Inishbofin, Inishdooey and tiny Inishbeg islands to the west; Sheep Haven Bay and the Rosguill Peninsula to the east; Malin Head to the northeast; and the coast of Scotland beyond. Take care in bad weather as the route can be perilous.

ARDS FOREST PARK

Anyone looking to stretch their legs will love this forested **park** (☎ 074-912 1139; admission free), which is criss-crossed by marked nature trails varying in length from 2km to 13km. It covers the northern shore of the Ards Peninsula and some of the best walks lead to its clean beaches. The woodlands are home to several native species, including ash, birch and sessile oak. Introduced species, both broadleaf and conifer, also proliferate, and you may even encounter foxes, hedgehogs and otters. In 1930 the southern part of the peninsula was taken over by Capuchin monks; the grounds of their friary are open to the public. It's 5km southeast of Dunfanaghy off the N56; daily closing times are posted at the entrance.

DUNFANAGHY WORKHOUSE

This grim building was the local workhouse, built to keep and employ the destitute. Conditions were excessively harsh. Men, women, children and the sick were segregated and their lives were dominated by gruelling

work. It was soon inundated with starving people as the Famine took grip. Two years after it opened in 1845, it accommodated some 600 people – double the number originally planned.

The workhouse, west of the centre, is now a **heritage centre** (☎ 074-913 6540; www.dunfanaghyworkhouse.ie; Main St; adult/child €4.50/2; ☺ 10.30am-5pm daily Jul & Aug, 11am-4pm Mon-Sat Mar-Jun & Sep, call for hours Oct-Feb), which tells the powerful tale of 'Wee Hannah' and her passage through the institution, and also hosts various temporary exhibitions and workshops. On some mornings the place is overrun with busloads of school children.

DUNFANAGHY GALLERY

Just up the road from the heritage centre, **Dunfanaghy Gallery** (☎ 074-913 6224; Main St; admission free; ☺ 10am-6pm Mon-Sat) started life as a fever hospital. The gallery has several rooms, which showcase paintings old and new, historic photos printed from original glass plates, hand-woven tweeds, pottery, jewellery and books.

DOE CASTLE

Although the interior of the early 16th-century **Doe Castle** (Caisleán na dTuath; Creeslough; ☺ approx 10am-6pm) isn't open to the public, locals open the gates each day, allowing you to wander through the grounds. The castle was the stronghold of the Scottish MacSweeney family until it fell into English hands in the 17th century. The castle is picturesquely sited on a low promontory with water on three sides and a moat hewn out of the rock on the landward side. The best view is from the Carrigart–Creeslough road. It's signposted 16km from Dunfanaghy on the Carrigart road.

CREESLOUGH & MUCKISH MOUNTAIN

When it's not shrouded in the cloud and mist that locals call *smir*, hulking Muckish Mountain (670m) makes a good climb. You can reach it via the village of Creeslough, 11km south of Dunfanaghy on the N56, and home to an extraordinary modern church, resembling a half-dissolved sugar cube that mirrors the mountain's shape. Turn right about 2km northwest of Creeslough and continue for about 6km, where a rough track begins the ascent.

BEACHES

The wide, sandy and virtually empty **Killyhoey Beach** leads right into the heart of Dunfanaghy village. **Marble Hill Beach**, about 3km east of

COUNTY DONEGAL

town in Port-na-Blagh, is more secluded but usually crammed in summer. Reaching Dunfanaghy's loveliest spot, **Tramore Beach**, requires hiking 20 minutes through the grassy dunes immediately south of the village.

Activities
WALKING
For an exhilarating hike, take the road from Dunfanaghy towards Horn Head until the bridge. After crossing, go through the gate on your left and stroll along the track until you reach the dunes. A well-beaten path will lead you to the magnificent **Tramore Beach**. Turn left and follow it to the end, where you can find a way up onto a path leading north to **Pollaguill Bay**. Continue to the cairn at the end of the bay and follow the coastline for a stupendous view of the 20m **Marble Arch**, carved out by the sea.

A shorter walk begins at Marble Hill Beach in Port-na-Blagh. Take the path on the left side of the beach past the cottage and work your way about 500m through the brush and along the top of the cliff until you reach **Harry's Hole**, a small crevice in the cliff that is popular with daredevil kids, who dive 10m into the water below.

GOLF
Dunfanaghy Golf Club (☎ 074-913 6335; www.dunfanaghy golfclub.com; green fees weekdays/weekends €30/40) is a stunning waterside 18-hole links course just outside the village on the Port-na-Blagh road.

HORSE RIDING
Exploring the expansive beaches and surrounding countryside on horseback can be arranged through **Dunfanaghy Stables** (☎ 074-910 0980; www.dunfanaghystables.com; Main St; adult/child per hr €30/25; ◷ hr vary seasonally).

SEA ANGLING
Richard Bowyer (☎ 074-913 6640; Port-na-Blagh) organises sea-angling trips from the small pier in Port-na-Blagh between Easter and September.

SURFING, WINDSURFING & KAYAKING
Windsurfing lessons and gear hire are available through **Marble Hill Windsurfing** (☎ 074-913 6231; richardharshaw@eircom.net; The Cottage, Marble Hill, Port-na-Blagh; ◷ daily Jul & Aug, by appointment May, Jun & Sep).

Jaws Watersports (☎ 086 173 5109; www.jawswater sports.com; Main St) rents surfboards (€20 per half day) and offers lessons (€30), and also has kayak rental (from €25 per half day) and runs kayaking trips (€35).

Sleeping
Corcreggan Mill Hostel (☎ 074-913 6409; www.corcreggan .com; Corcreggan Mill, Dunfanaghy; campsites per person €8-9, dm €18, s €35, d €50-55, tr €70; P ▣ ⌘) Spotless dorms, most with private bath, and private rooms are tucked into cosy corners of this former mill house, next to the stone ruins of the old mill. An organic vegetable garden provides the ingredients for soups and stews (€5 to €10) served of an evening, and you can add a continental/full breakfast for €5/7. Weary travellers can unwind with a massage (back/full-body €15/40). Look for signs on the roadside and in the car park reading 'Mill House'.

Carriage Hostel (☎ 074-910 0814; www.the-carriage -hostel-corcreggan.com; Corcreggan Mill, Dunfanaghy; dm €14-17, s €25-35, d €35-42; P) A 19th-century mahogany railway carriage (open year-round) and an old stone kiln house (open May to September) make up the sleeping quarters of this unique hostel. It's 4km southwest of Dunfanaghy on the Falcarragh road (N56), next door to the separately owned Corcreggan Mill Hostel. Ask the bus to stop outside.

Arnold's Hotel (☎ 074-913 6208; www.arnoldshotel .com; Main St; s €55-85, d €130; ◷ Apr-Oct; P ▣) Open since 1922, this 30-room hotel is run with tangible pride by the third generation of the Arnold family. Public areas with tartan carpeting are strewn with deep-red velour armchairs. Some front guestrooms have window seats where you can curl up with a book or simply gaze out over Sheep Haven Bay. Fine Irish food is served in the elegant bar (mains €16 to €30).

Shandon Hotel Spa & Wellness (☎ 074-913 6137; www.shandonhotel.com; Sheep Haven Bay, Dunfanaghy; d €184-244; ◷ Easter-Oct; P ⌘) Harried parents will love this 1950s hotel. You can drop off the kids at the free supervised playroom, and indulge at its award-winning spa or work out in the gym. Family-friendly facilities also include kids' and adults' swimming pools, a tennis court, minigolf, and laundry facilities. Most of the 70 spacious rooms have a spectacular vantage of Marble Hill Beach and all have in-room fridges. Dinner is available in the hotel restaurant (three-course menu €39).

Backpackers can enquire about cheaper annex rooms available on a room-only basis. Follow the signposts off the N56 along 3km of winding country lanes.

Eating

Muck 'n' Muffins (☎ 074-913 6780; Main Sq; sandwiches & snacks €3-9.50; ⓥ 9.30am-5pm Mon-Sat, 11am-5pm Sun, to 9pm Jul & Aug) A 19th-century rough-stone grain store now houses this waterfront cafe and craft shop. Even on rainy winter days, it's packed with locals tucking into healthy sandwiches, quiches and hot specials, tempting cakes and, of course, muffins.

Cove (☎ 074-913 6300; Rockhill, Port-na-Blagh; lunch menu €21, dinner mains €17.50-24; ⓥ lunch Sun, dinner Tue-Sun, closed Jan–mid-Mar) Owners Siobhan Sweeney and Peter Byrne are perfectionists who tend to every detail in Cove's art-filled dining room and on your plate. The seafood-skewed cuisine is inventive and deceptively simple with subtle Asian influences. After dinner, retire to the elegant lounge upstairs. It's on the main road in Port-na-Blagh.

Mill Restaurant & Guesthouse (☎ 074-913 6985; www.themillrestaurant.com; Figart, Dunfanaghy; 3-course menu €43.50; ⓥ dinner Tue-Sun mid-Mar–mid-Dec; Ⓟ) An exquisite country setting and perfectly composed meals make dining here a treat. It occupies an old flax mill that was for many years the home of renowned watercolour artist Frank Eggington. It also has six high-class guestrooms (single/double €70/100). It's just south of the town on the Falcarragh road.

Drinking

Molly's Bar (☎ 074-910 0739; Main St) Be sure to at least peek inside the cherry-red Molly's Bar, a wonderfully old-fashioned pub with proper snugs. It also hosts regular live music (traditional, jazz, blues and more) and events including quiz nights.

Getting There & Away

Feda O'Donnell (☎ 074-954 8114) buses from Crolly (€7, 40 minutes) to Galway (€20, five hours) stop in Dunfanaghy square twice daily Monday to Saturday and three times on Friday and Sunday.

John McGinley (☎ 074-913 5201) buses to Dublin stop in Dunfanaghy (€20, 4¾ hours).

The **Lough Swilly** (☎ 074-912 2863) bus from Dungloe stops in Dunfanaghy once daily Monday to Friday (€11.40, two hours) en route to Letterkenny and Derry.

EASTERN DONEGAL

LETTERKENNY
pop 17,586

You'd swear the Celtic Tiger was still prowling the traffic-snarled streets of Letterkenny (Leitir Ceanainn). Donegal's largest town continues to grow rapidly and is tracking towards city status. Huge new retail parks have recently opened on the town's fringe, and the traditional town centre is enjoying a cultural upswing with its theatre, pubs, clubs and stylish eateries all buzzing with students and young professionals.

Tourist attractions in the town itself, however, are few. Most passers-through will be on their way to Donegal's more alluring corners, but the town makes a central base for discovering the county's eastern and northern reaches. Visitors using public transport are likely to stop here for at least a short period.

Orientation

Main St, said to be the longest high street in Ireland, divides into Upper and Lower Main Sts. At the top of Upper Main St there is a Y-junction: High Rd veers left, while Port Rd goes right to the bus station and the road out to Derry.

Information

Check out www.letterkenny.ie for useful info on the town and surrounds.

AIB (Main St) Bank branch with ATM.
Bank of Ireland (Main St)
Cyberworld (☎ 074-912 0440; Lower Main St; per hr €2; ⓥ 9.30am-6pm Mon-Wed & Sat, 9.30am-8pm Thu & Fri) Internet cafe.
Duds 'n' Suds Laundrette (☎ 074-912 8303; Pearse Rd; load from €10; ⓥ 8am-7pm Mon-Fri, 8.30am-6.30pm Sat)
Post office (Upper Main St)
Tourist Office (☎ 074-912 1160; www.discoverireland .ie/northwest; Neil Blaney Rd; ⓥ 9am-5pm Mon-Fri, noon-3pm Sat & Sun Jun & Aug, 9am-5pm Mon-Fri Sep-May) Large, efficient office situated 1km southeast of town at the end of Port Rd.

Sights & Activities

Dominating the town's hillside profile, the enormous Gothic-style **St Eunan's Cathedral** (1901) thrusts skyward on Sentry Hill Rd (take Church Lane up from Main St) and contains much intricate Celtic carving.

Letterkenny's 19th-century workhouse, built to provide Famine relief, now houses the **Donegal County Museum** (☎ 074-9124613; High Rd; admission free; ☺ 10am-12.30pm & 1-4.30pm Mon-Fri, 1-4.30pm Sat). Temporary exhibits feature on the ground floor. Upstairs, the permanent collection is worth a peek for its 8000-strong artefacts from prehistoric times on.

Outside the town, salmon and trout populate the rivers and lakes. Equipment and information is available from **Top Tackle** (☎ 074-916 7545; 55 Port Rd; ☺ 9.30am-5.30pm Mon-Sat).

Festivals & Events

Theatre performances, concerts and art exhibits lure culture buffs to the diverse **Earagail Arts Festival** (☎ 074 916 8800; www.eaf.ie), held over two weeks in early to mid-July.

Sleeping

Port Hostel (☎ 074-912 5315; www.porthostel.ie; Port Rd; dm from €16, d €36-40; ☐) This IHO hostel's gregarious owner, Karen, is an unofficial ambassador to Donegal and often takes guests further afield in her minivan, as well as organising pub crawls, BBQs and summertime music sessions. Airy dorms and private rooms house 70 beds and well-equipped kitchens over two modern buildings in rambling gardens. It's up a crooked lane behind the An Grianán Theatre, a five-minute walk from the bus station and town centre.

Letterkenny Court Hotel (☎ 074-912 2977; www.letterkennycourthotel.com; Main St; s €59-99, d €78-158; ☐ ☎) Behind its rose-pink facade, this historic building on the main drag is deceptively large, housing 83 fresh-as-spring rooms. About a dozen pubs are within staggering distance of the front door. Some rooms and all public areas have wi-fi. There's discounted public parking out back.

ourpick Castle Grove (☎ 074-915 1118; www.castlegrove.com; s/d €70/110; ☐) Set on an enormous estate that rolls down to the estuary, this Georgian manor, filled with fragrant fresh flowers, manages to be at once grand, yet warm and personal. Its 15 rooms are elegantly arranged with antiques, and lawns are so neat they appear trimmed by nail clippers. The award-winning restaurant is renowned for seasonal dishes like its wild mushroom risotto with steamed asparagus (Sunday lunch €20 to €25, dinner menu €55). From Letterkenny, head 5km along the road to Rathmelton and turn right just before the Silver Tassie hotel.

Clanree Hotel (☎ 074-912 4369; www.clanreehotel.com; Derry Rd; s/d €115/150; ☐ ☒ ☎ ☒) Letterkenny is a popular conference venue, hence its substantial stock of upmarket hotels. Among the best is the sprawling, silvery-grey Clanree, just as you come off the main roundabout from Derry or Sligo. Its sweeping central staircase, bar and well-regarded restaurant have a timeless elegance, rooms are comfortable, there's a well-equipped leisure centre, and attentive staff.

Eating

The section of Port Rd by the An Grianán Theatre is carving out a niche as Letterkenny's dining strip, with a slew of hip new restaurants opening up.

Simple Simon's (☎ 074-912 2382; St Oliver Plunkett Rd; dishes €2.75-7; ☺ 9am-4.30pm Mon-Sat) Attached to a health food shop, this bohemian cafe serves up such delicious organic soups, wraps, paninis, salads and home-baked treats (plus enormous mugs of hot chocolate) that we'll pretend we didn't notice the Dan Quayle spelling of 'potatoe' on the specials board.

Oak Tree (☎ 074-912 5892; Port Rd; lunch mains €7-10.50, dinner mains €14-22.50; ☺ lunch Mon-Fri, dinner Mon-Sat, 1-9pm Sun) Chunky seafood chowder with brandy, and roast duck breast with Chinese spices are among the highlights of the select menu at this promising newcomer. The dining room opens to an aperitif-friendly alfresco terrace.

ourpick Yellow Pepper (☎ 074-912 4133; 36 Lower Main St; lunch mains €8-18, dinner mains €12-23; ☺ lunch & dinner) A 19th-century former shirt factory is the cosy home of this venerable restaurant. Despite being as comfy as a favourite shirt, it's regularly touted as Letterkenny's best restaurant. Stone walls, copper light fittings, a central cast-iron column and original hardwood floors give it a cosy atmosphere, and its menu, specialising in fresh fish, is outstanding value and offers plenty of vegetarian options.

Beetroot (☎ 074-912 9759; 41 Port Rd; lunch mains €9.50-12, dinner mains €16.50-25.50; ☺ lunch Mon-Fri, dinner nightly) The hottest new address in town, Beetroot's iridescent wallpaper, bare wood tables and sleek banquettes are a chic backdrop for its mod Irish cuisine. Try shredded beetroot salad with quail eggs, pork medallions on apple and cider mash or hake fillet with beetroot salsa, and a scrumptious 'messy meringue' for dessert.

Drinking

Cottage Bar (☎ 074-912 1338; 49 Upper Main St) Watch your head! All sorts of bric-a-brac hangs precariously from the ceiling of Letterkenny's most atmospheric pub.

McGinley's (☎ 074-912 1106; Main St) Trad sessions take place on Wednesday night at this central local stalwart.

Entertainment

An Grianán Theatre (☎ 074-912 0777; www.angrianan .com; Port Rd) An Grianán Theatre is both a community theatre and major arts venue for the northwest, presenting national and international drama, comedy and music. It also has a good cafe and bar.

Regional Cultural Centre (☎ 074-912 9186; www .donegalculture.com; Port Rd) In a stunning glass-and-aluminium structure, Letterkenny's cultural centre mounts performances, fine arts and multimedia exhibits, and film screenings.

Voodoo (☎ 074-910 9815; www.voodoolk.com; 21 Lower Main St) This vast club is the centre of Letterkenny's nightlife. Check the website for events.

Getting There & Away

Letterkenny is a major bus hub for northwestern Ireland. The bus station is by the roundabout at the junction of Ramelton Rd and the Derry road. **Left luggage** (per item €2.70; ⏱ 8.45am-5.45pm Mon-Sat) is available, though not overnight.

Bus Éireann (☎ 074-912 1309) express bus 32 runs to Dublin (€19.50, four hours) nine times daily via Omagh (€11.80, one hour) and Monaghan (€14.60, 1¾ hours). The Derry (€8.70, 35 minutes) to Galway (€21, 4¾ hours) bus 64 stops at Letterkenny four times daily (three times on Sunday) before continuing to Donegal (€8.90, 50 minutes), Bundoran (€13, 1½ hours), Sligo (€12, two hours) and Galway (€21, 4½ hours). Connections can be made in Galway for the hourly express bus 51 service to Limerick and Cork.

John McGinley (☎ 074-913 5201) buses run twice daily Sunday to Thursday (three on times Friday and once on Saturday) from Annagry to Dublin (€20, 3¾ hours) through Letterkenny and Monaghan.

Lough Swilly (☎ 074-912 2863) has one service from Derry Monday to Friday (€6.60, one hour) to Dungloe (€20, two hours), via Letterkenny and Dunfanaghy.

Feda O'Donnell (☎ 074-954 8114) runs a bus from Crolly (€7, 1½ hours) to Galway (€20, four hours) twice daily via Letterkenny, Donegal, Bundoran and Sligo. Buses stop on the road outside the bus station.

McGeehan Coaches (☎ 074-954 6150) runs a service from Letterkenny to Glencolumbcille (€12.50, 2¼ hours) once daily except Sunday.

Getting Around

Taxis can be ordered from **Letterkenny Cabs** (☎ 074-912 7000). There are taxi stands on Main St opposite the square, and opposite the bus station.

LOUGH GARTAN

The patriarch of Irish monasticism, St Colmcille (or Columba), was born in a lovely setting near the glassy Lough Gartan, and some isolated stone structures and crosses remain from his lifetime. The lake is 17km northwest of Letterkenny. It's beautiful driving country, but there's no public transport.

Colmcille Heritage Centre

Colmcille's Hall of Fame is this comprehensive **heritage centre** (☎ 074-913 7306; Gartan; adult/concession €3/2; ⏱ 10.30am-6.30pm Mon-Sat, 1-6.30pm Sun, May-Sep), on the shore of Lough Gartan, with a lavish display on the production of illuminated manuscripts.

Colmcille's mother, on the run from pagans, supposedly haemorrhaged during childbirth and her blood is believed to have changed the colour of the surrounding Gartan Clay to pure white. Ever since, the clay has been regarded as a lucky charm. Ask nicely and the staff may produce some from under the counter.

On the way to the heritage centre you'll also see signs to the stone pile that once was **Colmcille's Abbey**. Further down the road, on a hillside overrun by bleating sheep, is the **saint's birthplace**, marked by a hefty cross. Beside it is an intriguing prehistoric tomb strewn with greening coppers that's popularly known as the Flagstone of Loneliness, on which Colmcille supposedly slept. Some believe the chunky slab cures homesickness.

To reach the heritage centre, leave Letterkenny on the R250 road to Glenties and Ardara. After a few kilometres, turn right on the R251 to Churchill village and follow the signs. Alternatively, from Kilmacrennan on the N56, turn west and look for signs.

Gartan Outdoor Education Centre

Courses including rock climbing, sea kayaking, sailing, surfing, windsurfing, hill climbing and more are offered for both adults and children at this **adventure centre** (☎ 074-913

COUNTY DONEGAL

7032; www.gartan.com; Gartan, Churchill). It's located on a 35-hectare estate 18km northwest of Letterkenny on the shores of Lough Gartan.

Glebe Gallery & House

The English painter Derrick Hill bought historic **Glebe House** (☎ 074-913 7071; www.heritageireland .ie; Churchill; adult/child/concession €3/1/2; ◷ 10am-6.30pm daily Easter, 11am-6.30pm Sat-Thu Jun-Sep) in 1953, providing him with a mainland base close to his beloved Tory Island. Before Hill arrived, the house served as a rectory and then a hotel. The 1828-built mansion is sumptuously decorated with an evident love of all things exotic, but its real appeal is his astonishing art collection. In addition to paintings by Hill and Tory Island's 'naive' artists (see the boxed text, p481) are works by Picasso, Landseer, Hokusai, Jack B Yeats and Kokoschka. The woodland gardens are also wonderful. A guided tour of the house takes about 45 minutes.

DUNLEWEY & AROUND

pop 700

Blink and chances are you've missed the tiny hamlet of Dunlewy (Dún Lúiche) beside Lough Dunlewy. You won't miss Mt Errigal, however, whose bare face towers over the surrounding area.

Sights & Activities

DUNLEWEY LAKESIDE CENTRE

This hugely enjoyable **activity centre** (Ionad Cois Locha; ☎ 074-953 1699; www.dunleweycentre.com; Dunlewy; admission house & grounds or boat trip adult/child €5.95/3.95, combined ticket €9.50/7; ◷ 10.30am-6pm Mon-Sat, 11am-6pm Sun Easter-Oct) is a great place if you're travelling with the family in tow. Adults will be intrigued by the 30-minute tour of the thatched cottage that once belonged to local weaver Manus Ferry, who earned world renown for his tweeds (he died in 1975), while kids will adore the petting zoo. But the real highlight, for all ages, is an entertaining boat trip on the lake with a storyteller who vividly brings to life local history, geology and ghoulish folklore. Traditional music concerts (€8) take place on Tuesdays in July and August; you can also catch concerts on Sunday afternoons year-round in the new concert venue. There's a good cafe with a turf fire and craft shop.

STABLES DUNLEWEY

A range of pony and trap rides, treks, trail rides and lessons are available at Dunlewey's **stables** (☎ 087 320 8998; thestablesdunlewey@hotmail .com), situated across the car park from the Dunlewey Lakeside Centre.

MT ERRIGAL

The looming presence of Mt Errigal (752m) seemingly dares walkers to attempt the tough but beautiful climb to its pyramid-shaped peak. If you're keen to take on the challenge, pay close attention to the weather. It's a dangerous climb on misty or wet days, when the mountain is shrouded in cloud and visibility is minimal.

There are two paths to the summit: the easier route, which covers 5km and takes around two hours; and the more difficult 3.3km walk along the northwestern ridge, which involves scrambling over scree for about 2½ hours. Details of both routes are available at the Dunlewey Lakeside Centre.

POISONED GLEN

Legend has it that the stunning ice-carved rock face of the Poisoned Glen got its sinister name when the ancient one-eyed giant king of Tory, Balor, was killed here by his exiled grandson, Lughaidh, whereupon the poison from his eye split the rock and poisoned the glen. The less interesting truth, however, lies in a cartographic gaffe. Locals were inspired to name it An Gleann Neamhe (the Heavenly Glen), but when an English cartographer mapped the area, he carelessly marked it An Gleann Neimhe – the Poisoned Glen.

The R251 has several viewpoints overlooking the glen. It's possible to walk through it, although the ground is rough and boggy. From the lakeside centre a return walk along the glen is 12km and takes two to three hours. Watch out for the green lady – the resident ghost!

Sleeping

Errigal Hostel (☎ 074-953 1180; www.errigalhostel.com; Dunlewey; dm €20-21, d €52; **P**) At the base of Mt Errigal, this gleaming new 60-bed An Óige hostel has state-of-the-art facilities including a stainless steel self-catering kitchen, a large laundry room for your muddy climbing gear, light-filled common areas, and pristine dorms and private rooms. Green initiatives include wood-pellet heating. There's a petrol station that also sells groceries next door.

Radharc an Ghleanna (☎ 074-953 1835; http:// radharcanghleanna.littleireland.ie; Moneymore, Dunlewey; s/d with bathroom €50/70, without €45/66; ◷ Easter-Oct; **P**)

This county bungalow is aptly named: Radharc an Ghleanna translates as 'View of the Glen', and the views of the glen and lough are eye-popping. The four rooms are as clean as laboratories (but infinitely cosier). It's run by a friendly couple whose extended family enjoy staying here too, so be sure to book ahead. Follow the sign to Poisoned Glen down a small lane; it's a few metres ahead on your right.

GLENVEAGH NATIONAL PARK

Lakes shimmer like dew in the mountainous valley of **Glenveagh National Park** (Páirc Náisiúnta Ghleann Bheatha; www.glenveaghnationalpark.ie; admission free; ⓨ 10am-6pm mid-Mar–Oct, 9am-5pm Nov–mid-Mar). Alternating between great knuckles of rock, green-gold swaths of bog and scatterings of oak and birch forest, the 16,500 sq km protected area is magnificent walking country. Its wealth of wildlife includes the golden eagle, which was hunted to extinction here in the 19th century but was reintroduced in 2000.

Such serenity came at a heavy price. The land was once farmed by 244 tenants, who were forcibly evicted by landowner John George Adair in the winter of 1861 following what he called a 'conspiracy', but really because their presence obstructed his vision for the valley. Adair put the final touches on his paradise (1870–73) by building the spectacular lakeside Glenveagh Castle, while his wife, Adelia, introduced the park's definitive red deer and rhododendrons.

If anything, things got even more surreal after the Adairs' deaths. The castle was briefly occupied by the IRA in 1922. Then in 1929 the property was acquired by Kingsley Porter, professor of art at Harvard University, who mysteriously disappeared in 1933 (presumed drowned, but rumoured to have been spotted in Paris afterwards). Six years later the estate was bought by his former student, Henry McIlhenny, once described by Andy Warhol as 'the only person in Philadelphia with glamour'. In 1975, McIlhenny sold the whole kit and caboodle to the Irish government.

The park features nature trails along lakes, through woods and blanket bog, as well as a viewing point that's a short walk behind the castle.

The **Glenveagh Visitor Centre** (☎ 074-913 7090; Churchill) has a 20-minute audiovisual display on the ecology of the park and the infamous Adair. The restaurant serves hot food and snacks, and the reception sells the necessary midge repellent, as vital in summer as walking boots and waterproofs are in winter. Camping is not allowed.

Glenveagh Castle

This delightfully showy **castle** (adult/child €3/1.50) was modelled in miniature on Scotland's Balmoral Castle. Henry McIlhenny made it a characterful home with liberal reminders of his passion for hunting deer. In fact you'll be hard pressed to find a single room without a representation – or taxidermied remains – of a stag.

An entertaining 30-minute guided tour takes in a series of flamboyantly decorated rooms that remain as if McIlhenny has just stepped out. The most eye-catching, including the tartan-and-antler-covered music room and the pink candy-striped room demanded by Greta Garbo whenever she stayed here, are in the round tower.

The exotic gardens are similarly spectacular, boasting a host of terraces, an Italian garden, a walled kitchen garden, and the Belgian Walk, built by Belgian soldiers who stayed here during WWI. Their cultured charm is in marked contrast to the wildly beautiful landscape that enfolds the area.

The last guided tours of the castle leave about 45 minutes before closing time. **Minibuses** (adult/child return €2/1) shuttle between the visitor centre and the castle roughly every 15 minutes; the journey takes a mere five or so minutes; alternatively it's a scenic 3.6km walk.

DOON WELL & ROCK OF DOON

In centuries past, wells were commonly believed to cure afflictions. Judging by the shimmering rosaries, multicoloured rags and trinkets bejewelling nearby bushes, many still believe this to be true of the cupboard-like **Doon Well** (Tobar an Duin).

A sign points to the overgrown **Rock of Doon** (Carraig an Duin), which has some far-reaching views. This is where the O'Donnell kings were crowned – presumably so they could get a squiz at what they were inheriting.

Take the signposted turn-off from the N56 just north of Kilmacrennan. The well and rock are about 1.5km north of the village.

LIFFORD

pop 1448

It's hard to believe that dwindling little Lifford (Leifear), on the border of County Tyrone, is still Donegal's county town. While its powerful judicial past is long gone, its spirit lingers in the daunting 18th-century **Old Courthouse** (☎ 074-914 1733; www.liffordoldcourthouse .com; adult/concession €6/3; ☺ 10am-5pm Mon-Fri Jun-Aug, 10am-3pm Mon-Fri Sep-May, last tour 1hr prior to closing). The courthouse is home to an excellent **heritage centre** with creepily lifelike recreations that use actors' faces projected onto waxworks. In this manner, Manus O'Donnell tells the story of Donegal's Gaelic chieftains and several bona-fide trials are re-enacted in the austere courtroom (including that of Napper Tandy, John 'half-hanged' McNaughten and the Lord Leitrim murder). A guard will take you down to the prison cells, accompanied by sounds of banging doors and ominous footsteps, to be locked up for sheep-stealing or the like.

There are no stand-out places to stay or to dine, but it's a mere hop over the bridge to Strabane in County Tyrone, and within easy striking distance of Letterkenny.

Getting There & Away

Bus Éireann's (☎ 074-912 1309) express service 32 from Dublin (€17.60, 3¼ hours) to Letterkenny (€7.40, 20 minutes) stops in Lifford up to five times daily. Buses also connect Lifford with Ballybofey (€6.40, 30 minutes) at least twice daily, and Strabane (€1.60, five minutes).

NORTHEASTERN DONEGAL

ROSGUILL PENINSULA

The best way to appreciate Rosguill's rugged splendour is by driving, cycling or even walking the 15km **Atlantic Drive**. It's signposted to your left as you come into the sprawling village of **Carrigart** (Carraig Airt) from the south. There are plenty of thirst-quenching pubs in the village, and a pretty, secluded beach at **Trá na Rossan**. On no account should you swim in Mulroy Bay or the surrounding areas, as it's unsafe. Perhaps this is why the summer crowds don't linger here. Most prefer to travel 4km northward to **Downings** (often written as Downies), where the beach is spectacular, though it's much more built-up.

Activities

Designed by St Andrew's Old Tom Morris in 1891 and remodelled by Harry Vardon in 1906, the scenery at the **Rosapenna Golf Club**

(☎ 074-915 5301; www.rosapennagolflinks.ie; Downings; green fees €50-85) is as spectacular as the layout, which can challenge even the lowest handicapper.

Sleeping & Eating

Casey's Caravan Park (☎ 074-915 5301; rosapenna@ eircom.net; Downings; campsites €10-20; ☺ Apr-Sep) You won't get closer to Downing's Blue Flag beach than at this extremely popular campsite right beside the dunes. The village is just around the corner. Book ahead.

Trá na Rosann Hostel (☎ 074-915 5374; www.anoige .ie; Downings; dm €15; ☺ late May-Aug; **P**) Knockout views envelop this heritage-listed former hunting lodge, now an An Óige hostel. The trade-off for its tranquil setting is that it's 8km east of Downings and there's no public transport. Note that reception is generally closed from 10am to 5pm.

Beach Hotel (Óstán na Trá; ☎ 074-915 5303; www .beachhotel.ie; Downings; s/d €60/100; ☺ Apr-Oct; **P**) The former Beach Hotel burnt to the ground but gave rise to this brand-new incarnation of exposed stone, wood and glass. Most of its 30 rooms have ocean views; those that don't overlook the village centre and mountains beyond. The family-owners' personal touch is evident everywhere, especially in the dining room (dinner served nightly for guests; Friday to Sunday for nonguests), where everything is cooked to order (set menus €20 to €30).

Downings Bay Hotel (☎ 074-915 5586; www.downings bayhotel.com; Downings; s/d from €70/120; **P** 🛜) Just footsteps from the strand, rooms at this spacious, if slightly austere, hotel have subtle checked and striped fabrics. There's an adjacent nightclub, a couple of bars (bar food €12.50 to €23.50) and an excellent restaurant, the Haven (Sunday lunch €18.50, dinner €60 to €70 for two including wine).

ourpick Olde Glen Bar & Restaurant (☎ 074-915 5130; Glen, Carrigart; mains €18-24; ☺ dinner Tue-Sat late May–mid-Sep, Fri-Sun Easter-late May, Sat & Sun mid-Sep–Easter) Authentic down to its original 1700s uneven stone floor, this treasure of a traditional pub in the tiny hamlet of Glen serves a sensational pint. Out the back, its small farmhouse-style restaurant serves outstanding blackboard specials. It doesn't take reservations and is popular with locals – turn up by 5.30pm to get a table for the 6pm seating, or by 6.30pm for a table at the 7.30pm seating. By the time you leave, you'll feel like a local yourself.

Getting There & Around

A local bus connects Carrigart and Downings (contact Patrick Gallagher, ☎ 074-913 7037), but you really need your own transport for this area.

FANAD PENINSULA

The second-most northerly point in Donegal, Fanad Head thrusts out into the Atlantic to the east of Rosguill. The peninsula curls around the watery expanses of Mulroy Bay to the west, and Lough Swilly to the east, the latter trimmed by high cliffs and sandy beaches. Most travellers stick to the peninsula's eastern flank, visiting the beautiful beach and excellent golf course at Portsalon, and the quiet heritage towns of Rathmelton and Rathmullan. Accommodation is relatively limited, so book ahead in summer.

Portsalon & Fanad Head

Once named the second most beautiful beach in the world by British newspaper the *Observer*, the tawny-coloured Blue Flag **beach** in Ballymastocker Bay, which is safe for swimming, is the principle draw of tiny Portsalon (Port an tSalainn). For golfers, however, the main attraction is the marvellously scenic **Portsalon Golf Club** (☎ 074-915 9459; www .portsalongolfclub.ie; Portsalon; green fees weekdays/weekends €40/50).

It's another 8km to the lighthouse on the rocky tip of Fanad Head, the best part of which is the scenic drive there. Following the rollercoaster road that hugs the cliffs back to Rathmullan, you'll pass the early 19th-century **Knockalla Fort**, built to warn off any approaching French ships.

The peninsula has some crankin' surf – for lessons contact **Adventure One Surf School** (☎ 074-915 0262; www.adventureone.net; Ballyheirnan Bay, Fanad). Two-hour lessons, which include gear rental, cost €30.

The **Lough Swilly** (☎ 074-912 2863) bus leaves Letterkenny three times daily Monday to Friday, twice Saturday for Milford (€4.60, one hour).

Rathmullan

pop 520

The refined little port of Rathmullan (Ráth Maoláin) has a tranquillity that belies the momentous events that took place here from the 16th to 18th centuries. In 1587, Hugh O'Donnell, the 15-year-old heir to the power-ful O'Donnell clan, was tricked into boarding a ship here and taken to Dublin as a prisoner. He escaped four years later on Christmas Eve and, after unsuccessful attempts at revenge, died in Spain, aged only 30. In 1607, despairing of fighting the English, Hugh O'Neill, the Earl of Tyrone, and Rory O'Donnell, the Earl of Tyrconnell, boarded a ship in Rathmullan harbour and left Ireland for good. This decisive act, known as the Flight of the Earls, marked the effective end of Gaelic Ireland and the rule of Irish chieftains. Large-scale confiscation of their estates took place, preparing for the Plantation of Ulster with settlers from Britain. Also in Rathmullan, Wolfe Tone, leader of the 1798 Rising, was captured.

SIGHTS

The picturesque Carmelite **Rathmullan Friary** is so entangled in vines that it would probably crumble should they be cleared away. It was founded around 1508 by the MacSweeneys, and was still used in 1595 when English commander, George Bingham, raided the place and took off with the communion plate and priestly vestments. Bishop Knox then renovated the friary in 1618 in order to use it as his own residence.

SLEEPING & EATING

our pick **Rathmullan House** (☎ 074-915 8188; www.rath mullanhouse.com; s €80-100, d €160-240; P 🖳 🛜 🖭) This country house might be large and luxurious but the welcome from the family owners is so warm that you feel like you're staying with friends. Sprawled over wooded gardens on the shores of Lough Swilly, the original house dates from the 1780s, but extensions are sympathetic and stylish. Higher-priced rooms have claw-foot baths and some open to balconies or terraces. There's a tennis court, two genteel bars, and a glass-domed restaurant, the Weeping Elm, utilising organic produce from the property's walled gardens (menus €45 to €55).

Fort Royal (☎ 074-915 8100; www.fortroyalhotel .com; s €110-125, d €150-165, cottages per week €550-750; ⏲ Easter-Oct; P) This exclusive waterside country house has 15 old-fashioned rooms, an excellent restaurant and rambling gardens that feel as old as the house, built in 1805. The grounds extend to a private beach, and also include a tennis court and minigolf. Dinner is available for residents only (three-course menu €45).

Ań Stad T-Bar (☎ 074-915 8798; Major's Row; dishes €4-10; 🕑 10am-7pm mid-Jun–Aug, Easter & Christmas) Home-baked fare including tasty potato cakes are served up at Sandra Daly's cheerful little cafe just off the main street. This is also where breakfast's served for guests at Sandra's B&B diagonally opposite. The B&B's four rooms (single/double from €35/70) are painted in tutti-frutti shades like bright raspberry, lime green and custard yellow. Two have private bath (though shy types should note that one bathroom doesn't have a door).

GETTING THERE & AWAY
The **Lough Swilly** (☎ 074-912 2863) bus from Letterkenny arrives in Rathmullan (€4.40, 45 minutes) once daily Monday to Friday, twice Saturday, en route to Milford.

Rathmelton
pop 1088
The first community you come to if you're approaching the peninsula from the east is Rathmelton (Ráth Mealtain, also sometimes called Ramelton), a picture-perfect spot with rows of Georgian houses and rough-walled stone warehouses curving along the River Lennon.

The **National Irish Bank** (The Mall), by the River Lennon, has a bureau de change. You'll find an ATM at the Esso petrol station, and another on Main St next to the general store. The **post office** (Castle St) is off the Mall.

SIGHTS
One of the restored riverside warehouses is home to the **Donegal Ancestry Family Research Centre & Heritage Centre** (☎ 074-915 1266; www.donegal ancestry.com; The Quay; adult/child €4/2; 🕑 9am-4.30pm Mon-Thu, 9am-4pm Fri), which has an exhibition on the history of Rathmelton, and also does genealogical research. It costs €15 for an initial consultation.

The ruined **Tullyaughnish Church**, on the hill, is also worth a visit because of the Romanesque carvings in the eastern wall, which were taken from a far older church on nearby Aughnish Island, on the River Lennon. Coming from Letterkenny turn right at the river and follow it round for about 400m.

SLEEPING & EATING
Lennon Lodge (☎ 074-915 1227; www.lennonlodge .com; Market Sq; s/d €30/60; P 🛜) Above a lemon-yellow pub with duck-egg-blue trim, all but

three rooms at this family-run B&B have private bath (prices for all rooms are the same, so specify your preference). There are laundry facilities and a large common room. The pub has live music Friday and Saturday nights, and regular darts competitions.

Frewin House (☎ 074-915 1246; www.frewinhouse .com; s €75-100, d €130-180, cottage per week €550; 🕑 closed Christmas; P) Guests congregate for candlelit communal dinners (€45 to €50) at this vine-covered Victorian manor. Three of its exquisite rooms have private bath, and the fourth has a bathroom nearby. Take care entering the tight driveway.

Tanyard (☎ 074-915 1029; www.thetanyard.com; Bridgend, Rathmelton; 1-/2-bedroom apt per week from €350/400; P) Water laps the stonework of this converted Georgian warehouse, which sits right on the river. Its stylish self-catering apartments sleep up to seven people.

Bridge Bar (☎ 074-915 1119; Bridgend; mains €18-24; 🕑 dinner) Just over the bridge, about 100m from downtown, the Bridge Bar is one of those lovely old country pubs you came to Ireland for. Its cosy 1st-floor restaurant has good seafood dishes, such as roasted swordfish.

GETTING THERE & AWAY
Lough Swilly (☎ 074-912 2863) buses connect Rathmelton with Letterkenny twice daily from Monday to Friday and once on Saturday (€2.75, 30 minutes).

INISHOWEN PENINSULA
The Inishowen (Inis Eoghain) Peninsula reaches just far enough into the Atlantic to qualify as the northernmost point on the island of Ireland: Malin Head. It is remote, rugged, desolate and sparsely populated, making it a special and quiet sort of place. Ancient sites and ruined castles abound, as do traditional thatched cottages that aren't yet demoted to storage sheds.

Surrounded by vast estuarine areas and open seas, the Inishowen Peninsula naturally attracts a lot of birdlife. The variety is tremendous, with well over 200 species passing through or residing permanently on the peninsula. Inishowen regularly receives well-travelled visitors from Iceland, Greenland and North America. Irregular Atlantic winds mean rare and exotic species also blow in from time to time. Twitchers should check out *Ireland's Birds*, by Eric Dempsey and Michael O'Clery, or visit www.birdsireland.com.

Moville & Around

pop 1427

Essentially a couple of roads meeting beside a harbour, Moville (Bun an Phobail) is an elegant spot where nearly every building is old and well kept. It can be rather sleepy, but on holiday weekends tourists flood the town. Moville was a busy port during the 19th and early 20th centuries, when thousands of emigrants set sail for America from here. The **coastal walkway** from Moville to Greencastle takes in the stretch of coast where the steamers used to moor, and also affords some rewarding **birdwatching** opportunities. There's **fishing** off the pier for mackerel, mullet and coalfish.

Main St has several banks with ATMs and the post office.

SIGHTS

By the gate of the Cooley gravehouse is an unusual 3m-high **cross**. Note the ringhole in its head – through it, the hands of negotiating parties are said to have clasped to seal an agreement. Whether they were uncommonly tall or stood on boxes remains a mystery. In the graveyard is the **Skull House**, which is associated with St Finian, the monk who accused Colmcille of plagiarising one of his manuscripts in the 6th century. He lived in a monastery here that was founded by St Patrick and survived into the 12th century.

Approaching Moville from the south, look out for a turning on the left that has a sign on the corner for the Cooley Pitch & Putt (minigolf). If you pass a church, you've gone

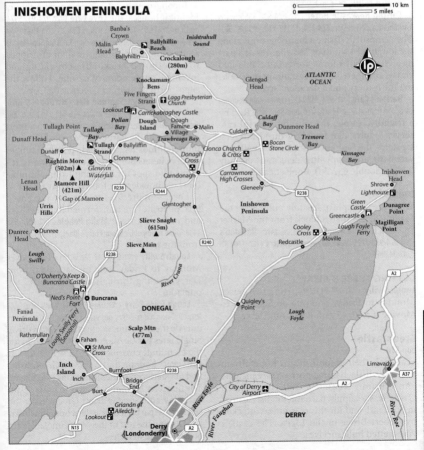

INISHOWEN PENINSULA

too far. The graveyard is just over 1km up this road on the right.

FESTIVALS

Summer sees a slew of music-oriented festivals, such the **Bob Dylan Festival** and the **Beatles Festival**, both held in July – check www.craicon.com for details.

SLEEPING & EATING

Moville Holiday Hostel (☎ 074-938 2378; Malin Rd; camping per person €10, dm €20, d €40; P) A private, unpaved road leads off the highway just west of town to a grove of trees and this secluded 20-bed hostel. It's in a nook-and-cranny-filled 18th-century farmhouse beside a river, with some gorgeous spots to pitch a tent. The owner is a fount of info on the area's rich history and folklore. Cash only.

Carlton Redcastle Hotel (☎ 074-938 5555; www.carltonredcastlehotel.ie; s €84-104, d €118-210; P ⏰ 🐾) The peninsula's flashiest luxury resort is along the lough, just south of Moville. Yes, it's part of a chain, but rooms are comfortable and classy, and there's a fine restaurant overlooking the estuary and a decadent spa.

Barron's Cafe (☎ 074-938 2472; Lower Main St; dishes €4-8; 🕙 9am-at least 7pm Easter–mid-Sep; 🛜) Run by a friendly couple, this cheap, cheerful cafe serves staples like freshly ground burgers. Upstairs, the four guestrooms, each with private bath, are happy little dens and very tidy (single/double €32/56). Book ahead.

DRINKING

There are a couple of friendly pubs along the Malin Rd, less than a block from the Market Sq, which have regular live music: **Rawdon's** (☎ 074-938 2225; Malin Rd) and **Rosato's** (☎ 074-938 2247; Malin Rd).

GETTING THERE & AWAY

Lough Swilly (☎ 074-912 2863) runs two buses Monday to Friday and one on Saturday to Moville (€6.60, 45 minutes) from Derry.

Greencastle
pop 530

Seals bob their smooth heads hopefully in the busy little fishing port of Greencastle (An Cáisleán Nua). The 1305-built Green Castle was a supply base for English armies in Scotland, and for this reason was attacked by Robert Bruce in the 1320s. The castle's vine-netted hulk survives.

A disarmingly eccentric collection of artefacts can be found at the **Inishowen Maritime Museum & Planetarium** (☎ 074-938 1363; www.inishowenmaritime.com; museum adult/child €5/3, museum & planetarium €10/6; 🕙 10am-5pm Mon-Sat, noon-5pm Sun Easter-Oct, 9am-5.15pm Mon-Fri Nov-Easter), in a former coastguard station next to the harbour. The most fascinating exhibits are from the sunken wrecks of Lough Foyle, including, in pride of place, a pair of perfectly preserved military-issue boxer shorts salvaged by marine archaeologists from a ditched WWII bomber. The demise of the Spanish Armada and the departure from these waters of Irish immigrants are two of the museums more compelling themes. Take care if visiting on a day when local children are testing their homemade rockets out front.

Incongruously set within a new estate of identikit houses, the **Cove Cafe** (☎ 074-932 5974; lunch mains €4.95-13, dinner mains €11-20; 🕙 10am-9pm Jun-Aug, noon-9pm Thu-Fri, 10am-9pm Sat & Sat Sep-May) is a surprisingly individualistic affair of stripped wood, exposed brick, alfresco seating and inventive contemporary cuisine. Follow the signs north of town to Greencastle Cove.

our pick **Kealy's Seafood Bar** (☎ 074-938 1010; lunch mains €8-14.50, dinner mains €16-50; 🕙 lunch Sun, dinner Fri-Sun) offers catches so fresh you almost have to fight the harbourside seals for it. The unpretentious nautical-style polished timber decor belies its numerous culinary awards. It's a splendid spot for anything from a humble bowl of chowder to a lobster extravaganza.

Local semiprecious stones (see the boxed text, opposite) are transformed into jewellery and unusual gifts at **Malin Pebbles** (☎ 074-938 1432; www.malinpebbles.com; Church Brae), 100m uphill from the ferry.

Lough Swilly (☎ 074-912 2863) has two buses Monday to Friday (one on Saturday) from Derry, passing through Greencastle (€7.90, one hour).

Lough Foyle Ferry (☎ 074-938 1901; www.loughfoyleferry.com) has a car-ferry service to Magilligan from outside the museum, saving you a 78km drive. Single fares per car/motorcycle/adult/child for the 15-minute crossing cost €12/7.50/2.20/1. It runs every hour on the hour from Greencastle, and at quarter past the hour from Magilligan. The first ferry is at 8am Monday to Friday, 9am Saturday and Sunday from Greencastle; the last ferry departs Greencastle at 6pm in winter, later during the rest of the year. Timetables are posted on the website.

Inishowen Head

A right turn outside Greencastle leads to Shrove; a sign indicating Inishowen Head is 1km along this road. It's possible to drive or cycle part of the way, but it's also an easy walk to the headland, from where you can see (on a clear day) the Antrim coast as far as the Giant's Causeway. A more demanding walk continues on to the sandy beach of **Kinnagoe Bay**.

Culdaff & Around

pop 155

Sheep vastly outnumber people around the secluded, resort village of Culdaff (Cúil Dabhcha) on the main Moville–Carndonagh road (R238).

Sheep now also wander the remains of the **Clonca church & cross**. Inside, an intricately carved tombstone sporting a sword and hurling-stick motif was erected by one Magnus MacOrristin. The carved lintel over the door is thought to come from an earlier church. Outside, the remains of the cross show the miracle of the loaves and fishes on the eastern face and geometric designs on the sides. Look for the turn-off to Culdaff, on the right if coming from Moville, on the left after about 6km if coming from Carndonagh. The Clonca church and cross are 1.5km on the right behind some farm buildings.

A necklace of around 30 prehistoric stones, called the **Bocan Stone Circle**, embroiders a farmer's field east of Clonca church. From Clonca, continue along the road until you reach a T-junction with a modern church facing you. Turn right here and after about 500m turn left (no sign). The Bocan Stone Circle is inside the first heather-covered field on the left.

The plain stumpy-armed **Carrowmore High Crosses** are all that remain of an ancient monastic site straddling a small lane. One is basically a decorated slab showing Christ and an angel, while the other is a taller, unadorned cross.

From Bocan Stone Circle and Clonca church, retrace the route back to the main Carndonagh–Moville road and turn left, then almost immediately right.

Culdaff has a Blue Flag beach that's great for **swimming** and **windsurfing**. From Bunagee Pier, **sea angling** and **diving** are popular – contact Geoff at Dive North (☎ 086 336 5699).

our pick **McGrory's of Culdaff** (☎ 074-937 9104; www.mcgrorys.ie; Culdaff; bar food €10.50-21, restaurant mains €15.50-22; ⏰ bar food 12.30-8pm, restaurant 6.30-9pm Tue-Sat, 1-3pm & 6-8.30pm Sun; P) is a raspberry-red village landmark. It's a good place to count sheep, with 17 spiffy rooms (single/double from €59/89) decorated with a contemporary eye. Before sleeping, however, head downstairs to catch live music in Mac's Backroom, which books international singer-songwriters and traditional music. McGrory's classic Irish cuisine is the best for miles around.

Malin Head

If you've already seen Ireland's southernmost point and its westernmost point, you'll still be impressed when you clap your eyes on Malin Head (Cionn Mhálanna), the island's northern extent. The head's rocky, weather-battered slopes feel like they're being dragged unwillingly into the sea. It's great for wandering on foot, absorbing the stark natural setting and pondering deep subjects as the wind tries to blow the clothes off your back. Bring cash with you, as there are no ATMs here.

On the northernmost tip, called **Banba's Crown** (Fíorcheann Éireann), stands a cumbersome cliff-top **tower** that was built in 1805 by the British admiralty and later used as a Lloyds signal station. Around it are unattractive concrete huts that were used by the Irish army in WWII as lookout posts. To the west from the fort-side car park, a path leads to **Hell's Hole**, a chasm where the incoming waters crash against the rocky formations. To the east a longer headland walk leads to the **Wee House of Malin**, a hermit's cave in the cliff face.

WASHED-UP TREASURES

Beachcombers will find more than empty shells along the Inishowen Peninsula. The area is renowned for its post-glacial strandlines, and its raised beaches continue to rise from the Ice Age. As a result, the beaches are littered with semiprecious stones: cornelian, agate, jasper and more. Good hunting grounds are the beaches along the northern coast of Malin Head, near Banba's Crown and Ballyhillin.

The stones make unique souvenirs, and you can buy these local treasures artfully polished and made into pendants, bracelets, earrings, brooches, candleholders and other quirky and beautiful items at the workshop of jeweller and craftsperson Petra Watzka at **Malin Pebbles** (opposite) in Greencastle.

COUNTY DONEGAL

Several endangered bird species thrive here. This is one of the few places in Ireland where you can still hear the call of the endangered corncrake in summer. Other birds to look out for are choughs, snow buntings and puffins.

The Plantation village of **Malin** (Málainn), on Trawbreaga Bay, 14km southeast of Malin Head, has a pretty movie-set quality. Walkers can head out from the tidy village green on a circular route that takes in **Knockamany Bens**, a local hill with terrific views, as well as **Lagg Presbyterian Church** (3km northwest from Malin), the oldest church still in use on the peninsula. The massive sand dunes at Five Fingers Strand, another 1km beyond the church, are a dog's dream.

SLEEPING & EATING

Sandrock Holiday Hostel (☎ 074-937 0289; www.sandrockhostel.com; Port Ronan Pier, Malin Head; dm €12, linen €1.50; P ⚭) The cinematically changing view from this IHH hostel – above a rocky bay on the western side of the headland – will take your breath away. Seafood can sometimes be bought straight off the boats out front. Inside you'll find 20 beds in two cosy dorms, musical instruments and laundry facilities. Bike rental (per day €10) is also available for nonguests, though you'll have to leave a deposit.

Malin Head Hostel (☎ 074-937 0309; www.malinheadhostel.com; Malin Head; dm/d €16/44; ☼ Mar–Oct; P) Owner Mary's great-great-grandfather built this farmhouse, which she's turned into a charming 20-bed IHH hostel. You can buy fruit and veggies straight from Mary's organic garden, eggs from her hens, and even carrageen moss (seaweed used as a gelatine substitute). Recipes for cooking up crab and lobster are stuck to the kitchen's fridge. If your batteries need recharging, ask Mary for a reflexology treatment (€35). There's a shop nearby and local buses stop at the hostel. No credit cards.

Malin Hotel (☎ 074-937 0606; www.malinhotel.ie; Malin; lunch mains €12-19, dinner menu €32.50; ☼ lunch & dinner; P ⚭) From the village green you'll first spot the old pub, but look beyond it and you'll also see a modern, boxlike hotel behind. Designer wallpapers adorn the lavish rooms (single/double from €90/150), and the pub-restaurant serves up good Irish standards. There's weekend entertainment.

DRINKING

McClean's (Malin) Easily spotted by the petrol pumps out front, this treasure of an old-time pub has the best craic in Malin and often has live music.

GETTING THERE & AROUND

The best way to approach Malin Head is by the R238/242 from Carndonagh, rather than up the eastern side from Culdaff.

Lough Swilly (☎ 074-912 2863) operates two buses Monday to Friday, three on Saturday, between Derry and Carndonagh (€7.40, 50 minutes).

Northwest Busways (☎ 074-938 2619) run connecting services from Carndonagh to Malin Head from Tuesday to Saturday.

Carndonagh
pop 1923

Carndonagh (Cardomhnach), surrounded by hills on three sides, is a busy commercial centre serving the local farming community. It's not a choice locale in these parts, but convenient for gathering information and provisions.

The locally run **Inishowen tourism office** (☎ 074-937 4933; www.visitinishowen.com; Chapel St; ☼ 9.30am-5pm Mon-Thu, 9.30am-4.30pm Fri year-round plus 11am-3pm Jun-Aug), southwest of the Diamond, also sells fishing licences. There are banks and an ATM on the Diamond; the post office is in the shopping centre halfway down Bridge St towards the Donagh Cross.

SIGHTS

Once an important ecclesiastical centre, Carndonagh has several early Christian stone monuments. The delightful 7th-century **Donagh Cross** stands under a shelter by an Anglican church at the Ballyliffin end of town. It's carved with a darling short-bodied, big-eyed figure of Jesus, smiling impishly. Flanking the cross are two small pillars, one showing a man, possibly Goliath, with a sword and shield, the other, David and his harp. In the graveyard there's a pillar with a carved marigold on a stem and nearby a crucifixion scene.

SLEEPING & EATING

Ashdale House (☎ 074-937 4017; www.ashdalehouse.net; s/d with bathroom €51/70, without €49/66; ☼ Mar-Nov; P ⚭) Carndonagh's best B&B is set on a working sheep farm, with other cute creatures including donkeys. A friendly family of seven share the lemon-yellow manor-style house with a clutch of stylish guestrooms. It's 1km out of town on the road towards Malin.

Simpson's (☎ 074-937 4499; Bridge St; mains €10.50-24; ✆ food served 12.30-9.30pm Mon-Sat, noon-9pm Sun) Dining options are few in Carndonagh — the solid surf, turf and international dishes at this busy bar, all made fresh on the premises, are your best bet.

GETTING THERE & AWAY
A **Lough Swilly** (☎ 074-912 2863) bus leaves Buncrana for Carndonagh (€5.40, 45 minutes) twice from Monday to Friday, once on Saturday.

Ballyliffin & Clonmany
pop 700

These two quaint villages and their surrounds have plenty to occupy visitors for a day or two. Both have post offices but no banks.

About 1km north of Ballyliffin (Baile Lifin) is the lovely, sandy expanse of **Pollan Strand**, but the crashing breakers make it unsafe for swimming. A walk north along the dunes brings you to **Doagh Island** (now part of the mainland),

where the matchbox ruin of 16th-century **Carrickbraghey Castle** (Carraic Brachaide) is continually battered by the ocean. Also here is the enthusiastically thrown-together **Doagh Famine Village** (☎ 074-937 8078; www.doaghfaminevillage .com; Doagh Island; adult/child €7/5; ✆ 10am-5.30pm Easter-late Sep & Christmas period), set in a reconstructed village of thatched cottages. Call ahead to book its tour, packed with entertaining titbits about a disappearing way of life, and insightful comparisons with famine-stricken countries today. In the lead-up to Christmas a cute 'Santa Village' sets up here.

The other beach is at **Tullagh Strand**. Although swimming's possible, the current can be strong and it isn't recommended when the tide's going out.

An 800m trail leads to the cascading 10m **Glenevin Waterfall**, with benches and picnic tables, and some fantastic walking into the mountainous landscape beyond. From Clonmany, follow the road signed to Tullagh Bay, cross the river and bear right at an inter-

---

WALK: GLENEVIN WATERFALL & RAGHTIN MORE

For tremendous panoramas, you can combine a visit to picturesque Glenevin Waterfall with a steady climb to the wild quartzite summit of Raghtin More (502m). Allow four hours for this 11km route.

From the waterfall, there are two options. Either locate a faint path that climbs steeply out of the eastern side of the gorge, around 10m back from the waterfall. Clamber up the steep peaty slope and cross a 50m section of heather to join a track. Alternatively, if the slope seems too steep for your liking, retrace your route downstream and take the first right at a junction of paths. This path climbs more gently over a lower part of the gorge wall, and will lead you to the same track.

Wherever you join the track, turn right and follow it as it climbs gradually southwest. Firm ground soon gives way to marshy terrain, and at times the track is more like a corridor of reeds and spongy mosses. The western edge of the track generally offers the firmest ground. Continue past a fenced area and climb until you are roughly level with the summit of Raghtin More, to the west. Leave the track here and head west, descending slightly to cross a stream before commencing the climb up the heather-clad slopes beyond.

Arc around to the northwest as you climb, aiming for the col between Raghtin More and Crockmain. Views over Mamore Gap and the Urris Hills become more extensive as you gain height. Heather begins to give way to jumbles of sharp quartzite as you near the wide summit plateau (2½ hours from the start). A high ring of rocks makes for a prominent summit cairn, although the views are better from the trig point, which is 50m to the west. From here, the sweeping panorama embraces Malin Head to the northeast, the Urris Hills to the southwest and a maze of coastal inlets backed by the profiles of north Donegal's mountains beyond.

Descend relatively steep ground northeast from the summit to the col between Raghtin More and Raghtin Beg. The summit of Raghtin Beg (418m) is a short distance to the north and can be readily visited for more good views, especially across the sandy beach at Tullagh Bay. Return to the col and begin to descend through short heather, heading for the fenced area beside the track that you passed on the outward journey. Cross the stream in front of the enclosure, turn left at the track, and follow this back to the car park at the start of the walk.

section. Butler's Bridge and the waterfall car park are about 1km further on.

With two championship courses, **Ballyliffin Golf Club** (☎ 074-937 6119; www.ballyliffingolfclub.com; Ballyliffin; green fees weekday/weekend Old Links €75/80, Glashedy €80/90; ☺ restaurant lunch & dinner) is among the best places to golf in Donegal. The scenery is so beautiful that it can distract even the most focused golfer. Its above-average restaurant, Linx, overlooks the fairways (mains €9.50 to €20).

SLEEPING & EATING

Tullagh Bay Camping & Caravan Park (☎ 074-937 8997; Tullagh Bay; campsites from €14; ☺ Easter-Sep) About 5km from Clonmany, this flat, windswept park is ideal for the bucket-and-spade brigade as it's just behind the vast, dune-backed Tullagh Strand.

our pick **Glen House** (☎ 074-937 6745; www.glenhouse.ie; Straid, Clonmany; menus from €17, ☺ tearoom 10am-6pm daily Jun-Aug, Sat & Sun Sep-May, restaurant lunch Sun, dinner Tue-Sun Jun-Aug, lunch Sun dinner Thu-Sun Sep-May) In a sparkling white manor house, the welcome couldn't be friendlier or more professional at this gem of a guesthouse (singles €40 to €80, doubles €70 to €90). Its eight airy rooms look like they've been decorated for an interior-design magazine spread, and two have stunning sea views. The walking trail to Glenevin Waterfall starts next door to the tearoom, which opens to a timber deck. From September to May there's a minimum two-night stay.

Ballyliffin Lodge (☎ 074-937 8200; www.ballyliffinlodge.com; s/d €120/250; P ☺ ☺) This elegant 40-room hotel has ultraspacious autumn-hued rooms. An extra €35 gets you a sublime view over the ocean. You can treat yourself at the state-of-the-art spa, golf course, sophisticated Holly Tree Restaurant (mains €16 to €26.50), or in the laidback Mamie Pat's (bar food €11.50 to €22.50).

GETTING THERE & AWAY

Lough Swilly (☎ 074-912 2863) buses run twice Monday to Friday, once Saturday, between Clonmany and Carndonagh (€2.50, 20 minutes).

Clonmany to Buncrana

There are two routes from Clonmany to Buncrana: the scenic coastal road via the Gap of Mamore and Dunree Head, and the speedier inland road (R238). The **Gap of Mamore** (elevation 262m) descends dramatically between Mamore Hill and Croaghcarragh on its way to Dunree (An Dún Riabhach), where the **Fort Dunree military museum** (☎ 074-936 1817; www.dunree.pro.ie; adult/child €6/4; ☺ 10.30am-6pm Mon-Sat, 1-6pm Sun Jun-Sep, 10.30am-4.30pm Mon-Fri, 1-6pm Sat & Sun Oct-May) sits on a rocky outcrop in a 19th-century fort. It's a beautiful spot. If the guns don't impress you, the scenery and birdlife will.

Buncrana
pop 3411

On the tame side of the peninsula, Buncrana (Bun Cranncha) is a busy but appealing town with its fair share of pubs and a 5km sandy beach on the shores of Lough Swilly.

INFORMATION

Bank of Ireland (Lower Main St) ATM and bureau de change.

Post office (Upper Main St)

Tourist office (☎ 074-936 2600; Derry Rd; ☺ Jun-Sep; hr vary annually) One kilometre south of the town centre.

Ulster Bank (Upper Main St) ATM and bureau de change.

Valu Clean (☎ 074-936 2570; Lower Main St; laundry from €6.60) Laundry service.

SIGHTS

At the northern end of the seafront, the early 18th-century, six-arched Castle Bridge leads to **O'Doherty's Keep**, a tower house built by the O'Dohertys, the local chiefs, in 1430. It was burned by the English and then rebuilt for their own use. At its side is the manorlike **Buncrana Castle**, built in 1718 by John Vaughan, who also constructed the bridge; Wolfe Tone was imprisoned here following the unsuccessful French invasion in 1798. Walking 500m further from the keep (turn left and stick to the shoreline) brings you to **Ned's Point Fort** (1812), built by the British and now under siege from graffiti artists.

SLEEPING & EATING

Tullyarvan Mill (☎ 074-936 1613; www.tullyarvanmill.com; Carndonagh Rd; dm/d/q €18/50/60; P) This excellent purpose-built hostel was recently attached to the historic Tullyarvan Mill. Amid riverside gardens, the mill also incorporates an inexpensive restaurant (open for breakfast, lunch and dinner, dishes from €5) and regular cultural events and art exhibits. Head north out of town on the R238 and follow the signs.

Lake of Shadows Hotel (☎ 074-936 1005; www.lakeofshadows.com; Grianán Park; s €40, d €90-100; P) A fine rose-coloured Victorian facade brings to mind past generations coming to 'take the sea air' at this 23-room hotel. Alas, while rooms are attractive, some have an unfortunate rising damp problem. The location is lovely, though, and staff helpful. Meals are available, with mains from €11 to €24. From Main St, head down Church St towards the bay.

our pick Beach House (☎ 074-936 1050; The Pier, Swilly Rd; lunch mains €6.50-17.50, dinner mains €16-26; ☻ 5pm-late Tue-Fri, noon-late Sat & Sun) With plate-glass windows facing the lough, this aptly named cafe/restaurant projects an elegant simplicity. Although the menu is also intrin-sically simple, the quality and preparation are a cut above: 'surf and turf', for example, comes with fillet steak, crab claws, langoustines and creamy bisque.

ENTERTAINMENT
Dating from 1792, the spearmint-and-moss-green **Atlantic Bar** (☎ 074-932 0880; Upper Main St) is Buncrana's oldest and most atmos-pheric pub.

GETTING THERE & AROUND
From Buncrana, **Lough Swilly** (☎ 074-912 2863) buses run several times daily to Derry and less often to Carndonagh.

The **Lough Swilly Ferry** (☎ 074-938 1901; www .loughfoyleferry.com) usually runs from Buncrana to Rathmullan (30 minutes) from mid-June to September, however, the continuation of this service was in doubt at the time of re-search – check for updates.

South of Buncrana
FAHAN
A monastery was founded in Fahan by St Colmcille in the 6th century. Among its ruins is the beautifully carved, 7th-century **St Mura Cross** in the graveyard beside the church. Each face is decorated with a cross, in intricate Celtic weave, and the barely discernible Greek inscription is the only one known from this early Christian period.

GRIANÁN OF AILEÁCH
This amphitheatre-like stone **fort** (admission free; ☻ 10am-6pm; **P**) encircles the top of Grianán Hill like a halo, 18km south of Buncrana near Burt, signposted off the N13. Locals open the gate each day, giving visitors the chance to take in eye-popping views of the surrounding loughs and all the way to Derry. Its mini-arena can resemble a circus whenever a tour bus rolls up and spills its load inside the 4m-thick walls.

The fort may have existed at least 2000 years ago, but it's thought that the site itself goes back to pre-Celtic times as a temple to the god Dagda. Between the 5th and 12th centuries it was the seat of the O'Neills, before being demolished by Murtogh O'Brien, king of Munster. Most of what you see now is a re-construction built between 1874 and 1878.

The merry-go-round-shaped **Burt Church** at the foot of the hill was modelled on the fort by Derry architect Liam McCormack and built in 1967.

INCH ISLAND
Few tourists make it to residential Inch Island, accessible from the mainland by a causeway, but it's worth a detour for its birdlife (espe-cially swans), two small beaches and remains of an old fort. **Inch Island Stables** (☎ 074-936 0335) organises horse-riding lessons and trips around the island.

Lenamore Stables (☎ 074-938 4022; www.lenamore stables.com), on the mainland in Muff, can also set you up for hacking in the area.

The Midlands

Rarely explored by those on their first visit to Ireland and wonderfully free of tour buses and souvenir stalls, the Midlands – the counties of Laois, Offaly, Roscommon, Leitrim, Longford, and Westmeath – may not have the scenic drama or sophisticated cities of coastal Ireland, but it's brimming with verdant pastoral landscapes, stately homes, archaeological remains and sleepy towns where the locals are genuinely glad to see you. The Midlands took longer than most parts to feel the effects of Ireland's economic boom, but its towns and cities have grown just as chaotically as elsewhere. The financial crisis has also taken its toll, but the locals aren't giving up their skinny lattes just yet.

The region is dominated by the River Shannon, which meanders through fields and forests, drawing boaters and fishers in hoards. Plush hotels and gourmet restaurants have sprung up along its banks, making it a wonderfully scenic and surprisingly cosmopolitan way to travel. The river drew early settlers to the area: the incredible Celtic site at Cruachan Aí is one of Europe's most significant, and the early Christians created Ireland's most magnificent monastic site at Clonmacnoise.

Outside the main centres, the Midlands is a wonderful place to get lost. It's one of the last regions in Ireland where you can wander into the local village shop-cum-pub/undertaker's/garage/post office and find it little changed from decades ago. If you're in search of a genuine slice of rural Irish life, this area makes the perfect retreat.

HIGHLIGHTS

- **Kick Back and Relax** Slow down a gear and discover the rolling landscapes along the banks of the Shannon–Erne Waterway at Carrick-on-Shannon (p521)

- **Backtrack** Discover the Iron Age oak track-way unearthed at Corlea in County Longford's bog land (p524)

- **Ecclesiastical Wonder** Contemplate the lost land of saints and scholars at Ireland's finest monastic site, Clonmacnoise (p511)

- **Pile on the Pounds** Enjoy the rising reputation of gourmet Ireland along the banks of the Shannon (p523), especially in Athlone and Carrick-on-Shannon

- **Georgian Gentility** Roam the tree-lined streets and explore the castle grounds before dropping in on a traditional session in elegant Birr (p507)

★ Carrick-on-Shannon

★ Corlea

★ Athlone

★ Clonmacnoise

★ Birr

- **POPULATION: 339,400**
- **AREA: 10,782 SQ KM**

COUNTY LAOIS

ittle-visited Laois (pronounced leash) is often verlooked as drivers zoom past to sexier ites in the west. Away from the main roads, hough, is a real hidden corner of Ireland, where historic towns and the unspoiled lieve Bloom Mountains squeeze in between patchwork of rivers and walkways.

For all you need to know about the county, heck out www.laoistourism.ie and pick up he excellent *Laois Heritage Trail* booklet at ourist offices, which does a good job of tying ogether the county's history. The handsome eritage town of Abbeyleix makes a much bet-er base than the busy but workaday county own of Portlaoise.

ABBEYLEIX
op 1568

Abbeyleix (abbey-*leeks*) is a pretty heritage own with a Georgian market house, grace-ul terraced housing and a wide leafy main treet. The town grew up around a 12th-entury Cistercian monastery, but problems with frequent flooding led local 18th-century andowner Viscount de Vesci to level the vil-age and create a new, planned estate town in he present location. During the Famine, de Vesci proved a kinder landlord than many, and the fountain obelisk in the square was rected as a thank you from his tenants.

The town's Georgian character remains in-act despite a near-constant flow of traffic. A bypass, which is due to open in late 2010, will ransform the town and return it to its former glory. Abbeyleix makes a good base for explor-ng Laois, with its wonderful food and accom-nodation options and a chance to sip a pint in one of Ireland's most atmospheric pubs.

Sights

In an old school building at the northern end of Main St is **Heritage House** (☎ 057-873 1653; www.heritagehousemuseum.com; adult/child €3/2.50; ☻ 9am-5pm Mon-Fri year-round & 1-5pm Sat & Sun May-Sep; **P**), a museum and tourist office that de-tails the town's colourful history. One room looks at the town's carpet-making legacy: the Turkish-influenced carpets once made here were chosen to grace the floors of the *Titanic*, but the factory closed soon after the ill-fated liner's demise.

In the town centre, the elegant 1836 **Market House** has been restored and now houses a library and exhibition space. Unfortunately for visitors, de Vesci's magnificent mansion, **Abbeyleix House**, is in private ownership and is not open to the public. Designed by James Wyatt in 1773, it's an elegant mansion set in roaming parklands 2km southwest of town.

Southeast of town, the lavish **Heywood Gardens** (☎ 057-873 3563; www.heritageireland.ie; ad-mission free; ☻ 8.30am-9pm May-Aug, to 7pm Apr & Sep, to 5.30pm Oct-Mar; **P**) were landscaped by Edwin Lutyens and Gertrude Jekyll and were com-pleted in 1912. The centrepiece is a sunken garden, where circular terraces lead down to an oval pool with a magnificent fountain. The gardens are 7km southeast of Abbeyleix, off the R432 to Ballinakill, in the grounds of Heywood Community School.

Garden lovers should also make their way to the **Abbey Sense Gardens** (☎ 057-873 1325; Dove House, Main St; admission by donation; ☻ 9am-4pm Mon-Fri year-round & 2-6pm Sat & Sun Jun-Sep; **P**). Set in the walled gar-dens of a Brigidine convent, the vibrant plant-ing, wind chimes, humming stone and fragrant blooms aim to stimulate all the senses.

Sleeping & Eating

Farran House Farm Hostel (☎ 057-873 4032; www .farmhostel.com; dm €20; **P**) In a beautifully re-stored limestone grain loft on a working fam-ily farm, this quirky independent hostel has 45 beds in rooms with a bathroom and up to five bunks. When you call, ask for direc-tions and about the possibility of meals, as the hostel is well secluded, about 6km west of Abbeyleix.

Sandymount House (☎ 057-873 1063; www.abbey leix.info; Oldtown; s/d €65/100; **P**) Once the home of the de Vesci estate manager, this lovely old country house has been beautifully re-stored to seamlessly blend modern style with period features. A grand sweeping staircase, marble fireplaces and mature gardens give it an elegant charm, while the spacious rooms are equipped with flat-screen TVs and indi-vidually designed bathrooms. Sandymount House is 2km from Abbeyleix down the R433 towards Rathdowney.

Preston House (☎ 057-873 1432; www.prestonhouse .ie; Main St; d €130, dinner mains €15-27; ☎) A restored Georgian town house on the main street, the grand rooms here are decked out in period style, with dark elegant furniture, big, comfy beds and lashings of charm. The restaurant follows the same lines and is a popular lunch

THE MIDLANDS

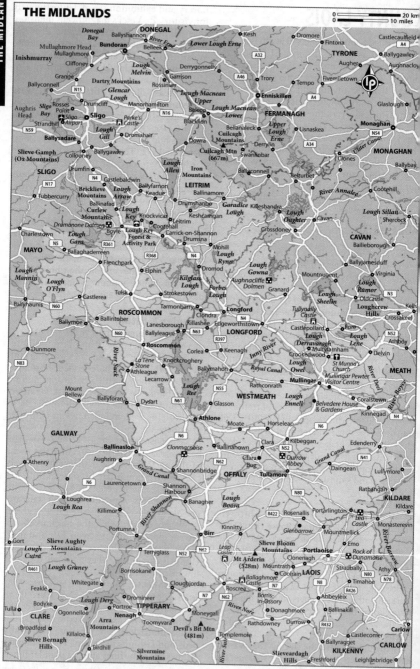

and dinner venue, serving an excellent choice of stylish European dishes.

Cafe Odhráan (☎ 057-875 7380; Main St; dishes €4-8; ✆ 9.30am-5.30pm Mon-Sat) Small and cosy, with a warm, friendly atmosphere, this simple little place serves up a tempting selection of salads, quiches, crostini, panini and wraps, as well as homemade cakes and scones. Ingredients are locally sourced and include such delicacies as Ballacolla blue brie and Mossfield goat's cheese.

Morrissey's (☎ 057-873 1281; Main St) This half-pub, half-shop is one of those increasingly rare places that has withstood the onslaught of modernisation. Ancient biscuit tins, jars of sweets, boxes of tea and a hodgepodge of oddities line the shelves above the pew seats and pot-belly stove. It's a wonderful place to soak up the atmosphere while you cradle a pint at the sloping counter.

Getting There & Away

Abbeyleix is on the Bus Éireann route to Dublin (€13, 1¾ hours) via Portlaoise, and Cork (€13, 2¾ hours) via Cashel and Cahir. There are six buses each way daily.

DURROW
pop 811

Another planned estate village, Durrow's neat rows of houses, pubs and cafes surround a manicured green. On the western side stands the imposing gateway to the 18th-century **Castle Durrow** (☎ 057-873 6555; www.castledurrow.com; d from €250; ℗), one of Ireland's top country-house hotels. The rooms here vary from opulent suites with four-poster beds and heavy brocades to more intimate oriental-style rooms. Even if you can't stay overnight, it's worth popping in for a coffee on the terrace overlooking the vast grounds. The excellent **restaurant** (5-course set menu €55; ✆ 7-8.45pm) is supplied by the castle's organic kitchen garden.

Durrow is 10km south of Abbeyleix and is accessible by bus (€3.40, 10 minutes, six buses daily in each direction).

SLIEVE BLOOM MOUNTAINS

One of the best reasons for visiting Laois is to explore the Slieve Bloom Mountains. Although not as spectacular as some Irish ranges, their sudden rise from a great plain and the absence of visitors make them highly attractive. You'll get a real sense of being away from it all as you tread the deserted blanket bogs, moorland, pine forests and isolated valleys.

The highest point is Mt Arderin (528m), south of the Glendine Gap on the Offaly border, from where, on a clear day, it's possible to see the highest points of all four of the ancient provinces of Ireland. East is Lugnaquilla in Leinster; west is Nephin in Connaught; north is Slieve Donard in Ulster; and southwest is Carrantuohil in Munster.

For leisurely walking, **Glenbarrow**, southwest of Rosenallis, has an interesting trail by the cascading River Barrow. Other spots to check out are **Glendine Park**, near the Glendine Gap, and the **Cut mountain pass**.

For something more challenging, you could try the **Slieve Bloom Way**, a 77km signposted trail that does a complete circuit of the mountains, taking in most major points of interest. The recommended starting point is the car park at Glenbarrow, 5km from Rosenallis, from where the trail follows tracks, forest firebreaks and old roads around the mountains. The trail's highest point is at Glendine Gap (460m).

You can walk alone or join a guided walk organised by the **Slieve Bloom Walking Club** (☎ 086 278 9147; www.slievebloom.ie; per person €5; ✆ Sun May-Nov). The website has lots of information on a variety of walks in the mountains and is a good place for initial planning. Alternatively, pick up a *Laois Walks Pack* at local tourist offices.

DETOUR: POVERTY'S LAST STOP AT DONAGHMORE

The farm village of Donaghmore is home to a grim survivor of the Famine. The **Donaghmore Workhouse** (☎ 086-829 6685; www.donaghmoremuseum.com; adult/child €5/3; ✆ 11am-5pm Mon-Fri, 2-5pm Sat & Sun Jun-Sep) opened as a last resort for the destitute in 1853. Conditions were intentionally grim, the idea being that if things were especially bad, the poor wouldn't stick around. Overcrowding was rife, families were separated, meals (no more than a bowl of gruel) were taken in silence, toilets were crude and bedding was limited. The loss of dignity that came with entering the workhouse was a tragic reality for many. It was a horrible time, recorded in a chilling fashion at this small museum. The workhouse is just off the R435, 20km west of Durrow.

GETTING AROUND LAOIS

Although the county town of Portlaoise does not merit a visit in itself, it's a useful transport hub. Direct trains run from Portlaoise to Dublin (€21.50, one hour, 12 daily); Cork (€20 to €44, two hours, three daily); and Limerick (€28.50, 1½ hours, five daily).

Bus Éireann runs frequent buses on three main routes from Portlaoise: to Cork (€11.70, three hours, six daily) via Abbeyleix, Cashel and Cahir; to Dublin (€11, 1½ hours, 12 daily) via Kildare city; and along the N7 to Limerick (€9.90, 2¼ hours, 12 daily) via Mountrath, Borris-in-Ossory and Roscrea.

JJ Kavanagh & Sons (☎ 081-833 3222; www.jjkavanagh.ie) runs two buses per day Monday to Saturday from Portlaoise to Carlow (€7.50, 70 minutes) and three to Limerick (€9, two hours).

For accommodation, Mountrath, to the south, and Kinnitty, to the northwest, are good bases. For something a little more regal, you could try **Ballaghmore Castle** (☎ 0505-21453; www.castleballaghmore.com; Ballaghmore; adult/child €5/3; ⏰ 10am-5pm), a 15th-century tower house with heavy, creaking wooden doors, cold stone walls and a mysterious sheila-na-gig. You can just take a look around, rent the whole place for a weekend (€2000), or stay in the grounds at **Manor Guest House** (per person from €60) or the self-catering **Rose Cottage** (per week €500). The castle is 3km west of Borris-in-Ossory.

Although there is no public transport across the Slieve Blooms, buses do stop in the nearby towns of Mountrath and Rosenallis.

MOUNTRATH & AROUND
pop 1435

A once-prosperous 18th-century linen centre, Mountrath is a low-key village, where the week's highlight is the cattle market. Both St Patrick and St Brigid are supposed to have established religious houses here, although no trace of either remains.

Today, the local place of pilgrimage is the 6th-century monastery of St Fintan at Clonenagh, 3km east of Mountrath on the Portlaoise road. Its claim to fame is **St Fintan's Tree**, a large sycamore; the water that collects in the groove in one of its lower branches is said to have healing properties.

Ballyfin House (8km north of Mountrath) is an architectural treasure, designed by Richard Morrison in 1850. Used for years as a college, work began (and was then suspended due to the credit crunch) on a painstaking restoration in order to transform the mansion into a luxury hotel. The original target date for completion was 2010 but it's likely it'll be at least a year behind schedule.

Instead, head for our pick **Roundwood House** (☎ 057-873 2120; www.roundwoodhouse.com; Slieve Blooms Rd; s/d from €110/170; ⏰ Feb-Dec; P ⏰), a lush country estate, family home and hotel where you'll feel like you're a family friend rather than a paying guest. Set in secluded woods, the rooms in this beautiful 17th-century Palladian villa are all elegantly decorated, but have a definite lived-in feel. Children will love all the outdoor space and the friendly dogs, and the communal dinner (€50 per person) is a chance to meet the amiable owners and enjoy a country treat of local foods. Try to get a room in the main house for the best atmosphere and value.

Mountrath is on the main Bus Éireann Dublin–Limerick route, with up to 14 buses daily in each direction.

MOUNTMELLICK
pop 2872

A quiet Georgian town on the River Owenass, Mountmellick was renowned for its linen production in the 19th century and owes much of its history to its Quaker settlers.

A 4km looped and signed **heritage trail**, beginning in the square, leads you on a walking tour of the most important landmarks. For an insight into the town's Quaker and industrial heritage, visit **Mountmellick Museum** (☎ 057-862 4525; Irishtown; adult/child €5/2; ⏰ 9am-1pm & 2-5pm Mon-Thu, to 4pm Fri), where you can also see a display of superbly subtle Mountmellick embroidery. Various linens and quilts still being made by locals are on sale here.

Mountmellick is on the N80, 10km north of Portlaoise.

PORTARLINGTON
pop 6004

Portarlington grew up under the influence of French Huguenot and German settlers and has some fine, but neglected, 18th-century buildings along French and Patrick Sts. The 1851 **St Paul's Church** (admission free; ⏰ 7am-7pm), on the site of the original 17th-century French church, was built for the Huguenots, some of whose tombstones stand in a corner of the churchyard. Portarlington is about 18km northwest of Portlaoise.

About 4km east of town are the impressive ivy-covered ruins of 13th-century **Lea Castle** on the banks of the River Barrow, once the stronghold of Maurice Fitzgerald, second Baron of Offaly. The castle consists of a fairly intact towered keep with two outer walls and a twin-towered gatehouse. Access is through a farmyard, 500m to the north off the main Monasterevin road (R420).

EMO COURT

The unusual, green-domed **Emo Court** (☎ 057-862 6573; www.heritageireland.ie; Emo; adult/child €3/1, grounds free; ☑ 10am-6pm Easter-Oct, last admission 5pm, grounds open daylight hr year-round) is an impressive house, designed in 1790 by James Gandon, architect of Dublin's Custom House (p116). It was originally the country seat of the first Earl of Portarlington. After many years as a Jesuit noviciate, the house, with its elaborate central rotunda, was impressively restored.

The extensive grounds, littered with Greek statues, contain over 1000 different trees, including huge sequoias, and shrubs from all over the world. Enjoy a picnic or a long walk through the woodlands to Emo Lake.

Emo is about 13km northeast of Portlaoise, just off the R422, 2km west of the M7.

ROCK OF DUNAMAISE

The **Rock of Dunamaise** (admission free; ☑ daylight hr; **P**) is an arresting sight: a craggy limestone outcrop rising dramatically out of the flat plains. The rock offered early settlers a superb natural defensive position with sweeping views across the surrounding countryside. It was first fortified in the Bronze Age and was recorded on Ptolemy's map of AD 140.

Over the centuries that followed, successive waves of Viking, Norman, Irish and English invaders fought over its occupation and control. The ruins you see today are those of a castle built in the 13th century. It was extensively remodelled in the 15th century and finally destroyed by Cromwell's henchmen in 1650.

You'll need some imagination to envisage the site as it once was, but the views from the summit are breathtaking on a clear day. If you're lucky, you'll be able to see Timahoe

round tower to the south, the Slieve Blooms to the west and the Wicklow Mountains to the east.

The rock is situated 6km east of Portlaoise along the Stradbally road (N80). **Portlaoise Taxi Service** (☎ 057-866 2270) will take you out there for about €25 return.

STRADBALLY
pop 1056

Strung out along the N80, the pretty village of Stradbally, 10km southeast of Portlaoise, is home to the annual **Electric Picnic** (www.elec tricpicnic.ie; 3-day pass €240), an open-air music festival held over three days in early September. Known for its eclectic line up, quality services and more mature attitude, it's attracted the likes of Björk, Jarvis Cocker, Sigur Rós, Franz Ferdinand and the Sex Pistols over the years.

Appealing to a rather different crowd, the **Stradbally Steam Museum** (☎ 057-864 1878; www .irishsteam.ie; admission €5; ☑ 2-5pm Sun or by arrangement) is a haven for steam enthusiasts, with a collection of lovingly restored fire engines, steam tractors and steamrollers. During the August bank-holiday weekend, the museum hosts a two-day rally where the 40-hectare estate of Stradbally Hall is taken over by steam-operated machinery and vintage cars. Visitors can also take a short trip on the **narrow-gauge railway** (admission varies; ☑ 2.30-5pm Sun & Mon bank holiday weekends only Easter-Oct) on the estate.

If you fancy staying in the area, **Tall Trees B&B** (☎ 057-862 5412; epcon@02.ie; Cork Rd; s €47-55, d €70-90; ☑ Feb-Oct; **P**) is a very friendly place, with simple, tranquil rooms in a modern house.

JJ Kavanagh & Sons (☎ 081-833 3222; www.jjkavanagh .ie) runs buses from Portlaoise to Carlow that pass through Stradbally (€5, 15 minutes, two daily Monday to Saturday).

Stradbally is also on the Bus Éireann Waterford–Longford service (two buses daily Monday to Saturday, one Sunday), which passes through Kilkenny, Carlow, Portlaoise (€3.50, 15 minutes) and Athlone.

TIMAHOE
pop 500

Tiny Timahoe casts a real charm, even if the village is nothing more than a handful of houses fronting a grassy triangle. Screened by a babbling stream and seemingly straight out of a fairy tale, is a tilting 30m-tall, 12th-century **round tower**. The tower, with its

THE GRAND & ROYAL CANALS

After much debate about linking Dublin to the Shannon by water, work began on the Grand Canal in 1757. The project was beset by problems from the start and encountered huge difficulties and delays. In the meantime, commercial rivals hatched a plan for the competing Royal Canal. The two canals revolutionised transport in Ireland in the early 19th century, but their heyday was short lived, as they were soon superseded by the railways. Today the canals are popular for cruising and fishing, and make wonderfully gentle territory for walking and cycling, with plenty of pretty villages along their banks.

Waterways Ireland (www.waterwaysireland.org) and the **Inland Waterways Association of Ireland** (www.iwai.ie) have a wealth of information on the canals. The former publishes *Ireland's Waterways, Map and Directory*. Other useful guides include the *Guide to the Grand Canal of Ireland* and the *Guide to the Royal Canal of Ireland,* both sold in tourist offices and bookshops in the region.

Grand Canal

The Grand Canal threads its way from Dublin through Tullamore to join the River Shannon at Shannonbridge (p511), a total of 131km in all. Along the way, the canal passes through relatively unpopulated countryside, with bogs, picturesque villages and 43 finely crafted locks lining the journey. Near the village of Sallins in County Kildare, the graceful seven-arched **Leinster Aqueduct** carries the canal across the River Liffey.

From nearby Robertstown (p180), a 45km spur turns south to join the River Barrow at the pretty town of Athy (p183).

Huge engineering difficulties, including the riddle of how to cross the Bog of Allen (p181), meant that the canal took 23 years to build. Passenger services continued until the 1850s and there was a trickle of commercial traffic until 1960.

For detailed information on the section of the canal between Robertstown and Lullymore, see p180.

Royal Canal

Fourteen years behind the Grand Canal and duplicating its purpose, the 145km Royal Canal was always a loss maker. It follows Kildare's northern border, flowing over a massive **aqueduct** near Leixlip, before it joins the River Shannon at Clondra (or Cloondara) in County Longford.

The canal has become a popular amenity for thousands of residents along the north Kildare commuter belt and, although the towpaths are open all the way to the Shannon, the canal itself is navigable only as far as Ballymahon in County Longford. Restoration continues and the final 18km to Clondra should reopen in 2010. It will then be possible to follow a triangular route from Dublin along the Royal Canal or the Grand Canal to the Shannon and back.

Barges & Boats

The canals offer a relaxing way to drift across the country in warmer months; you can hire narrow boats at several locations. Two-/six-berth boats cost from €892/1670 per week in September and about €992/1880 per week in July and August, but rates vary widely.

Both **Barrowline Cruisers** (☎ 057-862 660; www.barrowline.ie; Vicarstown Inn, Vicarstown, Co Laois) and **Canalways** (☎ 087 243 3879; www.canalways.ie; Spencer Bridge, Rathangan, Co Kildare) have boats for hire along the Grand Canal and River Barrow. Banagher (p510) is also a good place for Grand Canal rentals.

At the time of writing, there were no operators offering boats on the Royal Canal.

Walking the Towpaths

Canal towpaths are ideal for leisurely walkers and there are numerous access points along both canals. A variety of leaflets detailing the paths can be picked up at most regional tourist offices and you'll find information on suggested routes and descriptions of the trails on www.iwai.ie. Waterways Ireland is also a good source of information on the towpaths.

unusual carved Romanesque doorway high up on the side, is part of an ancient site that includes the ruins of a 15th-century church. The entire place has a certain magical quality, enhanced by a dearth of visitors.

Timahoe is 13km southeast of Portlaoise on the R426.

COUNTY OFFALY

Apart from the magnificent ecclesiastical city of Clonmacnoise, the green and watery county of Offaly doesn't feature on many tourists' itineraries, but this hidden gem of Ireland is also home to atmospheric Georgian towns, numerous castles and a burgeoning foodie culture.

Clonmacnoise, a monastic site overlooking the Shannon, is one of Ireland's most famous sights and a must-see attraction. But beyond this busy corner of Offaly, there's a county steeped in history, where the wonderful heritage town of Birr, with its excellent food and accommodation options, makes a rewarding base.

Geographically, Offaly is dominated by low-lying bogs. Enormous expanses like the Bog of Allen and the Boora Bog, where peat is extracted on an industrial scale, are horribly scarred. However, in the north of the county, Clara Bog is remarkably untouched and is recognised internationally for its plant and animal life. It's under consideration for Unesco recognition.

The rugged Slieve Bloom Mountains (p503) provide excellent walking, while fishing and water sports are popular on the River Shannon and the Grand Canal. Access www.offaly.ie and www.discoverireland.ie/offaly for more information.

BIRR
pop 4091

Feel-good Birr is one of the most attractive towns in the Midlands, with elegant pastel Georgian buildings lining its streets, a magnificent old castle, a good choice of restaurants and lively nightlife with excellent live music. Despite its appeal, Birr remains off the beaten track and you can enjoy its delights without jostling with the crowds.

In mid-August, the town celebrates its rich history during **Birr Vintage Week and Arts Festival** (www.birrvintageweek.com), with street parades, theatre, music, exhibitions, workshops, guided walks and a traditional fair.

History

Birr started life as a 6th-century monastic site founded by St Brendan. By 1208 the town had acquired an Anglo-Norman castle, home of the O'Carroll clan who reigned over the surrounding territory.

During the Plantation of 1620, the castle and estate were given to Sir Laurence Parsons. He changed the town's fate by carefully laying out streets, establishing a glass factory and issuing a decree that anyone who 'cast dunge rubbidge filth or sweepings in the forestreet' would be fined four pennies. He also banned barmaids, sentencing any woman caught serving beer to the stocks. The castle has remained in the family for 14 generations, and the present earl and his wife still live on the estate.

Orientation

All the main roads converge on Emmet Sq, with its erect column honouring martyred Irish patriot Robert Emmet. In one corner, Dooly's Hotel, dating from 1747, was once a coaching inn on the busy route to the west.

Information

The post office is in the northeastern corner of Emmet Sq.

Mid-Ireland Tourism (☎ 057-912 0923; www.midireland tourism.ie; Brendan St; ⓨ 9.30am-1pm & 2-5.30pm Mon-Fri) When the tourist office is closed, you'll find an info point with helpful staff and plenty of brochures here.

Tourist office (☎ 057-912 0110; Civic Offices, Wilmer Rd; ⓨ 9.30am-1pm & 2-5.30pm Mon-Sat mid-May–mid-Sep) Has good regional info, as well as info for Birr.

Sights

BIRR CASTLE DEMESNE

It's easy to spend half a day exploring the attractions and gardens of **Birr Castle Demesne** (☎ 057-912 0336; www.birrcastle.com; adult/child €9/5; ⓨ 9am-6pm mid-Mar–Oct, noon-4pm Nov-Feb). The castle is a private home, however, and cannot be visited. Most of the present building dates from around 1620, with alterations made in the early 19th century.

The 50-hectare castle grounds are famous for their magnificent **gardens** set around a large artificial lake. They hold over 1000 species of plants from all over the world; something always seems to be in bloom. Look for the world's tallest box hedges, planted in the 1780s and now standing 12m high, and the romantic Hornbeam cloister.

The Parsons were a remarkable family of pioneering Irish scientists, and their work is documented in the **historic science centre**. Exhibits include the massive **telescope** built by William Parsons in 1845. The 'leviathan of Parsonstown', as it was known, was the largest telescope in the world for 75 years and attracted a wide variety of scientists and astronomers. (It was used to make innumerable discoveries, including the spiral galaxies, and to map the moon's surface.) After the death of William's son, the telescope, unloved and untended, slowly fell to bits. A huge restoration scheme in the 1990s rebuilt the telescope: it's now fully operational, and demonstrations are held three times daily in high season.

OTHER BUILDINGS & MONUMENTS

Birr has no shortage of first-class Georgian houses; just stroll down tree-lined **Oxmantown Mall**, which connects Rosse Row and Emmet St, or **John's Mall**, to see some of the best examples.

The tourist office hands out a walking map that details the most important landmarks, including a **statue** of the third Earl of Rosse, the megalithic **Seffin Stone** (said to be the ancient marker for *Umbilicus Hiberniae* – the Navel of Ireland – used to mark the centre of the country) and **St Brendan's Old Churchyard**, reputedly the site of the saint's 6th-century settlement.

Activities

A beautiful leafy **riverside walk** runs east along the River Camcor from Oxmantown Bridge to Elmgrove Bridge.

If you're feeling more energetic, **Birr Outdoor Education Centre** (☎ 057-912 0029; www.oec.ie; Roscrea Rd) offers hill walking, rock climbing and abseiling in the nearby Slieve Blooms, as well as canoeing and kayaking on local rivers.

Birr Equestrian Centre (☎ 057-912 1961; www.birrequestrian.ie; Kingsborough House; treks per hr €35), 3km outside Birr on the Clareen road, runs hour-long treks in the surrounding farmland and half-day treks in the Slieve Bloom Mountains.

Sleeping

Spinners (☎ 057-912 1673; www.spinnerstownhouse.com; Castle St; s/d from €50/60; **P**) Bright, simple rooms with crisp white linen, wooden floors and neutral colour schemes make this restored Georgian guesthouse a good bet. The bathrooms are tight, but the rooms are quite spacious and good value. The courtyard restaurant downstairs is a treat.

Maltings Guesthouse (☎ 057-912 1345; themaltings birr@eircom.net; Castle St; s/d from €50/80; **P**) Based in an 1810 malt storehouse once used by Guinness, this place has a serene location right by the castle and the River Camcor. The 13 simple rooms are spotless, service is friendly and there's a popular restaurant downstairs.

Brendan House (☎ 057-912 1818; www.tinjugstudio.com; Brendan St; s/d €55/85) Gloriously eccentric and packed to the gills with knick-knacks, books, rugs, art and antiques, this Georgian town house is a bohemian delight. The three rooms share a bathroom, but the four-poster beds, period charm and artistic style of the place more than make up for this. The owners also run an artists' studio and gallery, offer evening meals on request and can arrange guided mountain walks, castle tours and holistic treatments.

Eating & Drinking

Emma's Cafe & Deli (☎ 057-912 5678; 31 Main St; meals €4-8; ☺ 9.30am-6pm Mon-Sat year-round, 12.30-5.30pm Sun Jun-Aug) Laid-back, relaxed and bursting with good food, Emma's is a popular local haunt, serving an interesting range of ciabatta, panini, salads and cakes. There are books and games for children and plenty of tempting deli options for picnics.

Spinners (☎ 057-912 1673; www.spinnerstownhouse.com; Castle St; mains €17-20; ☺ 6.30-9pm Wed-Mon, 12.30-2.30pm Sun) Hidden behind the thick walls of this beautifully restored woollen mill is a fine restaurant with a varied and seasonal menu, featuring locally sourced ingredients. Solid meaty fare mingles with seafood and veggie options. The courtyard terrace is a summertime delight.

Thatch (☎ 057-912 0682; www.thethatchcrinkill.com; Crinkill; mains €21-28; ☺ closed Mon) A traditional thatched Irish pub, just 2km southeast of Birr off the N62, this 200-year-old inn is a great place to sip a pint or enjoy a hearty meal. It's a hugely popular spot for Sunday lunch, when local families gather in force for the simply prepared meats and seafood. Bar food is also available; book in advance.

Craughwell's (☎ 057-912 1839; Castle St) Stop for a snootful at Craughwell's, renowned for its rollicking traditional session on Friday night and impromptu sing-along sessions on Saturday.

Chestnut (☎ 057-912 2011; Green St) Easily the most appealing pub in the centre, the

DETOUR: GHOSTS AT LEAP CASTLE

Ireland's most haunted castle, **Leap Castle** (☎ 057-913 1115; seanryan@mail2web.com; admission €6; ☒ call for opening times) originally kept guard over a crucial route between Munster and Leinster. The castle was the scene of many dreadful deeds and has quaint features like dank dungeons and a 'Bloody Chapel'. It's famous for its eerie apparitions – the most renowned inhabitant is the 'smelly ghost', a spirit that leaves a horrible stench behind after sightings.

Renovations are ongoing, but you can visit. It lies about 12km southeast of Birr between Kinnitty and Roscrea (in Tipperary) off the R421.

Chestnut dates to 1823, but has recently been refurbished. The current incarnation mixes dark furniture with a continental cafe style. Summer sees regular barbecue nights.

Entertainment

Besides the places listed above, you'll find many more humble boozers about Birr.

Melba's Nite Club (☎ 057-912 0032; Emmet Sq; ☒ Fri-Sun) In the basement of Dooly's Hotel, this popular club gives a fine insight into the potato-and-stout-fuelled mating habits of rural Ireland.

Birr Theatre & Arts Centre (☎ 057-912 2911; www .birrtheatre.com; Oxmantown Hall) A vibrant place with a regular line-up of films, local drama, well-known musicians and more.

Getting There & Away

Bus Éireann runs buses to Dublin (€16, 3½ hours, one daily) via Tullamore, and to Athlone (€9.80, one hour, four daily Monday to Saturday, two Sunday) and Limerick (€16.50, 1¼ hours, four daily Monday to Saturday, two Sunday)

Kearns Transport (☎ 057-912 0124; www.kearnstrans port.com) runs an early morning commuter bus to Dublin and a weekend service to Galway.

All buses depart from Emmet Sq; look for signs with the latest schedules.

KINNITTY
pop 333

Kinnitty is a quaint little village that makes a good base for exploring the Slieve Bloom Mountains (p503). Driving out of Kinnitty,

the roads across the mountains to Mountrath and Mountmellick, both in County Laois, are particularly scenic.

Look out for the bizarre 10m-high **stone pyramid** in the village graveyard behind the Church of Ireland. In the 1830s, Richard Bernard commissioned this scale replica of the Cheops pyramid in Egypt for the family crypt.

The shaft of the 9th-century **Kinnitty High Cross** was nabbed by Kinnitty Castle in the 19th century and is now displayed on the hotel's terrace. Adam and Eve and the Crucifixion are clearly visible on either face.

At the time of writing, **Kinnitty Castle** (www.kin nittycastle.com), one of Ireland's most renowned mansions, set on a vast estate, was embroiled in a bitter feud with its bankers. Operating as a luxury hotel, this former O'Carroll residence was rebuilt in neo-Gothic style in the 19th century, and was popular as a luxury wedding venue. The castle is 3km southeast of town off the R440. Check the website for the latest update.

If you wish to stay in Kinnitty proper, **Ardmore House** (☎ 057-913 7009; www.kinnitty.com; The Walk; s/d from €60/84; ℗), a lovely Victorian stone farmhouse, just oozes old-world charm. The rooms are full of character, with brass beds, subtle floral patterns, antique furniture and views of the nearby mountains. Turf fires and homemade brown bread complete the cosy, rustic atmosphere. The owners also organise walking tours in the nearby Slieve Bloom Mountains. The B&B is set off the R440, about 200m east of Kinnitty.

Alternatively try **Aaron House** (☎ 057-913 7040; www.aaronhouse.ie; Kinnitty; s/d €60/75; ℗), a more modern place with spacious, purpose-built rooms with king-size beds and sparkling bathrooms. Aaron House is on the R421 just outside the village.

BANAGHER & AROUND
pop 1636

Sleepy Banagher bursts into life in the summer months when the busy marina is awash with boaters. For the rest of the year, it's a pleasant backwater with pastel-fronted houses marching down the long main street to the banks of the River Shannon where there are some impressive fortifications.

Among its claims to fame: Charlotte Brontë had her honeymoon in Banagher in 1854, while thirteen years earlier, Anthony Trollope, fresh from inventing the pillar box, took up a

THE MIDLANDS

job as a post-office clerk in the village and, in his spare time, managed to complete his first novel, *The Macdermots of Ballycloran*.

Information

Inside an unusual bow-fronted Georgian town house, the helpful **tourist office** (☎ 057-915 2155; offalywest@hotmail.com; Crank House, Main St; ☺ 9am-1pm & 2-5pm Mon-Fri) provides information about Banagher and the surrounding region. Internet access is available for €1 per 15 minutes.

Sights

Situated at a crossing point over the River Shannon, Banagher was a place of enormous strategic importance during turbulent times, and a group of fortifications by the bridge remains as testimony to its turbulent past. Today you can still see the remains of **Cromwell's Castle**. Built in the 1650s, it was modified during the Napoleonic Wars, when **Fort Eliza** (a five-sided gun battery whose guardhouse, moat and retaining walls can still be seen), a **military barracks** and **Martello tower** were also built.

St Paul's Church at the far end of Main St contains a resplendent stained-glass window, originally intended for Westminster Abbey.

About 3km south of Banagher off the R439 in Lusmagh is **Cloghan Castle** (☎ 057-915 1650), in use for nearly 800 years. The castle has seen more than its fair share of bloodshed, beginning life as a McCoghlan stronghold and later becoming home to the mighty O'Carroll clan. Today the castle consists of a well-preserved Norman keep and an adjoining 19th-century house full of interesting antiques and armaments. Groups of up to five people can take an hour-long tour of the castle (€35) if you phone in advance. Occasional concerts are also held here. Ask at the tourist office.

From Lusmagh it's possible to take a tranquil walk down to picturesque **Victoria Lock**, where the Shannon splits into two channels. If you cross the lock and walk north along the west bank of the river, it's a lovely 2km walk to 15th-century **Meelick Church**, one of the oldest churches still in use in Ireland. You can also reach Meelick by road. It's about 8km south of Banagher, along tiny tracks on the County Galway side of the border.

Activities

You can rent canoes and cruisers in Banagher. During the summer, the placid waters and numerous islands and channels make it an ideal place for a paddle. Larger boats can cruise the Shannon from here or head out along the Royal and Grand Canals. The following include high season prices:

Carrick Craft (☎ 01-278 1666; www.cruise-ireland .com; The Marina) Four- to eight-person berths ranging from €1000 to €2560 per week.

Shannon Adventure (☎ 057-915 1411; www.iol .ie/~advcanoe/index.html; The Marina; per hr/day/week €15/60/332) Fully equipped Canadian canoes and free camping for canoers.

Silverline Cruisers (☎ 057-915 1112; www.silverline cruisers.com; The Marina) Two- to 12-person berths from €1100 to €3670 per week.

Sleeping & Eating

The tourist office keeps a full list of B&Bs in the area.

Charlotte's Way (☎ 057-915 3864; www.charlottesway .com; The Hill; s/d €45/80; P) This tastefully restored former rectory offers four comfy good-value rooms. Breakfasts star eggs fresh from the hens outside. A honeymooning Charlotte Brontë was a frequent visitor and, after her death, her husband Arthur lived here as the rector.

Brosna Lodge Hotel (☎ 057-915 1350; www .brosnalodge.com; Main St; s/d from €50/100; P) This family-run hotel in the centre of town has 14 spacious but rather soulless rooms. The restaurant (mains €9 to €16) serves pretty good food considering the lack of competition and you can get bar snacks in the pub.

Flynns Bar & Restaurant (☎ 057-915 1312; Main St; mains €9-20) Popular with locals for its grills, steak and pasta, this local bar also has a restaurant at the back serving a decent selection of reliable, if predictable, dishes. It's a good place to sip a pint if Houghs gets full of carousing boaters.

Drinking

JJ Houghs (☎ 057-915 1893; Main St) Rivalling the river as Banagher's most appealing feature, Hough's is a 250-year-old pub with vines of that vintage covering the front. Renowned for its music, there are traditional sessions most nights in summer and at weekends in winter. If there's no live music, you can entertain yourself by poring over the artefact-covered walls or counting stars in the pleasant beer garden.

Getting There & Away

Kearns Transport (☎ 057-912 0124; www.kearnstransport .com) links Banagher to Birr (€2, 15 mins),

TOP 10 TRADITIONAL MIDLANDS PUBS

These charming old-world pubs range from popular tourist haunts to undiscovered gems in little-visited backwaters where nothing has changed in decades.

Coffeey's (Lecarrow, County Roscommon) The centre of the village community and renowned for its craic, Coffeey's, on the N61 between Roscommon and Athlone, is all about the people.

Gunnings (Rathconrath, County Westmeath) Utterly unchanged and unadorned, Gunnings, on the R392 between Ballymahon and Mullingar, is kitted out with ancient stools, cracked lino and yellowing cereal packets; it doesn't get much more authentic than this.

JJ Houghs (opposite; Banagher, County Offaly) A 250-year-old pub hung with vines and plastered with knick-knacks, this is another place famed for its traditional music.

Killeens Village Tavern (below; Shannonbridge, County Offaly) Run by a family of music lovers, this bustling place is well known for its lively traditional sessions and warm welcome.

Magans (Killashee, County Longford) Delightful old bar, grocery and hardware store in a tiny village well off the beaten track, on the N63 between Lanesborough and Longford.

Mary Lynch's (Coralstown, County Westmeath) An unassuming old-fashioned pub off the N4 between Mullingar and Kinnegad, Lynch's is a perfect place for a pint overlooking the Grand Canal.

MJ Henry (Cootehall, County Roscommon) An unadulterated grocery store-cum-pub, Henry's, off the N4 between Boyle and Carrick-on-Shannon, is full of character and little changed since the '70s.

Morrissey's (p503; Abbeyleix, County Laois) Half-pub, half-shop, Morrissey's is a local institution, complete with a pot-belly stove, sloping counter and shelves decked out with a clutter of curios.

Sean's Bar (p527; Athlone, County Westmeath) Ancient pub with log fires, sawdust-strewn floors, a rickety piano and a riverside beer garden.

Village Inn (Coolrain, County Laois) This thatched old-style pub at the foot of the Slieve Bloom Mountains, off the N7 between Mountrath and Borris-in-Ossory, is renowned for its traditional music and set dancing.

Tullamore (€3, 45 mins) and Dublin (€10, 2¾ hours) once daily at 8.35am Monday to Saturday and at 6.35pm on Sunday. The Friday and Saturday service allows you to transfer in Birr for a bus to Galway.

SHANNONBRIDGE

pop 221

Perfectly picturesque, Shannonbridge gets its name from a narrow 16-span, 18th-century bridge that crosses the river into County Roscommon. It's a small, sleepy village with just one main street and two pubs.

You can't miss the massive 19th-century **fortifications** on the western bank, where heavy artillery was installed to bombard Napoleon in case he was cheeky enough to try to invade by river. The fort has been reincarnated as the **Old Fort Restaurant** (☎ 090-967 4973; www.theoldfortrestaurant.com; mains €19.50-29.50; ☒ 5-9.30pm Wed-Sat, 12.30-2.30pm Sun), which serves posh nosh in suitably grand surroundings. On a summer evening, a table outside offers beautiful river views.

Don't miss the opportunity to visit **Killeens Village Tavern**, an old-world pub-cum-shop that is renowned for its warm welcome and lively traditional music. The ceiling of the bar is plastered with old business cards left by cus-tomers over the years. There's a music session almost nightly in summer and at weekends during the rest of the year. Traditional pub grub is also available.

CLONMACNOISE

Gloriously placed overlooking the River Shannon, **Clonmacnoise** (☎ 090-967 4195; www.heritageireland.ie; adult/child €6/2; ☒ 9am-7pm mid-May-mid-Sep, 10am-6pm mid-Sep-Oct & mid-Mar-mid-May, 10am-5.30pm Nov-mid-Mar, last admission 45min before closing; ℗) is one of Ireland's most important ancient monastic cities. The site is enclosed in a walled field and contains numerous early churches, high crosses, round towers and graves in astonishingly good condition. The surrounding marshy area is known as the **Shannon Callows**, home to many wild plants and one of the last refuges of the seriously endangered corncrake (a pastel-coloured relative of the coot).

History

Roughly translated, Clonmacnoise (Cluain Mhic Nóis) means 'Meadow of the Sons of Nós'. The marshy land in the area would have been impassable for early traders, who instead chose to travel by water or on eskers (raised ridges formed by glaciers). When St

Ciarán founded a monastery here in AD 548, it was the most important crossroads in the country, the intersection of the north–south River Shannon, and the east–west Esker Riada (Highway of the Kings).

The giant ecclesiastical city had a humble beginning and Ciarán died just seven months after building his first church. Over the years, however, Clonmacnoise grew to become an unrivalled bastion of Irish religion, literature and art and attracted a large lay population. Between the 7th and 12th centuries, monks from all over Europe came to study and pray here, helping to earn Ireland the title of the 'land of saints and scholars'. Even the high kings of Connaught and Tara were brought here for burial.

Most of what you can see today dates from the 10th to 12th centuries. The monks would have lived in small huts scattered in and around the monastery, which would probably have been surrounded by a ditch or rampart of earth.

The site was burned and pillaged on numerous occasions by both the Vikings and the Irish. After the 12th century it fell into decline, and by the 15th century it was home only to an impoverished bishop. In 1552 the English garrison from Athlone reduced the site to a ruin: it was reported at the time that 'not a bell, large or small, or an image, or an altar, or a book, or a gem, or even glass in a window, was left which was not carried away'.

Among the treasures that survived the continued onslaughts are the crosier of the abbots of Clonmacnoise in the National Museum (p106),

in Dublin, and the 12th-century *Leabhar na hUidhre* (The Book of the Dun Cow), now in the Royal Irish Academy in Dublin.

Information

There's an excellent on-site museum and cafe, and there's a regional **tourist office** (☎ 090-967 4134; 10am-5.45pm Apr-Oct) near the entrance. If you want to avoid summer crowds, it's a good idea to visit early or late; the tiny country lanes nearby can get clogged with coaches. Leave at least a couple of hours for a visit.

Sights

MUSEUM

Three connected conical huts near the entrance, housing the museum, echo the design of early monastic dwellings. The centre's 20-minute audiovisual show is an excellent introduction to the site.

The exhibition area contains the original high crosses (replicas have been put in their former locations outside), and various artefacts uncovered during excavation, including silver pins, beaded glass and an Ogham stone. It also contains the largest collection of early Christian grave slabs in Europe. Many are in remarkable condition, with inscriptions clearly visible, often starting with *oroit do* or *ar* (a prayer for).

HIGH CROSSES

There's a real sense of drama as you descend to the foot of the imposing sandstone **Cross of the Scriptures**, one of Ireland's finest. It's very distinctive, with unique upward-tilting

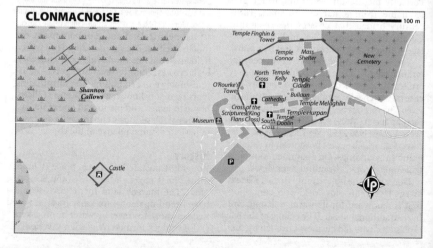

CLONMACNOISE

0 —————— 100 m

Temple Finghin & Tower
Temple Connor
Mass Shelter
New Cemetery
North Cross
Temple Kelly
Temple Ciarán
O'Rourke's Tower
Shannon Callows
Cathedral
Bullaun
Temple Melaghlin
Temple Hurpan
Cross of the Scriptures (King Flans Cross)
Temple Doolin
South Cross
Museum
Castle
P

DETOUR: SHANNON HARBOUR & AROUND

Just 1km east of where the Grand Canal joins the River Shannon, sleepy **Shannon Harbour** is a tiny but picturesque town that was once a thriving trading centre. A purpose-built village constructed to serve the waterways, it was home to over 1000 people in its heyday. Along with cargo boats, passenger barges ran from here, many of which took poor locals on their first leg of a long journey to North America or Australia.

Today the waterways are again teeming with boats and walking paths stretching in all directions, making Shannon Harbour an interesting stop for walkers, fishers, boaters and birders. The original 1806 **Harbour Master's House** (☎ 057-915 1532; gkirwan@iol.ie; s/d from €50/70; ☿ mid-Mar–Dec; ℗) is run by the daughter of a former harbour master and overlooks the canal. It has five guest rooms decked out in traditional style. Nearby are two lively pubs.

The village is about 10km northeast of Banagher off the R356. Nearby, 16th-century **Clonony Castle** (☎ 087 761 4034; www.clononycastle.ie) is enclosed by an overgrown castellated wall. Tales that Henry VIII's second wife, Anne Boleyn, was born here are unlikely to be true, but her cousins Elizabeth and Mary Boleyn are buried beside the ruins. The castle is open to visitors during the summer months when workers doing restoration are around; donations are appreciated.

Not far from the castle, **The Rectory** (☎ 090-645 7293; www.therectory.ie; Deerpark; s/d €45/70; ℗) is a really lovely old house set in mature gardens. The tranquil guest rooms are lovingly decorated in neutral tones, with crisp white linens and a touch of period style. Deerpark is off the R357, 1.5km from Clonony Castle.

---

arms and richly decorated panels depicting the Crucifixion, the Last Judgement, the arrest of Jesus, and Christ in the tomb.

Only the shaft of the **North Cross**, which dates from around AD 800, remains. It is adorned by lions, convoluted spirals and a single figure, thought to be the Celtic god Cernunnos (or Cernenus), who sits in a Buddha-like position. The richly decorated **South Cross** has mostly abstract carvings – swirls, spirals and fretwork – and, on the western face, the Crucifixion plus a few odd cavorting creatures.

CATHEDRAL

The biggest building at Clonmacnoise, the cathedral was originally built in AD 909, but was significantly altered and remodelled over the centuries. Its most interesting feature is the intricate 15th-century Gothic doorway with carvings of Sts Francis, Patrick and Dominic. A whisper carries from one side of the door to the other, and this feature was supposedly used by lepers to confess their sins without infecting the priests.

The last high kings of Tara – Turlough Mór O'Connor (died 1156) and his son Ruairí (Rory; died 1198) – are said to be buried near the altar.

TEMPLES

The small churches are called temples, a derivation of the Irish word *teampall* (church).

The little, roofed church is **Temple Connor**, still used by Church of Ireland parishioners on the last Sunday of the summer months. Walking towards the cathedral, you'll pass the scant foundations of **Temple Kelly** (1167) before reaching tiny **Temple Ciarán**, reputed to be the burial place of St Ciarán, the site's founder.

The floor level in Temple Ciarán is lower than outside because local farmers have been taking clay from the church for centuries to protect their crops and cattle. The floor has been covered in slabs, but handfuls of clay are still removed from outside the church in the early spring.

Near the temple's southwestern corner is a *bullaun* (ancient grinding stone), supposedly used for making medicines for the monastery's hospital. Today the rainwater that collects in it is said to cure warts.

Continuing round the compound you come to the 12th-century **Temple Melaghlin**, with its attractive windows, and the twin structures of **Temple Hurpan** and **Temple Doolin**.

ROUND TOWERS

Overlooking the River Shannon is the 20m-high **O'Rourke's Tower**. Lightning blasted the top off the tower in 1135, but the remaining structure was used for another 400 years.

Temple Finghin and its round tower are on the northern boundary of the site, also overlooking the Shannon. The building dates from

THE MIDLANDS

around 1160 and has some fine Romanesque carvings. The herringbone-patterned tower roof is the only one in Ireland that has never been altered. Most round towers became shelters when the monasteries were attacked, but this one was probably just used as a bell tower since the doorway is at ground level.

OTHER REMAINS

Beyond the site's boundary wall, about 500m east through the modern graveyard, is the secluded **Nun's Church**. From here the main site, including the towers, is not visible. The church has wonderful Romanesque arches with minute carvings; one has been interpreted as Ireland's earliest sheila-na-gig, in an acrobatic pose with feet tucked behind the ears.

To the west of the site, on the ridge near the car park, is a motte with the oddly shaped ruins of a 13th-century **castle**, built by John de Grey, bishop of Norwich, to watch over the Shannon.

Sleeping

If you want to stay near the ruins, your best option is **Kajon House** (☎ 090-967 4191; www.kajon house.ie; Creevagh; d from €70; ⍟ Mar-Oct; Ⓟ), just 1.5km from the ruins on the road signposted to Tullamore. It's an incredibly friendly place with cosy rooms, a spacious yard with a picnic table and evening meals on offer. You can even have pancakes for breakfast.

Shopping

On your way to Clonmacnoise, it's worth stopping off in Ballinahown to visit the **Core Craft Centre** (☎ 090-643 0222; Old School House, Ballinahown; ⍟ 10am-6pm Mon-Fri, 11am-6pm Sat) to browse the range of contemporary craftwork, bog oak sculpture and pottery on offer. There's an excellent range of items on display and prices are more reasonable than in city craft shops. Ballinahown is on the N62, about 10km from Clonmacnoise.

Getting There & Away

Clonmacnoise is 7km northeast of Shannonbridge on the R444 and about 24km south of Athlone in County Westmeath. By car you can explore this interesting and evocative area at leisure.

Silver Line (☎ 057-915 1112; www.silverlinecruisers .com; adult/child one-way €7/4) run three boat trips on Saturday and Sunday from June to September from Shannonbridge to Clonmacnoise.

There are also river cruises to Clonmacnoise from Athlone in County Westmeath (see p525).

A **taxi** (☎ 090-647 4400) from Athlone will cost roughly €50 to €70 round-trip, including an hour's wait.

TULLAMORE
pop 10,900

Tullamore, Offaly's county town, is a bustling but workaday place with a pleasant setting on the Grand Canal. The town is most famous for Tullamore Dew whiskey, although production has long since moved to County Tipperary. You can still visit the old distillery and have a dram of the amber liquid.

Information

My Office (☎ 057-932 9886; William St; per 15min €1; ⍟ 10.30am-10.30pm Mon-Fri, noon-8pm Sat & Sun) Internet access in a 1st-floor business centre.

Tourist office (☎ 057-935 2617; tullamoredhc@eircom .net; Bury Quay; ⍟ 9am-6pm Mon-Sat & noon-5pm Sun May-Sep, 10am-5pm Mon-Sat & noon-5pm Sun Oct-Apr).

Sights
TULLAMORE DEW HERITAGE CENTRE

Located in a 19th-century canalside warehouse, the **heritage centre** (☎ 057-932 5015; www .tullamore-dew.org; Bury Quay; adult/child €7/3.50; ⍟ 9am-6pm Mon-Sat & noon-5pm Sun May-Sep, 10am-5pm Mon-Sat & noon-5pm Sun Oct-Apr) mixes intriguing local history with booze propaganda. Fortunately, the emphasis is on the former and engaging exhibits show the role of the Grand Canal in the town's development. At the end of the tour you'll get to sample what is supposedly the easiest of Irish whiskeys to drink.

CHARLEVILLE CASTLE

Spires, turrets, clinging ivy and creaking trees combine to give this hulking structure a haunted feel. **Charleville Castle** (☎ 087 766 4110; www.charlevillecastle.com; adult/child €8/4, minimum 3 adults; ⍟ regular tours noon-6pm Apr-Aug, by appointment Sep-May) was the family seat of the Burys, who commissioned the design in 1798 from Francis Johnston, one of Ireland's most famous architects. The interior is spectacular, with stunning ceilings, one of the most striking Gothic-revival galleries in Ireland and a kitchen block built to resemble a country church.

Admission is by 35-minute tour only. If you'd like to help restore this pile, you can join groups of international volunteers; contact

---

DETOUR: LOUGH BOORA

Much of County Offaly's once extensive bogs were stripped of peat for electricity generation during the 20th century. One area, **Lough Boora** (www.loughbooraparklands .com), is now the focus of a scheme to restore its environment. Located 5km west of Blue Ball off the R357, there are over 50km of trails across the area with excellent birdwatching, rare flora, a mesolithic site and a series of impressive environmental **sculptures** (www.sculptureintheparklands.com) to explore.

---

the castle for details. The entrance is off the N52, south of Tullamore. Frustration ensues if you go too far and reach Blue Ball, a village with hairy traffic.

Sleeping & Eating

Ask at the tourist office for a list of local B&Bs.

Sea Dew (☎ 057-935 2054; www.seadewguesthouse .com; Clonminch Rd; s/d from €40/68; **P** 🖳) A purpose-built guesthouse just five minutes' walk from the town centre, this welcoming place has 12 spacious but cosy rooms. There's a lovely outdoor deck in the mature gardens and a play area for children. The guesthouse is just south of the town centre, off the N80.

Tullamore Court Hotel (☎ 057-934 6666; www .tullamorecourthotel.ie; O'Moore St; s/d from €75/110; **P** 🖳 🖳 🛜) This modern hotel on the edge of the centre has 104 elegant but corporate-style rooms at surprisingly reasonable rates. It has all the features you'd expect from a business hotel, including a great leisure centre.

Sirocco's (☎ 057-935 2839; Patrick St; mains €11-24; ⏱ noon-2.30pm Thu & Fri, 5-11pm Mon-Sat, 1-10.30pm Sun) Serving a good selection of fresh pasta and pizza, as well as meat, chicken and fish dishes, this simple little Italian bistro is a local favourite. Booking ahead is advised.

Getting There & Away
BUS

Bus Éireann stops at the train station, located south of town. From Tullamore there are buses to Dublin (€16, two hours, three daily), to Birr (€9.60, 30 minutes, one daily Monday to Friday) and to Waterford (€21, 3¼ hours, two daily) via Portlaoise, Carlow and Kilkenny.

Kearns Transport (☎ 057-912 0124; www.kearns transport.com) also serves Birr and Dublin with several buses daily.

TRAIN

There are fast trains east to Dublin (€15 to €26, 1½ hours, 11 daily) and west to Galway (€15 to €28.50, 1½ hours, six daily), as well as Westport and Sligo. The station is on the southwest edge of the centre on Cormac St.

DURROW ABBEY

Founded by St Colmcille (also known as St Columba) in the 6th century, Durrow Abbey is most famous for producing the illustrated *Book of Durrow*. The 7th-century text is the earliest of the great manuscripts to have survived – a remarkable feat considering it was recovered from a farm where it was dipped in the cattle's drinking water to cure illnesses. It can be seen at Trinity College, Dublin (p100).

The site contains five early-Christian gravestones and Durrow's splendid 10th-century **high cross**, whose complex, high relief carvings depict the sacrifice of Isaac, the Last Judgement and the Crucifixion; it was possibly created by the same stonemason who carved the Cross of the Scriptures at Clonmacnoise. A laborious process of restoration is underway and some areas may be closed to visitors.

The path north past the church leads to **St Colmcille's Well**, a place of pilgrimage marked by a small cairn.

Durrow Abbey is 7km north of Tullamore down a long lane west off the N52.

COUNTY ROSCOMMON

Studded with over 5000 megalithic tombs, ring forts and mounds, and home to a couple of excellent museums, Roscommon is a haven for history buffs. Add to the mix a couple of well-preserved mansions and some wonderful monastic ruins and it's hard to understand why the county sees so few visitors. Beyond the romance of times past, Roscommon has plenty of rolling countryside littered with lakes and cleaved by the Rivers Shannon and Suck – attributes much appreciated by visiting anglers.

STROKESTOWN & AROUND
pop 773

Strokestown's main street is a grand tree-lined avenue that remains a testament to the lofty

THE MIDLANDS

aspirations of one of the local landed gentry who wished it to be Europe's widest. It's a striking feature in what is a now a sleepy town most notable for its historic estate and famine museum

Over the May Day Bank Holiday weekend, the town bursts into life during the **International Poetry Festival** (www.strokestownpoetry.org).

Strokestown Park House & Famine Museum

At the end of Strokestown's main avenue, three Gothic arches lead to **Strokestown Park House** (☎ 071-963 3013; www.strokestownpark.ie; admission house, museum & gardens €14, house or museum or gardens €9.50; ☽ museum & grounds 10am-5.30pm mid-Mar–Oct, house tours 11.30am, 2pm & 4pm Mon-Fri, 5pm Sat & Sun mid-Mar–Oct, 2pm Mon-Fri Nov–mid-Mar).

The original 12,000-hectare estate was granted by King Charles II to Nicholas Mahon for his support in the English Civil War. Nicholas' grandson Thomas commissioned Richard Cassels to build him a Palladian mansion in the early 18th century. Over the centuries, the estate decreased in size along with the family's fortunes. When it was eventually sold in 1979, it had been whittled down to 120 hectares. The estate was bought as a complete lot, so virtually all of its remaining contents are intact.

Admission to the house is by a 50-minute **guided tour**, taking in a galleried kitchen with state-of-the-art clockwork machinery, and a child's bedroom complete with 19th-century toys and fun-house mirrors.

The **walled garden** contains the longest herbaceous border in Ireland and Britain, which blooms in a rainbow of colours in summer.

In direct and deliberate contrast to the splendour of the house and its grounds is the harrowing **Strokestown Famine Museum**, which sheds light on the devastating 1840s potato blight. There's a huge amount of information to take in, with long panels of text that require some concentration, but you'll emerge with an unblinking insight into the starvation of the poor, and the ignorance, callousness and cruelty of those who were in a position to help. Strokestown landlord Major Denis Mahon ruthlessly evicted starving peasants who couldn't pay their rent, chartering boats to transport them away from Ireland. Almost 600 of these 1000 emigrants died on the overcrowded 'coffin ships'. Perhaps unsurprisingly, Mahon was assassinated by some of his tenants in 1847. The museum also opens visitors' eyes to present-day famine around the world. Allow at least a half-day visit if your wish to see the house, museum and gardens.

Cruachan Aí Visitor Centre

Anyone with an interest in Celtic mythology will be enthralled by the area around the village of **Tulsk**, which contains 60 ancient national monuments including standing stones, barrows, cairns and fortresses, making it the most important Celtic royal site in Europe. The landscape and its sacred structures have lain largely undisturbed for the past 3000 years. It's hard to grasp just how significant the site is, as archaeological digs are still ongoing, but it has already been established that the site is bigger and older than Tara in County Meath (p539) and was at one time a major seat of Irish power.

The **Cruachan Aí Visitor Centre** (☎ 071-963 9268; www.cruachanai.com; Tulsk; adult/child €5/3; ☽ 9am-6pm Mon-Fri, 10am-6pm Sat, 1-6pm Sun Jun-Oct, 9am-5pm Mon-Sat Nov-May) has audiovisual displays and informative panels and maps that explain the significance of the sites, and can let you know the current status of access to the (privately owned) monuments.

According to the legend of Táin Bó Cúailnge (Cattle Raid of Cooley), Queen Maeve (Medbh) had her palace at Cruachan. The Oweynagat Cave (Cave of the Cats), believed to be the entrance to the Celtic otherworld, is also nearby. If you dare to enter, look closely at the stones by the entrance where you'll find the 1911 graffiti of Ireland's first president, Douglas Hyde.

Tulsk is 10km west of Strokestown on the N5. Bus Éireann's frequent Dublin to Westport route stops right outside the visitor centre.

BOYLE & AROUND
pop 1599

A quiet town at the foot of the Curlew Mountains, Boyle is a scenic and worthwhile stop, home to beautiful Boyle Abbey, a 4000-year-old dolmen, the hands-on King House Interpretive Centre, and an island-scattered forest park.

If you're here at the end of July, you can catch the lively **Boyle Arts Festival** (☎ 071-966 3085; www.boylearts.com), which features music, theatre, storytelling and contemporary Irish art exhibitions.

History

The history of Boyle is the history of the King family. In 1603 Staffordshire-born John King was granted land in Roscommon with the aim of 'reducing the Irish to obedience'. Over the next 150 years, through canny marriages and cold-blooded conquests, his descendants made their name and fortune, becoming one of the largest landowning families in Ireland. The town of Boyle grew around their estate.

King House was built in 1730, and in 1780 the family moved to the grander Rockingham House, built in what is now Lough Key Forest & Activity Park, but destroyed by fire in 1957.

Actress Maureen O'Sullivan (Mia Farrow's mother) was born in a house on Main St opposite the Bank of Ireland in 1911.

Information

Tourist office (☎ 071-966 2145; King House; ☽ 10am-5.30pm Mon-Sat Jun–early Sep)

Úna Bhán Tourism Centre (☎ 071-966 3033; www .unabhan.net; ☽ 9am-6pm daily May-Aug, 9am-5pm Mon-Fri Sep-Apr) A local cooperative in the grounds of King House.

Sights & Activities

KING HOUSE INTERPRETIVE CENTRE

After the King family moved to Lough Key, the imposing Georgian mansion King House became a military barracks for the fearsome Connaught Rangers. The county council bought the property in 1987, and spent several years and €3.8 million turning it into the inspired **King House Interpretive Centre** (☎ 071-966 3242; www.kinghouse.ie; Main St; adult/child/family €7/4/18; ☽ 10am-6pm Apr-Sep). Sinister-looking dummies from various eras tell the turbulent history of the Connaught kings, the town of Boyle and the King family, including a grim tale of tenant eviction during the Famine. Kids can try on replica ancient Irish cloaks, brooches and leather shoes, write with a quill, play a regimental drum and build a vaulted ceiling from specially designed blocks.

The mansion's sheltered walled courtyard hosts an **organic market** (☽ 10am-2pm Sat) selling a fantastic array of organic meat, fish, vegetables, cheeses, chutneys and breads, as well as hot soups to warm you up.

BOYLE ABBEY

Gracing the River Boyle is the finely preserved (and reputedly haunted) **Boyle Abbey** (☎ 071-966 2604; www.heritageireland.ie; adult/child/family €3/1/8; ☽ 10am-6pm Easter–late Oct, last admission 45 min before closing). Founded in 1161 by monks from Mellifont in County Louth (p552), the abbey captures the transition from Romanesque to Gothic style, best seen in the nave, where a set of arches in each style face each other. Unusually for a Cistercian building, figures and carved animals decorate the capitals to the west. After the Dissolution of the Monasteries, the abbey was occupied by the military and became Boyle Castle; the stone chimney on the southern side of the abbey, which was once the refectory, dates from that period.

Guided 40-minute tours of the abbey are available on the hour until 5pm.

LOUGH KEY FOREST PARK

Sprinkled with small islands, **Lough Key Forest Park** (☎ 071-967 3122; www.loughkey.ie; forest admission free, parking €4; ☽ 10am-6pm Mon-Fri, to 8pm Sat & Sun Jul & Aug, 10am-6pm Mar-Jun & Sep-Oct, 10am-4pm Wed-Sun Nov-Feb) has long been popular for its picturesque ruins, including a 12th-century abbey on tiny Trinity Island and a 19th-century castle on Castle Island. It's also a time-honoured favourite with families for its wishing chair, bog gardens, fairy bridge and viewing tower. There are plenty of marked walking trails and a deer enclosure.

The 350-hectare park was once part of the Rockingham estate, owned by the King family from the 17th century until 1957. Rockingham House, designed by John Nash, was destroyed by a fire in the same year; all that remains are some stables, outbuildings and eerie tunnels leading to the lake – built to hide the servants from view.

The park recently received a boost with the addition of a **visitor centre**, and the **Lough Key Experience** (adult/child €7.50/5), incorporating a panoramic, 250m-long treetop canopy walk, which rises 7m above the woodland floor and offers superb lake views. Other attractions include the **Boda Borg Challenge** (adult/child €16/12, min 3 people) – a series of rooms filled with activities and puzzles (great for sudden bursts of rain); and an outdoor **adventure playground** (adult/child free/€5).

In July and August, **Lough Key Boats** (☎ 071-966 7037; www.loughkeyboats.com) provides waterskiing lessons, hourly commentated boat trips, rowing-boat hire and fishing advice (record-breaking pike have been caught here).

Lough Key is 4km east of Boyle on the N4. The Bus Éireann Sligo to Dublin route has frequent services from Boyle to Lough Key.

CLOSE ENCOUNTERS

Maybe it's the wide open skies or the lack of evening entertainment, but Boyle and its surrounds have seen a rash of reported UFO sightings in recent years, particularly along the quiet little back road north to Ballinafad. The **UFO Society of Ireland** (☎ 071-966 2844; www.ufosocietyireland.com) was launched in Boyle in 1997 following a particularly mysterious crash in the nearby mountains. A few kilometres away, the Roscommon side of Carrick-on-Shannon is home to **Golden UFO Investigations** (☎ 086 684 7866). Of course, there are plenty of sceptics, but you might want to keep your eyes peeled – just in case.

DRUMANONE DOLMEN

This astonishing portal **dolmen**, one of the largest in Ireland, measures 4.5m by 3.3m and was constructed before 2000 BC. It can be tricky to find: follow Patrick St and then the R294 out of town for 5km, until you pass under a railway arch. A sign indicates the path across the railway line. Take care crossing as trains are frequent.

DOUGLAS HYDE INTERPRETIVE CENTRE

The life of Roscommon native Dr Douglas Hyde (1860–1949), poet, writer and first president of Ireland, is celebrated at the **Douglas Hyde Interpretive Centre** (Gairdín an Craoibhín; ☎ 094-987 0016; Frenchpark; admission free; ☷ 2-5pm Tue-Fri, 2-6pm Sat & Sun May-Sep). Outside the political arena, Hyde cofounded the Gaelic League in 1893 and spent a lifetime gathering Gaelic poems and folklore that might otherwise have been lost forever.

The centre is housed in the former Protestant church at Frenchpark, 12km southwest of Boyle on the R361. Call ahead to make sure it's open.

ARIGNA MINING EXPERIENCE

Ireland's first and last coal mine (1600s to 1990) is remembered at the **Arigna Mining Experience** (☎ 071-964 6466; www.arignaminingexperience.ie; adult/child €10/6; ☷ 10am-5pm), set in the hills above Lough Allen. The highlight is the 40-minute underground tour, which takes you 400m down to the coal face. Tours are led by ex-miners who really bring home the gruelling working conditions and dangers of their job. Wear sturdy shoes as it can be wet and muddy underfoot.

ARIGNA MINERS WAY & HISTORICAL TRAIL

Covering 118km of north Roscommon, east Sligo and mid-Leitrim, these well-signposted tracks and hill passes cover the routes taken by miners on their way to work. A guidebook with detailed maps is available from local tourist offices.

Sleeping

Boyle is blessed with a clutch of great B&Bs to choose from.

Lough Key Caravan & Camping Park (☎ 071-966 2212; campsites from €10; ☷ Apr–mid-Sep) Right inside the picturesque Lough Key Forest Park, excellent facilities at this campground include a recreation room, a laundry and a children's play area.

Cesh Corran (☎ 071-966 2265; www.marycooney.com; Abbey Tce; s/d €55/80; P) Overlooking the abbey ruins, this immaculately kept place has bright, simple rooms and a very warm welcome. There's a garden, wholesome breakfasts and even a separate bait fridge for anglers.

our pick **Lough Key House** (☎ 071-966 2161; www .loughkeyhouse.com; Rockingham; s/d €55/90; P ⌨) This beautifully restored Georgian country house is a wonderfully atmospheric place to stay, with three guest rooms, each individually decorated with period furniture and tasteful, elegant style. Eggs for breakfast come from the owner's hens, there are bikes to borrow and, if you arrive by bus, you can get picked up from town. Lough Key House is 5km east of town on the N4.

Forest Park House (☎ 071-966 2227; www.bed-and -breakfast-boyle.com; Rockingham; s/d €60/80; P) Slightly out of town near the entrance to Forest Park, this purpose-built guesthouse has spacious modern rooms with pine woodwork and crisp white linens. The B&B is 4km east of town on the N4.

Eating

Boyle has the usual array of Chinese and fast-food restaurants, but not a lot of choice apart from that. Carrick-on-Shannon is a much better place to eat out.

Stone House Cafe (☎ 087 375 5005; Bridge St; lunch €5-8; ☷ 10am-6pm Mon-Sat) This little building on the river was once the gate lodge to the private mansion Frybrook House. It serves a selection of soups, sandwiches, panini and cakes, which you can enjoy as the water rushes by.

Royal Hotel (☎ 071-966 2016; Main St; mains €9-19; ☷ 12.30-9.30pm) Boyle's traditional country

---

HARP & SOUL

The blind harpist Turlough O'Carolan (1670–1738) is celebrated as the last of the Irish bards, though his influence may have been more far-reaching: many attest that he composed the tune (adopted as a drinking song in England) that would later be used for 'The Star-Spangled Banner'.

Most of O'Carolan's life was spent in Mohill (County Leitrim), where his patron Mrs MacDermott-Roe lived. He later moved to the pretty village of Keadue (County Roscommon), where the **O'Carolan International Harp Festival & Summer School** (☎ 071-964 7204; www.keadue.harp.net; ☺ late Jul–early Aug) is held in his honour. Over the course of a week, the festival's program includes harp workshops, recitals and lectures. The festival is preceded by a week-long summer school of music and dancing classes.

O'Carolan is buried in the 12th-century Kilronan church just west of the village on the R284 to Sligo.

---

hotel serves decent but predictable bar food, ranging from steaks, grills and salmon fillets to toasted sandwiches.

Drinking & Entertainment

Moving Stairs (☎ 071-966 3586; The Crescent) The most lively evening joint in Boyle has a great line-up of live music – everything from jazz and traditional music to rock, depending on the night.

Wynne's Bar (☎ 086 821 4736; Main St) This quaint old bar in the centre of town is famous for its traditional music sessions on Friday nights. Come early if you want a seat.

Getting There & Away

Bus Éireann (☎ 01-836 6111) runs coaches between Dublin (€19, three hours) and Sligo (€11.50, 50 minutes), stopping off at Boyle en route. There are six buses in each direction Monday to Saturday and five on Sunday. Buses pull up near the Royal Hotel on Bridge St.

Boyle **train station** (☎ 071-966 2027) is on Elphin St. Trains leave eight times daily to Sligo (€13, 40 minutes) and Dublin (€39, 2½ hours) via Mullingar.

ROSCOMMON TOWN

pop 5017

The county town of Roscommon is very much a place of local business and commerce, but it has a small, stately centre, some significant abbey and castle ruins and a couple of really lovely accommodation options that make it well worth a stop.

Roscommon's seasonal **tourist office** (☎ 090-662 6342; www.irelandwest.ie; The Square; ☺ 10am-1pm & 2-5pm Mon-Sat Jun-Aug) is in the County Museum next to the post office. You can pick up a map of the town and heritage trail here.

Internet access is available upstairs in **Easons** (☎ 090-662 5049; The Square; ☺ 9am-7pm) for €3 per hour.

Sights & Activities

In the former Presbyterian church, **Roscommon County Museum** (☎ 090-662 5613; The Square; adult/child €2/1; ☺ 10am-3pm Mon-Fri Jun–mid-Sep) contains some interesting pieces, including an inscribed 9th-century slab from St Coman's monastery and a superb medieval sheila-na-gig. The unusual Star of David window supposedly represents the Trinity.

The impressive ruins of Norman **Roscommon Castle** stand alone in a field to the north of town, beautifully framed by the landscaped lawns and small lake of the new town park. Built in 1269, the castle was almost immediately destroyed by Irish forces, and its turbulent history continued until the final surrender to Cromwell in 1652. The massive walls and round bastions are a reminder of how significant this fortress once was.

At the southern end of town, the 13th-century **Dominican priory**, off Circular Rd, merits a quick visit for its unusual 15th-century carving of eight *gallógli* ('gallowglasses', who were mercenary soldiers). Wielding seven swords and an axe, they protect an earlier effigy of the priory's founder, Felim O'Conor, set in the north wall.

Roscommon's central square is dominated by its former courthouse (now the Bank of Ireland). Opposite, the facade of the **old jail** survives. Ask any local about the grim tale of Lady Betty, its infamous hang woman.

You can pick up a brochure and map of the **Suck Valley Way**, a 75km walking trail along the River Suck, at the tourist office. The river has an abundance of rudd, tench, pike and perch. En route you pass the rare **La Tène Stone**, an Iron Age spiral-inscribed stone in Castlestrange, 7km southwest of town on the R366.

Sleeping & Eating

Jacksons (☎ 090-663 4140; www.jacksons.ie; The Square; s/d €50/95, lunch mains €5-12, dinner mains €14-24; ⊗ 12.30-4.30pm daily & 5-9pm Wed-Sun) The top spot to eat in town, this modern restaurant is run by an award-winning chef keen to make the most of seasonal local produce. The menu features local meat, fish and game in interesting combinations. Upstairs there are 10 big, modern rooms with warm wood furniture and plenty of light.

Gleeson's (☎ 090-662 6954; www.gleesonstownhouse.com; The Square; s/d from €75/125, cafe mains €8-14, restaurant mains €11-20; ⊗ cafe 8am-6pm, restaurant noon-3pm & 6.30-9.15pm; P □) There's a wonderfully warm welcome at this listed 19th-century town house, set back from the square in its own courtyard, full of fairy lights. Rooms are decorated in bright Mediterranean colours and exude a cosy, country-house feel. There's a bustling cafe downstairs, as well as the popular Manse restaurant which serves solid but rather staid fare.

Castlecoote House (☎ 090-666 3794; www.castlecootehouse.com; Castlecoote; s/d €119/178; P) About 8km southwest of Roscommon, this Georgian mansion has five impossibly romantic rooms with antique furnishings and views over the orchard, croquet lawn, ruined castle or river. A couple also come with four-poster beds and chandeliers. You can play tennis on two courts on the grounds. From Roscommon town, take the R366 signposted to Fuerty and follow it to Castlecoote. As you go over the bridge into the village, the double gates of Castlecoote House are on your right.

Drinking & Entertainment

JJ Harlow's (☎ 090-663 0869; The Square) Untouched until recently, the front bar at this old-world pub still has shelves full of provisions and hardware items, though it has lost much of its original character. The modern back bar hosts regular live music including bluegrass and jazz.

Roscommon Arts Centre (☎ 090-662 5824; www.roscommonartscentre.ie; Circular Rd) There's an impressive range of independent cinema and touring comedy, theatre and music at this auditorium. Check the website for listings.

Getting There & Away

Bus Éireann (☎ 090-648 4406) express services between Westport (€16, 2¼ hours) and Dublin (€19, three hours) via Athlone stop in Roscommon three times daily (once on Sunday). Buses stop outside Regan's Bar on the square.

Roscommon train station is in Abbeytown, just south of the town centre near the Galway road; there are three trains daily (four Friday) on the line from Dublin (€15 to €40, two hours) to Westport (€15 to €26, 1½ hours).

COUNTY LEITRIM

The delights of the unassuming county of Leitrim are a well-kept secret, and it seems the locals like it that way. The untamed landscape and authentic rural charm are genuinely cherished by those who call it home and there's a reluctance to let anyone or anything spoilt it. Despite this, there's an enormous welcome for visitors – just don't bank on being let in on secrets about favourite fishing spots or watering holes until you've been here at least a generation.

Leitrim was ravaged by the famine in the 19th century and spent subsequent generations struggling with mass emigration and unemployment, but today it has a spark all of its own and has become a beloved hideout for artists, writers and musicians as well as a huge boating centre.

Water is everywhere in Leitrim: when locals say that land is sold by the gallon, they're only half joking. The county is split almost in two by Lough Allen, and the mighty River Shannon remains the area's biggest draw. Carrick-on-Shannon, the county town, is a lively centre that makes a great base for exploring the region by water or by road. To the west is the wonderfully atmospheric Parke's Castle and further north, the tranquil Organic Centre at Rossinver.

CARRICK-ON-SHANNON
pop 3163

Carrick-on-Shannon is a charming town with a riverside location and a thriving community. Since the completion of the Shannon–Erne Waterway, the marina here has become incredibly busy. The town is a hugely popular weekend destination with a good choice of accommodation and restaurants and a great

---

THE SHANNON–ERNE WATERWAY

Ireland's two main river systems, the Shannon and the Erne, were linked in the mid-1800s as part of a much-needed drainage scheme for the poor soil in the area. The canal was never a success however, and had already begun to deteriorate by the 1870s. In 1994 a far-sighted renovation project created a symbolic link between Northern Ireland and the Republic when the canal was reopened as the Shannon–Erne Waterway. It creates an amazing 750km network of rivers, lakes and artificial navigations. The waterway runs from the River Shannon beside the village of Leitrim, 4km north of Carrick-on-Shannon, through northwestern County Cavan to the southern shore of Upper Lough Erne, just over the Northern Ireland border in County Fermanagh.

---

music and arts scene. Plan your visit in advance, especially in summer.

During the 17th and most of the 18th centuries Carrick was a Protestant enclave, and the local residents' wealth can still be seen in the graceful buildings around the town. Catholics were permitted to live in the area known as the 'Liberty' on the Roscommon side of the river.

Orientation & Information

Carrick's main L-shaped layout (Main St, then the right-angled turn onto Bridge St) is in County Leitrim; the town's continuation over the bridge is in County Roscommon. Market Yard is situated at the corner of the 'L'.

AIB (Allied Irish Bank; Main St)

D Internet Cafe (☎ 071-965 0819; Main St; €5 per hr; ⏰ 10am-10pm Mon-Fri, 10am-8pm Sat, noon-8pm Sun)

Post office (St George's Tce) Opposite Market Yard.

Tourist office (☎ 071-962 0170; www.leitrimtourism .com; Old Barrel Store, Carrick-on-Shannon Marina; ⏰ 9.30am-5pm Easter-Oct) Has a walking-tour booklet, which takes in Carrick's places of interest.

Trinity Rare Books (☎ 071-962 2144; Bridge St) Stocks over 20,000 antique and second-hand books, including some hard-to-come-by first editions and a huge collection of Irish-interest titles.

Sights

Europe's smallest chapel is the teensy **Costello Chapel** (Bridge St), measuring just 5m by 3.6m. It was built by Edward Costello in 1877, dis-

traught at the early death of his wife Mary. Both husband and wife now rest within the grey limestone interior lit by a single stained-glass window. Their embalmed bodies were placed in lead coffins, which sit on either side of the door under slabs of glass. If the door is locked, ask the tourist office for a key.

Carrick has some wonderful examples of early-19th-century architecture on St George's Terrace. Have a glance at **Hatley Manor**, home of the St George family; and the **Old Courthouse** (now the seat of the county council), whose underground tunnel led convicts from the dock to the now demolished jail; and stop by the craft shops and cafes in the recently refurbished **Market Yard**.

Activities

The 110-seater boat **Moon River** (☎ 071-962 1777; www.moon-river.net; The Quay) runs one-hour cruises on the Shannon. There are one or two sailings per day (€15) between mid-March and October, increasing to four sailings during July and August; check the information board on the quay for details. The boat also has late-night cruises; see p523.

If you prefer to sail under your own steam, Carrick is the Shannon–Erne Waterway's **boat-hire** capital, with several companies based at the Marina. The canal's 16 locks are fully automated, you don't need a licence, and you're given full instructions on handling your boat before you set off. Make sure you pick up a chart of the waterway (available from bookshops and boat-hire companies), showing the depths and locations of locks. High-season prices start at around €1000 per week for a four-berth cruiser.

Hire companies:

Carrick Craft (☎ central reservations 01-278 1666, Carrick office 071-962 0236; www.carrickcraft.com; The Marina)

RIVER'S WISDOM

According to Irish mythology, the River Shannon's name comes from Princess Sinann, granddaughter of Lír (father god of the sea). According to the legend, Sinann plunged into a well where the salmon of wisdom swam in pursuit of its mystic knowledge, causing the well to boil up into a raging flood which created the great river.

A plaque on Carrick-on-Shannon's main street opposite Market Yard commemorates the legend.

Emerald Star (☎ 071-962 7633; www.emeraldstar.ie; The Marina)

The annual regatta run by **Carrick Rowing Club** (www.carrickrowingclub.com) takes place on the first Sunday in August and draws a big crowd.

For information on fishing, contact the **Carrick-on-Shannon Angling Club** (☎ 071-962 0313; Ashleigh House).

Sleeping

Carrick has a good choice of accommodation, with plenty of B&Bs and a selection of large, rather characterless hotels. Ask at the tourist office for details. Camping is free on the Roscommon side of the riverbank, though there are no facilities. Tokens for the showers at the nearby Marina can be purchased from the Marina office.

An Oiche Hostel (☎ 071-962 1848; Bridge St; dm €25; P) The town's only budget option is this basic hostel, hidden away above a vet's surgery on Main St. There are four plain, single-sex dorms that are comfortable but pricey. There's a small kitchen and sitting room for guest use.

Caldra House (☎ 071-962 3040; www.caldrahouse .ie; Caldragh; s/d €55/78; P ⌨) This creeper-clad Georgian house offers exceptional value, with four period-style rooms decorated with antiques and subtle floral patterns. Set in mature gardens overlooking the Arigna Mountains, it's a very tranquil spot, 3km from town. Follow the R280 north out of town, turning left after 2km, then right at the T-junction.

Ciúin House (☎ 071-967 1488; www.ciuinhouse.com; Hartley; s €64.50-85, d €99-130; P ⌨) On the edge of town but within walking distance of the main street, this lovely purpose-built guesthouse has 15 spacious rooms with simple but stylish furnishings. Orthopaedic beds, Jacuzzi baths and crisp linens make it feel more like a hotel than a B&B. There's also a restaurant on site (dinner mains €17 to €28) if you don't feel like going out. To get here, follow Main St to its end, veering left onto Leitrim Rd and left again at the fork for Hartley.

Hollywell (☎ 071-962 1124; hollywell@esatbiz.com; Liberty Hill; r €90-110; ⌚ mid-Feb–mid-Nov; P) This beautiful ivy-covered Georgian country house, on the Roscommon side of the river, has spacious, restful bedrooms with huge beds. The two superior rooms each have a generous sitting area, with splendid views of the Shannon and its ever-changing light. Hollywell's hosts are full of local knowledge and put on superb breakfasts. The antique furnishings and proximity to the water mean the house isn't suitable for children.

For extra romance and old-world elegance, there are two luxury castle hotels within a few miles of Carrick. Check their websites for special offers.

Lough Rynn Castle (☎ 071-963 2700; www.lough rynn.ie; Mohill, Co Leitrim; r €135-185) A 19th-century pile set on 300 acres on the shores of Lough Rynn, about 10km east of Carrick.

Kilronan Castle (☎ 071-961 8000; www.kilronan castle.ie; Ballyfarnon, Co Roscommon; r €179-240) An imposing castle overlooking Lough Meelagh, about 10km northwest of Carrick.

Eating

Larder Cafe (☎ 071-965 0525; www.thelarder.ie; 4 Market Yard; dishes €4.50-7; ⌚ 9am-5pm Tue-Fri, 10am-5pm Sat) Set in one of the restored stone buildings in Market Yard, this modern cafe is a popular lunch spot and serves a good selection of soups, sandwiches, cakes, gourmet coffees and fairtrade teas.

Vittos (☎ 071-962 7000; www.vittosrestaurant.com; Market Yard; mains €12-22; ⌚ Tue-Sat) In a wood-beamed barn, this family-friendly restaurant has an extensive menu of classic Italian and more traditional Irish dishes, including great pastas and pizzas and some less-inspired grills. Service is fast and friendly and the atmosphere is warm and cosy.

Victoria Hall Restaurant (☎ 071-962 0320; www .victoriahall.ie; Victoria Hall, Quay Rd; mains €19-28; ⌚ 12.30-10pm; 🛜) The locals' favourite for food, this graceful old parochial hall has had a thoroughly modern makeover and now has a stylish minimalist interior, with a lovely 1st-floor dining area. The open kitchen churns out excellent Asian- and European-inspired dishes, with bento boxes (€15.50) and boxty (a traditional potato pancake) wraps with Thai fillings (€11), the speciality at lunch.

The Oarsman (☎ 071-962 1733; www.theoarsman.com; Bridge St; lunch mains €9-13, dinner €22-28; ⌚ noon-3pm & 5-8.30pm Tue-Sat) It may look like a pub from the outside, but The Oarsman serves restaurant-quality food in relaxed, informal surroundings. The menu ranges from traditional Irish with a contemporary twist to Asian-inspired dishes, cooked equally well. Snacks and bar food are served between lunch and dinner, and they pull a good pint, too.

GRAZING YOUR WAY ALONG THE SHANNON

Cruising along the Shannon is a wonderful way to see some hidden corners of Ireland and attracts a leisurely crowd of boaters keen to relax, enjoy the views and eat well. Gastro pubs and gourmet restaurants have popped up all along the river banks, making a cruise along the Shannon a tempting way to sample the spoils of the lush Midlands pastures. Try Athlone and Carrick-on-Shannon for a great choice of fine-dining options or venture further afield to try some of the following:

Glasson Village Restaurant (p527; ☎ 090-648 5001; michaelrosebrooks@gmail.com; Glasson, Co Westmeath; mains €21-30; ☺ 6-9.30pm Tue-Sun, 12.30-2.30pm Sun) Pioneering gourmet restaurant with an informal atmosphere, specialising in seafood.

Keenans (☎ 043-332 6052; www.keenans.ie; Tarmonbarry, Co Roscommon; mains €16-28; ☺ 12.30-2.30pm daily & 6.30-8.30pm Mon-Sat) Spacious, modern restaurant with high ceilings, river views and wholesome, unpretentious food.

Old Fort (p511; ☎ 090-967 4973; www.theoldfortrestaurant.com; Shannonbridge, Co Roscommon; mains €19.50-29.50; ☺ 5-9.30pm Wed-Sat, 12.30-2.30pm Sun) Posh nosh in the grand surroundings of a massive bridgehead, built as defence against Napoleon.

Purple Onion (☎ 043-335 9919; www.purpleonion.ie; Tarmonbarry, Co Roscommon; mains €15-28; ☺ 5.30-9.30pm Tue-Sun, 12.30-3.30pm Sun) Popular old-world pub with great service and solid food.

Wineport Restaurant (p527; ☎ 090-643 9010; www.wineport.ie; Glasson, Co Westmeath; mains €25-37; ☺ 6-10pm Mon-Sun, 3-5pm Sun) A deservedly popular fine-dining spot, serving an ambitious international menu.

Yew Tree (☎ 090-666 1255; gerald.aherne@hotmail.com; Lecarrow, Co Roscommon; mains €15-28; ☺ 12.30-5pm & 6-9pm Wed-Sun) A surprising find in a tiny village, this place dishes up generous portions of traditional dishes brought bang up to date.

Drinking

Flynn's Corner House (☎ 071-962 1139; cnr Main & Bridge Sts) This authentic old-world pub serves a good pint of Guinness and has live music on Friday nights. Savour it before it's modernised.

Cryan's (☎ 071-967 2066; Bridge St) A traditional little pub with few frills, this is another good bet for traditional music sessions on Saturday and Sunday nights.

Moon River (☎ 071-962 1777; www.moon-river.net; The Quay; admission €15; ☺ mid-Mar–Sep) Local bands make Saturday nights aboard this 110-seat cruiser a great alternative to hitting the pubs. Boarding is at 9.30pm; the boat then sets sail along the Shannon from 10pm to midnight.

Entertainment

Carrick's **cinema** (Carrick Cineplex; ☎ 071-967 200; www.carrickcineplex.ie; Boyle Rd) screens new releases. In your travels around the area, you may also spot the **mobile cinema** (www.leitrimcinema.ie): a capsule that contains a full set of seats as well as a giant screen. The tourist office can tell you where you can catch it and what's playing.

The **Dock Arts Centre** (☎ 071-965 0828; www.thedock.ie; St George's Tce; ☺ 10am-6pm Mon-Sat) is set in the 19th-century former courthouse and hosts performances, exhibitions, workshops and artists' studios. Also here is the **Leitrim Design House** (www.leitrimdesignhouse.ie), which features the work of local artists, designers and craftspeople.

Getting There & Away

Bus Éireann (☎ 01-836 6111) express service 23 between Dublin (€19, 2¾ hours) and Sligo (€13, one hour) stops here six times in each direction Monday to Saturday (five Sunday). The service stops at several large towns en route, including Boyle, Longford and Mullingar. The bus stop is outside Coffey's Pastry Case on Bridge St.

The **train station** (☎ 071-962 0036) is a 15-minute walk, over on the Roscommon side of the river. Turn right across the bridge, then left at the petrol station onto Station Rd. Carrick has three trains daily to Dublin (€39, 2¼ hours) and Sligo (€17, 55 minutes), with an additional one to Sligo on Friday.

WEST LEITRIM

North and west of Carrick-on-Shannon, the Leitrim landscape comes into its own, its ruffled hills, steel-grey lakes and isolated cottages exuding a genuine rural charm, unadulterated for the tourist market. You'll also find a clutch of attractions in this seemingly forgotten part of the country that make it well worth the effort it takes to get there. All are easily accessible on a day trip from Sligo.

If you fancy taking to the hills on foot, the **Leitrim Way** walking trail begins in Drumshanbo and ends in Manorhamilton, a distance of 48km. For more-detailed information get a copy of *Way-Marked Trails of Ireland*, by Michael Fewer, from the tourist office.

Creevelea Abbey

A short riverside walk from Dromahair village leads to the ruinous remains of this unfortunate Franciscan friary. A monument to bad timing, the abbey was founded just a few decades before the orders were suppressed in 1539. Yet despite the abbey being gutted by fire on several occasions and desecrated by Richard Bingham and later Cromwell, the hardy monks kept coming back. The cloister has some curious carvings of St Francis, one displaying stigmata and another depicting the saint preaching to birds.

The abbey is off the R288, 3km from Dromahair.

Parke's Castle

The tranquil surrounds of **Parke's Castle** (☎ 071-916 4149; www.heritageireland.ie; Fivemile Bourne; adult/child €3/1; ☺ 10am-6pm mid-Mar–Oct; ℗), with swans drifting by on Lough Gill and neat grass cloaking the old moat, belie the fact that its early Plantation architecture was created out of an unwelcome English landlord's insecurity and fear.

The thoroughly restored, three-storey castle forms part of one of the five sides of the bawn, which also has three rounded turrets at its corners. Join one of the entertaining guided tours after viewing the 20-minute video. Last admission is at 5.15pm.

You can take a 1½-hour cruise on Lough Gill from the castle. Trips aboard the **Rose of Innisfree** (☎ 071-916 4266; www.roseofinnisfree.com; adult/child €15/7.50; ☺ 11am, 12.30pm, 1.30pm, 3.30pm & 4.30pm Easter-Oct) offer live recitals of Yeats' poetry accompanying music. The company runs a bus from Sligo to the castle. Call for departure times and location. To get to Parke's Castle from Creevelea Abbey, continue north along the R288.

Ard na Hoo

Cleanse the mind and spirit and get back to basics at **Ard na Hoo** (☎ 071-913 4939; www.ardnahoo .com; Mullagh, Dromahair; 4-bed cabin weekend/week €550/750), a rustic eco-retreat where you can rent a self-catering eco-lodge, join a yoga retreat or detox program, take a course in alternative living or natural healthcare, or simply sign up for some pampering in the spa. Facilities are simple but comfortable and are designed to relieve you of the stress of city living.

Rossinver Organic Centre

All things good and wholesome come together at the **Rossinver Organic Centre** (☎ 071-985 4338; www.theorganiccentre.ie; Rossinver; adult/child €5/free; ☺ 10am-5pm Feb-Nov), which aims to promote organic horticulture and sustainable living at its beautiful grounds in north Leitrim. You can simply come and tour the beautiful display gardens, or take a course in anything from organic growing to sustainable design, cheese-making, willow sculpture, bread baking or silk painting. The **cafe** (☺ 11am-4pm Sat & Sun) serves wonderful vegetarian fare baked with ingredients from the garden.

COUNTY LONGFORD

A solidly agrarian region, County Longford is a quiet place of low hills and pastoral scenes. It has few tourist sights but is a haven for anglers who come for the superb fishing around Lough Ree and Lanesborough.

Longford suffered massive emigration during the Famine of the 1840s and 1850s and it has never really recovered. Many Longford migrants went to Argentina, where one of their descendants, Edel Miro O'Farrell, became president in 1914.

Longford's eponymous county town is a decidedly workaday place, but there's a friendly **tourist office** (☎ 043-334 2577; www.longfordtourism .ie; Market Sq; ☺ 9am-5.30pm Mon-Sat May-Sep, hr vary Oct-Apr) and plenty of places to eat.

The county's main attraction is the magnificent **Corlea Trackway** (☎ 043-332 2386; www .heritageireland.ie; Keenagh; admission free; ☺ 10am-6pm Apr-Sep), an Iron Age bog road that was built in 148 BC. An 18m stretch of the historic track has now been preserved in a humidified hall at the visitor centre, where you can join a 45-minute tour that details the bog's unique flora and fauna, and fills you in on how the track was discovered, and methods used to preserve it. Wear a windproof jacket as the bog land can get blowy. The centre is 15km south of Longford on the Ballymahon road (R397).

Longford is also home to one of the three biggest portal dolmens in Ireland. The **Aughnacliffe dolmen** has an improbably balanced top stone and is thought to be around 5000 years old. Aughnacliffe is 18km north of Longford town off the R198.

There are regular **Bus Éireann** (☎ 01-836 6111) services from Longford town to numerous destinations, including Dublin (€15, two hours, 13 daily Monday to Saturday, 11 Sunday) and Sligo (€13, 1½ hours, six daily Monday to Saturday, five Sunday). Buses stop outside Longford train station.

Longford **train station** (☎ 043-334 5208), off New St, has trains to Dublin (€34, one hour and 40 minutes, four daily) and Sligo (€26, 1¼ hours, three daily Monday to Saturday, four Sunday).

COUNTY WESTMEATH

Characterised by lakes and pastures grazed by beef cattle, Westmeath has a wealth of attractions, ranging from a wonderful whiskey distillery and the miraculous Fore Valley, to the country's oldest pub in the confident county town, Athlone. The rivers and lakes attract a steady stream of visitors and a host of gourmet restaurants and fine accommodation options have sprung up in recent years to cater for the discerning crowds.

ATHLONE
pop 14,347
Set on the banks of the Shannon, the thriving town of Athlone is a magnet for river traffic and is a solid manufacturing base for international companies. It's one of Ireland's most vibrant towns, with a mix of stylish modern developments, big shopping centres and small winding streets, home to independent businesses.

The Shannon splits this former garrison town in two, with most businesses and services sitting on its eastern bank. In the shadow of Athlone Castle, the western bank is an enchanting jumble of twisting streets, colourfully painted houses, historic pubs, antique shops and old book binders, as well as some outstanding restaurants.

Orientation & Information
Athlone is on the main Dublin–Galway road (N6). The Shannon flows through the centre, with Athlone Castle and Sts Peter and Paul Cathedral prominently situated on the river's western bank. The websites www.athlone.ie and www.discoverireland.ie/westmeath are good sources of information. You'll find most of the main banks along Church St.

Netcafe (☎ 090-647 8888; 1 Paynes Lane; per hr €3.50; ✆ 11am–11pm)

Post office (Barrack St) Beside the cathedral.

Tourist office (☎ 090-649 4630; Athlone Castle; ✆ 9.30am–1pm & 2–5.15pm Mon-Fri May–Sep) Inside the castle guardhouse.

Sights & Activities
ATHLONE CASTLE
The ancient river ford at Athlone was an important crossroads on the Shannon and was the cause of many squabbles over the centuries. By 1210, the Normans had asserted their power and built a castle here. In 1690 the Jacobite town survived a siege by Protestant forces, but it fell a year later – under a devastating bombardment of 12,000 cannonballs – to William of Orange's troops. The castle was soon remodelled and further major alterations took place over the following centuries.

The **Athlone Castle Visitor Centre** (☎ 090-649 2912; adult/child/family €6/1.70/12.50; ✆ 9.30am-4.30pm May–Sep) contains some informative displays on the Siege of Athlone, the flora and fauna of the Shannon, and the Shannon's role in the production of hydroelectricity. Other highlights are an old gramophone that belonged to the great Athlone tenor John McCormack (1884–1945); and a military and folk museum with two sheila-na-gigs. An hour is probably enough time to take it all in.

RIVER CRUISES
If you fancy taking to the water, **Viking Tours** (☎ 086 262 1136; vikingtours@ireland.com; 7 St Mary's Pl; ✆ May–Sep) offers cruises on the Shannon aboard a replica Viking longship, complete with costumed staff and dress-up clothes, including helmets, swords and shields for kids. Tours sail north to Lough Ree (adult/child/family €12/10/40, 75 minutes), and south to Clonmacnoise (adult/child/family €20/15/60, 4½ hours) in County Offaly. A round trip to Clonmacnoise allows a 90-minute stop at the ruins. There are usually daily sailings in June, July and August, plus sailings most days in

THE MIDLANDS

THROW AWAY YOUR GUIDEBOOK

Whether you're on the water or travelling by road, there's a host of interesting small towns and villages along and around the Shannon and the Royal and Grand Canals that make wonderfully tranquil stops. Most are rarely visited by touring motorists but are brimming with history, picturesque views and fine pubs.

In Leitrim you'll find **Ballinamore**, a lively spot on the Shannon–Erne Waterway, and **Drumshanbo**, a wonderfully traditional town with an interesting visitor centre. Just to the south is **Keshcarrigan**, home to a collapsed dolmen and some unusual St Patrick's Day festivities. Further west, **Cootehall**, on the River Boyle, has a fine restaurant and a lovely old-world pub. Nearby **Knockvicar** has a riverfront restaurant at its busy marina. Heading south, **Drumsna** is a lovely traditional country village, while nearby **Dromod** is well known for its excellent fishing. **Tarmonbarry** is another good stop, with a good choice of interesting restaurants and pubs, a swish hotel and a lively vibe. Nearby **Clondra**, where the Shannon meets the Royal Canal, is a stunning little place with lovely walks and **Keenagh**, further along the canal, is a sleepy but quaint little town.

May and September; call or ask the tourist office about schedules.

New outfit **Shannon Safari** (☎ 086 284 9108; www.shannonsafari.ie; 36 Silverquay) offers private hour-long powerboat cruises year-round for €200 per hour. Boats depart beside the Radisson hotel.

FISHING

Information and permits are available from the friendly **Strand Tackle Shop** (☎ 090-647 9277; powell@iol.ie; The Strand), on the eastern bank of the river opposite the castle.

Sleeping

Bastion B&B (☎ 090-649 4954; www.thebastion.net; 2 Bastion St; s €45-60, d €65-85) In a converted draper's shop, this funky B&B's white-on-white interiors are a canvas for eclectic artwork, cactus collections and Indian wall hangings. The five rooms (three with private bathroom) are crisp and clean, with neatly folded fluffy towels, and there's an arty lounge–breakfast room, where you can kick-start your day with cereal, fruit, ground coffee, fresh bread and a cheeseboard.

our pick **Coosan Cottage Eco Guesthouse** (☎ 090-647 3468; www.ecoguesthouse.com; Coosan Point Rd; s/d €50/100; P) This beautiful ecofriendly cottage was a labour of love for its owners, blendsing traditional style with modern thinking. Triple glazed windows, a wood pellet burner and a heat recovery system are just some of its green credentials. For visitors, though, it's the tranquil surroundings and great breakfasts that will stick in the mind. The cottage is 2.5km from the town centre, with free pick-up if you're coming by train or bus. Credit cards aren't accepted.

Athlone Springs (☎ 090-644 4444; www.athlonespringshotel.com; Monksland; d from €120; P) This sleek, modern hotel on the outskirts of town makes a good alternative to the more predictable offerings elsewhere. Retro style carpets, designer furniture, slick finishes and a gleaming, split-level restaurant make it an attractive option. The spacious rooms are flooded with natural light and are suitably plush. The hotel is 3km west of town on the R362.

Eating

You'll be spoilt for choice when it comes to dining in Athlone, which has established itself as the culinary capital of the Midlands. Scout around the western bank's backstreets and you'll unearth some gems.

our pick **Left Bank Bistro** (☎ 090-649 4446; www.leftbankbistro.com; Fry Pl; lunch mains €5-14, dinner mains €22-29; noon-5pm & 5.30-10.30pm Tue-Sat) With airy, white-washed interiors, shelves of gourmet goods, and a menu combining superior Irish ingredients with Mediterranean and Asian influences, this sophisticated deli-bistro attracts those in the know. Lunch features bowls of steaming pasta, big salads and chunky open sandwiches, while dinner dishes up beautifully grilled meat and fish and some extraordinary desserts.

Olive Grove (☎ 090-647 6946; www.theolivegrove.ie; Custume Pl; lunch mains €6.50-12.50, dinner mains €17-27; noon-4pm & 5.30-10pm Tue-Sun) This slick waterside restaurant gets rave reviews from happy punters keen on the stylish design and creative menu. Go for prawn laska or baked camembert followed by chilli-garlic pork rack with a bean ragout or duck breast with poached pear flavoured with star anise.

Kin Khao (☎ 090-649 8805; www.kinkhaothai.ie; Abbey Lane; mains €16-22; ⏲ 12.30-2.30pm Wed-Fri, 5.30-10.30pm Mon-Sat, 1.30-10.30pm Sun) What is possibly the best Thai restaurant in Ireland is tucked away near the castle and is renowned for its extensive menu of authentic dishes. All the chefs and staff are Thai (with the exception of one half of the husband and wife team who run the place) and you'd be advised to book ahead if you want to join the band of loyal Kin Khao devotees.

Le Château (☎ 090-649 4517; Peter's Port; mains €17-25; ⏲ 5.30-10pm Tue-Sat, 12.30-9.30pm Sun) Another Athlone favourite, this classy joint has a split-level timber dining room glowing with flickering candles. The menu features traditional Irish favourites spiced up with speciality and local produce. Expect plenty of meat dishes. Sunday lunch is particularly popular.

Drinking & Entertainment

Sean's Bar (☎ 090-649 2358; 13 Main St) Age certainly hasn't wearied Sean's Bar. Dating way back to AD 900, Sean's stakes its claim as Ireland's oldest pub. Its log fires, uneven floors (to help flood waters run back down to the river), sawdust, rickety piano and curios collected over the years attest to the theory. The riverside beer garden has live music most nights in summer; to really see things in full swing, turn up at about 5.30pm on a Saturday.

Dean Crowe Theatre (☎ 090-649 2129; www.dean crowetheatre.com; Chapel St) This refurbished theatre has wonderful acoustics and runs a broad program of theatrical and musical events year-round.

Getting There & Around

Athlone's **bus depot** (☎ 090-648 4406) is beside the train station. Express buses stop there on many east–west routes. There are 15 buses daily to Dublin (€12, two hours) and Galway (€12, 1¼ hours); three from Monday to Saturday (one Sunday) to Westport (€11.50, 2¾ hours) in County Mayo; and three Monday to Saturday (one Sunday, plus an extra bus Friday) to Mullingar (€10.30, one hour).

From **Athlone train station** (☎ 090-647 3300), there are 11 trains daily Monday to Saturday (nine Sunday) to Dublin (€15 to €34, 1¾ hours); three or four daily to Westport (€15 to €32, two hours); and five to eight daily to Galway (€15 to €21.50, 1¼ hours).

The train station is on the eastern bank, on Southern Station Rd. To get here, follow Northgate St up from Custume Pl. Its extension, Coosan Point Rd, joins Southern Station Rd near St Vincent's Hospital.

You can order a taxi on ☎ 090-647 4400.

LOUGH REE & AROUND

Many of the 50-plus islands within **Lough Ree** were once inhabited by monks and their ecclesiastical treasures, drawing Vikings like moths to a flame. These days, the visitors are less bloodthirsty, with sailing, trout fishing and birdwatching the most popular pastimes. Migratory birds that nest here include swans, plovers and curlews.

Poet, playwright and novelist Oliver Goldsmith (1728–74), author of *The Vicar of Wakefield*, is closely associated with the area running alongside the eastern shore of Lough Ree. Known as **Goldsmith Country**, the region is beautifully captured in his writings. The *Lough Ree Trail: A Signposted Tour*, by Gearoid O'Brien, is available from the tourist offices in Athlone and Mullingar. Ideal for cycling, this 32km tour runs through Glasson (which Goldsmith called the 'loveliest village of the plain') and around the shores of Lough Ree, and into County Longford.

Situated 8km northeast of Athlone on the N55, the little village of **Glasson** is these days well worth a stop for its outstanding restaurants and lively pubs. The **Glasson Village Restaurant** (☎ 090-648 5001; michaelrosebrooks@gmail .com; mains €21-30; ⏲ 6-9.30pm Tue-Sun, 12.30-2.30pm Sun) is a wonderfully informal place serving excellent food. The nearby **Wineport Restaurant** (☎ 090-643 9010; www.wineport.ie; d €150-350, mains €25-37; ⏲ 6-10pm Mon-Sat, 3-5pm & 6-10pm Sun), in a lakeside cedar lodge, has a reputation for the finest modern Irish cuisine. The lodge's 10 luxurious rooms are named after wines and Champagnes.

Getting There & Away

Bus Éireann (☎ 090-648 4406) service 466 from Athlone to Longford has two trips daily from Monday to Saturday, stopping outside Grogan's pub in Glasson.

KILBEGGAN & AROUND

Little Kilbeggan has two big claims to fame: a restored distillery-turned-museum and Ireland's only National Hunt racecourse.

Whiskey buffs and industrial technology enthusiasts will get a kick out of **Locke's Distillery** (☎ 057-933 2134; www.lockesdistillery

museum.ie; Kilbeggan; adult/child €7/free; ⊙ 9am-6pm Apr-Oct, 10am-4pm Nov-Mar). Established in 1757, this whiskey producer is believed to have been the oldest licensed pot still in the world before it ceased operation two centuries later. Today you can marvel at hulking machinery, visit a cooper's room and warehouse, and listen to the creaks and groans of the working mill wheel. Guided tours last 50 minutes, finishing off with a whiskey tasting.

Punters from all over the country attend the old-time evening meetings at the **Kilbeggan Races** (☎ 057-933 2176; www.kilbegganraces.com; tickets €15; ⊙ approx fortnightly May-Sep). The town is transformed on race nights into a buzzing equine centre, where the thrill of the chase is matched by the craic in the pubs.

About 6.5km west of Kilbeggan (1.5km west of Horseleap), just off the N6, is the blissful spa retreat **Temple House & Health Spa** (☎ 057-933 5118; www.templespa.ie; s €95-155, d €130-350, 2/3-course dinner €39/48; ⊙ day spa Wed-Sun, restaurant 7-9pm Tue-Thu, 7-9.30pm Fri & Sat, 12.30-2pm Sun; P ⬛). The 250-year-old house is set on 40 hectares of grounds on the site of an ancient monastery. Rooms are blissfully tranquil with a mix of period charm and modern style and, although there are plenty of healthy options on the restaurant menu, it's a fine dining experience with locally sourced, organic ingredients topping the bill. Both the restaurant and the day spa are open to nonguests.

MULLINGAR & AROUND
pop 8940

A prosperous regional town, Mullingar hums with the activity of locals going about their daily lives. Nearby there are fish-filled lakes, a pewter factory, and a fantastical mansion with an odious history.

James Joyce visited the town in his youth and it appears in both *Ulysses* and *Finnegans Wake*. Restored sections of the Royal Canal (p506) extend in either direction from Mullingar.

Information

There are several banks on the main street (which changes name five times).

Laundrette (☎ 044-934 3045; Dublin Bridge; ⊙ 8.45am-6.15pm Mon-Sat)

Post office (Dominick St)

Tourist office (☎ 044-934 8650; Market Sq; ⊙ 9am-6pm Mon-Sat May-Sep, 9.30am-1pm & 2-5.15pm Sun Jul & Aug, 9.30am-1pm & 2-5.15pm Mon-Fri Oct-Apr)

Sights

Most of Mullingar's interesting sights lie a few kilometres outside the town centre.

In town, at the northern end of Mary St, the immense **Cathedral of Christ the King** was built just before WWII and has large mosaics of St Anne and St Patrick by Russian artist Boris Anrep, as well as a small ecclesiastical museum.

MULLINGAR PEWTER

Pewterware is Mullingar's best-known export. At the **Mullingar Pewter Visitor Centre** (☎ 044-934 8791; www.mullingarpewter.com; Great Down, The Downs; ⊙ 9.30am-6pm Mon-Sat), you can tour the **factory floor** (⊙ 9.30am-4pm Mon-Thu, 9.30am-3.30pm Fri) and see artisans turning the matt-grey metal into goblets, tankards, candle sticks and *objets d'art*. The centre is about 6km southeast of Mullingar on the Dublin road (N4).

BELVEDERE HOUSE & GARDENS

Don't miss the magnificent **Belvedere House Gardens & Park** (☎ 044-934 9060; www.belvedere-house.ie; adult/child €8.75/4.75; ⊙ house 9.30am-5pm Mar-Oct, 10am-4pm Nov-Feb, gardens 9.30am-8pm May-Aug, 9.30am-6pm Mar-Apr & Sep-Oct, 10am-4.30pm Nov-Feb), an immense 18th-century hunting lodge set in 65 hectares of gardens overlooking Lough Ennell. More than a few skeletons have come out of Belvedere's closets: the first earl, Lord Belfield, accused his wife and younger brother Arthur of adultery. She was placed under house arrest here for 30 years, and Arthur was jailed in London for the rest of his life. Meanwhile, the earl lived a life of decadence and debauchery. On his death, his wife emerged dressed in the fashion of three decades earlier, still protesting her innocence.

Lord Belfield also found time to fall out with his other brother, George, who built a home nearby. Ireland's largest folly, a ready-made 'ruin' called the **Jealous Wall**, was commissioned by the earl so he wouldn't have to look at George's mansion.

Designed by Richard Cassels, Belvedere House contains some delicate rococo plasterwork in the upper rooms. The gardens, with their Victorian glasshouses and lakeshore setting, make for wonderful walking on a sunny day. Kids will enjoy tram rides around the grounds, the **animal sanctuary** and themed play areas.

Note that the last admission to both the house and gardens is one hour prior to closing.

Belvedere House is 5.5km south of Mullingar on the N52 to Tullamore.

LOUGH ENNELL

This lough is renowned for its brown trout and coarse fishing. It's also the area where Jonathan Swift first dreamed up *Gulliver's Travels* (1726), hence its park's name, **Jonathan Swift Park**.

The park is 10km south of Mullingar on the N52.

Activities

Trout fishing is popular in the lakes around Mullingar. The fishing season runs from 1 March or 1 May (depending on the lake) to 12 October. Contact the tourist office or the **Shannon Regional Fisheries Board** (☎ 044-934 8769; www.shannon-fishery-board.ie) for further information.

If you fancy some horse riding, try the **Mullingar Equestrian Centre** (☎ 044-934 8331; www.mullingarequestrian.com; Athlone Rd; **P**).

You can kayak on Lough Ennell from the **Lilliput Adventure Centre** (☎ 044-26789; www.lilliputadventure.com; Jonathan Swift Park). The centre also organises land-based activities such as gorge walking and abseiling courses.

Sleeping & Eating

There are few B&Bs in the centre, but you'll find plenty on the approach roads from Dublin and Sligo.

Lakeshore (☎ 044-934 0618; www.lakeshorebnb.com; s/d from €45/70; **P**) This lovely B&B is on an organic farm just south of town. The four rooms have pine furniture and patchwork quilts as well as lovely views. You can sample the farm's own milk, yogurt and cheese at breakfast and there is a kitchenette for guest use. Lakeshore is 7km south of Mullingar. Head out along the N52, turning right onto the R390 just after the ring road.

Annebrook House Hotel (☎ 044-935 3300; www.annebrook.ie; Pearse St; s/d from €99/150; **P** 🖳 🛜) Right in the town centre, the hub of this modern hotel is a lovely 19th-century house with strong connections to local author Maria Edgworth. Accommodation is in a new annexe, where modern rooms in neutral colours are extremely comfortable but lack soul.

Ilia Tapas (☎ 044-934 5947; 37 Dominick St; tapas €3.95-12.95; ☽ 6-10pm Tue-Sat, 5-9pm Sun) Book in advance for one of Mullingar's most popular haunts. This modern restaurant serves generous portions of international-style tapas that are great for sharing. Go for beetroot and whipped goat's cheese with roast pine nuts or chickpea and baby spinach bacon salad with black pudding boudin. You'll be back for more.

Oscar's (☎ 044-934 4909; 21 Oliver Plunkett St; mains €15-22; ☽ 6-9.30pm Mon-Thu, 6-10pm Fri & Sat, 12.30-2.15pm & 6-8.15pm Sun) This perennially popular spot is the place to go for wholesome comfort food in a lively atmosphere. Bright colours, a menu that skirts the Mediterranean (think pastas, pizzas and French-inspired meat and poultry) and a decent wine list make it a good evening option.

Drinking & Entertainment

Con's (☎ 044-934 0925; 22 Dominick St; mains €8-14; ☽ carvery noon-3pm Mon-Fri) Con's is a traditional Irish pub that serves a good pint and decent, hearty grub, such as carvery lunches and doorstop sandwiches. It's a local favourite, so it can get busy.

Yukon Bar (☎ 044-934 0251; 11 Dominick St) A good live-music venue famous for its resident fortune teller, this bar has a great atmosphere and a range of soul, blues and rock music on offer.

Mullingar Arts Centre (☎ 044-934 7777; www.mullingarartscentre.ie; County Hall, Lower Mount St) The centre runs a regular program of music, comedy, drama and art exhibitions.

Getting There & Away

Bus Éireann (☎ 01-836 6111) runs services to Dublin (€14.30, 1½ hours, six Monday to Saturday, five Sunday) and Athlone (€10.30, one hour, three Monday to Saturday, one Sunday).

The **train station** (☎ 044-934 8274) has direct services to Dublin (€21.50, one hour, up to 10 Monday to Friday, seven Saturday, five Sunday) and Sligo (€34, two hours, eight Monday to Saturday, six Sunday).

NORTH OF MULLINGAR
Crookedwood & Around

The small village of Crookedwood hugs the shore of Lough Derravaragh. The 8km-long lake is associated with the legend of the children of Lír, who were turned into swans here by their jealous stepmother. Each winter the legend is recalled by thousands of snow-white migratory swans who flock here from as far away as Russia and Siberia.

About 3km west of Crookedwood is the **Multyfarnham Franciscan friary**. In the present church, the remains of a 15th-century church still stand, and there are outdoor Stations of the Cross set beside a stream.

East of Crookedwood, a small road leads 2km to the ruins of the fortified 15th-century **St Munna's Church**, built in a lovely location on the site of a 7th-century church founded by St Munna. Keys to the church are available from the nearby bungalow.

For a little bit of old-world luxury, you could stay at the tranquil **Mornington House** (☎ 044-937 2191; www.mornington.ie; Multyfarnham; s/d from €95/150; ☒ closed Nov-Mar; ℗), a lovely Victorian home set in mature gardens near the shore of Lough Derravaragh. The whole house is furnished with period charm. Antique furniture, log fires, brass beds and subtle florals give it a pleasingly lived-in atmosphere.

Tullynally Castle Gardens

The imposing Gothic revival **Tullynally Castle** (☎ 044-966 1159; www.tullynallycastle.com; Castlepollard; gardens adult/child/family €6/3/16; ☒ 2-6pm daily Jul–mid-Aug, Sat & Sun May & Jun) is the seat of the Pakenham family. The castle itself is closed to visitors, but you can roam its 12 hectares of gardens and parkland containing ornamental lakes, a Chinese and a Tibetan garden, and a wonderful stretch of 200-year-old yews.

To get here, take the N4 from Mullingar, then the R394 to Castlepollard, from where the castle and gardens are signposted 2km to the northwest.

Fore Valley

Near the shores of Lough Lene, the emerald-green Fore Valley is a superb place to explore by bicycle or on foot. In AD 630, St Fechin founded a monastery just outside the village of Fore. There's nothing left of this early settlement, but three later buildings in the valley are closely associated with 'seven wonders' said to have occurred here. It's a highly atmospheric place, even in the dead of winter, with sweeping views across a gentle valley.

The **Fore Abbey Coffee Shop** (☎ 044-966 1780; fore abbeycoffeeshop@oceanfree.net; ☒ 11am-6pm daily Jun-Sep, 11am-5pm Sun Oct-May), on the edge of Fore village, acts as a tourist information office and screens a 20-minute video about the wonders. Guided tours of Fore can be arranged by contacting the coffee shop in advance.

From Mullingar, take the N4 then the R394 northeast to Castlepollard. The road to Fore is signposted from there.

THE SEVEN WONDERS OF FORE

The oldest of the three buildings is **St Fechin's Church**, containing an early-13th-century chancel and baptismal font. Over the Cyclopean entrance is a huge lintel stone carved with a Greek cross and thought to weigh about 2.5 tonnes. It's said to have been put into place by St Fechin's devotions – the wonder of the **stone raised by prayer**.

A path runs from the church to the attractive little **anchorite cell** – the **anchorite in a stone** – which dates back to the 15th century and was lived in by a succession of hermits. The Seven Wonders pub in the village holds the key.

On the other side of the road near the car park is **St Fechin's Well**, filled with **water that will not boil**. Cynics should beware of testing this claim, as it's said that if you try it, doom will come to your family. Nearby is a branch from the **tree that will not burn**; the coins pressed into it are a more contemporary superstition.

Further over the plain are the extensive remains of a **13th-century Benedictine priory**, the **Monastery of the Quaking Scraw**, miraculous because it was built on what once was a bog. In the following century it was turned into a fortification, hence the loophole windows and castlelike square towers. The western tower is in a dangerous state – keep clear.

The last two wonders are the **mill without a race** and the **water that flows uphill**. The mill site is marked, and legend has it that St Fechin caused water to flow uphill, towards the mill, by throwing his crosier against a rock near Lough Lene, about 1.5km away

Counties Meath, Louth, Cavan & Monaghan

Stretching north and west of Dublin, the counties of Meath and Louth are now firmly on the capital's commuter belt, but it was their lush, fertile fields that attracted the very first of Ireland's settlers to the region, sealing its fate as the birthplace of Irish civilisation. Their legacy remains in the magnificent tombs at world-famous Brú na Bóinne and mysterious Loughcrew, both of which predate the Egyptian pyramids.

At Tara, gateway to the otherworld and seat of the high kings of Ireland, massive earthworks, passage graves and a 'stone of destiny' hint at the importance of the site for the early Celts. St Patrick put an end to all that with the introduction of Christianity, and the faithful built abbeys, high crosses and round towers to educate the worthy and protect their treasured manuscripts. Magnificent ruins at Monasterboice, Mellifont and Kells still whisper tales of a time when Ireland was known as the Land of Saints and Scholars.

Further north and west, the two counties of Monaghan and Cavan, bordering Northern Ireland, have a very different flavour, their rolling hills and copious lakes offering a far quieter pace of life. There's a refreshing lack of tourists in this area save for fishing enthusiasts flocking to Cavan's trout-filled lakes, boaters enjoying the lush scenery along the Erne Waterway and walkers savouring the wild scenery and expansive views of the Cuilcagh Mountains. Much of the attraction here is the outdoors, making it a perfect place for visitors seeking an unspoilt corner of Ireland.

HIGHLIGHTS

- **Prehistoric Wonders** Explore the extraordinary prehistoric remains at the ancient burial sites of Brú na Bóinne (p533)
- **Happy Days** Soak up the views, enjoy the oysters and kick back in the charming village of Carlingford (p555)
- **Ancient Ireland** Ramble around the evocative ruins and mighty castle of the unassuming town of Trim (p541)
- **Stony Grey Soil** Follow in the footsteps of poet and author Patrick Kavanagh on the quiet roads around Inniskeen (p115)
- **Mystical Past** Shun the crowds and make your way to the hilltop tombs of the Loughcrew Cairns (p547)

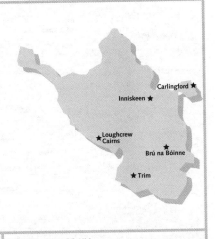

Carlingford ★

Inniskeen ★

★ Loughcrew Cairns

★ Brú na Bóinne

★ Trim

- POPULATION: 394,000
- AREA: 6387 SQ KM

COUNTY MEATH

One of the five provinces of ancient Ireland, Meath, 'the Middle Kingdom', attracted Ireland's first settlers and was at the centre of Irish politics for centuries. Although their purpose is not quite understood, the magnifi-

cent Neolithic monuments in the Boyne Vall were of enormous significance to the peop of the time. Meath was home to Ireland's hig kings, and the massive castle in Trim is a test mony to the power and the wealth of the are up until Norman times.

Today, Meath's fertile land and plentif water supply make it an important centr

COUNTIES MEATH, LOUTH, CAVAN & MONAGHAN

f agriculture, while its proximity to Dublin as meant unchecked growth for the county's owns in the last decade: Navan, Slane and Kells are blighted with soulless housing estates and the resulting traffic can be hellish.

For visitors though, the attractions are plentiful and Meath's tourism authority is one of the best in Ireland. Its publications are of a high standard, and you'll find loads of info at www.meathtourism.ie.

History

Meath's rich soil, laid down during the last Ice Age, attracted settlers as early as 8000 BC. They worked their way up the banks of the River Boyne, transforming the landscape from forest to farmland. The extensive necropolis at Brú na Bóinne lies on a meandering section of the Boyne between Drogheda and Slane. West of here there's a group of smaller passage graves in the Loughcrew Hills near Oldcastle.

For a thousand years the Hill of Tara was the seat of power for Irish high kings, until the arrival of St Patrick in the 5th century. Later, Kells, to the northwest, became one of the most important and creative monastic settlements in Ireland, and lent its name to the famed *Book of Kells*, a 9th-century illuminated manuscript now displayed at Trinity College, Dublin (see the boxed text, p103).

BRÚ NA BÓINNE

The vast Neolithic necropolis known as Brú na Bóinne (the Boyne Palace) is one of the most extraordinary sites in Europe and shouldn't be missed. A thousand years older than Stonehenge, this is a powerful and evocative testament to the mind-boggling achievements of prehistoric humans.

The complex was built to house the remains of those who were at the top of the social heap and its tombs were the largest artificial structures in Ireland until the construction of the Anglo-Norman castles 4000 years later. The area consists of many different sites, with the three principal ones being Newgrange, Knowth and Dowth.

Over the centuries the tombs decayed, were covered by grass and trees, and were plundered by everybody from Vikings to Victorian treasure hunters, whose carved initials can be seen on the great stones of Newgrange. The countryside around the tombs is littered with countless other ancient tumuli (mounds) and standing stones.

Orientation & Information

In an effort to protect the tombs and preserve the mystical atmosphere around them, all visits to Brú na Bóinne must start at the **Brú na Bóinne visitor centre** (☎ 041-988 0300; www.heritageire land.ie; Donore; adult/child visitor centre €3/2, visitor centre, Newgrange & Knowth €11/6; ⏰ 9am-6.30pm May, 9am-7pm

Jun-Sep, 9.30am-5pm Oct-Apr), from where a shuttle bus will take you to the tombs. Happily, this is a superb interpretive centre, its spiral design echoing that of Newgrange. The centre houses an extraordinary series of interactive exhibits on prehistoric Ireland and its passage tombs, and has regional tourism info, a good cafe and a bookshop.

You should allow plenty of time to visit Brú na Bóinne. Plan on an hour's visit for the interpretive centre alone, two hours if you wish to include a trip to Newgrange or Knowth, and a half day to see all three in one go (Dowth is not open to tourists).

In summer, particularly at weekends, and during school holidays, the place gets very crowded, and you will not be guaranteed a visit to either of the passage tombs. There are only 750 tour slots and on peak days 2000 people show up. Tickets are sold on a first-come, first-served basis (no advance booking) so the best advice is to arrive early in the morning or visit midweek and be prepared for a wait.

The important thing to note is that if you turn up at either Newgrange or Knowth first, you'll be sent to the visitor centre. Tours depart from a bus stop that you reach by walking across a spiral bridge over the River Boyne, and the buses take just a few minutes to reach the sites. Technically you can walk the 4km to either site from the visitor centre, but you're discouraged from doing so as you might get mowed down on the very narrow lanes by the tour bus you've chosen not to take.

The visitor centre is on the south side of the river. It's 2km west of Donore and 6km east of Slane, where bridges cross the river from the N51.

Sights
NEWGRANGE

Even from afar, you know that **Newgrange** (adult/child incl visitor centre €6/3) is something special. Its white, round stone walls topped by a grass dome look otherworldly, and just the size is impressive: 80m in diameter and 13m high. But underneath it gets even better. Here lies the finest Stone Age passage tomb in Ireland, and one of the most remarkable prehistoric sites in Europe. It dates from around 3200 BC, predating the Pyramids by some six centuries. No one is quite sure of its original purpose. It could have been a burial place for kings or a centre for ritual – although the tomb's pre-

cise alignment with the sun at the time of th winter solstice also suggests it was designe to act as a calendar.

The name derives from 'New Granary (the tomb did in fact serve as a repositor for wheat and grain at one stage), although more popular belief is that it comes from th Irish for 'Cave of Gráinne', a reference to popular Celtic myth. *The Pursuit of Diarmui and Gráinne* tells of the illicit love betwee the woman betrothed to Fionn McCumhai (or Finn McCool), leader of the Fianna, an Diarmuid, one of his most trusted lieuten ants. When Diarmuid was fatally wounded his body was brought to Newgrange by th god Aengus in a vain attempt to save him and the despairing Gráinne followed him int the cave, where she remained long after h died. This suspiciously Arthurian tale (su in Lancelot and Guinevere for Diarmuid an Gráinne) is undoubtedly a myth, but it's sti a pretty good story. Newgrange also play another role in Celtic mythology as the sit where the hero Cúchulainn was conceived.

Over time, Newgrange, like Dowth an Knowth, deteriorated and was at one stag even used as a quarry. The site was extensively restored in 1962 and again in 1975.

A superbly carved kerbstone with doubl and triple spirals guards the tomb's main en trance, but the area has been reconstructed s that tourists don't have to clamber in over it. Above the entrance is a slit, or roof box, which lets light in. Another beautifully decorated kerbstone stands at the exact opposite side o the mound. Some experts say that a ring o standing stones encircled the mound, forming a great circle about 100m in diameter, but only 12 of these stones remain, with traces of some others below ground level.

Holding the whole structure together are the 97 boulders of the kerb ring, designed to stop the mound from collapsing out-wards. Eleven of these are decorated with motifs similar to those on the main entrance stone, although only three have extensive carvings.

The white quartzite that decorates the tomb was originally obtained from Wicklow, 70km to the south – in an age before horse and wheel, it was transported by sea and then up the River Boyne – and there is also some gran-ite from the Mourne Mountains in Northern Ireland. Over 200,000 tonnes of earth and stone also went into the mound.

You can walk down the narrow 19m passage, lined with 43 stone uprights (some of them engraved), which leads into the tomb chamber about one-third of the way into the colossal mound. The chamber has three recesses, and in these are large basin stones that held cremated human bones. As well as the remains, the basins would have held funeral offerings of beads and pendants, but these were stolen long before the archaeologists arrived.

Above, the massive stones support a 6m-high corbel-vaulted roof. A complex drainage system means that not a drop of water has penetrated the interior in 40 centuries.

At 8.20am on the winter solstice (sometime between 19 and 23 December), the rising sun's rays shine through the roof box above the entrance, creep slowly down the long passage and illuminate the tomb chamber for 17 minutes. There is little doubt that this is one of the country's most memorable, even mystical, experiences. There is a simulated winter sunrise for every group taken into the mound, but to be in with a chance of witnessing the real thing add your name to the list that is drawn by lottery every 1 October.

KNOWTH

Northwest of Newgrange, the burial mound of Knowth (adult/child incl visitor centre €5/3; ☾ Easter-Oct) was built around the same time and seems set to surpass its better-known neighbour in both its size and the importance of the discoveries made here. It has the greatest collection of passage-grave art ever uncovered in Western Europe, and has been under excavation since 1962.

The excavations soon cleared a passage leading to the central chamber, which at 34m is much longer than the one at Newgrange. In 1968, a 40m passage was unearthed on the opposite side of the mound. Although the chambers are separate, they're close enough for archaeologists to hear each other at work. Also in the mound are the remains of six early-Christian souterrains (underground chambers) built into the side. Some 300 carved slabs and 17 satellite graves surround the main mound.

Human activity at Knowth continued for thousands of years after its construction, which accounts for the site's complexity. The Beaker folk, so called because they buried their dead with drinking vessels, occupied the site in the Bronze Age (c 1800 BC), as did the Celts in the Iron Age (c 500 BC). Remnants of bronze and iron workings from these periods have been discovered. Around AD 800 to 900, it was turned into a *ráth* (earthen ring fort), a stronghold of the very powerful O'Neill clan. In 965, it was the seat of Cormac MacMaelmithic, later Ireland's high king for nine years, and in the 12th century the Normans built a motte and bailey here. The site was finally abandoned in about 1400.

Further excavations are likely to continue for the next decade at least so you may see archaeologists at work when you visit.

DOWTH

The circular mound at Dowth is similar in size to Newgrange – about 63m in diameter – but is slightly taller at 14m high. It has suffered badly at the hands of everyone from road builders and treasure hunters to amateur archaeologists, who scooped out the centre of the tumulus in the 19th century. For a time, Dowth even had a tearoom ignobly perched on its summit. Relatively untouched by modern archaeologists, Dowth shows what Newgrange and Knowth looked like for most of their history. Because it's unsafe, Dowth is closed to visitors, though the mound can be viewed from the road between Newgrange and Drogheda. Excavations began in 1998 and will continue for years to come.

Dowth has two entrance passages leading to separate chambers (both sealed), and a 24m early-Christian underground passage at either end, which connect up with the western passage. This 8m-long passage leads into a small cruciform chamber, in which a recess acts as an entrance to an additional series of small compartments, a feature unique to Dowth. To the southwest is the entrance to a shorter passage and smaller chamber.

North of the tumulus are the ruins of **Dowth Castle** and **Dowth House**.

Tours

Brú na Bóinne is one of the most popular tourist attractions in Ireland, and there are oodles of organised tours transporting busloads of eager tourists to the visitor centre. Most depart from Dublin.

The **Mary Gibbons Tours** (☎ 01-283 9973; www.new grangetours.com; tour €35) are highly recommended. Tours depart from numerous Dublin hotels, beginning at 9.30am Monday to Saturday,

---

FIONN & THE SALMON OF KNOWLEDGE

One of the best-known stories in the Fenian Cycle tells of the Salmon of Knowledge, a fish that, once consumed, would bestow enormous wisdom on the eater, including the gift of foresight. An old Druid, Finegas, struggled for seven years to catch the salmon, but only managed to land the elusive fish at a time when a young Fionn McCumhaill was at his camp receiving tuition. As befits the inevitable tragedy of these stories, Finegas set the fish to cook and left Fionn to turn it over the fire, ordering him not to eat so much as the smallest bite. But as Fionn turned the spit a drop of hot oil from the fish landed on his thumb, which he quickly put in his mouth to soothe. Finegas returned, saw what had happened and knew that it was too late; he bade Fionn eat the rest of the fish and so it was that Fionn acquired wisdom and foresight.

---

and take in the whole of the Boyne Valley including Newgrange and the Hill of Tara. The expert guides offer a fascinating insight into Celtic and pre-Celtic life in Ireland, and you'll get access to Newgrange even on days when all visiting slots are filled.

Bus Éireann (☎ 01-836 6111; www.buseireann.ie; adult/child €30/25; ⊙ Mon-Thu, Sat & Sun mid-Mar–Sep) runs Newgrange and Boyne Valley tours departing from **Busáras** (Map pp92-3; Store St) in Dublin at 10am, returning at approximately 5.45pm.

Sleeping & Eating

Drogheda is close to Brú na Bóinne and has many hotels, while the nearby village of Slane is good for lunch. There are some excellent sleeping options close to the sites, and the visitor centre itself has a good cafe.

Newgrange Lodge (☎ 041-988 2478; www.new grangelodge.com; dm/s/d €18/45/70; ℗ 🖳) Just east of the Brú na Bóinne visitor centre, you'll find this converted farmhouse with a choice of cosy rooms varying from dorms with four to 10 beds, to hotel-standard rooms with TVs and internet access. Reception is open 24 hours, there's a kitchen for guest use, two outdoor patios, and a barbecue area.

Glebe House (☎ 041-983 6101; www.theglebehouse.ie; Dowth; s/d €60/120; ℗) This charming, wisteria-clad 17th-century country house has four lovely rooms with log fires, purple carpet and a cosy atmosphere. It's a really beautiful spot, set in mature gardens with wonderful views of the Boyne Valley. Glebe House is 7km west of Drogheda on the road between Newgrange and Dowth.

Rossnaree (☎ 041-982 0975; www.rossnaree.ie; Newgrange; s/d €100/160; ⊙ Apr-Dec; ℗) At a sharp corner on the narrow road between Donore and Slane is this magnificent Italianate country house overlooking the Boyne and

surrounded by a working farm. The lavish bedrooms are luxuriously furnished, and you can book dinner (€45) a day in advance. The events related in *Fionn and the Salmon of Knowledge* (above) are said to have taken place on this very spot.

Getting There & Away

From Drogheda, **Bus Éireann** (☎ 041-983 5023 runs a service that drops you off at the entrance to the visitor centre (€3.50, 20 minutes, five daily).

Newgrange Shuttlebus (☎ 1800 424 252; www.ove thetoptours.com; return ticket €18) runs one or two trips daily to the Brú na Bóinne visitor centre from central Dublin. Book in advance.

BATTLE OF BOYNE SITE

More than 60,000 soldiers of the armies of King James II and King William III fought on this patch of farmland on the border of counties Meath and Louth in 1690. In the end, William prevailed and James sailed off to France. Today, the **battle site** (☎ 041-980 9950 www.battleoftheboyne.ie; adult/child €4/2; ⊙ 10am-6pm May-Sep, 9.30am-5pm Oct-Apr, last admission one hr before closing) is part of the Oldbridge Estate farm. At the visitor centre you can watch a short show about the battle, see original and replica weaponry of the time and explore a laser battlefield model. Self-guided walks through the parkland and battle site are eerily low key, allowing ample time to think about the events that saw Protestant interests remain in Ireland. The site, 3km north of Donore, is signposted off the N51.

LAYTOWN

Most famous as the site for the only official beach-run horse race in Europe, Laytown is a sleepy seaside village for most of the year. In late August or early September, though, the ookies, punters and jockeys descend in force. Laytown races have been held here for over 140 years; for one day Laytown's 3km of golden sand are transformed into a racecourse, attracting a diverse crowd of locals, celebrities and die-hard racing fans.

Just outside Laytown on the road to Julianstown is **Sonairte** (☎ 041-982 7572; www sonairte.org; The Ninch, Laytown; adult/child €3/1, free if arriving on foot or by bike; ⓨ 10.30am-5pm Wed-Sun), the National Ecology Centre. Dedicated to promoting ecological awareness, it's a wonderful place to learn about sustainable living and organic horticulture. You can take a guided tour of the organic gardens and 200-year-old orchard, follow the nature trail or river walk, or take a course in anything from beekeeping to foraging for wild food and organic gardening. There's a shop and organic cafe on site. The centre is five minutes walk from Laytown train station. Trains to Dublin run every half hour (€13, 50 minutes).

SLANE
pop 1099

The pretty village of Slane, with its pleasant 18th-century stone houses and cottages, slithers down a steep hill to the River Boyne. A planned estate village, Slane grew up around the enormous castle after which it was named. At the junction of the main roads are four identical houses facing each other: local lore has it that they were built for four sisters who had taken an intense dislike to one another and kept a beady-eyed watch from their individual residences. The massive grey gate to the privately owned castle lies southwest of the town centre.

Slane makes a convenient base for Brú na Bóinne, located 6km east. For more information visit www.slanetourism.com.

Orientation

Slane is perched on a hillside at the junction of the N2 and N51, some 15km west of Drogheda. To the south, at the bottom of the hill, the Boyne glides by under a narrow bridge.

Sights
HILL OF SLANE

About 1km north of the village is the Hill of Slane, a fairly plain-looking mound that only stands out for its association with a thick slice of Celto-Christian mythology. According to

legend, St Patrick lit a paschal (Easter) fire here in AD 433 to proclaim Christianity throughout the land. Patrick's fire infuriated Laoghaire, the pagan high king of Ireland, who had expressly ordered that no fire be lit within sight of the Hill of Tara. Thankfully – at least for the future of Irish Christians – he was restrained by his far-sighted druids, who warned that 'the man who had kindled the flame would surpass kings and princes'. Laoghaire went to meet Patrick, and all but one of the king's attendants – a man called Erc – greeted Patrick with scorn.

Here the story *really* gets far-fetched. During the meeting, Patrick killed one of the king's guards and summoned an earthquake to subdue the rest. After his Herculean efforts, Patrick calmed down a little and plucked a shamrock from the ground, using its three leaves to explain the paradox of the Holy Trinity – the union of the Father, the Son and the Holy Spirit in one. Laoghaire wasn't convinced, but he agreed to let Patrick continue his missionary work. Patrick's success that day – apart from keeping his own life, starting an earthquake and giving Ireland one of its enduring national symbols – was good old Erc, who was baptised and later became the first bishop of Slane. To this day, the local parish priest lights a fire here on Holy Saturday.

The Hill of Slane originally had a church associated with St Erc and, later, a round tower and monastery, but only an outline of the foundations remains. Later a motte and bailey were constructed, which are still visible on the western side of the hill. You can also see the remains of a ruined church and tower that were once part of an early-16th-century Franciscan friary. On a clear day, from the top of the tower, which is always open, you can see the Hill of Tara and the Boyne Valley, as well as (it's said) seven Irish counties.

SLANE CASTLE

The private residence of Lord Henry Conyngham, Earl of Mountcharles, **Slane Castle** (☎ 041-988 4400; www.slanecastle.ie; adult/child €7/5; ⓨ noon-5pm Sun-Thu mid-May–Aug) is west of the town centre along the Navan road and is best known in Ireland as the setting for major outdoor rock concerts.

Built in 1785 in the Gothic-revival style by James Wyatt, the building was later altered by Francis Johnson for George IV's visits to Lady Conyngham. She was allegedly his mistress, and it's said the road between Dublin and

Slane was built especially straight and smooth to speed up the randy king's journeys.

In 1991, the castle was gutted by a fire, whereupon it was discovered that the earl was underinsured. A major fundraising drive – of which the summer concerts were a part – led to a painstaking restoration and the castle finally reopened for tours in 2001.

Tours include the neo-Gothic Ballroom, completed in 1821, and the Kings Room, where the monarch stayed while visiting his mistress.

U2's 1984 album *The Unforgettable Fire* was recorded here (though the castle featured on the album cover is in Moydrum in County Westmeath) and the band have returned on several occasions to play massive open-air concerts in the castle grounds.

LEDWIDGE MUSEUM

Simple yet moving, the **Ledwidge Museum** (☎ 041-982 4544; www.francisledwidge.com; Janesville; adult/child €2.50/1; ⊙ 10am-1pm & 2-5pm) is located in the birthplace of poet Francis Ledwidge (1891–1917). He died on the battlefield at Ypres, having survived Gallipoli and Serbia. A keen political activist, Ledwidge was thwarted in his efforts to set up a branch of the Gaelic League in the area, but found an outlet in verse.

The museum provides an insight into Ledwidge's life and works and the cottage itself is a good example of how farm labourers lived in the 19th century. It is about 1.5km east of Slane on the Drogheda road (N51).

Sleeping & Eating

Slane Farm Hostel (☎ 041-988 4985; www.slanefarm hostel.ie; Harlinstown House, Navan Rd; campsites per adult/child €8/4, dm/s/d €18/25/50; P ⬛ 🛜) These former stables, built by the Marquis of Conyngham in the 18th century, have been converted into a great hostel that is part of a working farm. It's a wonderful place with dorms that sleep six to 12, camping, a kitchen and a games room. It's 2.5km west of Slane.

Millhouse Boutique Hotel (☎ 041-982 0723; www .themillhouse.ie; r from €200; P ⬛ 🛜) Old-world charm and character blend seamlessly with sleek contemporary design at this luxurious boutique hotel in Slane. Set in a Georgian manor house by the river, this place is a real stunner with 11 guestrooms decked out with four-poster beds, free-standing baths, silks and velvets. There's a sauna for guest use

and evening meals (three-course set menu €43) can be booked in advance. The hotel is 500m downhill from town, right before the N2 bridge.

Old Post Office (☎ 041-982 4090; www.theoldpost office.ie; lunch mains €5-11, dinner mains €14-22; ⊙ 9am-6pm Mon-Sat, 10am-5pm Sun & 6.30-9.30pm Wed-Sat) Owned by a couple who worked on the *QE2* for seven years, the Old Post Office is a tastefully restored restaurant and B&B with simple menus and honest homemade food. The restaurant features a good choice of pastas, fish and meat dishes, while the four guestrooms (single/double €45/80) are bright and airy with contemporary, neutral decor.

Poet's Rest (☎ 041-982 4493; www.thepoetsrest.com, Chapel St; ⊙ restaurant 8am-10pm Tue-Sat, 9am-5pm Sun, deli 9am-6pm Tue-Sat; mains €10-23, 3-course menu €27.50) Fairtrade and organic foods top the bill at the Poet's Rest, a deceptively simple little place serving up stylish, modern cuisine in relaxed surroundings. Although succulent meat and fish dishes feature strongly on the menu, there's plenty of choice for vegetarians, and a mouth-watering array of desserts from the adjoining deli-patisserie – a great spot to pick up the makings for a gourmet picnic.

Getting There & Away

Bus Éireann has four to six buses daily to Drogheda (€4.20, 35 minutes), Dublin (€11.40, one hour) and Navan (€3.90, 20 minutes).

NAVAN

pop 3710

You won't want to waste too much time in Navan, Meath's main town and the crossroads of the busy Dublin road (N3) and the Drogheda–Westmeath road (N51), but you might find yourself changing buses here.

If you need local information, the **tourist office** (☎ 046-909 7069; Railway St; ⊙ 10am-6pm Mon-Sat) is in the County Hall.

If you're hungry, head for the **Loft** (☎ 046-907 1755; 26 Trimgate St; mains €11-16; ⊙ 5.30-10.30pm) for a menu of international comfort food, or **Ryan's Pub** (☎ 046-902 1154; 22 Trimgate St; bar food from €5; ⊙ noon-8pm) for decent pub grub.

Bus Éireann has an hourly service to Dublin (€11.40, 50 minutes) and to Cavan (€11.30, one hour) via Kells (€4.20, 15 minutes).

AROUND NAVAN

The impressive and relatively intact **Athlumney Castle** lies about 2km southeast of Navan. It was built by the Dowdall family in the 16th century, with additions made a hundred years later. After King James' defeat at the Battle of the Boyne, Sir Lancelot Dowdall set fire to the castle to ensure that James' conqueror, William of Orange, would never shelter or confiscate his home. He watched the blaze from the opposite bank of the river before leaving for France and then Italy. As you enter the estate, take a right toward the Loreto Convent, where you can pick up the keys to the castle. In the convent yard is another **motte**, which at one time had a wooden tower on it.

There are some pleasant **walks** around Navan, particularly the one following the towpath that runs along the old River Boyne canal towards Slane and Drogheda. On the southern bank, you can go as far as Stackallen and the Boyne bridge (about 7km), passing the impressive red-brick **Ardmulchan House** (closed to the public) and, on the opposite bank, the ruins of 16th-century **Dunmoe Castle**.

TARA

The **Hill of Tara** is Ireland's most sacred stretch of turf, an entrance to the underworld, occupying a place at the heart of Irish history, legend and folklore. It was the home of the mystical druids, the priest-rulers of ancient Ireland, who practised their particular form of Celtic paganism under the watchful gaze of the all-powerful goddess Maeve (Medbh). Later it was the ceremonial capital of the high kings – 142 of them in all – who ruled until the arrival of Christianity in the 6th century. It is also one of the most important ancient sites in Europe, with a Stone Age passage tomb and prehistoric burial mounds that date back up to 5000 years.

Although little remains other than humps and mounds of earth on the hill, its historic and folkloristic significance is immense. However, history and preservation have run headlong into the demands of sprawl and convenience in the Tara Valley, with controversy around the construction of a new motorway. A battle between government and campaigners over the proposed route has been raging for years and work had to be halted on the first day of digging in 2007 when an ancient site that could rival Stonehenge was uncovered. Despite pleas from eminent historians and archaeologists around the world, the government looks set to ignore calls for a new route that would completely avoid the area and

plough ahead with its controversial plans for the M3. For an update on the current situation visit www.tarawatch.org.

History

The Celts believed that Tara was the sacred dwelling place of the gods and the gateway to the otherworld. The passage grave was thought to be the final resting place of the Tuatha dé Danann, the mythical fairyfolk – they were real enough, but instead of pixies and brownies, they were earlier Stone Age arrivals on the island.

As the Celtic political landscape began to evolve, the druids' power was usurped by warlike chieftains who took kingly titles; there was no sense of a united Ireland, so at any given time there were countless *rí tuaithe* (regional kings) controlling many small areas. The king who ruled Tara, though, was generally considered the big shot, the high king, even though his direct rule didn't extend too far beyond the provincial border. The most lauded of all the high kings was Cormac MacArt, who ruled during the 3rd century.

The most important event in Tara's calendar was the three-day harvest *feis* (festival) that took place at Samhain, a precursor to modern Halloween. During the festival, the high king pulled out all the stops: grievances would be heard, laws passed, and disputes settled amid an orgy of eating, drinking and partying.

When the early Christians hit town in the 5th century, they targeted Tara straight away. Although the legend has it that Patrick lit the paschal fire on the Hill of Slane (p537), some people believe that Patrick's incendiary act took place on Tara's sacred hump. The arrival of Christianity marked the beginning of the end for Celtic pagan civilisation, and the high kings began to desert Tara, even though the kings of Leinster continued to be based here until the 11th century.

In August 1843, Tara saw one of the greatest crowds ever to gather in Ireland. Daniel O'Connell, the 'Liberator' and the leader of the opposition to union with Great Britain, held one of his monster rallies at Tara, and up to 750,000 people came to hear him speak.

Information

A former Protestant church (with a window by the well-known artist Evie Hone) is home to the **Tara Visitor Centre** (☎ 046-902 5903;

www.heritageireland.ie; adult/child €3/1; 10am-6pm mid-May–mid-Sep, last admission 5pm), where a 20-minute audiovisual presentation about the site is shown. Entrance to Tara is free and the site itself is always open. There are good explanatory panels by the entrance.

Sights

RATH OF THE SYNODS

The names applied to Tara's various humps and mounds were adopted from ancient texts, and mythology and religion intertwine with the historical facts. The Protestant church grounds and graveyard spill onto the remains of the Rath of the Synods, a triple-ringed fort where some of St Patrick's early synods (meetings) supposedly took place. Excavations of the enclosure suggest that it was used between AD 200 and 400 for burials, rituals and living quarters. Originally the ring fort would have contained wooden houses surrounded by timber palisades.

During a digging session in the graveyard in 1810, a boy found a pair of gold torcs (crescents of beaten gold hung around the neck), which are now in the National Museum in Dublin. Later excavations discovered Roman glass, shards of pottery and seals, showing links with the Roman Empire even though the Romans never extended their power into Ireland.

The poor state of the enclosure is due in part to a group of British 'Israelites' who in the 1890s dug the place up looking for the Ark of the Covenant, much to the consternation of the local people. The Israelites' leader claimed to see a mysterious pillar on the enclosure that was unfortunately invisible to everyone else. After they failed to uncover anything, the invisible pillar moved to the other side of the road; before the adventurers had time to start work there, however, the locals chased them away.

ROYAL ENCLOSURE

To the south of the church, the Royal Enclosure is a large, oval Iron Age hill fort, 315m in diameter and surrounded by a bank and ditch cut through solid rock under the soil. Inside the Royal Enclosure are several smaller sites.

Mound of the Hostages

This bump in the northern corner of the enclosure is the most ancient known part of Tara and the most visible of its remains. Supposedly

a prison cell for hostages of the 3rd-century king Cormac MacArt, it is in fact a small Stone Age passage grave dating from around 1800 BC that was later used by Bronze Age people. The passage contains some carved stonework but is closed to the public.

The mound produced a treasure trove of artefacts, including some ancient Mediterranean beads of amber and faience (glazed pottery). More than 35 Bronze Age burials were found here, as well as a mass of cremated remains from the Stone Age.

Cormac's House & the Royal Seat

Two other earthworks found inside the enclosure are Cormac's House and the Royal Seat. Although they look similar, the Royal Seat is a ring fort with a house site in the centre, while Cormac's House is a barrow (burial mound) in the side of the circular bank. Cormac's House commands the best views of the surrounding lowlands of the Boyne and Blackwater Valleys.

Atop Cormac's House is the phallic **Stone of Destiny**, originally located near the Mound of the Hostages, which represents the joining of the gods of the earth and the heavens. It's said to be the inauguration stone of the high kings, although alternative sources suggest that the actual coronation stone was the Stone of Scone, which was removed to Edinburgh, Scotland, and used to crown British kings. The would-be king stood on top of the Stone of Destiny and, if the stone let out three roars, he was crowned. The mass grave of 37 men who died in a skirmish on Tara during the 1798 Rising is next to the stone.

ENCLOSURE OF KING LAOGHAIRE

South of the Royal Enclosure is the Enclosure of King Laoghaire, a large but worn ring fort where the king, a contemporary of St Patrick, is supposedly buried standing upright and dressed in his armour.

BANQUET HALL

North of the churchyard is Tara's most unusual feature, the Banquet Hall. This rectangular earthwork measures 230m by 27m along a north-south axis. Tradition holds that it was built to cater for thousands of guests during feasts. Much of this information comes from the 12th-century *Book of Leinster* and the *Yellow Book of Lecan*, which even includes drawings of the hall.

Opinions vary as to the site's real purpose. Its orientation suggests that it was a sunken entrance to Tara, leading directly to the Royal Enclosure. More recent research, however, has uncovered graves within the compound, and it's possible that the banks are in fact the burial sites of some of the kings of Tara.

GRÁINNE'S FORT

Gráinne was the daughter of King Cormac. Betrothed to Fionn McCumhaill (Finn McCool), she eloped with Diarmuid, one of the king's warriors, on her wedding night, becoming the subject of the epic *The Pursuit of Diarmuid and Gráinne*. Gráinne's Fort and the northern and southern **Sloping Trenches** off to the northwest are burial mounds.

Tours

The **Mary Gibbons Tour** (☎ 01-283 9973; www.new grangetours.com; tour €35) to Brú na Bóinne takes in the whole of the Boyne Valley, including the Hill of Tara.

Bus Éireann (☎ 01-836 6111; www.buseireann.ie; adult/child €30/25; ☯ Mon-Thu, Sat & Sun mid-Mar–Sep) tours to Newgrange and the Boyne Valley include a visit to Tara on certain days.

Drinking

If a walk on the hill has worked up a thirst, head for the nearby village of Skyrne, where **O'Connell's** (☎ 046-902 5122) is a wonderfully unspoilt and atmospheric country pub.

Getting There & Away

Tara is 10km southeast of Navan, just off the Dublin–Cavan road (N3). **Bus Éireann** (☎ 01-836 6111) services linking Dublin and Navan pass within 1km of the site (€8.20, 40 minutes, hourly Monday to Saturday and four times on Sunday). Ask the driver to drop you off at the Tara Cross, where you take a left turn off the main road and follow the signs.

DUNSANY CASTLE

See how the other 1% lives at **Dunsany Castle** (☎ 046-902 5198; www.dunsany.com; Dunsany; adult/child €20/free; ☯ May-Jul, Aug by appointment), the residence of the lords of Dunsany, and one of the oldest continually inhabited buildings in Ireland. Construction started on the castle in the 12th century with major alterations taking place in the 18th and 19th centuries.

Today the castle houses an impressive private art collection and many other treasures related to important figures in Irish history, such as Oliver Plunkett and Patrick Sarsfield, leader of the Irish Jacobite forces at the siege of Limerick in 1691. A guided tour takes almost two hours and offers a fascinating insight into the family history as well as that of the castle. It remains a family home and maintenance and restoration are ongoing so opening hours vary and different rooms are open to visitors at different times. Call for details.

Housed in the old kitchen and in part of the old domestic quarters is a **boutique** (☎ 046-902 6202; www.dunsany.com; ☯ 10am-5pm) that proudly sells the Dunsany Home Collection, which features locally made table linen and accessories, as well as various articles designed by Lord Dunsany himself.

The castle is about 5km south of Tara on the Dunshaughlin–Kilmessan road.

TRIM

pop 1375

Dominated by its mighty castle and littered with atmospheric ruins, the quiet town of Trim was an important settlement in medieval times. Five city gates surrounded a busy jumble of streets, and as many as seven monasteries were established in the immediate area.

It's hard to imagine nowadays, but a measure of Trim's importance was that Elizabeth I genuinely considered building Trinity College here. One student who did go to school here – at least for a short time – was Arthur Wellesley, the Duke of Wellington, who studied in Talbot Castle and St Mary's Abbey. Local legend has it that the duke was born in a stable round these parts, which would explain the duke's famous exclamation that simply being born in a stable doesn't make one a horse. Sadly for the legend, if he did say it – which is hardly definite – he didn't mean it literally: for 'stable' and 'horse' read 'Ireland' and 'Irish', for he was in fact born in Dublin.

The local burghers dedicated the **Wellington column**, at the junction of Summerhill Rd and Wellington Pl, to the duke in recognition of his impressive career. After defeating Napoleon at the Battle of Waterloo, the Iron Duke went on to become prime minister of Great Britain and in 1829 passed the Catholic Emancipation Act, repealing the last of the repressive penal laws.

Today, Trim's history is everywhere, with ruins scattered about the town. The streets, still lined with tiny old workers cottages, are

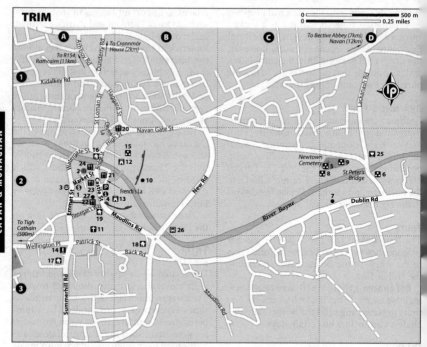

seeing a few new developments aimed at realising the area's huge tourism potential.

Orientation & Information

Almost everything commercial in Trim is on or near Market St. That huge steeple you see just south belongs to **St Patrick's Church**, parts of which date to the 15th century.

Bank of Ireland (Market St) Exchanges money and has an ATM.

Emmy's Internet (☎ 046-948 3498; Market St; per 20 min €1; ☒ 10.30am-8pm Mon-Sat, 2-4pm Sun)

Post office (cnr Emmet & Market Sts)

Tourist office (☎ 046-943 7227; Castle St; ☒ 9.30am-5.30pm Mon-Sat) Has a handy tourist trail map with information on the most important sights in town.

Sights

TRIM CASTLE

This remarkably preserved edifice was Ireland's largest Anglo-Norman fortification and is proof of Trim's medieval importance. Hugh de Lacy founded the truly impressive **Trim Castle** (King John's Castle; ☎ 046-943 8619; www .heritageireland.ie; adult/child €4/2, grounds only €3/1; ☒ 10am-6pm Easter-Oct, 9.30am-5pm Sat & Sun Nov-Easter, st admission one hr before closing) in 1173, but Rory)'Connor, said to have been the last high ing of Ireland, destroyed this motte and bai- ey within a year. The building you see today vas begun around 1200 and has hardly been nodified since.

Throughout Anglo-Norman times the castle ccupied a strategic position on the western dge of the Pale, the area where the Anglo- Normans ruled supreme; beyond Trim was he volatile country where Irish chieftains and ords fought with their Norman rivals and vied or position, power and terrain. By the 16th entury, the castle had begun to fall into de- line and in 1649, when the town was taken by Cromwellian forces, it was severely damaged.

In 1996, the castle briefly returned to its ormer glory as a location for Mel Gibson's Braveheart, in which it served as a 'castle dou-)le' for the castle at York. A small booklet old at the castle gives a fuller insight into its nistory and acts as a handy guide for touring he grounds.

The castle's grassy 2 hectare enclosure is dominated by a massive stone keep, 25m tall and mounted on a Norman motte. Inside are three levels, the lowest divided by a central wall. Just outside the central keep are the re- mains of an earlier wall.

The principal outer–curtain wall, some 500m long and for the most part still stand- ing, dates from around 1250 and includes eight towers and a gatehouse. It also has a number of sally gates from which defenders could exit to confront the enemy. The fin- est stretch of the outer wall runs from the River Boyne through Dublin Gate to Castle St. Within the northern corner was a church and, facing the river, the Royal Mint, which produced Irish coinage (called 'Patricks' and 'Irelands') into the 15th century.

In 1971, excavations in the castle grounds re- vealed the remains of 10 headless men, presum- ably hapless criminals who fell foul of Edward IV's 1465 decree that anyone who had robbed or 'who was going to rob' should be beheaded, their heads mounted on spikes and publicly displayed as a warning to other thieves.

In the car park is a Russian cannon, a tro- phy from the Crimean War, which bears the tsarist double-headed eagle.

TRIM VISITOR CENTRE

Sharing space in the town hall with the tourist office is the informative **Trim Heritage Centre**

(☎ 046-943 7227; Town Hall, Castle St; admission adult/child €3.20/1.50; ⏰ 9.30am-5.30pm Mon-Sat), where you can watch a 20-minute video outlining the medieval history of Trim. There's a coffee shop here, too.

The **Meath Heritage Centre** (☎ 046-943 6633; www.meathroots.com; Town Hall, Castle St; initial consulta- tion €30; ⏰ 9am-1pm & 1.30-5pm Mon-Thu, 9am-2pm Fri) has an extensive genealogical database for people trying to trace Meath ancestors. Write in advance for the best results.

TALBOT CASTLE & ST MARY'S ABBEY

Across the River Boyne from the castle are the ruins of the 12th-century Augustinian **St Mary's Abbey**, rebuilt after a fire in 1368, and once home to a wooden statue of Our Lady of Trim, which was revered by the faithful for its miraculous powers.

Part of the abbey was converted in 1415 into a fine manor house by Sir John Talbot, then viceroy of Ireland; it came to be known as **Talbot Castle**. The Talbot coat of arms can be seen on the northern wall. Talbot went to war in France where, in 1429, he was defeated at Orleans by none other than Joan of Arc. He was taken prisoner, released, and went on fighting the French until 1453. He became known as 'the scourge of France' and even got a mention in Shakespeare's Henry VI: 'Is this the Talbot so much feared abroad/That with his name still their babes?'

In 1649, Cromwell's soldiers invaded Trim and set fire to the abbey's revered statue, a rather poignant slap in the face of Catholic be- lief. Just in case the locals didn't get the sym- bolism of the gesture, the soldiers destroyed the remaining parts of the abbey as well.

In the early 18th century, Talbot Castle was owned by Esther 'Stella' Johnson, the mistress of Jonathan Swift. He later bought the property from her and lived there for a year. Swift was rector of Laracor, 3km southeast of Trim, from around 1700 until 1745, when he died. From 1713 he was also – and more significantly – dean of St Patrick's Cathedral in Dublin.

Just northwest of the abbey building is the 40m **Yellow Steeple**, once the bell tower of the abbey, dating from 1368 but damaged by Cromwell's soldiers. It takes its name from the colour of the stonework at dusk.

East of the abbey ruins is part of the 14th- century town wall, including the **Sheep Gate**, the lone survivor of the town's original five gates. It used to be closed daily between 9pm and 4am, and a toll was charged for sheep entering to be sold at market.

NEWTOWN

About 1.5km east of town on Lackanash Rd, Newtown Cemetery contains an interesting group of ruins. The former **Parish Church of Newtown Clonbun** contains the late-16th-century tomb of Sir Luke Dillon, Chief Baron of the Exchequer during the reign of Elizabeth I, and his wife Lady Jane Bathe. The effigies are known locally as the Jealous Man and Woman, perhaps because of the sword lying between them.

Rainwater that collects between the two figures is claimed to cure warts. Apparently you place a pin in the puddle and then jab your wart; when the pin becomes covered in rust your warts will vanish. Some say you should leave a pin on the statue as payment for the cure.

The other ruins here are the **Cathedral of Sts Peter and Paul** and the 18th-century **Newtown Abbey**. The cathedral was founded in 1206 and burned down two centuries later. Although parts of the cathedral wall were flattened by a storm in 1839, it throws a superb echo back to **Echo Gate** across the river.

Southeast of these ruins, and just over the river, is the **Crutched Friary**. There are ruins of a keep, and traces of a watchtower and other buildings from a hospital set up after the Crusades by the Knights of St John of Jerusalem, who wore a red crutch (cross) on their cassocks. **St Peter's Bridge**, beside the friary, is said to be the second-oldest bridge in Ireland.

Sleeping

Bridge House Tourist Hostel (☎ 046-943 1848; silvertrans@eircom.net; Bridge St; dm/d from €20/50; P) Well-loved and well-worn, this quirky old house right on the river has basic four-bed dorm rooms and a couple of doubles. It's a great place to meet other travellers and has a very atmospheric location.

Crannmór House (☎ 046-943 1635; www.crannmor.com; Dunderry Rd; s/d from €50/80; P wi-fi) Five acres of rolling farmland and paddocks surround this vine-covered old house about 2km along the road to Dunderry. Bright rooms and traditional hospitality are on offer, and if you're interested in fishing locally, the owner is an experienced *ghillie* (fishing guide).

Tigh Cathain (☎ 046-943 1996; www.tighcathaintrim.com; Longwood Rd; s/d €55/80; P) A mock–Tudor style country house about 1km southwest of the town centre, Tigh Cathain has three pretty, uncluttered pastel bedrooms. The house i surrounded by a handsome garden.

Highfield House (☎ 046-943 6386; www.highfieldguesthouse.com; Maudlins Rd; s/d from €55/80; P) Set hig on a hill, this 18th-century country hous has been restored with an eclectic mixture c styles. You'll find pine furniture and perio replicas side by side in the bedrooms, som swirly carpets and deep coloured walls. It's a bit overwhelming but the rooms are comfortable enough.

Castle Arch Hotel (☎ 046-943 1516; www.castlearc hotel.com; Summerhill Rd; s/d from €69/138; P internet) Th 22 rooms at this modern business-class hote have a posh, heavy-drapery design accente with vintage touches. It's a popular loca choice with very friendly service and a grea deal at the price.

Trim Castle Hotel (☎ 046-948 3000; www.trimcastl hotel.com; Castle St; s/d from €165/180; P internet wi-fi) This stylish new boutique hotel is part of a development that is spiffing up an area close tc the castle. The 68 rooms here have wi-fi and a compact but comfortable modern design. Check for special offers online.

Eating & Drinking

Silver Swan Cafe (046-943 8478; Market St; meals €5-9; 🕒 9am-7pm Mon-Sat) For a simple snack or cake and a coffee, head to this bright and cosy cafe in the centre of town. You'll also get a range of soups and sandwiches as well as more hearty but predictable mains.

Wau Asian (☎ 046-948 3873; Bridge St; mains €9-15; 🕒 5-11.30pm daily, 12.30-2.30pm Thu & Fri, 1.30-3.30pm Sun) Upstairs from the Sally Rodgers pub, this place serves an extensive menu of interesting Chinese, Malaysian, Indonesian and Thai food. After your meal pop into the pub below for a drink overlooking the river.

La Scala (☎ 046-948 3236; Finnegan's Way; mains €10-16; 🕒 5-10pm Mon-Thu, 1-10pm Fri-Sun) Trim's newest restaurant is a bright, modern place serving classic Italian food. Choose from a decent range of pizzas and pastas or go for the four-course early bird special (€18.95, 5pm to 7pm) to taste a full range of kitchen goodies.

Franzini O'Brien's (☎ 046-943 1002; French's Lane; mains €12-20; 🕒 6.30-10pm Tue-Sat, 1-8.30pm Sun) Modern and spacious, this relaxed but buzzing place is a local favourite, with an international menu featuring everything from nachos to teriyaki chicken and excellent seafood.

Brogan's Beacon (☎ 046-943 1237; www.brogans.ie; High St; mains €13-19; 🕒 noon-9pm) This popular estaurant serves country-style comfort food or adoring locals. The menu is fairly predict-ble with hearty chicken, salmon and pasta lishes, the odd risotto and the usual array of teaks and burgers. It won't win any awards, ut may just satisfy a niggling craving. There's lso a bar menu for lighter snacks.

Marcy Regan's (David's Lad; ☎ 046-943 6103; ackanash Rd, Newtown, Trim; 🕑 Thu-Tue) This small, raditional pub beside St Peter's Bridge claims o be Ireland's second-oldest. It's a no frills kind of place just steeped in old world atmos->here. There's often a trad music session on ‑riday nights.

Getting There & Around

Bus Éireann runs a bus at least once an hour >etween Dublin and Trim (€10.30, 70 min-utes). Buses stop on New Rd just beyond the >ridge.

If you fancy stretching your legs to see the sights, **Country Cycles** (☎ 046-948 3838; Unit 4, Emmet St Car Park; per hr/day €5/20) has a variety of bikes for hire.

AROUND TRIM

There are a couple of evocative Anglo-Norman remains in the area around Trim. **Bective Abbey** was founded in 1147 and was the first Cistercian offspring of magnificent Mellifont Abbey in Louth (p552). The abbey at Bective was much changed in the following years and the remains seen today are 13th- and 15th-century additions, consisting of the chapter house, church, ambulatory and cloister. In 1543, after the Dissolution of the Monasteries, the abbey was used as a fortified house and the tower was built. Bective is 7.5km northeast of Trim on the way to Navan.

Some 12km northwest of Trim, on the road to Athboy, is **Rathcairn**, the smallest Gaeltacht (Irish-speaking) district in Ireland. Rathcairn's population is descended from a group of Connemara Irish speakers who were settled on an estate here as part of a social experiment in the 1930s.

KELLS
pop 2257

Kells is best known for the magnificent illu-minated manuscript that bears its name, and which so many visitors queue to see on their visit to Trinity College in Dublin. Although the great book wasn't created here, it was stashed in Kells, one of the leading monas-teries in the country, from the end of the 9th century until 1541, when it was removed by the Church. Today Kells is a sleepy little town, but the remnants of the once great monastic site include some interesting high crosses and a 1000-year-old round tower.

On older maps you may see Kells labelled as Ceanannus Mór or just Ceanannus, once its official name; locally it is always known as Kells.

Information

The **tourist office** (☎ 046-924 7840; Kells Heritage Centre, Headfort Pl; 🕑 10am-6pm Mon-Sat, 1.30-6pm Sun May-Sep, 10am-5pm Mon-Fri Oct-Apr) is in the heritage centre, located behind the town hall. It's a useful place for information on some of Meath's remote sights, such as Loughcrew Cairns.

Sights
KELLS HERITAGE CENTRE

Spread across two detail-packed floors, the town's **heritage centre** (☎ 046-924 7840; Headfort Pl; admission free; 🕑 10am-6pm Mon-Sat, 1.30-6pm Sun May-Sep, 10am-5pm Mon-Fri Oct-Apr, last admission one hr before closing) has a rather beautiful copy of the area's most famous object, the *Book of Kells*, which was brought here from the monastery on Iona in Scotland in 807 after a Viking raid. Surrounding the book are various 6th- to 12th-century relics and artefacts, as well as a highly detailed scale model of the town in the 6th century. There's also a small cafe.

MARKET CROSS

Until 1996, the Market Cross had stood for centuries in Cross St, at the heart of the town centre. Besides inviting the pious admiration of the faithful, the cross was used as a gallows in the aftermath of the 1798 revolt; the British garrison hanged rebels from the crosspiece, one on each arm so the cross wouldn't fall over. But what 1000 years of foul weather and the sacrilegious British couldn't do, a care-less bus driver did in 1996 and with one bad turn the cross was toppled. It was eventu-ally repaired and re-erected outside the Kells Heritage Centre.

On the eastern face of the Market Cross are depictions of Abraham's sacrifice of Isaac, the brothers Cain and Abel, the Fall of Adam and Eve, guards at the tomb of Jesus, and a won-derfully executed procession of horsemen. On the western face, the Crucifixion is the only discernible image. On the northern side is a panel of Jacob wrestling with the angel.

ROUND TOWER & HIGH CROSSES

The Protestant church of **St Columba** (admission free; ☉ 10am-1pm & 2-5pm Mon-Sat, services only Sun), west of the town centre, has a 30m-high 10th-century round tower on the southern side. It's without its conical roof, but it's known to date back at least as far as 1076, when the high king of Tara was murdered in its confined apartments.

Inside the churchyard are four 9th-century high crosses in various states of repair. The **West Cross**, at the far end of the compound from the entrance, is the stump of a decorated shaft, which has scenes of the baptism of Jesus, the Fall of Adam and Eve, and the Judgement of Solomon on the eastern face, and Noah's ark on the western face. All that is left of the **North Cross** is the bowl-shaped base stone.

Near the tower is the best preserved of the crosses, the **Cross of Patrick and Columba**, with its semi-legible inscription, *Patrici et Columbae Crux,* on the eastern face of the base. Above it are scenes of Daniel in the lion's den, the fiery furnace, the Fall of Adam and Eve, and a hunting scene. On the opposite side of the cross are depictions of the Last Judgement, the Crucifixion, and riders with a chariot, as well as a dog on the base.

The other surviving cross is the unfinished **East Cross**, with a carving of the Crucifixion and a group of four figures on the right arm.

ST COLMCILLE'S HOUSE

From the churchyard exit on Church St, **St Colmcille's House** (admission free; ☉ 10am-5pm Sat & Sun Jun-Sep) is left up the hill, among the row of houses on the right side of Church Lane. This squat, solid structure is a survivor from the old monastic settlement. Its name is a misnomer, as it was built in the 10th century and St Colmcille was alive in the 6th century. Experts have suggested that it was used as a scriptorium, a place where monks illuminated books.

The site is usually locked except during the summer months, but ask at the tourist office about the keys or phone **Mrs Carpenter** (☎ 046-924 1778; 1 Lower Church View) for access.

Sleeping & Eating

Kells Hostel (☎ 046-924 9995; The Carrick; dm from €18; **P**) Right in the centre of town and close to

the bus stop and shops, this makes a convenient base for the surrounding sights. There's large basic kitchen and lounge, three- to eigh bed dorms and lots of local info on display.

Teltown House B&B (☎ 046-902 3239; teltownhouse eircom.net; Teltown; s/d €50/100; **P**) This lovingly re stored old stone farmhouse is full of characte and history, with period-style rooms and a incredibly warm welcome. The farm was th location of the Irish equivalent of the Olympi games 2000 years ago, and 2000 years befor *that,* rock art was carved on stones that sti stand next to the B&B. Teltown House is 6kr southeast of Kells, east of the N3 at the Silve Tankard pub.

Headfort Arms Hotel (☎ 046-924 0063; www.headfo arms.ie; John St; s/d from €95/160; **P** **Q** **?**) Famil run and right in the town centre, the Headfor Arms has 45 comfortable, modern rooms with classic styling. Rooms in the charming ol building have the most character, but there' wi-fi throughout and a small spa for indulgen treatments.

Vanilla Pod (☎ 046-924 0084; Headfort Arms Hote John St; mains €17-28; ☉ 5.30-10pm daily & noon-3pr Sun) Bright and modern but rather soulless this restaurant in the Headfort Arms Hotel i independently run and features an ambitiou bistro-style menu. The food is well-prepare and sourced locally, but for the best deal ain for the set three-course dinner at €21.95.

Getting There & Away

Bus Éireann (☎ 01-836 6111) has services fro Kells to Dublin (€12.70, 90 minutes, hourly via Navan. There are also buses to Cavar (€11.80, 45 minutes, hourly).

AROUND KELLS
Hill of Lloyd Tower

It's easy to see why this 30m-high tower or the Hill of Lloyd became known as the 'inland lighthouse'. Built in 1791 by the Earl of Bective, in memory of his father, it has been renovated, and has fantastic views from the top. Access can be arranged by appointment through the **Kells Heritage Centre** (☎ 046-924 7840; €20 minimum charge), or you can just enjoy the views and a picnic in the surrounding park.

The tower is 3km northwest of Kells, off the Crossakeel road.

Crosses of Castlekeeran

Lost in the ruins of an ancient hermitage are the Crosses of Castlekeeran. They're

ot overly impressive in themselves – three
lainly carved, early-9th-century crosses (one
 the river) – but there's something invitingly
eaceful about the quiet, overgrown cemetery
at surrounds them. The **ruined church** in the
entre has some early grave slabs and an
gham stone (rock slab inscribed with Ireland's
arliest form of writing).

To get to the crosses, head through a farm-
ard about 2km further down the Crossakeel
oad from the Hill of Lloyd tower.

OUGHCREW CAIRNS

Vith all the hoopla over Brú na Bóinne, the
mazing Stone Age passage graves strewn
bout the Loughcrew Hills are often over-
oked. There are 30-odd tombs here but
ey're hard to get to and relatively few people
ver bother, which means you can enjoy this
oody and evocative place in peace.

It's well worth making the effort to get
o the three hills, Carnbane East (194m),
arnbane West (206m) and Patrickstown
279m) – although the last has been so ruined
y 19th-century builders that there's little to
ee other than splendid views of the surround-
ng countryside.

Like Brú na Bóinne, the graves were all
uilt around 3000 BC, but, unlike their better-
nown and better-excavated peers, the
oughcrew tombs were used at least until 750
C. As at Newgrange, larger stones in some
of the graves are decorated with spiral pat-
erns. Some of the graves look like large piles
of stones, while others are less obvious, their
airn having been removed. Archaeologists
ave unearthed bone fragments and ashes,
tone balls and beads.

The cairns are west of Kells, along the R154,
ear Oldcastle.

Carnbane East

Carnbane East has a cluster of sites; **Cairn T**
(☎ 049-854 1240; www.heritageireland.ie; admission free;
(☺) 10am-6pm mid-Jun–Aug; (P)) is the biggest at
about 35m in diameter, with numerous carved
stones. One of its outlying kerbstones is called
the Hag's Chair, and is covered in gouged
holes, circles and other markings. You need
the gate key to enter the passageway and a
torch to see anything in detail. It takes about
half an hour to climb Carnbane East from
the car park. From the summit on a reasonably clear day, you should be able to see the
Hill of Tara to the southeast, while the view

north is into Cavan, with Lough Ramor to
the north, and Oldcastle and Lough Sheelin
to the northwest.

In summer, access to Cairn T is controlled by the Heritage Service, which provides
guides. But locals are passionate about the
place and at any time of the year you can arrange for guides who will not only show you
Cairn T but take you to some of the other
cairns as well. Enquire at the Kells tourist
office.

Carnbane West

From the car park, it takes about an hour to
reach the summit of Carnbane West, where
Cairn D and L, both some 60m in diameter,
are located. Cairn D has been disturbed in
an unsuccessful search for a central chamber. Cairn L, northeast of Cairn D, is also
in poor condition, though you can enter the
passage and chamber, where there are numerous carved stones and a curved basin stone in
which human ashes were placed.

Cairn L is administered by the Heritage
Service, which only gives out the key to those
with an authentic research interest.

Loughcrew Gardens

A labour of love, the recently restored **Loughcrew
Historic Garden** (☎ 049-854 1060; www.loughcrew.com;
adult/child €7/3.50; (☺) noon-6pm Mar-Oct, 1-4pm Sun Oct-Apr)
incorporates 6 acres of lawns, terraces and herbaceous borders along with a lime avenue, yew
walk, canal and parterre. There's also a medieval moat, tower house and St Oliver Plunkett's
family church. At the end of May each year the
gardens play host to the Loughcrew Opera,
where guests are encouraged to dress in period
costume and bring a picnic or stay for dinner.
Loughcrew Gardens are northwest of Kells,
along the R154, near Oldcastle.

COUNTY LOUTH

The Wee County, as it's known locally, has
prospered greatly in recent years thanks to
its proximity to Dublin, but along with a welcome increase in activities, restaurants and
nightlife comes commuter congestion and
urban sprawl.

Louth's most appealing town is Drogheda,
a bustling place steeped in history that makes
a good base for visiting Brú na Bóinne, just
over the border in County Meath. Nearby are

the evocative ruins of Mellifont Abbey and Monasterboice, and to the north the county town of Dundalk. From here it's a quick trip to the lonely and evocative Cooley Peninsula to enjoy the mountainous landscape and the implausibly picturesque village of Carlingford.

Louth can easily be explored as a day trip from Dublin, but you'll get more from your visit by spending some time exploring the county.

History

As part of the ancient kingdom of Oriel, Louth is the setting for perhaps the most epic of all Irish mythological tales, the Táin Bó Cúailnge (Cattle Raid of Cooley), which includes a star-ring role for Ireland's greatest mythological hero, Cúchulainn. *The Táin*, by Thomas Kinsella, is a modern version of this compelling and bloody tale.

In the 5th and 6th centuries, Louth was at the centre of ecclesiastical Ireland with wealthy religious communities at the monastery at Monasterboice and the Cistercian abbey at Mellifont.

However, the arrival of the Normans in the 12th century ushered in a period of great change and upheaval. Attracted by the fertile plains of the Boyne, the Anglo-Norman gentry set about subduing the local population and building mighty houses and castles. The Norman invaders were responsible for the development of Dundalk and the two towns on opposite banks of the Boyne that united in 1412 to become what is now Drogheda.

DROGHEDA
pop 28,973

Ongoing development and a rising population of commuters have begun to breathe new life into Drogheda, a historic fortified town straddling the River Boyne. A clutch of fine old buildings, a handsome cathedral and a riveting museum give it plenty of cultural interest, while its wonderful old pubs, fine restaurants, good transport and numerous sleeping options make it an excellent base for exploring the world-class attractions that surround it.

History

This bend in the fertile Boyne Valley has been desirable right back to 910, when the Danes built a fortified settlement here. In the 12th century, the Normans added a bridge and expanded the two settlements on either side of the river. They also built a large defen-

sive motte and bailey on the southern side Millmount. By the 15th century, Droghed was one of Ireland's four largest walled tow and a major player in Irish affairs.

The 17th century brought devastation, hov ever, when in 1649, Drogheda was the scer of Cromwell's most notorious Irish slaught (see p550). Things went from bad to worse i 1690 when the town backed the wrong hors at the Battle of the Boyne and surrendered th day after the defeat of James II.

Despite a boom in the 19th century, whe Drogheda became a textile and brewing cen tre, the town never really hit its stride an suffered a century-long torpor. Today, ne money and an influx of commuters hav spruced things up with plenty of new devel opments along the riverfront.

Orientation

Drogheda sits astride the River Boyne, with the principal shopping area on the norther bank along West and Laurence Sts. South o the river is Millmount mound and the best o the trendy new developments. Traffic in tow is always slow, but there are small car park scattered everywhere.

Information
Post office (West St)
Talk & Net (☎ 041-984 9838; 1 Dominic St; per hr €1.60; ⏰ 10am-10pm) Internet access.
Tourist office (☎ 041-983 7070; www.drogheda.ie; Mayoralty St; ⏰ 9am-5pm Mon-Fri, 9am-4.30pm Sat) On the northern side of the river, just off the docklands.
Wise Owl Bookshop (☎ 041-984 2847; Laurence Centre; ⏰ 9.30am-6pm Mon-Sat, to 7.45pm Thu & Fri) A large store with good local books and maps.

Sights
ST PETER'S ROMAN CATHOLIC CHURCH
The shrivelled little head of the martyr St Oliver Plunkett (1629–81) is the main draw at the 19th-century **Catholic church** (West St), which is actually two churches in one: the first, designed by Francis Johnston in classical style and built in 1791; and the newer addition, built in the Gothic style visible today. Plunkett's head – from which the rest of him was separated at his hanging in 1681 – is in a glittering brass-and-glass case in the north transept.

ST LAURENCE'S GATE
Astride the eastwards extension of the town's main street is St Laurence's Gate, the finest

urviving portion of the city walls. This impos-
ng pile of stone is not in fact a gate but instead
a barbican, a fortified structure used to defend
he gate, which was further behind it.

Dating from the 13th century, the structure
was named after St Laurence's Priory, which
once stood outside the gate; no traces of it
now remain. The barbican consists of two
lofty towers, a connecting curtain wall and
the entrance to the portcullis. When the town
walls were completed in the 13th century,
they ran for 3km around the town, enclosing
52 hectares.

HIGHLANES GALLERY

This impressive **gallery** (☎ 041-980 3311; www
.highlanes.ie; Laurence St; admission free; ☺ 10am-6pm

Mon-Sat, to 8pm Thu, noon-5pm Sun) is set in a beautifully converted 19th-century monastery. All
the visual arts can be found here, as well as a
good permanent collection of paintings. There
are regular special exhibitions and the entire
complex is worth a look – as is the view down
to the Boyne. Attached is a well-stocked shop
featuring the best of Louth craftwork.

MILLMOUNT MUSEUM & TOWER

Across the river from town, in a villagelike enclave amid a sea of dull suburbia, is Millmount,
an artificial hill overlooking the town. The
mound may have been a prehistoric burial
ground along the lines of Newgrange, but it
has never been excavated. Legend has it that it
is the burial place of Amergin, a warrior-poet

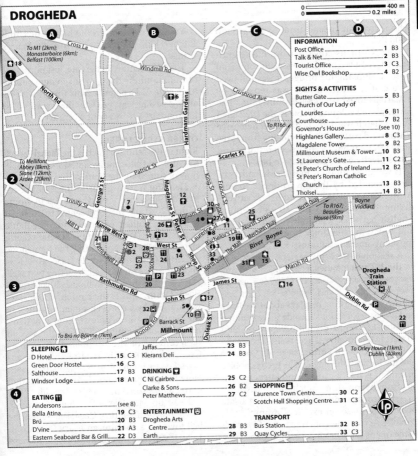

DROGHEDA

0 ___ 400 m
0 ___ 0.2 miles

INFORMATION		
Post Office	1	B3
Talk & Net	2	B3
Tourist Office	3	C3
Wise Owl Bookshop	4	B2

SIGHTS & ACTIVITIES		
Butter Gate	5	B3
Church of Our Lady of Lourdes	6	B1
Courthouse	7	B2
Governor's House	(see 10)	
Highlanes Gallery	8	C3
Magdalene Tower	9	B2
Millmount Museum & Tower	10	B3
St Laurence's Gate	11	C2
St Peter's Church of Ireland	12	B2
St Peter's Roman Catholic Church	13	B3
Tholsel	14	B3

SLEEPING		
D Hotel	15	C3
Green Door Hostel	16	C3
Salthouse	17	B3
Windsor Lodge	18	A1

EATING		
Andersons	(see 8)	
Bella Atina	19	C3
Brú	20	B3
D'vine	21	A3
Eastern Seaboard Bar & Grill	22	D3
Jaffas	23	B3
Kierans Deli	24	B3

DRINKING		
C Ní Cairbre	25	C2
Clarke & Sons	26	B2
Peter Matthews	27	C2

ENTERTAINMENT		
Drogheda Arts Centre	28	B3
Earth	29	B3

SHOPPING		
Laurence Town Centre	30	C2
Scotch Hall Shopping Centre	31	C3

TRANSPORT		
Bus Station	32	B3
Quay Cycles	33	C3

BE GOOD OR CROMWELL WILL GET YOU

Lauded as England's first democrat and protector of the people, Oliver Cromwell (1599–1658) was an Irish nightmare. Cromwell hated the Irish. To him, they were treacherous infidels, a dirty race of papists who had sided with Charles I during the Civil War. So when 'God's own Englishman' landed his 12,000 troops at Dublin in August 1649, he immediately set out for Drogheda, a strategic fort town and bastion of royalist support.

When Cromwell arrived at the walls of Drogheda, he was met by 2300 men led by Sir Arthur Aston, who boasted that 'he who could take Drogheda could take hell'. After Aston refused to surrender, Cromwell let fly with heavy artillery and after two days the walls were breached. Hell, it seems, was next.

In order to set a terrifying example to any other town that might resist his armies, Cromwell taught the defenders a brutal lesson. Over a period of hours, an estimated 3000 people were massacred, mostly royalist soldiers but also priests, women and children. Aston was bludgeoned to death with his own (wooden) leg. Of the survivors, many were captured and sold into slavery in the Caribbean.

Cromwell defended his action as God's righteous punishment of treacherous Catholics; he was quick to point out that he had never ordered the killing of noncombatants: it was the 17th century's version of 'collateral damage'.

---

who arrived in Ireland from Spain around 1500 BC.

The Normans constructed a motte-and-bailey fort on top of this convenient command post overlooking the bridge. It was followed by a castle, which in turn was replaced by a **Martello tower** (adult/child €3/2) in 1808. The tower played a dramatic role in the 1922 Civil War, when it was Drogheda's chief defensive feature and suffered heavy shelling from Free State forces. It has recently been restored and offers great views over the town below.

It was at Millmount that the defenders of Drogheda, led by the governor Sir Arthur Ashton, made their last stand before surrendering to Cromwell. Later, an 18th-century English barracks was built round the base, and today the buildings house craft shops, museums and a restaurant.

A section of the army barracks is now used as the **Millmount Museum** (☎ 041-983 3097; www.millmount.net; adult/child museum €3.50/2.50, tower €5.50/3; ⏱ 9.30am-5.30pm Mon-Sat, 2-5pm Sun), which has interesting displays about the town and its history. Exhibits include three wonderful late-18th-century guild banners, perhaps the last in the country. There is also a room devoted to Cromwell's brutal siege of Drogheda and the Battle of the Boyne. The pretty cobbled basement is full of gadgets and kitchen utensils from bygone times, including a cast-iron pressure cooker and an early model of a sofa bed. There's also an excellent example of a coracle. Across the courtyard, the **Governor's House** opens for temporary exhibitions.

You can drive up to the hilltop or climb Pitcher Hill via the steps from St Mary's Bridge.

The 13th-century **Butter Gate**, just northwest of Millmount, is the only surviving genuine town gate in Drogheda. This tower, with its arched passageway, predates the remains of St Laurence's Gate by about a century.

OTHER STRUCTURES

Right in the centre of town is the **Tholsel** (cnr West & Shop Sts), an 18th-century limestone town hall, now occupied by the Bank of Ireland.

Heading northwest from here is the restored 19th-century **courthouse** (Fair St), home to the sword and mace presented to the town council by William of Orange after the Battle of the Boyne. To the north is **St Peter's Church of Ireland** (William St), containing the tombstone of Oliver Goldsmith's uncle Isaac, as well as another image on the wall depicting two skeletal figures in shrouds, dubiously linked to the Black Death. This is the church whose spire was burned by Cromwell's men, resulting in the death of 100 people seeking sanctuary inside. Today's church (1748) is the second replacement of the original destroyed by Cromwell. It stands in an attractive close approached through lovely wrought-iron gates. Note the old 'Blue School' (for the education of freemen's sons) of 1844 on one side.

Head up Magdalene St from the church to see the 14th-century **Magdalene Tower**, the bell tower of a Dominican friary founded in 1224. It was here that England's King Richard

I, accompanied by a great army, accepted he submission of the Gaelic chiefs with suit-ble ceremony in 1395. Peace lasted only a ew months however, and Richard's return o Ireland led to his overthrow in 1399. Treasonous connections with the Gaelic Irish also lead to the Earl of Desmond's demise; he was beheaded here in 1468.

Keep making your way uphill from here to see the rather charming and more recent **Church of Our Lady of Lourdes** off Hardmans Gardens.

Finally, you can't help but admire the 1855 **Boyne Viaduct** carrying trains over the river east of the centre. Each of the 18 beautiful stone arches has a 20m span; erecting the piers bankrupted one company.

Sleeping

Green Door Hostel (☎ 041-983 4422; www.greendoorireland.com; 13 Dublin Rd; dm/d from €17/64) Set in a grand Georgian house near the train station, this hostel has five- to 12-bed dorm rooms as well as some private rooms, the best of which have their own TVs and bathrooms.

Salthouse (☎ 041-983 4426; 46 John St; s/d €35/70) This basic guesthouse makes a good option if you're looking for something slightly more cosy than the hostel. It has simple but clean rooms with pine furniture and white linens, and a bar with lively music sessions. Breakfasts go on almost all day so you can enjoy a sleep in without missing the fry up.

Windsor Lodge (☎ 041-984 1966; www.barwindsorlodge.com; The Court, North Rd; s/d €50/70; P wi-fi) This large purpose-built guesthouse has a good choice of modern, spacious rooms with country-style decor and new bathrooms. There's a lovely conservatory, a large lounge and an outdoor seating area to relax in at the end of your day.

D Hotel (☎ 041-987 7700; www.thed.ie; Scotch Hall, Marsh Rd; s/d from €70/130; P internet wi-fi) Slick, hip and unexpected, this is Drogheda's top dog when it comes to accommodation. The luxurious but minimalist rooms are bathed in light and decked out with designer furniture and cool gadgets. There's a stylish bar and restaurant, and great views of the city. Book in advance online and you could nab a fantastic deal.

Orley House (☎ 041-983 6019; www.orleyhouse.com; Bryanstown, Dublin Rd; r from €80; P) This spick-and-span B&B has large comfortable rooms and a warm welcome for families. It's a well-run place with excellent service and hearty breakfast served in a sun-filled conservatory. Orley House is about 2km out of town on the Dublin road.

Eating

Jaffas (☎ 041-980 2804; Fitzwilliam Court, Dyer St; meals €4.50-9; 8.30am-6pm Mon-Sat, to 7pm Thu & Fri, 11am-6pm Sun) Big, bright and modern with giant windows overlooking the river, this popular place serves a bumper range of soups, sandwiches, panini, bagels, crepes, and baked potatoes with a choice of interesting fillings. Service is swift and there are tables outside for alfresco dining on fine days.

Andersons (☎ 041-980 3295; Highlanes Gallery, Laurence St; meals €5-10; 10am-6pm Mon-Sat, noon-5pm Sun; wi-fi) Located in the impressive new Highlanes Gallery, this modern cafe serves a tempting range of soups, salads, sandwiches and wraps, as well as continental-style platters of luscious cheeses and cured meats. There's free wi-fi.

Eastern Seaboard Bar & Grill (☎ 041-980 2570; 1 Bryanstown Centre, Dublin Rd; mains €9-16; noon-10pm Mon-Sat, to 8pm Sun; wi-fi) Despite the swish, contemporary design, this popular new eatery manages to exude a warm, relaxed atmosphere with plenty of quirky details adding to its allure. The menu features all-American classics from sweet potato fries to burgers and New England clam chowder. Book ahead – it's been packed since opening.

Bella Atina (☎ 041-984 4878; The Mall; mains €10-15; 6-10.30pm Mon-Sat) Old-school country charm combines with new ideas at this excellent Italian place down by the river. It's all exposed brick arches and red walls inside, and the menu features classic Italian pastas as well as deftly prepared meat and fish dishes. The cannelloni is a treat.

D'vine (☎ 041-980 0440; Patrickswell Lane; mains €11-15; noon-3pm Mon-Sat & 6-10pm Wed-Mon) A little wine-bar-cum-restaurant with a cosy atmosphere and a great selection of Mediterranean foods, this place has excellent platters to start, followed by a largely Italian menu with an emphasis on rustic pasta dishes. It has an excellent wine menu and sometimes has live jazz on Sunday evenings.

Other options worth trying include:

Kierans Deli (☎ 041-983 8728; 15 West St; meals €6-12; 8.30am-5.30pm Mon-Sat) A renowned deli with a great selection of picnic options and a decent cafe at the back.

Brú (☎ 041-987 2784; Haymarket, Dyer St; noon-10pm; mains €10-16) Despite its slick appearance this contemporary bar and bistro is very child-friendly and serves a good but predictable menu of comfort food.

Drinking & Entertainment

Drogheda has dozens of bars and pubs, many with live music. Check the event guide at www.drogheda.ie for listings.

our pick **C Ní Cairbre** (Carberry's; ☎ 041-984 7569; North Strand) A national treasure, this pub has been owned by the same family since 1880. Old newspaper clippings and long-faded artwork cover most surfaces and it's a great place to catch some traditional music. You might find a session going on any night of the week but Tuesday nights and Sunday afternoons are your best bet.

Peter Matthews (McPhail's; ☎ 041-983 7371; Laurence St) One of Drogheda's top spots for live music, McPhail's (as it's always called, no matter what the sign says) is popular with a younger crowd and features everything from heavy metal cover bands to trad sessions. There's a traditional bar at the front and a beer garden out the back.

Clarke & Sons (☎ 041-983 6724; Peter St) This wonderful old boozer is right out of a time capsule. The unrestored wooden interior features snugs and leaded-glass doors that read Open Bar. The pints just taste better at this corner classic.

Earth (☎ 041-983 0969; Stockwell Lane; ◷ Thu-Sun) Drogheda's biggest nightclub attracts a fairly young crowd and can be a bit of a cattle mart, but the music ranges from club classics to hip hop, house and techno, and it's always buzzing.

Drogheda Arts Centre (☎ 041-983 3946; www .droichead.com; Stockwell Lane) Drama, music, comedy, film and visual art take to the stage at Drogheda's lively arts centre.

Shopping

Large glitzy malls are coming to Drogheda. Located on the south bank with the D Hotel is **Scotch Hall Shopping Centre** (Marsh Rd), while down close to the middle of town is the equally large **Laurence Town Centre** (Laurence St), which was once a grammar school.

Getting There & Away

BUS

Drogheda is only 48km north of Dublin, on the main M1 route to Belfast. The bus station is just south of the river on the corner of Rathmullan Rd and Donore Rd. This is one of the busiest bus routes in the country, and **Bus Éireann** (☎ 041-983 5023) regularly serves

Drogheda from Dublin (€6, one hour, one t four hourly). Drogheda to Dundalk is anothe busy route (€5, 30 minutes, hourly).

From Drogheda you can get a bus that drop you off at the entrance of the Brú na Bóinne vis itor centre (€2, 15 minutes, four to six daily).

TRAIN

The **train station** (☎ 041-983 8749) is just south of the river and east of the town centre, o Dublin Rd. Drogheda is on the main Belfast Dublin line (Dublin €15, 35 minutes; Belfas €27.50, 1½ hours), and there are six expres trains (and many slower ones) each way, with five on Sunday. This is the best line in Ireland with excellent on-board service.

Getting Around

Drogheda itself is excellent for walking, and many of the surrounding region's interesting sites are within easy cycling distance. **Quay Cycles** (☎ 041-983 4526; 11A North Quay; per day from €14), near the bridge, rents bikes between May and October.

AROUND DROGHEDA
Beaulieu House

Before Andrea Palladio and the ubiquitous Georgian style that changed Irish architecture in the early decades of the 18th century, there was the Anglo-Dutch style, a simpler, less ornate look that is equally handsome. **Beaulieu House** (☎ 041-983 8557; www.beaulieu.ie; admission house €8, garden €6, museum €6, combined ticket €20; ◷ 11am-5pm Mon-Fri May–mid-Sep, 1-5pm Sat & Sun Jul & Aug), about 5km northeast of Drogheda on the Baltray road, is a particularly good example of the style and – apparently – the first unfortified mansion to be built in Ireland. It was built between 1660 and 1666 on lands confiscated from the Plunkett family (the family of the headless Oliver) by Cromwell, and given to the marshal of the army in Ireland, Sir Henry Tichbourne. The red-brick mansion, with its distinctive steep roof and tall chimneys, has been owned by the same family ever since.

The interiors are stunning and house a superb art collection ranging from lesser Dutch masters to 20th-century Irish painters. There's also a wonderfully elegant garden and a classic car museum.

Mellifont Abbey

In its Anglo-Norman prime, **Mellifont Abbey** (☎ 041-982 6459; www.heritageireland.ie; Tullyallen;

dult/child €3/2; ☺ visitor centre 10am-6pm May-Sep; Ⓟ)
was the Cistercians' first and most magnificent centre in the country. Although the ruins are highly evocative and well worth exploring, they still don't do real justice to the site's former splendour.

In the mid-12th century, Irish monastic orders had grown a little too fond of the good life and were not averse to a bit of corruption. In 1142, Malachy, bishop of Down (later canonised for his troubles), was at the end of his tether; he invited a group of hard-core monks from Clairvaux in France to set up shop in a remote location, where they would act as a sobering influence on the local clergy. The Irish monks didn't quite get on with their French guests, and the latter soon left for home. Still, the construction of Mellifont – named for the Latin *mellifons* (honey fountain) – continued, and within 10 years, nine more Cistercian monasteries were established. Mellifont eventually became the mother house for 21 lesser monasteries; at one point as many as 400 monks lived here.

Mellifont not only brought fresh ideas to the Irish religious scene, it also heralded a new style of architecture. For the first time in Ireland, monasteries were built with the formal layout and structure that was being used on the Continent. Only fragments of the original settlement remain, but the plan of the extensive monastery can easily be traced.

Like many other Cistercian monasteries, the buildings clustered around an open cloister. To the northern side of the cloister are the remains of a principally 13th-century cross-shaped church. To the south, the chapter house has been partially floored with medieval glazed tiles, originally found in the church. The refectory, kitchen and warming room – the only place where the austere monks could enjoy the warmth of a fire – would also have been here. The eastern range would once have held the monks' sleeping quarters.

Mellifont's most recognisable building, and one of the finest pieces of Cistercian architecture in Ireland, is the lavabo, an octagonal washing house for the monks. It was built in the early 13th century and used lead pipes to bring water from the river. A number of other buildings would have surrounded this main part of the abbey.

After the Dissolution of the Monasteries, a fortified Tudor manor house was built on the site in 1556 by Edward Moore, using materials scavenged from the demolition of many of the buildings.

In 1603, this house was the scene of a poignant and crucial turning point in Irish history. After the disastrous Battle of Kinsale, the vanquished Hugh O'Neill, last of the great Irish chieftains, was given shelter here by Sir Garret Moore until he surrendered to the English lord deputy Mountjoy. After his surrender, O'Neill was pardoned but, despairing of his position, fled to the Continent in 1607 with other old-Irish leaders in the Flight of the Earls. In 1727, the site was abandoned altogether.

The visitor centre next to the site describes monastic life in detail. The ruins themselves are always open and there's good picnicking next to the rushing stream. The abbey is about 1.5km off the main Drogheda–Collon road (R168). A back road connects Mellifont with Monasterboice. There is no public transport to the abbey.

Monasterboice

Crowing ravens lend just the right atmosphere to **Monasterboice** (admission free; ☺ sunrise-sunset; Ⓟ), an intriguing monastic site containing a cemetery, two ancient church ruins, one of the finest and tallest round towers in Ireland, and two of the best high crosses. The site can be reached directly from Mellifont via a winding route along narrow country roads.

Down a leafy lane and set in sweeping farmland, Monasterboice has a special atmosphere, particularly at quiet times. The original monastic settlement here is said to have been founded in the 5th or 6th century by St Buithe, a follower of St Patrick, although the site probably had pre-Christian significance. St Buithe's name somehow got converted to Boyne, and the river is named after him. It's said that he made a direct ascent to heaven via a ladder lowered from above. An invading Viking force took over the settlement in 968, only to be comprehensively expelled by Donal, the Irish high king of Tara, who killed at least 300 of the Vikings in the process.

The high crosses of Monasterboice are superb examples of Celtic art. The crosses had an important didactic use, bringing the gospels alive for the uneducated, and they were probably brightly painted originally, although all traces of colour have long disappeared.

The cross near the entrance is known as **Muirdach's Cross**, named after a 10th-century

---

DETOUR: THE COAST ROAD

Most people just zip north along the M1 motorway but if you want to meander along the coast and see a little of rural Ireland, opt for the R166 from Drogheda north along the coast.

The picturesque little village of **Termonfeckin** was, until 1656, the seat and castle of the primate of Armagh. The 15th-century **castle** (admission free; ☽ 10am-6pm), or tower house, is tiny and worth a five-minute stop.

About 2km further north is the busy seaside and fishing centre of **Clogherhead**, with a good, shallow Blue Flag beach at Lurganboy. Try to ignore the caravan parks and concentrate on the lovely views of the Cooley and Mourne Mountains instead.

The 33km route comes to an end in **Castlebellingham**. The village here grew up around an 18th-century crenulated **mansion**, and generations of mud farmers served the landlord within. Buried in the local graveyard is Dr Thomas Guither, a 17th-century physician who allegedly reintroduced frogs to Ireland by releasing imported frog spawn into a pond in Trinity College, Dublin. Frogs, along with snakes and toads, had supposedly received their marching orders from St Patrick a thousand years earlier.

From here you can continue 12km north to Dundalk along the suburban R132 or join the M1 and zip off.

---

abbot. The subjects of the carvings have not been positively identified. On the eastern face, from the bottom up, are thought to be the Fall of Adam and Eve, the murder of Abel, the battle of David and Goliath, Moses bringing water from the rock to the waiting Israelites, and the three wise men bearing gifts to Mary and Jesus. The Last Judgement, with the risen dead waiting for their verdict, is at the centre of the cross, and further up is St Paul in the desert.

The western face relates more to the New Testament, and from the bottom depicts the arrest of Christ, Doubting Thomas, Christ giving a key to St Peter, the Crucifixion, and Moses praying with Aaron and Hur. The cross is capped by a representation of a gabled-roof church.

The **West Cross** is near the round tower and stands 6.5m high, making it one of the tallest high crosses in Ireland. It's much more weathered, especially at the base, and only a dozen or so of its 50 panels are still legible. The more distinguishable ones on the eastern face include David killing a lion and a bear, the sacrifice of Isaac, David with Goliath's head, and David kneeling before Samuel. The western face shows the Resurrection, the crowning with thorns, the Crucifixion, the baptism of Christ, Peter cutting off the servant's ear in the Garden of Gethsemane, and the kiss of Judas.

A third, simpler cross in the northeastern corner of the compound is believed to have been smashed by Cromwell's forces

and has only a few straightforward carvings. Photographers should note that this cross makes a great evening silhouette picture, with the round tower in the background.

The **round tower**, minus its cap, is over 30m tall, and stands in a corner of the complex Records suggest the tower interior went up in flames in 1097, destroying many valuable manuscripts and other treasures. It's closed to the public.

The church ruins are from a later era and are of less interest, although the modern gravestones are often quite sad.

There's a small gift shop outside the compound in summer. There are no set hours but come early or late in the day to avoid the crowds. It's just off the M1 motorway, about 8km north of Drogheda.

DUNDALK
pop 29,037

An industrial hub, Dundalk is all business and always has been. Although there's not a lot for the visitor here, it's a pleasant enough place with a couple of interesting sites.

In the Middle Ages, Dundalk was at the northern limits of the English-controlled Pale, and with partition in 1921 it once again became a border town, this time providing a quick escape from the 'bandit country' of South Armagh.

The **tourist office** (☎ 042-933 5484; dundalk@failteire land.ie; Jocelyn St; ☽ 9am-6pm Mon-Sat Jun–mid-Sep, 9.30am-5.15pm Mon-Fri mid-Sep–May) is next to the County Museum.

Right in the centre, the richly decorated 9th-century **St Patrick's Cathedral** was modelled on King's College Chapel in Cambridge, England. Also here is the interesting **County Museum Dundalk** (☎ 042-932 7056; Jocelyn St; adult/concession €4/2.50; ☽ 10.30am-5.30pm Mon-Sat, 2-6pm un, closed Mon Oct-Apr). Different floors in the museum are dedicated to the town's early history and archaeology, and to the Norman period. One floor deals with the growth of industry in the area, from the 1750s up to the 1960s – including the cult classic Heinkel Bubble Car, which was manufactured in the area.

The **courthouse** (cnr Crowe & Clanbrassil Sts) is a fine neo-Gothic building with large Doric pillars designed by Richard Morrison. In the front square is the stone **Maid of Éireann**, commemorating the 1798 Rising.

Should you need sustenance, **Rosso** (☎ 042-935 6502; 5 Roden Pl; cafe mains €6-9, restaurant lunch €9-15, dinner mains €17.50-24.50; ☽ cafe 10am-5pm, restaurant noon-2.30, 5.30-9.30pm Sun-Fri) is a trendy modern place opposite St Patrick's Cathedral. The slick downstairs restaurant features an ambitious international menu while the more informal cafe upstairs has cosy sofas and serves a tempting selection of salads, wraps and baguettes.

Bus Éireann (☎ 042-933 4075; Long Walk) runs an almost hourly service to Dublin (€8, 1½ hours) and a less frequent one to Belfast (€13, 80 minutes). The bus station is near the courthouse.

Clarke Train Station (☎ 042-933 5521; Carrickmacross Rd) is 900m west of the bus station. It has express trains to Dublin (€18 to €21.50, one hour, seven Monday to Saturday, five Sunday) and Belfast (€19, one hour, eight Monday to Saturday, five Sunday), as well as many slower services.

COOLEY PENINSULA

Unsettling, isolated and remote, the Cooley Peninsula has an arresting beauty with forested slopes and sun-dappled, multihued hills rising out of the dark waters of Carlingford Lough. Sweeping views lead the eyes across the water to Northern Ireland's Mourne Mountains, while tiny country lanes wind their way down to deserted stony beaches.

Carlingford
pop 623

Nestled dramatically between the hills and the water, Carlingford is a pretty three-street village littered with evocative ruins and white-washed houses. It's a really lovely place overlooking Carlingford Lough, but little of this was appreciated until the late 1980s, when the villagers got together to show what can be done to revive a dying community. The story of their efforts is vividly told in the heritage centre. Today the village is a wonderful stop with great pubs and restaurants, plenty of accommodation, a series of lively summer festivals and beautiful views.

INFORMATION

The **tourist office** (☎ 042-937 3033; www.carlingford .ie; ☽ 10am-5pm, closed Tue Oct-Mar) is in an old train station right next to the bus stop on the waterfront.

SIGHTS
Holy Trinity Heritage Centre

The **heritage centre** (☎ 042-937 3454; www.carlingford heritagecentre.com; Churchyard Rd; adult/concession €3/1.50; ☽ 10am-12.30pm & 2-4pm Mon-Fri) is in the former Holy Trinity Church. A mural shows what the village looked like in its heyday, when the Mint and Taafe's Castle were right on the waterfront, and a short video describes the village history and explains what has been done to give it new life in recent years.

King John's Castle

Carlingford was first settled by the Vikings, and in the Middle Ages became an English stronghold under the protection of the castle, which was built on a pinnacle in the 11th to 12th centuries to control the entrance to the lough. On the western side, the entrance gateway was built to allow only one horse and rider through at a time.

King John spent a couple of days here in 1210 en route to a battle with Hugh de Lacy at Carrickfergus Castle in Antrim. It's suggested by some that the first few pages of the Magna Carta, the world's first constitutional bill of rights, were drafted while he was here.

Other Sights

Near the tourist office is **Taafe's Castle**, an imposing 16th-century tower house that stood on the waterfront until the land in front was reclaimed to build a short-lived train line. The **Mint**, near the square, is of a similar age and has some interesting Celtic-inspired carvings around the windows. Although Edward IV is thought to have granted a charter to a mint in 1467, no coins were produced here. Near the Mint is the **Tholsel**, the only surviving gate to the original town, although it was much altered in the 19th century, when its defensive edge was softened in the interests of letting traffic through.

West of the village centre are the remains of a **Dominican friary**, built around 1305 and used as a storehouse by oyster fishermen after 1539.

Carlingford is the birthplace of Thomas D'Arcy McGee (1825–68), one of Canada's founding fathers. A bust commemorating him stands opposite Taafe's Castle.

ACTIVITIES

For a wide range of activities including sailing, kayaking, windsurfing, rock climbing and archery contact the **Carlingford Adventure Centre** (☎ 042-937 3100; www.carlingfordadventure.com; Tholsel St).

Carlingford is the starting point for the 40km **Táin Trail**, which makes a circuit of the Cooley Peninsula through the Cooley Mountains. The route is a mixture of surfaced roads, forest tracks and green paths. For more information contact the tourist office.

Much of the Cooley Peninsula is protected and is home to various species of birds including godwits, red-breasted mergansers, buzzards, tits and various finches. Ask at the tourist office for information on the **Cooley Birdwatching Trail**.

You'll also find information on angling tours at the tourist office, or try www.carling ford.ie.

FESTIVALS & EVENTS

Almost every weekend from June to September, Carlingford goes event crazy: there are summer schools, medieval festivals, leprechaun hunts, homecoming festivals and anything that'll lure folks in off the M1. The mid-August **Oyster Festival** is a favourite.

SLEEPING & EATING

You'll be spoilt for choice when it comes to food and accommodation in Carlingford, but it's a popular spot and can be crowded during summer, especially at weekends; book well in advance.

Carlingford Adventure Centre (☎ 042-937 3100; www.carlingfordadventure.com; Tholsel St; dm/s/d €20/25/50) Popular with school groups taking activity courses, the rooms here are often booked up;

things can be quieter outside term time. Th dorms are pretty simple with four to six beds but there are some doubles with private bath rooms on the second floor.

Belevedere House (☎ 042-938 3828; www.belveder house.ie; Newry St; s/d €50/100; ⓦ) An excellent deal the rooms at this lovely B&B are modern bu cosy with antique pine furniture, subtle light ing and pretty colour schemes. Guests have access to leisure facilities at the local Fou Seasons hotel and breakfast is served in the downstairs Bay Tree restaurant.

Ghan House (☎ 042-937 3682; www.ghanhouse.com Main Rd; s/d from €85/190; ☽ restaurant 7-9.30pm Mon Sat, 1-3.30pm Sun; P 🔲 ⓦ) This 18th-century Georgian house has 12 guestrooms, each tastefully decorated with period antiques and original artworks. Book one of the four rooms in the main house for plenty of character and old-world charm – the annexe just doesn't have the same appeal and its rooms are overpriced. The restaurant is renowned for its excellent, classical food (five-course set menu from €55) and themed banquet nights There's also a cookery school.

McKevitt's Village Hotel (☎ 042-937 3116; www .mckevittshotel.com; Market Sq; s/d €105/160; P) With 17 modern rooms all kitted out in light creams and whites, this hotel offers quality accommodation and decent rates. It's a bit old school, but you get more for your money than at some of the pricier options around town.

Kingfisher (☎ 042-937 3716; www.kingfisherbistro .com; Dundalk St; lunch mains €6-16, dinner mains €16-27; ☽ 11.30am-10pm) Set in a beautifully restored grain store, the Kingfisher serves up modern Irish food with a hint of Asian influence. Go for Thai spiced pork with sticky rice and sweet Asian salad, John Dory with a lime and lemongrass risotto or more traditional oven-baked salmon or duck confit. It's all extremely good.

Food for Thought (☎ 042-938 3838; Dundalk St; mains €10-12) A popular lunch stop with locals, this relaxed deli-cum-cafe serves a range of delicious down-to-earth dishes such as lasagne, pizza, sandwiches and salads in very generous portions. It's also a great place to pick up the makings of a tasty picnic.

Bay Tree (☎ 042-938 3828; www.belvederehouse.ie; Newry St; mains €20-25; ☽ 6-9pm Mon-Sat & 1-3pm Sun summer, closed Mon & Tue winter) Simple, modern food made from seasonal local ingredients is on the menu at the Bay Tree, a lovely little place featuring plenty of fresh fish as well as more exotic meats such as wild boar.

Other popular spots for food:

Magee's Bistro (☎ 042-937 3751; www.mageesbistro om; Tholsel St; mains €18-24; ☻ 10am-3.30pm Tue-Fri 7-9pm Tue-Sun) A local favourite serving honest, down->-earth steaks, seafood, chicken and fish.

ystercatcher Bistro (☎ 042-937 3922; www.the ystercatcher.com; Market Sq; mains €19-22; ☻ 6.30-.30pm Mon-Sat, 5-8.30pm Sun) Renowned for the superb uality of its oysters, this white-tablecloth restaurant does ocal seafood just right.

DRINKING

PJ O'Hares (☎ 042-937 3106; Newry St) Behind the old-style grocery at the front is a classic, stone-floor pub with a blazing fire. There's music most nights in summer and the owners have recently opened a restaurant (mains €13 to €20) upstairs serving excellent oysters and the likes of steak-and-Guinness pie and shellfish linguine.

GETTING THERE & AROUND

Bus Éireann (☎ 042-933 4075) has services to Dundalk (€6.50, 50 minutes, four to five daily Monday to Saturday).

There's great cycling around the Cooley Peninsula; rent a bike and pick up maps of cycling routes at **On Your Bike** (☎ 087 239 7467; per day/week €20/80). Bikes can be delivered to your accommodation or the tourist office.

COUNTY CAVAN

Cavan is paradise for boaters, anglers, walkers, cyclists and painters. Known as the 'Lake Country', there's supposedly a lake for every day of the year; between the steely grey waters is a gentle landscape of meandering streams, bogs and drumlins. Famed for its excellent fishing, Cavan also has some spectacular paths leading through the wild Cuilcagh Mountains, which are the source of the 300km River Shannon. The county's quiet, rural charm is best appreciated from the water, no more so than from the tranquil confines of the Shannon–Erne Waterway.

History

Magh Sleacht, a plain in northwest Cavan near the border village of Ballyconnell, was a hugely important Druidic centre in the 5th-century when St Patrick was busy converting the pagan Irish to Christianity. St Patrick won the converts and the area soon diminished in

significance, but it is still littered with tombs, standing stones and stone circles from this time.

In the 12th century, the Anglo-Normans tried to get a foothold in Cavan, but the land-scape foiled them and the region remained under the control of the Gaelic O'Reilly clan. The O'Reillys ruled until the 16th century, when they joined the other Ulster lords to fight the Nine Years' War (1594–1603) against the English and were defeated.

As part of the Ulster Plantation, Cavan was divided up among English and Scottish settlers. In the 1640s, taking advantage of England's troubles, Owen Roe O'Neill led a rebellion against the settlers. O'Neill died in 1649 of suspected poisoning in Clough Oughter Castle near Cavan.

After the War of Independence in 1922, the Ulster counties of Cavan, Monaghan and Donegal were incorporated into the Republic. With the border so close, Republicanism is strong here, but with border points now removed you may not even notice crossing between the two.

Activities

FISHING

Cavan's exceptional lake fishing reels in anglers from all over Europe to the county's southern and western borders. It's primarily coarse fishing, but there's also some game angling for brown trout in Lough Sheelin. Most lakes are well signposted, and the types of fish available are marked.

For more information, contact **Cavan Tourism** (☎ 049-433 1942; www.cavantourism.com) or the **Northern Regional Fisheries Board** (☎ 049-433 7174; www.nrfb.ie), both in Cavan town.

You can also pick up a copy of the *Angler's Guide to Cavan* from tourist offices.

WALKING

The highlight for many walkers in the region is the **Cavan Way**, a 26km trail between the hamlets of Blacklion and Dowra through the Cuilcagh Mountains. Heading south from Blacklion, it takes you through an area known locally as the Burren, and its ancient burial site Magh Sleacht, which is dotted with prehis-toric monuments – court cairns, ring forts and tombs – and was one of the last strongholds of Druidism. It continues past the Shannon Pot, the source of Ireland's longest river, then by road to Dowra, passing over the Black Pigs

Dyke, an ancient fortification that once divided Ireland in two.

From Blacklion it's mainly hill walking; from Shannon Pot to Dowra it's mainly road. The highest point on the walk is Giant's Grave (260m). You'll need OS map No 26 and the *Cavan Way* map guide. Maps are on display in Blacklion and Dowra. Detailed route information (including downloadable PDF maps) is available online at www.cavantourism.com. The route can be boggy, so take spare socks!

At Blacklion you can pick up the Ulster Way (p685) and at Dowra you can join the Leitrim Way, which runs between Manorhamilton and Drumshanbo.

CAVAN TOWN
pop 3934

Cavan's county town is a solidly workaday place with some handsome Georgian houses and a famous crystal showroom. There's not much here for the visitor, but it's a useful place to stock up on essentials or make a transport connection.

The **tourist office** (☎ 049-433 1942; www.cavantourism .com; Farnham St; ☒ 9.45am-1.30pm & 2-5pm Mon-Fri) is above the library. You can check your email at **Chapter One** (☎ 049-437 3488; 24 Main St; per hr €5; ☒ 8.30am-6pm Mon-Fri, 9am-6pm Sat).

All that remains of the 13th-century Franciscan friary the town grew up around is an ancient **bell tower**, next to the **grave** of 17th-century rebel leader Owen Roe O'Neill in Abbey St's cemetery.

The town's famous crystal is displaye at the **Cavan Crystal Showroom** (☎ 049-433 18C www.cavancrystaldesign.com; Dublin Rd; admission fre ☒ 9.30am-6pm Mon-Fri, 10am-5pm Sat, noon-5pm Sur It also sells a wide variety of local crafts. Th showroom is about 2km southeast of the tow centre on the N3.

If you're interested in tracing your Cava roots, **Cavan Genealogy** (☎ 049-436 1094; cavangen alogy@eircom.net; Central Library, Farnham St; assessme fee €95, single search €25; ☒ 9.15am-5pm Mon-Fri) ca pore over one million records for you, bu you cannot perform a search of the archive yourself.

Sleeping & Eating

Ballycloone House (☎ 049-436 2310; michaelobrien53@ eircom.net; Golf Links Rd; s/d €51/76; **P**) This larg modern house surrounded by gardens ha bright, cosy rooms with country-style fur nishings and plenty of space. It's on a quie road close to the hospital about 2km from the town centre.

Farnham Estate (☎ 049-437 7700; www.farnhamestat .ie; Cavan; d from €130; **P** ☒ ☒) Set in misty woodlands, this sprawling 16th-century es tate is part of the Radisson SAS group. The luxurious rooms blend contemporary style with period features and character, there's garden-view restaurant, an indoor/outdoo swimming pool and a fantastic spa (also open to non-guests). The estate's 3km west of towr on the R198.

Chapter One (☎ 049-437 3488; 24 Main St; mains €6-8 ☒ 8.30am-6pm Mon-Fri, 9am-6pm Sat; ☒) Heaving at

---

LAKE ESCAPES

Favoured by renegades, rebels and reclusive royals, *crannógs* (meaning 'small islands built with young trees') were the escapists' homes of choice. These artificial islands, particularly popular in times of political instability, had a surprisingly long life, and were made throughout the 6th to the 17th centuries.

Overgrown now with trees and brambles, it's sometimes hard to see *crannóg* remains as the amazingly dogged pieces of engineering that they are. Using the simplest tools, the islands were built from scratch from layers of wood, peat, stone, heather and soil. *Crannóg* dwellers made access even trickier by palisading the islands, and by using zigzagging causeways or submerged stepping stones as a front path. Sometimes canoe-like boats were the only way to get across.

Crannógs were used as defended farmsteads, craft centres and storage places for valuables (for example, during 9th-century Viking raids) and became important rebel hideouts during the Nine Years' War.

There are over 1200 *crannógs* in Ireland (mainly in Cavan, Monaghan, Leitrim and Fermanagh), but few have been properly excavated. Those that have give tantalising glimpses of turbulent *crannóg* life with the remains of the manacled, mutilated skeletons of slaves and hostages turning up with alarming regularity.

nchtime when locals sweep in to dine on the uge range of filled bagels, this place is one of ne town's most popular cafes. As well as the agels you'll find soups, lasagne and various pecials such as quesadillas in this friendly, formal spot.

Oak Room (☎ 049-437 1414; www.theoakroom.ie; 62 ain St; mains €18-30; ✆ 5.30-9.30pm Tue-Sat) You'll nd fine modern Irish cuisine on offer at this opular restaurant. The decor is minimalist rith eclectic art on the walls, but the menu is mbitious and relies heavily on local ingredi-nts with suppliers listed for each dish.

etting There & Around

uses arrive at and depart from the small **bus tation** (☎ 049-433 1353; Farnham St). There are 10 ervices daily to Dublin (€13.50, two hours), pur daily to Donegal (€17.50, two hours), nd three daily (one on Sunday) to Belfast €20, three hours) and Galway (€21.50, 3¼ ours).

There are also various services to small owns throughout the county including three ervices daily to Ballyconnell and Belturbet, nd buses leaving on the hour to Virginia nd Kells.

ROUND CAVAN TOWN
ough Oughter & Killykeen Forest Park

Rod-wielding anglers congregate at Lough Oughter, which splatters across the map like pilt liquid. Coarse fishing aside, the wildlife-rich lough is also idyllic for naturalists, walkers and anyone wanting to vanish into a andscape of shimmering waters and cathedral-ike aisles of trees. It's best accessed via Killykeen Forest Park (☎ 049-433 2541; www.coillteout loors.ie; car €5, pedestrians & cyclists free), 12km north-west of Cavan, where various nature trails (from 1.5km to 5.8km) lead you through the woods and along the shore. Keep an eye out for stoats, badgers, foxes, grey squirrels and hedgehogs, as well as some amazing birdlife.

Many of the low overgrown islands in the lake were *crannógs* (fortified, artificial islands, see opposite for more detail). The most spec-tacular is home to **Clough Oughter Castle**, a 13th-century circular tower perched on a tiny speck of land. It was used as a lonely prison, then as a stronghold by rebel leader Owen Roe O'Neill, who was (probably) poisoned there in 1649, before it was destroyed by Cromwell's army in 1653. Although the castle lies out of reach over the water, it's worth getting near

for the view: go on foot via the forest trails, or get a closer look by car by turning left out of the Killykeen park exit and following the narrow road running north from the village of Garthrattan.

Butlersbridge & Cloverhill

Heading north from Cavan along the N3 and N54 you'll pass the two pretty villages of Butlersbridge and Cloverhill. Set on the banks of the River Annalee, Butlersbridge is a good place for a riverside picnic. If it's not picnic weather, pop into the **Derragarra Inn** (☎ 049-433 1003), an ivy-covered pub with a wood-beamed interior, beer garden, live music at weekends and good bar food.

The lovely little village of Cloverhill is home to the award-winning **Olde Post Inn** (☎ 047-55555; www.theoldepostinn.com; 5-course din-ner €56; ✆ 6.30-9pm Tue-Sat, 12.30-2.30pm & 6.30-8.30pm Sun; **P**). This restaurant serves outstanding modern Irish cuisine based on traditional ingredients such as suckling pig, venison, pheasant and steak. The rooms (single/dou-ble €60/100) are modern and tasteful, but rather cramped.

Belturbet
pop 1395

In a prime position on the Shannon–Erne Waterway (see p521), this charming, old-fashioned village, 16km northwest of Cavan, is a fisherman's favourite. It's also a busy base for cruise boats, and a good starting point for a cycling trip along the canal and river system.

You can hire a boat from **Emerald Star** (☎ 049-952 2933; www.emeraldstar.ie; per week two-/five-berth €1043/1510; ✆ Apr-Oct) to cruise between Belturbet and Belleek. Alternatively, bike hire and route advice is available at **Fitz Hire** (☎ 049-952 2866; fitzpatrickhire@eircom.net; Belturbet Business Park, Creeney; per day/week €15/45).

The beautifully restored **Belturbet Railway Station** (☎ 049-952 2074; www.belturbet-station.com; Railway Rd; admission by donation; ✆ by appointment) houses a visitor centre exploring the history of rail travel in the area. Trains used the sta-tion from 1885 until 1959, after which it lan-guished for 40 years. Call in advance if you'd like to visit.

The cosiest accommodation option in town is the cherry-coloured **Church View Guest House** (☎ 049-952 2358; www.churchviewguesthouse.com; 8 Church St; s\d €40\70; **P**), but book ahead as it's

CHEESE MAKING

Hard pasteurised goat's cheese is something of a rarity, and prize-winning **Corleggy Cheese** (☎ 049-952 2930; www.corleggy.com; Belturbet) is particularly rare due to its small production runs. Corleggy uses vegetarian rennet and is washed in sea brine, with subtle flavours thanks to the grassy grazing pastures surrounding the farmhouse where the cheese is handmade. A number of other cheeses including cow's- and sheep's-milk cheeses are also produced here, with flavours including garlic and red pepper, smoked cheese, cumin, and green peppercorn.

You can stop by the farmhouse to buy Corleggy cheese direct from the source (but call in advance to check someone is around), pick some up at **Belturbet Farmers Market** on Fridays from 4pm to 6pm or Dublin's Meeting House Sq Market in Temple Bar (p149).

If you want to learn how to make cheese yourself, cheesemaker Silke Cropp runs several **cheese-making courses** each summer. Courses take place on Sundays from 10am to 5pm and cost €150, which includes an organic lunch with wine. Afterwards you'll have your own kilo of cheese to take with you. BYO bucket.

Corleggy's farmhouse is located 2.5km north of Belturbet village. Coming along the N3 from Cavan into Belturbet village, turn right at the point the main road takes a sharp left, then take your first left and follow it for just on 2.5km; you'll see Corleggy's sign on your left.

perennially busy with anglers thanks to its cold storeroom and proximity to the lakes.

For food head to **Le Rendezvous** (☎ 049-952 4089; Main St; mains €16-25; ⌚ 5.30-9.30pm daily & 12.30-2.30pm Sun), a deceptively simple-looking French restaurant that serves classic dishes such as *boeuf bourguignon* and braised lamb shank. For something simpler the atmospheric bar at the **Seven Horseshoes** (☎ 049-952 2166; Main St; bar food €6-14; ⌚ 1-3pm & 5-9pm) has old-world charm and a decent menu of hearty steaks and grills.

Bus Éireann (☎ 049-433 1353) services run through Belturbet, stopping outside the post office six times per day Monday to Saturday (four Sunday). The main towns on this route are Dublin (€15.50, two hours), Cavan (€5, 15 minutes) and Donegal (€17, 2¼ hours).

SOUTHERN CAVAN
Ballyjamesduff
pop 1690

A sleepy market town, Ballyjamesduff was the one-time home of the Earl of Fife, James Duff, an early Plantation landlord. His descendant, Sir James Duff, commanded English troops during the suppression of the 1798 Rebellion.

These days the town is best known as the home of the **Cavan County Museum** (☎ 049-854 4070; www.cavanmuseum.ie; Virginia Rd; adult/child €3/1.50; ⌚ 10am-5pm Tue-Sat year-round & 2-6pm Sun Jun-Sep), located inside a former convent. Highlights of the impressive collection include a huge array of 18th-, 19th- and 20th-century costumes

and folk items and relics from the Stone Bronze, Iron and Middle Ages, including the Celtic Killycluggin stone and the three-face Corleck Head, as well as a 1000-year-old boa excavated from Lough Errill. There's also large feature on Irish sports.

The area's other main attraction is **Lough Sheelin**, which is famous for its trout fishing May and June are the best months for anglers but it's a scenic place for horse riding, walking or boating year round.

You can relax in the tranquil surround of **Ross House** (☎ 049-854 0218; www.ross-house.com Mountnugent; d €90, apt €200; Ⓟ), a refined period farmhouse on the lakeshore. Rooms here are tastefully decorated, some with their own fireplaces and/or conservatories. You can also go horse riding (from €18 per hour) and hire boats (from €25 per day).

There are no buses to Ballyjamesduff; the closest bus stop is in Virginia and from there it costs around €12 by taxi.

EASTERN CAVAN

Many settlements in the county's east, such as the handsome town of **Virginia**, were laid out as 17th-century Plantation estates. While in the area, it's worth stopping at **Kingscourt** to visit **St Mary's Catholic Church**, with its superb 1940s stained-glass windows made by artist Evie Hone.

Just northeast of Kingscourt is the 225-hectare **Dún an Rí Forest Park** (☎ 042-966 7320; www.coillteoutdoors.ie; car/pedestrian €5/free). There are colour-coded forest walks (all under 4km

ng), with picnic places and a wishing well.
long the river, look out for mink and otters.
ordering the forest, the 19th-century **Cabra**
stle (☎ 042-966 7030; www.manorhousehotels.com;
d from €110/160; P &) is now a deluxe hotel
ecked out in plush period furnishings.
he hotel is 3km out of Kingscourt on the
arrickmacross road.

ORTHWESTERN CAVAN

et against the dramatic backdrop of the
uilcagh Mountains, the remote northwest-
rn edges of Cavan are some of its most scenic.
here's little in the way of public transport in
he area but the express Donegal–Dublin buses
ass through Ballyconnell and Bawnboy four
mes daily. The Westport–Belfast bus stops
n Blacklion five times Monday to Saturday
twice Sunday). Contact **Bus Éireann** (☎ 049-433
353) in Cavan for schedules.

Ballyconnell
op 747

he pretty canal-side village of Ballyconnell is
popular angling centre and a bustling place
n summer with visitors making their way
long the Shannon–Erne Waterway, which
vends its way through town.

You can stay at the simple but cheerful
andville House (☎ 049-952 6297; http://homepage.eircom
net/~sandville; dm from €15, d from €40; P), Cavan's only
1ostel. Set in a converted farmhouse, rooms
1ave two to 10 beds and there's a meditation
oom as well as a self-catering kitchen. The hos-
el is 3.5km southeast of the village (signposted
off the N87). The Dublin to Donegal bus stops
on request at the Slieve Russell Hotel, from
where you can pre-arrange for a pick up. Check
ahead as it's often closed for private retreats.

For relaxation of a more luxurious kind,
the **Slieve Russell Hotel** (☎ 049-952 6444; www.slieve
russell.ie; Cranaghan; s/d from €110/160; P ▣ ☎), 2km
southeast of town, is famed for its marble
columns, fountains, restaurants, bars, and
an 18-hole golf course. Spa treatments include flotation tanks, a herbal sauna and a
salt grotto.

Blacklion & Around
pop 174

Traversed by the Cavan Way (p557), the
area between Blacklion and Dowra is littered
with prehistoric monuments, including the
remains of a *cashel* (stone-walled circular fort)
and the ruins of several sweathouses, used
mostly in the 19th century.

Dedicated foodies make the pilgrimage to
Blacklion's **MacNean House & Restaurant** (☎ 071-985
3022; www.macneanrestaurant.com; Main St; five-course dinner
menu €50-70, four-course Sunday lunch €35; ☺ 6.30-9.30pm
Thu-Sat, 7-8.30pm Sun, 12.30 & 2.30pm Sunday lunch sitting,
closed Jan; P), run by award-winning TV chef
Neven Maguire, who grew up in this gorgeous
country house and has turned it into one of
the country's finest restaurants. The food here
is a celebration of local and seasonal produce,
and is truly outstanding. Feast on chestnut and
mushroom soup, carpaccio of beetroot and
goats cheese, or wild sea bass with truffle ravioli. From April to September you can also stay
overnight in one of the beautiful rooms (single/
double €80/140). Book well in advance.

Westport–Belfast buses stop in Blacklion
five times daily from Monday to Saturday
(twice on Sunday). Buses stop in front of
Maguire's pub.

Cuilcagh Mountain Park

The border between the Republic and
Northern Ireland runs along the ridge of
Cuilcagh Mountain, the distinctive table-
top summit of this park. Its lower slopes are

BALLY WHO?

All over Ireland you'll see the town prefix 'Bally' (and variations thereof, such as Ballyna and Ballina).
The ubiquitous term originates from the Irish phrase 'Baile na'. It's often mistranslated as 'town',
but there were very few towns in Ireland when the names came about. A closer approximation
is 'place of' (similar to the French expression *chez*). Hence Ballyjamesduff, for example, means
Place of James Duff (or James Duff's place). Dublin's Irish name was Baile Átha Cliath (Place of the
Hurdle Ford). If it was anglicised, it too would be a Bally; spelt something like 'Ballycleeagh'.

Other common place names – especially in the central northern counties – include Carrick
(or Carrig), meaning 'rock' in Irish, such as Carrickmacross (Rock of MacRoss/MacRoss' rock) in
County Monaghan; and Dun, from the Irish *dún* (meaning 'fort'), such as Dundalk (Dún Dealgan,
the Fort of Dalga) and Dunderry (Dún Doire, Fort of the Oak Grove).

DETOUR: JAMPA LING BUDDHIST CENTRE

If you're on a quest for enlightenment, or just seeking some time out, the **Jampa Ling Buddhist Centre** (☎ 049-952 3448; www.jampaling.org; Owendoon House, Bawnboy; dm/s self-catering €20/30, incl meals €35/40), in a beautiful country setting, is peace on earth. Jampa Ling, meaning 'Place of Infinite Loving Kindness', offers courses, retreats and workshops (about €45 to €60 per day, €215 to €275 per weekend) on Buddhist teachings, philosophy, meditation, yoga, and medicinal and culinary herbs. Though you don't have to take part in a course to stay here, accommodation may not be available if there is an event on. All meals, which are included in the day courses and for overnight guests, are vegetarian.

From Ballyconnell, follow the signs to Bawnboy. In the village, turn left at the petrol station and follow the small road for 3km. Continue past the lake and a series of bends; you'll see the centre's stone gates a further 250m ahead on your right.

---

important protected peatland habitats, while the upper slopes have dramatic sweeping cliffs. The visitor centre and the park's biggest attraction, the Marble Arch Caves (p689), lie a short hop over the border from Blacklion, in County Fermanagh.

COUNTY MONAGHAN

Monaghan's quiet, undulating landscape is littered with lakes and tiny rounded hills resembling bubbles in badly pasted wallpaper. Known as drumlins, the bumps are the result of debris left by retreating glaciers during the last Ice Age. The county's steely grey lakes attract plenty of anglers, but few others make it here, making it a tranquil place to roam.

Unlike much of the province, Monaghan was largely left alone during the Ulster Plantation. After the Cromwellian wars though, local chieftains were forced to sell their land for a fraction of its true value, or have it seized and redistributed to Cromwell's soldiers.

In the early 19th century, lace making became an important facet of the local economy, providing work and income for women. Clones and Carrickmacross were the two main centres of the industry and you can still see the fine needlework on display in both towns.

More recently however, Monaghan has been made famous by poet Patrick Kavanagh (1905–67), who was born in Inniskeen. The village's literary resource centre now offers an evocative insight into his life and work.

MONAGHAN TOWN
pop 6221

It may be the county town, but Monaghan's residents live their lives utterly unaffected by tourism. The main visitor attraction is th county museum, containing an extensiv regional collection, but it's also pleasant t wander the streets admiring the elegant 18th and 19th-century limestone buildings.

Orientation & Information

Monaghan is squashed between two sma lakes, Peter's Lake to the north, and Conver Lake in the southwest. Its principal stree form a rough arc, broken up by the town three main squares. From east to west thes are Church Sq, the Diamond (the Ulster nam for a town square) and Old Cross Sq, all o which are prone to traffic congestion.

To the west of this arc, at the top of Par St, is Clones Rd and the **tourist office** (☎ 047 81122, 047-73718; www.monaghantourism.com; Clones Rd ⊙ 10am-5pm Mon-Fri mid-May–mid-Sep).

Sights & Activities

Monaghan County Museum and Gallery (☎ 047-82928; comuseum@monaghancoco.ie; 1-2 Hill St; admission free; ⊙ 11am-5pm Mon-Fri, noon-5pm Sat) is an excellent regional museum, containing over 70,000 artefacts from the Stone Age to modern times. Its crowning glory is the 14th-century **Cross of Clogher**, an oaken altar cross encased in decorative bronze panels. Other impressive finds include the Lisdrumturk and Altartate Cauldrons, medieval *crannóg* artefacts, and some frightening knuckle-dusters and cudgels relating to the border with the North.

As you wander around town, look out for the **Dawson Monument** (1857), in Church Sq – a hefty obelisk commemorating Colonel Dawson's unfortunate demise in the Crimean War. Overlooking it is the Gothic **St Patrick's Church** and a stately Doric **courthouse** (1829). Heading west you'll find the **Rossmore Memorial**

: 1875), an over-the-top Victorian drinking ountain that dominates the Diamond. The wn also has a number of buildings with ently rounded corners, which is an unusual rchitectural feature in Ireland.

Just out of the centre of town on the Dublin oad is another piece of Victorian whimsy, le mock-14th-century **St Macartan's Catholic athedral** (1861), topped by a teetering 77m-igh, needle-sharp spire.

Fine fishing abounds in the area; contact **enture Sports** (☎ 047-81495; 71 Glaslough St) for ermits, tackle and local knowledge.

leeping & Eating

shleigh House (☎ 047-81227; 37 Dublin St; s/d €50/80; 🅿 💻 🛜) Right in the centre of town, this 0-room B&B has been recently refurbished nd offers good value rooms. All rooms have a rivate bathroom and are tastefully decorated; here's a small garden area for guests.

Hillgrove Hotel (☎ 047-81888; www.hillgrovehotel om; Old Armagh Rd; s\d from €100\140; 🅿 🐆) This arge, corporate-style hotel has 87 bright, modern rooms that are tastefully decorated out lack a little character. There's a great pool nd leisure centre and a spa boasting a herbal auna, mud chamber and hydro pool.

Andy's Bar & Restaurant (☎ 047-82277; www.andys nonaghan.com; 12 Market St; mains €15-25; 🕑 restaurant -10.15pm Tue-Sat, 5-10pm Sun) A local favourite, Andy's is an old-school place still proudly erving the likes of deep fried brie, prawn ocktails and pavlova. There's a good choice of more modern mains though, with a house peciality of monkfish and crab claws sautéed n lime. The Victorian pub downstairs serves good bar food.

Squealing Pig (☎ 047-84562; The Diamond; mains €16-7; 🕑 noon-4pm & 5-10pm Mon-Sat, 4-9pm Sun) This popular bar and restaurant is one of the town's iveliest spots, with a young, fun vibe. It's all comfort food here with steaks, burgers, rich pastas and stir-frys dominating the menu. By night the Pig really takes off with three bars and a nightclub keeping the energy and noise levels pumped up.

Drinking & Entertainment

Sherry's (☎ 047-81805; 24 Dublin St) Walking into Sherry's, one of Monaghan's oldest bars, is like stepping back into a spinster's parlour from the 1950s. The old tiled floor, beauty board and dusty memorabilia probably haven't been touched in decades.

Market House (☎ 047-38162; Market St) This restored 18th-century market hall-turned-arts-venue hosts exhibitions, concerts and drama. Ring for event listings. The centre acts as the main stage for the annual May **traditional music festival** (www.feileoriel.com) and the September **blues festival** (www.harvest blues.com).

Getting There & Around

From the **bus station** (☎ 047-82377; North Rd), there are numerous daily intercity services within the Republic and into the North. These include 10 buses daily to Dublin (€13.50, two hours); 11 to Derry (€13, two hours) via Omagh; and three (one Sunday) to Belfast (€11.30, two hours). There are also frequent daily local services to Carrickmacross.

ROSSMORE FOREST PARK

Crumbling remains of the Rossmore family's 19th-century castle, including its entrance stairway, buttresses and the family's pet cemetery can be seen at **Rossmore Forest Park** (☎ 047-433 1046; www.coillteoutdoors.ie; car/pedestrian €5/free), where rhododendrons and azaleas blaze with colour in early summer.

Along with forest walks and pleasant picnic areas, the park contains several giant redwoods, a fine yew avenue and Iron Age tombs. A gold collar (known as a lunula) from 1800 BC was found here in the 1930s and is now on display in the National Museum in Dublin. The park is located 3km southwest of Monaghan on the Newbliss road (R189).

CLONES & AROUND
pop 1517

Once the site of an important 6th-century monastery that later became an Augustinian abbey, Clones' main sights are ecclesiastical. There's a well-preserved 10th-century **high cross** on the Diamond, decorated with drama-charged biblical stories such as Daniel in the lion's den.

Along with the remains of the **abbey** founded by St Tiernach on Abbey St, there's a truncated 22m-high **round tower**, which dates from the early 9th century, in the cemetery south of town. Nearby is the supposed burial place of Tiernach himself, a chunky 9th-century **sarcophagus** with worn animal-head carvings.

More recently, Clones found fame as a lace-making centre. To learn about the history of

Clones lace, see it on display or purchase samples, visit the **Ulster Canal Stores** (☎ 047-52125; www.cloneslace.com; Cara St; ☿ 8.30am-5pm Easter-Sep, 9am-5pm Mon-Fri Oct-Easter).

For a small town, Clones has produced its fair share of famous names. It is the hometown of both heavyweight Kevin McBride, whose defeat of Mike Tyson in 2005 was so crushing that it prompted Tyson's immediate retirement; and former featherweight boxer Barry McGuigan, who won the world championship in 1985.

Clones-born writer Patrick McCabe set his dark novel *The Butcher Boy* in the town, and in 1997 Neil Jordan filmed the twisted tale here.

Clones' greatest secret however, is the **Flat Lake Literary and Arts Festival** (www.theflatlakefestival .com). A 'no-brow' event in mid-August, it aims to mix high art and popular culture. Expect heavyweight poets and authors discussing or reading their work along with top-notch comedy, film and theatre, as well as an art auction that in previous years featured work by Damian Hirst. Go now before it's discovered.

The bus stop, post office and banks are in the central Diamond.

Sleeping & Eating

Greenjoy (☎ 047-56042; www.greenjoyclones.com; Scotshouse; s/d €40/70; ℗) Set on a hill overlooking Clones golf course, this modern house has

three immaculate guestrooms decked out in cosy but contemporary style. Neutral colour quality furniture and sparkling bathroom make it a very good deal. The B&B is 4k south of town on the R212.

our pick Hilton Park (☎ 047-56007; www.hilto park.ie; s €165-190, d €250-300; ☿ Apr-Sep; ℗) Th spellbinding country-house retreat stands ou from competitors long since taken over b faceless hotel groups. Hilton Park has bee in the same family since 1734 and guests fre quently comment that they leave feeling like close friend rather than a guest. It's a magnif cent place just oozing old-world charm. Th six spacious guestrooms are bathed in ligh and offer stunning views of the 240-hectar estate. Original furniture, free-standing bath four-poster or half-tester beds and a wonder fully warm, lived-in atmosphere make then very special indeed. Top-class cuisine, muc of it produced in the estate's organic garden is served in regal surroundings (dinner €5 book 24 hours ahead). You can also come fo kitchen gardening or art weekends. Hilto Park is 5km south of Clones along the R21 towards Scotshouse.

Getting There & Around

Bus Éireann (☎ 047-82377) runs a service from Clones to Monaghan (€5.50, 30 minutes, fiv buses Monday to Saturday, one Sunday), wit connections on to Carrickmacross, Slane and Dublin.

DETOUR: CASTLE LESLIE

The ancestral home of the eccentric Leslie family, **Castle Leslie** (☎ 047-88100; www.castleleslie.com; Glasslough; d €160-480) is a Victorian pile with all the faded grandeur of a well-loved home. The family (who trace their ancestors back to Attila the Hun) acquired the castle in 1665 and its kooky history makes it an entertaining detour for both guests and non-guests. And yes, this is where Sir Paul McCartney and Heather Mills' doomed nuptials took place.

There are 20 guestrooms in the main house, each with a unique character and story to tell. The Red Room, used by WB Yeats, contains the first bath plumbed in Ireland; in Uncle Norman's Room, guests claim to have been levitated in the Gothic four-poster bed; and Desmond's Room recalls this particularly eccentric member of the Leslie family. A bon vivant who palled around with Mick Jagger and Marianne Faithful, Desmond made sci-fi films, composed experimental early electronic music and wrote several novels including the early 1950s bestseller *Flying Saucers Have Landed*.

All the rooms are sumptuous in their design and offer few concessions to modern living – you won't find telephones or TVs in any of them. The recently renovated Hunting Lodge provides a further 30 rooms with decor ranging from rich traditional drapery to more minimalist contemporary style.

Non-guests can come to dine on delicious Mediterranean cuisine in the open-plan Snaffles Brasserie (mains €18 to €25) or hearty bar food in the snug Conor's Bar (mains €8.50 to €16.50). You can also enjoy pampering treatments at the Victorian spa, take a jaunt around the estate on horseback (from €35 per hour) or attend a cookery course (one-/two-day course €185/350).

Ulsterbus (☎ 048-9066 6630) has one direct service per day between Clones and Belfast (€15, 2¼ hours), and two others that require a change in Monaghan, running Monday to Friday.

CARRICKMACROSS & AROUND
pop 1973

Carrickmacross was first settled by early English and Scottish Planters, and its broad main street is dotted with some elegant Georgian houses. It's most famous as the home of delicate Carrickmacross lace, an industry revived in 1871 by the St Louis nuns. The town is a peaceful spot to wander and a great base for anglers.

Father Ted fans may know Carrickmacross as the birthplace of Ardal O'Hanlon aka Father Dougal McGuire in the TV series. O'Hanlon's first novel *The Talk of the Town* was set in 'Castlecock', a thinly veiled version of the town.

There's no tourist office, but the tourism section of the town's website, www.carrickmacross.ie, has visitor information.

Sights & Activities

In the town's former cattle yards, a local cooperative runs the **Carrickmacross Lace Gallery** (☎ 042-966 2506; www.carrickmacrosslace.ie; Market Sq; ⓧ 9.30am-5.30pm Mon-Thu, 9.30am-4.30pm Fri), which sells the distinctive gossamerlike designs. Unlike Clones' crocheted lace, designs here are appliquéd on organza using thick thread and close stitches. Excess organza is cut away and the work is embellished with a variety of point stitches, guipure, pops and the lace's distinctive loop edge. Most famously, Carrickmacross lace graced the sleeves of Princess Diana's wedding dress.

Craftsmanship also shines at **St Joseph's Catholic Church** (O'Neill St), with 10 windows designed by Harry Clarke, Ireland's most renowned stained-glass artist.

There's fantastic **fishing** in many of the lakes around Carrickmacross, including Loughs Capragh, Spring, Monalty and Fea. For more information and contact details for guides, boat hire and tackle see the angling section on www.monaghantourism.com.

Sleeping & Eating

Lakewood (☎ 042-966 3207; www.irelandfishing.net; Kingscourt Rd; s/d €40/70; Ⓟ 🖳) This modern B&B has lovely, bright rooms with a simple contemporary style and a warm welcome. Although it caters mainly for anglers – boat hire, guides, bait fridge and tackle shop are available on site – this shouldn't put non-fishers off as it's one of the best deals in the area.

Shirley Arms (☎ 042-967 3100; www.shirleyarmshotel.ie; Main St; s/d from €85/120; Ⓟ 🖳) Recently refurbished and slap bang in the centre of town, the Shirley Arms is a sleek modern hotel with spacious rooms and decent food. White linens, walnut floors and modern bathrooms make the rooms contemporary but rather corporate in style, while the open-plan bar and lounge make an informal setting for some excellent bar food (€8 to €16). The more formal restaurant is pricey (mains €21 to €29).

Getting There & Away

Bus Éireann (☎ 01-836 6111) services connect with Dublin (€13.50, 1¾ hours, five daily). There are also several private operators on the route. The bus stop is outside O'Hanlon's shop on Main St.

INNISKEEN
pop 292

Acclaimed poet Patrick Kavanagh (1904–67) was born in the village of Inniskeen, 10km northeast of Carrickmacross. The **Patrick Kavanagh Rural and Literary Resource Centre** (☎ 042-937 8560; www.patrickkavanaghcountry.com; adult/child under 12 €5/free; ⓧ 11am-4.30pm Tue-Fri year-round & 3-5pm Sun Jun-Sep) is housed in the old parish church where he was baptised; the staff have a passion for his life and work that is contagious.

Kavanagh's long work, *The Great Hunger* (1942), blasted away the earlier clichés of Anglo-Irish verse and revealed Ireland's poor farming communities as half-starved, 'broken-backed' and sexually repressed. His best-known poem, *On Raglan Road* (1946), was an ode to his unrequited love. It doubled as the lyrics for the traditional Irish air 'The Dawning of the Day', which has been performed by Van Morrison, Mark Knopfler, Billy Bragg, Sinéad O'Connor and countless others.

Actor Russell Crowe is a passionate fan of Kavanagh's work, and has recited the four-line 'Sanctity' (1937) as part of his acceptance speech at award ceremonies on several occasions. In 2002 he was so irate that his recital was cut from the telecast of the BAFTA awards that he later threatened the show's director, vowing that the man would never work in Hollywood again.

Information on **guided literary tours** around town is posted on the resource centre's website. Otherwise you can buy a copy of the *Patrick Kavanagh Trail Guide* (€0.70) and walk or drive around the sites in and around the village and the picturesque surrounding countryside (5.6km in all).

The centre hosts an annual **Patrick Kavanagh Weekend** in November and an annual **Writers Weekend** in August. Contact the centre for booking information.

Inniskeen is on the Bus Éireann route between Cavan and Dundalk via Carrickmacross, with four services Monday to Saturday.

Belfast

The countdown to 2012 has begun. No, not the London Olympics – 2012 in Belfast represents the 100th anniversary of the maiden voyage of RMS *Titanic*, the iconic ocean liner that was built by Belfast's Harland and Wolff shipyards. And 2012 is also the year that Belfast has chosen to showcase its heritage to the world.

It may seem strange for a city to identify with a ship that is famous for sinking on its maiden voyage, but Belfast built what was the most advanced piece of technology in the world at that time and takes pride in the innovation, skill and engineering genius that went into making the *Titanic*. And as the locals constantly remind you, 'She was fine when she left here'.

Once lumped with Beirut, Baghdad and Bosnia as one the four 'B's for travellers to avoid, Belfast has pulled off a remarkable transformation from bombs-and-bullets pariah to a hip-hotels-and-hedonism party town. The city's skyline is in a constant state of flux as redevelopment continues apace. The old shipyards are giving way to the luxury waterfront apartments of the Titanic Quarter, and Victoria Sq, Europe's biggest urban regeneration project, has added a massive city-centre shopping mall to a list of tourist attractions that includes Victorian architecture, a glittering waterfront lined with modern art, foot-stomping music in packed-out pubs, and the UK's second-biggest arts festival.

So as 2012 approaches, it seems somehow fitting that Belfast should celebrate the *Titanic's* creation, building new pride and optimism out of the wreckage of past disaster. Get here early and enjoy it before the rest of the world arrives.

BELFAST

HIGHLIGHTS

- **Ah Go On, Take a Drink** Sup on a Guinness or three in some of Belfast's beautiful Victorian pubs (p592)
- **The Writing on the Walls** Ruminate on the powerful political murals in West Belfast (p582)
- **Titanic Town** Learn about the shipyards that gave birth to the *Titanic* on a boat trip around Belfast's docklands (p585)
- **Head for the Hills** Enjoy a panoramic view over the city from the top of Cave Hill (p581)
- **Back to the Future** Check out the iconic DeLorean DMC at the Ulster Transport Museum (p601)

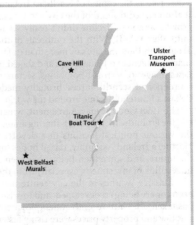

Ulster Transport Museum ★

Cave Hill ★

Titanic Boat Tour ★

★ West Belfast Murals

■ TELEPHONE CODE: 028 FROM UK; 048 FROM REPUBLIC OF IRELAND   ■ POPULATION: 277,000

HISTORY

Belfast is a relatively young city, with few reminders of its pre-19th-century history. The city takes its name from the River Farset (from the Gaelic *feirste,* meaning sandbank, or sandy ford), which flows into the River Lagan at Donegall Quay (it is now channelled through a culvert). The old Gaelic name, Béal Feirste, means 'Mouth of the Farset'.

In 1177, the Norman lord John de Courcy built a castle here, and a small settlement grew up around it. Both were destroyed in battle 20 years later, and the town did not begin to develop in earnest until 1611 when Baron Arthur Chichester built a castle and promoted the growth of the settlement.

The early-17th-century Plantation of Ulster brought in the first waves of Scottish and English settlers, followed in the late 17th century by an influx of Huguenots (French Protestants) fleeing persecution in France; they laid the foundations of a thriving linen industry. More Scottish and English settlers arrived, and other industries such as rope making, tobacco, engineering and shipbuilding developed.

With its textile mills and shipyards, Belfast was the one city in Ireland that truly rode the wave of the Industrial Revolution. Sturdy rows of brick terrace houses were built for the factory and shipyard workers, and a town of around 20,000 people in 1800 grew steadily into a city of 400,000 by the start of WWI, by which time Belfast had nearly overtaken Dublin in size.

The partition of Ireland in 1920 gave Belfast a new role as the capital of Northern Ireland. It also marked the end of the city's industrial growth, although decline didn't really set in until after WWII. With the outbreak of the Troubles in 1969, the city saw more than its fair share of violence and bloodshed, and shocking news images of terrorist bombings, sectarian murders and security forces' brutality made Belfast a household name around the world.

The 1998 Good Friday Agreement, which laid the groundwork for power-sharing among the various political factions in a devolved Northern Ireland Assembly, raised hopes for the future, and since then Belfast has seen a huge influx of investment, especially from the EU. Massive swathes of the city centre have been (or are being) redeveloped, and tourism has taken off. Until recently, unemployment was low and property prices were rising faster than in any other UK city, but Belfast was hit hard by the economic downturn – that meteoric rise was followed by a devastating tumble as house prices fell by 33% in 2008.

A historic milestone was passed on 8 May 2007 when the Reverend Ian Paisley (firebrand Protestant preacher and leader of the Democratic Unionist Party) and Martin McGuinness (Sinn Féin MP and former IRA commander) were sworn in at Stormont as first minister and deputy first minister of a new power-sharing government.

There are still plenty of reminders of the Troubles – notably the 'peace lines' that still divide Protestant and Catholic communities – and the passions that have torn Northern Ireland apart over the decades still run deep. But despite occasional setbacks, there is an atmosphere of determined optimism that will hopefully propel Belfast towards a peaceful future.

ORIENTATION

Belfast sits at the head of Belfast Lough, straddling the lower reaches of the River Lagan and hemmed in to the west by the steep slopes of Black Mountain and Cave Hill. The city centre lies on the west bank of the Lagan, with the imposing City Hall in Donegall Sq as a convenient central landmark. The principal shopping district is north of the square along Donegall Pl and Royal Ave. North again, the once run-down area around Donegall St and St Anne's Cathedral forms the bohemian Cathedral Quarter.

South of Donegall Sq, the so-called Golden Mile stretches for 1.5km along Great Victoria St, Shaftesbury Sq and Botanic Ave to Queen's University and the leafy suburbs of South Belfast. This area (now dubbed Queens Quarter) has dozens of restaurants and bars and most of the city's budget and midrange accommodation. Northwest of Donegall Sq, Divis St leads across the Westlink Motorway to Falls Rd and West Belfast (Gaeltacht Quarter). East of the river rise the massive cranes of the Harland and Wolff shipyards in East Belfast, an area undergoing major redevelopment (now known as the Titanic Quarter).

The Europa BusCentre and Great Victoria St train station are behind the Europa Hotel on Great Victoria St, 300m southwest of City Hall (access through Great Northern Mall); the Laganside BusCentre is near the Albert Memorial Clock Tower, 600m northeast of City Hall. Belfast Central train station (which isn't very central!) is 800m east of City Hall on East Bridge St.

BELFAST IN...

One Day
Start your day with breakfast in one of the many cafes on Botanic Ave – **Maggie May's** (p591) will do nicely – then stroll north into the city centre and take a free guided tour of **City Hall** (p573). Take a black taxi tour of the **West Belfast murals** (p582), then ask the taxi driver to drop you off at the **John Hewitt Bar & Restaurant** (p591) for lunch. Catch a 2pm **Titanic Tour** (p585) boat trip around the harbour, then walk across the **Lagan Weir** (p577) to visit the **Titanic Quarter** (p577). Round off the day with dinner at **Deane's Restaurant** (p590) or **Menu by Kevin Thornton** (p590).

Two Days
On your second day, take a look at **Queen's University** (p578), wander around the Early Ireland exhibit in the **Ulster Museum** (p579) and stroll through the **Botanic Gardens** (p579), then walk south along the river for lunch at **Cutters Wharf** (p592). In the afternoon either continue walking south along the **Lagan Towpath** (p576) to Shaw's Bridge and catch a bus back to town, or go for a hike up **Cave Hill** (p581). Have dinner at **Shu** (p592) or **Molly's Yard** (p591) then spend the evening crawling traditional pubs such as the **Crown Liquor Saloon** (p592), **Kelly's Cellars** (p593) and the **Duke of York** (p593).

Steam Packet ferries dock at Donegall Quay, 1km north of City Hall. The Stena Line car-ferry terminal is 2km north of the city centre, and the Norfolkline ferry terminal is 5km north of the city centre (see p597).

Maps

The Belfast Welcome Centre provides a free map of the city centre. The more detailed *Collins Belfast Streetfinder Atlas* (available at most bookshops) includes a full index of street names. Most detailed of all, but in the form of an unwieldy folded sheet, is the Ordnance Survey of Northern Ireland's 1:12,000 *Belfast Street Map* (available at TSO bookshop).

INFORMATION
Bookshops

Bookfinders (Map pp570-1; ☎ 9032 8269; 47 University Rd, South Belfast; ☯ 10am-5.30pm Mon-Sat) A studenty second-hand bookshop and book-finding service with a gallery, cafe and regular poetry readings.

Bookshop at Queen's (Map pp570-1; ☎ 9066 6302; www.queensbookshop.co.uk; 91 University Rd, South Belfast; ☯ 9am-5.30pm Mon-Fri, to 5pm Sat) Irish literature, travel, history and politics.

Eason (Map pp570-1; ☎ 9023 5070; 20 Donegall Pl; ☯ 8.30am-7pm Mon-Wed & Fri, to 9pm Thu, 9am-6pm Sat, 1-5pm Sun) Books, maps, magazines and stationery.

TSO Bookshop (Map pp570-1; ☎ 9023 8451; 16 Arthur St; ☯ 9am-5pm Mon-Fri) Good for Ordnance Survey maps and street plans.

Waterstones (Map pp570-1; ☎ 9024 0159; 44-46 Fountain St; ☯ 9am-6pm Mon-Wed, Fri & Sat, to 9pm Thu, 1-5.30pm Sun) General fiction, non-fiction and Lonely Planet guidebooks; good cafe on the first floor.

Emergency

For national emergency phone numbers, see the inside front cover.

Rape Crisis & Sexual Abuse Centre (☎ 9032 9002; www.rapecrisisni.com; ☯ 10am-midnight)

Victim Support (☎ 0845 30 30 900; www.victim support.org)

Internet Access

You can use British Telecom's blue, internet-enabled phone boxes around Donegall Sq and at Central Station for 10p per 90 seconds (£1 minimum for up to 15 minutes).

Ark Internet (Map pp570-1; ☎ 9032 9626; 44 University St; per min from 2.1p) High-speed broadband, no minimum charge. At the Ark Hostel.

Belfast Welcome Centre (Map pp570-1; ☎ 9024 6609; www.gotobelfast.com; 47 Donegall Pl; per 20 min £1; ☯ 9am-7pm Mon-Sat, 11am-4pm Sun Jun-Sep, 9.30am-5.30pm Mon-Sat, 11am-4pm Sun Oct-May)

Ground@Waterstones (Map pp570-1; ☎ 9024 0159; 44-46 Fountain St; per 20min £1; ☯ 9am-6pm Mon-Wed, Fri & Sat, to 9pm Thu, 1-5.30pm Sun; ☜) Three computers in the bookshop cafe; free wi-fi – ask at the counter for password.

Linen Hall Library (Map pp570-1; ☎ 9032 1707; cnr Fountain St & Donegall Sq; per 30min £1.50 minimum; ☯ 9.30am-5.30pm Mon-Fri, to 4.30pm Sat; ☜) One

BELFAST

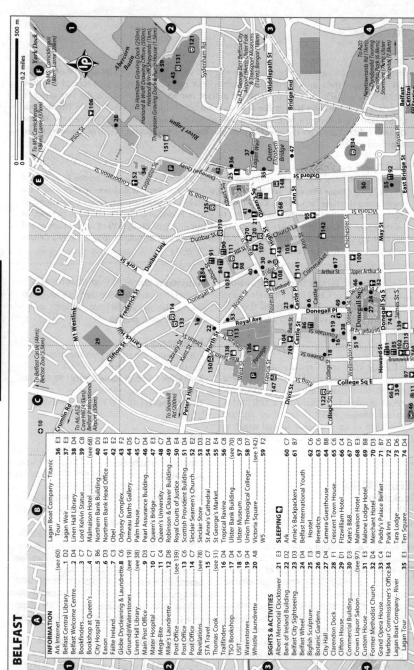

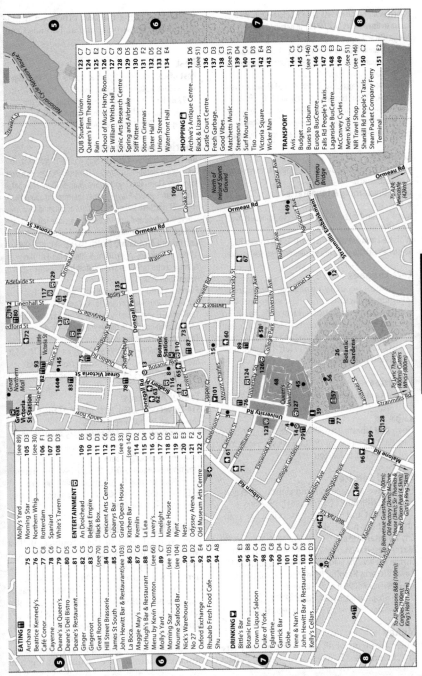

QUB Student Union 123 C7
Queen's Film Theatre 124 C7
Rain 125 E2
School of Music Harty Room 126 C7
Sir William Whitla Hall 127 C8
Sonic Arts Research Centre 128 C8
Spring and Airbrake 129 D5
Stiff Kitten 130 D5
Storm Cinemas 131 F2
Ulster Hall 132 D5
Union Street 133 D2
Waterfront Hall 134 E4

SHOPPING 🛍
Archive's Antique Centre 135 D6
Black & Lizars ....(see 51)
Castle Court Centre 136 C3
Fresh Garbage 137 D3
Good Vibes 138 C3
Matchetts Music ....(see 51)
Steensons 139 D4
Surf Mountain 140 C4
Tiso 141 D3
Victoria Square 142 E4
Wicker Man 143 D3

TRANSPORT
Avis 144 C5
Budget 145 C4
Buses to Lisburn ....(see 146)
Europa BusCentre 146 C4
Falls Rd People's Taxis 147 C3
Laganside BusCentre 148 E3
McConvey Cycles 149 E7
Metro Kiosk ....(see 51)
NIR Travel Shop ....(see 146)
Shankill Rd People's Taxis 150 C2
Steam Packet Company Ferry
    Terminal 151 E2

EATING 🍴
Archana 75 C5
Beatrice Kennedy's 76 C7
Café Conor 77 C8
Cayenne 78 C6
Deane's at Queen's 79 C7
Deane's Deli Bistro 80 D5
Deane's Restaurant 81 C4
Ginger 82 C5
Gingeroot ....(see 70)
Great Room ....(see 30)
Hill Street Brasserie 84 D3
James St South 85 C4
John Hewitt Bar & Restaurant..(see 103)
La Boca 86 D3
Maggie May's 87 C6
McHugh's Bar & Restaurant 88 E3
Menu by Kevin Thornton...........(see 66)
Molly's Yard ....(see 105)
Morning Star ....(see 104)
Mourne Seafood Bar 90 D3
Nick's Warehouse 91 D2
No 27 ....92 E4
Oxford Exchange 93 C5
Rhubarb Fresh Food Cafe 94 A8
Shu ....(see 142)

DRINKING 🍺
Bittle's Bar 95 E3
Botanic Inn 96 B8
Crown Liquor Saloon 98 D3
Duke of York 99 C8
Eglantine 100 D4
Garrick Bar 101 C7
Globe 102 C4
Irene & Nan's 103 D3
John Hewitt Bar & Restaurant 103 D3
Kelly's Cellars 104 D3

Molly's Yard ....(see 89)
Morning Star 105 D3
Northern Whig 106 F1
Rotterdam 107 D3
Spaniard 108 D3
White's Tavern 108 D3

ENTERTAINMENT 🎭
An Droichead 109 E6
Belfast Empire 110 C6
Black Box 111 D3
Crescent Arts Centre 112 C6
Dubarrys Bar 113 D3
Grand Opera House ....(see 33)
Kitchen Bar 114 D2
Kremlin 115 D4
La Lea 116 C6
Lavery's 117 C6
Limelight 118 D5
Movie House 119 E3
Mynt 120 E3
Nest 121 F2
Odyssey Arena 122 E2
Old Museum Arts Centre ......(see 142)

To All Seasons B&B (100m);
Bienvenue Guesthouse (100m);
Old Rectory (2km); Malone
Guesthouse (3km); Thomas
House (3.5km); Cutters
Wharf (4.5km); Lady
Dixon Park (4.5km);
Giant's Ring (5km)

To Lyric Theatre
(400m); Cutters
Wharf (800m)

Windsor Ave
To Mackie's
Ave; Falls Rd (5km);
King's Hall (1.5km)

computer on each floor; ask at desk before using. Wi-fi £3 for up to three hours (ask for log-in details).

Mega-Bite (Map pp570-1; ☎ 9031 1423; Great Northern Mall, Great Victoria St; per 15min £1; ⏰ 8.30am-8pm Mon-Fri, 10am-8pm Sat, 11am-8pm Sun) Convenient internet cafe.

Revelations (Map pp570-1; ☎ 9032 0337; www.revelations.co.uk; 27 Shaftesbury Sq; per 15min £1.10; ⏰ 8am-10pm Mon-Fri, 10am-6pm Sat, 11am-7pm Sun) Nineteen PCs, laptop access and printers available. Concession rate of £1 per 20 minutes for holders of student and hostelling ID cards.

Laundry

Expect to pay around £5 total to wash and dry one load.

Globe Drycleaning & Laundrette (Map pp570-1; 37 Botanic Ave)

Mike's Laundrette (Map pp570-1; 46 Agincourt Ave, South Belfast)

Whistle Laundrette (Map pp570-1; 160 Lisburn Rd, South Belfast) Offers service washes only; no self-service.

Left Luggage

Because of security concerns, there are no left-luggage facilities at Belfast's airports, train stations and bus stations. However, most hotels and hostels allow guests to leave their bags for the day, and the Belfast Welcome Centre (right) also offers a daytime left-luggage service (£4.50 per item).

Libraries

Belfast Central Library (Map pp570-1; ☎ 9050 9150; Royal Ave; ⏰ 9am-8pm Mon-Thu, to 5.30pm Fri, to 4.30pm Sat)

Linen Hall Library (Map pp570-1; ☎ 9032 1707; cnr Fountain St & Donegall Sq; ⏰ 9.30am-5.30pm Mon-Wed & Fri, to 7pm Thu, to 4pm Sat)

Medical Services

For advice on medical and dental emergencies, call **NHS Direct** (☎ 0845 4647; ⏰ 24hr).

Accident and emergency services are available at these hospitals:

City Hospital (Map pp570-1; ☎ 9032 9241; 51 Lisburn Rd)

Mater Hospital (Map pp570-1; ☎ 9074 1211; 45-51 Crumlin Rd) Near the junction of Antrim Rd and Clifton St.

Royal Victoria Hospital (Map p580; ☎ 9024 0503; 274 Grosvenor Rd) West of the city centre.

Ulster Hospital (Map p600; ☎ 9048 4511; Upper Newtownards Rd, Dundonald) Near Stormont Castle.

Money

There are plenty of ATMs around town. There are currency-exchange facilities at the Belfast

Welcome Centre, the post offices on Bridge St and Shaftesbury Sq, and at Thomas Cook branches.

Post

Post office Main post office (Map pp570-1; 12-16 Bridge St; ⏰ 9am-5.30pm Mon-Sat); Bedford St (Map pp570-1; 16-22 Bedford St); Botanic Gardens (Map pp570-1; cnr University Rd & College Gardens, South Belfast); Shaftesbury Sq (Map pp570-1; 1-5 Botanic Ave)

Tourist Information

Belfast Welcome Centre (Map pp570-1; ☎ 9024 6609; www.gotobelfast.com; 47 Donegall Pl; ⏰ 9am-7pm Mon-Sat, 11am-4pm Sun Jun-Sep, 9am-5.30pm Mon-Sat, 11am-4pm Sun Oct-May) Provides information about the whole of Northern Ireland, and books accommodation anywhere in Ireland and Britain. Services include left luggage (not overnight), currency exchange and internet access.

Cultúrlann McAdam Ó Fiaich (Map p580; ☎ 9096 4188; 216 Falls Rd; ⏰ 9.30am-5.30pm Mon-Fri) This cultural centre (p580) in West Belfast has a tourist information desk.

Fáilte Ireland (Irish Tourist Board; Map pp570-1; ☎ 9026 5500; www.ireland.ie; 53 Castle St; ⏰ 9am-5pm Mon-Fri year-round & 9am-12.30pm Sat Jun-Aug) Can book accommodation in the Republic of Ireland.

Tourist information desks George Best Belfast City Airport (Map p600; ☎ 9093 5372; ⏰ 8am-7pm Mon-Sat, to 5pm Sun); Belfast International Airport (off Map p600; ☎ 9448 4677; ⏰ 7.30am-7pm Mon-Sat, 8am-5pm Sun)

Travel Agencies

STA Travel (Map pp570-1; ☎ 0871 702 9803; 92-94 Botanic Ave; ⏰ 10am-6pm Mon-Sat)

Thomas Cook (Map pp570-1; ☎ 0845 308 9139; 10 Donegall Sq West; ⏰ 9am-5.30pm Mon-Wed & Fri, to 8pm Thu, 10am-5.30pm Sat)

Trailfinders (Map pp570-1; ☎ 9027 1888; 47-49 Fountain St; ⏰ 9am-7pm Mon-Fri, to 6pm Sat, 10am-6pm Sun)

USIT (Map pp570-1; ☎ 9032 7111; 13B Fountain Centre, College St; ⏰ 10am-5pm Mon-Fri)

DANGERS & ANNOYANCES

Even at the height of the Troubles, Belfast wasn't a particularly dangerous city for tourists, and today you're less at risk from crime here than you are in London. It's best, however, to avoid the so-called 'interface areas' – near the peace lines in West Belfast, Crumlin Rd and the Short Strand (just east of Queen's Bridge) – after dark; if in doubt about any area, ask at your hotel or hostel.

One irritating legacy of the Troubles is the absence of left-luggage facilities at bus and train stations. You will also notice a more obvious security presence than elsewhere in the UK and Ireland, in the form of armoured police Land Rovers, fortified police stations, and security doors on some shops (mostly outside the city centre) where you have to press the buzzer to be allowed in. There are doormen on many city-centre shops and pubs.

If you want to take photos of fortified police stations, army posts or other military or quasi-military paraphernalia, get permission first, just to be on the safe side. In the Protestant and Catholic strongholds of West Belfast it's best not to photograph people without permission; always ask first and be prepared to accept a refusal. Taking pictures of the murals is not a problem.

SIGHTS
City Centre
CITY HALL
The Industrial Revolution transformed Belfast in the 19th century, and its rapid rise to muck-and-brass prosperity is manifested in the extravagance of **City Hall** (Map pp570-1; ☎ 9027 0456; www .belfastcity.gov.uk; Donegall Sq; admission free; ☒ guided tours 11am, 2pm & 3pm Mon-Fri, 2pm & 3pm Sat). Built in classical Renaissance style in fine, white Portland stone, it was completed in 1906 and paid for from the profits of the gas supply company. It is equipped with facilities for the disabled.

The hall is fronted by a statue of a rather dour 'we are not amused' **Queen Victoria**. The bronze figures on either side of her symbolise the textile and shipbuilding industries, while the child at the back represents education. At the northeastern corner of the grounds is a statue of **Sir Edward Harland**, the Yorkshire-born marine engineer who founded the Harland & Wolff shipyards and who served as mayor of Belfast from 1885 to 1886. To his south stands a memorial to the victims of the *Titanic*.

The Marquess of Dufferin (1826–1902), whose career included postings as ambassador to Turkey, Russia, Paris and Rome, governor-general of Canada, and viceroy of India, has an ornate, temple-like **memorial** flanked by an Indian and a Turkish warrior, on the western side of the City Hall. There are proposals to add a memorial to George Best (1946–2005), Northern Ireland's most famous footballer. Belfast's City Airport has already been renamed in his honour.

The highlights of the free **guided tour** of City Hall include the sumptuous, wedding-cake Italian marble and colourful stained glass of the entrance hall and rotunda; an opportunity to sit on the mayor's throne in the council chamber; and the idiosyncratic portraits of past lord mayors. Each lord mayor is allowed to choose his or her own artist, and the variations in personal style are intriguing.

The **Belfast Wheel** (Map pp570-1; ☎ 9031 0607; City Hall, Donegall Sq; adult/child £6.50/4.50; ☒ 10am-9pm Sun-Thu, to 10pm Fri, 9am-10pm Sat), the city's answer to the London Eye, towers over the east end of City Hall. Originally intended as a temporary attraction while City Hall was closed for renovations, in May 2009 local councillors voted for it to remain in place for at least another two years. A spin in the wheel provides a panoramic view over the city centre, allowing you to see the extent of Belfast's fast-moving redevelopment.

LINEN HALL LIBRARY
Opposite City Hall, on Donegall Sq N, is the **Linen Hall Library** (Map pp570-1; ☎ 9032 1707; www.linen hall.com; 17 Donegall Sq N; admission free; ☒ 9.30am-5.30pm Mon-Wed & Fri, to 7pm Thu, to 4pm Sat). Established in 1788 to 'improve the mind and excite a spirit of general inquiry', the library was moved from its original home in the White Linen Hall (the site is now occupied by City Hall) to the present building a century later. Thomas Russell, the first librarian, was a founding member of the United Irishmen and a close friend of Wolfe Tone – a reminder that this movement for independence from Britain had its origins in Belfast. Russell was hanged in 1803 after Robert Emmet's abortive rebellion.

The library houses some 260,000 books, more than half of which are part of its important Irish and local-studies collection. The political collection consists of pretty much everything that has been written about Northern Irish politics since 1966. The library also has a small **coffee shop** (☒ 10am-4pm Mon-Fri, to 12.30pm Sat). The visitors' entrance is on Fountain St, around the corner from the main door.

OTHER DONEGALL SQ BUILDINGS
On Donegall Sq W is the ornate **Scottish Provident Building** (Map pp570–1; 1897–1902). It's decorated with a veritable riot of fascinating statuary, including several allusions to the industries that assured Victorian Belfast's prosperity, as well as sphinxes, dolphins and lions' heads. The building was the work of the architectural partnership of Young and MacKenzie, who counterbalanced it in 1902 with the red

BELFAST

BELFAST

RED HAND OF ULSTER

According to legend, the chief of a raiding party – O'Neills or O'Donnells, take your pick – approaching the coast by boat decided to fire up his troops by decreeing that Ulster would belong to the first man to lay his right hand upon it. As they neared land one particularly competitive chap cut off his own right hand and lobbed it to the shore, thus claiming Ulster as his own. The O'Neill clan later adopted the Red Hand as their emblem and it went on to become the symbol of the Irish province of Ulster.

You'll see the Red Hand of Ulster in many places: on the official Northern Irish flag, in the Ulster coat of arms, above the entrance to the Linen Hall Library (p573) on Donegall Sq, and laid out in red flowers in the garden of Mount Stewart House and Gardens (p611) in County Down. It also appears in many political murals in the badges of Loyalist terrorist groups, and as a clenched red fist in the badge of the Ulster Volunteer Force (UVF).

---

sandstone **Pearl Assurance Building** (Map pp570–1) on Donegall Sq E. Also on the east side of the square is the classical Greek portico of the **Former Methodist Church** (Map pp570–1; 1847), now occupied by the Ulster Bank.

On the square's north side is the equally fine **Robinson & Cleaver Building** (Map pp570–1; 1888), once the Royal Irish Linen Warehouse and later home to Belfast's finest department store (now occupied by Marks & Spencer). There are 50 busts adorning the facade, representing patrons of the Royal Irish Linen company – look out for Queen Victoria and the Maharajah of Cooch Behar, both former customers.

CROWN LIQUOR SALOON

There are not too many historical monuments that you can enjoy while savouring a pint of beer, but the National Trust's **Crown Liquor Saloon** (Map pp570–1; ☎ 9024 3187; www.crownbar.com; 46 Great Victoria St; admission free; ☑ 11.30am–11pm Mon-Sat, 12.30-10pm Sun) is one of them. Belfast's most famous bar was refurbished by Patrick Flanagan in the late 19th century and displays Victorian decorative flamboyance at its best (he was looking to pull in a posh clientele from the new-fangled train station and Grand Opera House across the street).

The exterior (1885) is decorated with ornate and colourful Italian tiles, and boasts a mosaic of a crown on the pavement outside the entrance. Legend has it that Flanagan, a Catholic, argued with his Protestant wife over what the pub's name should be. His wife prevailed and it was named the Crown in honour of the British monarchy. Flanagan took his sneaky revenge by placing the crown mosaic underfoot where customers would tread on it every day.

The interior (1898) sports a mass of stained and cut glass, marble, ceramics, mirrors and mahogany, all atmospherically lit by genuine gas mantles. A long, highly decorated bar dominates one side of the pub, while on the other is a row of ornate wooden snugs. The snugs come equipped with gunmetal plates (from the Crimean War) for striking matches, and bell-pushes that once allowed drinkers to order top-ups without leaving their seats (alas, no longer).

Above the Crown is **Flannigan's** (☎ 9027 9901), another interesting bar with *Titanic* and other maritime memorabilia.

GRAND OPERA HOUSE

One of Belfast's great Victorian landmarks is the **Grand Opera House** (Map pp570–1; ☎ 9024 1919; www.goh.co.uk; Great Victoria St; guided tours adult/child £5/3; ☑ tours by arrangement), across the road from the Crown Liquor Saloon. Opened in 1895, and completely refurbished in the 1970s, it suffered grievously at the hands of the IRA, having sustained severe bomb damage in 1991 and 1993. It was said that as the Europa Hotel next door was home to the media during the Troubles, the IRA brought the bombs to them so they wouldn't have to leave the bar.

The interior has been restored to its original, over-the-top Victorian pomp, with swirling wood and plasterwork, fancy gilt-work in abundance and carved elephant heads framing the private boxes in the auditorium. See also p596.

ORMEAU BATHS GALLERY

Housed in a converted 19th-century public bathhouse, the **Ormeau Baths Gallery** (Map pp570–1; ☎ 9032 1402; www.ormeaubaths.co.uk; 18A Ormeau Ave; admission free; ☑ 10am-5.30pm Tue-Sat) is Northern Ireland's principal exhibition space for contemporary visual art. The gallery stages changing exhibitions of work by Irish and international artists, and has hosted controversial showings of works by Gilbert and George, and Jake and Dinos Chapman. The gallery is a few blocks south of Donegall Sq.

THE ENTRIES

The oldest part of Belfast, around High St, suffered considerable damage from WWII bombing. The narrow alleyways running off High and Ann Sts, known as the Entries, were once bustling commercial and residential thoroughfares: **Pottinger's Entry**, for example, had 34 houses in 1822.

Joy's Entry is named after Francis Joy, who founded the *Belfast News Letter* in 1737, the first daily newspaper in the British Isles (it's still in business). One of his grandsons, Henry Joy McCracken, was executed for supporting the 1798 United Irishmen revolt.

The United Irishmen were founded in 1791 by Wolfe Tone in Peggy Barclay's tavern in **Crown Entry**, and used to meet in Kelly's Cellars (1720; p593) on Bank St, off Royal Ave.

White's Tavern (1630; p593), on **Wine Cellar Entry**, is the oldest tavern in the city and is still a popular lunchtime meeting spot.

Cathedral Quarter

The district north of the centre around St Anne's Cathedral, bounded roughly by Donegall, Waring, Dunbar and York Sts, has been promoted as Belfast's Left Bank, a bohemian district of restored red-brick warehouses and cobbled lanes lined with artists studios, design offices, and stylish bars and restaurants. It's home to the Cathedral Quarter Arts Festival (p586).

Built in imposing Hiberno-Romanesque style, **St Anne's Cathedral** (Map pp570–1; ☎ 9033 2328; www.belfastcathedral.org; Donegall St; admission free, donations accepted; ⏰ 10am-4pm Mon-Fri) was started in 1899 but did not reach its final form until 1981. As you enter you'll see that the black-and-white marble floor is laid out in a maze pattern – the black route leads to a dead end, the white to the sanctuary and salvation. The 10 pillars of the nave are topped by carvings symbolising aspects of Belfast life; look out for the Freemasons' pillar (the central one on the right, or south, side). In the south aisle is the tomb of Unionist hero Sir Edward Carson (1854–1935). The stunning mosaic of *The Creation* in the baptistry contains 150,000 pieces of coloured glass; it and the mosaic above the west door

are the result of seven years' work by sisters Gertrude and Margaret Martin.

A 10-minute walk northwest from the cathedral along Donegall and Clifton Sts leads to **Clifton House** (Map pp570-1; 2 N Queen St, Carlisle Circus), built in 1774 by Robert Joy (Henry Joy McCracken's uncle) as a poorhouse. The finest surviving Georgian building in Belfast, it now houses a nursing home.

South of the cathedral at the end of Donegall St lies the elegant Georgian **Commercial Building** (Map pp570-1; 1822), easily identified by the prominent name of the Northern Whig Printing Company, with a modern bar on the ground floor. Opposite is the **Northern Bank Building** (Map pp570-1), the oldest public building in the city. It started life as the one-storey Exchange in 1769, became the Assembly Rooms with the addition of an upper storey in 1777, and was remodelled in Italianate style in 1845 by Sir Charles Lanyon, Belfast's pre-eminent Victorian architect, to become a bank.

The most flamboyant legacy of Belfast's Victorian era is the grandiose **Ulster Bank Building** (Map pp570-1; 1860), now home to the Merchant Hotel (p587). This Italianate extravaganza has a portico of soaring columns and sculpted figures depicting Britannia, Justice and Commerce, and iron railings decorated with the Red Hand of Ulster and Irish wolfhounds.

To the west of the cathedral, at the junction of Royal Ave and North St, is the **Bank of Ireland Building** (Map pp570-1; 1929), a fine example of art-deco architecture. The former **Sinclair Store** (Map pp570-1; 1935), diagonally opposite the bank, is also in deco style.

Laganside & Lanyon Place

The ambitious **Laganside Project** (www.laganside.com) to redevelop and regenerate the centre of Belfast saw the building of the Waterfront Hall, British Telecom's Riverside Tower and the Belfast Hilton in the 1990s. Projects completed since then include several clusters of riverside apartments, the Lanyon Quay office development next to the Waterfront Hall and the restoration of listed buildings such as McHugh's bar on Queen's Sq, the ornate Victorian warehouses now housing the Malmaison Hotel on Victoria St and the Albert Memorial Clock Tower.

The latest stage is the 28-storey **Obel** (Map pp570–1), Belfast's tallest building, which dominates the waterfront at Donegall Quay. All 182 apartments in the building were sold

---

WALK: LAGAN TOWPATH

Part of Belfast's Laganside redevelopment project was the restoration of the towpath along the west bank of the River Lagan. You can now walk or cycle for 20km along the winding riverbank from central Belfast to Lisburn. The Belfast Welcome Centre provides the *Lagan Valley Regional Park – Towpath Leaflet*, which has a detailed map.

A shorter walk (10km) that you can easily do in half a day starts from **Shaw's Bridge** (Map p600) on the southern edge of the city. Take bus 8A or 8B from Donegall Sq E to the stop just before the Malone roundabout (where Malone Rd becomes Upper Malone Rd). Bear left at the roundabout (signposted Outer Ring A55) and in five minutes or so you will reach the River Lagan at Shaw's Bridge.

Turn left and follow the cycle/walkway downstream on the left bank of the river (waymarked with red '9' signs), passing a restored lock-keeper's cottage and canal-side cafe at lock number 3. After 30 minutes you will arrive at the most attractive part of the walk: **Lagan Meadows** (Map p600), a tree-fringed loop in the river to the right of the path and a good place for a picnic on a summer's day. Another half-hour will bring you to **Cutters Wharf** (p592), a great place for a lunch break. From the pub it's another hour of pleasant walking to **Lagan Weir** (Map pp570–1) in the city centre.

---

in advance, within 48 hours of being released; it's due for completion by the end of 2010.

A few blocks to the south is the brand new £320 million shopping mall, **Victoria Square** (Map pp570-1; www.victoriasquare.com), whose centrepiece is a soaring atrium topped by a vast glass dome.

CLARENDON DOCK

Near the ferry terminal on Donegall Quay is the Italianate **Harbour Commissioner's Office** (Map pp570–1; 1854). The striking marble and stained-glass interior features art and sculpture inspired by Belfast's maritime history. The captain's table built for the *Titanic* survives here – completed behind schedule, it never made it on board. Guided tours of the office are available during the Belfast Maritime Festival in early July. It's also open on European Heritage Open Days, which take place over a weekend in September or October (see the Events section on www.ni-environ ment.gov.uk).

Sinclair Seamen's Church (Map pp570-1; ☎ 9071 5997; Corporation Sq; admission free; ⏰ 2-4pm Wed), next to the Harbour Commissioner's Office, was built by Charles Lanyon in 1857–58 and was intended to meet the spiritual needs of visiting sailors. Part church, part maritime museum, it has a pulpit in the shape of a ship's prow (complete with red-and-green port and starboard lights), a brass ship's wheel and binnacle (used as a baptismal font) salvaged from a WWI wreck and, hanging on the wall behind the wheel, the ship's bell from HMS *Hood*.

North of the Harbour Commissioner's Office is the restored **Clarendon Dock** (Map pp570–1).

Leading off it are the dry docks where Belfast's shipbuilding industry was born – No 1 Dry Dock (1796–1800) is Ireland's oldest, and remained in use until the 1960s; No 2 (1826) is still used occasionally. Between the two sits the pretty little **Clarendon Building**, now home to the offices of the Laganside Corporation.

CUSTOM HOUSE SQUARE

South along the river is the elegant **Custom House** (Map pp570–1), built by Lanyon in Italianate style between 1854 and 1857; the writer Anthony Trollope once worked in the post office here. On the waterfront side, the pediment carries sculpted portrayals of Britannia, Neptune and Mercury. The Custom House steps were once Belfast's equivalent of London's Speakers' Corner, a tradition memorialised in a bronze statue preaching to an invisible crowd.

Looking across the River Lagan from the Custom House, East Belfast is dominated by the huge yellow cranes of the Harland and Wolff shipyards. The modern Queen Elizabeth Bridge crosses the Lagan just to the south, but immediately south again is **Queen's Bridge** (Map pp570–1; 1843), with its ornate lamps; this was Sir Charles Lanyon's first important contribution to Belfast's cityscape.

QUEEN'S SQUARE

At the east end of High St is Belfast's very own leaning tower, the **Albert Memorial Clock Tower** (Map pp570–1). Erected in 1867 in honour of Queen Victoria's dear departed husband, it is not as dramatically out of kilter as the more famously tilted tower in Pisa but does, nevertheless, lean noticeably to the south – as the locals say, 'Old Albert not only has the time, he also has the inclination.' Restoration work has stabilised its foundations and left its Scrabo sandstone masonry sparkling white.

Many of the buildings around the clock tower are the work of Sir Charles Lanyon. The white stone building immediately north of the clock tower was completed in 1852 by Lanyon as head office for the **Northern Bank** (Map pp570–1).

South of the tower on Victoria St is the **Malmaison Hotel** (Map pp570–1; 1868), formerly two seed warehouses – look for the friezes of exotic birds, plants and nut-munching squirrels on the left half of the facade.

LAGAN WEIR

Across the street from the Custom House is *Bigfish* (Map pp570–1; 1999), the most prominent of the many modern artworks that grace the riverbank between Clarendon Dock and Ormeau Bridge. The giant ceramic salmon – a symbol of the regeneration of the River Lagan – is covered with tiles depicting the history of Belfast.

It sits beside **Lagan Weir** (Map pp570–1), the first stage of the Laganside Project, completed in 1994. Years of neglect and industrial decline had turned the River Lagan, the original lifeblood of the city, into an open sewer flanked by smelly, unsightly mudflats. The weir, along with a program of dredging and aeration, has improved the water quality so much that salmon, eels and sea trout migrate up the river once again.

For details of the boat tours that depart from here, see p585.

LANYON PLACE

A five-minute walk south from the Lagan Weir leads to Lanyon Pl, the Laganside Project's flagship site, dominated by the 2235-seat Waterfront Hall (p595). Across Oxford St lie the neoclassical **Royal Courts of Justice** (Map pp570–1; 1933), bombed by the IRA in 1990 but now emerging from behind the massive security screens that once concealed them.

South of the courts is the elegant Victorian **St George's Market** (Map pp570–1; ☎ 9043 5704; cnr Oxford & May Sts; admission free; ⊙ 6am-1pm Fri, 9am-3pm Sat), built in 1896 for the sale of fruit, butter, eggs and poultry; it's the oldest continually operating market in Ireland. Restored in 1999,

it now hosts a variety market on Friday, selling fresh flowers, fruit, vegetables, meat and fish, plus general household and second-hand goods, and the City Food and Garden Market on Saturday, which often has live music. There's also a two-day Christmas Fair and Market in early December.

Titanic Quarter

Belfast's former shipbuilding yards – the birthplace of RMS *Titanic* – stretch along the east side of the River Lagan, dominated by the towering yellow cranes known as Samson and Goliath. The area is currently undergoing a £1 billion regeneration project known as **Titanic Quarter** (www.titanicquarter.com), which plans to develop the long-derelict docklands over the next 15 to 20 years.

There are plans to build an 'iconic attraction' in the Titanic Quarter (at the head of the *Titanic* slipways) in time for the centenary of the *Titanic*'s launch in 2012 although, at the time of research, work had not yet begun. In the meantime, the informative and entertaining commentary on the Lagan Boat Company's Titanic Tour (p585) is the best way to learn about the history of the shipyards.

ODYSSEY COMPLEX

The Odyssey Complex is a huge sporting and entertainment centre on the eastern side of the river across from Clarendon Dock. The complex features a hands-on science centre, a 10,000-seater sports arena (home to the Belfast Giants ice-hockey team), a multiplex cinema with an IMAX screen, a video-games centre and a dozen restaurants, cafes and bars.

Also known as whowhatwherewhenwhy, **W5** (Map pp570–1; ☎ 9046 7700; www.w5online.co.uk; adult/child £6.80/4.90, 2 adults & 2 children £20; ⊙ 10am-5pm Mon-Thu, to 6pm Fri & Sat, noon-6pm Sun, last admission 1hr before closing) is an interactive science centre aimed at children of all ages. Kids can compose their own tunes by biffing the 'air harp' with a foam rubber bat, try to beat a lie detector, create cloud rings and tornadoes, and design and build their own robots and racing cars.

The Odyssey Complex is a five-minute walk across the weir from the *Bigfish* sculpture. Metro bus 26 from Donegall Sq W to Holywood stops at the complex (£1.30, 5 minutes, hourly Monday to Friday only); the rather inconspicuous bus stop is on Sydenham Rd.

BELFAST

TITANIC TRAIL

Queens Rd strikes northeast from the Odyssey Complex into the heart of the Titanic Quarter, a massive redevelopment area that is part industrial wasteland, part building site and part hi-tech business park. Not much remains of the time when the *Titanic* was built, but a series of information boards along Queen's Rd point out items of interest.

You can hire a hand-held multimedia device from the Belfast Welcome Centre, which leads you on a self-guided walking tour of the **Titanic Trail** (☎ 9024 6609; per device for up to 3hr £8), complete with GPS technology, audio commentary and video presentations.

First up is the **Hamilton Graving Dock** (off Map pp570–1), which is slated to be the permanent mooring for the **SS Nomadic** (☎ 9027 7652; www .nomadicbelfast.com) – the only surviving vessel of the White Star Line (the shipping company that owned the *Titanic*). In 2006 she was rescued from the breaker's yard and brought to Belfast. The little steamship, which once served as a tender ferrying 1st- and 2nd-class passengers between Cherbourg Harbour and the giant Olympic Class ocean liners (which were too big to dock at the French port), was undergoing restoration work in Barnett Dock at the time of research, but should have moved to Hamilton Dock and be open to the public by summer 2010.

Just along the road are the original **Harland and Wolff Drawing Offices** (off Map pp570–1), where the designs for the *Titanic* were first drawn up (not open to the public); behind them, and best seen from a boat tour on the river, are the two massive **slipways** where the *Titanic* and her sister ship *Olympic* were built and launched.

A few hundred metres further on you'll reach the most impressive monument to the days of the great liners – the huge **Thompson Graving Dock** (off Map pp570–1), where the *Titanic* was fitted out. Its vast size gives you some idea of the scale of the ship, which could only just fit into it. Beside the dock is the **Thompson Pump House** (off Map pp570–1; ☎ 9073 7813; www.titanicsdock .com; admission free, guided tour £5; ☼ visitor centre 10.30am-4pm, tours 11am & 2pm), which houses an exhibition on Belfast shipbuilding, and a cafe. The guided tour includes a video of original film footage from the shipyards, and a visit to the inner workings of the pump house and dock.

In the dock on the far side of the pump house, naval history buffs can ogle **HMS Caroline**, a WWI Royal Navy cruiser built in 1914, now serving as a Royal Naval Reserve training ship (not open to the public).

South Belfast (Queen's Quarter)

The Golden Mile – the 1.5km stretch of Great Victoria St and Shaftesbury Sq that links the city centre to the university district – was once the focus for much of Belfast's nightlife. These days, with the regeneration of the city centre, it's more tarnished brass than gold, but it still has several decent pubs and eateries.

Metro buses 8A, 8B and 8C run from Donegall Sq E along Bradbury Pl and University Rd to Queen's University.

QUEEN'S UNIVERSITY

If you think that Charles Lanyon's Queen's College (1849), a Tudor Revival building in red brick and honey-coloured sandstone, has something of an Oxbridge air about it, that may be because he based the design of the central tower on the 15th-century Founder's Tower at Oxford's Magdalen College. Northern Ireland's most prestigious university was founded by Queen Victoria in 1845, one of three Queen's colleges (the others, still around but no longer called Queen's colleges, are in Cork and Galway) created to provide a nondenominational alternative to the Anglican Church's Trinity College in Dublin. In 1908, the college became the Queen's University of Belfast (Map pp570–1), and today its campus spreads across some 250 buildings. Queen's has around 25,000 students and enjoys a strong reputation in medicine, engineering and law.

Just inside the main entrance is a small **visitor centre** (☎ 9097 5252; www.qub.ac.uk/vcentre; University Rd; admission free; ☼ 9.30am-4.30pm Mon-Sat, 10am-1pm Sun) with exhibitions and a souvenir shop. Guided tours (£5 per person) depart at noon on Saturday.

The university quarter is an attractive district of quiet, tree-lined streets. Georgian-style **University Square** (1848–53), on the northern side of the campus, is one of the most beautiful terraced streets in Ireland. Opposite its eastern end is the grand, neo-Renaissance **Union Theological College** (Map pp570–1; 1853), originally the Presbyterian College and yet another Lanyon design. It housed the Northern Ireland Parliament from the partition of Ireland until 1932, when the Parliament Buildings at Stormont were opened.

BOTANIC GARDENS

The green oasis of Belfast's **Botanic Gardens** (Map pp570-1; ☎ 9031 4762; Stranmillis Rd; admission free; ⏰ 7.30am-sunset) is a short stroll away from the university. Just inside the Stranmillis Rd gate is a **statue** of Belfast-born William Thomson, Lord Kelvin (Map pp570-1), who helped lay the foundation of modern physics and who invented the Kelvin scale that measures temperatures from absolute zero (−273°C or 0°K).

The gardens' centrepiece is Charles Lanyon's beautiful **Palm House** (Map pp570-1; admission free; ⏰ 10am-noon & 1-5pm Mon-Fri, 1-5pm Sat, Sun & bank holidays, to 4pm Mon-Fri Oct-Mar), built in 1839 and completed in 1852, with its birdcage dome, a masterpiece in cast-iron and curvilinear glass. Nearby is the unique **Tropical Ravine** (Map pp570-1; admission free; ⏰ same as Palm House), a huge red-brick greenhouse designed by the garden's curator Charles McKimm and completed in 1889. Inside, a raised walkway overlooks a jungle of tropical ferns, orchids, lilies and banana plants growing in a sunken glen.

ULSTER MUSEUM

If the weather washes out a walk in the gardens, head instead for the nearby **Ulster Museum** (Map pp570-1; ☎ 9038 3000; www.ulstermuseum.org.uk; Stranmillis Rd; admission free; ⏰ 10am-5pm Mon-Fri, 1-5pm Sat, 2-5pm Sun). The museum was closed for redevelopment at the time of research, but should be open again by the time you read this.

Don't miss the **Early Ireland gallery**, a series of tableaux explaining Irish prehistory combined with a spectacular collection of prehistoric stone and bronze artefacts that help provide a cultural context for Northern Ireland's many archaeological sites. The exhibits are beautifully displayed – the Malone Hoard, a clutch of 16 polished, Neolithic stone axes discovered only a few kilometres from the museum, looks more like a modern sculpture than a museum exhibit.

Other highlights include the **Industrial History gallery**, based around Belfast's 19th-century linen industry, and the **Treasures of the Armada**, a display of artefacts and jewellery recovered from the 1588 wreck of the *Girona* (see the boxed text, p654) and other Spanish Armada vessels. Among the treasures is a ruby-encrusted golden salamander.

The centrepiece of the **Egyptian collection** is the mummy of Princess Takabuti. She was unwrapped in Belfast in 1835, the first mummy ever to be displayed outside Egypt; more recently, her bleached hair has led the locals to dub her 'Belfast's oldest bleached blonde'.

The top floors are given over to 19th- and 20th-century **Irish and British art**, notably the works of Belfast-born Sir John Lavery (1856–1941), who became one of the most fashionable and expensive portraitists of Victorian London.

West Belfast (Gaeltacht Quarter)

Though scarred by three decades of civil unrest, the former battleground of West Belfast is one of the most compelling places to visit in Northern Ireland. Recent history hangs heavy in the air, but there is a noticeable air of optimism and hope for the future.

The main attractions are the powerful murals that chart the history of the conflict as well as the political passions of the moment and, for visitors from mainland Britain, there is a grim fascination to be found in wandering through the former 'war zone' in their own backyard.

West Belfast grew up around the linen mills that propelled the city into late-19th-century prosperity. It was an area of low-cost, working-class housing, and even in the Victorian era was divided along religious lines. The advent of the Troubles in 1968 solidified the sectarian divide, and since 1970 the ironically named 'Peace Line' has separated the Loyalist and Protestant Shankill district from the Republican and Catholic Falls district.

Despite its past reputation, the area is safe to visit. The best way to see West Belfast is on a black taxi tour (see p585). The cabs visit the more spectacular murals as well as the Peace Line (where you can write a message on the wall) and other significant sites, while the drivers provide a colourful commentary on the history of the area.

There's nothing to stop you visiting under your own steam, either walking or using the shared black taxis along the Falls or Shankill Rds (see the boxed text, p599). Alternatively, buses 10A to 10F from Queen St will take you along the Falls Rd; buses 11A to 11D from Wellington Pl go along Shankill Rd.

You can also pick up a range of free leaflets at the Belfast Welcome Centre that describe walking tours around the Falls and Shankill districts.

FALLS ROAD

Although the signs of past conflict are inescapable, the Falls today is an unexpectedly lively, colourful and optimistic place. Local people are friendly and welcoming, and community ventures such as Conway Mill, the Cultúrlann centre and black taxi tours have seen tourist numbers increase dramatically.

The focus for community activity is the Irish language and cultural centre **Cultúrlann McAdam Ó Fiaich** (Map p580; ☎ 9096 4180; www.cultur lann.ie; 216 Falls Rd; ☒ 9am-9pm Mon-Fri, 10am-6pm Sat). Housed in a red-brick, former Presbyterian church, it's a cosy and welcoming place with a tourist information desk, a shop selling a wide selection of books on Ireland, Irish-language material, crafts, and Irish music CDs, and an excellent cafe-restaurant (p592). The centre also has an art gallery and a theatre that stages music, drama and poetry events.

A few blocks away is **Conway Mill** (Map p580; ☎ 9024 7276; www.conwaymill.org; 5-7 Conway St; admission free; ☒ 10am-5pm Mon-Fri, to 3pm Sat), a 19th-century flax mill that now houses an art gallery, an exhibition on the mill's history and more than 20 small shops and studios making and selling arts, crafts and furniture. (Redevelopment works mean that parts of the mill complex will be closed until completion in June 2010.) The mill also houses the **Irish Republican History Museum** (☒ 10am-2pm Tue-Sat), a collection of artefacts, newspaper articles, photos and archives relating to the Republican struggle from 1798 to the Troubles.

Also see the Belfast Walking Tour, p583.

SHANKILL ROAD

Although the Protestant Shankill district (from the Irish *sean chill*, meaning 'old church') has received less media and tourist attention than the Falls, it also contains many interesting murals. The people here are just as friendly, but the Shankill has far fewer tourists than the Falls. Loyalist communities seem to have more difficulty in presenting their side of the story than the Republicans, who have a far more polished approach to public relations.

To reach Shankill Rd on foot, set off north from City Hall along Donegall Pl and Royal Ave, then turn left on North St and continue straight on across the Westlink dual carriageway.

Beyond Shankill Rd, about 500m up Glencairn Rd, is **Fernhill House: The People's Museum** (Map p600; ☎ 9071 5599; www.fernhillhouse.co.uk;

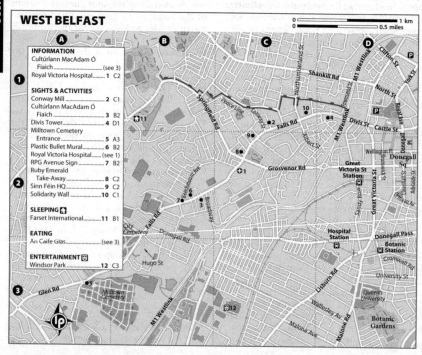

WEST BELFAST

0 ———— 1 km
0 ———— 0.5 miles

INFORMATION
Cultúrlann MacAdam Ó
   Fiaich .... (see 3)
Royal Victoria Hospital 1 C2

SIGHTS & ACTIVITIES
Conway Mill 2 C1
Cultúrlann MacAdam Ó
   Fiaich 3 B2
Divis Tower 4 D1
Milltown Cemetery
   Entrance 5 A3
Plastic Bullet Mural 6 B2
Royal Victoria Hospital ... (see 1)
RPG Avenue Sign 7 B2
Ruby Emerald
   Take-Away 8 C2
Sinn Féin HQ 9 C2
Solidarity Wall 10 C1

SLEEPING
Farset International 11 B1

EATING
An Caife Glas .... (see 3)

ENTERTAINMENT
Windsor Park 12 C3

Glencairn Rd; adult/child £2/1; ☻ 10am-4pm Mon-Sat, 1-4pm Sun). Set in a wealthy Victorian merchant's villa, the museum contains a recreation of a 1930s working-class terraced house, exhibitions detailing the history of the Shankill district and the Home Rule crisis, and the largest collection of Orange Order memorabilia in the world. To get there, take bus 11B, 11C or 11D from Wellington Pl, at the northwest corner of Donegall Sq.

Outside the Centre
CAVE HILL
The best way to get a feel for Belfast's natural setting is to view it from above. In the absence of a private aircraft, head for Cave Hill (Map p600; 368m), which looms over the northern fringes of the city. The view from its summit takes in the whole sprawl of the city, the docks and the creeping fingers of urbanisation along the shores of Belfast Lough. On a clear day you can even spot Scotland lurking on the horizon. For information on climbing to the summit, see the boxed text, p584.

The hill was originally called Ben Madigan, after the 9th-century Ulster king, Matudhain. Its distinctive, craggy profile, seen from the south, has been known to locals for two centuries as 'Napoleon's Nose' – it supposedly bears some resemblance to Bonaparte's shnoz, but you might take some convincing. On the summit is an Iron Age earthwork known as McArt's Fort where members of the United Irishmen, including Wolfe Tone, looked down over the city in 1795 and pledged to fight for Irish independence.

Cave Hill Country Park (Map p600; ☎ 9077 6925; Antrim Rd; admission free; ☻ 7.30am-dusk) spreads across the hill's eastern slopes, with several waymarked walks and an adventure playground for kids aged three to 14 years.

To get there, take buses 1A to 1H from Donegall Sq W to Belfast Castle or Belfast Zoo.

BELFAST CASTLE
Built in 1870 for the third Marquess of Donegall, in the Scottish Baronial style made fashionable by Queen Victoria's then recently built Balmoral, the multi-turreted pomp of **Belfast Castle** (Map p600; ☎ 9077 6925; www.belfast castle.co.uk; Antrim Rd; admission free; ☻ 9am-10pm Mon-Sat, to 6pm Sun) commands the southeastern slopes of Cave Hill. It was presented to the City of Belfast in 1934.

Extensive renovation between 1978 and 1988 has left the interior comfortably modern rather than intriguingly antique, and the castle is now a popular venue for wedding receptions. Upstairs is the **Cave Hill Visitor Centre** with a few displays on the folklore, history, archaeology and natural history of the park. Downstairs is the Cellar Restaurant and a small **antiques shop** (☻ noon-5pm Sun-Fri, to 10pm Sat).

Legend has it that the castle's residents will experience good fortune only as long as a white cat lives there, a tale commemorated in the beautiful formal gardens by nine portrayals of cats in mosaic, painting, sculpture and garden furniture – a good game for the kids is getting them to find all nine.

BELFAST ZOO
Belfast Zoo (Map p600; ☎ 9077 6277; www.belfastzoo .co.uk; Antrim Rd; adult/child Apr-Sep £8.30/4.40, Oct-Mar £6.80/3.50, children under 4, senior & visitors with disabilities free; ☻ 10am-7pm Apr-Sep, to 4pm Oct-Mar, last admission 2hr/90min before closing in summer/winter) is one of the most appealing zoos in Britain and Ireland, with spacious enclosures set on an attractive, sloping site; the sea lion and penguin pool with its underwater viewing is particularly good. Some of the more unusual animals include tamarins, spectacled bears and red pandas, but the biggest attractions are the ultra-cute meerkats, the colony of ring-tailed lemurs and 'Jack', the blue-eyed white tiger.

MALONE HOUSE
Malone House (Map p600; ☎ 9068 1246; www.malone house.co.uk; Upper Malone Rd; admission free; ☻ 9am-5pm Mon-Sat, 11am-5pm Sun) is a late-Georgian mansion in the grounds of Barnett Demesne. Built in the 1820s for local merchant William Legge, the house is now used mainly for social functions and conferences, with art exhibitions staged in the Higgin Gallery. The surrounding gardens are planted with azaleas and rhododendrons, with paths leading down to the Lagan Towpath (see boxed text, p576).

The house is about 5km south of the centre; take bus 8A or 8B to Dub Lane, Upper Malone Rd.

SIR THOMAS & LADY DIXON PARK
This **park** (Map p600; Upper Malone Rd; admission free; ☻ 7.30am-dusk) consists of rolling meadows, woodland, riverside fields and formal gardens. The main draw is its spectacular **Rose Garden**, which contains more than 45,000 blooms.

BELFAST

MURALS OF BELFAST

Belfast's tradition of political murals is a century old, dating from 1908 when images of King Billy (William III, Protestant victor over the Catholic James II at the Battle of the Boyne in 1690) were painted by Unionists protesting against home rule for Ireland. The tradition was revived in the late 1970s as the Troubles wore on, with murals used to mark out sectarian territory, make political points, commemorate historical events and glorify terrorist groups. As the 'voice of the community' the murals were rarely permanent, but changed to reflect the issues of the day.

Republican Murals

The first Republican murals appeared in 1981, when the hunger strike at the Maze Prison saw the emergence of dozens of murals supporting the hunger strikers. In later years, Republican muralists broadened their scope to cover wider political issues, Irish legends and historical events. After the Good Friday Agreement of 1998, the murals came to demand police reform and the protection of nationalists from sectarian attacks.

Common images seen in Republican murals include the phoenix rising from the flames (symbolising Ireland reborn from the flames of the 1916 Easter Rising), the face of hunger-striker Bobby Sands, and scenes and figures from Irish mythology. Common slogans include 'Free Ireland', the Irish Gaelic 'Éirí Amach na Cásca 1916' (The Easter Rising of 1916) and 'Tiocfaidh Ár Lá' (Our Day Will Come).

The main areas for Republican murals are Falls Rd, Beechmount Ave, Donegall Rd, Shaw's Rd and the Ballymurphy district in West Belfast; New Lodge Rd in North Belfast; and Ormeau Rd in South Belfast.

Loyalist Murals

Whereas Republican murals were often artistic and rich in symbolic imagery, the Loyalist ones have traditionally been more militaristic and defiant in tone. The Loyalist battle cry of 'No Surrender!' is everywhere, along with red, white and blue painted kerbstones, paramilitary insignia and images of King Billy, usually shown on a prancing white horse.

You will also see the Red Hand of Ulster, sometimes shown as a clenched fist (the symbol of the Ulster Freedom Fighters, UFF), and references to the WWI Battle of the Somme in 1916 in which many Ulster soldiers died; it is seen as a symbol of Ulster's loyalty to the British crown, in contrast to the Republican Easter Rising of 1916. Common mottoes include 'Quis Separabit' (Who Shall Divide Us?), the motto of the Ulster Defence Association (UDA); and the defiant 'We will maintain our faith and our nationality'.

Murals Today

In recent years there has been a lot of debate about what to do with Belfast's murals. Some see them as an ugly and unpleasant reminder of a violent past, while others claim they are a vital part of Northern Ireland's history. There's no doubt they have become an important tourist attraction, but there is now a move to replace the more aggressive and militaristic images with murals dedicated to local heroes and famous figures such as footballer George Best and *Narnia* novelist CS Lewis.

There are also some off-beat and amusing artworks, including one that has been baffling passers-by for years. A gable-end on Balfour Ave, off Ormeau Rd, asks the question 'How can quantum gravity help explain the origin of the universe?'. It was part of an art installation in 2001, one of 10 questions selected by scientists as the most important unsolved problems in physics. Perhaps it has survived so long as it reflects the still unsolved – and, to outsiders, equally baffling – problem of Northern Ireland's sectarian divide.

If you want to find out more about Northern Ireland's murals, look out for the books *Drawing Support* (three volumes) by Bill Rolston, *The Peoples' Gallery* by the Bogside Artists and the Mural Directory website (www.cain.ulst.ac.uk/murals).

Among other displays, a spiral-shaped garden traces the development of the rose from early shrub roses up to modern hybrids; the roses are in bloom from mid-July, when **Rose Week** (☎ 9091 8768; www.belfastcity.gov.uk) offers six days of rose competitions, music, plant and craft stalls, gardening workshops and kids activities. The park also contains a walled garden, a Japanese-style garden, a children's playground and a cafe.

The park is 1.5km southwest of Malone House.

GIANT'S RING

This huge **prehistoric earthwork** (admission free; ⏰ 24hr), nearly 200m in diameter, is a circular Neolithic ritual complex with a dolmen (known as the Druid's Altar) in the centre. Prehistoric rings were commonly believed to be the home of fairies and consequently treated with respect, but this one was commandeered in the 19th century as a racetrack, the 4m-high embankment serving as a natural grandstand. The site is 6.5km south of Belfast city centre, off Milltown Rd near Shaw's Bridge.

STORMONT

The dazzling white neoclassical facade of the **Parliament Buildings** (Map p600; ☎ 9052 1362; www .niassembly.gov.uk; admission free; ⏰ grounds 7.30am-dusk, buildings 9am-4pm Mon-Fri) at Stormont is one of Belfast's most iconic buildings; in the North, 'Stormont' carries the same connotation as 'Westminster' does in Britain and 'Washington' in the USA – the seat of power. For 40 years, from its completion in 1932 until the introduction of direct rule in 1972, it was the seat of the parliament of Northern Ireland. More recently, on 8 May 2007, it returned to the forefront of Irish politics when Ian Paisley and Martin McGuinness – who had been the best of enemies for decades – laughed and smiled as they were sworn in as first minister and deputy first minister respectively.

The building occupies a dramatic position at the end of a gently rising, 1.5km-long avenue and is fronted by a defiant statue of the arch Unionist Sir Edward Carson. Tours of Parliament Buildings are not available to the general public, but you can visit the Public Gallery (from noon on Monday, from 10.30am Tuesday) and are free to walk around the extensive grounds, or you can take a virtual tour at www.niassembly.gov.uk. Nearby, 19th-century **Stormont Castle** (Map p600) is, like Hillsborough

in County Down, an official residence of the Secretary of State for Northern Ireland.

Stormont is 8km east of the city centre, off Upper Newtonards Rd. Take bus 4A or 4B from Donegall Sq W.

WALKING TOUR

> **WALK FACTS**
>
> **Start** City Hall
> **End** Milltown Cemetery
> **Distance** 4km
> **Duration** one hour

This walk leads through the heart of Republican West Belfast (Map p580) from the city centre to Milltown Cemetery. Starting from **City Hall** (p573), go north along Donegall Pl and turn left on Castle St. Keep straight ahead along Divis St.

After you cross the busy Westlink dual carriageway, look along Townsend St, the first street on the right, and you'll see the steel gates that mark the beginning of the so-called **Peace Line**, the 6m-high wall of corrugated steel, concrete and chain link that has divided the Protestant and Catholic communities of West Belfast for almost 40 years. Begun in 1970 as a 'temporary measure', it has outlasted the Berlin Wall and zigzags for some 4km from the Westlink to the lower slopes of Black Mountain. These days the gates in the wall remain open during the day, but most are still closed from 5pm to 8am. There are now more than 20 such barriers in Belfast, and a total of more than 40 throughout Northern Ireland, the most visible sign of the divisions that have scarred the province for so long.

Ahead on the left rises the infamous **Divis Tower**, a 20-storey apartment block. The security forces took over the top two floors of the tower block as an observation post in the 1970s, and continued to use it to monitor people's movements until it was decommissioned in 2005.

Next, you'll pass the **Solidarity Wall**, a collection of murals expressing Republican sympathies with, among others, the Palestinians, the Kurds and the Basques, along with several anti–George W Bush murals. Just past here, Divis St becomes Falls Rd, and Conway St, on the right at the Celtic Bar, leads to **Conway Mill** (p580).

BELFAST

WALK: CAVE HILL

Start from the public car park just before the gates of Belfast Castle. Take the path that leads up from the car park. After 150m you'll reach a horizontal path at a T-junction; go right and follow this trail as it continues uphill through the woods. After about 800m you'll emerge from the trees beneath Cave Hill's eastern crags. Fork left beneath the obvious caves that give the hill its name (if you keep straight on here, the path continues north for 1km to the Belfast Zoo car park) and traverse to the north (right) beneath the cliffs then climb up to a shoulder (which can be muddy). The path then doubles back to the south (left) and follows the cliff tops to the summit.

A little bridge and some steps lead up to the summit proper, an Iron Age fort surrounded by crags. There's a superb view across the city, harbour and lough, with Scrabo Hill and Tower prominent on the eastern horizon, and the rounded forms of the Mourne Mountains far away to the south.

Continue south then west on a broad, well-made trail for almost 1km. At a sharp bend to the right, beside a wooden bench, leave the trail on the left via a stile, and go downhill on a faint path through a field. Pass over another stile at an old quarry and turn left, keeping the quarry on your left. The path then descends more steeply through woods; at a T-junction go left on a better path, which leads to the T-junction above the castle car park; turn right here to finish. (Total distance 5.5km; allow two hours.)

On the corner of Falls Rd and Sevastopol St is the red-brick **Sinn Féin headquarters**, with its famous mural of a smiling Bobby Sands, the hunger striker who was elected MP for West Belfast just a few weeks before he died in 1981. The text reads, in Sands' own words, 'Our revenge will be the laughter of our children'. A few blocks further on, on the right between Waterford St and Springfield Rd, look out for the **Ruby Emerald Take-Away** at 105 Falls Rd – it was on the pavement outside this shop (known as Clinton's Hot Food from 1996 to 2003) that the historic handshake between Sinn Féin leader Gerry Adams and US president Bill Clinton took place in November 1995.

On the left now are the artwork railings of the **Royal Victoria Hospital**, dating from 1906; it claims to be the world's first air-conditioned building. Known locally as the RVH, it played an important role in creating the first ever portable defibrillator and, in the 1970s and '80s, developed a well-earned reputation for expertise in the treatment of gunshot wounds. The wavy form of the railings mimics the structure of DNA – look for the little yellow Xs and Ys for X- and Y-chromosomes – and the portraits (laser-cut in sheet steel) chart the progress of a human life from birth to the age of 100. Just beyond the hospital is the **Cultúrlann MacAdam Ó Fiaich** (p580).

All along Falls Rd you'll see Republican murals, as well as memorials in honour of people who have died during the conflict. At Islandbawn St on the right, the **Plastic Bullet Mural** commemorates the 17 people, including eight children, who were killed by plastic baton rounds (now banned) fired by the security services. Two streets on, on the right, is **Beechmount Ave**. Look at the street name – a hand-painted sign reads 'RPG Avenue'. 'RPG' stands for 'rocket-propelled grenade'; the street earned its nickname because it offered a line of sight for IRA rocket attacks on the security forces base in nearby Springfield Rd.

Another 15 minutes of walking will take you past the **City Cemetery** and Falls Park to **Milltown Cemetery** where the 1981 hunger strikers are buried. You'll see green Hs attached to lamp posts (in memory of the H-blocks at the Maze Prison where the hunger strikers were incarcerated); at Hugo St, opposite the City Cemetery, there's a large mural entitled 'St James's Support the Hunger Strikers'.

The Republican plot in Milltown Cemetery is halfway along the southern wall – from the entrance head straight on until you reach a crossroads with a circular Stonehenge-like memorial. Turn right and keep straight on all the way to the end of the path.

Return by the same route or catch any bus or taxi back to the city centre. There's a bus stop across the road from the Milltown Cemetery entrance.

BELFAST FOR CHILDREN

W5 (p577) is the city's biggest draw for kids – it's hard to drag them away once they get started with the hands-on exhibits. The Odyssey Complex houses other attractions including a video-games arcade, a ten-pin bowling rink and an IMAX cinema. **Belfast Zoo** (p581) is a perennial favourite, and the **Ulster Museum** (p579) also has plenty of exhibits and special events designed for children of all ages.

For outdoor fun, head for the **Botanic Gardens** (p579) or the adventure playground in **Cave Hill Country Park** (p581). Or you can try crazy golf with a difference at **Pirates Adventure Golf** (☎ 9048 0220; www.piratesadventuregolf.com; 111A Dundonald Touring Caravan Park, Dundonald Rd; adult/child £6/4; ⏱ 10am-10pm), a landscaped, 36-hole course decked out with waterfalls, fountains and a giant pirate ship.

Sweeties may not be at the top of parents' shopping lists these days, but you might be prepared to make an exception for **Aunt Sandra's Candy Factory** (Map p600; ☎ 9073 2868; www.auntsan dras.com; 60 Castlereagh Rd; tours adult/child £3.50/2.50; ⏱ 9.30am-5pm Mon-Fri, 10am-4.30pm Sat). This 1950s-style shop sells fudge, candy, chocolates, toffee apples and other traditional sweets, which have been made by hand, and you can get a tour of the workshop before buying the goods.

Located outside of town but near enough for a day trip, you'll find the **Ulster Folk & Transport Museums** (p601), and the **Ark Open Farm** (p612), both of which are hugely popular with kids.

The free monthly *Whatabout?* booklet (available from the Belfast Welcome Centre) has a 'Family Fun' section, which lists events and attractions of interest to travellers with children. If you're in town in late May, look out for the **Belfast Children's Festival** (www.belfast childrensfestival.com), which is packed with cultural and educational events.

TOURS

You can find full details of organised tours at the Belfast Welcome Centre (p572). If you want to hire a personal guide, call the Welcome Centre or contact the **Northern Ireland Tourist Guide Association** (☎ 9753 3370; www .bluebadgeireland.org; half-/full-day tours £75/140).

Boat Tours

Lagan Boat Company (Map pp570-1; ☎ 9033 0844; www .laganboatcompany.com; adult/child/family £10/8/28) offers two 1¼-hour boat tours: the **River Lagan Tour** (⏱ 2pm & 3.30pm Mon, 12.30pm, 2pm & 3.30pm Sat & Sun Jun-Sep, 12.30pm & 2pm Sat & Sun Oct) heads upstream to Stranmillis, departing from the Lagan Lookout; the excellent **Titanic Tour** (⏱ 12.30pm, 2pm & 3.30pm daily Apr-Sep, 12.30 & 2pm Oct, Sat & Sun only Nov, Feb & Mar) explores the derelict docklands downstream of the weir, taking in the slipways

where the liners *Titanic* and *Olympic* were launched and the huge dry dock where they could fit with just nine inches to spare. The Titanic Tour departs from Donegall Quay near the *Bigfish* sculpture.

At the time of writing, **Belfast Duck Tours** (☎ 9032 1321; www.belfastducktours.com) was about to begin offering city tours in amphibious buses, part on road, part on river – check the website for details.

These tours are popular – it's safest to book in advance.

Bus Tours

Belfast City Sightseeing (Map pp570-1; ☎ 9045 9035; www.belfastcitysightseeing.com; adult/child £12.50/8.50) Runs 1¼-hour open-top bus tours that take in City Hall, the Albert Clock, the Titanic Quarter, the Botanic Gardens, and the Falls Rd and Shankill Rd murals in West Belfast. There are departures from Castle Pl every 30 minutes from 10am to 5pm from May to September, every 45 minutes from 10am to 4pm from October to March.

Belfast International Youth Hostel (☎ 9032 4733; www.minicoachni.co.uk; 22 Donegall Rd; tour adult/child £10/7) Recommended by many readers for its two-hour minibus tour that takes in all the city's main sights. Tours depart from the hostel (p587) daily at noon, and can be booked at the hostel or the Belfast Welcome Centre.

Taxi Tours

Black taxi tours of West Belfast's murals – known locally as the 'bombs and bullets' or 'doom and gloom' tours – are offered by a large number of taxi companies and local cabbies. These can vary in quality and content, but in general they're an intimate and entertaining way to see the sights and can be customised to suit your own interests. There are also historical taxi tours of the city centre. For a one-hour tour expect to pay from £25 total for one or two people, and £10 per person for three to six. Call and they will pick you up from anywhere in the city centre.

The following are recommended:

Harpers Taxi Tours (☎ 07711 757178; www.harpers taxitours.co.nr)

Official Black Taxi Tours (☎ 9064 2264, toll-free 0800 052 3914; www.belfasttours.com)

Original Belfast Black Taxi Tours (☎ 07751 565359)

Walking Tours

Belfast Pub Tours (☎ 9268 3665; www.belfast pubtours.com; per person £6; ⏱ 7pm Thu & 4pm Sat May-Oct) A two-hour tour (not including drinks) taking in six of the city's historic pubs, departing from the Crown

---

KEN HARPER, BLACK TAXI DRIVER

What do you do for a living? I do black taxi tours. I started work in Belfast in 1968 – that was just the start of the so-called Troubles – and qualified as a taxi driver in 1979. I remember, just before the ceasefires of 1994, the odd tourist coming through Belfast and asking me for a tour. Now it's a major industry.

What do people want to see? The most popular sights, without doubt, are the Shankill Rd and Falls Rd areas. For example, the murals, the so-called 'Peace Line' and the general area around those roads which the Troubles affected greatly.

Do visitors understand the situation here? Some tourists do and some don't understand the conflict and divisions in Northern Ireland, but I can explain to the majority of my tourists the background to the problem. The daftest question I have been asked was, 'Who is Sinn Féin?', thinking it was a person. Another tourist asked, on seeing a statue of Queen Victoria, 'Is that the bad Queen?'

Dining Rooms, above the Crown Liquor Saloon (p592) on Great Victoria St.

Blackstaff Way (☎ 9029 2631; billy.dickson@ntlworld .com; per person £6; ⊗ 11am Sat) A fascinating 1½-hour historical tour through the city along the route of the Blackstaff River, which was channelled underground in 1881. Departs from the Belfast Welcome Centre.

Historic Belfast Walk (☎ 9024 6609; per person £6; ⊗ 2pm Wed & Fri-Sun) A 1½-hour tour that explores the architecture and history of the Victorian city centre and Laganside. Departs from the Belfast Welcome Centre.

Titanic Tours (☎ 9065 9971; 07852 716655; www .titanictours-belfast.co.uk; per person £25) A two-hour tour led by the great-granddaughter of one of *Titanic*'s crew, visiting various *Titanic*-related sites, for groups of two to five people; includes pick-up and drop-off at your accommodation.

FESTIVALS & EVENTS

The **Belfast City Council** (☎ 9024 6609; www.belfastcity .gov.uk/events) organises a wide range of events throughout the year, covering everything from the St Patrick's Day parade to the Lord Mayor's Show, and has a very useful online events calendar.

March

Between the Lines (Crescent Arts Centre; ☎ 9024 2338; www.crescentarts.org) Ten-day literary festival.

St Patrick's Carnival (☎ 9043 4767; www.belfastcar nival.com) A celebration of Ireland's patron saint marked by various community festivals and culminating in a grand city-centre parade on 17 March.

Belfast Film Festival (☎ 9032 5913; www.belfastfilm festival.org) A weeklong celebration of Irish and international film making held in late March.

April

Titanic Made In Belfast Festival (☎ 9024 6609; www.belfastcity.gov.uk/titanic) A weeklong celebration held in early/mid April of the world's most famous ship,

and the city that built her, with special exhibitions, tours, lectures and film screenings.

May

Belfast Marathon (☎ 9060 5922; www.belfastcity marathon.com) First Monday in May. Runners from across the globe come to compete, but it's also a people's event, with a walk and fun run as well.

Cathedral Quarter Arts Festival (☎ 9023 2403; www.cqaf.com) Twelve days of drama, music, poetry, street theatre and art exhibitions in and around the Cathedral Quarter. Held in early May.

June

City Dance (Crescent Arts Centre; ☎ 9024 2338; www .crescentarts.org) Free one-day dance festival.

July

Belfast Maritime Festival (☎ 9024 6609; www .belfastcity.gov.uk/maritimefestival) A two-day festival at the beginning of July centred on Queen's Quay and Clarendon Dock, with sailing ships, street entertainment, a seafood festival and live music.

August

Féile an Phobail (☎ 9031 3440; www.feilebelfast .com) Said to be the largest community festival in Ireland, the Féile takes place in West Belfast over 10 days in early August. Events include an opening carnival parade, street parties, theatre performances, concerts, and historical tours of the City and Milltown cemeteries.

October

Belfast Festival at Queen's (☎ 9097 1197; www .belfastfestival.com) The UK's second-largest arts festival held in and around Queen's University over three weeks in late October and early November.

Halloween Carnival (☎ 9024 6609) Held from 27 to 31 October, with special events across the city, including a carnival parade, ghost tours and fireworks.

December

Christmas Festivities (☎ 9024 6609) A range of events from late November to 31 December, including carol singing, lamplight processions and a street carnival.

SLEEPING

From backpacker hostels to boutique hotels, the range of places to stay in Belfast gets wider every year. The traditional accommodation scene – red-brick B&Bs in the leafy suburbs of South Belfast and city-centre business hotels – has been lent a splash of colour in the form of stylish hotel-restaurant-nightclub combos such as Benedicts, and elegant but expensive boutique hotels set in refurbished historic buildings such as Ten Square and the Merchant Hotel.

Most of Belfast's budget and midrange accommodation is south of the centre, in the university district around Botanic Ave, University Rd and Malone Rd. This area is also crammed with good-value restaurants and pubs, and is mostly within a 20-minute walk of City Hall. You can expect to pay around £12 to £15 for a dorm bed in a hostel, approximately £50 to £70 for a double room in a good B&B or guesthouse, and about £80 to £100 for a double in a luxurious midrange hotel. The top-end and more expensive midrange places attract a business clientele during the week, and usually offer lower rates at weekends (Friday to Sunday nights).

Book ahead in summer or during busy festival periods. The Belfast Welcome Centre will make reservations for a fee of £2. You can also book accommodation through the **Lonely Planet website** (http://hotels.lonelyplanet.com).

City Centre

BUDGET

Belfast International Youth Hostel (Map pp570-1; ☎ 9031 5435; www.hini.org.uk; 22-32 Donegall Rd; dm £11-15; s/d from £21/29; 🖳 🛜) Belfast's modern Hostelling International (HI) hostel is conveniently located just off Shaftesbury Sq, which means it can be a bit noisy at night when the pubs and clubs empty. The hostel has a kitchen, a laundry, a cafe and free linen; rates are slightly higher on Friday and Saturday nights. Take bus 9A or 9B from Donegall Sq East or Great Victoria St (across from the Europa BusCentre) to Bradbury Pl.

MIDRANGE

Park Inn (Map pp570-1; ☎ 9067 7710; www.belfast.parkinn .co.uk; 4 Clarence St W; r from £60; 🛜) This brand new hotel boasts a bright and breezy atmosphere, with slick styling and splashes of bold primary colours. It has a top location, too – only five minutes from City Hall and close to loads of good pubs and restaurants – and is excellent value. There are eight wheelchair-accessible rooms, and family rooms can be arranged.

Benedicts (Map pp570-1; ☎ 9059 1999; www.benedicts hotel.co.uk; 7-21 Bradbury Pl; s/d from £70/80; 🖳 🛜) Set bang in the middle of the Golden Mile, Benedicts is a modern, style-conscious hotel at the heart of Belfast's nightlife. The rooms, complete with Egyptian cotton sheets and feather-bedded mattresses, are above a huge Gothic bar and restaurant (where you also have breakfast), so don't expect peace and quiet till after 1am.

ourpick Malmaison Hotel (Map pp570-1; ☎ 9022 0200; www.malmaison-belfast.com; 34-38 Victoria St; r from £95, ste from £315; 🖳 🛜) Housed in a pair of beautifully restored Italianate warehouses (originally built for rival firms in the 1850s), the Malmaison is a luxurious haven of king-size beds, deep leather sofas and roll-top baths big enough for two, all done up in a decadent decor of black, red, dark chocolate and cream. The massive, rock-star Samson suite has a giant bed (almost 3m long), a bathtub big enough for two and, wait for it…a billiard table, with purple baize.

TOP END

Fitzwilliam Hotel (Map pp570-1; ☎ 9044 2080; www.fitzwil liamhotelbelfast.com; 1-3 Great Victoria St; r from £110; 🖳 🛜) A brand new hotel in a truly central location, the Fitzwilliam pushes all the right style buttons with its use of designer fabrics, cool colours and mood lighting. Bedrooms have crisp linen sheets, fluffy bathrobes and powerful showers, and the staff are unstintingly helpful. There's an excellent restaurant, too (p590).

Merchant Hotel (Map pp570-1; ☎ 9023 4888; www .themerchanthotel.com; 35-39 Waring St; r/ste from £160/240; 🅿 🖳 🛜) Belfast's most flamboyant Victorian building, the old Ulster Bank head office, has been converted into the city's most flamboyant boutique hotel, a fabulous fusion of contemporary styling and old-fashioned elegance.

Ten Square (Map pp570-1; ☎ 9024 1001; www.ten square.co.uk; 10 Donegall Sq S; r from £170; 🖳 🛜) A former bank building to the south of City Hall that has been given a designer feng-shui makeover, Ten Square is an opulent, Shanghai-inspired boutique hotel with friendly and attentive service. Magazines such

BELFAST

as *Cosmopolitan* and *Conde Nast Traveller* drool over the dark lacquered wood, cream carpets, low-slung futon-style beds and sumptuous linen, and the list of former guests includes Bono, Moby and Brad Pitt.

South Belfast

To get to places on or near Botanic Ave, take bus 7A or 7B from Howard St. For places on or near University and Malone Rds, take bus 8A or 8B, and for places on or near Lisburn Rd, take bus 9A or 9B; both depart from Donegall Sq E, and from the bus stop on Great Victoria St across from the Europa BusCentre.

BUDGET

Paddy's Palace Belfast (Map pp570–1; ☎ 9033 3367; www.paddyspalace.com; 68 Lisburn Rd; dm £7.50-13.50, d £37; P 🖳 🛜) Paddy's offers clean and comfortable dorms, a big, well-equipped kitchen and a bright and homely common room, though the dorms are a bit gloomy. It has free wi-fi and friendly staff who are happy to point you to the best local pubs. There's no sign outside, so it's easy to miss – bang on the door on Fitzwilliam St, at the corner of Lisburn Rd.

Arnie's Backpackers (Map pp570–1; ☎ 9024 2867; www.arniesbackpackers.co.uk; 63 Fitzwilliam St; dm £9-12; 🖳) This long-established hostel is set in a quiet terraced house in the university area, with plenty of lively bars and restaurants nearby. It's a bit on the small side, but real coal fires, a friendly crowd, and the ever-helpful Arnie himself (and his two cute Jack Russell terriers) make it more cosy than cramped.

ourpick Ark (Map pp570–1; ☎ 9032 9626; www.arkhostel.com; 44 University St; dm £12, s/d £20/32; 🖳 🛜) The Ark is on the corner of University St and Botanic Ave (look for the tiny sign above the door), bang in the heart of Queen's student quarter. It's small, convivial and kitted out with all the mod cons. It has its own internet cafe, and is more family friendly than other hostels; there's also a 2am curfew.

Kate's B&B (Map pp570–1; ☎ 9028 2091; www.katesbnb.com; 127 University St; per person £25) Kate's is a homey kind of place, from the window boxes bursting with colourful flowers to the cute dining room crammed with bric-a-brac and a couple of resident cats. The bedrooms are basic but comfortable, and the showers are a bit cramped, but at this price – and only a few minutes' walk from Botanic Ave – we're not complaining.

MIDRANGE

All Seasons B&B (off Map p570–1; ☎ 9068 2814; www.allseasonsbelfast.com; 356 Lisburn Rd; s/d/f £35/55/65; P) Away from the centre, but right in the heart of trendy Lisburn Rd, All Seasons is a red-brick villa with bright, colourful bedrooms, modern bathrooms, a stylish little breakfast room and a comfortable lounge. Take bus 9A or 9B from the city centre; a taxi will cost around £7. The house is between Cranmore Ave and Cranmore Gardens, 150m past the big police station.

Bienvenue Guesthouse (off Map pp570–1; ☎ 9066 8003; bienvenueguesthouse@hotmail.com; 8 Sans Souci Park; s/d £45/64; P 🖳 🛜) Set in a grand Victorian house with a tree-lined garden in a quiet side street off Malone Rd, the Bienvenue's four rooms offer hotel-standard accommodation, with period antiques (including a half-tester bed in one room), direct-dial phones, 24-hour reception and daily newspapers.

Camera Guesthouse (Map pp570–1; ☎ 9066 0026; www.cameraguesthouse.com; 44 Wellington Park; s/d £48/62; 🛜) A cosy, welcoming Victorian B&B with an open fire in the drawing room, the Camera is set in yet another of South Belfast's peaceful, tree-lined terraced streets. The friendly young couple who own the place manage to create a family-friendly atmosphere, and are a fount of knowledge on what to see and do in town.

ourpick Old Rectory (off Map pp570–1; ☎ 9066 7882; www.anoldrectory.co.uk; 148 Malone Rd; s/d £50/80; P 🖳 🛜) A lovely red-brick Victorian villa with lots of original period features, this former rectory has four spacious bedrooms, a comfortable drawing room with a leather sofa and fancy breakfasts (wild boar sausages, scrambled eggs with smoked salmon, freshly squeezed OJ). It's a 10-minute bus ride from the centre – the inconspicuous driveway is on the left, just past Deramore Park South.

Tara Lodge (Map pp570–1; ☎ 9059 0900; www.taralodge.com; 36 Cromwell Rd; s/d £70/85; P 🖳 🛜) This B&B is a cut above your average South Belfast guesthouse, and feels more like a boutique hotel with its stylish, minimalist decor, friendly, efficient staff, delicious breakfasts, and 28 bright and cheerful rooms. Great location too, on a quiet side street just a few paces from the buzz of Botanic Ave.

Malone Lodge Hotel (Map pp570–1; ☎ 9038 8060; www.malonelodge.com; 60 Eglantine Ave; s/d/apt from £75/85/100; P 🛜) The centrepiece of a tree-lined Victorian terrace, the modern Malone Lodge has pulled in many plaudits for its large, luxurious rooms with elegant gold and navy

---

AIRPORT ACCOMMODATION

Park Plaza Hotel (off Map p600; ☎ 9445 7000; www.parkplazabelfast.com; Belfast International Airport, Aldergrove; r from £70; P ◻ 🛜) Immediately opposite the terminal at Belfast International Airport, the 106-room Park Plaza has a business centre, conference facilities and free courtesy transport to the city centre.

   Park Avenue Hotel (Map p600; ☎ 9065 6520; www.parkavenuehotel.co.uk; 158 Holywood Rd; s/d from £79/99; P 🛜) The classy 56-room Park Avenue is the nearest hotel to Belfast City Airport (3km away), and only 3km east of the city centre.

---

decor, good food and pleasant, helpful staff. It also offers five-star self-catering apartments (both one and two bedroom).

Crescent Town House (Map pp570-1; ☎ 9032 3349; www.crescenttownhouse.com; 13 Lower Cres; s/d/tr from £75/85/110; ◻ 🛜) Another stylish boutique hotel with a perfect location, the Crescent is an elegant Victorian town house transformed into a den of designer chic, with its finger on the pulse of the city's party zone. Rooms have silky, Ralph Lauren–style decor and luxury bathrooms with Molton Brown toiletries and walk-in rain-head showers.

Outside the Centre

Dundonald Touring Caravan Park (Map p600; ☎ 9080 9100; www.theicebowl.com; 111 Old Dundonald Rd, Dundonald; tent/caravan sites £12/20; 🕑 Mar-Oct) This small site (22 pitches) in a park next to the Dundonald Icebowl is the nearest camping ground to Belfast, 7km east of the city centre and south of the A20 road to Newtownards.

   Farset International (Map p580; ☎ 9089 9833; www.farsetinternational.co.uk; 446 Springfield Rd; s/d £34/48; P 🛜) This community-run venture in West Belfast is best described as a posh hostel. The bright, cheerful, modern complex, set in grounds overlooking a small lake, has 38 rooms with private bathroom and TV. Rates include breakfast, and in the evening you can eat in the restaurant or use the self-catering kitchen.

EATING

In recent years, Belfast's restaurant scene has been totally transformed by a wave of new restaurants whose standards compare with the best eating places in Europe.

City Centre

The main shopping area north of Donegall Sq becomes a silent maze of deserted streets and steel shutters after 7pm, but during the day the many pubs, cafes and restaurants do a roaring trade. In the evening, the liveliest part of the city centre stretches south of Donegall Sq to Shaftesbury Sq.

BUDGET

Rhubarb Fresh Food Cafe (Map pp570-1; ☎ 9020 0158; 2 Little Victoria St; mains £3.50-7; 🕑 8am-5pm Mon-Sat & 6pm-late Thu-Sat) Tucked away in a quiet corner, Rhubarb is a great place for tasty, freshly prepared food that's a cut above your usual cafe fare, from breakfasts (banana pancakes, omelettes, scrambled eggs with smoked salmon) to tuna-filled tortilla wraps to hot lunches such as Mediterranean chicken pasta. The dinner menu (mains £12 to £16) takes things up a notch, with dishes like pork and honey sausages with mash and onion gravy or seared scallops with chorizo risotto.

   Archana (Map pp570-1; ☎ 9032 3713; 53 Dublin Rd; mains £6-10; 🕑 noon-2pm & 5pm-midnight Mon-Sat, 5-11pm Sun) A cosy and unpretentious Indian restaurant, Archana offers a good range of vegetarian dishes from its separate 'Little India' menu. The thali – a platter of three curries with rice, naan bread, pakora and dessert – is good value at £14/10 for the meat/veg version.

   Morning Star (Map pp570-1; ☎ 9023 3976; 17 Pottinger's Entry; mains £6-15; 🕑 food served noon-9pm Mon-Sat) This former coaching inn is famed for its all-you-can-eat lunch buffet (£6). The upstairs restaurant features traditional Irish beef (big 700g steaks cost £15), mussels, oysters and eels as well as more unusual things like alligator and ostrich. See also p593.

   La Boca (Map pp570-1; ☎ 9032 3087; 6 Fountain St; mains £7-13; 🕑 10.30am-7pm Mon-Wed, to 9pm Thu, to 10pm Fri & Sat; 🛜) Named for the dockside district in Buenos Aires, this lively, high-ceilinged bistro is decked out with Latin American flags and local art, and has an Argentine-themed menu that includes grilled steak with *chimichurri* (a sauce of oil, garlic, herbs and spices), and grilled swordfish with chorizo, red pepper and olive dressing.

   Gingeroot (Map pp570-1; ☎ 9031 3124; 73-75 Great Victoria St; mains £8-12; 🕑 noon-3pm & 5.30-11.30pm Mon-Sat, 5.30-10.30pm Sun) A bright, modern restaurant that serves fresh and flavourful Indian dishes – the *jeera* (cumin) chicken is particularly tasty. Gingeroot offers an exceptionally good-value two-course lunch, available noon to 3pm Monday to Saturday (£6.50).

MIDRANGE

Oxford Exchange (Map pp570-1; ☎ 9024 0014; 1st fl, St George's Market, Oxford St; mains £9-18; ✆ noon-3pm & 5-11pm Tue-Sat) Smart and stylish with bare pine floors, chocolate brown chairs, white linen napkins and a yellow tulip on each table, the Oxford has breezy charm and a menu of high-end comfort food – try the beer-battered cod with mushy peas, and chunky chips served in a twist of newspaper, or pea, parsley and chervil risotto.

Deane's Deli Bistro (Map pp570-1; ☎ 9024 8800; 44 Bedford St; mains £10-16; ✆ noon-3pm & 5-9pm Mon & Tue, noon-3pm & 5-10pm Wed-Fri, noon-10pm Sat) Enjoy top-notch nosh by celebrity chef Michael Deane without breaking the bank at this relaxed and informal bistro, with gourmet burgers and posh fish and chips on the menu, or just grab a sandwich at the next-door deli.

our pick **Mourne Seafood Bar** (Map pp570-1; ☎ 9024 8544; 34-36 Bank St; mains £10-17; ✆ noon-6pm Mon, to 9.30pm Tue & Wed, to 10.30pm Thu-Sat, 1-6pm Sun) This informal, publike place, all red brick and dark wood with old oil lamps dangling from the ceiling, is tucked behind a fishmonger's shop, so the seafood is as fresh as it gets. On the menu are oysters served au naturel or Rockefeller, meltingly sweet scallops, lobster, langoustines, gurnard and John Dory. Hugely popular, so best book ahead, especially on Sunday.

Ginger (Map pp570-1; ☎ 9024 4421; 7-8 Hope St; mains £12-20; ✆ noon-3pm Tue-Sat & 5-9pm Mon-Sat) Ginger is one of those places you could walk right past without noticing, but if you do you'll be missing out. It's a cosy and informal little bistro with an unassuming exterior, serving food that is anything but ordinary – the flame-haired owner/chef (hence the name) really knows what he's doing, sourcing top-quality Irish produce and turning out exquisite dishes such as salad of seasoned pork belly with fennel and apple, and tempura of hake with pineapple salsa, roast cashews and pickled ginger dressing.

Cayenne (Map pp570-1; ☎ 9033 1532; 7 Ascot House, Shaftesbury Sq; mains £12-20, 2-/3-course lunch £12/15.50; ✆ noon-2.15pm Thu & Fri, 6-11pm Mon-Sat, 5-11pm Sun) Behind an anonymous frosted-glass facade lurks a funky, award-winning restaurant operated by TV celebrity chef, Paul Rankin, decked out in designer black and amber, and clad in conceptual art. The menu concentrates on Irish produce prepared with an Asian or

TOP FIVE BELFAST RESTAURANTS

- Deane's Restaurant (below)
- Menu by Kevin Thornton (below)
- Molly's Yard (opposite)
- Mourne Seafood Bar (left)
- Shu (p592)

Mediterranean twist; the set three-course dinner menu (£20 or £25), available Sunday to Friday, is good value.

TOP END

James St South (Map pp570-1; ☎ 9043 4310; 21 James St S; 2-/3-course lunch £14.50/16.50, dinner mains £15-20; ✆ noon-2.45pm & 5.45-10.45pm Mon-Sat, 5.30-9pm Sun) A starkly beautiful white dining room with crisp white table linen creates a perfect stage for the presentation of some of Belfast's finest food – the French-inspired menu offers dishes such as crisp calamari with tomato and caper dressing, and roast gurnard with leek, fennel and spring onion, while the service is relaxed yet highly professional.

our pick **Deane's Restaurant** (Map pp570-1; ☎ 9033 1134; 34-40 Howard St; mains £15-23, 2-/3-course lunch £18/22; ✆ noon-2.30pm & 6-9.30pm Tue-Sat) Chef Michael Deane heads the kitchen in Northern Ireland's only Michelin-starred restaurant, where he takes the best of Irish and British produce – beef, game, lamb, seafood – and gives it the gourmet treatment. Typical dishes include pan-fried scallops with apple black pudding, glazed pork belly and butternut squash purée, and saddle of rabbit wrapped in bacon with macaroni gratin, roast cep mushrooms and caramelised salsify. The ultra-cool dining room is open-plan and minimalist.

Menu by Kevin Thornton (Map pp570-1; ☎ 9044 2130; Fitzwilliam Hotel, 1-3 Great Victoria St; mains £15-23; ✆ lunch & dinner) The decor in the first-floor restaurant at the new Fitzwilliam Hotel is a bit 'boutique' overload, with tables and floors of polished oak, white linen and lampshades, a black wall, and strikingly tall, slender-backed chairs in bright cerise. But the food is superb, with the freshest Irish produce given the French gourmet treatment – a lunch of celeriac velouté with truffle-scented cream, followed by confit duck with a simple but exquisite mustard sauce, got 10 out of 10 from us.

Great Room (Map pp570-1; ☎ 9023 4888; Merchant Hotel, 35-39 Waring St; mains £16-25; ✆ 7am-11pm) Set in the former banking hall of the Ulster Bank office, the Great Room is a jaw-dropping extravaganza of gilded stucco, red plush, white marble cherubs and a vast crystal chandelier glittering beneath a glass dome. The menu matches the decor: decadent but delicious, a French-influenced catalogue of political incorrectness laced with foie gras, veal, truffles and caviar. A set three-course dinner menu (£25) is available from 6pm to 10pm Monday to Thursday.

Cathedral Quarter & Around

McHugh's Bar and Restaurant (Map pp570-1; ☎ 9050 9999; 29-31 Queen's Sq; mains lunch £7, dinner £10-16; food served noon-10pm Mon-Sat, noon-9pm Sun) This restored pub has a traditional feel with its old wooden booths and benches, and boasts one of the city's best bar-restaurants, serving traditional pub grub downstairs (till 7pm) and fancier dishes in the mezzanine restaurant upstairs (from 5pm).

John Hewitt Bar & Restaurant (Map pp570-1; ☎ 9023 3768; 51 Donegall St; mains £7-9; food served noon-3pm Mon-Sat) Named for the Belfast poet and socialist, this is a modern pub with a traditional atmosphere and a well-earned reputation for excellent food. The menu changes weekly, but includes inventive dishes such as pork and black pepper sausages with buttery mash and red wine gravy, and vegetable fritters with spicy bean casserole. It's also a great place for a drink; see p593.

Hill Street Brasserie (Map pp570-1; ☎ 9058 6868; 38 Hill St; mains lunch £7-9, dinner £13-16; noon-2.30pm Mon-Sat & 5-11pm Tue-Sun) In keeping with the design studios and art galleries that throng the nearby streets, this little brasserie is desperately trendy, from the slate-and-wood floor to the aubergine-and-olive colour scheme. The lunch menu is a bargain, offering a choice of homemade burgers, risotto of the day and a flavoursome and filling seafood chowder.

Nick's Warehouse (Map pp570-1; ☎ 9043 9690; 35-39 Hill St; mains £11-22; food served noon-3pm Mon-Sat & 6-10pm Tue-Sat) A Cathedral Quarter pioneer (opened in 1989), Nick's is an enormous red-brick and blond-wood wine bar and restaurant, buzzing with happy drinkers and diners. The menu is strong on inventive seafood and veggie dishes, such as grilled cod fillet on a king prawn, mussel and noodle laksa, and butternut squash, sage and blue cheese risotto.

No 27 (Map pp570-1; ☎ 9031 2884; 27 Talbot St; mains £15-22; noon-3pm Mon-Fri & 6-10pm Tue-Sat) One of the Cathedral Quarter's most stylish new restaurants, No 27 is a cool confection of red brick and white pillars scattered with locally produced art (most of it for sale). As much thought has gone into the food as the decor, with carefully crafted dishes such as scallop thermidor, and honey-roast duck with stir-fried Asian greens, glass noodles and spicy orange sauce.

South Belfast

BUDGET

Maggie May's (Map pp570-1; ☎ 9032 2662; 50 Botanic Ave; mains £4-6; 8am-10.30pm Mon-Sat, 10am-10.30pm Sun) This is a classic little cafe with two rows of cosy wooden booths, colourful murals of old Belfast, and a host of hungover students wolfing down huge Ulster fries at lunchtime. The all-day breakfast menu runs from tea and toast to eggy bread and maple syrup, while lunch can be soup and a sarnie or steak-and-Guinness pie; puddings include Dime Bar and sticky toffee. BYOB.

Cargoes (off Map pp570-1; ☎ 9066 5451; 613 Lisburn Rd; mains £7-8; 9am-4.30pm Mon-Fri, to 5pm Sat, 10am-3pm Sun) An award-winning deli and cafe neatly dressed up in nautical blue and white decor, Cargoes prides itself on the freshness of its food. The breakfast menu includes waffles, muesli and freshly baked scones, while lunch runs to leek and cheddar tart, and tagliatelle with meatballs.

Cafe Conor (Map pp570-1; ☎ 9066 3266; 11A Stranmillis Rd; mains £9-11; 9am-11pm) Set in the glass-roofed former studio of William Conor, a Belfast artist, this is a laid-back bistro with a light and airy dining area dominated by a portrait of Conor himself. The menu offers a range of pastas, salads, burgers and stir-fries, along with favourites such as fish and chips with mushy peas. The breakfast menu, which includes waffles with bacon and maple syrup, is served till noon on weekdays, 3pm at weekends.

MIDRANGE

Molly's Yard (Map pp570-1; ☎ 9032 2600; 1 College Green Mews; bistro mains £7-9; 2-/3-course dinner £22/27; noon-9pm Mon-Thu, to 9.30pm Fri & Sat) A restored Victorian stables courtyard is the setting for this quirky restaurant, with a cosy bar-bistro on the ground floor, outdoor tables in the yard and a rustic dining room in the airy roof space upstairs. The menu is seasonal and sticks to half a dozen each of starters and mains, ranging from gourmet confections such as warm salad of black pudding with roast apple in curry oil, to hearty comfort food such as homemade hamburgers topped with smoked cheddar and onion jam. It also has its own microbrewery; see p594.

Deane's at Queen's (Map pp570-1; ☎ 9038 2111; 1 College Gardens; mains £12-15; ⊙ noon-3pm Mon-Sat, 5.30-9pm Mon & Tue, 5.30-10pm Wed-Sat) A chilled-out bar and grill from Belfast's top chef, Michael Deane, this place focuses on what could be described as good-value, gourmet pub grub: salt and chilli squid, sirloin steak with blue cheese gratin, green beans and red wine sauce, and smoked haddock and leek fishcake with curried mayonnaise.

ourpick Shu (Map pp570-1; ☎ 9038 1655; 253 Lisburn Rd; mains £14-17; ⊙ noon-2.30pm & 6-9pm Mon-Fri, 7-9.30pm Sat) If you want to know who to blame for all those copycat designer restaurants with the dark-wood-and-chocolate-brown-leather decor, then look no further. Lording it over the hipper-than-than-thou Lisburn Rd since 2000, Shu is the granddaddy of Belfast chic, a stylish restaurant that is still winning awards for its food. The French-influenced menu includes smoked Lough Neagh eel with horseradish cream and beetroot purée, and crispy pork belly with cauliflower purée, potato gratin and cider soaked raisins.

Beatrice Kennedy's (Map pp570-1; ☎ 9020 2290; 44 University Rd; mains £16-19; ⊙ 5-10.15pm Tue-Sat, 12.30-2.30pm & 5-8.15pm Sun) This is where Queen's students take their parents for a smart dinner. It offers a candle-lit Edwardian drawing-room decor of burgundy, bottle green and bare red brick, with polished floorboards, starched white linen and brown leather chairs, and a simple menu of superb cuisine, including homemade bread and ice cream. Enjoy dishes such as smoked haddock and prawn chowder, or pan-fried salmon with basil mash and roast red pepper sauce. There's even a separate vegetarian menu, with dishes such as crispy potato rösti with fine beans, poached egg and truffle hollandaise. From 5pm to 7pm you can get a two-course dinner for £14.

Outside the Centre

An Caife Glas (Map p580; ☎ 9096 4184; Cultúrlann MacAdam Ó Fiaich, 216 Falls Rd, West Belfast; mains £5-7; ⊙ 9am-9pm Mon-Sat, 10am-6pm Sun) If you're exploring West Belfast, drop in to the cafe in this Irish language and arts centre (see p580) for some good home-cooked food – the menu includes stews, soups, pizzas, cakes, scones and fresh pastries.

Cutters Wharf (Map p600; ☎ 9080 5100; 4 Lockview Rd, Stranmillis; bar meals £6-11, dinner mains £9-16; ⊙ food served noon-10pm) One of the few bar-restaurants in Belfast with a waterside setting, Cutters Wharf has a terrace overlooking the River Lagan where you can enjoy a bar meal – try wild boar sausage with champ and gravy, or chicken caesar salad – while watching sculls and eights from the nearby rowing club messing about on the river.

DRINKING

Belfast's pub scene is lively and friendly, with the older traditional pubs complemented – and increasingly threatened – by a rising tide of stylish designer bars.

Standard opening hours are 11am or 11.30am to midnight or 1am, and 12.30pm to 11pm or midnight Sunday; some pubs remain closed all day Sunday, or don't open till 4pm or 6pm.

The worst thing about drinking in Belfast is getting past the bouncers on the door – the huge number of security staff employed in the city means that polite, well-trained doormen are a rarity. Some of the flashier bars have a dress code – usually no sneakers, no jeans, no baseball caps (so that the security cameras can get a clear shot of your face) and definitely no football colours. A few even specify 'No political tattoos'.

City Centre

Crown Liquor Saloon (Map pp570-1; ☎ 9024 9476; 46 Great Victoria St) Belfast's most famous bar has a wonderfully ornate Victorian interior. Despite being a tourist attraction (see p574), it still fills up with crowds of locals at lunchtime and in the early evening.

Garrick Bar (Map pp570-1; ☎ 9032 1984; 29 Chichester St) Established in 1870 but recently refurbished, the Garrick hangs on to a traditional atmosphere with acres of dark wood panelling, tiled floors, a pillared bar and old brass oil lamps. There are snug booths with buttoned leather benches, and a real coal fire in each room. There are traditional music sessions in the front bar from 9.30pm on Wednesday, 5pm to 9pm Friday and 3pm Sunday.

Irene & Nan's (Map pp570-1; ☎ 9023 9123; 12 Brunswick St) Named after two pensioners from a nearby pub who fancied themselves as glamour queens, Irene & Nan's typifies the new breed of Belfast bar, dripping with designer chic and tempting your taste buds with an in-bar bistro. It's a laid-back place with a 1950s

---

TOP FIVE TRADITIONAL PUBS

- Bittle's Bar (below)
- Crown Liquor Saloon (opposite)
- Duke of York (right)
- Kelly's Cellars (below)
- Morning Star (below)

---

retro theme (check out the cool clocks behind the bar), good tunes and good cocktails.

Morning Star (Map pp570-1; ☎ 9023 5986; 17 Pottinger's Entry) One of several traditional pubs hidden away in the pedestrian alleys off High St, the Morning Star dates back to at least 1810 when it was mentioned in the *Belfast News Letter* as a terminal for the Dublin to Belfast stagecoach. It has a big sweeping horseshoe bar, and cosy snugs for privacy. See also p589.

White's Tavern (Map pp570-1; ☎ 9024 3080; 1-4 Wine Cellar Entry) Established in 1630 but rebuilt in 1790, White's claims to be Belfast's oldest tavern (unlike a pub, a tavern provided food and lodging). Downstairs is a traditional Irish bar with an open peat fire, upstairs is all red brick, pine and polished copper, with live trad music Friday to Sunday.

Kelly's Cellars (Map pp570-1; ☎ 9032 4835; 1 Bank St) Kelly's is Belfast's oldest pub (1720) – as opposed to tavern; see White's Tavern above – and was a meeting place for Henry Joy McCracken and the United Irishmen when they were planning the 1798 Rising. The story goes that McCracken hid behind the bar when British soldiers came for him. A bit rough around the edges (a description that could apply to some of the regulars too), it remains resolutely old-fashioned, but pulls in a broad cross-section of Belfast society and is a good bet for impromptu traditional music sessions.

Bittle's Bar (Map pp570-1; ☎ 9031 1088; 103 Victoria St) A cramped and staunchly traditional bar that occupies Belfast's only 'flat iron' building, Bittle's is a 19th-century triangular red-brick building decorated with gilded shamrocks. The wedge-shaped interior is covered in paintings of Ireland's literary heroes by local artist Joe O'Kane. Pride of place on the back wall is a large canvas depicting Yeats, Joyce, Behan and Beckett at the bar with glasses of Guinness, and Wilde pulling the pints on the other side.

Cathedral Quarter & Around

our pick **John Hewitt Bar & Restaurant** (Map pp570-1; ☎ 9023 3768; 51 Donegall St) Named for the Belfast poet and socialist, the John Hewitt is one of those treasured bars that has no TV and no gaming machines; the only noise here is the murmur of conversation. As well as Guinness, the bar serves Hilden real ales from nearby Lisburn, plus Hoegaarden and Erdinger wheat beers. There are regular sessions of folk, jazz and bluegrass from 9pm most nights. See also p591.

Northern Whig (Map pp570-1; ☎ 9050 9888; 2 Bridge St) A stylish modern bar set in an elegant Georgian printing works, the Northern Whig's airy interior is dominated by three huge Socialist-Realist statues rescued from Prague in the early 1990s. Its relaxing sofas and armchairs encourage serious afternoon loafing, though the pace hots up considerably after 5pm on Friday and Saturday when the stag- and hen-party crowd starts knocking back the vodka tonics and alcopops.

Duke of York (Map pp570-1; ☎ 9024 1062; 11 Commercial Ct) Hidden away down an alley in the heart of the city's former newspaper district, the snug, traditional Duke was a hang-out for print workers and journalists and still pulls in a few hacks. One claim to fame is that the Sinn Féin leader, Gerry Adams, worked behind the bar here during his student days.

Spaniard (Map pp570-1; ☎ 9023 2448; 3 Skipper St) Forget 'style': this narrow, crowded bar, which looks as if it's been squeezed into someone's flat, has more atmosphere in one battered sofa than most 'style bars' have in their shiny entirety. Friendly staff, good beer, an eclectic crowd and cool tunes played at a volume that still allows you to talk: bliss. On Sunday from 9pm to midnight is You Say We Play, with the DJ playing requests only.

Rotterdam (Map pp570-1; ☎ 9074 6021; 54 Pilot St) Saved from demolition in 2008 by the credit crunch (which halted construction of the surrounding apartment development), the Rotterdam is a purist's pub, unrepentantly old-fashioned and wonderfully atmospheric, with stone floors, an open fire, low ceilings and a perfectly poured pint of Guinness. It's famed for the quality of its live-music sessions – jazz, folk, rock or blues plays most nights, and in summer the tables, and the gigs, spill outdoors. Get here before the bulldozers do – the Rott's long-term future is far from certain.

BELFAST

South Belfast

Eglantine (Map pp570-1; ☎ 9038 1994; 32 Malone Rd) The 'Eg' is a local institution, and widely reckoned to be the best of Belfast's student pubs. It serves good beer and good food, and there are DJs spinning most nights. Wicked Wednesday pulls in the crowds with an electric rodeo bull, bouncy boxing, sumo-wrestler suits and other fun; Tuesday is the big music and entertainment quiz night. Expect to see a few stag and hen parties stagger through at weekends.

Botanic Inn (Map pp570-1; ☎ 9050 9740; 23-27 Malone Rd) The 'Bot' is the second pillar of Malone Rd's unholy trinity of student pubs, along with the 'Eg' and the 'Welly Park' (Wellington Park). The latter has sadly been renovated into airport-departure-lounge anonymity, but the Bot is still a wild place, with dancing in the upstairs Top of the Bot club Wednesday to Saturday (people queue down the street to get in), live acoustic music in the Back Bar on Monday and Wednesday, and big-screen sport when there's a match on.

Globe (Map pp570-1; ☎ 9050 9848; 36 University Rd) This popular student pub seems to be the karaoke capital of Belfast, with sing-it-yourself sessions six nights a week; the pseudo-1970s decor goes well with the wild retro sessions on Monday nights. On Saturday afternoons sport is the order of the day with football or rugby blaring on half a dozen giant screens.

Molly's Yard (Map pp570-1; ☎ 9032 2600; 1 College Green Mews; ☺ closed Sun) This atmospheric restaurant-bar (see also p591) is home to Northern Ireland's first microbrewery, producing three varieties of real ale – Belfast Blonde (a continental-style lager), Molly's Chocolate Stout and Headless Dog, a dark amber ale with a refreshingly hoppy and slightly flowery flavour.

ENTERTAINMENT

The Belfast Welcome Centre issues *Whatabout?*, a free monthly guide to Belfast events, with pub, club and restaurant listings. The Thursday issue of the *Belfast Telegraph* has an Entertainment section with club, gig and cinema listings, as does the Scene section in Friday's *Irish News*.

The **Big List** (www.thebiglist.co.uk) is a weekly freesheet, published on Wednesday, that covers pubs, clubs and music events all over Northern Ireland, although the emphasis is heavily on Belfast. The **Belfast Beat** (www.adman publishing.com) is a free monthly guide listing what's on where on Friday and Saturday. **ArtsListings** (www.culturenorthernireland.org) is another free monthly that covers the arts scene throughout the whole of Northern Ireland.

Clubbing

Club hours are generally 9pm to 3am, with no admittance after 1am; bouncers can be really picky about who they let in, especially if you're under 21.

QUB Student Union (Map pp570-1; ☎ 0870 241 0126; www.qubsu-ents.com; Mandela Hall, Queen's Students Union, University Rd) The student union has various bars and music venues hosting club nights, live bands and stand-up comedy. The monthly Shine (www.shine.net, admission £10, first Saturday of the month) is one of the city's best club nights with resident and guest DJs pumping out harder and heavier dance music than most of Belfast's other clubs.

Stiff Kitten (Map pp570-1; ☎ 9023 8700; www .thestiffkitten.com; Bankmore Sq, Dublin Rd; admission £10; ☺ 11am-1am Mon-Wed, to 2am Thu, to 2.30am Fri, to 3am Sat, to midnight Sun) If the student union is too grungy a venue for your tastes, head for the Stiff Kitten, a stylish bar and club under the same management as Shine. Same serious attitude to the music, but it's distinctly glitzier, appealing to an over-25 crowd.

Rain (Map pp570-1; ☎ 9032 7308; www.rainnightclub .co.uk; 10-14 Tomb St; admission £5/10 Sun-Fri/Sat; ☺ 9pm-3am) Set in a converted red-brick warehouse, the former Milk has had a stylish makeover and is now operating as a mainstream nightclub with DJs pumping out commercial music for a mixed, over-21s crowd.

La Lea (Map pp570-1; ☎ 9023 0200; www.lalea.com; 43 Franklin St; admission £5; ☺ from 9pm Wed-Sat) Billed as Belfast's most prestigious nightclub, La Lea caters to a cocktail-sipping, style-conscious over-23 crowd (which translates as 'no students'), with a strict door policy to keep out the riff-raff. Impressive decor with space-age lighting and huge Cambodian stone heads.

Gay & Lesbian Venues

Belfast's gay scene is concentrated in the Cathedral Quarter. For information on what's happening, check out www.gaybelfast.net.

Kremlin (Map pp570-1; ☎ 9031 6060; www.kremlin-bel fast.com; 96 Donegall St; ☺ 10pm-2.30am Mon, 9pm-2.30am Tue, 9pm-3am Thu-Sun) Gay-owned and operated, the Soviet-kitsch-themed Kremlin is the heart and soul of Northern Ireland's gay scene. A statue of Lenin guides you into Tsar, the pre-club bar, from where the Long Bar leads into the main clubbing zone, Red Square. There's something going on seven nights a week – Revolution (admission £5) on Saturdays is the flagship event, with DJs mixing up dance, house, pop and commercial till 3am.

Dubarrys Bar (Map pp570-1; ☎ 9032 3590; www .dubarrysbar.co.uk; 10-14 Gresham St) One of Belfast's newest gay venues, Dubarrys is aimed at a slightly older, more sophisticated crowd who are looking for designer decor, cool tunes and conversation, rather than flashing lights and banging dance music.

Mynt (Map pp570-1; ☎ 9023 4520; www.myntbelfast .com; 2-16 Dunbar St) A complex with a vast, luxurious lounge bar and two club spaces, Mynt provides entertainment throughout the week, culminating in hilarious Friday-night game shows hosted by Belfast's favourite drag queen, Baroness Titti von Tramp. Kitty Killer (admission £5; first Friday of the month) is a ladies-only lesbian club night.

Union Street (Map pp570-1; ☎ 9031 6060; www.union streetpub.com; 8-14 Union St) A stylish modern bar with retro styling and lots of bare brick and dark wood – check out the Belfast sinks in the loo – Union Street pulls in a mixed gay and straight crowd, attracted by the laid-back atmosphere and good food.

Other gay-friendly pubs include the **Nest** (Map pp570-1; ☎ 9032 5491; 22-28 Skipper St), the John Hewitt (p593) and the Spaniard (p593).

Live Music & Comedy

Big-name bands and performers play to sell-out crowds at the Ulster Hall, Waterfront Hall, Odyssey Arena or King's Hall.

MAJOR VENUES

Waterfront Hall (Map pp570-1; ☎ 9033 4455; www .waterfront.co.uk; 2 Lanyon Pl) The impressive 2235-seat Waterfront is Belfast's flagship concert venue, hosting local, national and international performers from pop stars to symphony orchestras.

Ulster Hall (Map pp570-1; ☎ 9033 4455; www.ulster hall.co.uk; Bedford St) Ulster Hall (built in 1862) is a popular venue for a range of events including rock concerts, lunchtime organ recitals, boxing bouts and performances by the Ulster Orchestra (www.ulster-orchestra.org.uk).

Odyssey Arena (Map pp570-1; ☎ 9073 9074; www .odysseyarena.com; 2 Queen's Quay) The home stadium for the Belfast Giants ice-hockey team is also the venue for big entertainment events such

as rock and pop concerts, stage shows and indoor sports.

King's Hall (Map p600; ☎ 9066 5225; www.kingshall .co.uk; Lisburn Rd) Northern Ireland's biggest exhibition and conference centre hosts a range of music shows, trade fairs and sporting events. It's accessible by any bus along Lisburn Rd or by train to Balmoral Station.

ROCK

Belfast Empire (Map pp570-1; ☎ 9024 9276; www .thebelfastempire.com; 42 Botanic Ave; admission live bands £5-20) A converted late-Victorian church with three floors of entertainment, the Empire is a legendary live-music venue. The regular Thursday night Gifted session showcases the best of new talent, both local and UK-wide, while Saturday is either big-name bands or tribute bands. There's stand-up comedy every Tuesday at 8pm (admission £7).

Limelight (Map pp570-1; ☎ 9032 5942; www.the-lime light.co.uk; 17-19 Ormeau Ave) This combined pub and club, along with next-door venue the Spring and Airbrake (under the same management), is one of the city's top venues for live rock and indie music, having hosted bands from Oasis to Franz Ferdinand, the Manic Street Preachers and the Kaiser Chiefs. It's also home to alternative club night Helter Skelter (admission £5, from 10pm every Saturday) and Belfast's biggest student night, Shag (admission £3, from 10pm every Tuesday).

Lavery's (Map pp570-1; ☎ 9087 1106; www.laverys belfast.com; 14 Bradbury Pl) Managed by the same family since 1918, Lavery's is a vast, multilevel, packed-to-the-gills boozing emporium, crammed with drinkers young and old, from students to tourists, businessmen to bikers. The Back Bar has live acoustic music from local singer-songwriters on Wednesday and live indie and alternative bands on Thursday, while the Bunker stages various local and touring bands Sunday to Thursday and DJs Friday and Saturday.

FOLK, JAZZ & BLUES

Pubs with regular live sessions of traditional Irish music include the Botanic Inn, the Garrick Bar, White's Tavern, the John Hewitt, Kelly's Cellars and the Rotterdam (see pp592-3).

For jazz and blues, head for the John Hewitt, McHugh's, the Rotterdam, the Crescent Arts Centre (p596) or the **Kitchen Bar** (Map pp570-1; ☎ 9032 4901; www.thekitchenbar.com; 38 Victoria Sq).

BELFAST

GETTING INTO IRISH CULTURE

An Droichead (Map pp570-1; ☎ 9028 8818; www.androichead.com; 20 Cooke St; tickets £8.50-15) is a new centre in South Belfast, dedicated to Irish language, music and culture. It offers courses in Irish Gaelic, stages traditional dance and ceilidh workshops, hosts art exhibitions and also serves as a live music venue – it's a great place to hear live Irish folk music, not only big names from around the country, but also up-and-coming local talent. Check the website, or pick up a flyer from the Belfast Welcome Centre.

CLASSICAL MUSIC

Queen's University's **School of Music** (Map pp570-1; ☎ 9097 5337; www.music.qub.ac.uk; University Rd) stages free lunchtime recitals on Thursday and regular evening concerts in the beautiful, hammer-beam-roofed Harty Room (School of Music, University Sq), and at the Sonic Arts Research Centre (Cloreen Park), with occasional performances in the larger Sir William Whitla Hall (University Rd). Download a Music at Queen's program from the website.

COMEDY

There's no dedicated comedy club in the city, but there are regular comedy nights at various venues including the **Spring and Airbrake** (Map pp570-1; Ormeau Ave), the Belfast Empire (p595), and the QUB Student Union (p594).

Opera & Theatre

Grand Opera House (Map pp570-1; ☎ 9024 1919; www .goh.co.uk; 2-4 Great Victoria St; ☒ box office 8.30am-9pm Mon-Fri, to 6pm Sat) This grand old venue plays host to a mixture of opera, popular musicals and comedy shows. The box office is across the street on the corner of Howard St.

Lyric Theatre (Map p600; ☎ 9038 1081; www.lyrictheatre .co.uk; 55 Ridgeway St) The old Lyric Theatre, where Hollywood star Liam Neeson first trod the boards (he is now a patron), has been demolished; a new theatre is being built on the same site, and should be open by early 2011.

Old Museum Arts Centre (Map pp570-1; ☎ 9023 3332; www.oldmuseumartscentre.org; 7 College Sq N; ☒ box office 9.30am-5.30pm Mon-Sat, to 7.30pm before a performance) The Old Museum stages an exciting program of drama and comedy, with occasional prose and poetry readings and dance performances.

Crescent Arts Centre (Map pp570-1; ☎ 9024 2338 www.crescentarts.org; 2-4 University Rd) The Crescent hosts a range of concerts, plays, workshops, readings and dance classes. The Crescent also stages a 10-day literary festival called Between the Lines each March, and a dance festival, City Dance, in June.

Black Box (Map pp570-1; ☎ 9024 4400; www.black boxbelfast.com; 18-22 Hill St) Describing itself as a 'home for live music, theatre, literature, comedy, film, visual art, live art, circus, cabaret and all points in between', Black Box is an intimate venue in the heart of the Cathedral Quarter.

Cinemas

Movie House (Map pp570-1; ☎ 9024 5700; www .moviehouse.co.uk; 14 Dublin Rd) A convenient city-centre 10-screen multiplex.

Queen's Film Theatre (Map pp570-1; ☎ 9097 1097; www.queensfilmtheatre.com; 20 University Sq) A two-screen art-house cinema close to the university, and a major venue for the Belfast Film Festival.

Storm Cinemas (Map pp570-1; ☎ 9073 9134; www .stormcinemas.co.uk; Odyssey Pavilion) Belfast's biggest multiplex, with 12 screens and stadium seats throughout; part of the Odyssey Complex.

Sport

Rugby, soccer, Gaelic football and hockey are played through the winter, cricket and hurling through the summer.

Windsor Park (Map p580; ☎ 9024 4198; off Lisburn Rd) International soccer matches take place here, south of the centre; for details of Northern Ireland international matches, see www .irishfa.com.

Casement Park (Map p600; ☎ 9038 3815; www .antrimgaa.net; Andersonstown Rd) In West Belfast; you can see Gaelic football and hurling here.

Odyssey Arena (Map pp570-1; ☎ 9073 9074; www.odyssey arena.com; 2 Queen's Quay) The Belfast Giants ice hockey team draws big crowds to the arena at the Odyssey Complex; the season is September to March. The arena also hosts indoor sporting events including tennis and athletics.

SHOPPING

For general shopping you'll find all the usual high-street chains and department stores in the compact central shopping area north of City Hall. The main shopping malls are the **Castle Court Centre** (Map pp570-1; Royal Ave) and the new **Victoria Square** (Map pp570-1; btwn Ann & Chichester St). There's late-night shopping till 9pm on Thursdays.

Other shopping districts include the ultra-hip Lisburn Rd (from Eglantine Ave out to Balmoral Ave) – a long strip of red-brick and mock-Tudor facades lined with fashion boutiques, interior-design shops, art galleries, delicatessens, espresso bars, wine bars and chic restaurants – and the unexpected concentration of designer fashion shops (about a dozen of them) on Bloomfield Ave in East Belfast.

Items particular to Northern Ireland that you may like to look out for include fine Belleek china, linen (antique and new) and Tyrone crystal.

Wicker Man (Map pp570-1; ☎ 9024 3550; 44-46 High St; 🕑 9am-5.30pm Mon-Wed & Fri, to 9pm Thu, to 5.30pm Sat, 1-5.30pm Sun) This shop sells a wide range of contemporary Irish crafts and gifts, including silver jewellery, glassware and knitwear.

Fresh Garbage (Map pp570-1; ☎ 9024 2350; 24 Rosemary St; 🕑 10.30am-5.30pm Mon-Wed, Fri & Sat, to 8pm Thu) Easily recognised by the glumfest of Goths hovering outside the door, this place has been around for more than 20 years but remains a cult favourite for hippie and Goth clothes, band T-shirts and Celtic jewellery.

Steensons (Map pp570-1; ☎ 9024 8269; Bedford House, Bedford St; 10am-5.30pm Mon-Sat, to 7pm Thu) Showroom selling a range of stylish handmade jewellery in contemporary designs in silver, gold and platinum, from a workshop in Glenarm, County Antrim (p665).

Archive's Antique Centre (Map pp570-1; ☎ 9023 2383; 88 Donegall Pass; 🕑 10.30am-5.30pm Mon-Fri, 10am-6pm Sat) This is a warren of curios and collectables spread over three floors, with Irish silver, brass, pub memorabilia, militaria, books and light fittings.

Tiso (Map pp570-1; ☎ 9023 1230; 12-14 Cornmarket; 🕑 9.30am-5.30pm Mon, Tue, Fri & Sat, 10am-5.30pm Wed, 9.30am-8pm Thu, 1-5pm Sun) Make tracks to Tiso for hiking, climbing and camping gear and outdoor clothing.

Surf Mountain (Map pp570-1; ☎ 9024 8877; 12 Brunswick St; 🕑 9am-5.30pm Mon-Sat) Yo dude – come and join the goatee-stroking, nad-scratching crew checking out Surf Mountain's skate and snowboard gear.

Black & Lizars (Map pp570-1; ☎ 9032 1768; 8 Wellington Pl; 🕑 9am-5.30pm Mon-Sat) The place to go for all your photographic needs, both film and digital.

Matchetts Music (Map pp570-1; ☎ 9026 8661; 6 Wellington Pl; 🕑 9am-5.30pm Mon-Sat) Stocks a range of acoustic instruments, from guitars and mandolins to penny whistles and bodhráns,

as well as books of lyrics and guitar chords for traditional Irish songs.

Good Vibes (Map pp570-1; ☎ 9023 9308; 13 Winetavern St; 10am-5pm Mon-Sat) Owned by music producer Terry Hooley, the man who released *Teenage Kicks* by the Undertones on his Good Vibrations label back in 1978, this is Belfast's best alternative record shop and a source of tickets and info on the latest gigs.

Other good places to shop for Irish crafts and traditional Irish music include Cultúrlann MacAdam Ó Fiaich (p580; open 9am to 5.30pm Monday to Friday, 10am to 5.30pm Saturday) and Conway Mill (p580; open 10am to 4pm Monday to Friday).

GETTING THERE & AWAY
Air
Flights from North America, continental Europe and several major UK airports land at **Belfast International Airport** (off Map p600; ☎ 9448 4848; www.belfastairport.com; Aldergrove), 30km northwest of the city. For further information, see p714.

There are direct flights from Cork and most British cities to the convenient **George Best Belfast City Airport** (Map p600; ☎ 9093 9093; www.belfastcityairport.com; Airport Rd), just 6km northeast of the city centre.

Boat
The terminal for **Stena Line** (Map p600; ☎ 08705 707070; www.stenaline.co.uk) car ferries from Belfast to Stranraer in Scotland is 2km north of the city centre; head north along York St, and turn right into Dock St (just past the Yorkgate Centre). Other car ferries to and from Scotland dock at Larne, 37km north of Belfast (see p717).

Norfolkline (Map p600; ☎ 0844 499 0007; www.norfolkline-ferries.co.uk) ferries between Belfast and Liverpool dock at the Victoria Ferry Terminal, 5km north of town. Take the M2 motorway north and turn right at junction No 1.

The **Steam Packet Company** (Map pp570-1; ☎ 0871 222 1333; www.steam-packet.com) operates car ferries between Belfast and Isle of Man (two or three a week, April to September only). They dock at Donegall Quay, a short distance from the city centre.

For more information on ferry routes and prices, see p717.

Bus
Belfast has two bus stations. The main **Europa BusCentre** (Map pp570-1; ☎ 9066 6630) is behind the Europa Hotel and next door to Great

BELFAST

Victoria St train station, reached via the Great Northern Mall beside the hotel. It's the main terminus for buses to Derry, Dublin and destinations in the west and south of Northern Ireland. The smaller **Laganside BusCentre** (Map pp570-1; ☎ 9066 6630; Oxford St), near the river, is mainly for buses to County Antrim, eastern County Down and the Cookstown area.

There are **information desks** (7.45am-6.30pm Mon-Fri, 8am-6pm Sat) at both bus stations, where you can pick up regional bus timetables, and you can contact **Translink** (☎ 9066 6630; www.translink.co.uk) for timetable and fares information.

Typical one-way fares from Belfast:

Service	Fare (£)	Duration (hr)	Frequency
Armagh	8	1¼	hourly Mon-Fri, 6 Sat, 4 Sun
Ballycastle	9	2	3 daily Mon-Fri, 2 Sat
Bangor	3.30	¾	half-hourly Mon-Sat, 8 Sun
Derry	10	1¾	half-hourly Mon-Sat, 11 Sun
Downpatrick	5.10	1	at least hourly Mon-Sat, 6 Sun
Dublin	13	3	hourly Mon-Sun
Enniskillen	10	2¼	hourly Mon-Sat, 2 Sun
Newcastle	7	1¼	hourly Mon-Sat, 8 Sun

National Express (☎ 0870 580 8080; www.nationalexpress .com) runs a daily coach service between Belfast and London (£38, 14 hours) via the Stranraer ferry, Dumfries, Carlisle, Preston, Manchester and Birmingham. The ticket office is in the Europa BusCentre.

For information on bus fares, durations and frequencies in Ireland, see p719.

Train

Trains to Dublin and all destinations in Northern Ireland depart from **Belfast Central Station** (Map pp570-1; East Bridge St), east of the city centre. **Great Victoria St Station** (Map pp570-1; Great Northern Mall), next to the Europa BusCentre, has trains for Portadown, Lisburn, Bangor, Larne Harbour and Derry.

For information on train fares and timetables, contact **Translink** (☎ 9066 6630; www.translink.co .uk). The **NIR Travel Shop** (Map pp570-1; ☎ 9023 0671; Great Victoria St Station; 9am-5pm Mon-Fri, to 12.30pm Sat) books train tickets, ferries and holiday packages.

If you arrive by train at Central Station, your rail ticket entitles you to a free bus ride into the city centre.

Typical train fares from Belfast:

Service	Fare (£)	Duration (hr)	Frequency
Bangor	5	½	half-hourly Mon-Sat, hourly Sun
Derry	10	2¼	7 or 8 daily Mon-Sat, 4 Sun
Dublin	28	2	8 daily Mon-Sat, 5 Sun
Larne Harbour	6	1	hourly
Newry	9	¾	8 daily Mon-Sat, 5 Sun
Portrush	10	1¾	7 or 8 daily Mon-Sat, 4 Sun

On Sundays you can buy a Sunday Day Tracker ticket (£5), which allows unlimited travel on all scheduled train services within Northern Ireland.

For more information on the train network in Ireland, see p723.

GETTING AROUND

Belfast possesses a rare but wonderful thing – an integrated public-transport system, with buses linking both airports to the central train and bus stations.

To/From the Airports

The Airport Express 300 bus runs from Belfast International Airport to the Europa BusCentre (one way/return £7/10, 30 minutes) every 10 or 15 minutes between 7am and 8pm, every 30 minutes from 8pm to 11pm, and hourly through the night; a return ticket is valid for one month. A taxi costs about £25.

The Airport Express 600 bus links George Best Belfast City Airport with the Europa BusCentre (one way/return £1.50/2.60, 15 minutes) every 15 or 20 minutes between 6am and 10pm. The taxi fare to the city centre is about £7.

For details of the Airporter bus linking both airports to Derry, see p646.

To/From the Ferry Terminals

You can walk from Donegall Quay to City Hall in about 15 minutes. Alternatively, Laganside BusCentre is only a five-minute walk away. There is no public transport to the Stena Line and Norfolk Line ferry terminals.

Trains to the ferry terminal at Larne Harbour depart from Great Victoria St Station.

Bicycle

National Cycle Network route 9 runs through central Belfast, mostly following the western bank of the River Lagan and the north shore of Belfast Lough.

You can hire bikes from **McConvey Cycles** (Map pp570-1; ☎ 9033 0322; www.mcconveycycles.com; 183 Ormeau Rd; ◷ 9am-6pm Mon-Sat, to 8pm Thu) for around £15 a day, or £60 a week.

Bus

Metro (☎ 9066 6630; www.translink.co.uk) operates the bus network in Belfast. An increasing number of buses are low-floor, 'kneeling' buses with space for one wheelchair.

Buy your ticket from the driver (change given); fares range from £1.30 to £1.90 depending on distance. The driver can also sell you a Metro Day Ticket (£3.50), giving you unlimited bus travel within the City Zone all day Monday to Saturday. Cheaper versions allow travel any time after 10am Monday to Saturday (£2.70), or all day Sunday (£2.70).

Most city bus services depart from various stops on and around Donegall Sq, at City Hall. You can pick up a free bus map (and buy tickets) from the **Metro kiosk** (Map pp570-1; ◷ 8am-5.30pm Mon-Fri) at the northwest corner of the square.

If you plan on using city buses a lot, it's worth buying a Smartlink Travel Card (available from the Metro kiosk, the Belfast Welcome Centre, and the Europa and Laganside BusCentres). The card costs an initial fee of £1.50, plus £5.50/11 per five/ten journeys – you can get it topped up as you want. Alternatively, you can get seven days' unlimited travel for £16. When you board the bus, you simply place the card on top of the ticket machine, and it automatically issues a ticket.

Car & Motorcycle

A car can be more of a hindrance than a help in Belfast, as parking is restricted in the city centre. For on-street parking between 8am and 6pm Monday to Saturday, you'll need to buy a ticket from a machine. For longer periods, head for one of the many multistorey car parks that are dotted around the city centre.

Major car hire agencies in Belfast:

Avis (www.avis.co.uk) City (Map pp570-1; ☎ 0870 608 6374; 69-71 Great Victoria St); George Best Belfast City Airport (☎ 0844 544 6028); Belfast International Airport (☎ 0844 544 6012)

Budget (www.budget-ireland.co.uk) City (Map pp570-1; ☎ 9023 0700; 96-102 Great Victoria St); George Best Belfast City Airport (☎ 9045 1111); Belfast International Airport (☎ 9442 3332)

Europcar (www.europcar.co.uk) George Best Belfast City Airport (☎ 9073 9400); Belfast International Airport (☎ 9442 2285)

Hertz (www.hertz.co.uk) George Best Belfast City Airport (☎ 9073 2451); Belfast International Airport (☎ 9442 2533)

The Ireland-wide agency **Dooley Car Rentals** (☎ 0800 0778 774; www.dooleycarrentals.com; Airport Rd,

---

PEOPLE'S TAXIS

The black taxis that cruise along the Falls and Shankill Rds in West Belfast have more in common with Turkey's 'dolmuş' minibuses than the black cabs of London. These are shared taxis that operate along fixed routes, departing only when full, then dropping off and picking up passengers as they go, more like buses than traditional taxis.

Indeed, the 'People's Taxis', as they became known, were introduced in the 1970s to replace local bus services that had been disrupted or cancelled as a result of street riots at the height of the Troubles. The drivers' associations that ran the taxis were community-based ventures that provided much-needed employment during difficult times, and often gave jobs to ex-internees and prisoners who could not find work elsewhere. More than 30 years on, the black taxis are an accepted part of Belfast's public transport infrastructure. There is even a black taxi 'bus station' at Castle Junction.

Falls Rd People's Taxis (www.wbta.net) depart from Castle Junction at the corner of King and Castle Sts. During the day a sign in the windscreen shows their route; after 5.30pm the first person in the queue dictates the destination. You can hail a taxi anywhere; when you want to get out, knock on the window, and then pay the driver from the footpath.

Shankill Rd People's Taxis depart from North St. You can hail them at bus stops; when you want to get out, say 'next stop' to the driver, and pay before you get out. Fares on both services are around £1 to £2 per person.

Belfast International Airport, Aldergrove) is reliable and offers good rates – around £130 a week for a compact car, with no extra charge for driving cross-border to the Republic. You have to pay an extra £55 up front for a full tank of petrol, but if you return the car with an almost empty tank they're cheaper than the big names.

Taxi

For information on the black cabs that ply the Falls and Shankill Rds, see boxed text, p599. Regular black taxis have yellow plates back and front and can be hailed on the street.

Minicabs are cheaper, but you have to order one by phone. Companies to call include **Fona Cab** (☎ 9033 3333) and **Value Cabs** (☎ 9080 9080).

Train

There are local trains every 20 or 30 minutes connecting Great Victoria St and Central Stations via City Hospital and Botanic Stations. There's a flat fare of £1.30 for journeys between any of these stops.

AROUND BELFAST

LISBURN & AROUND

The southwestern fringes of Belfast extend as far as Lisburn (Lios na gCearrbhach), 12km southwest of the city centre. **Lisburn Tourist Information Centre** (☎ 9266 0038; Lisburn Sq; 9.30am-5pm Mon-Sat) is on the town's main square.

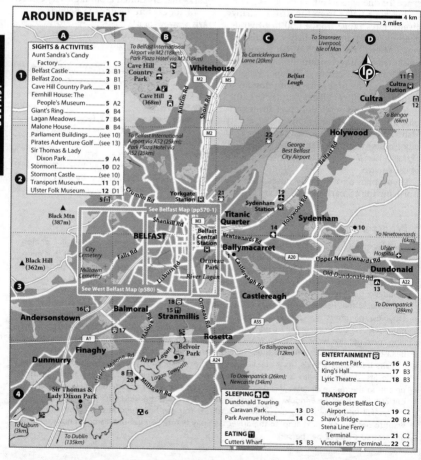

Like Belfast, Lisburn grew rich on the proceeds of the linen industry in the 18th and 19th centuries. This history is celebrated in the excellent **Irish Linen Centre & Lisburn Museum** (☎ 9266 3377; Market Sq; admission free; ☯ 9.30am-5pm Mon-Sat), housed in the fine 17th-century Market House.

The museum on the ground floor has displays on the cultural and historic heritage of the region, while upstairs the award-winning 'Flax to Fabric' exhibition details the fascinating history of the linen industry in Northern Ireland – on the eve of WWI Ulster was the largest linen-producing region in the world, employing some 75,000 people.

There are plenty of audiovisual and hands-on exhibits – you can watch weavers working on Jacquard looms and even try your hand at spinning flax.

Buses 523, 530 and 532 from Belfast's Upper Queen St go to Lisburn (£2.60, 40 minutes, half-hourly Monday to Friday, hourly Saturday and Sunday), or catch the train (£3.50, 30 minutes, at least half-hourly Monday to Saturday, hourly Sunday) from either Belfast Central or Great Victoria St Stations.

ULSTER FOLK & TRANSPORT MUSEUMS

Two of Northern Ireland's finest **museums** (Map p600; ☎ 9042 8428; www.uftm.org.uk; Cultra, Holywood; per museum adult/child £5.40/3.40, combined ticket £6.80/3.90; ☯ 10am-6pm Mon-Sat, 11am-6pm Sun Jul-Sep, 10am-4pm Mon-Fri, 10am-5pm Sat, 11am-5pm Sun Oct-Feb, 10am-5pm Mon-Fri, 10am-6pm Sat, 11am-6pm Sun Mar-Jun) lie close to each other on either side of the A2.

On the south side is the Folk Museum, where farmhouses, forges, churches and mills, and a complete village have been reconstructed, with human and animal extras combining to give a strong impression of Irish life over the past few hundred years. From industrial times, there are red-brick terraces from 19th-century Belfast and Dromore. In summer, thatching and ploughing are demonstrated and there are characters dressed in period costume.

On the other side of the road is the Transport Museum, a sort of automotive zoo with displays of captive steam locomotives, rolling stock, motorcycles, trams, buses and cars.

The highlight of the car collection is the stainless steel–clad prototype of the ill-fated DeLorean DMC, made in Belfast in 1981. The car was a commercial disaster but achieved fame in the *Back to the Future* films.

Most popular is the **RMS Titanic display** (www.titanicinbelfast.com), which includes the original design drawings for the *Olympic* and the *Titanic*, photographs of the ship's construction and reports of its sinking. Most poignant are the items of pre-sailing publicity, including an ad for the return trip that never was.

Buses to Bangor stop nearby. Cultra Station on the Belfast to Bangor train line is within a 10-minute walk.

BELFAST

Counties Down & Armagh

From the hilltop viewpoint of Scrabo Tower, the treasures of County Down lie scattered around you like jewels on a table. The sparkling, island-fringed waters of Strangford Lough stretch to the south, with the bird-haunted mudflats of Castle Espie and Nendrum's ancient monastery on one shore, and the picturesque Ards Peninsula with the elegant country house of Mount Stewart on the other.

On a clear day you can see the Mourne Mountains in the distance, their velvet curves sweeping down to the sea, above the Victorian-era seaside resort of Newcastle. This compact range of granite and heather peaks offers the best hill walking in the North, with expansive views of mountain, crag and sea. Nearby are Downpatrick and Lecale, the old stamping grounds of Ireland's patron saint.

Down is a region of lush fields and fertile farmland, a rich landscape in more ways than one – this is Belfast's wealthy hinterland, studded with expensive villas and endowed with more than its fair share of top golf courses and gourmet restaurants. It's easily reached from the capital, and at weekends you'll find city folks browsing the antique shops in Saintfield and Greyabbey, or slurping down fresh oysters in Dundrum and Strangford.

Down's neighbour County Armagh is largely rural, from the low, rugged hills of the south to the lush apple orchards and strawberry fields of the north, with Ireland's ecclesiastical capital, the neat little city of Armagh, in the middle. With the army watchtowers gone, south Armagh is once again a peaceful backwater, where you can wander back and forth across the border with the Republic without even noticing.

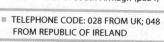

HIGHLIGHTS

- **Head for the Hills** Tempting trails among the granite peaks of the Mourne Mountains (p620)

- **A Taste of Ulster** Top-notch restaurants in Hillsborough (opposite), Warrenpoint (p623) and Strangford (p616)

- **To the Manor Born** The stately halls and exquisite gardens of Mount Stewart House (p611)

- **Wildlife Encounter** Birdwatching at Castle Espie (p612) and seal spotting near Portaferry (p609)

- **Rural Retreat** Off the beaten track on the back roads of South Armagh (p624)

■ TELEPHONE CODE: 028 FROM UK; 048 FROM REPUBLIC OF IRELAND	■ POPULATION: 652,000	■ AREA: 3702 SQ KM

COUNTY DOWN

CENTRAL COUNTY DOWN

Rich farmland spreads to the south of Belfast, with only the rough moorland of Slieve Croob, southwest of Ballynahinch, breaking the flatness of the terrain. The attractive towns of Hillsborough and Banbridge lie on the main A1 road from Belfast to Newry.

Hillsborough

pop 2400

Hillsborough is a name familiar to British ears, as it is the official residence of the Secretary of State for Northern Ireland – Hillsborough Castle is also used to entertain visiting heads of state (US presidents George W Bush and Bill Clinton have both enjoyed its hospitality). This is the Queen's official residence when she is in Northern Ireland.

The elegant little town of Hillsborough (Cromghlinn) was founded in the 1640s by Colonel Arthur Hill, who built a fort here to quell Irish insurgents. Fine Georgian architecture rings the square and lines Main St.

The **tourist information centre** (☎ 9268 9717; tic.hillsborough@lisburn.gov.uk; The Square; ☾ 9am-5.30pm Mon-Sat year-round, 2-6pm Sun Jul & Aug) is in the Georgian courthouse in the centre of the village.

SIGHTS & ACTIVITIES

The town's main attraction is **Hillsborough Castle** (☎ 9268 1309; Main St; guided tour adult/family £5/12.50, grounds only adult/family £2.50/7.50; ☾ 11am-4.30pm Sat May & Jun only), a rambling, two-storey late-Georgian mansion built in 1797 for Wills Hill, the first Marquess of Downshire, and extensively remodelled in the 1830s and 1840s. The guided tour takes in the state drawing room and dining rooms, and the Lady Grey Room where UK prime minister Tony Blair and US president George W Bush had talks on Iraq in 2003.

Hillsborough Courthouse (☎ 9268 9717; tic.hillsborough@lisburn.gov.uk; The Square; admission free; ☾ 9am-5.30pm Mon-Sat year-round, 2-6pm Sun Jul & Aug), a fine old Georgian building, houses various displays describing the working of the courts in the 18th and 19th centuries.

At the bottom of Main St is a statue of Arthur Hill, fourth Marquess of Downshire, opposite a tree-lined avenue leading to **St Malachy's Parish Church** (Main St; admission free; ☾ 9am-5.30pm Mon-Sat), one of Ireland's most splendid 18th-century churches, with twin towers at the ends of the transepts and a graceful spire at the western end.

Close to the church is **Hillsborough Fort** (☎ 9268 3285; Main St; admission free; ☾ 10am-7pm Tue-Sat, 2-7pm Sun Apr-Sep, 10am-4pm Tue-Sat, 2-4pm Sun Oct-Mar). It was built as an artillery fort by Colonel Hill in 1650 and remodelled as a Gothic-style tower house in 1758.

FESTIVALS

Each year in late August/early September, around 10,000 people – plus 6000 oysters from Dundrum Bay – converge on Hillsborough for a three-day **Oyster Festival** (www.hillsboroughoysterfestival.com), a celebration of local food, drink and general good fun, which includes an international oyster-eating competition.

SLEEPING & EATING

Hillsborough is a bit of a culinary hot spot, with several excellent restaurants. These are popular places, so book a table at weekends to avoid disappointment.

our pick **Fortwilliam Country House** (☎ 9268 2255; www.fortwilliamcountryhouse.com; 210 Ballynahinch Rd; s/d £50/70; P 🖳 🛜) The Fortwilliam offers B&B in four luxurious rooms stuffed with period furniture – our favourite is the Victorian room, with its rose wallpaper, huge antique mahogany wardrobe and view over the garden. Your host's hospitality knows no bounds, and breakfast includes fresh eggs from the chickens in the yard, with the smell of home-baked wheaten bread wafting from the Aga. Book well in advance.

our pick **Plough Inn** (☎ 9268 2985; 3 The Square; mains bar £7-9, restaurant £13-18; ☾ bar lunches noon-2.30pm, restaurant 6-9.30pm) This fine old pub, with its maze of dark wood-panelled nooks and crannies, has been offering 'beer and banter' since 1758. It serves gourmet bar lunches – how about seared pheasant breast with mushroom mash and green peppercorn sauce? – and also offers fine dining in the restaurant around the back, where stone walls, low ceilings and a roaring fireplace make a cosy setting for an adventurous menu ranging from sushi to steak.

Hillside Bar & Restaurant (☎ 9268 2765; 21 Main St; bar meals £8-11, 3-course dinner £30; ☾ bar meals noon-2.30pm & 4.30-9pm, restaurant 7.30-9.30pm Fri & Sat) This is a homely pub serving real ale (and mulled wine beside the fireplace in winter), with live jazz Sunday evenings and a dinky wee beer garden in a cobbled courtyard out the back. The upstairs restaurant offers formal dining, with crisp white table linen and sparkling crystal, and a menu offering dishes such as lobster tart, roast quail, venison and steak.

GETTING THERE & AWAY
Goldline Express bus 238 from Belfast's Europa BusCentre to Newry stops at Hillsborough (£3, 25 minutes, at least hourly Monday to Saturday, eight Sunday).

Banbridge & Around
Banbridge (Dróichead na Banna) is another handsome 18th-century town, whose fortunes were founded on the linen trade.

The **tourist information office** (☎ 40623322; tic@ban bridge.gov.uk; 200 Newry Rd; ☺ 10am-5pm Mon-Sat & 1-5pm Sun Oct-May, to 6pm Jun-Sep) is in the new

McWilliam Gallery on the southwest edge of town.

The town's broad main drag, Bridge St, climbs a steep hill from the bridge across the River Bann (from which the town takes its name) to the unusual **Downshire Bridge** at the top of the hill. A cutting was made in the middle of the street in the 19th century to lower the crest of the hill and make the climb easier for the Royal Mail coaches, who had threatened to boycott the town because of the difficulty of scaling the incline.

On the opposite side of the river stands the **Crozier Monument**, which is adorned with four idiosyncratically sculpted polar bears. Captain Francis Crozier (1796–1848), a native of Banbridge, was commander of HMS *Terror*

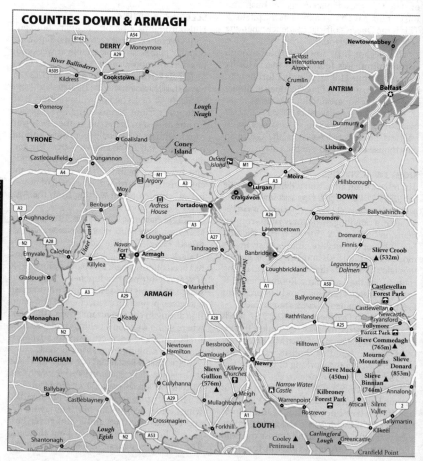

COUNTIES DOWN & ARMAGH

and froze to death in the Arctic during Sir John Franklin's ill-fated expedition in search of the Northwest Passage. Crozier lived in the fine blue and grey Georgian house across the road from the statue.

Banbridge is the starting point for the **Brontë Homeland Drive**, a signposted route along the Bann valley to Rathfriland, 16km to the southeast. Patrick Brontë, father of the famous literary sisters, was born and brought up here, and the locals like to think that her father's tales of the Mourne Mountains inspired the bleak setting for Emily's classic *Wuthering Heights*.

Milking this tenuous connection for all it's worth is the **Brontë Homeland Interpretive Centre** (☎ 4062 3322; Drumballyroney; adult/child £3/2;

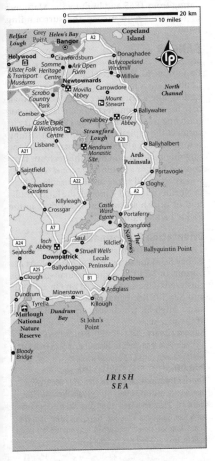

noon-4.30pm Fri-Sun Apr-Sep) in the former Drumballyroney School and Church, off the B10 road 13km southeast of Banbridge, where Patrick taught and preached. His birthplace is at Emdale, 6km west of here, near the B3 road between Rathfriland and Loughbrickland.

Goldline Express bus 238 from Belfast's Europa BusCentre to Newry stops at Banbridge (£6, 45 minutes, at least hourly Monday to Saturday, eight Sunday).

Saintfield & Around
pop 3000
Saintfield is a pretty and prosperous little town, a popular weekend destination for visitors from Belfast who come to browse its dozen or so antique shops and tearooms.

Rowallane Garden (☎ 9751 0131; Crossgar Rd, Saintfield; adult/child £5/2.50; 10am-8pm May-Aug, 6pm Mar & Apr, Sep & Oct, to 4pm Nov-Feb), 2km south of Saintfield, is renowned for its spectacular spring displays of rhododendrons and azaleas, which thrive behind a windbreak of Australian laurels, hollies, pines and beech trees. The walled gardens feature rare primulas, blue Himalayan poppies, plantain lilies, roses, magnolias and delicate autumn crocuses.

For lunch, try the **March Hare** (☎ 9751 9248; 2 Fairview; mains £3-6; 9am-5.30pm Mon-Sat) at the west end of the main street, a cosy little tearoom serving hearty, homemade soups, sandwiches and cakes.

Saintfield is 16km south of Belfast, and is a stop on the Goldline Express bus 215 service from Belfast to Downpatrick.

Legananny Dolmen
Ulster's most famous Stone Age monument is a strangely elegant tripod dolmen, looking as if a giant's hand has placed the capstone delicately atop the three slim uprights. Its elevated position on the western slopes of Slieve Croob (532m) gives it an impressive view to the Mourne Mountains.

Legananny is a challenge to find without the aid of a 1:50,000 scale map. Heading south from Ballynahinch along the B7 to Rathfriland, go through the hamlets of Dromara and Finnis, then look out for a minor road on the left (signposted Legananny Dolmen). Continue for a further 3km, through a crossroads, and look for another road on the left (a signpost is there, but it's difficult to spot). Continue over the hill for 2km, then turn left again at a farm. There's a parking place 50m along, and the dolmen is 50m uphill on the adjacent farm track.

BELFAST TO BANGOR

The coastal region stretching east from Belfast to Bangor and beyond is commuter territory for the capital, and home to many of the North's wealthiest citizens – it's known locally as the 'Gold Coast'. The attractive **North Down Coastal Path** follows the shore from Holywood train station to Bangor Marina (15km), and continues east to Orlock Point.

For the Ulster Folk and Transport Museums, see p601.

Crawfordsburn

pop 500

The pretty little conservation village of Crawfordsburn lies just over 3km west of Bangor on the B20. The picturesque our pick **Old Inn** (☎ 9185 3255; www.theoldinn.com; 15 Main St, Crawfordsburn; r £115-160; P 🖵 🤶) here was once a resting place on the coach route between Belfast and Donaghadee (formerly the main ferry port for mainland Britain). As a result, it has been patronised by many famous names, including the young Peter the Great (tsar of Russia), Dick Turpin (highwayman), former US president George HW Bush, and a veritable roll call of literary figures, including Swift, Tennyson, Thackeray, Dickens, Trollope and CS Lewis. Established in 1614, the Old Inn claims to be Ireland's oldest hotel, with the original thatched cottage (now the bar) flanked by 18th-century additions. The atmosphere is cosy and welcoming, with log fires, low ceilings and wood panelling, and there's a lovely garden terrace at the back. The rooms, dressed up with Arts and Crafts–style wallpaper and mahogany woodwork, have bags of character, and the inn's oak-panelled **Restaurant** (3-course dinner Mon-Thu £30, Fri & Sat £35, 4-course lunch Sun £19; 🕑 7-9.30pm Mon-Sat, noon-3pm Sun) is one of Northern Ireland's best.

The scenic glen behind the Old Inn runs through **Crawfordsburn Country Park** (☎ 9185 3621; South Bridge Rd, Helen's Bay; admission free; 🕑 9am-9pm Easter-Sep, to 5pm Oct-Easter) to reach the coast at one of County Down's best beaches; the park offers a number of good woodland and coastal walks. To the west lies **Grey Point Fort** (☎ 9185 3621; admission free; 🕑 10am-6pm Wed-Sun Easter-Sep, noon-4pm Sun Oct-Easter), an early-20th-century gun emplacement with command post and lookout station. The 30-tonne 6in coastal

---

TOP FIVE ROMANTIC HIDEAWAYS IN NORTHERN IRELAND

- Bushmills Inn (p655)
- Galgorm Resort & Spa (p667)
- Malmaison Hotel (p587)
- Westville Hotel (p681)
- Old Inn (left)

---

defence gun has been trained on Belfast Lough since 1904, though never fired in anger.

Ulsterbus service 1 from Belfast to Bangor stops at Crawfordsburn village (hourly); alternatively, you can take the train to Helen's Bay Station, a wonderful little Victorian halt dating from 1865 and built by the Marquess of Dufferin, who owned the surrounding estate.

BANGOR

pop 76,800

Bangor is to Belfast what Brighton is to London – a Victorian seaside resort that is undergoing a renaissance as an out-of-town base for city commuters. The Belfast–Bangor train line was built in the late 19th century to connect the capital with the then flourishing resort. The opening of a huge marina and the ongoing redevelopment of the seafront have boosted Bangor's fortunes in recent years – it's widely regarded as the most desirable address in Northern Ireland – though the kitsch tradition of British seaside towns survives in the Pickie Family Fun Park.

Orientation & Information

The bus and train stations are together on Abbey St, at the uphill end of Main St. At the bottom of Main St is the marina with B&Bs clustered to the east and west on Queen's Pde and Seacliff Rd. Bangor has both a Main St and a High St, which converge on Bridge St at the marina.

Bangor Library (☎ 9127 0591; 80 Hamilton Rd; 🕑 9am-9pm Mon-Wed, to 10pm Thu, to 5pm Fri & Sat) Internet access costs £1.50 for 30 minutes.

Post Office (☎ 9145 0150; 143 Main St)

Tourist Information Centre (☎ 9127 0069; www .northdown.gov.uk; 34 Quay St; 🕑 9am-6pm Mon, Tue, Thu & Fri, 10am-6pm Wed, 10am-5pm Sat & 1-5pm Sun Jul & Aug, 9am-5pm Mon, Tue, Thu & Fri, 10am-5pm Wed, 10am-4pm Sat, closed Sunday Sep-Jun) Housed in a tower built in 1637 as a fortified customs post.

Sights & Activities

Apart from strolling along the seafront, Bangor's main attraction is the **Pickie Family Fun Park** (☎ 9185 7030; Marine Gardens; per ride £1.50; ☼ 10am-10pm daily Easter-Sep, to sunset Sat & Sun Oct-Easter). It's an old-fashioned seaside entertainment complex famous for its swan-shaped pedal boats, complete with kids adventure playground, karts and miniature steam train. **Ballyholme Bay**, to the east of the town centre, has a long sandy beach and wide green spaces for the kids to run around in.

The **Blue Aquarius** (☎ 07779 600607; www.bangorboat.com; ☼ departures from 2pm daily Jul & Aug, Sat & Sun Apr-Jun & Sep) offers **pleasure cruises** (adult/child from £5/2) around Bangor Bay, departing from the marina pontoon next to the Pickie Family Fun Park. In July and August there are family-friendly **fishing trips** (per adult/child incl tackle & bait £14/10) departing at 9.30am and 7pm daily from the Eisenhower Pier (the right-hand side of the harbour, looking out to sea).

Housed in the converted laundry, stables and stores of Bangor Castle, the **North Down Heritage Centre** (☎ 9127 1200; Castle Park Ave; admission free; ☼ 10am-4.30pm Tue-Sat, 2-4.30pm Sun year-round, plus 10am-4.30pm Mon Jul & Aug) displays, among other historical curiosities, a facsimile of *The Antiphonary of Bangor*, a small 7th-century prayer book and the oldest surviving Irish manuscript (the original is housed in Milan's Ambrosian Library). There's also an interesting section on the life of William Percy French (1854–1920), the famous entertainer and songwriter (Bangor is also home to the Percy French Society; www.percyfrench.org). The centre is in Castle Park, west of the train and bus stations.

The fishing village of Groomsport on the eastern edge of town has a picturesque harbour, overlooked by **Cockle Row Cottages** (☎ 9145 8882; admission free; ☼ 11.30am-5.30pm Jun-Aug), one of which has been restored as a typical fisherman's home of 1910.

Sleeping

Ennislare House (☎ 9127 0858; www.ennislarehouse.com; 7-9 Princetown Rd; s/d £35/60; P ☞) Set in a lovely Victorian town house just 300m north of the train station, the Ennislare has big, bright rooms, stylish decor, and a friendly owner, who can't do enough to make you feel welcome.

Cairn Bay Lodge (☎ 9146 7636; www.cairnbaylodge.com; 278 Seacliff Rd; s/d from £45/80; P ☞) This lovely seaside villa overlooking Ballyholme Bay, 1km east of the town centre, oozes Edwardian elegance with its oak-panelled lounge and dining room. There are three bedrooms with private bathrooms that blend antique charm with contemporary style, beautiful gardens, gourmet breakfasts and sea views.

our pick **Hebron House** (☎ 9146 3126; www.hebron-house.com; 68 Princetown Rd; s/d £55/80; P ☐ ☞) Breakfast around the communal dining table is a highlight at the Hebron, where landlady Ilona gets inventive with organic produce, dishing up oat-crusted potato cakes with your bacon and eggs, or adding Bushmills whiskey and clotted cream to your porridge. The three bedrooms combine traditional Victorian fittings with elegant modern decor, and there are plush towels, bathrobes and Molton Brown toiletries in the stylish bathrooms.

Clandeboye Lodge Hotel (☎ 9185 2500; www.clandeboyelodge.com; 10 Estate Rd, Clandeboye; s/d from £85/100; P ☐ ☞) Looking a little like a modern, red-brick church set amid landscaped gardens on the southwest edge of town, the Clandeboye offers informal luxury – big bedrooms, polished granite bathrooms, fluffy bathrobes, Champagne and chocolates – plus a log fire in winter and a drinks terrace in summer.

Eating

Red Berry Coffee House (☎ 9147 3373; 2-4 Main St; mains £3-5; ☼ 9am-10pm Mon-Sat, 1-9pm Sun) A chilled-out fairtrade coffee shop that serves big breakfasts (including a stack of pancakes with bacon and maple syrup) till 11.30am, and deli sandwiches and salads thereafter.

Phezulu (mains £9-15; ☼ 5-8.45pm Thu-Sat, noon-3pm Sat, 1-5pm Sun) The upstairs bistro of the Red Berry, Phezulu boasts a South African–inspired menu with dishes such as Cape Malay Curry and *boerewors* (pork and coriander sausages) with mash and gravy.

our pick **Jeffers by the Marina** (☎ 9185 9555; 7 Gray's Hill; mains £13-17; ☼ 10am-10pm Tue-Sat, 11am-8pm Sun) This chic little cafe-restaurant is immediately likeable, with its laid-back jazzy tunes, cool art, granite table tops and view of the marina. It serves coffee, cakes and snacks all day and also has a fresh and interesting dinner menu that features local organic produce – from Strangford Lough oysters to their signature Irish beef, slow cooked for five hours, with roast beetroot and horseradish mash.

Coyle's Bistro (☎ 9127 0362; 44 High St; mains £13-18; ☼ 5-9pm Tue-Sat, to 8pm Sun) Despite being upstairs from a busy bar, this place is surprisingly intimate and inviting, with wood panelling, mirrored walls and subdued lighting. The menu won a mention in Michelin's 2008 pub food guide, with dishes such as pan-fried rabbit with roast apple and game chips, and lavender-and-thyme-crusted rump of lamb. The two-course set menu for two (available 5pm to 7pm) includes a bottle of wine and costs £30.

Rioja (☎ 9147 0774; 119 High St; mains £15-17; ⏲ 5-9pm Tue-Sat, noon-2pm Fri) Rioja is a relaxed Mediterranean bistro. With terracotta tiles and candle-lit tables, it offers a range of Iberian, French and Italian dishes, including *cataplana*, a Portuguese seafood casserole. Although it's licensed, you can bring your own wine if you want to (corkage £1); the early bird menu (5pm to 7pm Tuesday to Friday) offers any main course for £9.95.

Entertainment

Jenny Watts (☎ 9127 0401; 41 High St) A traditional pub with a beer garden out back, Jenny's pulls in a mixed-age crowd, offering folk music on Tuesday night, easy listening on Thursday, cool tunes (in the upstairs lounge) on Friday and Saturday, and jazz and blues Sunday lunchtime and evening. It also serves good pub grub, and kids are welcome at meal times.

Café Ceol (☎ 9146 8830; www.cafeceolbangor.com; 17-21 High St; admission free-£5; ⏲ 7pm-1am Wed-Fri, to 1.45am Sat) Bangor's biggest and busiest nightclub has a sleek cocktail bar, an intimate lounge and a stylish club venue, Mint, which features hip hop and R&B on Thursday, '80s and '90s music on Friday and dance, house, funk and R&B on Saturday.

Getting There & Away

Ulsterbus (☎ 9066 6630; www.translink.co.uk) services 1 and 2 run from Belfast's Laganside BusCentre to Bangor (£3, 55 minutes, half-hourly Monday to Saturday, eight Sunday). From Bangor, bus 3 goes to Donaghadee (25 minutes, four Sunday) Monday to Saturday, four Sunday), and bus 6 goes to Newtownards (20 minutes, half-hourly Monday to Saturday, seven Sunday).

There's also a regular train service from Belfast's Great Victoria St and Central stations to Bangor (£5, 30 minutes, half-hourly Monday to Saturday, hourly Sunday).

ARDS PENINSULA

The low-lying Ards Peninsula (An Aird) is the finger of land that encloses Strangford

Lough, pinching against the thumb of the Lecale Peninsula at the Portaferry Narrows. The northern half of the peninsula has some of Ireland's most fertile farmland, with large expanses of wheat and barley, while the south is a landscape of neat fields, white cottages and narrow, winding roads. The eastern coast has some good sandy beaches.

Donaghadee
pop 6500

Donaghadee (Domhnach Daoi) was the main ferry port for Scotland until 1874, when the 34km sea crossing to Portpatrick was superseded by the Stranraer–Larne route. Now it's a pleasant harbour town that's fast becoming part of Belfast's commuter belt.

The town is home to **Grace Neill's**, which dates from 1611 and claims to be Ireland's oldest pub. Among its 17th-century guests was Peter the Great, tsar of Russia, who stopped in for lunch in 1697 on his grand tour of Europe. In the 19th century, John Keats found the place 'charming and clean' but was 'treated to ridicule, scorn and violent abuse by the local people who objected to my mode of dress and thought I was some strange foreigner'.

In July and August, **MV The Brothers** (☎ 9188 3403; www.nelsonsboats.co.uk) runs boat trips to Copeland Island (adult/child £5/3, departs 2pm daily, weather permitting), which was abandoned to the seabirds at the turn of the 20th century. There are also sea-angling trips (£10 per person, departures at 10am and 7pm), with all tackle and bait provided.

SLEEPING & EATING

Pier 36 (☎ 9188 4466; 36 The Parade; s/d £50/70, mains £8-18; ⏲ food served 12.30-2.30pm & 5-9.30pm Wed-Sun) An excellent pub with a red-brick and terracotta-tiled restaurant at the back, dominated by a yellow Rayburn stove that turns out home-baked bread and the daily roast. The hearty menu includes soups, stews, sausage and champ, mussels and other seafood, steaks and a good range of veggie dishes, and there are a couple of comfortable B&B rooms upstairs.

ourpick Grace Neill's (☎ 9188 4595; 33 High St; mains £9-16; ⏲ food noon-3pm & 5.30-9pm Mon-Fri, noon-9.30pm Sat, 12.30-8pm Sun) At the back of Ireland's oldest pub is one of the North's best modern bistros, its sea-green, khaki and red-brick walls decked with arty photos of old Donaghadee. The menu can best be described as upmarket comfort food, from beer-battered fish with chunky, hand-cut chips, and beef-and-Guinness pie, to wicked desserts such as Toblerone and Malteser cheesecake. There's live music on Sunday afternoons, too.

East Coast
The A2 runs along the east coast of the peninsula, through the seaside villages and caravan parks of Millisle (Oileán an Mhuilinn), Ballywalter and Ballyhalbert, and the ugly fishing harbour of Portavogie. The best **beaches** are the Long Sand, immediately south of Ballywalter, and the seawater lagoon (enclosed by a stone dyke for safe bathing) at Millisle.

Approximately 1.5km northwest of Millisle is **Ballycopeland Windmill** (☎ 9054 6552; Moss Rd; admission free; ⏲ 10am-6pm Jul & Aug), a late-18th-century corn mill that remained in commercial use until 1915 and has been restored to full working order.

Portaferry
pop 3300
Portaferry (Port an Pheire), a neat huddle of streets around a medieval tower house, enjoys the most attractive setting on the Ards Peninsula, looking across the turbulent Narrows to a matching tower house in Strangford. A renowned marine biology station on the waterfront uses the lough as an outdoor laboratory, and you can investigate the local marine life yourself at the nearby Exploris aquarium.

The town hit the headlines in 2008 when SeaGen – the world's first commercial-scale tidal energy turbine, built at Belfast's Harland & Wolff shipyard – was installed in the Narrows. The generator is clearly visible, squatting in the channel just south of town like a stumpy red and black lighthouse. The business end is underwater, where two giant turbine blades spin in the tidal currents, generating around 1.2 megawatts of electricity for 18 to 20 hours a day.

The **tourist information centre** (☎ 42729882; tourism-portaferry@ards-council.gov.uk; Castle St; ⏲ 10am-5pm Mon-Sat, 2-6pm Sun Easter-Sep) is in a restored stable near the tower house.

SIGHTS & ACTIVITIES
You can take a look around **Portaferry Castle** (admission free; ⏲ 10am-5pm Mon-Sat, 2-6pm Sun Easter-Sep), a small 16th-century tower house beside the

tourist information centre, which, together with the tower house in Strangford, used to control sea traffic through the Narrows.

Next to the tower house is the outstanding state-of-the-art aquarium, **Exploris** (☎ 4272 8062; www.exploris.org.uk; Castle St; adult/child £7/4.50; ⏲ 10am-6pm Mon-Fri, 11am-6pm Sat, noon-6pm Sun Apr-Aug, 10am-5pm Mon-Fri, 11am-5pm Sat, 1-5pm Sun Sep-Mar), with displays of marine life from Strangford Lough and the Irish Sea. Touch tanks allow visitors to stroke and hold rays, starfish, sea anemones and other sea creatures. Exploris also has a seal sanctuary, where orphaned, sick and injured seals are nursed back to health before being released into the wild.

Walk up to **Windmill Hill** above the town, topped by an old windmill tower, for a good view over the Narrows to Strangford. The Vikings named this stretch of water Strangfjörthr, meaning 'powerful fjord', because when the tide turns, as it does four times a day, 400,000 tonnes of water per minute churn through the gap at speeds of up to eight knots (15km/h). You get some idea of the tide's remarkable strength when you see the ferry being whipped sideways by the current.

There are pleasant **walks** on the minor roads along the shore, north for 2.5km to Ballyhenry Island (accessible at low tide), and south for 6km to the National Trust nature reserve at Ballyquintin Point, both good for birdwatching, seal spotting, or just admiring the views of the Mourne Mountains.

From May to September, **Des Rogers** (☎ 4272 8297; desmondrogers@netscapeonline.co.uk) and **John Murray** (☎ 4272 8414) organise fishing and birdwatching trips, as well as pleasure cruises on the lough (per half-/full day around £75/150) for up to six people. Book in advance.

SLEEPING & EATING
Barholm (☎ 4272 9598; www.barholmportaferry.co.uk; 11 The Strand; dm/s/d from £14/18/40; ⏲ year-round; **P**) Barholm offers B&B and hostel-style accommodation in a Victorian villa in a superb seafront location opposite the ferry slipway, with a spacious kitchen, laundry facilities and a big, sunny conservatory that doubles as a tearoom. It's popular with groups, so be sure to book ahead.

Adair's B&B (☎ 4272 8412; 22 The Square; s/d £20/42, f per person £20) Mrs Adair's friendly and good-value B&B is an anonymous-looking house right on the main square (there's no sign

---

LORD CASTLEREAGH

As you wander around Mount Stewart, spare a thought for Robert Stewart, Lord Castlereagh (1769–1822), who spent his childhood here. Despite going down in history as one of Britain's most accomplished foreign secretaries, during his lifetime he was enormously unpopular with the public, who saw him as the spokesman for a violently repressive government. He was savagely attacked in print by liberal reformers, including Daniel O'Connell – who denounced him as 'the assassin of his country' – and the poets Percy Bysshe Shelley and Lord Byron. The latter's notorious *Epitaph for Lord Castlereagh* could hardly be bettered for withering contempt:

Posterity will ne'er survey
A nobler scene than this:
Here lie the bones of Castlereagh;
Stop, traveller, and piss!

Castlereagh's father, the first Marquess of Londonderry, primed his son's political career in 1790 by buying him a place in the Irish parliament as member for County Down. The campaign cost a cool £60,000, leaving the marquess unable to afford various planned improvements to Mount Stewart.

As Chief Secretary for Ireland in the government of William Pitt, Castlereagh was responsible for quelling the 1798 Rising and for passing the 1801 Act of Union. Later he served as foreign secretary during the Napoleonic Wars, and represented Britain at the Congress of Vienna in 1815 (the 22 chairs on which European leaders sat during the congress are on show in Mount Stewart House). Political success did not bring happiness, however; while still in office, Castlereagh succumbed to paranoia and depression, and committed suicide by slitting his own throat with a letter knife.

---

outside; look for No 22), with three spacious rooms – a single (shared bathroom), a twin (with private bathroom), and a family room (with private bathroom; for up to four people).

Fiddler's Green (☎ 4272 8393; www.fiddlersgreen portaferry.com; 10-12 Church St; s/d £45/65; P) This popular pub and restaurant provides B&B in four homely rooms – one has a four-poster bed (per night £75) – neatly decorated with pine furniture and paintings, and serves up a stonking cooked breakfast. The pub has traditional music sessions every Friday, Saturday and Sunday night.

Portaferry Hotel (☎ 4272 8231; www.portaferry hotel.com; 10 The Strand; s/d £65/110; P) Converted from a row of 18th-century terrace houses, this charming seafront hotel has an elegant, Georgian look to its rooms – ask for one with a sea view (£10 extra) – and has a good, family-friendly restaurant (mains £15 to £19) with a French-influenced menu.

GETTING THERE & AWAY

Ulsterbus services 9 and 10 travel from Belfast to Portaferry (£6, 1¼ hours, six daily Monday to Saturday, two Sunday) via Newtownards, Mount Stewart and Greyabbey. More frequent services begin from Newtownards (some buses go via Carrowdore and don't stop at Mount Stewart and Greyabbey; check first).

The **ferry** (☎ 4488 1637) between Portaferry and Strangford sails every half-hour between 7.30am and 10.30pm Monday to Friday, 8am to 11pm Saturday and 9.30am to 10.30pm Sunday; the journey time is about 10 minutes. The one-way/same-day return fares are £5.30/8.50 for a car and driver; £3.40/5.30 for motorcyclists and their bikes; and £1.10/1.80 for car passengers and pedestrians.

Greyabbey
pop 1000

The village of Greyabbey is home to the splendid ruins of **Grey Abbey** (☎ 9054 6552; Church Rd; admission free; ☼ 10am-6pm daily Easter-Sep, noon-4pm Sun only Oct-Easter). The Cistercian abbey was founded in 1193 by Affreca, wife of the Norman aristocrat John de Courcy (the builder of Carrickfergus Castle), in thanks for surviving a stormy sea crossing from the Isle of Man. The small visitor centre explains Cistercian life with paintings and panels.

The abbey church, which remained in use as late as the 18th century, was the first in Ireland to be built in the Gothic style. At the east end is a carved tomb, possibly depicting Affreca; the effigy in the north transept may be her husband. The grounds, overlooked by 18th-century Rosemount House, are awash with trees and flowers on spreading lawns, making this an ideal picnic spot.

Hoops Courtyard, off Main St in the village centre, has a cluster of 18 little shops selling antiques and collectables; opening times vary, but all are open on Wednesday, Friday and Saturday afternoons. **Hoops Coffee Shop** (☎ 4278 8541; Hoops Courtyard, Main St; mains £4-6; ♥ 10am-5pm Tue-Sat Sep-Jun, daily Jul & Aug) is a traditional tea-room with outdoor tables in the courtyard in fine weather, serving good lunches and wicked cream teas.

Mount Stewart House & Gardens

The magnificent 18th-century **Mount Stewart** (☎ 4278 8387; house tour & gardens adult/child £7.40/3.70, gardens only £5.60/2.80; ♥ house noon-6pm daily Jul & Aug, Wed-Mon Sep, Thu-Sun Apr & Oct, Sat & Sun Mar, 1-6pm daily Jun, Wed-Mon May) is one of Northern Ireland's grandest stately homes. It was built for the Marquess of Londonderry and is decorated with lavish plasterwork, marble nudes and priceless artworks.

Lady Mairi (born 1920) – daughter of the seventh marquess – still lives and entertains guests in part of the house; the family is related by marriage to the Goldsmiths via Annabel (born 1934), daughter of the eighth marquess, after whom the famous London nightclub was named. The house's treasures include the chairs used at the Congress of Vienna in 1815 (embroidery added in 1918–22), and a painting of the racehorse Hambletonian by George Stubbs, one of the most important paintings in Ireland.

Much of the landscaping of the beautiful **gardens** (♥ 10am-8pm May-Sep, to 6pm Apr & Oct, to 4pm Mar) was supervised in the early 20th century by Lady Edith, wife of the seventh marquess, for the benefit of her children – the Dodo Terrace at the front of the house is populated with unusual creatures from history (dinosaurs and dodos) and myth (griffins and mermaids), accompanied by giant frogs and duck-billed platypuses. The 18th-century **Temple of the Winds** (♥ 2-5pm Sun Apr-Oct) is a folly in the classical Greek style built on a high point above the lough.

Mount Stewart is on the A20, 3km northwest of Greyabbey and 8km southeast of Newtownards. Buses from Belfast and Newtownards to Portaferry stop at the gate. The ground floor of the house and most of the gardens are wheelchair accessible. Last admission one hour before closing time.

NEWTOWNARDS & AROUND
pop 27,800

Founded in the 17th century on the site of the 6th-century Movilla monastery, Newtownards (Baile Nua na hArda) today is a busy but unexceptional commercial centre. The **tourist information centre** (☎ 9182 6846; tourism@ards-council .gov.uk; 31 Regent St; ♥ 9.15am-5pm Mon-Fri, 9.30am-5pm Sat) is next to the bus station.

There's some fine 18th- and 19th-century architecture in the town, especially along Church St. Most striking of all is the 18th-century **Market House**, which once housed the town's prison – you can ask to see an original cell – and is now home to the **Ards Arts Centre** (☎ 9181 0803; Conway Sq; admission free; ♥ 9am-5pm Mon-Thu, to 4.30pm Fri & Sat), which hosts changing art exhibitions. The square in front of the Market House hosts a lively **market** every Saturday, and a traditional harvest fair in September.

The remains of **Movilla Abbey** and its 13th-century church have been almost swallowed up by the forest of gravestones in Movilla Cemetery (on Old Movilla Rd, on the B172 towards Millisle). There are some interesting 12th- and 13th-century grave slabs (thought by some to be those of Knights Templar) amid the abbey ruins.

The bus station is on Regent St, near the tourist office. Bus 5 goes to Belfast (£2.60, 35 minutes, seven daily Monday to Saturday, two Sunday).

Scrabo Country Park

Newtownards is overlooked by the prominent landmark of Scrabo Hill, located 2km southwest of town. It was once the site of extensive prehistoric earthworks, which were largely removed during construction of the 41m **1857 Memorial Tower** (☎ 9181 1491; admission free; ♥ 10am-6pm Easter-Sep, noon-4pm Sun only Oct-Easter), built in honour of the third Marquess of Londonderry. Inside there's an audiovisual display on the tower's history and a 122-step climb to the superb viewpoint at the top – on a clear day you can see Scotland, the Isle of Man, and even Snowdon in Wales. The disused sandstone quarries nearby provided material for many famous buildings, including Belfast's Albert Memorial Clock Tower (p576).

COUNTIES DOWN & ARMAGH

Somme Heritage Centre

The grimly fascinating **Somme Heritage Centre** (☎ 9182 3202; www.irishsoldier.org; 233 Bangor Rd; adult/child £4.25/3.25; ✹ 10am-5pm Mon-Fri, noon-5pm Sat & Sun Jul & Aug, 10am-4pm Mon-Thu, noon-4pm Sat Apr-Jun & Sep, 10am-4pm Mon-Thu, noon-4pm 1st Sat of month Oct-Mar) vividly illustrates the horrors of the WWI Somme campaign of 1916 from the perspective of men of the 10th (Irish), 16th (Irish) and 36th (Ulster) divisions. It's a high-tech show with short films and reconstructions of the trenches, but there's nothing celebratory about the exhibits, which are intended as a memorial to the men and women who died. A photographic display commemorates the suffragette movement and the part that women played in WWI.

The centre is 3km north of Newtownards on the A21 towards Bangor. Bus 6 from Bangor to Newtownards passes the entrance every half-hour or so.

Ark Open Farm

Opposite the Somme Heritage Centre, on the other side of the dual carriageway, is the **Ark Open Farm** (☎ 9182 0445; www.thearkopenfarm.co.uk; 296 Bangor Rd; adult/3 to 16 years/under 3 years £4.40/3.70/free; ✹ 10am-6pm Mon-Sat, 2-6pm Sun Apr-Sep, closes 5pm Oct-Mar). Hugely popular with families, the farm has displays of rare breeds of sheep, cattle, poultry, llamas and donkeys. Kids get to stroke and handfeed the lambs, piglets and ducklings.

STRANGFORD LOUGH

Almost landlocked, Strangford Lough (Loch Cuan; www.strangfordlough.org) is connected to the open sea by a 700m-wide strait (the Narrows) at Portaferry. Its western shore is fringed by humpbacked islands – half-drowned mounds of boulder clay (called drumlins) left behind by ice sheets at the end of the last ice age. On the eastern shore, the drumlins have been broken down by the waves into heaps of boulders that form shallow tidal reefs (known locally as 'pladdies').

Large colonies of grey seals frequent the lough, especially at the southern tip of the Ards Peninsula where the exit channel opens out into the sea. Birds abound on the shores and tidal mudflats, including brent geese wintering from Arctic Canada, eider ducks and many species of wader. Strangford Lough oysters are a local delicacy.

Castle Espie Wildfowl & Wetlands Centre

About 2km southeast of Comber, off the Downpatrick road (A22), is the **Castle Espie Wildfowl & Wetlands Centre** (☎ 9187 4146; www.wwt.org.uk; Ballydrain Rd, Comber; adult/child £5.95/2.95; ✹ 10.30am-5.30pm Mon-Fri, 11am-5.30pm Sat & Sun Jul & Aug, to 5pm Mar-Jun, Sep & Oct, 11am-4pm Mon-Fri, 11am-4.30pm Sat & Sun Nov-Feb). At the time of research, a new visitor centre was under construction, and redevelopment work will continue till December 2010.

The reserve is a haven for huge flocks of geese, ducks and swans – around 75% of the world's population of light-bellied brent geese spend the winter here – and is a paradise for fledgling ornithologists. The best time to visit is in May and June, when the grounds are overrun with goslings, ducklings and cygnets.

SLEEPING & EATING

our pick Anna's House B&B (☎ 9754 1566; www.annashouse.com; Tullynagee, 35 Lisbarnett Rd, Lisbane; s/d from £55/85; P ⊚) Just west of Lisbane, Anna's is an ecofriendly country house set in a superb garden with views over a little lake (free angling for residents). The hospitality is second to none, the food is almost all organic and the bread is home baked, with a breakfast menu that ranges from an Ulster Fry or smoked salmon omelette to fresh fruit salad.

Old Schoolhouse Inn (☎ 9754 1182; www.theoldschoolhouseinn.com; Ballydrain Rd, Comber; s/d £55/80; P) Just south of Castle Espie on the road to Nendrum, the characterful Old Schoolhouse has seven luxurious, modern rooms, each named for a former US president. The former classroom, now swathed in shades of deep claret and decorated with old musical instruments, houses an award-winning restaurant (three-course dinner costs £24; open 7pm to 10pm) serving local produce cooked in French country-kitchen style.

Old Post Office Tearoom (☎ 9754 3335; 191 Killinchy Rd, Lisbane; breakfast £3-5, lunch mains £7; ✹ 9.30am-5pm Mon-Sat) The thatched cottage that once housed the village post office has been lovingly converted into a tearoom and art gallery, with walls of cream plaster and bare stone, pine furniture and a wood-burning stove. It serves great coffee and home-baked scones, plus lunch specials such as lasagne and salad.

Nendrum Monastic Site

The Celtic monastic community of **Nendrum** (admission free; ✹ 24hr) was built in the 5th century under the guidance of St Mochaoi (St Mahee). It is much older than the Norman monastery at Grey Abbey on the opposite shore and couldn't be more different. The scant remains provide a clear outline of its early plan, with the foundations of a number of churches, a round tower, beehive cells and other buildings, as well as three concentric stone ramparts and a monks' cemetery, all in a wonderful island setting. A particularly interesting relic is the stone sundial that has been reconstructed using some of the original pieces. The minor road to Mahee Island from the lough's western shore crosses a causeway to Reagh Island and then a bridge guarded by the ruined tower of 15th-century Mahee Castle.

The small **visitor centre** (☎ 9754 2547; admission free; ⏰ 10am-6pm daily Easter-Sep, noon-4pm Sun only Oct-Easter) screens an excellent video comparing Nendrum with Grey Abbey, and there's some interesting material about the concept of time and how we measure it, presented in a child-friendly fashion.

The site is signposted from Lisbane, on the A20, 5km south of Comber.

Killyleagh
pop 2200

Killyleagh (Cill O Laoch) is a former fishing village dominated by the impressive **castle** (closed to the public) of the Hamilton family. Built originally by John de Courcy in the 12th century, the Scottish-baronial-style reconstruction of 1850 sits on the original Norman motte and bailey. Outside the gatehouse, a plaque commemorates Sir Hans Sloane, the naturalist, born in Killyleagh in 1660, whose collection was the basis for the founding of the British Museum (London's Sloane Square is named after him). The parish church houses the tombs of members of the Blackwood family (marquesses of Dufferin), who married into the Hamiltons in the 18th century.

In September the **Magnus Barelegs Viking Festival** (www.killyleagh.org/boatrace) features processions, craft fairs, live music and a Viking boat race on nearby Strangford Lough.

SLEEPING & EATING

ourpick **Dufferin Coaching Inn** (☎ 4482 1134; www .dufferincoachinginn.com; 35 High St; s/d from £45/70; Ⓟ 🛜) The comfortable lounge in this lovely Georgian house, complete with coal-fired stove and free Sunday papers, was once the village bank – the manager's office in the cor-

ner now houses a little library. The six plush rooms have crisp linen and fluffy towels, and some have four-poster beds; unusually, the smallest double has the bath *in* the bedroom, charmingly hidden behind a curtain. The excellent breakfasts include freshly squeezed orange juice, good coffee and scrambled eggs with smoked salmon.

Killyleagh Castle Towers (☎ 4482 8261; polly@killy leagh.plus.com; High St; 4-person apt per weekend/week £210/429; Ⓟ) If you've ever fancied staying in a castle, Killyleagh's three gatehouse towers (complete with spiral staircases and roof terraces) are available for weekly rental, including use of the castle gardens, swimming pool and tennis court. The two smaller towers sleep two or four and the largest sleeps five.

Dufferin Arms (☎ 4482 1182; www.dufferinarms.co.uk; 35 High St; mains £8-15; ⏰ noon-3pm & 5.30-8.30pm Mon-Thu, noon-8.30pm Fri-Sun) This comfortably old-fashioned pub, and the larger Stables Bar downstairs, serves decent pub grub, while the cosy, candle-lit Kitchen Restaurant offers a more intimate atmosphere. Bands play on Friday and Saturday nights from 9pm, with traditional sessions on Saturday afternoons.

GETTING THERE & AWAY

Ulsterbus service 11 runs from Belfast to Killyleagh (£4, one hour, 10 daily Monday to Friday, five Saturday, two Sunday) via Comber. Bus 14 continues from Killyleagh to Downpatrick (£3, 20 minutes, 10 daily Monday to Friday, five Saturday).

DOWNPATRICK
pop 10,300

St Patrick's mission to spread Christianity to Ireland began and ended in Downpatrick. Ireland's patron saint is associated with numerous places in this corner of Down – he made his first convert at nearby Saul, and is buried at Down Cathedral – and, on St Patrick's Day (17 March), the town is crammed with crowds of pilgrims and revellers.

Downpatrick – now County Down's administrative centre – was settled long before the saint's arrival. His first church here was constructed inside the earthwork *dún* (fort) of Rath Celtchair, still visible to the southwest of the cathedral. The place later became known as Dún Pádraig (Patrick's Fort), anglicised to Downpatrick in the 17th century.

In 1176 the Norman John de Courcy is said to have brought the relics of St Colmcille and

St Brigid to Downpatrick to rest with the remains of St Patrick, hence the local saying, 'In Down, three saints one grave do fill, Patrick, Brigid and Colmcille'. Later the town declined along with the cathedral until the 17th and 18th centuries, when the Southwell family developed the old town centre you see today. The best of its Georgian architecture is centred on English St and the Mall, which lead up to the cathedral, but the rest of the town is a bit bedraggled and looking a little down at heel.

Orientation & Information

The bus station is on Market St (the main A25 road south towards Newcastle), on the southern edge of the town centre.

The **tourist information centre** (☎ 4461 2233; www.visitdownpatrick.com; 53A Market St; ☺ 9.30am-6pm Mon-Sat & 2-6pm Sun Jul & Aug, 10am-5pm Mon-Sat Sep-Jun) is in the St Patrick Centre, just north of the bus station.

Sights

The **Mall** is the most attractive street in Downpatrick, with some lovely 18th-century architecture, including Soundwell School, built in 1733, and a courthouse with a finely decorated pediment.

SAINT PATRICK CENTRE

This centre houses a multimedia exhibition called **Ego Patricius** (☎ 4461 9000; www.saintpatrickcentre.com; 53A Market St; adult/child £4.95/2.55; ☺ 9.30am-6pm Mon-Sat & 10am-6pm Sun Jun-Aug, 9.30am-5.30pm Mon-Sat & 1-5.30pm Sun Apr, May & Sep, 10am-5pm Mon-Sat Oct-Mar, 9.30am-7pm St Patrick's Day), charting the life and legacy of Ireland's patron saint. Occasionally filled with parties of school kids, the exhibition uses audio and video presentations to tell St Patrick's story, often in his own words (taken from his *Confession*, written in Latin around the year AD 450, which begins with the words *'Ego Patricius'*, meaning 'I am Patrick'). At the end is a spectacular widescreen film that takes the audience on a swooping, low-level helicopter ride over the landscapes of Ireland.

DOWN CATHEDRAL

According to legend St Patrick died in Saul, where angels told his followers to place his body on a cart drawn by two untamed oxen, and that wherever the oxen halted, was where the saint should be buried. They supposedly stopped at the church on the hill of Down, now the site of the Church of Ireland's **Down Cathedral** (☎ 4461 4922; The Mall; admission free; ☺ 9.30am-4.30pm Mon-Sat, 2-5pm Sun).

The cathedral is a testimony to 1600 years of building and rebuilding. Viking attacks wiped away all trace of the earliest churches, and the subsequent Norman cathedral and monasteries were destroyed by Scottish raiders in 1316. The rubble was used in a 15th-century church finished in 1512, but after the Dissolution of the Monasteries it was razed to the ground in 1541. Today's building dates largely from the 18th and 19th centuries, with a completely new interior installed in the 1980s.

In the churchyard immediately south of the cathedral is a slab of Mourne granite with the inscription 'Patric', placed there by the Belfast Naturalists' Field Club in 1900, marking the traditional site of **St Patrick's grave**.

To reach the cathedral, go up the stairs to the right of the Saint Patrick Centre and turn left at the top, opposite Down County Museum.

DOWN COUNTY MUSEUM

Downhill from the cathedral is **Down County Museum** (☎ 4461 5218; www.downcountymuseum.com; The Mall; admission free; ☺ 10am-5pm Mon-Fri, 1-5pm Sat & Sun), housed in the town's restored 18th-century jail. In a former cell block at the back are models of some of the prisoners once incarcerated there, and details of their sad stories. Displays cover the story of the Norman conquest of Down, but the biggest exhibit of all is outside – a short signposted trail leads to the **Mound of Down**, a good example of a Norman motte and bailey.

INCH ABBEY

Built by de Courcy for the Cistercians in 1180 on an earlier Irish monastic site, **Inch Abbey** (☎ 9181 1491; admission free; ☺ 24hr) is visible across the river from the cathedral. The English Cistercians had a strict policy of non-admittance for Irishmen and maintained this until the end in 1541. Most of the ruins are just foundations and low walls; the neatly groomed setting beside the marshes of the River Quoile is its most attractive feature.

To get there, head out of town on the A7 Belfast road for about 1.5km, then take the first left after crossing the river.

DOWNPATRICK & COUNTY DOWN RAILWAY

From mid-June to mid-September, plus December, St Patrick's Day, Easter, May Day and Halloween, this working **railway museum**

(☎ 4461 5779; www.downrail.co.uk; Market St; adult/child £5/4; ⏱ 2-5pm Sat & Sun) runs steam-hauled trains over a restored section of the former Belfast–Newcastle line. There is a western terminus near Ballydugan, and a northern one close to Inch Abbey, plus a halt next to the grave of King Magnus Barefoot, a Norwegian king who died in battle on this spot in 1103. The ticket price includes a return journey on the train and a tour around the engine shed and signal cabin.

QUOILE COUNTRYSIDE CENTRE
A tidal barrier was built at Hare Island, 3km downstream from Downpatrick, in 1957 to control flooding. The waters enclosed by the barrier now form the Quoile Pondage Nature Reserve, whose ecology is explained at the **Quoile Countryside Centre** (☎ 4461 5520; 5 Quay Rd; admission free; ⏱ reserve 24hr, visitor centre 10am-6pm daily Easter-Sep, noon-4pm Sun only Oct-Easter). The centre is housed in a little cottage beside the ruins of **Quoile Castle**, a 17th-century tower house. There's a wheelchair-accessible **birdwatching hide** (⏱ 10am-4pm daily) on Castle Island, downstream from the centre.

Sleeping & Eating
Ardpatrick Country House (☎ 4483 9434; www.ardpatrick countryhouse.com; 108 Ballydugan Rd; s/d £33/56; P 🖥 🛜) You'll get a warm welcome and a hearty breakfast at this luxurious, modern villa, set in open countryside about 4km southwest of the town centre on the A25. All three rooms are neat as a pin, and all have private bathrooms.

Denvir's Hotel & Pub (☎ 4461 2012; www.denvirshotel .com; 14 English St; s/d £40/70) Recently taken over by Botanic Inns and awaiting a makeover, Denvir's is an old coaching inn dating back to 1642 and is the only accommodation in the town centre. It offers B&B in six idiosyncratic rooms with pine floorboards, Georgian windows and period fireplaces. The rustic restaurant (mains £8 to £14; open noon to 2.30pm and 5pm to 9pm) has an enormous, original stone fireplace and serves hearty dishes such as smoked trout and Cashel Blue cheese tart, and homemade lasagne.

Mill at Ballydugan (☎ 4461 3654; www.ballyduganmill .com; Drumcullen Rd, Ballydugan; s/d/f £55/75/85; P) This giant, eight-storey, 18th-century mill building overlooking Ballydugan Lake has been restored as a hotel and restaurant, housing 11 atmospheric rooms with lots of exposed stone and timber, and an attractive stone-floored lobby with a huge, roaring fire. It's 3km southwest of Downpatrick, off the A25.

> **GUITAR MAKER TO THE GREATS**
>
> Belfast-born George Lowden has been creating guitars in Northern Ireland since the 1970s, and his hand-built instruments have gained a worldwide reputation for excellence – satisfied Lowden owners include Eric Clapton, Van Morrison, Richard Thompson, Mark Knopfler and the Edge. If you're interested in buying one, you can get a tour of the workshop at **Lowden Guitars** (☎ 4461 9161; www.georgelowden.com; 34 Down Business Park, Belfast Rd, Downpatrick; ⏱ by prior arrangement Mon-Fri). However, be prepared to shell out upwards of £4000.

Getting There & Away
Downpatrick is 32km southeast of Belfast. Buses 15, 15A and 515 depart from the Europa BusCentre in Belfast for Downpatrick (£5, one hour, at least hourly Monday to Saturday, six Sunday). There's also the Goldline Express bus 215 (50 minutes, hourly Monday to Saturday).

Goldline Express bus 240 runs from Downpatrick to Newry (£5, 1¼ hours, six daily Monday to Saturday, two Sunday) via Dundrum, Newcastle, Castlewellan and Hilltown.

AROUND DOWNPATRICK
According to popular tradition, the young St Patrick was kidnapped from Britain by Irish pirates and spent six years as a slave tending sheep (possibly on Slemish, p668) before escaping back home to his family. After religious training, he returned to Ireland to spread the faith and is said to have landed on the shores of Strangford Lough near Saul, northeast of Downpatrick. He preached his first sermon in a nearby barn, and eventually retired to Saul after some 30 years of evangelising.

Saul
On landing near this spot in AD 432, St Patrick made his first convert: Díchú, the local chieftain, gave the holy man a sheep barn (*sabhal* in Gaelic, pronounced sawl) in which to preach. West of Saul village is the supposed site of the *sabhal*, with a replica 10th-century **church and round tower** built in 1932 to mark the 1500th anniversary of his arrival.

East of the village is the small hill of **Slieve Patrick** (120m), with stations of the cross along

COUNTIES DOWN & ARMAGH

the path to the top and a massive 10m-high statue of St Patrick, also dating from 1932, on the summit. The hill is the object of a popular pilgrimage on St Patrick's Day.

Saul is 3km northeast of Downpatrick off the A2 Strangford road.

Struell Wells

These supposedly curative spring waters are traditionally associated with St Patrick – it is said he scourged himself here, spending 'a great part of the night, stark naked and singing psalms' immersed in what is now the **Drinking Well**. He must have been a hardy soul – the well-preserved but chilly 17th-century **bathhouses** here look more likely to induce ill health than cure it! The site has been venerated for centuries, although the buildings are all post-1600. Between the bathhouses and the ruined chapel stands the **Eye Well**, whose waters are said to cure eye ailments.

The wells are in a scenic, secluded glen 2km east of Downpatrick. Take the B1 road towards Ardglass, and turn left after passing the hospital.

LECALE PENINSULA

The low-lying Lecale Peninsula is situated east of Downpatrick, isolated by the sea and Strangford Lough to the north, south and east, and the marshes of the Quoile and Blackstaff Rivers to the west. In Irish it's called Leath Chathail (lay-ca-*hal*), meaning 'the territory of Cathal' (an 8th-century prince), and is a region of fertile farmland that is fringed by fishing harbours, rocky bluffs and sandy beaches.

Lecale is a place of pilgrimage for Van Morrison fans – Coney Island, immortalised in his song of the same name, is between Ardglass and Killough in the south of the peninsula.

Strangford

pop 550

The picturesque fishing village of Strangford (Baile Loch Cuan) is dominated by **Strangford Castle** (☎ 9181 1491; Castle St), a 16th-century tower house (not open to the public) that faces its counterpart across the Narrows in Portaferry. At the end of Castle St is a footpath called the **Squeeze Gut**, which leads over the hill behind the village, with a fine view of the lough, before looping back to Strangford via tree-lined Dufferin Ave (1.5km), or continuing around the shoreline to Castle Ward Estate (4.5km).

Strangford is located 16km northeast of Downpatrick. See p610 for details of the car ferry between Strangford and Portaferry.

SLEEPING & EATING

Castle Ward Estate Campsite (☎ 4488 1204; jacqueline .baird@nationaltrust.org.uk; 19 Castle Ward Rd; tent/caravan sites £10/15; ☿ mid-Apr–Oct) The entrance to this wooded, lough-shore National Trust site is separate from the main estate entrance (closer to Strangford village).

our pick **Cuan** (☎ 4488 1222; www.thecuan.com; The Square; s/d £53/85, mains £9-15; ☿ food noon-9pm Mon-Thu, to 9.30pm Fri & Sat, to 8.30pm Sun; **P**) You can't miss the Cuan's duck-egg-green facade, just around the corner from the ferry slip, or the warm welcome from Peter and Caroline, the husband and wife team who run the place. The atmospheric, wood-panelled restaurant here is the main attraction, serving giant portions of local seafood, lamb and beef, but there are also nine neat, comfortable and well-equipped rooms if you want to stay the night.

Castle Ward Estate

Castle Ward house enjoys a superb setting overlooking the bay to the west of Strangford, but it has something of a split personality. It was built in the 1760s for Lord and Lady Bangor – Bernard Ward and his wife, Anne – who were a bit of an odd couple. Their widely differing tastes in architecture resulted in an eccentric country residence – and a subsequent divorce. Bernard favoured the neoclassical style seen in the front facade and the main staircase, while Anne leant towards the Strawberry Hill Gothic of the rear facade, which reaches a peak in the incredible fan vaulting of her Gothic boudoir.

The house is now part of the National Trust's **Castle Ward Estate** (☎ 4488 1204; Park Rd; adult/child grounds & wildlife centre £5/2.50, house tour £2.80/1.90; ☿ house 1-5pm daily Easter Week, Jul & Aug, 1-5pm Sat, Sun & public hols Mar-Jun, Sep & Oct; grounds 10am-8pm daily Apr-Sep, 10am-4pm daily Oct-Mar). While in the grounds you can visit a Victorian laundry museum, the Strangford Lough Wildlife Centre, Old Castle Ward (a fine 16th-century Plantation tower) and Castle Audley (a 15th-century tower house), and explore a range of walking and cycling trails.

Kilclief Castle

Square jawed and thickset, **Kilclief Castle** (☎ 9181 1491; Kilclief; admission free; ☿ 10am-6pm Jul & Aug) sprouts incongruously from a rural farmyard, framed between house and rickety barn. This is the oldest tower house in the county, built between 1413 and 1441 to guard the seaward entrance to the Narrows. It has some elaborate details and is thought to have been the prototype for Ardglass, Strangford and other castles in Lecale.

Kilclief Castle is on the A2, 4km south of Strangford.

Ardglass
pop 2900

Ardglass (Ard Ghlais) today is a small village with a busy fishing harbour, but in medieval times it was a major port and an important trading centre. The legacy of its heyday is the seven tower houses, dating from the 14th to the 16th centuries, that punctuate the hillside above the harbour.

The most prominent is **Jordan's Castle**, a four-storey tower near the harbour, built by a wealthy 15th-century merchant at the dawn of Ulster's economic development. At the time of research it was closed to the public, but may reopen in the future.

Ardglass is on the A2, 13km south of Strangford. Ulsterbus services 16A and 16F run from Downpatrick to Ardglass (20 minutes, eight daily Monday to Saturday, two on Sunday).

SLEEPING & EATING
Margaret's Cottage (☎ 4484 1080; www.margaretscot tage.com; 9 Castle Pl; s/d £30/60; P) A dinky little flower-bedecked 18th-century cottage (with a modern upper floor), Margaret's is squeezed between Aldo's Restaurant and the ruins of Margaret's Castle and offers luxurious B&B accommodation, with four cosy rooms and an open fire in the lounge.

Aldo's Restaurant (☎ 4484 1315; 7 Castle Pl; mains £9-14; ⏰ 5-10pm daily Jun-Aug, Thu-Sun Sep-May, plus 12.30-2pm Sun year-round) A local institution, this cosy Italian restaurant serves excellent seafood, pasta and vegetarian dishes, and is famed for its excellent Sunday lunches (best to book in advance, though).

Curran's Bar (☎ 4484 1332; 83 Strangford Rd, Chapeltown; mains £10-19; ⏰ food 12.30-9pm) This popular pub, 2.5km north of Ardglass on the A2 towards Strangford, has an atmospheric restaurant with worn wooden floors, a crackling open fire and old family photographs. It specialises in local seafood (try the smoked haddock with pea risotto and chorizo butter) and prime Irish beef accompanied with potatoes and other vegetables fresh from farmer Doyle along the road.

SOUTH DOWN & THE MOURNE MOUNTAINS
Newcastle
pop 7500

In recent years the Victorian seaside resort of Newcastle (An Caisleán Nua) has undergone a multimillion-pound makeover, and now sports a snazzy new promenade, stretching for more than a kilometre along the seafront, complete with modern sculptures and an elegant footbridge over the Shimna River. The facelift makes the most of Newcastle's superb setting on a 5km strand of golden sand at the foot of the Mourne Mountains, and there are hopes that it will transform the town's fortunes from fading bucket-and-spade resort to outdoor activities capital and gateway to the proposed Mourne National Park.

One short stretch of main street is still a gauntlet of amusement arcades and fast-food takeaways, which can get a bit raucous on Friday and Saturday nights, but the town is still a good base for exploring Murlough National Nature Reserve and the Mourne Mountains – accessible from here on foot, by car or by public transport. Golfers from around the globe flock to the Royal County Down golf course, voted the 'best in the world outside the US' by the magazine Planet Golf in 2007.

ORIENTATION
As you exit the bus station, Main St stretches ahead towards the mountains, becoming Central Promenade (with the tourist office on the left) and then South Promenade. Turning left out of the bus station leads to a mini-roundabout; straight ahead is the beach, on the right is Downs Rd and the youth hostel, and to the left is the Slieve Donard Resort & Spa.

If you're driving, be aware that the town can be a major traffic bottleneck on summer weekends.

INFORMATION
Coffee-Net (☎ 4372 7388; 5-7 Railway St; per 15 min £1; ⏰ 9am-6pm Mon-Sat) Internet access in the coffee shop in the bus station.
Mourne Heritage Trust (☎ 4372 4059; www.mourne live.com; 87 Central Promenade; ⏰ 9am-5pm Mon-Fri)

Books, maps and brochures on the Mourne region, plus information on walking in the Mournes.

Post office (☎ 4372 2651; 6 Railway St) Opposite the bus station.

Tourist information centre (☎ 4372 2222; newcastle.tic@downdc.gov.uk; 10-14 Central Promenade; 🕑 9.30am-7pm Mon-Sat, 1-7pm Sun Jul & Aug, 10am-5pm Mon-Sat, 2-6pm Sun Sep-Jun) Sells local-interest books and maps, and a range of traditional and contemporary crafts.

SIGHTS & ACTIVITIES

Newcastle's main attraction is the **beach**, which stretches 5km northeast to **Murlough National Nature Reserve** (admission free, car park May-Sep £3; 🕑 24hr), where footpaths and boardwalks meander among the grassy dunes, with great views back towards the Mournes.

Back in town, **Tropicana** (☎ 4372 5034; Central Promenade; adult/child £3.50/3; 🕑 11am-7pm Mon & Wed-Fri, 11am-5pm Tue & Sat, 1-5.30pm Sun Jul & Aug) is a family entertainment centre with outdoor heated fun pools, giant water slides, and paddling pools for toddlers.

At the south end of the seafront is the **Rock Pool** (☎ 4372 5034; South Promenade; adult/child £1.80/1.50; 🕑 10am-6pm Mon-Sat & 2-6pm Sun Jul & Aug), an outdoor seawater swimming pool that dates from the 1930s. If it's too cold for outdoor bathing, you can simmer away in a hot seaweed bath at nearby **Soak** (☎ 4372 6002; www.soakseaweedbaths.co.uk; 5A South Promenade; 🕑 11.30am-8pm Thu-Mon Sep-Jun, daily Jul & Aug), where a one-hour session costs £25.

The little **harbour** at the south end of town once served the 'stone boats' that exported Mourne granite from the quarries of Slieve Donard. The **Granite Trail**, which begins across the road from the harbour, is a waymarked footpath that leads up a disused funicular railway line that once carried granite blocks to the harbour. The view from the top is worth the steep, 200m climb.

Stretching north of town is the **Royal County Down Golf Course** (☎ 4372 3314; www.royalcountydown.org; green fees weekday/weekend £160/180 May-Oct, £75/80 Nov-Mar). The challenging Championship Links – venue for the 2007 Walker Cup – is full of blind tee shots and monster rough, and is regularly voted one of the world's top 10 golf courses. It's open to visitors on Monday, Tuesday, Thursday, Friday and Sunday.

SLEEPING

Tollymore Forest Park (☎ 4372 2428; 176 Tullybranigan Rd; tent/caravan sites £9/13) Many of Newcastle's 'camping sites' are for caravans only; the nearest place where you can pitch a tent is amid the attractive scenery of Tollymore Forest Park, 3km northwest of the town centre. You can hike here (along Bryansford Ave and Bryansford Rd) in 45 minutes.

Newcastle Youth Hostel (☎ 4372 2133; www.hini.org.uk; 30 Downs Rd; dm £14; 🕑 daily Mar-Oct, Fri & Sat nights only Nov & 1-22 Dec, closed 23 Dec-Feb) This hostel is only a few minutes' walk from the bus station, housed in an attractive 19th-century villa with sea views. It has 37 beds, mostly in six-bed dorms, a kitchen, a laundry and a TV room.

our pick **Briers Country House** (☎ 4372 4347; www.thebriers.co.uk; 39 Middle Tollymore Rd; s/d from £40/60; P) A peaceful farmhouse B&B with a country setting and views of the Mournes, Briers is just 1.5km northwest of the town centre (signposted off the road between Newcastle and Bryansford). Huge breakfasts – vegetarian if you like – are served with a view over the garden, and evening meals are available by prior arrangement.

Beach House (☎ 4372 2345; beachhouse22@tiscali.co.uk; 22 Downs Rd; s/d £50/90; P wi-fi) Enjoy a sea view with your breakfast at the Beach House, an elegant Victorian B&B with three rooms (all with private bathroom) and a balcony (open to all guests) overlooking the beach.

Harbour House Inn (☎ 4372 3445; www.harbourhouseinn.co.uk; 4 South Promenade; s/d £60/90; P wi-fi) The Harbour House is a family-friendly pub and restaurant with four recently redecorated rooms upstairs that are clean and comfortable. It's next to the old harbour, almost 2km south of the bus station, a perfect base for climbing Slieve Donard.

Slieve Donard Resort & Spa (☎ 4372 1066; www.hastingshotels.com; Downs Rd; s/d from £80/100; P swimming pool wi-fi) Established in 1897, the Slieve Donard is a magnificent, Victorian red-brick pile overlooking the beach, equipped with several restaurants and a luxurious spa. This is where golf legends Tom Watson, Jack Nicklaus and Tiger Woods stay when they're in town.

EATING

Maud's (☎ 4372 6184; 106 Main St; mains £3-7; 🕑 9am-9.30pm) Maud's is a bright, modern cafe with picture windows framing a stunning view across the river to the Mournes. It serves breakfast, good coffee, a range of tempting scones and sticky buns, plus salads, crêpes, pizzas and pastas; there's a kids menu, too.

WALK: SLIEVE DONARD

The rounded form of Slieve Donard (853m), the highest hill in Northern Ireland, looms above Newcastle like a slumbering giant. You can hike to the summit from various starting points in and around Newcastle, but remember – it's a stiff climb, and you shouldn't attempt it without proper walking boots, waterproofs and a map and compass.

On a good day the view from the top extends to the hills of Donegal, the Wicklow Mountains, the coast of Scotland, the Isle of Man and even the hills of Snowdonia in Wales. Two cairns near the summit were long believed to have been cells of St Donard, who retreated here to pray in early Christian times.

The shortest route to the top is via the Glen River from Newcastle. Begin at Donard Park car park, at the edge of town, 1km south of the bus station. At the far end of the car park, turn right through the gate and head into the woods, with the river on your left. A gravel path leads up the Glen River valley to the saddle between Slieve Donard and Slieve Commedagh. From here, turn left and follow the Mourne Wall to the summit (see p621 for more on the Mourne Wall). Return by the same route (round trip 9km, allow at least three hours).

Sea Salt (☎ 4372 5027; 51 Central Promenade; mains £4-6; ☷ 10am-5pm Mon-Fri, 9am-5pm Sat & Sun, 7-9pm Fri & Sat) Both delicatessen and bistro, Sea Salt serves everything from a morning cappuccino to a lunchtime seafood platter, with an evening menu that ranges from Spanish tapas to themed menus from around the world.

Strand Restaurant & Bakery (☎ 4372 3472; 53-55 Central Promenade; mains £5-9; ☷ 8.30am-11pm Jun-Aug, 9am-6pm Sep-May) The Strand has been around since 1930, and dishes up great homemade ice cream and cakes, as well as serving all-day breakfast (£2 to £5), lunch and dinner in its traditional, seaside, chips-with-everything restaurant.

Mourne Café (☎ 4372 6401; 107 Central Promenade; mains £6-8; ☷ 11am-9pm Mon-Thu, to 10pm Fri-Sun) A new venture by the owners of the Mourne Seafood Bar (right), this informal, family-friendly cafe dishes up a kids menu (mains £5) as well as seafood chowder and beer-battered haddock and chips for mum and dad.

Campers can stock up on provisions at the **Lidl Supermarket** (3 Railway St; ☷ 9am-7pm Mon-Wed & Fri, to 9pm Thu, to 6pm Sat, 1-6pm Sun) in the red-brick former train station beside the bus station.

SHOPPING

Hill Trekker (☎ 4372 3842; 115 Central Promenade; ☷ 10am-5.30pm Tue-Sun), at the far south end of town, sells hiking, climbing and camping equipment.

GETTING THERE & AROUND

The bus station is on Railway St. Ulsterbus 20 runs to Newcastle from Belfast's Europa BusCentre (£7, 1¼ hours, at least hourly Monday to Saturday, eight Sunday) via Dundrum. Bus 37 continues along the coast road from Newcastle to Annalong and Kilkeel (£4, 35 minutes, hourly Monday to Saturday, eight Sunday).

Goldline Express bus 240 takes the inland route from Newry to Newcastle (£5, 50 minutes, six daily Monday to Saturday, two Sunday) via Hilltown and continues on to Downpatrick. You can also get to Newry along the coast road, changing buses at Kilkeel.

Wiki Wiki Wheels (☎ 4372 3973; 10B Donard St; ☷ 9am-6pm Mon-Sat, 2-6pm Sun), near the bus station, and **Ross Cycles** (☎ 4377 8029; 44 Clarkhill Rd, Castlewellan; ☷ 9.30am-6pm Mon-Sat, 2-5pm Sun), near Castlewellan, both hire out bikes for around £10/50 per day/week.

Around Newcastle

DUNDRUM

Second only to Carrickfergus as Northern Ireland's finest Norman fortress is **Dundrum Castle** (☎ 9181 1491; Dundrum; admission free; ☷ 10am-6pm daily Easter-Sep, noon-4pm Sun only Oct-Easter), founded in 1177 by John de Courcy of Carrickfergus. The castle overlooks the sheltered waters of Dundrum Bay, famous for its oysters and mussels.

Set in a wood-panelled Victorian house with local art brightening the walls, ᴏᴜʀ ᴘɪᴄᴋ **Mourne Seafood Bar** (☎ 4375 1377; 10 Main St; mains £9-17; ☷ noon-9.30pm daily, closed Mon & Tue Nov-Mar) is a friendly and informal fishmonger-cum-restaurant. As well as a choice of local oysters served five different ways, the menu includes seafood chowder, crab, langoustines and daily fish specials, all sourced locally.

WALK: THE BRANDY PAD

The Brandy Pad is an ancient smugglers' trail across the Mourne Mountains, used in the 18th century to carry brandy, wine, tobacco and coffee to Hilltown, thereby avoiding the excise officer at Newcastle.

The trail begins at the car park at Bloody Bridge on the A2 coast road, 5km south of Newcastle (any bus to Kilkeel will drop you there). From here, the path leads up the valley of the Bloody Bridge River, past old granite workings, to the Mourne Wall at the saddle south of Slieve Donard (3.5km).

On the far side of the wall a wide path contours north (to your right) across the lower slopes of Slieve Donard, then continues traversing west below the Castles, a huddle of weathered granite pinnacles. Beyond the peaty col beneath Slieve Commedagh, the path descends slightly into the valley of the Kilkeel River (or Silent Valley) and continues traversing with Ben Crom reservoir down to your left to reach Hare's Gap and a reunion with the Mourne Wall.

Go through the gap in the wall and descend to the northwest, steeply at first, then more easily on a broad and stony trail known as the Trassey Track, which leads down to a minor road and the Trassey Bridge car park near Meelmore Lodge (12km from Bloody Bridge; allow three to five hours).

From here you can return to Newcastle on foot through Tollymore Forest Park, along the trail that begins immediately above the car park (8km; allow two to three hours), or you can catch the *Mourne Rambler* bus (July and August only) from either the car park or Meelmore Lodge.

Dundrum is 5km north of Newcastle. Bus 17 from Newcastle to Downpatrick stops in Dundrum (£2, 12 minutes, eight daily Monday to Friday, four Saturday, two Sunday).

TOLLYMORE FOREST PARK

This scenic **forest park** (☎ 4372 2428; Bryansford; car/pedestrian £4/2; ☼ 10am-dusk), 3km west of Newcastle, has lengthy walks along the Shimna River and across the northern slopes of the Mournes. The park is littered with Victorian follies including **Clanbrassil Barn**, which looks more like a church, and grottoes, caves and stepping stones. An electronic kiosk at the car park provides information on the flora, fauna and history of the park. Note: mountain biking is not allowed in the park.

CASTLEWELLAN

A less rugged outdoor experience is offered by **Castlewellan Forest Park** (☎ 4377 8664; Main St, Castlewellan; car/pedestrian £4/2; ☼ 10am-dusk), with gentle walks around the castle grounds and **trout fishing** in its lovely lake (a three-day permit costs £8.50).

In July Castlewellan village is the focus of the **Celtic Fusion Festival** (www.celticfusion.co.uk), a 10-day celebration of Celtic music, art, drama and dance at venues around County Down, including Castlewellan, Newcastle and Downpatrick.

Mourne Mountains

The humpbacked granite hills of the Mourne Mountains dominate the horizon as you head south from Belfast towards Newcastle. This is one of the most beautiful corners of Northern Ireland, with a distinctive landscape of yellow gorse, grey granite and whitewashed cottages, the lower slopes of the hills latticed with a neat patchwork of drystone walls cobbled together from huge, rounded granite boulders.

The hills were made famous in a popular song penned by Irish songwriter William Percy French in 1896, whose chorus, 'Where the Mountains of Mourne sweep down to the sea', captures perfectly their scenic blend of ocean, sky and hillside. In recent years a debate has raged about the possible creation of Mourne National Park, with tourism and environmental lobbies for the project, and farmers against; at the time of research, no decision had yet been taken.

The Mournes offer some of the best hill walking and rock climbing in the North. Specialist guidebooks include *The Mournes: Walks* by Paddy Dillon and *A Rock-Climbing Guide to the Mourne Mountains* by Robert Bankhead. You'll also need an Ordnance Survey map, either the 1:50,000 Discoverer Series (Sheet No 29: *The Mournes*), or the 1:25,000 Activity Series (*The Mournes*). You can buy maps at the tourist information centre in Newcastle.

HISTORY

The crescent of low-lying land on the southern side of the mountains is known as the Kingdom of Mourne. Cut off for centuries by its difficult approaches (the main overland route passed north of the hills), it developed a distinctive landscape and culture. Neither St Patrick nor the Normans (their nearest strongholds were at Greencastle and Dundrum) ventured here and, until the coast road was built in the early 19th century, the only access was on foot or by sea.

Smuggling provided a source of income in the 18th century. Boats carrying French spirits would land at night and packhorses would carry the casks through the hills to the inland road, avoiding the excise men at Newcastle. The Brandy Pad (see the boxed text, opposite), a former smugglers' path from Bloody Bridge to Tollymore, is a popular walking route today.

Apart from farming and fishing, the main industry here was the quarrying of Mourne granite. The quarried stone was carried down from the hills on carts to harbours at Newcastle, Annalong and Kilkeel where 'stone boats' shipped it out; kerbstones of Mourne granite are found in Belfast, Liverpool, London, Manchester and Birmingham. There are still several working quarries today, and Mourne granite has been used in the 9/11 British Memorial Garden in New York.

SIGHTS

At the heart of the Mournes is the beautiful **Silent Valley Reservoir** (☎ 08457 440088; car/motorcycle £4.50/2, plus per adult/child £1.60/0.60; ☼ 10am-6.30pm Apr-Oct, to 4pm Nov-Mar), where the Kilkeel River was dammed in 1933. There are scenic, waymarked walks around the grounds, a **coffee shop** (☼ 11am-5.30pm Sat & Sun Apr-Sep), and an interesting exhibition on the building of the dam. From the car park a shuttle bus (adult/child return £1.40/1) will take you another 4km up the valley to the Crom Dam. It runs daily in July and August, weekends only in May, June and September.

The dry-stone **Mourne Wall** was built between 1904 and 1922 to keep livestock out of the catchment area of the Kilkeel and Annalong Rivers, which were to be dammed to provide a water supply for Belfast. (Poor geological conditions meant the Annalong could not be dammed, and its waters were diverted to the Silent Valley Reservoir via a 3.6km-long tunnel beneath Slieve Binnian.) The spectacular wall, 2m high, 1m thick and over 35km long, marches across the summits of 15 of the surrounding peaks including the highest, Slieve Donard (853m).

ACTIVITIES

If you fancy a shot at hill walking, rock climbing, canoeing or a range of other outdoor activities, **Bluelough Mountain & Water Sports Centre** (☎ 4377 0714; www.mountainandwater.com; Grange Courtyard, Castlewellan Forest Park) offers one-day, have-a-go sessions for individuals, couples and families (around £60 to £100 per person), as well as Sunday afternoon taster sessions. They also rent canoes for £30/45 per half-day/day.

If the weather is wet, you can still go rock climbing at **Hotrock** (☎ 4372 5354; www.hotrockwall.com; adult/child £4.50/2.50; ☼ 10am-5pm Mon, to 10pm Tue-Fri, to 6pm Sat & Sun), the indoor climbing wall at Tollymore Mountain Centre; you can hire rock boots and harness for £3.50. The entrance is on the B180, 2km west of the Tollymore Forest Park exit gate.

Surfin' Dirt (☎ 07739 210119; www.surfindirt.co.uk; Tullyree Rd, Bryansford; ☼ 10am-6pm Tue-Sun Jul & Aug, 11am-6pm Sat & Sun Apr-Jun & Sep-Nov) is a mountainboarding track off the B180, 3km west of Bryansford village. A three-hour beginner's session, including board, safety gear and instruction, costs £17.50.

More sedate outdoor activities are offered by the **Mount Pleasant Pony Trekking & Horse Riding Centre** (☎ 4377 8651; www.mountpleasantcentre.com; Bannonstown Rd, Castlewellan; per hr £12-15), which caters for both experienced riders and beginners, and offers various guided treks into the park. Short rides, beach rides and pony trekking can also be arranged.

Mourne Cycle Tours (☎ 4372 4348; www.mournecycletours.com; 13 Spelga Ave, Newcastle) provide mountain- and touring-bike hire (from £10/15/80 per half-day/full day/week) and can arrange self-guided tours and family cycling weekends, including accommodation.

FESTIVALS

The Mournes are the venue for various hiking festivals, including the **Mourne International Walking Festival** (www.mournewalking.co.uk) in late June, and the Down District Walking Festival in early August.

SLEEPING

Meelmore Lodge (☎ 4372 6657; www.meelmorelodge.co.uk; 52 Trassey Rd, Bryansford; camping per adult/child £5/3, dm/tw £17/50; Ⓟ) Set on the northern slopes of the Mournes, 5km west of Bryansford village, Meelmore has hostel accommodation with a cosy lounge and kitchen, a campsite (tents only) and a good coffee shop.

Cnocnafeola Centre (☎ 4176 5859; www.mournehos tel.com; Bog Rd, Atticall; dm/tw/f £15/36/55; P 🖳) This modern, purpose-built hostel is in the village of Atticall, 6km north of Kilkeel, off the B27 Hilltown road, and 3km west of the entrance to Silent Valley. As well as a self-catering kitchen, there's a restaurant that serves breakfast, lunch and dinner.

GETTING THERE & AWAY
In July and August only, the Ulsterbus 405 *Mourne Rambler* service runs a circular route from Newcastle, calling at a dozen stops around the Mournes, including Bryansford (8 minutes), Meelmore (17 minutes), Silent Valley (40 minutes), Carrick Little (45 minutes) and Bloody Bridge (one hour). There are six buses daily – the first leaves at 9.30am, the last at 5pm; a £5 all-day ticket allows you to get on and off as many times as you like.

Bus 34A (July and August only) runs from Newcastle to the Silent Valley car park (45 minutes, two daily), calling at Donard Park (five minutes) and Bloody Bridge (10 minutes).

Mournes Coast Road
The scenic drive south along the A2 coast road from Newcastle to Newry is the most memorable journey in Down. Annalong, Kilkeel and Rostrevor offer convenient stopping points from which you can detour into the mountains.

ANNALONG
The harbour at the fishing village of Annalong (Áth na Long) desperately wants to be picturesque, with an early 19th-century **Corn Mill** (☎ 4376 8736; Marine Park; adult/child £2.10/1.20; 🕑 call to check opening times) overlooking the river mouth on one side. (Alas, the effect is spoiled a bit by graffiti and ugly buildings on the other side.)

You can overnight at the family-oriented **Cornmill Quay Hostel** (☎ 4376 8269; www.cornmillquay .com; Marine Park; dm adult/child £17/12, d £46; P), set in a pretty little cottage courtyard above the harbour. There are also four self-catering cottages (from £375 a week in high season).

The **Harbour Inn** (☎ 4376 8678; 6 Harbour Dr; mains £7-16; 🕑 food 12.30-2.30pm, 5-8pm Sun-Fri, 12.30-9pm Sat) has an attractive lounge bar with sofas

arranged along the picture windows beside the harbour, and an upstairs restaurant with a great view of the Mournes.

KILKEEL
Kilkeel (Cill Chaoil, meaning 'church of the narrow place') takes its name from the 14th-century **Church of St Colman**, whose ruins stand in the graveyard across the street from the tourist office. The town has a busy commercial fishing harbour and a quayside fish market supplied by Northern Ireland's largest fishing fleet.

The **tourist information centre** (☎ 4176 2525; kdakilkeel@hotmail.com; Rooney Rd; 🕑 9am-1pm & 2-5.30pm Easter-Dec) is in the Nautilus Centre next to the harbour.

ROSTREVOR
Rostrevor (Caislean Ruairi) is a pretty Victorian seaside resort famed for its lively pubs. Each year in late July, folk musicians converge on the village for the **Fiddler's Green International Festival** (☎ 4173 9819; www.fiddlersgreen festival.co.uk).

Most of the town's other noted pubs also have regular live music on offer. The best ones to eat in are the **Kilbroney** (☎ 4173 8390; 31 Church St) and the **Celtic Fjord** (☎ 4173 8005; 8 Mary St).

To the east is **Kilbroney Forest Park** (☎ 4173 8134; Shore Rd; admission free; 🕑 9am-10pm Jun-Aug, to 5pm Sep-May). From the car park at the top of the forest drive, a 10-minute hike leads up to a superb view over the lough to Carlingford Mountain, as well as to the **Cloughmore Stone**, a 30-tonne granite boulder inscribed with Victorian graffiti.

Warrenpoint
pop 7000
Warrenpoint (An Pointe) is a Victorian resort at the head of Carlingford Lough, its seaside appeal somewhat diminished by the large industrial harbour at the west end of town. Its broad streets, main square and renovated prom are pleasant enough, though, and it has better sleeping and eating options than either Newry or Rostrevor, including a couple of excellent restaurants.

The **tourist information centre** (☎ 4175 2256; Church St; 🕑 9am-1pm & 2-5pm Mon-Fri Oct-May, also Sat & Sun Jun-Sep) is in the town hall.

About 2km northwest of the town centre is **Narrow Water Castle** (☎ 9181 1491; admission free;

TOP 10 RESTAURANTS IN NORTHERN IRELAND (OUTSIDE BELFAST)

- 55 Degrees North (p653)
- Copper (below)
- Grace Neill's (p608)
- Jeffers by the Marina (p607)
- Lime Tree (p648)
- Mourne Seafood Bar (p619)
- Terrace Restaurant (p682)
- Plough Inn (p603)
- Restaurant 23 (below)
- Uluru Bistro (p629)

10am-6pm Fri only Jul & Aug), a fine Elizabethan tower house built in 1568 to command the entrance to the Newry River.

SLEEPING & EATING

Whistledown Hotel (☎ 4175 4174; www.thewhistledown hotel.co.uk; 6 Seaview; s/d £80/120; ☐) This former guesthouse on the waterfront has been given a boutique-style makeover, with scarlet and pistachio crushed velvet, bathrooms with triple shower heads and large flat-screen TVs. It also has a stylish bar and restaurant (mains £9 to £19; open noon to 5pm & 7.30pm to 10pm Monday to Saturday, plus 12.30pm to 3.30pm Sunday).

our pick Restaurant 23 (☎ 4175 3222; 23 Church St; mains £8-13, 3-course dinner £18; 12.30-3pm & 5.30-9pm Wed-Sat, 12.30-8.30pm Sun) Set in Bennet's Bar on Warrenpoint's main drag, the new kid on the block has already garnered a Michelin Bib Gourmand. It's also helping turn this corner of County Down into a foodie destination with dishes such as Kilkeel crab and prawn cocktail with avocado sauce, and Fermanagh roast pork with apple chutney, black pudding beignet and calvados jus.

Copper (☎ 4175 3047; 4 Duke St; mains £16-18, 2-/3-course dinner Sun & Tue-Thu £22/28; noon-3pm Wed-Sat, 5.30-9.30pm Tue-Thu, 5.30-10.30pm Fri & Sat, noon-8.30pm Sun) A stalwart of Warrenpoint's fine-dining scene, Copper is an elegant, white-linen-tablecloth kind of restaurant that combines food sourced from local farms and fish bought from the quayside at Kilkeel with Mediterranean and Asian flavours. There's a separate vegetarian menu (mains £12.50) with inventive dishes such as sweet-potato pancake with shiitake mushrooms, scallions and black bean sauce.

GETTING THERE & AWAY

Bus 39 runs between Newry and Warrenpoint (£2, 20 minutes, at least hourly Monday to Saturday, 10 on Sunday), with some services continuing on to Kilkeel (one hour).

Newry
pop 22,975

Newry has long been a frontier town, guarding the land route from Dublin to Ulster through the 'Gap of the North', the pass between Slieve Gullion and the Carlingford hills, still followed by the main Dublin–Belfast road and railway. Its name derives from a yew tree (An tIúr) supposedly planted here by St Patrick.

The opening of the Newry Canal in 1742, linking the town with the River Bann at Portadown, made Newry a busy trading port, exporting coal from Coalisland on Lough Neagh, as well as linen and butter from the surrounding area.

Newry today is a major shopping centre, with a busy market on Thursday and Saturday; it's invaded at weekends by shoppers from the South taking advantage of the euro exchange rate and the relative bargains available across the border.

INFORMATION

Coffee-Net (☎ 3026 3531; Newry BusCentre, The Mall; per 15min £1; 8.30am-6pm Mon-Fri, 9am-6pm Sat, 5-8pm Sun) Internet access.

Tourist information centre (☎ 3031 3170; newry tic@newryandmourne.gov.uk; Bagenal's Castle, Castle St; 9am-5pm Mon, to 6pm Tue-Fri mid-Jun–Sep, to 5pm Mon-Fri Oct–mid-Jun, plus 10am-4pm Sat Apr-Sep)

SIGHTS

So fierce was the rivalry between counties Down and Armagh in the 19th century that when the new red-brick **town hall** was built in 1893, it was erected right on the border – on a three-arched bridge across the Newry River. The cannon outside was captured during the Crimean War (1853–56) and given to the town in memory of local volunteers who fought in the war.

Bagenal's Castle is the town's oldest surviving building, a 16th-century tower house built for Nicholas Bagenal, grand marshal of the English army in Ireland. Recently rediscovered, having been incorporated into more recent buildings, the castle has been restored and now houses the **Newry and Mourne Museum** (☎ 3031 3178; www .bagenalscastle.com; Castle St; admission free; ☺ 10am-4.30pm Mon-Sat & 1-4.30pm Sun), with exhibits on the Newry Canal and local archaeology, culture and folklore. The castle also houses the tourist information centre and an excellent **cafe** (☺ 9am-5pm Mon-Sat, 1-4.30pm Sunday).

The **Newry Canal** runs parallel to the river through the town centre, and is a focus for the city's redevelopment. A cycle path runs 30km north to Portadown, following the route of the canal. **Newry Ship Canal** runs 6km south towards Carlingford Lough, where the Victoria Lock has been restored to working order as part of a long-term project to reopen the whole canal to leisure traffic. Designed by Sir John Rennie, the civil engineer who designed Waterloo, Southwark and London Bridges in London, the ship canal allowed large, sea-going vessels to reach Albert Basin in the centre of Newry.

SLEEPING

Marymount (☎ 3026 1099; patricia.ohare2@btinternet .com; Windsor Ave; s/d £35/60; Ⓟ 🛜) A modern bungalow in a quiet location up a hill off the A1 Belfast road, Marymount is only a 10-minute walk from the town centre. Only one of the three bedrooms comes with a private bathroom.

Canal Court Hotel (☎ 3025 1234; www.canalcourtho tel.com; Merchants Quay; s/d from £85/135; Ⓟ 🖥 🛜) You can't miss this huge, yellow building opposite the bus station. Although it's a modern hotel, it affects a deliberately old-fashioned atmosphere, with leather sofas dotted around the vast wood-panelled lobby and a restaurant that veers dangerously close to chintzy.

EATING & DRINKING

Café Krem (☎ 3026 6233; 14 Hill St; mains £3-4; ☺ 8.30am-6pm Mon-Sat; 🛜) A friendly, community atmosphere and the best coffee in town make Café Krem stand out from the crowd. There's also wicked hot chocolate, tasty soups, sandwiches, pasta and panini and a couple of big, soft sofas to sink into.

Brass Monkey (☎ 3026 3176; 1-4 Sandy St; mains £7-16; ☺ bar meals noon-9pm Mon-Sat, 12.30-8.30pm Sun) Newry's most popular pub, with Victorian brass, brick and timber decor, serves good bar meals ranging from lasagne and burgers to seafood and steaks. At weekends you can get a full Irish fried breakfast for £5 (9am till noon).

Table Bistro (☎ 3025 1935; 3 Monaghan St; mains £10-14; ☺ 8am-10pm) This stylish cafe-bistro is decked out in identikit Northern Ireland restaurant decor of blonde wood with leather chairs in shades of chocolate and cream. It dishes up big breakfasts (till 11.30am), light lunches (gourmet sandwiches, Caesar salad, pasta carbonara) and delicious dinners from a menu that ranges from steak and chips to prawn and shellfish tagliatelle with cream and white wine sauce.

GETTING THERE & AWAY

Newry BusCentre is on the Mall, opposite the Canal Court Hotel. Goldline Express bus 238 runs regularly to Newry from Belfast's Europa BusCentre (£8, 1¼ hours, at least hourly Monday to Saturday, eight Sunday) via Hillsborough and Banbridge.

Bus 44 runs from Newry to Armagh (£5, 1¼ hours, twice daily Monday to Saturday), and Goldline Express bus 295 goes from Newry to Enniskillen (£9, 2¾ hours, twice daily Monday to Saturday, July and August only) via Armagh and Monaghan. Bus 39 departs for Warrenpoint (20 minutes, at least hourly Monday to Saturday, 10 on Sunday) and Rostrevor (30 minutes), with 10 a day continuing to Kilkeel (£4, one hour).

The train station is 2.5km northwest of the centre, on the A25; bus 341 (free for train passengers) goes there hourly from the bus station. Newry is a stop on the train service between Dublin (£17, 1¼ hours, eight daily) and Belfast (£9, 50 minutes, eight daily).

COUNTY ARMAGH

SOUTH ARMAGH

Rural and staunchly Republican, South Armagh is known to its inhabitants as 'God's Country'. But to the British soldiers stationed there in the 1970s it had another, more sinister nickname – 'Bandit Country'. With the Republic only a few miles away, South Armagh was a favourite area for IRA cross-border attacks and bombings. For more than 30 years, British soldiers on foot patrol in village streets and the constant clatter of army helicopters were a part of everyday life.

The peace process has probably had more visible effect here than anywhere else in Northern Ireland. As part of the UK government's 'normalisation process', the army ulled out in 2007 – the hilltop watchtowers ave all been removed (their former location marked here and there by a defiant Irish tricolour) and the huge barracks at Bessbrook Mill nd Crossmaglen have been closed down.

Hopefully, a part of Ireland that was once notorious for its violence will again be known or its historic sites, enchanting rural scenery nd traditional music.

Bessbrook

op 3150

Bessbrook (An Sruthán) was founded in the mid-19th century by Quaker linen manufacturer John Grubb Richardson as a 'model village' to house the workers at his flax mill. Rows of pretty terraced houses made from local granite line the two main squares, Charlemont and College, each with a green in the middle, and are complemented by a town hall, school, bathhouse and dispensary. It is said that Bessbrook was the inspiration for Bournville (near Birmingham in England), the model village built by the Cadbury family for their chocolate factory.

At the centre of the village is the massive **Bessbrook Mill**. Requisitioned by the British Army in 1970, it served as a military base for more than 30 years – the helipad here was reputedly the busiest in Europe – until the troops moved out in 2007. Plans to convert the mill building into social housing and a new cultural complex were thwarted when it was given listed status in 2008. Its future is now uncertain.

Just south of Bessbrook is **Derrymore House** (☎ 8778 4753; house tour £3.70; ☺ gardens 10am-6pm May-Sep, to 4pm Oct-Apr), an elegant thatched cottage built in 1776 for Isaac Corry, the Irish MP for Newry for 30 years; the Act of Union was drafted in the drawing room here in 1800. The house is only open on a handful of days each year – call or check the National Trust website (www.nationaltrust.org.uk) – but the surrounding parkland, laid out by John Sutherland (1745–1826), one of the most celebrated disciples of English landscape gardener Capability Brown, offers scenic trails with views to the Ring of Gullion.

Bessbrook is 5km northwest of Newry. Bus 41 runs from Newry to Bessbrook (15 minutes, hourly Monday to Saturday), while buses 42 (to Crossmaglen) and 44 (to Armagh) pass the entrance to Derrymore House on the A25 Camlough road.

Ring of Gullion

The Ring of Gullion is a magical region steeped in Celtic legend, centred on Slieve Gullion (Sliabh gCuilinn; 576m), where the Celtic warrior Cúchulainn is said to have taken his name after killing the dog (cú) belonging to the smith Culainn. The 'ring' is a necklace of rugged hills strung between Newry and Forkhill, 15km to the southwest, encircling the central whaleback ridge of Slieve Gullion. This unusual concentric formation is a geological structure known as a ring dyke.

KILLEVY CHURCHES

Surrounded by beech trees, these ruined, conjoined **churches** (admission free; ☺ 24hr) were constructed on the site of a 5th-century nunnery that was founded by St Moninna. The eastern church dates from the 15th century, and shares a gable wall with the 12th-century western one. The west door, with a massive lintel and granite jambs, may be 200 years older still. At the side of the churchyard, a footpath leads uphill to a white cross that marks St Moninna's holy well.

The churches are 6km south of Camlough, on a minor road to Meigh. Look out for a crossroads with a sign pointing west to the churches and east to Bernish Rock Viewpoint.

SLIEVE GULLION FOREST PARK

A 13km scenic drive through this **forest park** (admission free; ☺ 8am-dusk) provides picturesque views over the surrounding hills. From the parking and picnic area at the top of the drive, you can hike to the summit of Slieve Gullion, the highest point in County Armagh, topped by two early Bronze Age cairns and a tiny lake (1.5km round trip). The park entrance is 10km southwest of Newry on the B113 road to Forkhill.

MULLAGHBANE & FORKHILL

In the village of Mullaghbane (Mullach Bán), just west of Slieve Gullion, is **Tí Chulainn** (☎ 3088 8828; www.tichulainn.com; admission free; ☺ 9am-5pm Mon-Fri, 11am-12.30pm Sat), a cultural activities centre that promotes the Irish language, local folklore, traditional music and storytelling. The centre houses an exhibition, craft shop and cafe. It also offers hostel-type accommodation (£45 for a room sleeping up to three people).

The pubs in nearby Forkhill hold traditional music sessions on Tuesday nights and alternate Saturdays, and a folk music festival in October.

Crossmaglen

pop 1600

Crossmaglen (Crois Mhic Lionnáin), arranged around one of Ireland's biggest market squares, is a strongly Republican village just 4km inside the border. At the height of the Troubles, the barracks at 'Cross' (or 'XMG', as it was known) was the most feared posting in the British Army.

Now the army has gone and, for today's visitors, Crossmaglen is a friendly place with a reputation for Gaelic football (Crossmaglen Rangers were the All-Ireland Club Champions in 2007, and Ulster champions in 2008 and 2009), horse breeding and lively pubs known for their excellent music sessions.

You can get tourist information at **RoSA** (☎ 3086 8900; 25-26 O'Fiaich Sq; ☉ 9am-5pm Mon-Fri).

Murtagh's Bar (☎ 3086 1378; aidanmurtagh@hotmail .com; 13 North St; s/d £30/50) offers good craic, traditional music, bar meals and B&B, while the modern **Cross Square Hotel** (☎ 3086 0505; www.cross squarehotel.com; 4-5 O'Fiaich Sq; s/d £45/70, mains £6-11; ☉ food served 9am-9pm) serves bar meals all day and an à la carte menu at lunch and dinner. There's live music on Friday, Saturday and Sunday nights.

Bus 42 runs from Newry to Crossmaglen (£4, 50 minutes, five daily Monday to Friday, four Saturday) via Camlough and Mullaghbane.

ARMAGH CITY

pop 14,600

The little cathedral city of Armagh (Ard Macha) has been an important religious centre since the 5th century, and remains the ecclesiastical capital of Ireland, the seat of both the Anglican and Roman Catholic archbishops of Armagh, and Primates of All Ireland. Their two cathedrals, both named for St Patrick, stare each other out from their respective hilltops.

Despite having a number of attractive Georgian buildings, the town has a bit of a dreary, run-down feel to it, with gap sites, wasteland and boarded-up windows spoiling the streetscape, but it's still worth a visit for the fascinating Armagh Public Library and nearby Navan Fort.

History

When St Patrick began his mission to spread Christianity throughout Ireland, he chose a site close to Emain Macha (Navan Fort), the nerve centre of pagan Ulster, for his power base. In AD 445 he built Ireland's first stone church on a hill nearby (now home to the Church of Ireland cathedral), and later decreed that Armagh should have pre-eminence over all the churches in Ireland.

By the 8th century Armagh was one of Europe's best-known centres of religion, learning and craftwork. The city was divided into three districts (called *trians*), centred around English, Scottish and Irish streets. Armagh's fame was its undoing, however, as the Vikings plundered the city 10 times between AD 831 and 1013.

The city gained a new prosperity from the linen trade in the 18th century, a period whose legacy includes a Royal School, an astronomical observatory, a renowned public library and a fine crop of Georgian architecture.

Armagh is associated with some prominent historical figures. James Ussher (1580–1655), Archbishop of Armagh, was an avid scholar who is best known for pinning down the day of the Creation to Sunday 23 October 4004 BC by adding up the generations quoted in the Bible, a date that was accepted as fact until the late 19th century. His extensive library became the nucleus of the great library at Trinity College, Dublin. Jonathan Swift (1667–1745), Dean of St Patrick's Cathedral, Dublin, and author of *Gulliver's Travels*, was a frequent visitor to Armagh, while the architect Francis Johnston (1760–1829), responsible for many of Dublin's finest Georgian streetscapes, was born in the city.

Information

Armagh City Library (☎ 3752 4072; Market St; ☉ 9.30am-5.30pm Mon, Wed & Fri, to 8pm Tue & Thu, to 5pm Sat) Internet access for £1.50 per 30 minutes.

Tourist information centre (☎ 3752 1800; www .visitarmagh.com; 40 Upper English St; ☉ 9am-5pm Mon-Sat year-round, also noon-5.30pm Sun Jul & Aug, 2-5pm Sun Sep-Jun) Part of the St Patrick's Trian complex.

Sights

ST PATRICK'S TRIAN

The old Presbyterian church behind the tourist office has been turned into a heritage centre and visitor complex known as **St Patrick's Trian** (☎ 3752 1801; 40 Upper English St; adult/child £5/3.25; ☉ 10am-5pm Mon-Sat, 2-5pm Sun). There are three exhibitions: the Armagh Story explores the history of Armagh from pagan prehistory to the present day; Patrick's Testament takes an interactive look at the ancient *Book of Armagh*; and for the kids there's the Land of Lilliput, where Gulliver's adventures in Lilliput are recounted by a gigantic model of Jonathan Swift's famous creation.

ST PATRICK'S CHURCH OF IRELAND CATHEDRAL

The city's **Anglican cathedral** (☎ 3752 3142; Cathedral Close; admission free; ⏱ 9am-5pm Apr-Oct, to 4pm Nov-Mar) occupies the site of St Patrick's original stone church. The present cathedral's ground plan is 13th century but the building itself is a Gothic restoration dating from 1834 to 1840. A stone slab on the exterior wall of the north transept marks the burial place of Brian Ború, the high king of Ireland, who died near Dublin during the last great battle against the Vikings in 1014.

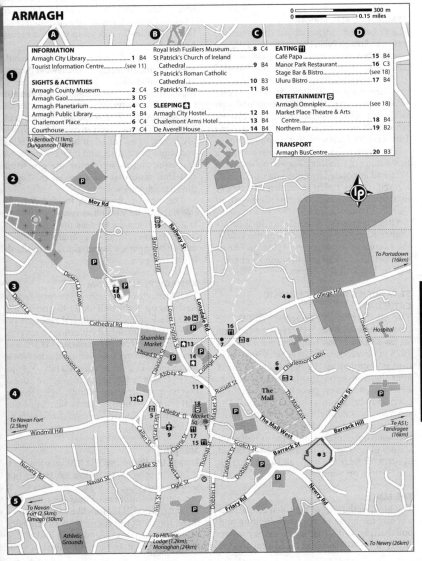

ARMAGH

0 — 300 m
0 — 0.15 miles

INFORMATION
Armagh City Library	**1** B4
Tourist Information Centre	(see 11)

SIGHTS & ACTIVITIES
Armagh County Museum	**2** C4
Armagh Gaol	**3** D5
Armagh Planetarium	**4** C3
Armagh Public Library	**5** B4
Charlemont Place	**6** C4
Courthouse	**7** C4
Royal Irish Fusiliers Museum	**8** C4
St Patrick's Church of Ireland Cathedral	**9** B4
St Patrick's Roman Catholic Cathedral	**10** B3
St Patrick's Trian	**11** B4

SLEEPING ᐃ
Armagh City Hostel	**12** B4
Charlemont Arms Hotel	**13** B4
De Averell House	**14** B4

EATING ᐃ
Café Papa	**15** B4
Manor Park Restaurant	**16** C3
Stage Bar & Bistro	(see 18)
Uluru Bistro	**17** B4

ENTERTAINMENT ᐃ
Armagh Omniplex	(see 18)
Market Place Theatre & Arts Centre	**18** B4
Northern Bar	**19** B2

TRANSPORT
Armagh BusCentre	**20** B3

To Benburb (11km); Dungannon (18km)

Moy Rd

Banbrook Hill

Railway St

Desert La Lower

Desert La

Cathedral Rd

Convent Rd

Lower English St

Lonsdale Rd

Shambles Market

Edward St

Dawson St

Abbey St

College St

Russell St

Cathedral Cl

Vicar's Hill

Callan St

Castle St

Chapel La

Thomas St

Market Sq

Market St

The Mall

The Mall East

Charlemont Gdns

College Hill

Lower Hill

Hospital

Victoria St

The Mall West

Barrack Hill

Scotch St

Barrack St

Linenhall St

Dobbin St

Dobbin La

Newry Rd

To Portadown (16km)

To A51; Tandragee (16km)

To Navan Fort (2.5km)

Windmill Hill

Nursery Rd

Navan St

Culdee St

Ogle St

Irish St

Friary Rd

To Navan Fort (2.5km); Omagh (50km)

Athletic Grounds

To Hillview Lodge (1.2km); Monaghan (24km)

To Newry (26km)

Within the church are the remains of an 11th-century **Celtic Cross** that once stood nearby, and the **Tandragee Idol**, a curious granite figure dating back to the Iron Age. In the south aisle is a **memorial to Archbishop Richard Robinson** (1709–94), who founded Armagh's observatory and public library. Guided tours, which should be arranged in advance, cost £2 per person.

ARMAGH PUBLIC LIBRARY

The Greek inscription above the main entrance to **Armagh Public Library** (☎ 3752 3142; www.armaghrobinsonlibrary.org; 43 Abbey St; admission free, guided tour £2; ☒ 10am-1pm & 2-4pm Mon-Fri), founded in 1771 by Archbishop Robinson, means 'the medicine shop of the soul'. Step inside and you'd swear that the archbishop had just swept out of the door, leaving you to browse among his personal collection of 17th- and 18th-century books, maps and engravings.

The library's most prized possession is a first edition of *Gulliver's Travels*, published in 1726 and annotated by none other than Swift himself. It was stolen in an armed robbery in 1999, but was recovered, undamaged, in Dublin 20 months later.

Other treasures of the library include Sir Walter Raleigh's 1614 *History of the World*, the *Claims of the Innocents* (pleas to Oliver Cromwell) and a large collection of engravings by Hogarth and others.

ST PATRICK'S ROMAN CATHOLIC CATHEDRAL

The other **St Patrick's Cathedral** (☎ 3752 2802; Cathedral Rd; admission free; ☒ 9am-6pm Mon-Fri, to 8pm Sat, 8am-6.30pm Sun) was built between 1838 and 1873 in Gothic Revival style, with huge twin towers dominating the approach up flight after flight of steps. Inside it seems almost Byzantine, with every piece of wall and ceiling covered in brilliantly coloured mosaics. The sanctuary was modernised in 1981 and has a very distinctive tabernacle holder and crucifix that seem out of place among the mosaics and statues of the rest of the church. Mass is said at 10am Monday to Friday, and at 9am, 11am and 5.30pm on Sunday.

THE MALL

The Mall, to the east of the town centre, was a venue for horse racing, cock fighting and bull baiting until the 18th century when Archbishop Robinson decided that was all a tad vulgar for a city of learning, and transformed it into an elegant Georgian park.

At its northern end stands the **courthouse**, rebuilt after being destroyed by a huge IRA bomb blast in 1993. It originally dates from 1809, designed by local man Francis Johnston, who later became one of Ireland's most famous architects. At the southern end, directly opposite the courthouse, is the forbidding **Armagh Gaol**. Built in 1780 to the design of Thomas Cooley, it remained in use until 1988; there are plans to redevelop it into a luxury hotel.

The east side of the park is lined with handsome Georgian terraces. **Charlemont Place** is another creation of Francis Johnston, as is the portico fronting **Armagh County Museum** (☎ 3752 3070; www.armaghcountymuseum.org.uk; The Mall East; admission free; ☒ 10am-5pm Mon-Fri, 10am-1pm & 2-5pm Sat). The museum displays prehistoric axe heads, items found in bogs, corn dollies and straw-boy outfits, and military costumes and equipment. Don't miss the gruesome cast-iron skull that once graced the top of the Armagh gallows.

The nearby **Royal Irish Fusiliers Museum** (☎ 3752 2911; The Mall East; admission free; ☒ 10am-12.30pm & 1.30-4pm Mon-Fri) tells the story of the 'Eagle Takers', the first regiment to capture one of Bonaparte's imperial eagle standards in 1811.

ARMAGH PLANETARIUM

The Armagh Observatory was founded by Archbishop Robinson in 1790 and is still Ireland's leading astronomical research institute. Aimed mainly at educating young people, the nearby **Armagh Planetarium** (☎ 3752 3689; www.armaghplanet.com; College Hill; admission to exhibition area per person £2, shows per adult/child £6/5; ☒ 1-5pm Mon-Fri, 11.30am-5pm Sat) has an interactive exhibition on space exploration, and a digital theatre that screens a range of spectacular half-hour shows on its domed ceiling (check website for show times).

Sleeping

Armagh City Hostel (☎ 3751 1800; www.hini.org.uk; 39 Abbey St; dm/tw £16/34; ☒ open daily Mar-Oct, Fri & Sat only Nov-Feb, closed 23 Dec-2 Jan; ℗) This modern, purpose-built hostel near the Church of Ireland Cathedral is more like a small hotel – there are six comfortable twin rooms with private bathrooms, TV and tea-and-coffee facilities, as well as 12 small dorms, a well-equipped kitchen, a laundry, a lounge and a reading room.

Hillview Lodge (☎ 3752 2000; www.hillviewlodge.com; 33 Newtownhamilton Rd; s/d £38/58; P 🛜) Just 1.5km south of Armagh, Hillview is a welcoming, family-run guesthouse with a self-contained accommodation block containing six appealing rooms with great countryside views. And there's a driving range next door if you feel like improving your golf swing.

De Averell House (☎ 3751 1213; www.deaverellhouse .net; 47 Upper English St; s/d £45/75; P 🛜) A converted Georgian town house with four spacious rooms and a self-catering apartment, the De Averell is run by a friendly landlord who can't do enough to help. Rooms at the front can be noisy; the twin at the back is the quietest.

Charlemont Arms Hotel (☎ 3752 2028; www.charle montarmshotel.com; 57-65 Lower English St; s/d £55/90; P) This hotel dates from the 19th century, but has been renovated in charming period decor – oak-panelled dining room, Victorian fireplaces, flagstone-floored cellar restaurant. The bedrooms, in contrast, are modern and stylish.

Eating

Café Papa (☎ 3751 1205; 15 Thomas St; mains £4-8; 🕒 9am-5.30pm Mon-Sat, 6-9pm Fri & Sat) This deli-cum-cafe serves good coffee, cakes, home-baked bread and gourmet sandwiches, and does bistro dinners on Friday and Saturday evenings when you can bring your own wine.

Stage Bar & Bistro (☎ 3752 1828; Market Sq; mains £5-12; 🕒 food noon-4pm Mon-Sat, 5-9pm Thu-Sat, cafe menu from 9.30am Mon-Sat) This stylish little place is a chilled-out haven of coffee- and cream-coloured sofas and chairs in the theatre lobby, with a menu that offers some tasty vegetarian dishes – try the brie, red onion and spinach tart – as well as the steak sandwich with cara-melised onions, and baked sea bass with cur-ried mango dressing.

our pick Uluru Bistro (☎ 3751 8051; 16-18 Market St; mains £14-18; 🕒 noon-3pm & 5-9.30pm Tue-Fri, noon-3pm & 5-10.30pm Sat, 4-10pm Sun) The Aussie chef at Uluru brings a bit of antipodean flair to Armagh, with a fusion menu that ranges from Balinese chicken with ginger and lemongrass to mari-nated, chargrilled medallions of kangaroo with sweet-potato chips, plus lobster, monkfish and other seafood freshly landed at Kilkeel.

Manor Park Restaurant (☎ 3751 5353; 2 College Hill, The Mall; mains £15-25; 🕒 noon-9.30pm) Crisp white linen and silver candlesticks complement a cosy old-world decor of red-brick walls, par-quet floors and Persian rugs in this atmos-pheric French restaurant. The menu runs the gastronomic gamut from sautéed scallops to tournedos Rossini, with a wine list as long as the Loire. There's a three-course early evening menu for £20, available 5pm to 6.30pm.

Entertainment

Market Place Theatre & Arts Centre (☎ 3752 1821; www .marketplacearmagh.com; Market St; 🕒 box office 9.30am-4.30pm Mon-Sat) Armagh's main cultural venue hosts a 400-seat theatre, exhibition galleries, a restaurant, a cafe and the Stage Bar & Bistro, which has live bands on Saturday nights.

Armagh Omniplex (☎ 08717 200400; www.omniplex .ie; Market St; adult/child £6/4) Four-screen cinema next door to the arts centre.

Northern Bar (☎ 3752 7315; 100 Railway St) The Northern is your best bet for live bands, with traditional music sessions on Tuesday eve-nings, and local rock bands and DJs on Friday and Saturday nights.

You may be lucky enough to catch a game of **road bowling** (www.irishroadbowling.ie), a traditional Irish game now played mostly in Armagh and Cork. Contestants hurl small metal bowls weighing 750g along quiet country lanes to see who can make it to the finishing line with the least number of throws. Games usually take place on Sunday afternoons in summer, with the Ulster Finals held at Armagh in late June. Ask for details at the tourist informa-tion centre.

Getting There & Away

Buses stop at Armagh BusCentre on Lonsdale Rd, north of the town centre.

Goldline Express bus 251 runs from Belfast's Europa BusCentre (£8, one to 1½ hours, hourly Monday to Friday, six Saturday, four Sunday) to Armagh. Bus 44 runs from Armagh to Newry (£5, 1¼ hours, twice daily Monday to Saturday), and Goldline Express 295 runs to Enniskillen (£7, two hours, twice daily Monday to Saturday, July and August only) via Monaghan.

There are no direct services from Armagh to Derry – the fastest route (three hours) is via Dungannon (buses 72 and 273).

Armagh is a stop on the once-daily bus 278 from Coleraine to Monaghan (change here for Dublin) and the once-daily bus 270 from Belfast to Galway.

AROUND ARMAGH CITY
Navan Fort

Perched atop a drumlin a little over 3km west of Armagh is Navan Fort (Emain Macha), the most important archaeological site in Ulster. It was probably a prehistoric provincial capital and ritual site, on a par with Tara in County Meath.

The Irish name Emain Macha means 'the twins of Macha', Macha being the same mythical queen or goddess after whom Armagh itself is named (from Ard Macha, 'heights of Macha'). The site is linked in legend with the tales of Cúchulainn and named as capital of Ulster and the seat of the legendary Knights of the Red Branch.

It was an important centre from around 1150 BC until the coming of Christianity; the discovery of the skull of a Barbary ape on the site indicates trading links with North Africa. The main circular earthwork enclosure is no less than 240m in diameter, and encloses a smaller circular structure and an Iron Age burial mound. The circular structure has intrigued archaeologists – it appears to be some sort of temple, whose roof was supported by concentric rows of wooden posts, and whose interior was filled with a vast pile of stones. Stranger still, the whole thing was set on fire soon after its construction around 95 BC, possibly for ritual purposes.

The nearby **Navan Centre** (☎ 3752 9644; www .navan.com; 81 Killylea Rd, Armagh; adult/child £5.15/3.45; ☼ 10am-7pm Jul-Sep, to 4pm Oct-Dec & Easter-Jun) has exhibitions placing the fort in its historical context, and a recreation of an Iron Age settlement.

You can walk to the site from Armagh (45 minutes), or you can take bus 73 to Navan village (10 minutes, 10 daily Monday to Friday).

NORTH ARMAGH

North Armagh, 'the orchard of Ireland', is the island's main fruit-growing region, famed for its apples and strawberries. In May the countryside is awash with pink apple blossoms.

Ardress House

Starting life as a farmhouse, **Ardress House** (☎ 8778 4753; 64 Ardress Rd; adult/child £4.60/2.30; ☼ 2-6pm Thu-Sun Jul & Aug, 2-6pm Sat & Sun mid-Mar–Jun & Sep) was extended and converted to a manor house in 1760. Much of the original neoclassical interior remains, including a table made in 1799 on which King George V signed the Constitution of Northern Ireland in 1921. The farmyard houses a vast collection of machinery, along with a piggery and a smithy. The walled garden has been planted with a selection of the old apple varieties for which north Armagh's orchards are famous, and there are pleasant walks around the wooded grounds.

Ardress House is 15km northeast of Armagh, on the B28, halfway between Moy and Portadown.

Argory

A fine country house above the River Blackwater, the **Argory** (☎ 8778 4753; Derrycaw Rd; adult/child grounds & tour £5.80/2.90, grounds only £2.50/1; ☼ house 1-5.30pm daily Easter week, Jul & Aug, 1-5.30pm Sat, Sun & public hols mid-Mar–Jun & Sep) retains most of its original 1824 fittings; some rooms are still lit by acetylene gas from the house's private plant. There are two formal gardens

COUNTIES DOWN & ARMAGH

LOUGH NEAGH

Lough Neagh (pronounced nay) is the largest freshwater lake in all of Britain and Ireland, big enough to swallow the city of Birmingham (West Midlands, UK, or Alabama, USA – either one would fit). Though vast (around 32km long and 16km wide), the lough is relatively shallow – never more than 9m deep – and is an important habitat for waterfowl. Its waters are home to the pollan, a freshwater herring found only in Ireland, and the dollaghan, a subspecies of trout unique to Lough Neagh. Connected to the sea by the River Bann, the lough has been an important waterway and food source since prehistoric times, and still has an eel fishery that employs around 200 people.

The main points of access to the lough include Antrim Town (p667) on the eastern shore, Oxford Island (opposite) in the south, and Ardboe (p693) in the west. The **Loughshore Trail** (www.loughshoretrail.com) is a 180km cycle route that encircles the lough. For most of its length it follows quiet country roads set back from the shore; the best sections for actually seeing the lough itself are west of Oxford Island and south from Antrim town.

featuring roses, Victorian clipped-yew arbours and a lime walk by the river, and an excellent tearoom.

The Argory is 3.5km northeast of Moy on the Derrycaw road (off the B28), and 5km northwest of Ardress.

Oxford Island

Oxford Island National Nature Reserve protects a range of habitats – woodland, wildflower meadows, reedy shoreline and shallow lake margins – on the southern edge of Lough Neagh (see boxed text, opposite). It's crisscrossed with walking trails, information boards and birdwatching hides.

The **Lough Neagh Discovery Centre** (☎ 3832 2205; www.oxfordisland.com; Oxford Island, Lurgan; admission free; ⓨ 9am-5pm Mon-Fri, 10am-5pm Sat & Sun Sep-Jun, to 6pm daily Jul & Aug), set in the middle of a reed-fringed pond inhabited by waterfowl, has a tourist information desk, a gift shop and a great little **cafe** (ⓨ 10am-4.30pm year-round, to 5.30pm Easter-Sep) with lake-shore views.

One-hour **boat trips** (☎ 3832 7573; adult/child £5/2.50; ⓨ 1.30-5pm Sat & Sun Apr-Oct) on the lough depart from nearby Kinnego Marina, aboard the 12-seater cabin cruiser *Master McGra*.

Oxford Island is just north of Lurgan, signposted from Junction 10 on the M1 motorway.

COUNTIES DOWN & ARMAGH

Counties Derry & Antrim

The north coast of Northern Ireland, from Carrickfergus to Coleraine, is like a giant geology classroom. Here the patient workmanship of the ocean has laid bare the black basalt and white chalk that underlie much of County Antrim, and dissected the rocks into a scenic extravaganza of sea stacks, pinnacles, cliffs and caves, bordered by broad, sandy beaches swept by Atlantic surf. This rugged seaboard has some of the most beautiful coastal scenery in Ireland, but bring your boots and wetsuit as well as your camera – it's also an outdoor adventure playground that offers challenging coastal walks, extreme rock-climbing on the 100m-high crags of Fair Head, and the North's best surf breaks.

Tourists flock to the surreal geological centrepiece of the Giant's Causeway, its popularity challenged only by the test-your-nerve tightrope of the Carrick-a-Rede rope bridge nearby. But you can also escape the crowds amid the more sedate scenery of the Glens of Antrim, where the picturesque villages of Cushendun, Cushendall and Carnlough lie beneath lush green valleys and foaming waterfalls.

To the west, County Derry's chief attraction is the historic city of Derry, nestled in a broad sweep of the River Foyle. It is the only surviving walled city in Ireland, and a walk around it is one of the highlights of a visit to Northern Ireland. Derry's other draws include the powerful political murals in the Bogside district and the lively music scene in its many pubs. Northeast along the coast there are vast sandy beaches at Magilligan Point, Portstewart and Portrush, and from the basalt escarpment of Binevenagh, which overlooks the coast, superb views across Lough Foyle beckon you towards the blue-hazed hills of County Donegal.

HIGHLIGHTS

- **City Lights** Ancient walls, modern murals and foot-stomping music in the historic city of Derry (opposite)

- **Catch A Wave** Surfing or body-boarding the Atlantic breakers at the beaches around Portrush (p653)

- **Coastal Challenge** A 16.5km hike along the spectacular Causeway Coast from Carrick-a-Rede to the Giant's Causeway (p658)

- **Test Your Nerve** The slender, swaying Carrick-a-Rede Rope Bridge (p658)

- **Away From It All** Seabirds and seals at the remote western end of Rathlin Island (p660)

- TELEPHONE CODE: 028 FROM UK; 048 FROM REPUBLIC OF IRELAND
- POPULATION: 532,000
- AREA: 4918 SQ KM

COUNTY DERRY

DERRY/LONDONDERRY
pop 83,700

Northern Ireland's second city comes as a pleasant surprise to many visitors. Derry (or Londonderry; see the boxed text, p637) may not be the prettiest of cities, and it certainly lags behind Belfast in terms of investment and redevelopment, but it has a great riverside setting, several fascinating historical sights and a determined air of can-do optimism that has made it the powerhouse of the North's cultural revival.

There's lots of history to absorb, from the Siege of Derry to the Battle of the Bogside – a stroll around the 17th-century city walls is a must, as is a tour of the Bogside murals – and the city's lively pubs are home to a burgeoning live-music scene. But perhaps the biggest attraction is the people themselves: warm, witty and welcoming.

History

The defining moment of Derry's history was the Siege of Derry in 1688–89, an event whose echoes reverberate around the city's walls to this day. King James I granted the city a royal charter in 1613, and gave the London livery companies (trade guilds) the task of fortifying Derry and planting the county of Coleraine (soon to be renamed County Londonderry) with Protestant settlers.

In Britain, the Glorious Revolution of 1688 saw the Catholic King James II ousted in favour of the Protestant Dutch prince, William of Orange. Derry was the only garrison in Ireland that was not held by forces loyal to King James, and so, in December 1688, Catholic forces led by the Earl of Antrim arrived on the east bank of the River Foyle, ready to seize the city.

They sent emissaries to discuss terms of surrender, but in the meantime troops were being ferried across the river in preparation for an assault. On seeing this, 13 apprentice boys barred the city gates with a cry of 'There'll be no surrender!'

And so, on 7 December 1688, the Siege of Derry began. For 105 days the Protestant citizens of Derry withstood bombardment, disease and starvation (the condition of the besieging forces was not much better). By the time a relief ship burst through and broke the siege, an estimated half of the city's inhabit-

ants had died. In the 20th century the Siege of Derry became a symbol of Ulster Protestants' resistance to rule by a Catholic Irish Republic, and 'No surrender!' remains a Loyalist battle-cry to this day.

In the 19th century Derry was one of the main ports of emigration to the USA, a fact commemorated by the sculptures of an emigrant family standing in Waterloo Pl. It also played a vital role in the transatlantic trade in linen shirts: supposedly, local factories provided uniforms for both sides in the American Civil War. Even now, Derry still supplies the US president with 12 free shirts every year.

Orientation

The centre of old Derry is the walled city on the western bank of the River Foyle. The bus station is just outside the walls at its north end; the modern city centre stretches north from here along Strand Rd. The train station is on the east bank of the River Foyle, across Craigavon Bridge, in a district known as the Waterside. The Bogside lies to the west of the walled city.

Information

BOOKSHOPS

Eason (Map p638; ☎ 7137 7133; Foyleside Shopping Centre, Foyle St; ☽ 9am-6pm Mon & Tue, to 9pm Wed-Fri, to 7pm Sat, 1-6pm Sun) The city's biggest bookshop, on level 3 of the shopping centre.

Foyle Books (Map p638; ☎ 7137 2530; 12A Magazine St; ☽ 11am-5.15pm Mon-Fri, 10am-5pm Sat) Stocks a good selection of second-hand books.

INTERNET ACCESS

Central Library (Map p638; ☎ 7127 2310; 35 Foyle St; per 30min £1.50; ☽ 9.15am-8pm Mon & Thu, to 5.30pm Tue, Wed & Fri, to 5pm Sat)

Derry Tourist Information Centre (p634) Internet access for £1 per 20 minutes.

MONEY

Bank of Ireland (Map p638; ☎ 7126 4992; 12 Ship-quay St)

First Trust Bank (Map p638; ☎ 7136 3921; 15-17 Shipquay St)

Thomas Cook (Map p638; ☎ 7185 2552; 34 Ferryquay St)

POST

Post office (☽ 8.30am-5.30pm Mon, 9am-5.30pm Tue-Fri, 9am-12.30pm Sat); Main post office (Map p638; Custom House St); Bishop St Within (Map p638)

TOURIST INFORMATION
Derry Tourist Information Centre (Map p636; ☎ 7137 7577; www.derryvisitor.com; 44 Foyle St; ☼ 9am-7pm Mon-Fri, 10am-6pm Sat, 10am-5pm Sun Jul-Sep, 9am-5pm Mon-Fri & 10am-5pm Sat Mar-Jun & Oct, 9am-5pm Mon-Fri Nov-Feb) Covers all of Northern Ireland and the Republic as well as Derry. Sells books and maps, can book accommodation throughout Ireland and has a bureau de change.

Sights

WALLED CITY
Derry's walled city is Ireland's earliest example of town planning. It is thought to have been modelled on the French Renaissance town of Vitry-le-François, designed in 1545 by Italian engineer Hieronimo Marino; both are based on the grid plan of a Roman military camp, with two main streets at right angles to each other, and four city gates, one at either end of each street.

City Walls
Completed in 1619, Derry's **city walls** (www .derryswalls.com) are 8m high and 9m thick, with a circumference of about 1.5km, and are the only city walls in Ireland to survive almost intact. The four original gates (Shipquay, Ferryquay, Bishop's and Butcher's) were rebuilt in the 18th and 19th centuries, when three new gates (New, Magazine and Castle) were added. Derry's nickname, the Maiden City, derives from the fact that the walls have never been breached by an invader.

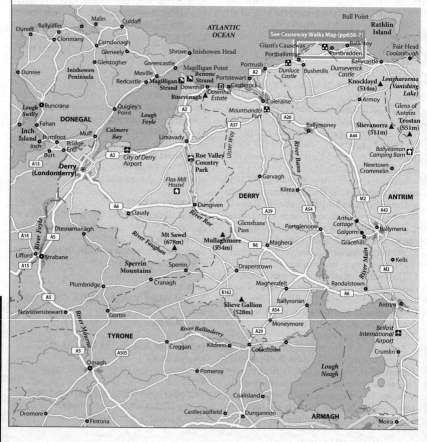

COUNTIES DERRY & ANTRIM

The walls were built under the supervision of the Honourable The Irish Society, an organisation created in 1613 by King James and the London livery companies to fund and oversee the fortification of Derry and the plantation of the surrounding county with Protestant settlers. The society still exists today (though now its activities are mainly charitable) and it still owns Derry's city walls.

See p640 for a self-guided walk around the walls.

Tower Museum

Inside the Magazine Gate is the award-winning **Tower Museum** (Map p638; ☎ 7137 2411; Union Hall Pl; adult/child £4/2; ⏰ 10am-5pm Mon-Sat & 11am-3pm Sun Jul & Aug, 10am-5pm Tue-Sat & bank holidays

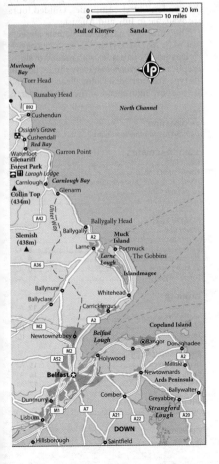

Mon Sep-Jun), housed in a replica 16th-century tower house. Head straight to the fifth floor for a view from the top of the tower, then work your way down through the excellent **Armada Shipwreck** exhibition, which tells the story of *La Trinidad Valenciera* – a ship of the Spanish Armada that was wrecked at Kinnagoe Bay in Donegal in 1588. It was discovered by the City of Derry Sub-Aqua Club in 1971 and excavated by marine archaeologists. On display are bronze guns, pewter tableware and personal items – a wooden comb, an olive jar, a shoe sole – recovered from the site, including a 2.5-tonne siege gun bearing the arms of Phillip II of Spain showing him as king of England.

The museum's other exhibition is the **Story of Derry**, where well-thought-out exhibits and audiovisuals lead you through the history of the city from the founding of the monastery of St Colmcille (Columba) in the 6th century to the Battle of the Bogside in the late 1960s. Allow a good two hours to do the museum justice.

St Columb's Cathedral

Built between 1628 and 1633 from the same grey-green schist as the city walls, **St Columb's Cathedral** (Map p638; ☎ 7126 7313; www.stcolumbs cathedral.org; London St; admission £2; ⏰ 9am-5pm Mon-Sat Easter-Oct, 9am-1pm & 2-4pm Mon-Sat Nov-Easter) was the first post-Reformation church to be built in Britain and Ireland, and is Derry's oldest surviving building.

In the **porch** (under the spire, by the St Columb's Court entrance) you can see the original foundation stone of 1633 that records the cathedral's completion, inscribed:

> If stones could speake
> Then London's prayse
> Should sounde who
> Built this church and
> Cittie from the grounde.

The smaller stone inset, inscribed '*In Templo Verus Deus Est Vereo Colendus*' (The True God is in His Temple and is to be truly worshipped), comes from the original church built here in 1164 and dedicated to the city's patron saint, Colmcille.

Also in the porch is a hollow mortar shell fired into the churchyard during the Great Siege of 1688–89; inside the shell were the terms of surrender. The neighbouring **chapter house** contains more historical artefacts, including paintings, old photos and the four huge padlocks used to secure the city gates in the 17th century.

The **nave**, built in a squat, solid style known as Planter's Gothic, shares the austerity of many Church of Ireland cathedrals, with thick walls, small windows, and an open-timbered roof (from 1823) resting on corbels depicting the heads of past bishops and deans. The bishop's throne, at the far end of the nave, is an 18th-century mahogany chair in ornate, Chinese Chippendale style.

The **chancel** and the stained-glass east window depicting the Ascension, date from 1887. The flags on either side of the window were captured from the French during the Great Siege; although the yellow silk has been re-newed several times since, the poles and gold wirework are original.

OUTSIDE THE WALLS

Standing just outside the city walls opposite the Tower Museum, the neo-Gothic **Guildhall** (Map p638; ☎ 7137 7335; Guildhall Sq; admission free; ☷ 9am-5pm Mon-Fri) was originally built in 1890, then rebuilt after a fire in 1908. As the seat of the old Londonderry Corporation, which institutionalised the policy of discriminating against Catholics over housing and jobs, it incurred the wrath of Nationalists and was bombed twice by the Irish Republican Army (IRA) in 1972. From 2000 to 2005 it was the seat of the Bloody Sunday Inquiry (see the boxed text, p639). The Guildhall is noted for its fine stained-glass windows, presented by the London Livery companies. Guided tours are available in July and August.

The small, old-fashioned **Harbour Museum** (Map p638; ☎ 7137 7331; Harbour Sq; admission free; ☷ 10am-1pm & 2-5pm Mon-Fri), with models of ships, a replica of a *currach* – an early sailing boat of the type that carried St Colmcille to Iona – and the bosomy figurehead of the *Minnehaha*, is

DERRY

DERRY-STROKE-LONDONDERRY

Derry/Londonderry is a town with two names. The settlement was originally named Doíre Calgaigh (Oak Grove of Calgach), after a pagan warrior-hero; in the 10th century it was renamed Doíre Colmcille (Oak Grove of Columba), in honour of the 6th-century saint who established the first monastic settlement here.

In the following centuries the name was shortened and anglicised to Derrie or Derry. Then in 1613, in recognition of the Corporation of London's role in the 'plantation' of northwest Ulster with Protestant settlers, Derry was granted a royal charter and both town and county were renamed Londonderry. However, people generally continued to call it Derry in everyday speech.

When Nationalists gained a majority on the city council in 1984, they voted to change its name from Londonderry City Council to Derry City Council. This infuriated Unionists, and the name remains a touchstone for people's political views. Nationalists always use Derry, and vandals often deface the 'London' part of the name on road signs. Staunch Unionists insist on Londonderry, which is still the city's (and county's) official name, used in government publications, Ordnance Survey maps, rail and bus timetables and Northern Ireland Tourist Board (NITB) literature.

On radio and TV, to avoid giving offence to either side, some announcers use both names together – 'Derry-stroke-Londonderry' – while the BBC uses Londonderry at its first mention in a report, and Derry thereafter (the local radio station avoids the dilemma by calling itself BBC Radio Foyle). Road signs in Northern Ireland point to Londonderry, those in the Republic point to Derry (or Doíre in Irish), and some tourism industry promotional material covers all bases, using Derry-Londonderry-Doíre.

In 2006 Derry City Council asked for a judicial review in the High Court of Belfast, claiming that the renaming of the council in 1984 effectively amended the charter of 1613, but in January 2007 the judge rejected the claim, saying that only new legislation or royal prerogative could change the city's official name.

Luckily, not everyone takes the Derry/Londonderry controversy too seriously. One local radio presenter opted instead for the simpler 'Stroke City'! In fact, the majority of people in Northern Ireland, no matter what their political persuasion, still use 'Derry' in everyday speech, which is why we use the shorter version in this book.

housed in the old Harbour Commissioner's Building next to the Guildhall.

As you enter the city across Craigavon Bridge, the first thing you see is the **Hands Across the Divide** (Map p636) monument. This striking bronze sculpture of two men reaching out to each other symbolises the spirit of reconciliation and hope for the future; it was unveiled in 1992, 20 years after Bloody Sunday.

Outside the city walls to the southwest is **Long Tower Church** (Map p636; ☎ 7126 2301; Long Tower St; admission free; ☼ 9am-8.30pm Mon-Sat, 7.30am-7pm Sun), Derry's first post-Reformation Catholic church. Built in 1784 in neo-Renaissance style, it stands on the site of the medieval Teampall Mór (Great Church), built in 1164, whose stones were used to help build the city walls in 1609. Long Tower was built with the support of the Anglican bishop of the time, Frederick Augustus Harvey, who presented the capitals for the four Corinthian columns framing the ornate high altar.

The Roman Catholic **St Eugene's Cathedral** (Map p636; ☎ 7126 2894; Great James St; admission free; ☼ 9am-8.30pm) was begun in 1851 as a response to the end of the Great Famine, and dedicated to St Eugene in 1873 by Bishop Kelly; the handsome east window (1891) is a memorial to the bishop. The bells of St Eugene's still ring every night at 9pm as a reminder of the Penal Laws (in force from 1691 until the early 19th century) which forbade Catholics from attending mass and subjected them to a 9pm curfew.

BOGSIDE

The Bogside district, to the west of the walled city, developed in the 19th and early 20th centuries as a working-class, predominantly Catholic, residential area. By the 1960s, its serried ranks of small, terrace houses had become an overcrowded ghetto of poverty and unemployment, a focus for the emerging civil rights movement and a hotbed of Nationalist discontent.

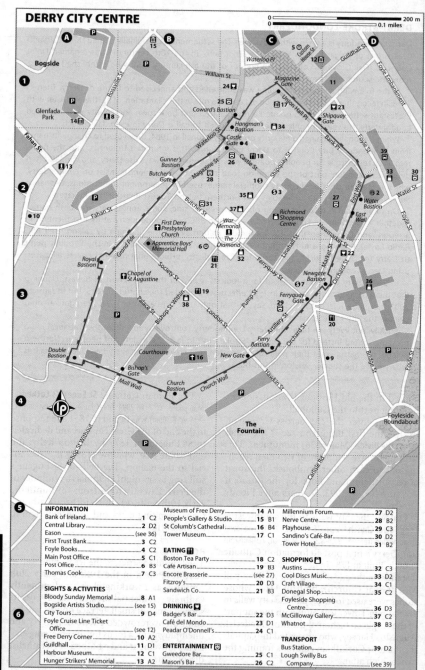

DERRY CITY CENTRE

In August 1969, the three-day 'Battle of the Bogside' – a running street battle between local youths and the Royal Ulster Constabulary (RUC) – prompted the UK government to send British troops into Northern Ireland. The residents of the Bogside and neighbouring Brandywell districts – 33,000 of them – declared themselves independent from the civil authorities, and barricaded the streets to keep the security forces out. 'Free Derry', as it was known, was a no-go area for the police and army, its streets patrolled by IRA volunteers. In January of 1972 the area around Rossville St witnessed the horrific events of Bloody Sunday (see the boxed text, below). 'Free Derry' ended with Operation Motorman on 31 July 1972, when thousands of British troops and armoured cars moved in to occupy the Bogside.

Since then the area has been extensively redeveloped, the old houses and flats demolished and replaced with modern housing, and the population is now down to 8000. All that remains of the old Bogside is **Free Derry Corner** (Map p638) at the intersection of Fahan and Rossville Sts, where the gable end of a house painted with the famous slogan 'You Are Now Entering Free Derry' still stands. Nearby is the H-shaped **Hunger Strikers' Memorial** (Map p638; see also p46) and, a little further north along Rossville St, the **Bloody Sunday Memorial** (Map p638), a simple granite obelisk that commemorates the 14 civilians who were shot dead by the British Army on 30 January 1972.

The **Museum of Free Derry** (Map p638; ☎ 7136 0880; www.museumoffreederry.org; 55-61 Glenfada Park; adult/child £3/2; 🕙 9.30am-4.30pm Mon-Fri year-round, 1-4pm Sat Apr-Sep, 1-4pm Sun Jul-Sep), just off Rossville St, chronicles the history of the Bogside, the civil rights movement and the events of Bloody Sunday through photographs, newspaper reports, film clips and the accounts of first-hand witnesses, including some of the original photographs that inspired the murals of the People's Gallery.

People's Gallery

The 12 murals that decorate the gable ends of houses along Rossville St, near Free Derry Corner, are popularly referred to as the People's

---

SUNDAY, BLOODY SUNDAY

Tragically echoing Dublin's Bloody Sunday of November 1920, when British security forces shot dead 14 spectators at a Gaelic football match in Croke Park, Derry's Bloody Sunday was a turning point in the history of the Troubles.

On Sunday, 30 January 1972, the Northern Ireland Civil Rights Association organised a peaceful march through Derry in protest against internment without trial, which had been introduced by the British government the previous year. Some 15,000 people marched from Creggan through the Bogside towards the Guildhall, but they were stopped by British Army barricades at the junction of William and Rossville Sts. The main march was diverted along Rossville St to Free Derry Corner, but a small number of youths began hurling stones and insults at the British soldiers.

The exact sequence of events is disputed, but it now seems clear that soldiers of the 1st Battalion the Parachute Regiment opened fire on unarmed civilians. Fourteen people were shot dead, some of them shot in the back; six were aged just 17. Another 14 people were injured, 12 by gunshots and two from being knocked down by armoured personnel carriers. The Catholic population of Derry, who had originally welcomed the British troops as a neutral force protecting them from Protestant violence and persecution, now saw the army as enemy and occupier. The ranks of the Provisional Irish Republican Army (IRA) swelled with a fresh surge of volunteers.

The Widgery Commission, set up in 1972 to investigate the affair, failed to find anyone responsible. None of the soldiers who fired at civilians, nor the officers in charge, were brought to trial or even disciplined; records disappeared and weapons were destroyed.

Long-standing public dissatisfaction with the Widgery investigation led to the massive **Bloody Sunday Inquiry** (www.bloody-sunday-inquiry.org.uk), headed by Lord Saville, which sat from March 2000 till December 2004. The inquiry heard from 900 witnesses, received 2500 witness statements, and allegedly cost British taxpayers £400 million; its final report, originally due to be published in 2007, was, at the time of writing, not expected until 2010.

The events of Bloody Sunday inspired rock band U2's most overtly political song, 'Sunday Bloody Sunday' (1983), and are commemorated in the Museum of Free Derry, the People's Gallery and the Bloody Sunday Monument, all in the Bogside (p637).

Gallery. They are the work of Tom Kelly, Will Kelly and Kevin Hasson, known as 'The Bogside Artists' (see boxed text, p642). The three men have spent most of their lives in the Bogside, and lived through the worst of the Troubles.

Their murals, mostly painted between 1997 and 2001, commemorate key events in the Troubles, including the Battle of the Bogside, Bloody Sunday, Operation Motorman (the British Army's operation to re-take IRA-controlled no-go areas in Derry and Belfast in July 1972) and the 1981 hunger strike. The most powerful images are those painted largely in monochrome, consciously evoking journalistic imagery – *Operation Motorman*, showing a British soldier breaking down a door with a sledgehammer; *Bloody Sunday*, with a group of men led by local priest Father Daly carrying the body of Jackie Duddy (the first fatality on that day); and *Petrol Bomber*, a young boy wearing a gas mask and holding a petrol bomb.

The most moving image is *The Death of Innocence*, which shows the radiant figure of 14-year-old schoolgirl Annette McGavigan, killed in crossfire between the IRA and the British Army on 6 September 1971, the 100th victim of the Troubles. Representing all the children who died in the conflict, she stands against the brooding chaos of a bombed-out building, the roof beams forming a crucifix in the top right-hand corner. At the left, a downward-pointing rifle, broken in the middle, stands for the failure of violence, while the butterfly symbolises resurrection and the hope embodied in the peace process.

The final mural in the sequence, completed in 2004, is the *Peace Mural*, a swirling image of a dove (symbol of peace, and also of Derry's patron saint, Columba), rising out of the blood and sadness of the past towards the sunny yellow hope of a peaceful future.

The **People's Gallery & Studio** (Map p638; ☎ 7137 3842; www.bogsideartists.com; cnr Rossville St & William St; admission free; ☾ 9am-6pm daily) opened in 2008 on 'Aggro Corner', the street intersection once notorious as the kicking-off point for confrontations between Bogsiders and security forces. It provides an exhibition space for local and international artists, and runs art workshops for young people. You can buy prints of the murals, and the Bogside Artists themselves are usually in residence – they are happy to sign books and posters, and offer guided tours of the murals (see opposite).

The murals can be seen online at www.cain .ulst.ac.uk/bogsideartists, and in the book *The People's Gallery* (available from the gallery shop and the artists' website).

THE WATERSIDE

Across the river from the walled city lies the largely Protestant Waterside district. At the height of the Troubles, many Protestants living in and around the Bogside moved across the river to escape the worst of the violence.

Here you'll find the **Workhouse Museum** (Map p636; ☎ 7131 8328; 23 Glendermott Rd; admission free; ☾ 10am-5pm Mon-Thu & Sat), housed in Derry's original 1840–1946 workhouse. Daily life at the workhouse for the 800 inmates was designed to encourage them to leave as soon as possible, alive or dead. One of the exhibits is the grisly horse-drawn hearse used to carry away the corpses.

Other displays cover the Potato Famine, while the excellent Atlantic Memorial exhibition tells the story of the WWII Battle of the Atlantic and the major role that Derry played.

Walking Tour

You can make a complete circuit of Derry's walled city, walking along the top of the walls, in around 30 minutes. There are frequent sets of steps where you can get on and off.

This walk starts from the Diamond, Derry's central square, dominated by the **war memorial (1)**.

From the Diamond, head along Butcher St to **Butcher's Gate (2)**. At the height of the Troubles the gate reverted to its original, 17th-century role, serving as a security checkpoint controlling entry to the city centre from the Bogside. Turn right before the gate and climb the steps up onto the top of the city walls.

Stroll downhill across **Castle Gate (3)**, added in 1865, to **Magazine Gate (4)**, named for the powder magazine that used to be close by. Inside the walls is the modern **O'Doherty's Tower (5)**, based on a 16th-century castle that once stood nearby. It houses the excellent **Tower Museum (6**; p635). Outside the walls is the red-brick, neo-Gothic **Guildhall (7**; p636).

The River Foyle used to come up to the northeastern wall here, and the stretch from Coward's Bastion to the Water Bastion (demolished 1844) once had ships moored just outside. In the middle is the **Shipquay Gate (8)**, which originally linked the port with the mar-

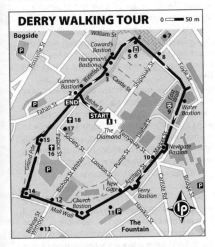

WALK FACTS

Start The Diamond
Finish The Diamond
Distance 2km
Duration 30 to 40 minutes

ket area; it was rebuilt in its present form in 1805. Symbols above the arch show the cornucopia (horn of plenty) and the rod of Mercury (a symbol of trade and commerce).

The walls then turn southwest and begin a steep climb beside the modern **Millennium Forum** (9; p645) theatre and concert venue. At the top of the hill is the **Ferryquay Gate** (10), where the apprentice boys barred the gate at the start of the Great Siege of 1688–89. In those days there would have been a drawbridge as well as a padlock on the gate. Both padlock and key can be seen in the chapter house of St Columb's Cathedral (p635).

Above the gate is the image of the Reverend George Walker. Below, in the arches to either side, are metal rings; these were used to tether horses, which were not allowed into the inner city on market days.

The stretch of wall beyond overlooks the **Fountain housing estate** (11), the last significant Protestant community on the western bank of the Foyle (the vast majority of Derry's Protestants have moved across the river to the Waterside area or further afield). The round, brick-paved area on the ground outside New Gate is where a 10m-high bonfire is lit on the night before the annual Apprentice Boys' march.

Bishop's Gate (12), which bisects the southern flank of the wall, was rebuilt in 1789 for the 100th anniversary of the Great Siege. Bishop Harvey, a keen antiquarian, had a hand in the reconstruction and requested a triumphal arch in honour of King William I. During the Great Siege, it was here that King James II demanded the surrender of the city.

Outside the gate on Bishop St Without is the one remaining turret of the 1791 **Old Gaol** (13). Theobald Wolfe Tone, founder of the United Irishmen, spent some time in prison here following the failed rebellion of 1798.

The **Double Bastion** (14) at the southwestern corner of the walls is home to Roaring Meg, the most famous of the cannons used during the Siege of Derry; the noise it made was said to be more terrifying than any physical damage it managed to inflict.

The next section of wall is known as the Grand Parade, and offers an excellent view over the Bogside estate. The prominent murals on the houses below were painted by the Bogside Artists (see the boxed text, p642).

An empty plinth on **Royal Bastion** (15) marks the former site of a monument to the Reverend George Walker, joint governor of the city during the Great Siege. The 27m-tall column, erected in 1826 and seen by local Nationalists as a symbol of Unionist domination, was blown up by the IRA in 1973. The restored statue of Walker now stands in a memorial garden next to the Apprentice Boys' Memorial Hall.

Behind the Royal Bastion is the 1872 Church of Ireland **Chapel of St Augustine** (16), built on the site of St Colmcille's 6th-century monastery. A little further along is the **Apprentice Boys' Memorial Hall** (17), its windows protected by steel grilles and splashed with paint bombs hurled from below. Behind it is the grand Corinthian temple of the **First Derry Presbyterian Church** (18).

Just past the church is the Butcher's Gate, from where you can return to the Diamond, head down Magazine St to the Tower Museum, or descend Fahan St to the Bogside (p637) and the People's Gallery (p639).

Tours

Bogside Artists Tours (Map p638; ☎ 7137 3842; www.bogsideartists.com; People's Gallery & Studio, cnr Rossville & William Sts; per person £4; ☼ tours start

---

VOICES: THE BOGSIDE ARTISTS

The Bogside Artists – brothers Will and Tom Kelly, and friend Kevin Hasson – are famous as the creators of the murals that make up the People's Gallery. Tom and Kevin were 10 and 11 years old when the Troubles broke out in 1969, Will in his early 20s.

What was it like growing up in Derry during the Troubles? Kevin: 'One minute nobody knows about us or Derry or even Northern Ireland; the next thing, we are all over the international news. You could watch the daily riot later on TV in your own front room. As kids, you must understand we were still on fantasy island, as most kids are. Soldiers were, to us, aliens from another planet. We painted the soldier as such on our Bloody Sunday mural depicting the death of Jackie Duddy for that reason. That was our perception at the time and kids tend to see things bereft of all historical or other considerations. All in all, our growing up in Derry at that time could be described as very intense and very bitter-sweet.'

Will: 'We felt that our destiny had come. We were well clued-up on Marxist doctrine and, what with the riots in Paris and the struggle of the black population in America for democratic rights, we truly believed we were part of a global working-class revolution. A new world order was coming into being and we were in the front line. As a young man, the unfolding events faced one with questions of ultimate concern at a time when, in other circumstances, we would likely have been thinking of finding a secure job and starting a family. Individualistic pursuits had to be shelved in the face of imminent threats to oneself and one's family. In retrospect, the whole experience was very hyper-real. During the Hunger Strikes of 1980–81 it became surreal.'

Whose art do you admire? Will: 'Those old masters like Raphael, Mantegna, the Tiepolos and Michelangelo cannot be equalled when it comes to mural art. Diego Rivera was summoned from Paris 20 years or so *after* the revolution, so we are not as impressed by his work as those who have bought into the myth of Rivera as a contemporary freedom fighter. Incidentally, he did not portray Mexico's history as it was. What he did was offer a Marxist *interpretation* of that history. Not that we compare ourselves to Rivera. His body of work far exceeds our own. But we do recall one lady who came to our studio and told us that she had just returned from Mexico and considered our murals to be better than his! Go figure, as they say.'

Which of the Bogside murals means the most to you? Tom: '*The Death of Innocence*, for me, is the one that stands out, both the pictorial content of it and the fact that it is a peace and antiwar mural painted long before any of us in Derry thought peace was even possible.'

10am, noon, 2pm & 4pm daily) Guided walking tours of the famous People's Gallery murals led by the artists themselves. Minimum of five preferred, though singles can tag along with bigger groups. Best to book ahead on the website.

City Tours (Map p638; ☎ 7127 1996; www.irishtour guides.com; Carlisle Stores, 11 Carlisle Rd) Runs one-hour Historic Derry walking tours starting from Carlisle Stores at 10am, noon and 2pm year-round and costing £4/2 per adult/child. There are also tours of the Bogside and of Derry's murals.

Derry Tourist Information Centre (Map p636; ☎ 7126 7284; 44 Foyle St) Offers 1½-hour guided walking tours of the walled city for £6/4 per adult/child, starting from the bureau at 11.15am Monday to Friday year-round. The price includes admission to St Columb's Cathedral.

Foyle Cruise Line (Map p636; ☎ 7136 2857; www .foylecruiseline.com; Harbour Museum, Harbour Sq) Oper-

ates daily cruises on the Foyle estuary. Trips to Culmore Bay (1¼ hours) cost £8/5 per adult/child and depart at 2pm; four-hour evening cruises to Greencastle with bar and entertainment cost £12/10 per adult/child, and depart at 8pm.

Festivals & Events

City of Derry Jazz Festival (☎ 7137 6545; www.city ofderryjazzfestival.com; early May) Four days of jazz at various venues.

Foyle Days (☎ 7137 6504; www.derrycity.gov.uk/foyle days; mid Jun) River-based festival with visiting navy ships, yacht races, boat trips, live music and shore-side street entertainment.

Gasyard Wall Féile (☎ 7136 6931; Jul) A major cultural festival that features live music, street performers, carnival, theatre and Irish-language events.

City of Derry Guitar Festival (☎ 7137 5550; www .cityofderryguitarfestival.com; late Aug) The grounds of

Kevin: 'Our *Peace Mural* means most to me, as we decided to do that 10 years before we were actually able to get around to realising it. Also, it had a strong community input where both Catholic and Protestant kids worked together to help design it. The dove, in fact, is not just a cliché – it refers to our city's patron saint, St Columba, whose Latin name Columbanus means 'dove'.'

Will: 'They're like our children – it's unfair to single any one out at the expense of the others. That said, it would be dishonest not to admit that our first-born, *The Petrol Bomber*, is a wee bit special.'

What is Derry like to visit? Will: 'We all agree that Derry is a very special city that is fast becoming the cultural focus of not only the North of Ireland but Ireland as a whole. It is a big city with the ambience and character of a village. The sense of freedom of the people, young and old, is truly infectious. You could pick any Derryman or woman and put them on stage for their wit alone. In short, Derry is fun. The girls here are very pretty, too!

Above all, get to meet the locals, whom you will likely find enjoying a Guinness or two in the pubs. Have they got stories to tell! There's also a great view of the city and the lough from the hill of Creggan.'

Tom: 'Peadar O'Donnell's (p645) is the best place for traditional Irish music. The Craft Village (p646) I would recommend for lunch or a quiet drink.'

Kevin: 'For older visitors, the **Tower Hotel** (Map p638; ☎ 7137 1000; www.towerhotelderry.com; Butcher St) has good Irish music sessions that are very popular.'

Will: 'A short trip over the border to Buncrana will present you with more options, as well as a neat little beach where you can nurse your hangover the next morning.'

How do you see the future of Derry over the next 10 years? Will: 'There is a covert rivalry going on between Derry and Belfast with regards to the creative arts that is reminiscent of the rivalry between Rome and Florence during the High Renaissance. It is a healthy rivalry that will bring out the very best in both cities. Alas, Dublin has sacrificed its old-world charm to commercialism, to the extent that neither Joyce, Beckett nor Behan would be able to recognise it if they came back. Dublin has painted itself out of the picture, frankly. It is fast becoming another Blackpool.'

Tom: 'With massive investment from Britain and America, the rapid growth of tourism and stronger economic relations between North and South, things can only get better for the people of Derry, especially for those of us who have lived through over 30 years of conflict. When you know how bad it can really get, you become grateful for what you have. Thankfully, we have plenty here to enjoy.'

University of Ulster host performances and master classes from guitar greats around the world, including classical, acoustic, electric, flamenco and bass.

Halloween Carnival (☎ 7137 6545; www.derrycity.gov .uk/halloween; 27-31 Oct) Ireland's biggest street party has the entire city dressing up and dancing in the streets.

Foyle Film Festival (☎ 7126 7432; www.foylefilm festival.com; Nov) This week-long event is the North's biggest film festival.

Sleeping

It's best to book accommodation in advance during festival events.

BUDGET

our pick Derry City Independent Hostel (Map p636; ☎ 7128 0542; www.derry-hostel.co.uk; 44 Great James St; dm/d from £12/36; 🖵) Run by experienced backpackers

and decorated with souvenirs from their travels around the world, this small, friendly hostel is set in a Georgian town house, just a short walk northwest of the bus station. They have an annexe nearby called Dolce Vita, with stylishly decorated double rooms aimed at couples.

Derry Palace Hostel (Map p638; ☎ 7130 9051; www .paddyspalace.com; 1 Woodleigh Tce, Asylum Rd; dm from £12; P 🖵 🛜) Part of the Ireland-wide Paddy's Palace chain, this hostel is central, comfortable and as friendly as they come. There's a sunny garden, a good party atmosphere and the staff regularly organise nights out at local pubs with traditional music.

MIDRANGE

Laburnum Lodge (Map p636; ☎ 7135 4221; www.laburnum lodge.com; 9 Rockfield, Madam's Bank Rd; s/d £35/50;

P ▢ ☎) Readers recommended this suburban villa on a quiet street on the northern edge of town, impressed by the friendly welcome, spacious bedrooms and hearty breakfasts. If you don't have your own transport, the owner can pick you up from the train or bus station.

Sunbeam House (Map p636; ☎ 7126 3606; www .sunbeamhouse.com; 147 Sunbeam Tce, Bishop St; s/d £38/60; ☎) This attractive red-brick terrace house is a five-minute walk southwest of the walled city. The four cheerfully decorated rooms are a bit on the small side, but there's nothing cramped about the hospitality – or the size of the breakfasts!

Arkle House (☎ 7127 1157; www.derryhotel.co.uk; 2 Coshquin Rd; s/d £40/58; P ▢ ☎) Located 2km northwest of the city centre, this grand Victorian house is set in private gardens and offers five large, lush bedrooms and a private kitchen for guests to use.

Abbey B&B (Map p636; ☎ 7127 9000; www.abbey accommodation.com; 4 Abbey St; s/d £45/60; ▢) There's a warm welcome waiting at this family-run B&B just a short walk from the walled city, on the edge of the Bogside. The six rooms are stylishly decorated and include family rooms with up to four beds.

our pick Merchant's House (Map p636; ☎ 7126 9691; www.thesaddlershouse.com; 16 Queen St; s/d £45/60; ▢ ☎) Run by the same couple as the Saddler's House, this historic, Georgian-style town house is a gem of a B&B. It has an elegant lounge and dining room with marble fireplaces and antique furniture, TV, coffee-making facilities and even bathrobes in the bedrooms (only one has an en-suite bathroom), and homemade marmalade at breakfast. Call at the Saddler's House first to pick up a key.

Saddler's House (Map p636; ☎ 7126 9691; www .thesaddlershouse.com; 36 Great James St; s/d from £50/60; ▢ ☎) Centrally located within a five-minute walk of the walled city, this friendly B&B is set in a lovely Victorian town house. All seven rooms have private bathrooms, and you get to enjoy a huge breakfast in the family kitchen.

Da Vinci's Hotel (☎ 7127 9111; www.davincishotel .com; 15 Culmore Rd; r from £75, ste from £100; P ▢ ☎) This sleek boutique hotel on the west bank of the Foyle is the accommodation of choice for visiting celebrities, businesspeople and politicians, offering spacious, stylish rooms and a hip cocktail bar and restaurant. It's 1.5km north of the city centre.

Eating
BUDGET

Boston Tea Party (Map p638; 15 Craft Village; snacks £2-4; ☺ 9am-5.30pm Mon-Sat) Homemade soups, hot lunches, freshly baked cakes, friendly service and the best apple pie in town – what more could you want from a cafe?

Café Artisan (Map p638; ☎ 7128 2727; 18-20 Bishop St Within; mains £2-5; ☺ 9.30am-5.30pm Mon-Sat; ☎) This cool little cafe serves delicious homemade soups, deli sandwiches, panini and excellent cappuccinos.

Sandwich Co (sandwiches & salads £3-5; ☺ 9am-5pm Mon-Sat); The Diamond (Map p638; ☎ 7137 2500); Strand Rd (Map p636; 61 Strand Rd) White bread, brown bread, baguettes, panini, ciabatta – this place offers good-value, choose-your-own sandwiches and salads.

MIDRANGE

Spice (Map p636; ☎ 7134 4875; 162-164 Spencer Rd, Waterside; mains £9-19; ☺ 12.30-2.30pm Tue-Fri & Sun, 5.30-10pm Tue-Sat, 5-9pm Sun) If you can't decide what cuisine you fancy, this pleasantly chilled-out eatery offers a range of culinary influences, from warm duck salad with hoisin dressing, to tarragon chicken with wild mushrooms, to Madras-spiced bean stew with coriander rice. There's a separate vegetarian menu, and a three-course dinner deal for £14.

Encore Brasserie (Map p638; ☎ 7137 2492; Millennium Forum, Newmarket St; mains £10-15; ☺ noon-3pm & 5-9pm Mon-Sat, 1-4pm & 5-9pm Sun) Set in the lobby of the city's main cultural venue, the Encore is a stylish little place with friendly, efficient service and a crowd-pleasing menu of perennial favourites from chicken Caesar salad to slow braised-steak-and-Guinness pie.

Fitzroy's (Map p638; ☎ 7126 6211; 2-4 Bridge St; mains £10-15; ☺ 11am-10pm Mon-Sat, noon-8pm Sun) Informal Fitzroy's does cafe-style burger-and-chips lunches till 5.30pm, and then bistro-style dinners, including Thai chicken curry, herb-crusted salmon, and Mediterranean vegetable tagliatelle. The set two-/three-course dinner for £12/15 (available from 8pm Monday to Thursday) is good value. There's a second entrance on Carlisle Rd.

Mange 2 (Map p636; ☎ 7136 1222; 110-115 Strand Rd; mains £13-19; ☺ noon-2.30pm Tue-Fri, noon-3.30pm Sun & 5-10pm Tue-Sun) Mange 2 may have moved from its old Georgian home to a shiny, new, glass-fronted venue on the riverfront, but the menu is still faithful to top-quality Irish produce served plain or with an Asian- or French-fusion twist – try Finnebrogue venison with sweet potato purée, pan-seared spinach and redcurrant jus; or Donegal smoked cod with champ, buttered cabbage and chive sauce.

SELF-CATERING

Tesco (Map p636; ☎ 0845 677 9639; Quayside Shopping Centre, Strand Rd; ✆ 9am-9pm Mon-Thu, 8.30am-9pm Fri, 8.30am-8pm Sat, 1-6pm Sun) Self-caterers can stock up at this big supermarket, just north of the walled city.

Drinking

Whatever you do in Derry, don't miss an evening in the city's lively pubs – for the craic rather than the beer, which is nothing to write home about. They're friendly and atmospheric, mostly open until 1am, and are within easy walking distance of each other – there are six within dancing distance along Waterloo St.

Peadar O'Donnell's (Map p638; ☎ 7137 2138; 63 Waterloo St) A backpackers' favourite, Peadar's goes for traditional music sessions every night and often on weekend afternoons as well. It's done up as a typical Irish pub-cum-grocer, down to the shelves of grocery items, shopkeepers scales on the counter and a museum's-worth of old bric-a-brac.

Badgers Bar (Map p638; ☎ 7136 0763; 16-18 Orchard St) A fine polished-brass and stained-glass Victorian pub crammed with wood-panelled nooks and crannies, Badgers overflows at lunchtime with shoppers enjoying quality pub grub, and offers a quiet haven in the evenings when it attracts a crowd of more mature drinkers.

Café del Mondo (Map p638; ☎ 7126 8228; 4 Shipquay St; ✆ 8.30am-5pm Mon-Sat) A newly opened Bohemian cafe that serves excellent fairtrade coffee, at the time of research del Mondo was planning a Sunday-night music club – call in to see what's on the program.

Entertainment

Check out the Entertainment/Northern Beats page at www.derryjournal.com for news of what's coming up on Derry's live music scene.

CLUBS & LIVE MUSIC

Sandino's Café-Bar (Map p638; ☎ 7130 9297; www.sandinos .com; 1 Water St; admission free, live bands £4; ✆ 11.30am-1am Mon-Sat, 1pm-midnight Sun) From the posters of Ché to the Free Palestine flag to the fairtrade coffee, this relaxed cafe-bar exudes a liberal, left-wing vibe. There are live bands on Friday nights and occasionally midweek, and DJ sessions on

Saturdays. On Sundays there's a traditional Irish music session at 5pm, and live jazz/soul or DJs from 9pm, plus regular theme nights, fundraising nights and political events.

Mason's Bar (Map p638; ☎ 7136 0177; 10 Magazine St; admission free-£12) The city that spawned the Undertones is still turning out raw, rumbustious live music;Mason's Wednesday- and Friday-night sessions, kicking off at 6pm, are the place to catch the latest offerings from local talent. There are three or four acts each week, as well as open-mic nights on Mondays, occasional live bands on Saturdays and trad music sessions on Sundays at 6pm.

Earth@Café Roc (Map p636; ☎ 7136 0556; 129-135 Strand Rd) Derry's main nightclub and bar complex, close to the university, was closed for a major refurbishment at the time of research; check out www.bebo.com/earth_roc for what's on when it re-opens.

Gweedore Bar (Map p638; ☎ 7126 3513; 59-61 Waterloo St; admission £6-10) Next door to Peadar O'Donnell's and part of the same complex, the Gweedore Bar hosts live rock bands most nights, while the DJ bar upstairs is home to Jika Jika, the city's best house-music club (last Friday of month).

CONCERTS, THEATRE & CINEMA

Millennium Forum (Map p638; ☎ 7126 4455; www .millenniumforum.co.uk; Newmarket St) Ireland's biggest theatre auditorium is a major venue for dance, drama, concerts, opera and musicals.

Nerve Centre (Map p638; ☎ 7126 0562; www.nerve -centre.org.uk; 7-8 Magazine St) The Nerve Centre was set up in 1990 as a multimedia arts centre to encourage young, local talent in the fields of music and film. The centre has a performance area (live music at weekends), a theatre, a cinema (with an art-house program), a bar and a cafe.

Playhouse (Map p638; ☎ 7126 8027; www.derryplay house.co.uk; 5-7 Artillery St; ✆ box office 10am-5pm Mon-Fri) Housed in beautifully restored former school buildings with an award-winning modern extension at the rear, this community arts centre stages music, dance and theatre performances by local and international performers. It's also home to the Context Gallery (open 11am to 5.30pm Tuesday to Saturday), which hosts exhibitions by local artists.

Waterside Theatre (☎ 7131 4000; www.waterside theatre.com; Ebrington Centre, Glendermott Rd; ✆ box office 9am-4.30pm Mon-Fri) Housed in a former factory 500m east of the River Foyle, this theatre stages drama, dance, comedy, children's theatre and live music.

Magee College (Map p636; ☎ 7137 5679; www.culture .ulster.ac.uk; University of Ulster, Northland Rd) The college hosts a variety of arts, theatre and classical-concert performances throughout the year.

Derry Omniplex (Map p636; ☎ 08717 200400; www .omniplex.ie; Quayside Shopping Centre, Strand Rd) This seven-screen multiplex is the place for mainstream movies.

Shopping

Ogmiós (Map p636; ☎ 7126 4132; www.gaelaras.ie/shop .htm; 34 Great James St) Housed in the An Gaeláras Gaelic language centre, this craft shop stocks a good range of Irish-language books, traditional music CDs, musical instruments, pottery, prints and jewellery.

Donegal Shop (Map p638; ☎ 7126 6928; 8 Shipquay St) A long-established craft shop, the Donegal is crammed with Irish knitwear, Celtic jewellery, Donegal tweeds, Irish linen and souvenirs.

McGilloway Gallery (Map p638; ☎ 7136 6011; 6 Shipquay St) A commercial gallery that provides a showcase for the best of contemporary Irish art, the McGilloway sells work by local artists and stages around half a dozen exhibitions each year.

Whatnot (Map p638; ☎ 7128 8333; 22 Bishop St Within) The Whatnot is an interesting little antique shop crammed with jewellery, militaria, bric-a-brac and collectables.

Cool Discs Music (Map p638; ☎ 7126 0770; www .cooldiscsmusic.com; 6/7 Lesley House, Foyle St) One of Northern Ireland's best independent record shops, Cool Discs has a wide selection of music by Irish artists old and new.

Austins (Map p638; ☎ 7126 1817; 2 The Diamond) The world's oldest independent department store (established 1830), Austins is a good place to shop for Irish linen (they can ship your purchases overseas).

Foyleside Shopping Centre (Map p638; ☎ 7137 7575; Orchard St; ☼ 9am-6pm Mon & Tue, to 9pm Wed-Fri, to 7pm Sat, 1-6pm Sun) This is a huge, four-level mall just outside the eastern city walls that contains a Marks & Spencer, Eason bookshop and other high-street chain stores.

The little courtyard of **Craft Village** (Map p638) is home to a handful of craft shops selling Derry crystal, hand-woven cloth, ceramics, jewellery and other local craft items. Enter from Shipquay St, Magazine St or Tower Museum.

Getting There & Away

AIR

City of Derry Airport (Map pp634-5; ☎ 7181 0784; www.city ofderryairport.com) is about 13km east of Derry along the A2 towards Limavady. There are direct flights daily to Dublin (Aer Arann), London Stansted, London Luton, Liverpool, Birmingham and Glasgow Prestwick (Ryanair).

BUS

The **bus station** (Map p638; ☎ 7126 2261) is on Foyle St, just northeast of the walled city.

Bus 212, the Maiden City Flyer, is a fast and frequent service between Derry and Belfast (£10, 1¾ hours, every 30 minutes Monday to Saturday, 11 on Sunday), calling at Dungiven. Goldline Express 274 goes from Derry to Dublin (£16, four hours, every two hours daily).

Other useful Ulsterbus services include the 273 to Omagh (£8, 1¼ hours, hourly Monday to Saturday, six Sunday) and the 234 to Limavady and Coleraine (£6, one hour, five daily Monday to Saturday, two Sunday), continuing to Portstewart and Portrush on weekday evenings.

Lough Swilly Bus Company (Map p638; Foyle St; ☎ 7126 2017) has an office upstairs at the bus station, and runs buses to Buncrana, Carndonagh, Dungloe, Letterkenny (£5, 30 to 45 minutes, eight daily Monday to Friday, five on Saturday) and Greencastle (one hour, two daily Monday to Friday, one on Saturday) in County Donegal. There's also a bus from Derry to Malin Head (£6, 1¼ hours) via Carndonagh on Saturdays only – it's a very scenic trip.

Bus Éireann (☎ in Donegal 353-742 1309) service 64 runs from Derry to Galway (£18, 5¼ hours, three daily, two on Sundays) via Letterkenny, Donegal and Sligo; another four a day terminate at Sligo.

The **Airporter** (Map p636; ☎ 7126 9996; www .airporter.co.uk; Quayside Shopping Centre, Strand Rd) bus service runs direct from Derry to Belfast International (one-way/return £18/28, 1½ hours) and George Best Belfast City (same fare, two hours) airports. Buses depart every 90 minutes Monday to Friday, every two hours on Saturday and Sunday.

TRAIN

Derry's train station (always referred to as Londonderry in Northern Ireland timetables) is on the eastern side of the River Foyle; a free

Rail Link bus connects it with the bus station on Foyle St. Trains to Belfast (£10, 2¼ hours, seven or eight daily Monday to Saturday, four on Sunday) are slower but more comfortable than the bus, and the section of line between Derry and Coleraine is very scenic. There are also frequent trains to Coleraine (£7.50, 45 minutes, seven daily), with connections to Portrush (£9, 1¼ hours).

Getting Around

Bus 143A to Limavady stops at City of Derry airport (30 minutes, seven daily Monday to Friday, three Saturday, one Sunday); otherwise a taxi costs about £12.

The local Ulsterbus Foyle buses leave from Foyle St, outside the bus station, with 13 routes leading to the suburbs and surrounding villages; a day ticket giving unlimited travel on these buses costs £1.50.

The **Derry Taxi Association** (☎ 7126 0247) and **Foyle Delta Cabs** (☎ 7127 9999) operate from the city centre to all areas.

The Foyle Valley cycle route runs through Derry, along the west bank of the river, on the way to Strabane.

LIMAVADY & AROUND

pop 12,000

Enchanted by a folk tune played by a blind fiddler outside her window in 1851, Limavady resident Jane Ross (1810–79) jotted down the melody – then known as O'Cahan's Lament, and later as the Londonderry Air. She had written down for the first time the tune that came to be known around the world as 'Danny Boy' – probably the most famous Irish song of all time.

Limavady was granted to Sir Thomas Phillips, the organiser of the Plantation of County Londonderry, by James I in 1612,

after the last ruling chief, Sir Donnell Ballagh O'Cahan, was found guilty of rebellion (see p45 for more on the Plantation). Its original Gaelic name Léim an Mhadaidh means 'The Dog's Leap', and it commemorates one of the O'Cahans' dogs that jumped a gorge across the River Roe to bring warning of an unexpected enemy attack.

The **tourist office** (☎ 7776 0307; 7 Connell St; ⏰ 9am-5pm Mon-Fri Sep-Jun, to 5.45pm Jul & Aug, also 9.30am-5.30pm Sat May-Sep) is northeast of the town centre in the Limavady Borough Council Offices.

Sights & Activities

Today Limavady is a quiet and prosperous small town. There's not much to see except the **blue plaque** on the wall at 51 Main St, opposite the Alexander Arms, commemorating the home of Jane Ross. The town hosts a **jazz and blues festival** (www.limavadyjazzandblues.com) in June.

The lovely **Roe Valley Country Park**, about 3km south of Limavady, has riverside walks stretching for 5km either side of the River Roe. The area is associated with the O'Cahans, who ruled the valley until the Plantation. The 17th-century settlers saw the flax-growing potential of the damp river valley and the area became an important linen-manufacturing centre.

The **Dogleap Centre** (☎ 7772 2074; Roe Valley Country Park, 41 Dogleap Rd; admission free; ⏰ 10am-6pm Easter-Sep, to 5pm Oct-Easter) houses a visitor centre and tearoom. Next door is Ulster's first domestic **hydroelectric power station**, opened in 1896; it opens by request at the visitor centre. The nearby **Green Lane Museum** (admission free; ⏰ 1-5pm daily Easter-Sep) contains old photographs and relics of the valley's flax industry. The scutch mill, where the flax was pounded, is a 20-minute walk away, along the river, past two watchtowers built to guard the linen when it was spread out in the fields for bleaching.

The River Roe is famous for its **sea trout and salmon fishing** (www.roeangling.com). Day tickets cost £15, and are available from **SJ Mitchell & Co** (☎ 7772 2128; Main St, Limavady), the Dogleap Centre and the Alexander Arms Hotel. The season runs from the third week in May until 20 October.

The park is signposted off the B192 road between Limavady and Dungiven. Bus 146 from Limavady to Dungiven will drop you at the turn-off; the park is about a 3km walk from the main road.

Sleeping & Eating

Alexander Arms Hotel (☎ 7776 3443; 34 Main St; s/d £30/50; Ⓟ) A long-established hotel and pub dating from 1875, the centrally located Alexander Arms is a friendly, family-run place that offers B&B and serves pub grub and restaurant meals.

Hunter's Bakery & Oven Door Café (☎ 7772 2411; 5 Market St; mains £3-7; ☺ 9am-5.30pm Mon-Sat) If you fancy a quick snack, this homely bakery has a comfy cafeteria at the back, serving good coffee, cakes and light meals. It's a local institution, patronised by a broad cross-section of the community, with a pleasantly old-fashioned feel.

ourpick **Lime Tree** (☎ 7776 4300; 60 Catherine St; mains £15-20; ☺ 6-9pm Tue-Fri, to 9.30pm Sat) Unfussy decor in shades of burgundy and beige softened by flickering tea-lights makes for a relaxing atmosphere in Limavady's top eatery. The menu promotes local produce – from succulent Malin Head crab cakes and seafood thermidor made with Donegal fish to fillet steak from award-winning butcher Hunter's of Limavady, served with red wine and tarragon sauce – and includes vegetarian dishes that are a cut above the usual, such as spinach and sun-dried tomato roulade with red pepper dressing. There's also an early-bird menu (two/three courses £13.50/16.50) available before 7pm Tuesday to Friday.

Getting There & Away

Bus 143A runs between Derry and Limavady hourly (four daily on Sunday). There's no direct bus to Belfast from Limavady but connections can be made at Coleraine or Dungiven. Bus 146 goes from Limavady to Dungiven (40 minutes, five daily Monday to Friday).

DUNGIVEN
pop 3000

As the main road from Belfast to Derry sweeps down from the bleak moors of the Glenshane Pass it sweeps right through the small market town of Dungiven (Dún Geimhin), 14km south of Limavady. The traffic-choked main street is almost as bleak as the moors, but it's worth stopping to take a look at the old priory.

Sights

The remains of the Augustinian **Dungiven Priory**, off the A6 on the eastern edge of town, date back to the 12th century when it replaced a pre-Norman monastery.

In the chancel of the church is the magnificent **tomb of Cooey-na-Gal**, a chieftain of the O'Cahans, who died in 1385. It's difficult to see in the dark of the blocked-off chancel (bring a torch if you're really keen), but the tomb bears figures of six kilted *gallowglasses*, Scottish mercenaries hired by Cooey O'Cahan as minders – they earned him the nickname 'na-Gal' ('of the Foreigners'). It's topped by a beautifully sculpted canopy of Gothic tracery.

Near the entrance to the churchyard is a **bullaun** – a mossy, hollowed stone originally used by the monks for grinding grain – which now collects rainwater and is used as a site of pilgrimage and prayer by people seeking cures for illnesses. A nearby tree is covered in prayer rags left by visiting pilgrims.

Sleeping

Flax Mill Hostel (☎ 7774 2655; www.flaxmill-textiles.com; Mill Lane, Derrylane; dm £6; ☺ Mar-Oct; Ⓟ) The owners of this converted 18th-century flax mill grow their own organic veggies and generate their own electricity, but their main business is creating hand-woven textiles. There's basic hostel accommodation, too. The mill is 5km north of Dungiven, signposted off the B192 road to Limavady.

Dungiven Castle (☎ 7774 2428; www.dungivencastle.com; 145 Main St, Dungiven; s/d £55/100; Ⓟ) The ancestral home of the O'Cahan clan has been given a luxurious Laura Ashley makeover and now offers a lovely romantic getaway in a most unexpected spot. Don't be put off by the car park and ugly buildings on the street side – the far side of the castle is another world, looking out across beautiful gardens to the Sperrin Mountains.

Getting There & Away

The half-hourly Maiden City Flyer bus 212 between Derry and Belfast stops in Dungiven, as does the 146 from Limavady (£3.50, 25 minutes, five daily Monday to Friday).

COASTAL COUNTY DERRY
Magilligan Point

The huge triangular spit of land that almost closes off the mouth of Lough Foyle is mostly taken up by a military firing range, and is home to a once-notorious prison. Still, it's worth a visit for its vast sandy beaches – **Magilligan Strand** to the west, and the 9km sweep of **Benone Strand** to the northeast, the latter providing a superb venue for kite buggies and mini land yachts. On the point itself, watching over the entrance to Lough Foyle, stands a **Martello tower**, built during the Napoleonic Wars in 1812 to guard against French invasion.

Benone Tourist Complex (☎ 7775 0555; 59 Benone Ave; campsites £10, caravans £13-16; ♥ 9am-10pm Jul & Aug, to dusk Apr-Jun & Sep, to 4pm Oct-Mar), adjacent to Benone Strand, has an outdoor heated pool, a children's pool, tennis courts and a putting green. Note that dogs are not allowed on the beach from May to September.

The **Lough Foyle Ferry** (☎ in the Republic 074-938 1901; www.loughfoyleferry.com; car/motorcycle/pedestrian £10/5/2) runs between Magilligan Point and Greencastle in County Donegal all year round. The trip takes 10 minutes and runs hourly from 8am Monday to Friday, 9am Saturday and Sunday, departing on the hour from Greencastle, 15 minutes past from Magilligan. The last ferry is at 9.15pm June to August, 8.15pm May, 7.15pm April and September, and 6.15pm October to March.

Downhill

In 1774 the eccentric Bishop of Derry and fourth Earl of Bristol, Frederick Augustus Hervey, built himself a palatial home, Downhill, on the coast west of Castlerock. It burnt down in 1851, was rebuilt in 1876, and was finally abandoned after WWII. The ruins of the house now stand forlornly on a cliff top.

The original demesne covered some 160 hectares, which is now part of the National Trust's **Downhill Estate** (☎ 2073 1582; adult/child £2.50/1.70, parking £3; ♥ temple & facilities 10am-5pm daily Apr-Sep, grounds dawn-dusk). The beautiful landscaped gardens below the ruins of the house are the work of celebrated gardener Jan Eccles, who became custodian of Downhill at the age of 60 and created the garden over a period of 30 years. She died in 1997 aged 94.

The main attraction here is the little **Mussenden Temple**, built by the bishop to house either his library or his mistress – opinions differ! The randy old clergyman continued an affair with the mistress of Frederick William II of Prussia well into old age.

The main access is from the car parks at the Lion's Gate and Bishop's Gate on the coast road. A more peaceful alternative is the pleasant, 20-minute walk to the temple from Castlerock village, with fine views west to the beach at Benone and Donegal, and east to Portstewart and the shadowy outlines of the Scottish hills. Begin at the path along the seaward side of the caravan park; halfway there, you have to descend into

a steep-sided valley and climb the steps on the far side of the little lake. On the beach below the temple, the bishop used to challenge his own clergy to horseback races, rewarding the winners with lucrative parishes.

On the main road 1km west of the temple, opposite the Downhill Hostel, the scenic **Bishop's Road** climbs steeply up through a ravine and heads over the hills to Limavady. There are spectacular views over Lough Foyle, Donegal and the Sperrin Mountains from the **Gortmore** picnic area, and from the cliff top at **Binevenagh Lake**.

our pick **Downhill Hostel** (☎ 7084 9077; www.downhillhostel.com; 12 Mussenden Rd; dm/d from £11/35, f from £40 plus per child £5; P ◻) is a beautifully restored late-19th-century house, tucked beneath the sea cliffs and overlooking the beach, offering very comfortable accommodation in six-bed dorms, doubles and family rooms. There's a big lounge with an open fire and a view of the sea, and you can hire wetsuits and body boards when the surf's up. You can even paint your own mugs, plates and bowls in the neighbouring pottery. There are no shops in Downhill so bring supplies with you.

Bus 134 between Limavady and Coleraine (20 minutes, nine daily Monday to Friday, six Saturday) stops at Downhill, as does the 234 between Derry and Coleraine.

Castlerock

Castlerock is a small seaside resort with a decent beach. At the turn-off from the main coast road towards Castlerock is the late-17th-century **Hezlett House** (☎ 2073 1582; guided tour adult/child £3.50/2.40; ♥ 11am-5pm Fri-Tue Jul & Aug, 11am-5pm Sat & Sun Easter, Jun & Sep), a thatched cottage noted for its cruck-truss roof gables of stone and turf strengthened with wooden crucks, or crutches. The interior decor is Victorian.

Bus 134 between Limavady and Coleraine (20 minutes, nine daily Monday to Friday, six

---

TOP FIVE VIEWPOINTS IN NORTHERN IRELAND

- Binevenagh Lake (above)
- Fair Head (p661)
- Cuilcagh Mountain (p691)
- Scrabo Hill (p611)
- Slieve Donard (p619)

Saturday) stops at Castlerock, as does the 234 between Derry and Coleraine.

There are nine trains a day from Castlerock to Coleraine (£2, 10 minutes) and Derry (£7.50, 35 minutes) Monday to Saturday, and four on Sunday.

COLERAINE
pop 25,300

Coleraine (Cúil Raithin), on the banks of the River Bann, is an important transport hub and shopping centre. It was one of the original Plantation towns of County Londonderry, founded in 1613. The University of Ulster was established here in 1968 much to the chagrin of Derry, which had lobbied hard to win it.

There's not much to see in town, but it's a pleasant enough place for a wander on your way between Derry and the Antrim Coast.

Orientation & Information

The mostly pedestrianised town centre is on the east bank of the River Bann. From the combined train and bus station turn left along Railway Rd to find the **tourist information centre** (☎ 7034 4723; info@northcoastni.com; Railway Rd; ☷ 9am-5pm Mon-Sat), then turn right at King's Gate St for the main shopping area and **Coleraine Library** (☎ 7034 2561; Queen St; ☷ 9.30am-8pm Mon-Thu, to 5pm Fri & Sat, 1-5pm Sun), which has public internet access for £1.50 per 30 minutes.

Sights & Activities

The tourist office has a *Heritage Trail* leaflet that will guide you around what little remains of the original Plantation town, including **St Patrick's Church**, parts of which date from 1613, and fragments of the town walls.

On the second Saturday of each month the **Causeway Speciality Market** (☷ 9am-2.30pm) is held in the Diamond, selling a range of local crafts and organic produce, from hand-turned wooden bowls and homemade candles to farmhouse jam from Ballywalter, County Down, and sheep-milk cheese from County Derry.

Just 1.5km south of the town centre, on the east bank of the river, is **Mountsandel Fort** (admission free; ☷ dawn-dusk), a massive and mysterious earthwork that may have been an early Christian stronghold or a later Anglo-Norman fortification. From the Mountsandel Forest parking area on Mountsandel Rd, a 2.5km circular walk leads high above the River Bann to the fort, where you descend steeply down

to the riverbank and return upstream past the Victorian lock and weir at Cutts.

You can take a 1½-hour river cruise on the **Lady Sandel** (☎ 07798 786955; www.riverbanncruises .com; adult/child £8.50/5.50) from the jetty on Strand Rd (across the river from the town centre) upstream to Macfinn via the lock at Cutts, or downstream to the river mouth. Boats depart at 2pm Saturday and Sunday from Easter to mid-September, plus 3pm Monday to Friday in July and August.

Sleeping & Eating

There's not much accommodation in the town centre; most B&Bs are on the fringes.

Camus Country House (☎ 7034 2982; 27 Curragh Rd, Castleroe; s/d £33/60; **P**) This lovely, ivy-clad, 17th-century house with views over the River Bann occupies the site of an 8th-century monastery, with an old Celtic cross in the adjacent cemetery. The owner can organise fishing trips on the river. It's on the A54, 5km south of town.

Lodge Hotel & Travelstop (☎ 7034 4848; www .thelodgehotel.com; Lodge Rd; s/d from £65/85; **P** ☎) The Lodge offers a choice of rooms with all the mod cons in the main hotel, or slightly more basic rooms in the motel-style annexe (family rooms that sleep two adults and two kids from £63 per room without breakfast). It's fairly central too – less than 1km southeast of the town centre.

Ground (☎ 7032 8664; 25 Kings Gate St; mains £2-5; ☷ 9am-5.30pm Mon-Sat; ▢ ☎) This cheerful and child-friendly coffee shop serves excellent fairtrade coffee and tasty organic grub, including soups, sandwiches, panini and home-baked cakes, as well as offering organic baby food, bibs, wipes and a baby-changing room.

Getting There & Away

Goldline Express bus 218 links Coleraine to Belfast (£9, 1¾ hours, hourly Monday to Friday, six on Saturday, two on Sunday), while bus 234 goes to Derry (£6, one hour, five daily Monday to Saturday) via Limavady. See also Getting There & Away, p652.

There are regular trains from Coleraine to Belfast (£9, two hours, seven or eight daily Monday to Saturday, four on Sunday) and Derry (£7.50, 45 minutes, same frequency). A branch line links Coleraine to Portrush (£2, 12 minutes, hourly Monday to Saturday, 10 on Sunday).

PORTSTEWART

pop 7800

Ever since Victorian times, when English novelist William Thackeray described it as having an 'air of comfort and neatness', the seaside and golfing resort of Portstewart has cultivated a sedate, upmarket atmosphere that distinguishes it from populist Portrush, 6km further east. However, there's also a sizeable student community from the University of Ulster in Coleraine.

The fantastic beach is the main attraction, along with a couple of world-class golf courses – a combination that has created the North's highest property prices and a large demand for holiday homes. Concerns about overdevelopment were realised when the economic downturn of 2008 hit the North – you'll see no shortage of half-built houses and For Sale signs.

Orientation & Information

Central Portstewart consists of a west-facing promenade with a harbour at the north end. A coastal walk, paralleled by Strand Rd, runs south for 1.5km to the beach of Portstewart Strand.

The **tourist information office** (☎ 7083 2286; Town Hall, The Crescent; ☺ 10am-1pm & 2-4.30pm Mon-Sat Jul & Aug) is in the library in the red-brick town hall at the south end of the promenade.

Sights & Activities

The central promenade is dominated by the castellated facade of a Dominican college, looming over the seaside fun and games like a Catholic conscience. The broad, 2.5km beach of **Portstewart Strand** is a 20-minute walk south of the centre, or a short bus ride along Strand Rd. Parking is allowed on the firm sand, which can accommodate over 1000 cars (open all year round, £5 per car from Easter to October).

Heading in the opposite direction, the **Port Path** is a 10.5km coastal footpath (part of the Causeway Coast Way) that stretches from Portstewart Strand to White Rocks, 3km east of Portrush.

Portstewart is within a few kilometres of three of Northern Ireland's top **golf courses** – the championship links at Portstewart Golf Club (green fees weekday/weekend £80/95), Royal Portrush (£125/140) and Castlerock (£65/80).

In early May the **North West 200 motorcycle race** (www.northwest200.org) is run on a road circuit taking in Portrush, Portstewart and Coleraine – you can see the starting grid painted on the main road on the eastern edge of town. This classic race – Ireland's biggest outdoor sporting event – is one of the last to be run on closed public roads anywhere in Europe, and attracts up to 150,000 spectators; if you're not one of them, it's best to avoid the area on the race weekend.

Sleeping

Don't even think about turning up without a booking during the North West 200 weekend in May.

BUDGET

Causeway Coast Independent Hostel (☎ 7083 3789; rick@causewaycoasthostel.fsnet.co.uk; 4 Victoria Tce; dm/tw from £11/35; ☐ ☎) This neat terrace house just northeast of the harbour has spacious four-, six- and eight-bed dorms plus a double room, and good power showers. It has its own kitchen, laundry and welcoming open fire in winter.

Millfield Holiday Village (☎ 7083 3308; 80 Mill Rd; tent & caravan sites £15) This is the nearest place to the promenade (a 15-minute walk away) that you can pitch a tent; great views. Coming from Coleraine on the A2, turn right at the Mill Rd/Strand Rd roundabout.

MIDRANGE

Cul-Erg B&B (☎ 7083 6610; www.culerg.co.uk; 9 Hillside, Atlantic Circle; s/d £40/70; ℗ ☎) This family-run B&B is in a modern, flower-bedecked terrace house just a couple of minutes' walk from the promenade. Warm and welcoming, it's set in a quiet cul-de-sac; the rooms at the back have a view of the sea.

Cromore Halt Inn (☎ 7083 6888; www.cromore.com; 158 Station Rd; s/d £55/80; ℗ ☎) Located about 1km east of the harbour, on the corner of Station Rd and Mill Rd, the motel-style Cromore has a dozen modern, businesslike rooms, along with friendly, helpful staff and a good restaurant.

The York (☎ 7083 3594; www.theyorkportstewart .co.uk; 2 Station Rd; s/d from £79/110; ℗ ☎) The York brings a bit of boutique chic to Portstewart's mostly staid accommodation scene, with designer rooms in shades of chocolate, cream and cappuccino, red leather chairs, spacious bathrooms with rain-head showers, and big breakfasts served in a glass-lined dining room with stunning views along the coast.

Eating & Drinking

Morelli's (☎ 7083 2150; 53 The Promenade; mains £4-8; ✆ 9am-11pm, food to 8pm) Morelli's is a local institution, founded by Italian immigrants and famous for its mouth-watering ice cream since 1911. The menu includes pasta, pizza, sandwiches, omelettes, and fish and chips, as well as good coffee and cakes, and there's a great view across the bay to Mussenden Temple, Benone Strand and Donegal.

Anchor Bar & Skippers Restaurant (☎ 7083 2003; 87-89 The Promenade; mains £8-15; ✆ food noon-9pm) The liveliest of Portstewart's traditional pubs, famed for its Guinness and hugely popular with students from the University of Ulster, the Anchor serves decent pub grub, opens till 1am and has karaoke on Tuesday, quiz nights on Wednesday, trad Irish music on Thursday and live bands Friday and Saturday, plus DJ club nights from 9.30pm Thursday to Sunday. There's also Skippers Restaurant, which serves more sophisticated dishes such as mussels in garlic and basil butter, roast duckling, and vegetable stir-fry.

Preference Brasserie (☎ 7083 3959; 81 The Promenade; mains £15-21; ✆ 6-9.30pm Tue-Sat, 12.30-3.30pm Sun) A welcome new addition to Portstewart's prom, this stylish brasserie prides itself on a seasonal menu of fresh local produce served with continental flair – dishes include medallions of Irish beef with creamed haricot beans and pancetta, roast cod fillet with braised puy lentils and Dijon mustard vinaigrette, and stilton and red pepper frittata with seasonal leaves.

Getting There & Away

Bus 140 plies between Coleraine and Portstewart (£2, 20 to 30 minutes) roughly every half-hour (fewer on Sunday). Also see Getting There & Around, below.

COUNTY ANTRIM

Getting There & Around

Translink (☎ 9066 6630; www.translink.co.uk) operates several bus services specially designed for tourists visiting the popular Antrim coast and Giant's Causeway areas.

The *Antrim Coaster* (bus 252/256) links Coleraine with Belfast (£10, four hours, two daily Monday to Saturday) via Portstewart, Portrush, Bushmills, the Giant's Causeway, Ballycastle, the Glens of Antrim, and Larne,

departing Belfast at 9.05am and 3pm. Southbound buses leave Coleraine at 9.35am and 3.40pm. A Sunday service operates from July to September only.

From June to mid-September the *Causeway Rambler* (bus 402) links Bushmills Distillery and Carrick-a-Rede (£4.50, 25 minutes, seven daily) via the Giant's Causeway, White Park Bay and Ballintoy. The ticket allows unlimited travel in both directions for one day.

In July and August only, the *Bushmills Bus* (bus 177), an open-topped (weather permitting) double-decker, runs from Coleraine to the Giant's Causeway (one way/day return £3/4.50, one hour, four daily) via Portstewart, Portrush, Dunluce Castle, Portballintrae and Bushmills Distillery.

PORTRUSH

pop 6300

The bustling seaside resort of Portrush (Port Rois) bursts at the seams with holiday-makers in high season and, not surprisingly, many of its attractions are focused unashamedly on good, old-fashioned family fun. However, it is also one of Ireland's top surfing centres, and is home to the North's hottest nightclub.

The **tourist information centre** (☎ 7082 3333; portrsuhtic@btconnect.com; Dunluce Centre, 10 Sandhill Dr; ✆ 9am-7pm Jul-Aug, 9am-5pm Mon-Fri, noon-5pm Sat & Sun Apr-Jun & Sep, noon-5pm Sat & Sun Mar & Oct) books accommodation and has a bureau de change.

Sights & Activities

Portrush's main attraction is the beautiful sandy beach of **Curran Strand** that stretches for 3km to the east of the town, ending at the scenic chalk cliffs of White Rocks.

The town is also famous for **Barry's** (☎ 7082 2340; www.barrysamusements.com; 16 Eglinton St; admission free, per ride 50p-£2; ✆ 12.30-10.30pm Jul & Aug, 10am-6pm Mon-Fri, 12.30-10.30pm Sat & 12.30-9.30pm Sun Jun, 12.30-10.30pm Sat & 12.30-9.30pm Sun Apr & May), Ireland's biggest amusement park, filled with classic, family-friendly rides, including a carousel, ghost train and dodgems.

There's more family-oriented fun at the **Dunluce Centre** (☎ 7082 4444; www.dunlucecentre.co.uk; 10 Sandhill Dr; admission £3.50-4.50; ✆ 10am-7pm Jul & Aug, noon-5pm Sat & Sun Apr-Jun & Sep), a hi-tech, indoor adventure playground especially for kids, with interactive games, a computerised treasure hunt and a 'turbo-tour' motion-simulator ride.

Waterworld (☎ 7082 2001; The Harbour; ✆ 10am-7pm Mon-Sat, noon-7pm Sun Jul & Aug, 10am-3pm Mon-Fri,

10am-5pm Sat & noon-5pm Sun Jun), by the harbour, has indoor swimming pools, waterslides and spa baths for children to play in (adult/child under eight years £4.50/2.50, family tickets for three/four/five persons £11.75/15.60/19.50), and ten-pin bowling (from £8 per lane; open till 9pm).

You'll find even more activities for kids at **The Coastal Zone** (☎ 7082 3600; 8 Bath Rd; admission free; 🕑 10am-5pm Easter week & Jun-Aug, 10am-5pm Sat & Sun Sep), including marine-life exhibits, a touch pool, rock-pool rambles and fossil hunts.

In summer, boats depart regularly for **cruises** or **fishing trips**; the tourist office has a list of operators. For horse riding, contact the **Maddybenny Riding Centre** (☎ 7082 3394; Maddybenny Farm, Atlantic Rd; lessons & hacking per hr £12); beginners are welcome.

Portrush is the centre of Northern Ireland's **surfing** scene – the Portrush Open in March is a regular feature on the Irish Surfing Association competition calendar, and the UK Pro Surf Tour held a contest here for the first time in 2007. From April to November the friendly **Troggs Surf Shop** (☎ 7082 5476; www .troggssurfshop.co.uk; 88 Main St; 🕑 10am-6pm) offers bodyboard/surfboard hire (per day £5/10) and wetsuit hire (per day £7), surf reports and general advice. A two-hour lesson including equipment hire costs £25 per person.

Sleeping

Places fill up quickly during summer so it's advisable to book in advance.

BUDGET

Carrick Dhu Caravan Park (☎ 7082 3712; 12 Ballyreagh Rd; camp & caravan sites from £14; 🕑 Apr-Sep) This is a small site 1.5km west of Portrush on the A2 towards Portstewart. Facilities include a children's playground and restaurant.

MIDRANGE

ourpick Clarmont (☎ 7082 2397; www.clarmont.com; 10 Landsdowne Cres; per person £35-40) Our favourite among several guesthouses on Landsdowne Cres, the Clarmont has great views and, from polished pine floors to period fireplaces, has a decor that tastefully mixes Victorian and modern styles. Ask for a room with a bay window overlooking the sea.

A Pier View (☎ 7082 3234; www.apierview.co.uk; 53 Kerr St; s/d £35/60; P) Any closer to the harbour and you'd be in it! This cosy B&B has three snug rooms, and great views over the harbour

and beach from the luxurious lounge and conservatory-style breakfast room.

Albany Lodge Guest House (☎ 7082 3492; www.albany lodgeni.co.uk; 2 Eglinton St; s/d from £60/90; P ☐ 🛜) This elegant, four-storey Victorian villa has a great location close to the beach, with spectacular views along the coast. The rooms are spacious and welcoming, with pine furniture and warm colours, and the owners are friendly without being in your face. It's worth shelling out a few extra quid for the four-poster suite on the top floor, where you can soak up the view while reclining on your chaise longue.

Eating
BUDGET

Café 55 (☎ 7082 2811; 1 Causeway St; mains £4-7; 🕑 9am-5pm Sep-Jun, to 10pm Jul & Aug) Tucked beneath 55 Degrees North, this licensed cafe serves good coffee plus breakfast bagels and pancakes (10am to 11.30am) on an outdoor terrace; it also has daily lunch specials such as fish pie, and an evening menu in summer.

Coast (☎ 7082 3311; The Harbour; mains £5-10; 🕑 5-9.30pm Wed-Fri, 4-10.30pm Sat, 3-9.30pm Sun) Coast is another waterfront place, overlooking the harbour, offering stone-baked pizzas, pasta dishes and a range of steak, chicken and fish dishes.

MIDRANGE

Harbour Bistro (☎ 7082 2430; The Harbour; mains £8-15; 🕑 5-10pm Mon-Fri, 5-10.30pm Sat, 4-9pm Sun) Quality grub – juicy steaks, homemade burgers, spicy chicken, oriental dishes and vegetarian meals – a family-friendly atmosphere (there's a kids menu) and a harbour-side location make the Harbour one of Portrush's most popular eating places.

ourpick 55 Degrees North (☎ 7082 2811; 1 Causeway St; mains £11-16; 🕑 5-9pm Mon-Sat, 12.30-2.30pm & 5-7.30pm Sun) One of the north coast's most stylish restaurants, 55 Degrees North boasts a wall of floor-to-ceiling windows allowing diners to soak up a spectacular panorama of sand and sea. The food is excellent, concentrating on clean, simple flavours and unfussy presentation, with dishes such as grilled sea bass with new potatoes and leek and chorizo cream. There's an early-bird menu (mains £7 to £9) available before 7pm.

Entertainment

Kelly's Complex (☎ 7082 6633; www.kellysportrush .co.uk; 1 Bushmills Rd) The North's top clubbing

---

WRECK OF THE GIRONA

The little bay 1km to the northeast of the Giant's Causeway is called Port na Spaniagh – Bay of the Spaniards. It was here, in October 1588, that the *Girona* – a ship of the Spanish Armada – was driven onto the rocks by a storm.

The *Girona* had escaped the famous confrontation with Sir Walter Raleigh's fleet in the English Channel, but along with many other fleeing Spanish ships had been driven north around Scotland and Ireland by bad weather. Though designed for a crew of 500, when she struck the rocks she was loaded with 1300 people – mostly survivors gathered from other shipwrecks – including the cream of the Spanish aristocracy. Barely a dozen survived.

Somhairle Buidhe (Sorley Boy) MacDonnell (1505–90), the constable of nearby Dunluce Castle, salvaged gold and cannons from the wreck, and used the money to extend and modernise his fortress – cannons from the ship can still be seen on the castle's landward wall. But it was not until 1968 that the wreck site was excavated by a team of archaeological divers. They recovered a magnificent treasure of gold, silver and precious stones, as well as everyday sailors' possessions, which are now on display in Belfast's Ulster Museum (p579).

---

venue regularly features DJs from London and Manchester, and attracts clubbers from as far afield as Belfast and Dublin. Plain and small-looking from the outside, the TARDIS effect takes over as you enter a wonderland of seven bars and three dance floors, which was undergoing a £1.5 million refurbishment at the time of research. It's been around since 1996, but Lush!@Kellys (admission £7 to £12, open 9pm to 2am Saturday) is still one of the best club nights in Ireland.

The complex is on the A2 just east of Portrush, beside the Golf Links Holiday Park.

Getting There & Around

The bus terminal is near the Dunluce Centre. Bus 140 links Portrush with Coleraine (£2, 20 minutes) and Portstewart (£2, 20 to 30 minutes) every 30 minutes or so. Also see Getting There & Around, p652.

The train station is just south of the harbour. Portrush is served by trains from Coleraine (£2, 12 minutes, hourly Monday to Saturday, 10 on Sunday), where there are connections to Belfast or Derry.

For taxis call **Andy Brown's** (☎ 7082 2223) or **North West Taxis** (☎ 7082 4446). Both are near the town hall. A taxi to Kelly's is around £6, and it's £12 to the Giant's Causeway.

DUNLUCE CASTLE

Views along the Causeway Coast between Portrush and Portballintrae are dominated by the ruins of **Dunluce Castle** (☎ 2073 1938; 87 Dunluce Rd; adult/child £2/1; ☺ 10am-6pm Easter-Sep, 10am-4pm Oct-Easter, last admission 30 min before closing), perched atop a dramatic basalt crag. In the

16th and 17th centuries it was the seat of the MacDonnell family (the earls of Antrim from 1620), who built a Renaissance-style manor house within the walls. Part of the castle, including the kitchen, collapsed into the sea in 1639, taking seven servants and that night's dinner with it.

A narrow bridge leads from the mainland courtyard across a dizzying gap to the main part of the fortress. Below, a path leads down from the gatehouse to the Mermaid's Cave beneath the castle crag.

Dunluce is 5km east of Portrush, a one-hour walk away along the coastal path. All the buses that run along the coast stop at Dunluce Castle; see p652.

PORTBALLINTRAE
pop 750

During WWI, Portballintrae was the only place in the UK to be shelled by a German submarine. And that's pretty much its only claim to fame. A once-pretty village set around a sand-fringed, horseshoe bay with a tiny harbour, today it suffers from rampant overdevelopment, with modern holiday apartments everywhere (fewer than half of the houses are permanently occupied). The village is an easy 2km walk from Bushmills, and 2.5km from the Giant's Causeway. The fine sandy beach of Bushfoot Strand stretches for 1.5km to the northeast.

BUSHMILLS
pop 1350

The small town of Bushmills has long been a place of pilgrimage for connoisseurs of Irish whiskey. A good youth hostel and a restored ail link with the Giant's Causeway have also made it an attractive stop for hikers exploring the Causeway Coast.

Sights

Bushmills Distillery (☎ 2073 3218; www.bushmills.com; Distillery Rd; adult/child £6/3; ☺ 9.15am-5pm Mon-Sat & noon-5pm Sun Apr-Oct, 9.15am-5pm Mon-Sat & noon-4pm Sun Mar, 9.30am-3.30pm Mon-Fri & 12.30-3.30pm Sat & Sun Nov-Feb) is the world's oldest legal distillery, having been granted a licence by King James I in 1608. Bushmills whiskey is made with Irish barley and water from St Columb's Rill, a tributary of the River Bush, and matured in oak barrels. During ageing, the alcohol content drops from around 60% to 40%; the spirit lost through evaporation is known, rather sweetly, as 'the angels' share'. After a tour of the distillery you're rewarded with a free sample (or a soft drink), and four lucky volunteers get a whiskey-tasting session to compare Bushmills with other brands. Tours begin every 30 minutes, and there's late opening (last tour 6pm) on Wednesday and Thursday in August.

The **Giant's Causeway & Bushmills Railway** (☎ 2073 2844; www.freewebs.com/giantscausewayrailway; adult/child return £6.75/4.75) follows the route of a 19th-century tourist tramway for 3km from Bushmills to below the Giant's Causeway visitor centre. The narrow-gauge line and locomotives (two steam and one diesel) were brought from a private line on the shores of Lough Neagh. Trains run hourly between 11am and 5.30pm, departing on the hour from the Causeway, on the half-hour from Bushmills, daily in July and August, weekends only from Easter to June and September and October.

Sleeping & Eating

Mill Rest Youth Hostel (☎ 2073 1222; www.hini.org .uk; 49 Main St; dm £16-17, d £39; ☺ closed 11am-2pm Jul & Aug, 11am-5pm Mar-Jun, Sep & Oct; 🖥 ♿) This modern, purpose-built and child-friendly hostel is just off the Diamond in the centre of town. Accommodation is mostly in four- to six-bed dorms with one twin room with private bathroom. There's also a kitchen, restaurant, laundry and bike shed. The hostel is open daily March to October, Friday and Saturday nights only November to February.

Ballyness Caravan Park & B&B (☎ 2073 2393; www.bally nesscaravanpark.com; 40 Castlecatt Rd; campervan & caravan sites incl car & 2 persons £20, B&B s/d £35/55; ☺ mid-Mar–Oct; 🖥 🛜) This ecofriendly caravan park (no tents) is about 1km south of Bushmills town centre on the B66. The farmhouse at the entrance offers B&B accommodation March to October.

Bushmills Inn Hotel (☎ 2073 2339; www.bushmillsinn .com; 9 Dunluce Rd; s/d from £168/178; 🅿 🖥 🛜) One of

---

THE MAKING OF THE CAUSEWAY

The Mythology

The story goes that the Irish giant, Finn McCool, built the Causeway so he could cross the sea to fight the Scottish giant Benandonner. When he got there he found his rival asleep and, seeing that the Scot was far bigger than he, fled back to Ireland. Soon, Finn's wife heard the angry Benandonner come running across the Causeway, so she dressed Finn in a baby's shawl and bonnet and put him in a crib. When the Scottish giant came hammering at Finn's door, Mrs McCool warned him not to wake Finn's baby. Taking a glance in the cot, Benandonner decided that if this huge baby was Finn's child, then McCool himself must be immense, and fled in turn back to Scotland, ripping up the causeway as he went. All that remains are its ends – the Giant's Causeway in Ireland, and the island of Staffa in Scotland (which has similar rock formations).

The Geology

The more prosaic scientific explanation is that the causeway rocks were formed 60 million years ago, when a thick layer of molten basaltic lava flowed along a valley in the existing chalk beds. As the lava flow cooled and hardened – from the top and bottom surfaces inward – it contracted, creating a pattern of hexagonal cracks at right angles to the cooling surfaces (think of mud contracting and cracking in a hexagonal pattern as a lake bed dries out). As solidification progressed towards the centre of the flow, the cracks spread down from the top, and up from the bottom, until the lava was completely solid. Erosion has cut into the lava flow, and the basalt has split along the contraction cracks, creating the hexagonal columns.

Northern Ireland's most atmospheric hotels, the Bushmills is an old coaching inn complete with peat fires, gas lamps and a round tower with a secret library. There are no longer any bedrooms in the old part of the hotel – the luxurious accommodation is in the neighbouring, modern Mill House complex.

Copper Kettle (☎ 2073 2560; 61 Main St; mains £3-6; ⏰ 8.30am-5pm Mon-Sat, from 10am Sun) This rustic tearoom serves breakfast fry-ups till 11.30am, and has daily lunch specials as well as good tea, coffee, cakes and scones.

our pick **Bushmills Inn restaurant** (lunch mains £7-12, dinner mains £15-20; ⏰ noon-9.30pm Mon-Sat & 12.30-9pm Sun) The inn's excellent restaurant, with intimate wooden booths set in the old 17th-century stables, specialises in fresh Ulster produce and serves everything from sandwiches to full á-la-carte dinners.

Getting There & Away

See Getting There & Around, p652 for transport information.

GIANT'S CAUSEWAY

When you first see it you'll understand why the ancients did not think the causeway was a natural feature. The vast expanse of regular, closely packed, hexagonal stone columns dipping gently beneath the waves looks for all the world like the handiwork of giants.

This spectacular rock formation – a national nature reserve and Northern Ireland's only Unesco World Heritage Site – is one of Ireland's most impressive and atmospheric landscape

features, but it is all too often swamped by visitors – 750,000 of them in 2008. If you can, try to visit midweek or out of season to experience it at its most evocative. Sunset in spring and autumn is the best time for photographs.

Orientation & Information

Visiting the Giant's Causeway itself is free of charge but the overcrowded, council-run car park charges £6 per car. It's an easy 1km walk from the car park down to the Causeway; minibuses with wheelchair access ply the route every 15 minutes (adult/child £2/1 return). Guided tours of the site (June to August only) cost £3.50/2.25 per adult/child.

Although plans for a new, world-class visitor centre for the Giant's Causeway were announced in 2005, at the time of research there was still no sign of it appearing; the latest estimate is for completion in spring 2011. Meanwhile, a 'temporary' **visitor centre** (☎ 2073 1855; www.giantscausewaycentre.com; admission free, audiovisual show £1; ⏰ 10am-6pm Jul & Aug, to 5pm Sep-Jun), which has been around since 2000, is housed in a wooden building beside the National Trust's gift shop and tearoom.

Sights & Activities

From the car park it's an easy 10- to 15-minute walk downhill on a tarmac road (wheelchair accessible) to the Giant's Causeway itself. However, a much more interesting approach is to follow the cliff-top path northeast for 2km to the **Chimney Tops** headland, which has an excellent view of the Causeway and the

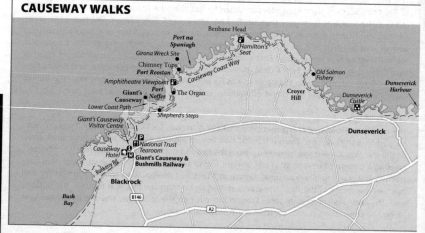

CAUSEWAY WALKS

Benbane Head
Port na Spaniagh
Hamilton's Seat
Girona Wreck Site
Chimney Tops
Port Reostan
Causeway Coast Way
Old Salmon Fishery
Amphitheatre Viewpoint
Dunseverick Harbour
Giant's Causeway
Port Noffer
The Organ
Croyer Hill
Dunseverick Castle
Lower Coast Path
Giant's Causeway Visitor Centre
Shepherd's Steps
Dunseverick
National Trust Tearoom
Causeway Hotel
Giant's Causeway & Bushmills Railway
Rinkerry Rd
Blackrock
Bush Bay
B146
A2

coastline to the west, including Inishowen and Malin Heads.

This pinnacled promontory was bombarded by ships of the Spanish Armada in 1588, who thought it was Dunluce Castle, and the wreck of the Spanish galleon *Girona* (see the boxed text, p654) lies just off the tip of the headland. Return towards the car park and about halfway back descend the Shepherd's Steps (signposted) to a lower-level footpath that leads down to the Causeway. Allow 1½ hours for the round trip.

Alternatively, you can visit the Causeway first, then follow the lower coastal path as far as the Amphitheatre viewpoint at Port Reostan, passing impressive rock formations such as the **Organ** (a stack of vertical basalt columns resembling organ pipes), and return by climbing the Shepherd's Steps.

You can also follow the cliff-top path east as far as Dunseverick or beyond (see the boxed text, p658).

Sleeping & Eating

Causeway Hotel (☎ 2073 1226; www.giants-causeway -hotel.com; 40 Causeway Rd; s/d £60/90; **P**) You can't beat it for location – the National Trust's Causeway Hotel is within a stone's-throw of the Causeway, a useful base if you want to explore the Causeway early or late in the day when the crowds are not around. Rooms 28 to 32 are the best, with outdoor terraces that enjoy sunset views over the Atlantic.

National Trust tearoom (☎ 2073 1582; snacks £2-5; 10am-5.30pm Jul & Aug, to 4.30pm Sep-Jun) Serves tea, coffee and light meals.

Getting There & Away

Bus 172 from Coleraine and Bushmills to Ballycastle passes the site year round. Also see Getting There & Around, p652.

GIANT'S CAUSEWAY TO BALLYCASTLE

Between the Giant's Causeway and Ballycastle lies the most scenic stretch of the Causeway Coast, with sea cliffs of contrasting black basalt and white chalk, rocky islands, picturesque little harbours and broad sweeps of sandy beach. It's best enjoyed on foot, following the 16.5km of waymarked **Causeway Coast Way** between the Carrick-a-Rede car park and the Giant's Causeway (see the boxed text, p658), although the main attractions can also be reached by car or bus.

About 8km east of the Giant's Causeway is the meagre ruin of 16th-century **Dunseverick Castle**, spectacularly sited on a grassy bluff. Another 1.5km on is the tiny seaside hamlet of **Portbradden**, with half a dozen harbourside houses and the tiny, blue-and-white **St Gobban's Church**, said to be the smallest in Ireland. Visible from Portbradden and accessible via the next junction off the A2 is the spectacular **White Park Bay**, with its wide, sweeping sandy beach.

A few kilometres further on is **Ballintoy** (Baile an Tuaighe), another pretty village tumbling down the hillside to a picture-postcard harbour. The restored limekiln on the quayside once made quicklime using stone from the chalk cliffs and coal from Ballymoney.

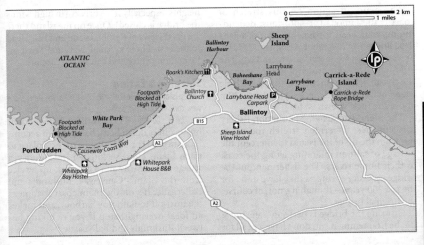

WALK: CAUSEWAY COAST WAY

The official **Causeway Coast Way** (www.walkni.com) stretches for 53km from Portstewart to Ballycastle, but the most scenic section – the 16.5km between Carrick-a-Rede and the Giant's Causeway – can be done in a day and offers one of the finest coastal walks in Ireland.

There are cafes and public toilets at Larrybane, Ballintoy Harbour and the Giant's Causeway, and bus stops at Larrybane, Ballintoy village, Whitepark Bay Youth Hostel, Dunseverick Castle and the Giant's Causeway. Note that parts of the walk follow a narrow, muddy path along the top of unfenced cliffs, and can be dangerous in wet and windy weather. Also, high tides can temporarily block the way at either end of White Park Bay; check tide times at any tourist office.

Begin at Larrybane, the car park for Carrick-a-Rede. The path starts off along a cliff top with views of Sheep Island, then cuts inland straight towards Ballintoy church. At the church turn right and follow the road down to the harbour. Continue along the shoreline past a series of conical sea stacks and arches, and scramble around the foot of a limestone crag to reach the 2km-long sandy sweep of White Park Bay.

The going here is easiest at low tide, when you can walk on the firm sand. At the far end of the bay (the building with the yellow gable above the dunes is Whitepark Bay Hostel), scramble over rocks and boulders at the bottom of a high limestone cliff for 250m (slippery in places) to Portbradden. If you've timed it wrong and the way is blocked by high tide, you can detour up to the hostel and reach Portbradden by walking along the road.

Beyond Portbradden white limestone gives way to black basalt, and the path threads through a natural tunnel in the rocks before weaving around several rocky coves with the high cliffs of Benbane Head visible in the distance. At tiny Dunseverick Harbour you follow a minor road for 200m before descending steps on the right at a waymark. The path then wanders along the grassy foreshore, rounds a headland and crosses a footbridge above a waterfall before reaching the car park at Dunseverick Castle.

From here the cliff-top path, narrow in places, climbs steadily, passing an old salmon fishery (the little rusty-roofed cottage on the shore far below). Near Benbane Head, the highest and most northerly point on the walk, a wooden bench marks the viewpoint known as Hamilton's Seat (William Hamilton was an 18th-century clergyman and amateur geologist from Derry, who wrote one of the earliest descriptions of the Causeway Coast's geology). Soak up the spectacular panorama of 100m-high sea cliffs, stacks and pinnacles stretching away to the west, before you set off on the final stretch. If you want to visit the causeway itself, descend the Shepherd's Steps (signposted), about 1km before the visitor centre and the end of the walk. Total: 16.5km. Allow five to six hours.

The main attraction on this stretch of coast is the famous (or notorious, depending on your head for heights) **Carrick-a-Rede Rope Bridge** (☎ 2076 9839; Ballintoy; adult/child £4/2; ⏱ 10am-7pm Jun-Aug, to 6pm Mar-May, Sep & Oct). The 20m-long, 1m-wide bridge of wire rope spans the chasm between the sea cliffs and the little island of Carrick-a-Rede, swaying gently 30m above the rock-strewn water.

The island has sustained a salmon fishery for centuries; fishermen stretch their nets out from the tip of the island to intercept the passage of salmon migrating along the coast to their home rivers. The fishermen put the bridge up every spring as they have done for the last 200 years – though it's not, of course, the original bridge.

Crossing the bridge is perfectly safe, but it can be frightening if you don't have a head for heights, especially if it's breezy (in high winds the bridge is closed). Once on the island there are good views of Rathlin Island and Fair Head to the east. There's a small National Trust information centre and cafe at the car park.

Sleeping & Eating

Sheep Island View Hostel (☎ 2076 9391; www.sheepisland view.com; 42A Main St, Ballintoy; campsites £6, dm from £14, d £30; P 🖳 🛜) This excellent independent hostel offers dorm beds, basic shared accommodation in the camping barn, or a place to pitch a tent. There's a kitchen and laundry, a village store nearby and a free pick-up service from the Giant's Causeway, Bushmills and Ballycastle. It's on the main coast road near the turn-off to Ballintoy harbour, and makes an ideal overnight stop if you're hiking between Bushmills and Ballycastle.

Whitepark Bay Hostel (☎ 2073 1745; www.hini.org
.uk; 157 White Park Rd, Ballintoy; dm/tw £17/40; ☺ Apr-Oct;
Ⓟ) This modern, purpose-built hostel, near
the west end of White Park Bay, has mostly
four-bed dorms, plus twin rooms with TV, all
with private bathroom. There is a common
room positioned to soak up the view, and
the beach is just a few minutes' walk through
the dunes.

our pick **Whitepark House B&B** (☎ 2073 1482; www
.whiteparkhouse.com; 150 Whitepark Rd, Ballintoy; s/d £75/100;
Ⓟ 🖳 🛜) A beautifully restored 18th-century
house overlooking White Park Bay, this B&B
has traditional features such as antique furniture and a peat fire complemented by Asian
artefacts gathered during the welcoming owners' oriental travels. There are three rooms –
ask for one with a sea view.

Roark's Kitchen (☎ 2076 3632; Ballintoy Harbour; mains
£3-6; ☺ 11am-7pm Jun-Aug, Sat & Sun only May & Sep) This
cute little chalk-built tearoom on the quayside at Ballintoy serves teas, coffees, ice cream,
home-baked apple tart and lunch dishes such
as Irish stew or chicken and ham pie.

Getting There & Away

Bus 172 between Ballycastle, Bushmills and
Coleraine (eight daily Monday to Friday, two
on Saturday, three Sunday) is the main, year-
round service along this coast, stopping at
the Giant's Causeway, Ballintoy and Carrick-
a-Rede. Also see Getting There & Around,
p652.

BALLYCASTLE

pop 4000

The harbour town and holiday resort of
Ballycastle (Baile an Chaisil) marks the eastern end of the Causeway Coast. It's a pretty
town with a good bucket-and-spade beach,
but apart from that, there's not a lot to see. It's
also the port for ferries to Rathlin Island.

The **tourist information office** (☎ 2076 2024; tourism
@moyle-council.org; 7 Mary St; ☺ 9.30am-7pm Mon-Fri,
10am-6pm Sat & 2-6pm Sun Jul & Aug, 9.30am-5pm Mon-Fri
Sep-Jun) is in the district council building at the
east end of town. There are a couple of banks
with ATMs on Ann St, near the Diamond.

Sights & Activities

The town has a family-friendly **promenade**,
with a giant sandpit for kids overlooking the
marina. A footbridge leads east across the
mouth of the River Glenshesk to a good sandy
beach.

The tiny **Ballycastle Museum** (☎ 2076 2942; 61A
Castle St; admission free; ☺ noon-6pm Jul & Aug), in the
town's 18th-century courthouse, has a collection of Irish arts and crafts works.

In the harbour car park is the **Marconi
Memorial**, a plaque at the foot of a rock pinnacle. Guglielmo Marconi's assistants con-
tacted Rathlin Island by radio from Ballycastle
in 1898 to prove to Lloyds of London that
wireless communication was a viable proposi-
tion. The idea was to send notice to London
or Liverpool of ships arriving safely after a
transatlantic crossing – most vessels on this
route would have to pass through the channel
north of Rathlin.

Just east of town are the ruins of **Bonamargy
Friary**, founded in 1485. It's an attractive site to
explore, but sadly the vault – which contains
the tombs of MacDonnell chieftains, including
Sorley Boy MacDonnell of Dunluce Castle – is
not open to the public.

Aquasports (☎ 7082 3563, 07962 309670; www.aqua
sports.biz) offers a range of high-speed boat trips
out of Ballycastle harbour, including wildlife
tours, cruises along the coast to the Giant's
Causeway and tours around Rathlin Island
from £25 per person.

You can go sea-angling with **Ballycastle
Charters** (☎ 2076 2074); three-hour trips depart
at 7pm Monday, Wednesday and Friday in
summer, and cost £15/10 per adult/child including tackle, bait and lessons.

Festivals

Ballycastle's **Ould Lammas Fair**, held on the last
Monday and Tuesday of August, dates back
to 1606. Thousands of people descend on the
town for the market stalls and fairground
rides, and to sample 'yellowman' and dulse.
Yellowman is a hard chewy toffee that's available from a few months before the fair. Dulse
is dried edible seaweed. The fruit shop on the
Diamond often stocks both delicacies.

Sleeping

BUDGET

Watertop Open Farm (☎ 2076 2576; www.watertopfarm
.co.uk; 188 Cushendall Rd; tent sites per person £4, caravan
sites from £14; ☺ Apr-Oct) About 10km east of
Ballycastle on the road to Cushendun, child-
friendly Watertop is based in a working farm
and activity centre, offering pony trekking,
sheepshearing and farm tours.

Glenmore Caravan & Camping Park (☎ 2076 3584;
www.glenmore.biz; 94 White Park Rd; camp/caravan sites from

£10/12; Apr–Oct) Glenmore is a small and peaceful camping ground with its own trout-stocked fishing lough, about 4.5km west of Ballycastle on the B15 road to White Park Bay.

Ballycastle Backpackers (2076 3612; www.ballycastlebackpackers.net; 4 North St; dm/tw £15/40; P) This is a small and homely hostel set in a terrace house overlooking the harbour, with one six-bed dorm, a family room and a couple of twin and double rooms. There's also a cosy self-catering cottage in the backyard, with two twin rooms with private bathroom (£25 per person per night, also available for rental by the week).

MIDRANGE

Glenluce Guesthouse (2076 2914; www.glenluce.com; 42 Quay Rd; s/d £30/60; P) Recently taken over by an enthusiastic young couple, Glenluce is our favourite among several B&Bs on Quay Rd. It has a luxurious lounge, its own tea shop, and a warm and welcoming family atmosphere. Rooms are spacious and comfortable, if a bit creaky in the floorboard department, and the house is only a few minutes' walk from the beach.

Crockatinney Guest House (2076 8801; www.crockatinneyguesthouse.co.uk; 80 Whitepark Rd; s/d £50/65; P) This large, purpose-built guesthouse enjoys a superb location on the coast road 3km west of Ballycastle, with a panoramic view of Rathlin Island, Fair Head and the Scottish coast. All six rooms have en-suite bathrooms – the upstairs rooms have the best views, while the ground floor room is equipped for guests with limited mobility.

Eating

Pantry (2076 9993; 41A Castle St; mains £2-5; 9am-5pm Mon-Sat) Housed in a former printer's shop with a lovely original black-and-white mosaic floor, this brisk and cheerful cafe serves a wide range of sandwiches, from pitta to panini and bagels to baguettes, as well as cappuccino and homemade cakes. It's uphill from the Diamond.

our pick Cellar Restaurant (2076 3037; 11 The Diamond; mains £9-16; noon-10pm Mon-Sat, from 5pm Sun Jun-Aug, 5-10pm Sep-May) This cosy little basement restaurant with intimate wooden booths and a big fireplace is the place to sample Ulster produce – locally caught crab claws grilled with garlic butter, and Carrick-a-Rede salmon are both on the menu, along with Irish beef and lamb, and lobster from Rathlin Island. There are also good vegetarian dishes such as baked peppers stuffed with mushroom and shallot.

Quay 26 (2076 1133; Bayview Rd; mains £10-16; noon-3pm & 5-9pm) Seafood is the main item on the menu at this minimalist, modern restaurant with a view across the marina to the cliffs of Fair Head – mussels in white wine and garlic, grilled sea bream, and smoked haddock with bacon, chive and cheese mash. There's also Irish venison, lamb shank, and roast veggie linguini for those who don't fancy the fish.

Getting There & Away

The bus station is on Station Rd, just east of the Diamond. Ulsterbus Express 217 links Ballycastle with Ballymena, where you change to Goldline Express 218 or 219 for Belfast (£9, two hours, three daily Monday to Friday, two Saturday).

Bus 172 goes along the coast to Coleraine (£4, one hour, eight daily Monday to Friday, two on Saturday, three Sunday) via Ballintoy, the Giant's Causeway and Bushmills. Also see Getting There & Around, p652.

The ticket office for the Rathlin Island Ferry is beside the harbour.

RATHLIN ISLAND
pop 110

In spring and summer, rugged Rathlin Island (Reachlainn), 6km offshore from Ballycastle, is home to hundreds of seals and thousands of nesting seabirds. An L-shaped island just 6.5km long and 4km wide, Rathlin is famous for the coastal scenery and bird life at Kebble National Nature Reserve at its western end. **RSPB West Light Viewpoint** (2076 0062; admission free; 11am-3pm Apr–mid-Sep) provides stunning views of the neighbouring sea stacks, thick with guillemots, kittiwakes, razorbills and puffins from mid-April to August. During the summer a minibus service runs there from the harbour; public toilets and binocular hire are available.

If you don't have time to visit Kebble, the best short walk on the island is through the National Trust's Ballyconagan Nature Reserve to the **Old Coastguard Lookout** on the north coast, with great views along the sea cliffs and across to the Scottish islands of Islay and Jura.

The **Boathouse Visitor Centre** (2076 2024; admission free; 10.30am-4pm May-Aug), south of the harbour, details the history, culture and ecology of the island, and can give advice on walks and wildlife. **Paul Quinn** (7032 7960, 07745 566924; www.rathlinwalkingtours.com) offers guided walking tours of the island.

WALK: FAIR HEAD

From the National Trust car park at Coolanlough, a waymarked path leads north past a small lake dotted with tiny islands, one of which is a *crannóg* (Neolithic island settlement). After 1.5km you arrive at the top of the impressive 180m-high basalt cliffs that mark Fair Head. The cliffs, one of Ireland's most important rock-climbing areas, are split here by a spectacular gully bridged by a fallen rock, known as the Grey Man's Path. The panorama of sea and islands extends from Rathlin Island in the west (to your left), with the Scottish island of Islay to its right, followed by the three pointed hills of Jura, to the dark mass of the Mull of Kintyre and the tiny island of Sanda. To the east is the squat cone of Ailsa Craig with the coast of Ayrshire far beyond.

Turn right and follow the faint trail south along the cliff tops for 1.5km until you reach the upper car park on the Murlough Bay road. From here, another faint path, marked by yellow paint marks, strikes west for 1km back to Coolanlough. (Total 4km. Allow one to two hours.)

The island's most illustrious visitor was Scottish hero Robert the Bruce, who spent some time here in 1306 while hiding out after being defeated by the English king. Watching a spider's resoluteness in repeatedly trying to spin a web gave him the courage to have another go at the English, whom he subsequently defeated at Bannockburn. The cave where he is said to have stayed is beneath the **East Lighthouse**, at the northeastern tip of the island.

Sleeping & Eating

The island has a pub and restaurant, two shops and a handful of accommodation options; it is essential to book your accommodation in advance. You can camp for free on the eastern side of Church Bay in a field not far from the harbour.

Kinramer Camping Barn (☎ 2076 3948; alison .mcfaul@rspb.org.uk; Kinramer; dm £9) This is a basic bunkhouse located on an organic farm, 5km (a one-hour walk) west from the harbour, where you bring your own food and bedding; book in advance. You might be able to get a lift there on one of the island minibuses.

Soerneog View Hostel (☎ 2076 3954; www.n-ireland holidays.co.uk/rathlin; Ouig; s/d £12.50/20; ◷ Apr-Sep) A private house, a 10-minute walk south of the harbour, Soerneog offers basic hostel-style accommodation in one double and two twin rooms.

Coolnagrock B&B (☎ 2076 3983; Coolnagrock; s/d £30/50; ◷ closed Dec) This well-appointed guesthouse is in the eastern part of the island, with great views across the sea to Kintyre. It's a 15-minute walk from the ferry, but you can arrange for the owner to pick you up.

Manor House (☎ 2076 3964; www.rathlinmanorhouse .co.uk; Church Quarter; s/d £40/70) Restored and run by the National Trust, the 18th-century Manor House, on the north side of the harbour, is the island's biggest (12 rooms) and most pleasant place to stay. Evening meals are available by arrangement.

The restaurant at the Manor House is open to non-residents from May to September (11am to 4pm and 6.30pm to 9pm, booking necessary), and there's a cafe/chip shop at **McCuaig's Bar** (☎ 2076 3974), just east of the harbour. There's a tiny grocery shop a few paces to the west of the ferry berth (turn left as you come off the pier).

Getting There & Around

A **ferry** (☎ 2076 9299; www.rathlinballycastleferry.com) operates daily (adult/child/bicycle return £11/5/3) from Ballycastle; advance booking is recommended in spring and summer. From April to September there are eight or nine crossings a day, half of which are fast catamaran services (20 minutes), the rest via a slower car ferry (45 minutes); in winter the service is reduced.

Only residents can take their car to Rathlin (except for disabled drivers), but nowhere on the island is more than 6km (about 1½ hours' walk) from the ferry pier. You can hire a bicycle (£8 per day) from Soerneog View Hostel, or take a minibus tour with **McGinn's** (☎ 2076 3451), who also shuttle visitors between the ferry and Kebble Nature Reserve from April to August.

GLENS OF ANTRIM

The northeastern corner of Antrim is a high plateau of black basalt lava overlying beds of white chalk. Along the coast, between Cushendun and Glenarm, the plateau has been dissected by a series of scenic, glacier-gouged valleys known as the Glens of Antrim.

Two waymarked footpaths traverse the region: the Ulster Way (p685) sticks close to the sea, passing through all the coastal villages; while the 32km Moyle Way runs inland across the high plateau from Glenariff Forest Park to Ballycastle.

Torr Head Scenic Road

A few kilometres east of Ballycastle, a minor road signposted Scenic Route branches north off the A2. This alternative route to Cushendun is not for the faint-hearted driver (nor for caravans), as it clings, precarious and narrow, to steep slopes high above the sea. Side roads lead off to the main points of interest – Fair Head, Murlough Bay and Torr Head. On a clear day, there are superb views across the sea to Scotland, from the Mull of Kintyre to the peaks of Arran.

The first turn-off ends at the National Trust car park at Coolanlough, the starting point for a hike to Fair Head (see the boxed text, p661). The second turn-off leads steeply down to **Murlough Bay**. From the parking area at the end of this road, you can walk north along the shoreline to some ruined miners' cottages (10 minutes); coal and chalk were once mined in the cliffs above, and burned in a limekiln (south of the car park) to make quicklime.

The third turn-off leads you past some ruined coastguard houses to the rocky headland of **Torr Head**, crowned with a 19th-century coastguard station (abandoned in the 1920s). This is Ireland's closest point to Scotland – the Mull of Kintyre is a mere 19km away across the North Channel. In late spring and summer, a salmon fishery like the one at Carrick-a-Rede operates here, with a net strung out from the headland. The ancient ice house beside the approach road was once used to store the catch.

Cushendun
pop 350

The pretty seaside village of Cushendun is famous for its distinctive, Cornish-style cottages, now owned by the National Trust. Built between 1912 and 1925 at the behest of the local landowner, Lord Cushendun, they were designed by Clough Williams-Ellis, the architect of Portmeirion in north Wales. There's a nice sandy beach, various short coastal walks (outlined on an information board beside the car park), and some impressive **caves** cut into the overhanging conglomerate sea cliffs south of the village (follow the trail around the far end of the holiday apartments south of the river mouth).

Another natural curiosity lies 6km north of the village on the A2 road to Ballycastle – **Loughareema**, also known as the Vanishing Lake. Three streams flow in but none flow out. The lough fills up to a respectable size (400m long and 6m deep) after heavy rain, but then the water gradually drains away through fissures in the underlying limestone, leaving a dry lake bed.

SLEEPING

Cushendun Caravan Park (☎ 2176 1254; 14 Glendun Rd; camp/caravan sites from £9/17; ☼ Easter-Sep) The local council-run camping ground enjoys a pleasant woodland setting just north of the village and a mere five-minute walk from the beach.

Villa Farmhouse (☎ 2176 1252; maggie.scally@hotmail .co.uk; 185 Torr Rd; s/d from £35/60; P ☐) This lovely old whitewashed farmhouse is set on a hillside 1km north of the village, with great views over the sea and down to Cushendun Bay. The owner is an expert chef and breakfast will be a highlight of your stay – best scrambled eggs in Northern Ireland!

Cloneymore House (☎ 2176 1443; ann.cloneymore@ btinternet.com; 103 Knocknacarry Rd; s/d £40/50; P ☎) A traditional family B&B on the B92 road 500m southwest of Cushendun, Cloneymore has three spacious and spotless rooms named after Irish and Scottish islands – Aran is the biggest. There are wheelchair ramps and a stairlift, and all rooms are equipped for visitors with limited mobility.

Mullarts Apartments (☎ 2176 1221; www.mullarts apartments.co.uk; 114 Tromra Rd; d per weekend/week £140/375; P) An unusual alternative, Mullarts offers three luxury, self-catering apartments housed in a converted 19th-century church, 2.5km south of the village. There are two double apartments, and one that can sleep up to six people.

EATING & DRINKING

Theresa's Tearoom (☎ 2176 1506; 1 Main St; mains £3-9; ☼ 11am-7pm Easter-Sep, to 6pm Sat & Sun Oct-Easter) The cosy village tearoom beside the bridge offers tea and cakes, sandwiches and salads, and hot lunch dishes such as fish and chips, grilled chicken and vegetable tortilla wraps.

Mary McBride's Pub (☎ 2176 1511; 2 Main St; mains £5-9; ☼ food noon-9pm Apr-Sep, to 8pm Oct-Mar) The original bar here (on the left as you go in) is the smallest in Ireland (2.7m by 1.5m) but there's plenty of elbow-bending room in the rest of the pub. It has lost some of its charm in recent years, and the food – standard pub grub –

...s not as good as it used to be, but it's the only place in the village for an evening meal.

GETTING THERE & AWAY
Bus 150 runs from Ballymena to Cushendun (one hour, six daily Monday to Friday, four Saturday) via Glenariff Forest Park and Cushendall; Ballymena can be reached by train from Belfast and Derry. Also see the *Antrim Coaster* service, p652.

Cushendall
pop 1250
Cushendall is a holiday centre (and traffic bottleneck) at the foot of Glenballyeamon, overlooked by the prominent flat-topped hill of Lurigethan. The beach is small and shingly, though; there are better ones at Waterfoot and Cushendun.

The **tourist office** (☎ 2177 1180; 24 Mill St; ☺ 10am-1pm & 2-5.30pm Mon-Fri, 10am-1pm Sat Jul-Sep, 10am-1pm Tue-Sat Oct-Jun) is run by the Glens of Antrim Historical Society, which also offers public internet access.

SIGHTS
The unusual red sandstone **Curfew Tower** at the central crossroads was built in 1817, based on a building the landowner had seen in China. It was originally a prison 'for the confinement of idlers and rioters'.

From the car park beside the beach, a coastal path leads 1km north to the picturesque ruins of **Layde Old Church**, with views across to Ailsa Craig (a prominent conical island also known as 'Paddy's Milestone') and the Scottish coast. Founded by the Franciscans, it was used as a parish church from the early 14th century until 1790. The graveyard contains several grand MacDonnell memorials. Near the gate stands an ancient, weathered ring-cross (with the arms missing), much older than the 19th-century inscription on its shaft.

In Glenaan, 4km northwest of Cushendall, is **Ossian's Grave**, a Neolithic court tomb romantically, but inaccurately, named after the legendary 3rd-century warrior-poet. The site is signposted off the A2; you can park at the farm and walk up.

SLEEPING & EATING
Cushendall Caravan Park (☎ 2177 1699; 62 Coast Rd; camp/caravan sites £9/17; ☺ Easter-Sep) This camping ground overlooks the sea, just over 1km south of the town centre.

Village B&B (☎ 2177 2366; alexmckillop@hotmail.com; 18 Mill St; s/d £35/50; ☺ Apr-Sep; P) Bang in the middle of town, the Village offers three spotless rooms with en-suite bathrooms and huge hearty breakfasts, and is just across the road from McCollams, the best pub in Cushendall for traditional music.

Cullentra House (☎ 2177 1762; www.cullentrahouseireland.com; 16 Cloughs Rd; s/d £30/66; P ☺) This modern bungalow sits high above the village at the end of Cloughs Rd, offering good views of the craggy Antrim coast. The three rooms are spacious and comfy, and the breakfasts (accompanied by home-baked wheaten bread) are as big as the owners' hospitality.

Harry's Restaurant (☎ 2177 2022; 10 Mill St; bar meals £6-9, dinner mains £9-13; ☺ bar meals noon-9.30pm, dinner from 6.30pm) With its cosy lounge-bar atmosphere and friendly welcome, Harry's is a local institution, serving pub grub throughout the day – battered cod with mushy peas, or steak and onion ciabatta, for example – plus an á-la-carte dinner menu in the evenings.

Upstairs@Joe's (☎ 2177 2630; 23 Mill St; mains lunch £6-8, dinner £11-15; ☺ noon-9pm) This new restaurant above McCollams pub prides itself on promoting local produce, with dishes such as seafood chowder with wheaten bread, medallions of Irish beef with Béarnaise sauce, and lamb chops with parsnip puree and rosemary jus – all sourced within County Antrim. Actor Liam Neeson has eaten here during visits to his home town of Ballymena.

GETTING THERE & AWAY
Bus 162 travels from Larne to Cushendall (£7, one hour, three daily Monday to Friday), stopping at Glenarm and Carnlough; there are frequent trains and buses from Belfast to Larne. Bus 150 goes to Cushendun (left) and Glenariff Forest Park.

Glenariff
About 2km south of Cushendall is the village of **Waterfoot**, with a 2km-long sandy beach, the best on Antrim's east coast. From here the A43 Ballymena road runs inland along Glenariff, the loveliest of Antrim's glens. Views of the valley led the writer Thackeray to exclaim that it was a 'Switzerland in miniature', a claim that makes you wonder if he'd ever been to Switzerland!

At the head of the valley is **Glenariff Forest Park** (☎ 2175 8232; car/motorcycle/pedestrian £4/2/1.50; ☺ 10am-dusk), where the main attraction is

---

WALK: THE GLENARIFF CIRCUIT

This varied 7.5km hike, which ranges from the mossy depths of a waterfall-filled ravine to the edge of the high Antrim Plateau, is one of the best forest-park walks in Northern Ireland. Begin at the Laragh Lodge restaurant, and follow the boardwalk upstream (admission £1.50 Easter-Oct) along the Glenariff River to the foaming cascade of Ess-na-Larach, then continue steeply up the zigzags beyond. There's a junction at a wooden bench – the path to the left leads down to the forest park visitor centre (signposted), but go right on the trail heading upstream with the river down to your right.

At the next junction (signposted Hermit's Fall to the right), turn left and follow the path uphill to reach a road, where you turn right. The path now parallels the road for 600m until you reach a sign marked Scenic Trail pointing back the way you came. Go left across the road and, a few metres further on, cross a second road and follow the obvious path up through the forest. You eventually emerge from the trees to get your first open view along Glenariff. Beyond, the path slowly curves around to the right (south; there are more Scenic Trail waymarks, but you are following them in reverse). As you near the head of the next valley (that's the River Inver down below), the path forks near a wooden shelter, the left branch descending steeply; keep right here and continue right to the top of the glen.

The trail then curves left and crosses the three streams that feed the River Inver, then switchbacks up the far side and into thick pine forest, only to emerge into a clearing on a cliff top with a stunning view down Glenariff – the valley floor is slung like a green hammock between steep, black basalt crags. A short distance further on there's a very steep zigzag descent, followed by a level traverse to the left. When you reach a forest road, turn right. After 1km it descends steeply leftwards down to a gate; take the path on the left and cross a footbridge over the river. Turn right, then right again and you'll find yourself back at your starting point. (Total 7.5km. Allow three to four hours.)

Ess-na-Larach Waterfall, an 800m walk from the visitor centre. You can also walk to the waterfall from Laragh Lodge, 600m downstream. There are various good walks in the park; the longest is a 10km circular trail.

There's hostel accommodation for hikers at **Ballyeamon Camping Barn** (☎ 2175 8451; www .ballyeamonbarn.com; 127 Ballyeamon Rd; dm £10; ☐), 8km southwest of Cushendall on the B14 (1km north of its junction with the A43), close to the Moyle Way and about 1.5km walk from the main entrance to the forest park.

Laragh Lodge (☎ 2175 8221; 120 Glen Rd; mains £9-11, 4-course Sun lunch £15; ☺ 10.30am-11pm, food noon-9pm) is a restaurant and bar on a side road off the A43, 3km northeast of the main park entrance. A recently renovated Victorian tourist lodge with assorted bric-a-brac dangling from the rafters, the Laragh dates from 1890 and serves hearty pub-grub style meals – beef and Guinness pie, fish and chips, sausage and mash (with a couple of vegetarian options) – and offers a traditional roast lunch on Sunday.

You can reach Glenariff Forest Park from Cushendun (£4, 30 minutes, six daily Monday to Friday, four Saturday) and Ballymena (£4, 30 minutes) on Ulsterbus 150.

Carnlough
pop 1500

Carnlough is an attractive little town with a pretty harbour and a historic hotel. Many of the buildings, made of local limestone, were commissioned by the Marquess of Londonderry in 1854. The limestone quarries were in use until the early 1960s – the white stone bridge across the main street once carried a railway line that brought stone down to the harbour. The line is now a walkway that leads to the local beauty spot, Cranny Falls.

The **tourist information centre** (☎ 2888 5236; 14 Harbour Rd; ☺ 10am-10pm daily Easter-Sep, to 8pm Mon-Sat Oct-Easter) is in McKillop's general store, next to the Londonderry Arms Hotel.

SLEEPING & EATING

Londonderry Arms Hotel (☎ 2888 5255; www.glensofan trim.com; 20 Harbour Rd; s/d from £65/110; ℗ ⊛) Dating from 1848, this atmospheric coaching inn was briefly owned by Winston Churchill, who sold it in 1921 (he once stayed in room 114). It has a wonderfully crusty, old-fashioned atmosphere, with various bits of antique furniture, wing-back armchairs and lots of polished mahogany, spoiled a little by 1970s avocado bathroom suites. The hotel's Frances Anne restaurant (mains £15 to £20) serves local lamb and seafood, while the wood-panelled bar is a shrine to the famous Irish racehorse Arkle.

GETTING THERE & AWAY

Bus 162 runs from Larne to Glenarm and Carnlough (£4, 40 minutes, eight daily Monday to Friday, six Saturday); three buses a day on weekdays continue north to Cushendall. Bus 128 goes to Ballymena (£4, one hour, five daily Monday to Friday, one Saturday). Also see Getting There & Around, p652.

Glenarm
pop 600

Since 1750 Glenarm (Gleann Arma), the oldest village in the glens, has been the family seat of the MacDonnell family; the present 14th Earl of Antrim lives in **Glenarm Castle** (☎ 2884 1203; www.glenarmcastle.com), on a private estate hidden behind the impressive wall that runs along the main road north of the bridge. The castle itself is closed to the public, except for two days in July when a Highland Games competition is held, but you can visit the lovely **walled garden** (adult/child £4/2; ☼ 10am-5pm Mon-Sat & noon-6pm Sun May-Sep, closed Tue May & Sep).

The **tourist office** (☎ 2884 1705; 2 The Bridge; glenarm@ nacn.org; ☼ 9.30am-5pm Mon-Fri, 2-6pm Sun) is beside the bridge on the main road. It has internet access for £2 per 30 minutes.

Take a stroll into the old village of neat Georgian houses (off the main road, immediately south of the river). Where the street opens into the broad expanse of Altmore St, look right to see the **Barbican Gate** (1682), the entrance to Glenarm Castle grounds. On the left is **Steensons** (☎ 2884 1445; Toberwine St; ☼ 9.30am-5.15pm Mon-Sat year-round, plus 1-5.30pm Sun Easter-Sep), a designer jewellery workshop and visitor centre where you can watch craftspeople at work.

Turn left here and climb steeply up Vennel St, then left again immediately after the last house along the Layde Path to the **viewpoint**, which has a grand view of the village and the coast.

Riverside House B&B (☎ 2884 1474; faith.pa@btopen world.com; 13 Toberwine St; s/d £35/50; ☐ ☎) is a nicely restored Georgian house in the heart of the old village. The two double rooms have chunky pine furniture and views over the river to Glenarm Castle. The B&B doubles as a cafe, and there's another good tearoom in Glenarm Castle's walled garden.

See Carnlough section (left) for details of bus services.

LARNE
pop 17,600

As a major port for ferries from Scotland, Larne (Lutharna) is one of Northern Ireland's main points of arrival. However, with its concrete overpasses and the huge chimneys of Ballylumford power station opposite the harbour, poor old Larne is a little lacking in the charm department. After a visit to the excellent tourist information centre, there's no real reason to linger.

Larne Harbour train station is in the ferry terminal. It's a short bus ride or a 15-minute walk from here to the town centre – turn right on Fleet St and right again on Curran Rd, then left on Circular Rd. At the big roundabout, Larne Town train station is to your left, the **tourist information centre** (☎ 2826 0088; larnetourism@ btconnect.com; Narrow Gauge Rd; ☼ 9am-5pm Mon-Fri & 10am-4pm Sat Easter-Sep, 9am-5pm Mon-Fri Oct-Easter) is to the right, and the bus station is ahead (beneath the road bridge).

Getting There & Away
BOAT

For information on ferries from Larne to Scotland and England, see p717.

BUS

Bus 256 provides a direct service between the town centre and Belfast (£4, one hour, hourly Monday to Friday, six Saturday, plus two on Sunday July to September only).

Heading north to the Glens of Antrim, take bus 162 (see left) or the *Antrim Coaster* (see p652).

TRAIN

Larne has two train stations, Larne Town and Larne Harbour. Trains from Larne Town to Belfast Central (£6, one hour) depart at least hourly; those from the harbour are timed to connect with ferries. From Belfast Central you can continue to Botanic, City Hospital and Great Victoria St stations.

ISLANDMAGEE

Islandmagee (Oileán Mhic Aodha) is the finger of land that encloses Larne Lough to the east. There's a popular sandy beach at **Brown's Bay** at the northern end of the peninsula. Nearby is the picturesque little harbour of **Portmuck** and, just 300m offshore, the North's second-largest seabird nesting colony on **Muck Island**.

On the east coast lie the rugged basalt sea cliffs known as the **Gobbins**. The cliffs were developed as a tourist attraction in 1902, when a railway company engineer built a spectacular footpath along the coast from Whitehead, complete with steps, iron bridges and tunnels cut from the rock. By WWII the path had fallen into disrepair, and was closed for safety reasons. You can see photographs of the walkway in its heyday at the Ulster Museum (p579) in Belfast.

There's a good coastal walk from the car park at the north end of the promenade in **Whitehead**. It follows a walkway around the sea cliffs beneath Black Head lighthouse, past several deep caves, then climbs a steep flight of stairs to the lighthouse itself. From here you can descend a zigzag path to rejoin the shoreline trail back to the car park (3.5km in total).

From May to December the high-speed launch *North Irish Diver* offers two-hour **boat trips** (☎ 9338 2246; www.northirishlodge.com) from Whitehead harbour to the Gobbins and Muck Island (adult/child £20/15, minimum six people, arrange in advance).

There are also boat trips to the Gobbins from Bangor (p606). **Blue Aquarius** (☎ 07779 600607; www.bangorboat.com) offers trips from Bangor Harbour to the Gobbins on Fridays in late May and June only (adult/child £16/10).

CARRICKFERGUS
pop 28,000

Northern Ireland's most impressive medieval fortress commands the entrance to Belfast Lough from the rocky promontory of Carrickfergus (Carraig Fhearghais). The old town centre opposite the castle has some attractive 18th-century houses and you can still trace a good part of the 17th-century city walls.

The **tourist information centre** (☎ 9335 8049; www.carrickfergus.org; Heritage Plaza, Antrim St; ☺ 10am-6pm Mon-Sat & 1-6pm Sun Apr-Sep, 10am-5pm Mon-Sat & 1-5pm Sun Oct-Mar; ☎) has a bureau de change and books accommodation.

Sights

The central keep of Ireland's first and finest Norman fortress, **Carrickfergus Castle** (☎ 9335 1273; Marine Hwy; adult/child £3/1.50; ☺ 10am-6pm Easter-Sep, to 4pm Oct-Easter), was built by John de Courcy soon after his 1177 invasion of Ulster. The mas-

sive walls of the outer ward were completed in 1242, while the red-brick gun ports were added in the 16th century. The keep houses a museum and the site is dotted with life-size figures illustrating the castle's history.

The castle overlooks the harbour where **William of Orange** landed on 14 June 1690, on his way to the Battle of the Boyne; a blue plaque on the old harbour wall marks the site where he stepped ashore, and a bronze statue of the man himself stands on the shore nearby.

The glass-fronted Heritage Plaza on Antrim St houses **Carrickfergus Museum** (☎ 9335 8049; 11 Antrim St; admission free; ☺ 10am-6pm Mon-Sat & 1-6pm Sun Apr-Sep, 10am-5pm Mon-Sat & 1-5pm Sun Oct-Mar), which has a small collection of artefacts relating to the town's history, and a pleasant coffee shop.

The parents of the seventh US president left Carrickfergus in the second half of the 18th century. His ancestral home was demolished in 1860, but the **Andrew Jackson Centre** (Boneybefore; admission free; ☺ by appointment only – contact the tourist office in advance) is housed in a replica thatched cottage complete with fireside crane and earthen floor. It has displays on the life of Jackson, the Jackson family in Ulster and Ulster's connection with the USA. Next door is the **US Rangers Centre**, with a small exhibition on the first US rangers, who were trained during WWII in Carrickfergus before heading for Europe. The centre is on the coast, 2km north of the castle.

Sleeping & Eating

Keep Guesthouse (☎ 9336 7007; www.thekeepguesthousecarrickfergus.co.uk; 93 Irish Quarter S; s/d £35/50; ☎) Just across the main road from the marina, and close to the town centre, the Keep has four rooms with attractive, modern decor and original art on the walls; go for the spacious double/family room on the first floor if possible.

Dobbin's Inn Hotel (☎ 9335 1905; www.dobbinsinnhotel.co.uk; 6-8 High St; s/d £54/78, mains £7-13; ☺ food 9am-9pm; ☐) In the centre of the old town, Dobbin's is a friendly and informal place with 15 small and creaky-floored but comfortable rooms. The building has been around for over three centuries, and has a priest's hole and an original 16th-century fireplace to prove it. The hotel bar serves food all day.

Courtyard Coffee House (☎ 9335 1881; 38 Scottish Quarter; mains £4-6; ☺ 9am-4.45pm Mon-Sat) This cafe serves tasty homemade soups and light

---

DETOUR: GALGORM

About 6km west of Ballymena is the **Galgorm Resort & Spa** (☎ 2588 1001; www.galgorm.com; 136 Fenaghy Rd, Galgorm; d/f from £85/175; P 🖥 🛜), a 19th-century manor house in a lovely setting on the bank of the River Main. Refurbished by the owners of Belfast's boutique hotel Ten Square (p587), the Galgorm has been redeveloped and extended to create one of Ireland's top country-house hotels.

The rustic atmosphere of the original **Gillie's Bar** (mains £7-16; 🕓 food served 7am-10pm), set in the former stables, has been retained with bare stone walls, huge timber beams, a log fire and cosy sofas, but it has been extended into a spectacular, high-roofed barn with a huge, central free-standing chimney and a monumental staircase framed by crouching sphinxes – all in all, a pretty jaw-dropping setting for some of the fanciest pub grub in Ireland.

---

lunches as well as coffee and cakes, and has a second branch inside Carrickfergus Castle.

our pick Wind Rose (☎ 9335 1164; Rodgers Quay; mains £8-16; 🕓 food noon-9pm) This stylish, modern bar-bistro, with a more formal restaurant upstairs (mains £13 to £25, dinner only), serves a range of dishes from lasagne and lamb shank to steaks and stir-fries. The outdoor terrace overlooking the forest of yacht masts in the marina is a real sun-trap on a summer afternoon.

Getting There & Away
There's an hourly train service between Carrickfergus and Belfast (£4, 30 minutes).

INLAND COUNTY ANTRIM
To the west of the high moorland plateau above the Glens of Antrim, the hills slope down to the agricultural lowlands of Lough Neagh and the broad valley of the River Bann. This region is rarely visited by tourists, who either take the coast road or speed through on the way from Belfast to Derry, but there are a few places worth seeking out if you have time to spare.

Antrim Town
pop 19,800
The town of Antrim (Aontroim) straddles the River Sixmilewater, close to an attractive bay on the shores of Lough Neagh. During the 1798 Rising, the United Irishmen fought a pitched battle along the length of the town's High St.

The **tourist information centre** (☎ 9442 8331; info@antrim.gov.uk; 16 High St; 🕓 9am-5.30pm Mon-Fri & 10am-3pm Sat Jul & Aug, 9am-5pm Mon-Fri & 10am-1pm Sat May, Jun & Sep, 9am-5pm Mon-Fri Oct-Apr) provides a free, self-guided heritage trail leaflet, and has internet access for £1.50 per 30 minutes.

The town centre is dominated by a bleakly modern shopping mall, but a few older buildings survive, including the fine **courthouse**, which dates back to 1762. Beyond the courthouse is the **Barbican Gate** (1818) and a portion of the old castle walls.

Pass through the gate and the underpass beyond to reach **Antrim Castle Gardens** (admission free; 🕓 9.30am-dusk Mon-Fri, 10am-5pm Sat, 2-5pm Sun). The castle burned down many years ago, but the grounds remain as one of the few surviving examples of a 17th-century ornamental garden.

Lough Rd leads west from the town centre to **Antrim Lough Shore Park**, where the vast size of Lough Neagh (see the boxed text, p630) is apparent. There are picnic tables and lakeside walking trails.

The vintage launch **Maid of Antrim** (☎ 2582 2159; www.loughneaghcruises.co.uk), built on Scotland's River Clyde in 1963, offers cruises on the lough on Sunday afternoons from Easter to October.

Goldline Express 219 from Belfast to Ballymena stops in Antrim (£4, 40 minutes, hourly Monday to Friday, seven on Saturday). There are also frequent trains from Belfast to Antrim (£5, 25 minutes, 10 daily Monday to Saturday, five on Sunday) continuing to Derry.

Ballymena
pop 29,200
Ballymena (An Baile Meánach) is the home turf of Ian Paisley, the founder of the Free Presbyterian Church and the stridently anti-Nationalist and anti-Catholic Democratic Unionist Party (DUP), who served as First Minister of Northern Ireland until 2008. The town council was the first to be controlled by the DUP in 1977 and voted unanimously to remove all mention of Darwin's theory of

evolution from religious education in Ballymena's schools. The town is also the birthplace of the actor Liam Neeson, of *Schindler's List* and *Star Wars* fame.

The **Ecos Environmental Centre** (☎ 2566 4400; www.ecoscentre.com; Broughshane Rd; admission free; ☼ 9am-4pm Mon-Fri, noon-4pm Sat & Sun Easter week & Jun-Aug, 9am-4pm Mon-Fri Sep & Oct), on the eastern edge of town, is a visitor centre dedicated to alternative energy sources and sustainable technology – the centre's waste water is filtered through reed beds, and used to irrigate nearby willow coppices, which provide fuel for heating and electricity, supplemented by solar panels. There are lots of hands-on exhibits to keep the kids amused, plus a picnic-and-play area, a pond with ducks to feed, and radio-controlled boats to play with.

Goldline Express 219 goes to Ballymena from Belfast (£6, one hour, hourly Monday to Friday, seven Saturday). Bus 128 goes to Carnlough on the coast (£4, one hour, five daily Monday to Friday, one Saturday).

Trains from Belfast run more frequently (£7, 10 daily Monday to Saturday, five on Sunday); Ballymena is on the Derry–Belfast train line.

Slemish

The skyline to the east of Ballymena is dominated by the distinctive craggy peak of Slemish (438m). The hill is one of many sites in the North associated with Ireland's patron saint – the young St Patrick is said to have tended goats on its slopes. On St Patrick's Day, thousands of people make a pilgrimage to its summit; the rest of the year it's a pleasant climb, though steep and slippery in wet weather, rewarded with a fine view (allow one hour return from the parking area).

Arthur Cottage

The ancestors of Chester Alan Arthur (1830–86), 21st president of the USA, lived in an 18th-century thatched **cottage** (☎ 2563 5900; Dreen, Cullybackey; adult/child £2/1; ☼ 10.30am-4pm Thu-Sat Easter-Sep) in Cullybackey, about 6km northwest of Ballymena.

Cullybackey is a stop on the Belfast–Derry railway line.

Ireland
Outdoors

GARETH MCCORMACK

It may not always have full cooperation from the weather, but Ireland is a country best appreciated out of doors. Whether you're a hiker, a cyclist, a surfer or an angler, it's merely a question of donning the right gear and going for it: there is something extraordinarily invigorating – never mind refreshing – about hiking in a summer storm or cycling into the teeth of a blowing gale. Then, the clouds break and the sun appears, and you can while away a long summer's evening with a fishing pole by the banks of a river, or catch a tidy late wave when the rest of Europe has already turned in.

The Beara Way, County Cork (p282)

For more information on activities, see also p698.

WALKING & CYCLING

There is simply no better way of experiencing this wildly beautiful country than on foot or on two wheels – and the rewards can be spectacular. From rolling hills of green to lush riparian woods, from rugged limestone escarpments to broad sandy beaches, and from dramatic sea cliffs to blankets of bog stretching as far as the eye can see, Ireland's landscapes will never disappoint.

Cyclists, alas, will have to share the road with the motorised bully, but they can find solace in the scenic routes that wend their way through sparsely populated countryside or along rugged coasts.

What goes up the Gap of Dunloe (p297) must come down

Where the mountains meet the sea: Mt Mweelrea, Leenane, County Galway (p421)

GARETH MCCORMACK

Day Walks

In just about any part of Ireland you can take a leisurely day hike. The wooded trails around Glendalough (p165) in County Wicklow lure many a traveller from nearby Dublin for a few hours. Along the River Barrow in Counties Kilkenny and Carlow, perfectly pleasant walks can be had along the towpath from Borris (p225) to Graiguenamanagh (p238). Also in County Kilkenny, the prettiest section of the South Leinster Way (p240) is a 13km hike between the charming villages of Graiguenamanagh and Inistioge. In either direction, a pleasant meal awaits at the end of the trail. In County Galway, Clifden's Sky Road (p418) yields views of the Connemara coast; it's suitable for walking or cycling. Anyone roaming the woods around Lough Key (p517), in County Roscommon, should take advantage of the park's unique canopy walk.

Day Cycles

There are some stunning cycleways, including the 70km-long, signposted West Clare Cycleway that stretches from Killimer on the Shannon Estuary (where you can get the Shannon Ferry to Tarbert in County Kerry; p369) to Lahinch (p373). The coastal route goes through Kilrush and Cappa, and offers stunning views of the estuary and beautiful Scattery Island (p370). Equally stunning is the Beara Way Cycle Route (p281), a 138km path that forms a loop around the

Mt Brandon, County Kerry (p325) GARETH MCCORMACK

peninsula, shadowing the famous walking route (see Waymarked Ways, p673). For more routes, look for cycling information on www.discoverireland.ie.

The Coast

Ireland's coastlines are naturally conducive to long and reflective walks with or without shoes. If that sounds like your particular nirvana, the coast of County Galway's Connemara and the pristine beaches of Counties Mayo and Sligo beckon. Some coastal

Taking in the views along the Wicklow Way, County Wicklow (p166)

EOIN CLARKE

walks, however, present unexpected challenges. County Antrim, in Northern Ireland, is rife with rocky trails above the surf. Particularly spectacular is the final 16.5km, starting from Carrick-a-Rede, on the Causeway Coast Way (p657). The Wexford Coastal Walk (p192) isn't quite so treacherous, but it is long, following 221km of trails overlooking the bones of old shipwrecks.

Mountains

Ireland's mountain ranges aren't as magnificent as the Alps, but they do offer gratifying hillwalking opportunities, many of which can be done in a day. County Donegal's Blue Stack Mountains (p467) encompass varied terrain and dramatic peaks. The Brandon Way (p240), in County Kilkenny, wends up through woodlands and moorlands from the River Barrow to picturesque Brandon Hill (516m). Mt Leinster (p204) in County Wexford affords views of five counties from its 796m-high summit. You'll find Northern Ireland's best hill-walking in the Mourne Mountains (p620) of County Down. In this range, Northern Ireland's highest peak, Slieve Donard (853m; p619), is good for a day walk from the town of Newcastle.

Killarney National Park in County Kerry offers superb and challenging routes for both walkers and cyclists. The top walk, of course, is up Mt Carrantuohil (1039m; p298), the highest peak in all Ireland. The park also has an adventurous 55km bike route. On the

Kayaking, a great way to see the coast (p674)

RICHARD WAREHAM FOTOGRAFIE / ALAMY

TOP ADVENTURE CENTRES

Adventure centres can be found around Ireland, especially near the coast. These centres make it easy for a traveller to indulge in such activities as canoeing, surfing, kayaking, orienteering, hiking, climbing and other sports. Some also provide accommodation. Here's a select list:

- Killary Adventure Centre, County Galway (p421)
- Delphi Mountain Resort, County Galway (p433)
- Dunmore East Adventure Centre, County Waterford (p210)
- Donegal Adventure Centre, County Donegal (p470)
- University of Limerick Activity Centre, County Clare (p367)

Bundoran, County Donegal (p469) is one of Ireland's top surfing spots

GARETH MCCORMACK

nearby Dingle Peninsula, Mt Brandon (951m; p325) offers spectacularly rugged trails that yield jaw-dropping views.

Waymarked Ways

The country's network of 31 long-distance 'waymarked ways' can keep a traveller walking for a week or longer. Though many of these run for several hundred kilometres, you can jump in or jump out as you see fit. The Beara Way (p282), in West Cork, is an unstrenuous loop of 196km that follows historic routes and tracks. The Burren Way (p378), at 35km, is far shorter and takes in County Clare's unique, rocky landscape, the Cliffs of Moher and the musical town of Doolin.

Cavan Way (p557) is not long, either – just 26km – but it boasts impressive topographic variety, taking in bogs, Stone Age monuments and the source of the River Shannon. In County Kerry, the 168km Dingle Way (p317) loops round one of Ireland's most beautiful peninsulas. Starting in County Tipperary and ending up in County Waterford, the East Munster Way (p352) is a 70km walk through forest and open moorland, and along the towpath of the River Suir. The 214km Kerry Way (p300) takes in the spectacular Macgillycuddy's Reeks (p298) and the Ring of Kerry coast.

To the north, the Ulster Way (p685) makes a circuit around the six counties of Northern Ireland and Donegal. In total, the footpath covers more than 900km, but it can easily be broken down into smaller sections. The popular 132km Wicklow Way (p166) starts in southern Dublin and ends in Clonegal in County Carlow; the most scenic bit of Ireland's most famous walk is between Glendalough and Aughrim.

The Kingfisher Trail (p679) is a waymarked, long-distance cycling trail stretching some 370km along the back roads of Counties Fermanagh, Leitrim, Cavan and Monaghan.

WATERSPORTS

Ireland has 3100km of coastline and numerous rivers and lakes, so no matter where in the country you may be, you're never far from a place to surf, windsurf, scuba dive, paddle a canoe, swim or simply cast a line into a cool stream ribboned with salmon. Outfitters and information sources abound.

Surfing & Windsurfing

Surfing is all the rage on the coast, especially in the west. Bundoran (p469) in County Donegal is home to the Irish national championships each April. Down in County Sligo, Easkey (p458) and Strandhill (p455) are famous for their year-round surf, and have facilities for travellers who seek room and board. County Clare has nice breaks at Kilkee (p370), Lahinch (p373) and Fanore (p383).

Over on the east coast, some fine surfing can be had at County Waterford's Tramore Beach (p211), a coastal resort that's home to Ireland's largest surf school. In County Wexford, surfing is popular at Rosslare Strand (p194). The beaches around Portrush (p652), County Antrim, afford good surfing and body-surfing. The swells are highest and the water warmest in September and October.

Windsurfing is also gathering momentum along Ireland's coasts, especially in the shallow bay off County Wexford's Rosslare Strand (p194) and off Achill Island (p439) in County Mayo. Windsurfing and kite-surfing are equally popular around Port-na-Blagh (p483), County Donegal.

Canoeing & Kayaking

Ireland's serrated coastline makes it ideal for canoeing and kayaking expeditions. The type of canoeing in Ireland and degree of difficulty varies from gentle paddling to white-water canoeing and canoe surfing. The best time for white water is winter (December to February), when the heavier rainfall swells the rivers. In County Carlow, the River Barrow (p221) is a dream setting for canoeists and kayakers. A canoe and paddle also provide the only means for exploring the backwaters of Lough Erne (p688).

HORSE RIDING

There are hundreds of centres throughout Ireland, offering possibilities ranging from a one-hour ride (from €25/£15) to fully packaged, residential equestrian holidays. Short sessions – anything from one hour to a half-day – are pretty straightforward, but they can also involve lessons, ponycraft courses for the kids, and rides over a variety of terrain, from gentle, sandy beaches to tougher, cross-country treks. You can ride almost everywhere, but most wannabe jockeys favour the west, where the landscapes are more conducive to the kind of romantic equestrianism riders have in mind.

Surprisingly, there is no legislation governing the set-up and conduct of horse yards, but the **Association of Irish Riding Establishments** (AIRE; ☎ 045-850 800; www.aire.ie; Beech House, Millennium Pk, Naas, Co Kildare) has over 200 member schools and centres spread throughout the country; membership ensures that they have qualified instructors, a resident first-aider and child-protection schemes, are certified by insurance and, crucially, that all of the horses are maintained according to an acceptable standard of care. We recommend that you stick to AIRE-approved centres.

Although most yards offer rides on Irish hunters or cobs, many a traveller seeks the opportunity to ride Connemara ponies (see the boxed text, p74), and this can be arranged at Errislannan Manor (p418), near Clifden in County Galway.

The AIRE website has a complete list of reputable outfits, including Donegal Equestrian Holidays (p470) in Bundoran, County Donegal, and Killarney Riding Stables (p291), which offers multiday rides through County Kerry's stunning Iveragh Peninsula.

Scuba Diving

With little sewage from cities to obscure the waters, Ireland's west coast has some of the best scuba diving in Europe. The offshore islands and rocks host especially rich underwater life. The best period for diving is roughly March to October. Visibility averages more than 12m, but can increase to 30m on good days. Scuba Dive West (see the boxed text, p422), in Letterfrack, County Galway, is one of the country's best outfitters and can organise diving expeditions along the west coast.

Fishing

Ireland is justly famous for its coarse fishing (which is generally free), covering bream, pike, perch, roach, rudd, tench, carp and eel. Freshwater game fish include salmon, sea trout and brown trout. Some managed fisheries also stock rainbow trout.

The enormous Shannon and Erne river systems, which stretch southwards from Counties Leitrim and Fermanagh, are prime angling spots, and County Cavan (p557), the 'Lake County', is a favourite with hardcore fishers. In the west, the great lakes of Corrib (p416), Mask (p429) and Conn (p445) have plenty of lakeshore B&Bs, good sturdy boats and knowledgeable boaters.

WATCHING WILDLIFE

Spotting animals in the wild is often a highlight on a walk through Ireland's diverse natural settings. The country's forests, lakes, bogs, wetlands and coastal islands are rife with birds, furtive furry creatures and sea mammals. In many parts of the country your chances of spotting wildlife are quite high.

Land Mammals

Killarney National Park (p295), in County Kerry, has been designated a Unesco Biosphere Reserve for its bounty of intriguing plant and animal species. It is home to the only wild herd of red deer, Ireland's most

The steely-nerved Irish hare (p73) RICHARD MILLS

Red deer run wild in Killarney NP (p295) RICHARD MILLS

Seals (p73) are a common coastal sight RICHARD MILLS

magnificent native mammal. Steely-nerved hares are commonly observed along many of Ireland's rural walkways.

Water Mammals

Whales, including fin whales, humpbacks and minke whales, are often spotted off the coast of West Cork during summer, when they come to feed offshore. Dolphins and porpoises are year-round residents of Irish waters, particularly favouring the natural harbours of Counties Kerry and Cork.

Seals live all around Ireland's perimeter. You're likely to encounter them on the island of Inishbofin (p419) off the coast of Galway; near Portaferry (p609) in County Down; on Rathlin Island (p660) off the Antrim coast; and around Greencastle (p494) in Donegal's Inishowen Peninsula. One of Ireland's most prized animals is the river otter, which has survived here long after disappearing from much of the rest of Europe. They are extremely shy, but a sharp-eyed walker may get lucky along the streams of Connemara (p411) in County Galway.

Birds

Birds, of course, proliferate in huge numbers and are not generally shy, making Ireland a hot destination for birders. For a description of some birds found in Ireland, see p73.

There are more than 70 reserves and sanctuaries in Ireland, many of them open to the public. Good places to go are the Inishowen Peninsula (p492) in County Donegal; the Skellig Islands (p305) off the coast of County Kerry; the Cooley Birdwatching Trail (p556) in County Louth; and Castle Espie (p612) in County Down.

The formally attired puffin (p73)

RICHARD MILLS

The fierce peregrine falcon (p73)

RICHARD MILLS

TOP SPOTS FOR BIRDWATCHING

Ireland may be a birdwatcher's paradise, but there are some spots that are more heavenly than others:

- Castle Espie, Strangford Lough, County Down (p612) – In May and June it's overrun with goslings, ducklings and cygnets.
- Saltee Islands, County Wexford (p197) – Gannets, gulls, puffins and Manx shearwaters, and a vast colony of cormorants.
- Cape Clear, County Cork (p272) – Fulmars, great black backed gulls, storm petrels, gannets and shearwaters can be seen in large numbers.
- Rathlin Island, County Derry (p660) – Best during the early winter months, when you'll see brent geese, whooper swans and wigeons.
- Skellig Islands, County Kerry (p305) – Storm petrels, kittiwakes, fulmars, puffins and the ubiquitous gannet reign supreme.

Counties Fermanagh & Tyrone

The ancient landscape of Fermanagh is shaped by ice and water, with rugged hills rising above quilted plains of half-drowned drumlins and shimmering, reed-fringed lakes. A glance at the map shows the county is around one-third water – as the locals will tell you, the lakes are in Fermanagh for six months of the year; for the other six, Fermanagh is in the lakes.

This watery maze is a natural playground for anglers – the loughs and rivers are stuffed with trout and pike – and for boaters. You can hire a motor cruiser and spend a week or two navigating the scenic waterways of Lough Erne and the River Shannon, which together form a 750km network of rivers, lakes and canals. If you prefer your boats without engines, the 50km Lough Erne Canoe Trail is a paddler's paradise.

The limestone ridges to the south of Lough Erne are riddled with caves – at Marble Arch you can explore an underground river – while the higher hills are swathed with blanket bog, a rare and endangered habitat. This is all grand walking country, but there are also rainy-day attractions, such as the contrasting stately homes of Florence Court and Castle Coole, and the world-famous pottery at Belleek.

County Tyrone – from Tír Eoghain (Land of Owen, a legendary chieftain) – is the homeland of the O'Neill clan, and is dominated by the tweed-tinted moorlands of the Sperrin Mountains, whose southern flanks are dotted with prehistoric sites. Apart from the hiking opportunities offered by these heather-clad hills, the county's main attraction is the Ulster American Folk Park, a fascinating outdoor museum celebrating Ulster's historic links with the USA.

HIGHLIGHTS

- **Climb to the Lost World** Hike over rare blanket bog to the remote summit of Cuilcagh Mountain (p691)

- **Faces from the Past** Ponder the meaning of the strange stone figures on White Island (p686) and Boa Island (p686)

- **River of Adventure** Follow the course of an underground river as it flows through the Marble Arch Caves (p689)

- **Blazing Paddles** Hire a canoe and explore the reed-fringed backwaters of Lough Erne (p688)

- **The American Connection** Learn about the historical links between Ireland and the USA at the Ulster American Folk Park (p690)

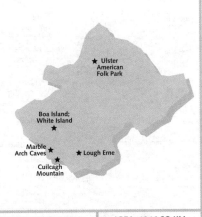

- TELEPHONE CODE: 028 FROM UK; 048 FROM REPUBLIC OF IRELAND
- POPULATION: 227,000
- AREA: 4846 SQ KM

COUNTY FERMANAGH

ENNISKILLEN
pop 13,600

Perched amid the web of waterways that link Upper and Lower Lough Erne, Enniskillen (Inis Ceithleann, meaning Ceithleann's Island, after a legendary woman warrior) is an appealing town with a mile-long main street that rides the roller-coaster spine of the island's drumlin. (The locals say you're only a true Enniskilliner if you were born 'between the bridges'; that is, on the town's central island.) Its attractive waterside setting, bustling with boats in summer, plus a range of lively pubs and restaurants, make Enniskillen a good base for exploring Upper and Lower Lough Erne Florence Court and the Marble Arch Caves.

Though neither was born here, both Oscar Wilde and Samuel Beckett were pupils at Enniskillen's Portora Royal School (Wilde from 1864 to 1871, Beckett from 1919 to 1923) it was here that Beckett first studied French, a language he would later write in. The town's name is also prominent in the history of the Troubles – on Poppy Day (11 November) in 1987 an IRA bomb killed 11 people during a service at Enniskillen's war memorial.

Orientation

The main street changes name half a dozen times between the bridges at either end; the prominent clock tower marks the town centre.

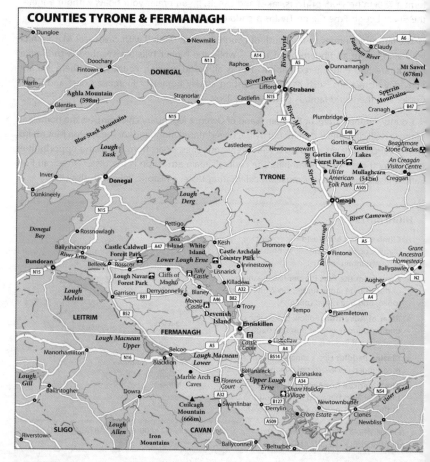

The other principal street is Wellington Rd, south of and parallel to the main street, where you'll find the bus station, tourist office and car parking. If you're driving, try to avoid rush hour – the bridge at the west end is a traffic bottleneck.

Information

Bank of Ireland (☎ 6632 2136; 7 Townhall St) ATM.

Eason (☎ 6632 4341; 10 High St; ☼ 8am-6pm Mon-Sat, 10am-5pm Sun) Local-interest books and maps.

Enniskillen Library (☎ 6632 2886; Hall's Lane; ☼ 8.30am-5.15pm Mon & Fri, 8.30am-8pm Tue-Thu, 9am-1pm & 2-5pm Sat) Internet access £1.50 per 30min.

Post office (3 High St) In Dolan's Centra grocery store.

Tourist Information Centre (☎ 6632 3110; www .fermanagh.gov.uk; Wellington Rd; ☼ 9am-7pm Mon-Fri, 10am-6pm Sat, 11am-5pm Sun Jul & Aug, 9am-5.30pm Mon-Fri, 10am-6pm Sat, 11am-5pm Sun Easter-Jun & Sep, 9am-5.30pm Mon-Fri & 10am-2pm Sat & Sun Oct, 9am-5.30pm Mon-Fri Nov-Easter) Books accommodation, changes money, sells fishing licences and provides a postal and fax service.

Ulster Bank (☎ 6632 4034; 16 Darling St) ATM.

Sights

Enniskillen Castle (☎ 6632 5000; www.enniskillencastle .co.uk; Castle Barracks; adult/child £2.95/1.95; ☼ 2-5pm Mon & 10am-5pm Tue-Fri year-round, also 2-5pm Sat May-Sep & 2-5pm Sun Jul & Aug), a former stronghold of the 16th-century Maguire chieftains, guards the western end of the town's central island, its twin-turreted **Watergate** looming over passing fleets of cabin cruisers. Within the walls you'll find the **Fermanagh County Museum**, which has displays on the county's history, archaeology, landscape and wildlife. The 15th-century keep contains the **Royal Inniskilling Fusiliers Regimental Museum**, full of guns, uniforms and medals – including eight Victoria Crosses awarded in WWI; it's dedicated to the regiment that was raised at the castle in 1689 to support the army of William I.

In Forthill Park, at the eastern end of town, stands **Cole's Monument** (admission free; ☼ 1.30-3pm mid-Apr–Sep). It commemorates Sir Galbraith Lowry-Cole (1772–1842), who was one of Wellington's generals and the son of the first Earl of Enniskillen. Climb the 108 steps inside the column for a good view of the surrounding area.

Activities

The **Kingfisher Trail** is a waymarked, long-distance cycling trail that starts in Enniskillen and wends its way through the back roads of Counties Fermanagh, Leitrim, Cavan and Monaghan. The full route is around 370km long, but a shorter loop, starting and finishing in Enniskillen, and travelling via Kesh, Belleek, Garrison, Belcoo and the village of Florencecourt, is only 115km – easily done in two days with an overnight stay at Belleek. You can get a trail map from the Enniskillen Tourist Information Centre. There's no bicycle hire available in Enniskillen, though; the nearest is in Castle Archdale Country Park (p685).

You can hire canoes and kayaks from the **Lakeland Canoe Centre** (☎ 6632 4250; www.thehigh pointgroup.com; Castle Island; per 2hr £20).

You can buy **fishing** permits and licences from the tourist information office, or Home, Field and Stream (p682).

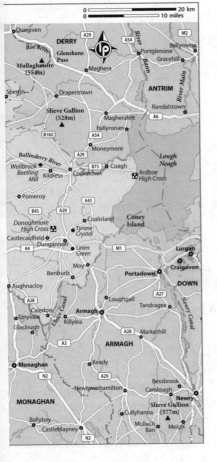

ENNISKILLEN

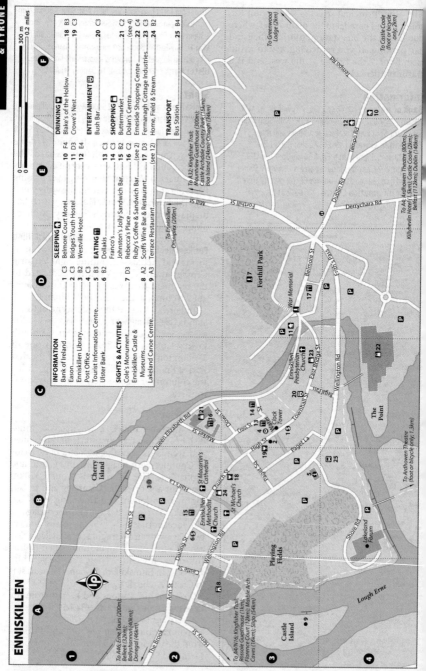

0 — 300 m
0 — 0.2 miles

INFORMATION	
Bank of Ireland	1 C3
Eason	2 C3
Enniskillen Library	3 B2
Post Office	4 C3
Tourist Information Centre	5 B3
Ulster Bank	6 C3

SIGHTS & ACTIVITIES	
Cole's Monument	7 D3
Enniskillen Castle &	
Museums	8 A2
Lakeland Canoe Centre	9 A3

SLEEPING	
Belmore Court Motel	10 F4
Bridges Youth Hostel	11 D3
Westville Hotel	12 E4

EATING	
Dollakis	13 C3
Franco's	14 C3
Johnston's Jolly Sandwich Bar	15 B2
Rebecca's Place	16 C2
Ruby's Coffee & Sandwich Bar	(see 2)
Scoffs Wine Bar & Restaurant	17 D3
Terrace Restaurant	(see 12)

DRINKING	
Blake's of the Hollow	18 B3
Crowe's Nest	19 C3

ENTERTAINMENT	
Bush Bar	20 C3

SHOPPING	
Buttermarket	21 C2
Dolan's Centra	(see 4)
Erneside Shopping Centre	22 C4
Fermanagh Cottage Industries	23 C3
Home, Field & Stream	24 B2

TRANSPORT	
Bus Station	25 B4

See p684 and p688 for boat-hire options, and the boxed text, p689, for information on **cruising** the lakes.

Tours

Blue Badge Tours (☎ 6862 1430; breegemccusker@btopenworld.com) offers guided tours of Enniskillen and the Lough Erne area with local historian Breege McCusker, a registered tourist guide. Special interest tours include prehistoric sites, monastic sites, carved stones and plantation castles.

Erne Tours (☎ 6632 2882; www.ernetoursltd.com; Round 'O' Quay, The Brook; adult/child £10/6; 🕑 10.30am, 2.15pm & 4.15pm daily Jul & Aug, 2.15pm & 4.15pm daily Jun, 2.15pm & 4.15pm daily Tue, Sat & Sun May, Sep & Oct) operates 1¾-hour cruises on Lower Lough Erne aboard the 56-seat waterbus MV *Kestrel*, calling at Devenish Island along the way. It departs from the Round 'O' Quay, just west of the town centre on the A46 to Belleek. There are also **Saturday evening cruises** (adult/child £29/15; 🕑 6.30pm May-Sep) that include a three-course dinner at the Killyhevlin Hotel, departing from the hotel jetty.

Sleeping
BUDGET

Bridges Youth Hostel (☎ 6634 0110; www.hini.org.uk; Belmore St; dm/s/tw £17/22/39; 🅿 💻 🛜) This modern, purpose-built hostel is in a great location overlooking a river in the centre of town. It has mostly four-bed dorms, each with en suite bathroom, plus six twin rooms, a kitchen, restaurant, laundry and bike shed. Consult the website for daytime closing hours (when check-in is not available).

MIDRANGE

Rossole Guesthouse (☎ 6632 3462; nora.sheridan@btinternet.com; 85 Sligo Rd; s/d from £30/50; 🅿) A modern Georgian-style house with a sunny conservatory overlooking a small lake, the five-room Rossole is an angler's delight – you can fish in the lake, and there are rowing boats for guests at the bottom of the garden. It's 1km southwest of the town centre on the A4 Sligo road.

Greenwood Lodge (☎ 6632 5636; www.greenwoodlodge.co.uk; 17 Killyvilly Ct, Tempo Rd; s/d from £35/50; 🅿) The owners of this spacious and modern villa, set on a quiet side street 3km northeast of town off the B80, go out of their way to make you feel welcome. The three homely bedrooms all have en suite bathrooms, the breakfasts are freshly prepared, and there is secure storage available for bikes.

Mountview Guesthouse (☎ 6632 3147; www.mountviewguests.com; 61 Irvinestown Rd; s/d from £45/65; 🅿 🛜) Indulge in a spot of country-house comfort in this large, ivy-clad Victorian villa set in wooded grounds. There are three bedrooms with private bathrooms, a luxurious lounge and even a snooker room with a full-size table. The Mountview looks out over Race Course Lough, just a 10-minute (800m) walk north from the town centre.

Belmore Court Motel (☎ 6632 6633; www.motel.co.uk; Tempo Rd; d from £60, apt £85-140; 🅿 🛜) Recently expanded from its original row of terrace houses into a huge modern extension, the friendly Belmore offers stylish and spacious 'superior' rooms in the new building (single/double from £80/95) and, in the old, family 'mini-apartments' with self-catering facilities.

our pick **Westville Hotel** (☎ 6632 0333; www.westvillehotel.co.uk; 14-20 Tempo Rd; s/d from £80/95; 🅿 💻 🛜) A dash of style arrived on Enniskillen's rather staid accommodation scene with the opening of the Westville in 2008. Designer fabrics, cool colour combinations, good food and welcoming staff make this our favourite place to stay in town.

TOP END

Killyhevlin Hotel (☎ 6632 3481; www.killyhevlin.com; Killyhevlin; s/d from £95/130; 🅿 💻 🛜) Enniskillen's top hotel is 1.5km south of town on the A4 Maguiresbridge road, in an idyllic setting overlooking Upper Lough Erne. Many of its 43 effortlessly elegant rooms enjoy stunning views over landscaped gardens to the lough; there are also 13 two-bedroom lakeside chalets (£275 per weekend April to June, £225 per weekend November to March, £595 per week July to October).

Eating
BUDGET

Johnston's Jolly Sandwich Bar (☎ 6632 2277; 3 Darling St; sandwiches £2-4; 🕑 8am-4pm Mon-Fri, 8.30am-4pm Sat) A traditional bakery selling excellent pick-and-mix sandwiches, soup, pies and cakes to take away or eat in.

Rebecca's Place (☎ 6632 4499; Buttermarket; snacks £2-5; 🕑 9.30am-5.30pm Mon-Sat) A traditional cafe with pine tables and chairs, Rebecca's is set in a craft shop (see p682) and serves good sandwiches, salads and pastries.

Ruby's Coffee & Sandwich Bar (☎ 6632 9399; 10 High St; snacks £2-5; 🕑 9am-5.30pm Mon-Sat) Tucked upstairs in Eason's bookshop is this comfy nook furnished with sofas and armchairs, offering breakfast bagels and croissants, sandwiches and salads, soups and baked potatoes. Free newspapers, too.

MIDRANGE

Dollakis (☎ 6634 2616; 2 Cross St; lunch £5-7, dinner £13-19; 10am-4pm Tue, to 10pm Wed-Sat, noon-4pm Sun) Our prize for best coffee in town goes to this very chic little cafe-bistro. And, as well as serving coffee, cakes and snacks through the day, it transforms into a Greek-Mediterranean restaurant in the evening. The menu includes things such as seafood-and-leek tart topped with hollandaise sauce, chicken breast with a poppy-seed crust stuffed with olive tapenade and mozzarella, and souvlaki and vegetarian moussaka.

Scoffs Wine Bar & Restaurant (☎ 6634 2622; 17 Belmore St; mains £9-19; 4.30pm-late Mon-Sat, to 10pm Sun) This busy restaurant has a modern vibe with shades of chocolate-brown and burgundy, dark wood and dim candlelight, and an international menu that includes braised lamb shank with creamy mash and redcurrant and rosemary gravy, and spicy vegetable and sunflower seed tortillas with tomato sauce and créme fraiche. The downstairs wine bar offers lighter meals. Three-course Sunday lunch costs £18.

Franco's (☎ 6632 4424; Queen Elizabeth Rd; pizza £10-11, mains £12-22; noon-11pm) An atmospheric warren of wood-panelled, candlelit nooks set in a former blacksmith's forge, Franco's is always bustling and noisy, and serves a range of Italian, Asian and seafood dishes as well as filling pizzas and pasta.

TOP END

our pick Terrace Restaurant (☎ 6632 0333; Westville Hotel, 14-20 Tempo Rd; 2-/3-course dinner £30/35; dinner only) The restaurant at the new Westville Hotel combines understated elegance in the dining room with a deft touch in the kitchen – candlelight creates a romantic atmosphere, while delightful dishes such as ballotine of quail stuffed with smoked-bacon mousse, and pan-fried turbot with white beans, asparagus, parmesan crisps and chive velouté, make for a memorable meal.

Drinking

our pick Blake's of the Hollow (William Blake; ☎ 6632 2143; 6 Church St) Ulster's best pint of Guinness awaits you in this traditional Victorian pub, almost unchanged since 1887, complete with marble-topped bar, four huge sherry casks, antique silver lamp holders and ancient wood panelling kippered by a century of cigarette smoke. There's traditional music from 9pm on Fridays.

Crowe's Nest (☎ 6632 5252; 12 High St) A lively bar with a conservatory and patio out the back for those sunny summer afternoons, the Nest has live music most nights from 9pm in the back bar and traditional music sessions downstairs on Tuesday nights during summer.

Entertainment

Bush Bar (☎ 6632 5210; www.thebushbar.com; 26 Townhall St) The nearest Enniskillen comes to a nightclub, with leather chairs and banquettes in various shades of coffee, from dark roast to cafe au lait, a reasonable cocktail menu, and an upstairs lounge that hosts DJs or live bands on Friday and Saturday.

Ardhowen Theatre (☎ 6632 5440; www.ardhowentheatre.com; Dublin Rd; box office 11am-4.30pm Mon-Fri, 10am-7pm before a performance, 11am-1pm, 2-5pm & 6-7pm Sat) The program here includes concerts, local amateur and professional drama and musical productions, pantomimes and films. The theatre is about 2km southeast of the town centre on the A4, in an impressive glass-fronted building overlooking a lake.

Enniskillen Omniplex (☎ 08717200400; www.omniplex.ie; Factory Rd) A seven-screen cinema, 700m north of the town centre on Race Course Lough.

Shopping

Buttermarket (☎ 6632 4499; Down St) The refurbished buildings in the old marketplace house a variety of craft shops and studios selling paintings, ceramics, jewellery and even fishing flies.

Erneside Shopping Centre (☎ 6632 5705; The Point; 9am-6pm Mon, Tue & Sat, to 9pm Wed-Fri & Sat, 1-6pm Sun) A modern complex of shops, cafes and a supermarket. The Millets store stocks camping and outdoor equipment.

Fermanagh Cottage Industries (☎ 6632 2260; 14 East Bridge St) A craft shop selling linen, lace and tweed.

Home, Field & Stream (☎ 6632 2114; 18 Church St) Has a wide range of fishing tackle and also sells fishing licences and permits.

Dolan's Centra (3 High St; 7.30am-9pm Mon-Sat, 9am-9pm Sun) A handy, late-opening minimarket and post-office counter; also sells Sunday newspapers.

Getting There & Away

Ulsterbus service 261 runs from Enniskillen to Belfast (£10, 2¼ hours, hourly Monday to Saturday, two on Sunday) via Dungannon. Bus 296 runs to Omagh (£5, one hour, one daily Monday to Saturday) and, in the other direction, to Cork (8¼ hours; change at Longford) via Athlone (3½ hours). In July and August only, bus 99 goes from Enniskillen to Bundoran (£6, 1¼ hours, four daily Monday to Friday, three Saturday, one on Sunday) via Belleek (45 minutes). Bus 64 goes to Bundoran year round, twice on Thursdays and once on Sundays.

Bus Éireann's 66 service runs to Sligo (£8, 1½ hours, five daily Monday to Saturday, two on Sundays) via Belcoo, and bus 30 between Dublin (£13, 2½ hours, seven daily Monday to Saturday, four Sunday) and Donegal (one hour) also stops in at Enniskillen and Belleek.

AROUND ENNISKILLEN

Castle Coole

When King George IV visited Ireland in 1821, the second Earl of Belmore had a state bedroom specially prepared at Castle Coole in anticipation of the monarch's visit. The king, however, was more interested in dallying with his mistress at Slane Castle and never turned up. The bedroom, draped in red silk and decorated with paintings depicting *The Rake's Progress* (the earl's sniffy riposte to the king's extramarital shenanigans), is one of the highlights of the one-hour guided tour around **Castle Coole** (☎ 6632 2690; Dublin Rd, Enniskillen; adult/child £5/2; ☺ house noon–6pm daily Jul & Aug, 1-6pm Fri-Wed Jun, 1-6pm Sat, Sun & public hols mid-Mar–May & Sep; grounds 10am-8pm mid-Mar–Sep).

Designed by James Wyatt, this Palladian mansion was built between 1789 and 1795 for Armar Lowry-Corry, the first Earl of Belmore, and is probably the purest expression of late-18th-century neoclassical architecture in Ireland. It is built of silvery-white Portland stone, which was brought in at great expense from southern England – first sent by ship to Ballyshannon, then overland to Lough Erne, by boat again to Enniskillen, and finally by bullock cart for the last 3km.

Building costs of £70,000 nearly bankrupted the first earl, but that didn't stop his son Somerset Lowry-Corry, the second earl, spending another £35,000 on exuberant Regency furnishings and decoration, best seen in the opulent, oval saloon where the family and friends would gather before dinner. The eighth Earl of Belmore, John Armar Lowry-Corry, reserves part of the house for his private use, but most of the building is under the care of the National Trust.

The 600 hectares of landscaped **grounds** (car/pedestrian £3.50/free) contain a lake that is home to the UK's only nonmigratory colony of greylag geese. It is said that if the geese ever leave, the earls of Belmore will lose Castle Coole.

Castle Coole is on the A4 Dublin road, 2.5km southeast of Enniskillen. You can easily walk there in 30 minutes – beyond Dunnes Stores, fork left on Tempo Rd and keep straight on along Castlecoole Rd.

Sheelin Irish Lace Museum

This **museum** (☎ 6634 8052; www.irishlacemuseum .com; Bellanaleck; adult/child £4/1.50; ☺ 10am-6pm Mon-Sat) houses a collection of beautiful Irish lace dating from 1850 to 1900. Lace-making was an important cottage industry in the region both before and after the Famine – prior to WWI there were at least 10 lace schools in County Fermanagh. The museum is just over 6km southwest of Enniskillen in the village of Bellanaleck.

UPPER LOUGH ERNE

About 80km long, Lough Erne is made up of two sections: the Upper Lough to the south of Enniskillen, and the Lower Lough to the north. The two are connected by the River Erne, which begins its journey in County Cavan and meets the sea at Donegal Bay west of Ballyshannon.

Upper Lough Erne is not so much a lake as a watery maze of islands (more than 150 of them), inlets, reedy bays and meandering backwaters. Bird life is abundant, with flocks of whooper swan and goldeneye overwintering here, great crested grebes nesting in the spring, and Ireland's biggest heronry in a 400-year-old oak grove on the island of Inishfendra, just south of Crom Estate.

Lisnaskea is the main town, with shops, pubs, ATMs and a post office. An island at the north end of the lough, near Lisbellaw, is home to the **Belle Isle School of Cookery** (☎ 6638 7231; www.irish-cookery-school.com), which offers a range of cookery and wine courses lasting from one day to four weeks, with luxurious accommodation in Belle Isle Castle and its estate cottages. One-day courses cost £120-140, not including accommodation.

Crom Estate

Home to the largest area of natural woodland in Northern Ireland, the National Trust's beautiful **Crom Estate** (☎ 6773 8118; Newtownbutler; adult/child £3/1; ◷ grounds 10am-7pm Jun-Aug, to 6pm mid-Mar–May & Sep-Nov; visitor centre 10am-6pm Easter–mid-Sep, 10am-6pm Sat & Sun late Mar & late Sep–early Oct, Sun only late Oct) is a haven for pine martens, rare bats and many species of bird.

You can walk from the visitor centre to the ruins of old Crom Castle, with its ancient walled garden, abandoned bowling green and gnarled yew trees, and views over the reed-fringed lough to an island folly. There are rowing boats for hire (£6 per hour).

Check the **National Trust website** (www.ntni.org.uk) for details on bat-watching and other wildlife events.

The estate is on the eastern shore of the Upper Lough, 5km west of Newtownbutler.

Tours

The **Inishcruiser** (☎ 6772 2122; adult/child/family £7.50/5.50/21; ◷ 2.30pm Sun & public hols Easter-Sep) offers 1½- to two-hour cruises on the lough leaving from the Share Holiday Village, 5km southwest of Lisnaskea.

Activities

Day boats can be hired for fishing or exploring from **Knockninny Marina** (☎ 6774 8590; near Derrylin) on the west shore of the lough; rates are £50/70 per half-/full-day for a six-seater motor boat with cabin. The marina also rents bikes for £7/12 a half-/full-day. It's signposted from the main road just north of Derrylin.

Guests and day visitors at the **Share Holiday Village** (☎ 6772 2122; www.sharevillage.org) near Lisnaskea can take part in canoeing, windsurfing, dinghy sailing, archery, orienteering and other activities for £12 per person per 2½-hour session.

Sleeping & Eating

Lisnaskea Caravan Park (☎ 6772 1040; Gola Rd, Mullynascarty; tent/caravan sites £9/13; ◷ Apr-Oct) This local council–run site enjoys a beautiful wooded setting on the banks of the Colebrooke River about 2km northwest of Lisnaskea, on the B514 road towards Enniskillen.

Share Holiday Village (☎ 6772 2122; www.sharevillage.org; Smiths Strand, Lisnaskea; tent/caravan sites £10/15; ◷ Easter-Sep) Share is a charity that work towards the integration of people with an without disabilities through a range of activities and courses. The holiday village i mostly occupied by groups, but it also has touring site with space for nine caravans an 24 tents. Booking is strongly recommended The village is 5km southwest of Lisnaskea off the B127.

Donn Carragh Hotel (☎ 6772 1206; www.donncarragh hotel.com; Main St, Lisnaskea; s/d from £45/80; P) There' not too much in the way of hotel or B&B accommodation around Upper Lough Erne; this pleasant but unexceptional 18-room hotel in the middle of Lisnaskea is the best of what there is.

Knockninny House (☎ 6774 8590; www.knockninny house.com; near Derrylin; r per person from £45; P ⊛) A Victorian villa built in the 1870s and Lough Erne's first hotel, Knockninny House enjoys an idyllic lakeside setting, and now offers accommodation in seven country-style bedrooms. There's also a restaurant with an outdoor terrace overlooking the marina, where you can take afternoon tea, and a tiny sandy beach.

Kissin Crust (☎ 6772 2678; 125 Main St, Lisnaskea; mains £3-6; ◷ 8.30am-5pm Mon-Sat) Very popular with local people, this friendly coffee shop is stacked with home-baked apple pie, lemon meringue pie, quiches and scones, and serves up a lunch menu of homemade soup, freshly made sandwiches and a hot dish of the day.

Getting There & Away

From Enniskillen, Ulsterbus service 95 runs along the east side of the lough to Lisnaskea (£3, 30 minutes, five daily Monday to Friday, three on Saturdays, plus one on Sundays in July and August only), while bus 58 goes down the west side to Derrylin (£3, 40 minutes, five daily Monday to Friday, two on Saturdays), and continues to Belturbet in County Cavan.

LOWER LOUGH ERNE

Lower Lough Erne is a much more open expanse of water than the Upper Lough, with its 90-odd islands clustered mainly in the southern reaches. In early Christian times, when overland travel was difficult, Lough Erne was an important highway between the Donegal coast and inland Leitrim, and there are many ancient religious sites and other antiquities dotted around its shores. In medieval times the lough was part

---

ULSTER WAY

The Ulster Way long-distance walking trail makes a circuit around the six counties of Northern Ireland and Donegal. In total the route covers just over 900km, so walking all of it might take four to five weeks. However, much of the way is on minor roads rather than footpaths, a criticism which has been taken on board by the Northern Ireland Tourist Board (NITB), who are 'relaunching' the Ulster Way and dividing it into 'Quality Sections' – good, scenic, off-road walking – separated by Link Sections which can be covered by public transport. Check the **WalkNI website** (www.walkni.com) for the latest info.

Short sections of the Ulster Way that make good day walks include Cuilcagh Mountain (boxed text, p691) and the Causeway Coast Way (boxed text, p658).

---

of an important pilgrimage route to Station Island in Lough Derg, County Donegal.

The following sights are described travelling anticlockwise around the lough from Enniskillen.

Devenish Island

Devenish Island (from Daimh Inis, meaning Ox Island) is the biggest of several 'holy islands' in Lough Erne. The remains of an **Augustinian monastery**, founded here in the 6th century by St Molaise, include a superb 12th-century **round tower** in near perfect condition, the ruins of St Molaise's Church and St Mary's Abbey, an unusual 15th-century high cross, and many fascinating old gravestones. Four ladders allow you to climb to the top of the round tower for a cramped view out of the five tiny windows.

A speedboat **ferry** (☎ 6862 1588; adult/child return £3/2; ☻ 10am, 1pm, 3pm & 5pm daily Apr-Sep) crosses to Devenish Island from Trory Point landing. From Enniskillen, take the A32 towards Irvinestown and after 5km look for the sign on the left, just after a service station and immediately before the junction where the B82 and A32 part company. At the foot of the hill by the lough, turn left for the jetty.

You can also visit as part of a cruise with Erne Tours (p681) from Enniskillen.

Killadeas

The churchyard at Killadeas, 11km north of Enniskillen on the B82, contains several unusual carved stones. Most famous is the 1m-high **Bishop's Stone**, dating from between the 7th and 9th centuries, which has a Celtic head reminiscent of the White Island figures (see p686) carved on its narrow western edge, and an engraving of a bishop with bell and crozier on the side. Located nearby is a slab set on edge, with several deep cup-marks – possibly

bullauns (ancient grinding stones) – on one side, and a cross within a circle on the other. You will also find a broken phallic column and a large, perforated stone.

SLEEPING & EATING

The **Manor House Country Hotel** (☎ 6862 2211; www.manor-house-hotel.com; Killadeas; s/d from £105/130; Ⓟ �ⓢ) is a grand, 19th-century country house overlooking Lough Erne. It has had a thorough makeover in neoclassical style, complete with a Greek temple–style lobby, Romanesque pool and Jacuzzis with a view over the lough. The public areas are impressive but the rooms, though luxurious, are a bit on the bland side. The hotel's **Watergate Lounge** serves decent pub grub (mains £9 to £17), and has live music at weekends.

Castle Archdale Country Park

This **park** (☎ 6862 1588; Lisnarick; admission free; ☻ 9am-dusk) has pleasant woodland and lakeshore walks and cycle tracks in the former estate of 18th-century Archdale Manor. The island-filled bay was used in WWII as a base for Catalina flying boats, a history explained in the **visitor centre** (admission free; ☻ 10am-6pm Easter-Sep, noon-4pm Sun Oct-Easter).

You can hire bikes for £4/8/12 per hour/half-day/full-day, or swap two wheels for four legs – the park offers pony trekking (£15 per hour), as well as short rides (£5 per 15 minutes) for beginners. There are also boats for hire (£55/80 per half-day/full-day), and you can also rent fishing rods (£5 per day including bait).

The park is 16km northwest of Enniskillen on the B82, near Lisnarick.

SLEEPING & EATING

Castle Archdale Caravan Park (☎ 6862 1333; www.castlearchdale.com; Castle Archdale Country Park; tent sites

£15-20, caravan sites £20-25; Easter-Oct) This attractive, tree-sheltered site is dominated by onsite caravans, but has good facilities, including a shop, launderette, playground and restaurant.

ourpick Cedars Guesthouse (6862 1493; www .cedarsguesthouse.com; Drummal, Castle Archdale; s/d from £40/70; P) Set in a former rectory just south of the park entrance, this peaceful 10-room guesthouse goes for a Victorian country-house feel, with rose-patterned bedspreads and antique-style furniture.

Rectory Bistro (mains £11-17; 6-9pm Wed-Sat, 12.30-3pm & 5-9pm Sun) Adjoining the Cedars Guesthouse, this bistro has a welcoming open fireplace, lots of golden pine lit by chunky candles and a sprinkling of Gothic motifs, with a hearty menu that ranges from a fresh crab and smoked salmon wrap to beef and Guinness pie with creamy mash, peas and onions.

White Island

White Island, in the bay to the north of Castle Archdale Country Park, is the most haunting of Lough Erne's monastic sites. At the eastern tip of the island are the ruins of a small 12th-century church with a beautiful Romanesque door on its southern side. Inside are six extraordinary Celtic stone figures, thought to date from the 9th century, lined up along the wall like miniature Easter Island statues.

This line-up is a modern arrangement; most of them were discovered buried in the walls of the church in the 19th century, where the medieval masons had used them as ordinary building stones. The six main figures, all created by the same hand, are flanked on the left by a sheila-na-gig, which is probably contemporary with the church, and flanked on the right by a scowling stone face. The age and interpretation of these figures has been the subject of much debate; it has been suggested that the two central pairs, of equal height, were pillars that once supported a pulpit, and that they represent either saints or aspects of the life of Christ.

The first figure is holding a book (Christ as Evangelist?) and the second holds a bishop's crozier and bell (Christ as Bishop?). The third has been identified as the young King David, author of the Psalms. The fourth is holding the necks of two griffins (symbols of Christ's dual nature as both human and divine?). The fifth bears a sword and shield (Christ's Second Coming?) and the sixth is unfinished.

A **ferry** (6862 1892; per person £4; 11am-6pm da Jul & Aug, to 5pm Sat & Sun Apr-Jun & Sep) crosses to th island hourly, on the hour (except for 1pm from the marina in Castle Archdale Countr Park; buy your ticket from the Billieve Boa Hire office. The crossing takes 15 minutes, and allows you around half an hour on the island

Boa Island

Boa Island, at the northern end of Lowe Lough Erne, is connected to the mainland a both ends – the main A47 road runs along it length. Spooky, moss-grown Caldragh grave yard, towards the western end of the island contains the famous **Janus Stone**. Perhaps 200 years old, this pagan figure is carved with tw grotesque human heads, back to back. Nearb is a smaller figure called the **Lusty Man**, brough here from Lusty More island. Their origin and meaning have been lost to the mists of time.

There's a small sign indicating the grave-yard about 1.5km from the bridge at the west-ern tip of the island.

SLEEPING & EATING

Lusty Beg Island (6863 3300; www.lustybegisland.com; Boa Island, Kesh; s/d £70/100; P   ) This private island retreat, reached by ferry (on demand from 8.30am to 11pm) from a jetty halfway along Boa Island, has self-catering chalets that sleep four to six people (£485 to £795 per week in July and August) but also offers B&B in its rustic 37-room Courtyard Motel. There's a tennis court, nature trail and canoeing on the lough for guests.

Lusty Beg's informal **Island Restaurant** (6863 1342; mains £9-17; 1-9pm Jul & Aug) is open to all, and serves everything from burgers and lasagne to beef Wellington and salmon en croute. Booking is necessary; you can summon the ferry from a telephone in the block-house on the slipway.

Castle Caldwell Forest Park

Castle Caldwell, built between 1610 and 1619, is nothing but a ruin, but the **park** (admission free; 24hr), about halfway between Boa Island and Belleek, has a nature reserve full of bird life, and is a major breeding ground for the common scoter.

At the entrance to the park is the **Fiddle Stone** (in the shape of a fiddle). The inscription, now too worn to read, once commemorated a favourite musician who fell out of a boat while drunk:

On firm land only exercise your skill;
there you may play and safely drink
your fill. To the memory of Denis Mc-
Cabe, Fiddler, who fell out of the St
Patrick Barge belonging to Sir James
Caldwell Bart. and Count of Milan and
was drowned off this point August ye
13 1770.

Belleek
pop 550

Belleek's (Beal Leice) village street of colourful, flower-bedecked houses slopes up from a
bridge across the River Erne, where it flows
out of the Lower Lough towards Ballyshannon
and the sea. The village is right on the border – the road south across the bridge passes
through a finger of the Republic's territory for
about 200m before leaving again – and shops
accept both pounds sterling and euros.

The imposing Georgian-style building
beside the bridge houses the world-famous
Belleek Pottery (☎ 6865 9300; www.belleek.ie; Main
St; ⏰ 9am-6pm Mon-Fri, 10am-6pm Sat, noon-6pm Sun
Jul-Oct, 9am-5.30pm Mon-Fri & 10am-5.30pm Sat Mar-Jun,
Nov & Dec, 9am-5.30pm Mon-Fri Jan & Feb), founded in
1857 to provide local employment in the wake
of the Potato Famine. It has been producing
fine Parian china ever since, and is especially
noted for its delicate basketware. The visitor
centre houses a small museum, showroom
and restaurant, and there are **guided tours**
(adult/child £4/free) of the pottery every half-hour
from 9.30am to 12.15pm and 1.45pm to 4pm
(till 3pm on Friday) Monday to Friday year
round.

SLEEPING & EATING

Moohan's Fiddlestone (☎ 6665 8008; 15-17 Main St; s/d from
£35/60; P) This is a traditional Irish pub offering B&B in five rooms with private bathrooms
upstairs. The lively bar downstairs is a popular
venue for impromptu music sessions, so don't
expect peace and quiet in the evenings.

Best Western Hotel Carlton (☎ 6865 8282; www.hotel
carlton.co.uk; Main St; s/d from £60/90; P 🛜) Though
the rooms are plush and luxurious, the family-
friendly Carlton has a welcoming and informal feel to it, and a lovely setting on the
banks of the River Erne. There are frequent
live music sessions in the hotel's Potters Bar.

Thatch Coffee Shop (☎ 6865 8181; 20 Main St; mains
£3-7; ⏰ 9am-5pm Mon-Sat) This cute little thatched
cottage may be Belleek's oldest building (late
18th century), but it serves a thoroughly mod-

ern cup of coffee, a delicious smoked-salmon
toastie, and excellent homemade cakes and
scones.

Black Cat Cove (☎ 6865 8942; 28 Main St; mains £7-
10; ⏰ noon-9pm) This friendly, family-run pub
with antique furniture and an open fire serves
good bar meals. It also has music on Tuesday,
Wednesday and Thursday nights from May
to September.

Lough Navar Forest Park

This **forest park** (car £3; ⏰ 10am-dusk) lies at the
western end of Lower Lough Erne, where the
Cliffs of Magho – a 250m-high and 9km-long
limestone escarpment – rise above a fringe of
native woodland on the south shore. An 11km
scenic drive through the park leads to the
Magho Viewpoint. The panorama from the cliff
top here is one of the finest in Ireland, especially
before sunset: it looks out over the shimmering
expanse of lough and river to the Blue Stack
Mountains, the sparkling waters of Donegal
Bay and the sea cliffs of Slieve League.

The hiking trail from the lough shore to the
Magho Viewpoint has been blocked by a land-
slide, but you can get there by car or bike. The
vehicle entrance to Lough Navar Forest Park
is on the minor Glennasheevar road between
Garrison and Derrygonnelly, 20km southeast
of Belleek (take the B52 towards Garrison, and
fork left after 2.5km).

Activities
FISHING

The lakes of Fermanagh are renowned for
both coarse and game fishing. The Lough Erne
trout-fishing season runs from the beginning
of March to the end of September. Salmon
fishing begins in June and also continues to the
end of September. The mayfly season usually
lasts a month from the second week in May.
There's no closed season for coarse fish.

You'll need both a licence (issued by the
Fisheries Conservancy Board) and a permit
(from the owner of the fishery). Licences and
permits can be purchased from the tourist
information centre (p679) and Home, Field &
Stream (p682), both in Enniskillen, and from
the marina in Castle Archdale Country Park
(p685), which also hires out fishing rods. A
combined licence and permit for game fishing on Lough Erne costs £8.50/24 for three/14
days.

The **Belleek Angling Centre** in the Thatch Coffee
Shop (left) in Belleek sells fishing tackle and can

arrange boat hire for anglers, and you can get expert instruction in fly-casting from **Michael Shortt** (☎ 6638 8184; fish.teach@virgin.net).

Enniskillen's tourist information centre also provides a free guide to angling in Fermanagh and South Tyrone, which has full details of lakes and rivers, fish species, seasons and permit requirements.

BOAT HIRE

A number of companies hire out day boats at Enniskillen, Killadeas and Castle Archdale Country Park. Rates range from about £10 to £15 per hour for an open rowing boat with outboard motor to £60/90 per half-/full-day for a six-seater with cabin and engine. The tourist information centre in Enniskillen has a full list of companies and costs.

CANOEING

The **Lough Erne Canoe Trail** (www.canoeni.com) highlights the attractions along the 50km of lough and river between Belleek and Belturbet. The wide open expanses of the Lower Lough can build up big waves in a strong breeze and are best left to experts, but the sheltered backwaters of the Upper Lough are ideal for beginners and families.

You can pick up a map and guide (£1.50) showing public access points, camping sites and other facilities along the trail from the tourist information office in Enniskillen (p679). Canoe hire is available from the Lakeland Canoe Centre (p679), also in Enniskillen, and Ultimate Watersports (below).

WATERSPORTS

Working out of Castle Archdale marina and Lusty Beg island, **Ultimate Watersports** (☎ 07808 736818, 07863 344172; www.ultimatewatersports.co.uk) offers equipment hire and instruction in waterskiing, wakeboarding, jet-skiing, canoeing, dinghy sailing and power-boating.

Getting There & Away

On the eastern side of the lough, Ulsterbus service 194 from Enniskillen to Pettigo via Irvinestown (four or five daily Monday to Saturday) stops near Castle Archdale Country Park (35 minutes) and Kesh (one hour). In July and August only, bus 99 goes from Enniskillen to Belleek (£4, 45 minutes, four daily Monday to Friday, three on Saturday, one on Sunday) along the western shoreline via Blaney, Tully

Castle and the Cliffs of Magho car park, terminating at Bundoran.

Bus 64 travels from Enniskillen to Belcoo (£2, 25 minutes, seven or eight daily Monday to Friday, three on Saturdays, one on Sundays); the Sunday bus and two of the Thursday buses continue to Garrison, Belleek and Bundoran.

WEST OF LOUGH ERNE
Florence Court

Part of the motivation for the first Earl of Belmore to build Castle Coole (near Enniskillen) was to keep up with the Joneses – in the 1770s his aristocratic neighbour William Willoughby Cole, the first Earl of Enniskillen, had overseen the addition of grand Palladian wings to the beautiful, baroque country house called Florence Court, named after his Cornish grandmother Florence Wrey.

Set in lovely wooded grounds in the shadow of Cuilcagh Mountain, and not to be confused with the nearby, single-worded village of Florencecourt, **Florence Court** (☎ 6634 8249; Swanlinbar Rd, Florencecourt; house tour adult/child £5/2, grounds £2.50/1; ⏰ noon-6pm daily Jul & Aug, 1-6pm Wed-Mon Jun, 1-6pm daily early Sep, 1-6pm Sat, Sun & public hols Mar-May & late Sep-Oct) is famous for its rococo plasterwork and antique Irish furniture. The house was badly damaged by fire in 1955 and much of what you see on the one-hour guided tour is the result of meticulous restoration, but the magnificent plasterwork on the ceiling of the dining room is original.

Florence Court feels more homely and lived-in than the rather cold and austere Castle Coole, especially since the family belongings of the sixth earl were returned. (The earl had a falling out with the National Trust in 1974 and stomped off to Scotland with all his stuff; it was returned after the death of his widow in 1998.) The library, in particular, feels as if the last earl has just nipped out for a stroll and could return at any minute.

In the **grounds** (⏰ 10am-8pm Apr-Oct, to 6pm late Feb-Apr, to 4pm Oct-early Feb) you can explore the walled garden and, on the edge of Cottage Wood, southeast of the house, admire an ancient Irish yew tree. It's said that every Irish yew around the world is descended from this one.

The house is 12km southwest of Enniskillen. Take the A4 Sligo road and fork left onto the A32 to Swanlinbar. Ulsterbus service 192 from Enniskillen to Swanlinbar can drop you at Creamery Cross, about 2km from the house.

CRUISING HOLIDAYS ON LOUGH ERNE

If you fancy exploring Lough Erne as captain of your own motor cruiser, well, you can – and without any previous experience or qualification. Several companies in Fermanagh hire out self-drive, live-aboard cabin cruisers by the week, offering a crash course (not literally, you hope) in boat-handling and navigation at the start of your holiday. Weekly rates in high season (July and August) range from about £800 for a two-berth to £1300 for a four-berth and £1800 for an eight-berth boat. Low- and mid-season rates are around 70% to 90% of the high-season rates.

The main cruiser hire companies in Fermanagh are:

Aghinver Boat Company (☎ 6863 1400; www.abcboats.com; Lisnarick, Lower Lough Erne)

Carrick Craft (☎ 3834 4993; www.cruise-ireland.com; Tully Bay, Lower Lough Erne)

Carrybridge Boat Company (☎ 6638 7034; Carrybridge, Lisbellaw, Upper Lough Erne)

Corraquill Cruising Holidays (☎ 6774 8712; www.corraquill.co.uk; Drumetta, Aghalane, Derrylin, Upper Lough Erne)

Manor House Marine (☎ 6862 8100; www.manormarine.com; Killadeas, Lower Lough Erne)

Marble Arch Caves

To the south of Lower Lough Erne lies a limestone plateau, where Fermanagh's abundant rainwater has carved out a network of subterranean caverns. The largest of these are the **Marble Arch Caves** (☎ 6634 8855; www.marblearchcaves.net; Marlbank Scenic Loop, Florencecourt; adult/child £8/5; ⏰ 10am-5pm Jul & Aug, to 4.30pm Easter-Jun & Sep), first explored by the French caving pioneer Edouard Martel in 1895, but not opened to the public until 1985.

The 1¼-hour tour of the caves begins with a short boat trip along the peaty, foam-flecked waters of the underground River Cladagh to Junction Jetty, where three subterranean streams – the Owenbrean, the Aghinrawn and the Sluh Croppa, which drain the northern slopes of Cuilcagh Mountain – meet up. You then continue on foot past the Grand Gallery and Pool Chamber, regaled all the time with food-related jokes from your guide. An artificial tunnel leads into the New Chamber (pioneering cave explorers originally wriggled through a natural tunnel high above here), from which the route follows the underground Owenbrean River, through the Moses Walk (a walled pathway sunk waist-deep into the river) to the Calcite Cradle, where the most picturesque formations are to be found. The caves are very popular, so it's wise to phone ahead and book a tour, especially if you're in a group of four or more. (The listed closing time is the starting time of the last tour.)

The caves take their name from a natural limestone arch that spans the River Cladagh where it emerges from the caves; you can reach it via a short walk along a signposted footpath from the visitor centre.

Unexpected serious flooding of the caves in the 1990s was found to have been caused by mechanised peat-cutting in the blanket bog – one of Ireland's biggest – on the slopes of Cuilcagh Mountain, whose rivers feed the caves. **Cuilcagh Mountain Park** (www.cuilcaghmountainpark.com) was then established to restore and preserve the bog environment, and in 2001 the entire area was designated a Unesco Geopark. The park's geology and ecology are explained in the caves' visitor centre.

The Marble Arch Caves are 16km southwest of Enniskillen, and some 4km from Florence Court (an hour's walk), reached via the A4 Sligo road and the A32.

Loughs Melvin & Macnean

Lough Melvin and Lough Macnean are situated along the border with the Republic, on the B52 road from Belcoo to Belleek. Lough Melvin is famous for its salmon and trout fishing, and is home to two unusual trout species – the sonaghan, with its distinctive black spots, and the crimson-spotted gillaroo – that are unique to the lough, as well as brown trout, ferox trout and char.

Corralea Activity Centre (☎ 6638 6123; www.activityireland.com; Belcoo), based on Upper Lough Macnean, hires out bicycles (half-/full-day £10/15) and two-person canoes (half-/full-day £15/20). It also offers instruction in activities such as caving, canoeing, climbing, windsurfing and archery from £22 per day.

The lakeside **Lough Melvin Holiday Centre** (☎ 6865 8142; www.melvinholidaycentre.com; Garrison; tent sites £12, caravan sites £20, dm £20) offers caving, canoeing, walking and fishing holidays, and also has a campsite, dorm accommodation, rooms with private bathrooms and a restaurant and coffee shop.

The **Customs House Country Inn** (☎ 6638 6285; www.customshouseinn.com; Main St, Belcoo; s/d from £60/80; mains £9-15; P 🛜) is a welcoming pub decked out in acres of waxed oak and pine, with a cosy, candlelit restaurant and nine bedrooms with en suite bathrooms, many with good views of Lough Macnean.

There is also gourmet dining a few hundred metres across the border in Blacklion, County Cavan (p561).

COUNTY TYRONE

OMAGH
pop 20,000

Situated at the confluence of the Rivers Camowen and Drumragh, which join to form the River Strule, Omagh is a busy market town that serves as a useful base for exploring the surrounding area by car.

Sadly, for a long time to come, Omagh (An Óghmagh) will be remembered for the devastating 1988 car bomb that killed 29 people and injured 200. Planted by the breakaway group Real IRA, the bomb was the worst single atrocity in the 30-year history of the Troubles. A memorial garden on Drumragh Avenue, 200m east of the bus station, remembers the dead.

The **tourist information centre** (☎ 8224 7831; info@omagh.gov.uk; Strule Arts Centre, Town Hall Sq, Bridge St; 🕓 10am-5.45pm Mon-Sat) is in the new arts centre, just across the river from the bus station. It has a Town Trail leaflet that guides you around Omagh's remaining historic buildings.

Sleeping & Eating
Omagh Independent Hostel (☎ 8224 1973; www.omagh hostel.co.uk; 9a Waterworks Rd; dm/tw from £12.50/30, 2-person tent sites £20; 🕓 Mar-Oct; P 🖳) This peaceful, family-friendly and ecofriendly hostel is 4km northeast of town, tucked away on a back road off the B48 to Gortin. The lovely, rural setting is awash with flowers in summer; if you prefer, you can pitch a tent outside. If you ring from the bus station someone will come and pick you up.

ourpick Mullaghmore House (☎ 8224 2314; www .mullaghmorehouse.com; Old Mountfield Rd; s/d £42/78; P 🖳 🛜) Offering affordable country-house luxury, this beautifully restored Georgian villa boasts a gleaming mahogany-panelled library, billiards room and marble-lined steam room.

The bedrooms have period cast-iron fireplaces and antique furniture, and the owners run courses on antique restoration and traditional crafts. It's 1.5km northeast of the town centre.

Riverfront Coffee Shop (☎ 8225 0011; 38 Market St; sandwiches £3-5; 🕓 9am-5.30pm Mon-Sat) This lively little eatery serves up excellent coffee, cakes, quiche, homemade soup, and choose-your-own sandwiches on baguettes, panini or ciabatta rolls, and also provides vegetarian, coeliac-friendly and low-carb options.

Grant's of Omagh (☎ 8225 0900; 29 George's St; mains £8-16; 🕓 4-10pm Mon-Fri, 3-10.30pm Sat, noon-10pm Sun) Grant's – as in US president Ulysses S Grant – bathes in a golden glow of Irish emigrant nostalgia, from the fiddle and bodhrán on the wall above the smoke-blackened fireplace in the front bar to the American-themed restaurant in the back, with a menu that ranges from steak, burgers and lasagne to Cajun chicken and spicy enchiladas.

Getting There & Away
The bus station is on Mountjoy Rd, just north of the town centre along Bridge St.

Goldline Express bus 273 goes from Belfast to Omagh (£10, 1¾ hours, hourly Monday to Saturday, six on Sundays) via Dungannon and on to Derry (£8, 1¼ hours). Bus 94 goes to Enniskillen (£7, one hour, six or seven daily Monday to Friday, three on Saturdays, one on Sundays) where you can change for Donegal, Bundoran or Sligo. Goldline Express bus 274 runs from Derry to Omagh (£8, one hour, every two hours), and continues to Dublin (£13, three hours) via Monaghan.

AROUND OMAGH
Ulster American Folk Park
In the 18th and 19th centuries thousands of Ulster people left their homes to forge a new life across the Atlantic; 200,000 emigrated in the 18th century alone. Their story is told here at one of Ireland's best museums, the **Ulster American Folk Park** (☎ 8224 3292; www.folkpark.com; Mellon Rd; adult/child £4.90/2.90; 🕓 10.30am-6pm Mon-Sat, 11am-6.30pm Sun & public holidays Apr-Sep, 10.30am-5pm Mon-Fri Oct-Mar). Last admission is 1½ hours before closing.

The Exhibition Hall explains the close connections between Ulster and the USA – the American Declaration of Independence was signed by several Ulstermen – and includes a genuine Calistoga wagon. But the real appeal of the folk park is the outdoor museum, where

WALK: CUILCAGH MOUNTAIN VIA THE LEGNABROCKY TRAIL

Rising above Marble Arch and Florence Court like a miniature Mount Roraima, Cuilcagh (*cull*-kay) Mountain (666m) is the highest point in Counties Fermanagh and Cavan, its summit right on the border between Northern Ireland and the Republic.

The mountain is a geological layer cake, with a cave-riddled limestone base, shale and sandstone flanks draped with a shaggy tweed skirt of blanket bog, and a high gritstone plateau ringed by steep, craggy slopes, all part of the **Marble Arch Caves European Geopark** (www.europeangeoparks.org).

Hidden among the sphagnum moss, bog cotton and heather of the blanket bog, you can find the sticky-fingered sundew, an insect-eating plant, while the crags echo to the 'krok-krok-krok' of ravens and the mewing of peregrine falcons. The otherworldly summit plateau, strewn with boulders and riven by deep fissures in the gritstone bedrock, is a breeding ground for golden plover and is rich in rare plants such as alpine clubmoss.

The hike to the summit is a 15km round trip (allow five or six hours); the first part is on an easy gravel track, but you'll need good boots to negotiate the boggy ground and steep slopes further on. Start at the Cuilcagh Mountain Park car park, 300m west of the entrance to Marble Arch Caves visitor centre (grid reference 121335; you'll need the Ordnance Survey 1:50,000 Discovery series map, sheet 26). Right next to the car park is the Monastir sink hole, a deep depression ringed by limestone cliffs where the Aghinrawn River disappears underground for its journey through the Marble Arch Caves system. (Note that the OS map has wrongly labelled this river the Owenbrean.)

Climb the stile beside the gate and set out along the Legnabrocky Trail, a 4WD track that winds through rich green limestone meadows before climbing across the blanket bog on a 'floating' bed of gravel and geotextiles – boardwalks off to one side offer a closer look at bog regeneration areas. The gravel track comes to an end at a gate about 4.5km from the start. From here you follow a line of waymarked wooden posts, squelching your way across spongy bog (don't stray from the route – there are deep bog holes where you can get stuck) before climbing steeply up to the summit ridge, with great views west to the crags above little Lough Atona. The waymarkers come to an end here, so you're on your own for the final kilometre across the plateau, aiming for the prominent cairn on the summit (a map and compass are essential in poor visibility).

The summit cairn is actually a Neolithic burial chamber; about 100m south of the summit you will find two rings of boulders, the foundations of prehistoric huts. On a clear day the view extends from the Blue Stack Mountains of Donegal to Croagh Patrick, and from the Atlantic Ocean to the Irish Sea. Return the way you came.

---

the 'living history' exhibits are split into Old World and New World areas, cleverly linked by passing through a mock-up of an emigrant ship. Original buildings from various parts of Ulster have been dismantled and re-erected here, including a blacksmith's forge, a weaver's thatched cottage, a Presbyterian meeting house and a schoolhouse. In the 'American' section of the park you can visit a genuine 18th-century settler's stone cottage and a log house, both shipped across the Atlantic from Pennsylvania.

Costumed guides and artisans are on hand to explain the arts of spinning, weaving, candlemaking and so on, and various events are held throughout the year, including reenactments of American Civil War battles, a festival of traditional Irish music in May, American Independence Day celebrations in July, and the Appalachian and Bluegrass Music Festival

in September. There's almost too much to absorb in one visit and at least half a day is needed to do the place justice.

The park is 8km northwest of Omagh on the A5. Goldliner bus 273 from Belfast to Derry (hourly Monday to Saturday, five on Sunday) stops in Omagh, and will stop on request at the park gates.

SPERRIN MOUNTAINS

When representatives of the London guilds visited Ulster in 1609 the Lord Deputy of Ireland made sure they were kept well away from the Sperrin Mountains, fearing that the sight of these bleak, moorland hills would put them off the idea of planting settlers here. And when it rains there's no denying that the Sperrins can be dismal, but on a sunny spring day, when the russet bogs and yellow gorse stand out against a clear blue sky, they can offer some grand

> **TOP FIVE TRADITIONAL PUBS IN NORTHERN IRELAND**
>
> - Bittle's Bar (p593)
> - Blake's of the Hollow (p682)
> - Grace Neill's (p608)
> - Dufferin Arms (p613)
> - Peadar O'Donnell's (p645)

walking. The area is also dotted with thousands of standing stones and prehistoric tombs.

The main ridge of the Sperrins stretches for 30km along the border with County Derry. The highest summit is Mt Sawel (678m), rising above the B47 road from Plumbridge to Draperstown, a right little roller-coaster of a road that undulates across the southern slopes of the Sperrins. Halfway along it you'll find the **Sperrin Heritage Centre** (☎ 8164 8142; 274 Glenelly Rd, Cranagh; adult/child £2.70/1.65; ⏰ 11.30am-5.30pm Mon-Fri, to 6pm Sat, 2-6pm Sun Easter-Oct) which offers an insight into the culture, natural history and geology of the region. Gold has been found in the Sperrins, and for a bit extra (adult/child 85/45p) you can try your luck at panning for gold in a nearby stream. (At the time of research there was some doubt over the centre's future – call ahead to make sure it's open.)

If you're thinking of walking up Mt Sawel, enquire at the Sperrin Heritage Centre about the best route. The climb is easy enough in good weather, but some farmers are not as accommodating as others about hikers crossing their land.

Gortin

The village of Gortin, about 15km north of Omagh, lies at the foot of Mullaghcarn (542m), the southernmost of the Sperrin summits (unfortunately capped by two prominent radio masts). Hundreds of hikers converge for a mass ascent of the hill on **Cairn Sunday** (the last Sunday in July), a revival of an ancient pilgrimage that first petered out in the 19th century. There are several good walks around the village, and a scenic drive to **Gortin Lakes**, with views north to the main Sperrin ridge.

A few kilometres south of Gortin, towards Omagh, is **Gortin Glen Forest Park** (☎ 8167 0666; Gortin Rd; car/pedestrian £3/1; ⏰ 10am-dusk), whose dense conifer woodland is home to a herd of Japanese sika deer. An 8km scenic drive

offers the chance to enjoy the views without breaking into a sweat.

There is hostel accommodation at the **Gortin Accommodation Suite** (☎ 8164 8346; www.gortin.net; 62 Main St; dm/f £10/50), a modern outdoor activity centre in the middle of Gortin village; it also has family rooms with one double and two single beds and en suite bathrooms.

Creggan

About halfway along the A505 between Omagh and Cookstown (20km east of Omagh) is **An Creagán Visitor Centre** (☎ 8076 1112; www.an-creagan .com; Creggan; admission free; ⏰ 11am-6.30pm Apr-Sep, to 4.30pm Oct-Mar), with an exhibition covering the ecology of the surrounding bogs and the archaeology of the region. There's also a restaurant and gift shop.

There are 44 prehistoric monuments within 8km of the centre, including the **Beaghmore Stone Circles**. What this site lacks in stature – the stones are all less than 1m tall – it makes up for in complexity, with seven stone circles (one filled with smaller stones, nicknamed 'dragon's teeth') and a dozen or so alignments and cairns. The stones are signposted about 8km east of Creggan, and 4km north of the A505.

Getting Around

Ulsterbus service 403, the *Sperrin Rambler*, runs twice daily Monday to Saturday between Omagh and Magherafelt, stopping at Gortin, the Sperrin Heritage Centre and Draperstown (in County Derry). The morning bus leaves Omagh at 10.05am, arriving at the Sperrin Heritage Centre at 11am; the return bus leaves the centre at 2.40pm.

COOKSTOWN & AROUND

Cookstown boasts the longest (2km) and widest (40m) street in Ireland, the legacy of an over-ambitious 18th-century town planner, but apart from that there's not much to see in town. The main sights here are in the surrounding countryside.

The **tourist information centre** (☎ 8676 9949; www .cookstown.gov.uk; Burn Rd, Cookstown; ⏰ 9am-5pm Mon-Sat, plus 2-4pm Sun Jul & Aug) is in the Burnavon Arts and Cultural Centre, west of the main street.

Wellbrook Beetling Mill

Beetling, the final stage of linen making, involves pounding the cloth with wooden hammers, or beetles, to give it a smooth sheen. Restored to working order by the National

Trust, the 18th-century **Wellbrook Beetling Mill** (☎ 8674 8210; 20 Wellbrook Rd, Corkhill; adult/child £4/2.30; ☺ 2-6pm Sat-Thu Jul & Aug, 2-6pm Sat, Sun & public hols mid-Mar–Jun & Sep, closed Oct–mid-March) still has its original machinery, and stages demonstrations of the linen-making process led by guides in period costume. The mill is on a pretty stretch of the Ballinderry River, 7km west of Cookstown, just off the A505 Omagh road.

Ardboe High Cross

A 6th-century monastic site overlooking Lough Neagh is home to one of Ireland's best-preserved and most elaborately decorated Celtic stone crosses. The 10th-century **Ardboe high cross** stands 5.5m tall, with 22 carved panels depicting biblical scenes. The western side (facing the road) has New Testament scenes: (from the bottom up) the Adoration of the Magi; the Miracle at Cana; the miracle of the loaves and fishes; Christ's entry into Jerusalem; the arrest (or mocking) of Christ; and, at the intersection of the cross, the Crucifixion.

The more weathered eastern face (towards the lough) shows Old Testament scenes: Adam and Eve; the Sacrifice of Isaac; Daniel in the Lions' Den; the Three Hebrews in the Fiery Furnace. The panels above may show the Last Judgement, and/or Christ in Glory. There are further scenes on the narrow north and south faces of the shaft.

Ardboe is 16km east of Cookstown. Take the B73 through Coagh and ignore the first (white) road sign for Ardboe. Keep straight on until you find the brown sign (on the right) for Ardboe High Cross.

Sleeping & Eating

Drum Manor Forest Park (☎ 8676 2774; Drum Rd, Oaklands; tent & caravan sites £9.50-11) This is a pleasant site 4km west of Cookstown on the A505, with lakes, forest trails, a butterfly farm and an arboretum.

Avondale B&B (☎ 8676 4013; www.avondalebb.co.uk; 31 Killycolp Rd; r per person £30; P ☎) Set in a spacious Edwardian house with a large garden, patio and sun lounge, Avondale offers B&B in two family rooms (one double and one single bed in each), each with private bathroom. It's 3km south of Cookstown, just off the A29 Dungannon road.

ourpick Tullylagan Country House (☎ 8676 5100; www.tullylagan.com; 40b Tullylagan Rd; s/d £65/95; P ☎) Set amid beautiful riverside gardens 4km south of Cookstown (just off the A29), the ivy-clad Tullylagan goes for the Victorian country manor feel, with shabby-chic sofas, gilt-framed mirrors on deep red walls, and marble-effect bathrooms with period taps. The restaurant (mains £14 to £23; open for lunch daily and for dinner Monday to Saturday) specialises in locally produced seafood, game and beef.

Getting There & Away

The bus station is on Molesworth St, east of the main street. Bus 210 connects Cookstown with Belfast's Europa BusCentre (£8, 1¾ hours, four daily Saturday, two Sunday to Friday). Bus 80 shuttles between Cookstown and Dungannon (£3, 45 minutes, hourly Monday to Friday, eight Saturday).

DUNGANNON & AROUND

Dungannon is a pleasant enough market town halfway between Cookstown and Armagh, worth a brief stop in passing if you want to do a spot of shopping.

Killymaddy Tourist Information Centre (☎ 8776 7259; www.flavouroftyrone.com; 190 Ballygawley Rd; ☺ 9am-5pm Mon-Fri, 10am-4pm Sat & Sun) is at a caravan site 10km west of Dungannon on the A4 road towards Enniskillen.

Tyrone Crystal

Ireland's first crystal factory was established in Dungannon in 1771 by Benjamin Edwards from Bristol. It closed down in 1870, but Tyrone's crystal industry was revived in 1968 by a local priest, Father Austin Eustace, who raised funding to establish a new factory to help relieve local unemployment.

Today, **Tyrone Crystal** (☎ 8772 5335; www.tyrone crystal.com; Coalisland Rd, Killybrackey; tours adult/child £5/free; ☺ 9am-5pm Mon-Sat) continues to produce high-quality lead crystal. The factory offers guided tours (11am, noon and 2pm weekdays only) of the manufacturing process, from the furnace where molten glass is prepared, through hand-blowing and moulding, to cutting and polishing. Admission to the showroom is free, and the tour price is reimbursed if you buy something.

The factory is 2.5km northeast of Dungannon on the A45 towards Coalisland – it's clearly signposted. Bus 80 to Cookstown stops nearby.

Linen Green

Housed in the former Moygashel Linen Mills, the **Linen Green** (☎ 8775 3761; Moygashel; ☺ 10am-5pm Mon-Sat) complex includes a range of designer shops and factory outlets, plus a visitor centre with an exhibition covering the history of the local linen industry. It's a good place to shop for bargain men's and women's fashion, shoes, accessories and linen goods or to stop for lunch at the Deli on the Green (see right).

Donaghmore High Cross

The village of Donaghmore, 8km northwest of Dungannon on the B43 road to Pomeroy, is famed for its 10th-century Celtic high cross. It was cobbled together from two different crosses in the 18th century (note the obvious join halfway up the shaft) and now stands outside the churchyard. The carved biblical scenes are similar to those on the Ardboe cross (see p693). The nearby **heritage centre** (☎ 8776 7039; Pomeroy Rd; admission free; ☷ 9am-5pm Mon-Fri) is based in a converted 19th-century school.

Grant Ancestral Homestead

Ulysses Simpson Grant (1822–85) led Union forces to victory in the American Civil War and later served as the USA's 18th president for two terms, from 1869 to 1877. His maternal grandfather, John Simpson, emigrated from County Tyrone to Pennsylvania in 1760, but the farm he left behind at Dergina has now been restored in the style of a typical Ulster smallholding, as it would have been during the time of Grant's presidency.

The furnishings in the **Grant Ancestral Homestead** (Dergina, Ballygawley; admission free; ☷ 9am-5pm Mon-Sat) are not authentic, but the original field plan of the farm survives together with various old farming implements. There's also an exhibition on the American Civil War, a picnic area and children's playground. Confirm opening times by calling the Killymaddy tourist information centre (p693).

The site is 20km west of Dungannon, south of the A4; look out for the signpost 5.5km west of Killymaddy tourist information centre.

Sleeping & Eating

Dungannon Park (☎ 8772 8690; dpreception@dungannon .gov.uk; Moy Rd; tent/caravan sites £8/12; ☷ Mar-Oct) This small (20 pitches) council-run campsite is in a quiet, wooded location complete with its own trout-fishing lake, 2.5km south of Dungannon on the A29 towards Moy and Armagh.

Grange Lodge (☎ 8778 4212; www.grangelodge countryhouse.com; 7 Grange Rd; s/d from £65/89; ℗ ☏)

The five-room Grange is a period gem se in its own 20-acre grounds. Parts of the house, which is packed with antiques, dat from 1698, though most are Georgian with Victorian additions. The landlady is an award-winning chef, and the Grange runs cookery courses. A four-course dinner (£35 is available (except Sundays) as long as you book at least 48 hours in advance. It's 5km southeast of Dungannon, signposted off the A29 Moy road.

our pick Deli on the Green (☎ 8775 1775; 2 Linen Green, Moygashel; mains £6-10; ☷ 10am-5pm Mon-Sat) Take a break from browsing the designer goodies in the Linen Green shops to relax over breakfast or lunch in this stylish little bistro. As well as the sandwiches and salads on offer at the deli counter, there are succulent homemade steakburgers and seared salmon fillet with champ (potatoes mashed with spring onions), while the breakfast menu includes organic porridge with cream, and pancakes with bacon and maple syrup.

Viscounts Restaurant (☎ 8775 3800; 10 Northland Row, Dungannon; mains £9-15; ☷ noon-9.30pm) Set in a converted church, child-friendly Viscounts offers carvery lunches, snacks and á la carte dinners. You can feast on steaks, pasta, stir-fries and vegetarian dishes in a mock medieval setting of knights' armour, swords and jousting banners. Booking is advisable at weekends.

Getting There & Away

Dungannon's bus station is just southwest of the town centre; turn right, cross the bridge and follow Scotch St to reach the main square. Bus 261 runs from Belfast's Europa BusCentre to Dungannon (£8, one hour, hourly Monday to Saturday, four on Sundays) and continues to Enniskillen (£8, 1½ hours). Bus 273 travels from Belfast to Derry via Dungannon (£8, one hour, hourly Monday to Saturday, five on Sundays) and Omagh .

Bus 80 shuttles between Cookstown and Dungannon (£3, 45 minutes, hourly Monday to Friday, eight on Saturdays). Bus 278 runs from Coleraine (County Derry) to Dungannon (£8, 1½ hours, two a day Monday to Friday, one daily on Saturdays and Sundays) and continues to Armagh (£4, 30 minutes), Monaghan and Dublin.

Directory

CONTENTS

> **BOOK ACCOMMODATION ONLINE**
>
> For more accommodation reviews and recommendations by Lonely Planet authors, check out the online booking service at www.lonelyplanet.com. You'll find the true, insider lowdown on the best places to stay on the island. Reviews are thorough and independent. Best of all, you can book online.

ACCOMMODATION

Sleeping entries listed in this book are categorised by the price of a double room and then ordered by budget. Our favourites are selected because they have a little something – or in some cases, a lot of something – that makes a stay there that bit more memorable; we've also endeavoured, where possible, to highlight properties that walk the green walk and are committed to eco-responsibility (see also the GreenDex, p754).

Rates are per *room* per night, unless otherwise stated: budget (under €60/£40), mid-range (€60 to €150/£40 to £100) and top end (over €150/£100), and high-season rates are given throughout. Where a range of prices is given, it refers to rates for different rooms during high season. Prices are cheaper online and off-peak. Room prices in Dublin are disproportionately high and can be double what you would pay elsewhere in the country.

Caveat emptor: the global financial crisis has hit Irish tourism very hard and price structuring is not nearly as predictable as it was as recently as 2008. B&B rates have more or less remained steady since 2008 and many hoteliers – particularly at the upper end of the scale – are in a desperate struggle to stay alive. Consequently, they're doing the previously unthinkable in an effort to sell rooms, slashing rates dramatically and offering a plethora of incentive deals to get you into their hotels: free add-ons like dinners and spa treatments are increasingly standard, as are 'three nights for the price of two' offers.

Rack rates at the top hotels are no longer to be trusted and the standard prices quoted on the brochure or the website have become increasingly pie-in-the-sky – it's quite the norm these days to pay half the quoted rate in some of the country's top properties, particularly out of season. The key, however, is to ask: when making a booking, don't settle for the first rate quoted, and be sure to ask for a better deal. More often than not, you'll get one.

Generally speaking, the majority of accommodation providers will still raise their rates during 'special' weekends – bank holidays or during major sporting events and festivals – when tourist numbers are their highest and hoteliers can take a breather from worrying about empty rooms. Expect to be charged

DIRECTORY

PRACTICALITIES

- Ireland uses the metric system for weights, measures, speed limits and most signposting, except for the old-style black-on-white signs which still use miles (as does Northern Ireland).

- DVD players take Region 2 discs, as with the rest of Europe.

- Electrical appliances use a three flat-pin socket and a 220V/50Hz AC power supply.

- Get an insight into Irish life with one of the world's best newspapers, the *Irish Times*, or Ireland's biggest-selling *Irish Independent*.

- Relish Irish political satire in the fortnightly magazine *Phoenix*, or brush up on current affairs in *Magill* magazine.

- Check both sides of Northern Irish current affairs with Loyalist tabloid *News Letter* or the pro-Republican *Irish News*.

- TV addicts should tune into *Questions and Answers* (RTE 1), a hard-hitting current affairs program on Monday nights, or catch a great documentary on TG4, the national Irish-language station (subtitles available).

- Tune into RTE Radio One (88-90 FM or 252 kHz LW) for culture and politics; Today FM (100-102 FM) for pop, rock and alternative music; or Newstalk (106-108 FM) for music, chat and some current affairs.

---

anything up to 15% to 20% more than usual at these times.

In low season (November to March) you can simply drop in or ring ahead in rural areas. In peak season it's best to book ahead. Fáilte Ireland (Irish Tourist Board) or the Northern Ireland Tourist Board (NITB) will book serviced (€5 to €13 booking fee, depending on the size of your party) or self-catering accommodation (€7 booking fee) through their booking system, **Gulliver Ireland** (☎ 066-9792030; www.gulliver.ie).

Much of the accommodation closes during Christmas and New Year, especially in rural areas.

B&Bs

The ubiquitous bed and breakfasts are small, family-run houses, farmhouses and period country houses with fewer than five bedrooms. Standards vary enormously, but most have some bedrooms with private bathroom at a cost of roughly €35 to €40 (£20 to £25) per person per night. In luxurious B&Bs, expect to pay €55 (£38) or more per person. Facilities in budget-range B&Bs may be very limited; TVs, telephones, kettles and the like are the trappings of midrange to top-end establishments, while the hand-held credit card machine is increasingly common (although don't be surprised in remote rural areas if they insist on cash).

Camping & Caravan Parks

Camping and caravan parks aren't as common in Ireland as they are in Britain or on the continent. Some hostels have camping space for tents and also offer house facilities, which makes them better value than the main camping grounds. At commercial parks the cost is typically somewhere between €12 and €20 (£7 to £10) for a tent and two people. Prices for campsites in this book are for two people unless stated otherwise. Caravan sites cost around €15 to €25 (£11 to £15). Most parks are open only from Easter to the end of September or October.

Guesthouses

Essentially, guesthouses are much like upmarket B&Bs. The difference lies in their size, with guesthouses having between six and 30 bedrooms. Prices vary enormously according to the standard but the minimum you can expect to shell out is €35 (£22) per person (€40 in Dublin), and up to about €100 (£35) in upmarket places. Unlike hotels, the majority of guesthouses are unlicensed, but many have restaurants and good facilities, and can take credit-card payment.

Hostels

The prices quoted in this book for hostel accommodation are for those aged over 18. A

WEBSITE ACCOMMODATION RESOURCES

www.allgohere.com This website lists accommodation in Northern Ireland suitable for travellers with (and without) a disability.

www.corkkerry.ie A useful resource for accommodation and information throughout the southwest.

www.daft.ie Online classified paper for short- and long-term rentals.

www.discoverireland.ie Fáilte Ireland's main site, which has a database of various types of accommodation all over the Republic.

www.discovernorthernireland.com Northern Ireland Tourist Board's (NITB) accommodation booking site.

www.elegant.ie Specialises in self-catering castles, period houses and unique properties.

www.familyhomes.ie Lists (you guessed it) family-run guesthouses and self-catering properties.

www.gulliver.ie Fáilte Ireland and the NITB's web-based accommodation reservation system.

www.hostelworld.com A useful website for comparing hostels and booking beds.

www.irishlandmark.com Not-for-profit conservation group that rents self-catering properties of historical and cultural significance, such as castles, gate lodges and lighthouses.

www.stayinireland.com Lists guesthouses and self-catering options.

---

dorm bed in high season generally costs €13 to €25 (£8 to £14).

An Óige and Hostelling International Northern Ireland (HINI) are the two associations that belong to Hostelling International (HI). About half of the hostels have family and smaller rooms. An Óige has 23 hostels scattered around the Republic and HINI has six in the North.

An Óige (☎ 01-830 4555; www.anoige.ie; 61 Mountjoy St, Dublin; ☯ 9.30am-5.30pm Mon-Fri)

HINI (☎ 9032 4733; www.hini.org.uk; 22-32 Donegall Rd, Belfast; ☯ 24hr)

Ireland also has a large number of independent hostels, some excellent, but many high

---

SOMETHING DIFFERENT

An alternative to normal caravanning is to hire a horse-drawn caravan with which to wander the countryside. In high season you can hire one for around €800 a week. Search www .discoverireland.ie for a list of operators, or see www.irishhorsedrawncaravans.com.

Another unhurried and pleasurable way to see the countryside (with slightly less maintenance) is by barge on one of the country's canal systems. As above, contact Fáilte Ireland for a list of rental companies.

Another option is to hire a boat, which you can live aboard while cruising Ireland's inland waterways. One company offering boats for hire on the Shannon-Erne Waterway is **Emerald Star** (☎ 071-962 0234; www. emeraldstar.ie).

---

on character and low on facilities. The following associations, with hostels in the Republic and in the North, do their best to offer reliable accommodation:

Independent Holiday Hostels of Ireland (IHH; ☎ 01-836 4700; www.hostels-ireland.com; 57 Lower Gardiner St, Dublin 1)

Independent Hostel Owners of Ireland (IHO; ☎ 074-973 0130; www.independenthostelsireland; Dooey Hostel, Glencolumbcille, Co Donegal)

Hotels

Hotels range from the local pub to medieval castles, and prices fluctuate accordingly. In most cases, you'll get a better rate than the one published if you go online or negotiate directly with the hotel, especially out of season. The explosion of bland midrange chain hotels (many Irish-owned) has proved a major challenge to the traditional B&B or guesthouse: they mightn't have the same personalised service but their rooms are clean and their facilities generally quite good.

House Swapping

House swapping has become a popular and affordable way to visit a country and enjoy a real home away from home. There are several agencies in Ireland that, for an annual fee, facilitate international swaps. The fee pays for access to a website and a book giving house descriptions, photographs and the owner's details. After that, it's up to you to make arrangements. Use of the family car is sometimes included.

Homelink International House Exchange (☎ 01-846 2598; www.homelink.ie)

DIRECTORY

Intervac International Holiday Service (☎ 041-983 7969; www.intervac.com; Frank & Hillary Kelly, Drogheda, Co Dublin; ✆ 7-9.30pm Mon-Fri)

Rental Accommodation

Self-catering accommodation is often rented on a weekly basis and usually means an apartment or house where you look after yourself. The rates vary from one region and season to another. Fáilte Ireland publishes a guide for registered self-catering accommodation; you can check listings at their website www .discoverireland.ie.

ACTIVITIES

There are plenty of cheap and relaxing activities on offer in Ireland that provide a unique experience of the country. See also Ireland Outdoors, p669.

Birdwatching

The variety and size of the flocks that visit or breed in Ireland make it of particular interest to birdwatchers. It's also home to some rare and endangered species. For descriptions of some of the birds found in Ireland, see p73.

There are more than 70 reserves and sanctuaries in Ireland, but some aren't open to visitors and others are privately owned, so you'll need permission from the proprietors before entering.

More information on birdwatching can be obtained from the tourist boards and from the following organisations:

Birds of Ireland News Service (☎ 01-830 7364; www.birdsireland.com)

BirdWatch Ireland (☎ 01-281 9878; www.bird watchireland.ie) Runs birdwatching field courses, all of which take place on Cape Clear Island in County Cork.

National Parks & Wildlife Service (☎ 01-888 2000; www.npws.ie)

Royal Society for the Protection of Birds (RSPB; ☎ 9049 1547; www.rspb.org.uk; Belvoir Park Forest, Belfast)

Some useful publications on birdwatching are Dominic Couzens' *Collins Birds of Britain and Ireland* and the slightly out-of-date *Where to Watch Birds in Ireland* by Clive Hutchinson.

Cycling

The tourist boards can supply you with a list of operators who organise cycling holidays. For more on the practicalities of travelling around Ireland with a bike, see p718.

Both **Irish Cycling Safaris** (☎ 01-260 0749; www .cyclingsafaris.com; Belfield Bike Shop, UCD, Dublin) and **Go Ireland** (☎ 066-976 2094; www.goactivities.com; Old Orchard House, Killorglin, Co Kerry) organise tours for groups of cyclists in the southwest, the southeast, Connemara and Counties Clare, Donegal and Antrim.

Fishing

Ireland is justly famous for its (generally no-fee) coarse fishing, eg bream, pike, perch, roach, rudd, tench, carp and eel. The killing of pike over 6.6lb (3kg) in weight is prohibited, so anglers are limited to one pike; the killing of coarse fish is frowned upon and anglers are encouraged to return coarse fish to the water alive. Freshwater game fish available here include salmon, sea trout and brown trout. Some managed fisheries also stock rainbow trout.

The enormous Shannon and Erne river systems, stretching southwards from Leitrim and Fermanagh, are prime angling spots, and Cavan, the 'Lake County', is a favourite with hardcore fishermen. In the west, the great lakes of Corrib, Mask and Conn have plenty of lakeshore B&Bs, good sturdy boats and knowledgeable boatmen. These lakes can be dangerous, as they tend to be littered with hidden rocks and shoals.

While Ireland is a land of opportunity for the angler, intensive agriculture and the growth of towns have brought about a general reduction in water quality in many areas, markedly so in some. Fáilte Ireland and the NITB produce several information leaflets on fishing, accommodation, events and licences required.

Licences in the Republic are available from the local tackle shop or direct from the **Central Fisheries Board** (☎ 01-884 2600; www.cfb.ie). An all-district license costs €31.74/£15, while a single district license costs €15.23/£12; both are valid for one year.

In the North, rod licences for coarse and game fishing are obtainable from the **Foyle, Carlingford & Irish Lights Commission** (☎ 7134 2100; www.loughs-agency.org) for the Foyle and Carlingford areas, and from the **Fisheries Conservancy Board** (☎ 3833 4666; www.fcbni. com) for all other regions. You also require a permit from the owner, which is usually the **Department of Culture, Arts & Leisure, Inland Waterways & Inland Fisheries Branch** (☎ 9025 8825; www.dcalni.gov.uk).

Golf

There are over 300 golf courses and links in Ireland. Despite the spread of new, American-style parkland courses over the last decade, golf in Ireland is best played on a links course, which can be found along the entirety of its coastline. Contact Fáilte Ireland, the NITB, the **Golfing Union of Ireland** (☎ 01-505 4000; www .gui.ie), or the **Irish Ladies Golf Union** (☎ 01-293 4833; www.ilgu.ie) for information on golfing holidays.

Green fees for 18 holes start from around €25 (£15) on weekdays, but top-notch places charge up to €200 (£150). Courses are tested for their level of difficulty; many are playable year round, especially links.

Hang-gliding & Paragliding

Some of the finest hang-gliding and paragliding in the country is found at Mt Leinster (p204) in Carlow, Great Sugarloaf Mountain (p171) in Wicklow, Benone and Magilligan Beaches (p648) in Derry and Achill Island (p676) in Mayo. Check the websites of the **Irish Hang Gliding & Paragliding Association** (www .ihpa.ie) and the **Ulster Hang Gliding & Paragliding Club** (www.uhpc.co.uk) for local pilots.

Horse Riding

Unsurprisingly, considering the Irish passion for horses, riding is a popular pastime. There are dozens of centres throughout Ireland, offering possibilities ranging from hiring a horse for an hour (from €25/£15) to fully packaged, residential equestrian holidays.

Recommended outfits are Canadian-based **Hidden Trails** (www.hiddentrails.com) and **Ballycumisk Riding School** (☎ 028-37246, 087 961 6969; Ballycumisk, Schull, Co Cork)

Walking

There are many superb walks in Ireland, including 31 'waymarked ways' (designated long-distance paths of varying lengths). Individual chapters have details of recommended walks; for more inspiration see the boxed text, p700, or p670.

There are, however, some issues that have made what should be some of the best walking in Europe a frustrating or even disappointing experience. Some trails run through miles and miles of tedious forestry tracks and bitumen roads. The ways are marked with signposts showing the standard yellow arrow and hiker – in theory at least: waymarking is often variable and in some cases totally nonexistent. Ireland has a tradition of relatively free access to open country but the growth in the number of walkers and the carelessness of a few have made some farmers less obliging. Unfortunately it's not uncommon to find unofficial signs on gateways barring access, or physical barriers blocking ways. If you come across this problem, refer to the local tourist office.

The maintenance and development of the ways is administered in the Republic by the **National Trails Office** (☎ 01-860 8800; www.walk ireland.ie) and in the North by **Countryside Access & Activities Network** (CAAN; ☎ 9030 3930; www.countryside recreation.com).

Some useful guides are Lonely Planet's *Walking in Ireland*, Michael Fewer's *Irish Long-Distance Walks*, or *Best Irish Walks* by Joss Lynam.

For mountain rescue call ☎ 999.

MAPS

EastWest Mapping (☎ /fax 053-937 7835; www.east westmapping.ie) has good maps of long-distance walks in the Republic and the North. Tim Robinson of **Folding Landscapes** (☎ 095-35886; www.foldinglandscapes.com) produces superbly detailed maps of the Burren, the Aran Islands and Connemara. His and Joss Lynam's *Mountains of Connemara: A Hill Walker's Guide* contains a useful detailed map.

ORGANISED WALKS

If you don't have a travelling companion you could consider joining an organised walking group.

Go Ireland (☎ 066-976 2094; www.goactivities.com; Old Orchard House, Killorglin, Co Kerry) Offers walking tours of the west.

South West Walks Ireland (☎ 066-712 8733; www.southwestwalksireland.com; 6 Church St, Tralee, Co Kerry) Provides a series of guided and self-guided walking programs around the southwest, northwest and Wicklow.

Rock Climbing

Ireland's mountain ranges aren't high – Mt Carrantuohil in Kerry's Macgillycuddy's Reeks is the tallest mountain in Ireland at only 1039m – but they're often beautiful and offer some excellent climbing possibilities (see p298). The highest mountains are in the southwest.

Adventure centres around the country run courses and organise climbing trips. For

---

MORE WALKS IN IRELAND

- The Wicklow Way – Glendalough To Aughrim (p166), County Wicklow
- The Great Sugarloaf (p172), County Wicklow
- Mt Seefin (p281), County Cork
- Reeks Ridge (p299), County Kerry
- Mt Brandon (p325), County Kerry
- Tipperary Heritage Trail (p349), County Tipperary
- South Leinster Way (p240), County Kilkenny
- Killary Harbour (p424), County Galway
- Inisheer (p410), County Galway
- Blue Stack Mountains (p467), County Donegal
- Slieve Donard (p619), County Down
- Fair Head (p661), County Antrim
- Causeway Coast (p658), County Antrim
- The Cliffs Of Magho (p687), County Fermanagh
- Cuilcagh Mountain via the Legnabrocky Trail (p691), County Fermanagh
- The Ulster Way (p685), County Donegal and Northern Ireland

---

further information contact the **Mountaineering Council of Ireland** (☎ 01-625 1115; www.mountaineering .ie), which also publishes climbing guides and the quarterly magazine *Irish Mountain Log*, or check the forums on **Irish Climbing Online** (www.climbing.ie).

Water Sports

CANOEING
Ireland has canoeing for all levels, from novice to expert; winter is the best time, when heavy rains swell the rivers. Check out the **Irish Canoe Union** (☎ 01-625 1105; www.irishcanoe union.com).

SAILING
There is a long history of sailing in Ireland and the country has more than 120 yacht and sailing clubs, including the **Royal Cork Yacht Club** (☎ 021-483 1023; www.royalcork.com) at Crosshaven, which, established in 1720, is the world's oldest. The most popular areas for sailing are the southwestern coast, especially between Cork Harbour and the Dingle Peninsula; the coast of Antrim; along the sheltered coast north and south of Dublin; and some of the larger lakes such as Loughs Derg, Erne and Gill.

The **Irish Association for Sail Training** (☎ 01-605 1621; www.irishmarinefederation.com) watches over professional schools; the national governing body is the **Irish Sailing Association** (☎ 01-280 0239; www.sailing.ie). A recommended publication, available from most booksellers, is *Irish Cruising Club Sailing Directions*. It contains details of port facilities, harbour plans and coast and tidal information.

SCUBA DIVING
Ireland has some of the best scuba diving in Europe, found almost entirely off the western coast among its offshore islands and rocks. The best period for diving is roughly March to October. Visibility averages more than 12m but can increase to 30m on good days. For more details about scuba diving in Ireland, contact Comhairle Fó-Thuinn (CFT), also known as the **Irish Underwater Council** (☎ 01-284 4601; www.cft.ie); Ireland's diving regulatory body, it publishes the dive magazine *SubSea* (also available online).

Divecology (☎ 028-28943; www.divecology.com; Cooradarrigan, Schull, Co Cork) is a good dive school, with trips to local wrecks.

SWIMMING & SURFING
Ireland has some magnificent coastline and some great sandy beaches: the cleaner, safer ones have EU Blue Flag awards. Get a list from the government agency **An Taisce** (National Trust for Ireland; ☎ 01-454 1786; www.antaisce.org) or check online with the **Blue Flag Programme** (www .blueflag.org).

Surfers should visit www.surfingireland .net or www.victorkilo.com for beach reports and forecasts. **Donegal Adventure Centre** (☎ 074-984 2418; www.donegal-holidays.com; Bay View Ave, Bundoran, Co Donegal) is an excellent youth-oriented surf school and **Bundoran Surf Co** (☎ 984 1968; www.bundoransurfco.com; Bundoran, Co Donegal) conduct surf lessons, kite-surfing and power-kiting.

The best months for surfing in Ireland – when the swells are highest – are September (when the water is warmest because of the Gulf Stream) and October. Some of the best locations are on the south and southwest coasts, such as Tramore (p212) in Waterford,

nd there are also big surfing schools in Sligo
p452) and Donegal (p467 and p469), where
ou can also have a blast at kite-surfing.

See also p669.

VATERSKIING

here are waterski clubs all over Ireland of-
ering tuition, equipment and boats. A full list
s available from the **Irish Water Ski Federation**
vww.iwsf.ie).

VINDSURFING

he windsurfer has plenty of locations to
idulge in this popular sport – even on the
irand Canal in Dublin! The western coast is
ie most challenging and the least crowded.
he bay at Rosslare (see p194) in County
Vexford is ideal for windsurfing, with equip-
ient and tuition available in summer. The
ish Sailing Association (☎ 01-280 0239; www.sailing
e) is the sport's governing authority and has
etails of particular activity centres.

USINESS HOURS

he standard business hours are generally
ie same for both the Republic and Northern
eland and are shown below, with any vari-
ions noted:

anks 10am to 4pm Monday to Friday (to 5pm Thursday)

ffices 9am to 5pm Monday to Friday

ost offices Northern Ireland 9am to 5.30pm Monday to
iday, 9am to 12.30pm Saturday; Republic 9am to 6pm
onday to Friday, 9am to 1pm Saturday. Smaller post
ices may close at lunch and one day per week.

ubs Northern Ireland 11.30am to 11pm Monday to
turday, 12.30pm to 10pm Sunday. Pubs with late
ences open until 1am Monday to Saturday, and midnight
nday; Republic 10.30am to 11.30pm Monday to Thursday,
.30am to 12.30am Friday and Saturday, noon to 11pm
nday (30 min 'drinking up' time allowed). Pubs with bar
tensions open to 2.30am Thursday to Saturday. All pubs
se Christmas Day and Good Friday.

estaurants Noon to 10.30pm; many close one day of
e week.

ops 9am to 5.30pm or 6pm Monday to Saturday (until
m on Thursday and sometimes Friday), noon to 6pm
nday (in bigger towns only). Shops in rural towns may
se at lunch and one day per week.

urist offices 9am to 5pm Monday to Friday, 9am to
m Saturday. Many extend their hours in summer, and
en fewer hours/days or close from October to April.

HILDREN

iccessful travel with young children requires
fort, but can be done. Try not to overdo things

and consider using some sort of self-catering
accommodation. It's sometimes easier to eat in
(or to at least have the option), rather than be
restricted by the relatively confined space of a
hotel or B&B room. On the whole you'll find
that restaurants and hotels, especially in the
countryside, will go out of their way to cater
for you and your children – with the exception
of a few places, generally in the capital, where
children aren't allowed after 6pm. Children are
allowed in pubs until 7pm.

Most attractions sell cheaper family tickets, and family passes are available on public
transport. It's always a good idea to talk to
fellow travellers with (happy) children and
locals on the road for tips on where to go.
For further general information see Lonely
Planet's *Travel with Children*.

Practicalities

Most hotels will provide cots at no extra charge
and restaurants will have high chairs. Car seats
(around €50/£25 per week) are mandatory for
children in hire cars between the ages of nine
months and four years. Bring your own seat
for infants under about nine months as only
larger, forward-facing child seats are generally
available. Remember not to place baby seats in
the front if the car has an airbag.

Remarkably, baby changing facilities are
scarce, even in city centres.

Ireland has one of the lowest rates of breast-
feeding in the world; nevertheless, you should
be able to feed your baby in all but a few public
places without jaws dropping.

Two great websites are www.eumom.ie,
for pregnant women and parents with young
children, and www.babygoes2.com, which is
an excellent travel site about family-friendly
accommodation worldwide.

CLIMATE CHARTS

Thanks to the moderating effect of the Atlantic
Gulf Stream, Ireland's climate is relatively mild
for its latitude, with a mean annual temperature of around 10°C (50°F). The temperature
drops below freezing only intermittently during winter, and snow is scarce – perhaps one
or two brief flurries a year. The coldest months
are January and February, when daily temperatures range from 4° to 8°C (39 to 46°F),
with 7°C (44°F) the average. In summer, temperatures during the day are a comfortable
15° to 20°C (59 to 68°F). During the warmest
months, July and August, the average is 16°C

DIRECTORY

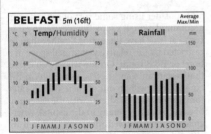

BELFAST 5m (16ft)

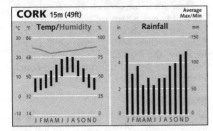

CORK 15m (49ft)

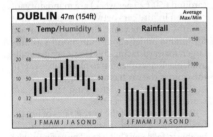

DUBLIN 47m (154ft)

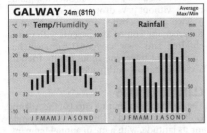

GALWAY 24m (81ft)

(61°F). A hot summer's day in Ireland is 22° to 24°C (72 to 75°F), although it can sometimes reach 30°C (86°F). There are about 18 hours of daylight daily during July and August and it's only truly dark after about 11pm.

One thing you can be sure of about Irish weather is how little you can be sure of. It may be shirtsleeves and sunglasses in February, but winter woollies in March and even during the summer.

And then there's the rain. Ireland receives a lot of rain, with certain areas getting a soaking for as many as 270 days a year. County Kerry is the worst affected. The southeast is the driest, enjoying a more continental climate.

See also p20 for information about when to go.

COURSES

Ireland offers myriad courses, from archery classes to learning how to play the harp. Adventure centres, where you can do everything from hill-walking to raft-building, are increasingly popular; we have listed them throughout the book. For cookery courses – a very popular pastime – check out the Food & Drink chapter (p65). Below are only guidelines to courses; for greater details, see the relevant sections in the destination chapters or check out www.discoverireland.ie.

Arts & Crafts

Rockfield Ecological Estate (☎ 043-76024; Rathaspick, Rathowen, Co Westmeath; tour €5, mains €18-25; ☿ by appointment) gives you an inspiring insight into sustainable living as well as traditional Irish culture and crafts. In addition to two-hour tours of the working farm, you can dine on nutritious homemade food made with organic produce from the rambling gardens (while sitting on a chair fashioned from fallen tree branches), and take part in full-day craft courses (€100 per person including lunch) such as spinning, weaving, basket-making, woodcarving and stone-sculpting.

English Language

Fáilte Ireland (see p711) publishes a list of recognised schools for teaching English as a foreign language. Most – but certainly not all – English-language schools are in and around Dublin.

Centre of English Studies (☎ 01-671 4233; www.ces-schools.com; 31 Dame St, Dublin)

Dublin School of English (☎ 01-677 3322; www.dse.ie; 10-12 Westmoreland St, Dublin)

English Language Institute (☎ 01-475 2965; www.englishlanguage.com; 99 St Stephen's Green, Dublin)

Language Centre of Ireland (☎ 01-671 6266; www.lci.ie; 45 Kildare St, Dublin)

Irish Language

There are plenty of Irish language courses, especially (but not exclusively) in the Gaeltacht (Irish-speaking) areas. Check with **Údarás**

Gaeltachta (Gaeltacht Authority; www.gaelsaoire.ie), the government agency charged with maintaining the Gaeltacht; or **Foras na Gaeilge** (Irish Language Board; ☎ 1850 325 325; www.gaeilge.ie), the body responsible for the promotion of Irish throughout the country. Also try:
Oideas Gael (☎ 074-973 0248; www.oideas-gael.com; Glencolumbcille, Donegal; 3-/7-day courses €100/230; ✷ Mar-Oct) Irish language courses and cultural activity holidays.

Meditation

Jampa Ling Buddhist Centre (☎ 049-952 3448; www.jampaling.org; Owendoon House, Bawnboy, Co Cavan; self catering dm/s €20/30, dm/s incl meals €35/40) offers meditation courses. See p562 for details.

Music

In July and August, **Dingle Music School** (☎ 086-319 0438; www.dinglemusicschool.com; Dykegate Lane, Dingle, Co Kerry) offers beginners' workshops in bodhrán (from €15; noon Tuesday, Wednesday and Thursday, 11am on Saturday) and tin whistle (€25, 11am Monday). Bodhráns are supplied.

Harp workshops are conducted as part of the O'Carolan International Harp Festival & Summer School. For details, see the boxed text, p519.

CUSTOMS

Duty-free sales are not available when travelling within the EU. Goods for personal consumption purchased in and exported within the EU incur no additional taxes if duty has been paid somewhere in the EU. Over certain limits you may have to show that they are for personal use. The amounts that officially constitute personal use are 3200 cigarettes (or 400 cigarillos, 200 cigars or 3kg of tobacco) and either 10L of spirits, 20L of fortified wine, 60L of sparkling wine, 90L of still wine or 110L of beer. There are no customs inspections apart from those concerned with drugs and national security.

Travellers coming from outside the EU are allowed to import the following duty-free: 200 cigarettes, 1L of spirits or 2L of wine, 60ml of perfume and 250ml of eau de toilette.

Dogs and cats from anywhere outside Ireland and the UK are subject to strict quarantine laws. The EU Pet Travel Scheme, whereby animals are fitted with a microchip, vaccinated against rabies and blood-tested six months *prior* to entry, is in force in the

---

FOR THE RECORD:

- The legal voting age in Ireland is 18
- You can leave school when you're 16
- The legal drinking age is 18
- Smoking is legal at 16
- You can ride a moped when you're 16
- You can drive a car when you're 17

UK and the Republic of Ireland. No preparation or documentation is necessary for the movement of pets directly between the UK and the Republic. Contact the **Department of Agriculture, Food & Rural Development** (☎ 01-607 2000; www.agriculture.gov.ie) in Dublin for further details.

DANGERS & ANNOYANCES

Ireland is safer than most countries in Europe, but normal precautions should be observed. In Dublin, drug-related crime is not uncommon and the city has its fair share of pickpockets and thieves (see p99).

Northern Ireland is as safe as anywhere else, but there are areas where the sectarian divide is bitterly pronounced, most notably in parts of Belfast. For the foreseeable future, it's probably best to ensure your visit to Northern Ireland doesn't coincide with the climax of the Orange marching season on 12 July; sectarian passions are usually inflamed and even many Northerners leave the province at this time.

DISCOUNT CARDS
Heritage Discounts

Heritage Card (☎ 01-647 6587; www.heritageireland.com; adult/child & student/senior/family €21/8/16/55) Entitles you to free access to over 75 sites for one year.
National Trust (☎ 0870 458 4000; www.nationaltrust.org.uk; adult/under 25/family £47.50/21.50/82) Entitles you to free admission to its 18 properties in Northern Ireland, but only really makes financial sense if you're touring its British sites, too. It's cheaper to join online.

Senior Cards

Senior citizens are entitled to many discounts in Ireland on things such as public transport and museum admission fees, provided they show proof of age. The minimum qualifying age is usually 60 to 65 for men and 55 to 65 for women. In your home country, a lower age may already entitle you to travel packages and discounts (on car hire, for instance).

Car hire companies usually won't rent to drivers aged over 70 or 75.

Student & Youth Cards

The **International Student Identity Card** (ISIC; www.isiccard.com) allows discounts on transport, commercial goods and services, and admission to theatres, cinemas, museums and sights. The **International Youth Travel Card** (IYTC; www.isiccard.com) and **European Youth Card** (Euro<26 card; www.euro26.org) offer similar discounts for nonstudents under 26. All these cards are issued by hostelling organisations, student unions and student travel agencies.

EMBASSIES & CONSULATES
Irish Embassies & Consulates

Irish diplomatic offices overseas:

Australia Embassy (☎ 02-6273 3022; www.embassyofireland.au.com; 20 Arkana St, Yarralumla, Canberra, ACT 2600)

Canada Embassy (☎ 613-233 6281; www.embassyofireland.ca; 130 Albert St, Suite 1105, Ottawa, Ontario K1P 5G4)

France Embassy (☎ 01 44 17 67 00; www.embassyofireland.fr; 4 rue Rude, 75116 Paris)

Germany Embassy (☎ 030-220 720; Friedrichstrasse 200, 10117 Berlin)

Italy Embassy (☎ 06 697 9121; www.embassyofireland.it; Piazza di Campitelli 3, 00186 Rome)

Netherlands Embassy (☎ 070-363 0993; www.embassyofireland.nl; Dr Kuyperstraat 9, 2514BA The Hague)

New Zealand Consulate (☎ 09-977 2252; www.ireland.co.nz; Level 7, Citibank Bldg, 23 Customs Street East, Auckland)

UK Embassy (☎ 020-7235 2171; www.embassyofireland.co.uk; 17 Grosvenor Pl, London SW1X 7HR, England); Consulate (☎ 0131-226 7711; www.irishconsulatescotland.co.uk; 16 Randolph Crescent, Edinburgh EH3 6TT, Scotland); Consulate (☎ 029-2066 2000; Brunel House, 2 Fitzalan Rd, Cardiff CF24 0EB, Wales)

USA Embassy (☎ 202-462 3939; www.embassyofireland.org; 2234 Massachusetts Ave NW, Washington, DC 20008) There are also consulates in Boston, Chicago, New York and San Francisco.

United Kingdom (for Northern Ireland) diplomatic offices abroad:

Australia High Commission (☎ 02-6270 6666; www.ukinaustralia.fco.gov.uk; Commonwealth Ave, Yarralumla, Canberra, ACT 2600)

Canada High Commission (☎ 613-237 1530; www.ukincanada.fco.gov.uk; 80 Elgin St, Ottawa, Ontario K1P 5K7)

France Embassy (☎ 01 44 51 31 00; www.ukinfrance.fco.gov.uk; 35 rue du Faubourg St Honoré, 75383 Paris)

Germany Embassy (☎ 030-204 570; www.ukingermany.fco.gov.uk; Wilhelmstrasse 70, 10117 Berlin)

Italy Embassy (☎ 06 4220 0001; www.ukinitaly.fco.gov.uk; Via XX Settembre 80a, 00187 Rome)

Netherlands Embassy (☎ 070-427 0427; www.ukinnl.fco.gov.uk; Lange Voorhout 10, 2514ED The Hague)

New Zealand High Commission (☎ 04-924 2888; www.ukinnewzealand.fco.gov.uk; 44 Hill St, Wellington 6011)

USA Embassy (☎ 202-588 6500; www.ukinusa.fco.gov.uk; 3100 Massachusetts Ave NW, Washington, DC 20008)

Embassies & Consulates in Ireland

If you're even remotely responsible for any kind of trouble, your country's embassy won't be of any help to you – you're bound by Irish (and in the North, British) law. In genuine emergencies you might get some assistance: a free ticket is exceedingly unlikely but embassies might assist you with getting a new passport.

Foreign embassies in Dublin:

Australia (Map p90; ☎ 01-664 5300; www.ireland.embassy.gov.au; 7th fl, Fitzwilton House, Wilton Tce, Dublin 2)

Canada (Map p90; ☎ 01-234 4000; 7-8 Wilton Tce, Dublin 2)

France (☎ 01-277 5000; www.ambafrance.ie; 36 Ailesbury Rd, Dublin 4)

Germany (☎ 01-269 3011; www.dublin.diplo.de; 31 Trimleston Ave, Booterstown, Blackrock, County Dublin)

Italy (Map p90; ☎ 01-660 1744; www.ambdublin.esteri.it; 63-65 Northumberland Rd, Ballsbridge, Dublin 4)

Netherlands (☎ 269 3444; www.netherlandsembassy.ie; 160 Merrion Rd, Ballsbridge, Dublin 4)

UK (Map p90; ☎ 01-205 3700; www.britishembassy.ie; 29 Merrion Rd, Ballsbridge, Dublin 4)

USA (Map p90; ☎ 01-668 8777; www.usembassy.ie; 42 Elgin Rd, Ballsbridge, Dublin 4)

The following countries have consular representation in Northern Ireland:

Germany (☎ 9024 4113; Chamber of Commerce House, 22 Great Victoria St, Belfast)

Netherlands (☎ 9077 9088; c/o All-Route Shipping Ltd, 14-16 West Bank Rd, Belfast)

USA (☎ 9038 6100; Danesfort House, 223 Stranmillis Rd, Belfast)

FESTIVALS & EVENTS

There are literally hundreds of festivals held throughout the year, but the summer months are the most popular; listed here is a thumbnail sketch of the major events. Local tourist offices will have additional information, as will **Fáilte Ireland** (www.discoverireland.ie). Also, the Association of Irish Festival Events (AOIFE) maintains a very useful website at www.aoifeonline.com; www.art.ie is worth perusing, too. For regional festivals, see individual destination chapters.

FEBRUARY

Jameson Dublin International Film Festival (☎ 01-872 1122; www.dubliniff.com) The island's biggest film festival, with local flicks, arty international films and advance releases of mainstream movies, runs during the last two weeks of the month.

MARCH

St Patrick's Day (17 March; ☎ 01-676 3205; www.stpatricksday.ie) Ireland erupts into one giant celebration on 17 March. The biggest party is in Dublin, where the streets reverberate with a cacophony of parades, fireworks and light shows for five days around 17 March. Over 250,000 attend. Cork, Armagh and Belfast also have parades; elsewhere, festivities are less ostentatious.

APRIL

Circuit of Ireland International Rally (www.circuitofireland.net) Known locally as 'the Circuit', this rally car race, held over the Easter weekend, begins and ends in Northern Ireland but takes in chunks of the Republic, too.

Irish Grand National (www.fairyhouseracecourse.ie) The showcase race in the national hunt season takes place at the County Meath racetrack on Easter Monday.

World Irish Dancing Championships (☎ 01-475 2220) About 4000 dancers from all over the globe compete in late March or early April. The location varies from year to year.

MAY

Cork International Choral Festival (☎ 021-421 5125; www.corkchoral.ie) One of Europe's premier choral festivals, with the winners going on to the Fleischmann International Trophy Competition; held over four days from the first Monday of May.

North West 200 (☎ 9076 0066; www.northwest200.org) Ireland's most famous road race is also the country's biggest outdoor sporting event; 150,000-plus people line the triangular route to cheer on some of the biggest names in motorcycle racing. Held in mid-May.

Fleadh Nua (☎ 01-280 0295; www.comhaltas.ie) Absorb a week of traditional music as Ennis, County Clare, hosts one of the country's most important festivals during the third week of the month.

Irish Open Golf Championship (☎ 041-988 1530; www.countylouthgolfclub.com) Not as prestigious as the European Open, it still manages to attract its fair share of top European names. Takes place over four days around late May at the County Louth Golf Club, Baltray.

Cat Laughs (☎ 056-776 3837; www.thecatlaughs.com) Kilkenny gets very, very funny from late May into early June with the country's best comedy festival, attracting the cream of local and international talent.

JUNE

Irish Derby (☎ 045-441 205; www.curragh.ie) The best flat race in the country is run during the first week of the month at the County Kildare course. A great occasion for racing fans and people with fancy hats.

Bloomsday (☎ 01-878 8547; www.jamesjoyce.ie) Edwardian dress and breakfast of 'the inner organs of beast and fowl' are but two of the elements of the Dublin festival celebrating June 16th, the day on which Joyce's *Ulysses* takes place; the real highlight is retracing Leopold Bloom's daily steps.

Wexford Opera Festival (☎ 053-912 2400; www.wexfordopera.com) Ireland's premier festival of classical music and opera runs for two weeks in early June in Johnstown Castle.

Lismore Festival of Travel Writing (☎ 058 53803; www.lismoreimmrama.com) Although clearly impossible to teach(!), heaven's gift is explained in mid-June through presentations and workshops by top international writers (none of whom worked on this particular book).

JULY

Killarney Summerfest (☎ 064-667 1560; www.killarneysummerfest.com) From kayaking to street theatre and gigs by international artists, this two-week extravaganza in the first half of July literally has something for everybody.

Willie Clancy Summer School (☎ 065-708 4281; www.setdancingnews.net/wcss/) Six days of intense traditional music workshops, gigs and pub sessions in Miltown Malbay, County Clare; the best players in the world generally show up.

Oxegen (www.oxegen.ie) Four-day super-gig in mid-July at Punchestown Racecourse in County Kildare featuring top international rock, dance and pop acts.

Galway Film Fleadh (☎ 091-751 655; www.galwayfilmfleadh.com) Irish and international releases make up the program at one of the country's premier film festivals, held in early July.

Galway Arts Festival (☎ 091-509 700; www.galwayartsfestival.ie) The most important arts festival in the country sees Galway City go mental for the last two weeks of the month, with lots of music and drama to go with the merriment.

Earagail Arts Festival (☎ 074-916 8800; www.eaf.ie) The most prominent Irish-language festival in the country runs over three weeks in July, with a bilingual program of music, literature, theatre and children's events.

AUGUST

Electric Picnic (☎ 01-478 9093; www.electricpicnic.ie) A boutique festival of alternative music in the grounds of Stradbally Hall, County Laois; late August. Comedy, art, and a strong ecofriendly buzz complement the terrific music.

Féile An Phobail West Belfast (☎ 9031 3440; www.feilebelfast.com) Europe's largest community arts festival takes place on the Falls Rd in West Belfast over two weeks.

Fleadh Cheoil na hÉireann (☎ 01-280 0295; www.comhaltas.ie) The mother of all Irish music festivals attracts in excess of 250,000 to whichever town is playing host; it usually takes place over a week toward the end of the month.

Galway Races (☎ 091-753 870; www.galwayraces.com) The biggest horse racing festival west of the Shannon draws massive crowds. It's held the first week of the month.

Mary from Dungloe (☎ 074-952 1254; www.maryfromdungloe.com) Ireland's second-most important beauty pageant takes place in Dungloe, County Donegal at the beginning of the month – although it's really an excuse for a giant party, the young women really do want to be crowned the year's 'Mary'.

Puck Fair (☎ 066-976 2366; www.puckfair.ie) Three days of what must be one of the quirkiest festivals in Europe see Killorglin, County Kerry, celebrating the crowning of a goat amidst plenty of mayhem. Held in mid-August.

Rose of Tralee (☎ 066-712 1322; www.roseoftralee.ie) The County Kerry town plays host to *the* Irish beauty pageant, which attracts women with Irish links from all over the world. For everyone else, it's just an opportunity to drink, dance and have fun. It's held in the third week of the month.

SEPTEMBER

Lisdoonvarna Matchmaking Festival (☎ 065-707 4005; www.matchmakerireland.com) The County Clare town hosts this famous festival that attracts hopefuls from all over; it's all a bit of fun throughout the month.

Dublin Fringe Festival (☎ 01-872 9016; www.fringefest.com) Comedy and alternative fringe theatre precedes the main theatre festival and is often a hell of a lot more fun. Runs for two weeks from late September to early October.

Ballinasloe Horse Fair (☎ 090-964 3453; www.ballinasloe.com) Europe's oldest horse fair in this Galway town comes with a 10-day family festival that is a highlight of the calendar. Deals are made with just spit and a handshake!

OCTOBER

Dublin Theatre Festival (☎ 01-677 8439; www.dublintheatrefestival.com) The cream of Irish theatre festivals sees all manner of theatrics at venues throughout the capital.

Cork Film Festival (☎ 021-427 1711; www.corkfilmfest.org) With a strong emphasis on local and short films, this excellent festival is held in Cork's three cinemas in early October.

Cork Jazz Festival (www.corkjazzfestival.com) Over the last weekend of the month, the city goes mad for all kinds of jazz in one of the country's most popular festivals.

All-Ireland Finals (☎ 01-8363222; www.gaa.ie) The second and fourth Sundays of the month see the finals of the hurling and Gaelic football championships, respectively, with 80,000-plus thronging into Dublin's Croke Park for the biggest sporting days of the year.

Belfast Festival at Queens (☎ in UK 020-9097 1197; www.belfastfestival.com) Northern Ireland's top arts festival attracts performers from all over the world; on offer is everything from visual arts to dance.

Irish Conker Championship (☎ 056-776 7219; www.irishconkerchampionship.com) The most important game of many an Irish youth – threading a chestnut (conker) with a piece of string and then hitting your opponent's conker until it breaks – has been turned into an intense competition; held at the end of October in Kilkenny.

DECEMBER

Christmas This is a quiet affair in the countryside, though on 26 December the ancient custom of Wren Boys is reenacted, most notably in Dingle, County Kerry, when groups of children dress up and go about singing hymns.

FOOD

Our cafe and restaurant listings appear in order of price, with the cheapest appearing first. We've used the following price ranges: budget (under €10/£10), midrange (€10 to €20/£10 to £20) and top end (above €20/£20). Please note that our hierarchies of favourite places aren't written in stone (as authors, we can crave caviar on a Monday and cod and chips on a Friday).

For explanations of peculiarities of Irish menus and further reading on Irish food and drink, see the Food & Drink chapter (p65).

GAY & LESBIAN TRAVELLERS

Irish laws on homosexuality are among the most liberal in Europe, and the margin of tolerance between the laws and prevalent attitudes is getting narrower all the time. Gays and lesbians are a comfortably visible presence on the streets of the bigger urban centres, but even outside of Dublin, Cork and Galway there is a growing acceptance of homosexuality as a fact of life.

Generally the Irish couldn't care less what you do behind closed doors, and neither gays nor lesbians (in the Republic) are excluded from the armed forces. Although the Vatican maintains its position that being gay is a crime against God, the Catholic Church here maintains an air of discreet silence on gay and lesbian issues.

The monthly *Gay Community News* (www .gcn.ie), found in clubs and bars and online, is a free publication of the **National Lesbian & Gay Federation** (NLGF; ☎ 01-671 9076; www.nlgf.ie). Aimed at younger members of the gay, lesbian and transgender community, **BeLonG To** (Map p94; ☎ 01-670 6223; www.belongto.org; 13 Parliament St, Dublin) offers advice and support to people aged 14 to 23 and facilitates support groups throughout the country.

Other online resources and organisations for the gay and lesbian community:

Gaire (www.gaire.com) Message board and info for a host of gay-related issues.

Gay & Lesbian Youth Northern Ireland (www.glyni .org.uk)

Northern Ireland Gay Rights Association (Nigra; ☎ 9066 5257; nigra@dnet.co.uk)

Outhouse (Map pp92-3; ☎ 01-873 4932; www .outhouse.ie; 105 Capel St, Dublin) A gay, lesbian and transgender community centre.

The following helplines can be called from anywhere in Ireland:

Gay Men's Health Project (☎ 01-660 2189) Practical advice on men's health issues.

Gay Switchboard Dublin (☎ 01-872 1055; ⏱ 7.30am-9.30pm Mon-Fri, 3.30-6pm Sat)

Lesbian Line Belfast (☎ 9023 8668; ⏱ 7.30-10pm Thu)

Lesbian Line Dublin (☎ 01-872 9911; ⏱ 7-9pm Thu)

Mensline Belfast (☎ 9032 2023; ⏱ 7.30-10pm Mon-Wed)

HOLIDAYS

Public holidays can cause road chaos as everyone tries to get somewhere else for the break. It's also wise to book accommodation in advance around these times.

Public Holidays

Public holidays in both the Republic and Northern Ireland:

New Year's Day 1 January
St Patrick's Day 17 March
Easter (Good Friday to Easter Monday inclusive) March/April
May Holiday 1st Monday in May

Christmas Day 25 December
St Stephen's Day (Boxing Day) 26 December

NORTHERN IRELAND
Spring Bank Holiday Last Monday in May
Orangeman's Day 12 July
August Holiday Last Monday in August

REPUBLIC
June Holiday 1st Monday in June
August Holiday 1st Monday in August
October Holiday Last Monday in October

St Patrick's Day and St Stephen's Day holidays are taken on the following Monday when they fall on a weekend. In the Republic, nearly everywhere closes on Good Friday even though it isn't an official public holiday. In the North, most shops open on Good Friday but close the following Tuesday.

School Holidays

In the Republic, standardised primary and secondary school holidays include Christmas, Easter and the summer (July and August for primary schools, and also June for secondary pupils) and two midterm breaks, usually in October and February. For specific dates, check out www.citizensinformation.ie.

In the North, holidays for primary and secondary schools vary. Visit www.deni.gov.uk for more comprehensive information.

INSURANCE

Insurance is important: it covers you for everything from medical expenses and luggage loss to cancellations or delays in your travel arrangements, depending on your policy.

If you're an EU citizen, a European Health Insurance Card (EHIC; available from health centres, or from post offices in the UK) covers you for most medical care. While other countries, such as Australia, also have reciprocal agreements with Ireland and Britain, many do not.

If you do need health insurance, remember that some policies offer lower and higher medical-expense options, and that the higher one is chiefly for countries that have extremely high medical costs. Ensure that you're covered for the worst possible case, such as an accident requiring an ambulance, hospital treatment or an emergency flight home. You may prefer a policy that pays health-care providers directly rather than having you pay on the spot and claim later. See p724 for health insurance details.

All cars on public roads must be insured. If you are bringing your own vehicle check that your insurance will cover you in Ireland.

INTERNET ACCESS

Most laptops these days are dual-voltage and should work with just a plug adapter (Ireland uses the same triple flat-pin plug as the UK), but if your computer isn't equipped to handle 220 volts AC, you'll need a universal AC adapter, as well. All hotel rooms have phone lines and you can plug the phone cord into your laptop's modem; although most have direct-dial services, you'll most likely have to dial an outside line access number (usually 9) to get online. Provided you're dialling a local access number, you'll be charged the price of a local call (which from a hotel is usually timed and 50% more than usual).

Major internet service providers (ISPs) such as **AOL** (www.aol.com), **CompuServe** (www .compuserve.com) and **AT&T Business Internet Services** (www.attbusiness.net) have dial-in nodes in Ireland. If you access your email account through an ISP based at home, your best option is to open an account with a local ISP provider: the most reliable ones are **Eircom** (☎ 1890 260 260; www.eircom.ie) or **O2** (☎ 1850 200 741; www.o2.ie).

Although Ireland has one of the lowest rates of broadband penetration in Europe (26% in 2009), 60% of Irish households have broadband, including most B&Bs in and around the major towns of Ireland; you'll also find wi-fi (wireless internet) in many midrange and top-end hotels. Most towns also have internet cafes, although many are closing as the rate of household broadband goes up. You can log on for €4 to €10 per hour in the Republic, or about £4 per hour in the North.

LEGAL MATTERS

If you need legal assistance contact the **Legal Aid Board** (☎ 066-947 1000; www.legalaidboard.ie), which also has a number of local law centres listed in the phone book. In the North, contact the **Northern Ireland Legal Services Commission** (www .nilsc.org.uk).

The possession of small quantities of marijuana attracts a fine or warning, but harder drugs are treated more seriously. Public drunkenness is illegal but commonplace. Be aware that you will undoubtedly attract police attention if you're way out of line. Fighting is treated more harshly – you could easily end up in a cell for the night, or worse.

MAPS

Many publishers produce some good-quality maps of Ireland. Michelin's 1:400,000-scale Ireland map (No 923) is a decent single sheet map, with clear cartography and most of the island's scenic roads marked. The four maps – North, South, East and West – that make up the Ordnance Survey Holiday map series at 1:250,000 scale are useful if you want more detail. Collins also publishes a range of maps covering Ireland.

For greater detail, map aficionados and walkers should look out for the Ordnance Survey Discovery series, which covers the whole island in 89 maps at a scale of 1:50,000. They're available at the **National Map Centre** (Map p96; ☎ 01-476 0471; www.mapcentre.ie; 34 Aungier St, Dublin), through www.osi.ie and many bookshops around Ireland.

MONEY

To get a general idea of food and accommodation costs in Ireland, see p706 and p695, respectively. Tips of around 10% are expected for metered cabs and in restaurants where the service charge isn't included.

ATMs & Credit Cards

Most banks have ATMs that are linked to international money systems such as Cirrus, Maestro or Plus. Each transaction incurs a currency conversion fee and credit cards can incur immediate and exorbitant cash-advance interest rate charges.

Charge cards such as Amex and Diners Club don't have credit limits, but may not be accepted in smaller establishments. Visa and MasterCard are more widely accepted, though some rural B&Bs and some smaller or remote petrol stations still deal only in cash.

Remember to keep a note of the emergency telephone number to ring if your cards are lost or stolen.

Cash & Travellers Cheques

Most major brands of travellers cheques are accepted in Ireland. Amex and Thomas Cook travellers cheques are widely recognised; branches don't charge a fee for cashing their own cheques. Travellers cheques are rarely accepted outside banks or used for everyday transactions. Eurocheques can be cashed in Ireland, but special arrangements must be made with your home bank before you travel if you are thinking of using personal cheques.

As for cash, we suggest you arrive with some cash in the local currency (both euros and sterling, if travelling to the North) to tide you over.

Currency

Ireland's currency is the euro (€), which is divided into 100 cents. While the notes are all the same throughout the 12 countries of the euro zone, the Irish coins feature a harp on the reverse side – though of course all non-Irish euro coins are also legal tender. (Remember that the UK is not a participant, so if you're travelling to Northern Ireland you'll have to change euros into pounds.)

The British pound sterling (£) is used in Northern Ireland, where it is known as the Northern Irish pound. Northern Ireland notes, while equivalent in value to British pound notes, are not readily accepted in Britain, but British banks will swap them for you.

The best exchange rates are obtained at banks. Bureaus de change and other exchange facilities usually open for longer hours but the rate and/or commission will be worse. Many post offices operate a currency-exchange facility and open on Saturday morning. Exchange rates at the time of writing are on the inside front cover of this book.

Taxes & Refunds

Value-added tax (VAT) is a sales tax of 21.5% that applies to most luxury goods in Ireland, excluding books, second-hand clothing, and children's footwear. Visitors from non-EU countries can claim back most of the VAT on purchases that are subsequently exported from the EU within three months of purchase.

Most shops in the Republic and Northern Ireland operate a taxback scheme – the most popular are Cashback and Ireland Tax Free – which operate roughly as follows: if you're a resident of a country outside the EU and buy something from a store displaying a Cashback or Ireland Tax Free sticker, you'll be given a relevant voucher with your purchase which can be refunded directly on to your credit card or in US, Canadian or Australian dollars, British pounds or euros at Dublin or Shannon

airport; one advantage of Ireland Tax Free is that you can reclaim your tax at the nearest Travelex office, usually Thomas Cook.

If you claim more than €250 on any of your vouchers you'll need to get the voucher stamped at the customs booth in the arrivals hall at Dublin or Shannon airport before you can get your refund from the Cashback desk.

In Northern Ireland, shops participating in the Tax-Free Shopping refund scheme will give you a form or invoice on request to be presented to customs when you leave. After customs have certified the form, it will be returned to the shop for a refund and the cheque sent to you at home.

PHOTOGRAPHY

Natural light in Ireland can be very dull, so use faster film, such as 400ASA, to capture the sombre atmosphere (though 200ASA should do in most situations). Lonely Planet's full-colour *Travel Photography: A Guide to Taking Better Pictures,* written by internationally renowned travel photographer Richard I'Anson, is full of handy hints and is designed to take on the road. Film and digital memory cards are readily available in all tourist centres.

In regard to taking photos in Northern Ireland, if you want to take photos of fortified police stations, army posts or other military or quasi-military paraphernalia, get permission first to be on the safe side. In the Protestant and Catholic strongholds of West Belfast it's best not to photograph people without permission: always ask first and be prepared to accept a refusal.

POST

The Irish postal service, **An Post** (www.anpost.ie), is reliable, efficient and usually on time. Some rates for StandardPost service:

Type	Ireland	UK/Europe	Other
letter/postcard (<100g)	€0.55	€0.82	€0.82
packet (100–250g)	€2.70	€3.50	€3.50
packet (1kg)	€6	€7.50	€10.40

In Northern Ireland, post offices are operated by Royal Mail; letters sent by 1st-/2nd-class mail to Britain cost £0.39/0.30 as long as they weigh less than 100g. Airmail letters under 20g cost £0.56 to continental Europe and £0.90 to the rest of the world (£0.62 to the rest of the world for under 10g).

For post office opening hours, see p701.

SOLO TRAVELLERS

Travelling alone in Ireland is easy. People are extremely sociable, especially in the countryside, and will be more than keen to chat with you in pubs or public places – sometimes whether you like it or not! Hostels and internet cafes are always good places to meet fellow travellers, or you might consider combining independent travel with a short course or activity where you have more chance of meeting people. One disadvantage of solo travel is the extra cost of accommodation: many places charge per room, and if they charge per person, they also slap a single supplementary charge (up to 30%) on to the room rate.

TELEPHONE

You shouldn't have any problems in Ireland making phone calls to anyone, anywhere.

Prices are lower during evenings after 6pm and weekends. Phone calls from hotel rooms cost twice the standard rate. You can send and receive faxes from post offices or most hotels. Local telephone calls from a public phone in the Republic cost €0.30 for around three minutes (around €0.60 to a mobile), regardless of when you call.

The number for local and national directory enquiries in the Republic is ☎11811 or ☎11850; for international enquiries it's ☎11818. In the North, call ☎118118.

Pre-paid phonecards from Eircom and private operators can be purchased at both newsagencies and post offices, and work from all payphones for both domestic and international calls.

Direct Home Call Codes

Instead of placing reverse-charge calls through the Irish operator, you can dial direct to your home-country operator and then reverse the charges or charge the call to a credit card. To use the home-direct service, dial the codes listed here, the area code and, in most cases, the number you want. Your home-country operator will come on the line before the call goes through.

Australia (☎ 1800 550 061 + number)
France (☎ 1800 551 033 + number)
Italy (☎ 1800 550 039 + number)
New Zealand (☎ 1800 550 064 + number)
Spain (☎ 1800 550 034 + number)
UK – BT (☎ 1800 550 044 + number)
USA – AT&T (☎ 1800 550 000 + number)

USA – MCI (☎ 1800 551 001 + number)
USA – Sprint (☎ 1800 552 001 + number)

Mobile Phones

Virtually everyone in Ireland has a mobile phone. Ireland uses the GSM 900/1800 cellular phone system, which is compatible with European and Australian, but not North American or Japanese, phones. SMS is a national obsession, especially with young people (who communic8 mostly by txt).

There are four Irish service providers: Vodafone, O2, Meteor and 3. There are three mobile codes – 085, 086 and 087. All have links with most international GSM providers, which allow you to 'roam' onto a local service on arrival. This means you can use your mobile phone to text and make local calls, but note that you'll be charged at a much higher rate. You can also purchase a pay-as-you-go package with a local provider using your own GSM mobile phone (check that it can handle the frequencies mentioned above). As you use up your airtime, you simply buy a top-up card (€10 to €35) at a newsagency or petrol station. Similar schemes exist in Northern Ireland.

Phone Codes

To call the Republic of Ireland from abroad, you'll need to dial your country's international access code, followed by 353 (the Republic's country code), then the domestic number including the area code (minus the initial '0').

When calling Northern Ireland from abroad, dial your international access code, then 44 (the UK country code), then 28 (the North's area code), and then the local number. To call Northern Ireland from Britain, simply dial 028, then the local number. This changes to 048 when calling from the Republic.

The area code for the whole of Northern Ireland is 028, so domestic callers need only dial the eight-digit local number.

To call UK numbers from the Republic dial 00-44, then the area code minus the initial '0', then the local number. Do the same for international calls, replacing 44 with the country code.

To call Britain from Northern Ireland, dial the area code followed by the local number. To place an international call or to call the Republic from Northern Ireland, dial 00 followed by the country code, then the area code (dropping any leading '0') and the local number.

TIME

In winter, Ireland is on Greenwich Mean Time (GMT), also known as Universal Time Coordinated (UTC), the same as Britain. In summer, the clock shifts to GMT plus one hour, so when it's noon in Dublin and London, it's 4am in Los Angeles and Vancouver, 7am in New York and Toronto, 1pm in Paris, 7pm in Singapore, and 9pm in Sydney.

TOILETS

Forget about the few public facilities on the street: they're dirty and usually overrun with drug dealers and addicts. All shopping centres have public toilets – often marked with the Irish *Fir* (Men) and *Mná* (Women); if you're stranded, go into any bar or hotel.

TOURIST INFORMATION

Fáilte Ireland (☎ in the Republic 1850 230 330, in the UK 0800 039 7000; www.discoverireland.ie) and the **Northern Irish Tourist Board** (NITB; head office ☎ 9023 1221; www.discovernorthernireland.com) are mines of information.

Both websites include an accommodation booking service; reservations can also be made via the tourist boards' system **Gulliver Ireland** (☎ 066-9792030; www.gulliver.ie).

Fáilte Ireland has an office in **Belfast** (☎ 9032 7888) and NITB has an office in **Dublin** (☎ within the Republic 01-679 1977, 1850 230 230).

In both the Republic and the North there's a tourist office in almost every big town; most can offer a variety of services including accommodation and attraction reservations, currency changing services, map and guidebook sales and free publications. Fáilte Ireland also has six regional offices, which can give more in-depth information on specific areas.

Main Regional Tourist Offices in the Republic

Cork & Kerry (☎ 021-425 5100; www.discoverireland .ie/southwest; Cork Kerry Tourism, Áras Discover, Grand Pde, Cork)

Dublin (☎ 01-605 7700; www.visitdublin.com; Dublin Tourism Centre, St Andrew's Church, 2 Suffolk St, Dublin)

East Coast & Midlands (☎ 044-934 8761; www.dis coverireland.ie/eastcoast; East Coast & Midlands Tourism, Dublin Rd, Mullingar) For Kildare, Laois, Longford, Louth, Meath, North Offaly, Westmeath and Wicklow.

Ireland North West & Lakelands (☎ 071-916 1201; www.discoverireland.ie/northwest; Temple St, Sligo) For Cavan, Donegal, Leitrim, Monaghan and Sligo.

Ireland West (☎ 091-537 700; www.discoverireland .ie/west; Ireland West Tourism, Áras Fáilte, Forster St, Galway) For Galway, Roscommon and Mayo.

Shannon Region (☎ 061-361 555; www.discoverire land.ie/shannon; Shannon Development, Shannon, Clare) For Clare, Limerick, North Tipperary and South Offaly.

South East (☎ 051-875 823; www.discoverireland .ie/southeast; South East Tourism, 41 The Quay, Waterford) For Carlow, Kilkenny, South Tipperary, Waterford and Wexford.

Tourist Offices Abroad

Outside Ireland, Fáilte Ireland and the NITB unite under the banner Tourism Ireland. More information about offices around the world can be found at the international website, www.discoverireland.com.

TRAVELLERS WITH DISABILITIES

Travelling in Ireland with a disability can be a frustrating experience, as facilities and access are quite poor by European standards. Improvements are being made, but progress is quite slow in some areas. If you have a physical disability, get in touch with your national support organisation (preferably the travel officer if there is one) before you go. It often has libraries devoted to travel and can put you in touch with agencies that specialise in tours for travellers with disabilities.

Guesthouses, hotels and sights in Ireland are gradually being adapted for people with disabilities. Fáilte Ireland and NITB's accommodation guides indicate which places are wheelchair accessible.

Public transportation can be a bit hit-and-miss. In the big cities, most buses now have low-floor access and priority space on board, but the number of kneeling buses on regional routes is still relatively small.

Trains are accessible with help. In theory, if you call ahead, an employee of Iarnród Éireann (Irish Rail) will arrange to accompany you to the train. Newer trains have audio and visual information systems for visually impaired and hearing-impaired passengers.

The **Citizens' Information Board** (☎ 01-605 9000; www.citizensinformationboard.ie) in the Republic and **Disability Action** (☎ 9066 1252; www.disabilityaction.org) in Northern Ireland can give some advice, although most of their information concerns the rights of Irish citizens with disabilities. Travellers to Northern Ireland can also check out the website www.allgohere.com.

DIRECTORY

VISAS

UK nationals don't need a passport to visit the Republic, but are advised to carry one (or some other form of photo identification) to prove that they *are* a UK national. It's also necessary to have a passport or photo ID when changing travellers cheques or hiring a car. European Economic Area (EEA) citizens (that is, citizens of EU states, plus Iceland, Liechtenstein and Norway) can enter Ireland with either a passport or a national ID card. Visitors from outside the EEA will need a passport that is valid for at least six months after their intended arrival.

For EEA nationals and citizens of most Western countries, including Australia, Canada, New Zealand and the USA, no visa is required to visit either the Republic or Northern Ireland; citizens of India, China and many African countries do need a visa for the Republic. Full visa requirements for visiting the Republic are available online at www.dfa.ie; for Northern Ireland's visa requirements, see www.ukvisas.gov.uk.

EEA nationals can stay for as long as they like, but other visitors can usually remain for up to three months in the Republic and up to six months in the North. To stay longer in the Republic, contact the local *garda* (police) station or the **Garda National Immigration Bureau** (Map pp92-3; ☎ 01-666 9100; www.garda.ie; 13-14 Burgh Quay, Dublin). To stay longer in Northern Ireland, contact the **Home Office** (UK Border Agency; ☎ 0870-606 7766; www.ukba.homeoffice.gov.uk).

Citizens of member states of the EEA do not need a work visa to work in the Republic. Non-EEA nationals are allowed to work for up to one year in the Republic, if they have a specific job to come to and their employer has obtained permission from the Department of Enterprise, Trade and Employment (see right for Commonwealth exceptions).

Although you don't need an onward or return ticket to enter Ireland, it could help if there's any doubt that you have sufficient funds to support yourself during your stay.

VOLUNTEERING

Prosperous Western democracies don't afford the same volunteering opportunities as you'd find elsewhere, but that doesn't mean there aren't projects where you can lend a volunteering hand. From painting walls in Wicklow to helping out in hospitals in Galway and guiding visitors in Dublin museums, your time and effort will be put to good use. Check out www.volunteeringireland.ie for all relevant information, including how to sign up and where to go.

WOMEN TRAVELLERS

Except for the occasional wolf whistle from a building site or a ham-fisted attempt at a chat-up by some drunken guy, women will probably find travelling in Ireland a blissfully relaxing experience. Walking alone at night, especially in certain parts of Dublin, and hitching are probably unwise. Should you have serious problems, be sure to report them to the local tourist authorities.

There's little need to worry about what you wear in Ireland, and the climate is hardly conducive to topless sunbathing. Finding contraception is not the problem it once was, although anyone on the pill should bring adequate supplies.

Rape Crisis Network Ireland (www.rcni.ie) runs a 24-hour helpline at ☎ 1800 77 88 88. In the North, try the **Rape Crisis & Sexual Abuse Centre** (☎ 9032 9002).

WORK

The collapse of the Irish economy in 2008 means that even low-paid seasonal work in the tourist industry (usually restaurants and pubs) is increasingly hard to come by. Sometimes volunteer work is available in return for bed and board, such as from the **Burren Conservation Trust** (☎ 065-707 6105; jdmn@iol.ie; Fanore, Co Clare).

Citizens of other EU countries can work legally in Ireland. If you don't come from an EU country but have an Irish parent or grandparent, it's fairly easy to obtain Irish citizenship without necessarily renouncing your own nationality, and this opens the door to employment throughout the EU. Obtaining citizenship isn't an overnight procedure, though; enquire at an Irish embassy or consulate in your own country.

To work in the North, citizens of Commonwealth countries who are aged 17 to 27 can apply for a Working Holiday Entry Certificate, which allows them to spend two years in the UK (and therefore Northern Ireland) and to take work that's 'incidental' to a holiday. You need to apply – before you travel – at the British consulate or high commission in your country. In the Republic, a similar system, the Working Holiday Authorisation, allows citizens of Australia,

New Zealand and Canada to work casually so they can take an extended holiday; again, you must apply while still in your own country.

Commonwealth citizens with a UK-born parent may be eligible for a Certificate of Entitlement to the Right of Abode, which entitles them to live and work in the UK free of immigration control. Commonwealth citizens with a UK-born grandparent, or a grandparent born before 31 March 1922 in what's now the Republic, may qualify for a UK Ancestry Employment Certificate, allowing them to work full time for up to four years in the UK; check with the UK Border Agency, part of the Home Office, at www.ukvisas.gov.uk.

Full-time US students aged 18 and over can get a four-month work permit for Ireland, plus insurance and support information, through the **Work & Travel Ireland** (☎ 01-602 1788; www.work andtravelireland.org).

Nixers (www.nixers.com) is a useful noticeboard site for those in search of casual labour.

Transport

CONTENTS

GETTING THERE & AWAY

ENTERING THE COUNTRY

An increase in the number of foreign nationals seeking asylum during the last decade has meant a far more rigorous questioning at customs for those from African and Asian countries or from certain parts of Eastern Europe. The border between the Republic and Northern Ireland still exists as a political reality, but there are few if any checkpoints left; for non-EU nationals it is assumed the screening process occurred upon entry to the UK. For information on visa requirements, see p712.

Passport

EU citizens can travel freely to and from Ireland if bearing official photo ID. Those from outside the EU, however, must have a passport that remains valid for six months after entry.

AIR
Airports & Airlines

There are scheduled nonstop flights from Britain, continental Europe and North America to Dublin and Shannon, and good nonstop connections from Britain and continental Europe to Cork.

Cork (ORK; ☎ 021-431 3131; www.corkairport.com)
Dublin (DUB; ☎ 01-814 1111; www.dublinairport.com)

THINGS CHANGE...

The information in this chapter is particularly vulnerable to change. Check directly with the airline or a travel agent to make sure you understand how a fare (and ticket you may buy) works and be aware of the security requirements for international travel. Shop carefully. The details given in this chapter should be regarded as pointers and are not a substitute for your own careful, up-to-date research.

Shannon (SNN; ☎ 061-712 000; www.shannonairport.com)

Other airports in the Republic with scheduled services from Britain:
Donegal (CFN; ☎ 074-954 8284; www.donegalairport.ie; Carrickfinn)
Kerry (KIR; ☎ 066-976 4644; www.kerryairport.ie; Farranfore)
Knock (NOC; ☎ 094-936 8100; www.irelandwestairport.com)
Waterford (WAT; ☎ 051-875 589; www.flywaterford.com)

In Northern Ireland there are flights to **Belfast International** (BFS; ☎ 028-9448 4848; www.belfastairport.com) from Britain, continental Europe and the USA.

Other airports in Northern Ireland that operate scheduled services from Britain:
Belfast City (BHD; ☎ 028-9093 9093; www.belfastcityairport.com)
Derry (LDY; ☎ 028-7181 0784; www.cityofderryairport.com)

The main Irish airlines:
Aer Árann (☎ 1890 462 726; www.aerarann.ie) A small carrier that operates flights within Ireland and also to Britain.
Aer Lingus (☎ 01-886 8888; www.aerlingus.com) The main Irish airline, with direct flights to Britain, continental Europe and the USA.

FARE GO

Travel costs throughout this book are for single (one-way) adult fares, unless otherwise stated.

CLIMATE CHANGE & TRAVEL

Climate change is a serious threat to the ecosystems that humans rely upon, and air travel is the fastest-growing contributor to the problem. Lonely Planet regards travel, overall, as a global benefit, but believes we all have a responsibility to limit our personal impact on global warming.

Flying & Climate Change

Pretty much every form of motor travel generates CO_2 (the main cause of human-induced climate change) but planes are far and away the worst offenders, not just because of the sheer distances they allow us to travel, but because they release greenhouse gases high into the atmosphere. The statistics are frightening: two people taking a return flight between Europe and the US will contribute as much to climate change as an average household's gas and electricity consumption over a whole year.

Carbon Offset Schemes

Climatecare.org and other websites use 'carbon calculators' that allow jetsetters to offset the greenhouse gases they are responsible for with contributions to energy-saving projects and other climate-friendly initiatives in the developing world – including projects in India, Honduras, Kazakhstan and Uganda.

Lonely Planet, together with Rough Guides and other concerned partners in the travel industry, supports the carbon offset scheme run by climatecare.org. Lonely Planet offsets all of its staff and author travel.

For more information check out our website: lonelyplanet.com.

Ryanair (☎ 01-609 7800; www.ryanair.com) Ireland's no-frills carrier with inexpensive services to Britain and continental Europe.

Nearly all international airlines use Dublin as their hub within Ireland. Airlines flying into and out of Ireland:

Adria Airways (www.adria.si)
Aer Árann (☎ 1890 462 726; www.aerarann.com)
Aer Lingus (☎ 01-886 8888; www.aerlingus.com)
Air Baltic (www.airbaltic.com)
Air Canada (☎ 1800 709 900; www.aircanada.ca)
Air France (☎ 01-605 0383; www.airfrance.com)
Air Malta (☎ 1800 397 400; www.airmalta.com)
Air Southwest (www.airsouthwest.com)
Air Transat (www.airtransat.com)
American Airlines (☎ 01-602 0550; www.aa.com)
BMI (☎ 01-407 3036; www.flybmi.com)
British Airways (☎ 1800 626 747; www.britishairways .com)
City Jet (☎ 01-870 0300; www.cityjet.com)
Continental (☎ 1890 925 252; www.continental.com)
Delta Airlines (☎ 1800 768 080; www.delta.com)
EasyJet (☎ 048-9448 4929; www.easyjet.com; Knock only)
Etihad Airways (☎ 01-477 3479; www.etihadairways.com)
Flybe (☎ 1890 925 532; www.flybe.com)
Flyglobespan (☎ 01-874 7666; www.flyglobespan.ie)
German Wings (☎ 01-865 0125; www.germanwings.com)
Iberia (☎ 01-407 3017; www.iberia.com)
Lufthansa (☎ 01-844 5544; www.lufthansa.com)

Luxair (☎ 01-477 3479; www.luxair.co.uk)
Malev Hungarian Airlines (☎ 01-844 4303; www .malev.com)
Ryanair (☎ 0818 30 30 30; www.ryanair.com)
S7 Airlines (☎ 01-663 3933; www.s7.ru)
Scandinavian Airlines (☎ 01-844 5440; www.flysas .com)
Swiss Airlines (☎ 1890 200 515; www.swiss.com)
Turkish Airlines (☎ 01-844 7920; www.turkishairlines .com)
US Airways (☎ 1890 925 065; www.usairways.com)

Tickets

The emergence of the no-frills, low-fares model as the future of European air travel has made cheap tickets the norm rather than the exception. For point-to-point travel, the best deals are almost always available online – indeed, Europe's largest carrier, Ryanair, will penalise passengers who don't avail themselves of the online services (including check-in) – but more complicated travel arrangements are best handled by a real live travel agent, who knows the system, the options and the best deals. Be sure to check the terms and conditions of the cheapest fares before purchasing.

ONLINE BOOKING AGENCIES

Best Fares (www.bestfares.com) American site offering discounted airfares and hotel rooms.

Cheap Flights (www.cheapflights.com) American- and British-based site that lists discounted flights and packages.

ebookers (www.ebookers.com) Irish, web-based internet travel agency.

Expedia (www.expedia.co.uk) Microsoft's travel site.

Opodo (www.opodo.com) Joint booking service for nine European airlines.

Priceline (www.priceline.com) American, web-based travel agency.

STA Travel (www.statravel.com) International student travel agency.

Travelocity (www.travelocity.com) American, web-based travel agency.

Australia & New Zealand

There are no nonstop scheduled air services from Australia or New Zealand to Ireland; generally it's cheapest to fly to London or Amsterdam and continue from there. Most fares to European destinations can have a return flight to Dublin tagged on at little or no extra cost. Round-the-world (RTW) tickets are another good bet and are often better value than standard return fares.

The Saturday travel sections of the *Sydney Morning Herald* and Melbourne *Age* newspapers advertise cheap fares; in New Zealand, check the *New Zealand Herald* travel section.

Recommended agencies:

AUSTRALIA
Flight Centre (☎ 133 133; www.flightcentre.com.au)
Shamrock Travel (☎ 03-9602 3700; www.irishtravel.com.au)
STA Travel (☎ 1300 733 035; www.statravel.com.au)

NEW ZEALAND
Flight Centre (☎ 0800-243 544; www.flightcentre.co.nz)
STA Travel (☎ 0508-782 872; www.statravel.co.nz)

Canada

Air Canada is the only carrier flying directly to Ireland, from Toronto to both Dublin and Shannon. Your best bet for cheaper fares may be to connect to transatlantic gateways in the USA or to fly to London and continue on to Ireland from there. Check the travel sections of the *Globe & Mail, Toronto Star, Montreal Gazette* or *Vancouver Sun* for the latest offers.

Recommended agencies:

Canadian Affair (☎ 1604-678 6868; www.canadianaffair.com) Cheap one-way fares to British cities.

Flight Centre (☎ 1877-967 5302; www.flightcentre.ca)
Travel CUTS (☎ 866-246 9762; www.travelcuts.com)

Continental Europe

Price wars have cut the price of flights to Ireland from continental Europe to their lowest rates ever. The two biggest players in the market are the one-time national airline, **Aer Lingus** (www.aerlingus.com), now a low-frills airline in virtually every respect, offering competitive prices to over 40 destinations; and the king of all low-fares airlines, **Ryanair** (www.ryanair.com), which serves over 80 European destinations from Dublin and over 100 from its (now) main hub at London Stansted. Ryanair's success is predicated on using secondary airports in or around major cities, which can make for expensive and time-consuming transfers. Check when you book.

UK

There is a mind-boggling array of flights between Britain and Ireland. The best deals are usually available online, and it's not unusual for airport taxes to exceed the base price of the ticket on the lowest fares (generally for early morning or late-night flights midweek).

Most regional airports in Britain have flights to Dublin and Belfast and some also provide services to Shannon, Cork, Kerry, Knock and Waterford.

USA

In the USA, discount travel agencies (consolidators) sell cut-price tickets on scheduled carriers. Aer Lingus is the chief carrier between the USA and Ireland, with flights from New York, Boston, Chicago, San Francisco and Washington, DC, to Shannon, Dublin and Belfast. Heavy competition on transatlantic routes into London might make it cheaper to fly there and then continue on to Ireland. The Sunday travel sections of the *New York Times, San Francisco Chronicle-Examiner, Los Angeles Times* and *Chicago Tribune* list cheap fares.

Some of the more popular travel agencies:
Ireland Consolidated (☎ 212-661 1999; www.irelandair.com)
STA Travel (☎ 800-781 4040; www.statravel.com)

LAND

Eurolines (www.eurolines.com) has a three-times-daily coach and ferry service from London's Victoria Station to Dublin Busáras. For information on border crossings, see p719.

SEA

There are many ferry and fast-boat services from Britain and France to Ireland. Prices quoted throughout this section are one-way fares for a single adult on foot/up to two adults with a car, during peak season.

UK & Ireland

There are numerous ferry and fast-boat services between Britain and Ireland but it's definitely wise to plan ahead as fares can vary considerably, depending on the season, day, time and length of stay. Often, some return fares don't cost that much more than one-way fares and it's worth keeping an eye out for special offers. International Student Identity Card (ISIC) holders and Hostelling International (HI) members get a reduction on the normal fares.

These shipping lines operate between Britain and Ireland:

Irish Ferries (☎ in the UK 0870-517 1717, in the Republic 1890 31 31 31; www.irishferries.com) For ferry and fast-boat services from Pembroke to Dublin, and ferry services from Pembroke to Rosslare.

Isle of Man Steam Packet Company/Sea Cat (☎ in the UK 1800 805 055, in the Republic 01-836 4019; www.steam-packet.com) Ferry and fast-boat services from Liverpool to Dublin or Belfast via Douglas (on the Isle of Man).

Norfolkline (☎ in the UK 0870-600 4321, in the Republic 01-819 2999; www.norfolkline.com) Ferry services from Liverpool to Belfast and Dublin.

P&O Irish Sea (☎ in the UK 0870-242 4777, in the Republic 01-407 3434; www.poirishsea.com) Ferry and fast-boat services from Larne to Cairnryan and Troon, and ferry services from Liverpool to Dublin.

Stena Line (☎ 0870-570 7070; www.stenaline.com) Ferry services from Holyhead to Dun Laoghaire, Fleetwood to Larne and Stranraer to Belfast, and fast-boat services from Holyhead to Dublin, Fishguard to Rosslare, and Stranraer to Belfast.

The main routes from the UK to the Republic include the following (for a foot passenger/vehicle):

Fishguard & Pembroke to Rosslare These popular, short ferry crossings take 3½ hours (from Fishguard) or four hours (from Pembroke) and cost around £25/119; the cost drops significantly outside peak season. The fast-boat crossing from Fishguard takes just under two hours and costs around £30/135.

Holyhead to Dublin & Dun Laoghaire The ferry crossing takes just over three hours and costs from £25/95. The fast-boat service from Holyhead to Dun Laoghaire takes a little over 1½ hours and costs £25/130.

Liverpool to Dublin The ferry service takes 8½ hours from Liverpool and costs £25/180. Cabins on overnight sailings cost more. The fast-boat service takes four hours and costs up to £40/240.

The main routes from mainland Britain to the North (for a foot passenger/vehicle):

Cairnryan to Larne The fast boat takes one hour and costs £21/170. The ferry takes 1¾ hours and costs £15/120.

Fleetwood to Larne The six-hour crossing costs £122; no foot passengers are carried.

Liverpool to Belfast The 8½-hour crossing costs £40/155 (including meals) during the day and £30/235 (including cabin and meals) at night.

Stranraer to Belfast The fast boat takes 1¾ hours and costs £20/130. The ferry takes 3¼ hours and costs £16/85.

It's possible to combine bus and ferry tickets from major UK centres to all Irish towns on the bus network, which mightn't be as convenient as flying on a budget airline, but leaves less of a carbon footprint. The journey between London and Dublin takes about 12 hours and costs about £43 one way. The London to Belfast trip takes 13 to 16 hours and costs £38 one way. For details in London

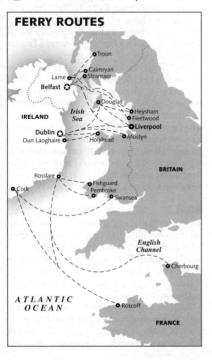

FERRY ROUTES

contact **Eurolines** (☎ 0870-514 3219; www.eurolines .com).

France

Two companies operated on the France–Ireland route:

Brittany Ferries (☎ in the Republic 021-427 7801, in France 02 98 29 28 00; www.brittany-ferries.com) Weekly service from Roscoff to Cork from early April to late September. The crossing takes 14 hours and costs up to €85/490 without accommodation.

Irish Ferries (☎ in Rosslare 053-33158, in Cherbourg 02 33 23 44 44, in Roscoff 02 98 61 17 17; www.irishferries .com) One to three times a week from Roscoff to Rosslare from late April to late September; the crossing time is 17½ hours. Ferries from Cherbourg to Rosslare sail two to four times per week year-round, except in late January and all of February; crossing time is 20½ hours. Both services cost up to €150/625 without accommodation.

GETTING AROUND

Travelling around Ireland is short, simple and sweet – or maddeningly long and infuriatingly complicated. Distances are relatively short and there's a good network of roads, but public transportation can be infrequent, expensive or both and – especially with trains – not reach many of the more interesting places.

Having your own transport is a major advantage and it's worth considering car hire for at least part of your trip. The growing network of motorways have cut journey times considerably, but the huge network of secondary and tertiary roads are much better if you want to 'experience' Ireland as you travel – although it is still true that smaller, rural roads can make for difficult driving conditions.

If you opt not to drive, a mixture of buses, the occasional taxi, plenty of time, walking and sometimes hiring a bicycle will get you just about anywhere.

AIR
Airlines in Ireland

Ireland's size makes domestic flying unnecessary unless you're in a hurry, but there are flights between Dublin and Belfast, Cork, Derry, Donegal, Galway, Kerry, Shannon and Sligo, as well as a Belfast–Cork service. Most flights within Ireland take around 30 to 50 minutes.

The only domestic air carriers are the following:

Aer Árann (☎ 1890-462 726, in Dublin 01-814 5240, in Galway 091-593 034, in Cork 021-814 1058; www .aerarann.com) Operates flights from Dublin to Belfast, Cork, Derry, Donegal, Galway, Knock and Sligo; and a Belfast to Cork route.

Aer Lingus (☎ information & bookings 01-886 8844, flight information 01-705 6705, in Belfast 028-9442 2888; www.aerlingus.com) Operates flights between Dublin and Shannon.

Ryanair (www.ryanair.com) Operates flights between Dublin and Cork.

BICYCLE

Ireland is a great place for bicycle touring, despite bad road surfaces in places and inclement weather. If you intend to cycle in the west, the prevailing winds mean it's easier to cycle from south to north. Both **Irish Cycling Safaris** (☎ 01-260 0749; www.cyclingsafaris.com; Belfield Bike Shop, UCD, Dublin 4) and **Go Ireland** (☎ 066-976 2094; www .govisitireland.com; Old Orchard House, Killorglin, Co Kerry) organise tours for groups of cyclists in the southwest, the southeast, Clare, Connemara, Donegal and Antrim.

Bicycles can be transported by bus if there's enough room; the charge varies. By train the cost varies from €4 to €8 for a one-way journey, but bikes are not allowed on certain train routes, including the Dublin Area Rapid Transit (DART); check with **Iarnród Éireann** (☎ 01-836 3333).

Typical bicycle hire costs are €20 to €25 per day or €60 to €100 per week plus a deposit of around €100. There are many local independent outlets, but several dealers have outlets around the country:

Irish Cycle Hire (☎ 041-685 3772; www.irishcyclehire .com; Unit 6, Enterprise Centre, Ardee, Co Louth)

Raleigh Ireland (☎ 01-626 1333; www.raleigh.ie; Raleigh House, Kylemore Rd, Dublin) Ireland's biggest rental dealer.

Rent-a-Bike Ireland (☎ 061-416 983; www.ireland rentabike.com; 1 Patrick St, Limerick, Co Limerick)

BOAT

There are many boat services to islands lying off the coast, including to the Aran and Skellig Islands to the west, the Saltee Islands to the southeast, and Tory and Rathlin Islands to the north. Ferries also operate across rivers, inlets and loughs, providing useful short cuts, particularly for cyclists.

Cruises are very popular on the 258km-long Shannon–Erne Waterway and on a variety of other lakes and loughs. The tourist offices only recommend operators that are registered with them. Details of non-tourist-board-affiliated boat trips are given under the relevant sections throughout this book.

BORDER CROSSINGS

Security has been progressively scaled down in Northern Ireland in recent years and all border crossings with the Republic are now open and generally unstaffed. Permanent checkpoints have been removed and ramps levelled. On major routes your only indication that you have crossed the border will be a change in road signs and the colour of number plates and postboxes.

BUS

Bus Éireann (☎ 01-836 6111; www.buseireann.ie; Busáras, Store St, Dublin) is the Republic's bus line and offers an extensive network throughout the South. Private buses compete – often very favourably – with Bus Éireann in the Republic and also run where the national buses are irregular or absent. **Ulsterbus** (☎ 028-9066 6600; www.ulsterbus.co.uk; Milewater Rd, Belfast) is the only bus service in Northern Ireland.

In Belfast, the bus service is operated by **Metro** (☎ 9066 6630; www.translink.co.uk), while Dublin has **Dublin Bus** (☎ 01-872 000; www.dublinbus.ie).

The larger bus companies will usually carry bikes for free but you should always check in advance to avoid surprises.

Bus Passes

Details of special deals and passes are given in the boxed text, p720.

Costs

Bus travel is much cheaper than train travel, and private buses often charge less than Bus Éireann. Generally, return fares cost little more than a one-way fare.

Some sample one-way bus fares include the following:

Service	Cost	Duration (hrs)	Services per Day (Mon-Sat)
Belfast-Dublin	£13	3	7
Derry-Belfast	£10	1¾	10+
Derry-Galway	£26.10	5¼	4
Dublin-Cork	€11.70	4½	6
Dublin-Donegal	€17.60	4	5
Dublin-Rosslare	€16.70	3	12
Dublin-Tralee	€23	6	12
Dublin-Waterford	€12.20	2¾	7
Killarney-Cork	€15.30	2	12
Killarney-Waterford	€21.20	4½	12

Reservations

Bus Éireann bookings can be made online, but you can't reserve a seat for a particular service.

CAR & MOTORCYCLE

Ireland has more cars than ever and the building of new roads and the upgrading of existing ones just hasn't kept pace. Be prepared for delays, especially at holiday weekends. **AA Roadwatch** (☎ 1550 131 811; www .aaroadwatch.ie) provides traffic information in the Republic.

In the Republic, speed-limit and distance signs are in kilometres (although the occasional older white sign shows distances in miles); in the North, speed-limit and distance signs are in miles.

You'll need a good road map and a sense of humour to deal with the severe lack of signposts in the Republic, and on minor roads be prepared for lots of potholes.

Petrol is considerably cheaper in the Republic than in the North. Most service stations accept payment by credit card, but some small, remote ones may take cash only.

All cars on public roads must be insured. If you are bringing your own vehicle in to the country, check that your insurance will cover you in Ireland.

Bring Your Own Vehicle

It's easy to take your own vehicle to Ireland and there are no specific procedures involved, but you should carry a vehicle registration document as proof that it's yours.

Automobile Association members should ask for a Card of Introduction entitling you to services offered by sister organisations (including maps, information, breakdown assistance, legal advice etc), usually free of charge. **Automobile Association** (AA; www.aaireland.ie) Northern Ireland (☎ 0870-950 0600, breakdown assistance 0800-667 788); Republic (☎ Dublin 01-617 9999, Cork 021-425 2444, breakdown assistance 1800 667 788) **Royal Automobile Club** (RAC; www.rac.ie) Northern Ireland (☎ 0800 029 029, breakdown assistance 0800 828 282); Republic (☎ 1890 483 483)

Driving Licence

Unless you have an EU licence, which is treated like an Irish one, your driving licence is valid for 12 months from the date of entry to Ireland, but you should have held it for two years prior to that. If you don't

TRANSPORT

TRANSPORT

FERRY, BUS & TRAIN DISCOUNT DEALS

For Travel Across Europe

Eurail (www.eurail.com) passes are for non-Europeans who have been in Europe for less than six months. They are valid on trains in the Republic, but not in Northern Ireland, and offer discounts on Irish Ferries crossings to France. Passes are cheaper when purchased outside Europe. In the USA and Canada try **Europrail International** (☎ 1888-667 9734; www.europrail.net). In London contact **Rail Europe** (☎ 0870-584 8848; 179 Piccadilly).

    InterRail (www.interrail.com) passes give you a 50% reduction on train travel within Ireland and discounts on Irish Ferries and Stena Line services. Passes can be purchased at most major train stations and student travel outlets.

For Travel Within Ireland

Holders of the new Student Travel Card (www.studenttravelcard.ie) are entitled to a 40% discount on Irish trains and 25% off Bus Éireann services. The card is available from Usit offices (www.usit.ie).

Unlimited-Travel Tickets For Buses & Trains

The Open-Road Pass covers bus-only travel within the Republic, allowing for a variety of travel options, from three days' travel out of six consecutive days (€54) to 15 days' travel out of 30 (€234).

    Irish Rover tickets combine services on Bus Éireann and Ulsterbus. They cost €83.50 (for three days' travel out of eight consecutive days), €190 (eight days out of 15) and €280 (15 days out of 30).

    Iarnród Éireann Explorer tickets cover train travel in the Republic. They cost €160 (for five days travel out of 15 consecutive days). The Irish Explorer rail and bus tickets (€245) allow eight days' travel out of 15 consecutive days on trains and buses within the Republic.

    Freedom of Northern Ireland passes allow unlimited travel on NIR, Ulsterbus and Citybus services for £15 for one day, £36 for three out of eight consecutive days, and £53 for seven consecutive days.

    Children aged under 16 pay half price for all these passes and for all normal tickets. Children aged under three travel for free on public transport. You can buy the above passes at most major train and bus stations in Ireland. Although they're good value, many of them make economic sense only if you're planning to travel around Ireland at the speed of light.

---

hold an EU licence, it's a good idea to obtain an International Driving Permit (IDP) from your home automobile association before you leave. Your home-country licence is usually enough to hire a car for three months.

You must carry your driving licence at all times.

Hire

Car hire in Ireland is expensive, so you're often better off making arrangements in your home country with some sort of package deal. For travel in July and August it's wise to book well ahead. Most cars are manual; automatic cars are available, but they're more expensive to hire.

The international hire companies and the major local operators have offices all over Ireland. **Nova Car Hire** (www.rentacar-ireland.com) acts as an agent for Alamo, Budget, European and National, and offers greatly discounted rates.

In the Republic typical weekly high-season hire rates with Nova are around €150 for a small car, €185 for a medium-sized car, and €320 for a five-seater people carrier. In the North, similar cars are marginally more expensive.

When hiring a car, be sure to check whether the price includes collision-damage waiver (CDW), insurance (eg for car theft and windscreen damage), value-added tax (VAT) and unlimited mileage.

If you're travelling from the Republic into Northern Ireland, it's important to be sure that your insurance covers journeys to the North. People aged under 21 aren't allowed to hire a car; for the majority of hire companies, you have to be aged at least 23 and have had a valid driving licence for a minimum of one year. Some companies in the Republic won't rent to you if you're aged 74 or over; there's no upper age limit in the North.

Motorbikes and mopeds are not available for rent in Ireland.

Parking

Ireland is tiny and the Irish love their cars; the numbers just don't add up and parking is an expensive and difficult nightmare. Parking in towns and cities is either by meter, 'pay and display' tickets or disc parking (discs, which rotate to display the time you park your car, are available from newsagencies).

Purchase

It's more expensive to buy a car in Ireland than in most other European countries. If you do buy a car (or intend to import one from another country), you must pay vehicle registration tax and motor tax, and take out insurance.

Road Rules

Copies of Ireland's road rules are available from tourist offices. Here are some of the most basic rules:

- Drive on the left; overtake to the right.
- Safety belts must be worn by the driver and all passengers.
- Children aged under 12 aren't allowed to sit in the front passenger seat.
- Motorcyclists and their passengers must wear helmets.
- When entering a roundabout, give way to the right.
- Speed limits are 120km/h on motorways, 100km/h on national roads, 80km/h on regional and local roads and 50km/h or as signposted in towns.
- The legal alcohol limit is 80mg of alcohol per 100ml of blood or 35mg on the breath (roughly two pints of beer an hour for a man, one for a woman). Note: three pints (1½ for a woman) will put you over the limit.

HITCHING

Hitching is becoming increasingly less popular in Ireland, even though it's still pretty easy compared to other European countries. Travellers who decide to hitch should understand that they are taking a small but potentially serious risk, and we don't recommend it. If you do plan to travel by thumb, remember it's illegal to hitch on motorways.

TRANSPORT

ROAD DISTANCES (KM)

	Athlone	Belfast	Cork	Derry	Donegal	Dublin	Galway	Kilkenny	Killarney	Limerick	Rosslare Harbour	Shannon Airport	Sligo	Waterford	Wexford
Athlone	---														
Belfast	227	---													
Cork	219	424	---												
Derry	209	117	428	---											
Donegal	183	180	402	69	---										
Dublin	127	167	256	237	233	---									
Galway	93	306	209	272	204	212	---								
Kilkenny	116	284	148	335	309	114	172	---							
Killarney	232	436	87	441	407	304	193	198	---						
Limerick	121	323	105	328	296	193	104	113	111	---					
Rosslare Harbour	201	330	208	397	391	153	274	98	275	211	---				
Shannon Airport	133	346	128	351	282	218	93	135	135	25	234	---			
Sligo	117	206	336	135	66	214	138	245	343	232	325	218	---		
Waterford	164	333	126	383	357	163	220	48	193	129	82	152	293	---	
Wexford	184	309	187	378	372	135	253	80	254	190	19	213	307	61	---

LOCAL TRANSPORT

Dublin and Belfast have comprehensive local bus networks (see p719), as do some other larger towns. The Dublin Area Rapid Transport (DART; p151) line runs roughly the length of Dublin's coastline, while the Luas (p151) tram system has two popular lines. Taxis tend to be expensive – for daytime rates, flagfall is €4.10 and fares start at €1.03 per km after that (nighttime rates are a bit higher).

TOURS

If your time is limited, it might be worth considering an organised tour, though it's cheaper to see things independently, and Ireland is small enough for you to get to even the most remote places within a few hours. Tours can be booked through travel agencies, tourist offices in the major cities, or directly through the tour companies themselves.

Bus Éireann (☎ 01-836 6111; www.buseireann.ie; 59 Upper O'Connell St, Dublin) Runs day tours to various parts of the Republic and the North.

CIE Tours International (☎ 01-703 1888; www .cietours.ie; 35 Lower Abbey St, Dublin) Runs four- to 11-day coach tours of the Republic and the North, including accommodation and meals. The Taste of Ireland tour (five days) takes in Blarney, Ring of Kerry, Killarney, Cliffs of Moher and the region around the River Shannon (€715 in high season).

Grayline Tours (☎ 01-872 9010; www.irishcitytours .com; 33 Bachelor's Walk, Dublin) Located in Dublin, it offers half- and full-day tours (€25) from Dublin to Newgrange, Glendalough and north Dublin, and three- and four-day trips to the Ring of Kerry (€219 to €369).

TRAIN ROUTES

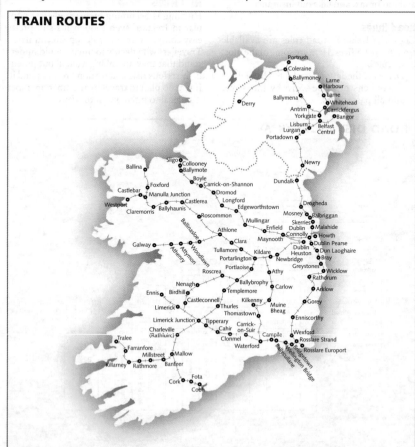

Paddywagon Tours (☎ 01-672 6007; www.paddy wagontours.com) Activity-filled three- and six-day tours all over Ireland with friendly tour guides. Accommodation is in IHH hostels.

Ulsterbus Tours (☎ 028-9033 7004; www.ulsterbus .co.uk) Runs a large number of day trips throughout the North and the Republic.

It's worth checking **GoIreland.com** (☎ 1800 668 668; www.goireland.com) for holiday packages.

For train enthusiasts, **Railtours Ireland** (☎ 01-856 0045; www.railtoursireland.com) organises a series of one- and two-day train trips in association with Iarnród Éireann. A three-day trip from Dublin to Cork, Blarney Castle and Kerry costs €339.

TRAIN

Iarnród Éireann (Irish Rail; ☎ 1850 366 222; www .irishrail.ie; 35 Lower Abbey St, Dublin) operates trains in the Republic on routes that fan out from Dublin. The system is limited though: there's no north–south route along the western coast, no network in Donegal, and no direct connections from Waterford to Cork or Killarney.
Northern Ireland Railways (NIR; ☎ 028-9089 9411; www.nirailways.co.uk; Belfast Central Station) runs four routes from Belfast. One links with the system in the Republic via Newry to Dublin; the other

three go east to Bangor, northeast to Larne and northwest to Derry via Coleraine (see the map, p722).

Costs

Train travel is more expensive than bus travel and one-way fares are particularly poor value – a midweek return ticket is often about the same as a one-way fare. First-class tickets cost around €5 to €10 more than the standard fare for a single journey.

Some sample one-way fares:

Service	Cost (€)	Duration (hrs)	Frequency/Service per Day (Mon-Sat)
Dublin-Belfast	38	2	half-hourly
Dublin-Cork	66	3¼	8
Dublin-Galway	34.50	3¼	5
Dublin-Limerick	50	2½	13
Dublin-Sligo	32	3	3
Dublin-Tralee	68.50	4½	8
Dublin-Waterford	27	2½	7

Reservations

Iarnród Éireann takes reservations for all its train services. You need to fax your details (name, number of passengers, date and time of service, credit-card number and expiry date) to ☎ 01-703 4136.

TRANSPORT

Health

CONTENTS

BEFORE YOU GO

While Ireland has excellent health care, prevention is the key to staying healthy while abroad. A little planning before departure, particularly for pre-existing illnesses, will save trouble later. Bring medications in their original, clearly labelled containers. A signed and dated letter from your physician describing your medical conditions and medications, including generic names, is also a good idea. If carrying syringes or needles, be sure to have a physician's letter documenting their medical necessity. Carry a spare pair of contact lenses and glasses, and take your optical prescription with you.

INSURANCE

If you're an EU citizen, a European Health Insurance Card (EHIC), available from health centres or, in the UK, post offices, covers you for most medical care. The EHIC won't cover you for non-emergencies, or emergency repatriation home. Citizens from other countries should find out if there is a reciprocal arrangement for free medical care between their country and Ireland. If you do need health insurance, make sure you get a policy that covers you for the worst possible case, such as an accident requiring an emergency flight home. Find out in advance if your insurance plan will make payments directly to providers, or reimburse you later for overseas health expenditures.

RECOMMENDED VACCINATIONS

No jabs are required to travel to Ireland. The World Health Organization recommends, however, that all travellers should be covered for diphtheria, tetanus, measles, mumps, rubella, polio and hepatitis B, regardless of their destination.

IN TRANSIT

DEEP VEIN THROMBOSIS (DVT)

Blood clots may form in the legs during plane flights, chiefly because of prolonged immobility. The longer the flight, the greater the risk. The chief symptom of deep vein thrombosis is swelling or pain of the foot, ankle, or calf, often on just one side. When a blood clot travels to the lungs, it may cause chest pain and difficulty breathing. Travellers with any of these symptoms should immediately seek medical attention.

To prevent the development of DVT on long flights, you should walk about the cabin, contract the leg muscles while sitting, drink plenty of fluids and avoid alcohol and tobacco.

JET LAG & MOTION SICKNESS

To avoid jet lag (quite common when crossing more than five time zones), try drinking plenty of nonalcoholic fluids and eating light meals. Upon arrival, get exposure to natural sunlight and readjust your schedule (for meals, sleep etc) as soon as possible.

Antihistamines such as dimenhydrinate (Dramamine) or meclizine (Antivert, Bonine) are quite often the first choice for treating motion sickness. A herbal alternative is ginger.

IN IRELAND

AVAILABILITY & COST OF HEALTH CARE

Excellent health care is readily available. For minor, self-limiting illnesses, pharmacists can give valuable advice and sell over-the-counter medication. They can also advise when more specialised help is required and point you in the right direction.

TRAVELLER'S DIARRHOEA

If you develop diarrhoea, be sure to drink plenty of fluids, preferably in the form of an oral rehydration solution, such as dioralyte. If diarrhoea is bloody, persists for more than 72 hours or is accompanied by fever, shaking, chills or severe abdominal pain you should seek urgent medical attention.

ENVIRONMENTAL HAZARDS
Heatstroke

Heat exhaustion (yes, even in Ireland it can still happen!) occurs following excessive fluid loss with insufficient replacement of fluids and salt. Symptoms include headache, dizziness and tiredness. Dehydration is already happening by the time you feel thirsty – aim to drink sufficient water to produce pale, diluted urine. To treat heat exhaustion, drink water and/or fruit juice, and cool the body with cold water and fans.

Hypothermia

Hypothermia occurs when the body loses heat faster than it can produce it. As ever, proper preparation will reduce the risks of getting it. Even on a hot day in the mountains the weather can change rapidly, so carry waterproof garments, warm layers and a hat, and inform others of your route.

Hypothermia starts with shivering, loss of judgment and clumsiness. Without rewarming, the sufferer deteriorates into apathy, confusion and coma. Prevent further heat loss by seeking shelter, warm dry clothing, hot sweet drinks and shared body warmth.

Language

CONTENTS

In 2003 the government introduced the Official Languages Act, whereby all official documents, street signs and official titles must be either in Irish (Gaeilge) or in both Irish and English. While Irish is the official language, it's only spoken in isolated pockets of rural Ireland known as Gaeltachtaí, the main ones being Cork (Chorcaí), Donegal (Dhún na nGall), Galway (Gaillimhe), Kerry (Chiarraí) and Mayo (Mhaigh Eo).

Irish is a compulsory subject in schools for those aged six to 15, but Irish classes have traditionally been thoroughly academic and unimaginative, leading most kids to resent it as a waste of time. Ask people outside the Gaeltachtaí if they can speak Irish and nine out of 10 of them will probably reply, 'ah, cupla focal' (a couple of words), and they generally mean it. It's a pity that the treatment of Irish in schools has been so heavy-handed because many adults say they regret not having a greater grasp of it. At long last, and for the first time since the formation of the state, a new Irish curriculum has recently been introduced that will cut the hours devoted to the subject but make the lessons more fun, practical and celebratory.

If you'd like a witty insight into the quirks of language in Ireland, get a copy of Lonely Planet's pocket-sized Irish Language & Culture.

PRONUNCIATION

Irish has three main dialects: Connaught Irish (Galway and northern Mayo), Munster Irish (Cork, Kerry and Waterford) and Ulster Irish (Donegal). The pronunciation guidelines given here are an anglicised version of modern standard Irish, which is essentially an amalgam of the three.

Vowels

Irish divides vowels into long (those with an accent) and short (those without) and, more importantly, broad (**a**, **á**, **o**, **ó**, **u** and **ú**) and slender (**e**, **é**, **i** and **í**), which can affect the pronunciation of preceding consonants.

a	as in 'cat'
á	as in 'saw'
e	as in 'bet'
é	as in 'hey'
i	as in 'sit'
í	as in 'marine'
o	as in 'son'
ó	as in 'low'
u	as in 'put'
ú	as in 'rule'

Consonants

Other than a few odd-looking clusters, like **mh** and **bhf**, consonants are generally pronounced as they are in English.

bh	as the 'v' in 'voice'
bhf	as the 'w' in 'well'
c	as the 'c' in 'cat'
ch	as the 'ch' in Scottish loch
d	as in 'do' when followed by a broad vowel; as the 'j' in 'jug' when followed by a slender vowel
dh	as the 'g' in 'gap' when followed by a broad vowel; as the 'y' in 'year' when followed by a slender vowel
mh	as the 'w' in 'well'
s	as in 'said' before a broad vowel; as the 'sh' in ship before a slender vowel and at the end of a word
t	as the 't' in 'toast' before a broad vowel; as the 'ch' in 'church' before a slender vowel
th	as the 'h' in 'house'; as the 't' in 'mat'; silent at the end of a word

MAKING CONVERSATION

Hello.	Dia duit.	dee·a gwit
(lit: God be with you)		
Hello. (reply)	Dia is Muire duit.	dee·as moyra gwit
(lit: God and Mary be with you)		
Good morning.	Maidin mhaith.	maw·jin wah
Good night.	Oíche mhaith.	eek·heh wah

Goodbye.	*Slán leat.*	slawn lyat
(said by person leaving)		
Goodbye.	*Slán agat.*	slawn agut
(said by person staying)		
Welcome.	*Ceád míle fáilte.*	kade meela fawlcha
(lit: 100,000 welcomes)		
How are you?	*Conas a tá tú?*	kunas aw taw too

CUPLA FOCAL

Here are a few cheeky phrases *os Gaeilge* (in Irish) to help you impress the locals:

amadáin – fool
Dún do chlab! – Shut your mouth!
Ní ólfaidh mé go brách arís!
(knee ohl-hee mey gu brawkh u-reeshch)
I'm never ever drinking again!
Póg ma thóin! – Kiss my arse!
Slainte! (slawn-cha) – Your health! (cheers)
Táim go maith! (thawm go mah) – I'm good!

Thank you (very) much.		
Go raibh (míle)	goh rev (meela)
maith agat.	mah agut
…, (if you) please.	
…, más é do thoil é.	… maws ay do hall ay
(I'm) fine/good/OK.	
(Tá mé) go maith.	(taw may) goh mah
What's your name?	
Cad is ainm duit?	kod is anim dwit?
My name is (Sean Frayne).	
(Sean Frayne) is	(shawn frain) is
ainm dom.	anim dohm
Excuse me.	
Gabh mo leithscéal.	gamoh lesh scale
another/one more	
ceann eile	kyawn ella

Yes./It is.	*Tá./Sea.*	taw/sheh
No./It isn't.	*Níl./Ní hea.*	neel/nee heh
nice	*go deas*	goh dyass

Also available from Lonely Planet:
Irish Language & Culture phrasebook

SIGNS

Fir	*fear*	Men
Gardaí	*gardee*	Police
Leithreas	*lehrass*	Toilet
Mna	*m'naw*	Women
Oifig An Phoist	*iffig ohn fwisht*	Post Office

BASIC WORDS & PHRASES

What is this/that?	
Cad é seo/sin?	kod ay shoh/shin
I don't understand.	
Ní thuigim.	nee higgim
I'd like to go to …	
Ba mhaith liom	baw wah lohm
dul go dtí …	dull go dee …
I'd like to buy …	
Ba mhaith liom …	bah wah lohm …
a cheannach	a kyanukh

DAYS & MONTHS

Monday	*Dé Luáin*	day loon
Tuesday	*Dé Máirt*	day maart
Wednesday	*Dé Ceádaoin*	day kaydeen
Thursday	*Déardaoin*	daredeen
Friday	*Dé hAoine*	day heeneh
Saturday	*Dé Sathairn*	day sahern
Sunday	*Dé Domhnaigh*	day downick

NUMBERS

1	*haon*	hayin
2	*dó*	doe
3	*trí*	tree
4	*ceathair*	kahirr
5	*cúig*	koo-ig
6	*sé*	shay
7	*seacht*	shocked
8	*hocht*	hukt
9	*naoi*	nay
10	*deich*	jeh
11	*haon déag*	hayin jague
12	*dó dhéag*	doe yague
20	*fiche*	feekhe

LANGUAGE

Glossary

12 July – the day the *Orange Order* marches to celebrate Protestant King William III's victory over the Catholic King James II at the Battle of the Boyne in 1690

An Óige – literally 'the Youth'; Republic of Ireland Youth Hostel Association
An Taisce – National Trust for the Republic of Ireland
Anglo-Norman – Norman, English and Welsh peoples who invaded Ireland in the 12th century
Apprentice Boys – *Loyalist* organisation founded in 1814 to commemorate the Great Siege of Derry in August every year
ard – literally 'high'; Irish place name
Ascendancy – refers to the Protestant aristocracy descended from the Anglo-Normans and those who were installed here during the *Plantation*

bailey – outer wall of a castle
bawn – area surrounded by walls outside the main castle, acting as a defence and as a place to keep cattle in times of trouble
beehive hut – see *clochán*
Black & Tans – British recruits to the Royal Irish Constabulary shortly after WWI, noted for their brutality
Blarney Stone – sacred stone perched on top of Blarney Castle; bending over backwards to kiss the stone is said to bestow the gift of gab
bodhrán – hand-held goatskin drum
Bord Na Móna – the Irish turf board, charged with harvesting peat for use in power plants
boreen – small lane or roadway
Bronze Age – earliest metal-using period, around 2500 BC to 300 BC in Ireland; after the Stone Age and before the *Iron Age*
B-Specials – Northern Irish auxiliary police force, disbanded in 1971
bullaun – stone with a depression, probably used as a mortar for grinding medicine or food, often found at monastic sites

CAC IRA – Continuity Army Council of the *IRA*, a breakaway group
caher – circular area enclosed by stone walls
cairn – mound of stones heaped over a prehistoric grave
cashel – stone-walled *ring fort*; see also *ráth*
céilidh – session of traditional music and dancing; also called 'ceili'
Celtic Tiger – nickname of the Irish economy during the growth years from 1990 to about 2002
Celts – *Iron Age* warrior tribes that arrived in Ireland around 300 BC and controlled the country for 1000 years
ceol – music

cha – slang term for tea, as in a 'cup of cha'
chancel – eastern end of a church, where the altar is situated, reserved for the clergy and choir
chipper – slang term for fish 'n' chips fast-food restaurant
cill – literally 'church'; Irish place name; also known as 'kill'
cillín – literally 'little cell'; a hermitage, or sometimes a small, isolated burial ground for unbaptised children and other 'undesirables'
Claddagh ring – ring worn in much of *Connaught* since the mid-18th century, with a crowned heart nestling between two hands; if the heart points towards the hand then the wearer is partnered or married, if towards the fingertip he or she is looking for a mate
clochán – circular stone building, shaped like an old-fashioned beehive, from the early Christian period
Connaught – one of the four ancient provinces of Ireland, made up of Counties Galway, Leitrim, Mayo, Roscommon and Sligo; sometimes spelled 'Connacht'; see also *Leinster, Munster* and *Ulster*
Continuity IRA – anti-Agreement splinter *Republican* group, opposed to any deal not based on a united Ireland
craic – conversation, gossip, fun, good times; also known as 'crack'
crannóg – artificial island made in a lake to provide habitation in a good defensive position
crios – multicoloured woven woollen belt traditionally worn in the Aran Islands
cú – dog
culchie – derogatory nickname used by Dubliners for anyone not from the capital
currach – rowing boat made of a framework of laths covered with tarred canvas; also known as 'cúrach'

Dáil – lower house of the parliament of the Republic of Ireland; see also *Oireachtas* and *Seanad*
DART – Dublin Area Rapid Transport train line
delft – glazed blue-and-white earthenware from Holland; in Ireland the word refers to any kind of dishware
demesne – landed property close to a house or castle
diamond – town square
dolmen – tomb chamber or portal tomb made of vertical stones topped by a huge capstone; from around 2000 BC
drumlin – rounded hill formed by retreating glaciers
Dúchas – government department in charge of parks, monuments and gardens in the Republic; formerly known as the Office of Public Works
dún – fort, usually constructed of stone
DUP – Democratic Unionist Party; founded principally by Ian Paisley in 1971 in hard-line opposition to Unionist policies held by the *UUP*

Éire – Irish name for the Republic of Ireland
esker – raised ridge formed by glaciers

Fáilte Ireland – literally 'Welcome Board'; Irish Tourist Board
Fianna – mythical band of warriors who feature in many tales of ancient Ireland
Fianna Fáil – literally 'Warriors of Ireland'; a major political party in the Republic, originating from the *Sinn Féin* faction opposed to the 1921 treaty with Britain
Fine Gael – literally 'Tribe of the Gael'; a major political party in the Republic, originating from the *Sinn Féin* faction that favoured the 1921 treaty with Britain; formed the first government of independent Ireland
fir – men (singular 'fear'); sign on men's toilets; see also *leithreas* and *mná*
fleadh – festival

GAA – Gaelic Athletic Association; promotes Gaelic football and hurling, among other Irish games
Gaeltacht – Irish-speaking
gallery grave – tunnel-shaped burial chamber
gallóglí – mercenary soldiers of the 14th to 15th century; anglicised to 'gallowglasses'
garda – Irish Republic police; plural 'gardaí'
ghillie – fishing or hunting guide; also known as 'ghilly'
gob – mouth; from Irish word 'gob', meaning bird's beak or bill
gort – literally 'field'; Irish place name

Hibernia – literally 'Land of Winter'; Roman name for Ireland (the Romans had confused Ireland with Iceland)
hill fort – a hilltop fortified with ramparts and ditches, usually dating from the *Iron Age*
HINI – Hostelling International of Northern Ireland
hurling – Irish sport similar to hockey
Hunger, the – colloquial name for the Great Famine of 1845–51

Iarnród Éireann – Republic of Ireland Railways
INLA – Irish National Liberation Association; formed in 1975 as an *IRA* splinter group unhappy with the ceasefire; it has maintained its own ceasefire since 1998
IRA – Irish Republican Army; the largest Republican paramilitary organisation, founded 80 years ago with the aim to fight for a united Ireland; in 1969 the IRA split into the Official IRA and the Provisional IRA; the Official IRA is no longer active and the PIRA has become the IRA
IRB – Irish Republican Brotherhood; a secret society founded in 1858 and revived in the early 20th century; believed in independence, through violence if necessary, and was a precursor to the *IRA;* also known as the Fenians
Iron Age – metal-using period that lasted from the end of the *Bronze Age,* around 300 BC (the arrival of the Celts), to the arrival of Christianity, around the 5th century AD

jackeen – derogatory nickname used to describe anyone from Dublin or Dublin *GAA* players or supporters; originally used to describe Dubliners who waved Union Jacks during Queen Victoria's visit in 1901
jarvey – driver of a *jaunting car*
jaunting car – Killarney's traditional horse-drawn transport; see also *jarvey*

knackered – slang for tired or worn out

Leinster – one of the four ancient provinces of Ireland, made up of Counties Carlow, Dublin, Kildare, Kilkenny, Laois, Longford, Louth, Meath, Offaly, West Meath, Wexford and Wicklow; see also *Connaught, Munster* and *Ulster*
leithreas – toilets; see also *mná* and *fir*
leprechaun – mischievous elf or sprite from Irish folklore
lough – lake, or long narrow bay or arm of the sea
Loyalist – person, usually a Northern Irish Protestant, insisting on the continuation of Northern Ireland's links with Britain
Luas – light-rail transit system in Dublin; Irish for 'speed'
LVF – Loyalist Volunteer Force; an extreme *Loyalist paramilitary* group opposed to the current peace process. It has been on ceasefire since 1998

marching season – *Orange Order* parades, which take place from Easter and throughout summer to celebrate the victory by Protestant King William III of Orange over Catholic James II in the Battle of the Boyne on 12 July 1690, and the union with Britain
Mesolithic – also known as the Middle Stone Age; time of the first human settlers in Ireland, about 8000 BC to 4000 BC; see also *Neolithic*
midden – refuse heap left by a prehistoric settlement
mná – women; sign on women's toilets; see also *fir* and *leithreas*
motte – early Norman fortification consisting of a raised, flattened mound with a keep on top; when attached to a *bailey* it is known as a motte-and-*bailey* fort, many of which were built in Ireland until the early 13th century
Munster – one of the four ancient provinces of Ireland, made up of Counties Clare, Cork, Kerry, Limerick, Tipperary and Waterford; see also *Connaught, Leinster* and *Ulster*

naomh – holy or saint
Nationalism – belief in a reunited Ireland
Nationalist – proponent of a united Ireland
Neolithic – also known as the New Stone Age; a period characterised by settled agriculture lasting from around 4000 BC to 2500 BC in Ireland; followed by the *Bronze Age;* see also *Mesolithic*
NIR – Northern Ireland Railways

NITB – Northern Ireland Tourist Board
NNR – National Nature Reserves
North, the – political entity of Northern Ireland, not the northernmost geographic part of Ireland
NUI – National University of Ireland; made up of branches in Dublin, Cork, Galway and Limerick

Ogham stone – a stone etched with Ogham characters, the earliest form of writing in Ireland, with a variety of notched strokes placed above, below or across a keyline
Oireachtas – Parliament of the Republic of Ireland, consisting of the *Dáil,* the lower house, and the *Seanad,* the upper house
Orangemen – members of the *Orange Order;* must be male
Orange Order – the largest Protestant organisation in Northern Ireland, founded in 1795, with a membership of up to 100,000; name commemorates the victory of King William of Orange in the Battle of the Boyne
óstán – hotel

Palladian – style of architecture developed by Andrea Palladio (1508–80), based on ancient Roman architecture
paramilitaries – armed illegal organisations, either *Loyalist* or *Republican,* usually associated with the use of violence and crime for political and economic gain
Partition – division of Ireland in 1921
passage grave – Celtic tomb with a chamber reached by a narrow passage, typically buried in a mound
penal laws – laws passed in the 18th century forbidding Catholics from buying land and holding public office
Plantation – settlement of Protestant immigrants (sometimes known as Planters) in Ireland in the 17th century
poitín – illegally brewed whiskey, also spelled 'poteen'
Prod – slang for Northern Irish Protestant
provisionals – Provisional IRA, formed after a break with the official *IRA* (who are now largely inconsequential); named after the provisional government declared in 1916, they have been the main force combating the British army in *the North;* also known as 'provos'
PSNI – Police Service of Northern Ireland
PUP – Progressive Unionist Party; a small Unionist party seen as a political front for the *UVF,* who support the Good Friday Agreement

rashers – Irish bacon
ráth – *ring fort* with earthen banks around a timber wall; see also *cashel*
Real IRA – splinter movement of the *IRA* and opposed to *Sinn Féin's* support of the Good Friday Agreement; the Real IRA was responsible for the Omagh bombing in 1998 in which 29 people died; subsequently called a ceasefire but has been responsible for bombs in Britain and other acts of violence
Red Hand Commandos – illegal *Loyalist paramilitary* group

Red Hand Defenders – breakaway *Loyalist paramilitary* group formed in 1998 by dissident *UFF* and *LVF* members
Republic of Ireland – the 26 counties of *the South*
Republican – supporter of a united Ireland
Republicanism – belief in a united Ireland, sometimes referred to as militant nationalism
ring fort – circular habitation area surrounded by banks and ditches, used from the *Bronze Age* right through to the Middle Ages, particularly in the early Christian period
RTE – Radio Telefís Éireann; the national broadcasting service of the Republic of Ireland, with two TV and four radio stations
RUC – Royal Ulster Constabulary, the former name for the armed Police Service of Northern Ireland *(PSNI)*

sassenach – Irish word for Saxon, used to refer to anyone from England
SDLP – Social Democratic and Labour Party; the largest nationalist party in the Northern Ireland Assembly, instrumental in achieving the Good Friday Agreement; its goal is a united Ireland through nonviolent means; mostly Catholic
Seanad – upper house of the parliament of the Republic of Ireland; see also *Oireachtas* and *Dáil*
seisiún – music session
shamrock – three-leafed plant said to have been used by St Patrick to illustrate the Holy Trinity
shebeen – from the Irish 'síbín'; illicit drinking place or speakeasy
sheila-na-gig – literally 'Sheila of the teats'; female figure with exaggerated genitalia, carved in stone on the exteriors of some churches and castles; various explanations have been offered for the iconography, ranging from male clerics warning against the perils of sex to the idea that they represent Celtic war goddesses
shillelagh – stout club or cudgel, especially one made of oak or blackthorn
shinners – mildly derogatory nickname of members of *Sinn Féin*
Sinn Féin – literally 'We Ourselves'; a *Republican* party with the long-term aim of a united Ireland; seen as the political wing of the *IRA* but it maintains that both organisations are completely separate
slí – hiking trail or way
snug – partitioned-off drinking area in a pub
souterrain – underground chamber usually associated with *ring* and *hill forts;* probably provided a hiding place or escape route in times of trouble and/or storage space for goods
South, the – Republic of Ireland
standing stone – upright stone set in the ground, common across Ireland and dating from a variety of periods; some are burial markers

taoiseach – Republic of Ireland prime minister
TD – *teachta Dála;* member of the lower house *(Dáil)* of the parliament of the Republic of Ireland

teampall – church

Tinkers – derogatory term used to describe Irish itinerant communities that roam the country; see also *Travellers*

trá – beach or strand

Travellers – the term used today to describe Ireland's itinerant communities

Treaty – Anglo-Irish Treaty of 1921, which divided Ireland and gave relative independence to *the South;* cause of the 1922–23 Civil War

trian – district

Tricolour – green, white and orange Irish flag designed to symbolise the hoped-for union of the 'green' Catholic Southern Irish with the 'orange' Protestant Northern Irish

turlough – a small lake that often disappears in dry summers; from the Irish 'turlach'

UDA – Ulster Defence Association; the largest *Loyalist paramilitary* group; it has observed a ceasefire since 1994

UDP – Ulster Democratic Party; a small fringe *Unionist* party with links to the banned *Loyalist UFF*

UFF – Ulster Freedom Fighters, aka the Ulster Defence Association; this group supports the Good Friday Agreement and has been on ceasefire since 1994

uillean pipes – Irish bagpipes with a bellow strapped to the arm; 'uillean' is Irish for 'elbow'

Ulster – one of the four ancient provinces of Ireland; a term sometimes used to describe the six counties of *the North,* despite the fact that Ulster also includes Counties Cavan, Monaghan and Donegal (all in the Republic); see also *Connaught, Leinster* and *Munster*

Unionism – belief in the political union with Britain

Unionist – person who wants to retain Northern Ireland's links with Britain

United Irishmen – organisation founded in 1791 aiming to reduce British power in Ireland; it led a series of unsuccessful risings and invasions

UUP – Ulster Unionist Party; the largest *Unionist* party in Northern Ireland and the majority party in the Assembly; founded in 1905 and led by Unionist hero Edward Carson from 1910 to 1921; from 1921 to 1972 the sole Unionist organisation but is now under threat from the *DUP*

UVF – Ulster Volunteer Force; an illegal *Loyalist* Northern Irish *paramilitary* organisation

Volunteers – offshoot of the *IRB* that came to be known as the *IRA*

The Authors

FIONN DAVENPORT
Coordinating Author; Dublin, Counties Wicklow & Kildare

Born and partly bred in Dublin, it took Fionn years before he understood that though part of the same nation, Ireland beyond the pale was often a different country. Which made for some great exploring, but in the end he settled for the bits he knew best – and discovered a whole bunch of stuff on his doorstep he didn't know about. Which makes writing about his country year after year never get boring. Over the years he's also expanded his travel bag to include TV and radio – catch him on Newstalk 106-108FM (www.newstalk.ie).

CATHERINE LE NEVEZ
Counties Wexford, Waterford, Carlow, Kilkenny, Mayo, Sligo, Donegal

Catherine's wanderlust kicked in when she roadtripped across Europe aged four, and she's been hitting the road at every opportunity since, completing a Doctorate of Creative Arts in Writing, Masters in Professional Writing, and postgrad qualifications in Editing and Publishing along the way. Her Celtic connections include Irish and Breton heritage, as well as Irish mates who warned her that Ireland would be a grand country if it had a roof (and that the Guinness tastes better there than anywhere else on earth). She's since crisscrossed Ireland for several Lonely Planet gigs (including this book's previous edition), discovering that the Guinness tastes *so* much better it more than makes up for the rain.

ETAIN O'CARROLL
The Midlands, Counties Meath, Louth, Cavan & Monaghan

Born and bred in the boggy hinterlands of rural Ireland, it was almost inevitable that Etain's youthful quests for more exotic pastures would translate into a career as a travel writer and photographer. Although work often takes her far from home, Etain has written about Ireland's landscape and culture for a wide variety of publications, and the lure of untouched pubs, meandering rivers and genuine craic never quite goes away. Work on this guide provided a cherished opportunity to traipse around her own backyard searching for hidden treats, revisit some of her favourite places and quiz friends and family on the best spots in the country to eat, drink and be merry.

LONELY PLANET AUTHORS

Why is our travel information the best in the world? It's simple: our authors are passionate, dedicated travellers. They don't take freebies in exchange for positive coverage so you can be sure the advice you're given is impartial. They travel widely to all the popular spots, and off the beaten track. They don't research using just the internet or phone. They discover new places not included in any other guidebook. They personally visit thousands of hotels, restaurants, palaces, trails, galleries, temples and more. They speak with dozens of locals every day to make sure you get the kind of insider knowledge only a local could tell you. They take pride in getting all the details right, and in telling it how it is. Think you can do it? Find out how at **lonelyplanet.com**.

RYAN VER BERKMOES
Counties Cork, Kerry, Limerick, Tipperary, Clare & Galway

From Galway to Cork, with plenty of diversions in between, Ryan Ver Berkmoes has delighted in this great swath of Ireland. He first visited the latter in 1985, from when he remembers a grey place where the locals wandered the muddy tidal flats for fun and frolic. Times have changed! From lost rural pubs to lost memory, he's revelled in a place where his first name brings a smile and his surname brings a 'huh?' Catch up with him at www.ryanverberkmoes.com.

NEIL WILSON
Belfast, Counties Down, Armagh, Derry, Antrim, Fermanagh & Tyrone

Neil's first visit to Northern Ireland was in 1994, during the first flush of post-ceasefire optimism, and his interest in the history and politics of the place intensified a few years later when he found out that most of his mum's ancestors were from Ulster. Working on recent editions of the Ireland guidebook has allowed him to witness firsthand the progress being made towards a lasting peace, as well as enjoying some excellent hiking on the Causeway Coast and in the Mourne Mountains. Neil is a full-time travel writer based in Edinburgh, Scotland, and has written more than 45 guidebooks for half a dozen publishers.

Behind the Scenes

THIS BOOK

This 9th edition of the Ireland guide was written by Fionn Davenport, Catherine Le Nevez, Etain O'Carroll, Ryan Ver Berkmoes and Neil Wilson. It was commissioned in Lonely Planet's London office and produced by the following people:

Commissioning Editor Clifton Wilkinson
Coordinating Editor Ali Lemer
Coordinating Cartographer Mark Griffiths
Coordinating Layout Designer Jacqui Saunders
Managing Editor Bruce Evans
Managing Cartographers Corey Hutchison, Alison Lyall, Herman So
Managing Layout Designer Sally Darmody
Assisting Editors Elizabeth Anglin, Cathryn Game, Liz Heynes, Robyn Loughnane, Anne Mulvaney, Charlotte Orr, Angela Tinson, Saralinda Turner
Assisting Cartographers Diana Duggan, Khanh Luu, Anthony Phelan
Cover Image research provided by lonelyplanetimages.com
Project Manager Eoin Dunlevy
Language Content Coordinator Annelies Mertens

Thanks to Lucy Birchley, Jessica Crouch, Kirsten Rawlings, Dianne Schallmeiner, Trent Paton

THANKS
FIONN DAVENPORT

Thanks first and foremost to my fellow authors: Ryan, Catherine, Etain and Neil, who yet again came up with trumps and made this book every bit as good as it is. It's always a pleasure to work with you. Thanks to Mark French, Una Mullally & Sinéad Gleeson for your expertise. Thanks to Cathy Kelly, who submitted to my pestering with a smiling friendliness. Thanks to Cliff in London, who served as sounding board and agony aunt in equal measure. Thanks to Tracy, Billy, Paul and Anto, who provided advice, suggestion and direction. Thanks finally to Caroline, whose cups of tea, quips and hugs were what made it all worthwhile.

CATHERINE LE NEVEZ

Sláinte to all of the locals, fellow travellers and tourism professionals in counties Wexford, Waterford, Carlow, Kilkenny, Mayo, Sligo and Donegal who provided insights and inspiration. To thank everyone individually would run for pages, but a particular shout-out to Declan Murphy, Rosie in Carlow, Donal Lehane from Slow Food, surfer Fergal Smith, woodcarver Michael Quirke, bodhrán player Junior Davey and the locals in Gurteen, chef Paul Flynn, and Brian and all in Graiguenamanagh.

THE LONELY PLANET STORY

Fresh from an epic journey across Europe, Asia and Australia in 1972, Tony and Maureen Wheeler sat at their kitchen table stapling together notes. The first Lonely Planet guidebook, *Across Asia on the Cheap*, was born.

Travellers snapped up the guides. Inspired by their success, the Wheelers began publishing books to Southeast Asia, India and beyond. Demand was prodigious, and the Wheelers expanded the business rapidly to keep up. Over the years, Lonely Planet extended its coverage to every country and into the virtual world via lonelyplanet.com and the Thorn Tree message board.

As Lonely Planet became a globally loved brand, Tony and Maureen received several offers for the company. But it wasn't until 2007 that they found a partner whom they trusted to remain true to the company's principles of travelling widely, treading lightly and giving sustainably. In October of that year, BBC Worldwide acquired a 75% share in the company, pledging to uphold Lonely Planet's commitment to independent travel, trustworthy advice and editorial independence.

Today, Lonely Planet has offices in Melbourne, London and Oakland, with over 500 staff members and 300 authors. Tony and Maureen are still actively involved with Lonely Planet. They're travelling more often than ever, and they're devoting their spare time to charitable projects. And the company is still driven by the philosophy of *Across Asia on the Cheap*: 'All you've got to do is decide to go and the hardest part is over. So go!'

Major thanks to Cliff Wilkinson for the gig, as well as Eoin Dunlevy, Herman So, Fionn and all at Lonely Planet. As ever, *merci surtout* to my family.

ETAIN O'CARROLL

Huge thanks to all the helpful staff in tourist offices around my area who answered endless questions and offered some great advice. If you have a great meal, discover an untouched pub or village, wander into a session in full swing or chance on a great B&B because of this book then thanks go to my family and friends who have been sampling the delights of the region for years and let me in on their best-kept secrets. Thanks to Sinéad Killeen, Róisín McSharry, Aoife Farnon, Breda McGuigan, Claire Cunningham and Sinéad Culbert for all their hot tips and to Mary, Madeleine, Lisa, Oda and Luan O'Carroll for advice on where to go, what to see and how to get there without getting lost, not to mention all the hot dinners, freshly made beds, babysitting and entertainment. Thanks to Fionn and Cliff for guidance and inspiration along the way, and Mark and Osgur for company on the road and support on return.

RYAN VER BERKMOES

Like a conversation over nothing in particular in an Irish pub, thanks to those who helped me on this book threaten to go on and on and on... But a few: Charlie Adley and his cohorts had me ready to move to Galway, where Geraldine Bray knows her cheese. Bernadette McCarthy hit the right notes in Galway. Ben Greensfelder didn't save my bacon (a good thing) but he did fluff up my Fungie. Fionn Davenport again guided this book to spectacular completion (and did a fine job dealing with groupies) while Claudia Stehle and Alevtina Chernorukova guided me down the road. While Annah and Erin always guide me home.

NEIL WILSON

Thanks to the Belfast Welcome Centre, to friendly and helpful tourist office staff all over Northern Ireland, and to Tom and Will Kelly and Kevin Hasson (the Bogside Artists).

OUR READERS

Many thanks to the travellers who used the last edition and wrote to us with helpful hints, useful advice and interesting anecdotes:

Peter Addison, Carmen Arce, Borut Bajzelj, Jochen Beier, Ann Brophy, Seán Brosnan, Helen Browne, Dan Bullock, Sally Burnett,

SEND US YOUR FEEDBACK

We love to hear from travellers – your comments keep us on our toes and help make our books better. Our well-travelled team reads every word on what you loved or loathed about this book. Although we cannot reply individually to postal submissions, we always guarantee that your feedback goes straight to the appropriate authors, in time for the next edition. Each person who sends us information is thanked in the next edition and the most useful submissions are rewarded with a free book.

To send us your updates – and find out about Lonely Planet events, newsletters and travel news – visit our award-winning website: **lonelyplanet.com/contact**.

Note: we may edit, reproduce and incorporate your comments in Lonely Planet products such as guidebooks, websites and digital products, so let us know if you don't want your comments reproduced or your name acknowledged. For a copy of our privacy policy visit lonelyplanet.com/privacy.

BEHIND THE SCENES

Jean Carey, Fergal Carroll, Beatriz Castedo, Donal Cawley, Sarah Chambers, Liz Chorlton, Malcolm Clark, Janine Coetzee, Robert Coffey, Shaun Connor, Jennita Dankelman, Aaron Dawson, Caluide Decarie, Philip Dew, Karen Dodd, Ilka Doehler, Colm Doyle, Martina Feige, Chad Fenton-Smith, Lisa Fitzsimons, Cian Foley, Kenny Foster, Daniel Giesbrecht, Conor Hanlon, Carmel Hawkins, Paul Heaney, Barbara Helm, Mairin Herman, Nicole Hessels, Miras Hugo, Massoud Javadi, KWS Kane, Bridget King, Bradley King, Terry King, Cath Lanigan, Ida Milton Larsen, Deirdre Little, William Lucia, Janet Martin, Esme Martinez, Brian McCaul, Katy McClure, Paul McKeever, Niocla Meenan, Heather Monell, Dan Moreland, James Moroney, Richard Norman, Michael Nürnberger, Daniel Obrist, Dave Olson, Kitty Ott, Mic Porter, Grace Poutch, Juan Manuel Álvarez Quicler, Mikaela Ring, Brian Roberts, Michael Roche, Tomás Alonso Román, Jessie Sampson, Matthew Sampson, Alicia San Mateo, Marianne Schmidt, Anne Sheehan, Jerome Simpson, Matthew Skeffington, Paul Smith, Allison Speers, Kathie Sullivan, Dan Tasse, Ingrid Thorstensen, Jean Tracey-Bower, Annette Turner, Niall Twamley, Margaret Wakefield, Melissa Watson, Rosemary West, Ariane Witt

ACKNOWLEDGMENTS

Many thanks to the following for the use of their content:

Globe on title page ©Mountain High Maps 1993 Digital Wisdom, Inc.

Index

INDEX

000 Map pages
000 Photograph pages

INDEX

INDEX

INDEX

000 Map pages
000 Photograph pages

GreenDex

GOING GREEN

The following attractions, accommodation, cafés, pubs and restaurants have been selected by Lonely Planet authors because they demonstrate a commitment to sustainability. We've selected hotels, pubs and restaurants for their support of local producers or their devotion to the 'slow food' cause – so they might serve only seasonal, locally sourced produce on their menus. We've also highlighted farmers markets and the local producers themselves. In addition, we've covered accommodation that we deem to be environmentally friendly, for example for their commitment to recycling or energy conservation. Attractions are listed because they're involved in conservation or environmental education or have been given an ecological award (for example, Blue Flag beaches).

For more tips about travelling sustainably in Ireland, turn to the Getting Started chapter (p21).

We want to keep developing our sustainable-travel content. If you think we've omitted someone who should be listed here, or if you disagree with our choices, email us at talk2us@lonelyplanet .com.au and set us straight for next time. For more information about sustainable tourism and Lonely Planet, see www.lonelyplanet.com/responsibletravel.

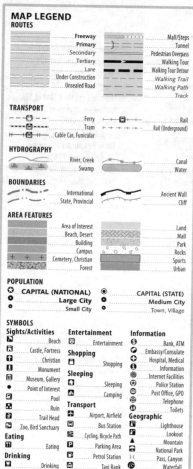

MAP LEGEND

ROUTES
- Freeway
- Primary
- Secondary
- Tertiary
- Lane
- Under Construction
- Unsealed Road
- Mall/Steps
- Tunnel
- Pedestrian Overpass
- Walking Tour
- Walking Tour Detour
- Walking Trail
- Walking Path
- Track

TRANSPORT
- Ferry
- Tram
- Cable Car, Funicular
- Rail
- Rail (Underground)

HYDROGRAPHY
- River, Creek
- Swamp
- Canal
- Water

BOUNDARIES
- International
- State, Provincial
- Ancient Wall
- Cliff

AREA FEATURES
- Area of Interest
- Beach, Desert
- Building
- Campus
- Cemetery, Christian
- Forest
- Land
- Mall
- Park
- Rocks
- Sports
- Urban

POPULATION
- **CAPITAL (NATIONAL)**
- **Large City**
- **Small City**
- CAPITAL (STATE)
- Medium City
- Town, Village

SYMBOLS

Sights/Activities
- Beach
- Castle, Fortress
- Christian
- Monument
- Museum, Gallery
- Point of Interest
- Pool
- Ruin
- Trail Head
- Zoo, Bird Sanctuary

Eating
- Eating

Drinking
- Drinking

Entertainment
- Entertainment

Shopping
- Shopping

Sleeping
- Sleeping
- Camping

Transport
- Airport, Airfield
- Bus Station
- Cycling, Bicycle Path
- Parking Area
- Petrol Station
- Taxi Rank

Information
- Bank, ATM
- Embassy/Consulate
- Hospital, Medical
- Information
- Internet Facilities
- Police Station
- Post Office, GPO
- Telephone
- Toilets

Geographic
- Lighthouse
- Lookout
- Mountain
- National Park
- Pass, Canyon
- Waterfall

LONELY PLANET OFFICES

Australia (Head Office)
Locked Bag 1, Footscray, Victoria 3011
☎ 03 8379 8000, fax 03 8379 8111
talk2us@lonelyplanet.com.au

USA
150 Linden St, Oakland, CA 94607
☎ 510 250 6400, toll free 800 275 8555
fax 510 893 8572
info@lonelyplanet.com

UK
2nd fl, 186 City Rd,
London EC1V 2NT
☎ 020 7106 2100, fax 020 7106 2101
go@lonelyplanet.co.uk

Published by Lonely Planet Publications Pty Ltd
ABN 36 005 607 983

© Lonely Planet 2009

© photographers as indicated 2009

Cover photograph: Giant's Causeway rock formations, County Antrim, Northern Ireland, Richard Cummins/Lonely Planet Images. Many of the images in this guide are available for licensing from Lonely Planet Images: lonelyplanetimages.com.

Printed by Hang Tai Printing Company, Hong Kong.
Printed in China.

Mixed Sources
Product group from well-managed forests and other controlled sources
www.fsc.org Cert no. SGS-COC-005002
© 1996 Forest Stewardship Council
FSC

Although the authors and Lonely Planet have taken all reasonable care in preparing this book, we make no warranty about the accuracy or completeness of its content and, to the maximum extent permitted, disclaim all liability arising from its use.